THE ENCYCLOPEDIA OF
Witches, Witchcraft and Wicca

THIRD EDITION

Also by Rosemary Ellen Guiley

The Encyclopedia of Angels, Second Edition

The Encyclopedia of Ghosts and Spirits, Third Edition

The Encyclopedia of Magic and Alchemy

The Encyclopedia of Saints

*The Encyclopedia of Vampires, Werewolves,
and Other Monsters*

THE ENCYCLOPEDIA OF
Witches, Witchcraft and Wicca

THIRD EDITION

Rosemary Ellen Guiley

Facts On File
An imprint of Infobase Publishing

The Encyclopedia of Witches, Witchcraft and Wicca, Third Edition

Copyright © 1989, 1999, 2008 by Visionary Living, Inc.

Facts On File, Inc.
An imprint of Infobase Publishing
132 West 31st Street
New York NY 10001

Library of Congress Cataloging-in-Publication Data

Guiley, Rosemary.
The encyclopedia of witches, witchcraft and wicca / Rosemary Ellen Guiley. — 3rd ed.
    p. cm.
Rev. ed. : The encyclopedia of witches and witchcraft . 1999.
Includes bibliographical references and index.
ISBN-13: 978-0-8160-7103-6 (hardcover : alk. paper)
ISBN-10: 0-8160-7103-9 (hardcover : alk. paper)
1. Witchcraft—Encyclopedias. 2. Witches—Encyclopedias. I. Guiley, Rosemary.
Encyclopedia of witches and witchcraft. II. Title.
    BF1566.G85 2008
    133.4'303—dc22   2008008917

Facts On File books are available at special discounts when purchased in bulk quantities for businesses, associations, institutions, or sales promotions. Please call our Special Sales Department in New York at (212) 967-8800 or (800) 322-8755.

You can find Facts On File on the World Wide Web at http://www.factsonfile.com

Text design by Cathy Rincon
Cover design by Salvatore Luongo

Printed in the United States of America

VB Hermitage 10 9 8 7 6 5 4 3 2 1

This book is printed on acid-free paper and contains
30 percent postconsumer recycled content.

For Jo Clark

⸬ CONTENTS ⸬

❧ Acknowledgments ❧

For the third edition of this encyclopedia, I would like especially to thank the following individuals for their help: Laurie Cabot, Selena Fox, Raymond Buckland, Z Budapest, Marion Weinstein, Oberon Zell-Ravenheart, Orion Foxwood, Christopher Penczak, Raven Digitalis, Gavin Bone, Janet Farrar, Gavin and Yvonne Frost, Isaac Bonewits, Deborah Lipp and Carl Weschke.

❧ INTRODUCTION ❧

Centuries ago, the inquisitors and witch-hunters who executed witches as servants of the Devil believed they were doing a service to God and humanity. They envisioned a society free of witchcraft, which they viewed as heresy, a scourge, an evil and a blight. They would be astonished today to find that Witchcraft—with a capital *W*—has become one of the fastest-growing religions in Western culture.

How did this 180-degree turn take place?

The road from sorcery to spirituality is a colorful one, full of secrets, twists, rituals and compelling personalities. In its short half century as a religion, Witchcraft has a history rivaling that of any of the world's great faiths in drama, intrigue, pathos and triumph. Witchcraft has taken its place in the ecumenical religious theater.

Traditionally, witchcraft—with a small *w*—is a form of sorcery, concerned with spells and divination. The magical witch, the sorcerer witch, was not practicing a religion of witchcraft, but was practicing a magical art, passed down through families or taught by adepts.

Witches have never enjoyed a good reputation. Almost universally since ancient times, witchcraft has been associated with malevolence and evil. Witches are thought to be up to no good, interested in wreaking havoc and bringing misery to others. Individuals who used the magical arts to divine and to heal often took great pains to call themselves something other than "witch."

In Christianity, witchcraft became interpreted as serving the Devil in his plan to subvert and destroy souls. A witch hysteria mounted in Europe, Britain and even the American colonies and was seized upon by the church as a way of eliminating rival religious sects, political enemies and social outcasts. From the 14th to 18th centuries, thousands of people—perhaps hundreds of thousands—were tortured, jailed, maimed and executed on charges of witchcraft. Many of them were innocent, framed by personal enemies or tortured into confessions.

They told lurid stories of signing pacts with the Devil in blood, of being given demons in the form of animal familiars that would do their malevolent bidding and of attending horrid feasts called sabbats, where they would kiss the anus of the Devil and roast babies for a meal. None of these tales was ever substantiated by fact, but they served as sufficient evidence to condemn those who confessed to them.

The accused also admitted to doing evil to their families, friends, neighbors, rivals and enemies. How much of that was true is uncertain. Folk magic practices were part of everyday life, and casting a spell against someone, especially to redress a wrong, was commonplace. Since most confessions were extracted under fear and torture, it is likely that a great deal of untruth and exaggeration spilled out.

In the American colonies, the Puritans were obsessed with evil and believed the Devil had followed them across the ocean from England to destroy them. No wonder this paranoia erupted into witch hunts, including those in Salem, Massachusetts, in 1692, when the tales of hysterical girls were enough to send people to their deaths.

The stigma upon witchcraft left by the Inquisition and witch hunts lingers to this day, perpetuated by lurid films and novels of baby-eating hags and Satan worshipers gathered in candlelit circles intoning ominous chants.

Witchcraft as a religion was born in Britain after World War II and came out of the closet when the anti-witchcraft laws there were repealed in 1953. It is argued that Gerald B. Gardner, the man who more or less invented the religion, should have chosen another term besides *witchcraft* for the mix of pagan, ceremonial magic and occult material he assembled. Perhaps *witchcraft* sounded secretive, exotic and forbidden. It certainly struck the right chord with the public, who suddenly could not get enough of witches.

Gardner may not have envisioned a worldwide religious movement, but that is what unfolded, first with the export of Witchcraft to the United States, Canada and Europe, and then around the world. The "Gardner tradition," as it became known, quickly mutated into offshoots.

A spiritual tradition that reinvented pagan deities and rituals, combined with folk magic and ceremonial magic, proved to be what many people wanted. Alienated by the dry, crusty rituals and somber dogma of patriarchal mainstream Christianity and Judaism, people were hungry for a spirituality that was fresh and creative. Witchcraft—as well as reborn Paganism, reconstructions of pre-Christian and non-Christian traditions—offered just that, along with independence, autonomy, a connection to Nature and direct contact with the Divine. No need for meddling priests, ministers and clergy to guard the gates to the Godhead—or the afterlife. Another appeal was the top billing given to the feminine aspect of deity—the Goddess. And, sensuality was honored and celebrated, not punished.

Witchcraft the religion, along with its Pagan cousins, flourished in the blooming New Age counterculture of the 1960s and 1970s and then took hold on the edges of mainstream society. In the years since its birth, Witchcraft has solidified some in uniform codes, values and core beliefs. But at heart it remains fluid, constantly evolving in practice and interpretation. Practitioners find Witchcraft empowering and believe it provides a powerful spiritual path on a par with all other mystical, spiritual and religious paths. Dozens and dozens of Witchcraft and Pagan traditions exist, and new ones are born all the time.

Witchcraft and Paganism have survived the first tests of time. The movements took hold in the baby boom generation. Now, the children and grandchildren of those people are growing up Wiccan and Pagan, and new young people are attracted to the fold in increasing numbers.

But there remains that pesky word *witchcraft,* which still evokes Satan, evil and black magic to many outsiders.

For decades now, Witches have argued about whether or not *Witch* ought to be replaced with a term that doesn't come with so much negative baggage. Some have adopted the terms *Wicca* and *Wiccan* to describe themselves and their religion and also to distinguish who they are and what they do from folk magic.

Today, most Witches stand firm by the terms *Witch* and *Witchcraft,* believing that the public can and should be reeducated about both. They have made headway, for Witchcraft/Wiccan churches are recognized legally, Witch holidays have gained some official recognition, and, in the United States, Wiccan military veterans have won the right to have the pentacle, their religious symbol, placed on their tombstones.

The different kinds and definitions of witchcraft present a challenge in putting together an encyclopedia. First, there is witchcraft the magical art, which deals with sorcery, spell-casting for good or ill, healing and divination. Then there is the Inquisition witchcraft, the alleged Devil worship. And then there is Witchcraft the religion. All three overlap, and all three are covered in this volume. Most of the topics deal with the history and evolution of witchcraft in the West, though there are entries of cross-cultural interest.

I have used a lower-case *w* to describe folk and Inquisition witches and witchcraft, and a capital *W* to refer to the modern religion. I have also used the terms *Wicca* and *Wiccan* for the modern religion. Likewise, a lowercase *p* in pagan and paganism are used for pre- and non-Christian references, while a capital *P* refers to modern religious traditions. Witchcraft the modern religion is considered a form of Paganism, but there are many forms of Paganism that are not Witchcraft.

Topics include folklore, historical cases and events, biographies, descriptions of beliefs, rites and practices and related topics. For the third edition, I have added entries in all categories and have updated entries to reflect changes and developments. Students of the Salem witch hysteria will find individual biographies on the key victims.

Witchcraft is a topic of enduring interest and study. In one respect, it peeks into a shadow side of the occult and the dark underbelly of human nature. In another respect, it opens into a realm of spiritual light.

The church may never officially apologize for the Inquisition, which destroyed many people other than accused witches. Perhaps the success of Witchcraft the religion is karmic payback for a campaign of terror in the name of religion.

—Rosemary Ellen Guiley

abracadabra A magical spell consisting of a single word, which was popular in medieval times to get rid of illness, misfortune or DEMONS. The word is inscribed on an amulet (see AMULETS) or written out on paper in a magical inverted triangle, in which one letter of the word is dropped in each succeeding line, until nothing is left. The evil is supposed to fade away just as the word does. The diminishing word technique is used in many other SPELLS for the same purposes.

In medieval times, *abracadabra* was believed to ward off the plague. The triangle was written on a piece of paper, which was tied around the neck with flax and worn for nine days, then tossed backwards over the shoulder into a stream of water running toward the east.

The word's origin is unknown. It is said by some to have been invented around 208 by Quintus Serenus Sammonicus, physician to the Roman emperor Severus, as a cure for fever. Some hold that Sammonicus merely borrowed a formula that was much older.

According to others, the word comes from the old Aramaic phrase, *abhadda kedhabhra,* "disappear like this word," or the Hebrew phrase *abreq ad habra,* "hurl your thunderbolt even unto death." It is also said to be derived from the name Abraxas, the Gnostic god who appears on charms against the evil eye dating from the second century. Another possibility is that it is the name of some long-forgotten demon. INCREASE MATHER dismissed it as a "hobgoblin word" that had no power at all. ALEISTER CROWLEY, on the other hand, said it is a

magical word of great power and that its true form is *abrahadabra.*

See CHARMS.

FURTHER READING:
Farrar, Janet, and Stewart Farrar. *A Witches Bible Compleat.* New York: Magickal Childe, 1984.

Abramelin the Mage (1362–1460) A Jew from Würzburg, Germany, Abraham, or Abramelin (also spelled Abra-Melin), created a body of magical works that for centuries influenced magicians, including ALEISTER CROWLEY. An expert on the KABBALAH, Abramelin said he learned his magical knowledge from angels, who told him how to conjure and tame DEMONS into personal servants and workers, and how to raise storms (see STORM RAISING). He said that all things in the world were created by demons, who worked under the direction of angels, and that each individual had an angel and a demon as FAMILIARS. The basis for his system of magic, he said, may be found in the Kabbalah.

According to lore, Abramelin created 2,000 spirit cavalrymen for Frederick, elector of Saxony. He also is said to have aided an earl of Warwick in his escape from jail and helped save the antipope John XXIII (1410–15) from the Council of Constance.

The MAGIC of Abramelin allegedly is contained in a manuscript, *The Sacred Magic of Abramelin the Mage,* actually a collection of three books. The manuscript was written in French in the 18th century but claims to be

1

a translation of Abramelin's original manuscript in Hebrew, dated 1458. It was translated into English around the turn of the 20th century by S. L. MacGregor Mathers, one of the early and most influential members of the HERMETIC ORDER OF THE GOLDEN DAWN. Crowley borrowed from the book for his own rituals to master demons, and GERALD B. GARDNER used it as a source for his BOOK OF SHADOWS.

Abramelin magic is similar to that found in *The Key of Solomon,* considered the leading magical grimoire (see GRIMOIRES). It is based on the power of numbers and sacred names and involves the construction of numerous magical squares for such purposes as invisibility, FLYING, commanding spirits, NECROMANCY, shape shifting (see METAMORPHOSIS) and scores of other feats. Rituals for conjuring spirits, creating magic squares and making seals and SIGILS are elaborate and must be followed exactly in accordance with astrological observances.

FURTHER READING:
MacGregor-Mathers, S. L. *The Book of the Sacred Magic of Abra-Melin the Mage.* Wellingborough, England: The Aquarian Press, 1976.

Adler, Margot (1946–)   American Pagan, author and journalist, Adler is the first writer to chronicle in detail the emergence and evolution of PAGANISM in the United States. The results of her research, *Drawing Down the Moon* (1979; 1986; 1995), make up a meticulous landmark study of a highly complex and diversified religious movement.

Adler's interest in Paganism began with an early fascination with ancient Greek deities. Born April 16, 1946, in Little Rock, Arkansas, she grew up in New York City as the only child in a nonreligious household: her father was an atheist and her mother a Jewish agnostic. Psychiatry was a significant influence: her father and an aunt are psychiatrists; her grandfather was renowned psychiatrist Alfred Adler. Her mother was a radical educator.

At age 12, Adler became acquainted at grammar school with the pantheon of ancient Greek deities. She was particularly drawn to ARTEMIS and ATHENA for their images of strength and power.

While a student at the High School of Music and Art, Adler made a religious search, visiting different churches. She was attracted to the Quakers and their practice of speaking from the heart, and to the moving, ritual splendor of Catholic Mass in Latin.

Religion then took a back seat to politics for a few years. From 1964 to 1968, Adler attended the University of California at Berkeley, where she earned a bachelor's degree in political science, and became increasingly involved in political activities. She participated in the Free Speech Movement and was jailed for demonstrating. She helped to register black voters in civil rights activities in Mississippi in 1965. She was an activist against the Vietnam War, and demonstrated at the Democratic convention in Chicago in 1968.

Margot Adler (COURTESY OF MARGOT ADLER)

In 1968, she entered broadcast journalism, first as a volunteer for the radical/alternative radio stations in Berkeley and New York owned by the Pacifica Foundation. From 1969 to 1970, she earned a master's degree in journalism from the Graduate School of Journalism at Columbia University in New York, and then went to work for WBAI, Pacifica's station in Manhattan. In 1971, WBAI sent Adler to Washington, D.C., to manage its news bureau operation there.

In Washington, politics and religion came together for Adler. She devoted extensive coverage to environmental issues, which stimulated her interest in nature writers such as Thoreau. She saw a connection between environmental issues and religion: the Judeo/Christian view that it is humans' right to have dominion over the earth seemed flawed and had led to exploitation of nature and the earth. In contrast, Paganism and animistic religions viewed humankind as a part of nature equal with all other creatures and parts.

On a trip to England, Adler investigated the history of the DRUIDS, and in the process discovered numerous Pagan organizations. She subscribed to *The Waxing Moon,* which led to her introduction to WITCHCRAFT and WICCA.

WBAI relocated Adler back to New York, where she worked as a producer and then hosted her own live program, *Hour of the Wolf,* which aired for two hours in the early morning five days a week. Her show dealt with cutting edges in such topics as politics, women's issues, the arts, ecology and religion. She hosted two other radio shows: *Unstuck in Time* and *The Far Side of the Moon.*

She received a letter from two Witches in Essex, England, who were selling tapes of rituals to *Waxing Moon* subscribers. At first, the idea of Witchcraft rituals on tape struck Adler as a joke. She replied that she might air them on her radio program.

The first tape she received was of the DRAWING DOWN THE MOON ritual and the CHARGE OF THE GODDESS. It evoked childhood memories of beautiful Greek goddesses, and in a powerful moment, Adler realized that the idea of becoming the Goddess as an empowering image was not only permissible but was being done by others. She began to search for such people.

In the early 1970s, contemporary Witchcraft was rapidly gaining adherents in the United States. Imported from England under the aegis of RAYMOND BUCKLAND and Rosemary Buckland, followers of GERALD B. GARDNER, the Craft was modified by numerous American covens. Adler joined a study group in Brooklyn run by the New York Coven of Welsh Traditional Witches. Another group hived off from that coven to observe the Gardnerian tradition, and Adler followed. She was initiated as a first degree Gardnerian priestess in 1973.

Adler stayed in the coven about three years, then moved off in new directions. She formed a PAGAN WAY grove in Manhattan, which became an informal recruiting center for persons interested in Witchcraft and Paganism.

A friend introduced Adler to New York literary agent Jane Rotrosen, who suggested writing a book. Adler was uncertain at first, then realized she was "on a nexus point . . . standing on a crack in the universe." The time for such a book was right. With Rotrosen's help, Adler developed and sold a proposal.

She spent three years researching and writing *Drawing Down the Moon.* She traveled around the country, interviewing about 100 persons and groups involved in the Pagan/Wiccan communities. Originally, she intended to include Britain in her survey, but British groups and individuals proved reluctant to participate.

To her surprise, Adler discovered that the Pagan movement is not what she had imagined: an integrated spiritual movement with environmental concerns. Some segments did fit that image, while others were radically different. A decade later, the movement had become much more integrated and concerned with ecological issues, in part, perhaps, due to the influence of books by Adler and STARHAWK.

Adler also was the first to note the connection between the revival of Wicca and the women's spirituality movement. In later editions of *Drawing Down the Moon,* she chronicled the growing number of Pagans who entered the Unitarian Universalist churches. For some 10

years, she was on the board of directors of CUUPS, the Covenant of Unitarian Universalist Pagans.

Though she acknowledges that she is a Witch in the Wiccan religion, Adler prefers to call herself a Pagan. She feels the term Witch has so many negative associations that it may never be reclaimed as a term of female power and independence. Furthermore, what is now practiced as "Witchcraft" has nothing to do with the heretical "witchcraft" of the Inquisition.

In 1977, two years into the book project, Adler left WBAI. Upon completing *Drawing Down the Moon,* she worked as a freelance reporter for National Public Radio (NPR) in Manhattan, then joined the NPR staff in 1979. She was priestess of a Gardnerian coven for five years until 1981, when she was awarded a prestigious one-year Neiman fellowship to Harvard University. Following the Neiman, she returned to NPR in New York, but did not rejoin a coven or pagan group.

On June 19, 1988, Adler married her longtime companion, Dr. John Gliedman, in a handfasting held outdoors on Martha's Vineyard, Massachusetts. SELENA FOX officiated at the legal ceremony, conducted within a magic circle made of flowers and greens. Adler and Gliedman then jumped the broom, according to tradition. A reception followed. The wedding was the first Wiccan handfasting to be written up in the society pages of the *New York Times.* A son, Alexander Gliedman-Adler, was born in 1990.

In 1997, her book *Heretic's Heart: A Journey Through Spirit & Revolution* was published. It chronicles her upbringing as a "red diaper baby" and her involvement in the radical issues and movements of the 1960s, including the emergence of Paganism. Adler sees that period more as a ferment of ideas and ideals and of creative risk-taking rather than as an indulgent drug-and-sex party portrayed by most media. *Heretic's Heart* also includes perhaps the only known correspondence between a radical student in Berkeley and an American soldier in Vietnam.

Adler is chief of the New York bureau of NPR. She is a correspondent for *All Things Considered* and *Morning Edition* and hosts *Justice Talking,* a national show on constitutional issues. She presents lectures and workshops, represents Paganism and women's spirituality at conferences and leads rituals at gatherings. She has especially emphasized the importance of RITUAL, not only as part of worship and rites of passage, but as an important way for the human soul to commune with and understand creation.

African witchcraft   In African tribal traditions, witchcraft is part of the accepted supernatural landscape and is generally something to be feared.

Study of African tribal religions illustrates the African ancestry of modern VODUN, SANTERÍA and Candomblé. There is a fairly universal belief in a supreme God, who manifests himself in light and brightness: a shining, snowcapped mountain, or the light streaming through a sacred grove of trees. But such a God is remote, accessible only to the priests or elders. God inspires great awe in his people, causing them to fear and avoid his symbols, such as thunder and lightning. The birth of twins is also a sign from God, creating reverence for the twins' divinity and their isolation from the rest of the community.

The spirits of the dead, or the "shades," however, are regarded as alive and able to communicate the needs of humans to the divines. They are always about, participating in daily living, evident in the rustling of leaves, dust spirals in the earth, currents in the river. Southern Africans divide the shades into two categories: the deceased relatives of any particular family and the founding heroes, male or female, who define a community, chiefdom or region.

To keep the ancestors happy, living relatives offer food, drink and animal sacrifice. Offering feasts must be attended by the ancestor's kin, since the meal itself is a communion between the living and the dead. Family members air and resolve any quarrels before the offering, since Africans believe that festering, unspoken anger is the root of witchcraft.

For the tribal African, the power of evil is everywhere, abetted by witches and their FAMILIARS but brought on by anger, hate, jealousy, envy, lust and greed—all the vices men observe in themselves and their neighbors. It can even be brought on by laziness, as certain evil persons raise the dead to do their work for them (see ZOMBIE). Evil does not come from the shades, nor do the shades possess a living person. Both are outside influences caused by witchcraft.

Members of the Nyakyusa tribes describe witchcraft as a "python in the belly," while the Pondo people call it a "snake of the women." As in Europe, most witches come from the ranks of women, poor men and young people. Others depict witchcraft as a baboon, and members of the Xhosa tribes see it as a fantastic hairy beast with exaggerated sexual organs. People accused of witchcraft within a tribe often confess, attributing their evil to quarrels with wives, children or co-workers. If witchcraft has caused sickness, no recovery is possible without the witch's confession and subsequent goodwill toward the victim.

In his groundbreaking studies of the Azande tribes in the late 1920s, Professor E. E. Evans-Pritchard found that the Azande believe witchcraft, or *mangu*, is a hereditary trait found in the stomach of a witch. Such an abdominal condition results in an oval, blackish swelling or sac containing small objects located near the bile tract. The Azande admit not seeing this sac while a person is alive but claim to have extracted it in autopsy. Professor Evans-Pritchard speculated that the Azande were describing the gall-bladder.

Nevertheless, the Azande attribute any misfortune, however, small, to *mangu*. Many people who possess *mangu* do not know it; since the spirit of witchcraft leaves the witch at night to attack the victim's spirit, such dirty work

could occur while the perpetrator is asleep and unaware. Nightmares are considered witch attacks. Sons of male witches inherit the condition from their fathers, while daughters receive *mangu* from their mothers. Children's *mangus* are small and inexperienced, so children cannot be accused of witchcraft until they are older. The Azande also believe that witchcraft emits a small, bright light, similar to that of fireflies or sparks, which is invisible except to other witches or to witch doctors, who are trained witch-hunters (see WITCHES' LIGHT).

The Azande attribute little witchcraft activity to SORCERY. Sorcery is possible, but unlikely unless a man has seen an *adandala*—a species of wildcat associated with witchcraft, the sight of which is fatal—or has touched his wife's menstrual BLOOD or seen her anus.

Witches among the Azande call each other to meetings where they learn each other's techniques, discuss crimes and rub their bodies with a special ointment called *mbiro mangu*. A particularly successful supernatural killing may be celebrated by feasting on the revived body of the victim. Their familiars, both animal and human, accompany them and goad them on to greater evil. Whereas European witches were said to prefer CATS, dogs and TOADS as familiars, African witches chose owls, bats, hyenas, baboons, zombies or, among the Xhosa, "hairy dwarves."

To identify a witch, relatives of the sick first consult the iwa oracle, a rubbing board operated with a wooden instrument. The names of possible suspects are placed before the *iwa*, and the oracle selects the culprit and his or her accomplices. Then the family verifies the witch's name via the *benge* oracle: chickens are given poison while a list of names is read aloud. If a chicken dies while a particular person's name is called, that person is guilty.

At that point, a wing from the unlucky chicken is cut off and attached to a stick like a fan. One of the sick man's relatives takes it to a deputy of the neighboring chief, to maintain impartiality, and the deputy carries the fan to the home of the suspected witch. The suspect's reaction and apparent sincerity are most important; if the suspect claims innocence and begs his *mangu* to stop bothering the sick person, recovery may occur. If not, the procedure is repeated. If the suspect is a respected figure in the community, the relatives may announce they know witchcraft is behind their relative's illness without naming names. Their discretion in the affair appeals to the pride and honor of the suspected witch, and he may stop the spell in appreciation.

Members of the Tswana peoples deny the possibility of an uncontrollable *mangu*; for them, all witchcraft involves malice aforethought. They do, however, distinguish between "night witches" and "day sorcerers." Day sorcerers, called *baloi ba motshegare*, use magic to inflict harm through the use of herbs and other medicinal preparations on a specific enemy and do not practice witchcraft habitually.

Night witches, or *baloi ba bosigo,* are mainly elderly women who gather at night in small groups and then travel about the countryside bewitching the unfortunate. Instead of wearing clothes, they smear their bodies with white ashes or the blood of the dead. Admission is open to anyone, but the applicant must profess her zeal by causing the death of a close relative, usually a first-born child. Initiates receive an ointment that allows them to wake instantly and join their colleagues when called. Some tribes say that a special medicine is injected into the witch's thumb, and when her thumb itches, she will awake and depart.

Among their alleged activities is the exhumation of newly buried corpses, which the night witches accomplish by using a special magic that makes the body float to the surface. The witches then take whatever body parts they need for their spells and medicines. Walls and locked doors cannot keep a witch from entering a victim's house; once inside, the witch cuts her victim and inserts small stones or fragments of flesh that will sicken him and eventually cause death unless treated.

Night witches choose OWLS as their familiars and ride on hyenas to cover great distances, with one foot on the hyena's back and one on the ground. Members of the BaKgatla tribe say that the witches make their own hyenas from porridge and then activate them with special medicines.

Although beliefs in night witches are widely held, many Africans take such stories lightly, acknowledging that no one has seen *baloi ba bosigo* at work. But the activities of day sorcerers are taken seriously, as many people have seen the results of *go jesa* ("to feed"), or the practice of putting poison in food or drink. In some accounts the poison changes into a miniature crocodile, gnawing away at the victim's insides until he dies in pain. But most accounts describe true poison, acting so slowly that suspicions are not aroused until the victim is seriously ill or dying, and making identification and indictment of the poisoner very difficult.

FURTHER READING:

Evans-Pritchard, E. E. *Witchcraft, Oracles and Magic Among the Azande* (abridged). Oxford: Clarendon Press, 1983.

Mair, Lucy. *Witchcraft.* New York: McGraw-Hill World University Library, 1969.

Middleton, John, ed. Magic, *Curing & Witchcraft.* Austin: University of Texas Press, 1967.

Parrinder, Geoffrey. *Witchcraft European and African.* London: Faber & Faber, 1970.

aiguillette   A knotted loop of thread, also called a *ligature,* which witches were said to use to cause impotence, and perhaps even castration, in men; barrenness in women; and general discontent in marriage. The *aiguillette* also served to bind couples in illicit amatory relationships.

The phobia of the ligature, or fear of satanic castration, was widespread in 16th-century France. It was believed that at the instant when a priest blessed a new marriage, the witch slipped behind the husband, knotted a thread and threw a coin on the ground while calling the Devil. If the coin disappeared, which all believed to mean that the Devil took it and kept it until Judgment Day, the couple was destined for unhappiness, sterility and adultery.

Couples living in Languedoc were so fearful of satanic castration that not 10 weddings in 100 were performed publicly in church. Instead, the priest, the couple and their parents went off in secret to celebrate the sacrament. Only then could the newlyweds enter their home, enjoy the feasting and go to bed. At least one physician, Thomas Platter, concluded that the panic was so bad that there was a local danger of depopulation.

See also MALEFICIA.

Aix-en-Provence Possessions   The burning alive of Father Louis Gaufridi for BEWITCHMENT of the nuns at Aix in 1611 formed the legal precedent for the conviction and execution of Urbain Grandier at Loudun more than 20 years later. This case was one of the first in France to produce a conviction based on the testimony of a possessed demoniac. Prior to the 17th century in France, accusations from a demoniac were considered unreliable, since most clerics believed that any words spoken by one possessed by the Devil were utterances from "the father of lies" (John 8:44) and would not stand up to accepted rules of evidence. As in Loudun, sexual themes dominated the manifestations of the nuns' possession (see POSSESSION).

In *The World of the Witches* (1961), historian Julio Caro Baroja comments that "in the history of many religious movements, particularly those which have to struggle against an Established Church, an important part is played by men who have a physical and sexual power over groups of slightly unbalanced women in addition to strong spiritual powers." By the 17th century, the Catholic Church was fighting to stem the tide of Reformation through miraculous cures and demonstrations of faith and by the TORTURE of heretics and WITCHES. Baroja continues: "At a later stage [in the religious movement] we find such people formally accused of being sorcerers and magicians . . . and causing the women they had abused [or seduced] to be possessed by the Devil." Baroja finds Father Gaufridi to be the perfect example, concluding that if he indeed was guilty of sexual crimes, he certainly was not a Satanist (see SATANISM).

Nevertheless, Father Gaufridi was convicted by his own confession following torture and the accusations of two nuns: Sister Madeleine Demandolx de la Palud and Sister Louise Capel. Gaufridi recited his DEVIL'S PACT for the inquisitors, in which he renounced all spiritual and physical goodness given him by God, the Virgin Mary and all the saints, giving himself body and soul to Lucifer. Sister Madeleine also recited her pact, renouncing God and the saints and even any prayers ever said for her.

Gaufridi was burned alive, and the two nuns were banished from the convent.

Two years later, in 1613, the possession epidemic at Aix spread to nearby Lille, where three nuns accused Sister Marie de Sains of bewitching them. Most notable about Sister Marie's testimony, in many ways a copy of Sister Madeleine's earlier pact, was her detailed description of the witches' SABBAT: The witches copulated with devils and each other in a natural fashion on Mondays and Tuesdays, practiced sodomy on Thursday, and bestiality on Saturdays and sang litanies to the Devil on Wednesdays and Fridays. Sunday, apparently, was their day off.

FURTHER READING:
Baroja, Julio Caro. *The World of the Witches.* 1961. Reprint, Chicago: University of Chicago Press, 1975.

allotriophagy   The vomiting or disgorgement of strange or foul objects, usually associated with someone possessed by or obsessed with the DEVIL or other DEMONS (see POSSESSION). Such actions also once were seen as illusions or SPELLS caused by witches or as attempts at suicide by the mentally deranged. Most treatises on possession written during the Renaissance and later included the vomiting of unusual objects as an indication that the Devil had entered a person's body. The objects vomited by the victim could be anything from live animals, such as toads, snakes, worms or butterflies, to pieces of iron, nails, small files, pins, needles, feathers, stones, cloth, shards of glass, hair, seaweed or foam.

Simon Goulart, a 15th-century historian, tells of a young girl whose abdomen continually swelled as if she were pregnant. Upon receiving drugs, the girl began vomiting a huge mass of hair, food, wax, long iron nails and brass needles. In another account, Goulart says a man named William, succumbing to the fervent prayers of his master's wife, Judith, began vomiting the entire front part of a pair of shepherd's trousers, a serge jacket, stones, a woman's peruke (hairpiece), spools of thread, needles and a peacock feather. William claimed that the Devil had placed the items in his throat. Finally, Goulart relates the case of 30 children in Amsterdam in 1566 who became frenzied, vomiting pins, needles, thimbles, bits of cloth and pieces of broken jugs and glass. Efforts by doctors, exorcists and sorcerers had no effect, and the children suffered recurrent attacks.

Alrunes   In German and Scandinavian myth, the Alrunes are sorceresses or female DEMONS who can change shape; they are believed to be the mothers of the Huns. As late as the 19th century in some rural areas, they were personified by small statues, which were kept in the home, clothed and made offerings of food and drink. It was believed that the Alrunes could divine the future by responding to questions with motions of the head. If the statues were not properly cared for, they were said to cry out, which would bring great misfortune to the household.

altar   Elevated place where religious ceremonies are conducted and where offerings are made to a deity or deities. The altar has ancient associations with the GODDESS and Mother Earth, who rule the wheel of birth-death-rebirth.

In WICCA and PAGANISM, the altar is placed within a MAGIC CIRCLE. It usually faces either east or north, depending on the tradition and practices of the COVEN. There are no set rules in the Craft for the construction of the altar. If the ceremonies take place out of doors, rocks or tree stumps may be used. Indoors, the altar may be a table, a wooden box or a board placed on boxes or bricks. Whatever the form or materials, the altar should not contain conductive metals such as iron or steel, since they could interfere with the energy of the ritual tools made of iron or steel (see WITCHES' TOOLS). Since many covens meet in homes or apartments where space is at a premium, the altar may not be permanent but erected only during ceremonies.

The objects of RITUAL and worship placed on the altar vary, depending upon the practices of the coven and the rituals to be performed. They may include an athame (a black-handled knife that is the Witch's primary magical tool), a white-handled knife, a sword, a wand, CANDLES, a cup or goblet of wine, anointing OILS, dishes for SALT and WATER, a necklace without beginning or end, a censer, BELLS, scourges, dishes for offering food and drink to the deities and images of the deities, such as figurines, wax statues or drawings. If a BROOM and CAULDRON are needed in rituals, they are placed on either side of the altar.

The altar is never used for blood SACRIFICE, which is prohibited in Wicca and Paganism.

In the GREAT RITE, which is actual or symbolic ritual sex, the body of the high priestess is considered an altar of the sacred forces of life, which echoes back to the ancient connection of altar to the Mother GODDESS.

During the witch hunts, it was believed that at witches' SABBATS, the woman who was high sorceress or high priestess served as both living altar and sacrifice to the DEVIL. "On her loins a demon performed Mass, pronounced the *Credo,* deposited the offertory of the faithful," observes historian Jules Michelet in *Satanism and Witchcraft.* According to Michelet, the eucharist at these sabbats consisted of a cake baked upon the altar of the woman: "It was her life, her death, they ate. The morsel was impregnated already with the savour of her burning flesh."

These accounts of sabbats were extracted under TORTURE and were fiction to satisfy inquisitors.

FURTHER READING:
Buckland, Raymond. *Buckland's Complete Book of Witchcraft.* St. Paul: Llewellyn Publications, 1986.

Crowley, Vivianne. *Wicca: The Old Religion in the New Millennium.* Revised ed. London: Thorsons/Harper Collins, 1996.
Farrar, Stewart. *What Witches Do: A Modern Coven Revealed.* Custer, Wash.: Phoenix Publishing Co., 1983.

amber A yellow-gold, fossilized resin with electrical properties, highly prized since prehistoric times and worn as jewelry to protect against WITCHCRAFT, SORCERY and POISONS. Only the pearl is older than amber in use as jewelry and AMULETS. Amber was heavily traded by the Phoenicians. The ancient Romans used it to cure headaches and throat infections, and considered a phallus made of amber to be the ultimate protection against the EVIL EYE.

Amber also is considered a bringer of good luck and a protector of health. It is believed to help women in labor, to keep a person cool in the hot sun and to remedy failing eyesight, earaches and a host of intestinal and kidney ailments. Jet, or black amber, has similar properties. In Iceland, jet serves as a protective amulet. In medieval Europe, jet was burned to drive away evil spirits.

FURTHER READING:
Farrar, Janet, and Stewart Farrar. *A Witches Bible Compleat.* New York: Magickal Childe, 1984.

amulets Objects imbued with magical properties that protect against bad luck, illness and evil. Amulets are universal and are answers to age-old needs: to be healthy; to be virile and fertile; to be powerful and successful; to have good fortune. To ancient humans, these needs were controlled by the invisible forces of good and evil. PRAYERS, SACRIFICES and offerings induced the good spirits to grant blessings; amulets prevented the evil spirits from taking them away.

Early amulets were natural objects whose unusual shapes or colors attracted attention. The magical properties of such objects were presumed to be inherent. As civilization advanced, amulets became more diverse. They were fashioned into animal shapes, symbols, RINGS, seals and plaques, and were imbued with magical power with inscriptions or SPELLS (see ABRACADABRA).

The term *amulet* comes from either the Latin word *amuletum* or the Old Latin term *amoletum,* which means "means of defense." The Roman naturalist, Pliny, defined three basic types of amulets: those offering protection against trouble and adversity; those providing a medical or prophylactic treatment; and substances used in medicine. Within these three general categories are many subdivisions, for no one amulet is broadly multipurpose. Amulets with inscriptions are also called CHARMS. An amulet typically is worn on the body—usually hung around the neck—but some amulets guard tombs, homes and buildings.

The ancient Egyptians, Assyrians, Babylonians, Arabs and Hebrews placed great importance in amulets. The Egyptians used them everywhere. The frog protected fertility; ankhs were linked to everlasting life and generation; the *udjat,* or eye of Horus, was for good health, comfort and protection against evil; the scarab beetle was for resurrection after death and protection against evil magic. Some Egyptian amulets are huge: a stone beetle mounted on a pedestal at Karnak (now at the British Museum) measures five feet long by three feet wide, and weighs more than two tons.

The Assyrians and Babylonians used cylinder seals that were imbedded with semiprecious and precious stones, each stone having its own unique magical powers (see STONES). Various animal shapes served as amulets; for example, the ram for virility, and the bull for virility and strength.

The Arabs gathered dust from tombs and carried it in little sacks as protection against evil. They also wore pieces of paper on which were written prayers, spells, magical names or the highly powerful attributes of God, such as "the compassionate" and "the forgiver."

Hebrews wore crescent moons to ward off the EVIL EYE and attached BELLS to their clothing to ward off evil spirits.

The natives of the west coast of Africa carry amulets which Western explorers named fetishes (see FETISH). A fetish consists of a pouch or box of "medicine" such as plants, fruits or vegetables, animal hair, paws, dung or livers, snake heads, SPITTLE and URINE. Natives believe that the fetish also contains a god or spirit who will help the wearer of the fetish obtain his or her desire.

Two amuletic symbols that are nearly universal throughout history are eyes and phallic symbols. Eyes protect against evil spirits and are found on many tombs and walls, and on utensils and jewelry. The phallic symbol, as represented by horns and hands, protects against the evil eye.

The names of God and gods, and magical words and numbers, have provided amuletic protection since antiquity; they were particularly popular from the Renaissance to the early 19th century, when the GRIMOIRES, books of magical instruction, were written. In MAGIC, using the name of a deity taps into divine power. In the Old Testament, the Hebrews gave the personal name of God as a four-letter word called the tetragrammaton, transliterated as YHWH and pronounced "Yahweh." This name appeared in different spellings on many amulets and TALISMANS to help magicians conjure DEMONS and protect them from attack by the spirits (see NAMES OF POWER).

Some magical words and numbers are arranged in patterns of squares. One of the best known of these is the "Sator square":

S	A	T	O	R
A	R	E	P	O
T	E	N	E	T
O	P	E	R	A
R	O	T	A	S

Although numerous attempts have been made to translate the Sator square into something that makes sense, it remains nonsensical. It was inscribed on walls and vessels as early as ancient Rome and was considered an amulet against SORCERY, poisonous air, colic and pestilence, and for protecting cow's milk from witchcraft.

Holy books such as the Koran, Torah and Bible are considered to have protective powers. Bits of parchment with scripture quotes, carried in leather pouches or silver boxes, are amulets in various religions. Ancient pagans wore figurines of their gods as amulets. This custom was absorbed into the Catholic Church.

In Wicca, the most powerful amulet is the silver pentacle, the religious symbol of the Craft (see PENTACLE AND PENTAGRAM). SILVER has amuletic properties and is used in jewelry along with various crystals and gems. The sign of the pentacle, called a *pentagram,* is traced in the air in rituals done to protect sacred sites, homes and other places. Other amulets are made from herbs and various ingredients, which are placed in a charm bag (also called a GRIS-GRIS).

FURTHER READING:

Budge, E. A. Wallis. *Amulets and Superstitions.* 1930. Reprint, New York: Dover Publications, 1978.

Lockhart, J. G. *Curses, Lucks and Talismans.* 1938. Reprint, Detroit: Single Tree Press, 1971.

Thomas, Keith. *Religion and the Decline of Magic.* New York: Charles Scribner's Sons, 1971.

Anderson, Victor (1917–2001)   Cofounder of the Feri (formerly Faery) Tradition of Witchcraft. Victor H. Anderson was born on May 21, 1917, in Clayton, New Mexico. When he was a young child, his family moved to Bend, Oregon. An uncorrected condition or ailment left him nearly blind for life.

In Oregon, Anderson met and was initiated at about age nine into the Craft by Witches who called themselves FAERIES. He came upon a small, old woman sitting naked in the center of a circle alongside brass bowls filled with herbs (see MAGIC CIRCLE). She told him he was a Witch. Instinctively, he took off his clothes and was sexually initiated. He experienced a vision, which he could see clearly despite his nearblindness, in which he floated in black space, holding on to the woman (who became the GODDESS), until he suddenly found himself in a junglelike setting under a vast sky filled with stars and a green moon. Coming toward him was the HORNED GOD, a beautiful and powerful man, yet effeminate, with an erect phallus. His head was horned, and from his head came a blue flame. After some communications with the deities, the vision vanished and Anderson returned to the present. He sat in the circle with the old woman and was taught the ritual use of the herbs and teas in the brass bowls. She washed him in butter, oil and SALT. He dressed and returned home.

Anderson worked in a COVEN; most of the coveners hailed from the American South and practiced a type of Witchcraft (there were no "traditions" then) that was not so much a religion but more a "devotional science," a way of living that emphasized harmony with nature, MAGIC, celebration, music and ecstatic dancing. They revered Pagan deities, which they called "The Old Gods" and "The Old Powers," but did not have the developed theologies of more modern Craft traditions.

In 1944, Anderson married a northern Alabama woman, Cora, who came from a family of Christians who practiced folk MAGIC. The two had meetings on the astral plane for several years before meeting in the physical. In the 1950s the Andersons broke up a fistfight between their only son and a neighbor boy. The boy, who years later changed his name to GWYDION PENDDERWEN, became a good friend of the family and was initiated into Witchcraft by the Andersons. The publication of GERALD B. GARDNER's book, *Witchcraft Today,* inspired Anderson to form his own coven. He and Pendderwen cofounded and wrote most of the rituals for the Faery Tradition, named after the Faery Witches Anderson worked with as a child. After Pendderwen's meeting with Alexandrian-tradition Witches in England, he and Anderson incorporated material from the Alexandrian BOOK OF SHADOWS into the Faery Tradition, later renamed Feri.

Anderson lived with his wife in the Bay Area of California. He authored a book of Craft poems, *Thorns of the Blood Rose.* Anderson initiated STARHAWK into the Craft. He also was a Kahuna and a bokor shaman. He earned his living as a musician, playing the accordion and singing.

FURTHER READING:

"Victor H. Anderson." Witchvox.com. URL: http:www.witchvox.com/va/dt_va.html?a=usca&c=passages&id=3624. Downloaded October 17, 2007.

ankh   The Egyptian symbol of life, regeneration, the universe and immortality, the ankh, which means "life" and "hand mirror," is a tau, or looped cross. Wiccans and Pagans wear it as an AMULET against negativity and as a TALISMAN for good fortune and benevolent forces. It also represents the union of the male principle (the staff) and the female principle (the closed loop).

Egyptian art shows the ankh being carried as a scepter in the right hand of deities and being applied to the nostrils of the dead in order to bring them back to life. Ankh amulets were made of faience, semiprecious and precious stones, wax, metal and wood. Tutankhamen had a hand mirror in the shape of an ankh.

Egyptians who converted to Christianity from the first century on used both the ankh and the Christian cross as their signs.

anointing oils   See OILS.

apples   Apples, cultivated in Britain as early as 3000 B.C.E., have had a long association with MAGIC, WITCHES and goddesses. Magic apple lands, whose fruit gave eternal life, were cultivated by various Western pagan goddesses, among them the Greek Hera, the Scandinavian Idun (Idhunn), the Teutonic Freya and the Norse Hel, Queen of the Underworld. In Iroquois myth, the apple is the central tree of heaven. In Christianity, the apple offered Eve by the serpent is the fruit of life but becomes equated with sin.

Games and DIVINATION with apples were part of the Celtic/Druidic harvest festival of Samhain (All Hallow's Eve), now celebrated on October 31 (see WHEEL OF THE YEAR). A surviving custom is the dunking for apples on this night. According to another custom, peeling an apple in front of a candlelit mirror on Samhain will reveal an image of one's future spouse.

Magical fermented cider may have been used in other pagan rites. In parts of England, another name for strong cider is *witches' brew*. Apples and apple peel are used in divination methods common in the British Isles.

In English lore, the apple tree is synonymous with enchantment and associated with figures in the Arthurian legends. Arthur, upon being mortally wounded, was spirited by three fairy queens to the magical place of Avalon, "Isle of the Apples" or "appleland," ruled by MORGAN LE FAY, the crone or Mother Death aspect of the Triple Goddess. Arthur's knight Lancelot fell asleep under a grafted apple tree and was carried off by four fairy queens. Queen Guinevere gave an apple to St. Patrick, who died; she was accused of WITCHCRAFT and condemned to burn at the stake, but was rescued by Lancelot.

Witches who wished to bewitch or poison others were often said to use apples, as in the folktale of Snow White, who was put to sleep by the poisoned apple of the black witch-queen. In 1657 Richard Jones, a 12-year-old boy in Shepton Mallet in the county of Somerset in England, was said to be bewitched by a girl who gave him an apple. Jones suffered fits, and neighbors said they saw him fly over his garden wall. The girl, Jane Brooks, was charged with witchcraft, convicted and hanged on March 26, 1658.

According to English folklore, it is bad luck to pick all the apples in a harvest: some must be left for the FAIRIES.

The apple is a love charm in VODUN, and in English, Danish and German folklore.

See POSSESSION.

FURTHER READING:
Leach, Maria, ed., and Jerome Fried, assoc. ed. *Funk & Wagnall's Standard Dictionary of Folklore, Mythology and Legend.* New York: Harper & Row, 1972.
Opie, Iona, and Moira Tatem. *A Dictionary of Superstitions.* New York: Oxford University Press, 1989.

Aquarian Tabernacle Church   Interfaith church of WICCA and Earth Religions, formed in 1979 in Index, Washington, by Pete "Pathfinder" Davis, to support the Wiccan and Pagan communities. The Aquarian Tabernacle Church, or "Tab," as it is known, is recognized as a church in the United States, Canada, Australia, Ireland and South Africa. David is Archpriest and Deborah K. Hudson is Archpriestess. Membership is open.

Davis, a native of Jersey City, New Jersey, was initiated into the Dorpat tradition, a small and secretive tradition of the Craft, on August 14, 1974, in Patterson, New Jersey. In 1976, he relocated to the Seattle area and established the Tab based on English Traditional Wicca. In 1983, he was initiated into the Coven of the Stone and Staff of the New Wiccan Church.

The Tab grew in size, attracting Wiccans and Pagans from diverse traditions. In 1984, a Moonstone Circle of tall standing menhirs was constructed and dedicated for the Tab. Liturgy was formalized the following year. Tax status as a church was obtained in 1988.

The role of the church has expanded, and it has been involved in gaining acceptance for Wicca as a religion in Washington prisons; coordinating Wiccan and Pagan interests in the Interfaith Council of Washington State (Davis has served as president); establishing SpiralScouts for youth; and establishing the Woolston-Steen Seminary for the training of clergy.

JANET AND STEWART FARRAR established the ATC-Eire church in Ireland in 1999. The church was a leader in the PENTACLE QUEST campaign to allow Wiccan and Pagan veterans to put symbols of their faith on their headstones.

In 2006, Davis and his working partner, E'bet Tennis, were initiated into the third degree in Alexandrian and British Traditional Wicca.

FURTHER READING:
The Aquarian Tabernacle Church Web site. URL: http://www.aquattabch.org/about/atc/pagantree.php. Downloaded October 12, 2007.

Aradia   The Tuscan legend of Aradia, daughter of the moon goddess DIANA who was dispatched to earth to establish witchcraft and teach it to witches, was published by the American folklorist, CHARLES GODFREY LELAND, in 1889. Leland said the legend had been passed on to him by a hereditary Etruscan witch named Maddalena. Godfrey said the name *Aradia* is a corruption of *Herodias,* or Queen Herodias, the wife of Herod, with whom Diana came to be identified by the 11th century.

Leland went to Tuscany in northern Italy in the 1880s. There he met a "sorceress" named Maddalena, whom he employed to collect from her witch "sisters" old spells and traditions. In 1886, he heard about a manuscript that supposedly set down the old tenets of witchcraft. He told Maddelana to find it. A year later, she gave him a document in her own handwriting, an alleged copy of this manuscript.

Leland translated it into English and published it as *Aradia, or the Gospel of the Witches.* He was struck by the references to Diana and Lucifer, and offered it as evidence of witchcraft as an old religion. In his preface, he acknowledged drawing from other, unspecified sources. He never produced Maddalena or any documentation to verify her existence.

Aradia recounts the story of Diana's daughter and of Diana's rise to become Queen of the Witches. Diana is created first among all beings and divides herself into light and darkness. She retains the darkness and makes the light into Lucifer (whose name means "light-bearer"), her brother and son. She falls in love with him and seduces him by changing herself into a cat. Their daughter from that union, Aradia, is destined to become "the Messiah of witches." Aradia lives for a while in heaven and then is sent to earth by Diana to teach the arts of witchcraft, especially poisoning and malevolent acts against "oppressors":

> And thou shalt be the first of witches known;
> And thou shalt be the first of all i' the world;
> And thou shalt teach the art of poisoning,
> Of poisoning those who are the great lords of all;
> Yea, thou shalt make them die in their palaces;
> And thou shalt bind the oppressor's soul (with power);
> And when ye find a peasant who is rich,
> Then ye shall teach the witch, your pupil, how
> To ruin all his crops with tempests dire,
> With lightning and with thunder (terrible),
> And with the hail and wind . . .
> And when a priest shall do you injury
> By his benedictions, ye shall do to him
> Double the harm, and do it in the name
> Of me, Diana, Queen of witches all!

When Aradia's task is finished, Diana recalls her daughter to heaven and gives her the power to grant the desires of the meritorious witches who invoke Aradia. Such requests include success in love, and the power to bless friends and curse enemies, as well as:

> To converse with spirits.
> To find hidden treasures in ancient ruins.
> To conjure the spirits of priests who died leaving treasures.
> To understand the voice of the wind.
> To change water into wine.
> To divine with cards.
> To know the secrets of the hand [palmistry].
> To cure diseases.
> To make those who are ugly beautiful.
> To tame wild beasts.

The invocation for Aradia is given as follows:

> Thus do I seek Aradia! Aradia! Aradia! At midnight, at midnight I go into a field, and with me I bear water, wine, and salt, *I bear water, wine, and salt,* and my talisman—*my talisman, my talisman,* and a red small bag which I ever hold in my hand—*con dentro, con dentro, sale,* with salt in it, *in it.* With water and wine I bless myself, *I bless myself* with devotion to implore a favor from Aradia, Aradia.

Frontispiece to Aradia

The truth about the origins of *Aradia* may never be known. Some skeptics believe that Leland fabricated the entire story, or that he was duped by Maddalena, who made it up. A more likely scenario, put forward by scholar RONALD HUTTON, is that Maddalena, pressed to deliver, collected some authentic bits of lore and embellished them. Leland, who is known to have embellished his other folklore accounts, probably added his own flourishes. Contemporary folklore scholars do not accept *Aradia* as authentic.

Aradia had little impact on contemporary European Witchcraft, but enjoyed more prominence in America.

In contemporary Witchcraft, *Aradia* is one of the most often used names for the GODDESS.

FURTHER READING:
Adler, Margot. *Drawing Down the Moon.* Revised ed. New York: Viking, 1986.
Clifton, Chas S., ed. *Witchcraft Today: Book One The Modern Craft Movement.* St. Paul: Llewellyn Publications, 1993.

Farrar, Janet, and Stewart Farrar. *A Witches Bible Compleat.* New York: Magickal Childe, 1984.

Leland, Charles G. *Aradia: Gospel of the Witches.* Custer, Wash.: Phoenix Publishing, 1990.

Arianrod   Welsh goddess of the dawn, famed for her beauty, whose name means "silver wheel" or "silver circle." Arianrod is a significant figure in WICCA and PAGANISM. She was worshiped as a virgin/fertility goddess and as a lunar goddess. She was the mistress of GWYDION THE WIZARD and bore twin sons, Llew Llaw Gyffes (the counterpart to the Irish Lugh) and Dylan, a god of the sea. She is associated with the constellation Corona Borealis, which is also known as Caer Arianrod.

Ár nDraíocht Féin (ADF)   The largest Pagan Druid organization and church in the world. *Ár nDraíocht Féin* is Irish Gaelic for "Our Own Druidism."

The ADF has no direct links to the ancient Druids but is a reconstruction of Druidic and Indo-European pagan rituals and religious traditions. It was founded in 1983 by P. E. I. ISAAC BONEWITS, former Archdruid of several groves within the now defunct Reformed Druids of North America. Bonewits served as Archdruid for 10 years and remains active in the organization.

In an open letter in 1983, Bonewits outlined his vision for creating a modern, Neopagan Druidic religion. "I see Druids as being artists and intellectuals, magicians and clergy, holders of the highest wisdom their cultures (or subcultures) have to offer," he said.

ADF integrates religion with alternate healing arts, ecology-consciousness, psychic development and artistic expression. It is organized in groves, many of them named after trees. The oak tree is sacred, as it was to the ancient Druids. The groves observe eight seasonal High Days that coincide with the SABBATS observed in WICCA and conduct regular study and discussion groups and a wide range of artistic activities. Through study and training, members advance through a series of five circles, the fourth of which is the equivalent of a master's degree, and the fifth the equivalent of a doctorate. The idea of the circle structure was borrowed from the CHURCH OF ALL WORLDS.

Worship and rituals usually are conducted outdoors. ADF is polytheistic, and recognition of various deities depends on the individual grove and the purpose of the rites. The one deity who is worshiped at every ritual is the Earth-Mother (Mother Nature). The Three Kindreds of deities, ancestors and nature spirits of the Three Worlds—Land, Sea and Sky—are invoked. The Waters of Life, passed or asperged in rites, represent the spark of immanent deity.

Liturgy and rituals are based upon scholarly research of old Indo-European religious, folk magic, art and social customs. The research is ongoing and involves translation of numerous foreign and archaic language texts. The

ADF claims no unbroken lineages or traditions and does not promote any "one right and true way" of Druidism.

Bonewits identified five phases of liturgical design common in the religions of related Indo-European cultures:

1. The consecration of time and space; the psychic centering, grounding and unifying of the participants into a "groupmind."
2. The opening of the Gates Between the Worlds and the starting of a flow of energy back and forth between participants and deities.
3. The raising and sending of the major part of the congregation's energy to the deities being worshiped.
4. The returning of power from the deities to the congregation.
5. The reversing of the rite's beginnings and the closing down of the psychic, magical and spiritual energy fields that were created.

ADF rituals are not conducted within barriers such as a MAGIC CIRCLE, and participants can come and go while rituals are in progress.

Sacrifices made to the deities include tree branches, fruits, flowers and vegetables. Although animal, even human, sacrifices were performed in most paleo-Pagan religions, they are strictly forbidden in ADF rituals, as well as in neo-Paganism in general.

Clergy wear long white robes; members of the congregation are encouraged to dress in paleo-Pagan garb. Bonewits introduced the white beret as a signature of ADF; the berets and any headcoverings are removed upon entrance to a ritual site, except during very hot weather. The ADF's sigil, a circle pierced by two vertical parallel lines, was first associated with neo-Pagan Druidism by David Fisher, the founder of the Reformed Druids of North America. The sigil may have been taken from the shape of a foundation of an old Roman-Celtic temple. The logo, a branch sprouting from an oak tree stump, is a Celtic rendition inspired by the badge of the Scottish MacEwen clan.

The only piece of dogma espoused by the ADF is the Doctrine of Archdruidic Fallibility. The Archdruid does not have all the answers and can make mistakes.

FURTHER READING:

Ár nDraíocht Féin Web site. URL: http://www.adf.org. Accessed July 15, 2008.

Bonewits, Isaac. "*Ár nDraíocht Féin*: A Druid Fellowship." Witchvox.com. Available online. URL: http://www.witchvox.com/va/dt_va.html/a=usny&c=trads&id=3209. Downloaded August 14, 2007.

Arnold, Charles (1947–)   Wiccan priest and author, and a key figure in legal battles for the decriminalization of WICCA as a religion in Canada and for the right of Wiccan priests to perform legal marriages in the province of Ontario.

Born in Washington, D.C., in 1947, Charles Arnold served in the Vietnam War with the U.S. Army Security Agency. He moved to Canada after his discharge. He began practicing Witchcraft as a SOLITARY in the late 1970s, intuiting RITUALS and sensing innately that he had always been a Witch. He later was initiated in several traditions.

In Canada, Arnold became involved in the Wiccan Church of Canada for about two and a half years, serving on its board of directors and as secretary-treasurer. He left that organization in 1984 to found the Spendweik Coven, of which he later was named Elder. He resigned from that to help found and serve as executive director of Wicca Communitas, a nonprofit support and network organization for Wiccans and Pagans in southern Ontario. Wicca Communitas oversees the Temple of the Elder Faiths, a public organization of which Arnold was high priest until 1988. The Temple of the Elder Faiths was founded in 1986 as a non-initiatory public temple whose rituals and services are based largely on the PAGAN WAY. Its priesthood come from diverse traditions, including the well-established Gardnerian and Alexandrian traditions.

In 1986, Arnold undertook legal measures to have Wicca decriminalized by the Canadian government. The issue revolved around the granting of paid leave for two religious holidays, Beltane (April 30) and Samhain (October 31). Arnold had been denied paid leave by his employer, Humber College of Applied Arts and Technology in Toronto, where he worked as a secretary in the Equine Center. The college's contract with the Ontario Public Service Employees Union, of which Arnold was a member and officer, stated that time off with pay could be granted for religious reasons and could not be unduly withheld.

The process was long, contentious and stressful. The case went to the Ministry of Labor for arbitration. Arnold was backed by his union, and also received support from a Christian minister, Rev. Donald Evans of the United Church of Canada. Arnold was called upon to refute commonly held misconceptions about SATANISM, Devil-worship and animal or human SACRIFICE. He testified about the GODDESS, the HORNED GOD, the fundamentals of Wicca and its holidays, and his own involvement in the religion. His pastoral responsibilities, he told the arbitrators, were similar to those of a pastor or priest in any other religion, including planning and conducting worship services, teaching and counseling.

Evans testified that Wicca met his definition of a religion, as "a set of beliefs and practices of a community pertaining to a spiritual dimension in the cosmos and the practice of rituals designed to enable the participants to live their daily lives in relation to that spiritual dimension."

On December 9, 1987, the arbitrators found in favor of Arnold, awarding him two religious holidays each year with paid leave. They issued a 21-page statement that declared, "Wicca is obviously a religion. We are of the view that it would be unreasonable for the employer to continue its refusal to grant religious leave." The ruling noted that Wicca is "the modern survival of the ancient pagan religions of Western Europe which were suppressed following the conversion, in Roman times, to Christianity." It is secret and misunderstood, "which is not surprising," the ruling said, given "the well-known persecution to which its adherents were subjected by Christianity."

The ruling further said that "had the parties [to the college's collective bargaining agreement] intended to restrict this provision to leave for the purposes of majority or well-established religions, it is our view that they should have said so in much clearer language." That, however, probably would have violated human rights laws, the ruling observed.

At the same time, Arnold pursued another legal quest in applying to the Ministry of Consumer and Commercial Relations for a license to perform marriages. That was turned down on March 15, 1988, on the grounds that the application did not satisfy criteria of the Marriage Act: the denomination or tradition of the applicant must have been in existence for at least 25 years. Though Arnold provided information on his tradition and initiation as a high priest, the ministry said it did not sufficiently demonstrate "that his denomination had been permanently established both as to the continuity of its existence as well as its rites and ceremonies."

Arnold filed complaints about the application procedures with the Ontario Human Rights Commission and the Office of the Ontario Ombudsman. Years later, the province revised its rules for obtaining the license to marry, and Wiccans and Pagans may now qualify.

The legal issues took a heavy toll on Arnold, who had to contend with criticism from inside his own spiritual community that he had taken on these battles for personal publicity. By 1988, he had resigned from all offices and positions he held in various organizations across North America and withdrew to a more private life. In 1993, he and his second wife, Vykki, moved back to the United States, settling in Vykki's home state of Vermont.

By the late 1990s, Arnold resumed public speaking and activism work within the Wiccan-Pagan community. He was involved in the founding of The New Temple of Astarte, becoming high priest, and helped to organize other groups, among them The Temple of Our Lady of the Green Mountains (a branch of The Temple of Astarte) and the Temple Star Cloak—A Pagan Congregation.

Arnold moved to Perth Amboy, New Jersey. He has served as national coordinator of the Pagan Veterans Headstone Campaign, to gain the right of Wiccans and Pagans in the military to have symbols of their faiths on their tombstones, and as chairman of the United Pagan Temples of America.

Arnold is the author of articles and books, including *Goddessborn* (1987); *Ritual Art—Drawing the Body* (1997); and *Ritual Art—Drawing the Spirit* (2001).

FURTHER READING:
Bradley, Jeff. "Canada's Most Visible Witch." Available online. URL: http://www.holysmoke.org/wb/wb0037.htm. Downloaded September 14, 2007.
"Charles Arnold." Witchvox.com. Available online. URL: http://www.witchvox.com/vn/vn_detail/dt_pa.html'a= usnj&id=65436. Downloaded October 1, 2007.

Arras witches (1459–1460) A mass witch hunt in Arras, northern France. The accused were brutally tortured and promised their lives, then burned at the stake. The incident roused the ire of the duke of Burgundy, and eventually those executed were posthumously exonerated.

The witch hunt was one of the earliest in the region. Inquisitors used charges of witchcraft against heretics such as the Waldenses, or VAUDOIS, a religious sect under persecution. The Arras affair began at Langres in 1459, when a hermit, who may have been suspected of being one of the Vaudois, was arrested. Under TORTURE, he admitted attending a SABBAT (the Vaudois were said to hold nocturnal revelries in worship of the DEVIL) and named a prostitute and an elderly poet of Arras as his companions. The hermit was burned at the stake, and the inquisitors arrested and tortured his accomplices. They, in turn, confessed and named others.

A widening pool of accusations, arrests, tortures and confessions spread through Arras, including not only poor and feebleminded women but persons of importance. The inquisitor of Arras was spurred on by his zealous superiors, two Dominican monks. The Dominicans believed that one-third of the population of Europe were secret WITCHES, including numerous bishops and cardinals in the church. Anyone who was against burning witches was also a witch.

The accused were put on the rack and tortured. The soles of their feet were put into flames, and they were made to swallow vinegar and oil. They confessed to whatever the judges wanted, specifically, to attending the sabbat, where they bowed to the Devil and kissed his backside (see KISS OF SHAME), and then indulged in a sexual orgy. They also named others in accordance with the inquisitors' leading questions. The inquisitors lied to them, promising that in exchange for their confessions, they would be spared their lives and given only the mild punishment of a short pilgrimage. Instead they were sent to the stake, where they were publicly denounced and burned alive. As they died, some of them shrieked out to the onlookers, protesting their innocence and how they had been framed, but to no avail.

Some of the richer prisoners bribed their way out, but most were not so lucky. Their estates and possessions were seized. Eventually, the witch hunt took a severe toll on the commerce of the city. Arras was a trading and manufacturing center, and many ceased doing business there, out of fear that the merchants they dealt with would be arrested and have their monies seized.

At the end of 1460, Philip the Good, the duke of Burgundy, intervened, and the arrests stopped. In 1461 the Parlement of Paris demanded the release of some of those imprisoned; the remainder were freed by the bishop of Arras, who had been absent during the hysteria. Thirty years later, in 1491, the Parlement of Paris condemned the cruelty of the tortures and said the Inquisition had acted without due process.

See INQUISITION.

FURTHER READING:
Parrinder, Geoffrey. *Witchcraft European and African.* London: Faber & Faber, 1970.
Robbins, Rossell Hope. 1959. Reprint, *The Encyclopedia of Witchcraft & Demonology.* New York: Bonanza Books, 1981.
Summers, Montague. *The Geography of Witchcraft.* London: Kegan Paul, Trench, Truner & Co. Ltd., 1927.

Artemis See DIANA.

Astarte (also Ashtart, Ashtoreth) In ancient Phoenicia, the great GODDESS of fertility, motherhood and war. She is the counterpart to the Babylonian goddess ISHTAR and is one of the oldest Middle Eastern aspects of the Goddess, dating to the Neolithic and Bronze Ages. Tammuz is identified as her son/consort, as he is with Ishtar. According to myth, Astarte descended to earth as a fiery star, landing near Byblos in a lake at Alphaca, the site where the original Tammuz is said to have died.

The Phoenicians portrayed Astarte with cow horns, representing fertility. Ancient Assyrians and Babylonians portrayed her caressing a child. She was associated with the moon and called the Mother of the Universe, giver of all life on Earth. She was ruler of all spirits of the dead, who lived in heaven in bodies of light and were visible on earth as stars. Her other counterparts are ISIS and Hathor of Egypt, Kali of India and Aphrodite and DEMETER of Greece.

The first recorded mention of Astarte's name dates back to 1478 B.C.E., but her cult was already well established by then. The cult of Astarte spread westward from Phoenicia into ancient Greece, Rome and as far as the British Isles. The goddess was worshiped with sexual rituals that were condemned by the prophets of the Old Testament. Sacrifices made to her included firstborn children and newborn animals.

Christians turned Astarte into a male DEMON, Astaroth.

Athena Greek GODDESS of wisdom, war, the arts, industry, justice and skill, and an important deity in WICCA and PAGANISM. Athena's mother was Metis, the goddess of wisdom, and her father was Zeus.

When Metis was pregnant, Zeus was afraid that she would bear a son who would be greater than he, so he swallowed Metis. Inside him, she began to hammer out a helmet for her daughter and make a robe. The hammering gave him a headache. His son Hephaestus, god of thunder and the forge, split his skull open, and out came a fully grown and clothed Athena.

Athena's symbols are the olive tree and the OWL.

Avebury   The most important and oldest megalithic henge in Britain, predating the DRUIDS with active use between 2600–1600 B.C.E. Avebury is said to be the largest henge in the world, covering 28.5 acres and including most of the village of Avebury, located six miles west of Marlborough in Wiltshire, southern England. The site may have served Neolithic GODDESS worship and is considered a center of Earth and psychic power by WICCANS, PAGANS and others. The original purpose of the stones is shrouded in mystery.

Site and layout.   The henge is surrounded on three sides by the Marlborough chalk downs and consists of a 15-foot-high bank, 1,200 feet in diameter, encircling an outer ditch. The bank is intersected by four roads, three of which, and possibly the fourth, are thought to have been causeways to provide access to and from the henge. From the air, Avebury looks like a Celtic, or circled, cross.

Within the large outer circle stand the ruins of two and perhaps three smaller circles. The outer Great Stone Circle once contained about 100 upright sarsen stones which are hard, sandstone rocks found in the downs. Only 27 remain, due to massive destruction by the Puritans in the 17th and 18th centuries. The largest of these weigh about 60 tons and stand around 25 feet tall.

The circle to the north is known as the Central Circle and was composed of about 30 stones, four of which still stand. In the center were three stones forming a ring called a Cove or Devil's Den; only two of the stones survive. The Cove may have been used for funeral rites for bodies that were buried elsewhere.

Standing alone between the main circle and the South Circle at the other end is a stone with a natural hole. It is now referred to as Stukeley's Ring Stone for William Stukeley, the 18th-century antiquarian-archaeologist whose investigations provided much of what is known about the site before modern developments.

The South Circle has two large stones still upright at its entrance. Originally there were about 32 stones, five of which remain, and there are markings where others once stood. Some theorists believe that this inner circle was the site of fertility ceremonies during which human bones were used.

A large stone, called the Obelisk, stands in the center with smaller stones, called Z stones, surrounding it. The Obelisk may have been the site for an ancestor cult, for human bones were found at its base. At this end are also some tall standing stones and smaller stones in triangle or diamond shapes, perhaps depicting the male and female forms.

A double row of stones forms West Kennet Avenue and leads toward the Kennet valley from the South Circle. Originally, the avenue comprised about 200 standing stones set in pairs and was the link between the Great Stone Circle and another small circle known as the Sanctuary, one mile away on Overton Hill. One researcher, Alexander Keiller, excavated the site in 1934 and found burials at the bases of four of the large stones. Keiller also learned that the avenue was crossed by early Iron Age and Roman field boundaries.

The Sanctuary might have been built on the site where wooden rings stood and where corpses were stored until the flesh decayed. The dead may have been carried along the avenue to this circle. The Sanctuary also was part of Stukeley's theory that the Druids were serpent worshipers and Avebury, like Stonehenge, was a serpent temple of 'Dracontia.' The Sanctuary was the head of a snake, the West Kennet Avenue stone paths formed the neck, and the sarsen circles were the coils of the body.

At the western entrance of the henge once stood Beckhampton Avenue. It was destroyed by the Puritans and now only two stones, known as Adam and Eve or the Longstones, stand. No one knows where the avenue ended, but it is thought to have extended a mile and a half. Stukeley claims that it stretched from the two stones to the sarsen circles. Sir Norman Lockyer, a 20th-century astronomer, asserted that the Beckhampton Avenue and Cove features were orientated to the May sunrise and May ceremonials, and the West Kennet Avenue was once used to observe the morning rise of Alpha Centauri in November.

Silbury Hill is built on a natural chalk ridge covering about five acres and rising 130 feet in height. It is the largest man-made mound in Europe, and while its purpose and relationship to Avebury have not been determined, the carbon date for its first phase of use is c. 2600 B.C.E. and suggests it was built about the time of the first construction stages of Avebury. However, West Kennet Long Barrow, a mound about 350 feet long with a long passage and five burial chambers, was built c. 2700 B.C.E.

Windmill Hill, 1.5 miles northwest of Avebury, has an earthwork on the top that was built around 2500 B.C.E. Animal bones uncovered here suggest it may have been a cattle market, trading post and ritual site.

The antiquarian John Aubrey visited Avebury in 1648 and observed that the stones were either standing in their original places or had fallen nearby. Shortly after, the Puritans began destroying sarsens by breaking them with hammers or by burning them. In 1649, stones were removed to clear the land for farming. Local inhabitants used them in their own buildings; fragments can still be seen in the village manor house, church and homes. Aubrey's notes provide modern investigators with their only clues for defining the stones' original positions.

Purpose and uses of the stones.   Excavations at Avebury and monuments in the surrounding area have failed to determine a definite origin, purpose or interrelationship among the stones. According to various theories, the entire site may have comprised a single religious, magical or psychic center, or one specific set of stones may have served as sites for fertility, religious or burial rites or for astronomical purposes.

The most widely accepted theory holds that Avebury was built by prehistoric Beaker folk, so named for their beaker pottery, over a period of five centuries. Beaker pottery has been found in the area, and timber buildings were uncovered at the site, suggesting that Avebury might have once been a settlement of huts. The name Avebury, however, implies that at some time in its history, it was a burial site and was referred to as such in the 10th-century charter of King Athelstan.

One scenario holds that Avebury was built for seasonal festivals, and the stones were arranged for processionals. Some observers see male and female aspects to the pillars and diamond shapes of the stones. Silbury Hill may be an image of the pregnant Goddess, another fertility symbol. Still another symbol is the Devil's Chair, a huge stone that measures 14 feet wide by 13 feet high and contains a ledge. In folk tradition, Avebury village girls would sit on Devil's Chair on Beltane (May Eve) to make wishes.

The stones of Avebury are widely believed to be the collectors and repositories of Earth and psychic energy, which supposedly was known to the original users of the site and which can be dowsed. The area around Avebury has been popular with the makers of crop circles.

See MEGALITHS.

FURTHER READING:
Burl, Aubrey. *Rites of the Gods*. London: J.M. Dent & Sons Ltd., 1981.
———. *Rings of Stone*. New York: Ticknor & Fields, 1979.
Hadingham, Evan. *Circles and Standing Stones*. New York: Anchor Books, 1976.

Awen   In Druidry, divine inspiration. "Awen" is Welsh for "gift of the gods" or "inspiration." Awen is especially associated with the poetic inspiration that comes to the bard in trance or altered state of consciousness. In Celtic lore, the goddess CERRIDWEN brews Awen in her CAULDRON. Three drops fall upon the fingers of Gwion, a youth who was her assistant, giving him great and magical knowledge.

In Druidry, Awen is chanted in ceremonies to receive divine inspiration and knowledge. It is part of making magic, the ability to manifest dreams and goals.

Baba Yaga In Russian folklore, a female witch who loved to roast and eat people, preferably children. She was as likely to pop a niece in the oven as she was a stranger. She lived in a little hut beyond a river of fire in the "thrice tenth kingdom." The hut was ringed with stakes topped by human heads. It stood on chickens' legs and dogs' heels and turned on command. Those who were brave enough to enter the hut usually found Baba Yaga lying on the floor with her right leg in one corner and her left leg in another, sometimes with her nose growing into the ceiling.

The Bony-Legged One, as Baba Yaga often was called, would cackle at her guests, "Fie! Fie! I smell a Russian bone!" If she didn't try to get them into the oven, she gave them advice.

Baba Yaga possessed a magic wand and flew in an IRON mortar (CAULDRON) that she spurred on with a pestle as she swept away her tracks with a BROOM. She had two or three sisters, also called Baba Yaga.

FURTHER READING:
Leach, Maria, ed., and Jerome Fried, assoc. ed. *Funk & Wagnall's Standard Dictionary of Folklore, Mythology and Legend.* New York: Harper & Row, 1972.

Babylonian Devil trap A terra-cotta bowl inscribed with CHARMS or magical texts to drive away evil. Babylonian Devil traps were common between the third to first centuries B.C.E. and sixth century C.E. They were adopted by captive Hebrews.

Baba Yaga

The bowls were inverted and buried under the four corners of the foundations of houses and buildings. Their magic was believed to protect against an assortment of evils, including male and female DEMONS, illness, CURSES and the EVIL EYE. Some inscriptions invoked God or quoted from Hebrew scriptures. One bowl from the 3rd century B.C.E. proclaims a "bill of divorce" to the DEVIL and all his night-monsters, ordering them to leave the community.

See AMULETS.

Baldrey, Tilly   See TOAD-WITCH.

Bamberg Witches   At the center of the worst witch tortures and trials in Germany was Bamberg, a small state ruled by Gottfried Johann Georg II Fuchs von Dornheim. The *Hexenbischof* (Witch Bishop) von Dornheim, as he was known, ruled the state from 1623 to 1633 and established an efficient witch-burning machine aided by the INQUISITION.

By the time von Dornheim reached power, witch-hunting had already been established in Bamberg, and at least 400 persons had been executed since 1609. Von Dornheim established an operation of lawyers, full-time torturers and executioners, led by Suffragan Bishop Friedrich Forner. A witch prison, a *Drudenhaus,* was built, with a capacity of 30 to 40 prisoners. A network of informers was encouraged, and the hunts began afresh in 1624. Accusations were not made public, and the accused were denied legal counsel.

Torture was the rule, not the exception, and was rigorously applied to all suspects. No one subjected to torture avoided confessing to attending SABBATS, desecrating the cross, having intercourse with DEMONS, poisoning persons (see POISONS) and other crimes. Victims were put in thumbscrews and vises, dumped in cold baths and in scalding lime baths, whipped, hung in the strappado (see TORTURE), burned with feathers dipped in sulphur, put in iron-spiked stocks and subjected to other forms of excruciating abuse. The torture did not stop even after condemnation. As they were led to the stake, prisoners had their flesh ripped with hot pincers or had their hands cut off.

Many prominent persons in Bamberg fell victim to the "machine," including all the burgomasters. Von Dornheim, meanwhile, confiscated their property and lined his own coffers. Anyone who showed sympathy for the victims or expressed doubt about their guilt became a victim as well, including the vice-chancellor of the diocese, Dr. George Haan. Haan tried to check the trials but was himself tried as a witch and burned at the stake along with his wife and daughter in 1628.

In 1627 von Dornheim built a *Hexenhaus* (Witch House), a larger, special prison for witches that contained both cells and torture chambers.

Some managed to escape Bamberg and went to appeal to Emperor Ferdinand for help. The emperor made an effort to intercede in one case but was defied by von Dornheim. Finally, political pressure forced Ferdinand to issue mandates opposing the persecutions in 1630 and 1631. The situation also was changed by the deaths of Forner in 1621 and von Dornheim in 1632.

As a result of the Bamberg trials, Ferdinand's son, Ferdinand II, decreed that in future trials, the accusations were to be made public, the defendants were to be allowed attorneys and no property could be confiscated.

Von Dornheim's cousin, Prince-Bishop Philipp Adolf von Ehrenberg, ruled over Würzburg, another small state, and subjected his citizens to the same type of terror. Between 1623 and 1631, when he died, von Ehrenberg tortured, beheaded and burned 900 persons, including at least 300 children three to four years of age.

See JOHANNES JUNIUS.

FURTHER READING:

Midelfort, H. C. Erik. *Witch Hunting in Southwestern Germany 1562–1684.* Stanford, Calif.: Stanford University Press, 1972.

Summers, Montague. *The Geography of Witchcraft.* London: Kegan Paul, Trench, Trubner & Co. Ltd., 1927.

Baphomet   The symbol of the "sabbatic goat," portrayed as a half-human, half-goat figure, or a goat head. It is not a symbol of modern WITCHCRAFT.

Baphomet by Eliphas Levi

The origin of the name *Baphomet* is unclear. It may be a corruption of *Mahomet* (Muhammad). The English witchcraft historian MONTAGUE SUMMERS suggested it was a combination of two Greek words, *baphe* and *metis,* meaning "absorption of knowledge." Baphomet has also been called the Goat of Mendes, the Black Goat and the Judas Goat.

In the Middle Ages the Baphomet was believed to be an idol, represented by a human skull, a stuffed human head or a metal or wooden human head with curly black hair. The idol was said to be worshiped by the Order of the KNIGHTS TEMPLAR as the source of fertility and wealth. In 1307 King Philip IV of France accused the Order of the Knights Templar of heresy, homosexuality and, among other things, worshiping this idol and anointing it with the fat of murdered children. However, only 12 of the 231 knights interrogated by the church admitted worshiping or having knowledge of the Baphomet. Novices said they had been instructed to worship the idol as their god and savior, and their descriptions of it varied: it had up to three heads and up to four feet; it was made of either wood or metal, or was a painting; sometimes it was gilt.

In 1818 a number of idols called *heads of Baphomet* were discovered among forgotten antiquities of the Imperial Museum of Vienna. They were said to be replicas of the Gnostic divinity Mete, or "Wisdom."

Perhaps the best-known representation of Baphomet is the drawing by the 19th-century French magician Eliphas Levi, called "the Baphomet of Mendes." Levi combined elements of the Tarot Devil card and the he-goat worshiped in antiquity in Mendes, Egypt, which was said to fornicate with its women followers (as the church claimed the Devil did with witches). Levi's Baphomet has a human trunk with rounded, female breasts, a caduceus in the midriff, human arms and hands, cloven feet, wings and a goat's head with a pentagram (see PENTACLE AND PENTAGRAM) in the forehead and a torch on top of the skull between the horns. The attributes, Levi said, represented the sum total of the universe—intelligence, the four ELEMENTS, divine revelation, sex and motherhood and sin and redemption. White and black crescent moons at the figure's sides represent good and evil.

ALEISTER CROWLEY named himself Baphomet when he joined the Ordo Templis Orientalis, a secret sexual magic order formed around 1896 in Germany.

FURTHER READING:
Thomas, Keith. *Religion and the Decline of Magic.* New York: Charles Scribner's Sons, 1971.
Waite, A. E. *The Book of Black Magic and of Pacts.* 1899. Reprint, York Beach, Me.: Samuel Weiser, 1972.

Bargarran Witches (1696–1697)   Scottish witchcraft hysteria started by a girl. The case bears similarities to the WARBOYS WITCHES and to the SALEM WITCHES, in which the fits of supposedly possessed children led to the executions of accused witches.

The cause of the hysteria was Christine Shaw, the 11-year-old daughter of John Shaw, the laird of Bargarran, near Paisley in Renfrewshire. On August 17, 1696, Shaw caught another girl, Catherine Campbell, stealing some of the Shaws' milk and threatened to expose her. Campbell responded by wishing Shaw would go to hell.

Possibly Shaw brooded about the insult and thought of ways to get back at Campbell. She apparently was in an ill humor, for on August 21 she sassed a woman, Agnes Naismith, who asked her how she was doing.

On August 22, Shaw fell into violent fits. She swallowed her tongue and went into extreme contortions. She claimed that the specters of Naismith and Campbell were torturing her and had forced her to swallow vile items that she then vomited up: wild bird feathers, soiled hay, eggshells, crooked PINS, hot cinders, small bones, hairballs and wads of candle grease. She showed this evidence on her bed, and the items were found to be exceptionally dry, as though they could not have come out of a stomach.

When in her fits, Shaw argued with the witches' specters and quoted Bible verses at them. She was examined by two doctors, who could not explain her affliction. She was sent away by her family to recover, and while away she was fine. As soon as she returned home, the fits and vomiting resumed.

Shaw widened her accusations, naming other people in a family who supposedly were witches tormenting her, cutting her body: Elizabeth Anderson, 17; her father, Alexander, a beggar; her grandmother, Jean Fulton; and two of her cousins, James, 14, and Thomas Lindsay, 11 or 12. Emboldened, Shaw also named two upper-class women, Margaret Lang and her daughter Martha Semple, 17.

The accusations and Shaw's ongoing afflictions caused an investigation to be launched on January 19, 1697. Lang and Semple were indignant. Some of the others readily confessed to being witches and in turn named others. Elizabeth Anderson admitted that she had often seen the DEVIL appear to her in the shape of a black man, accompanied by her grandmother. Furthermore, Elizabeth said she had attended local meetings of witches for at least seven years and said her father and another man were among Shaw's tormentors.

Thomas Lindsay at first protested his innocence and then admitted his guilt, saying he had signed a DEVIL's PACT. He said the Devil was his father and that he could fly like a crow whenever he pleased. He could cast SPELLS by uttering magical words and turning WIDDERSHINS, causing a plough to stand on its own and horses to break their yokes. Thomas said his brother James was with him at meetings with the Devil and the witches. James confessed. In all, 21 people were named by Shaw and then formally accused. Members of the Lindsay family were already thought to be witches, and examinations showed them to have WITCH's MARKS.

The investigators assembled the accused witches and brought Shaw before them. She gave more stories of torments, claiming she was levitated down her stairs, that objects were lifted as though by invisible hands and that her body was being harmed. She recoiled and fell into fits if any of the accused touched her.

Meanwhile, some of the accused confessed to more crimes than tormenting Shaw. They took credit for previous deaths, among them a minister, two children found strangled in their beds and two drowning victims on a ferryboat that sank.

On April 5, 1697, a new commission of judges was appointed. The accused were indicted and turned over to a jury on April 13. After seven hours of deliberation, the jury convicted seven of the 21 accused: three men, including James Lindsay, and four women, Lang, Semple, Naismith and the unfortunate Campbell, whose CURSE started the entire tragedy.

The seven were executed by hanging in Paisley. Their bodies were burned. According to lore, some were not quite dead when taken down from the gallows and thrown into the fire. A walking stick was borrowed from a spectator to poke their moving limbs back into the flames. The owner of the stick refused to take it back, saying he did not want it after it had touched witches.

After the executions, Shaw recovered and had no more fits. She married a minister in 1718. He died seven years later. She helped to bring Dutch machinery into Scotland for the manufacture of a high-quality thread, which was named after her family name, Bargarran. As a result, Paisley prospered as a wool center.

A HORSESHOE was set in Paisley to commemorate the execution place. Shaw's home eventually became a historical attraction.

In 1839, a small hole was discovered in Shaw's bedroom wall. It was speculated that perhaps she had had an accomplice who passed the "vomit" into her bedroom. The vomited items were suspiciously dry.

FURTHER READING:
Grant, James. *The Mysteries of All Nations: Rise and Progress of Superstition, Laws Against and Trials of Witches, Ancient and Modern Delusions, Together With Strange Customs, Fables and Tales.* Edinburgh: Leith, Reid & Son, n.d.
Robbins, Rossell Hope. *The Encyclopedia of Witchcraft & Demonology.* New York: Bonanza Books, 1981 (first published 1959).

bees   According to the demonologists of the INQUISITION, witches or sorceresses who managed to eat a queen bee before they were arrested would be able to withstand TORTURE and trial without confessing. This is one of the many ready explanations witch-hunters had for victims who refused to buckle under, thus enabling them to condemn the accused to death without confessions.

bell, book and candle   A phrase from the Roman Catholic ritual for excommunication that sometimes is used to denote a WITCH or WITCHCRAFT. Excommunication, or exclusion from the religious fellowship of the church, represents a condemnation to spiritual darkness, with repercussions in society. The excommunicated becomes an outcast in secular as well as religious life.

The rite is the equivalent of a CURSE and involves a BELL, the holy Book and a candle or CANDLES. The priest reads the following sentence:

> We exclude him from the bosom of our Holy Mother the Church, and we judge him condemned to eternal fire with Satan and his angels and all the reprobate, so long as he will not burst the fetters of the demon, do penance and satisfy the Church.

The priest then closes the book, rings a bell—a symbolic toll for death—extinguishes the candle and throws it down, which symbolizes the removal of the victim's soul from the sight of God.

The phrase "bell, book and candle" became associated with witches because the church believed them to be Devil-worshipers who should be excommunicated.

bells   Repellers of witches and evil spirits. Bells are associated with the divine: their sound is symbolic of creative power, their shape a symbol of the female force and the celestial vault. The sound vibrations created by the ringing of bells have been believed for centuries to possess magical and/or spiritual power. Bells are used in many religious rites. In WICCA and PAGANISM, small hand bells may be rung in rituals to enhance harmony and augment power. In African religions and VODUN, bells and dancing are used to invoke the gods and *loas* (see AFRICAN WITCHCRAFT). Shamans have long used magical bells in their rituals to chase away evil spirits.

In folk magic, the ringing of bells drives away evil spirits, witches and the DEVIL himself, and wards off the EVIL EYE. Bells have been attached to clothing, worn as AMULETS, tied to children and hung from the necks of horses, camels, cows, asses and other animals important to a community.

As fertility CHARMS, bells have been worn on human phalluses in certain rites. Bells are sometimes said to have curative powers; medicine is drunk from them. In the Middle Ages, bell ringing was believed to clear the air of disease and was prescribed by some doctors. Bells also have been used to raise the spirits of the dead and FAIRIES.

Since the fifth century C.E., Christian church bells have been ascribed a special magical potency to combat evil and chase off the wicked spirits that lurked on every church threshold. In the Middle Ages, on nights when witches were believed to be about, such as Samhain (All Hallow's Eve) and Beltane (also known as WALPURGISNACHT), church bells were rung to keep the witches from FLYING over a village. The townspeople also turned out and added to the noise by banging on pots and pans and ringing their own bells. In witch trials, accused witches testified to being transported through the air to SABBATS on the backs of DEMONS or the Devil, and to being thrown off to fall to the ground when a church bell sounded in the night.

Thunder and lightning storms were believed to be the work of witches and demons, and church bells also would be rung at an approaching storm in an attempt to dispel it. At someone's death, the tolling of the church bells helped the departing soul on its way to heaven and prevented evil spirits from interfering with the journey.

Church bells were baptized, named for saints and in some cases, ascribed human characteristics. Some were said to talk, ring on their own and sweat BLOOD at the invasion of their community. Medieval Europeans believed that their church bells traveled to Rome on Good Friday; everyone stayed inside so as not to witness their flight from the belfries. A bell that missed the Good Friday pilgrimage brought bad luck to the community.

Shopkeepers hung bells over their thresholds, not so much to alert them to the entry of customers but to keep evil spirits from entering their premises.

The Necromantic Bell of Giradius. Bells have been used in rituals for summoning the dead. One such necromantic bell is that of Giradius. Eighteenth-century French instructions specified that the bell be cast from an alloy of gold, SILVER, fixed mercury, tin, IRON and lead at the exact day and hour of birth of the person who intends to use it. The bell was to be inscribed with various astrological symbols and the magical words of Adonai, Jesus and the Tetragrammaton (see NAMES OF POWER).

The bell was to be wrapped in green taffeta and placed in the middle of a grave in a cemetery. It was to be left for seven days, during which time it absorbed certain vibrations and emanations. At the end of a week, the bell was properly "cured" for NECROMANCY rituals.

FURTHER READING:

Farrar, Janet, and Stewart Farrar. *A Witches Bible Compleat.* New York: Magickal Childe, 1984.

Thomas, Keith. *Religion and the Decline of Magic.* New York: Charles Scribner's Sons, 1971.

benandanti   Participants in the lingering remnants of an ancient agrarian cult in northern Italy, which came to the attention of the INQUISITION in the late 16th century because of the cult's nocturnal battles with witches and WARLOCKS over the fertility of the crops and livestock.

The term *benandanti* means "good walkers." The cult flourished in the Friuli region of Italy, an isolated area where Italian, German and Slavic traditions met and mingled. The *benandanti* were comprised of men and women born of the CAUL, that is, with the inner fetal membrane still covering the body, especially the head. This was a sign not only of the *benandanti* but of supernatural powers of HEALING the bewitched and the power to see witches.

Some *benandanti* saved their cauls and wore them about their necks as AMULETS or TALISMANS.

The *benandanti* were compelled to serve their villages during the Ember Days, the changing of the seasons marked by the solstices and equinoxes. At midnight, usually on Thursday but sometimes on Friday or Saturday of the Ember Days, they were summoned, sometimes by drums or, tradition has it, by angels. If they did not respond promptly and were late, they were severely beaten. They left their bodies, and their spirits assumed the shapes of butterflies, mice, cats and hares (see METAMORPHOSIS). They went to the valley of Josaphat in the center of the world, where they met the army of witches and warlocks, also in spirit guises. The *benandanti* would be armed with stalks of fennel, renowned for its healing properties; the witches would be armed with sorghum stalks, a type of millet perhaps identified with BROOMS.

For an hour or several hours, the opposing spirit armies engaged in battle, beating each other with their stalks. If the *benandanti* won, the year's crops would be abundant. If the witches won, storms would plague the growing and harvesting seasons, and famine would ensue. After the "games," as the battles were called, the *benandanti* and the witches passed by houses looking for clean water to drink. If they found none, the witches entered the cellars and either overturned the wine casks, or drank the wine and urinated in the casks.

The spirits had to return to their bodies by cock's crow. If they did not, or if their bodies had been turned over onto their stomachs while their spirits were gone, they either had great difficulty re-entering them, or could not get back in at all. The spirits then were forced to wander the earth until their bodies' destined time of death arrived.

The origins of the *benandanti* cult are unknown; the roots are probably ancient. The leaving of the body and doing battle in spirit, in the guise of animals, is shamanic in nature. The *benandanti* may be an offshoot of the cult of DIANA, which was known in Italy from the end of the 14th century. Followers of Diana held peaceful SABBATS at night and were not associated with diabolical rites until later by the church. The rites of the *benandanti* had no similarities to the celebrated witches' sabbat but were entirely agricultural in intent, and were emotionally intense. The *benandanti* considered themselves soldiers of the good fight, preserving their crops and protecting their villages from the evildoing of witches. The cult persisted in spite of the magical/holy measures provided by the church to protect crops, such as the sprinkling of holy water over the fields, the erection of a cross and the processions and prayers on Rogation Days. Apparently, the *benandanti* believed their ways were more effective.

Though pagan, the cult had acquired Christian elements by the late 16th century. The *benandanti* went out in the service of Christ and God, to battle the agents of the Devil.

The *benandanti* came to the attention of the church in 1575, when a priest in Brazzano heard rumors of a man in Civdale, Paolo Gasparutto, who could cure bewitched persons and who "roamed about at night with witches and goblins." Summoned and questioned by the priest, Gasparutto admitted the Ember Days' outings, adding that in addition to fighting, there was leaping about, dancing and riding on animals. To the priest, this sounded ominously like a witches' sabbat, and he involved the inquisitors.

Various interrogations and trials of *benandanti* were conducted in the region from 1575 to 1644. The church inquisitors made efforts to associate the *benandanti* with witches and to get them to confess that they participated in witches' sabbats (said to occur every Thursday night, not just during the Ember Days), and were forced to abjure Christ and gave their souls to the Devil.

With few exceptions, the *benandanti* staunchly deflected these efforts. They also insisted that being *benandanti* did not at all interfere with their regular churchgoing and Christian prayers. They said they were forced to go out in service because they had been born with the caul. They were initiated at maturity, and after some 10 or 20 years in service, were relieved of their obligations. While some *benandanti* claimed to go out during each of the Embers Days, others said they went out only once every few years. Still others said they were called out whenever witches "did evil." Some said they knew who were other *benandanti* and who were witches, while others said they did not know anyone but recognized the spirit forms as one side or the other. Most protested that they could not reveal names or even details about the battles, lest they be severely beaten in punishment. The inquisitors, however, often succeeded in eliciting names of members of both factions.

One aspect of the *benandanti's* nocturnal travels that puzzled inquisitors the most was the leaving behind of the body. By the late 16th century, inquisitors and demonologists were beginning to question the actuality of the witches' sabbat, contending instead that it was all hallucinatory. But the *benandanti* insisted that their spirit battles were very real; that they did leave the body and travel in spirit, and could assume the shapes of animals. They did not feel pain in the fighting, they said. Some said they left the body after rubbing on an OINTMENT or oil, while others fell into a faint that resembled a cataleptic state. Beyond that, the peasants were at a loss to explain. One description of the spirit travel to the valley of Josaphat, offered in 1591 by Menechino della Nota as a dream in order to dodge the inquisitors, is described in *Night Battles* by Carlo Ginzburg:

> . . . I had the impression there were many of us together as though in a haze but we did not know one another, and it felt as if we moved through the air like smoke and that we crossed over water like smoke . . . everyone returned home as smoke . . .

No inquisitors could accept that the soul could leave the body while it was living and return. That the *ben-* *andanti* took the shapes of animals led the inquisitors to believe that they were physically led off on animals, and they tried to ascertain that the Devil did the leading.

Until the Inquisition, little had been known about the secretive *benandanti,* even in their own villages. Some who were known for their healing and spell-breaking abilities were sought out. The public attention, plus the persistent efforts of the church to ally the *benandanti* with witches, eventually did lead to increasing association of the *benandanti* with witches. By 1623 the church had obtained confessions from *benandanti* that they participated in witches' SABBATS. This led to more damning confessions of DEVIL'S PACTS, desecration of the cross, vampirism and abjuration of the Christian faith. What had once been a purely agricultural rite became transformed into a rite of Devil worship.

Despite its success, the church put little effort into prosecuting the *benandanti*. Many trials were never concluded, and TORTURE was not used. Punishment, when meted out, was mild—prison sentences or banishment. The *benandanti* apparently came to light when skepticism about witches was gaining ground in parts of Europe. The last major *benandanti* trial took place in 1644. A few scattered inquisitional efforts occurred into the late 1600s, but trials were abandoned.

See WILD HUNT.

FURTHER READING:
Barstow, Anne Llewellyn. *Witchcraze: A New History of the European Witch Hunts.* San Francisco: Pandora, 1994.
Ginzburg, Carlo. *Night Battles, Witchcraft & Agrarian Cults in the Sixteenth & Seventeenth Centuries.* New York: Penguin Books, 1983.
Russell, Jeffrey Burton. *Witchcraft in the Middle Ages.* Ithaca and London: Cornell University Press, 1972.

Berkeley Witch   In English folklore, the Berkeley Witch was a wealthy woman who lived during the time of the Norman Conquest in the town of Berkeley in England's heartland. She was wealthy and well liked, and lived luxuriously. Her secret, kept until she was close to death, was that her wealth was given her by the DEVIL, in a pact for her soul (see DEVIL'S PACT). Apparently, she earned the name *witch* because she sold her soul to the Devil, which reflects the once-common belief that all WITCHES made diabolic pacts.

According to lore, one evening as the Berkeley Witch ate at her dining table, her pet raven gave a single, harsh note and dropped dead. The woman recognized this as a sign that her end was near and that she would have to live up to her end of the bargain with the Devil. The beginning of the end was an onslaught of bad news, the first being the death of her oldest son and his entire family. She was so overwhelmed that she took to bed and grew weaker by the day. She confessed her pact to her two other children, who were a monk and a nun. It was determined that the only way to keep her out of the Devil's clutches was to wrap her body in a stag's skin, place it in a stone coffin bound with three magic IRON chains—for iron drives away the Devil and his hordes—and place the coffin upright in church. Psalms and masses were to be sung and said over the coffin for 40 days and 40 nights. Meanwhile, if the coffin were not violated by the Devil by the third day, her body could be buried in the church's graveyard.

On the first night after her death, a horde of DEMONS appeared and broke one iron chain. They reappeared on the second night and broke a second chain. But the third chain remained impervious to the demons' efforts, despite the fact that the very church shook on its foundation, and doors splintered on their hinges.

Then a hideous figure appeared—the Devil himself—and bade the Berkeley Witch follow him. From inside the coffin she replied she could not, for she was bound. "I will unbind you, to your great loss," the Devil answered. He tore away the chain, smashed the coffin and seized the living corpse of the witch. He strode outside, where there waited a huge, demonic black horse covered with spikes. He threw the witch on the horse, and her corpse was pierced through with spikes. Her screams reportedly could be heard for miles, but for naught: the Devil leaped up on the horse and rode away into the night.

FURTHER READING:

Briggs, Katharine. *British Folktales.* New York: Dorset Press, 1977.

Russell, Jeffrey Burton. *Witchcraft in the Middle Ages.* Ithaca and London: Cornell University Press, 1972.

bewitchment   See BLASTING; CURSE; HEX; ILL-WISHING; MALEFICIA; SPELL.

bibliomancy   The use of the Bible for DIVINATION. The Bible served as an important instrument of magical divination, particularly during medieval and Reformation times in Britain and parts of Europe. It was believed that the Bible, opened at random, would reveal one's fortunes or answer questions. Bibles laid on a child's head would induce sleep. Reading from the Bible to a pregnant woman would give her a safe delivery. Persons accused of WITCH-CRAFT and SORCERY were weighed against the great Bible in the local church. If the accused weighed less than the Bible, she or he was innocent. A method of Bibliomancy to determine guilt in a crime was the "key and book" method, still used in some rural parts of Britain as late as the 19th century. In that procedure, a key was placed randomly within the pages of the Bible. The names of the suspects were written on small pieces of paper and inserted up the hollow end of the key. When the paper bearing the name of the guilty party was inserted, the Bible would fall out of the grasp of the person holding it.

Biddy Early (1798–1874)   Irish seer and healer, often described as a witch. Most of what is known about Biddy

Early has been collected from oral tradition, and many of the stories about her have numerous variations. Nonetheless, Biddy seemed to have possessed real powers, and many people from all over Ireland and even England came to her for cures. She was widely believed to be "of the FAIRIES."

She was born Biddy O'Connor. Her birthplace is accepted as Faha, but Carrowroe is also given. She was of a farming family, small in stature and described as good-looking throughout her life. When she was 16 or 17 years of age, Biddy left her home to work as a serving girl in either Feakle or Ayle. She entered into her first marriage in 1817 to Pat Malley, who later died. She married Tom Flannery in the 1840s, and they had one son, also named Tom.

Biddy's powers were credited to a mysterious dark bottle that had been given to her either by husband Tom after his death or by the fairies, via her son prior to his own death. She was instructed that by looking into the bottle with one eye and keeping the other eye open, she would be able to see what ailed people and view the future. In exchange for this ability, she was never to charge money for her services, or she would lose the powers. She could accept gifts, however, but was to give away whatever was left over from her own needs. She was not to allow others to look into the bottle, or else they would either die or go mad.

One of the first stories about Biddy concerns a mean-tempered landlord who set about to evict her and others from their homes. Biddy agreed to go, but told the landlord he would never leave his home. A fire subsequently broke out in the landlord's home and he perished in it.

After the landlord disaster, Biddy moved to Kilbarron. At this point in her life, she already was in possession of the mysterious bottle. A man offered to move her possessions in exchange for a look inside the bottle. Biddy agreed. He did, and went mad.

Biddy lived the rest of her life in Kilbarron. Her various husbands were tenant farmers; some allegedly died of drink. She spooked people who came to visit her by announcing their names, the purpose of their visit, and their specific ailment or problem before they ever said a word.

She was sought out for three primary reasons: to cure human ailments, to cure animal ailments (farm animals often meant the difference between starvation and comfort for a family) and to relieve fairy molestations. In terms of the last reason, people would be made ill or otherwise troubled by the fairies for inadvertently disturbing their invisible forts, paths or nighttime play areas. Biddy could see these and prescribe remedial action. Sometimes, she said, she would receive a terrible "gruelling" from the fairies for her help to humans.

Biddy could also know when someone had been made ill by an unhappy ghost or evil spirit or by another witch.

After healing, people also sought out Biddy for fortune-telling or the answers to mysteries, such as who committed a crime and where something was lost.

She often made up potions for people from her own well water. These were given with complex instructions which had to be followed precisely in order for a cure to happen. Medicines could not be used for any other purpose, or disaster would strike. Some of her cures resemble the miraculous healings of Jesus and saints of various religions, such as instantly curing cripples.

Biddy accepted mostly food and whiskey for her services, although some reports tell of her asking for a "shilling for the bottle." Otherwise, she had no set fees of any sort. Sometimes she would ask for whatever a person had a surplus of, such as butter or bacon.

Sometimes she required penance of people in order to be healed, or a demonstration of their sincere desire for healing. Occasionally, she sent people away without help. In these cases, their problems were beyond her powers, or they had angered the fairies too much for reprieve, she said.

Biddy did not keep a CAT, but did have a dog (named either Spot or Fedel) that acted as a FAMILIAR. She would tie messages in a sock around the dog's neck and send him out to people, reputedly controlling him via her bottle.

The Catholic clergy felt threatened by a peasant woman who was credited with having greater powers than they. Although village priests scorned her and told people not to pay her any heed, most people—either out of awe or fear—respected her and valued her over more traditional doctors. She was counted on by her neighbors as a "good Christian" who always shared whatever she had and who did not misuse her powers. Nonetheless, the church labeled her a wicked witch whose powers came from the DEVIL. Although they denounced her from their pulpits, they were not above dressing up as ordinary people and consulting her themselves when in need. She apparently didn't hold grudges against them, even curing one priest of cancer.

In 1865, she was charged with witchcraft and appeared in court in Ennis. Apparently she was not convicted, for there is no record of her being jailed.

Biddy was married four times. The last was in 1869, when she was more than 70 years of age. A young man named either O'Brien or Meaney from Limerick came to her to be cured. She asked him if he would marry her if she did. He agreed, she did and they wed.

In April of 1874, Biddy became seriously ill and asked a friend to see to it that she received the rites of the church and was properly buried. She apparently was living alone—it is not known what happened to her fourth husband—and was too poor to pay for her own burial. The friend, Pat Loughnane, agreed. She died during the night of April 21/22. Lore has it that a mysterious ball of fire went out the front door of the house at her passing. She was buried in Feakle churchyard in an unmarked grave.

As for her bottle, Biddy reportedly gave it to the priest who administered last rites, telling him he would now possess the same powers. He threw it into Kilbarron Lake. People went diving in an effort to recover it, but found scores of bottles and could not determine which one had been hers.

See WITCH BOTTLE.

FURTHER READING:
Lenihan, Edmund. *In Search of Biddy Early.* Dublin: Mercier Press, 1987.

Bishop, Bridget (d. 1692)   The first victim of the SALEM WITCHES hysteria in Massachusetts in 1692–93. Bridget Bishop was the first to be accused and examined, and the first to be tried and executed.

Bishop was an easy target when the hysteria began. She was not well regarded by her neighbors, for she owned a tavern and exhibited "loose" behavior. She dressed provocatively, and some of her younger tavern patrons were known to stay well past closing, drinking and playing games.

According to the testimony lodged against Bishop, she had bewitched a baby and a girl to death, paid a man in disappearing money, caused various mishaps with carts and horses and paid nocturnal visits to a man as a glowing apparition that hopped around his room in a cloak. She also had bewitched people into serious illnesses, caused people to argue violently and bewitched animals.

John Lowder, 24, a laborer, testified that Bishop tormented him numerous times after they argued over her chickens damaging the gardens of Lowder's employer. Lowder said he woke up one night to find Bishop sitting on his chest. She tried to choke him.

Lowder also said that he had other dark bedroom visitors: a black pig and a flying DEMON that had the body of a monkey, the feet of a rooster and the face of an old man. The demon told him he was sent by the Devil and promised him money if he would pledge himself. Lowder chased the creature out of his room. It disappeared, but he saw Bishop in the distance. When he returned to his room, the demon came back. Lowder invoked God and it flew out, causing apples to fall from trees. It kicked gravel into Lowder's stomach, and he was unable to eat for three days.

COTTON MATHER said that when Bishop was brought to trial, he had no doubt of her guilt. With a look, she brought in an invisible demon who damaged part of the courthouse.

Bishop was executed by hanging on June 10, 1692.

black animals   A favored shape-shifted form of the DEVIL and DEMONS, especially demons who serve as the FAMILIARS of witches.

Dogs and cats were the most common black animals mentioned as demons and familiars in the trials of the witch hysteria. Black birds, especially crows and ravens, were also thought to be forms taken often by demons.

In the CHELMSFORD WITCHES trial of 1566, Joan Waterhouse was accused of sending a black dog familiar with a short tail, the face of an ape, a pair of horns on his head and a silver whistle about his neck. In 1577, during a storm in East Anglia, a demonic black dog tore through a church in Bungay, leaving behind two people strangled and a third "as shrunken as a piece of leather scorched in a hot fire."

In 1945, a phantom black dog was associated with the alleged witchcraft murder of CHARLES WALTON in the Cotswolds. Walton himself had seen such a dog, which metamorphosed into a headless woman, as an omen of death.

Black spectral animals in ghost lore are associated with witches (see HECATE) and demons (see WILD HUNT). The best-known black dog in England's ghost lore is Black Shuck, also called Old Shuck. *Shuck* comes from the Anglo-Saxon term *scucca,* meaning "demon." Black Shuck lurks about graveyards, lonely country roads, misty marshes and the hills around villages. Anecdotal accounts describe him as big as a calf, with glowing red or green eyes. Black Shuck follows travelers and also darts out on roads in front of automobiles that pass right through him.

Black Shuck is also a death omen. To see him means that one or a member of one's family will soon die.

Black Goat   See BAPHOMET.

Black Mass   An obscene parody of the Catholic Holy Mass firmly entrenched in the popular notion of DEVIL worship. Black Masses are erroneously associated with all WITCHES. They are not performed by Wiccans and Pagans, who do not worship the Devil, and it is doubtful that they were ever performed, at least in any significant numbers, by anyone in centuries past. The Black Mass exists more in fiction and film than it does in reality, though it is performed by various modern satanic groups (see SATANISM).

There is no one Black Mass ritual. The general purpose of the mass is to mock the Catholic Holy Mass by performing it or parts of it backwards, inverting the cross, stepping or spitting on the cross, stabbing the host and other obscene acts. URINE is sometimes substituted for the holy water used to sprinkle the attendees; urine or WATER is substituted for the wine; and rotted turnip slices, pieces of black leather or black triangles are substituted for the host. Black CANDLES are substituted for white ones. The service may be performed by a defrocked priest, who wears vestments that are black or the color of dried BLOOD, and embroidered with an inverted cross, a goat's head (see BAPHOMET), or magical symbols.

The magical significance of the Black Mass lies in the belief that the Holy Mass involves a miracle: the transubstantiation of the bread and wine into the body and blood of Christ. If the priest, as magician, can effect a miracle in a Holy Mass, then he surely can effect MAGIC in a mass used for other purposes. Priests who attempted to subvert the Holy Mass for evil purposes, such as cursing a person to death (see CURSE), were condemned by the Catholic church as early as the 7th century.

One such famous form of the Black Mass was the Mass of St. Secaire, said to have originated in the Middle Ages in Gascony. The purpose of the mass was to curse an enemy to death by a slow, wasting illness. MONTAGUE SUMMERS provided a colorful description of it in *The History of Witchcraft and Demonology:*

> The mass is said upon a broken and desecrated altar in some ruined or deserted church where owls hoot and mope and bats flit through the crumbling windows, where toads spit their venom upon the sacred stone. The priest must make his way thither late, attended only by an acolyte of impure and evil life. At the first stroke of eleven he begins; the liturgy of hell is mumbled backward, the canon said with a mow and a sneer; he ends just as midnight tolls.

The Mass of St. Secaire required a triangular, black host and brackish water drawn from a well in which the corpse of an unbaptized baby was tossed.

The beginnings of the Black Mass as it is known in modern times date back to the 14th century, when the church was persecuting heretics. Most of the Black Mass cases centered in France. In 1307 the KNIGHTS TEMPLAR were accused of conducting blasphemous rites in which they renounced Christ and worshiped idols made of stuffed human heads. They also were accused of spitting and trampling upon the cross, and worshiping the Devil in the shape of a black cat. Through arrests and trials, the order was destroyed.

In the 15th century, Gilles de Rais, a French baron, was arrested and accused of conducting Black Masses in the cellar of his castle in order to gain riches and power. He was accused of kidnapping, torturing and murdering more than 140 children as sacrifices and was executed in 1440.

In the 16th and 17th centuries numerous priests in France were arrested and executed for conducting Black Masses. In 1500 the cathedral chapter of Cambrai held Black Masses in protest against their bishop. A priest in Orleans, Gentien le Clerc, tried in 1614–15, confessed to performing a "Devil's mass" which was followed by drinking and a wild sexual orgy. In 1647 the nuns of Louviers said they had been bewitched and possessed, and forced by chaplains to participate nude in masses, defiling the cross and trampling upon the host.

During the same period, the Black Mass was associated with witchcraft. Witches tortured and tried by witch-hunters and inquisitors confessed to participating in obscene rituals at SABBATS, in which the cross was defiled and the Devil served as priest. It is unlikely that these took place.

The height of the Black Mass was reached in the late 17th century, during the reign of Louis XIV, who was criticized for his tolerance of witches and sorcerers. It became fashionable among nobility to hire priests to perform erotic Black Masses in dark cellars. The chief organizer of these rites was Catherine Deshayes, known as "La Voisin," said to be a witch who told fortunes and sold love philtres. La Voisin employed a cadre of priests who performed the masses, including the ugly and evil Abbé Guiborg, who wore gold-trimmed and lace-lined vestments and scarlet shoes.

The mistress of Louis XIV, the Marquise de Montespan, sought out the services of La Voisin because she feared the king was becoming interested in another woman. Using Montespan as a naked altar, Guiborg said three Black Masses over her, invoking Satan and his demons of lust and deceit, Beelzebub, Asmodeus and Astaroth, to grant whatever Montespan desired. It was said that while incense burned, the throats of children were slit and their blood poured into chalices and mixed with flour to make the host. Whenever the mass called for kissing the altar, Guiborg kissed Montespan. He consecrated the host over her genitals and inserted pieces in her vagina. The ritual was followed by an orgy. The bodies of the children were later burned in a furnace in La Voisin's house.

When the scandal of the Black Masses broke, Louis arrested 246 men and women, many of them among France's highest-ranking nobles, and brought them to trial. Confessions were made under torture. Most of the nobility got off with jail sentences and exile in the countryside. Thirty-six of the commoners were executed, including La Voisin, who was burned alive in 1680.

The Black Mass was a decadent fashion into the 19th century, when it began to wane. The Hellfire Club, a fraternal group in London in the late 19th century, was said to perform a Black Mass regularly in worship of the Devil, though it is likely that the rites were little more than sexual escapades with liberal quantities of alcohol. In 1947 a Black Mass was performed at the graveside of ALEISTER CROWLEY. When the Church of Satan was founded in 1966, a Black Mass was not included among the rituals; it was the opinion of the church's founder, Anton Szandor LaVey, that the Black Mass was outmoded. Nevertheless, Church of Satan and other satanic groups perform their own versions of Black Masses.

FURTHER READING:
Baroja, Julio Caro. *The World of the Witches.* 1961. Reprint, Chicago: University of Chicago Press, 1975.
Michelet, Jules. *Satanism and Witchcraft.* Secaucus, N.J.: Citadel Press, 1939 (reprint).
Russell, Jeffrey B. A *History of Witchcraft.* London: Thames and Hudson, 1980.

Black Shuck   See BLACK ANIMALS.

blasting   The ability of WITCHES to interfere with or destroy the fertility of man, beast and crop. This malicious destruction was considered a common activity among witches, and remedies and preventive actions circulated in folklore and MAGIC. Blasting is the antithesis of rituals to enhance fertility, and accusations of it date to the second century C.E. Witches also were credited with the power to produce abundant harvests and ensure healthy offspring of livestock and humans, but during the witch hunts this ability was largely ignored in favor of *MALEFICIA*; witches could not be prosecuted by inquisitors for good acts.

Since fertility was vital to prosperity, it was believed that a witch who wanted to harm a neighbor would cast a SPELL on his generative ability or that of his livelihood (see ILL-WISHING). If cows didn't calve, if the corn failed to sprout, if the wife miscarried, then the household had been bewitched. The bewitchment could be done with a look (see EVIL EYE) or touch but usually involved incantations and magic powders. According to the church, God allowed the DEVIL to have power over the generative act because the first sin of corruption was sex; a serpent tempted Eve; therefore, witches—the alleged agents of the Devil—could use snakes to impair fertility.

To blast crops, witches were said to take a flayed CAT, TOAD, lizard and viper and lay them on live coals until they were reduced to ashes. From this, they made a powder and sowed it in the crop fields. To disrupt conception and cause miscarriages, stillbirths and the births of deformed young, they placed serpents under barns, stables and houses. A medieval male witch named Stadlin in Lausanne, France, confessed (perhaps with the aid of TORTURE) that he had for seven years caused miscarriages in the wife and animals of a certain household simply by placing a serpent under the threshold of the outer door of the house. Fertility, he said, could be restored by removing it. But the serpent had long since decayed into dust, and so the owners excavated an entire piece of ground. After that, fecundity was restored to humans and animals alike.

In a story recounted in the *MALLEUS MALEFICARUM* (1486), a pregnant noblewoman in Reichshofen was warned by her midwife not to speak to or touch any witches if she ventured outside her castle. She did go out and after awhile sat down to rest. A witch came up and put both hands on her stomach, causing her immediately to begin aborting the fetus. She returned home in great pain. The fetus did not come out whole, but in little pieces.

Witches reportedly could blast generations of a family with such CURSES as "a heavy pox to the ninth generation" or "pox, piles and a heavy vengeance."

With regard to humans, the Devil and witches also were believed to interfere with fertility by obstructing the sex act in several ways: by preventing bodies from coming together by interposing a demon in a bodily shape; by destroying desire; by preventing an erection, and by

Witches brewing up trouble (WOODCUT FROM *NEWES OF SCOTLAND*, 1591)

shutting off the seminal ducts so that no ejaculation oc-curred. These bewitchments were directed mostly at men because, it was said, most witches were women who lusted after men. The Devil preferred to work through witches rather than directly because that offended God more and increased the Devil's power.

The "removal" of the male organ by a witch was ex-plained as illusion, though the Devil was said to have the power actually to take the organ away physically. A spurned mistress, for example, might be a witch who cast a spell to make her lover believe he had lost his penis—he couldn't see or feel it. The only way to restore it was to get the witch to remove the curse; if she didn't or couldn't, the effect was permanent. One story attributed to a Dominican priest tells of a young man who came to confession and proved to the father that he was missing his penis by stripping off his clothes. The priest could scarcely believe his eyes. The young man convinced the witch who'd bewitched him to remove her curse, and his penis was restored.

This type of bewitchment allegedly affected only those persons who were "sinful" fornicators and adulter-ers. The Devil, apparently, could not disturb the organs of the pious.

Some witches were said to collect male organs and keep them in boxes, where they wiggled and moved and ate corn and oats. The *Malleus Maleficarum* also tells of a man who lost his member and went to a witch to ask for it back:

> She told the afflicted man to climb a certain tree, and that he might take which he like out of a nest in which there were several members. And when he tried to take a big one, the witch said: You must not take that one; add-ing, because it belonged to a parish priest.

Given the prevalence of folk magic in daily life in cen-turies past, and given the jealous and vengeful aspects of human nature, it is likely that individuals cast or paid to have cast blasting spells against neighbors and competitors. The INQUISITION used blasting to its own ends, as one of many justifications for the crushing of pagans, heretics and political enemies of the Church.

In PAGANISM and WICCA, blasting and all other acts of harmful magic are considered unethical, a violation of the law, "An' it harm none, do what ye will." According to tenets of the Craft, Witches must use their powers for good, to help others and work in harmony with nature (see WICCAN REDE).

In many tribal cultures, however, such ethical distinctions are not made, and blasting continues to be among the acts of SORCERY carried out against people, animals, crops and possessions.

FURTHER READING:
Guazzo, Francesco Maria. *Compendium Maleficarum*. Secaucus, N.J.: University Books, 1974.
Remy, Nicolas. *Demonolatry*. Secaucus, N.J.: University Books, 1974.
Summers, Montague, ed. *The Malleus Maleficarum of Heinrich Kramer and James Sprenger*. 1928. Reprint, New York: Dover Publications, 1971.

blessed be   In WICCA and PAGANISM, "blessed be" is a widely used salutation and parting in conversation and correspondence. A common variation is "bright blessings."

Blight, Tamsin (1798–1856)   Famous witch, healer and PELLAR of Cornwall, England, known as "the Pellar of Helston." Stories about her were recorded by the Cornish folklorist William Bottrell in the 19th century.

Tamsin Blight was born in Redruth in 1798, probably to a poor family. Her first name is sometimes given as Tamson in records. She also was called Tammy Blee (*blee* is Cornish for "wolf"). Little is known about her early life. Later, it was said that she was a descendant of the true pellar blood of Matthew Lutey of Cury.

In 1835, at age 38, she married a widower, James (Jemmy) Thomas, a copper miner who claimed to be a pellar. While Blight enjoyed a good reputation, Thomas did not. Reputedly, he was a drunk who repelled SPELLS for young men in return for sexual favors. One newspaper story described him as "a drunken, disgraceful, beastly fellow, and ought to be sent to the treadmill."

His outrageous conduct damaged Blight's reputation. When a warrant was issued for his arrest for wanting to commit "a disgraceful offence" (i.e., an act of homosexuality), Blight separated from him. Thomas fled and was gone from Cornwall for about two years.

Blight continued her career as a pellar. People from far away would make pilgrimages to see her; sailors would get protective CHARMS from her prior to making voyages. She especially healed people who believed they suffered because of ill-wishing. Even when she was ill and confined to bed prior to her death, people still came to see her. According to stories, people would lie on stretchers by her bedside, and walk away healed.

Blight also divined the future, and expelled bewitchments of animals. She reportedly conjured spirits and the dead.

She evidently did not hesitate to curse those who angered her, however. One story tells of the village cobbler refusing to mend her shoes because she was not good about paying her bills. She told him, "You'll be sorry for that, for in a short while I will see to it that you have no work to do." The cobbler's business went into a tailspin, and he left the area.

At some point, Blight may have renewed her relationship with Thomas. She had a son, and Thomas may have been the father. She reportedly passed on her powers to her son.

Blight died on October 6, 1856.

Little was heard about Thomas until his death in 1874 in the parish of Illogan. An obituary described him as a WIZARD of great ability and repute.

FURTHER READING:
Jones, Kelvin I. *Seven Cornish Witches*. Penzance: Oakmagic Publications, 1998.

blood   Called the "river of life," blood is identified with the soul and is the vehicle that carries the vital energy of the universe through the body. In MAGIC, blood is revered and feared for the miraculous power it possesses and confers. Blood that is let is believed to unleash power: sacrificial blood scattered on the earth regenerates the crops. Animals, fowl and humans are sacrificed in religious and some magical rites (see SACRIFICE). The blood of executed criminals is said to be a powerful protector against disease and bad luck, because of the energy of resentment and fury that is released upon execution.

Blood is used to bind oaths and brotherhood, either by mingling or in signing. Blood oaths are considered inviolate. According to lore, Devil's pacts are always signed in blood (see DEVIL'S PACT).

In folklore, the magical power of witches is neutralized or destroyed by burning their blood in fires—hence the common European method of execution by burning at the stake—or a practice called "blooding." Witches were "scored above the breath" (cut above the mouth and nose) and allowed to bleed, sometimes to death. Shakespeare made use of the blooding custom in Part I of *King Henry VI*, when Talbot sees Joan of Arc:

Devil, or devil's dam, I'll conjure thee;
Blood will I draw from thee, thou art a witch,
And straightway give thou soul to him thou serv'st.

A few drops of blood of a person used in magical CHARMS and SPELLS, sprinkled in potions and WITCH BOTTLES or on effigies, is said to give a witch or magician power over that person, in the same manner as do HAIR AND NAIL clippings. Animal blood also is used in folk charms and spells. The blood of a black CAT is said to cure pneumonia.

Menstrual blood. Menstrual blood is particularly potent and is sacred to the GODDESS. Menstrual flow is linked to the phases of the MOON. The blood of the Goddess, also called "wine," "milk," "mead" and "wise blood," appears universally in mythologies; it is drunk for wisdom, fertility, regeneration and immortality. The menstrual blood of the Goddess is valued as a healing charm. The blood of Iris, symbolized in an ambrosia drink, conferred divinity on pharaohs. According to Taoism, red yin juice, as menstrual blood was called, confers long life or immortality. A pagan custom that has survived Christianity is the carrying of seeds to the field in a cloth stained with menstrual blood. In some shamanic cultures, menstrual periods are said to be accompanied by prophetic dreams that guide the shamaness-to-be to her path of power.

In patriarchies, such as Christianity and Judaism, men traditionally feared menstrual blood, which was associated with uncleanliness and evil. Contact with menstrual blood, or even being in the presence of a menstruating woman was considered dangerous, even fatal. In some societies, menstruating women are still shunned or isolated, lest they pollute the earth and harm others with their blood. In the first century, ancient Romans believed the touch of a menstruating woman could blunt knives, blast fruit (see BLASTING), sour wine, rust iron and cloud mirrors.

In the Old Testament, Leviticus 18:19 states, "You shall not come near a woman while she is impure by her uncleanliness to uncover her nakedness." In orthodox Judaism, the Talmud specifies that husband and wife are to be sexually separated, and sleep in different beds, for 12 days a month (an average of five days for menstruation, followed by seven "clean days" to make sure the woman is free of every drop of pollutant). Sex may be resumed after a ritual bath, called a *mikveh*, in which the woman is to scrub every part of her body. It is still the custom among some orthodox Jews not to shake hands with a woman, lest she be menstruating, and never to use the same wash water as a woman, for the same reason.

In Christianity, menstrual blood has been similarly scorned and feared. Early church scholars shamed women for their uncleanliness. At various times, up to the late 17th century, menstruating women were forbidden to partake in communion, or in some cases, even to enter church. Menstrual blood was believed to spawn DEMONS. Some factions within the Catholic Church continue to believe menstruating women would defile an altar, one reason why they should not be admitted into the priesthood.

In some magical ceremonies, menstruating women are barred from participation, because it is believed their flux interferes with the raising of psychic power and the effectiveness of spells.

In folk magic, menstrual blood is believed to be a powerful ingredient in love PHILTRES and charms. A few drops of menstrual blood mixed in a man's meal supposedly will secure his undying love. Conversely, menstrual blood also is used in charms to cause impotency.

bloodstone   A semiprecious stone with magical or healing properties. Perhaps the best known is green jasper with red flecks, used in rituals and CHARMS by sorcerers and witches. It is considered an enabling stone, bringing about the wishes of the user. It protects health, drives away night DEMONS (see LAMIA), guards against deception and pacifies. It is also used in the DIVINATION of natural disasters, such as storms, earthquakes and floods. Powdered, it has been used in medicines throughout history, particularly by women as an aid to pregnancy and lactation.

Bloodstone also refers to red coral, red marble, red jasper, carnelian, red agate and heliotrope. The ancient Egyptians associated red jasper with the blood of ISIS. Ancient Greek believed bloodstones fell from heaven and could stop internal and external bleeding.

In Europe, especially in the Mediterranean area, bloodstones have long been regarded as protection against the EVIL EYE.

See HEALING; RED.

Blymire, John (b. 1895)   In the secret world of Pennsylvania Dutch witchcraft, John Blymire became the central figure in a celebrated murder trial in York, Pennsylvania, in 1929. Blymire, a witch of mediocre repute, and two other men were charged with the murder of a well-known witch, Nelson Rehmeyer, known as "The Witch of Rehmeyer's Hollow." After a trial that attracted journalists from all over the world—much to the consternation of the quiet, rural residents—all three men were found guilty. The trial was colored by the deliberate suppression of evidence in a collusion between the judge and district attorney, which, in more modern times, would have resulted in a mistrial.

Blymire was born in York County, an area of Pennsylvania steeped in the superstition and lore of the Pennsylvania Dutch folk. His family and neighbors were primarily farmers, descendants of early German settlers who brought their own culture and language with them from the Old World.

In the "hex belt," as this part of the state is still called, belief in witches, witchcraft and folk magic runs strong. At the turn of the century, many persons ran profitable businesses as witches or "powwowers," curing illnesses by faith healing and magical powders, potions and charms; hexing people; and removing hexes (see HEX; POWWOWING). The country folk often preferred to consult a local witch rather than a medical doctor for such things as warts, flu, colds, minor disorders and even serious illnesses. Every powwower consulted as the bible of the craft a book by JOHN GEORGE HOHMAN called *Pow-wows, or Long Lost Friend,* which was a grimoire of sorts, containing remedies and charms for all sorts of afflictions (see GRIMOIRES).

Blymire was born into a family of witches. Both his father and grandfather were skilled in powwowing. True to lore, little John inherited their supernatural ability. Blymire gradually absorbed knowledge about his family's peculiar powers from his father and grandfather. When the older men could not cure one of their own family of an illness, they took them to a neighbor witch who lived eight miles away. The witch, Nelson Rehmeyer, was a brooding giant of a man who reportedly could conjure Beelzebub, one of the major DEMONS of hell. Blymire's first visit to Rehmeyer took place the winter when he was five and was suffering from *opnema,* a wasting away that was often believed to be the result of a hex but usually was due to malnutrition.

Rehmeyer took the sick boy off to his dark basement and emerged half an hour later. He told John's father to make the boy urinate into a pot before sunrise, then boil an egg in the urine. They were to take a needle and punch THREE small holes in the egg, then leave it on an anthill. John would be cured when the ants ate the egg, Rehmeyer promised. The elder Blymire followed the instructions, and the boy was cured by the following spring.

At age seven, the boy successfully "tried for" his first cure, enabling his grandfather to overcome difficulty in urinating. At age ten, he was sent back to Rehmeyer not as a patient but as an employee, digging potatoes for 25 cents a day.

As he grew older, Blymire had modest successes as a witch. He was a dull boy, however, of limited intelligence. He was homely, with a long, pointy nose, and he was extremely twitchy and nervous. All of these factors caused others to shun him except when seeking out his ability as a witch. Blymire was thus extremely lonely.

In 1908, at age 13, he left school and took a job in a cigar factory in York. He lived by himself in a series of rooming houses. He kept to himself, but word gradually got around that he could heal. A coworker who suffered from a wheal in his right eye had heard that Blymire's family did powwowing and asked him if someone could help cure the wheal. Blymire offered to do it himself. He instructed the coworker, Albert Wagner, to bring a dirty supper plate to work, which Wagner did the next morning. Blymire pressed the dirty side against the inflamed eye while he muttered something unintelligible. Then he threw the plate to the ground and stomped it to pieces. He made the sign of the cross three times on Wagner's eye and stated it would be better the next day. To Wagner's astonishment, the eye was healed when he awoke the following morning.

Others started coming to Blymire with their health problems. As was customary in powwowing, Blymire charged no fees but accepted whatever "voluntary" offerings his clients cared to give him.

One hot summer day in 1912 at quitting time, Blymire and the other men were heading out of the factory onto the streets of York. All of a sudden, someone screamed, "Mad dog!" A rabid collie, foaming at the mouth, was charging straight for them. Everyone scrambled to get back inside the factory, but they were blocked by the men who were coming out. But Blymire put himself in front of the collie, murmured an incantation and made the sign of the cross over the collie's head. The dog stopped foaming at the mouth. Miraculously, it seemed cured of rabies. Blymire patted its head. The dog licked his hand and followed him down the street, wagging its tail.

That incident should have clinched Blymire's fame as a powwower. Instead, it plummeted him into poor health and financial ruin, and an obsession that followed him for nearly 20 years. Shortly after his glory with the dog, Blymire began suffering from opnema. He lost his appetite and couldn't sleep. Already thin, he lost even more weight. He became convinced that someone had put a hex on him, perhaps an envious competitor who didn't want him to become too popular as a powwower.

In Pennsylvania Dutch belief, a hex cannot be removed until the identity of the one who cast the hex is discovered. Neither Blymire's father nor his grandfather was able to unmask the hexer and break the SPELL. Blymire consulted other witches, spending all of his meager pay but failing to get rid of the hex. The longer he was unable to break the mysterious CURSE, the more obsessed he became with doing so. He spent more and more time consulting witches further and further afield of York.

In the winter of 1913, shortly before he turned 18, he quit his job at the cigar factory in order to devote more time to breaking the hex on him. He moved from rooming house to rooming house, eking out a living with his own powwowing and odd jobs as a janitor, busboy and assistant to the sexton in a Presbyterian church. He spent all of his money on "voluntary offerings" to other witches, some of whom took him for hundreds of dollars before giving up. By the time he was 19, Blymire was a wreck. He weighed less than 100 pounds and suffered from real and imagined pains and illnesses, and nearly constant headaches.

At one rooming house, he fell in love with Lily Halloway, the landlord's 17-year-old daughter. They were married in 1917, and the relationship seemed to provide the cure he sought. Blymire's health improved, he gained weight, he got a steady job and his powwowing clientele increased.

The illusion was broken with the birth of their first child, a son who died within five weeks. A second child was born prematurely and lived only three days. Blymire was convinced the hex was back. His health declined, the headaches returned and he lost his job. He vowed he would not stop until he discovered his unknown hexer and removed the curse.

By 1920 Blymire had consulted more than 20 witches, none of whom was able to help him. One of them was

Andrew C. Lenhart, a powerful witch who struck fear into the hearts of the police, who gave Lenhart a wide berth. It was said that if Lenhart hexed someone, only the Devil himself could remove the spell. Lenhart was known to advise his clients to take violent action in order to break spells cast by enemies. He told Blymire he had been hexed by someone "very close." Blymire, half out of his mind by this time, immediately suspected his wife. Lily began fearing for her life. Her father hired a lawyer and was able to get Blymire examined by a psychiatrist. He was evaluated as a "borderline psychoneurotic" and was committed to the state mental hospital in Harrisburg. After 48 days, Blymire escaped by walking out the door. He returned to York, and no one made an effort to have him recommitted. Lily divorced him.

In 1928 Blymire went back to work at the cigar factory in York. He met 14-year-old John Curry, who had suffered a harsh childhood, with an apathetic mother and an abusive stepfather. Curry thought he himself had been hexed. In misfortune, he and Blymire had something in common, and became friends.

In June of 1928, Blymire consulted Nellie Noll, a witch of formidable reputation in her nineties, who lived in Marietta. At their sixth session, Noll identified Nelson Rehmeyer as the villain who had hexed Blymire. At first he didn't believe it. To prove it, Noll told him to take out a dollar bill and stare at George Washington's picture. He did and saw Washington's face dissolve into that of Rehmeyer. Noll told him there were only two ways to break Rehmeyer's hex: to take Rehmeyer's copy of the *Long Lost Friend* and burn it, or to cut a lock of his hair and bury it six to eight feet in the ground.

About this time, a farmer named P. D. Hess, who was convinced he was hexed, consulted Blymire for help. Hess and his family, their crops and livestock all were wasting away. Blymire tried to identify the source of the hex but failed. So as not to lose Hess as a client, Blymire secretly consulted Noll, who named Rehmeyer as the hexer not only of Hess but of John Curry as well.

Blymire recruited Curry and Hess' son, Wilbert, to accompany him to Rehmeyer's isolated cabin, where they would somehow wrest away his copy of the *Long Lost Friend* or a lock of his hair. It was a rainy, pitch-black November night, and all three men were nervous about confronting Rehmeyer.

Rehmeyer was not at home. The men went next to the cabin of his estranged wife, who told them he was probably at the home of a woman he was seeing. The three returned to Rehmeyer's Hollow, and by this time—close to midnight—a light was on inside. They knocked, and Rehmeyer invited them inside.

The four men sat up for hours making small talk. Blymire was too frightened to reveal his real purpose in coming, sensing the greater power possessed by Rehmeyer, and fearing that Rehmeyer was able to guess what he wanted. At last Rehmeyer excused himself and went upstairs to bed, telling the others they could spend the night. In the morning, he fed them breakfast, and they left.

Hess returned to his father's farm. Blymire and Curry hitched a ride to York. Blymire had already hatched a new plan of attack. The two went straight to a hardware store, where Blymire bought rope. They took it to Curry's room, where they cut it into 14 foot-and-a-half lengths. Then they went to the Hess farm, where they fetched Wilbert for a return visit to Rehmeyer's Hollow. It was the night of November 27, clear and bright under a full moon.

Once again, Rehmeyer invited them inside. Blymire immediately demanded "the book." Rehmeyer acted as though he didn't know what they meant. He denied having "the book," which incited Blymire to violence. Blymire shrieked and grabbed at Rehmeyer, and Curry and Hess joined in the fight. It took all three of them to hold down the huge, strong man. Curry got out a length of rope and struggled to tie up Rehmeyer's legs.

Rehmeyer then offered to give them "the book" if they would let him up. They did, and he threw out his wallet. That made Blymire even angrier, and he attacked Rehmeyer once again. The three of them managed to get Rehmeyer down, and Blymire tied a piece of rope around his neck and began choking him and beating him. Hess kicked and beat him. Curry picked up a block of wood and hit him three times on the head until blood poured out his ear. The men continued to kick and pummel Rehmeyer until his face was beaten beyond recognition. No one ever admitted who dealt the fatal blow, but at last Rehmeyer groaned and died. It was just after midnight. Blymire exulted, "Thank God! The witch is dead!" They ransacked the house and divided up what little money they found, which ranged from 97 cents, according to Wilbert, to $2.80, as the district attorney claimed later.

Rehmeyer's body was discovered on November 30 by a neighbor who heard his hungry mule braying and went to check to see what was wrong. It didn't take the authorities long to trace the deed of Blymire and his accomplices, through information supplied by Rehmeyer's estranged wife. Blymire, Curry and Hess were arrested. Blymire readily confessed, bragging that he had killed the witch who had hexed him.

The press had a field day with the case, dubbing it "voodoo murder" and writing about the backward ways and superstitions of the private Pennsylvania Dutch folk. The case came before Judge Ray P. Sherwood, a man who thought witches, powwowing and hexes constituted a lot of nonsense. He was greatly disturbed at the negative publicity generated by the case. Sherwood instructed all the attorneys involved that the case would be dispensed with as quickly as possible, and under no circumstances would he entertain any evidence or discussions about witchcraft. The motive for the murder was to be nothing more than robbery, a ridiculous notion considering that Rehmeyer's poverty was widely known. In an area where

$100,000 estates were common, he had left an estate of only $500 to $1,000. The entire amount taken by his murderers was less than $3.

Sherwood appointed the attorneys for Curry and Blymire, who were too poor to afford their own, but the Hess family was able to hire their own counsel. The trials began on January 9, 1929. As a result of Sherwood's instructions, all references to witchcraft and hexes were edited out of the confessions before they were admitted into the record. All of the defense attorneys' efforts to circumvent the judge were defeated. The jury of peers, who undoubtedly believed in witchcraft and would have understood Blymire's motive, and perhaps even sympathized with him, did what the judge wanted and found all three guilty—Blymire and Curry of murder in the first degree and Hess of murder in the second degree.

They were sentenced on January 14. Blymire and Curry were given life in prison. Hess was given 10 to 20 years. In 1934 Curry and Hess were paroled. Both resumed quiet, respectable lives in the York area. Curry died in 1962. Blymire petitioned for parole several times and was refused. Finally, in 1953, at the age of 56 and after 23 years and five months in prison, he was released. He returned to York and got a job as a janitor. He bought a modest house with the money he had saved in prison, determined to live quietly for the rest of his life.

FURTHER READING:
Hohman, John George. *Pow-wows or Long Lost Friend.* 1820.
    Reprint, Brooklyn, N.Y.: Fulton Religious Supply Co., n.d.
Lewis, Arthur H. *Hex.* New York: Pocket Books, 1970.

Bodin, Jean (1529–1596)   French demonologist and political theorist who encouraged the vicious persecution of witches and helped fan the fires of the INQUISITION throughout Europe. Jean Bodin said that people who denied the existence of WITCHCRAFT were witches themselves and said that, with rare exceptions, no accused witch should go unpunished.

Bodin was born in Angers, France. For a time, he served as a Carmelite monk. He left the monastery for the University of Toulouse, where he became a professor of Roman law. Bodin possessed a brilliant intellect and distinguished himself in his studies of philosophy, law, classics and economics. In 1561 he left Toulouse for Paris, where he worked in the service of the king. But his book *Six livres de la république,* published in 1576, caused him to fall out of favor with the king because of its concept that sovereign power belonged to the people.

Bodin wrote other works of political theory, but he is best known for his treatise on witchcraft, *De la démonomanie des sorciers (The Demonomania of Witches),* published in 1580. The book was an immediate success and was reprinted frequently throughout Europe. Like the *MALLEUS MALEFICARUM* published nearly 100 years earlier, it served as a guide to witch-hunters and judges in the matters of identifying, prosecuting and executing

Jean Bodin (OLD ENGRAVING)

witches. Bodin drew on his own experience as a judge at numerous witchcraft trials.

Démonomanie describes witches, their methods of diabolic acts and their abilities, such as pacts with Satan (see DEVIL'S PACT), FLYING through the air to their SABBATS, copulating with incubi and succubi and casting evil SPELLS. It also acknowledges that there are good daemons as well as evil DEMONS, and that good daemons can communicate with man and provide inspiration. He himself had such a daemon, who whispered instructions in his ear.

Bodin believed that authorities were too soft in prosecuting witches, whom he saw less as heretics and more as social deviants. He condoned convicting the accused on the basis of lies by informants, confessions made under TORTURE, secret accusations and false promises of leniency. He urged local authorities to encourage secret accusations by placing a black box in the church for anonymous letters.

He was adamant about torturing and punishing witches, saying that God would reject those who did not do so:

Those too who let the witches escape, or who do not punish them with the utmost rigor, may rest assured that they will be abandoned by God to the mercy of the witches. And the country which shall tolerate this will be scourged with pestilences, famines, and wars; and those which shall take vengeance on the witches will be blessed by him and will make his anger cease.

Even children and invalids were not to be spared torture, as Bodin demonstrated time and again by his own example as judge. Children, he said, should be forced to testify against their accused parents. One of his favored methods was cauterizing flesh with a red-hot iron and then cutting out the putrefied flesh. That torture, he said, was mild compared to the hell that awaited the condemned witch.

Bodin took exception with EXORCISM, however, which he said was both ineffective and dangerous to the exorcist. Music was preferable as a form of exorcism; in the Old Testament, Saul's possession had been calmed by music. Bodin did not believe that a person could cause another to become possessed (see POSSESSION).

Bodin savagely criticized JOHANN WEYER, a Lutheran physician and contemporary, who opposed the burning of witches and maintained they were helpless victims. Bodin said Weyer's books should be burned.

Except for *Démonomanie,* which served the purpose of the church, all of Bodin's other books on political theory were condemned by the Inquisition. Bodin died in Laon, a victim of the bubonic plague.

See NICHOLAS RÉMY.

FURTHER READING:
Baroja, Julio Caro. *The World of the Witches.* Chicago: University of Chicago Press, 1975. First published 1961.
Kors, Alan C., and Edward Peters. *Witchcraft in Europe, A Documentary History 1100–1700.* Philadelphia: University of Pennsylvania Press, 1972.

Boguet, Henri (1550–1619)   French grand judge, lawyer and demonologist, known for his cruelty and TORTURE. Boguet presided over witch trials in Saint-Claude, Burgundy, France.

Boguet exhibited a preoccupation with lurid accounts of witches' SABBATS and copulations with the DEVIL. His interrogations focused on these aspects, and he was successful in coercing confessions from his victims. He said he wished that all witches could be united into a single body, so that they all could be executed at once in a single fire. Many of those he condemned were sent to the stake without the mercy of being strangled first. One victim, a woman, struggled so violently that she broke free of the fire three times, and three times Boguet had her thrown back in, until she was burned alive.

He did not hesitate to burn children, declaring that once they were contaminated by the Devil, they could not be reformed.

In 1598, Boguet presided over a famous werewolf case, the Gandillon family, said to shape-shift into howling, ravenous wolves. Boguet tortured them until they confessed to having sex with the Devil. Three family members were convicted, hanged and burned.

Boguet wrote a legal handbook on witchcraft, *Discours des Sorciers* (1610), which rivaled the *MALLEUS MALEFICARUM* in authority and popularity and went into 12 editions in 20 years.

Bone, Eleanor "Ray" (1910–2001)   English Witch, one of the original high priestesses initiated by GERALD B. GARDNER. Eleanor "Ray" Bone followed Gardner's footsteps in the media attention and was sometimes called the Matriarch of British Witchcraft.

Bone was born in London; her mother was a school headmistress. As a child, she saw the ghost of a pet, which stimulated her interest in reincarnation, folklore, magic and the occult.

During World War II, Bone served in the military and was sent to Cumbria, where she met a couple who revealed themselves to be hereditary witches. They initiated her into their tradition in 1941, and she practiced with them for four years before returning to London.

After the war, Bone married a man named Bill and took a job running a home for the elderly. She was introduced to Gardner and was initiated into his coven. She became acquainted with DOREEN VALIENTE, PATRICIA CROWTHER and others and became a close friend of DAFO.

Bone established a flourishing coven in South London and was an active public proponent of the Craft. She made numerous public appearances and posed skyclad (nude) for the media. She went to the United States on a media tour. On one television show, where she appeared with a testy SYBIL LEEK, she was asked to turn Leek into a TOAD. She retorted, "Why should I improve on nature?"

In 1966, Bone and Crowther joined forces to publicly denounce ALEX SANDERS as an imposter. They and others were incensed that Metro-Goldwyn-Mayer studios in Hollywood had hired Sanders to consult on a film about witchcraft.

In 1968 Bone went to Tunis to visit the grave of Gardner. She learned that the government planned to turn the cemetery into a park. Bone took up a collection among Witches and had the remains of Gardner moved to Carthage, Tunisia.

Over time, Bone preferred to practice the folk magic–oriented tradition she learned from the Cumbrian couple rather than the Gardnerian tradition. She had many pupils, among them VIVIANNE CROWLEY and her husband, Chris Crowley.

In 1972, Bone retired to Alston, a village in Cumbria.

In 2001, the PAGAN FEDERATION (PF) invited Bone to be an honorary member, but she declined, saying that she did not recognize several of the traditions with the PF, believing them to be spurious.

Her final public appearance was in the summer of 2001, when she gave an address over the telephone to the Occulture Festival, speaking about the Craft revival and divulging personal information about the New Forest CO-

VEN that had initiated Gardner. In August 2001, in failing health, she announced that she would soon be "called back to the Old Gods," and she got her affairs in order. She died on September 21, 2001.

FURTHER READING:

"Eleanor Bone." Witchvox. Available online. URL: http://www.witchvox.com/va/dt_va.html?a=usfl&c=passages&id=4227. Downloaded September 30, 2007.

Hutton, Ronald. *The Triumph of the Moon: A History of Modern Pagan Witchcraft.* Oxford: Oxford University Press, 1999.

Valiente, Doreen. *The Rebirth of Witchcraft.* London: Robert Hale, 1989.

Bone, Gavin (1964–)   Wiccan and author and companion/partner with JANET FARRAR. In his work with Janet and her late husband, STEWART FARRAR, Gavin Bone has advocated a "progressive" and more shamanic trance Craft based on direct relationship with deities.

Bone was born in Portsmouth, Hampshire, England, in 1964. He trained as a registered nurse and studied complementary healing, such as herbal remedies and reflexology.

Drawn to MAGIC and the Craft, Bone joined an eclectic ceremonial magic group whose members included Pagans. In 1986 he was initiated into the Seax-Wicca Tradition founded by RAYMOND BUCKLAND and then was initiated into a Celtic Wiccan COVEN. He studied shamanic techniques and runes.

In 1989, Bone became a contact for the PAGAN FEDERATION after attending the Pagan-Link Groby Festival. The same year, he met the Ireland-based Farrars at a Pagan festival in Leicester, England, and struck up a friendship with them. They invited him to come with them on their tour of the United States in 1992. They visited Salem, Massachusetts, to attend a remembrance of the SALEM WITCHES hysteria.

In 1993, Bone moved to Ireland, where he entered a polyamorous marriage with the Farrars and collaborated in their work and writing. He served as webmaster and production manager for their videography work.

Stewart suffered a stroke in 1995, and Bone provided care for him.

After Stewart's death in 2000, Bone and Janet Farrar continued development of their ideas about the practice of WICCA. They are priest and priestess to Freya as trance goddess, who has a direct relationship with them in daily life, not just in ceremony, as their muse and life guide. They are eclectic, recognizing different pantheons of deities, and different approaches to worship. According to Bone, Wicca is inherently a shamanic path and is evolving away from the duotheistic and even polytheistic traditions of its early and more structured years.

Bone and Farrar do not label themselves with a tradition, but follow Seith, the tradition of trance-prophecy in the Northern Tradition. They are honorary members of

Janet and Gavin Bone (COURTESY JANET AND GAVIN BONE)

several traditions, among them Strega, Eclectic Eclectic Eleusinian Kuven, The Elusinian Mysteries of the AQUARIAN TABERNACLE CHURCH and The Order of Bill the Cat.

In 2003, Bone and the Farrars were jointly recognized with the Gerald B. Gardner Lifetime Achievement Award.

Bone collaborated with both Stewart and Janet on *The Pagan Path: The Wiccan Way of Life* (1995), *The Healing Craft: Healing Practices for Witches, Pagans and the New Age* (1999) and *The Complete Dictionary of European Gods and Goddesses* (2001). With Janet, he coauthored *Progressive Witchcraft: Spirituality, Training and the Mysteries in Modern Wicca* (2004).

Bonewits, P. E. I. (Isaac) (1949–)   American Pagan, author and scholar, and a leader in contemporary Druidry and PAGANISM.

Philip Emmons Isaac Bonewits was born October 1, 1949, in Royal Oak, Michigan—the perfect place, he likes to joke, for a future Archdruid. The fourth of five children (three girls, two boys), he spent most of his childhood in

Ferndale, a suburb of Detroit. When he was nearly 12, the family moved to San Clemente, California.

From his mother, a devout Roman Catholic, Bonewits developed an appreciation for the importance of religion; from his father, a convert to Catholicism from Presbyterianism, he acquired skepticism. His first exposure to magic came at age 13, when he met a young Creole woman from New Orleans who practiced "voodoo." She showed him some of her magic, and so accurately divined the future that he was greatly impressed. During his teen years, he read extensively about magic and parapsychology, and was fascinated by the power of the mind. He also read science fiction, which often has strong magical and psychic themes.

In his second semester of ninth grade, Bonewits entered a Catholic high school seminary because he wanted to become a priest. He soon realized that he did not want to be a priest in the Catholic faith. He returned to public school and graduated a year early. After spending a year in junior college to get foreign-language credits, he enrolled at the University of California at Berkeley in 1966. At about the same time, he began practicing magic, devising his own rituals by studying the structure of rituals in books, and by observing them in various churches.

His roommate at Berkeley, Robert Larson, was a self-professed Druid, an alumni of Carleton College, where

Isaac Bonewits (COURTESY ISAAC BONEWITS)

the Reformed Druids of North America (RDNA) had been born in 1963. Larson interested Bonewits in Druidism, and initiated him into the RDNA. The two established a grove in Berkeley. Bonewits was ordained as a Druid priest in October 1969. The Berkeley grove was shaped as a contemporary Pagan religion; other RDNA groves considered the order a philosophy.

During college, Bonewits spent about eight months as a member of the Church of Satan, an adventure which began as a lark. The college campus featured a spot where evangelists of various persuasions would lecture to anyone who would listen. As a joke, Bonewits showed up one day to perform a satirical lecture as a Devil's evangelist. He was so successful that he did the act repeatedly, and soon was approached by a woman who said she represented Anton LaVey, the founder of the Church of Satan. Bonewits attended the church's meetings and improved upon some of their rituals—he was never seduced, as the woman had promised—but dropped out after personality conflicts with LaVey. The membership, he found, was largely middle-class conservatives who were more "right-wing and racist" than satanist.

At Berkeley, Bonewits created his own degree program, graduating in 1970 with a bachelor of arts degree in magic—the first person ever to do so at a Western educational institution. He also was the last to do so in the United States. College administrators were so embarrassed over the publicity about the degree that magic, witchcraft and sorcery were banned from the individual group study program.

His first book, *Real Magic,* about magic, ritual and psychic ability, was published in 1971.

In 1973, Bonewits met a woman named Rusty. They moved to Minneapolis, where they were married. For a year and a half, Bonewits edited *Gnostica,* a Pagan journal published by CARL WESCHCKE of Llewellyn Publications, but his scholarly approach was not popular with many of the readers.

Bonewits remained in Minneapolis for about another year. He established a Druid grove called the Schismatic Druids of North America, a schism of the RDNA. He also joined with several Jewish Pagan friends and created the Hasidic Druids of North America, the only grove of which existed briefly in St. Louis, where its membership overlapped with that of the CHURCH OF ALL WORLDS. In 1974–75, Bonewits wrote, edited and self-published *The Druid Chronicles (Evolved),* a compendium of the history, theology, rituals and customs of all the reformed Druid movements, including the ones he invented himself.

He also founded the Aquarian Anti-Defamation League (AADL), a civil liberties and public relations organization for members of minority belief systems, such as the Rosicrucians, Theosophists, Pagans, Witches, occultists, astrologers and others. Bonewits served as president of the AADL and devoted most of his income—unemployment insurance—to running it. The organization scored several small victories in court—such as restoring an astrologer to her apartment after she had been evicted because a neighbor told her landlord that her astrology classes were "black magic seances."

Bonewits and Rusty divorced in 1976 and he returned to Berkeley. The AADL disintegrated shortly after his departure.

In Berkeley, Bonewits rejoined the RDNA grove and was elected Archdruid. He established *The Druid Chronicler* (which later became *Pentalpha Journal*) as a national Druid publication in 1978. After a few clashes with members, he left the organization. *Pentalpha Journal* folded.

In 1979, he was married for a second time, to a woman named Selene. That relationship ended in 1982. In 1983, he was initiated into the New Reformed Order of the Golden Dawn. The same year, he married again, to Sally Eaton, the actress who created the role of the hippie witch in the Broadway musical *Hair*. They moved to New York City in 1983.

Since the late 1960s, Bonewits had worked as a freelance journalist, and, since college, had earned a sporadic living from writing and editing. In 1983, he entered the computer technology field as a technical writer for a firm in Manhattan. He left that over an ethical matter and became a self-employed computer consultant for small businesses.

In 1983 in New York, Bonewits met Shenain Bell, a fellow Pagan, and discussed the idea of starting a Druidic organization. The religious fellowship, *Ár nDraíocht Féin* ("Our Own Druidism" in Gaelic), was born, with no ties to the ancient Druids or to the RDNA. Bonewits became Archdruid and Bell became Vice Archdruid.

Bonewits and Eaton parted company in 1986. He moved to Nyack, New York, in November 1987 with his intended fourth wife, Deborah, a Wiccan high priestess. He continued work as a computer consultant and worked on the building of the ADF. He and Deborah married; a son, Arthur, was born in 1990.

The ADF grew, but more slowly than Bonewits had envisioned. A clergy training program was launched, but a seminary facility was not created. A prolific author, Bonewits wrote numerous articles and essays on Druidry, magic and Paganism. He predicted that Paganism would become a mainstream religion with millions of members.

In 1996 he resigned as Archdruid of the ADF due to the debilitating effects of eosinophilia myalgia syndrome, which also prevented him from working as a computer consultant. He retained his life membership in the ADF and devoted himself to his writing. His *Authentic Thaumaturgy 2.0*, a new edition of *Real Magic* (revised in 1979) designed for players of fantasy games, was published in 1998.

Bonewits and Deborah separated in 1999 and divorced in 2007. In 2004 he handfasted, then in 2007 married, Phaedra Heyman, a former vice president of the Covenant of Unitarian Universalist Pagans. The couple live in Nyack, New York, but they plan to move to Ashland, Oregon, in 2008.

Bonewits' other published books are *Rites of Worship* (2003), *The Pagan Man* (2005), *Bonewits' Essential Guide to Druidism* (2006), *Bonewits' Essential Guide to Wicca and Witchcraft* (2006) and *Neopagan Rites* (2007). With Phaedra, he coauthored *Real Energy: Systems, Spirits and Substances to Heal, Change and Grow* (2007).

Bonewits is also songwriter and singer and has performed at Pagan gatherings.

Bonewits has had involvements with Santería, the Caliphate Line of the Ordo Templi Orientis, Gardnerian Wicca, and the New Reformed Orthodox Order of the Golden Dawn, as well as others.

FURTHER READING:
"Isaac Bonewits." Controverscial.com. Available online. URL: http://www.controverscial.com/Isaac%20Bonewits.htm. Downloaded October 1, 2007.
"Isaac Bonewits' Cyberhenge." Available online. URL: http://www.neopagan.net/. Downloaded October 1, 2007.

book of shadows In contemporary WITCHCRAFT and WICCA, a book of beliefs, rituals, Witchcraft laws and ethics, herbal and HEALING lore, incantations, chants, dances, SPELLS, DIVINATION methods, rituals and miscellaneous topics that serves as a guide for Witches in practicing their Craft and religion. There is no definitive book of shadows for Witchcraft in general; each tradition may have a standard book of shadows, which may be added to or adapted by separate covens (see COVEN). In addition, individual Witches add their own personal material. The book is to be kept secret, but some Witches have gone public with their books of shadows over the years (see LADY SHEBA).

Traditionally, only one copy existed for an entire coven, kept by the high priestess or high priest. That rule has proved unfeasible, and it is commonplace for all Witches to have their own copies. In the early days of Wicca, a newly initiated Witch copied the coven's master copy, held by the high priestess or high priest, in her or his own handwriting, and added original material as inspired. Today, many books of shadows are kept on computers.

Material is given according to the Witch's position in the hierarchy. As a Witch advances in skill and in the hierarchy—the most common system is one of three degrees—more material is provided. The book of shadows cannot be kept by a Witch if he or she leaves the coven.

GERALD B. GARDNER, considered the father of contemporary Witchcraft, claimed that when he was initiated into his coven in 1939, he inherited a fragmentary book of shadows representing the coven's alleged historical tradition. Gardner, who believed MARGARET ALICE MURRAY's ideas about an unbroken lineage of witchcraft as a religion since ancient times, claimed his coven was part of this heritage. Murray's theories were later proved to be without merit, and similarly Gardner's claim of an ancient Witch religion evaporated.

The true origins of his book of shadows have been disputed for decades. It is unlikely that such books existed in earlier times, as folk MAGIC generally was passed orally through the generations.

Gardner wrote down some rituals in an unpublished manuscript called *Ye Bok of ye Art Magical,* and published some rituals allegedly taken from his book of shadows in a pseudonymous novel, *High Magic's Aid* (1949). There is evidence that he drew from a variety of sources, including Murray, *The Greater Key of Solomon* (a magical GRIMOIRE), James G. Frazer, Robert Graves, the ARADIA legend of CHARLES LELAND, various classicists, ALEISTER CROWLEY, Rosicrucianism, Freemasonry, and the HERMETIC ORDER OF THE GOLDEN DAWN and other sources. Most likely, most of this material—to which Gardner probably made his own additions—was assembled between 1947 and 1950.

In 1952, Gardner met DOREEN VALIENTE and initiated her into his coven in 1953. Valiente, a good writer with a poetic flair, helped him revise the rituals and write additional ones; she accepted the book as a product of a long witchcraft heritage but objected to the Crowley material and removed most of it, substituting simpler wording, including her own poetry. She also gave more emphasis to the GODDESS. It is estimated that she may have contributed up to half of the book of shadows by the mid-1950s.

Valiente and Gardner parted company in 1957, and Gardner revised the book of shadows on his own. He died in 1964. When Gardnerian Witchcraft was exported to other countries, such as the United States, the book of shadows became the guide and rule book.

Regardless of its origins, the book of shadows is a living text in contemporary Witchcraft. It reflects the practices and beliefs of each individual coven and the interests or specialties of the individual Witch. It can be a dynamic collection of information, with additions being made as necessary.

According to tradition, a Witch's book of shadows is destroyed upon death. Gardner's original book of shadows, however, was passed to Valiente after his death. Other books of shadows are passed on as keepsakes and documents of historical significance.

FURTHER READING:
Adler, Margot. *Drawing Down the Moon.* Revised ed. New York: Viking, 1986.
Farrar, Janet, and Stewart Farrar. *The Witches' Way: Principles, Rituals and Beliefs of Modern Witchcraft.* Custer, Wash.: Phoenix Publishing, 1988.
Gardner, Gerald B. *Witchcraft Today.* 1954. Reprint, New York: Magickal Childe, 1982.
Kelly, Aidan A. *Crafting the Art of Magic Book I: A History of Modern Witchcraft, 1939–1964.* St. Paul: Llewellyn Publications, 1991.
Kemp, Anthony. *Witchcraft and Paganism Today.* London: Michael O'Mara Books, 1993.
Lady Sheba. *Book of Shadows.* St. Paul: Llewellyn Publications, 1971.
Valiente, Doreen. *The Rebirth of Witchcraft.* London: Robert Hale, 1989.

Bovet, Richard (b. 1641)   English demonologist. Richard Bovet is known for his book *Pandaemonium* (1684), a rehash of prevailing opinions about the diabolical nature and activities of witches, and a collection of stories about psychic phenomena, apparitions and ghosts.

Little is known about Bovet. He was born around 1641 and lived in Somerset, England. He was educated at Wadham College, Oxford, from 1657 to 1658. He was an admirer of Joseph Glanvil, an Anglican, royalist and writer on witchcraft, best known for *Saducismus Triumphatis: or Full and Plain Evidence Concerning Witches and Apparitions.*

Pandaemonium is a rare book, with only nine copies known in existence, held in libraries in England, Scotland, France and the United States.

Bovet is believed to have died in the early 18th century.

Bowers, Roy   See COCHRANE, ROBERT.

Bradley, Marion Zimmer (1930–1999)   Best-selling science fiction and fantasy author and mentor of women in WICCA. Marion Zimmer Bradley's novels carry such Wiccan themes as the power of women and worship of the Earth GODDESS.

Bradley was sometimes called a witch or Wiccan priestess, which she publicly disavowed. She described herself as an occultist and student of ceremonial MAGIC, but not a witch. "That is not my path in this life," stated Bradley, who was an ordained priest in the New Catholic Church. "I myself am unalterably Christian."

Bradley was interested and involved with the occult most of her life. She was born on June 3, 1930, in Albany, New York, to a Lutheran family. She had an early interest in poetry and writing and dictated poetry to her mother before she could write. At age 11, she started an alternative school newspaper, *The Columbia Journal,* because she did not like the official school paper. She also had an early and intense interest in classical history, classical ceremonial magic, the mystery religions and the Arthurian legends.

Bradley spent three years at New York State Teachers College in Albany (now part of the State University of New York) but did not graduate. In October 1949, she married Robert A. Bradley, a railroad man, and had a son. The Bradleys moved to Texas, living in what Bradley termed "a succession of small towns and smaller towns," including Levelland and Rochester. For a period in the early 1950s, Bradley joined the Rosicrucians, which put structure into her interest in the occult.

Bradley started her writing career in the 1950s by writing short stories for the pulp and confession magazines and then original paperback novels, most of them science fiction. Her first novel was *Seven from the Stars,* published in 1955.

In 1959, Bradley left her husband and went to Abilene, where she finished college at Hardin Simmons University, majoring in education, psychology and Spanish and earning a teaching certificate. She financed her tuition by writing confession and romance novels and was selling so well by the time she finished that she never had to use the teaching certificate.

In 1963, Bradley moved to Berkeley, where she remained for the rest of her life. She undertook graduate work in psychology at the University of California at Berkeley from 1965 to 1967, but did not complete it for a degree.

In February 1964, she married Walter Breen, a leading authority on rare coins. Breen became the first member of an occult order Bradley had conceived while still in Texas, the Aquarian Order of the Restoration. The purpose of the order was to restore worship of the Goddess, long before it became fashionable to do so. At its height, the order had about 18 members. The order eventually dissolved, feeling that its purpose had been accomplished. The last meeting took place in 1982.

Between 1965 and 1969, Bradley occasionally took LSD as a religious experience. She had read about the uses of LSD in psychology. Typically, she would spend a day or two preparing for the experience, a day immersed in the experience and then a day or two integrating the insights from it. She stopped taking the drug in 1978, because it lowered her blood sugar.

Of Bradley's novels, the one that identified her most closely with witchcraft is *The Mists of Avalon,* published in 1983. Bradley had long been interested in creating a novel for Morgan Le Fay, the sorceress/fairy said to be the sister of King Arthur. The opportunity came in 1977, when Bradley's editors, Lester and Judy Del Rey, suggested that she write *The Acts of Sir Lancelot,* which would be a companion to *The Acts of King Arthur* by John Steinbeck. Bradley said she would rather write about Morgan Le Fay. The Del Reys agreed to the idea and offered her a contract.

Bradley began work on the book in 1978. She took what was to be her last LSD experience, which provided her with a flood of ideas that coalesced into the central vision of the book. *The Mists of Avalon* tells the story of Arthur through the viewpoints of the women around him. The central narrator is Morgan (Morgaine), priestess of the Goddess and the Mysteries, schooled for seven years in the magical arts by Viviane, the Lady of the Lake. The other key women are Viviane, Igraine, Arthur's mother, and Guinevere (Gwenhwyfar), his wife and queen. As part of her research, Bradley took a flat in London and traveled around to various Arthurian sites in Britain.

Mists, which portrays the ancient ways of the Goddess, the mysterious world of Faerie, and the conflict between paganism and Christianity, gained a wide following in the Wiccan and PAGAN communities.

Bradley herself became involved with Wiccans in the late 1970s. She joined a women's group (STARHAWK was one of the leaders). Bradley, DIANA L. PAXSON and other women formed the Dark Moon Circle, of which Bradley was a member for about four to five years. The group was described as "part coven, part women's consciousness-raising and part sewing circle." Bradley dropped out shortly after *The Mists of Avalon* was published in 1983. She found herself besieged by people who wanted her to speak on female consciousness, crystals and how much of the book had been "channeled" (none, she said). Also, some of the members of the Dark Moon Circle wanted to open it to men. Bradley had joined in the interest of learning how to relate better to women.

Bradley took exception to some of the values and aspects of the Craft that she felt were "intellectually dishonest." For example, she said, modern witchcraft is a fertility religion, yet many feminist witches lobbied for abortion rights. Bradley said that "witchcraft is too tied up in people's minds with medieval witchcraft, which is a form of satanism. Witches do not even believe in, let alone worship, satan." Also, she said, trying to return to the old Earth religions in a society that is intertwined with technology does not make sense.

Bradley followed Christianity all her life, occasionally attending Episcopal services (an aunt was Episcopalian) and singing in the Unitarian Church. She became involved in the New Catholic Church through Breen, an archbishop, and a friend, also an archbishop. After taking classes, Bradley was ordained in 1980. For about five years, she worked with a gay counseling service in Berkeley, California.

In addition to her son by Robert Bradley, she had a son and a daughter by Breen and a foster daughter and a foster son. Robert Bradley died of lung cancer in 1966. Bradley separated from Breen in 1979, but they remained married and best friends.

Bradley died on September 25, 1999. Bradley was a believer in reincarnation and had her first spontaneous past-life recall as a teenager. She said she had past lives with her two husbands. She recalled lives as a Spanish soldier, a male cowherd of the 13th or 14th century, an official in the Roman Empire under Tiberius and a schoolboy in Belgium during World War I who died in a bombing. She also thought she might have been the writer and poet Charlotte Brontë.

FURTHER READING:
"Encyclopedia of World Biography on Marion Zimmer Bradley." Available online. URL: http://www.bookrags.com/biography/marion-zimmer-bradley/. Downloaded July 27, 2007.
Guiley, Rosemary Ellen. *Tales of Reincarnation.* New York: Pocket Books, 1991.

brass In folk MAGIC, brass is considered to be effective in repelling witches and evil spirits. It has been used in the making of numerous kinds of AMULETS. Brass BELLS hung on the necks of horses, cows and other animals protect them from the EVIL EYE.

See IRON.

bright blessings   See BLESSED BE.

broom   A primary means of travel for witches, enabling them to travel at tremendous speed, according to lore.

There are different origins of the association of brooms with witches. One is old pagan fertility rites, in which brooms, poles and pitchforks were ridden like hobbyhorses in fields and in dances. In some lore, witches are afraid of horses and ride brooms. In other lore, brooms are a natural tool for witches, in accordance with a custom of putting a broom outside a house to indicate a woman is away.

During the witch hysteria, the belief that witches traveled by broom was more prevalent in continental Europe. English witchcraft laws never specifically outlawed flying, and brooms are mentioned only once in English witch trials.

Accused witches on trial said they were able to fly thanks to a magical OINTMENT they rubbed on themselves or on chairs or brooms. If they wished, they could travel invisibly. However, not all authorities agreed that this was possible. JEAN BODIN, a 16th-century French demonologist, maintained that only a witch's spirit could fly, not her physical body.

The broom was not always the "steed of the Devil." In early 16th-century German woodcuts, witches are shown astride forks, sticks, shovels and demons in the form of animals. By the late 16th and early 17th centuries, witches were more often shown riding either brooms or demonanimals. The position of the faggot of twigs changed over time. Initially, the faggot was held down, so that the witch could sweep her tracks from the sky; this is the image that has prevailed into the 20th century. But by the late 17th century, art showed witches riding with the faggot end up. The faggot held a candle to light the way.

According to one folklore belief, the Devil gave every newly initiated witch a broom and flying ointment. Other lore held that he dispensed those items only to weak witches who needed help.

Before mounting their broomsticks, witches first had to anoint themselves or the sticks with the flying ointment, a concoction that often included hallucinogenic and/or toxic ingredients. If they were inside a house, they supposedly rose up through the chimney, though few witches brought to trial actually acknowledged doing that. Sorcerers as well as witches flew brooms, though men were more often depicted riding on pitchforks.

According to lore, witches flew their brooms to SABBATS, sometimes carrying along DEMONS or their FAMILIARS in the shapes of animals. They also rode their brooms to fly out to sea for STORM RAISING. Novices sometimes fell

Witches flying up chimney on broomsticks (THOMAS ERASTUS, *DEUX DIALOGUES TOUCHANT LE POUVOIR DES SORCIÈRES ET DE LA PUNITION QU'ELLES MÉRITENT,* 1579)

off. On witch festival nights such as WALPURGISNACHT, townspeople laid out hooks and scythes to kill witches who fell off their brooms. People also rang church BELLS, which had the power to ground broomsticks and knock witches off them.

In the SALEM WITCH hysteria in colonial Massachusetts, accused witch Mary Lacy confessed that she and another accused witch Martha Carrier rode on sticks when they attended witches' meetings in Salem Village (now Danvers). She said that witches from other states, even Maine and Connecticut, would fly into the pasture behind Reverend Samuel Parris' house.

Witches were believed to deceive their husbands by substituting a broom for themselves in bed so that they could slip off and attend sabbats. ISOBEL GOWDIE, a famous Scottish witch of the 17th century, said her husband never knew the difference, which might have been more of a comment on their marriage than a confession of witchcraft.

In WICCA and PAGANISM, the broom is used in rituals and may be placed at the altar with other tools and objects. A coven's high priestess or maiden takes a broom to symbolically sweep away evil, as in clearing the space for a MAGIC CIRCLE, and to sweep away the old and worn. In a handfasting, the bride and groom traditionally jump over a broom, which is similar to an old Welsh custom that calls for newlyweds to enter their new home by stepping over a broom.

In other folklore, it is bad luck to take one's broom in a move to a new home. In India, brooms are tied to ships' sails to sweep storms out of the sky. In Chinese lore, the Broom Goddess is the deity of fine weather, who sweeps the skies clean.

FURTHER READING:
Buckland, Raymond. *Buckland's Complete Book of Witchcraft.* St. Paul, Minn.: Llewellyn Publications, 1986.
Cahill, Robert Ellis. *Strange Superstitions.* Danvers, Mass.: Old Saltbox Publishing, 1990.

bruja/brujo   The feminine and masculine names, respectively, for the witches of Mexico, Mesoamerica and Hispanic communities in the United States. Of the two, the *bruja,* the woman, is more prevalent and considered the more powerful. The *bruja* holds a visible, important function: she is sought for remedies for physical illness, and SPELLS and CHARMS to remedy emotional, romantic and social problems. *Brujas* work in many open-air markets in Mexico, selling herbs, charms and other objects from which customized AMULETS and charms may be made. Many of their remedies for physical ailments are based on folk cures handed down through the centuries.

See also *CURANDERO/CURANDERA*; DEVIL FISH; GARLIC.

Buckland, Raymond (1934–)   English Witch called "the Father of American Witchcraft," who introduced Witchcraft to America. After moving to the United States in 1962, Raymond Buckland became a leading authority on witchcraft and WICCA and enjoys a career as a prolific author, public speaker, media consultant and media personality. He has written more than 50 books translated into 17 languages.

Buckland was born in London on August 31, 1934, to Stanley Thomas Buckland and Eileen Lizzie Wells. His father was a Romani (Gypsy) who worked in the British Ministry of Health as Higher Executive Officer. A *poshrat,* or half Gypsy, Buckland was raised in the Church of England. Around age 12, a Spiritualist uncle interested him in Spiritualism and the occult, and the interest expanded over time to include witchcraft, MAGIC and the occult.

Buckland was educated at King's College School in London and served in the Royal Air Force from 1957 to 1959. He earned a doctorate in anthropology from Brantridge Forest College in Sussex, England. He performed in theaters, taught himself to play the trombone and led his own Dixieland band.

He married his first wife, Rosemary Moss, in 1955. The couple had two sons. They immigrated to the United States in 1962 and settled in Brentwood, Long Island. Buckland went to work for British Airways (then BOAC), first in reservations service and then as a sales manual editor.

His decision to embrace Witchcraft as his religion was influenced by two books, *The Witch-cult in Western Europe,* by Margaret Murray, and *Witchcraft Today,* by GERALD B. GARDNER. They helped him realize that Witchcraft was the religion for which he had been searching. Buckland wrote to Gardner, who was living on the Isle of Man, and struck up a mail and telephone relationship. He became Gardner's spokesperson in the United States;

whenever Gardner received a query from an American, he forwarded the letter to Buckland.

Buckland went to England in 1963, where he met Gardner. Buckland was initiated into the Craft by one of Gardner's high priestesses, MONIQUE WILSON, or Lady Olwen. The initiation took place in Perth, Scotland, where Wilson lived. Rosemary was initiated at a later time. It was the first and last time Buckland would ever see Gardner, who died in February 1964.

Interest in witchcraft caught on quickly in America, but the Bucklands built their own coven slowly and cautiously. They were later criticized for their caution; people who did not want to wait to be witches by traditional INITIATION simply started their own covens. Initially, Buckland kept his real name and address out of the media. The information eventually was published in the *New York Sunday News,* which focused more attention on him as a spokesperson for the Craft.

Buckland was inspired by Gardner's MUSEUM OF WITCHCRAFT AND MAGIC on the Isle of Man and began collecting pieces for his own museum, the first Museum of Witchcraft and Magic in the United States. The collection

Raymond Buckland (COURTESY RAYMOND BUCKLAND)

began in a bookcase, spilled out into the Bucklands' basement and eventually needed a separate building.

In 1969, Buckland published his first book, *A Pocket Guide to the Supernatural*, followed in 1970 by *Witchcraft Ancient and Modern* and *Practical Candleburning Rituals*. Also in 1970, he published a novel *Mu Revealed*, written under the pseudonym Tony Earll, an anagram for not really. The novel was written tongue in cheek, inspired by the successful books on the lost continent of Mu by James Churchward. *Witchcraft from the Inside* was published in 1971.

The year 1973 was transitional. The museum collection was big enough to fill a rented building, and Buckland quit his job to run it full time. However, the Bucklands' marriage broke up, and they turned the leadership of their coven over to Theos and Phoenix of Long Island. Buckland moved to Weirs Beach, New Hampshire, where in 1974 he married Joan Helen Taylor and reopened the museum.

At about the same time, Buckland left the Gardnerian tradition and founded Seax-Wica, a new open and democratic tradition based on Saxon heritage. He had two primary reasons for making this move: Gardnerian witchcraft no longer met his religious needs, and he had been dismayed at some of the ego and power trips exhibited within the Craft. His book *The Tree: The Complete Book of Saxon Witchcraft* was published in 1974.

Four years later, the couple moved to Virginia Beach, Virginia, where Buckland became educational director of the Poseidia Institute. He and Joan established the Seax-Wica Seminary, a correspondence school that grew to have more than 1,000 students worldwide. Plans to establish a campus, however, did not materialize.

After nearly 10 years of marriage, Buckland and Joan divorced in 1982. In 1983, he married Tara Cochran of Cleveland. They moved to Charlottesville, Virginia, where they operated the seminary school and Taray Publications. In December 1984, they moved to San Diego, and the seminary correspondence course was phased out. Seax-Wica covens remain established around the world.

In San Diego, Buckland withdrew from having a high profile in witchcraft, practicing with his wife with a small coven and as solitaries. In 1986, his 11th book on witchcraft was published, *Buckland's Complete Book of Witchcraft*, which comprised everything Buckland felt he had to say on the subject. Some witches criticized him for revealing too much. While the book does not reveal Gardnerian secrets, it does reflect his view that the Craft should be more open.

In the late 1980s, Buckland turned to new creative avenues, writing books on other topics, plus screenplays and novels in comedy, mystery and Tolkien-style fantasy genres. In addition, he wrote numerous magazine and newspaper articles on witchcraft and appeared on talk shows and lectured at universities. He also served as technical adviser for Orson Welles' movie *Necromancy* and for a stage production of *Macbeth*, working with

William Friedkin, the director of *The Exorcist*. Buckland acted in small parts in several films, including the role of the crazy psychiatrist in *Mutants in Paradise*.

In 1992, Buckland and his family moved to a small farm in north-central Ohio. He retired from active involvement in the Craft, save for occasional public appearances. He continues his solitary practice in Seax-Wica and PectiWita, a Scottish tradition inspired by Aidan Breac and developed by Buckland.

In 1999, Buckland sold his Museum of Witchcraft and Magic, a collection of about 500 pieces, to Monte Plaisance and Tolia-Ann, a Gardnerian high priest and high priestess couple in Houma, New Orleans. The metaphysical store "Crossroads" housed the museum and also serves as the location of the Church of Thessaly.

Buckland continues to make public appearances, lecturing, teaching workshops and working as a medium at Lily Dale Assembly Spiritualist camp in New York.

His other nonfiction books are *Witchcraft . . . the Religion* (1966); *Amazing Secrets of the Psychic World* (1975); *Here Is the Occult* (1974); *Anatomy of the Occult* (1977); *The Magic of Chant-O-Matics* (1978); *Practical Color Magick* (1983); *Secrets of Gypsy Fortunetelling* (1988); *Secrets of Gypsy Love Magic* (1990); *Secrets of Gypsy Dream Reading* (1990); *Scottish Witchcraft* (1991); *Witchcraft Yesterday and Today*, a video (1990); *The Book of African Divination* (1992); *Doors to Other Worlds* (1993); *Ray Buckland's Magic Cauldron* (1995); *Truth About Spirit Communication* (1995); *Advanced Candle Magic* (1996); *Buckland Gypsies Domino Divination Cards* (1995); *Gypsy Fortune Telling Tarot Kit* (1998); *Gypsy Witchcraft and Magic* (1998); *Gypsy Dream Dictionary* (1999); *Coin Divination* (2000); *Buckland Romani Tarot Deck and Book* (2001); *Wicca for Life* (2001); *The Witch Book* (2001); *The Fortune-Telling Book* (2003); *Signs, Symbols and Omens* (2003); *Cards of Alchemy* (2003); *Wicca for One* (2004); *Buckland's Book of Spirit Communications* (2004); *The Spirit Book* (2006); *Buckland Spirit Board and Ouija—Yes! Yes!* (2006); *Mediumship and Spirit Communication* (2005); *Face to Face With God?* (2006); *"Death, Where Is Thy Sting?"* (2006); and *Dragons, Shamans and Spiritualists* (2007). Other novels are *The Committice* (1993); *Cardinal's Sin* (1996); and *The Torque of Kernow* (2008).

FURTHER READING:
Buckland, Raymond. *Buckland's Complete Book of Witchcraft*. St. Paul, Minn.: Llewellyn Publications, 1986.
———. *The Witch Book: The Encyclopedia of Witchcraft, Wicca, and Neo-paganism*. Detroit: Visible Ink Press, 2002.
Raymond Buckland Web site. Available online. URL: http://www.raybuckland.com. Downloaded July 13, 2007.

Budapest, Z (1940–) Founder of the first feminist witches' coven and the main branch of Dianic Wicca.

Z Budapest (her feminist name) was born Zsusanna Mokcsay in Budapest, Hungary, on January 30, 1940. Her mother, Masika Szilagyi, was a medium and ceramics artist whose work was GODDESS-inspired. Her grandmother Ilona was a herbalist and healer.

At age three, Budapest had her first psychic experience, an apparition of Ilona at the time of her death. According to Hungarian tradition, a death apparition portends that the departed one will assume the role of guardian spirit in the life of the one who has observed him or her. Ilona has served in that capacity throughout Budapest's life.

In childhood, Budapest appreciated nature, "playing priestess" and conducting her own rituals. By age 12, she had met a 14-year-old boy, Tom, who was to become her husband.

Following the Hungarian Uprising in 1956, Budapest joined the 65,000 political refugees who left the country. She completed her high school education in Innsbruck, Austria, and won a scholarship to the University of Vienna, where she studied languages.

Tom located her through relatives, and the two were engaged by the time Budapest was 18. She was awarded a scholarship to the University of Chicago in 1959. Three weeks after her arrival there, she and Tom were married. Budapest had two sons, Laszo and Gabor, by the time she was 21.

Budapest studied improvisational acting with the Second City theatrical school for about two years, learning skills she later put to use in conducting rituals and training priestesses. She began her practice as a SOLITARY, worshiping the Goddess at a home altar.

After a move to New York in 1964, Budapest enrolled in the American Academy of Dramatic Arts and Tom took a teaching job as a mathematics professor. The family lived in Port Washington, Long Island. The marriage ended in 1970, and Budapest moved to California, where she became involved in the feminist movement and worked at the Women's Center.

Budapest saw a need to develop a female-centered theology that not only would help women but would answer opponents of the feminist movement who claimed that feminism was "against God." Drawing on her own heritage and her improvisational skills, she collected six friends and began holding SABBATS. A COVEN was born on the winter solstice, 1971, named the Susan B. Anthony Coven No. 1 after the leader of the women's suffrage movement.

The sabbats were uplifting and empowering, and Budapest's message of revolution, women-only covens and the crushing of an oppressive and aggressive patriarchy drew more participants. The expanding group was moved to the beach and then to a mountaintop in Malibu. Within nine years, membership was at 700 and sister covens had formed across the country. The Dianic Wicca movement (also called "wimmin's religion") grew to a major force both in Witchcraft and feminism.

For 10 years, Budapest led sabbats and full MOON circles, initiating priestesses and teaching women to bless each other and connect with the Goddess through Mother Nature. One of Budapest's pupils was STARHAWK.

Z Budapest

Budapest opened a shop, The Feminist Wicca, in Venice, California, and self-published a book that became a basic text of Dianic Wicca, *The Feminist Book of Lights and Shadows* (1975), a collection of rituals, spells and lore. The book later was sold to a publisher and was released as *The Holy Book of Women's Mysteries: Feminist Witchcraft, Goddess Rituals, Spellcasting and Other Womanly Arts* (1989).

Budapest was arrested in 1975 for giving a Tarot reading to an undercover policewoman. She was put on trial and lost, but the law prohibiting psychic readings was repealed nine years later.

In the early 1980s, Los Angeles' air pollution caused Budapest to close the shop, turn the Susan B. Anthony Coven No. 1 over to another leader, and move to Oakland. She formed a new coven, the Laughing Goddess, but it did not succeed due partly to internal politics and friction.

Budapest did not form or join another coven but developed herself as a speaker, teacher, media personality, author and psychic reader. For a time, she hosted a radio program in the Bay Area, then became director of the Women's Spirituality Forum in Oakland. She also continues to lead rituals, and hosts her own cable television show, *13th Heaven*, a title suggested to her by her deceased mother. She lives in the San Francisco Bay Area.

Her other books are *Grandmother Moon: Lunar Magic in Our Lives: Spells, Rituals, Goddesses, Legends, and Emotions*

Under the Moon (1991); *The Goddess in the Office: A Personal Energy Guide for the Spiritual Warrior at Work* (1993); *The Goddess in the Bedroom: A Passionate Woman's Guide to Celebrating Sexuality Every Night of the Week* (1995); *The Grandmother of Time: A Woman's Book of Celebrations, Spells, and Sacred Objects for Every Month of the Year* (1989); *Celestial Wisdom for Every Year of Your Life: Discover the Hidden Meaning of Your Life* (2003); and *Summoning the Fates: A Guide to Destiny and Transformation* (2nd ed. 2007). Her novel *Rasta Dogs* was self-published in 2003.

The impact of Dianic Wicca may be seen in the increase of literature and college courses devoted to the Goddess and women's spirituality. Budapest termed religion as the "supreme politics" because it influences everything people do. Patriarchal monotheism has worked to the detriment of women; it has glorified war and has permitted suffering for all. Her vision for the future is that of peace and abundance, expressed in female values, to dominate the world's consciousness. Then, Budapest said, "both sexes will be free to flourish according to their natural inclinations and abilities. Global Goddess Consciousness means acknowledging the oneness of all as children of one Mother, our beloved blue planet, the Earth."

burning times   A term used by Wiccans and Pagans to refer to the period in Western history of intense witch hunting and executions, generally the mid-15th to mid-18th centuries.

Burning, one of the most extreme forms of execution, was urged by St. Augustine (354–430), who said that pagans, Jews and heretics would burn forever in eternal fire with the DEVIL unless saved by the Catholic Church. During the INQUISITION, charges of WITCHCRAFT were used against heretics, social outcasts and enemies of the church. Such individuals were declared to have renounced God and formed a compact with the Devil (see DEVIL'S PACT).

Fire is the element of purification, so nothing less than fire could negate the evil of witchcraft. Jean Bodin, a 16th-century demonologist, stated in *De la démonomanie des sorciers:*

> Even if the witch has never killed or done evil to man, or beast, or fruits, and even if he has always cured bewitched people, or driven away tempests, it is because he has renounced God and treated with Satan that he deserves to be burned alive . . . Even if there is no more than the obligation to the Devil, having denied God, this deserves the most cruel death that can be imagined.

Not all witches were burned at the stake; hanging was the preferred means of execution in some countries, including England and the American colonies. In France, Scotland and Germany, it was customary to strangle (worry) condemned witches first, as an act of mercy, by either hanging or garroting, and then burn them to ashes. Nonetheless, many were burned alive, especially if they recanted their confession at the last moment or were unrepentant for their "crimes." The expenses of the burning—along with all the expenses of the trial and the stay in jail—were billed to the deceased's relatives or estate. Witch lynchings and burnings continued sporadically into the late 19th century in England, Europe and Latin America. There are no reliable figures of the numbers of persons burned or otherwise executed for witchcraft. Estimates by historians range from 200,000 to 1 million. Wiccan and Pagan authors have cited 9 million as the number of victims, but this is an inflated figure without evidence of support.

The burning of a witch was a great public occasion. The execution took place shortly after the sentencing, just long enough to hire an executioner, construct the execution site and gather the fuel. In Scotland, a witch burning was preceded by days of fasting and solemn preaching. The witch was strangled first, and then her corpse—or sometimes her unconscious or semiconscious body—was tied to a stake or dumped into a tar barrel and set afire. If the witch was not dead and managed to get out of the flames, onlookers shoved her back in. Records of trials in Scotland report that burning a witch consumed 16 loads of peat plus wood and coal. In 1608 witches in Brechin, Scotland were executed in the following manner, according to original records as cited in *Enemies of God: The Witch hunt in Scotland* (1981) by Christine Larner:

> . . . they were brunt quick [alive] eftir sic ane crewell maner, than sum of thame deit in despair, renunceand and blasphemeand; and utheris, half brunt, brake out of the fyre, and wes cast quick in it agane, quhill they wer brunt to the deid.

The term *burning times* also refers to any threatened prejudice against or persecution of Wiccans and Pagans by other religious groups, law enforcement agencies, employers, politicians and others (see HELMS AMENDMENT).

FURTHER READING:
Barstow, Anne Llewellyn. *Witchcraze: A New History of the European Witch Hunts.* San Francisco: Pandora/HarperCollins, 1994.

Burroughs, George (d. 1692)   Minister accused of witchcraft and executed in the SALEM WITCHES hysteria in Massachusetts in 1692 to 1693.

George Burroughs served as minister of Salem Village from 1680 to 1982. He was a man of good reputation, having graduated from Harvard in 1670. He had distinguished himself as a preacher in Maine, especially in the face of hostilities from Indians. Invited to Salem Village, he had no idea of the hornet's nest of social and political infighting that awaited him. Not everyone was pleased to have him.

After moving, Burroughs and his wife lived for a time with Thomas and Rebecca Putnam. Later, when the witch hysteria broke out, the Putnams alleged that Burroughs had treated his wife cruelly.

Burroughs' wife died in September 1681. By then, Burroughs had not been paid his salary for some time, a casualty of the local infighting. He went into debt to pay for his wife's funeral. Perhaps it was the combination of grief over his loss and frustration at the sentiments raging in the village, but Burroughs decided not to pursue the monies owed him and quit his job. He returned to Maine, where he became a pastor in Wells.

In 1683, a suit was brought against Burroughs for the unpaid debt for funeral expenses. The suit was dropped when Burroughs demonstrated that the village owed him back salary, which could be applied to the debt. The situation fomented ill will against the minister.

Burroughs was long gone from Salem Village when the witchcraft hysteria erupted in 1692. Burroughs was decried as a witch. Twelve-year-old Ann Putnam said that on April 20 the specter of a minister appeared and tortured and choked her, urging her to write in his devil's book. She identified the specter as Burroughs. She said he told her he had three wives and that he had bewitched the first two to death. He also said he had killed Mrs. Lawson and her daughter Ann; he had bewitched many soldiers to death; and he had turned Abigail Hobbs into a witch. He claimed to be a conjurer, which was above a witch.

On May 4, Burroughs was arrested at his home in Wells, Maine—while he sat at his dinner table with his family, according to lore—and brought immediately to Salem. In his examination on May 9, he was accused of witchcraft, of not attending communion on some occasions and of not baptizing all but his eldest child. These were grave sins for a minister. Like others who had been cried out against, Burroughs was simply astounded both at the accusations and the girls falling into fits claiming that he was tormenting and biting them.

Putnam said that on May 8, the apparition of Burroughs appeared to her again and told her that she would soon see his dead two wives, who would tell her lies. She saw two ghosts of women in burial shrouds. They said that Burroughs had been cruel to them and had killed them. The first wife said she had been stabbed beneath the armpit and the wound covered with sealing wax. She pulled aside her burial shroud to show Putnam the wound. Putnam also said that the ghosts of Lawson and her child appeared and said they, too, had been murdered by Burroughs. Later, Putnam saw the ghost of Goody Fuller, who said Burroughs had killed her over a dispute with her husband.

Others, including eight confessed witches, came forward against him. Burroughs was a man of small stature but had exceptional strength for his size. It was alleged that his unusual strength came from the Devil, and that he reveled in letting others know of his occult powers, also granted by the Devil. By the time the testimonies were done, Burroughs was the ringleader of all the witches, tempting and seducing them, giving them POPPETS for evil SPELLS.

Burroughs was tried on August 5. Found guilty, he was condemned to death by hanging. On August 19, he and four others were driven to GALLOWS HILL in an open cart. He mounted the gallows and then preached a sermon, ending with the LORD'S PRAYER. His flawless recitation of the prayer upset the onlookers, for it was strongly believed that a witch could not say the prayer without stumbling. COTTON MATHER, watching astride his white horse, kept the execution on track by telling the crowd that Burroughs was not an ordained minister and, thus, the Devil could help him recite the prayer. The executions proceeded.

Burroughs and the others were cut down and dragged by halters to a shallow hole about two feet deep. Burroughs' shirt and pants were pulled off, and an old pair of pants belonging to one of the executed were put on him. The bodies were barely covered with dirt. Burroughs' chin and one hand stuck out from the ground, along with a foot of one of the others.

After his execution, more stories of his dealings with the Devil circulated through Salem. The citizens seemed to need a sense of justification at having killed the man who once led their church. Mather made special effort to spread disparaging stories. Filled with loathing of Burroughs, Mathers said he could hardly speak his name and would not have done so except that the state of Massachusetts asked for accounts of the Salem trials to be included in Mather's book, *On Witchcraft: Being the Wonders of the Invisible World*.

FURTHER READING:

Demos, John Putnam. *Entertaining Satan: Witchcraft and the Culture of Early New England*. New York: Oxford University Press, 2004.

Hansen, Chadwick. *Witchcraft at Salem*. New York: New American Library, 1969.

Mather, Cotton. *On Witchcraft: Being the Wonders of the Invisible World*. Mt. Vernon, N.Y.: The Peter Pauper Press, 1950. First published 1693.

Upham, Charles. *History of Witchcraft and Salem Village*. Boston: Wiggin and Lunt, 1867.

Bury St. Edmonds Witches   Of the various witch trials of Suffolk, England, conducted in Bury St. Edmonds during the 17th century, two episodes stand out. In 1645, 68 WITCHES went to their deaths on the gallows, victims of the witch-hunting zeal of MATTHEW HOPKINS and John Stearne. Seventeen years later, in 1662, Sir Matthew Hale presided over trials that led to the condemnation and execution of two witches based on the flimsy spectral evidence of hysterical, "possessed" children. The 1662 trials heavily influenced officials of the Salem witch trials in 1692–93, the worst witch incident in the history of America (see SALEM WITCHES).

The Hopkins trials. In 1645 Matthew Hopkins, England's most notorious WITCH-HUNTER, and his associate, John Stearne, a rigid Puritan, were storming about the countryside routing out "witches" in exchange for exorbitant fees. Using unscrupulous methods to extract confessions, the witch-hunters, according to surviving records, charged at least 124 Suffolk men and women with witchcraft, who were tried at Bury St. Edmonds in August. (There probably were more persons charged than surviving records indicate.) Most of the "confessions" concerned the possession by evil imps (see IMP), the making of compacts with the Devil (see DEVIL'S PACT) and having carnal relations with the Devil, the latter of which was guaranteed to inflame Puritan outrage. Some of the witches also were charged with the murder of livestock and people.

Victims were thoroughly searched for witch's marks (see WITCH'S MARK), a most humiliating ordeal for women, since the "marks" usually were found in or on the genitals. These marks, which were said to be supernumerary teats from which imps sucked, were discovered in the folds of the labia or were sometimes the clitoris itself. Stearne had a particular fondness for searching for witch's marks and boasted that 18 of the Bury St. Edmonds witches "all were found by the searchers to have teats or dugs which their imps used to suck. . . . And of these witches some confessed that they have had carnal copulation with the Devil, one of which said that she had conceived twice by him, but as soon as she was delivered of them, they ran away in most horrid, long and ugly shapes."

Men also were said to have these teats. John Bysack confessed that he had been compromised 20 years earlier by the Devil who came in through his window in the shape of a sandy-colored, rugged dog and demanded that Bysack renounce God, Christ and his baptism. Bysack agreed, and the Devil used his claw to draw BLOOD from Bysack's heart. The Devil gave him six imps in the forms of snails, who sustained themselves by sucking Bysack's blood. Each snail was an assassin with a particular assignment: Atleward killed cows, Jeffry pigs, Peter sheep, Pyman fowls, Sacar horses and Sydrake Christians. Stearne claimed he found snail marks on Bysack's body.

Margaret Wyard confessed to having seven imps, including flies, dogs, mice and a spider. She had only five teats, however, which forced her imps to fight "like pigs with a sow." Wyard said the Devil had come to her seven years earlier in the likeness of a calf, saying he was her husband. She would not submit sexually to him (a comment, perhaps, on the state of her marriage) until the Devil returned as "a handsome young gentleman." Imps of other accused witches included a chicken named Nan; two "heavy and hairy" mice; and three imps "like chickens."

Stearne recorded that 68 witches were executed; one who was tried at Ipswich instead of Bury St. Edmonds reportedly was burned to death. Dozens more may have been hanged—records are uncertain—and still others died in prison.

Ironically, Parliament had established a special commission to oversee witch-hunting activities, in response to reports of excesses. The commission, however, benignly accepted the "evidence" for Devil's pacts and the existence of imps, leaving Hopkins and Stearne free to wreak their havoc for another two years.

The hysterical children of 1662. Rose Cullender and Amy Duny of Lowestoft, Suffolk, were two old widows who were accused of bewitching seven children, one of them to death, and performing various other malicious acts upon their neighbors over a period of years. Sir Matthew Hale (later Chief Justice), who heard the trials, was a believer in witchcraft and did nothing to discourage the most outrageous accusations. The trials of the two unfortunates were recorded by COTTON MATHER in *On Witchcraft: Being the Wonders of the Invisible World* (1692).

Duny's fate as a witch was sealed when she was hired as a baby-sitter by Dorothy Durent for her infant. Duny tried to nurse the baby, William, contrary to Durent's instructions, and was reprimanded, much to her (obvious) displeasure. Not long after, the baby began having fits that went on for weeks. Durent took it to a "white witch" doctor (a man), who told her to hang the child's blanket in a corner of the chimney for a day and a night, then wrap the infant in it and burn anything that fell out. According to Mather:

> . . . at Night, there fell a great Toad out of the Blanket, which ran up and down the Hearth. A Boy catch't it, and held it in the Fire with the Tongs: where it made a horrible Noise, and Flash'd like to Gun-Powder, with a report like that of a Pistol: Whereupon the Toad was no more to be seen.

The child recovered. The next day, Duny reportedly was seen with burn marks. Now labeled a witch, Duny was accused of causing fits in other children who had had contact with her. The Durents's 10-year-old daughter, Elizabeth, fell into fits, complaining that the specter of Duny plagued her. The girl became lame in both legs and died within three days. Mrs. Durent herself went lame and had to walk about with crutches. Another Durent child, Ann, suffered fits and swooning spells and vomited pins (see ALLOTRIOPHAGY), blaming her maladies on the specter of Rose Cullender.

The nine- and 11-year-old daughters of Samuel Pacy, Deborah and Elizabeth, suffered fits that included lameness, extreme stomach pain as though being stabbed with pins and "shrieking at a dreadful manner, like a Whelp, rather than a rational creature." They also vomited crooked pins and a two-penny nail. These girls cried out against Duny and Cullender, claiming to see them as specters, and saying that the witches threatened them not to talk, lest they be tormented 10 times greater than before. The Pacy girls could not pronounce the names of Lord, Jesus or Christ without falling into fits. But the names of Satan or the Devil made them say, "This bites, but it makes me speak right well!"

The Pacy children also saw invisible mice, one of which they threw on the fire, and it "screeched like a Rat." Another invisible mouse thrown on the fire "Flash'd like to Gun-Powder" just like the toad of Durent. The specter of Duny, meanwhile, tempted one of the girls to destroy herself.

Jane Bocking was so afflicted with fits and pain caused by the specters of Duny and Cullender that her mother had to testify in her place.

Another girl, Susan Chandler, said Cullender would come into her bed, and that she was accompanied by a great dog. Chandler had fits and vomited pins. Cullender was searched for a witch's mark. According to Mather.

> . . . they found on her Belly a thing like a Teat, of an inch long; which the *said Rose* ascribed to a strain. But near her Privy-parts, they found Three more, that were smaller than the former. At the end of the long Teat, there was a little Hole, which appeared, as if newly Sucked; and upon straining it, a white Milky matter issued out.

To bolster the testimony of the girls and their families, the court heard "evidence" from others. John Soam testified that one day, while he was bringing home his hay in three carts, one cart wrenched the window of Cullender's house. She flew out in a rage, shouting threats against Soam. The cart that wrenched the window later overturned two or three times the same day. The men had such difficulty with the carts—one got stuck in a gate, so that the gateposts had to be cut down—and were so exhausted that their noses bled.

Robert Sherringham testified to a similar incident, in which the axle-tree of his cart broke off a part of Cullender's house. (Perhaps Cullender's house was in an unfortunate position on a roadway; if these accidents happened regularly, it is understandable that she would lose her temper.) In an angry fit, Cullender told him his horses should suffer for it. Within a short time, his four horses died, followed by many of his cattle. Sherringham also was afflicted with lameness and was "so vexed with Lice of an extraordinary Number and Bignes, that no Art could hinder the Swarming of them, till he burnt up two Suits of Apparel."

As for other testimony against Duny, she was said to have been overheard saying the Devil would not let her rest until she revenged herself on the wife of one Cornelius Sandswel. The Sandswels' chimney collapsed and their chickens died suddenly.

Sir Thomas Browne, a respected physician, testified that the victims were bewitched and commented that witches discovered in Denmark afflicted their victims in the same manner, with fits and vomitings of pins.

Mather wrote of Hale's instructions to the jury:

> He made no doubt, there were such Creatures as Witches; for the Scriptures affirmed it; and the Wisdom of all Nations had provided Laws against such persons. He pray'd the God of Heaven to direct their Hearts in

the weighty thing they had in hand; for, *To Condemn the Innocent, and let the guilty go free, were both an Abomination to the Lord.*

The jury took exactly half an hour to convict Duny and Cullender on 19 counts of witchcraft. The next morning, the children were miraculously restored to good health. Duny and Cullender confessed nothing, and were hanged.

When the witch hysteria broke out in Salem in 1692, the authorities took their cue from the 1662 Bury St. Edmonds trials and Hale's reputation as a judge. As Mather wrote in *Wonders of the Invisible World:*

> It may cast some Light upon the Dark things now in *America,* if we just give a glance upon the *like things* lately happening in *Europe.* We may see the *Witchcrafts* here most exactly resemble the *Witchcrafts* there; and we may learn what sort of Devils do trouble the World.

FURTHER READING:

Deacon, Richard. *Matthew Hopkins: Witch Finder General.* London: Frederick Muller, 1976.

Hole, Christina. *Witchcraft in England.* London: B.T. Batsford Ltd., 1947.

Mather, Cotton. *On Witchcraft: Being the Wonders of the Invisible World.* 1692. Reprint, Mt. Vernon, N.Y.: The Peter Pauper Press, 1950.

Pennick, Nigel. *Secrets of East Anglican Magic.* London: Robert Hale, 1995.

Butters, Mary (late 18th–early 19th centuries) An attempt to cure a cow of bewitchment with white MAGIC ended in disaster for Mary Butters, the "Carmoney Witch," who narrowly escaped a trial in Carricfergus, Ireland, in March 1808. Butters was a reputed wise woman, skilled in herbal knowledge and various SPELLS.

In August 1807 Butters was hired by Alexander Montgomery, a tailor who lived in Carmoney, to cure a cow that gave milk from which no butter could be made. Montgomery's wife was convinced that the cow was bewitched. On the appointed night of the exorcism (see SPIRIT EXORCISM), Butters arrived with her CHARM bag of magical ingredients. She ordered Montgomery and an onlooker, a young man named Carnaghan, out to the barn, where they were to turn their waistcoats inside out and stand by the cow's head until she sent for them. Butters, Mrs. Montgomery, the Montgomery's son and an old woman named Margaret Lee remained with her in the house.

Montgomery and Carnaghan waited until dawn, growing increasingly worried. They returned to the house, where they were shocked to find all four persons collapsed on the floor. The smoky air smelled of sulphur; on the fire was a big pot containing milk, needles, PINS and crooked nails. The windows and door were sealed tight, and the chimney was covered. The wife and son were dead, and Butters and Lee were close to death; Lee died moments after the men arrived. In a fury, Montgomery threw

Butters out onto a dung heap and began kicking her to consciousness.

On August 19 an inquest was held in Carmoney, at which it was determined that the victims had died of suffocation from Butters's "noxious ingredients" and smoke. Butters, terrified, claimed that during her spell-casting, a black man appeared inside the house wielding a huge club. He knocked everyone down, killing the other three and stunning Butters to unconsciousness.

Butters was put forward for trial at the spring assizes, but the charges against her were dropped. The community's reaction to the tragedy was one of derision. The incident was made the subject of a humorous ballad.

FURTHER READING:
Seymour, St. John D. *Irish Witchcraft and Demonology*. Dublin: Hodges, Figgis & Co., 1913.

Cabot, Laurie (1933–) Witch, author, artist, businesswoman, civil rights watchdog and founder of two traditions of contemporary Witchcraft. Known as "the Official Witch of Salem" in Salem, Massachusetts, Laurie Cabot has attracted attention for her dramatic dress of flowing black garments and PENTACLE pendants, which she always wears when in public.

Cabot (her maiden name) is descended from a line of Cabots from the Isle of Jersey off the coast of England, a place renowned for its witchcraft. An only child, she was born March 6, 1933, in Wewoka, Oklahoma, during a family move from Boston to Anaheim, California. Her father was a businessman. From an early age she felt an affinity with witches, although she did not know exactly what a witch was. According to Cabot, her heritage includes a long line of witches, including a mysterious woman who lived some 4,000–5,000 years ago whose genetic memory Cabot feels she possesses nearly intact.

By age six, her psychic gifts became apparent, and she constantly was in trouble for discussing information she picked up through extrasensory perception. From her father, a science-oriented man who did not believe in the Devil, Cabot developed a lifelong interest in science, which she dovetailed with her interest in witchcraft, the occult and the paranormal.

From Anaheim, Cabot returned to Boston at age 14 with her mother in order to finish high school. She embarked on a comparative study of religions and spent much time in the library. There she met a woman on the staff who encouraged her to look beyond Christianity for information on paranormal phenomena. The woman eventually revealed she was a Witch and introduced Cabot to two other female Witches, one of them elderly. The three women helped to school Cabot in the Craft. When she was 16, the Witches initiated her in a profoundly transformational experience. She was anointed with oil and dubbed with a sword. She took the sword, impaled it in the earth, and said, "I return to earth my wisdom and I call myself Witch."

Cabot made a life's projection for herself, in which she asked the GODDESS and God to enable her to teach Witchcraft as a science.

After high school, Cabot did not follow through on plans to attend Smith College, but instead became a dancer in Boston's Latin Quarter. She was married twice, first to an Italian and then to a Greek, and had a daughter by each husband: Jody in 1963 and Penny in 1965. After her second divorce, in the late 1960s, Cabot and her daughters moved to the north end of Boston. She made a vow that she would live her life "totally as a Witch": she would wear nothing but traditional Witch clothing (which she says is long black robes), wear her pentacle displayed, and would emulate the Goddess by outlining her eyes in black makeup, according, she says, to an ancient tradition.

She admits she was naive in not realizing how such attire would provoke people and in thinking that as soon as she explained herself, others would understand and

Laurie Cabot (COURTESY LAURIE CABOT)

accept her. Over the years, she has had to deal with jokes, aversion and accusations that her dress is for purposes of commercial exploitation.

At the urging of a friend, Cabot moved to Boston, where she and the friend rented a house that was the first house built on Salem's historic Chesnut Street, and had been home to NATHANIEL HAWTHORNE for a year. Three years earlier, Cabot had gone through a past-life regression to see the life of a Susan Sarah Prescott who supposedly had lived in Salem during the 1700s. Cabot believes she picked up on traces of a genetic memory. She discovered that Prescott had indeed existed and that her father had been the builder of their house. She stayed in the house one year.

Cabot also discovered that Salem had little idea what to think of modern Witches. Members of the public derided her for believing "in all that," and other Witches criticized her for her appearance. Through a new friend, she began teaching "Witchcraft as a Science" classes for the public, forming the beginnings of her Science Tradition of Witchcraft. She also taught classes for seven years in the Salem State College continuing education program.

She opened The Witch Shop in Salem, which did not do well and closed; a second venture, Crow Haven Corner, was successful and has become a tourist attraction in Salem. Cabot turned the shop over to daughter Jody in the late 1970s.

In 1973, Cabot established the annual Witches' Ball, a costume party to celebrate Samhain (All Hallow's Eve) in Salem, which each year draws an international crowd of participants and media.

Since 1971, Cabot had sought to be named "the Official Witch of Salem," but was turned down by local government; then-Mayor Samuel Zoll was quoted saying he thought it would be "improper" and that "the historical recognition of the city would be internationally demeaned by allowing a commercial capitalization by one individual." In 1977, Michael Dukakis, then governor of Massachusetts, signed a citation granting Cabot the title. The "Paul Revere" citation, as it is called, is recognition given to various citizens courtesy of members of the legislature. Cabot received hers for her work with dyslexic children.

Cabot has long urged Witches to take a stronger stand for their civil rights and public image. In 1986, she founded the WITCHES LEAGUE OF PUBLIC AWARENESS to serve as a media watchdog and civil rights advocate for Witchcraft.

She entered the Salem mayoral race in 1987 after incumbent Anthony V. Salvo made derogatory comments about Witchcraft and Witches in the press. One of Salvo's opponents, Robert E. Gauthier, a friend of Cabot's, was rumored to be a "WARLOCK," a term not favored by Witches of either sex. Gauthier denied this and blamed the Salvo camp for spreading the rumors. Salvo denied the accusation, saying he discounted witchcraft, and no one with "average intelligence" believed in it. Cabot jumped into the race "to prove that Witches have civil rights" and ran a spirited campaign that attracted local support and national media attention. But on August 11, the deadline for returning nominating papers, she dropped out of the race, citing business commitments, including work on a book. Cabot continued to serve Salem as a member of the executive board of the Chamber of Commerce, which she joined in 1980.

In 1988 she established the Temple of Isis, a chapter of the National Alliance of Pantheists. Through the National Alliance of Pantheists, she was ordained Reverend Cabot and may perform legal marriages.

In 1955, Cabot founded the Cabot Tradition of the Science of Witchcraft (originally called Witchcraft as a Science), which she described as Celtic and "pre-Gardnerian" (see GERALD B. GARDNER). It teaches practical magic and adheres to the WICCAN REDE ("Do what you will and harm none") and the THREEFOLD LAW OF KARMA (everything one does returns threefold). Classes and workshops in the science tradition continue; one of Cabot's premier students is CHRISTOPHER PENCZAK. Cabot also teaches classes in Witchcraft as religion and art.

Cabot's books include *Practical Magic: A Salem Witch's Handbook* (1986); *The Power of the Witch,* with Tom Cowan (1990); *Love Magic,* with Tom Cowan (1992); *Celebrate the Earth: A Year of Holidays in the Pagan Tradition,* with Jean

Mills and Karen Bagnard (1994); and *The Witch in Every Woman: Reawakening the Magical Nature of the Feminine to Heal, Protect, Create and Empower,* with Jean Mills (1997).

Cabot maintains a full schedule of teaching classes, giving readings and making public appearances. She is active in community work, including a tree-planting program for the Salem area. She continues to host the annual Witches' Ball at Samhain, and she is involved in Wiccan/Pagan civil rights issues. In 2007, she founded the Project Witches Protection, an educational organization "dedicated to correcting misinformation and Witches and Witchcraft."

The Cabot Tradition

This tradition holds that Witchcraft is a science as well as a religion and an art. As a science, it may be applied to harness and expand psychic potential. The key to extrasensory perception is the harnessing of light energy and the sensitivity to alpha waves, which are part of the aura surrounding every living thing. Cabot says her method of controlling alpha waves is based on an ancient Pythagorean method of using colors and numbers.

Cabot teaches that each individual is responsible for all his or her thoughts and actions. The WICCAN REDE, "An' it harm no living thing, do what you will," is extended to defending oneself against evil energy or psychic attack. While other traditions hold that it is acceptable to boomerang psychic attack back to the sender, the Cabot Tradition considers this a violation of the Rede. Instead, practitioners are taught to erect a psychic neutralizing shield, which enables them to either transform the energy so that it can be used in a positive fashion or distintegrate it so that it harms no one, including the sender.

The Cabot Tradition includes practitioners of all other traditions; therefore, rituals are eclectic. Practitioners wear black, which the tradition considers to be the traditional witch's color. Cabot notes that black absorbs light while white reflects it; this absorption of light facilitates psychic power. To further augment power, practitioners wear gold jewelry for psychic strength, usually in the form of a pentacle pendant. At least one piece of silver jewelry is worn for its psychic power properties.

In addition to Craft basics and history, instruction includes parapsychology; physiology; astrology; geometric structure; sociology; anthropology; meditation; aura reading, balancing and healing; the use of crystals; and the psychic arts. The Cabot Tradition traces the origins of the Craft to the Celts. The tradition teaches past-life regression and Cabot's theory of the Root Races of humankind, which holds that humans come from other planetary systems. According to Cabot, alpha waves store all knowledge of the universe, and a person who enters an alpha trance may pick up on vibrations from the past.

FURTHER READING:
Cabot, Laurie, with Tom Cowan. *Power of the Witch.* London: Michael Joseph, 1990.

Laurie Cabot Web site. URL: http://www.cabotwitchcraft. com. Downloaded October 2, 2007.

cakes-and-wine (also cakes-and-ale)   In WICCA and PAGANISM, a relaxed sharing of refreshments, conversation, dancing and singing that follows rituals, circles, seasonal celebrations (see WHEEL OF THE YEAR), RITES OF PASSAGE and other sacred occasions. The food and drink, which help to replenish energy after psychic work has been done, are consecrated and blessed by the high priest and priestess, which imbues the refreshments with divine energy of the Goddess and God. An offering is made to the deities as a thanks for the basic necessities of life. The high priest and high priestess sample the food and drink then share them with the group. Some of the refreshments may be scattered upon the earth as an offering, or be left for the FAIRIES or ELEMENTALS.

FURTHER READING:
Crowley, Vivianne. *Wicca: The Old Religion in the New Millennium.* Revised ed. London: Thorsons/HarperCollins, 1996.

Calling Down the Moon   See DRAWING DOWN THE MOON.

candles   Candles have a long history in religious worship, MAGIC and folklore. Candlelight repels evil spirits while attracting benevolent ones. In liturgy, they are offerings of fealty to a deity. In magic, candles are used in various rituals and SPELLS.

Beeswax candles were used in Egypt and Crete as early as 3000 B.C.E. Egyptians of about the 3rd century C.E. used lamps and possibly candles in a magic ritual for "dreaming true," or obtaining answers from dreams. The individual retired to a dark cave facing south, and stared into a flame until he saw a god. He then lay down and went to sleep, anticipating that the god would appear in his dreams with the answers he sought.

Ancient pagans used candles and lamps in religious observances, a practice which the Roman Christian theologian Tertullian (ca. 200) vehemently protested as "the useless lighting of lamps at noonday." By the fourth century, both candles and lamps were part of Christian rituals, but it was not until the latter part of the Middle Ages that candles were placed on church altars. The Catholic Church established the use of consecrated holy candles in rituals of blessings and absolving sins, and in exorcising demons (see EXORCISM). Medieval farmers used holy candles to protect their livestock from danger and bewitchment. During the INQUISITION, inquisitors' handbooks such as the *MALLEUS MALEFICARUM* (1486) prescribed holy candles as among those consecrated objects "for preserving oneself from the injury of witches."

During the witch hunts, witches were said to light candles at their SABBATS as offerings of fealty to the DEVIL, who was often portrayed as wearing a lighted candle between his horns. The witches lit their candles from the Devil's candle; sometimes he lit the candles and handed them to his followers. Witches also put lighted candles in the faggots of their brooms, which they rode through the air to their sabbats.

It was believed that witches made perverse use of holy candles in putting CURSES on individuals. According to an English work, *Dives and Pauper* (1536), "it hath oft been known that witches, with saying of the Paternoster and dropping of the holy candle in a man's steps that they hated, hath done his feet rotten of."

In contemporary Witchcraft, consecrated white candles are placed on altars and at the four quarters of a MAGIC CIRCLE. If a ritual calls for it, candles are placed at the points of a pentagram (see PENTACLE AND PENTAGRAM). Candles are burned in all religious ceremonies. Colored candles are used in magical SPELLS; each color has its own vibration, attribute, symbolism and influence.

See HAND OF GLORY.

FURTHER READING:
Marlbrough, Ray L. *Charms, Spells & Formulas.* St. Paul, Minn.: Llewellyn Publications, 1987.

Canewdon Witches   According to a prophecy by the famous 19th-century CUNNING MAN JAMES MURRELL, the Essex village of Canewdon, located in England's "witch country" of East Anglia, would be populated with witches "forever." Indeed, the village and the surrounding area have been steeped in witch lore since at least 1580, when a woman named Rose Pye was accused of witchcraft, tried and acquitted. Legend has it that every time a stone falls from the tower of St. Nicholas Church, one witch will die but another will take her place. At midnight, a headless witch sometimes materializes near the church and floats down to the river. Anyone who encounters her is lifted into the air and let down in the nearest ditch.

Many of the witches of Canewdon were said to keep white mice FAMILIARS, or IMPS. A blacksmith, who became a witch when he sold his soul to the DEVIL, was given mice familiars. When he reached the end of his life—in fear of his eventual fate—he confessed on his deathbed that he could not die until he had passed on his powers to a successor. All of his imps climbed up on the bed and sat before him as he spoke. His wife refused them, but at last he was able to persuade his daughter to accept them, and he died.

Canewdon witches were usually described as old, ugly women with unpleasant personalities, true to the HAG stereotype. In the late 19th century, their bewitchments were countered by a white witch, known as Granny, with such folk-magic CHARMS as a knife or pair of scissors under the doormat, which would keep witches out, and potions made for WITCH BOTTLES that would break BEWITCHMENTS.

See OLD GEORGE PICKINGILL.

FURTHER READING:
Folklore, Myths and Legends of Britain. London: Reader's Digest Assoc. Ltd., 1977.
Maple, Eric. *The Dark World of Witches.* New York: A. S. Barnes & Co., 1962.
Pennick, Nigel. *Secrets of East Anglican Magic.* London: Robert Hale, 1995.

Canon Episcopi   One of the most important ecclesiastical documents of the Middle Ages was the *Canon Episcopi,* ca. 900, which defined witchcraft as Devil-worship but declared it to be nothing more than a foolish delusion. The origin of the canon is unknown. When it was made public at the beginning of the 10th century by Regino of Prüm, Abbot of Treves, it was erroneously presented as an ancient authority dating back to the fourth century. Around 1140, the Italian monk, Gratian, incorporated the *Canon Episcopi* into his authoritative text of canon law, the *Concordance of Discordant Canons* (usually called the *Decretum*). Thus the *Episcopi* became entrenched in the highest canonical law.

The *Canon Episcopi* denied that witches had the ability to fly through the air and metamorphose themselves into animals and birds (see FLYING; METAMORPHOSIS). Whoever was "so stupid and foolish" as to believe such fantastic tales was an infidel. While such *physical* feats were impossible, the canon acknowledged that they could be accomplished *in spirit.*

The *Canon Episcopi* presented a dilemma for the demonologists of the 12th century and later, who accepted the physical reality of metamorphosis and transvection. Convoluted theories were put forth in order to skirt the *Canon Episcopi.* It was reasoned that, even if witches flew with DIANA and DEMONS in spirit or imagination only, they were just as guilty as if they had done so in the flesh. It was then easy to propose that all heretics (including witches) were guilty of having pacts with the Devil (see DEVIL'S PACT) just by virtue of being heretics.

With its portrayal of hordes of women riding upon beasts through the air at night, following their goddess Diana, the *Canon Episcopi* helped promote the idea of the demonical sabbat, the descriptions of which became increasing lurid in the writings of demonologists (see SABBATS).

The text of the *Canon Episcopi* is as follows:

Bishops and their officials must labor with all their strength to uproot thoroughly from their parishes the pernicious art of sorcery and malefice invented by the Devil, and if they find a man or woman follower of this wickedness to eject them foully disgraced from their parishes. For the Apostle says, "A man that is a heretic after the first and second admonition avoid." Those are held captive by the Devil who, leaving their creator, seek the aid of the Devil. And so Holy Church must be cleansed of this pest. It is also not to be omitted that some wicked women, perverted by the Devil, seduced by illusions and phantasms of demons, believe and profess themselves, in the hours of the night, to ride upon certain beasts with Diana, the goddess of pagans, and an innumerable multitude of women, and in the silence of the dead of the night to traverse great spaces of earth, and to obey her commands as of their mistress, and to be summoned to her service on certain nights. But I wish it were they alone who perished in their faithlessness and did not draw many with them into the destruction of infidelity. For an innumerable multitude, deceived by this false opinion, believe this to be true, and so believing, wander from the right faith and are involved in the error of the pagans when they think that there is anything of divinity or power except the one God. Wherefore the priests throughout their churches should preach with all insistence to the people that they may know this to be in every way false and that such phantasms are imposed on the minds of infidels and not by the divine but by the malignant spirit. Thus Satan himself, who transfigures himself into an angel of light, when he has captured the mind of a miserable woman and has subjugated her to himself by infidelity and incredulity, immediately transforms himself into the species and similitudes of different personages and deluding the mind which he holds captive and exhibiting things, joyful or mournful, and persons, known or unknown, leads it through devious ways, and while the spirit alone endures this, the faithless mind thinks these things happen not in the spirit but in the body. Who is there that is not led out of himself in dreams and nocturnal visions, and sees much when sleeping which he has never seen waking? Who is so stupid and foolish as to think that all these things which are only done in spirit happen in the body, when the Prophet Ezekiel saw visions of the Lord in spirit and not in the body, and the Apostle John saw and heard the mysteries of the Apocalypse in the spirit and not in the body, as he himself says "I was in the spirit"? And Paul does not dare to say that he was rapt in the body. It is therefore to be proclaimed publicly to all that whoever believes such things or similar to these loses the faith, and he who has not the right faith in God is not of God but of him in whom he believes, that is, of the Devil. For of our Lord it is written "All things were made by Him." Whoever therefore believes that anything can be made, or that any creature can be changed to better or to worse or be transformed into another species or similitude, except by the Creator himself who made everything and through whom all things were made, is beyond doubt an infidel.

By the mid-15th century, inquisitors and demonologists had begun to dismiss the *Canon Episcopi*. Its influence, however, lingered for at least another 200 years.

FURTHER READING:

Baroja, Julio Caro. *The World of the Witches.* Chicago: University of Chicago Press, 1975. First published 1961.

Lea, Henry Charles. *Materials Toward a History of Witchcraft.* Philadelphia: University of Pennsylvania, 1939.

Russell, Jeffrey Burton. *Witchcraft in the Middle Ages.* Ithaca and London: Cornell University Press, 1972.

Carmoney Witch   See MARY BUTTERS.

Carpenter, Dennis (1954–)   Prominent American Pagan scholar and, with his wife, SELENA FOX, codirector of CIRCLE SANCTUARY in Mt. Horeb, Wisconsin. Since the mid-1990s, Dennis Carpenter has served as a leading academic Pagan spokesperson, participating in interdisciplinary and interfaith networking and dialogue around the world.

Carpenter was born on January 16, 1954, in Hillsboro, Wisconsin, a farming community in southwestern Wisconsin, not far from his present home at Circle. He was raised on a dairy farm in a Protestant family and spent a great deal of time in childhood outdoors, learning to appreciate nature. A pivotal experience of finding the spiritual dimensions of nature came in high school, when he participated in the "Endu Club" (*Endu* was short for "Endurance"), a church-sponsored activity for boys featuring outdoors adventures.

Dennis Carpenter and Selena Fox on their wedding day in June 1986 at Circle Sanctuary (COURTESY CIRCLE SANCTUARY)

Carpenter attended the University of Wisconsin, graduating in 1977 with a bachelor's degree in psychology, and earning his master's degree in psychology in 1979. He began his career as a school psychologist. For five years he lived in a cabin by a lake, deepening his rapport with nature.

In the early 1980s, friends introduced Carpenter to a UW professor of philosophy who had Pagan interests and was involved with Circle, which had already been formed by Fox. He recommended books to Carpenter, and interested him in attending some Circle events. The first came in 1982, when Carpenter attended a program sponsored by Circle featuring STARHAWK. In 1983, he attended Circle's annual Pagan Spirit Gathering, followed by involvement in more of Circle's activities.

In 1984, Carpenter moved to Circle and became publications editor, a position he continues to hold. He and Fox were married in 1986 in a two-part Pagan handfasting ceremony.

In the first part, they were legally married in a ceremony at the June new moon, attended by family and a few friends. MARGOT ADLER officiated. The second part was a large ceremony at Circle's Pagan Spirit Gathering—again with Adler officiating—held in Eagle Cave, Wisconsin's largest onyx cave.

Around this time, Carpenter became interested in pursuing more academic work. Through his interests in humanistic and transpersonal psychologies, he met Stanley Krippner, a psychologist at the Saybrook Institute in San Francisco, California, who has long been involved in research into parapsychology, healing and altered states of consciousness. Carpenter enrolled in a doctoral program at Saybrook in 1988, focusing his academic work on Paganism, which was attracting the attention of scholars. He was nominated for "Best Essay of the Year" in 1992 and 1993 at Saybrook, and in 1993 received the Parker Scholarship for research.

In 1994 he was awarded a Ph.D. with distinction in psychology, Saybrook's highest graduate honor. His dissertation concerned the nature of Pagans' experiences with the Divine, how those experiences impacted life, and especially how they influenced ecological views and actions.

Carpenter is an author of essays and articles on various aspects of Paganism. With Fox, he participates in conferences, seminars and symposia, presenting papers and workshops. He views his role as helping to articulate the Pagan worldview, explore the relationship between humankind and nature, and build international bridges of understanding. Paganism remains too diverse to espouse a unified message, and so Carpenter focuses on the ripple effects of Paganism: how people change when they understand divine immanence and a reverence for nature.

In addition to his editorial functions at Circle, Carpenter oversees administrative affairs and groundskeeping.

Cassandra   In Greek mythology, a seer whose prophecies, including the fall of Troy, were ignored. She was the daughter of Priam and also was called the daughter of HECATE. Cassandra received the gift of clairvoyance by sleeping in the temple of Apollo and allowing snakes to lick her ears. When Apollo tried to seduce her, she rebuffed him, and he punished her by declaring that no one would pay attention to her forecasts. In another version of the myth Apollo fell in love with her and gave her the gift of prophecy in return for her promise of giving herself to him. She reneged. Apollo begged for a kiss, to which she consented. By breathing into her mouth, he gave her the gift of prophecy but took away her power of persuasion.

After the fall of Troy, Cassandra was taken prisoner by Agamemnon, whose death she prophesied, and which came to pass with his slaying by his wife, Clytemnestra. Another version of Cassandra's tale says she was killed in the fall of Troy.

She also was able to understand the language of animals.

cats   Cats have been associated with the supernatural since ancient times. Cats are associated with either good or bad luck, HEALING or harm. In folklore, the cat is one of the favored animal companions of witches, sorcerers (see SORCERY) and fortune-tellers. Superstitions about cats abound.

The cat was sacred to the ancient Egyptians, who associated it with the MOON and Bast, the goddess of marriage. It also was associated with the Mother Goddess, Isis. In Egyptian art, the sun god, Ra, was personified as a cat slaying the Serpent of Darkness. Black cats were associated with darkness and death.

According to lore, virtually every sorcerer, witch and Gypsy fortune-teller was supposed to have a cat—and sometimes an OWL and a TOAD as well. During the witch hunts, cats were FAMILIARS; they embodied DEMONS who performed the witches' tasks of MALEFICIA against their neighbors. Elizabeth Francis of Chelmsford, England, convicted as a witch in 1556, said she kept a white spotted cat named Sathan, which, whenever it performed a job for her, demanded a reward of a drop of her BLOOD (see CHELMSFORD WITCHES).

Witches were said to be able to assume the shape of a cat nine times, presumably because a cat has nine lives. Black cats were said to be the DEVIL himself. Throughout medieval Europe, black cats were routinely hunted down and burned, especially on Shrove Tuesday and Easter. A cat accused of being a witch's familiar usually was killed by being burned alive. Cats were also used in witches' SPELLS. In the trial of JOHN FIAN, Scotland's most famous witch, in 1590–91, Fian and his COVEN were accused of trying to drown James VI (JAMES I) and Queen Anne on their voyage to Denmark. The witches allegedly christened a cat, tied it to a dismembered human corpse and threw

A witch's cat familiar, described in the St. Osyth witches trial, 16th century

the bundle into the sea while they recited incantations. A great storm arose and forced the royal ship to return to Scotland, but the king and queen were unharmed.

In the lore of the Scottish Highlands, a large breed of wild cats, called Elfin Cats, are said to be witches in disguise. The Elfin Cats are about the size of dogs and are black with a white spot on the breast. They have arched backs and erect bristles—the stereotypical Halloween cat.

Though the black cat is associated with witchcraft, it is nevertheless considered good luck to own one in parts of Europe, England and the United States. But having one's path crossed by a black cat is always bad luck. In other folklore, if a cat jumps over a corpse, the corpse will become a vampire. To prevent this, the cat must be killed. Cats are fertility CHARMS—a cat buried in a field will ensure a bountiful crop.

The cat plays a role in VODUN in the southern United States. Cat charms, particularly those made with cats' whiskers, can bring bad luck, disease and death to the victim. Conversely, in folklore cats have many healing properties. A broth made from a black cat is said to cure consumption. In the 17th century, a whole cat boiled in oil was held to be good for dressing wounds. Illnesses could be transferred to cats, who were then driven from homes.

Cats' eyes are supposed to be able to see ghosts. In western Asia, a stone called the Cat's Eye—dull red with a white mark—is associated with trouble and evil.

In WICCA, the cat is a favored companion or familiar, valued for its psychic sensitivity and assistance in MAGIC and RITUAL.

FURTHER READING:

Howey, M. Oldfield. *The Cat in Magic, Mythology, and Religion.* New York: Crescent Books, 1989.

Larner, Christina. *Enemies of God.* London: Chatto & Windus, 1981.

Leach, Maria, ed., and Jerome Fried, assoc. ed. *Funk & Wagnall's Standard Dictionary of Folklore, Mythology and Legend.* New York: Harper & Row, 1972.

Russell, Jeffrey Burton. *Witchcraft in the Middle Ages.* Ithaca and London: Cornell University Press, 1972.

caul Amniotic fetal membrane that sometimes clings to a newborn's head or body after birth. Being born with a caul, or veil, has significance in folklore related to magical powers.

A person born with a caul was believed to have psychic gifts such as the ability to see ghosts and spirits and to divine the future. In seafaring lore, such a person can never drown. In earlier times, cauls were brought on board sailing ships as good luck charms against sinking. Cauls were traded and sometimes sold for large sums of money.

In certain parts of Europe, a person born with a caul was believed to be a natural vampire. To prevent this, the caul was broken immediately, and prayers were said. In areas where the caul was considered to be a good omen, it was dried and placed in a flask that was worn around the person's neck. Sometimes it was mixed into an elixir that was drunk when the person reached a certain age, in order to initiate the magical powers.

In northern Italy, the cult of the BENANDANTI included people born with cauls who could see invisible witches and fight them.

cauldron Usually an IRON pot, the cauldron is a tool of witches and sorcerers (see SORCERY). In European witch lore, the cauldron was the receptacle in which POISONS, OINTMENTS and PHILTRES were brewed. WICCANS may have cauldrons, but use them for burning fires and incense in RITUALS or for decoration in the home. If used in rituals, the cauldron is placed on the witches' ALTAR inside the MAGIC CIRCLE. As a vessel, it is a feminine symbol and is associated with the womb of the Mother GODDESS.

The cauldron has had a magical significance throughout history. In the lore of ancient Ireland, magic cauldrons never ran out of food at a feast. The early Celts associated cauldrons with fertility and abundance, and revival of the dead. Cauldrons were used in human SACRIFICE— the victims had their throats slashed over the bowls, or were drowned or suffocated in them. The Cauldron of Regeneration, of death and rebirth, the receptacle of souls and the source of inspiration, is associated with the Celtic goddesses CERRIDWEN and Branwen and with the Babylonian fate-goddess, Siris, who stirred the mead of regeneration in the cauldron of the heavens. Cerridwen's cauldron was said to provide the mead of wisdom and inspiration. Among the Celts, the priestess of the MOON goddess was required to sacrifice human victims by cutting off their heads over a SILVER cauldron. The BLOOD was boiled to produce a magical drink of inspiration. The Celtic god, CERNUNNOS, identified with the HORNED GOD, was torn apart and boiled in a cauldron, to be born again. Decorations on the Gundestrup cauldron, fashioned out of silver in about 100 B.C.E. and recovered from a peat bog in Gundestrup, Denmark, depict victims being plunged headfirst into a sacrificial cauldron. Sacrificial cauldrons

Witches stirring up brew in cauldron (ABRAHAM SAUR, *EIN KURTZE TREUE WARNING*, 1582)

also appear in some shamanic traditions. In Norse mythology, the patriarch god, Odin, drank magic blood from a cauldron of wisdom to obtain divine power. In Greek mythology, the witch goddess, Medea, could restore people to youth in a magic cauldron. The cauldron is linked to the chalice of the Holy Grail, which became incorporated into Christian myth.

In medieval art, literature and folktales, the cauldron was in every witch's house, set over a blazing fire. During the witch hunts, it was believed that witches stirred up vile brews made with ingredients such as bat's blood, decapitated and flayed toads, snakes and baby fat. Before a SABBAT witches prepared their flying ointments and drugs in cauldrons. They often carried their pots to their sabbats, where they used them to boil small children for the feast. Witches could cause storms at sea by dumping the contents of their cauldrons into the ocean (see STORM RAISING). One of the more bizarre cauldrons allegedly belonged to LADY ALICE KYTELER, an accused Irish witch of the 14th century. Lady Alice reportedly used the skull of a beheaded robber for mixing up her poisons and potions.

According to one tale with an ironic twist, a 14th-century Scottish WIZARD was executed in a cauldron. William Lord Soulis, described as a pernicious wizard and perpetrator of "the most foul sorceries," was convicted for various evil crimes and boiled to death in a cauldron (see HERMITAGE CASTLE).

The cauldron also was an important tool of the alchemist in the search for formulas to change lead into gold or silver, and mold small gems into big ones.

FURTHER READING:

Cavendish, Richard, ed. in chief. *Man, Myth & Magic: The Illustrated Encyclopedia of Mythology, Religion and the Unknown.* New York: Marshall Cavendish, 1983.
Valiente, Doreen. *An ABC of Witchcraft Past and Present.* 1973. Reprint, Custer, Wash.: Phoenix Publishing, 1986.

Cernunnos   The HORNED GOD of the Celts, associated with the hunt and with fertility. He was sometimes portrayed with serpent's legs, a man's torso and the head of a bull or ram; or he was shown with stags or wearing stag antlers. Cernunnos was ruler of the underworld or otherworld, the opener of the gates between life and death. He also was worshiped by the Romans and Gauls, who sometimes portrayed him as triple-headed. The name *Cernunnos* means simply "the horned."

The famous Gundestrup CAULDRON, a large, gilt silver cauldron dated ca. 100 B.C.E. and recovered from a bog near Gundestrup, Denmark, depicts a stag-horned Cernunnos in several scenes: as an antlered man attended by animals, including a boar, and grasping a ram-headed serpent; and grasping a stag in each hand. The cauldron is believed to be Celtic in origin, though some scholars say it is Gallic.

In WICCA and PAGANISM, the Horned God is often addressed as "Cernunnos" in rituals.

Cerridwen (also Keridwen)   Celtic goddess of wisdom, intelligence, MAGIC, DIVINATION and enchantment. She possesses the gifts of prophecy and shape-shifting (see METAMORPHOSIS) and presides over the mysteries of the Druidic bards. She is associated with water and the MOON, which represent the emotions, the unconscious and intuition. Her primary symbol is the CAULDRON, in which she makes a magical brew of herbs, roots and the foam of the ocean, prepared according to the movements of the heavenly bodies. The brew boils for a year and a day to yield three drops, which bestows knowledge, inspiration and science.

According to the *Book of Taliesin* (ca. 1275), a collection of poems and songs, some of which are attributed to the sixth-century Welsh bard, Taliesin, Cerridwen prepared her magic-cauldron brew for her ugly son, Avaggdu. She put a youth named Gwion in charge of stirring the contents. Gwion consumed the three magical drops and gained the wisdom meant for Avaggdu. The rest of the brew turned to poison and split the cauldron open. In a rage, Cerridwen pursued Gwion, intent on destroying him, but he possessed the wisdom to evade her. He changed into a hare, a fish, an otter and a bird, but she shapeshifted accordingly and kept up the pursuit. At last Gwion turned himself into a grain of wheat and hid himself among other grains. Cerridwen turned into a black hen and ate Gwion. Nine months later, she gave birth to a beautiful baby boy, Taliesin, whom she bound up in a leather sack and threw into the sea. Taliesin was rescued by Gwyddno and Elphin, who found the sack while fishing.

See AWEN; GODDESS.

chanting   In RITUAL, the repetition of sacred or magical words, names and phrases to alter consciousness and raise psychic power. Chanting, done in conjunction with dancing, drumming, visualization and body movements and postures, is one of the oldest and most universal techniques to align human consciousness with the realms of spirits and the gods.

The principle behind chanting is expressed in the Eastern mystical concept of the mantra, sacred words or the names of God/Goddess, which are chanted verbally or silently. The term *mantra* means "to protect," especially the mind. The mantra harnesses the power of the vibration of *shabda,* sacred sound. The repetition of mantras unleashes certain cosmic forces that drive deep into the consciousness, down to the level of the cells. When a name of God/Goddess is chanted or repeated, for example, a person thus aligns every cell in his or her being with the highest divine consciousness possible, imbuing that consciousness into his or her being. The alignment of consciousness raises a tremendous psychic power for creating change.

In magic, this power is utilized in spellcraft. When the power is raised, the SPELL (a desired goal or outcome) is chanted forcefully. The energy sent out into the spiritual realm thus works to manifest change in the physical realm.

Chanting has been an important part of magical rituals since ancient times. In ancient Greece, female sorcerers were said to howl their magical chants. Early and medieval sorcerers and magicians also chanted their incantations in forceful voices, a practice carried into modern times. Folk witches chanted their CHARMS and SPELLS.

The chants of contemporary Witches and Pagans may be names of Goddess or Horned God, rhymes, charms, allierative phrases, or sacred words or runes (chant-songs) derived from various spiritual traditions. In WICCA, chanting may be done during a ring dance that accelerates in tempo (thus contributing to the raising of power), or while working with cords.

The Witches' Rune, composed by English Witch DOREEN VALIENTE, is a traditional power-raising chant, the refrain of which is:

Eko Eko Azarak
Eko Eko Zomelak
Eko Eko Cernunnos
Eko Eko Aradia

In shamanic traditions, shamans chant power songs that follow rhythms and melodies that have been passed down through generations. The words vary according to the individual. Power songs help a shaman achieve an altered state of consciousness for healing or divining. The chanted songs are monotonous, short refrains, and have different purposes. Every shaman has at least one chant to summon his power animal or guardian spirit, which provides the source of his shamanic powers.

Native Americans have chants for the undertaking of many activities, such as hunts, battles and weather control, and funeral rites and initiations. Curing chants are important in Navaho ceremonies. The chants are long texts in which are entwined myths about how the chants were performed for the first time by deities or supernatural beings. The chanters must chant the texts perfectly, or else the cures are nullified. Incorrectly rendered chants also will strike the chanter with the illness they are supposed to cure. The chants may go on for days and nights. A chanter is assisted by helpers, all of whom are paid for their work. If a chanter of great repute does not err yet fails to cure an illness, he usually blames witchcraft as the reason. If sickness has been caused by a witch's spell, only Evil Way chants will be effective. Navaho chanters take care not to perform the same chant more than three times a year, lest they suffer the illness they cure.

See CONE OF POWER.

FURTHER READING:

Crowley, Vivianne. *Wicca: The Old Religion in the New Millennium.* Revised ed. London: Thorsons/HarperCollins, 1996.

Guiley, Rosemary Ellen. *Harpers Encyclopedia of Mystical and Paranormal Experience.* San Francisco: HarperSanFrancisco, 1991.

Starhawk. *The Spiral Dance.* Revised ed. San Francisco: HarperSanFrancisco, 1989.

Valiente, Doreen. *Witchcraft for Tomorrow.* 1978. Reprint, Custer, Wash.: Phoenix Publishing, 1985.

Charge of the Goddess   In WICCA, a poetic and inspiring address given by the GODDESS to her worshipers through her intermediary, the COVEN high priestess. The Charge of the Goddess is used primarily in the Gardnerian and Alexandrian traditions, but is not limited to them. It was authored and popularized in the 1950s by GERALD B. GARDNER and DOREEN VALIENTE, and is one of the best-loved and most oft-quoted writings in the Craft. Various versions have been written by other Witches, such as STARHAWK.

The charge customarily is delivered in DRAWING DOWN THE MOON, a ritual in which the high priest invokes the Goddess into the high priestess, who enters a trance state and allows the Goddess to speak through her.

Gardner wrote the first version of the Charge, in which he adapted Tuscan witches' rituals as recorded by CHARLES GODFREY LELAND in *Aradia: The Gospel of the Witches* (1889), and borrowed from ALEISTER CROWLEY's writings. Valiente rewrote Gardner's version in verse, retaining words from *Aradia* because they were traditional, but eliminating much of the Crowley material.

Aradia includes a "Charge of the Goddess," which consists of instructions given to mortal witches by Aradia, daughter of DIANA and Lucifer. Leland maintained that the legend possibly dated back to the Middle Ages and had been handed down orally from generation to generation. According to the legend, Diana charges Aradia with coming to earth to teach witchcraft to mortals. When Aradia is finished, Diana recalls her to heaven. As she prepares to leave earth, Aradia tells her witches:

When I have departed from this world,
Whenever ye have need of anything,
Once in the month, and when the moon is full,
Ye shall assemble in some desert place,
Or in a forest all together join
To adore the potent spirit of your queen
My mother, great *Diana.* She who fain
Would learn all sorcery yet has not won
Its deepest secrets, them my mother will
Teach her, in truth all things as yet unknown.
And ye shall all be freed from slavery,
And so ye shall be free in everything;
And as a sign that ye are truly free,
Ye shall be naked in your rites, both men
And women also: this shall last until
The last of your oppressors shall be dead; . . .

After writing her verse version of the Charge, Valiente found that most persons preferred a prose Charge. She wrote a final prose version which retains bits of *Aradia,* as well as phrases from Crowley's writings, such as "Keep pure your highest ideal," from *The Law of Liberty,* and "Nor do I demand [aught in] sacrifice," from *The Book of the Law.*

The following prose text of the Charge is as it appears in *Eight Sabbats for Witches* (1981) by Janet and Stewart Farrar. The Farrars, who call the Charge a "Wiccan Credo," made small changes in Valiente's wording, such as substituting "witches" for "witcheries":

The High Priest says:
"Listen to the words of the Great Mother; she who was of old also called among men Artemis, Astarte, Athene, Dione, Melusine, Aphrodite, Cerridwen, Dana, Arianrhod, Isis, Bride, and by many other names."

The High Priestess says:
"Whenever ye have need of any thing, once in the month, and better it be when the moon is full, then shall ye assemble in some secret place, and adore the spirit of me, who am Queen of all witches. There shall ye assemble, ye who are fain to learn all sorcery, yet have not won its deepest secrets; to these will I teach things that are yet unknown. And ye shall be free from slavery; and as a sign that ye be really free, ye shall be naked in your rites; and ye shall dance, sing, feast, make music and love, all in my praise. For mine is the ecstasy of the spirit, and mine also is joy on earth; for my law is love unto all beings. Keep pure your highest ideal; strive ever towards it; let naught stop you or turn you aside. For mine is the secret door which opens upon the Land of Youth, and mine is the cup of wine of life, and the Cauldron of Cerridwen, which is the Holy Grail of immortality. I am the gracious Goddess, who gives the gift of joy unto the heart of man. Upon earth, I give the knowledge of the spirit eternal; and beyond death, I give peace, and freedom, and reunion with those who have gone before. Nor do I demand sacrifice; for behold, I am the Mother of all living, and my love is poured out upon the earth."

The High Priest says:
"Hear ye the word of the Star Goddess, she in the dust of whose feet are the hosts of heaven, whose body encircles the universe."

The High Priestess says:

"I who am the beauty of the green earth, and the white Moon among the stars, and the mystery of the waters, and the desire of the heart of man, call unto thy soul. Arise, and come unto me. For I am the soul of nature, who gives life to the universe. From me all things proceed, and unto me all things must return; and before my face, beloved of Gods and of men, let thine innermost divine self be enfolded in the rapture of the infinite. Let my worship be within the heart that rejoiceth; for behold, all acts of love and pleasure are my rituals. And therefore let there be beauty and strength, power and compassion, honor and humility, mirth and reverence within you. And thou who thinkest to seek me, know thy seeking and yearning shall avail thee not unless thou knowest the mystery; that if that which thou seekest thou findest not within thee, thou wilt never find it without thee. For behold, I have been with thee from the beginning; and I am that which is attained at the end of desire."

See ARADIA.

FURTHER READING:

Adler, Margot. *Drawing Down the Moon.* Revised ed. New York: Viking, 1986.

Farrar, Janet, and Stewart Farrar. *A Witches Bible Compleat.* New York: Magickal Childe, 1984.

Kelly, Aidan A. *Crafting the Art of Magic Book I: A History of Modern Witchcraft, 1939–1964.* St. Paul: Llewellyn Publications, 1991.

Starhawk. *The Spiral Dance.* Revised ed. San Francisco: Harper-SanFrancisco, 1989.

Valiente, Doreen. *The Rebirth of Witchcraft.* London: Robert Hale, 1989.

charms   Magical words, phrases, chants (see CHANTING) and incantations used in the casting of SPELLS. Charms have been common since ancient times. Some charms are verbal—a phrase, formula or PRAYER—while others are inscriptions on paper, parchment, wood or other materials and are worn on the body. Still other charms combine phrases with actions, such as spitting (see SPITTLE).

Charms exist or can be composed for every desire and purpose: to secure or lose a lover; ensure chastity, fertility and potency; gain victory, riches and fame; and exact revenge. Other charms protect crops and farm animals, milking and churning butter and get rid of rats, vermin and weeds. One of the most important functions of the folk witch was to create charms that would repel or break the spells of other witches that were blamed for illness and bewitchment (see PELLAR).

Some of the oldest charms are magical words or phrases written on parchment and worn around the neck. The term ABRACADABRA, which dates back at least to 2nd-century Rome, and probably is older than that, is supposed to cure fever.

The church promoted the use of holy charms, including rosaries and holy relics. The most common charm was the *agnus dei,* a small wax cake, originally make out of paschal CANDLES, bearing images of the lamb and the flag. When blessed by the pope, the *agnus dei* protected the wearer against attacks by the DEVIL, thunder, lightning, fire, drowning, death in childbed and other dangers. In the 17th century, rosaries were similarly blessed as AMULETS against fire, tempest, fever and evil spirits.

Folk witches and WIZARDS who were renowned as healers employed many charms. These "charmers," as they were often called, used Christian prayers spoken or written in Latin, or debased Christian prayers. The church approved the use of prayers and the Scriptures as cures and as protection against evil but disapproved of the prescription of them by sorcerers and charmers—a rather contradictory position that blurred the line between religion and magic. In the 17th century, a Nottingham sorcerer, for example, sold copies of St. John's Gospel as a charm against witchcraft. To break witches' SPELLS, he prescribed herbs plus the recitation of five Paternosters, five Aves and one Creed.

Some charms were simple little verses, such as this 19th-century English charm against witchcraft:

He who forges images, he who bewitches
the malevolent aspect, the evil eye,
the malevolent lip, the finest sorcery,
Spirit of the heaven, conjure it! Spirit of the earth
conjure it!

Even witches had their good-luck charms, according to this old folk-magic verse:

The fire bites, the fire bites; Hogs-turd over it, Hogs-turd over it, Hogs-turd over it; the Father with thee, the Son with me, the Holy Ghost between us both to be: ter.

After reciting this verse, the witch spit once over each shoulder and three times forward.

Charms are recited during MAGIC-related activities, such as the gathering of medicinal herbs, the consecration of tools (see WITCHES' TOOLS) and the boiling of a pot of URINE to break a witch's spell.

With the advance of science in the late 17th century, the efficacy of magic charms was challenged, and folk magic in general began to diminish, especially in urban centers. Charms, though, are still part of folk culture. Some linger even in the industrialized West, such as the popular charm to divine love, "He/she loves me, he/she loves me not . . . ," spoken while pulling petals out of a daisy.

In WICCA, the term *charm* has been replaced by such terms as *chant, incantation* and *rune.* Some Witches carry "charm bags," little drawstring pouches containing items used in spells.

FURTHER READING:

Macfarlane, A. D. J. *Witchcraft in Tudor and Stuart England.* London: Routledge & Kegan Paul Lt., 1970.

Guazzo, Francesco Maria. *Compendium Maleficarum.* Secaucus, N.J.: University Books, 1974.

Marlbrough, Ray L. *Charms, Spells & Formulas.* St. Paul: Lewellyn Publications, 1987.

Remy, Nicolas. *Demonolatry.* Secaucus, N.J.: University Books, 1974.

Chelmsford witches   Four major witch trails in the 16th–17th centuries that resulted in numerous convictions and executions.

The first trial occurred in the summer of 1566, under the rule of Queen Elizabeth, whose Parliament had passed the second of England's three witchcraft acts in 1563. The Act of 1563 tightened penalties for witchcraft, making it a felony to invoke evil spirits for any purpose, regardless of whether or not harm resulted. It provided for mandatory jail sentences but did not provide for the death penalty unless a human being died because of MA-LEFICIA. Thus, the 1566 Chelmsford trials became the first significant witch trials to be tested under the new law. The outcome of the trials took on further weight because of the prestigious judge and prosecutors: John Southcote, a justice of the Queen's Bench; Rev. Thomas Cole, a rector of a church near Chelmsford; Sir John Fortescue, who later became chancellor of the Exchequer; and, most no-tably, Sir Gilbert Gerard, attorney general. The records of the trials were written up and distributed in pamphlets, which became popular reading.

Three women were charged with witchcraft: Elizabeth Francis, Agnes Waterhouse and Agnes' daughter, Joan Waterhouse. All lived in the little village of Hatfield Peverell. Their only connection was a white-spotted CAT named Sathan, which was alleged to be a FAMILIAR that talked. The most damning testimony in the two-day affair was given by a malicious 12-year-old girl. Francis and Agnes Waterhouse "confessed" to their charges, while Joan Waterhouse threw herself on the mercy of the court.

Francis was the first to be tried, on July 26. The wife of Christopher Francis, she was charged with bewitching the baby of William Auger, which "became decrepit." She confessed to that crime and also to some doings far racier and more nefarious, including illicit sex, murder and abortion.

Francis said she had been taught the art of WITCH-CRAFT at age 12 by her grandmother, Mother Eve, who counseled her to renounce God and give her BLOOD to the DEVIL. Mother Eve delivered the Devil to Francis in the likeness of a white-spotted cat, which was to be named Sathan, fed bread and milk and kept in a basket. According to the trial records:

> . . . this Elizabeth desired first of the said Cat (calling it Sathan) that she might be rich and to have goods, and he promised her that she should—asking her what she would have, and she said sheep (for this Cat spake to her as she confessed in a strange hollow voice, but as such she understood by use) and this Cat forthwith brought sheep into her pasture to the number of eighteen, black and white, which continued with her for a time, but in the end did all wear away she knew not how.
>
> Item, when she had gotten these sheep, she desired to have one Andrew Byles to her husband, which was a man of some wealth, and the Cat did promise her that she should, but that she must first consent that this Andrew should abuse her, and she so did.
>
> And after when this Andrew had thus abused her he would not marry her, wherefore she willed Sathan to waste his goods, which he forthwith did, and yet not being content with this, she willed him to touch his body which he forthwith did whereof he died. Item, that every time he did anything for her, she said that he required a drop of blood, which she gave him by pricking herself, sometime in one place and then in another, and where she pricked herself there remained a red spot which was still to be seen.
>
> Item, when this Andrew was dead, she doubting [believing] herself with child, willed Sathan to destroy it, and he bade her take a certain herb and drink it, which she did, and destroyed the child forthwith. Item, when she desired another husband he promised her another, naming this Francis whom she now hath, but said he is not so rich as the other, willing her to consent unto that Francis in fornication which she did, and thereof

Hanging of three Chelmsford witches (ENGLISH PAMPHLET, 1589)

conceived a daughter that was born within a quarter of a year after they were married.

After they were married they lived not so quietly as she desired, being storred (as she said) to much unquietness and moved to swearing and cursing, wherefore she willed Sathan her Cat to kill the child, being about the age of half a year old, and he did so, and when she yet found not the quietness that she desired, she willed it to lay a lameness in the leg of this Francis her husband, and it did in this manner. It came in a morning to this Francis' shoe, lying in it like a toad, and when he perceived it putting on his shoe, and had touched it with his foot, he being suddenly amazed asked of her what it was, and she bad him kill it and he was forthwith taken with a lameness whereof he cannot be healed.

After Elizabeth Francis had kept Sathan for 15 or 16 years, she grew tired of him. One day, she encountered Agnes Waterhouse en route to the oven and asked Waterhouse for a cake, in exchange for which she would give her "A thing that she should be the better for so long as she lived." Waterhouse agreed and gave her a cake. Francis then delivered Sathan to her and taught Waterhouse what she had been taught by Mother Eve, including feeding the cat her blood, bread and milk.

The records do not indicate whether or not testimony was given by William Auger, father of the bewitched child, nor do they explain why the confessions to murder did not lead to a death sentence. Francis was found guilty of bewitching the child and was sentenced to a year in prison.

The following day, July 27, Agnes Waterhouse, a 63-year-old widow, went on trial on the charge that she had bewitched one William Fynee, who deteriorated and died in November 1565. Agnes confessed to her guilt and acknowledged that she had also willed her cat to destroy her neighbors' cattle and geese. When she fell out with the widow Gooday, Agnes drowned the woman's cow. She also caused another neighbor to lose her curds when the woman denied Agnes' request for butter. At Agnes' command, Sathan caused another neighbor man to die. After all these acts of *maleficia*, Agnes said she rewarded Sathan, whom she kept at home as a TOAD. She denied that she gave the cat her blood, but court officials examined her and found numerous telltale spots on her face and nose (see WITCH'S MARK).

Agnes testified that she dispatched her daughter, Joan, to the home of Agnes Brown, a 12-year-old girl, to ask for bread and cheese. The girl refused the request. Angry, Joan went home and, in the words of her mother.

. . . remembered that her mother was wont to go up and down in her house and to call Sathan Sathan she said she would prove the like, and then she went up and down the house and called Sathan and then there came a black dog to her and asked her what she would have, and then she said she was afraid and said, I would have thee to make one Agnes Brown afraid, and then he asked her what she would give him and she said she would give

him a red cock, and he said he would have none of that, and she asked him what he would have then, and he said he would have her body and soul . . .

Agnes Brown was called to the stand. The girl testified that on the day in question she was churning butter at home when she saw a thing like a black dog with a face like an ape, a short tail, a chain and a silver whistle about his neck, and a pair of horns on his head. The dog carried the key to the milk-house door in his mouth. She asked the creature what he wanted, and he answered, "Butter," but she said no. The dog then took the key and opened the milk-house door and laid the key on a new cheese. After a while, he came out and told the girl he had made flap butter for her, and left.

Brown told her aunt, who immediately sent for a priest. The priest advised Brown to pray and call on the name of Jesus.

The next day, the dog reappeared carrying the milk-house key. Brown said, "In the name of Jesus what hast thou there?" The dog replied that she spoke "evil words" in using the name of Jesus, and left.

In subsequent visits, the dog came bearing a bean pod in its mouth and then a piece of bread. Each time, Agnes said, "In the name of Jesus what hast thou there?" and the dog spoke of "evil words" and left.

Finally, the dog showed up with a knife in its mouth and asked Agnes if she were not dead. Agnes replied she was not and thanked God. Then, she testified,

. . . he said if I would not die that he would thrust his knife to my heart but he would make me to die, and then I said in the name of Jesus lay down thy knife, and he said he would not depart from his sweet dame's knife as yet, and then I asked of him who was his dame, and then he nodded and wagged his head to your house Mother Waterhouse . . .

The court asked Agnes Waterhouse to produce the dog and offered to let her go if she could, but the old woman claimed to have no more power over the animal.

Joan Waterhouse, 18, was tried on the charge of bewitching Brown, who claimed to become "decrepit" in her right leg and arm on July 21. Joan was found not guilty, but her mother was sentenced to die by hanging. Agnes was executed on July 29.

Just before she went to the gallows, she made a final confession:

. . . that she had been a witch and used such execrable sorcery the space of fifteen years, and had done many abominable deeds, the which she repented earnestly and unfeignedly, and desired almighty God's forgiveness in that she had abused his most holy name by her devilish practises, and trusted to be saved by his most unspeakable mercy.

Waterhouse confessed she had sent Sathan one last time to destroy a neighbor and his goods, a tailor by the name of Wardol, but the cat returned saying Wardol's faith was so great he could not be harmed. She also admitted that she always prayed in Latin, not in English, which seemed to upset the townspeople more than her alleged witchcraft crimes, for it was considered "God's word" that prayers could be said in "the English and mother tongue that they best understand." Waterhouse replied that Satan would not allow her to pray in English.

While Joan remained free of trouble after the trial, Elizabeth Francis encountered more difficulty with the law. She was later indicted for bewitching a woman, who fell ill for 10 days. Francis pleaded innocent but was found guilty and sentenced to another year in jail plus four confinements to the public pillory.

The second and third mass trials at Chelmsford. In 1579 four women were charged with BEWITCHMENT; one case involved another evil black dog. One woman was a repeat offender: Elizabeth Francis, who was charged with causing the slow death of one Alice Poole in 1578. Francis pleaded innocent, but this time the court was out of patience. She was hanged.

Ellen Smith was charged with bewitching a four-year-old child, who cried out, "Away with the witch!" as she died. The child's mother then saw a large black dog go out the door of her house. Smith, whose mother had been hanged as a witch, threw herself on the mercy of the court and was hanged.

A third accused witch, Alice Nokes, was also hanged, but the fourth, Margery Stanton, accused of bewitching a gelding and a cow to death, was released because of the weakness of the case against her.

Ten years later, in 1589, nine women and one man were brought up on charges of bewitchment. The bulk of the evidence against them came from children, and once again, testimony as to the existence of familiars was accepted by the court. Trial records indicate the fate of only seven of the 10: four were hanged for bewitching others to death, and three were found not guilty on charges of bewitching persons and property.

Matthew Hopkins comes to Chelmsford. The fourth major trial took place in 1645, at the instigation of England's most notorious witch finder, MATTHEW HOPKINS. Hopkins made a substantial living traveling about the countryside whipping up antiwitch hysteria. He promised to find witches, bring them to trial and get them convicted—the last was most important, for his fees were based on numbers of persons convicted. His methods relied heavily upon establishing the existence of familiars and finding witch's marks, and he relied as well on TORTURE, such as walking and sleep deprivation, to extract confessions.

It is not known exactly how many people were charged by Hopkins at Chelmsford, but the jail calendar and pamphlets published after the trials listed 38 men and women, of whom Hopkins claimed 29 were condemned. Most were hanged; several died in jail. Hopkins amassed

evidence against them from 92 persons. Much of the testimony was coaxed from witnesses with plenty of suggestion added by Hopkins. For example, a child who spoke of nightmares and being bitten in bed was not bitten by fleas, which were in the bed, but by a witch's familiar, Hopkins suggested. Once the possibility of a familiar was established, Hopkins ordered a search of the suspect's premises and body. Any animal, from a toad to a rat to a cat, was immediately declared the said familiar, while any unusual marks upon the suspect's body added further proof.

For example, Hopkins succeeded in getting one Margaret Landish to admit that, while lying ill, "something" had come to her and "sucked her on her privy parts and much pained and tormented her." Landish was encouraged to speculate who sent this IMP, and she pointed the finger at Susan Cock, another defendant. The familiars soon multiplied to include a rat, mice, kittens, TOADS, cats, rabbits, dogs and frogs, which were alleged to have tormented many and killed children and adults. Margaret Moone admitted to harboring an army of 12 IMPS, which she dispatched to destroy bread in a bakery and to upset brewing. When her landlord evicted her in favor of a man who would pay a higher rent, Moone said she got her revenge by sending a plague of lice to the landlord's household. Anne Cate signed a confession admitting to sending her four mice familiars to bite the knees of a man who then died.

Hopkins went into great detail regarding the descriptions and activities of these malevolent imps, perhaps because he once claimed to have been frightened by a familiar, which he described as "a black thing, proportioned like a cat oneley it was thrice as big." It stared at him and then ran away, followed by a greyhound.

Of the 38 known accused in the Chelmsford trials, 17 were hanged; six were declared guilty but reprieved; four died in prison; and two were acquitted. The fate of the remainder is not certain.

FURTHER READING:
Deacon, Richard. *Matthew Hopkins: Witch Finder General.* London: Frederick Muller, 1976.
Hole, Christina. *Witchcraft in England.* London: B. T. Batsford Ltd., 1947.
Kors, Alan C., and Edward Peters. *Witchcraft in Europe, A Documentary History 1100–1700.* Philadelphia: University of Pennsylvania Press, 1972.
Macfarlane, A. D. J. *Witchcraft in Tudor and Stuart England.* London: Routledge & Kegan Paul Lt., 1970.

Children of Artemis (CoA)   Educational and networking organization for the promotion of WICCA based in the United Kingdom. Children of Artemis organizes the world's largest witch festival, Witchfest, held annually in London, Cardiff, Wales, and Glasgow, Scotland.

The CoA was formed in the early 1990s as a ritual group. In 1995 it became a public organization. Since

2000, it has grown rapidly. CoA publishes a magazine, *Witchcraft & Wicca,* and holds events in addition to the festival. The CoA assisted the PAGAN FEDERATION with its conference in 1998 and 1999. Witchfest was launched in 2002.

Until 2003, the CoA had a COVEN-finding service for people interested in joining the Craft, but had to discontinue it because there were not enough covens to accommodate the large number of applicants.

Church and School of Wicca   Religious and educational institutions founded by GAVIN AND YVONNE FROST, located in Hinton, West Virginia. The Church of Wicca, founded in 1968, is the oldest recognized church of Witchcraft in the United States, achieving federal recognition in 1972. Its teaching arm is the School of Wicca, which offers correspondence courses.

History. The Frosts, who were living in St. Louis, Missouri, developed correspondence courses out of their interest and involvement in Witchcraft and began advertising the courses as the School of Wicca. They followed with the founding of the church in 1968. Working with lawyers, Gavin Frost was able to win a "Letter of Determination" from the Internal Revenue Service giving religious recognition to "Wicca" and "Witchcraft." The ruling, which came in 1972, made the church the first Wiccan church to achieve this federal recognition, and the first to use "Wicca" to describe the religion of Witchcraft.

The same year, the Frosts began to work for the church and school full time. Gavin serves as archbishop and Yvonne as bishop. They obtained their doctorates of divinity from the church.

The Frosts moved to Salem, Missouri, and then to New Bern, North Carolina, in 1974. In New Bern, they attempted to establish a survival community, but it never matched their vision and after a few years, became inactive. In 1996, they moved their residence and church and school offices to Hinton, West Virginia.

In 1986, the Church of Wicca achieved another legal landmark by becoming the only federally recognized Wiccan church to have its status as a bona fide religion upheld in federal appeals court. In a prisoner's rights case decided in 1985, *Dettmer v. Landon,* the District Court of Virginia ruled that Witchcraft is a legitimate religion. The decision was appealed by Virginia prison authorities. In 1986, Judge J. Butzner of the Federal Appeals Court affirmed the decision. In his ruling, Butzner said, "The Church of Wicca is clearly a religion for First Amendment purposes. Members of the Church sincerely adhere to a fairly complex set of doctrines relating to the spiritual aspects of their lives, and in doing so they have 'ultimate concerns' in much the same way as followers of accepted religions."

Beliefs and tenets of the church. The roots of the church are Welsh Celtic, coming from Gavin Frost's own Welsh heritage. Its early philosophy, as expressed in *The Witch's Bible* (finally published in 1975), created controversy in the Craft. The church held that the Ultimate Deity is not definable, thus downplaying the emphasis given the Goddess by most other Witches, and maintained that the Craft is agnostic, as well as both monotheistic and polytheistic. Every life form contains a spark of Divine Fire—a piece of Deity. Lower-level polytheistic deities, or "stone gods," can be created in anthropomorphic form as storehouses of energy for use in magic rituals. In addition to the controversy, the church's early view that homosexuals did not fit into the Craft, a fertility religion, was criticized as prejudice.

The church's early view of homosexuality has evolved. The Church and School of Wicca does not discriminate against any member by reason of race, color, gender, sexual orientation, or national or ethnic origin. If any member of the association is proven to be discriminating for any of those reasons, that member is dismissed from the association. Beyond the controversy over homosexuality, there was much criticism of the church's early view that young adults should be fully aware sexually before initiation.

Over the years, the church's position has grown and changed. Elements of Eastern, Native American Indian and Afro-American practices have been recognized for their overlap with the Welsh Celtic tradition, and the church is now open to people of all sexual orientations. The church's view of the Ultimate Deity is still genderless; God is impersonal, treating all persons alike, transcending human emotions.

The church espouses five basic tenets of the Craft:

1. The WICCAN REDE—"If it harm none, do what you will."
2. Reincarnation as an orderly system of learning. This is not a tally of "sins" and punishments. Human experiences are comparable to term papers: a way of learning.
3. The Law of Attraction—What I do to other living creatures I will draw to myself. Shakespeare called this "measure for measure." It can also be expressed as "birds of a feather."
4. Power through Knowledge—Each living creature has the power (energy) within its body. The skill of directing that power can be taught and learned. Whether the power is "good" or "evil" depends on the intent in the mind of the worker.
5. Harmony—There are perceptible rhythms in the patterns of the Sun, the Moon, the Seasons. It makes sense to learn those rhythms and to live in harmony with them.

The church's view of reincarnation is that it is a steadily upward progress of development of the soul. The Frosts feel that excessive and careless sex has led to the incarnation of numerous, ill-prepared souls, one of the reasons for the increase in poverty, crime and warfare and other societal troubles around the world. They personally advocate more judicious contraception.

The use of "stone gods"—Yvonne Frost calls them "mascots"—is taught for magic RITUAL. The anthropomorphic deities are objects temporarily charged with psychic power; the object itself depends on the purpose of the ritual and/or the choice of the practitioner.

Craft observances in the church are held on full MOON nights. The four great seasonal holidays are observed at the appropriate full moon: Samhain, Imbolc, Beltane and Lugnasadh. The church occasionally conducts services open to the public, but which do not include power-raising rituals.

The church has chartered 28 independent subsidiary churches around the world. In the late 1970s, the Celtic Heritage Investigation Foundation was created under the auspices of the church to conduct "an archaeology of ideas, beliefs and practices that were lost in the 'Burning Times' when the books of shadows were destroyed."

Other major activities of the church include working for Wiccan rights, and bringing Craft teachings to those in the military, and to prisoners in state and federal penitentiaries. The church was among Wiccan and Pagan organizations which fought against the HELMS AMENDMENT, an attempt made in the U.S. Congress in 1985 to strip Wiccan and Pagan churches of their tax-exempt status.

The School of Wicca. The first and largest Witchcraft correspondence school in the United States, the School of Wicca offers numerous courses, among them Celtic Witchcraft, sorcery, Tantra, astrology, developing psychic ability, healing, use of herbs, dreams, Western sex magic, spells and rituals, sacred and mysterious sites, ufology, Egyptian and Native American Indian magic, and travel in the astral realm. There are three levels of study: theoretical, practical and initiatory.

The school publishes the longest-lived Wiccan newsletter, *Survival.*

In 1989, the school formulated a *Prisoner's Handbook for Wicca* for the state of Washington, which specifies religious tenets, observances and requirements. The handbook has become a model for other prison systems.

Since its beginnings, the school has introduced more than 200,000 people to the Craft. It also sponsors special interest groups, such as gay Wiccans and Wiccans in the military.

Students of the school, as well as followers of the church, are encouraged to keep their own BOOK OF SHADOWS—or, rather, "book of lights," as Yvonne Frost prefers to call the personal handbook, because it represents a reaching up to the Deity and the light of spiritual knowledge.

FURTHER READING:

Church and School of Wicca Web site. Available online. URL: http://www.wicca.org. Downloaded October 3, 2007.

Church of All Worlds   One of the first and most influential contemporary Pagan churches. The key founder was OBERON ZELL-RAVENHEART (formerly Tim Zell, Otter G'Zell, Otter Zell and Oberon Zell), president, and his wife, MORNING GLORY ZELL-RAVENHEART. The headquarters are in Cotati, California.

The Church of All Worlds (CAW) espouses pantheism but is not a belief-based religion. Rather, it is a religion of experience, in which members called Waterkin experience Divinity and honor the experiences and perspectives of others. Divinity is defined as "the highest level of aware consciousness accessible to each living being, manifesting itself in the self-actualization of that Being." The mission of CAW "is to evolve a network of information, mythology and experience that provides a context and stimulus for re-awakening Gaia, and re-uniting her children through tribal community dedicated to responsible stewardship and evolving consciousness."

CAW recognizes the Earth Mother GODDESS as well as the Green Goddess and the HORNED GOD, who represent the plant and animal kingdoms, respectively. In CAW, many forms and levels of Divinity are honored—from the universal and cosmic ("The Great Spirit," "Mother Nature"), to the polytheistic pantheons of various peoples and cultures, to the immanent divinity within each and every one. It is dedicated to the "celebration of life, the maximum actualization of human potential and the realization of ultimate individual freedom and personal responsibility in harmonious eco-psychic relationship with the total Biosphere of Holy Mother Earth." It celebrates the eight seasonal festivals of Paganism and the Craft (see WHEEL OF THE YEAR).

CAW may be the first religion to draw as much of its inspiration from the future as from the past. Its mythology includes science fiction, which played a significant role in the church's beginnings.

Formation of the Church

CAW began in 1961 with a group of high school friends, led by Richard Lance Christie of Tulsa, Oklahoma, who became immersed in the ideas of Ayn Rand and the self-actualization concepts of Abraham Maslow. After enrolling at Westminster College in Fulton, Missouri, Christie met fellow student Tim Zell; together, they began experiments in extrasensory perception. The Christie group, which Zell joined, read Robert A. Heinlein's science fiction novel *Stranger in a Strange Land* (1961), which became a catalyst and inspiration for CAW.

In the novel, Valentine Michael Smith is an Earthman born on Mars and raised by Martians. He eventually returns to Earth, where he finds that his upbringing renders him literally a "stranger in a strange land." Smith forms the Church of All Worlds, organized in nests. The church teaches "grokking," or the intuiting of the "fullness" of all things and beings, and joyful, coequal love between the sexes. God is immanent in all things; church members greet each other with "Thou art God." In a ceremony called the "waterbrotherhood," members share water and "grok," the divine that exists in each other.

Heinlein's book had a profound impact on the Christie-Zell group. They related it to Maslow's self-actualizers, whom Maslow described as being alienated from their own culture. In 1962, following a watersharing between Zell and Christie, the group formed a waterbrotherhood called *Atl,* a term derived from an Aztec word for "water" and also meaning "home of our ancestors." Atl remained a loose organization dedicated to innovative political and social change and attracted up to 100 members. ATL (now standing for Association for the Tree of Life) is still in existence and remains under the direction of Christie. Headquarters are in Moab, Utah.

From Atl, Zell founded CAW, and it evolved under his leadership. The church filed for incorporation in 1967 and was formally chartered on March 4, 1968, making it the first of the Pagan earth religions in the United States to obtain full federal recognition as a church. Zell coined the term *Neo-Pagan* to apply to the emerging, ecology-conscious Earth religions of the 1960s.

In 1968, CAW began publishing *Green Egg* under the editorship of Zell. The journal, one of three membership newsletters (the other two, *Scarlet Flame* and *Violet Void,* were short-lived), gained a reputation as one of the leading Pagan periodicals, providing a thought-provoking forum for the exchange of ideas in the Pagan community.

CAW initially was refused recognition as a church by the state of Missouri because of its lack of dogma concerning God, the hereafter, the fate of souls, heaven and hell, and sin and its punishment, among other matters. That decision was reversed in 1971.

Early Organization and Beliefs
Like Heinlein's fictional church, the early CAW was organized around nests. The church had nine circles of advancement, each named after a planet. One advanced by fulfilling reading and writing requirements and participating in psychic training systems such as a martial arts discipline. The process was intended to be continuous.

The basic dogma of the CAW was that there was no dogma; the basic belief was the lack of belief. The only sin was hypocrisy, and the only crime in the eyes of the church was interfering with another. The unofficial goal of CAW was to achieve union with all consciousness.

By 1970, CAW was placing greater emphasis on ecology and nature. The term *Pagan* was used less to identify non-Christians than to identify nature lovers of all religious persuasions. In 1970, Zell formulated and published what he called "the thealogy [sic] of deep ecology," concerning the interconnection of all living things to each other and to Mother Earth, a sentient being in her own right. Humankind's reconnection with nature is critical to the survival of the planet as a whole. Four years later, James Lovelock popularized this idea with his independent publication of the Gaia hypothesis.

Zell expresses impatience with contemporary religions because the sole interest of their followers is personal salvation, something he feels to be unworthy of primary attention in the greater context of the evolution of humanity—and all life—toward universal sentience. In Zell's own words:

> Religion means relinking. It should be about connecting one with everything else, integrating the individual into the greater scheme of things, the life flow, the universe, the cosmic vision. The connectedness of each individual with the whole of everything is in essence the religious quest, and this is what a religion should be about. This is what the Church of All Worlds is about.

Rather than personal salvation, people should be concerned with salvation of the planet and endangered species.

Evolution of the Church
The move toward nature-consciousness eventually led to a dissolution of the relationship between CAW and Atl. A brief collaboration followed with another early Pagan organization, Feraferia. CAW then remained on its own. By 1974, it had nests in more than a dozen states around the country.

The same year, Zell remarried, to Morning Glory (née Diana Moore). In 1976, he and Morning Glory left St. Louis, eventually settling in Eugene, Oregon, and then at the Coeden Brith land in northern California, adjacent to GWYDION PENDDERWEN's Annwfn. With Zell gone from the central leadership, CAW suffered internal conflict and in large part dissolved. The *Green Egg* ceased publication in 1976, after 80 issues over nine years. The nine-circle structure was revamped. By 1978, CAW was significantly changed. The focus of the organization shifted with the Zells to California, where for several years CAW served primarily as an umbrella organization for subsidiaries.

CAW Subsidiaries
In 1977, Morning Glory founded the Ecosophical Research Association (ERA) to research arcane lore and legends. The premise of the ERA is that all life on the planet originated from a single cell and is thus integrated, and that human archetypes are often reflected in material things, animals or places. Morning Glory coined the term *ecosophy,* meaning "wisdom of the home," to define research aimed at relating such archetypes to Earth.

The first project of note for the ERA was the creation of living unicorns in 1980. In their research, the Zells noted that in early art, unicorns resembled goats more than horses. They discovered the work of W. Franklin Dove, a biologist at the University of Maine who researched horn development in the 1930s and created a "taurine," or bull unicorn. The Zells reconstructed what they said was an ancient unicorning procedure and applied it to baby goats. During the first week of life, the horn buds of kids are not attached yet to the skull but are loose tissue beneath the skin. The tissue may be manipulated surgically so that the two buds become fused together and grow out as a single massive horn perpendicular to the forehead. The procedure is performed with local anesthetic.

The Zells created several unicorns, including pets Lancelot and Bedivere, and made appearances at Pagan festivals and medieval fairs. In 1984, they signed a contract to lease four unicorns to Ringling Brothers/Barnum and Bailey Circus. The animals caused a great deal of controversy and were denounced by the American Society for the Prevention of Cruelty to Animals (ASPCA), an accusation some consider ironic, as the Zells are animal lovers and volunteers for a wildlife rescue organization. Under the terms of their contract, the Zells were prohibited from publicly discussing the unicorns for a number of years.

Another ERA project was an expedition in 1985 to search for ri, unknown sea creatures associated with legends of the mermaids off the coast of Papua New Guinea. They discovered ri is the local term for *dugong*, a type of marine mammal, and concluded that the mermaid legends relate to dugongs.

In 1978, CAW merged with Nemeton, the Pagan organization founded by Pendderwen and Alison Harlow, and Nemeton became CAW's publishing arm. In 1987, CAW also absorbed Forever Forests, another of Pendderwen's organizations. Annwfn, Pendderwen's 55-acre land in Mendocino County, was deeded to CAW, which operates it as a wilderness retreat. Lifeways, a teaching order founded and directed by ANODEA JUDITH (past president of CAW), is no longer active. It was an outgrowth of Forever Forests and focused on healing, bodywork, magic, psychic development, dance, ritual, music and religion.

Another subsidiary is the Holy Order of Mother Earth (HOME), a group of individuals dedicated to magical living and working with the land.

CAWmunity, located in Brushwood, New York, is a campsite in Fairy Woods for CAW members and friends who are attending the Starwood and Sirius Rising Pagan festivals.

Renaissance of CAW
By 1988, CAW had all but ceased to exist outside of Ukiah, California, where the Zells had relocated in 1985. The structure of the organization was revamped and plans were launched for more nest meetings, training courses, new rituals and new publications. The *Green Egg* resumed publication in 1988 and became an award-winning Pagan periodical. In 1992, CAW became legally incorporated in Australia.

By the late 1990s, CAW had increased membership internationally and was particularly strong in Australia.

In 1996, there was a hostile takeover of *Green Egg*, with deep animosities between longtime water brothers. Oberon continued to contribute to the magazine, but was no longer editor. In 1998, profoundly disheartened, he took a sabbatical from his role as Primate in order to pursue his own creative projects—particularly Mythic Images, producing and marketing his series of God and Goddess altar statuary. At the same time, the church headquarters moved to Toledo, Ohio.

Phoenix Resurrection
In 2004, CAW underwent a serious shake-up as a result of growing antagonism toward Zell from the president, Jim Looman, and the Ohio board of directors. In August 2004, the entire board of directors resigned en masse and issued a resolution to disband the church as of June 1, 2005. Looman died on October 3, 2004.

In May 2005, Zell revived the California corporate status of CAW and reinstated himself as president, with Morning Glory as secretary. Lance Christie, still director of ATL, took on a more active role. Taking advantage of the unique opportunity provided by the complete dissolution of the former structure, old and new members rallied to begin a complete evaluation and overhaul of the entire church, rebuilding it carefully from the ground up and incorporating lessons learned from decades of experience, triumphs and mistakes. Zell calls this "The 3rd Phoenix Resurrection of the CAW"—the first having been in St. Louis and the second in Ukiah, California.

During this same period, Oberon finally began writing books and created the online GREY SCHOOL OF WIZARDRY—possibly his most ambitious and far-reaching venture.

FURTHER READING:
Church of All Worlds. Available online. URL: http://www.caw.org. Downloaded October 12, 2007.
Green Egg magazine. Available online. URL: http://www.GreenEggzine.com. Downloaded October 12, 2007.
The Grey School of Wizardry. Available online. URL: http://www.GreySchool.com. Downloaded October 12, 2007.
The Mythic Images Collection. Available online. URL: http://www.MythicImages.com. Downloaded October 12, 2007.
Oberon Zell website. Available online. URL: http://www.OberonZell.com. Downloaded October 12, 2007.

Circe In Greek mythology, a sorceress renowned for her enchantments, who turned Odysseus' men into swine. Described by Homer as fair-haired, she was sometimes said to be the daughter of HECATE, patron GODDESS of WITCHCRAFT and MAGIC. Homer said she controlled fate and the forces of creation and destruction with braids in her hair (see KNOTS). She is seen both as a MOON goddess—because she lived in the west of the isle of Aeaea—and as a goddess of degrading love.

Circe was married to the king of Sarmaritans, whom she poisoned. She was exiled to Aeaea, which means "wailing," built herself a palace and learned magic. She cast a SPELL over the entire island so that anyone who came there would be turned into an animal.

Odysseus' men were turned into swine, but Odysseus escaped with the help of a magical herb, *moly,* given to him by HERMES. He forced Circe to restore his men to their human form. Nevertheless, he was so taken with her that he spent a year with her. She was slain by Telemachus, who married her daughter, Cassiphone.

Circle Sanctuary One of the most active and well-established interfaith Pagan centers. Circle Sanctuary, a Wiccan church, is located on a 200-acre nature preserve and herb farm between Mt. Horeb and Barneveld, Wisconsin. Circle was formed in 1974 in Madison, Wisconsin, by SELENA FOX with the help of Jim Alan and a small group of Pagans. Fox continues to direct its activities with her husband, DENNIS CARPENTER.

Circle originally was formed as an informal coven, after Fox conceived the idea, name and logo in a meditation. Fox and Alan drew on their musical backgrounds to create a body of Pagan RITUAL chants and songs, which continue to be used by Wiccan and Pagan groups around the world. Circle quickly took a leadership role in the growing Pagan community, providing a national and international contact service, organizing and coordinating gatherings, and disseminating information to individuals and groups within the movement, the general public and the media.

In 1978, the networking activity led to formation of Circle Network, which has grown to include membership of thousands of organizations and individuals from Pagan and Wiccan traditions, magical traditions, animistic and shamanic traditions and others. Members are in more than 50 other countries. Circle's guide to Pagan resources has been published continuously since 1979.

Also in 1978, Circle Sanctuary was incorporated as a nonprofit religious organization and a legally recognized church at the state level. A newsletter, *Circle Network News,* was started. It expanded to a magazine format, *Circle Magazine,* in 1998 and remains one of the oldest and the largest of Pagan journals.

In 1980, Circle was recognized as a church at the federal level. The Pagan Spirit Alliance was organized as a special network within Circle Network devoted to fostering friendship among Wiccans and other Pagans through the mail. The Alliance eventually was folded into Circle Network.

Beginning in 1981, Circle began sponsoring the International Pagan Spirit Gathering, held each year at

Stone circle atop Ritual Mound at Circle Sanctuary Nature Preserve (PHOTO BY SELENA FOX; COURTESY CIRCLE SANCTUARY)

summer solstice at a private campground in the Midwest and one of Paganism's oldest and most established festivals. The church also coordinates or assists other Pagan gatherings held around the United States.

From 1974 to 1982, Circle was based in various homes. In 1983, the church used its own funds to purchase a 200-acre nature preserve in rural hill country west of Madison. The land has a rich spiritual heritage, and includes sites once used by ancient Indians. The region is said in local legends to be enchanted with trolls, FAIRIES and nature spirits. Sightings of ghosts, spirits, Bigfoot, UFOs and other unusual phenomena are often reported.

But a year later, in 1984, local residents who were fearful of possible "devil-worship" at Circle raised zoning issues. After four years of legal battles, Circle won the challenges, and Circle Sanctuary and its 200 acres were zoned for church use. Circle became the first Pagan organization to achieve the recognition of Witchcraft as a legal religion by a local government in a public hearing. Circle was assisted by the American Civil Liberties Union.

Numerous religious, educational, therapeutic and spiritual training activities take place on, or are coordinated from, the Circle Sanctuary land. As ministers, Fox, Carpenter and others perform HANDFASTINGS, child blessings, funerals and other "life passage" ceremonies at Circle and all over the United States. They also conduct Pagan seasonal festivals, full MOON ceremonies and a variety of training programs, including intensives for Pagan ministers and a School for Priestesses, established in 1986.

The church also does organic gardening, wild plant foraging activities and preservation work for frogs, toads, songbirds and other species, and for wetlands, woodlands and prairie.

Circle's Lady Liberty League, founded in 1985, formerly known as the Pagan Strength Web, includes Pagan religious freedom activists who help Pagans who are being harassed or discriminated against because of their religion. Fox and Circle played leading roles in 1985 in a lobbying campaign against the HELMS AMENDMENT in the U.S. Congress, which sought to prohibited Wiccan churches from having nonprofit, tax-free status.

Since the late 1980s, Circle has achieved greater public recognition and acceptance as has Paganism in general. In 1988, Circle became the first Wiccan church to be listed in the religious directory of Madison's leading newspapers. Fox also serves on the Board of Advisors of the Madison Area Interfaith Network.

In the same year, Circle established its growing interfaith presence with representation at the World Council of Churches International Interfaith Dialogue Conference, marking the first time that Goddess spirituality and Paganism were represented at an international interfaith conference. Fox was joined by MARGOT ADLER.

In 1991, Circle assisted other Pagan groups in defeating a proposed network television series unfriendly to Witches.

The Pagan Academic Network was formed within Circle Network in 1992, becoming Paganism's first intertradition network of Pagan scholars. Circle participates in numerous international academic seminars, conferences and networking, in response to the establishment of Paganism as an area of academic interest. Circle provides academic archives and research assistance for scholars.

Circle joined other Wiccan-Pagan groups to lobby for the right of Wiccan-Pagan military veterans to have symbols of their faiths on their tombstones. The campaign, started in 1997, took years. In 1995, Circle Cemetery was founded on Circle land for cremains, the cremated remains of Wiccans and Pagans. The cemetery is now 20 acres in size. In 2007, three veteran gravestones with pentacles, among the first to be issued by the U.S. Department of Veterans, were dedicated.

FURTHER READING:
Circle Sanctuary Web site. Available online. URL: http://www. circlesanctuary.org. Downloaded September 23, 2007.

Clan of Tubal Cain   Influential Witch mystery tradition founded by ROBERT COCHRANE in England in the 1950s. The Clan of Tubal Cain, named after the legendary Hebrew blacksmith, Tubal Cain, was never intended by Cochrane to become a religion. Its concepts were passed to America in the 1734 Tradition and also were absorbed into the Roebuck Tradition and Ancient Keltic Church.

Cochrane, who claimed to come from a long line of hereditary witches, worked for a while as a blacksmith and also lived on a canal boat. The Clan had its roots in his own family tradition, as well as in the folklore he absorbed from blacksmithing and canal life.

Cochrane viewed witchcraft as a mystery tradition, not a fertility religion. The heart of his views was expressed in an anonymous article he wrote for *Psychic News* on November 8, 1963, entitled "Genuine Witchcraft Is Defended." Cochrane said he was tired of tirades against real witchcraft written by uninformed journalists. He requested anonymity because of his wife and small son. Excerpts from the letter are:

> I am a witch descended from a family of witches. Genuine witchcraft is not paganism, though it retains the memory of ancient faiths.
>
> It is a religion mystical in approach and puritanical in attitudes. It is the last real mystery cult to survive, with a very complex and evolved philosophy that has strong affinities with many Christian beliefs. The concept of a sacrificial god was not new to the ancient world; it is not new to a witch.
>
> Mysticism knows no boundaries. The genuine witch is a mystic at heart. Much of the teaching of witchcraft is subtle and bound with poetical concept rather than hard logic.
>
> I come from an old witch family. My mother told me of things that had been told to her grandmother by her grandmother. I have two ancestors who died by hanging for the

practice of witchcraft. The desire for power may have been the motive behind the persecution of witches . . .

[Cochrane explains that during the Crusades in the 13th and 14th centuries, Islamic ideas infiltrated witch covens, and witches were members of the upper classes as well as the lower.]

One basic tenet of witch psychological grey magic is that your opponent should never be allowed to confirm an opinion about you but should always remain undecided. This gives you a greater power over him, because the undecided is always the weaker. From this attitude much confusion has probably sprung in the long path of history . . .

[Cochrane then explains that witches are not part of a premature Spiritualist movement and are not concerned primarily with messages or morality from the dead.]

. . . It [witchcraft] is concerned with the action of God and gods upon man and man's position spiritually.

Cochrane preferred the term *clan* to COVEN, and he openly despised GERALD B. GARDNER and his followers.

The structure of the Clan was loose; RITUALS, which were shamanic in nature, were conceived as Cochrane went along. Inner planes contacts and alignment with natural forces formed the basis of magical workings. The Clan worshiped the GODDESS and HORNED GOD and conducted rituals outdoors when possible, dressed in black hooded robes. The Clan observed the same SABBATS and ESBATS as Gardnerian and Alexandrian traditions, the dominant ones of the time. Principal working tools were a stang, a forked staff that represented the Horned God, a CAULDRON for the Goddess, a cup made of horn, a cord and a whetstone. There was only one degree of INITIATION.

Cochrane liked to use herbal psychedelics as part of his own practice; it is not known how many of the Clan followed suit. The sacred contents of the Cauldron were the *Aqua Vitae,* the Waters of Life, laced with fly agaric or peyote.

The Clan was never big. When DOREEN VALIENTE was initiated into it in 1964, members included Cochrane (as Magister) and his wife, Jane, and three men. A woman member had recently left. Two women joined later.

In the 1960s, Cochrane began writing articles for *The Pentagram,* a short-lived publication. *The Pentagram* attracted the attention of an American Witch named Joe Wilson, who placed an advertisement in it asking for correspondence from interested parties. Cochrane responded, and the two exchanged numerous letters for about six months until Cochrane's death by apparent ritual suicide at the summer solstice in 1966.

In his first letter to Wilson, dated December 20, 1965, Cochrane asked if Wilson understood the meaning of "1734." It was not a date, but a "grouping of numerals that means something to a 'witch,'" he said. He explained that 1734 is the witch way of saying YHVH (Yod He Vau He), the Tetragrammaton, or holiest name of God. One becomes seven states of wisdom, represented by the God-

dess of the Cauldron. Three are the Queens of the elements (water, air and earth—fire belongs to man); and four are the Queens of the Wind Gods.

Cochrane believed that America had the right mystical underpinnings—the stars on the American flag are PENTAGRAMS, he pointed out—and he liked the rapport with Wilson. He transmitted his philosophy and some of his rituals in his letters.

Cochrane was fond of teaching in riddles, poems, dream images and mysteries. "There is no hard and fast teaching technique, no laid down scripture or law, for wisdom comes only to those who deserve it, and your teacher is yourself seen through a mirror darkly," he told Wilson. He signed many of his letters "Flags Flax and Fodder," which he translated as a blessing by water, air and earth.

Toward the end of his life, Cochrane wrote a witch's code of ethics:

Do not do what you desire—do what is necessary.
Take all you are given—give all of yourself.
"What I have—I hold!"
When all is lost, and not until then, prepare to die with dignity . . . and return to the womb of the Dark Goddess to give life another try until the wheel of rebirth is finally broken.

After Cochrane's death, Wilson founded the 1734 Tradition. In 1969, he traveled to England while enlisted in the U.S. Air Force and was able to meet some of Cochrane's clan members. The 1734 Tradition is a family of covens with roots to the Clan of Tubal Cain, integrated with the teachings and ideas of other streams of WICCA and PAGANISM. It does not have an initiation lineage by authority; one can join without being initiated by an elder. Wilson died in 2004.

In 1976, Americans David and Ann Finnin founded the Roebuck Tradition based on the 1734 Tradition. In 1982, English magician William S. Gray, a friend of Cochrane's, put the Finnins in touch with Evan John Jones, one of the original Clan members. The Finnins served a two-year apprenticeship with Jones and were adopted into the Clan with the power to carry it to America. In 1989, the Roebuck incorporated as the Ancient Keltic Church, based in Tujunga, California.

FURTHER READING:
Clifton, Chas. A. "The 1734 Tradition in North America." Witchvox.com. Available online. URL: http://www.witch-vox.com/va/dt_va.html?a=usco&c=trads&id=3356. Posted March 18, 2001. Downloaded October 2, 2007.
Cochrane, Robert, and Evan John Jones. *The Robert Cochrane Letters: An Insight into Modern Traditional Witchcraft.* Somerset, England: Capall Bann Publishing, 2001.
Finnin, David. "The Roebuck Tradition." Witchvox.com. Available online. URL: http://www.witchvox.com/va/dt_va.html?a=usca&c=trads&id=3380. Posted April 7, 2001. Downloaded October 2, 2007.

Hutton, Ronald. *The Triumph of the Moon: A History of Modern Pagan Witchcraft.* Oxford: Oxford University Press, 1999.

Valiente, Doreen. *The Rebirth of Witchcraft.* London: Robert Hale, 1989.

Cleary, Bridget   See FAIRY WITCH OF CLONMEL.

Clutterbuck, Old Dorothy (1880–1951)   The alleged high priestess of a COVEN of hereditary Witches in the New Forest of England, who initiated GERALD B. GARDNER into Witchcraft in 1939. Little was known about Clutterbuck for many years, prompting some outside observers to speculate that she had never existed at all but was fabricated by Gardner. In 1980 DOREEN VALIENTE, English high priestess and an early initiate to Gardner's coven, undertook a search of records to prove that Old Dorothy Clutterbuck had indeed lived and died.

Clutterbuck was born January 19, 1880, in Bengal, to Thomas St. Quintin Clutterbuck, a captain (later major) in the Indian Local Forces, and Ellen Anne Clutterbuck. The Clutterbucks had been married in Bengal in 1877 at the ages of 38 and 20, respectively.

Virtually nothing is known about Clutterbuck's early years. At some point, she went to live in England, where she enjoyed an affluent life. Gardner said he became acquainted with her through the Fellowship of Crotona, a group that opened "The First Rosicrucian Theatre in England" in 1938 in the New Forest region, and performed plays with occult themes. Some of the members of the Fellowship revealed themselves to Gardner as Witches. In 1939, just after the start of World War II, Gardner said Clutterbuck initiated him in her home (see INITIATION). She was considered "a lady of note in the district" and had a large house, and a pearl necklace valued at 5,000 pounds, which she liked to wear often.

Clutterbuck died in 1951, leaving a considerable estate of more than 60,000 pounds.

Valiente began her search near Samhain (All Hallow's Eve), 1980. On the actual night of Samhain, Valiente said that she and three other Witches met in a wood in southern England and called upon Clutterbuck's spirit to show a sign that she wished Valiente to succeed in her search. An answer interpreted as affirmative came when the lantern at the south quarter of the MAGIC CIRCLE suddenly tipped over and broke its glass. Valiente also heard the deceased Gardner calling her name. It took Valiente two years to trace the documents proving the existence of Clutterbuck.

More recently, doubt has been cast on Clutterbuck's alleged role in Witchcraft. Scholar RONALD HUTTON researched Clutterbuck's life and background, and found no proof that she was or wasn't a Witch. Her diaries and the details of her life point to a woman who was a conservate Christian, a scion of society and active in supporting local charities. She was married to a Tory, Rupert Fordham, a retired landowner. (There is some question as to whether the marriage was legal.) Her diaries, full of poetry and art, make no references to the Craft in either word or image. She had no obvious relationship with Gardner and was not associated with the Rosicrucian theater.

The argument can be made that Clutterbuck was following the convention of the time to be careful and secret about her Craft involvement. But if this were the case, she led an amazingly complex double life that fooled both her family and her neighbors and risked exposure that would have caused a monumental scandal. She is remembered by others as being a sweet, kind, compassionate woman who had no marked intellectual pursuits.

Gardner claimed that his initiation took place at Clutterbuck's home. This, too, is improbable, given Clutterbuck's social standing and visibility.

Hutton says that Gardner may have used Clutterbuck as a blind to protect his real high priestess, a woman known only as DAFO. Gardner had promised Dafo that he would never reveal her identity. Clutterbuck, who died before Gardner went public as a Witch, may have provided a convenient means for him to keep the promise.

FURTHER READING:

Farrar, Janet, and Stewart Farrar. *The Witches' Way: Principles, Rituals and Beliefs of Modern Witchcraft.* Custer, Wash.: Phoenix Publishing, 1988.

Valiente, Doreen. *The Rebirth of Witchcraft.* London: Robert Hale, 1989.

Cochrane, Robert (1931–1966)   Controversial hereditary Witch at the forefront of the revival of Witchcraft in Britain in the 1960s. Robert Cochrane, whose real name was Roy Bowers, founded the CLAN OF TUBAL CAIN, which became the 1734 Tradition in America. Cochrane's flamboyant life ended in what may have been a ritual suicide. DOREEN VALIENTE called him "perhaps the most powerful and gifted personality to have appeared in modern witchcraft." Had his life been longer and more stable, said scholar RONALD HUTTON, a strain of "Cochranian" witchcraft may have emerged to rival the tradition founded by GERALD B. GARDNER.

Cochrane gave his birthdate as January 26, 1931, at 3 A.M., to a Methodist family in London. Little is known about his early life; his own accounts in his surviving letters have been vague. At the time of his death, Cochrane had set down his life and work only in letters and a few articles; his widow, Jane, destroyed most of his letters.

Cochrane claimed to come from a line of hereditary witches that included his great-grandfather, great-uncle, grandmother, aunt and mother. At different times he claimed to have learned the Craft from his great-uncle, his mother or his aunt.

In a letter written to the English ritual magician William S. Gray, founder of the Sangreal tradition of magic—with whom he collaborated later in life—Cochrane said his great-grandfather was the last of the Staffordshire witches, a family tradition going back to at least the 17th century. His grandparents renounced the old gods and became Methodists, causing his great-grandfather to curse them. The CURSE decimated the family, and "nearly all of them died in misery or violence," he said.

Cochrane said he had his first mystical awareness of the gods at age five. One windy night of a full MOON, he was alone upstairs in his house and went to the window to gaze out. The eerie atmosphere of broken clouds racing past the moon and the sounds of the wind enabled him to have a mystical experience in which he knew that the old gods were real and that the goddess of the Moon was real and alive.

After his father's death, his mother told him the truth about the family. He turned to his aunt Lucy, who taught him the hereditary tradition. He said that only witches can bear witches, and that witch blood, which reoccurs every second or third generation, must be possessed in order to gain the ear of the gods.

By his early teens he was fascinated by ancient Celtic and Druidic lore. He may have found a mentor or teacher. He was in his early 20s when Britain's Witchcraft Act was repealed in 1953, and he formed his own coven, the Clan of Tubal Cain. Cochrane had worked as a blacksmith, and Tubal Cain is in lore the first in the trade.

A talented poet, Cochrane loved to teach in stories, riddles and poems rather than in straight instruction. His coven worshiped the GODDESS and HORNED GOD and practiced their rituals outdoors in remote areas. Unlike the nude Witches in Gardner's skyclad tradition, members wore black hooded robes. They "called down the power" in rituals and used guided meditation to create astral temples. Cochrane was particularly close to a man who went by the name of "Taliesin," who said he was a West Country hereditary witch.

Cochrane was married for at least 14 years to Jane, and they had a son. Jane practiced his tradition with him and helped him to develop psychic and healing abilities. He had no interest in money and status, but, after the arrival of his son, took office work as a designer. They lived in the Thames Valley west of London.

Cochrane was charismatic and, if not for the emergence of Gardner, might have become the dominant figure in the Craft revival. He held Gardner in contempt and was an open critic of him. He called Gardner "an out and out fake, who through various degenerative habits first came into this field." Gardner was "driven by a desire to be whipped and to prance around naked" and "devised his own religion which he called 'witchcraft.'" No real authority except one ever accepted him as the genuine article, Cochrane said.

He was equally contemptuous of Gardner's followers, stating that they gave witches a bad name, were thoroughly disliked by real witches and might be responsible for starting a backlash against witches.

In 1962, Cochrane, Taliesin and another person placed a newspaper ad inviting people interested in Robert Graves' *White Goddess* to contact them. In 1963, Cochrane gained attention by writing an anonymous article for *Psychic News* in which he described himself as a hereditary witch and defended witchcraft against critics.

In 1964, Valiente met Cochrane, on the recommendation of friends. She had been looking for evidence of a pagan witchcraft tradition that was older than the one alleged by Gardner, and she initially was impressed by Cochrane's hereditary claims. She was initiated into the Clan of Tubal Cain. She went to his home and participated in rituals both outdoors and indoors.

Valiente, Cochrane and Taliesin were among the witches who became involved in the WITCHCRAFT RESEARCH ASSOCIATION, formed by SYBIL LEEK after the death of Gardner. Cochrane and Taliesin wrote for the WRA's journal, the *Pentagram*, which attracted the attention of an American witch Joe Wilson. Wilson wrote asking for correspondence, and Cochrane responded. Wilson founded the 1734 Tradition based on Cochrane's material.

Valiente soon became disillusioned with Cochrane, concluding that he was full of fiction about his hereditary lineage and probably made up rituals as he went along. She also grated at his sharp criticisms of her friend Gardner, his increasingly controlling and autocratic behavior and an extramarital affair with a coven member. And she discovered that Taliesin really had been a member of Gardner's tradition and was not a hereditary witch.

Cochrane said he was leery of Valiente and her intentions and engaged in an intellectual sparring with her via letters. He said she seemed pleasant enough, but she asked him so many questions about his interpretations of witch history, RITUALS, symbols and tools that he felt pressed to answer them and admitted dodging some of them. Exasperated, he said, "I shall have to work with the woman so that she will understand."

In his letters to Gray, Cochrane expressed an interest in giving Valiente fictitious material just to fool with her, ". . . each time I start fooling it up, she takes me seriously," he said. He shared secrets and rituals with Gray, but asked him not to pass certain information to Valiente because he did not want to see it in print. He did admit to passing fake material to Justine Glass, the pen name of a journalist sympathetic to witchcraft and the author of *Witchcraft, the Sixth Sense—and Us* (1965).

Valiente knew about the Glass situation and disapproved, and she also strongly disapproved of Cochrane and Taliesin's use of herbal psychedelics, which Cochrane referred to as "witch's potions." She was furious with Cochrane when he performed a handfasting for a young couple and gave them a drink laced with deadly nightshade, telling them that they should drink it to determine if they were accepted by the gods or would be rejected, in which case they would die. Fortunately for the couple, they only became violently ill.

Valiente said that the breaking point for her came one day when Cochrane was railing against the Gardnerians to his coven. She told him she was fed up with his malice and had better things to do. She stopped working with the coven. Soon thereafter, Jane left, and the coven stopped functioning. Jane started divorce proceedings, but the couple never actually divorced. Later, Cochrane wrote to Valiente and apologized for his arrogant behavior.

Cochrane's relationship with Gray was an important part of his life; they shared ideas, rituals and material. He told Gray that he felt the two of them were brought together for a purpose, children of the Sun and Moon seeking the same truth. He diagnosed Gray's health problems via clairvoyance and even performed a healing at a distance on him. Gray suffered from an abscessed tooth, which he had removed, but his health did not improve. Cochrane conducted a magical healing circle ritual. He told Gray to be asleep by midnight on a certain night, to take no sleeping aids and to not be surprised by any dreams he might recall. Gray did as instructed. Sometime during the night he became aware of a sensation of being tossed around like a small ball by the coven while they chanted or sang. He then felt a piercing pain under his ribs, which moved around his body and then faded. When he awoke, he was free of pain, and his health was restored.

Cochrane was not so good with his own health. He pushed physical, mental and spiritual limits, skirting insanity by his own admission. The sacred Water of Life drunk in his rituals sometimes was laced with fly agaric or peyote to induce visions. Much of his spiritual pursuits were devoted to accessing the Akashic Records, the universal repository of all thoughts, emotions and events, to recover mystical wisdom.

In his work on the inner planes, Cochrane met his spiritual master and had a powerful encounter with "the Power we call God, or at least a representative of Her." He said he awakened in the middle of the night to find himself half in and half out of his body. A dark form was in the room, and it frightened him. He then was forcefully taken out of his body to a wood, where he saw his master for the first time. He was dressed in 16th-century clothing and a cloak. The master announced the arrival of "the Lass" and said, "Let us worship Her." All the colors around Cochrane were brilliant. A white light came through the oak trees and revealed a naked woman on horseback in pure light. Flooded with mystical feelings, Cochrane was shot back into his body with a "thundering crash." He got out of bed, trembling and shaking. Years later, he realized that what he had seen was "the cosmic power we call truth."

Cochrane lamented England as "psychically dead" and felt that he was one of the last of his kind. In a bizarre offhand observation in one of his letters to Gray, he foreshadowed the 1980 shooting murder of John Lennon in New York City. The noise and sexual hysteria gener-ated by rock music was a dangerous force for teenagers to play with, he said, "and that is what the Beatles are doing. I would never be surprised to read that . . . one of the Beatles has come to a very bloody and untimely end, à la primitive magic as the God of Vegetation."

Cochrane came to an untimely end himself. Early in 1966, he began telling friends that he planned to commit ritual suicide on Midsummer's Eve. Few took the threat seriously, and Cochrane himself seemed to back off the threat a few days before the solstice. He followed through with it, though, and was found unconscious on June 21, 1966. He was taken to the hospital, where he died comatose. The cause was poisoning by belladonna leaves combined with sleeping pills. It is not known whether he intended to kill himself or his death was accidental. Some of his friends and supporters believed that he had committed ritual suicide by offering himself as a sacrifice on Midsummer Eve.

Valiente was not convinced that Cochrane actually intended to kill himself. Several days before the solstice, he wrote to her, saying that by the time she read the letter, he would be dead. Valiente believed that Cochrane intended for her to get the letter in time to send help, but it sat unread at home for several days while she was in the hospital. She also thought that he might have been playing a game to see if the gods accepted or rejected him. Either way, it was a gamble with a heavy price. Valiente composed "Elegy for a Dead Witch" in honor of Cochrane.

Cochrane's letters and papers that Jane kept were bequeathed upon her death in 2001 to Evan John Jones, one of Cochrane's original coven members; Jones died in 2003. Most have been published in two collections, *The Roebuck in the Thicket* (2001) and *The Robert Cochrane Letters* (2002).

Cochrane believed in an afterlife and in reincarnation. In a letter to Gray, he said, "When I am dead, I shall go to another place that myself and my ancestors created. Without their work it would not exist, since in my opinion, for many eons of time the human spirit had no abode, then finally the desire to survive created the pathway into the other worlds. Nothing is got by doing nothing, and whatever we do now creates the world in which we exist tomorrow. The same applies to death, that we have created in thought, we create in that other reality."

FURTHER READING:
Cochrane, Robert, and Evan John Jones. *The Robert Cochrane Letters: An Insight into Modern Traditional Witchcraft.* Somerset, England: Capall Bann Publishing, 2001.
Hutton, Ronald. *The Triumph of the Moon: A History of Modern Pagan Witchcraft.* Oxford: Oxford University Press, 1999.
Jones, Evan John, and Robert Cochrane. *The Roebuck in the Thicket: An Anthology of the Robert Cochrane Tradition.* Somerset, England; Capall Bann Publishing, 2002.
Jones, Evan John, with Chas. S. Clifton. *Sacred Mask, Sacred Dance.* St. Paul, Minn.: Llewellyn Publications, 1997.

Valiente, Doreen. *The Rebirth of Witchcraft.* London: Robert Hale, 1989.

cocks Symbols of light and goodness, cocks have been favored birds of SACRIFICE to the gods. The cock is sacred and is associated with sun deities; it has the power to banish evil. The cock is a bird of omen, both of luck (in Wales) and death and evil (in Hungary). It is also a symbol of fertility and has been used in DIVINATION for centuries around the world.

The cock is an embodiment of the corn-spirit, who guards the corn crop until it can be harvested. The last sheaf of corn is variously called the cock-sheaf, cock, harvest-cock, autumn-hen and harvest-hen. Traditionally, a cock is sacrificially killed at the end of harvest, in order to ensure a bountiful crop the following season. According to some customs, the cock is bound up in the cock-sheaf

Witches sacrificing cock and snake to raise hailstorm (ULRICH MOLITOR, *DE IANIJS ET PHITONICIUS MULIERIBUS,* 1489)

and then run through with a spit. Sometimes it is buried in the fields up to its neck and then beheaded. Or, it is whipped, beaten or stoned to death. It is either cooked, or the flesh is thrown out and the skin and feathers saved to be sprinkled on the new fields in the spring.

During the witch hunts, witches were said to sacrifice cocks as an offense to God. The cock represented God, light and goodness, the very things that the Devil's legions hated. Accused Irish witch Dame ALICE KYTELER in the 14th century supposedly sacrificed cocks to her FAMILIAR at a CROSSROADS. Witches also were said to sacrifice cocks over their cauldrons as part of their spells to raise rain and storms (see STORM RAISING).

The witches' SABBATS allegedly went on all night until cock-crow, at which point the revelers scattered. MONTAGUE SUMMERS observed in *The History of Witchcraft and Demonology* (1926):

That the crowing of a cock dissolves enchantments is a tradition of extremest antiquity. The Jews believed that the clapping of a cock's wing will make the power of demons ineffectual and break magic spells. . . . The rites of Satan ceased [at dawn] because the Holy Office of the Church began. In the time of S. Benedict Matins and Lauds were recited at dawn and were actually often known as *Gallicinium,* Cock-crow.

NICHOLAS RÉMY, 16th-century French demonologist and witch prosecutor, said that a witch confessed to him that cocks were hated by all witches and sorcerers. The cock heralds the dawn, which brings light to the sins of the night and rouses men to the worship of God.

Cocks were said to crow at the birth of Christ and at his death. During the Middle Ages, the cock became an important Christian symbol of vigilance and resurrection, and earned a place at the top of church steeples, domes and buildings.

FURTHER READING:
Leach, Maria, ed., and Jerome Fried, assoc. ed. *Funk & Wagnall's Standard Dictionary of Folklore, Mythology and Legend.* New York: Harper & Row, 1972.
Rémy, Nicolas. *Demonolatry.* Secaucus, N.J.: University Books, 1974.
Summers, Montague. *The History of Witchcraft and Demonology.* London: Kegan Paul, Trench, Trubner & Co. Ltd., 1926.

Cole, Ann (17th century) Accused witch in Hartford, Connecticut, who was believed to be under demonic POSSESSION. The case was recorded in a letter written by Reverend John Whiting, which in turn was published by INCREASE MATHER in *An Essay for the Recording of Illustrious Providences* (1684).

Ann Cole was described by Mather as a woman of great integrity and piety. In 1662, she was living in the house of her father—"a godly man"—when she began having bizarre fits, "wherein her Tongue was improved by a *Daemon* to express things which she herself knew nothing of," Mather wrote. Sometimes the discourses went on for hours. Cole named other persons as witches and described how they intended to carry out "mischievous designs" against herself and others, by afflicting bodies and spoiling names. The DEMONS told her to "run to the rock."

Cole's fits happened in public as well as in private. They were violent physically as well as verbally. She even disrupted church services, causing one person to faint.

At times Cole lapsed into gibberish. Then the demons said they would change her language so that she could tell no more tales. She began speaking English with a precise Dutch accent, describing how a woman who lived next to a Dutch family had been afflicted by a strange pinching of her arms at night. Cole's Dutch accent was so good that others pronounced it to be genuine and impossible for Cole to imitate on her own.

One of the alleged witches named by Cole was her next-door neighbor, REBECCA GREENSMITH, who was convicted and executed in 1693. A man and a woman named by Cole were given the SWIMMING test of being bound and thrown into water. They neither floated nor sank, but bobbed like buoys, half in and half out of the water. A witness, protesting that anyone bound with their hands to their feet would not sink (and therefore be guilty), underwent the test himself. He was lowered gently into the water, not thrown in as were the accused, and promptly sank.

It is not known how many others named by Cole were accused of witchcraft and executed; some fled Hartford and were never seen again. Once the accused were dead or gone, Cole recovered and had no more fits. She resumed her life as "a serious Christian." Twenty years later, Whiting reported that she was still devout and free of fits.

One possible explanation for Cole's fits is multiple personality disorder. More likely, her fits were brought on by intense fear of witchcraft, prevalent at the time.

FURTHER READING:
Karlsen, Carol F. *The Devil in the Shape of a Woman: Witchcraft in Colonial New England.* New York: W. W. Norton & Co, 1987.
Hansen, Chadwick. *Witchcraft at Salem.* New York: New American Library, 1969.
Mather, Cotton. *On Witchcraft: Being the Wonders of the Invisible World.* Mt. Vernon, N.Y.: The Peter Pauper Press, 1950. First published 1693.

Cole, Eunice (17th century)   New Hampshire woman accused repeatedly of witchcraft, who was staked like a vampire when she died.

Eunice Cole of Hampton, New Hampshire, was in her 70s when she was found guilty of witchcraft in 1656. She was sentenced to a flogging and life imprisonment in jail in Boston. Her 82-year-old husband, William, was too frail to take care of their farm by himself. He also could

not keep up with the eight pounds a year that he was being charged to pay for Eunice's keep in jail.

In 1662, he went to court to beg for the release of Eunice. The court refused. The selectmen of Hampton stepped in to pay her jail costs, but they also fell behind and were arrested for nonpayment. To avoid being put in jail himself, one of the selectmen, named Marston, confiscated the Cole property. William, thoroughly broken by then, died soon thereafter.

Eunice appealed to the court for her release, and the court this time agreed—provided that she live outside of the court's jurisdiction. In 1670, the selectmen of Hampton allowed her to live in a small hut by the river. The townspeople gave her food.

Barely a year later, Cole was charged with witchcraft once again. Her alleged crime was hurling a CURSE at a boat passing by on the river. The boat went asunder on rocks, and everyone aboard drowned. The incident was so heavily publicized that poet John Greenleaf Whittier wrote a poem about it, *The Wreck of Rivermouth.*

By the time the case came to court in 1673, Cole was in her 90s. This time she was found not guilty of witchcraft and sent back to her hut. However, she was shunned by the townspeople, who stopped giving her food and aid. Cole died soon thereafter.

Townspeople found her dead. Her body was carted to a roadside and a shallow pit was dug. A stake was pounded into her chest to prevent her spirit from walking about, and a HORSESHOE was tied to the stake in order to repel any evil spirits, such as FAMILIARS that might be lurking around her. Then her corpse was set afire. While her body burned, the townspeople danced and celebrated.

FURTHER READING:
Cahill, Robert Ellis. *Strange Superstitions.* Danvers, Mass.: Old Saltbox Publishing, 1990.

cone of power   The raising and directing of a spiral of psychic energy in RITUAL and spellcraft. GERALD B. GARDNER described the cone of power as one of the "old ways" of witches; most likely, he borrowed the concept from the various magical sources he used in constructing his rituals and BOOK OF SHADOWS. The raising of psychic energy is intrinsic to ritual and MAGIC in general, and many methods have been used since ancient times.

According to Gardner, witches raise a cone of power by dancing in a circle around a fire or candle, then linking hands and rushing toward the fire shouting the goal, until everyone is exhausted or someone faints, which indicates the energy has been sent off successfully.

Wiccans use variations of this, chanting and dancing in a circle to an increasing tempo, perhaps accompanied by drumming and perhaps employing visualizations of psychic energy moving up through the chakras from the base of the spine to the crown. The energy is projected over the group in a cone shape; it is visible to those with clairvoyant sight. The energy is controlled by the high priestess or high priest, who determines when the group should release it collectively for maximum effect.

The cone shape has symbolic significance for Witches. In parts of ancient Syria, the cone was the symbol of Astarte, the Phoenician goddess of motherhood, fertility and war. Tall, conical hats are associated with magicians and folk witches of old. The cone also is associated with the circle, symbol of the Sun, unity, eternity and rebirth, and with the triangle, which has associations with the elements and pyramids, and represents the upwards spiritual aspirations of all things. The triangle also represents the number three, which represents the energy of creation, and is associated with the Triple Goddess.

FURTHER READING:
Crowley, Vivianne. *Wicca: The Old Religion in the New Millennium.* Revised ed. London: Thorsons/Harper Collins, 1996.
Starhawk. *The Spiral Dance.* Revised ed. San Francisco: HarperSanFrancisco, 1989.
Valiente, Doreen. *An ABC of Witchcraft Past and Present.* 1973. Reprint, Custer, Wash.: Phoenix Publishing, 1986.

conjurer   See CUNNING MAN/CUNNING WOMAN.

Corey, Giles (d. 1692)   Executed in the SALEM WITCHES hysteria of 1692–93 by being pressed to death for not acknowledging the right of the court to try him on charges of witchcraft.

Giles Corey was a well-to-do man of Salem Town, in his 80s when the hysteria started. He owned a farm of 100 acres and other properties as well. Though hardworking, he was not entirely well regarded, having a reputation for being quarrelsome and "scandalous." Long before the hysteria, Corey was regarded as the reason for just about anything that went bad in Salem Town. In 1676, he was rumored to have beaten a farmhand who subsequently died. Corey was arrested and charged with murder, but the jury found him not guilty, believing the man to have died of a non-related disease. Corey paid a fine and was set free.

Two years later, Corey was in court again, this time in a lawsuit brought by a laborer over a wage dispute. The court found against Corey.

He was married to MARTHA COREY, his third wife, who was condemned as a witch and hung on September 22, 1692. When the hysteria began in early 1692, Corey believed in witches as the cause of the girls' afflictions. He differed with Martha, who was skeptical.

Corey did not distinguish himself as the hysteria spread and Martha became one of the victims. In fact, he even spoke against her and was willing to testify against her in her trial. Then he defended her innocence, denying things he'd said, thus making himself out to be a liar—one of the gravest of sins in Puritan eyes.

The tables turned on him when the afflicted girls cried out against him, calling him a WIZARD and saying they had seen his specter about town. Corey may have seen the handwriting on the wall, for he made out a will bequeathing his properties and possessions to two of his sons-in-law. He then refused to answer his indictment. Under the laws of New England, a person who refused to answer an indictment could not be tried. If Corey could not be tried and found guilty, then his properties could not be seized by the state.

However, the law allowed such a person to be tortured until they either answered or died. The torture method chosen for Corey was pressing. Corey was excommunicated on September 14, 1692. He was taken out into a field and staked to the ground. A wooden plank was placed over his body and then heavy stones were laid on top of the plank. The weight was increased until Corey literally was pressed to death. For two days he lay in agony, until at last he expired. The weight pushed his tongue out of his mouth. Sheriff Richard Corwin took his cane and pushed the tongue back in.

According to lore, Corey was asked repeatedly to answer the indictment, but replied only "More weight!" His ghost is said to haunt the area where he died.

Corey's excommunication was reversed on March 2, 1712.

FURTHER READING:
Hansen, Chadwick. *Witchcraft at Salem.* New York: New American Library, 1969.
Upham, Charles. *History of Witchcraft and Salem Village.* Boston: Wiggin and Lunt, 1867.

Corey, Martha (d. 1692)   The fourth person to be accused of witchcraft in the SALEM WITCHES hysteria of 1692–93, who was tried and executed.

Martha Corey was the wife of GILES COREY, who also was executed. The Coreys were well-to-do, pious residents of Salem Town. Martha's age at the time of the trials is not known. Presumably, she was beyond child-bearing years. She was Giles' third wife; the couple had no children of their own.

Corey was renowned for her piety, but she became a target after the slave TITUBA confessed to witchcraft. Tituba said that four women were hurting the afflicted girls, but named only two—SARAH GOOD and Sarah Osborne. The afflicted girls came up with no names. Then gossip circulated that the girls were talking about others as witches, including Martha Corey. Thirteen-year-old Ann Putnam broke the silence in March 1692 by naming Corey next as one of the four who was tormenting them. Corey, she said, appeared in spectral form and pinched and tormented her.

One of the girls' tricks was to claim that they could identify their tormentors, who came in spectral form, by their clothing, which they could see. Two representatives, Thomas Putnam (Ann's uncle) and Ezekiel Cheever, were chosen to visit Corey to ask her questions about the allegations of the girls. First, they asked Putnam to describe the clothing that Corey would be wearing when they arrived. But Putnam dodged the matter, claiming that Corey had struck her blind so that she could not see the clothing.

When Putnam and Cheever arrived at the Corey residence, Martha confidently denied any knowledge or role in the girls' afflictions. When told she had been cried out against by Putnam, she asked if Putnam had identified her clothing. Apparently, Corey was wise to the trick and thought she would expose it. Instead, her answer was taken as a sign of witchcraft, for how else would she know?

Corey was arrested on March 19 and taken to the Salem Town meetinghouse for examination by the magistrates. She seemed to be convinced that common sense would prevail. She denied being a witch and said she did not know if there were any witches in New England. She laughed at some of the questions. She said the magistrates were blind to the truth, and she could make them see it, but then declined to do so.

Days later, Putnam was sent for and, when in the presence of Corey, went into fits. If Corey bit her lip, the girl said she was being bitten. If Corey clenched her hands, she said she was being pinched.

Corey was sent to jail and tried in September. She continued to think that it would be impossible for a person such as herself to be found guilty of witchcraft. What could she do, she said, if others were against her? Unfortunately, her husband Giles contributed to the case against her. Giles had bought completely into the hysteria and said that Martha acted in strange ways "like the Devil was in her." He testified that some of their animals had been mysteriously hurt or sick, implying that Martha may have been responsible. Corey was condemned to death. She was excommunicated from the church in Salem Town on September 11. On September 22, she was hanged with seven others. She ended her life with prayer.

As Corey and the others swung at the ends of their ropes, Reverend Nicholas Noyes said, "What a sad thing it is to see eight firebrands of hell hanging there."

Corey's excommunication was reversed on February 14, 1703. In its statement, the brethren of the church said that "we were at that dark day under the power of those errors which then prevailed in the land" and that Corey's execution "was not according to the mind of God."

FURTHER READING:
Hansen, Chadwick. *Witchcraft at Salem*. New York: New American Library, 1969.
Karlsen, Carol F. *The Devil in the Shape of a Woman: Witchcraft in Colonial New England*. New York: W.W. Norton & Co, 1987.
Upham, Charles. *History of Witchcraft and Salem Village*. Boston: Wiggin and Lunt, 1867.

corn dolly   A RITUAL doll, or variation of a POPPET, used in traditional seasonal rites for fertility of the land. The corn dolly is a harvest figure made of either the last or first sheaves of grain. It is placed in the fields or used as a CHARM in fertility rites or as a centerpiece in seasonal celebrations (see WHEEL OF THE YEAR). Corn dollies are hung in homes or fed to livestock as a magical charm for their well-being.

Modern corn dollies are made in various shapes, especially for hanging in the home, such as bells, cornucopias, or plaited into intricate patterns.

Corn dollies have many names, such as corn-mother, grandmother, mother of the grain, harvest-mother, mother-sheaf, old woman, old wife, the Cailleach, the hag, the queen, the Bride, the maiden, the Ceres and the Demeter. The latter two are the Greek and Roman names, respectively, for the goddess of the grain and harvest.

corpse light   See JACK-O'-LANTERN.

Council of American Witches   An alliance of Wiccans from different traditions, which was active in 1973–74 in an effort to define the principles of WICCA. The effort was spearheaded by CARL WESCHCKE, a Wiccan priest and president of Llewellyn Publications in St. Paul, Minnesota. Weschcke believed that the formulation of a common set of principles and definitions would help dispel myths about WITCHCRAFT and distinguish it from SATANISM in the eyes of the public and press.

Under the sponsorship of Llewellyn Publications, 73 Wiccans from various traditions convened in Minneapolis in the fall of 1973 and formed the Council. Weschcke was named chair. A newsletter, *Touchstone*, was inaugurated, and the Council began collecting statements of principles from Wiccan traditions around the country. Differences were many, but by April 1974 the Council was able to unify them into a general set of 13 principles. Weschcke drafted "The Principles of Wiccan Belief," which many Wiccans continue to endorse, and which were later incorporated into one or more editions of the handbook for chaplains in the U.S. Army.

In adopting the principles, the Council stated:

In seeking to be inclusive, we do not wish to open ourselves to the destruction of our group by those on self-serving power trips, or to philosophies and practices contradictory to those principles. In seeking to exclude those whose ways are contradictory to ours, we do not want to deny participation with us to any who are sincerely interested in our knowledge and beliefs, regardless of race, color, sex, age, national or cultural origins or sexual preference.

Shortly after this landmark action, the Council disbanded, due in part to continuing differences among traditions.

The principles of Wiccan belief are as follows:

1. We practice rites to attune ourselves with the natural rhythm of life forces marked by the phases

of the Moon and the seasonal Quarters and Cross Quarters.

2. We recognize that our intelligence gives us a unique responsibility toward our environment. We seek to live in harmony with Nature, in ecological balance offering fulfillment to life and consciousness within an evolutionary concept.

3. We acknowledge a depth of power far greater than that apparent to the average person. Because it is far greater than ordinary it is sometimes called "supernatural," but we see it as lying within that which is naturally potential to all.

4. We conceive of the Creative Power in the universe as manifesting through polarity—as masculine and feminine—and that this same Creative Power lies in all people, and functions through the interaction of the masculine and the feminine. We value neither above the other, knowing each to be supportive of the other. We value sex as pleasure, as the symbol and embodiment of life, and as one of the sources of energies used in magickal practice and religious worship.

5. We recognize both outer worlds and inner, or psychological, worlds sometimes known as the Spiritual World, the Collective Unconsciousness, Inner Planes, etc.—and we see in the interaction of these two dimensions the basis for paranormal phenomena and magickal exercises. We neglect neither dimension for the other, seeing both as necessary for our fulfillment.

6. We do not recognize any authoritarian hierarchy, but do honor those who teach, respect those who share their greater knowledge and wisdom, and acknowledge those who have courageously given of themselves in leadership.

7. We see religion, magick and wisdom in living as being united in the way one views the world and lives within it—a world view and philosophy of life which we identify as Witchcraft—the Wiccan Way.

8. Calling oneself "Witch" does not make a Witch—but neither does heredity itself, nor the collecting of titles, degrees and initiations. A Witch seeks to control the forces within her/himself that make life possible in order to live wisely and well without harm to others and in harmony with nature.

9. We believe in the affirmation and fulfillment of life in a continuation of evolution and development of consciousness giving meaning to the Universe we know and our personal role within it.

10. Our only animosity towards Christianity, or towards any other religion or philosophy of life, is to the extent that its institutions have claimed to be "the only way" and have sought to deny freedom to others and to suppress other ways of religious practice and belief.

11. As American Witches, we are not threatened by debates on the history of the Craft, the origins of various terms, the legitimacy of various aspects of different traditions. We are concerned with our present and our future.

12. We do not accept the concept of absolute evil, nor do we worship any entity known as "Satan" or "the Devil," as defined by Christian tradition. We do not seek power through the suffering of others, nor accept that personal benefit can be derived only by denial to another.

13. We believe that we should seek within Nature that which is contributory to our health and well-being.

FURTHER READING:
Adler, Margot. *Drawing Down the Moon.* Revised ed. New York: Viking, 1986.

coven The formal organization and working unit of witches and Wiccans. The origin of the word *coven* is not clear. Most likely, it derives from the verb *convene,* which includes in its variant *convent,* which once referred both to a religious meeting and the place of a religious meeting. Chaucer used the term *covent* in *Canterbury Tales* to refer to the meeting of 13 people. The term *covine* was used in 1662 in the trials of the Auldearne, Scotland, witches to describe the witches' organizations. One of the witches, ISOBEL GOWDIE, likened the covines to squads. The witches were divided into these subdivisions because there were so many of them, Gowdie said.

Sir Walter Scott, in *Letters on Demonology and Witchcraft* (1830), notes that the term *Covine tree* was the common name for the tree that usually stood in front of a castle, probably so named because the lord of the castle met his guests there:

He is the lord of the hunting horn
And king of the Covine tree;
He's well loo'd in the western waters
But best of his ain minnie.

MONTAGUE SUMMERS referred to covens as *conventicles,* from the Latin *coventus,* (assembly or coming together) and also includes *covey, coeven* and *curving* as variations of the word.

Historical Beliefs about Covens
The existence of covens. References in literature to covens of witches date back to the 12th century. In Polycraticus, John of Salisbury describes organized groups of witches carrying on at wild SABBATS but adds the caveat that they are merely deceptions created by the DEVIL and are not to be believed. A story popular in the late Middle Ages concerns an episode in the life of St. Germain, the bishop of Auxerre (390–448), in which he encounters villagers preparing a dinner for "the good women who walked about

at night." St. Germain, expressing the dominant view of the Catholic Church, discredited these sabbats of covens as deceits of the Devil.

It was not until the INQUISITION that the existence of covens was taken more seriously. Accused witches were tortured into confessing that they were members of secret, subversive organizations, and were forced to implicate others (see TORTURE).

British anthropologist MARGARET A. MURRAY held that covens were far more prevalent and organized than the Church was willing to believe, though there is little evidence to support that contention. Many accused witches persecuted by the Inquisition were solitary old women, outcasts from society, who may have possessed special healing or clairvoyant powers.

The earliest known reference to a coven in a witch trial occurred in 1324 in Kilkenny, Ireland, when Dame ALICE KYTELER was accused of being part of a 13-member group. In the 16th and 17th centuries, more witches, though not a great number of them, confessed under torture to having joined covens. By the time witch-hunting died down in the early 1700s, the concept of the coven was firmly established.

Among Wiccans, it was once commonly believed that witchcraft had descended unbroken from prehistoric times as a pagan religion.

Some Witches claim to be members of covens that date back generations. SYBIL LEEK's New Forest coven claimed to be 800 years old. Some covens may indeed be old, but there is little evidence to indicate that covens have existed in unbroken lines throughout history. As of the 1980s, most witches had abandoned the unbroken tradition theory in favor of the view that modern Witchcraft reflects a reconstruction of old beliefs and practices.

Number in a coven. Traditionally, the number of witches in a coven is supposed to be 13: 12 followers plus a leader. Murray stated this unequivocally in *The God of the Witches* (1931), concerning medieval covens:

> The number in a coven never varied, there were always thirteen, i.e., twelve members and the god. . . . In the witch-trials the existence of covens appears to have been well known, for it is observable how the justices and the priests or ministers of religion press the unfortunate prisoners to inculpate their associates, but after persons to the number of thirteen or any multiple of thirteen had been brought to trial, or had at least been accused, no further trouble was taken in the matter.

The leader was believed to be either the DEVIL himself or a person, usually a man, who, witch-hunters said, represented the Devil and dressed himself in animal skins and horns at sabbats.

The evidence for a constancy of 13 members is slim, however, and is referenced in only 18 trials (see THIRTEEN). At her trial in 1662 Isobel Gowdie stated, "Ther ar threttein persons in ilk Coeven." In 1673 accused witch

Ann Armstrong of Newcastle-on-Tyne stated she knew of "five coveys consisting of thirteen persons in every covey," and of a large meeting or sabbat of many witches, and "every thirteen of them had a divell with them in sundry shapes." Such "testimony" may have been the result of leading questions posed by inquisitors, combined with torture.

Structure and activities of a coven. In *The History of Witchcraft and Demonology* (1926), Summers defined covens as:

> . . . bands of men and women, apparently under the discipline of an officer, all of whom for convenience' sake belonged to the same district. Those who belonged to a coven were, it seems from the evidence at the trials, bound to attend the weekly Esbat. The arrest of one member of a coven generally led to the implication of the rest.

COTTON MATHER, in writing on the Salem witchcraft trials of 1692, said "the witches do say that they form themselves much after the manner of Congregational Churches, and that they have a Baptism, and a Supper, and Officers among them, abominably resembling those of our Lord."

Murray also drew on witch trials to portray the alleged organization of a coven. According to old testimony, the titular head of each coven was the *grandmaster,* or deity worshiped. Most likely, this was a pagan deity with horns (see HORNED GOD), but in the Inquisition it became the Devil himself. Usually, the god/Devil was represented by a substitute man or woman who conducted rituals in the god/Devil's name. At sabbats, when the god/Devil was present in person, the grandmasters then became *officers.*

Each coven reputedly also had a *summoner,* a person who secretly gave notice to members regarding the next meeting time and location. Sometimes the officer and summoner were the same person; not uncommonly, this person was a Christian priest who still participated in pagan ceremonies. The duties of the officer/summoner included keeping attendance records, scouting for recruits and presenting initiates to the god/Devil.

Covens also had a high-ranking position called *maiden,* a comely young lass with primarily ceremonial duties. The maiden served mostly as consort and hostess at the right hand of the grandmaster, or Devil, at sabbats and led the dance with him. The witches of Auldearne, Scotland, in 1662 claimed to have a "Maiden of the Covine," described in Sir Walter Scott's *Letters on Demonology and Witchcraft* as "a girl of personal attractions, whom Satan placed beside himself, and treated with particular attention, which greatly provoked the spite of the old hags, who felt themselves insulted by the preference." In some accounts, this maiden was also called the *Queen of the Sabbat.*

Murray contended that JOAN OF ARC was a witch and that her appellation "the Maid" therefore had special significance.

Each coven was independent yet supposedly was linked to other covens in a region through a cooperative network. In the trial of the North Berwick witches in Scotland in 1591, three covens allegedly worked together to try to murder King James VI of Scotland (see NORTH BERWICK WITCHES). There is scant other historical evidence for formal networks of covens.

The Coven in Wicca

Existence and formation of covens. Many Wiccans belong to covens, although it is estimated that many more practice alone as solitaries (see SOLITARY). The number of covens is unknown, for most exist quietly, some even secretly.

Most Wiccans do not proselytize or seek converts; prospective joiners must seek out a coven and ask for admission. Novices are admitted at the coven's discretion; not everyone who wants to join a coven is admitted. Applicants are screened and trained in a "training circle," traditionally for a year and a day. They are evaluated as to their reasons for wanting to enter the Craft and how well they fit with the group. A coven is a close working group, the effectiveness of which depends heavily upon the rapport and trust of its members. Successful candidates are those who are interested in healing and spiritual development. Candidates who are accepted are formally initiated into the Craft and the coven.

Most covens follow a tradition that has its own BOOK OF SHADOWS, a set of rules, ethics, beliefs, rituals, songs and administrative procedures for running a coven. It is customary for new covens to be formed by "hiving off" from existing covens.

Wicca is fluid, and any witch can start a new tradition, as well as a coven. Smaller ones abound, even one-coven traditions. Some of them are short-lived. Some covens choose to be eclectic, blending various traditions together or incorporating elements of SHAMANISM or other religions. Even within traditions, covens vary in the emphasis given to aspects of the Craft (see WITCHCRAFT).

Some covens join together and incorporate in organizations that serve as sources for networking or as advocates in legal issues (see COVENANT OF THE GODDESS).

The regular, working meeting of a coven is the ESBAT or circle, which usually occurs at the full MOON but may be set at other lunar phases. Covens also meet to celebrate eight seasonal festivals (see WHEEL OF THE YEAR). The covenstead is the location of a coven's temple and the place where a coven meets. It may be an outdoor site or the basement or spare room in the home of one of the coven members. The covenstead is the epicenter of a circular area called the covendom, which extends out one league, or three miles, in all directions, and in which all coven members are supposed to live. Traditionally, covendoms are not to overlap, but this rule is not strictly observed.

Number in a coven. GERALD B. GARDNER considered 13 to be the ideal number of a coven, which would include six "perfect couples" of men and women, plus a leader. Ideally, the couples would be married or be lovers, in order to produce the best harmony and results in magic. SYBIL LEEK also said that all New Forest covens had 13 members: six men and six women plus a high priestess.

Thirteen is traditional, but not a rigid rule. Many covens vary in size from three to about 20 members. Size is important, for too few members means ineffective magic. Too many become unwieldy. Some witches consider nine to 13 the ideal range. Much depends upon the group rapport and harmony.

Most covens have both male and female members, which is in keeping with the male-female polarity required for a fertility religion. Some covens are all-women or all-men.

History of a coven. Members of a coven are called coveners. All are priests and priestesses, save the leaders, who are the high priestess and/or high priest. Some traditions call the leaders the Master and the Lady. Most traditions have a three-degree system of advancement that calls for a minimum of a year and a day at each degree. As the Witch advances, she or he learns more secrets of the Craft and is entrusted to perform higher-level duties and rituals. Third-degree witches are eligible to become high priestesses and high priests.

In most covens, the high priestess is the ranking leader of a coven and represents the GODDESS. The high priestess is sometimes called the *magistra* (and the high priest the *magister*). If a coven has both male and female members, the high priestess shares leadership with a high priest; however, she is still viewed as the titular head of the coven. A Witch may become high priestess by leaving a coven to start her own, or by group consensus, should a high priestess leave a coven or step down. The high priestess is responsible for the smooth running of the coven so that all members can work in spiritual harmony with one another.

Besides good leadership qualities, the high priestess should possess strong psychic powers and sharp intuition. Much of a coven's magic work involves the sensitive use of psychic abilities. The high priestess must be able to build and shape the group psychic powers and sense when they are at their peaks. In addition, she helps individual coveners develop their own psychic abilities. It is usually the role of the high priestess to cast and purify the MAGIC CIRCLE and invoke the GODDESS and the spirits of the four quarters and ELEMENTS. She also directs the chants, rituals and magic work. The high priestess may "pass the wand" or delegate these duties from time to time to other coveners, as part of their training.

The high priest represents the Horned God, who is the consort to the Goddess and performs certain rituals with the high priestess. In most traditions, only high priests and high priestesses may initiate others into the craft; men initiate women and women initiate men (see INITIATION).

There are no appointed or elected "kings" and "queens" of Witches, though some individuals have adopted those titles. A high priestess from whose coven others have hived off is entitled to be called a *Witch Queen,* which is entirely different.

Many covens have a maiden, who is at least a second-degree Witch and is the personal assistant of the high priestess. The maiden can substitute for the high priestess in certain tasks; she also handles various administrative duties. She is likely to be in charge of a "training circle" of potential initiates. According to tradition, the office of maiden is held by one woman, until she succeeds the high priestess or leaves to form her own coven. In some covens, the position may be rotated as a means of training for third degree.

Many covens have a summoner, also called a *fetch,* who is in charge of scheduling meetings and notifying members.

FURTHER READING:
Buckland, Raymond. *Buckland's Complete Book of Witchcraft.* St. Paul: Llewellyn Publications,1986.
Crowley, Vivianne. *Wicca: The Old Religion in the New Millennium.* Revised ed. London: Thorsons/Harper Collins, 1996.
Russell, Jeffrey Burton. *Witchcraft in the Middle Ages.* Ithaca and London: Cornell University Press, 1972.
Seymour, St. John D. *Irish Witchcraft and Demonology.* Dublin: Hodges, Figgis & Co., 1913.
Summers, Montague. *The Geography of Witchcraft.* London: Kegan Paul, Trench, Truner & Co. Ltd., 1927.

Covenant of the Goddess   One of the largest and oldest Wiccan religious organizations. The Covenant of the Goddess (COG) is an international nonprofit confederation of autonomous covens and solitary witches of various traditions and is based in Berkeley, California. COG states that its purpose is "to increase cooperation among Witches and to secure for witches and covens the legal protection enjoyed by members of other religions."

COG was formed in 1975 by elders from diverse Wiccan traditions in response to the rise of interest in witchcraft, feminism and environmentalism. The elders drafted a covenant among them, and bylaws for the new organization. The bylaws were ratified by 13 member covens at the summer solstice in 1975. Incorporation as a nonprofit religious organization came on October 31 (Samhain) the same year.

COG has a national board of directors but no hierarchy and is governed by consensus. It has the power to confer credentials upon clergy. Membership is open to all covens and individual Witches who worship GODDESS and "the Old Gods," believe in a code of ethics compatible with COG, and have been meeting or practicing for at least six months. About two-thirds of its clergy are women. There are 13 local councils, regional conferences, a national newsletter and an annual national conference, "Merry-Meet," that is open to all Pagans and Wiccans. In addition, COG participates in numerous interfaith, educational, environmental, charitable and community activities and provides educational resources for teen Wiccans.

COG recognizes the autonomy of each coven, and the variations in craft law among various traditions. The organization does not shape or direct policy. It does have a code of ethics, which states that:

- Witches must follow the WICCAN REDE, "An' it harm none, do as ye will."
- No fees can be charged for initiations or initiate training.
- "Reasonable fees" may be charged for services that earn a living.
- The autonomy and sovereignty of other Witches and covens must be respected.
- Witches should be mindful of both the unity and diversity of their religion.

FURTHER READING:
Covenant of the Goddess Web site. Available online. URL: http://www.cog.org. Downloaded August 17, 2007.

cowan   In Wicca, a non-witch, a person who has not been initiated into the Craft (see INITIATION). The word is an old Scottish term for a mason who has learned the trade without serving an apprenticeship. Cowans generally are not allowed to attend circles, or ESBATS, the regular meetings of covens in which magical work is performed. Cowans may be invited to attend seasonal festivals.

Craft name   In Wicca, a name taken upon INITIATION that reflects one's new identity as witch. A witch may keep a Craft name secret and use it only in meditation, or may disclose it only to members of the COVEN. Some witches choose to use their Craft names publicly, while others have both private and public Craft names. Some covens have strict rules against disclosing Craft names to outsiders.

During the witch hysteria, witch-hunters and inquisitors spread the notion that witches were given new names by the DEVIL after he had signed them to pacts and baptized them. In Wicca, Craft names have nothing to do with the Devil, who is neither recognized nor worshiped by witches.

Craft names are highly individualistic. They may reflect personal aspirations, ethnic heritage or an aspect of a deity with whom the Witch identifies. A Witch selects a Craft name through meditation, study or oracular DIVINATION. Some use trance to receive a name bestowed by the GODDESS. Others are given names by their high priestess or high priest. Witches may change their Craft names as they advance from first degree to third degree, the levels of knowledge in major traditions, or as their sense of identity and purpose changes.

FURTHER READING:
Buckland, Raymond. BUCKLAND'S COMPLETE BOOK OF WITCH-CRAFT. St. Paul, Minn.: Llewellyn Publications, 1986.

crosses   One of the oldest AMULETS in the world, pre-dating Christianity by many centuries. In the commonest form of a cross, all four arms are of equal length rather than in a T-shape. Crosses have been associated with sun deities and the heavens, and in ancient times they may have represented divine protection and prosperity. Crosses also are represented by the Y-shaped Tree of Life, the world-axis placed in the center of the universe, the bridge between the earth and the cosmos, the physical and the spiritual.

In Christianity, the cross transcends the status of amulet to become symbolic of the religion and of the suffering of Christ's crucifixion; yet, it still retains aspects of an amulet, protecting against the forces of evil. Even before the crucifixion of Christ, the cross was a weapon against the dark forces. According to legend, when Lucifer declared war upon God in an attempt to usurp his power, his army scattered God's angels twice. God sent to his angels a Cross of Light on which were inscribed the names of the Trinity. Upon seeing this cross, Lucifer's forces lost strength and were driven into hell.

Early Christians made the sign of the cross for divine protection and as a means of identification to each other. In the fourth century, Christ's wooden cross was allegedly found in excavations in Jerusalem by Empress Helena, mother of Constantine I. It is said that Helena found three buried crosses at the site of the crucifixion but did not know which belonged to Christ. She tested all three with the corpse of a man. Two crosses had no effect upon the body, but the third caused it to come to life. Helena sent part of the cross to Constantine, who sent a portion to Rome, where it is still preserved in the Vatican. The rest of the cross Helena reburied. Bits of the cross that were fashioned into amulets became highly prized.

As the Church grew in power, so did its symbol, the cross. According to belief, nothing unholy can stand up to its presence. The cross, and the sign of the cross, will help exorcise DEMONS and devils (see EXORCISM), ward off incubi and succubi, prevent bewitchment of man and beast, protect crops from being blasted by witches (see BLASTING), and force vampires to flee. During the INQUISITION, inquisitors wore crosses or made the sign of the cross while in the presence of accused witches, in order to ward off any evil SPELLS they might cast. People crossed themselves routinely, before the smallest task, just in case an evil presence was near.

FURTHER READING:
Thomas, Keith. Religion and the Decline of Magic. New York: Charles Scribner's Sons, 1971.

crossroads   A heavily charged place of MAGIC. The Greek goddess of witchcraft, HECATE, was also goddess of the crossroads, and animals were sacrificed to her at such locations. It was believed that Hecate appeared at crossroads on clear nights, accompanied by spirits and howling dogs. Offerings were placed there to propitiate her and ask for her intercession in cases of madness, which was believed to be caused by departed souls. In Ireland and Wales, it was traditional on Samhain (All Hallow's Eve), the Druidic new year, to sit at a crossroads and listen for the howling of the wind, which would prophesy the year to come.

During the witch hunts, sorcerers (see SORCERY) and WITCHES were said to frequent crossroads to conjure the DEVIL or his DEMONS or make SACRIFICES to them. In the sixth century, the sorcerer Salatin conjured the Devil for THEOPHILUS at a crossroads. In 1324 Dame ALICE KYTELLER, an accused Irish witch, was said to sacrifice COCKS to her familiar at a crossroads.

According to Carl G. Jung, a crossroads is a mother symbol; in that respect, it corresponds to the emphasis placed on the Mother GODDESS in contemporary WITCHCRAFT. The crossroads also represents the intersection of positive, neutral and negative forces. It is a place of flux and of change.

FURTHER READING:
Baroja, Julio Caro. The World of the Witches. 1961. Reprint, Chicago: University of Chicago Press, 1975.
Leach, Maria, ed., and Jerome Fried, assoc. ed. Funk & Wagnall's Standard Dictionary of Folklore, Mythology and Legend. New York: Harper & Row, 1972.

Crowley, Aleister (1875–1947)   The most controversial and perhaps least understood magician and occultist of his time, Aleister Crowley has been both vilified and idolized. He was a man of both low excesses and high brilliance. He considered himself to be the reincarnation of other great occultists: Pope Alexander VI, renowned for his love of physical pleasures; Edward Kelly, the notorious assistant to occultist John Dee in Elizabethan England; Cagliostro; and occultist Eliphas Levi, who died on the day Crowley was born. Crowley also believed he had been Ankh-f-n-Khonsu, an Egyptian priest of the XXVIth dynasty.

Crowley was born in Warwickshire, England. His father was a brewer and a preacher of Plymouthism, the beliefs of a sect founded of the Plymouth Brethren in 1830 that considered itself the only true Christian order. As a child, Crowley participated in the preaching with his parents, then rebelled against it. His behavior inspired his mother to call him "the Beast" after the Antichrist. Later, he called her "a brainless bigot of the most narrow, logical and inhuman type." His father died when he was 11.

As Crowley grew older, he became interested in the occult. He also discovered he was excited by descriptions of TORTURE and BLOOD, and he liked to fantasize about being degraded by a Scarlet Woman who was both wicked and independent.

He entered Trinity College at Cambridge, where he wrote poetry and pursued, on his own, his occult studies. He loved to climb rocks and mountains and attempted some of the highest peaks in the Himalayas. In 1898 he published his first book of poetry, *Aceldama, A Place to Bury Strangers in. A Philosophical Poem. By a Gentleman of the University of Cambridge,* 1898. In the preface, he described how God and Satan had fought for his soul: "God conquered—now I have only one doubt left—which of the twain was God?"

After reading Arthur Edward Waite's *The Book of Black Magic and of Pacts,* which hints of a secret brotherhood of adepts who dispense occult wisdom to certain initiates. Intrigued, Crowley wrote to Waite for more information and was referred to *The Cloud upon the Sanctuary,* by Carl von Eckartshausen, which tells of the Great White Brotherhood. Crowley determined he wanted to join this brotherhood and advance to the highest degree.

On November 18, 1898, Crowley joined the London chapter of the HERMETIC ORDER OF THE GOLDEN DAWN, which was the First or Outer Order of the Great White Brotherhood. He discovered he had a natural aptitude for MAGIC and rose quickly through the hierarchy. He began practicing yoga, in the course of which he discovered his earlier incarnations. He left Trinity College without earning a degree, took a flat in Chancery Lane, named him-

Aleister Crowley (HARRY PRICE COLLECTION; COURTESY MARY EVANS PICTURE LIBRARY)

self Count Vladimir and pursued his occult studies on a full-time basis. He advanced through the First Order and sought entry into the Second Order of the Great White Brotherhood, a Rosicrucian order also called the Order of the Red Rose and the Golden Cross. Beyond this was the top order, the Silver Star or A∴A∴ (*Argentum Astrum*), which had three grades: Master of the Temple, Magus and Ipissimus. The latter could be achieved only by crossing an unknown and uncharted Abyss.

Crowley was intensely competitive with S. L. Mac-Gregor Mathers, the chief of the Hermetic Order of the Golden Dawn and a ceremonial magician. Mathers taught Crowley Abra-Melin magic (see ABRAMELIN THE MAGE) but had not attained any of three grades in the A∴A∴. The two quarreled, and Mathers supposedly dispatched an army of ELEMENTALS to attack Crowley. Crowley also argued with other members of the Golden Dawn as well and as a result was expelled from the order. He pursued the attainment of Ipissimus on his own.

Crowley traveled widely. He studied Eastern mysticism, including Buddhism, Tantric Yoga and the *I Ching.* For a time he lived in Scotland, in an isolated setting near Loch Ness. In 1903 he married Rose Kelly, who bore him one child. Rose began to receive communications from the astral plane, and in 1904 she told Crowley that he was to receive an extremely important message. It came from Aiwass, a spirit and Crowley's Holy Guardian Angel, or True Self. Crowley also later identified Aiwass as a magical current or solar-phallic energy worshiped by the Sumerians as Shaitan, a "devil-god," and by the Egyptians as Set. On three consecutive days in April 1904, from noon until 1 P.M., Aiwass reportedly manifested as a voice and dictated to Crowley *The Book of the Law,* the most significant work of his magical career. It contains the Law of Thelema: "Do what thou wilt shall be the whole of the law." Though some have interpreted it to mean doing as one pleases, it actually means that one must do what one must and nothing else. Admirers of Crowley say the Law of Thelema distinguishes him as one of the greatest magicians of history.

Aiwass also heralded the coming of a new Aeon of Horus, the third great age of humanity. The three ages were characterized as Paganism/Christianity/Thelema, represented, respectively, by ISIS/OSIRIS/Horus. Crowley considered himself the prophet of the New Aeon.

From 1909 to 1913, Crowley published the secret rituals of the Golden Dawn in his periodical, *The Equinox,* which also served as a vehicle for his poetry. Mathers tried but failed to get an injunction to stop him. By 1912 Crowley had become involved with the *Ordo Templi Orientis,* a German occult order practicing magic.

In 1909 Crowley explored levels of the astral plane with his assistant, poet Victor Neuberg, using Enochian magic. He believed he crossed the Abyss and united his consciousness with the universal consciousness, thus becoming Master of the Temple. He described the astral journeys in *The Vision and the Voice,* published first in *The Equinox* and posthumously in 1949.

Crowley kept with him a series of "scarlet women." The best known of these was Leah Hirsig, the "Ape of Thoth," who indulged with him in drinking, drugs and sexual magic and who could sometimes contact Aiwass. Crowley apparently made several attempts with various scarlet women to beget a "magical child," none of which was successful. He later fictionalized these efforts in his novel, *Moonchild,* published in 1929.

From 1915 to 1919 Crowley lived in the United States. In 1920 he went to Sicily and founded the Abbey of Thelema, which he envisioned as a magical colony.

In 1921, when Crowley was 45, he and Hirsig conducted a ritual in which Crowley achieved Ipissimus and became, according to his cryptic description, a god ("As a God goes, I go"). He did not reveal attaining Ipissimus to anyone, only hinting at it in his privately published *Magical Record* much later, in 1929. After the transformation, however, Hirsig found him intolerable. Crowley later discarded her and acquired a new scarlet woman, Dorothy Olsen.

In 1922 Crowley accepted an invitation to head the *Ordo Templi Orientis.* In 1923 the bad press that he routinely received led to his expulsion from Sicily, and he had to abandon his abbey. After some wandering through France (where he suffered from a heroin addiction), Tunisia and Germany, he returned to England.

In 1929 he married his second wife, Maria Ferrari de Miramar, in Leipzig.

In his later years he was plagued with poor health, drug addiction and financial trouble. He kept himself financially afloat by publishing nonfiction and fiction. In 1945 he moved to a boardinghouse in Hastings, where he lived the last two years of his life, a dissipated shadow of his former vigorous self. During these last years, he was introduced to GERALD B. GARDNER by ARNOLD CROWTHER. According to Gardner, Crowley told him he had been initiated into the Craft as a young man. This claim is unlikely, as there is nothing in Crowley's published or unpublished writings referring to involvement in witchcraft. Crowley seemed disinterested in the Craft because of the authority of women; according to PATRICIA CROWTHER, he said he "refused to be bossed around by any damn woman." Crowley died in a private hotel in Hastings in 1947. His remains were cremated and sent to his followers in the United States.

Crowley's other published books include *The Diary of a Drug Fiend; Magick in Theory and Practice,* still considered one of the best books on ceremonial magic; *The Strategem,* a collection of fiction stories; *The Equinox of the Gods,* which sets forth *The Book of the Law* as mankind's new religion; and *The Book of Thoth,* his interpretation of the Tarot *Confessions* originally was intended to be a six-volume autohagiography, but only the first two volumes were published. He argued with the publishing company, which was taken over by his friends and then went out of business. The remaining galleys and manuscripts—he had dictated the copy to Hirsig while under the influence of heroin—were lost or scattered about. They were collected and edited by John Symonds and Kenneth Grant and published in a single volume in 1969.

Crowley referred to himself in some of his writings as "the Master Therion" and "Frater Perdurabo." He spelled *magic* as *magick* to "distinguish the science of the Magi from all its counterfeits." Some modern occultists continue to follow suit.

See OLD GEORGE PICKINGILL.

FURTHER READING:

Hutton, Ronald. *The Triumph of the Moon: A History of Modern Pagan Witchcraft.* Oxford: Oxford University Press, 1999.

Michaelsen, Scott, ed. *Portable Darkness: An Aleister Crowley Reader.* New York: Harmony Books, 1989.

Stephenson, P. R., and Israel Regardie. *The Legend of Aleister Crowley.* St. Paul, Minn.: Llewellyn Publications, 1970.

Symonds, John, and Kenneth Grant, eds. *The Confessions of Aleister Crowley, an Autobiography.* London: Routledge & Kegan Paul, 1979.

Crowley, Vivianne   Prominent Wiccan, best-selling author, psychologist and university lecturer, whose work has helped to build bridges between WICCA and PAGANISM and mainstream religions and society.

Vivianne Crowley is Irish but was raised mainly in the New Forest area of England where GERALD B. GARDNER has his beginnings in Witchcraft. She was educated at state, Catholic and Protestant schools, which opened her to different spiritual traditions. Her mother had strong psychic abilities, including precognitive dreams, and this helped to make Crowley aware at a young age that there is more to the world than meets the five senses.

As she played in the New Forest, she attuned to the intelligences of nature, the energy of trees and the spirit of the land; the world emerged as a magical place. Occasionally she would come across the evidence of a ritual, such as the place where a Witches' circle had been cast. By age eight, she was testing her abilities in practical magic, starting with a rain-making spell cast with friends, and which did produce rain. She taught herself how to read cards and gave readings to fellow students on the school bus.

By age 11, Crowley had learned about covens and Witchcraft from the media and decided to form her own coven at her all-girls school. She formulated her own initiation rite after modern rites she had seen in photographs. Representing Goddess, she stood with her legs apart and had initiates pass through to be reborn. Her coven eventually was brought to a halt by school officials, not because they were a "coven" of "witches" (the term never was mentioned), but because nearby residents complained of the noise they made.

Crowley was about 14 when she decided that she wanted to take a formal initiation as a Witch. Up to then, she had not seen Witchcraft as a spiritual path or religion, but as a way of practical magic—a craft. Publicity surrounding ALEX SANDERS and his wife Maxine, founders of the Alexandrian tradition, changed her perspective. She began to see Witchcraft as a spiritual tradition, one in which women could play a prominent role. However, the Sanders' coven informed her that she had to be 18 to be initiated.

Crowley waited, and upon turning 18 was initiated into the Sanders' coven in London. The coven underwent major changes after the Sanderses separated in 1973 and Alex moved to the south coast of England. Crowley left and joined a Gardnerian coven.

Crowley met her future husband, Chris, who was not involved in Wicca but through Crowley became interested and was initiated. They married in 1979 and established their own coven, which they have maintained to the present. Numerous covens have hived off, and the Crowleys have helped many individuals in Britain, Continental Europe and North America to start their own covens.

Professionally, Crowley is a psychologist who lectures in the psychology of religion at King's College, University of London, and is adjunct professor at the Union Institute in Cincinnati, Ohio. She also works in management consulting, plus some counseling. She describes herself as Jungian oriented but with an eclectic approach, including transpersonal psychology. She holds a bachelor's degree and Ph.D. in psychology from the University of London.

In 1988, the Crowleys formed the Wicca Study Group in London as a way of introducing interested people to the Craft. At the time, there were few venues for the public teaching of Witchcraft. Vivianne also began teaching in Germany, following up on work done there by Sanders. The success of the Wiccan Study group led the Crowleys to expand their teaching to other countries.

Also in 1988, the Crowleys became involved in the PAGAN FEDERATION, she as secretary and he as treasurer and then president. Crowley also served for a time as the federation's interfaith coordinator, and as the U.K. coordinator of Pagan chaplaincy services for prisons. Both helped to develop the federation's system of democratic elections. They have served on the council since 1991.

In 1989, Crowley entered a larger public spotlight with the publication of her book *Wicca: The Old Religion in the New Age*. A best-seller, the book was revised and updated in 1996 as *Wicca: The Old Religion in the New Millennium*. Like STARHAWK's *The Spiral Dance*, Crowley's *Wicca* has provided a clear and appealing introduction to Wicca as a spiritual tradition that facilitates personal growth, creativity and integration.

Crowley's spiritual perspective is as a panentheist, seeing the divine at the essential force present in the universe that is both transcendent and immanent. Her interests lie more in worshiping the gods and in achieving spiritual growth than in magical spellcraft. Wicca is a mystery religion oriented toward personal wholeness.

Crowley has been instrumental in the establishment of networking and peer group support for Wiccans and Pagans in Britain and Europe. In addition, one of her most significant contributions is her ability to bridge these traditions to other areas: religions, academia, psychology and popular culture, establishing the common multicultural, disciplinary and spiritual ground. She has been a prime spokesperson as Wicca and Paganism have become the subjects of serious academic and interfaith study.

Crowley's other books are: *Phoenix from the Flame: Pagan Spirituality in the Western World* (1994), *Principles of Paganism* (1996), *Principles of Wicca* (1997), *Principles of Jungian Spirituality* (1998), *Celtic Wisdom: Seasonal Festivals and Rituals* (1998), *A Woman's Guide to the Earth Traditions* (2001) and *The Magical Life: A Wiccan Priestess Shares Her Secrets* (2003). With Chris, she coauthored *Free Your Creative Spirit* (2001) and *Your Dark Side* (2001). In addition, she has published numerous articles and essays and has contributed to anthologies on Paganism and Wicca.

Crowther, Arnold (1909–1974) English Witch and skilled stage magician, friend of GERALD B. GARDNER and husband of PATRICIA C. CROWTHER. According to Patricia, Crowther, like Gardner, was an "old" soul who had lived many earthly lives. He discovered a past life as a Tibetan monk, and he experienced vivid dreams in which the secrets of ancient MAGIC were revealed to him.

Crowther was born on October 6, 1909, in Chatham, Kent, one of a pair of fraternal twin brothers. His mother was Scottish and his father, an optician, was from Yorkshire.

Crowther was fascinated with sleight-of-hand, magic tricks, ventriloquism and puppeteering. From the age of about eight on, he practiced tricks in secret in his bedroom. Both he and his twin planned to follow their father's footsteps as opticians, but magic led Crowther in another direction. By his early twenties, he was touring his professional magic act. He had a good stage persona and was very clever at sleight-of-hand.

He worked in cabaret, and in 1938–39, he entertained the then-Princesses Elizabeth and Margaret Rose at Buckingham Palace, which led to numerous engagements to entertain the titled gentry of England. He was a founder member of the Puppet Guild and made more than 500 puppets. He lectured on "curios of the world" to various societies and clubs and was himself a collector of odd items from around the world. An African witch doctor gave him the title "White Witch Doctor." Crowther was a Freemason and was interested in Buddhism, until he entered the Craft.

Crowther met Gardner and Gardner's wife, Donna, shortly before the start of World War II, probably at a lecture, and struck up a friendship with them.

Crowther became very interested in the Craft but was not initiated into it for about 18 years (see INITIATION). Gardner's coven was wary of adverse publicity and felt that Crowther might use the Craft in his act. Gardner assured Crowther that the time would come when a "very special person" would initiate him into the Craft. The Gardners kept a flat in London, and Crowther frequently met them there, especially at the Caledonian Market, an antique market where Gardner loved to browse. Crowther was often out of town during the summer season, but upon his return, he would drop by the Caledonian Market and often find Gardner, who would greet him as though he'd never been gone: "Oh, hello, old man, did I tell you . . . ?"

During the war, Crowther was in the Entertainers National Services Association and toured throughout Europe entertaining troops with his show, "Black Magic." The show's name derived from its African Basuto choir. Crowther performed wherever required, including in a DC 3 plane at 4,000 feet, en route from Tripoli to Malta on November 10, 1943.

While stationed in Paris, he learned of his past life as a beggar Tibetan monk when he and an officer visited a palmist, Madame Brux, who invited them to a séance and introduced them to a medium. The medium went into trance and began communicating with a masculine spirit who said he had been Crowther's teacher in a previous life and was his guide in the present life. The medium reported that Crowther had been a young student in a Tibetan lamasary and had been killed. She spoke the name "Younghusband," but Crowther knew no one of that name. "Your possessions will be returned to you," the medium said. With that, an object fell on the séance table. It was a Tibetan prayer wheel inscribed with the most holy of mantras, *"Om mani padme hum."* The medium said it was an apport.

After the war, other Tibetan articles found their way into Crowther's possession: a butter lamp, a trumpet made of a human thigh bone, a drum made of a human skull and a small rattle hand-drum. An expert told Crowther such articles were used by the *Z'i-jed-pa,* "The Mild Doer," a homeless medicant class of Yogi regarded as saints, who should attain Nirvana after death and not have to be born again.

If he had indeed been such a monk in a previous life, then he would not have reincarnated as Crowther, he reasoned. He discovered, however, that if he, as the monk, had killed someone, he would have had to be reincarnated to balance the karma. At an exhibition of Tibetan curios in London, Crowther discovered that a Colonel Younghusband had led a military attack against Tibet in 1904. Crowther believed he had killed one of the soldiers in the attack before being killed himself.

During his travels Crowther also met ALEISTER CROWLEY. He introduced Gardner to Crowley on May 1, 1947. Crowley's diary entry for that date reads "Dr. G.B. Gard-

Arnold Crowther (COURTESY PATRICIA C. CROWTHER)

ner, Ph.D. Singapore, Arnold Crowther Prof. G. a Magician to tea . . ."

After the war, Crowther returned to the public stage. Just as Gardner had predicted, he met a fair-haired woman, Patricia Dawson, who initiated him into the Craft. After their marriage in 1960, he and Patricia made their home in Sheffield and achieved prominence as spokespersons for the Craft.

Crowther died on Beltane (May 1), 1974. He was given the Passing Rite of the Old Religion at his funeral. A piper played a lament, as he had requested before his death. When the music ended, the sound of a running brook could be heard: the Brook of Love, said by DION FORTUNE to exist on the other side.

In addition to two books, numerous articles for a wide variety of magazines, and a radio series on Witchcraft written in collaboration with Patricia, Crowther's published credits include: *Let's Put on a Show* (1964), a how-to book of magic which he illustrated himself; *Linda and the Lollipop Man* (1973), a book on road safety for children; *Yorkshire Customs* (1974); and *Hex Certificate* (late 1970s), a collection of cartoons he drew on themes of Witchcraft. His autobiography, *Hand in Glove,* was not published but was serialized on B.B.C. Radio in Bristol, Sheffield, Medway and Leeds between 1975 and 1977.

Crowther, Patricia C. (1927–) A Witch and high priestess of Sheffield, Yorkshire, England, and one of the last surviving high priestesses initiated by GERALD B. GARDNER. Patricia Crowther has, since the 1960s, been a leading spokesperson for the Old Religion in books, the media and lecture appearances. Initiated formally into the Craft by Gardner, she is regarded by many as Gardner's spiritual heir. She has formed covens all over the United Kingdom.

She was born Patricia Dawson on October 27, 1927, in Sheffield. Her Breton great-grandmother was an herbalist and clairvoyant, who also told fortunes. Her grandmother, Elizabeth (Tizzy) Machen (her maiden name) was a very small woman whose surname means "fairy" (see FAIRIES).

The Dawsons lived next door to a palmist, Madame Melba, who accurately predicted that Patricia would develop great clairvoyant powers. During childhood, she experienced synchronistic associations with fairies and the Craft: at a children's birthday party, she was chosen

Patricia C. Crowther (PHOTO BY IAN MACGILL; COURTESY PATRICIA C. CROWTHER)

to be Fairy on the Moon, and was wheeled around seated on a huge, illuminated crescent moon (the GODDESS with crescent moon is often symbolic of DIANA); for a birthday present, she was given a gold snake bangle, symbol of wisdom, life and rebirth; she performed as Robin Hood in pantomime, and she was the leading lady in a revue which featured a tableau entitled *The Legend of the Moon Goddess.*

When Patricia was 30, a hypnotist regressed her to previous lives, including one as a Witch, Polly, an old crone of about 66 in the year 1670. Polly revealed that she lived in a hut with a CAT, frog, goat and hen, and worked spells for people, most of whom she held in contempt. Polly freely recited SPELLS, all in rhyme, with instructions on how to use them. Patricia had no knowledge of such spells, which experts determined were authentic. The regression proved to her that she had been a Witch in a previous life and that, in accordance with Witch lore, she would find her way back into the Craft in the present life. Since that experience, she has recalled, in clairvoyant visions, another past life in which she served as a priestess of the Goddess who had great power. She identifies more strongly with the spiritual priestess than with the spell-casting crone.

Patricia's parents had trained her in singing, dancing and acting for the stage, and she toured all over the United Kingdom. While playing a theater in Birmingham in 1954, she met a fortune-teller who predicted she would meet her future husband, a man named Arnold, two years later over water. The prediction seemed fantastic, but it was borne out. In 1956 Patricia took a summer job on the Isle of Wight, where she met ARNOLD CROWTHER, a stage magician and ventriloquist who was performing in the same show as she. When Arnold discovered her interest in Witchcraft, he offered to introduce her to Gardner, a personal friend since 1939. Several years earlier, Gardner had predicted that Arnold would meet a fair-haired woman who would initiate him into the Craft. This prediction proved to be true as well.

After several meetings with Gardner, Patricia was initiated by him on June 6, 1960. The INITIATION took place in Gardner's private Magic Room, the top floor of a barn, at his home in Castletown on the Isle of Man. Patricia in turn initiated Arnold. Gardner presented them with ritual tools and jewelry, including a coral necklace for Patricia.

During the rite, Patricia had a profound and powerful trance experience in which she saw herself being reborn into the priesthood of the Moon Mysteries, initiated by a line of howling, naked women who passed her, gauntlet-style, through their spread legs. Gardner posited that she had gone back in time to another previous life and relived an ancient initiation ceremony.

On November 8, 1960, Patricia and Arnold were married in a private HANDFASTING officiated by Gardner. The ceremony took place in a circle; participants were skyclad (nude). The following day, November 9, the Crowthers were married in a civil ceremony which the press found out about in advance and publicized heavily. The Crowthers established their home in Sheffield. They took the second-degree initiation on October 11, 1961; Patricia became high priestess on October 14, her birthday.

The Crowthers often were sought out by the media for interviews. One interview inadvertently led to the gradual formation of a COVEN. Asked by a reporter if she wanted to meet others who were interested in the Craft, Patricia answered yes. The reporter's story was headlined, "Witch Seeks Recruits for Coven," which prompted many inquiries from interested persons. The Crowthers initiated the first member of their coven in December 1961, with others following gradually over time.

The Crowthers continued their instruction in the Craft with Gardner. Patricia was taught an old secret, inner tradition by an old woman who lived in Inverness, who saw Patricia on a television program and wrote to her. Her name was Jean, and she told Patricia she considered her worthy of inheriting this knowledge, which she imparted over the course of a two-year correspondence.

The Crowthers' media exposure generated requests for more interviews and speaking engagements. Together, they authored two books, *The Witches Speak* (1965, 1976) and *The Secrets of Ancient Witchcraft* (1974). For B.B.C. Radio Sheffield, the Crowthers produced the first radio series in Britain on Witchcraft, *A Spell of Witchcraft,* which debuted on January 6, 1971. They performed services for people, including casting SPELLS and exorcising ghosts (see SPIRIT EXORCISM). They wrote RITUALS for the seasons of the year and introduced new music and poetry into the Craft.

Patricia's nonfiction books include *Witchcraft in Yorkshire* (1973), her autobiography, *Witch Blood!* (1974), *The Witches Speak* (1976), *Lid Off the Cauldron* (1981, 1985, 1989, 1992, 1998), *The Zodiac Experience* (1992, 1995), *One Witch's World* (1998) and *From Stagecraft to Witchcraft; The Early Years of a High Priestess* (2002). Her novel *Witches Were for Hanging* (1992) was reprinted in 1999. In addition, she wrote poetry and designed three cards (The Sun, Karma and The World) for *The Tarot of the Old Path* (1990).

In addition, she has written articles for periodicals, including *Prediction, Gnostica, New Dimensions, Zodiac,* and *The Lamp of Thoth.* She is a frequent guest on radio and television shows and lectures as well, working to dispel sensational misconceptions associated with the Old Religion and with the modern Craft. In 1978 she represented Wicca in the United Kingdom at an international occult conference in Barcelona.

In addition to her activities on behalf of the Craft, Crowther continued to work professionally as a singer, magician and puppeteer well her later years.

After her 70th birthday, Crowther received clairaudient guidance while meditating in a circle that she should call herself a "Grand-Mother of the Craft of the Wise."

She emphasized that the Craft concerns the evolution of the soul, and that its inner teachings should be transmitted orally.

"I am sure that the Craft/Paganism will have a big part to play in the centuries to come," she stated. "We must not forget that in the New Age, the ruler of Aquarius is none other than the Star Goddess, whose white hand, even now, beckons the Children of the Earth to become Children of the Stars."

FURTHER READING:
Crowther, Patricia. *Witch Blood!* New York: House of Collectibles, Inc., 1974.
———. *Lid Off the Cauldron: A Wicca Handbook.* York Beach, Me.: Samuel Weiser, 1989.
———. *From Stagecraft to Witchcraft: The Early Years of a High Priestess.* Milverton, Eng.: Capall Bann Publishing, 2002.

Cunningham, John   See JOHN FIAN.

Cunningham, Scott (1956–1993) Prolific Wiccan author and expert on earth and natural MAGIC, best known for his books on magical herbalism, earth power, crystals, gems and metals and "the truth about Witchcraft." Born June 27, 1956, in Royal Oak, Michigan, Cunningham lived in San Diego from 1961 until his death in 1993. He began practicing WICCA in 1971. A full-time writer, he authored more than 30 fiction and nonfiction books and wrote scripts for occult videocassettes.

Cunningham was introduced to the Craft in 1971 through a book purchased by his mother, *The Supernatural,* by Douglas Hill and Pat Williams. Early on in life, Cunningham had had a strong interest in plants, minerals and other natural earth products, and the book piqued his curiosity. He read it and was particularly fascinated by the book's descriptions of Italian hand gestures used to ward off the EVIL EYE.

In the next two days, two other incidents added impetus to his interest in the Craft: a movie about Witchcraft shown on television; and a female classmate in high school who was involved in an occult and magic study group. Meeting on the first day of drama class, the two began talking, and Cunningham unconsciously made the evil eye hand gestures. The classmate recognized them and asked, "Are you a Witch" "No," said Cunningham, "but I'd sure like to be one." The classmate introduced him to Wicca. Learning magic intensified his interest in the power of nature. Cunningham was initiated into several covens of various traditions (see INITIATION) but eventually opted to practice as a SOLITARY.

In 1974 he enrolled in San Diego State University and studied creative writing, intending to become a professional writer like his father, Chet, who has authored more than 170 nonfiction and fiction books. He wrote truck and automotive trade articles and advertising copy on a freelance basis. After two years in college, he realized he

Scott Cunningham (COURTESY LLEWELLYN PUBLICATIONS)

had more published credits than most of his professors, and decided to drop out and begin writing full-time.

The first book he wrote was *Magical Herbalism*, though it was not his first to be published. That book, *Shadow of Love*, an Egyptian romance novel, appeared in 1980. *Magical Herbalism* was published in 1982. Between 1980 and 1987, Cunningham published 21 novels in various genres, six nonfiction occult books and one nonfiction booklet. Besides *Magical Herbalism*, his credits include *Earth Power: Techniques of Natural Magic* (1983); *Cunningham's Encyclopedia of Magical Herbs* (1985); *The Magic of Incense, Oils and Brews* (1987); *The Magical Household* (1987; coauthored with David Harrington); and *Cunningham's Encyclopedia of Crystal, Gem and Metal Magic* (1987); *The Truth About Herb Magic* (1992); *Sacred Sleep* (1992); *The Art of Divination* (1993); *Spellcrafts* (1993); and *Hawaiian Magic* (1993).

Cunningham anonymously wrote a booklet, *The Truth About Witchcraft*, which explains folk magic as well as the Wiccan religion. An expanded, booklength version of *The Truth About Witchcraft*, as well as a second title, *Wicca: A Guide for the Solitary Practitioner,* were published in 1988. He also wrote *The Magic of Food* (1991), a book about the magical properties within foods.

Cunningham lectured to groups around the United States and occasionally made media appearances on behalf of the Craft. He viewed Wicca as a modern religion, created in the 20th century, incorporating elements of pagan folk magic. He said Wicca should be stripped of its quasi-historical and mythological trappings and presented to the public as a modern religion sprung from primeval concepts. The purpose of Wicca is to facilitate human contact with the GODDESS and God; the differences between traditions, he maintained, are petty and distracting.

Like others in the Craft, Cunningham believed in reincarnation, but said many people place too much importance on exploring past lives. He said the present is what counts, and one's attention should be given to learning the lessons of the here and now.

Cunningham's intense devotion to his work and his prolific outpouring of writing perhaps was fueled in part by his intuition that his time might be limited. In 1983, at age 27, he was diagnosed with lymphoma. After surgery, radiation, chemotherapy and healing rituals and spells, the cancer was in remission.

In 1990, during a publicity tour in the midwestern and eastern United States, Cunningham began to suffer increasingly painful migraine headaches. In Salem, Massachusetts, he collapsed, semi-conscious, and was rushed to the hospital. He was diagnosed with cryptococcal meningitis complicated by AIDS infections. He spent several weeks in the hospital and then was transferred to the University of California San Diego Medical Center. He had no medical insurance, and friends and family set up a fund to help pay staggering medical bills.

Cunningham recovered enough to resume writing and traveling, although his health was impaired and his prognosis was not good. In 1992, his vision began to fail, and he spent increasing time in the hospital. In January 1993, he sold some of his personal belongings and books and moved back home with his parents.

In February 1993, the spinal meningitis returned, along with an infection in the brain. Cunningham went into a coma for several days and lost his remaining vision. He returned home, where he passed away on March 28.

Cunningham left an autobiography unfinished at the time of his death. It was completed and published as *Whispers of the Moon* by David Harrington and deTraci Regula in 1996.

FURTHER READING:
Harrington, David, and deTraci Regula. *Whispers of the Moon: The Life and Work of Scott Cunningham.* St. Paul, Minn.: Llewellyn Publications, 1996.

cunning man/cunning woman   Village witch or healer who provided cures, remedies, CHARMS, SPELLS and divination, usually in exchange for a fee or gift.

Judith Phillips, an English cunning woman, 1595

"Cunning" comes from the Old English term kenning, meaning "wise" or "knowledgeable." Other terms for cunning man and cunning woman are *wise man, wise woman, sorcerer,* WIZARD, conjurer, charmer, blesser, white witch and WITCH.

Traditionally, cunning men and women came into their craft by heredity, such as JAMES MURRELL, one of England's most famous cunning men. Others acquired their gifts by supernatural intervention, such as from FAIRIES or the dead, or from divine intervention. Some, in fact, were revered in earlier times as semi-divine. Their abilities were from their gifts and knowledge, or "cunning," as opposed to any particular holy status in the church. The magic they practiced was a home-made amalgam of Christian prayers and rites mixed with pagan material, folk magic and occultism. Folk magical arts were passed along in oral tradition, embroidered, embellished and changed as time passed. Cunning men and women who could read possessed various magical texts, including famous grimoires such as *The Greater Key of Solomon* (see GRIMOIRES) or the *Fourth Book of Agrippa.*

Many cunning men and women were described as odd people, with strange or unusual appearances, or living alone or in semi-seclusion, who could "do a thing or two." Their animals were regarded as their FAMILIAR servants, or, when public opinion was charitable, as their "good angels."

Fees for magical services generally were small, as most clients were poor locals; thus, cunning men and women often lived on the edge of poverty themselves. The better ones were sought out by aristocrats, usually for procuring the love of someone or faithfulness from a wayward spouse. Court records in England show that not all cunning men and women worked cheaply. Some assessed the aristocracy for hefty 40- and 50-pound fees, even annuities. In 1492 a cunning man set a fee of 1,000 pounds for a charm to procure a husband for a widow, while a cunning woman of the same time period took 25 percent of all stolen goods she found through DIVINATION. By contrast, the Church of England took in slightly less than 100 pounds in offerings in a year. Some cunning men and women became wealthy enough to buy land and build homes.

Cunning men and women flourished up until about the late 17th century, when belief in magic was high. They served as a sort of unofficial police and as a deterrent to wrongdoing, for when crimes were committed, a cunning man or woman was consulted to divine the guilty party. Though magic declined in importance from the 18th century on, their presence in society continued even into modern times, especially in rural areas, albeit in a diminished status.

They practiced their magical arts as an open secret, conducting their business quietly so as to avoid prosecution under various anti-magic and anti-witchcraft laws. Sometimes they met with little interference from authorities, who looked the other way unless a client complained. Some, such as BIDDY EARLY, were regularly denounced from pulpits but were more or less not bothered because of their popularity.

During the INQUISITION, however, cunning men and women became vulnerable targets for charges of Devil-worship and evil witchcraft. A proliferation of laws made it illegal to divine, heal and cast spells for virtually any reason. If a cunning man or woman was quite successful and competed with the church for the locals' meager wages, the church got rid of them by bringing charges of witchcraft. Some cunning men and women (mostly women) simply became scapegoats for waves of witch hysteria. But even prosecution failed to dampen public support in some cases, and visitors would throng a jail to seek a fallen cunning woman's services before she was likely executed for her "crimes."

The art of the old cunning man and woman lives on in modern times in a variety of guises: the astrologer, psychic or intuitive counselor, energy healer and herbalist. Some of these individuals consider themselves part of WICCA or PAGANISM; others belong to mainstream religions; still others consider themselves part of no particular religion at all.

See CHARMS; OLD GEORGE PICKINGILL; PELLAR; POW-WOWING; SPELLS.

FURTHER READING:
Bottrell, William in Kelvin I. Jones, ed., *Cornish Witches & Cunning Men.* Penzance: Oakmagic Publications, 1996.
Maple, Eric. *The Dark World of Witches.* New York: A.S. Barnes & Co., 1962.
Thomas, Keith. *Religion and the Decline of Magic.* New York: Charles Scribner's Sons, 1971.

Re-creation of a country witch in her cottage, at the Museum of Witchcraft in Boscastle, Cornwall (PHOTO BY AUTHOR; COURTESY OF MUSEUM OF WITCHCRAFT)

curandero/curandera   Medicine men and women of Mexico, Mesoamerica and Hispanic communities. The *curandero* and *curandera* have a different healing function than their counterparts, the BRUJO and BRUJA (male and female witches). *Curanderos* are folk psychiatrists, providing magical cures for mental and emotional problems. For example, *a curandero* will "clean the soul," which may involve exorcising spirits believed responsible for problems. Both *curanderos* and *brujos* use herbal and folk remedies.

curse   A SPELL intended to bring misfortune, illness, harm or death to a victim. The most dreaded form of magic, curses are universal. They are "laid" or "thrown" primarily for revenge and power but also for protection, usually of homes, treasures, tombs and grave sites. A curse can take effect quickly or may be dormant for years. Curses have been laid upon families, plaguing them for generations.

Any person can lay a curse by expressing an intense desire that a particular person come to some kind of harm (see ILL-WISHING). However, the success of a curse depends upon the curser's station and condition. Curses are believed to have more potency—and therefore more danger—when they are laid by persons in authority, such as priests, priestesses or royalty; persons of magical skill, such as witches, sorcerers and magicians; and persons who have no other recourse for justice, such as women, the poor and destitute and the dying. Deathbed curses are the most potent, for all the curser's vital energy goes into the curse.

If a victim knows he has been cursed and believes he is doomed, the curse is all the more potent, for the victim helps to bring about his own demise, through sympathetic magic. However, curses work without such knowledge on the part of the victim. Some victims are not told a curse has been laid, lest they find another witch to undo the spell (see PELLAR).

Like a blessing, a curse is a calling upon supernatural powers to effect a change. Intent makes the difference between benefit and harm. Witches and sorcerers perform both blessings and curses as services to others, either to clients in exchange for fees, or in carrying out judicial sentences. As Plato noted in the *Republic,* "If anyone wishes to injure an enemy, for a small fee they [sorcerers] will bring harm on good or bad alike, binding the gods to serve their purposes by spells and curses."

The most universal method of cursing is with a figure or effigy that represents the victim. Waxen effigies were common in ancient India, Persia, Egypt, Africa and Europe, and are still used in modern times. Effigies are also made of clay, wood and stuffed cloth (see POPPET). They are painted or marked, or attached with something associated with the victim—a bit of hair, nail clippings (see HAIR AND NAILS), excrement, clothing, even dust from his footprints—and melted over, or burned in, a fire. As the figure melts or burns, the victim suffers, and dies when the figure is destroyed. The Egyptians often used wax figures of Apep, a monster who was the enemy of the sun. The magician wrote Apep's name in green ink on the effigy, wrapped it in new papyrus and threw it in a fire. As it burned, he kicked it with his left foot four times. The ashes of the effigy were mixed with excrement and thrown into another fire. The Egyptians also left wax figures in tombs.

Waxen images were popular during the witch hunts, and numerous witches were accused of cursing with them. JAMES I of England, writing in his book, *Daemonologie* (1597), described how witches caused illness and death by roasting waxen images:

> To some others at these times he [the Devil], teacheth how to make pictures of wax or clay. That by the roasting thereof, the persons that they beare the name of, may be continually melted or dried away by continual sicknesses.
>
> They can bewitch and take the life of men or women, by roasting of the pictures, as I spake of before, which likewise is verie possible to their Maister to performe, for although, as I said before, that instrument of waxe has no vertue in that turne doing, yet may he not very well, even by the same measure that his conjured slaves, melts that waxe in fire, may he not, I say at these times, subtily, as a spirite, so weaken and scatter the spirites of life of the patient, as may make him on the one part, for faintnesses, so sweate out the humour of his bodie. And on the other parte, for the not concurrence of these spirites, which causes his digestion, so debilitate his stomacke, that this humour radicall continually sweating out on the one part, and no new good sucks being put in the place thereof, for lacke of digestion on the other, he shall at last vanish away, even as his picture will die in the fire.

As an alternative to melting, effigies are stuck with pins, thorns or knives. Animal or human hearts may be substituted for effigies. Hearts, animal corpses or objects which quickly decompose, such as eggs, are buried with spells that the victim will die as the objects deteriorate.

In Ireland, "cursing stones" are stones that are stroked and turned to the left while a curse is recited. Gems and crystals are often said to have the power to hold curses; the Hope Diamond, purchased by Louis XVI from Tavernier in 1668, is deemed cursed because its owners have suffered illness, misfortune and death.

Curses in contemporary witchcraft. It is against Wiccan ethics and laws of the Craft to lay curses (see WICCAN REDE). Witches believe that a curse will come back on the curser in some form (see THREEFOLD LAW OF RETURN). Some, however, believe cursing is justified against one's enemies. Some witches approve certain types of curses, such as binding spells to stop acts of violence. Witches from ethnic cultures believe curses are justified.

Repelling curses. AMULETS that have been made according to various formulas are said to repel curses, as is dragon's blood, which is used in herbal mixes for protection. A cloth poppet stuffed with nettles, inscribed with the name of the curser (if known), then buried or burned, also breaks a curse. Nettles sprinkled about a

Poppet created for a curse, in the collection of the Museum of Witchcraft at Boscastle, Cornwall (PHOTO BY AUTHOR; COURTESY MUSEUM OF WITCHCRAFT)

room add protection. The OILS of rosemary and van-van, and various mixed VODUN oils, placed in baths or used to anoint the body, are other remedies. Burning a purple candle while reciting a spell is yet another method (see CANDLES). Hindu sorcerers turn curses in the opposite direction, "upstream," sending them back to slay their originators.

Traditionally, the most propitious time for both laying and breaking curses is during the waning moon.

See HEX.

FURTHER READING:

Ogden, Daniel. *Magic, Witchcraft, and Ghosts in the Greek and Roman Worlds: A Sourcebook.* New York: Oxford University Press, 2002.

Randolph, Vance. *Ozark Magic and Folklore.* New York: Dover Publications, 1964. First published 1947.

Russell, Jeffrey B. *A History of Witchcraft.* London: Thames and Hudson, 1980.

Thomas, Keith. *Religion and the Decline of Magic.* New York: Charles Scribner's Sons, 1971.

Dafo The pseudonym or magical name of the woman who initiated GERALD B. GARDNER into witchcraft around 1939–40. The identity of Dafo remains uncertain. She is sometimes confused with OLD DOROTHY CLUTTERBUCK, who was Gardner's first high priestess. He described her as his teacher and an authority on witchcraft.

Little is known about Dafo's life. She lived in Christchurch, Hampshire, and was a member of the New Forest COVEN, which Gardner always claimed was a line of hereditary witches practicing the Old Religion. Dafo was the leading lady and stage director of the Rosicrucian theater of the Fellowship of Crotona, a Mason group founded by Mabel Besant-Scott, the daughter of theosophist Annie Besant and actor G. A. Sullivan.

Dafo was probably a woman of considerable social repute who needed a pseudonym to conceal her involvement in what was, until 1951, an illegal practice under British law. From 1944 on, she was a frequent companion of Gardner's. In 1947, they became partners in Ancient Crafts Ltd., a company that bought a plot of land and built a replica of a 16th-century witch's cottage. Dafo and Gardner led their coven rites there until 1952, when Dafo withdrew, partly due to poor health, but also out of concern that Gardner's increasing publicity would jeopardize her secrecy.

Gardner introduced DOREEN VALIENTE to Dafo in 1952. Valiente described her "an elegant graceful lady with dark hair."

By 1958, Dafo was living with a niece who was a devout Christian. She turned down requests from three witch groups to validate Gardner's story of the New Forest coven. She would neither confirm nor deny Gardner's claims in her answers to two groups. To the third she said she had only a theoretical interest in the occult.

In researching the roots of Wicca, RONALD HUTTON decided not to approach Dafo's heirs and to leave her identity obscured. Author Philip Heselton makes a case for Edith Woodford-Grimes being Dafo.

FURTHER READING:
Heselston, Philip. *Wiccan Roots*. Milverton, Eng.: Capall Bann, 2000.
Hutton, Ronald. *The Triumph of the Moon: A History of Modern Pagan Witchcraft*. Oxford: Oxford University Press, 1999.

Darrell (also Darrel), Reverend John (16th century) The Puritan minister John Darrell, caught in religious infighting between moderate Catholics, English Anglicans and Puritans, was convicted of fraud in May 1599, as a result of exorcising the DEVIL from the demoniac William Sommers of Nottingham (see EXORCISM). Darrell was called to exorcise nine other people before Sommers: Katherine Wright in 1586, Thomas Darling in 1596, and seven possessed children in Lancashire in 1597. He was unsuccessful in exorcising Wright, and although a witch was accused of causing the possession, the Justice in charge refused to commit her and warned Darrell to desist from exorcisms or face imprisonment. In the case of Thomas Darling, Darrell advised fasting and PRAYER but was not present so as to avoid personal "glory."

The possession of the seven Lancashire children had already led to the execution of Edmund Hartley—originally brought in to cure the children but eventually found to be the witch responsible—but the children were still having fits and convulsions. Assisted by Derbyshire minister George More, Darrell exorcised the children in one afternoon, emphasizing that the greatest value of such Puritan exorcisms was in refuting the claim by the Papists that theirs was the only true Church, since they could cast out devils.

Darrell's last case, the exorcism of William Sommers, began in November 1597. Sommers, aged 20, suffered fits and had a lump the size of an egg which ran about his body. His behavior was obscene, including bestiality with a dog in front of onlookers. Darrell exorcised him in front of 150 witnesses, but Sommers suffered repossessions, eventually naming witches responsible. Although Sommers did not react consistently to the various witches' presence, Darrell had all 13 arrested. All but two were released, but Darrell claimed that Sommers's accusations were correct, and that Sommers could probably find all the witches in England. Eventually, one of the accused witch's powerful families charged Sommers with witchcraft, and Sommers confessed to having simulated his fits.

Fearful of the effect that talk of witchcraft had on the people, as well as the increasing power of the Puritans, or Calvinists, the Archbishop of Canterbury moved against Darrell. Katherine Wright and Thomas Darling were summoned as witnesses against Darrell and joined Sommers in confessing fraud. Wright and Sommers even accused Darrell of teaching them how to contrive fits. Based mainly on Sommers's detailed accusations, the ecclesiastical court found Darrell to be a counterfeit and deposed him from the ministry in May 1599. Darrell languished in prison for several months but was never really sentenced.

As a result of Darrell's conviction, the Anglican Church of England passed Canon 72 of the Episcopal Church, forbidding exorcism as a formal RITUAL. Some Anglican priests today practice exorcism on an informal basis with the approval of their bishops.

See POSSESSION.

FURTHER READING:
Hole, Christina. *Witchcraft in England.* London: B.T. Batsford Ltd., 1947.
Maple, Eric. *The Dark World of Witches.* New York: A.S. Barnes & Co., 1962.
Summers, Montague. *The History of Witchcraft and Demonology.* London: Kegan Paul, Trench, Trubner & Co. Ltd., 1926.

Davis, Pete "Pathfinder"   See AQUARIAN TABERNACLE CHURCH.

de Lancre, Pierre   See LANCRE, PIERRE DE.

Demeter   Greek goddess of the fertile soil and agriculture and an important aspect of the GODDESS. As a goddess of nature, Demeter also represents women, marriage, harmony and health. She controls the seasons, the dying of the earth in winter and its rebirth in spring. She is acknowledged in the spring and autumn equinox celebrations, just as she was worshiped in ancient times (see WHEEL OF THE YEAR).

Cults of Demeter were particularly strong in ancient Eleusis, and she was a central figure in the Eleusinian Mysteries of death and rebirth. According to myth, Demeter is the daughter of Cronos and Rhea, and the sister of Zeus and Poseidon. In an incestuous union with Zeus, she bore a daughter, Kore, "the maiden," also known as Persephone. Hades, the god of the underworld, lusted after Kore, and Zeus promised the maiden to him without telling Demeter.

Hades raped Kore and kidnapped her to his underworld kingdom. When Demeter learned of this, she went into profound mourning, donning black clothing and searching nine days for her daughter. On the tenth day she encountered HECATE, the patron goddess of witchcraft, who had heard Kore cry out. The two went to Helios, who had witnessed the abduction.

Upon hearing the entire story from Helios, Demeter went into a rage. She resigned from the company of the gods and neglected her duties. Crops failed and famine spread throughout the lands. The situation grew worse and worse, but Demeter could not be persuaded to act. Finally, HERMES succeeded in convincing Hades to let Kore go. But the crafty god of the underworld tricked Kore into eating part of a pomegranate before she left; this partaking of food in the underworld doomed her to spend at least part of her time with Hades forever. A compromise was struck: each year she would spend six months above the earth, six months below. The coming and going of Kore is signaled by the equinoxes.

Demeter was so grateful to have her daughter back at least part of the year that she initiated mankind into her mysteries and taught him agriculture, symbolized by corn. Many of the secret rites of her cults were practiced only by women, because of their power to bring forth life. In Attica, the rituals were performed by both men and women.

Demeter and Kore were sometimes considered as two aspects of the Corn Mother and were called the "Two Goddesses" or the "Great Goddesses." Sacrifices of fruit, honey cakes, bulls, pigs and cows were made to them.

The Romans identified Demeter with Ceres, their goddess of the earth, and incorporated Demeter's aspects into their own goddess. The concept of the earth goddess who governs the fertility of the earth exists around the world.

Abduction of Proserpine (Persephone) on a unicorn (ALBRECHT DÜRER, 1516)

demon   A lesser spirit that intervenes in the physical world. Demons usually are associated with evil, but in pre-Christian and non-Christian cultures, demons were, and are, not necessarily good or evil. There are good and bad demons, and demons capable of both kinds of behavior. The study of demons is called demonology.

The term *demon* means "replete with wisdom"; good demons once were called *eudemons,* and evil demons were called *cacodemons.* Demon is derived from the Greek term *daimon,* or "divine power," "fate" or "god." In Greek mythology, *daimon* included deified heroes. *Daimones* were intermediary spirits between man and the gods. A good *daimon* acted as a guardian spirit, and it was considered lucky to have one for guidance and protection. A guardian *daimon* whispered advice and ideas in one's ear. Evil *daimones* could lead one astray. Socrates claimed he had a daimon his entire life. The *daimon's* voice warned him of danger and bad decisions but never directed him what to do. Socrates said his guardian spirit was more trustworthy than omens from the flights and entrails of birds, two highly respected forms of divination at the time.

Demons are controlled by magicians and sorcerers. Solomon commanded demons called djinn to work for him. Demons have been exorcised as the causes of disease, misfortune and POSSESSION. In ancient Egypt, it was believed that a magician who exorcised a demon responsible for a possession would be just as likely to use the same demon to other ends. To the present day in many tribal societies, demons are blamed for a wide range of misfortunes and illnesses.

Jewish systems of demonology have long and complex histories and distinguish between classes of demons. According to the KABBALAH, evil powers emanate from the left pillar of the Tree of Life, especially from Geburah, the sephira (sphere) of the wrath of God. By the 13th century, the idea had developed of ten evil sephiroth to counter the ten holy sephiroth of the Tree. Another system of demons distinguishes those born of night terrors, and yet another system describes the demons that fill the sky between the earth and the moon. There are demons who, with angels, are in charge of the night hours and interpretations of diseases, and those who have seals that may be used to summon them.

In the development of Christian demonology, demons were associated only with evil; they are agents of the DEVIL. Good Christian spirits belong to the ranks of angels of the Lord. Demons are fallen angels who followed Lucifer when he was cast out of heaven by God. Their sole purpose is to tempt humankind into immoral acts and come between humans and God. As Christianity spread, the ranks of demons swelled to include the gods and spirits of the ancient Middle Eastern and Jewish traditions, and all pagan deities and nature spirits.

As agents of the Devil, demons especially became associated with witches during the witch hunts and INQUISITION. INCREASE MATHER, writing in *Cases of Conscience* (1693), said, "The Scriptures assert that there are Devils and Witches and that they are the common enemy of Mankind." George Giffard, an Oxford preacher of about the same period, said that witches should be put to death not because they kill others but because they deal with devils: "These cunning men and women which dealt with spirites and charme seeming to do good, and draw the people into manifold impieties, with all other which haue [have] familiarity with deuils [devils], or use conjurations, ought to bee rooted out, that others might see and feare."

Sex between Humans and Demons
Demons have sexual appetites for intercourse with humans. In *The Zohar* ("Book of Splendor"), the principal work of the Kabbalah, any pollution of semen results in the birth of demons, including intercourse with the night-terror demons such as LILITH. Demons in the shape of human males (*incubi*) prey on women, while demons in female shapes (*succubi*) prey on men. In Christianity, the possibility of intercourse with demons was denied prior to the 12th century. But as the Inquisition gained force, intercourse with demons was a focus of interest by the 14th century. In particular, witches and other heretics—enemies of the Church—were said not only to have sex with demons but also to copulate wildly and frequently with them, especially at SABBATS, and to worship them in their rites. In many cases, the distinction between the Devil himself and demons was blurry.

Inquisitors wrote a great deal on demonic sex. Sex with demons was portrayed as unpleasant and painful. Sometimes demons appeared to persons in the forms of their spouses or lovers. After copulation, they would reveal their true identities and blackmail the victims into continuing the sexual liaison.

Incubi, male demons, were especially attracted to women with beautiful hair, young virgins, chaste widows and all "devout" females. Nuns were among the most vulnerable and could be molested in the confessional as well as in bed. While the majority of women were forced into sex by the incubi, it was believed that some of them submitted willingly and even enjoyed the act. Incubi had huge phalluses, sometimes made of horn or covered with scales, and they ejaculated icy semen. When they appeared as demons and not as human impostors, they were described as ugly, hairy and foul-smelling.

Incubi were believed to have the ability to impregnate women. They did not possess their own semen but collected it from men in nocturnal emissions, masturbation or in coitus while masquerading as succubi. The demons preserved the semen and used it later on one of their victims. The children that resulted were considered the child of the man who unwittingly provided the semen; some horror stories held that the children came out half human and half beast.

In a small number of cases, claims of molestation by incubi were dismissed as the products of female melancholia or vivid imaginations. False pregnancies that arose from this state were chalked up to flatulence.

The wild copulation between witches and demons was lamented in the *MALLEUS MALEFICARUM* (1486), which noted that "in times long past the Incubus devils used to infest women against their wills [but] modern witches . . . willingly embrace this most foul and miserable servitude." Some incubi served as FAMILIARS to witches, who sent them to torment specific individuals.

Since sex with incubi was expected of witches, many accused witches were tortured until they confessed to this crime (see TORTURE). In 1485 the Inquisitor of Como sent 41 such women to their deaths at the stake. Their "confessions" were corroborated, incredibly, by eye-witness accounts, as well as by hearsay evidence "and the testimony of credible witnesses."

Incubi were believed to be always visible to witches but only occasionally visible to others—even the victims. Reports exist of people observed in the throes of passion with invisible partners. Husbands, however, could see incubi as they copulated with their wives who thought they were other men.

Succubi could appear in the flesh as beautiful, voluptuous women (perhaps an indication of male fantasies). They usually visited men in their sleep—especially men who slept alone—and their sexual activities caused erotic dreams and nocturnal emissions.

Succubi were not as prevalent as incubi. Because of the inherent evil of women, in the view of Christianity, women were morally weak and therefore more licentious than men. If a man were assaulted by a succubus, it was most likely not his fault.

The sex act itself with a succubus was often described as penetrating a cavern of ice. There are accounts of men being forced to perform cunnilingus on succubi, whose vaginas dripped urine, dung and other vile juices and smells.

Succubi appeared often in the records of witchcraft trials. Men accused of witchcraft sometimes were tortured until they confessed having sex with demons, among other diabolical crimes. In 1468 in Bologna, Italy, a man was executed for allegedly running a brothel of succubi.

The church prescribed five ways to get rid of incubi and succubi: 1) by making a Sacramental Confession; 2) by making the sign of the cross; 3) by reciting the Ave Maria; 4) by moving to another house or town; and 5) by excommunication of the demon by holy men. Sometimes the LORD'S PRAYER worked, as did a sprinkling of holy water.

It should be noted that cases of sexual molestation by demons did not die with the witch hunts; they continue to be reported to the present time, often in connection with poltergeist activities and POSSESSION. For example, *The Haunted* by Robert Curran (1988) tells of a family of Wilkes-Barre, Pennsylvania, who said they were tormented by a hideous demon for several years. The demon manifested in various forms, including a hag with scraggly, long white hair, scaly skin and vampirelike fangs, which sexually molested the husband. (See NIGHTMARE).

Demons in Contemporary Witchcraft

Demons are not courted or worshiped in contemporary WICCA and PAGANISM. The existence of negative energies is acknowledged.

Demons in Ceremonial Magic

Demons are powerful intelligences that may be summoned and controlled in rituals along with god-forms, elementals, angels, planetary and Zodiacal spirits and thought-forms. The GRIMOIRES give detailed instructions for conjuring and controlling demons. Demons are dangerous; hence the magician must be careful.

The Hierarchies and Functions of Demons

Demons have been catalogued, ranked and classified since at least 100–400, the period in which the *Testament*

Belial and djinn presenting their credentials to King Solomon (JACOBUS DE TERAMO, *DAS BUCH BELIAL,* 1473)

of Solomon appeared, describing Solomon's magic ring for commanding the djinn and listing the names and functions of various Hebrew, Greek, Assyrian, Babylonian, Egyptian and perhaps Persian demons. Christian demonologists of the 16th and 17th centuries catalogued demons into hierarchies of hell and ascribed to them attributes and duties, including ambassadorships to various nations. JOHANN WEYER, who devised the most complex hierarchy, estimated that there were 7,405,926 demons serving under 72 princes. The grimoires of ceremonial magic also give their own hierarchies. Some of the major demons important to witchcraft cases are:

Asmodeus. The demon of lechery, jealousy, anger and revenge. His chief objectives are to prevent intercourse between husband and wife, wreck new marriages and force husbands to commit adultery. He is also one of the chief demons involved in possession. Throughout history, he has been regarded as one of the most evil of Satan's infernal demons. He is usually portrayed as having three heads, those of an ogre, a ram and a bull, all sexually licentious creatures; having the feet of a cock, another sexually aggressive creature; and having wings. He rides on a dragon and breathes fire.

Asmodeus has his roots in ancient Persia. He is identified with the demon Aeshma, one of the seven archangels of Persian mythology. The Hebrews absorbed him into their mythology, where he attained the highest status and most power of all demons in Hebrew legends. According

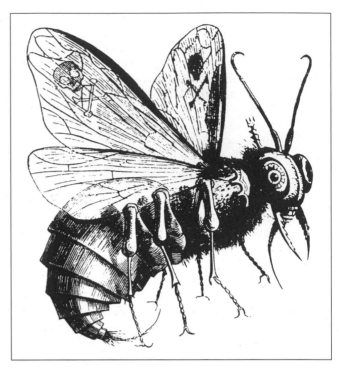

Beelzebub, "Lord of the Flies" (L. BRETON, IN COLLIN DE PLANCY'S *DICTIONNAIRE INFERNAL,* 1863)

to the Hebrews, he is the son of Naamah and Shamdon. He was part of the seraphim, the highest order of angels, but fell from grace. In other Hebrew legends, he is either associated with or is the husband of Lilith, the demon queen of lust. Sometimes he is said to be the offspring of Lilith and Adam.

Asmodeus migrated into Christian lore, becoming one of the Devil's leading agents of provocation. Witches were said to worship him, and magicians and sorcerers attempted to conjure him to strike out at enemies. Grimoires admonish anyone seeking an audience with Asmodeus to summon him bareheaded out of respect. Weyer said Asmodeus also ruled the gambling houses. He was one of the infernal agents blamed for the obscene sexual possession of the Louviers nuns in 17th-century France.

Astaroth (also Ashtaroth). A male demon who evolved from the ancient Phoenician mother goddess of fertility, ASTARTE or Ashtoreth. In his male incarnation, he has little to do with man's sexual nature. He is a teacher of the sciences and a keeper of the secrets of the past, present and future and is invoked in necromantic rituals of DIVINATION. He appears as an angel in human form, by some accounts ugly and by other accounts beautiful. He does, however, possess a powerful stench. Weyer said Astaroth was a grand duke of hell and commanded 40 legions of demons. Astaroth is listed as one of the three supreme evil demons, with Beelzebub and Lucifer, in the *Grimoire Verum* and *Grand Grimoire,* which date from about the 18th century.

Asmodeus, demon of lust and anger (L. BRETON, IN COLLIN DE PLANCY'S *DICTIONNAIRE INFERNAL,* 1863)

The demon is said to instigate cases of demonic possession, most notably that of the Loudun nuns in France in the 16th century. The nuns accused a priest, Father Urbain Grandier, of causing their possession. At Grandier's trial, a handwritten "confession" of his was produced detailing his pact with the Devil, witnessed and signed by Astaroth and several other demons.

Baal. Many small deities of ancient Syria and Persia carried this name, which means "the lord" (from the Hebrew *bá'al*), but the greatest Baal was an agricultural and fertility deity of Canaan. The son of El, the High God of Canaan, Baal was the lord of life and ruled the death-rebirth cycle. He engaged in a battle with Mot ("death") and was slain and sent to the underworld. The crops withered, until Baal's sister, Anath, the maiden goddess of love, found his body and gave it a proper burial. The Canaanites worshiped Baal by sacrificing children by burning. As a demon in Christianity, Baal was triple-headed, with a cat's head and a toad's head on either side of his human head. He imparted visibility and wisdom.

Beelzebub. Known as "Lord of the Flies," Beelzebub was the prince of demons in Hebrew belief at the time of Jesus. The Pharisees accused Christ of exorcising demons in Beelzebub's name. In medieval times, Beelzebub was regarded as a demon of great power. A sorcerer conjured him at his own risk of death by apoplexy or strangulation; once conjured, the demon was difficult to banish. When he manifested, it was as a gigantic, ugly fly.

Beelzebub was said to reign over witches' SABBATS. Witches denied Christ in his name and chanted it as they danced. There are many stories of his copulating with witches in wild orgies; to do this, he apparently appeared in other than fly form.

Beelzebub was among the demons blamed for the possession cases of the nuns of Loudun and Aix-en-Provence in 17th-century France, forcing the nuns into lewd behavior (see AIX-EN-PROVENCE POSSESSIONS).

Belial. One of Satan's most important and evil demons, who is deceptively beautiful in appearance and soft in voice, but full of treachery, recklessness and lies. He is dedicated to creating wickedness and guilt in mankind,

Belial (JACOBUS DE TERAMO, *DAS BACH BELIAL*, 1473)

especially in the form of sexual perversions, fornication and lust.

Belial's name probably comes from the Hebrew phrase *beli ya'al,* which means "without worth." The ancient Hebrews believed Belial was the next angel created after Lucifer and was evil from the start, being one of the first to revolt against God. After his fall from heaven, he became the personification of evil.

Weyer said Belial commanded 80 legions of demons (at 6,666 demons per legion) and served as infernal ambassador to Turkey. Magicians of that time believed that sacrifices and offerings were necessary to invoke him. Belial was reputed to break his promises to magicians, but those who managed to gain his true favor were handsomely rewarded.

Belial's name is sometimes used as a synonym for Satan or the Antichrist. In the Old Testament, the phrase "sons of Belial" refers to worthlessness and recklessness. Belial also is known as Beliar.

Lucifer. In Latin, his name means "light-bringer," and he originally was associated with Venus, the morning star. His rebellion against God caused him and his followers to be cast from heaven. The fallen angels lost their beauty and power and became "fiendes black." The name "Lucifer" was sometimes applied to Christ, as the light-bearer, but by the Middle Ages, both "Lucifer" and "Satan" were used as names for the Devil. Lucifer could apply to the Devil in either his pre-fall or post-fall state. In the hierarchies of demons, Lucifer is emperor of hell and ranks above Satan, one of his lieutenants (ranks and distinctions not made in theology). When conjured, he appears as a beautiful child. Lucifer was said to rule Europeans and Asiatics.

FURTHER READING:
Cavendish, Richard. *The Black Arts.* New York: Putnam, 1967.
Lea, Henry Charles. *Materials Toward a History of Witchcraft.* Philadelphia: University of Pennsylvania, 1939.
Russell, Jeffrey Burton. *Witchcraft in the Middle Ages.* Ithaca and London: Cornell University Press, 1972.
Summers, Montague, ed. *The Malleus Maleficarum of Heinrich Kramer and James Sprenger.* New York: Dover Publications, 1971. First published, 1928.

deosil (also deiseal)   Clockwise circular movement which in MAGIC and witchcraft is used in casting positive SPELLS and in casting the MAGIC CIRCLE. The clockwise rotation is associated with the movement of the sun across the heavens and with blessings and good fortune. *Deiseal* is the Irish term for "a turning to the right," or the "holy round." Deosil dances and circuits are done not only around magic circles but around festival fires (see WHEEL OF THE YEAR), holy objects such as sacred STONES, crops, fields, homes and buildings. The opposite of deosil is WIDDERSHINS.

de Rivera, Luis   See RIVERA, LUIS DE.

Devil   Christianity's Prince of Supreme Evil. The Devil, or Satan, is not a god of Wiccans and Pagans. The association of witches with the Devil grew in the Middle Ages and Reformation, when belief in a personal Satan as the agent of all evil was particularly strong. Accusations of Devil-worship were not limited to witches. Christians charged the same of Jews, Muslims, pagans, Cathars, Albigenses, Waldenses, "Red Indians" and other heretics, and Protestants and Catholics accused each other of it as well. Even Martin Luther was said by Catholics to have given himself over to the Devil.

Devil comes from the Greek *diabolos* ("slanderer" or "accuser"), translated from the Hebrew *satan.* The concept of the Devil as archfiend of evil developed slowly over many centuries, becoming a composite of Lucifer, the fallen angel whose pride and ego got him expelled from heaven; Satan, the tempter of man; and various pagan deities such as PAN and CERNUNNOS.

Satan plays a minor role in the Old Testament as the opponent of man, dispatched by God to test man's faith. He is not evil and is an angel in the kingdom of heaven. In Job, Satan follows God's instructions to destroy Job's family and possessions and cover him with running sores in an effort to tempt him into cursing God. In the New Testament, Satan becomes more personal and is the great antagonist of God as well as man. The book of Revelation forecasts that Christ, in his second coming, will bind the Devil for 1,000 years, at which time the Devil will reappear one final time, as the Antichrist, before being destroyed. The dualism of Christianity became firmly established, with a god of light and goodness and a god of evil and darkness.

By the ninth century, the Devil held a central position in Christianity. Satan, the Devil, was believed in as a real,

The Devil with his witches and demons (OLD WOODCUT)

potent being who possessed terrible supernatural powers and was intent upon destroying man by undermining his morals. In this pursuit, he was aided by an army of evil DEMONS (a corruption of the Greek term *daimon* or *daemon,* meaning "divine power"). This army was expanded to include heretics and sorcerers, who were considered outlaws of the church, and whose MAGIC posed a threat to the divine miracles of the church. Witches were included first as associates of sorcerers, then as heretics.

Preachers pounded fear of the Devil into their followers by constantly inveighing against his attempts to pervert people and turn them away from God. Satan's kingdom was the material world. He would tempt people with false riches, luxuries and carnal pleasures, only to claim their souls for eternal damnation in the end. His chief means of attacking others was through demonic possession. Pacts with the Devil, which date to the 6th century, became implied; any consort with the Devil automatically meant one had entered into a diabolic pact (see DEVIL'S PACT). John Stearne, the assistant to MATTHEW HOPKINS, England's notorious witch-hunter of the 17th century, was of the opinion that the preachers' obsession with Satan encouraged witches to worship him. Agnes Wilson, an accused witch of Northampton in 1612, was asked how many gods she believed in and replied, "Two—God the Father, and the Devil." Her answer was no surprise in light of the prevailing social-religious climate, but it was taken by her prosecutors as an admission of Devil-worship.

The Devil was said to appear in many guises in order to fool people. His most common human shape was that of a tall black man or a tall man, often handsome, dressed in black. Henri Boguet (1550–1619), a jurist in witch trials, stated in *Discourse des sorciers* (1602) that:

> Whenever he [the Devil] assumes the form of a man, he is, however, always black, as all witches bear witness. And for my part I hold that there are two principal reasons for this: first, that he who is the Father and Ruler of darkness may not be able to disguise himself so well that he may not always be known for what he is; secondly, as proof that his study is only to do evil; for evil, as Pythagoras said, is symbolized by black.

The Devil also could appear in disguises, such as a saint, the Virgin Mary, comely young women and preachers. He could appear in a multitude of animal shapes, most commonly a dog, a serpent or a goat (see METAMORPHOSIS). He also had ugly appearances: as the alleged god of witches, he was portrayed as half human, half animal, like Pan, with horns, cloven feet, hairy legs, a tail, a huge penis, glowing eyes and Saturnine features.

By the 18th century, literalist views of the Devil were losing power. Enlightenment philosophers and writers were questioning the origins of evil, and were looking within the human psyche for answers. The Devil became more a metaphor in literature.

Witches attending Satan (PIERRE BOAISTUAU, *HISTOIRES PRODIGIEUSES,* 1597)

In folklore, the Devil was often portrayed in a lighter fashion, perhaps to mitigate the fear inspired by the clergy. He was often buffoonish and called by nicknames such as Jack, Old Nick, Old Horny and Lusty Dick. He could be easily tricked.

The distinction between the Devil as Prince of Evil and his hordes of demons often blurs. The phrase "the Devil" has referred to both. Joseph Glanvil observed in *Saducismus Triumphatus* (1689) that "The Devil is a name for a body politic, in which there are very different orders and degrees of spirits, and perhaps in as much variety of place and state, as among ourselves."

The worship of Satan as a god of power and materialism is practiced by some groups.

Pagans and Wiccans do not worship the Devil. Pagan deities, and the HORNED GOD of witches, are often confused in the public mind with the Devil.

See INITIATION; SABBATS; SATANISM.

FURTHER READING:
O'Grady, Joan. *The Prince of Darkness: The Devil in History, Religion and the Human Psyche.* New York: Barnes & Noble Books, 1989.

Rudwin, Maximilian. *The Devil in Legend and Literature.* 1931. Reprint, La Salle, Ill.: Open Court Publishing Co., 1959.

Russell, Jeffrey Burton. *Lucifer: The Devil in the Middle Ages.* Ithaca and London: Cornell University Press, 1984.

———. *The Devil.* Ithaca and London: Cornell University Press, 1977.

———. *The Prince of Darkness.* London: Thames and Hudson, 1989.

devil fish   A type of ray fish used by Mexican witches (*brujas or brujos*) in the casting of SPELLS. When dried, the Devil fish resembles a man with a horned head, tail and webbed arms. It is considered effective in quieting up gossipy neighbors.

Devil's Dandy Dogs   See WILD HUNT.

Devil's mark   According to witch-hunters, the DEVIL always permanently marked the bodies of his initiates to seal their pledge of obedience and service to him. He marked them by raking his claw across their flesh or using a hot iron, which left a mark, usually blue or red, but not a scar. Sometimes he left a mark by licking them. The Devil supposedly branded WITCHES at the end of INITIATION rites, which were performed at nocturnal SABBATS.

The marks were always made in "secret places," such as under eyelids, in armpits and in body cavities. The mark was considered the ultimate proof of being a witch—all witches and sorcerers (see SORCERY) were believed to have at least one. All persons accused of witchcraft and brought to trial were thoroughly searched for such a mark. Scars, birthmarks, natural blemishes and insensitive patches of skin that did not bleed qualified as Devil's marks. Experts firmly believed that the mark of Satan was clearly distin-

Satan marking witch with claw (R. P. GUACCIUS, *COMPENDIUM MALEFICARUM*, 1626)

guishable from ordinary blemishes, but in actuality, that was seldom the case. Protests from the victims that the marks were natural were ignored.

Accounts of being marked by the Devil were obtained in the "confessions" of accused witches, who usually were tortured to confess (see TORTURE). Inquisitors stripped off the accused witch's clothes and shaved off all body hair so that no square inch of skin was missed. Pins were driven deeply into scars, calluses and thickened areas of skin (see PRICKING). Since this customarily was done in front of a jeering crowd, it is no surprise that some alleged witches felt nothing from the pricks.

Inquisitors believed that the Devil also left invisible marks upon his followers. If an accused witch had no likely natural blemishes that could be called a Devil's mark, pins were driven into her body over and over again until an insensitive area was found.

British anthropologist MARGARET A. MURRAY said that Devil's marks were actually tattoos, marks of identification, which she offered as support of her contention that witchcraft as an organized pagan religion had flourished in the Middle Ages. Murray's controversial ideas have been debunked.

Devil's marks were sometimes called WITCH'S MARKS.

FURTHER READING:
Barstow, Anne Llewellyn. *Witchcraze: A New History of the European Witch Hunts.* San Francisco: Pandora, 1994.

Cavendish, Richard. *The Black Arts.* New York: Putnam, 1967.

Lea, Henry Charles. *Materials Toward a History of Witchcraft.* Philadelphia: University of Pennsylvania, 1939.

Maple, Eric. *The Dark World of Witches.* New York: A.S. Barnes & Co., 1962.

Devil's pact   A pledge to serve the DEVIL or one of his DEMONS. The pact may be made orally, but according to lore it is best to write it on virgin parchment and sign it in BLOOD. The pact provides that in exchange for allegiance and one's soul, the Devil will grant whatever a person wishes. Pacts with the Devil or demons for personal gain appear in various cultures.

From the earliest days of Christianity, a pact with the Devil was tacitly understood to be part of any MAGIC, SORCERY or DIVINATION performed by an adept. Pacts also involved ordinary people: in legends, the Devil routinely appeared to people in distress and bartered love, money or power in exchange for souls. In the witch hysteria of the Middle Ages and Renaissance, the pact took on new significance as proof of heresy and became grounds for prosecution and condemnation of accused witches.

The collaboration between men and demons, which implies a pact, predates Christ by thousands of years. King Solomon, son of David, acquired his wisdom and riches with the help of an army of demons called djinn.

The Bible does not expressly deal with Devil's pacts, but Christian theologians have always assumed them to exist and have condemned them. If the worship of God required

Witches feasting with the Devil and demons (OLD WOODCUT)

a pledge of service and the soul, then surely those who followed God's opposite, Satan, would do the same. The prevailing view of the church was that worldly goods and the like could not be obtained without crime except by appealing directly to God, or to Him through one of his saints.

One of the earliest Christian stories of a pact with Satan concerns Theophilus, treasurer of the church of Adana, who allegedly sold his soul to the Devil around 538 in order to become bishop.

Two major early Christian theologians, Origen (185–254) and St. Augustine (354–430) claimed that divination and the practices of magic and sorcery required demonic pacts. Much later, this was affirmed by the influential theologian THOMAS AQUINAS (ca. 1227–1274), who stated

in *Sententiae,* "Magicians perform miracles through personal contracts made with demons."

Using the ritual instructions in a GRIMOIRE, the magician or sorcerer evoked demons for the purpose of attaining wealth, the power of invisibility, love or political power—but seldom to harm enemies. The belief was that sooner or later such demonic favors compromised the magician into selling his soul to Satan in return. If Satan himself was invoked instead of a lower-ranking demon, he always demanded the magician's soul as payment "up front."

The Key of Solomon, one of the major medieval grimoires whose authorship is attributed to King Solomon, offered the following instruction for making a pact with a demon:

Exactly at dawn, use a new knife to cut a fork-shaped wand from the twig of a wild nut tree that has never borne fruit. Take the wand, a magic bloodstone and consecrated candles to the site of the ritual, preferably a ruined castle or deserted house, where one will be undisturbed and receive whatever treasures the demon produces. With the bloodstone, draw a triangle on the ground or floor, and place the candles on the side of it. Stand in middle of the triangle, hold the wand and recite the required invocation. When the work is finished, recite another incantation to dismiss the demon.

Stories of Devil's pacts were common from the Middle Ages to the 16th and 17th centuries. Typically, the victim was not a witch but an ordinary person who was vulnerable to temptation. Satan or a demon would appear, sometimes as a man and sometimes as an animal, and offer to help. The pact would last for a specified number of years, at which time Satan would collect: the victim would die and his soul would go to hell. Perhaps the best-known tale is the story of Faust, a scientist and alchemist who sells his soul to the demon Mephistopheles in exchange for youth and lust. These moralistic stories were publi-

cized through pamphlets and portrayed Satan as a trickster. The victim, despite his or her supernatural favors, usually came to a dreadful demise. Sometimes the Virgin Mary would intercede for the victims and snatch the pacts away from the Devil.

During the witch hunts, the Devil's pact took on new resonance. Witches were said to derive their powers from Satan, which required entering into a pact with him. The purpose of the pact was portrayed less as personal gain than as the deliberate and malicious intent to harm others, and a renunciation of God and the Christian faith. Christian demonologists created a substantial body of literature on Devil's pacts and the alleged rituals surrounding them—and the punishment that should be meted out for such acts. A representative view was expressed by Johann Trithemius (1462–1516), abbot and scholar, in his work, *Liber Octo Quaestionum:*

> Witches are a most pestiferous class, who enter on pacts with demons, and, after making a solemn profession of faith, dedicate themselves, in lasting obedience, to some particular demon. No one can describe the evils of which this class of beings is guilty. Hence they

Devil's pact allegedly signed by Father Urbain Grandier of Loudon, countersigned by Lucifer, Beelzebub, Satan, Elimi, Leviathan, Astaroth and Baalbarith must nowhere be tolerated, but utterly and everywhere exterminated.

Demonologists and witch-hunters distinguished between two kinds of pacts: the private pact and the solemn public pact. The private pact was a vow made by a witch, sometimes with the help of another witch. It was assumed that eventually the initiate would declare his or her allegiance to the Devil publicly. The details of these pacts were obtained from accused witches through TORTURE.

The public pact was made in a ceremony, either in a Christian church or at a SABBAT, which always took place outdoors. If held in a church—an act of sacrilege—the Devil himself was not always present; at a sabbat, he was.

According to demonologists, the initiates renounced their Christian faith and baptism, swore allegiance to Satan and promised to sacrifice to him unbaptized children, pledged an annual tribute to him and gave him a token piece of their clothing. They signed a written pact in their own BLOOD. The Devil gave them new names and marked them with his claw (see DEVIL'S MARK). In some accounts, the Devil stripped off the initiates' clothing and forced them to pay homage to him by kissing him on the anus (see KISS OF SHAME).

All aspects of the ceremony were done in reverse, since Satan is the reverse of God. Crosses were held upside down and then trampled, pacts were written backwards, the initiates signed their names with their left hands and the Devil made his mark on the left side of the body.

Until the 14th century most witches were prosecuted only for the alleged harm they did to people and their animals—not just for worshiping and making pact with the Devil. The church began to press the idea that witches should be prosecuted for heresy as well. This view received a powerful impetus from the Bull of POPE INNOCENT VIII (1484), which, in addition to citing various MALEFICIA done by witches, adds, ". . . over and above this, they blasphemously renounce that Faith which is theirs by the Sacrament of Baptism . . ."

In order to prove this heresy in a witch trial, the existence of a formal pact with the Devil had to be established. Most inquisitors had little trouble with this—they simply tortured the accused until he or she confessed. Seldom was a document actually produced; it was said that the Devil conveniently took most of his pacts with him in order to protect his servants.

One notable exception to this was the trial of Father Urbain Grandier, parish priest of St.-Pierre-du-Marche in Loudun, France, in 1633. Grandier was accused of causing the nuns in Loudun to become possessed. At his trial, a Devil's pact, allegedly written backwards in Latin in his own hand and signed in blood, was produced and introduced as evidence. The pact stated:

We, the all-powerful Lucifer, seconded by Satan, Beelzebub, Leviathan, Elimi, Astaroth, and others, have today accepted the pace of alliance with Urbain Grandier, who is on our side. And we promise him the love of women, the flower of virgins, the chastity of nuns, worldly honors, pleasures, and riches. He will fornicate every three days; intoxication will be dear to him. He will offer to us once a year a tribute marked with his blood; he will trample under foot the sacraments of the church, and he will say his prayers to us. By virtue of this pact, he will live happily for twenty years on earth among men, and finally will come among us to curse God. Done in hell, in the council of the devils.

[Signed by] Satan, Beelzebub, Lucifer, Elimi, Leviathan, Astaroth.

Notarized the signature and mark of the chief Devil, and my lords the princes of hell.

[Countersigned by] Baalberith, recorder.

Grandier was convicted and burned.

Louis Gaufridi, a man who confessed to being a witch in 1611, recited his pact verbally for the inquisitors:

I, Louis Gaufridi, renounce all good, both spiritual as well as temporal, which may be bestowed upon me by God, the Blessed Virgin Mary, all the Saints of Heaven, particularly my Patron St. John-Baptist, as also S. Peter, S. Paul, and S. Francis, and I give myself body and soul to Lucifer, before whom I stand, together with every good that I may ever possess (save always the benefits of the sacraments touching those who receive them). And according to the tenor of these terms have I signed and sealed.

One of Gaufridi's victims was a woman named Madeleine de la Paud (see AIX-EN-PROVENCE POSSESSIONS) who also confessed her Devil's pact:

With all my heart and most unfeignedly and with all my will most deliberately do I wholly renounce God, Father, Son and Holy Ghost; the most Holy Mother of God; all the Angels and especially my Guardian Angel, the Passion of Our Lord Jesus Christ, His Precious Blood and the merits thereof, my lot in Paradise, also the good inspirations which God may give me in the future, all the prayers which are made or may be made for me.

The prosecution of witches solely for having pacts with the Devil increased slowly on the European continent, though convictions still required evidence of maleficia. Witch-hunting handbooks such as the MALLEUS MALEFICARUM (1486) discussed pacts in great detail.

In Protestant England, Devil's pacts were acknowledged to exist but did not play a major role in most trials, according to surviving records. The public cared little about pacts and more about what harm a witch did to her neighbors. Such maleficia were presumed possible without a pact. Of the three Parliamentary Witchcraft Acts, only the third (1604) outlawed pacts "with any evil or wicked spirit." The first oral Devil's pact was recorded in 1612, and Elizabethan witches in general were believed not to be in direct contact with Satan.

In 1645 MATTHEW HOPKINS began his infamous hunt of witches in England and obtained sworn evidence of written pacts. Some of his 230-plus victims may have been condemned largely on the basis of such "evidence."

Wiccans do not worship the Devil and have nothing to do with Devil's pacts.

See STACKER LEE.

FURTHER READING:

Lea, Henry Charles. *Materials Toward a History of Witchcraft.* Philadelphia: University of Pennsylvania, 1939.

Michelet, Jules. *Satanism and Witchcraft.* Reprint. Secaucus, N.J.: Citadel Press, 1939.

Rudwin, Maximilian. *The Devil in Legend and Literature.* La Salle, Ill.: Open Court Publishing Co., 1931, 1959.

Russell, Jeffrey B. *A History of Witchcraft.* London: Thames and Hudson, 1980.

Seligmann, Kurt. *The Mirror of Magic.* New York: Pantheon Books, 1948.

Diana (Artemis)   Classical goddess of the MOON and the hunt and one of the most important aspects of the GODDESS in Wicca. Diana (counterpart to he Greek Artemis) personifies the positive attributes of the moon, which is the source of Witches' magical power, as well as independence, self-esteem and fierce aggressiveness. A virgin goddess and maiden warrior, she is the eternal feminist, owned by no man, beholden to none. As a moon goddess, Diana shares the lunar trinity with SELENE and HECATE and serves as patron goddess of witches. In the trinity, she represents power over the earth.

Diana's origins as Artemis comprise a rich mythology. Her cult flourished throughout the Mediterranean region during the Bronze Age. The Amazons build a beehive-shaped temple to her at Ephesus circa 900 B.C.E., and it is considered the Seventh Wonder of the ancient world. The temple contained a statue of Black Diana, on which was implanted a magical stone. Emperor Theodosius closed the temple in 380, allegedly because he despised the religion of women. Early Christians sought to destroy the cult as Devil-worshipers, and Black Diana was smashed ca. 400.

According to myth, Artemis was born of Zeus and Leto, a nature deity and the twin sister of Apollo, who became the god of oracles and of the Sun. As soon as she was born, Artemis was thrust into the role of protector and helper of women. Though Artemis was born without pain, Apollo caused Leto great suffering. Artemis served as midwife. As a result, women have traditionally prayed to her to ease childbirth.

As a youth, Artemis exhibited a boyish taste for adventure and independence. At her request, Zeus granted her a bow and a quiver of arrows, a band of nymph maidens to follow her, a pack of hounds, a short tunic suitable for running and eternal chastity, so that she could run forever through the wilderness. She was quick to protect wildlife and animals, as well as humans who appealed

Apollo and Diana (ALBRECHT DÜRER, 1502)

to her for help, especially women who were raped and victimized by men.

She was equally quick to punish offending men. Actaeon, a hunter who spied Artemis and her nymphs bathing nude in a pool, was turned into a stag and torn to pieces by his own hounds. She killed Orion, whom she loved, with an arrow shot to the head. In one version, she was tricked into killing Orion by Apollo, who did not like Orion; in another version, she killed him out of jealousy over his feelings for Dawn. She sent a boar to ravage the countryside of Calydon as punishment to King Oeneus, because he forgot to include her in the sacrifice of the first fruits of harvest. (None of the bravest male warriors of Greece could slay the boar. It took another woman, Atalanta, to do it.)

In British myth, Diana directed Prince Brutus of Troy to flee to Britain after the fall of that city. Brutus, who then founded Britain's royalty, is said to have erected an altar to Diana at the site where St. Paul's Cathedral is located today. A surviving remnant of that altar is the London Stone.

As late as the fifth and sixth centuries, a Dianic cult flourished among European pagans. With the slow Christianization of Europe, Diana became associated with evil and Satan. In the early Middle Ages, she was believed to be the patroness of SORCERY (an evil) and to lead witches' processions and rites. Historian Jeffrey B. Russell notes that Dianic witches' processions were not known in classical times but probably grew out of the Teutonic myth of the WILD HUNT, a nocturnal spree of ghosts who destroyed the countryside. Clerical scholars may have substituted Diana, a familiar deity, for the Teutonic goddesses, Holda and Berta, who sometimes led the Wild Hunt and who were identified by the church as followers of the Devil.

The CANON EPISCOPI, an ecclesiastical law written ca. 900, reinforced the portrayal of a Devil Diana who leads the witches:

> It is not to be omitted that some wicked women, perverted by the Devil, seduced by illusions and phantasms of demons, believe and profess themselves, in the hours of the night, to ride upon certain beasts with Diana, the goddess of pagans, and an innumerable multitude of women, and in the silence of the dead of the night to traverse great spaces of earth, and to obey her commands as of their mistress, and to be summoned to her service on certain nights.

Diana also became associated with Herodias, wife of Herod, who was responsible for the execution of John the Baptist. Herodias took on the aspects of a demon, condemned to wander through the sky forever but allowed by God to rest in trees from midnight to dawn. In Italian lore, the name *Herodias* became ARADIA. In the 19th century, CHARLES GODFREY LELAND recorded oral legends told to him by witches of Etruscan heritage concerning Aradia, the daughter of Diana and her brother Lucifer. Diana dispatched Aradia to earth to teach witches their craft.

British anthropologist MARGARET A. MURRAY erroneously believed that an organized Dianic cult of witches had existed throughout the Middle Ages and the witch hunt centuries, though no evidence survives to prove it. Murray relied heavily upon the *Canon Episcopi* in developing these ideas. They were adopted by GERALD B. GARDNER, a key figure in the revival of witchcraft in the 1950s in Britain.

Diana in Wicca. Though most Wiccans no longer believe in Murray's medieval Dianic cult, they do revere Diana as a Pagan deity and an archetype. As part of the Triple Goddess aspect of the moon, Diana holds sway over the new and waxing moon, a two-week period that is auspicious for magic related to new beginnings, growth and achievement. Diana is invoked as nurturer and protector. At the full moon, she turns her power over to Selene.

As an archetype, Diana serves as a role model for feminist Witchcraft, called the Dianic tradition. She is a free spirit, an achiever, who knows what she wants and scores the mark with a single arrow shot. She is neither dependent upon nor subjugated by men. Though a lunar goddess, she walks the earth, and her domain is the wild; she is one with nature.

FURTHER READING:
Adler, Margot. *Drawing Down the Moon.* Revised ed. New York: Viking, 1986.
Crowley, Vivianne. *Wicca: The Old Religion in the New Millennium.* Revised ed. London: Thorsons/Harper Collins, 1996.
Starhawk. *The Spiral Dance.* Revised ed. San Francisco: HarperSan Francisco, 1989.
Thomas, Keith. *Religion and the Decline of Magic.* New York: Charles Scribner's Sons, 1971.

Digitalis, Raven (1983–) Pagan priest and empathic healer, noted for his teaching of "Goth Craft," a merger of Goth subcultures with Witchcraft and Pagan spiritual practices.

Raven Digitalis was born Colin Smith on July 29, 1983, in Missoula, Montana. As a youth, he identified with concepts in occultism, magic and Witchcraft. At age 16, he was introduced to the Craft by a friend and knew he had found his spiritual home, attracted to the Craft's emphasis on self-empowerment, independent thought and direct contact with the divine.

Raven Digitalis (COURTESY RAVEN DIGITALIS)

Digitalis graduated from the University of Montana in 2007 with a bachelor's degree in cultural anthropology. He works as a Gothic-industrial radio and club disc jockey and as a black-and-white photographic artist. He took his name Raven Digitalis from two of his spirit helpers, the raven and the plant digitalis (foxglove).

In 2003, several events took place that influenced Digitalis' spiritual path. He became a Pagan priest. He and his high priestess, Estha McNevin, founded the disciplined eclectic shadow magic occult tradition of Opus Aima Obscurae ("Work of the Great Dark Mother"). The tradition draws upon Gardnerian Wicca, the HERMETICA, the KABBALAH, SHAMANISM and chaos MAGIC and requires intense study, self-reflection, spiritual ordeals and sacraments such as fasting, tonsure and devotions as ways to progress spiritual development.

The same year, Digitalis undertook a psychedelic mushroom shamanic journey and had a vision to write a book on the growing convergence of the Goth and Witchcraft cultures. *Goth Craft: The Magickal Side of Dark Culture* was published in 2007. "Goth Craft" concerns spiritual exploration of one's shadow side; it is not about "evil." Dark aspects of deity are given more emphasis, and RITUALS encompass BLOOD magic, death energy and body art/modification. Goth Craft has gained increasing acceptance among Witches and Pagans.

A second book, *Shadow Magick Compendium: Exploring Darker Aspects of Magickal Spirituality,* not.specific to Goth, was published in 2008. The two books are intended as reference guides for working in the darker, yet progressive and evolutionary aspects of spirit and magical spirituality.

Digitalis sees Witchcraft/Paganism as an accessible, progressive spiritual community. Practitioners, he says, must live their magic and extend it to others in order for the community to realize its spiritual potential. Healing is an important aspect of Witchcraft and Paganism, and Digitalis uses his empathic healing ability to help others.

Digitalis, McNevin and their COVEN plan a metaphysical bookstore, café and resource center, Twigs and Brews, most likely for the Missoula area.

In addition to Witchcraft, Paganism and occultism, Digitalis has studied Buddhist philosophy and trained in Georgian Wicca, a tradition similar to the Gardnerian and Alexandrian traditions, founded in 1970 in California by George Patterson, Zanonia Silverknife and Tanith.

FURTHER READING:
Digitalis, Raven. *Goth Craft: The Magickal Side of Dark Culture.* St. Paul, Minn.: Llewellyn Publications, 2007.
———. *Shadow Magick Compendium: Exploring Darker Aspects of Magickal Spirituality.* St. Paul, Minn.: Llewellyn Publications, 2008.
"Opus Anima Obscura." Available online. URL: http://www.witchvox.com/vn/vn_detail/dt_gr.html?a=usmt&id=30426. Downloaded December 10, 2007.
Raven Digitalis Web site. Available online. URL: http://www.ravendigitalis.com. Downloaded November 30, 2007.

divination   Foretelling the future, finding objects and people, and determining guilt by means of information obtained from signs, omens, dreams, visions and divinatory tools. Divination traditionally is an important skill of the folk witch. In some societies, divination has been performed only by special classes of trained priests or priestesses. Divination is an important skill for many Wiccans and Pagans.

Since the earliest times in all known civilizations, people have looked to supernatural sources for help and advice, in personal affairs and particularly in matters of state. Methods of divination involve either interpretation of natural patterns in the environment or patterns that are formed by the tossing of objects such as sticks, stones or bones. Information is obtained from the way smoke curls from a fire, the shape of an animal bone, the formation of clouds, and the markings on organs and entrails of sacrificed animals. The ancient Romans favored augury, the interpretation of the flight pattern of birds, and haruspicy, the examination of the livers and entrails of sacrificed animals. The augurs were a special caste of priests who read the signs to deter-

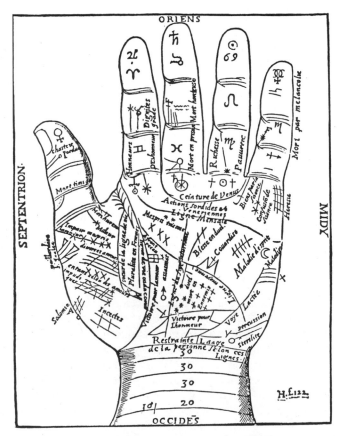

Lines, Zodiac signs in hand (JEAN-BAPTISTE BELOT, *OEUVRES,* 1640)

mine whether the gods approved or approved of coming events.

Dreams have always been an important medium for divining answers to questions, as has SCRYING. Oracles are persons who enter trance states.

Popular in the Middle Ages was the tossing of grain, sand or peas onto the earth to see what could be read from the patterns. Similarly, the Japanese set out characters of the syllabary in a circle, then scatter rice around them and let a cock pick at the rice. Whatever syllables are nearest the grain picked up by the cock are used to puzzle out messages. As far back as 1000 B.C.E., the Chinese have used the *I Ching,* an oracle which involves tossing and reading long and short yarrow sticks. Another ancient Chinese divinatory method, which is still in use, is *feng-shui,* or geomancy, the siting of buildings, tombs and other physical structures by determining the invisible currents of energy coursing through the earth.

Finding the guilty. Throughout history, divination has been used to identify parties guilty of crimes. Despite the true psychic ability no doubt employed by many diviners, it is certain that many innocent people have been punished along with the guilty. In the Pacific Islands, murderers have been identified through examining the marks of a beetle crawling over the grave of a victim. The Lugbara of western Uganda fill small pots with medicines that represent the suspects. The pot that does not boil over when heated reveals the culprit. In other methods, suspects are forced to eat or drink various substances and concoctions, such as the gruesome stew made from the boiled head of an ass. Whoever is unfortunate enough to choke or suffer indigestion—even a rumbling stomach—is guilty by divination.

During the witch hunts, witch suspects were bound and thrown in lakes and rivers to see if they would float (guilty) or sink (innocent). If the sinking innocent drowned, that was simply an unfortunate consequence (see SWIMMING).

Contemporary divinatory methods. Most Witches have a favored tool in divining that acts as a prompt to intuition and the tuning in to psychic forces and vibrations. The divined information comes in a variety of ways, depending on the individual. Some persons "hear" it with the inner ear; others see visual images on their mental screen. Divinatory information also comes through other senses, including taste, smell and tactile sensations.

Popular tools include the Tarot; rune stones; crystals, mirrors or bowls for scrying; dowsing; and the I Ching. Many Witches also use psychometry, which is the reading of objects or photographs by handling them. Astrology and numerology are often used in conjunction with divination.

Some Witches divine by reading auras, the layers of invisible energy that surround all living things.

Palmistry, the reading of lines on the hand, and TAS-SEOMANCY, the reading of tea leaves, are used by some Witches.

Nineteenth-century Tarot trumps

Divination is both art and skill, and one's proficiency depends on natural psychic gifts and regular practice. For some, divination comes fairly easily, while others must work harder and longer to attune the psychic faculties. Most covens offer training in developing psychic abilities and divinatory skills. Many Witches feel that the best time to divine is between midnight and dawn, when the psychic currents are supposed to be at their strongest.

FURTHER READING:
Guiley, Rosemary Ellen. *Harpers Encyclopedia of Mystical and Paranormal Experience.* San Francisco: HarperSanFrancisco, 1991.

Luhrmann, T. M. *Persuasions of the Witch's Craft: Ritual Magic in Contemporary England.* Cambridge: Harvard University Press, 1989.

Doctor John (19th century)   Famous American WITCH DOCTOR, Doctor John (also called Bayou John and Jean Montaigne) was a free black man who owned slaves in antebellum New Orleans.

A huge man, Doctor John claimed he was a prince in his homeland of Senegal, sent into slavery by the Spaniards and taken to Cuba. There he became an excellent cook and convinced his master to grant his freedom. Next he worked as a sailor, returning to Senegal, where he no longer felt at home. Returning to sea, he ended up in New

Orleans, where he found work as a cotton roller on the docks. He noticed he had the "power," and his bosses made him overseer.

Doctor John's fame spread, and he found he could get money for his tricks and services. He built a house on Bayou Road and bought female slaves. He married some of them, performing his own ceremonies, eventually boasting 15 wives and more than 50 children. New Orleanians stared at him in public, for he rode in a carriage with horses as fine as any white man. When Doctor John rode horseback alone, he wore a gaudy Spanish costume. Later he affected an austere black costume with a white, frilly shirt and grew a beard.

Leaving the Voodoo (see VODUN) meetings to the administration of the queens, Doctor John specialized in fortune-telling, healing and making GRIS-GRIS. His house was filled with snakes, lizards, toads, scorpions and human skulls stolen from graveyards. Blacks and whites came to him for advice, love potions and the placing or lifting of CURSES. Others followed his commands out of fear of Doctor John's secret knowledge. Most of his wisdom did not come from the spirits, however, but from a huge network of black servants placed all over town. He either bought or took information from them, thereby giving him an advantage when thickly veiled white girls came to him desiring to know if their lovers were faithful.

One of Doctor John's specialties was the starting or stopping of poltergeist phenomena, usually showers of rocks and stones on the victim's home (see LITHOBOLY). Policemen stood baffled as the rocks rained down, apparently from nowhere. Naturally, Doctor John could stop such harassment, for a fee. One case reports that the slaves of a Samuel Wilson paid $62 to stop a shower of rocks, but Wilson took Doctor John to court to retrieve the $62. A few days later, the rock showers began again.

Unable to read or write, Doctor John supposedly amassed a fortune, even burying $150,000 on his property, according to local stories. He never forgot his poorer neighbors, however, dispensing food to anyone who needed it. But by the end of his life, his poor business sense caused his financial demise. He didn't trust banks, convinced that once he gave a bank his money he would never see it again. His investments turned sour, and his wives and children were continually leaving with part of his assets. Others cheated him outright. Finally, Doctor John employed a young black to teach him to read and write, and he spent long hours learning to sign his name. One day, a con artist had him sign his name at the bottom of a long paper, and Doctor John lost all his Bayou Road property.

Doctor John tried to regain his prestige, but younger people—principally his protégée, MARIE LAVEAU, then her daughter of the same name—had taken over the voodoo business. At age 80, he was forced to move in with children from his white wife, though he despised mulattoes. New Orleanians gossiped that Doctor John was "fixed,"

or the victim of spells greater than his. He died in August 1885 at age 82, four years after the death of the first Marie Laveau.

FURTHER READING:
Rigaud, Milo. *Secrets of Voodoo.* San Francisco: City Lights Books, 1985.
Tallant, Robert. *The Voodoo Queen.* Gretna, La.: Pelican Publishing, 1983.

Drawing Down the Moon   An important ritual in some traditions of WICCA in which a COVEN's high priestess enters a trance and becomes the GODDESS, who is symbolized by the MOON. The transformation may be accomplished with the help of the high priest, who invokes, or draws down, the spirit of the Goddess into the high priestess.

The origins of Drawing Down the Moon can be found in classical times. Ancient Thessalian witches were believed to control the moon, according to an old tract: "If I command the moon, it will come down; and if I wish to withhold the day, night will linger over my head; and again, if I wish to embark on the sea, I need no ship, and if I wish to fly through the air, I am free from my weight."

In the modern rite, the high priestess may recite the CHARGE OF THE GODDESS, a poetic address written by DOREEN VALIENTE, high priestess in the Gardnerian tradition (see GERALD B. GARDNER), or she may deliver a spontaneous address.

Drawing Down the Moon is considered one of the most beautiful of all RITUALS in Wicca. Depending upon the high priestess's trance state and the energy raised, the words that come forth can be moving, poetic and inspiring. Through Drawing Down the Moon, many women connect with the power of the Goddess and therefore with the power within themselves.

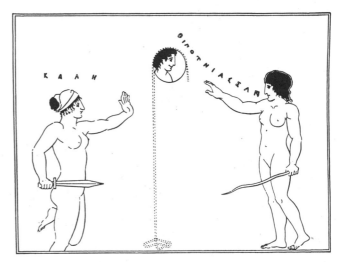

Greek vase ca. second century B.C.E. *depicts Drawing Down the Moon ceremony* (NEW YORK PUBLIC LIBRARY)

A similar rite for invoking the HORNED GOD into the high priest is called Drawing Down the Sun or Drawing Down of the Horned God. Similar Pagan rituals are called Calling Down the Moon.

FURTHER READING:

Adler, Margot. *Drawing Down the Moon.* Revised ed. New York: Viking, 1986.

Fitch, Ed, and Janine Renee. *Magical Rites From the Crystal Well.* St. Paul: Llewellyn Publications, 1984.

Starhawk. *The Spiral Dance.* Revised ed. San Francisco: HarperSanFrancisco, 1989.

Druids   An exalted caste of Celtic priests. Little is known about the Druids. Reconstructions of their tradition form a central part of PAGANISM.

The Celts were a tribal people who spread throughout Gaul, Britain, Ireland, Europe, Asia Minor and the Balkans by the fifth century B.C.E. In the first century C.E., the Romans launched a series of suppressions of the Celts, and their religion eventually was replaced by Christianity.

The rituals and teachings of the Druids were highly secret and passed on orally. Most of what is known comes from a few writings of Greeks and Romans between the second century B.C.E. and the fourth century C.E., archaeological evidence found in graves, shrines and temples, and iconography.

History

The exact role of the Druids in Celtic society is open to interpretation and varies according to geography. In the third century C.E., Diogenes Laertius said that the Druids were an ancient institution in the fourth century B.C.E., during the time of Aristotle. Julius Caesar said the Gaulish Druids were one of the two highest castes, along with the knights, and were organized under a single titular head. In Ireland, the Druids were the second highest of three castes, below the nobility and above the plebes, or landless ones.

By most accounts, the Druids were the keepers of traditional wisdom who were concerned with moral philosophy, natural phenomena and theology. They included both men and women, for women had a place of importance in Celtic society. The Druids influenced both the sacred and secular lives of the Celts. They conducted religious ceremonies, served as mediators between the people and gods, exercised influence over the moral, ethical and spiritual fabric of Celtic society through their teachings and divination and made political and judicial decisions. Their teachings included moral philosophy, ethics, astronomy, the law of nature, the power of the gods and the concept of immortality.

Druids were skilled in the interpretation of omens, the correct RITUALS of SACRIFICE, the construction of a calendar, the medicine of herbs, the science of astronomy and the composition of poems. Ammianus, quoting Tima-genes, said Druids "are uplifted by searchings into things most secret and sublime." Gaulish Druids were said to administer law and justice, though it is unknown how they did so in relation to tribal chiefs. Irish Druids were described as men of learning and art, who included seers, wise men, bards and jurists. The Druids of Gaul and Britain were said to be separate from others in the priesthood, including diviners, bards and seers. There seemed to be overlap, as Druids were said to read omens and prophesy the future. In the first century C.E., Dio Chrysostom equated the Druids with Hindu brahmins, Persian magi and Egyptian priests. More recently, Druids have been described as shamanic, based on their customs of night fires, drumming, chanting and ecstatic dancing.

Certain trees, plants and animals were believed to be endowed with sacred and curative powers, and the Druids used them in religious ceremonies and for remedial purposes. The mistletoe, believed to be a sign from heaven, was used as a remedy against poisons and infertility, even for animals. The robur oak tree was thought to have come from the sacred forest, and its foliage was used in ceremonies. *Druid* means "knowing the oak tree" in Gaelic.

Religious ceremonies were conducted in sacred woods or oak groves that served as temples. These sacred enclosures were also assembly sites where the Druids made decisions and administered justice in civil and criminal disputes. Other meetings took place at river sources and lakes because the Celts worshiped water gods and believed water to be sacred.

Ceremonies included prayers, libations and human and animal sacrifices. Victims were burned alive in wickerwork cages, stabbed, impaled on stakes and shot with arrows. The sacrifice of humans outraged the Romans, who outlawed it as barbaric by senatorial decree in 97 B.C.E. Later writers tried to excuse the Druids from participation in sacrifices, saying they did not do the actual killing. This is highly unlikely, given their roles as priests.

The only extant detailed account of a Druid ceremony comes from Pliny and concerns the harvesting of mistletoe. On the sixth day of the Moon, a Druid garbed in a white robe climbed an oak tree and, with his left hand, cut the mistletoe with a gold sickle (or, more likely, a gilded bronze sickle, since gold is too soft to cut mistletoe). The mistletoe, not supposed to fall to the ground, was caught in a white cloth. Two white bulls were sacrificed, and a feast held.

In interpreting omens, the Druids observed the hare or such birds as the crow and eagle to foretell events. They practiced DIVINATION by observing the death throes and entrails of their sacrificial victims. During religious festivals, the Druids divined by dreams. A man would be put to sleep with Druids chanting over his body. Upon awakening, the man would describe his dream and the Druids would interpret it.

Classical writings make some references to MAGIC, including CHARMS with herbs and mistletoe, and belief in a magical egg made from the SPITTLE of angry snakes that would ensure success in court and guarantee favors from princes.

The Druids' belief in the immortality of the soul and life after death have been equated with Pythagoras' belief in metempsychosis. The dead were cremated with all their possessions. Sometimes relatives committed suicide by jumping into the fire and holding the corpses so as to be with them in the next world. The Celts wrote letters to the dead and advanced loans that would be repayable after death. Julius Caesar said that this belief in immortality sustained the legendary Celtic courage in battle.

The Romans feared and were repulsed by the Celts, and in 43 C.E., the emperor Claudius banned Druidism throughout the empire. In 60 or 61, the Romans sacked and destroyed their holy stronghold on the island of Mona (also called Mon and Anglesey). According to Tacitus, black-clad Druidesses leaped among the Celtic warriors, howling to the gods and screaming CURSES at the Romans. The Romans were victorious and killed the warriors and the Druids and laid waste to the sacred groves. The loss sent Druidism into permanent decline; within several generations, the venerated and powerful priesthood was on a par with common sorcerers.

Antiquarian Druidic Revival

In the 16th and 17th centuries, interest in the Druids revived. Translators of the classical texts romanticized them and turned them into characters of folklore. John Aubrey, a leading British antiquarian of the 17th century, suggested the Druids had constructed Stonehenge, which has since been refuted. But the association of Druids with Stonehenge continued well into modern times.

Aubrey's views were endorsed in the 18th century by William Stukeley, who became known as the "Arch Druid" and the founder of modern Druidism. A meeting of "British Druids" is said to have taken place in 1717, organized by John Tolan and led by Stukeley. In 1781, the Ancient Order of Druids was founded by Henry Hurle, a carpenter. This order was inspired by Freemasonry and also was a benefit society. The issue of charity split the organization in 1833. The United Ancient Order of Druids continued purely as a benefit society, while the Ancient Order of Druids retained its mystical underpinnings.

Modern Druid Revivals

By the early 20th century, there were at least five modern Druidic organizations, including the Druidic Hermetists and the British Circle of the Universal Bond, but most did not survive more than a few decades. In 1964, the Order of Bards, Ovates and Druids, led by Ross Nichols, split away from the Ancient Order of Druids, drawing members from that group and the British Circle of the Universal Bond.

In 1979, the British Druid Order (BDO) was founded in England by Phillip Shallcrass. A Council of British Druid Orders was formed in England in 1989. Around 2006, the BDO went into a state of "transition" and was largely inactive, but still in existence.

In the United States, a modern Druidic movement with no connection to the ancient Druids or the modern Druids in England was formed in 1963. The Reformed Druids of North America (RDNA) initially was conceived as a hoax by a group of students at Carleton College, Northfield, Minnesota, who were protesting a school requirement that students attend religious services. The requirement was dropped in 1963–64, but the Reformed Druids decided to take themselves seriously and continue as an organization of autonomous "groves." Rituals were reconstructed from anthropological material and included non-bloody sacrifices. The founders of RDNA did not intend for it to become a religion, but rather viewed it as a philosophy. Some groves split off to form a separate branch, the New Reformed Druids of North America, which emphasized Paganism. Among these groves was the Berkeley grove, which was led by Archdruid P. E. I. (ISAAC) BONEWITS in the mid-1970s. Bonewits left the organization about 1978–79. In 1983, he formed his own Druidic organization, ÁR NDRAÍOCHT FÉIN ("Our own Druidism").

The Reformed Druids of North America ceased activity, though individual groves remained scattered around the country. *Ar nDraiocht Fein* grew to become the largest Pagan Druidic organization in the world.

FURTHER READING:
Carr-Gomm, Philip (ed.). *The Druid Renaissance*. London: Thorsons, 1996.
———. *Druidcraft: The Magic of Wicca and Druidry*. London: Thorsons, 2002.
Hutton, Ronald. *The Pagan Religions of the Ancient British Isles: Their Nature and Legacy*. London: Basil Blackwell Publishers, 1991.
Piggott, Stuart. *The Druids*. London: Thames and Hudson, 1975.
Shallcrass, Philip. *Druidry*. London: Piatkus Books, 2000.

Duncan, Helen (1898–1956) British Spiritualist whose conviction on flimsy charges of witchcraft led to the repeal of Britain's Witchcraft Act of 1736, thus clearing the way for the public practice of Witchcraft.

Helen Duncan, a Scotswoman, was renowned for her natural mediumistic abilities by the 1920s. During the 1930s and 1940s, she traveled around Britain giving seances. Audience members said she could produce materializations in which luminous ectoplasm would appear to emanate from her mouth and take on the form of the dead.

Like other mediums of her day, Duncan was investigated by authorities. In 1933, she was convicted of fraud over the materialization of a dead child. She was accused of manipulating a woman's vest in order to produce the appearance of ectoplasm.

Duncan continued to practice mediumship. After the start of World War II, she had a steady business of the bereaved seeking to contact their dead loved ones.

Duncan caught the attention of authorities again in 1941 when she allegedly conjured up a dead sailor at a seance in Portsmouth. She said that his hatband bore the name HMS *Barham*. The battleship *Barham* had been sunk off Malta—but not even family members knew about the disaster because the Admiralty had decided to keep it secret in the interests of morale.

Upset by the revelation from Duncan, people demanded an explanation from the Admiralty, which complicated matters by stalling for three months before making an official announcement.

As a result, authorities monitored Duncan for the next two years. With the approach of the D-Day invasion by Allied troops, it was feared that she might clairvoyantly "see" the planned landing sites in Normandy and make them public in advance.

Under the Witchcraft Act of 1735, Duncan was charged with witchcraft for pretending to conjure the dead. At her seven-day trial at the Old Bailey in 1944, more than 40 witnesses testified as to their belief in her powers. The Crown argued that she was a fraud and "an unmitigated humbug who could only be regarded as a pest to a certain of section of society."

Duncan was convicted and sentenced to nine months in Holloway prison. She declared as she was led to the cells, "Why should I suffer like this? I have never heard so many lies in my life." Her words echoed those of countless accused witches in Britain, Europe and America who in earlier times had gone to jail or to their executions under false accusations.

Her case became a cause célèbre, attracting the attention of Winston Churchill, who was interested in Spiritualism. Churchill was so angered by the trial that he wrote to the Home Secretary, "Let me have a report on why the 1735 Witchcraft Act was used in a modern court of justice. What was the cost to the state of a trial in which the Recorder was kept so busy with all this obsolete tomfoolery?"

In 1951 Parliament repealed the 1735 Witchcraft Act, making Duncan the last person in Britain to be convicted and jailed for the crime of witchcraft.

After the war Duncan resumed her mediumship. In November 1956, police raided a seance she was conducting at a private house in West Bridgford, Nottingham-shire. Duncan reportedly was shocked out of a trance, which her supporters claimed led to her death five weeks later. But she was also overweight and diabetic and had a history of heart trouble.

In 1998, the 100th anniversary of Duncan's birth, a campaign was launched to clear her name and have her pardoned. However, the Criminal Cases Review Commission examined the case but decided against referring it back to the Appeal Court. Spiritualists planned formal petitions.

The repeal of the 1736 Witchcraft Act is one of the most significant events in the emergence of WICCA. It enabled GERALD B. GARDNER to publish his groundbreaking books about his own practice of Witchcraft, and enabled interest in the subject to come out into the open. By the 1960s, Wicca was growing and expanding and was being exported to other countries.

FURTHER READING:
Cassirer, Manfred. *Medium on Trial: The Story of Helen Duncan and the Witchcraft Act.* Stanstead, Eng.: PN Publishing, 1996.
Johnston, Philip. "Campaign to clear name of wartime 'witch.'" *The Daily Telegraph.* Jan. 31, 1998, p. 3.
Valiente, Doreen. *The Rebirth of Witchcraft.* London: Robert Hall, 1989.

Duny, Amy (17th century) A Connecticut nanny accused of cursing the infant under her care. Amy Duny was an old woman who worked for a woman named Dorothy Duent, taking care of her infant child. In 1682, Duent accused Duny of being a witch and cursing her baby by suckling it. Duent consulted a doctor who said he was an expert on breaking the CURSES and SPELLS of witches. His solution was to wrap the baby in a blanket and hang it over a fire, which would cause the witch's FAMILIAR to fall out.

Duent did as ordered, hanging the wrapped infant over the fire in her hearth. The baby screamed in pain. Witnesses reported that a black TOAD fell out into the fire and burned up instantly, like a flash of gunpowder. According to reports, the baby was no longer cursed. No record exists of the fate of Duny.

egg tree A CHARM against witches. The egg tree is a dead bush with the limbs cropped, decorated with dozens or perhaps hundreds of blown eggs. The bush is set in the ground near a cabin and is said to ward off witches.

elder In PAGANISM and WICCA, one who has attained a high level of respect for his or her experience and skill. In Wicca, an elder does not necessarily have to be of the third, or highest, degree of rank; she or he may be a first-degree witch (see INITIATION; WITCHES). Most elders, however, are third-degree Witches who have been in the Craft a long time. Elders are consulted in policy decisions and interpretations of Craft laws and traditions.

See COVEN.

elementals Spirits that personify the four ELEMENTS—earth, air, fire and water. The term elementals also is applied to NATURE SPIRITS, which exist in all things in nature and look after animals, insects, birds, rocks and plants. Elementals are summoned to assist in MAGIC related to nature.

Earth elementals are known as gnomes; fire as salamanders; water as undines; and air as sylphs. They can be seen clairvoyantly if a person has good attunement to the nature realm. Numerous elemental sightings have been reported at the CIRCLE SANCTUARY at Mt. Horeb, Wisconsin. The pioneers of the Findhorn community in northern Scotland achieved remarkable gardening results reputedly by communicating with elementals.

Some elementals are said to be malicious and unpredictable, tricking human beings into accidents, setting traps for them and killing them. Wicca emphasizes working with friendly elementals in the creation of positive magic.

Artificial elemental is a term occasionally used for *thought-form,* a being of energy ritually created through intense will, which is programmed to carry out assignments and disintegrate once the work is done.

elements The four elements of nature—earth, air, water and fire—form the foundation of natural MAGIC. The elements are associated with the cardinal points of the MAGIC CIRCLE and with a hierarchy of spirits—beings called ELEMENTALS.

In Western occultism, the four elements are considered the basis of all life, not only on the planet but throughout the universe as well, linking humankind to nature, the heavens and the divine, and governing mankind's well-being. In the ancient Mysteries, the rays of celestial bodies become the elements when they strike the crystallized influences of the lower world. The elements figured prominently in the magic of the ancient Egyptians and Greeks, who ascribed to each one various attributes and characteristics. Plato divided all beings into four groups based on the elements—air/birds, water/fish, earth/pedestrians and fire/stars—all of which are interrelated. The magicians and alchemists of the Middle Ages ascribed elements to external and internal parts of the human body; various

Salamander, an elemental of fire (MICHAEL MAIER, *SCRUTINIUM CHYMICUM*, 1687)

gems, minerals and metals; planets and constellations; the Four Horsemen of the Apocalypse; various species of the animal and plant kingdoms; human personality traits; and geometrical shapes. Roger Flud (1574–1637), alchemist and astrologer, related the elements to harmonics, while another Renaissance alchemist, Sisismund Bactrom, believed that if all the elements could be harmonized and united, the result would be the Philosopher's Stone. This is represented by the fifth element, spirit, which Carl G. Jung called the *quinta essentia*.

The Mithraic Mysteries hold that man must rule the elements before he can attain spiritual wisdom; accordingly, he must successfully undergo the initiations of earth, air, water and fire, each of which test a different aspect of his nature and being.

Some of the major correspondences of the elements are:

Earth: The north; the pentacle; female principle; fertility; darkness, quiet; practicality; thrift; acquisition; patience; responsibility; boredom; stagnation; the materialization of cosmic powers; the color green; the metal gold.

Air: The east, the wand (in some traditions, the sword and athame); male principle; intellect, energy, endeavor; sociability; squandering, frivolity; the expression of the magician's will; the color yellow; the metal silver.

Water: The west; the cup, challice and cauldron; female principle; fecundity; body fluids; magical brews; the rhythms of nature; emotions, sensitivity, receptivity; instability, indifference; the color blue; the metal silver.

Fire: The south; the sword or athame (in some traditions, the wand); male principle; action, courage, defense against hostile forces; struggle, animosity, jealousy, anger; the color orange; the metal gold.

Center: Connection to cosmos; the Self; the Mystic Center; the All That Is.

FAMILIARS are considered sources of vital elemental energy. Ritual tools and objects are consecrated with the four elements, by placing them on or touching them with a pentacle, passing them over a candle flame and a censer (air) and sprinkling them with salted water (see WITCHES' TOOLS). When a magic circle is cast, it is consecrated and purified with the elements. Each element or its symbol is taken to its corresponding quarter, and its guardian spirit is invoked.

FURTHER READING:
Crowley, Vivianne. *Wicca: The Old Religion in the New Millennium.* Revised ed. London: Thorsons/Harper Collins, 1996.
Farrar, Janet, and Stewart Farrar. *A Witches Bible Compleat.* New York: Magickal Childe, 1984.

elf arrows　Arrowhead-shaped flints from the Stone Age found in many parts of the British Isles, Europe and northern Africa, which witches supposedly used as weapons against animals and people. Elf arrow superstitions predominate in Ireland, Scotland and parts of England, where fairy lore is strong (see FAIRIES). According to lore, many witches learn their craft from fairies and elves.

Elf arrows are said to be fatal to cattle, a common target of witches. Stricken cattle can be saved by touching them with the arrow, then dipping the arrow into water and giving the water to the cattle to drink. The term *elf-shot* is still applied to sick animals.

A person shot with an elf arrow supposedly comes down with mysterious and fatal supernatural illnesses. The use of elf arrows was among the accusations of witchcraft brought in 1560 against a Scottish woman, Catherine Ross, Lady Fowllis, and her son-in-law, Hector Munro. The two were part of a group of witches who conspired to kill Ross' husband and Marjory Campbell, Lady Balnagowan, so that Ross and Lord Balnagowan could marry. The witches were charged with "the making of two clay pictures, one for the destruction of the young Lady Balnagowan, and getting them enchanted, and shooting of elf-arrow heads at the said persons." Apparently the witches' plot was uncovered before the victims were killed.

See ISOBEL GOWDIE.

FURTHER READING:
Maple, Eric. *The Dark World of Witches.* New York: A.S. Barnes & Co., 1962.

esbat　The regular meeting of a COVEN of Witches at which religious worship is conducted, business is discussed and MAGIC and HEALING work is done.

The frequency of esbats depends on the coven. Most covens meet at the full MOON, which occurs 13 times a year. They may also meet at the new moon. Some meet weekly.

The esbat may take place indoors or outdoors. A coven may have a regular meeting place or rotate it among the homes of coveners. The coveners may wear loose clothing such as robes, or they may be skyclad (nude).

Animals belonging to coveners usually are allowed to be present at an esbat and to come and go as long as they do not disturb the energy flow of the RITUALS and magic work. Animals are not used as sacrifices.

At the end of the esbat, coveners share food and drink (see CAKES-AND-WINE).

The term *esbat* is a modern one. It may have been coined by MARGARET A. MURRAY, a British anthropologist who wrote about medieval witchcraft as an organized pagan religion. Most Wiccans use the term *circle* rather than *esbat* for their regular meeting; *esbat* is used formally.

FURTHER READING:
Buckland, Raymond. *Buckland's Complete Book of Witchcraft.* St. Paul: Llewellyn Publications, 1986.
Farrar, Janet, and Stewart Farrar. *A Witches Bible Compleat.* New York: Magickal Childe, 1984.

evil eye   The causing of illness, misfortune, calamity and death by the looks of strangers and by envious looks. AMULETS and incantations (see CHARMS) ward the danger off.

The evil eye exists around the world, dating to ancient times. The oldest recorded references to it appear in the cuneiform texts of the Sumerians, Babylonians and Assyrians, about 3000 B.C.E. The ancient Egyptians believed in the evil eye and used eye shadow and lipstick to prevent it from entering their eyes or mouths. The Bible makes references to it in both the Old and New Testaments. It is among ancient Hindu folk beliefs. Evil-eye superstitions have remained strong into modern times, especially in Mediterranean countries such as Italy and in Mexico and Central America.

There are two kinds of evil eye: deliberate and involuntary. Most cases of evil eye are believed to occur involuntarily; the person casting it does not mean to do it and probably isn't even aware of it. No revenge is sought for this hazard.

Malevolent, deliberate evil eye is called "overlooking" and is a form of witchcraft that can bring about misfortune or catastrophe: illness, poverty, injury, loss of love, even death. Witches were said to give anyone who crossed them the evil eye and to use it to bewitch judges from convicting them.

The involuntary evil eye typically occurs when someone, especially a stranger, admires one's children, livestock or possessions, or casts a lingering look on anyone. Unless immediate precautions are taken, the children get sick, the animals die, the possessions are stolen or good fortune in business turns sour. If the evil eye cannot be warded off, the victim must turn to an initiate—usually an older woman in the family—who knows a secret cure.

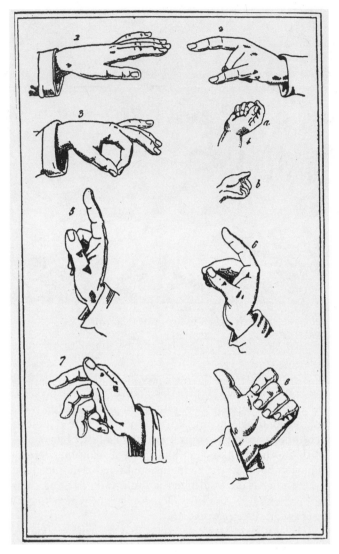

Hand positions to ward off the evil eye (FROM FREDERICK THOMAS ELWORTHY'S *THE EVIL EYE*, 1895)

Besides envious glances, the evil eye comes from strangers in town, or anyone who has unusual or different-colored eyes—a blue-eyed stranger in a land of brown-eyed people, for example. Some unfortunate souls are said to be born with permanent evil eye, laying waste to everything they see. High-ranking people such as noblemen or clergy sometimes are believed to be afflicted like this. Pope Pius IX (1846–78) was branded as having the evil eye shortly after his investiture as Pope in 1869. Driving through Rome in an open car, he glanced at a nurse holding a child in an open window. Minutes later, the child fell to its death, and from then on, it seemed that everything the Pope blessed resulted in disaster. Pope Leo XIII (1878–1903) was also said to possess the *mal occhio,* as the evil eye is known in Italy.

The evil eye is most likely to strike when one is happiest; good fortune, it seems, invites bad fortune. Small children and animals are especially vulnerable. In many villages, it is considered unwise to show children too much in public or to call attention to their beauty. Likewise, it is not advisable to display possessions or brag about successes.

In 19th-century Ireland, animals who were under the influence of the evil eye were said to have been "blinked." In order to save such animals, local wise women were sought for ritual cures.

The primary defense against the evil eye is an amulet, which may be fashioned from almost any kind of material. Common shapes are frogs and horns, the latter of which suggests both the powerful Mother Goddess (a bull is her consort) and the phallus. Another popular amulet is the "fig," a clenched fist with thumb thrust between the index and middle fingers, which also suggests a phallus.

The roots of the phallus amulet go back to the ancient Romans and their phallic god, Priapus. Another name for him was Fascinus, from *fascinum,* which means "witchcraft"; the evil eye is sometimes called "fascination." Romans employed phallic symbols as their protection against the evil eye. In Italy, it is still common for men to grab their genitals as a defense against the evil eye or anything unlucky.

The ancient Egyptians used an eye to fight an eye. The *udjat eye,* also called the Eye of God and Eye of Horus, appears on amulets, pottery and in art, warding off the forces of darkness.

Other defenses include BELLS and RED ribbons tied to livestock, horse harnesses and the underwear of children, which divert the attention of the evil eye. Gardens are surrounded by protective jack beans. Other plants act as amulets—the shamrock in Ireland and GARLIC in Greece. In Hindu lore, barley, a universal remedy supplied by the gods and the symbol of the thunderbolt of Indra, god of war, thunder and storms, will avert the evil eye.

Without an amulet, quick action is important when the evil eye strikes. One should make gestures such as the "fig" or "horns" (holding up the index and little finger). Spitting is a powerful remedy, a hold-over from the ancient Romans and Greeks.

Cures for the evil eye usually involve reciting secret incantations, which typically are passed on from mother to daughter within a family. In Italy, an initiate diagnoses the evil eye and performs the cure with a bowl of water, olive oil and, occasionally, SALT. A few drops of oil are dropped into the water (sometimes salted). The oil may scatter, form blobs or sink to the bottom. These formations are interpreted to determine the source of the attack. The initiate drops more oil into the water while reciting incantations and making the sign of the cross on the forehead of the victim. If that fails, the victim is sent to a sorceress for further treatment.

FURTHER READING:

Di Stasti, Lawrence. *Mal Occhio/The Underside of Vision.* San Francisco: North Point Press, 1981.

Elworthy, Frederick Thomas. 1895. Reprint. *The Evil Eye.* Secaucus, N.J.: University Books/Citadel Press.

exorcism   The expulsion of evil spirits by commanding them to depart. The expulsion is often done in the name of a deity, saints, angels or other intercessory figures.

Exorcism comes from the Greek *horkos,* meaning "oath," and translates as *adjuro,* or *adjure,* in Latin and English. To "exorcize," then, does not really mean to cast out so much as it means "putting the Devil on oath," or invoking a higher authority to compel the Devil to act in a way contrary to its wishes. Such compulsion also implies binding. The Anglican pamphlet *Exorcism* (1972) states, "Christian exorcism is the binding of evil powers by the triumph of Christ Jesus, through the application of the power demonstrated by that triumph, in and by his Church." Exorcism rituals often begin with the Latin words, "Adjure te, spiritus nequissime, per Deum omnipotentem," which translates as "I adjure thee, most evil spirit, by almighty God." Jesus, who cast out devils, did not exorcise, because he did not need to call on any higher authority than Himself.

Violence both physical and spiritual often dominates an exorcism. Furniture bangs and breaks, waves of heat

Priest exorcising demon from possessed woman (PIERRE BOAISTUAU, *HISTOIRES PRODIGIEUSES,* 1597)

and cold pour over the room, horrible cries emanate from the victim and often the victim suffers real physical pain and distress. The Devil seems to revel in spitting, vomiting (see ALLOTRIOPHAGY) and other, more disgusting bodily functions as well. Spiritually, the Devil and the exorcist battle for the soul of the victim, and while the Devil hurls invectives, the exorcist counters with the strongest demands for the demon's departure, vowing pain and penalty if it does not comply.

Exorcisms may also include the physical beating of a sufferer to force the demon to depart, or throwing stones at the possessed person. In extreme cases, such as that of Urbain Grandier in Loudun, the possessed person is killed and burned, or even burned alive, to remove all traces of the Devil's evil. Such punishments imply that the exorcist does not believe the victim suffered innocently at the hands of the Devil, but rather that in some say he or she invited trouble. As late as 1966, members of a fanatic cult in Zurich, Switzerland, ritually beat a young girl to death for being "the Devil's bride."

Priests and ministers perform most exorcisms, but clairvoyants and spiritualists also expel evil spirits. The ritual is not nearly as important as the exorcist himself (or herself); such talent is a gift that should be developed. The exorcist must be convinced of the victim's possession and have faith in the power of the Lord to work through the exorcist.

In his book *Hostage to the Devil* (1976), former Jesuit professor Malachi Martin describes the typical exorcist:

Usually he is engaged in the active ministry of parishes. Rarely is he a scholarly type engaged in teaching or research. Rarely is he a recently ordained priest. If there is any median age for exorcists, it is probably between the ages of fifty and sixty-five. Sound and robust physical health is not a characteristic of exorcists, nor is proven intellectual brilliance, postgraduate degrees, even in psychology or philosophy, or a very sophisticated personal culture. . . . Though, of course, there are many exceptions, the usual reasons for a priest's being chosen are his qualities of moral judgment, personal behavior, and religious beliefs—qualities that are not sophisticated or laboriously acquired, but that somehow seem always to have been an easy and natural part of such a man.

The exorcist as victim. Although most accounts of exorcism concentrate on the sufferings of the victim and the machinations of the Devil, little has been said about the effect on the exorcist. Yet an exorcist assumes a heavy risk when fighting evil. Not only can the ordeal go on for weeks, maybe months, but the exorcist must be prepared to have his entire life bared by the paranormal knowledge of the Devil. Secret sins are blurted out and ridiculed, and the demons may even mimic the voices of long-lost loved ones.

Becoming possessed himself ranks as the greatest danger to the exorcist, especially if he suffers from guilt and secretly feels the need to be punished.

Father Jean-Joseph Surin, Jesuit exorcist to the nuns at Loudun, became possessed while ministering to Jeanne des Anges after the death of Grandier. Reared in a cloister, Surin practiced self-denial during his early years as a priest, denying himself food, sleep and social contact. By the time he went to Loudun, Surin suffered from poor health, severe headaches, muscle pain, melancholy and attacks of depression and confusion. Unlike many of his fellow Jesuits, Surin firmly believed that Sister Jeanne and the others were truly possessed.

On January 19, 1635, Surin experienced his first possession, and by January 7 of the next year, the demon Isacaaron—devil of lust and debauchery—had left Sister Jeanne and entered Father Surin. Leviathan and other demons also tortured the priest. In May 1635 Father Surin wrote of his torments to his friend Father Datichi, a Jesuit in Rome:

Things have gone so far that God has permitted, for my sins, I think, something never seen, perhaps, in the Church: that during the exercise of my ministry, the Devil passes from the body of the possessed person, and coming into mine, assaults me and overturns me, shakes me, and visibly travels through me, possessing me for several hours like an energumen. . . . Some say that it is a chastisement from God upon me, as punishment for some illusion; others say something quite different; as for me, I hold fast where I am, and would not exchange my fate for anyone's, being firmly convinced that there is nothing better than to be reduced to great extremities.

Surin continued to be ill and tormented throughout 1637 and 1638, and by 1639 he could no longer dress himself, eat without difficulty, walk or read and write. In 1645 Surin attempted suicide. He would have probably died had not the kindly Father Bastide taken over as head of the Jesuit College at Saintes, where Surin lived, in 1648. He brought Surin back to health step by step, giving him the love and attention Surin had never experienced. Eventually Father Surin was able to walk again, and to read and write; he even attained enough inner strength to preach and hear confession. He wrote of his experiences at Loudun in his memoirs, *Science Experimentale*, and finally died, peacefully, in 1665.

The setting of an exorcism. There is a special connection between the spirit and its possessing location, most often the victim's bedroom or personal place. Anything hat can be moved is taken out, such as rugs, lamps, dressers, curtains, tables and trunks, to minimize flying objects. Only a bed or couch remains, accompanied by a small side table to hold a crucifix, candle, holy water and prayer book. Doors and windows are closed but cannot be nailed shut as air must be allowed to enter the room. Doorways must be kept covered, even if the door is open, or else the evil forces inside the room could affect the vicinity outside. Modern exorcists also employ a small tape recorder to validate the procedure. The priest-exorcist wears a white surplice and a purple stole.

Exorcists usually are assisted by a junior priest chosen by the diocese and in training to be an exorcist himself. The assistant monitors the exorcist, trying to keep him to the business at hand and not be misguided by the perversions of the demons, and provides physical aid if necessary. If the exorcist collapses or even dies during the ritual, the assistant takes over.

Other assistants may include a medical doctor and perhaps a family member. Each must be physically strong and be relatively guiltless at the time of the exorcism, so that the Devil cannot use their secret sins as a weapon against the exorcism. According to Martin:

> The exorcist must be as certain as possible beforehand that his assistants will not be weakened or overcome by obscene behavior or by language foul beyond their imagining; they cannot blanch at blood, excrement, urine; they must be able to take awful personal insults and be prepared to have their darkest secrets screeched in public in front of their companions.

Rites of exorcism. Rituals vary from a spiritual laying-on of hands by a clairvoyant exorcist, taking the entity into his or her own body and then expelling it, to the formal procedure outlined in the Catholic Rituale Romanum. Salt, which represents purity, and wine, which represents the blood of Christ, figure prominently in exorcisms as well as strong-smelling substances such as hellebore, attar of roses and rue.

Members of many faiths—Hasidic Jews, Muslims, Hindus, Protestant Christians and Pentacostal Christians—practice exorcism, but only the Roman Catholic church offers a formal ritual. In India, Hindu priests may blow cow-dung smoke, burn pig excreta, pull their or the victim's hair, press rock salt between their fingers, use copper coins, recite mantras or prayers, cut the victim's hair and burn it or place a blue band around the victim's neck to exorcise the demonic spirits. Trying another tack, the exorcist may offer bribes of candy or other gifts if the spirit leaves the victim. Early Puritans relied solely on prayer and fasting.

The official exorcism ritual outlined in the *Rituale Romanum* dates back to 1614, with two small revisions made in 1952. Cautioning priests to make sure a victim is truly possessed before proceeding, the rite includes prayers and passages from the Bible and calls upon the demons, in powerful Latin, to depart in the name of Jesus Christ.

While no two exorcisms are exactly alike, they tend to unfold in similar stages:

1. *The Presence.* The exorcist and his assistants become aware of an alien feeling or entity.

2. *Pretense.* Attempts by the evil spirit to appear and act as the victim, to be seen as one and the same person. The exorcist's first job is to break this Pretense and find out who the demon really is. Naming the demon is the most important first step.

3. *Breakpoint.* The moment where the demon's Pretense finally collapses. This may be a scene of extreme panic and confusion, accompanied by a crescendo of abuse, horrible sights, noises and smells. The demon begins to speak of the possessed victim in the third person instead of as itself.

4. *The Voice.* Also a sign of the Breakpoint, the Voice is, in the words of Martin, "inordinately disturbing and humanly distressing babel." The demon's voices must be ilenced for the exorcism to proceed.

5. *The Clash.* As the Voice dies out, there is tremendous pressure, both spiritual and physical. The demon has collided with the "will of the Kingdom." The exorcist, locked in battle with the demon, urges the entity to reveal more information about itself as the exorcist's holy will begins to dominate. As mentioned above, there is a direct link between the entity and place, as each spirit wants a place to be. For such spirits, habitation of a living victim is preferable to hell.

6. *Expulsion.* In a supreme triumph of God's will, the spirit leaves in the name of Jesus, and the victim is reclaimed. All present feel the Presence dissipating, sometimes with receding noises or voices. The victim may remember the ordeal or may have no idea what has happened.

See POSSESSION.

FURTHER READING:
Ebon, Martin. *The Devil's Bride, Exorcism: Past and Present.* New York: Harper & Row, 1974.
Huxley, Aldous. *The Devils of Loudun.* New York: Harper & Brothers, 1952.
Martin, Malachi. *Hostage to the Devil.* New York: Harper & Row, 1976.

eye-biters During the reign of queen Elizabeth I (1558–1603), an epidemic illness spread among cattle in Ireland which rendered them blind. Witches were accused of causing the blindness by malevolent SPELLS. Many of the eye-biters, as the witches were called, were arrested, tried and executed. Eye-biting was considered an involuntary form of EVIL EYE.

Faery (Feri) Tradition See VICTOR H. ANDERSON; GWYDION PENDDERWEN.

fairies A host of supernatural beings and spirits who exist between earth and heaven. Both good and evil, fairies have been associated with witches. During the witch hunts in Europe and the British Isles, accused witches often sought to save their lives by claiming they were taught their witch arts by fairies, which seemed less malevolent than if they had been taught by the DEVIL. For the most part, fairies have remained in a category of their own, though when convenient, the clergy allied them with the Devil.

Belief in fairies is universal and ancient and is especially strong in Europe and the British Isles. Fairies come in all shapes and sizes and are known by scores of names, among them in Western lore brownie, elf, dwarf, troll, gnome, pooka, kobold, leprechaun and banshee. In the colonization of America, fairy beliefs were transported across the Atlantic, where they survived in the Appalachians, the Ozarks and other remote mountainous areas.

The word *fairy* comes from the Latin term, *fata,* or "fate." The Fates were supernatural women who liked to visit newborn children. The archaic English term for fairy is *fay,* which means enchanted or bewitched; the state of enchantment is *fayerie,* which gradually became *faerie* and *fairy.*

There are four principal proposed origins of fairies:

1. *Fairies are the souls of the pagan dead.* Being unbaptized, the shades, or souls, are caught in a netherworld and are not bad enough to descend into hell nor good enough to rise into heaven.
2. *Fairies are fallen angels.* When God cast Lucifer from heaven, the angels who were loyal to Lucifer plunged down toward hell with him. But God raised his hand and stopped them in midflight, condemning them to remain where they were. Some were in the air, some in the earth and some in the seas and rivers. This belief is widespread in the lore of Ireland, Scotland and Scandinavia.
3. *Fairies are nature spirits.* Fairies are among the many spirits that populate all things and places on the planet. (See NATURE SPIRITS.)
4. *Fairies are diminutive human beings.* Evidence exists that small-statured races populated parts of Europe and the British Isles in the Neolithic and Bronze Ages, before the spread of the Celts. In Ireland a mythical race called the Tuatha de Danaan lived in barrows and in shelters burrowed under hills and mounds. They were shy and hard-working, and, as stronger races invaded and conquered with their iron weapons, they retreated into the woodlands to live secretive lives. They were pagan and continued to worship pagan deities. They were close to nature and had keen psychic senses. Some were skilled in metals and mining, and some were herdsmen, keeping stocks of diminutive cattle and horses.

Some maintained a guerilla warfare against invaders. The legends of Robin Hood and Rob Roy may be related to fairy lore.

The elusive fairy races were regarded with suspicion and superstition by the larger races and gradually became endowed in popular belief with magical attributes and characteristics. These races, such as the Lapps, Picts and Romano-British-Iberian peoples, were not so small as to be unable to mingle with the Celts, Normans and Saxons. Many were made into servants and serfs, while some married and mixed bloodlines. Prior to the 13th century, having fairy blood was admired.

Of the four main ideas, the latter two may be most likely: the small races became identified as fairies and were ascribed the supernatural abilities and characteristics of nature spirits in lore.

Fairy lore. Physical characteristics of fairies vary. Some are tiny, winged, gossamer creatures a few inches tall who can alight on a drop of water and barely make it tremble. Some are dwarfs and "little people" barely smaller than mortals. Others are giants. Fairies are both ugly and beautiful. They are usually mischievous and unpredictable and must be placated by gifts of food and spotlessly clean houses. The superstitious refer to them as "the good people" or "the good neighbors" in order to stay in the fairies' good graces.

When won over by a mortal, fairies may be very generous with gifts, either material or psychic such as clairvoyance or the ability to heal. Some are evil and malevolent. Many are lascivious and enjoy seducing mortals; some even marry mortals. In general, it is considered bad luck to talk about fairies and their activities. To do so invites a beating from them and the instantaneous disappearance of all the gifts bestowed by the fairies, such as wealth and possessions, and even the fairy lovers or spouses themselves.

Fairies are nocturnal creatures and like to drink, dance and sing. Their music is exquisite. Their color is green, which is also identified with witches. Green clothing perhaps helps them to blend into their forests; some are said to have green skin. They keep many animals, including dogs, cattle and sheep, which usually are red and white in color, but they do not keep cats or fowl. In Irish folklore, cats are regarded as fairies, generally as evil ones. The crowing of COCKS drives away fairies, as well as witches and DEMONS.

Like the Fates, fairies love to visit the newborn babies of mortals and will not hesitate to steal those that are unbaptized, or "little pagans," substituting in their place changelings—wizened fairy children. Fairies particularly desire fair-haired children, to improve their own hairy stock. To protect infants against kidnapping by fairies, an open pair of IRON scissors traditionally was hung over them in the cradle—for iron is believed to repel fairies—or an iron PIN was stuck in their clothes. Other measures

included laying the trousers of the child's father across the cradle; drawing a circle of fire around the cradle; making a sign of the cross over the child; sprinkling it and the cradle with holy water; and giving it a nickname. The latter relates to beliefs in the magic power of names (see NAMES OF POWER). If fairies do not know the true name of a child, they will not be able to cast a magical spell over it. In lore, witches were said to collude with fairies to steal babies or children for money, infants who were ugly, retarded or unruly were written off as changelings. It was believed that the changelings could be induced to confess if they were set afire, and many babies may have died that way.

In the early Middle Ages, fairies were said to be visible to all. As time went on, they acquired more and more supernatural powers and became invisible to all but those with second sight. Fairies who were captured by mortals were said to pine away and die quickly if they could not escape. Mortals who visited Fairyland, an enchanted land beneath the ground, discovered that time passes very slowly for fairies: what seemed like a few days translated into years when the mortals returned to the physical world.

Some fairies were said to suck human blood like vampires. On the Isle of Man, it was believed that if water was not left out for them, they would suck the blood of the sleepers in the house or bleed them and make a cake with the blood. The fairies would then leave some of the blood cake hidden in the house; it had to be found and given to the sleepers to eat, or they would die of a sleeping sickness. (See HORNED WOMEN for a description of blood cakes attributed to witches.)

Fairies and witches. According to British anthropologist MARGARET A. MURRAY and others, real "little people" gradually became identified with witches. In the 16th and 17th centuries, when fairy beliefs were at their height, fairies and witches were often blended together. Both could cast and break SPELLS, heal people and divine lost objects and the future. Both danced and sang beneath a full moon—often together—and trafficked with the Devil. Both could change shape, fly, levitate and cause others to levitate (see METAMORPHOSIS; FLYING; LEVITATION). Both stole unbaptized children and poisoned people. Both stole horses at night and rode them hard to their SABBATS, returning them exhausted by dawn. Both avoided SALT and both were repelled by iron. JAMES I of England, in *Daemonologie,* his book about witches, called DIANA, the goddess of witches, the "Queen of Faerie." Oberon, the name of the King of Fairies, was also the name of a demon summoned by magicians. Fairies were said to be the FAMILIARS of witches. It is no surprise, then, that fairies figured in numerous witch trials. Those richest in detail took place in the British Isles.

In 1566 John Walsh of Dorset was accused of witchcraft. He admitted being able to tell if a person was bewitched, a gift bestowed upon him partly by fairies, he said. The

A queen meets the Lion Fairy (FROM THE FAIRY TALE "THE FROG AND THE LION FAIRY" IN ANDREW LANG'S *THE ORANGE FAIRY BOOK*)

fairies, he claimed, lived in great heaps of earth in Dorsetshire and could be consulted for one hour, at either noon or midnight. Walsh also defined three kinds of fairies: green, white and black, and said the black were the worst.

Bessy Dunlop, a wise woman healer of Ayrshire, was accused of witchcraft and sorcery on November 8, 1576, She suddenly became a successful herbalist and healer and gained second sight, which helped her predict the recovery or death of patients and the location of lost objects.

In her trial, Dunlop testified that she had been taught these abilities by a phantom fairy named Thorne or Thome Reid. Reid told her that he had been ordered to be her attendant by the Queen of Elfhane. Many years before, when Dunlop was in childbirth, the Queen appeared before her as a stout woman, asked for a drink and was given one. Reid explained to Dunlop that afterwards, he had been killed in the battle of Pinkie on September 10, 1547, and had gone to Fairyland. He now served the Queen of Elfhane.

The ghostly Reid appeared many times before Dunlop, beseeching her to go away with him to Fairyland or to deny the Christian faith, in exchange for which he would grant her every wish. She denied him repeatedly, she testified. One day, Reid appeared with a company of eight women and four men. Reid explained that they were "good wights" (fairies) who lived in Elfland. They asked Dunlop to accompany them. When Dunlop remained silent, they left "with a hideous ugly howling sound, like that of a hurricane."

Reid continued to visit Dunlop, offering his assistance in healing sick animals and people. Eventually, he gave her herbal ointments and taught her how to use them and predict their effectiveness.

Dunlop would see Reid in town from time to time, though he remained invisible to others. He always appeared if she summoned him thrice. On every occasion, he begged her to come with him to Fairyland, sometimes tugging at her apron, but she always refused, which sometimes put him in an ill humor.

These supernatural visits went on for four years before Dunlop was brought down on charges of witchcraft. The fact that Dunlop had always used her new skills for good did not help her case; neither did her testimony that her benefactor was a fairy and not the Devil. Dunlop was convicted and burned at the stake.

A few years later, in 1588, Alison Pearson of Byrehill was charged with invoking the spirits of the Devil. She also was said to have a fairy familiar: her cousin, William Sympson, a physician who had been kidnapped by a Gypsy and had died. One day while Pearson was traveling, she felt ill and lay down. A green man (Sympson) appeared and said he would do her good if she would be faithful to him. The green man vanished and reappeared with a band of fairies, who cajoled Pearson into accompanying them and taking part in their drinking and merrymaking.

Pearson gradually became comfortable with her fairy friends. If she talked about their activities, however, she was tormented with blows that left insensitive spots on her skin. Sympson advised her of when the fairies were coming to her and of the fact that they usually arrived in a whirlwind. Sympson also taught her how to use herbal remedies and told her that every year, the Devil took one-tenth of the fairies away to hell as a tithe.

Like Dunlop, Pearson's confession only worsened her case. She also was convicted and burned.

ISOBEL GOWDIE, Scotland's renowned witch who voluntarily confessed in 1662, said she had frequent doings with fairies. Gowdie went often to Fairyland, entering through various caverns and mounds. The entrance of Fairyland was populated with elf-bulls, whose "roaring and skoilling" always frightened her. She often met with the King and Queen of Fairy, who were finely dressed and offered her more meat than she could eat. Gowdie, her fellow witches and the fairies would amuse themselves by metamorphosing into animals and destroying the homes of mortals.

Gowdie said the fairies manufactured their poisonous elf-arrow heads (see ELF ARROWS) in their caverns, and she had seen the Devil working alongside them, putting the finishing touches on the flints. Fairies taught her how to fly, by mounting cornstraws and beanstalks and crying, "Horse and Hattock, in the Devil's name!"

As late as 1894 beliefs in fairies and witches in Ireland caused the murder of Bridget Cleary of Clonmel, who was accused by her own husband and family of being a changeling wife. The trials of Michael Cleary and Bridget's relatives were Ireland's last involving witchcraft (see FAIRY WITCH OF CLONMEL).

Many contemporary Witches believe in fairies and some see them clairvoyantly. Some Witches say their Craft was passed down from fairies through the generations of their families.

FURTHER READING:

Briggs, K. M. *The Fairies in Tradition and Literature.* London: Routledge & Kegan Paul, 1978.

Briggs, Katharine. *An Encyclopedia of Fairies.* New York: Pantheon, 1976.

Evans-Wentz, W. Y. *The Fairy-Faith in Celtic Countries.* 1911. Reprint, Secaucus, N.J.: University Books, 1966.

Scott, Sir Walter. *Letters on Demonology and Witchcraft.* 1884. Reprint, New York: Citadel Press, 1968.

Yeats, W. B. *Irish Fairy and Folk Tales.* 1892. Reprint, New York: Dorset Press, 1986.

fairy light   See JACK-O'-LANTERN.

fairy ring   A natural mushroom fungus that grows in dark rings on grass and turf. In folklore it is said to be the site where FAIRIES and witches meet at night to dance and sing. The mushroom is inedible—and animals tend to shun it—and has a reddish, buff or tawny cap. It is common in Europe, the British Isles and North America and often appears after heavy rains. In Britain, fairy rings also are known as *hag tracks,* in the belief that they are created by the dancing feet of witches.

Because fairies are associated with MAGIC, fairy rings have magical superstitions attached to them. It is said that if one stands in the center of a fairy ring under a full MOON and makes a wish, the wish will come true. If one wishes to see and hear the fairies, who often are beyond the awareness of the five senses, one can run around a fairy ring nine times under a full moon. However, superstition holds, it is dangerous to do so on Samhain (All Hallow's Eve) or Beltane (May Eve), two major festivals of fairies (and witches), as the fairies may take offense and carry the mortal off to Fairyland.

Fairy rings are still associated with natural magic and are used by contemporary Witches as sites for meetings and seasonal festivals (see WHEEL OF THE YEAR.)

Fairies also are said to dance around stone circles.

FURTHER READING:

Briggs, Katherine. *An Encyclopedia of Fairies.* New York: Pantheon, 1976.

Fairy Witch of Clonmel (1894)   A young woman named Bridget Cleary, of Clonmel, County Tipperary, who was tortured and burned to death because her husband believed the fairies had spirited her away and substituted in her place a witch changeling.

Changelings are sickly fairy infants that fairies leave in the place of the human babies they are said to kidnap. However, many stories exist of fairies kidnapping mortal men and women—especially women—to be spouses of fairies in Fairyland.

Sometime in March 1894 Michael Cleary, a man who may have suffered from mental disturbances, began to think something was strange about his 26-year-old wife, Bridget. She seemed more refined. She suddenly appeared to be two inches taller. Cleary, whose mother had acknowledged going off with fairies, immediately suspected foul play by the "little people." He confronted his wife and accused her of being a changeling. When she denied it, he began to torture her with the help of three of her cousins, James, Patrick and Michael Kennedy; her father, Patrick Boland; her aunt, Mary Kennedy; and two local men named John Dunne and William Ahearne.

The townsfolk of Clonmel noticed that Bridget was missing for several days. Hearing that Bridget was sick, a neighbor, Johanna Burke, tried to pay a visit but found the door to the house barred. She encountered William Simpson and his wife, neighbors who also were attempting to pay a visit but were not admitted to the house. The three looked in a window and eventually convinced Cleary to let them in.

The neighbors were aghast to see Bridget, clad only in nightclothes, held spread-eagled on the bed by the Kennedy boys and Dunne, while Boland, Ahearne and Mark Kennedy looked on. Michael Cleary was attempting to coerce his wife into drinking a mixture of milk and herbs (probably a fairy antidote), saying, "Take it, you witch." Cleary repeatedly asked her, "Are you Bridget Boland, wife of Michael Cleary, in the name of God?" Bridget kept crying, "Yes, yes," but Cleary did not seem to believe her. Dunne suggested holding her over the kitchen fire, which Cleary and Patrick Kennedy did, while Bridget writhed and screamed and begged the visitors in vain for help. In fairy lore, setting fire to someone is considered a failproof way to expose changelings and induce the fairy parents to return the stolen human.

Bridget continued to insist that she was Bridget Boland, wife of Michael Cleary, and finally was put to bed. Everyone except Cleary seemed satisfied that Bridget was not a witch changeling.

The next day, Cleary approached William Simpson and asked to borrow a revolver, explaining that Bridget was with the fairies at Kylegranaugh Hill, a fairy fort, and he was going to go "have it out with them." Cleary also claimed that Bridget would ride up to the house at midnight on a big gray horse, bound with fairy ropes, which had to be cut before she could return as a mortal. Simpson told Cleary he had no revolver. Later, he saw Cleary heading for Kylegranaugh Hill, carrying a big knife.

That night, Johanna Burke returned to the Cleary house to find Bridget sitting by the fire talking to Boland, Cleary and Patrick Burke, Johanna's brother. Cleary flung his wife to the ground and forced her to eat bread and jam and drink tea—fairies do not have to eat mortal food—and threatened her with more punishment if she did not. He again demanded to know her true identity, and she insisted she was Bridget, not a witch changeling.

Cleary's rage increased. He tore off her clothes and grabbed a hot brand from the fire and held it up to her mouth. He refused to let anyone out of the house until he got his wife back. Then he threw lamp oil over Bridget and set her afire. Later Burke described what happened:

> She lay writhing and burning in the hearth, and the house was full of smoke and smell . . . she turned to me and screamed out, "Oh Han, Han." . . . When I came down Bridget was still lying on the hearth, smoldering and dead. Her legs were blackened and contracted with the fire. . . . Michale [sic] Cleary screamed out, "She is burning now, but God knows I did not mean to do it. I may thank Jack Dunne for all of it."

Cleary and Patrick Burke put Bridget's remains in a sack and buried them in a shallow grave about a quarter of a mile away. The remains, with the legs, abdomen, part of the back and the left hand nearly burned away, were found on March 22. Witnesses came forward. Cleary, Boland, the Kennedy boys and aunt, Ahearne and Dunne were charged with willful murder. In the investigation, two more men were charged: William Kennedy, another cousin, and Dennis Ganey, an herb doctor. The trial lasted two weeks.

A jury found all defendants guilty of manslaughter, a lesser charge, and the judge sentenced all to jail. Cleary received the harshest sentence: 20 years of hard labor. Even as he was sentenced, he still believed the fairies had stolen his wife and left a changeling witch in her place.

FURTHER READING:
Seymour, St. John D. *Irish Witchcraft and Demonology.* Dublin: Hodges, Figgis & Co., 1913.

familiars   In folklore, low-ranking DEMONS in constant attention to witches for the purpose of carrying out SPELLS and bewitchments. Familiars usually assumed animal forms—CATS, TOADS, OWLS, mice and dogs were the most common—though virtually any animal or insect could be suspected. In witchcraft trials, if so much as a fly buzzed in the window while a witch was being questioned or tried, it was said to be her familiar. The inquisitors took the Bible to heart: those who had familiars were

Three witches and their familiars (WOODCUT FROM THE *WONDERFUL DISCOVERIE OF THE WITCHCRAFTS OF MARGARET AND PHILIP [PA] FLOWER,* 1619)

"an abomination unto the Lord" (Deut. 23:10–12) and should be "put to death: they shall stone them with stones: their blood shall be upon them" (Lev. 20:27).

Familiars—also called IMPS—were said to be given to witches by the DEVIL or bought or inherited from other witches. A witch could have several of them. Cats were the favored forms, especially black ones. The fear that all cats were witches' familiars was one of the reasons for cat massacres that swept through medieval Europe.

Familiars were given names like any household pets, which most of them undoubtedly were. One 16th-century Essex woman accused of witchcraft admitted that she had three familiars in the form of mice: Littleman, Prettyman and Daynty. Another had four mice named Prickeare, James, Robyn and Sparrow. Elizabeth Clark, the first victim of MATTHEW HOPKINS, England's great witch-hunter of the 17th century, confessed to having five familiars, including unearthly ones: Holt, a kitten; Jamara, a fat, legless spaniel; Sack and Sugar, a black rabbit; Newes, a polecat; and Vinegar Tom, a long-legged, greyhoundlike creature with an ox's head and broad eyes, which could turn itself into a headless four-year-old child. Other familiars named in trials included Grizel, Greedigut, Peck in the Crown and Elemauzer. Perhaps the best-known familiar name is Pyewackett, the monicker of the witch's cat in the movie *Bell, Book and Candle,* and a name that dates to Renaissance England. Pyewackett, Hopkins stated, was a name "no mortal could invent."

Witches were said to take great care of their familiars. As Emile Grillot de Givry described in *Witchcraft, Magic and Alchemy* (1931) "they baptized their toads, dressed them in black velvet, put little bells on their paws and made them dance." Familiars were dispatched to bewitch people and animals into sickness and death. They also protected their witches. In return, witches gave them what they craved: BLOOD. ALICE KYTELER of Kilkenny, Ireland, convicted as a witch in 1324, confessed (or perhaps was made to confess) that she sacrificed red COCKS to her familiar. It was believed that witches allowed familiars to suck blood from their fingers or any protuberance or unnatural spot on the skin. The existence of WITCH'S MARKS was proof of suckling familiars and therefore of being a witch—enough evidence to get witches hanged.

Familiars also were said to assume more than one shape. Agnes Waterhouse, an Englishwoman accused of witchcraft in 1566, had a cat familiar named Satan that could change into a dog (see METAMORPHOSIS). Familiars also could vanish at will. It should be noted that the appearance of the Devil himself as an animal was not the same as the appearance of a familiar.

If a witch was arrested, she was often tied up and left in a cell, while inquisitors watched secretly to see if her familiars came to her aid. Even an ant or cockroach crawling toward her was called a familiar.

Religion was a CHARM against the familiar's infernal power. Waterhouse was said to be unable to harm one man through her familiar cat because of his religious beliefs.

During the witch hysteria, the obsession with familiars was most prevalent in England and Scotland, where they are mentioned in numerous trial records, especially those related to Hopkins. The Witchcraft Act of 1604 made it a felony to "consult, covenant with, entertain, employ, feed, or reward any evil and wicked spirit to or for any intent or purpose." But the *MALLEUS MALEFICARUM* (1486), the major witch inquisitor's handbook, offers no instructions concerning familiars in the interrogation and trial of witches. The book does acknowledge that an animal familiar "always works with her [witch] in everything." It also advises inquisitors never to leave witch prisoners unattended, because the Devil "will cause her to kill herself." The Devil might accomplish that through a familiar.

There is scant evidence of familiars in early American witch trials. In the Salem trials in 1692, John Bradstreet was indicted for "inciting a dog to afflict." The dog was tried and hanged as a witch (see SALEM WITCHES).

Outside of witch trials, more benevolent familiars were believed to exist, serving wizards and wise men and women who were magicians or village healers. The familiars helped diagnose illnesses and the sources of bewitchment and were used for divining and finding lost objects and treasures. Magicians conjured them with rituals, then locked them in bottles, RINGS and STONES. They sometimes sold them as charms, claiming the spirits would ensure success in gambling, love, business or whatever the customer wanted. This sort of familiar technically was not illegal; England's Witchcraft Act of 1604 specifically prohibited only evil and wicked spirits.

Some familiars were said to be FAIRIES. *Oberon* was a popular name for fairy familiars in 15th- and 16th-century England.

Familiars in contemporary witchcraft. Many modern witches have animal familiars, usually cats, which are their magical helpers. Some also have dogs, birds, snakes or toads. Witches do not believe the familiars are "demons" or spirits in animal form but simply animals whose psychic attunement makes them ideal partners in MAGIC. Some Witches say it is possible to endow pets with magical powers and turn them into familiars, though others don't believe it should be done. Still others believe familiars are never pets (and should not be treated as such) but are animals who volunteer to work as familiars and are karmically attracted to Witches. Witches who do not have familiars send out psychic "calls" to draw in the right animal.

Familiars reputedly are sensitive to psychic vibrations and power and are welcome partners inside the MAGIC CIRCLE for the raising of power, the casting of spells, SCRYING, spirit contact and other magical work. They also serve as psychic radar, reacting visibly to the presence of any negative or evil energy, whether it be an unseen force or a person who dabbles in the wrong kind of magic. Familiars are given psychic protection by their Witches.

Some Witches also use the term *familiar* to describe thought-forms created magically and empowered to carry out a certain task on the astral plane.

Familiars in sorcery and shamanism. Sorcerers and shamans around the world have helpers in the form of spirits (see SORCERY; SHAMANISM). Dispatching them on errands to harm or kill is called *sending.* The physical shape of a familiar varies. New Guinea sorcerers rely on snakes and crocodiles, while in Malaya, the familiar is usually an owl or badger passed down from generation to generation.

In Africa, the wild creatures of the bush are said to be witches' familiars: for the Lugbara, they are the toad,

A witch's familiar outside her door (WOODCUT FROM FRANCESCO MARIA GUAZZO'S *COMPENDIUM MALEFICARUM,* 1608)

snake, lizard, water frog, bat, owl, leopard, jackal and a type of monkey that screeches in the night; for the Dinka, they are black cobras and hyenas. The Zulus' familiars are said to be corpses dug up and reanimated with magic; they are sent out on night errands to scare travelers with their shrieking and pranks. The Ndembu of Zambia believe that evil men create spirit familiars out of the blood of their victims and send them out to kill others. The Pondo witches, also of Africa, are women who are said to have sex with their light-colored spirit familiars (see AFRICAN WITCHCRAFT).

In shamanism, a novice shaman acquires his familiar, or totem, spirits, usually manifested in animal, reptile or bird, shapes, when he completes his initiation. He may send them out to do battle in his place, but if they die, so does the shaman. Familiars usually stay with their shaman until death, then disappear. Among certain Eskimos, the familiar is embodied in an artificial seal, not a live animal.

See WITCH OF ENDOR.

FURTHER READING:

Howey, M. Oldfield. *The Cat in Magic, Mythology, and Religion.* New York: Crescent Books, 1989.

Maple, Eric. *The Dark World of Witches.* New York: A.S. Barnes & Co., 1962.

Thomas, Keith. *Religion and the Decline of Magic.* New York: Charles Scribner's Sons, 1971.

Valiente, Doreen. *An ABC of Witchcraft Past and Present.* 1973. Reprint, Custer, Wash.: Phoenix Publishing, 1986.

Farrar, Janet (1950–) and Stewart (1916–2000)

English witches whose "progressive witchcraft" work has had a major influence on the Craft. Janet and Stewart Farrar were initiated by the flamboyant Alex Sanders but were able to transcend the showmanship that surrounded Sanders and his COVEN, and went on to form their own covens in England and Ireland. Their Craft is sometimes called "reformed Alexandrian" and "post-Alexandrian," but the Farrars avoided applying a sectarian label to their work. They preferred to call themselves simply Wiccans working on the Pagan path.

Pre-Wiccan backgrounds. Janet Farrar was born Janet Owen in Clapton, London, on June 24, 1950. Her father, Ronald Owen, came from an English and Welsh background; her mother, Ivy (née Craddock), was Irish. Both parents were hospital workers and followers of the Church of England. Ivy Owen died when Janet was five.

Janet attended Leyton Manor School in London and Royal Wanstead High School for Girls in Sawbridgeworth, Hertfordshire. After graduation, she worked as a model and receptionist. In 1970, she was initiated into the coven of ALEX AND MAXINE SANDERS, which led to her meeting Stewart Farrar the same year.

Stewart Farrar was born on June 28, 1916, in Highams Park, Essex. His father, Frank Farrar, an Englishman,

Janet Farrar and Stewart Farrar (COURTESY JANET AND STEWART FARRAR)

worked as a bank official, and his mother, Agnes (née Picken), a Scotswoman, worked as a schoolteacher. Stewart was raised a Christian Scientist, but at 20 he turned agnostic until he was initiated into the Craft in 1970.

Stewart was educated at City of London School and University College, London, where he studied journalism. He served as president of the London University Journalism Union and as editor of *London Union Magazine.* He graduated in 1937.

In 1939, Stewart volunteered for the army and became an instructor in gunnery, antiaircraft. He served until discharged in 1946 with the rank of major. Following military service, he worked as a civilian public relations and press officer for the Allied Control Commission for Germany until 1947.

In 1947, he embarked on a career as journalist, author and scriptwriter. From 1947–50, he worked as sub-editor and then deputy night editor in the London office of Reuters. He joined the British Communist Party and from 1953 to 1954 worked as a reporter and editor for the party's *Daily Worker.* Disillusioned, he left it and the party in 1954. From 1956 to 1962, Stewart was a scriptwriter for

Associated British Pathé, where he worked on television documentaries and a feature film, and for the company's associate, A.B.C. Television (now known as Thames Television) where he worked on dramas. As a freelance writer, Stewart authored radio scripts for the British Broadcasting Corporation, short stories for magazines and books. His first book, a detective novel, *The Snake on 99,* was published in 1958.

From 1969 to 1974, Stewart worked as a feature writer for the weekly *Reveille,* a job that led to his introduction to witchcraft. Late in 1969, Stewart was sent to a press preview of the film *Legend of the Witches.* Alex and Maxine Sanders, who had given technical advice for the film, were to be present, and *Reveille* was interested in a story. Stewart was skeptical about Witchcraft, but was impressed with Sanders upon meeting him. Sanders invited Stewart to attend a witch's initiation, which Stewart did, and found it both dignified and moving. He wrote a two-part feature for the magazine, which gained him Sanders' trust. Sanders told him the publisher of his biography, *King of the Witches,* was looking for an author to write another book on modern witchcraft. Stewart got the contract for *What Witches Do* and began attending the Sanders' training classes. At first, he was a sympathetic but skeptical outsider. What he learned, however, struck a positive, personal chord, and on February 21, 1970, Maxine Sanders initiated him into the coven, where he met Janet Owen.

Wiccan and Pagan activities. On December 22, Stewart and Janet left the Sanders' coven to form their own coven in London. The Sanders separated shortly after that; the last time Stewart and Janet ever saw Alex again was in 1971. The same year, *What Witches Do* was published. Despite its inclusion of Sanders' fabricated stories about himself—and Stewart's assertion that Sanders ranked above GERALD B. GARDNER and alongside ALEISTER CROWLEY and Eliphas Levi in terms of magical achievement—the book helped to establish Stewart as a major voice in the Wiccan community. Though Stewart later admitted he had been too credulous and that he no longer put Sanders on the same or better footing with Crowley, Levi and Gardner, he refused to disparage "the enfant terrible of British witchcraft." Sanders, he said, made a significant contribution to the Craft.

From 1970 to 1976, Stewart and Janet developed their coven. On January 31, 1974, they were handfasted. They were legally married in a civil ceremony on July 19, 1975, with Stewart's two sons and two daughters from a previous marriage in attendance. In 1974, Stewart left *Reveille* to work full time as a freelance writer.

In 1976, the Farrars turned their coven over to Susan and David Buckingham and moved to Ireland, where they built up a new coven. Other Irish covens eventually hived off of it. About 75 percent of all Wiccans in Ireland have their origins with the Farrars or one of their initiates.

What Witches Do brought an unending stream of mail from people seeking help in joining the Craft. After nine years of running a coven and being sought out for advice, the Farrars jointly authored two books of ritual and nonritual material, *Eight Sabbats for Witches* (1981) and *The Witches' Way* (1984). The books were combined and published in the United States as *A Witches Bible Compleat* (1984). The books included rituals created by the Farrars, plus a wealth of material relating to the religion of the Craft. *The Witches' Way* provides the first thorough reconstruction of the evolution of the Gardnerian BOOK OF SHADOWS, as developed by Gardner and DOREEN VALIENTE and includes contributions from Valiente.

For years, the Farrars continued as leaders in dispelling myths and misconceptions about Wicca and in making it more available to the public. They stressed that their books were to be taken as guidelines for coven working and were not to be taken as traditional.

Until 1989, the Farrars' experiences with the broader Pagan movement were within the European theater. In 1991, they did their first tour in the United States, where they discovered progressive change and growth within the Pagan community. Stewart envisioned the emergence of a diverse "Pagan Global Village," with Wicca being but one path in it. The Farrars make frequent lecture tours to the States, as well as in Europe. In 1998 they became ministers with the United States–based AQUARIAN TABERNACLE CHURCH and were given the charter for the ATC in Ireland.

Their work has evolved along with Wicca and Paganism, reflecting less Kabbalistic ceremonial magic and more shamanic elements, the latter of which the Farrars view as part of the core of traditional Witchcraft. They advocated a progressive practice of the Craft, fluid and changing in accordance to need.

In 1989, the Farrars met GAVIN BONE, and in 1993 added him as a permanent member of their polyamorous family. Bone assumed the roles of webmaster and general business manager. Their Web site led to the formation of the Pagan Information Network, now operated under the aegis of the Aquarian Tabernacle Church.

In 1995, Stewart suffered a stroke, and Bone helped to nurse him back to health. Stewart suffered a heart attack on February 7, 2000, and died in his sleep at home in Kells, County Meath, Ireland. He was cremated, and his ashes were scattered at a undisclosed megalithic site close to his home at the summer solstice.

Janet and Bone were married on May 5, 2001. They continue their collaboration in writing and educational activities for the Craft.

Awards: The Presentation Shield from the WITCHES LEAGUE OF PUBLIC AWARENESS in 1991 for their educational books and the Gerald B. Gardner Lifetime Achievement Award (with Gavin Bone) in 2003.

Books: Other books the Farrars wrote are *The Witches' Goddess* (1987), *The Witches' God* (1989), *Spells and How They Work* (1990). With Bone they wrote *The Pagan Path* (1995), *The Healing Craft: Healing Practices for Witches,*

Pagans and the New Age (1999), and *The Complete Dictionary of European Gods and Goddesses* (2001). Janet and Bone coauthored *Progressive Witchcraft: Spirituality, Training and the Mysteries in Modern Wicca* (2004).

Stewart Farrar's other fiction works include two additional detective novels: *Zero in the Gate* (1960) and *Death in the Wrong Bed* (1963); a romance novel, *Delphine, Be a Darling* (1963); and seven occult novels: *The Twelve Maidens* (1974); *The Serpent of Lilith* (1976); *The Dance of Blood* (1977); *The Sword of Orley* (1977); *Omega* (1980); *Forcible Entry* (1986); and *Backlash* (1988).

fetish   An object, usually a West African wooden doll, that is possessed by spirits and represents those spirits to the fetish owner. Fetishes may also be animals' teeth, snake bones, beautiful stones or even the huts where WITCH DOCTORS commune with spirit guides. They are often worn as ornamental AMULETS or carried on the body.

A fetish is supposed to possess magical powers and be capable of bringing about the owner's designs or preserving him from injury (see MAGIC).

Possession of a fetish by a slave in the New World was punishable by sadistic torture and death. Not only were the fetishes graven images of a god other than the Catholic one, they represented tribal ways feared by white masters.

See AFRICAN WITCHCRAFT.

Fian, John (?–1591)   A young schoolmaster in Saltpans, Scotland, in the late 16th century, Dr. John Fian was the central figure in Scotland's most famous witch trials, which involved James VI (JAMES I) himself. Fian, also known as John Cunningham, was accused of leading a COVEN of witches in North Berwick who, among other charges attempted to assassinate the king. Fian was brutally tortured until he confessed and was burned at the stake in 1591.

The downfall of Fian was brought about by a young servant girl named Gillis Duncan, whose gift for natural HEALING was suspected by her master as the Devil's MAGIC. Under TORTURE, she accused several persons of witchcraft, including Fian (see NORTH BERWICK WITCHES). Fian, who had a reputation as a conjurer, was arrested on December 20, 1590, and charged with 20 counts of witchcraft and high treason.

The most important charge was that of the attempted murder of King James as he sailed to Denmark to fetch his bride-to-be. The witches allegedly raised a terrible storm at sea by tossing a CHARM of a dead CAT with human limbs tied to its paws into the ocean and crying "Hola!" On the return voyage, Satan then cast a "thing like a football" into the sea, raising a mist. The king's vessel was battered about but returned safely with no casualties (see STORM RAISING). Other charges against Fian included acting as

John Fian and his coven fly widdershins around the church (FROM F. ARMYTAGE IN SIR WALTER SCOTT'S *LETTERS ON DEMONOLOGY AND WITCHCRAFT*; COURTESY MARY EVANS PICTURE LIBRARY)

secretary at the COVEN meetings, at which he recorded the oaths of allegiance to Satan; kissing the Devil's anus (see KISS OF SHAME) and making a DEVIL'S PACT; falling into ecstasies and trances, during which his spirit was transported to various mountains; bewitching a man to have a spell of lunacy once every 24 hours because he loved the same woman as Fian; attempting to seduce the woman by bewitching her, but instead bewitching a heifer that followed him about "leaping and dancing . . . to the great admiration of all the townsmen of Saltpans"; robbing graves for body parts to use as CHARMS; and various acts of magic, such as FLYING through the air. He was also accused of putting magical CANDLES on the legs of his horse and upon his staff, which enabled him to turn night into day as he rode.

Upon his arrest, Fian was imprisoned. He refused to confess and was subjected to severe torture. After having his head "thrawed" with a rope (bound and twisted in various directions), he still denied the charges. Fian was then given a torture described as "the most severe and cruell paine in the world," the "boots," a vise that went around the legs from knee to ankle, and that was progressively tightened with blows from a hammer. Fian was given three hammer blows while in the boots, and passed out. His torturers "found" two pins under his tongue, thrust in up to their heads. The court declared that the pins were a witch's charm to prevent him from confessing.

Fian was released from the boots and taken before King James. Broken, he confessed in his own writing. He renounced the DEVIL and vowed to lead the life of a Christian. He was taken back to jail.

The following day, the jailors found Fian greatly distressed. He said the Devil had appeared before him in the night, dressed in black and carrying a white wand, and had demanded that he continue his service in accordance with his pact. Fian said he stood firm in his renunciation, but the Devil reminded him that he still would possess Fian's soul upon death. The Devil broke the wand and vanished.

All that day, Fian languished in depression. That night, he stole the key to the prison door and fled to Saltpans. The king had the area scoured. Fian was soon arrested and brought again before James. He recanted his confession.

James was convinced that Fian had entered into a new pact with the Devil. He had Fian's body searched for a new DEVIL'S MARK, but none could be found. Determined to get another confession out of the schoolmaster, James ordered more brutal torture, described as follows in a pamphlet, *Newes from Scotland* (1591):

> His nailes upon all his fingers were riven and pulled off with an instrument called in Scottish a turkas, which in England wee called a payre of pincers, and under everie nayle there was thrust in two needles over, even up to the heads; at all which tormentes, notwithstanding, the

Doctor never shronke anie wit, neither woulde he then confess it the sooner for all the tortures inflicted upon him.

Then was hee, with all convenient speed, by commandement, convaied againe to the torment of the bootes, wherein he continued a long time, and did abide so many blowes in them, that his legges were crusht and beaten together as small as might bee, and the bones and flesh so bruised, that the blood and marrow spouted forth in great abundance, whereby they were made unserviceable for ever.

Fian still would not confess, "so deeply had the Devil entered into his heart." The enraged king nevertheless condemned him to die. Fian was put into a cart and taken to Castle Hill in Edinburgh, where a great bonfire was prepared. On a Saturday at the end of January, 1591, he was strangled and thrown immediately into the flames.

FURTHER READING:
Kors, Alan C., and Edward Peters. *Witchcraft in Europe, A Documentary History 1100–1700.* Philadelphia: University of Pennsylvania Press, 1972.

Sharpe, C. K. *A History of Witchcraft in Scotland.* Glasgow: Thomas D. Morison, 1884.

Firth, Violet Mary   See DION FORTUNE.

Fitch, Ed   American Wiccan high priest and key founder of the PAGAN WAY. Born in Roxboro, North Carolina, to a family with Russian roots, Ed Fitch grew up in various locations around the country because of the moves required of his father, who worked in the construction trade. At age nine, he and his father sighted a UFO over their ranch in northern California. Fitch remembers that a circular object about 50 feet in diameter, with an aura of orange flames, rose up from a nearby mountain and cruised silently over the ranch.

Fitch spent four years at the Virginia Military Institute, where he began a lifelong research into the paranormal. After graduation, he entered the Air Force and was sent to Japan, where he ran a courier station, carrying secret documents from a spy organization that evesdropped on Soviet activities in Siberia. While there, he delved into Buddhism and Shinto.

After three years, Fitch returned to civilian life in the United States, working as a technical writer and electronics engineer in Washington, D.C. It was now the 1960s, and contemporary Witchcraft and Paganism were spreading around the country. Fitch was initiated into the Gardnerian tradition of Witchcraft by Raymond and Rosemary Buckland (see RAYMOND BUCKLAND) and rose to the rank of high priest. He also was trained in trance channeling by Spiritualist mediums from the CHURCH OF ALL WORLDS.

The Air Force called him back to duty during the Vietnam war and stationed him in Thailand, which provided him with another opportunity to learn about Eastern religions and mysticism. He obtained a black belt in Tae Kwon

Do, which introduced him to Zen thought and action, a discipline that has stuck with him throughout life.

In Thailand, Fitch wrote two books the were never formally published but that later circulated in the Pagan community and became "underground classics": *The Grimoire of the Shadows,* a book of magical training techniques, and *The Outer Court Book of Shadows,* which reconstructs the magical and seasonal rituals of ancient Crete, Greece and Druidic Europe (see also BOOK OF SHADOWS). Material from these books continues to be in new traditions and rituals, sometimes being labeled as an "ancient Celtic tradition from Ireland and Scotland."

After Thailand, Fitch was reassigned to North Dakota to work on the redesign of Minuteman rockets. During this time he became part of a informal group that created the Pagan Way. Fitch composed introductory and background materials and public rituals and was instrumental in the forming of the first Pagan Way grove, in Chicago.

The Air Force sent Fitch next to southern California. He left the military as a captain and obtained a master's degree in systems management from the University of Southern California. He went to work for a major aerospace firm as a research and development engineer.

In the growing Pagan movement, Fitch helped to organize and chair two Pagan Ecumenical Councils, which established the COVENANT OF THE GODDESS as an international umbrella organization for Pagans in 1975. Fitch also published for a time *The Crystal Well,* a magazine of neo-romantic Paganism, which resulted in a published book, *Magical Rites from the Crystal Well* (1984).

In the 1980s Fitch remained active as a Gardnerian high priest and became involved in Odinism, a form of Norse Paganism that stresses conservative, family-oriented values. Fitch's other books are *Castle of Deception: A Novel of Sorcery and Swords and Other-worldly Matters, with Seven Short Essays on the Reality of Matters Supernatural* (1983), *The Rites of Odin* (1990), and *A Grimoire of Shadows: Witchcraft, Paganism & Magic* (1996).

During the 1990s, Fitch held various jobs as a private detective, Disneyland shopkeeper and editor of a small publisher. He moved to Washington, D.C., to work for the Federal Aviation Administration. In 1997, he returned to southern California to work in the aerospace industry again.

Fitch turned his creative efforts to the dark Goddess, SHAMANISM, dance magick and Goth and to television and film projects.

fivefold kiss   A ritual kissing of five parts of the body, done in certain rites and ceremonies, such as HANDFASTING, in some traditions of contemporary Witchcraft. It is done within a MAGIC CIRCLE and is symbolic of the homage paid by the God and the GODDESS to each other. The fivefold kiss can be done man to woman or woman to man. The kisses may be given on the parts of the body which, with arms and legs outstretched, correspond to points of a pentacle: head, arms or hands; legs or feet. Or, eight kisses may be given in five body points: on each foot; on each knee; above the pubic hair; on each breast; on the lips. Each kiss is accompanied by a blessing, such as the following:

> Blessed be thy feet that have brought thee in these ways; blessed be thy knees that shall kneel at the sacred altar; blessed be thy womb [phallus], without which we should not be; blessed be thy breasts, formed in beauty [strength]; blessed be thy lips that shall utter sacred names.

FURTHER READING:
Farrar, Janet, and Stewart Farrar. *A Witches Bible Compleat.* New York: Magickal Childe, 1984.

flying   A belief during the witch hunts, that the DEVIL, his DEMONS and witches could transport themselves and others through the air. Flying (also called *transvection*) was done with the aid of a BROOM, fork or shovel, according to lore; some witches were said to ride demons who were transformed into animals such as goats, cows, horses and wolves (see METAMORPHOSIS). The Devil had the power to pick people up and whisk them through the air with no visible means of transport or support.

While a popular belief, flying was not accepted universally during the centuries of witch-hunting in Europe. As early as the 10th century, flying was disputed as impossible. The *CANON EPISCOPI* said that if witches flew, it was in their imaginations. But in the late 15th century, the *MALLEUS MALEFICARUM,* the bible of witch-hunters and judges, lamented this "erroneous" view, saying it allowed witches to go unpunished.

The Devil reputedly could transport whomever he pleased at whim. Stories tell of children and adults be-

Witch takes flight on demon (WOODCUT FROM FRANCESCO MARIA GUAZZO'S *COMPENDIUM MALEFICARUM,* 1608)

ing picked up in their sleep and flown through the air for miles. One 15th-century German priest claimed he saw a man "borne on high with his arms stretched out, shouting but not whimpering." The fellow, the priest said, had been drinking beer with friends. One of the men went fetch more beer, but upon opening the door of the tavern, saw a mysterious cloud, became frightened and refused to go. The man who was picked up and flown said he would go instead, "even if the Devil were there."

Witches, sorcerers and necromancers were said to be able to fly with the help of magical OINTMENTS consisting mostly of baby fat that had been boiled off the limbs of a young child who had been killed before baptism. Such ointments also contained various herbs and drugs, which doubtless put witches into hallucinatory states in which they really believed they were flying. One witch in Italy in 1560 rubbed herself with ointment and went into a trance. When she came out of it, she said she had been flying over mountains and seas. In 14th-century Italy, necromancers reportedly made beds fly with magical INCANTATIONS.

The speed of flight was great, and novices were prone to fall off their forks or broomsticks. Sometimes the demons who rode with them pushed them off. One story tells of a German man who convinced a sorcerer to fly him to a SABBAT. En route, the sorcerer threw him off the broom. The man fell into a strange country that was so far away, it took him three years to get home.

Church BELLS were supposed to be able to ground brooms, and in some towns, the church bells were run constantly during witch festivals to prevent witches from flying overhead.

While some demonologists and inquisitors did not believe that witches could actually fly, they accepted confessions of it, reasoning that if witches *thought* they could fly, it was just as incriminating as if they actually did so. Many witches did confess to flying. Some said it was possible to fly either bodily or by imagination. If a witch wanted to observe a sabbat without actually being there, all she had to do was lie down on her left side and breathe out a blue vapor, in which she could watch the activities—a medieval version of clairvoyance.

Flying is not mentioned much in English cases of witches. The various witchcraft acts in effect between 1542 and 1736 outlawed many witchcraft practices but did not prohibit flying.

Magical and mystical flight. Various magical and spiritual disciplines place importance on the ability to fly. The act of flying is not as important as what the flying signifies: the soul's breaking free of the bonds of earth and soaring into the cosmos, accessing realms that others reach only through death. Flying is a transcendent experience, a flight of the spirit.

Magical and mystical flight is attributed to alchemists, mystics, sorcerers, shamans, medicine men, yogis and fakirs, as well as Witches. In many shamanic rites, the shaman identifies with, or becomes, a bird in order to take flight. Each magical/spiritual system has its own techniques for achieving the ecstasy of flight,

A witch abducts a young woman on her broom (OLD WOODCUT)

though breathing, meditation, contemplation, dancing, drumming, chanting and/or hallucinogenic drugs (see SHAMANISM).

Mystical flight is attained by many modern Witches, many of whom blend Eastern and shamanic spiritual elements into contemporary Witchcraft.

FURTHER READING:
Lea, Henry Charles. *Materials Toward a History of Witchcraft.* Philadelphia: University of Pennsylvania, 1939.
Russell, Jeffrey Burton. *Witchcraft in the Middle Ages.* Ithaca and London: Cornell University Press, 1972.
Summers, Montague, ed. *The Malleus Maleficarum of Heinrich Kramer and James Sprenger.* 1928. Reprint, New York: Dover Publications, 1971.

footprints   Footprints are reputed to contain the essence of a person and may be used in magical CHARMS and SPELLS. Dust or dirt taken from a footprint may be used to obtain power over the person who made the print, just as clippings of HAIR AND NAILS, bits of clothing, URINE and excrement are believed to have magical potential. In the lore of Lithuania, footprint dirt buried in a graveyard will cause someone to fall fatally ill. Australian aborigines believe they can magically cause lameness by placing bits of glass or sharp stones in a footprint. In European folk MAGIC, lameness is caused by putting some earth from a footprint, a nail, a needle and broken glass into a kettle, and boiling the mixture until the kettle cracks. In VODUN magic, dirt from a footprint placed in a GRIS-GRIS, or charm bag, will cause a person to follow one. In parts of Africa, great care is taken to obliterate footprints, lest a witch or sorcerer use them for harmful magic.

FAIRIES also are associated with the magic of footprints. In Irish lore, if you are passed by fairies on All Hallow's Eve, you should throw the dirt from your footprint after them, which will force them to surrender any humans they have taken captive.

In cases of POSSESSION and poltergeist hauntings, strewing ashes about the house will help identify the demon from prints left in the ashes.

FURTHER READING:
Leach, Maria, ed., and Jerome Fried, assoc. ed. *Funk & Wagnall's Standard Dictionary of Folklore, Mythology and Legend.* New York: Harper & Row, 1972.

Fortress of Dumbarton   Legendary fortress at Dumbarton, Scotland, near Glasgow on the Clyde River, created by a band of angry WITCHES in pursuit of St. Patrick. Around the year 388, the DEVIL became so offended at the piety of St. Patrick that he incited "the whole body of witches in Scotland" against the saint. In an army, the witches attacked St. Patrick, who fled toward the Clyde. At the mouth of the river, he found a little boat, leaped into it and set off for Ireland. The witches were unable to cross running WATER—another folk belief—and in anger, they ripped off a huge chunk of rock from a nearby hill and hurled it after the saint. Their aim was so bad that the rock fell harmlessly to the ground. Later, the rock was turned into a fortress.

FURTHER READING:
Sharpe, C. K. *A History of Witchcraft in Scotland.* Glasgow: Thomas D. Morison, 1884.

Fortune, Dion (1891–1946)   The magical name of Violet Mary Firth, British occultist and author whose books continue to have an impact on modern WITCHCRAFT and PAGANISM. Considered one of the leading occultists of her time, Dion Fortune was an adept in ceremonial MAGIC and was perhaps one of the first occult writers to approach magic and hermetic concepts from the psychology of Jung and Freud (see HERMETICA). Some contemporary Witches and Pagans consider her fiction more important than her nonfiction, for her novels contain Pagan themes and are a rich source for rituals.

Fortune was born into a family of Christian Scientists and displayed mediumistic abilities in her teen years. In her early twenties, she worked as a law analyst at the Medico-Psychological Clinic in London. Her interest in exploring the human psyche resulted from an unpleasant episode in 1911, when, at age 29, she went to work in a school for a principal who took a great personal dislike to her. When Fortune went to see the woman to announce she was leaving her job, she was subjected to invective that she had no self-confidence and was incompetent. Fortune said later that the principal also conveyed this by psychic attack, using yogic techniques and hypnotism that left Fortune a "mental and physical wreck" for three years.

As a result, she studied psychology, delving into the works of both Freud and Jung. She preferred the ideas of Jung but eventually concluded that neither Freud nor Jung adequately addressed the subtleties and complexities of the mind. The answers, Fortune felt, lay in occultism.

In 1919 Fortune joined the Alpha and Omega Lodge of the Stella Matutina, an outer order of the HERMETIC ORDER OF THE GOLDEN DAWN, and studied under J. W. Brodie-Innes. She experienced clashes with the wife of S. L. MacGregor-Mathers, one of the founders of the Golden Dawn, which she again felt were forms of psychic attack. She left Stella Matutina in 1924 and founded her own order, the Community (later Fraternity) of the Inner Light. The order initially was part of the Golden Dawn but later separated from it.

Fortune worked as a psychiatrist, which brought her into contact with other cases of psychic attack. She was a prolific writer, pouring her occult knowledge into both novels and nonfiction. Her pen name was derived from the magical motto she adopted upon joining the Stella Matutina, "Deo Non Fortuna," ("by God, not chance"), which became shortened to Dion Fortune. Her books are considered classics and continue to enjoy wide readership.

For a time she lived in Glastonbury and became deeply interested in the Arthurian legends and magical-mystical lore centered there. She wrote about Glastonbury in *Avalon of the Heart*.

Fortune used her experiences with psychic attack to conclude that hostile psychic energy can emanate both deliberately and unwittingly from certain people and that one can mentally fend off such energy. Her book *Psychic Self-Defense* (1930) remains the best guide to detection and defence against psychic attack.

One of her most famous books is *The Mystical Qabbalah* (1936), in which she discusses the Western esoteric tradition and how the Qabbalah (see KABBALAH) is used by modern students of the Mysteries. The true nature of the gods, she said, is that of magical images shaped out of the astral plane by mankind's thought, and is influenced by the mind.

Her other major nonfiction works include *Sane Occultism* (1929); *The Training and Work of an Initiate* (1930); *Through the Gates of Death* (1932); *Applied Magic; Aspects of Occultism*; and *Spiritualism in the Light of Occult Science. Machinery of the Mind* (1922) was published under her given name. But it is her novels that have captured the most interest among modern Witches and Pagans. In particular, *The Goat-Foot God* (1936) concerns the powers of Pan, a HORNED GOD, and offers a wealth of details on LEYS; *The Sea-Priestess* (1938) concerns the power of Isis, the moon goddess, and has been used by modern witches as an inspiration for creating rituals and invocations. Her other novels are *The Secrets of Dr. Taverner* (1926), about an adept who runs an occult nursing home; *The Demon Lover* (1927); and *The Winged Bull* (1936).

Fortune was married to Dr. Thomas Penry Evans. She died in January 1946.

The Fraternity of the Inner Light remains based in London and now is known as the Society of the Inner Light. It offers techniques in the Western esoteric tradition. The Society stresses that Fortune was not a Witch and was not involved with any COVEN, and that the Society is not connected with Witchcraft in any way.

FURTHER READING:

Knight, Gareth. *Dion Fortune and the Three Fold Way*. London: S.I.L. (Trading) Ltd., 2002.

Richardson, Alan. *Priestess: The Life and Magic of Dion Fortune*. Wellingborough, Eng.: The Aquarian Press, 1987.

fox fire   See JACK-O'-LANTERN.

Fox, Selena (1949–)   American Wiccan high priestess, Pagan scholar, ecospiritual minister and ritual artist. Selena Fox is renowned for her leadership role in the international Wiccan-Pagan community and for founding CIRCLE SANCTUARY, a legally recognized Wiccan church with a worldwide Pagan ministry.

Selena Fox (PHOTO BY LYNNIE JOHNSTON; COURTESY NATIONAL FILM BOARD OF CANADA)

Born October 20, 1949, in Arlington, Virginia, Fox was raised in a fundamentalist Southern Baptist family. As a child, she began having mystical experiences, out-of-body travel and psychic visions. Upon reaching her teens, she pursued her interest in dreams, the psychic and parapsychology and learned how to give psychic readings with Tarot cards. She left the Southern Baptist Church while in high school, citing a number of reasons, including the church's disapproval of dancing and its refusal to allow women to become pastors.

Fox attended the College of William and Mary in Virginia, graduating cum laude in 1971 with a bachelor of science degree in psychology. At the age of 21, she led her first Pagan ritual as president of Eta Sigma Phi, the classics honor society. She led the society in a reenactment of a Dionysian rite of spring, which took place outdoors in the center of campus.

After college, she worked on an archaeological dig in nearby Hampton, Virginia, where she met a woman who was a hereditary Witch. Realizing her own spiritual orientation had much in common with her friend's Craft, Fox embraced Witchcraft as a religion and later was initiated as a high priestess in several Wiccan traditions.

Following the archaeological work, Fox spent several years in various jobs, including work as a photographer and publications editor for a large corporation.

In October 1974, Fox conceived the name, logo and central spiritual focus for Circle, also known as Circle Sanctuary. Fox, along with her partner, Jim Alan, and a group of friends, formed the beginnings of Circle Sanctuary, with periodic meetings at the Fox-Alan home in Sun Prairie, near Madison, Wisconsin. In 1978, Fox decided to devote herself full time to the Wiccan ministry. The same year, Circle Sanctuary was incorporated as a Wiccan church.

In 1979, Fox and Alan were evicted from their Sun Prairie farmhouse by a prejudiced landlord. After several moves to other farmhouses in the Madison area, they settled on land near Barneveld and Mt. Horeb, Wisconsin, and created Circle Sanctuary, a nature preserve, organic herb farm and church headquarters.

Fox and Alan ended their common-law relationship in 1984, and Alan eventually left Circle Sanctuary to devote himself to a writing career. In 1986, Fox married DENNIS CARPENTER, a Wiccan priest and former school psychologist and now a renowned Pagan scholar. Fox and Carpenter live on Circle Sanctuary and work together to coordinate Circle Sanctuary's diverse activities and responsibilities: networking, publishing, research, counseling, education and nature preservation.

In 1995, Fox earned a master's degree in counseling at the University of Wisconsin in Madison and became certified as a clinical psychotherapist. Soon after graduation, she was invited into a public practice in a mental health facility in Madison, where she works as a staff psychotherapist with a mainstream clientele. She also has a private spiritual counseling practice at Circle.

Fox travels extensively throughout the world, participating in interfaith dialogue and networking, and working for various environmental, peace, social, civil rights and women's studies efforts. She also works to preserve sacred sites in North America and elsewhere. Her involvement with the interfaith and academic communities has increased dramatically since the late 1980s, in response to interest in and study of contemporary Pagan traditions. In 1995, she was the first to publish a study on Pagans as a distinct cultural population with special needs in terms of recovery therapy.

In addition, her public work includes lectures, workshops and seminars on Paganism, spiritual growth and psychology to all kinds of audiences in colleges and universities, learning centers, conferences, churches and Pagan gatherings. She does nature therapy, psychic healing, Tarot readings, dream work, guided creative visualizations and other types of spiritual healing services. For the media, she is a leading spokesperson on Wicca and Paganism and was a leading activist in the veterans' PENTACLE QUEST .

Fox has been a prominent religious freedom activist in the Pagan movement. She has worked successfully on cases involving the right of Wiccans and Pagans to worship, allowing Wiccan priestesses to minister as clergy in prisons, securing paid Pagan holidays for a Canadian employee (see CHARLES ARNOLD) and helping Native American Indians protect sacred burial grounds and other types of sites, including rock art, in North America. In 1985, Fox was a leader in the effort to defeat the HELMS AMENDMENT in Congress, which sought to strip Wiccan churches of their tax-exempt status.

Fox founded WICCAN SHAMANISM, an interfaith blend of Wicca, cross-cultural shamanic practices and transpersonal psychology.

Through genealogical research, Fox has traced her Welsh and Scots family lines back several centuries and found a family tradition of "religious radicalism," which she feels she is part of and continues in her life. Ancestral land in Scotland includes caves decorated with Bronze Age artwork. Fox is descended from St. Margaret (ca. 1045–93), wife of King Malcolm III of Scotland.

Foxwood, Orion   Wiccan, author and CUNNING MAN in the Faery Faith. Orion Foxwood is founder of the Foxwood Temple of the Old Religion, a legal church in Maryland dedicated to the Elder Gods. He is well known for his teachings in WICCA, ritual, practical MAGIC and psychic development and the Faery Faith, a spiritual path of seership attunement with the faery realm.

Foxwood holds a master of human services degree from Lincoln University in Pennsylvania and a doctor of divinity degree from Ravenwood Church and Seminary of the Old Religion, Inc., in Atlanta, Georgia. He is trained in transactional analysis. He works as a licensed professional counselor and hyponotherapist, specializing in chemical dependency, AIDS and AIDS education and public health. Foxwood also works as a spiritual counselor, especially for life passages and grief and loss.

Foxwood is a high priest in Celtic/Traditional and Alexandrian Wicca as well as a priest in the Welsh Cymric Tradition. At Foxwood Temple, he teaches an oathbound and initiatory tradition. He is the elder and teacher to the groves and covens around the United States who have received their Wiccan lineage from him.

Foxwood has studied with R. J. Stewart and the Lady Circe, a hereditary witch and founder of Sisterhood and Brotherhood of Wicca in Toledo, Ohio. With Lady Circe, he established the Alliance of the Old Religion (AOTOR), a network of traditional covens and elders in the Craft that draw lineage from Lady Circe. The Alliance membership includes elders in eight states. Lady Circe named three mantle carriers: Foxwood (Lord Orion); Lady Meshalamthea of Toledo, Ohio; and Lord Malachi of Kewadin, Michigan. Lady Circe, who died in 2004, is the Queen of Foxwood Temple lineage.

Foxwood founded Foxwood Temple in 1990. The curriculum is a syncretic Mystery tradition, drawing from teachings, lore, and practices from Prytani Celtic, Strega, Alexandrian Wicca, Faery and Southern Conjure traditions. These are blended together into a unified spiritual path, Traditional Witchcraft or "The Old Religion."

The tradition emphasizes service to the divine through participation in sacred work, honoring of and communion with ancestors of the past, present, and future and adherence to a strict ethical code.

The Faery Faith teachings focus on reattunement to the spirits of the land, sea, wind, flame, human ancestry and the Elder race, known as the Faery. The attunement is achieved through the application of age-old lore, techniques, folk practices, inner contacts and wisdom of Faery Seership.

Foxwood was codirector of the Moonridge Center, a land-based nature sanctuary and mystical educational center located near Beltsville, Maryland. He also co-founded the Amber Web, an Internet spiritual resource for men.

Foxwood lectures widely. He is the author of *The Faery Teachings* (2003; 2007) and *The Tree of Enchantment: Wisdom of Faery Seership* (2008).

FURTHER READING:

Foxwood, Orion. *The Faery Teachings.* Arcata, Calif.: RJ Stewart Books, 2007.

———. *The Tree of Enchantment: Wisdom of Faery Seership.* York Beach, Me.: Samuel Weiser, 2008.

Frost, Gavin (1930–) and Yvonne (1931–) Witches, authors and founders of the CHURCH AND SCHOOL OF WICCA, located in Hinton, West Virginia. The Frosts have steadfastly followed their own path in the Craft, and whenever that took them out of mainstream views, they have weathered much criticism from others in the Wiccan/Pagan communities. Though the Frosts are Witches, they do not consider themselves Pagans, because they do not worship nature or named deities. They are

Gavin and Yvonne Frost (COURTESY GAVIN AND YVONNE FROST)

open about their Craft and view their work as a needed "information booth" to Pagans and non-Pagans alike.

Gavin Frost was born in 1930 in Staffordshire, England, to a Welsh family. The seeds of his interest in Witchcraft were planted in childhood, during which he spent holidays in Wales, a country steeped in folk magic, Witchcraft and the occult. From 1949 to 1952, he attended London University, graduating with a bachelor of science degree in mathematics and a doctorate in physics and math.

At the university, Gavin joined an informal group formed by T. C. Lethbridge, a demonstrator (laboratory assistant) who was interested in magic, the occult, dowsing and sacred stone sites (Lethbridge went on to write *Witches*, published in 1962, and other works). The group decided to undertake an INITIATION and sought the help of a pursuivant of the duke of Norfolk, who, as Earl Marshal, is the heraldic head of England. The duke's four pursuivants look after heraldic designs, and their offices correspond to the four directions. The initiation was carried out at a stone circle in Boskednan, Cornwall, in 1951. The initiates received a mark cut onto their wrists.

While working on infrared missiles in the Salisbury Plain for an aerospace company—a job which required nighttime hours—Frost had ample time to explore Stonehenge and its environs during the day. He became further intrigued about the megaliths and their mysterious builders and was led to the Craft.

Gavin lived in Germany from 1966 to 1968, where he joined the Zauberers, an occult group of sorcerers in the Bayrischen Naehe, south of Munich. The group's required initiation was to hike up to the top of a mountain in the middle of the night in winter. The test of this centered on one's ability to generate one's own body heat, like the *tumo* taught to Tibetan monks. Gavin was able to pass the snow line, but did not reach the mountaintop. Nonetheless, he qualified as a Zauberer.

Gavin was married from 1951 to 1969. He has two children, a son and a daughter, from that marriage.

Yvonne Frost was born Yvonne Wilson in 1931 in Los Angeles into a "foot-washing Baptist" family. After struggling through her childhood and teen years to come to terms with the Baptist faith, Yvonne began a comparative study of religions in her early adult years to find a more compatible faith. Her family heritage includes two long lines of Witches going back for generations to the Cumberland Gap of Kentucky and to Clan Gunn of Scotland.

In 1950 she married a military man and spent time in Germany. When the marriage ended 10 years later (there were no children), she enrolled in Fullerton Junior College in Fullerton, California, to earn an A.A. degree in secretarial skills. She graduated in 1962.

Meanwhile, Gavin's career in the aerospace industry had taken him to Ontario, Canada, and then to California. He and Yvonne met in the 1960s in the halls of their mutual employer, a major aerospace company in

Anaheim. She was involved in Spiritualism and was exploring spiritual alternatives, and he was involved in Witchcraft. Together they studied psychic development with a Spiritualist teacher. A career move took them to St. Louis, where they pursued the Craft and Yvonne was initiated into the Celtic tradition.

Seeing the confusion about Witchcraft and Wicca in the general population in the United States, and reading of negative behaviors being called Witchcraft, they decided they would try to change the popular image of the religion they had espoused. They coauthored a book, *The Witch's Bible,* but could not find a publisher for it. As an alternative, they organized the material as correspondence courses and advertised the School of Wicca in magazines. The federal recognition of the church followed in 1972. The Frosts married in 1970; they have one daughter, Bronwyn, who works with them at the church and school.

In 1972, Gavin left his aerospace career to devote himself full time, along with Yvonne, to the numerous activities of the church and school. They moved to Salem, Missouri, and then to New Bern, North Carolina, in 1974–75. In 1996 they moved to Hinton, West Virginia.

Both Gavin and Yvonne have doctor of divinity degrees from the Church of Wicca. Gavin serves as archbishop and Yvonne as bishop. They are the Arch-Flamen and Flamenca, respectively, of the Western Neighborhood, or high priest and high priestess of the eternal flame. They have taken vows of poverty.

The Frosts do healing work and have been active public speakers. They are prolific authors, with more than 22 books and monographs. *The Witch's Bible* remains one of their best-sellers and has been periodically updated. In 1991 it was retitled *Good Witch's Bible.* Other notable titles are *The Magic Power of Witchcraft* (1976), *Helping Yourself with Astromancy* (1980), *Astral Travel* (1982), *Tantric Yoga* (1989), the first Western book on the subject to be translated into Hindi, *Good Witch's Guide to Life* (1991), *The Prophet's Bible* (1991), *Who Speaks for the Witch?* (1991), *Witch Words* (1993), *Good Witch's Bible* (1999), *The Witch's Magical Handbook* (2000), *The Witch's Book of Magical Ritual* (2002), *A Witch's Guide to Psychic Healing: Applying Traditional Therapies, Rituals, and Systems* (2003), *The Solitary Wiccan* (2004) and *Good Witches Fly Smoothly: Surviving Witchcraft* (2006).

Gallows Hill The execution site of those condemned as witches in the infamous witch trails in Salem, Massachusetts. Gallows Hill has been believed to be haunted ever since the trials in 1692–93. Nineteen men and women were hanged from the trees at Gallows Hill. The site was long considered the meeting grounds for witches at annual SABBATS. It also was oracular: young persons who wished to know their future in marriage, and the identities of their future spouses, would go to Gallows Hill at night and listen for the answers to be revealed to them by the ghosts of the dead witches. Whenever an important event was about to happen, the neighborhood would be filled with the screechings and screamings of the haunting witches (see GHOSTS, HAUNTINGS AND WITCHCRAFT). Gallows Hill is now a residential area.

See SALEM WITCHES.

Gardner, Gerald B(rousseau) (1884–1964) English Witch and founder of contemporary Witchcraft as a religion. As much myth as truth surrounds Gerald B. Gardner. Some of the truth about his motivations and actions may never be known. The posthumous assessment of him is that he was a con man and an artful dissembler, yet he had great vision and creativity and was willing to try outrageous things. The religion that he helped to launch and shape has evolved far beyond what he is likely to have forseen.

Hereditary Witches and practitioners of family tradition witchcraft object to Gardner being credited as the "founder" of the religion of Witchcraft, claiming that family traditions have existed for centuries. Nonetheless, there is no evidence that an organized religion of Witchcraft—not simply traditions of folk and ceremonial magic mixed with occultism and fragments of pagan traditions—existed prior to Gardner.

Gardner was born into a well-to-do family in Blundellsands, near Liverpool, England, on Friday, June 13, 1884. His father was a merchant and justice of the peace, a member of a family that had made money in the timber trade. According to Gardner, the family's roots could be traced to Grissell Gairdner, who was burned as a witch in 1610 in Newburgh. Gardner's grandfather married a woman reputed to be a witch, and some of Gardner's distant relatives were purported to have psychic gifts. Gardner's ancestral family tree also included mayors of Liverpool and Alan Gardner, a naval commander and later vice admiral and peer, who distinguished himself as commander in chief of the Channel fleet and helped to deter the invasion of Napoleon in 1807.

The middle of three sons, the young Gardner was raised primarily by the family's nurse and governess, Josephine "Com" McCombie. He suffered severely from asthma. Com convinced his parents to let her take him traveling during the winters to help alleviate his condition. Com roamed about Europe, leaving Gardner to spend much time by himself reading. When Com married a man who lived in Ceylon, Gardner traveled there with her and worked on a tea plantation. Later, he moved to Borneo and then Malaysia to work.

Gerald B. Gardner, taken at the wedding of Arnold and Patricia C. Crowther on November 9, 1960 (PHOTO BY *DAILY EXPRESS;* COURTESY *DAILY EXPRESS* AND PATRICIA C. CROWTHER)

In the Far East, he became fascinated with the local religious and magical beliefs, and was drawn to ritual daggers and knives, especially the Mayalsian *kris,* a dagger with a wavy blade. He later wrote a book, *Kris and Other Malay Weapons,* published in Singapore in 1939. It was reprinted posthumously in England in 1973.

From 1923 to 1936, Gardner worked in the Far East as a civil servant for the British government as a rubber plantation inspector, customs official and inspector of opium establishments. He made a considerable sum of money in rubber, which enabled him to dabble in a field of great interest to him, archaeology. He claimed to have found the site of the ancient city of Singapura.

In 1927 he married an Englishwoman, Donna. The two returned to England upon his retirement from government work in 1936. Gardner spent much time on various archaeological trips around Europe and Asia Minor. In Cyprus he found places he had dreamed about previously, which convinced him he had lived there in a previous life.

His second book, *A Goddess Arrives,* a novel set in Cyprus and concerning the worship of the GODDESS as Aphrodite in the year 1450 B.C.E., was published in 1939.

In England Gardner became acquainted with the people who introduced him to the Craft. The Gardners lived in the New Forest region, where Gardner became involved with the Fellowship of Crotona, an occult group of Co-Masons, a Masonic order established by Mrs. Besant Scott, daughter of Theosophist Annie Besant. The group had established "The First Rosicrucian Theater in England," which put on plays with occult themes. One of the members told Gardner they had been together in a previous life and described the site in Cyprus of which Gardner had dreamed.

Within the Fellowship of Crotona was another, secret group, which drew Gardner into its confidence. The members claimed to be hereditary Witches who practiced a Craft passed down to them through the centuries, unbroken by the witch-hunts of the Middle Ages and Renaissance. The group met in the New Forest. Just days before World War II began in 1939, Gardner was initiated into the coven in the home of OLD DOROTHY CLUTTERBUCK.

Gardner was intensely interested in MAGIC and witchcraft and invested much time in extending his network of contacts in occultism. He collected material on magical procedures, especially ceremonial magic, which he put together in an unpublished manuscript entitled *Ye Bok of ye Art Magical.*

In 1946, he met CECIL WILLIAMSON, the founder of the Witchcraft Research Centre and MUSEUM OF WITCHCRAFT. In 1947, he was introduced to ALEISTER CROWLEY by ARNOLD CROWTHER. Gardner was especially interested in gleaning whatever he could from Crowley, who by then was in poor health and only months away from death. Gardner obtained magical material from Crowley. From this and other sources, he compiled his BOOK OF SHADOWS, a collection of rituals and Craft laws. Gardner claimed to have received a fragmentary book of shadows from his New Forest coven.

Crowley made Gardner an honorary member of the Ordo Templi Orientis (OTO), a Tantric sex magic order at one time under Crowley's leadership, and granted Gardner a charter to operate an OTO lodge.

Gardner was prevented from being too public about Witchcraft because it was still against the law in England. He disguised his book of shadows in a novel, *High Magic's Aid,* published in 1949 under the pseudonym Scire. The novel concerns worship of "the old gods" but mentioned by name only Janicot. The GODDESS had yet to make a major appearance in Gardner's Craft—although he said that his coven worshiped the Goddess by the name of Airdia or Areda (see ARADIA).

The anti-witchcraft law was repealed in 1951. Gardner broke away from the New Forest coven and established his own.

He became involved in Williamson's Museum of Witchcraft in Castletown on the Isle of Man, officiating at its opening and serving for a time as its "resident Witch." In 1952, he bought the museum buildings and display cases from Williamson and operated his own museum.

In 1953 Gardner initiated DOREEN VALIENTE into his coven. Valiente substantially reworked his book of shadows, taking out most of the Crowley material because his "name stank" and giving more emphasis to the Goddess. From 1954 to 1957 Gardner and Valiente collaborated on writing ritual and nonritual material, a body of work which became the authority for what became known as the Gardnerian tradition.

Gardner's first nonfiction book on the Craft, *Witchcraft Today*, was published in 1954. It supports anthropologist MARGARET A. MURRAY's now meritless theory that modern Witchcraft is the surviving remnant of an organized Pagan religion that existed during the witch-hunts. Murray wrote the introduction for Gardner's book. The immediate success of *Witchcraft Today* led to new covens springing up all over England and vaulted Gardner into the public arena. He made numerous media appearances, and the press dubbed him "Britain's Chief Witch." He loved being in a media spotlight, which cast him in the curious position of initiating people into a "secret" tradition that was then spread all over the tabloids. The publicity, much of it negative, led to a split in his coven in 1957, with Valiente and others going separate ways.

In 1959 Gardner published his last book, *The Meaning of Witchcraft*. In 1960 he was invited to a garden party at Buckingham Palace in recognition of his distinguished civil service work in the Far East. The same year, his wife (who never joined the Craft or participated in any of its activities) died, and he began to suffer again from asthma. In 1963, shortly before he left for Lebanon for the winter, he met RAYMOND BUCKLAND, an Englishman who had moved to America and who would introduce the Gardnerian tradition to the United States. Gardner's high priestess, MONIQUE WILSON (Lady Olwen), initiated Buckland into the Craft.

On Gardner's return home from Lebanon by boat in 1964, he suffered heart failure and died at the breakfast table on board the ship on February 12. He was buried ashore in Tunis on February 13.

In his will, Gardner bequeathed the museum, his ritual tools and objects, notebooks and the copyrights of his

Gardner's house in Malew Street, Castletown, Isle of Man. House is on right. The barn, at left, held Gardner's covenstead on the upper floor and a workshop on the ground floor, where Gardner made his magical tools. Patricia C. Crowther and others were initiated in the covenstead. (PHOTO BY IAN LILLEYMAN; COURTESY PATRICIA C. CROWTHER)

books to Wilson. Other beneficiaries of his estate were PATRICIA C. CROWTHER and Jack L. Bracelin, author of a biography on Gardner, *Gerald Gardner: Witch* (1960). Wilson and her husband operated the museum for a short time and held weekly coven meetings in Gardner's cottage. They then closed the museum and sold much of the contents to the Ripley organization, which dispersed the objects to its various museums. Some of the items have since been resold to private collections.

Valiente describes Gardner as a man "utterly without malice," who was generous to a fault and who possessed some real, but not exceptional, magical powers. His motives were basically good and he sincerely wanted to see "the Old Religion" survive. Others, such as Williamson, saw him as manipulative and deceitful, not above fabrication in order to accomplish his objectives: to establish an acceptable venue for his personal interests in naturism and voyeuristic sex. (Gardner was a nudist, and the ritual nudity in the Craft is likely to have been one of his inventions; hereditary Witches say they have worked robed.)

Unfortunately, Gardner's personal papers prior to 1957 no longer exist. He destroyed them at Valiente's urging during the aforementioned period of unfavorable publicity.

From the 1960s onward, Witchcraft, the religion, continued to grow and spread around the world. Initially, new Witches accepted Gardner's assertion of an old and unbroken heritage, but that was soon exposed as unfounded. The Gardnerian tradition has inspired other traditions, and Witchcraft has taken on a life of its own as a predominantly Goddess-centered mystery religion, part of a larger reconstruction and revival of PAGANISM.

Whatever his flaws and foibles, Gardner deserves respect and credit for what he started. As scholar Ronald Hutton notes, contemporary Witchcraft, or Wicca, is the only religion that England has ever given to the world.

FURTHER READING:
Adler, Margot. *Drawing Down the Moon*. Revised ed. New York: Viking, 1986.
Bracelin, J. L. *Gerald Gardner: Witch*. London: Octagon Press, 1960.
Crowther, Patricia. *Witch Blood!* New York: House of Collecticles, Inc., 1974.
Farrar, Janet, and Stewart Farrar. *The Witches' Way: Principles, Rituals and Beliefs of Modern Witchcraft*. Custer, Wash.: Phoenix Publishing, 1988.
Gardner, Gerald B. *Witchcraft Today*. London: Rider & Co., 1954, 1956.
———. *The Meaning of Witchcraft*. New York: Magickal Childe, 1982. First published 1959.
Hutton, Ronald. *The Triumph of the Moon: A History of Modern Pagan Witchcraft*. Oxford: Oxford University Press, 1996.
Kelly, Aidan A. *Crafting the Art of Magic Book I: A History of Modern Witchcraft, 1939–1964*. St. Paul: Llewellyn Publications, 1991.

Valiente, Doreen. *The Rebirth of Witchcraft*. London: Robert Hale, 1989.

garlic   A protection against witches, DEMONS, vampires, the EVIL EYE and other dark supernatural forces, and an ingredient in folk HEALING remedies. Garlands of garlic worn around the neck or hung in a house are said to ward off evil spirits, creatures and SPELLS. In Mexico, the *ajo macho* is a huge garlic, sometimes as big as a baseball, used exclusively as an AMULET against evil in general, but not against specific CURSES, which require their own special remedies. According to custom, the *ajo macho* will work only if it is given as a gift, not if it is bought. In Europe, the phrase "here's garlic in your eyes" is said to ward off the evil eye.

In times past, garlic was used to prove guilt. Suspects tossed garlic cloves into a fire; the one whose clove popped was guilty.

In healing folklore, garlic is widely reputed for its ability to cure and prevent colds and other ailments. It is baked in bread, ground into powder and made into liniment. Ancient Roman soldiers wore garlic into battle for extra courage. In ancient Greece and Rome, garlic was placed at CROSSROADS as an offering to HECATE, the goddess of WITCHCRAFT and the night. Odysseus used garlic as protection against the witchcraft of CIRCE, who turned his men into swine.

FURTHER READING:
Leach, Maria, ed., and Jerome Fried, assoc. ed. *Funk & Wagnall's Standard Dictionary of Folklore, Mythology and Legend*. New York: Harper & Row, 1972.

garters   Ornaments with magical properties, and in contemporary Witchcraft, sometimes worn in various rituals and as badges of rank. Garters may have been used in rituals in Paleolithic times: an ancient cave painting in northeastern Spain portrays nine women, wearing pointed headdresses, dancing in a circle around a naked man, who wears a cord or garter tied under each knee.

Garters are prominent in folklore and folk MAGIC. The color of a garter carries special meaning. Green, for example, is the color of FAIRIES and Robin Hood. Garters are worn by Morris dancers, and "Green Garters" is the name of an old tune used in Morris dancing. RED is protection against bewitchment; SILVER is associated with the MOON.

In witch trials, garter, or "pointes," were associated with the DEVIL. Accused witches often described the Devil's clothing as being tied with garters, as in this description by Margaret Johnson of Lancashire in 1633: ". . . a spirit or divell in the similtude and proportion of a man, apparelled in a suite of black, tyed about with silke pointes." MARGARET A. MURRAY, a British anthropologist, said that the garter was a secret symbol of identification among medieval witches; however, no evidence exists that witches were widely or uniformly organized.

In WICCA, the garter is the emblem of the high priest-ess of the Craft. Some garters are made of green snakeskin or leather, or green or blue velvet, and decorated with a silver buckle.

See ORDER OF THE GARTER.

FURTHER READING:

Farrar, Janet, and Stewart Farrar. *A Witches Bible Compleat.* New York: Magickal Childe, 1984.

Murray, Margaret A. *The Witch-Cult in Western Europe.* London: Oxford University Press, 1921.

Gaufridi, Father Louis See AIX-EN-PROVENCE POS-SESSIONS.

ghosts, hauntings and witchcraft Hauntings by ghosts and poltergeists are sometimes blamed on witches and witchcraft, particularly in areas where fear of MAGIC runs high. In Brazil, for example, where fear of magic is strong among the working class, many cases of poltergeist activity are attributed to witches' CURSES laid on families.

The notion that witches were responsible for ghosts and hauntings took root on the Continent and in the British Isles after the Protestant Reformation of the 16th century. The belief that dead men walk the earth as ghosts has been universal since ancient times. The Catholic Church used ghosts to its own ends, teaching that they were the souls of those stuck in purgatory, who could not rest until they atoned for their sins, and that they were sent by God to roam the realm of the living. The Reformation rejected the concept of purgatory and said all souls went straight to heaven or hell, from which they never emerged. This required a new explanation for ghosts. In general, the Prot-estant church denied their existence, claiming that ghosts were a Catholic fraud used to manipulate the masses. Those who did see ghosts were led to think that they were caused by the DEVIL, DEMONS and witches, who also were manipulating the populace in a battle for souls. Two camps formed: those who dismissed ghosts as foolishness and those who saw ghosts as proof of demonic forces.

JAMES I of England, who said there existed a "fearful abounding" of witches in the land, gave credit to the Dev-il for all ghosts. Witches, being viewed as the servants of the Devil, were automatically connected to apparitions and hauntings. During the 17th century, hauntings often were blamed on the witchcraft of malicious neighbors or relatives. It was not uncommon to call upon the services of another witch or WIZARD to exorcise the haunting (see EXORCISM).

The Drummer of Tedworth. One of the most famous cases of alleged witchcraft-caused hauntings was a poltergeist case, the Drummer of Tedworth, which took place in England in 1661. In March of that year, the drummer had been annoying the town of Ludgarshall, Wiltshire, with his drum beating. John Mompesson, of the neighbor-ing town of Tedworth (formerly Tidworth), had the man

Manifestations of the Devil (JOSEPH GLANVIL, *SADUCISMUS TRIUMPHATUS*, 1689 ED.)

taken before the justice of the peace. The drum was con-fiscated, and given to Mompesson to secure in his own home. The drummer persuaded the constable to release him, and he left the area.

In April, during Mompesson's absence, a violent storm of poltergeist activity erupted in his house, frightening his wife, children and servants. It began with a drum-ming noise heard outside the house and on top of it, which then moved indoors to the room where the confis-cated drum was kept. For more than two years, this and other bizarre phenomena occurred at irregular intervals, creating widespread interest and drawing curious visi-tors. The children and servants saw apparitions and the younger children were levitated in their beds. Some of the lesser phenomena—scratchings and pantings heard near the children's beds—were heard by Joseph Glanvil, who chronicled the case in *Saducismus Triumphatus* (1668).

Glanvil also reported the following: chairs walked about the room by themselves; a servant was chased by a stick of wood, while another was held by an invisible force; sulphurous and other foul odors filled the air, which became hot; clothing and children's shoes were thrown about; the sounds of coins jingling were heard; doors opened and shut violently by themselves; blue, glimmering lights were seen; footsteps and the rustling of invisible, silklike clothing were heard; clawlike marks were found in ashes, along with unintelligible letters and numerous circles; lighted candles floated up the chimney, and singing was heard in the chimney; a horse was found with its hind leg stuffed into its mouth so firmly that it took several men to pry it out with a lever; a servant saw "a great Body with two red glowring, or glaring eyes" standing at the foot of his bed; chamber pots were emptied onto beds, and a knife was found in one bed; and pocket money mysteriously burned black. The telltale phenomenon, however, was the words, "A Witch, A Witch," heard "for at least a hundred times" one morning in the children's room. The Mompesson household believed itself to be in the grip of a witch-sent demon or the Devil himself. Mompesson was approached by a wizard, who said the disturbances were caused by a "rendezvous of witches" and offered to perform an exorcism for 100 pounds. Mompesson apparently did not accept.

The vagrant drummer eventually surfaced in court again, this time at the Salisbury assizes where he was tried on theft charges, convicted and sent to the Gloucester goal. When a Wiltshire man visited the drummer, the drummer asked for news and was told there was none. The drummer reportedly replied, "No, do you not hear of the Drumming at a gentlemen's house in Tedworth? I have plagued him (or to that purpose) and he shall never be quiet, till he hath made me satisfaction for taking away my Drum." The drummer was swiftly charged with witchcraft and tried at Sarum. Numerous witnesses to the poltergeist activities testified against him.

The court banished the drummer and he left the area. Rumors surfaced later that in his wanderings he raised storms and frightened seamen. As long as he was gone, the Mompesson house was quiet, but whenever he returned to the area, the disturbances began again. Glanvil does not say if the Mompessons were plagued indefinitely or if the problem eventually went away.

Modern witchcraft, ghosts and hauntings. Witches are often blamed for hauntings in societies that have such expectations. In the industrialized West, only a small percentage of cases—less than 10 percent—are attributed to witchcraft.

Many contemporary witches exorcise haunting spirits. Like psychics, clerics and paranormal investigators, they are called into a home or building to send on the spirit of a departed animal or person. The witch contacts the spirit and either persuades it to depart or uses magical words of power to send it away.

Psychic energy also may manifest in artificially created forms that some Witches term "ghosts" and others call "thought-forms." In November of 1981 the coven of STEWART AND JANET FARRAR in Ireland acted to stop the illegal slaughter of gray seal pups by fisherman. The fisherman claimed the seals, which had their pups on the Ineshka Islands off the coast of Ireland, were a threat to salmon fishing. According to the Farrars, the COVEN magically created a gray-green thought-form named Mara (Gaelic for "of the sea") and instructed it to manifest as a ghost on the islands and frighten any seal-killers; she was not to harm any hunter unless he could be stopped no other way. At each full moon, the coven psychically recharged and reinstructed Mara. The Irish Wildlife Federation also sent volunteers to guard the seals. No massacres occurred in 1982 and 1983. Certainly the presence of the volunteers was a deterrent—but stories began to circulate about sightings of a mysterious woman, clad in a gray-green mackintosh, who moved among the seals without disturbing them.

According to Witches, ghostly remnants of thought-forms may also linger in a place where a great deal of psychic and magical work has been done, such as a Witches' covenstead. Unless banished by proper ritual, such energy is believed to be capable of poltergeistlike hauntings.

Another form of haunting, which may be exorcised by ritual magic, is that of nature spirits, or ELEMENTALS. Such beings are said occasionally to haunt newly constructed homes, buildings or roads, particularly if a secluded or wooded area was freshly cleared for the construction. Elemental hauntings are characterized by the presence of strange or uncomfortable sensations; invasions of pests; malfunctions of heating and electrical equipment; the unexplained failure of plants to grow or the wild overgrowth of plants; missing objects; and the appearance that the structure is askew.

FURTHER READING:

Finucane, R. C. *Appearances of the Dead: A Cultural History of Ghosts.* Buffalo, N.Y.: Prometheus Books, 1984.

Gauld, Alan, and A. D. Cornell. *Poltergeists.* London: Routledge & Kegan Paul, 1979.

Thomas, Keith. *Religion and the Decline of Magic.* New York: Charles Scribner's Sons, 1971.

girdle measuring   An old technique of magical HEALING by wise women and men, WIZARDS and witches involving the measuring of the patient's girdle or belt. Changes in girth revealed the presence of evil spirits or FAIRIES which had invaded the body to cause the illness. After exorcising the entity, usually through CHARMS, the witch took another measurement to verify that the spirit was gone. Some cures involved the recitation of charms, cutting up of the girdle and burying the pieces in the ground. Girdle measuring was a widespread practice in Europe and the British Isles through the end of the 16th century.

See SPIRIT EXORCISM.

Goat of Mendes   See BAPHOMET.

goblins   In French folklore, wandering sprites who attach themselves to households and both help and plague the residents. Goblins live in grottoes but are attracted to homes that have beautiful children and lots of wine. When they move in, they help by doing household chores at night and by disciplining children—giving them presents when they are good and punishing them when they are naughty. Goblins have an unpredictable, mischievous nature, and instead of doing chores at night will sometimes keep everyone awake by banging pots and pans, moving furniture, knocking on walls and doors and snatching bedclothes off sleeping persons. Goblins who become tiresome can be persuaded to leave by scattering flaxseed on the floor. The sprites get tired of cleaning it up every night.

Goblins are the equivalent of brownies in England and Scotland, *kobalds* in Germany, *domoviks* in Russia and other sprites in other countries. They have become associated with Halloween and are said to roam the night when the veil is thinnest between the world of the living and the world of the dead.

FURTHER READING:
Briggs, Katharine. *An Encyclopedia of Fairies.* New York: Pantheon, 1976.
Leach, Maria, ed., and Jerome Fried, assoc. ed. *Funk & Wagnall's Standard Dictionary of Folklore, Mythology and Legend.* New York: Harper & Row, 1972.

Goddess   In contemporary Witchcraft, the Goddess embodies the very essence of the Craft: she is the Great Mother, whose limitless fertility brings forth all life; she is Mother Nature, the living biosphere of the planet and the forces of the elements; she is both creator and destroyer; she is the Queen of Heaven; she is the MOON, the source of magical power; she is emotion, intuition and the psychic faculty. The Divine Force is genderless but is manifest in the universe in a polarity of the male and female principles. Most traditions of Witchcraft emphasize the Goddess aspect of the Divine Force, some almost to the exclusion of the HORNED GOD, the male principle. The Goddess is called by many names, each one representing a different facet or aspect. The Goddess also is recognized in Pagan traditions.

Worship of the Goddess, or at least the female principle, dates back to Paleolithic times. It has been suggested by some anthropologists that the first "God" was a female, who, according to the earliest creation myths, self-fertilized and created the universe from herself and reigned alone; that early agricultural religions were dominated by Goddess worship; that gods prospered only when graced with a beneficence and wisdom of the Goddess; and that early societies may have been matriarchal. "From me come all gods and goddesses who exist," says Isis in Apuleius's *The Golden Ass.* Robert Graves, in *The*

The Virgin on the Crescent. The Blessed Virgin absorbed pagan elements. Here she is both Virgin and Mother, with a crescent moon, symbol of the Goddess, at her feet. Note face of the Man in the Moon. (ALBRECHT DÜRER, CA. 1499)

White Goddess (1948), made a case for a widespread earth and moon Goddess cult, especially among the Celts, but his theory is not supported by evidence

Other scholars argue that existing evidence does not support those claims. While women have at times held status equal to men, there is no evidence that they have ever held superior status in a matriarchy. Goddess worship has been balanced by God worship and the worship of both male and female Supreme Deities. The sacred marriage of a Sky God and Earth Mother is a common theme in societies around the world.

Among the first human images found to date are the "Venus figures," naked female forms with exaggerated sexual parts, which date to the Cro-Magnons of the Upper Paleolithic period between 35,000 and 10,000 B.C.E. The Venus of Laussel, carved in basrelief on a rock shelter in southern France that apparently was once a hunting shrine, dates to ca. 19,000 B.C.E. She is painted in red ochre—perhaps suggesting BLOOD—and is holding a bison horn in one hand. Cro-Magnon cave paintings also depict women giving birth. A naked Goddess appeared to be patroness of the hunt to mammoth hunters in the Pyrenees and was also protectress of the hearth and lady of the wild things. Female figurines also have been found from the proto-Neolithic period of 7000–9000 B.C.E. In the Middle Neolithic period, ca. 6000–5000 B.C.E., figures of a mother holding a child appear. In the High Neolithic period, ca. 4500–3500 B.C.E., decorated female figurines presumably were objects of worship. In Africa, cave images of the Horned Goddess (later ISIS) date to 7000–6000 B.C.E. The Black Goddess was bisexual and self-fertilizing. In predynastic Egypt, prior to 3110 B.C.E., the Goddess was known as Ta-Urt ("Great One") and was portrayed as a pregnant hippopotamus standing on hind legs. In the Halaf culture on the Tigris River ca. 5000 B.C.E., Goddess figurines were associated with the cow, serpent, humped ox, sheep, goat, pig, bull, dove and double ax, symbols often connected to the Goddess in later historical periods. In the Sumerian civilization ca. 4000 B.C.E., the princess, or queen of a city was associated with the Goddess, and the king with the God.

The Goddess took on many aspects with the advance of civilization. She acquired a husband, lover or son who died or was sacrificed in an annual birth-death-rebirth rite of the seasons. She became creator, mother, virgin, destroyer, warrior, huntress, homemaker, wife, artist, queen, jurist, healer, sorcerer. She acquired a thousand faces and a thousand names. She has been associated with both the Sun and Moon, and Earth and sky.

The end of the Golden Age of the Goddess occurred between 1800 and 1500 B.C.E., when Abraham, the first prophet of the Hebrew God, Yahweh, is said to have lived in Canaan.

Many contemporary Witches feel the Goddess has been ignored and suppressed for too long by patriarchies. The powerful desire to worship the Goddess may be seen in the veneration accorded the Virgin Mary. Although officially the Virgin Mary is the human mother of the incarnate God, she is virtually deified by her many worshipers, who petition her in prayer.

Despite suppression by the Church, pagan Goddess cults, particularly of DIANA, flourished in Europe into and beyond the Middle Ages. The Church associated them, and all pagan deities, with evil and the DEVIL. Diana was said to be the Goddess of witches (see THE CANON EPISCOPI). As late as the 19th century, American folklorist CHARLES GODFREY LELAND claimed to have discovered material relating to a Diana/ARADIA cult of Tuscany.

In contemporary Witchcraft, the emphasis on the Goddess evolved out of the Witchcraft tradition developed by GERALD B. GARDNER, which he began publicly promoting in the 1950s, claiming an unbroken heritage along the lines of MARGARET MURRAY's unfounded theories. He said traditional and hereditary covens in Britain had emphasized the Horned God, and he himself seemed to prefer that. His earliest published writing, a novel of Witchcraft called *High Magic's Aid* (1949), makes no mention of the Goddess. In 1953, Gardner initiated DOREEN VALIENTE, who rewrote much of Gardner's rituals in his BOOK OF SHADOWS, and who gave more emphasis to the Goddess. Valiente maintained that both Goddess and God elements, interwoven, were present when she joined Gardner's coven. As for Gardner, he believed that the Horned God should have dominance and that women in the Craft should be subservient to men. He may have recognized, however, that a central figure of the Goddess would ultimately be more popular.

When Murray's witchcraft theory was shattered and some of the fallacies about Gardner's "ancient, unbroken religion" were exposed, Witchcraft was forced to look for a past. It grafted itself more firmly onto a reconstruction of Paganism and Goddess spirituality. This it did successfully with momentum from the growing feminist and environmental movements.

The Goddess in contemporary Witchcraft and Paganism is a mystery tradition. The Goddess represents Gaia, the living consciousness of the Earth; the Divine Feminine; the inner woman. The Goddess validates woman's power—her intuition, emotions, will, creativity, sexuality, body, desires and heritage. She is the cycle of life, death and rebirth, and the eternal spark in all of creation. Both men and women can find both the transcendent Goddess as cocreator of the universe and the immanent Goddess force within—the highest expression of anima, or the Great Mother archetype residing deep in the unconscious.

The Goddess is "She of a Thousand Names" who can be worshiped and petitioned in any of her numberless guises. In the Craft, her most common name is Aradia, and she is most frequently recognized in a trinity, the Triple Goddess, a personification of her three faces as Virgin, Mother and Crone. Trinities of goddesses (and gods) have been worshiped since antiquity in various cultures. The Morrigan of Ireland is personified by Ana, the virgin; Babd, the mother; and Macha, the crone.

The Triple Goddess of the modern Craft is personified by three Greek goddesses of the Moon: Artemis (usually called by her Roman name, DIANA), SELENE and HECATE. They are the new/waxing, full and waning/dark phases of the Moon, respectively. Diana, the Virgin and huntress, is associated with the new and waxing Moon, and rules the earth. She represents independence. Selene, the Mother, is associated with the full Moon and rules the sky. She represents nurturing and creation. Hecate, the Crone, is associated with the waning and dark of the Moon, and rules the underworld. She represents wisdom. Hecate herself was said to have three death aspects—Hecate, Circe and Persephone (Kore)—and also was part of a Greek Mother Goddess trinity that included Hebe as virgin, Hera as mother and Hecate as crone.

A Witch's magical powers are used to serve the Goddess. As her representatives on Earth, Witches must use magic for the greater good of humanity. The use of magic to harm is proscribed. The WICCAN REDE, a Witch's version of the Golden Rule, states, "An' it harm none, do what ye will."

The Goddess offers a source of wholeness and strength and an identification with the Divine that is missing from monotheism and that appeals to many women and men alike.

FURTHER READING:
Adler, Margot. *Drawing Down the Moon*. Revised ed. New York: Viking, 1986.
Crowley, Vivianne. *Wicca: The Old Religion in the New Millennium*. Revised ed. London: Thorsons/Harper Collins, 1996.
Harvey, Graham. *Contemporary Paganism: Listening People, Speaking Earth*. New York: New York University Press, 1997.
Larrington, Carolyn, ed. *The Feminist Companion to Mythology*. London: Pandora/HarperCollins, 1992.
Luhrmann, T. M. *Persuasions of the Witch's Craft: Ritual Magic in Contemporary England*. Cambridge: Harvard University Press, 1989.
Sjoo, Monica, and Barbara Mor. *The Great Cosmic Mother*. San Francisco: Harper & Row, 1987.

Good, Dorcas (17th century)   Youngest victim of the SALEM WITCHES hysteria of 1692–93.

Dorcas Good was the daughter of SARAH GOOD, one of the first persons to be accused of witchcraft in Salem, Massachusetts, in 1692. Only four years old, Dorcas was also accused of being a witch. In childlike fashion, she readily confessed to witchcraft, which she said she learned from her mother.

Dorcas was arrested about a month after her mother, in March 1692. She was cried out against by the afflicted girls along with REBECCA NURSE and ELIZABETH PROCTER. The girls accused Dorcas of tormenting them, saying she was taking supernatural revenge for the arrest of her mother.

When brought up for examination, Dorcas was confronted by three of the afflicted girls, Ann Putnam, Mary Walcott and Mercy Lewis. Putnam and Walcott fell into their fits, claiming Dorcas had bitten, pinched and choked them. They showed the marks of pinpricks and little teeth on their arms. The evidence was convincing to the magistrates and the onlookers.

Little Dorcas was an easy mark and became the second person after the slave TITUBA to confess to witchcraft. Asked if she had a FAMILIAR, Dorcas said yes, it was a small snake that sucked at the lowest joint of her forefinger. Dorcas showed the examiners a red mark at the spot, about the size of a flea bite. In all likelihood, it was a flea bite, but it was accepted as a WITCH'S MARK or DEVIL'S MARK by the examiners. Asked who gave her the familiar, the child replied that it was not the "Black Man," the Devil, but her mother.

Dorcas continued to give evidence against her mother, testifying at her trial that Sarah had three familiars in the shapes of birds that hurt the afflicted children and others. One was black and one was yellow.

Because of her confession, Dorcas was not tried for witchcraft. She was sent to prison in Boston, along with her mother, for about seven to eight months. There she was treated abominably, as were the other prisoners, and was confined in chains. They were too poor to pay for their upkeep, and "the country" was billed for their food and blankets.

Her father, William Good—who testified against his own wife—wrote a letter to the General Court in 1710 in which he protested the damage done to his family, including Dorcas. The child, he said, "hath ever since been very chargable, having little or no reason to govern herself."

FURTHER READING:
Hansen, Chadwick. *Witchcraft at Salem*. New York: New American Library, 1969.
Karlsen, Carol F. *The Devil in the Shape of a Woman: Witchcraft in Colonial New England*. New York: W.W. Norton & Co, 1987.
Upham, Charles. *History of Witchcraft and Salem Village*. Boston: Wiggin and Lunt, 1867.

Good, Sarah (d. 1692)   One of the first people to be accused of witchcraft in the SALEM WITCHES hysteria of 1692–93. Sarah Good was executed by hanging and on the gallows delivered a famous CURSE that seemed to bear true.

Good was married to her second husband, William Good. They had at least one child living at the time of the hysteria, four-year-old daughter, DORCAS GOOD. Sarah came from an unhappy background of debt and deprivation. Her father, John Solart, a prosperous innkeeper who ran up a lot of debt, committed suicide in 1672, leaving behind a small estate. Sarah never received her rightful though small inheritance. She married Daniel Poole, a former indentured servant. Poole died sometime after 1682, leaving Sarah in debt. She and William were held responsible for Poole's debt and had to sell their property to satisfy the court. This reduced the couple and their children to begging for shelter, work and food. The circumstances probably made them unpopular in the vicious Salem social politics leading up to the hysteria. When others refused to give aid to the Goods, Sarah reacted in anger, muttering to herself as she went away. Thus, she was readily seen as a good candidate for witchcraft—she was old and forlorn, and she had grudges, anger and reason to strike out at people.

The first people cried out against by the hysterical girls were Good, Sarah Osburn and Reverend Samuel Parris' slave TITUBA. Warrants were issued on February 29, 1692, and the three accused were examined by magistrates on March 1.

Good, the first to be examined, did little to help her case. She was indignant and evasive. She readily accused Osburn of being the one hurting the children, not her.

She denied having familiarity with evil spirits and said she had made no pact with the Devil.

The children accused Good to her face of tormenting them at a distance, appearing in spectral form. She denied it. The magistrates asked her what she muttered against people, and she replied that it was a psalm. No one believed her—everyone thought her to be muttering CURSES against others.

Even William turned against Sarah, apparently because their relationship had soured prior to the hysteria. William said he was afraid that Sarah either was a witch or would become one rather quickly. He admitted that he had no hard evidence of witchcraft practiced by her, but said that he considered her a witch because of "her bad carriage" to him. "Indeed," he said, "I may say with tears that she is an enemy to all good."

Tituba confessed to witchcraft and named Good and Osburn as two of four witches who were causing the afflictions and fits of the hysterical girls. Both women had signed marks in the Devil's book and rode on a pole through the air with Tituba to witches' meetings with the Devil.

Good and Osburn were sent to jail in Boston to be held for trial, along with a growing number of others accused by the girls of witchcraft. Dorcas followed Sarah by about a month, landing in jail with her mother after having testified against her.

Good and others were tried on June 29 and were sentenced to death. The executions were carried out by hanging on July 19. Prior to her hanging, Reverend Nicholas Noyes urged Good to confess, saying that she was a witch and knew she was witch. Good shot back, "You are a liar. I am no more a witch than you are a wizard; and if you take away my life, God will give you blood to drink."

Her words sounded like a curse, and strangely her prediction came true. Noyes later died of a hemorrhage in his throat, blood pouring from his mouth.

See HAWTHORNE, NATHANIEL.

FURTHER READING:
Hansen, Chadwick. *Witchcraft at Salem*. New York: New American Library, 1969.
Karlsen, Carol F. *The Devil in the Shape of a Woman: Witchcraft in Colonial New England*. New York: W.W. Norton & Co, 1987.
Upham, Charles. *History of Witchcraft and Salem Village*. Boston: Wiggin and Lunt, 1867.

Gowdie, Isobel (?–ca. 1662)   Scottish witch whose stories of wild sexual escapades with the DEVIL titillated and shocked her stern neighbors and reinforced the prevailing beliefs in witches as evil creatures bent on destroying their fellow man. Isobel Gowdie, an attractive woman with RED hair, a color associated with witches, voluntarily confessed to witchcraft on four occasions in April and May 1662. The confessions in themselves astonished the local folk, but what was even more aston-ishing was Gowdie's assertion that she had been engaging in obscene activities for 15 years. No one, apparently, had ever caught on, not even her husband.

According to her confessions, Gowdie's involvement with the Devil began in 1647, when she met him in the shape of a man in gray in Auldearne, the remote area in Morayshire where she lived. He enticed her into his service, and that very evening baptized her as a witch in the local church with her own BLOOD, which he sucked from her. He gave her a DEVIL'S MARK on her shoulder and renamed her Janet. Much of her witchcraft, she said, was taught to her by FAIRIES.

Gowdie said she joined a COVEN of 13 witches—thus bolstering the myth that all witches organize in groups of 13—which met regularly for SABBATS marked by sexual orgies with DEMONS and the Devil, feasting and dancing. She proudly explained how she sneaked away to attend these affairs without her husband knowing: she substituted a broomstick for herself in bed, and he never realized the difference.

She and her sister witches flew off to the sabbats on corn straws, beanstalks and rushes, which they charmed into flight by shouting, "Horse and Hattock, in the Devil's name!" If someone below spotted them and did not cross himself, they would shoot him down with ELF ARROWS.

Gowdie delighted in describing her intercourse with the Devil: how he plunged an enormous, scaly penis into her, causing excruciating pain, and how his semen was cold as ice. As painful as she made it sound, Gowdie also apparently enjoyed it. If she or the other witches displeased the Devil, he beat them with scourges and wool cards.

She also told how she and her coven members tormented their neighbors. They raised storms by beating wet rags upon stones while reciting incantations. They made farmland sterile by ploughing it with a miniature plough drawn by TOADS. They hexed children by sticking pins in dolls. They blasted one farmer's crops (see BLASTING) by digging up the body of an unchristened child and burying it in his manure heap. They shot elf arrows at people to injure or kill them. If they became bored with tormenting others, the witches amused themselves by metamorphosing into animals, usually hares and cats (see METAMORPHOSIS).

Stunned by these stories, the local authorities had Gowdie stripped and searched for the DEVIL'S MARK, which they found.

The records give no reason as to why Gowdie one day decided to confess these lurid tales, without any prompting or suspicion upon her. Furthermore, she welcomed punishment: "I do not deserve to be seated here at ease and unharmed, but rather to be stretched on an iron rack: nor can my crimes be atoned for, were I to be drawn asunder by wild horses."

In *Letters on Demonology and Witchcraft* (1830), Sir Walter Scott speculated that "this wretched creature

The Devil scourges witches, 17th century

was under the dominion of some peculiar species of lunacy." In *The Occult* (1971), Colin Wilson suggests she was a highly sexed woman with a vivid imagination, who turned to fantasies to alleviate the boredom of a dull existence; at some point, her fantasies became real to her. But after 15 years, the excitement of having a secret grew thin, and there was only one way to recharge it—by making a public confession.

The records also do not indicate what became of Gowdie or the other unfortunate Auldearne witches she named.

FURTHER READING:
Scott, Sir Walter. *Letters on Demonology and Witchcraft.* 1884. Reprint, New York: Citadel Press, 1968.

Sharpe, C. K. *A History of Witchcraft in Scotland.* Glasgow: Thomas D. Morison, 1884.

Wilson, Colin. *The Occult.* New York: Vintage Books, 1971.

Graves, William (17th century) Connecticut man accused of witchcraft over a dispute with his daughter and son-in-law. Though no legal action was taken against William Graves, his case indicates how easily personal squabbles could be turned into serious witchcraft charges.

Graves' daughter, Abigail, married a man named Samuel Dibble. Graves may not have approved of the match, for he refused to turn over his daughter's "portion" or inheritance to her after the marriage. Angry, Dibble got an attachment against Graves. Graves responded by telling Dibble that he would repent this attachment for as long as he lived; it sounded like a CURSE to Dibble. Graves also made angry remarks to Abigail, to the point where she and her husband were in fear that somehow Graves would harm them.

Abigail became pregnant and went into what became a difficult labor in February 1666. She reportedly experienced fits. Witnesses said that Graves told his daughter to prepare to meet the Lord; Graves claimed that his daughter looked so bad that he thought she was going to die.

After much suffering on the part of Abigail, the baby was finally delivered, but Abigail continued to have fits, and others feared for her life. Her tongue was black and protruding, and her eyes bulged. Graves reportedly remarked that Abigail would die and he would be hanged for her death.

The same month as the childbirth, Graves was brought to a hearing on charges of witchcraft. No legal action was taken. Whether Abigail and her husband ever got her inheritance is not known.

FURTHER READING:
Hall, David D, ed. *Witch-hunting in Seventeenth-Century New England: A Documentary History 1638–1692.* Boston: Northeastern University Press, 1991.

Great Rite   In contemporary Witchcraft, a powerful, magical rite of sexual intercourse that pays homage to the male/female polarity that exists in all things in the universe. The Great Rite expresses the physical, mental, spiritual and astral union between man and woman, and the union of the GODDESS and God.

The Great Rite is the *hieros gamos,* the Sacred Marriage or Holy Matrimony, which is union with a deity or godhead. It dates to the Neolithic era. Ancient kings required the *hieros gamos,* a union with a priestess representing the Goddess, in order to rule. The *hieros gamos* also was part of ancient women's mysteries, in which women sacrificed control of their feminine power to the Goddess and were renewed by her. It was part of the Mysteries of ISIS and reportedly was part of the Eleusinian Mysteries.

The Great Rite represents the inner marriage of the soul and spirit, Ego and Self. As an INITIATION, it represents the gateway to individuation, or becoming whole. It also releases great power, which may be directed for magical purposes; it is one of the Eightfold Paths to magical power in the Craft.

Depending on the tradition, the Great Rite is performed within a MAGIC CIRCLE at INITIATIONS (such as the third-degree initiations in the Gardnerian and Alexandrian traditions), seasonal festivals (see WHEEL OF THE YEAR) and HANDFASTINGS. The high priest and high priestess may perform the Great Rite together. As part of an initiation, the rite is done between initiate and high priest or high priestess. It is done either "in token," that is, symbolically with ritual tools (such as an athame inserted into a chalice), or "in true," as a sexual act. If done in true, the participating couple usually are intimate partners. An outer portion of the rite is done with the coven, and the sexual portion is done privately.

GERALD B. GARDNER had the Great Rite performed with the coven watching. Gardner also favored ritual scourging as part of the rite, a practice which has fallen out of favor.

FURTHER READING:
Crowley, Vivianne. *Wicca: The Old Religion in the New Millennium.* Revised ed. London: Thorsons/Harper Collins, 1996.
Farrar, Janet, and Stewart Farrar. *A Witches Bible Compleat.* New York: Magickal Childe, 1984.

Green Man   A pagan deity of the woodlands, usually represented as a horned man peering out from a mask of foliage, usually the sacred oak. The Green Man, also called "Green Jack," "Jack-in-the-Green" and "Green George," represents the spirits of the trees, plants and foliage. He is attributed with the powers of making rain and fostering the livestock with lush meadows. He appears often in medieval art, including carved church decorations.

In spring Pagan rites, Green George, as he is usually called then, is represented by a young man clad from head to foot in greenery, who leads the festival procession. In some festivals, Green George, or an effigy of him, is dunked into a river or pond in order to ensure enough rain to make the fields and meadows green.

As the woodlands deity, the Green Man shares an association with the forest-dwelling FAIRIES (green is the fairy color). In some locations in the British Isles, the fairies are called "Greenies" and "Greencoaties." "The Green Children" is a myth of two fairy children, a brother and a sister, whose skin is green, and who claim to be of a race with green skin.

See NATURE SPIRITS.

FURTHER READING:
Anderson, William, and Clive Hicks. *The Green Man: The Archtype of Our Oneness with the Earth.* San Francisco: HarperSanFrancisco, 1991.

Greensmith, Rebecca (17th century)   Hartford, Connecticut, woman accused of witchcraft, who confessed and was executed.

Rebecca Greensmith and her third husband, Nathaniel, lived next door to ANN COLE. The couple were reasonably affluent, but Rebecca was considered a "lewd and ignorant" woman. In 1662, when Cole was brought up on charges of witchcraft, Greensmith was already languishing in prison on charges of witchcraft, which she denied.

Cole named several accomplices, including Greensmith. Rebecca was brought before a magistrate and was confronted with the accusations of Cole that had been recorded by Reverend John Whiting and Joseph Haines. At first Greensmith was astonished and protested her innocence once again, but soon confessed that all Cole had said was true.

Greensmith said that she and others had familiarity with the DEVIL, but had not signed a DEVIL'S PACT with him. However, she had gone with him whenever he had called her. The Devil told her that at Christmas the witches would have a fine celebration and would all sign the pact with him.

Greensmith was questioned again on the following day by Haines. She told him that she was in such a rage that she could have torn him limb from limb. Haines persisted in his interrogation, and Greensmith broke down again, saying that she felt as if her own flesh was being pulled from her bones. She again confessed to the accusations.

She said that the Devil appeared to her in the shape of a deer or a fawn and skipped around her until she was not frightened. The Devil began conversing with her and then frequently had sexual intercourse with her. "I liked it very much," Greensmith stated.

She said she met with other witches at a place not far from her home. The witches all flew to the meetings in different animal shapes, one of them being a cow.

Greensmith was sentenced to death and was hanged in January 1663. Her husband, Nathaniel, was also accused of witchcraft by association and was executed, despite his lack of confession of guilt.

FURTHER READING:
Hansen, Chadwick. *Witchcraft at Salem.* New York: New American Library, 1969.
Jameson, J. Franklin, ed. *Narratives of the Witchcraft Cases 1648–1706.* New York: Charles Scribner's Sons, 1914.

Grey School of Wizardry   Online school of magickal and alchemical arts, founded in 2004 by OBERON ZELL-RAVENHEART. The Grey School of Wizardry offers courses taught by leading practitioners to students ages 11 and up.

The school is an outgrowth of the Grey Council, two dozen mages and sages who created the curriculum, and

The Grey School of Wizardry logo (COURTESY OBERON ZELL-RAVENHEART)

some of whom remain on the faculty. The school opened on Lughnasagh (August 1) 2004, and by early 2008 had more than 1,050 students enrolled. Its long-range vision is to make the wisdom of the ages available to new generations and the new millennium.

There are 16 departments of study: Wizardry, Nature Studies, Magickal Practice, Mind Magicks, Healing, Wortcunning, Divination, Performance Magicks, Alchemy and Magickal Sciences, Lifeways, Beast Mastery, Cosmology, Mathemagicks, Ceremonial Magick, Lore and Dark Arts. Zell serves as headmaster.

Youth students (11–17) are organized into elemental houses (Gnomes, Salamanders, Sylphs and Undines), and adult students (18 and older) are in elemental lodges (Flames, Stones, Waters and Winds).

In addition to online studies, there are events, personal internships and other activities.

Primary handbooks are *Grimoire for the Apprentice Wizard* (2004) and *Companion for the Apprentice Wizard* (2006), both written by Zell.

FURTHER READING:
Grey School of Wizardry Web site. Available online. URL: http://www.greyschool.com. Accessed June 4, 2008.

Grimassi, Raven (1951–)   American witch with a heritage and expertise in Italian Witchcraft. Raven Grimassi is the author of several books on the Craft, including the *Encyclopedia of Wicca & Witchcraft.*

Grimassi's mother came to the United States in 1946. Grimassi says one of his ancestors is a Neapolitan witch, Calenda Tavani, and that Italian Witchcraft absorbed elements of Catholicism in order to survive. He was raised Catholic, but at age 13 stopped attending services and turned his interest to Witchcraft.

In 1969, he was initiated into Gardnerian/Alexandrian Wicca by Lady Heather and studied under Lady Sara Cunningham. In 1975, he was initiated into Brittic Wicca, a blend of Basque Witchcraft and English Wicca. He also joined the Rosicrucians and First Temple of Tipareth. In 1983, he was initiated into the Pictish-Gaelic tradition.

Grimassi began his writing career in 1981, writing and editing *The Shadow's Edge,* a publication about Italian Witchcraft. He has contributed to the magazines *Moon Shadow* and *Raven's Call.* Booklets and books include *The Book of the Holy Strega* (1981), *The Book of Ways* (1981), *The Wiccan Mysteries* (1998), *Italian Witchcraft* (2000), *Hereditary Witchcraft* (1999), *Beltane* (2001), and *Wiccan Magick* (1998). The *Encyclopedia of Wicca and Witchcraft* was published in 2000.

Grimassi lives on Crow Haven Ranch in southern California.

grimoires   Handbooks of MAGIC, some reputedly dating back to ancient sources, popular from the 17th to early 19th centuries. Grimoires still are consulted by students of ceremonial magic in modern times, though newer

The Book of Spirits (FRANCIS BARRETT, *THE MAGUS*, 1801)

books have replaced them. In modern Witchcraft, some rituals may draw on ceremonial magic texts, but the Witch's personal handbook of Craft rituals and laws is called the BOOK OF SHADOWS.

The original purpose of the grimoires was to conjure and control DEMONS and spirits, in order to acquire great wealth and power or harm or kill enemies. Grimoires give precise and sometimes laborious instructions for various rituals, instructing the magician on what to wear, what tools to use and what PRAYERS and incantations to recite at precise astrological times and various hours of the day and night. They give recipes for incenses to burn, descriptions for the creation of MAGIC CIRCLES, AMULETS, TALISMANS, seals and SIGILS, instructions for the slaughtering and SACRIFICE of animals and ways to deal with unruly DEMONS. They admonish the magician to prepare with periods of fasting, sexual abstinence, cleanliness and prayer and to use only virgin materials in rituals. They describe the hierarchies of demons and spirits that may be summoned with the help of the grimoire's instructions.

Grimoires, or "black books," as they were often called, came into usage around the 13th century. They were possessed not only by magicians and sorcerers but also by physicians and noblemen—or anyone who thought he had something to gain with help from a DEMON. Ideally, the grimoire was copied by hand.

The material in grimoires is drawn largely from Hermetic texts dating to 100–400 C.E. and from Hebrew and Latin sources. Some grimoires are devoted to *theurgy,* or magic effected with divine intervention, while others concern *goety,* or sorcery. Some include both.

The writers and users of grimoires did not consider themselves Devil-worshipers or evil. The conjuring of demons was merely one of many means to an end. Doing business with demons often meant making pacts with

them. The magician's objective was to outwit the demon so that he did not have to fulfill his end of the bargain. The grimoires helped him do this (see DEVIL'S PACT).

The greatest grimoire is *The Key of Solomon,* which has provided material for many other grimoires. The book is attributed to the legendary King Solomon, who asked God for wisdom and commanded an army of demons to do his bidding and build great works. A book of incantations for summoning demons, attributed to the authorship of Solomon, was in existence in the first century and is mentioned in literature throughout the centuries. So many versions of this grimoire were written that it is virtually impossible to ascertain what constituted the original text; a Greek version that dates to ca. 1100–1200 is part of the collection in the British Museum. Around 1350 Pope Innocent VI ordered a grimoire called *The Book of Solomon* to be burned; in 1559 Solomon's grimoire was again condemned by the Church as dangerous. *The Key of Solomon* was widely distributed in the 17th century.

Another grimoire attributed to Solomon is the *Lemegeton,* or *Lesser Key of Solomon,* which includes both white and black magic information.

FURTHER READING:
Cavendish, Richard. *The Black Arts.* New York: Putnam, 1967.
Waite, A. E. *The Book of Black Magic and of Pacts.* 1899. Reprint, York Beach, Me.: Samuel Weiser, 1972.

gris-gris In VODUN, CHARMS or TALISMANS kept for good luck or to ward off evil. The original gris-gris were probably dolls or images of the gods, but most gris-gris today are small cloth bags filled with herbs, OILS, STONES, small bones, HAIR AND NAIL clippings, pieces of clothing soiled with perspiration and/or other personal items, gathered under the direction of a particular god and designed to protect the owner.

The origin of the word is unclear, but many scholars trace it to *juju,* the West African name for a FETISH, or sacred object. Juju may be a European translation of the native expression *grou-grou* (hence gris-gris), or it may refer to the French word *joujou,* which meant "doll" or "plaything." Most of the African fetishes were in the shape of dolls, and early Europeans on the African West Coast may have mistaken serious religious objects for innocent-looking poppets (see AFRICAN WITCHCRAFT).

In New Orleans, gris-gris are common. They are made to attract money and love, stop gossip, protect the home, maintain good health and achieve innumerable other ends. Even police officers have been known to carry gris-gris for protection. A gris-gris is ritually made at an altar and consecrated with the four ELEMENTS of earth (salt), air (incense), water and fire (a candle flame). The number of ingredients is always either one, three, five, seven, nine or 13 (see THIRTEEN). Ingredients can never be even in number or number more than 13. Stones and colored objects are selected for their occult and astrological properties, depending on the purpose of the gris-gris.

Legends about the famous New Orleans Vodun queen MARIE LAVEAU tell that her gris-gris contained bits of bone, colored stones, graveyard dust (also called *goofer dust*), salt and red pepper. More elaborate gris-gris might have been made of tiny birds nests or horsehair weavings.

A red-flannel bag containing a lodestone, or magnet, was a favorite gris-gris for gamblers, guaranteed to bring them good luck. Another gambler's gris-gris was made from a piece of chamois, a piece of RED flannel, a shark's tooth, pine-tree sap and a dove's blood. The blood and sap were mixed together, then used to write the amount the gambler wanted to win on the chamois. The chamois was covered with the red flannel, with the shark's tooth placed between the layers, and the whole thing was sewn together with cat's hair. The gris-gris was to be worn in the left shoe for best, if uncomfortable, results.

Gris-gris also can be used to cause someone else bad luck, known as "putting a gris-gris" on a person. Throwing a gris-gris bag filled with gunpowder and red pepper in someone's path or on their doorstep supposedly makes that person get into a fight. To get rid of someone, Marie Laveau would write that person's name on a small balloon, tie the balloon to a statue of St. Expedite, then release the balloon. The victim would depart in whichever direction the balloon flew. Just leaving a gris-gris, usually a powder, at someone's front door tells the person he is out of favor with "the voodoos" and should watch his step.

One of Marie Laveau's more horrible *wangas*, or bad-luck charms, reputedly was a bag made from the shroud of a person who had been dead nine days. Into the bag went a dried, one-eyed TOAD, the little finger of a black person who had committed suicide, a dried lizard, bat's wings, a cat's eyes, an owl's liver and a rooster's heart. If such a gris-gris were hidden in a victim's pillow, the unfortunate would surely die. Many white masters in old New Orleans who mistreated their black slaves found some kind of gris-gris in their handbags or pillows, such as a little sack of black paper containing saffron, salt, gunpowder and pulverized dog manure.

In SANTERÍA gris-gris bags are called *resguardos*, or "protectors." A typical *resguardo* under the protection of the thunder-god Chango might contain herbs, spices, brown sugar, garlic, aloes, stones or other small sacred relics, tied up in red velvet and stitched with red thread. Finally, the Santero attaches a tiny gold sword, the symbol of St. Barbara (Changó's image as a Catholic saint), and if the sword breaks, Changó has interceded on the owner's behalf.

Gurunfindas are talismans prepared by Santería's black witches, the *mayomberos*, to ward off evil from themselves and direct it magically to others. To make a *gurunfinda*, first the *mayombero* hollows out a *guiro*, a hard, inedible fruit found in the tropics, and fills it with the heads, hearts and legs of a turtle and various species of parrots; the tongue and eyes of a rooster; and seven live ants. Next, the *mayombero* adds seven teeth, the jawbone and some hair from a cadaver, along with the cadaver's name on a piece of paper, and seven coins to pay the dead spirit for his services. Then, the *mayombero* pours rum over the mixture and buries the *guiro* beneath a sacred ceiba tree for 21 days. When he disinters the *guiro,* the *mayombero* marks the outside of the fruit with chalk and then hangs the charm from a tree near his home.

Gruber, Bernardo (17th century) German trader accused of SORCERY by Pueblo Indians in northern New Mexico. Bernardo Gruber was imprisoned. He escaped but died a strange death.

In 1668, Gruber arrived in New Mexico with a pack train of mules bearing fine goods. It was said that he was fearless and traveled through the lands of the fierce Apache without harm. Perhaps it was his ability to avoid Apache attacks that led to his downfall. Soon after coming to New Mexico, several Pueblo Indians betrayed him to a priest for possessing sorcery skills that would make him invulnerable. According to the Indians, Gruber had given them instructions in sorcery that he had learned in his native Germany. They said that if certain SPELLS were written on the first day of the feast of the Nativity when the Gospel was being spoken and the person ate the writings they would become invulnerable for 24 hours and could not be harmed or killed by any weapon. Gruber reportedly claimed that this spell was undertaken whenever Germany went to war. Supposedly it was tried out on an Indian boy and an Indian adult from Las Salinas, both of whom could not be wounded with knives.

An investigation by the Franciscan prelate revealed that many Pueblo said they had been taught the magical formula by Gruber. Summoned to appear before church authorities, Gruber readily admitted that he did indeed possess such a spell, and he wrote it down:

†A. B. N. A. ɪ A. D. N. A.ɪ

Upon this confession and evidence, the church arrested Gruber, and he was put in irons in the Pueblo mission at Abo. While in jail, he talked freely of other magical things he had learned in Germany, evidently unaware of how folk magic was regarded by the Catholic Church authorities in New Mexico. His admissions only solidified the case against him as a sorcerer.

The authorities intended to transfer Gruber to the INQUISITION in Mexico City. Before this could happen, Gruber's servants sneaked into the mission and pried open the bars of his cell so that he could escape.

Gruber remained at large for several weeks. Then one day, Captain Andrés de Peralta made an odd discovery on a desert road in southern New Mexico. A dead roan horse was tied to a tree. Near the carcass were a blue cloth coat lined with otter skin and a pair of blue breeches, both severely decayed. The captain recognized the distinctive clothing as items worn by Gruber. He searched the area and found Gruber's hair and several of his bones, all widely scattered: the skull, three ribs, two long bones and two small bones.

It was assumed that Gruber had been killed by Indians, giving the case a bizarre twist. In the end, it seemed that his sorcery had failed him.

FURTHER READING:
Simmons, Marc. *Witchcraft in the Southwest: Spanish and Indian Supernaturalism on the Rio Grande.* Lincoln.: University of Nebraska Press, 1974.

Guazzo, Francesco-Maria (17th century)   Italian friar who became well known as a demonologist and opponent of witches. Francesco-Maria Guazzo is best known as the author of *Compendium Maleficarum (Handbook of Witches)*, a leading inquisitor's guide.

Little is known about Guazzo's life. He joined the Brethren of St. Ambrose ad Nemus and St. Barnabas in Milan. He wrote the *Compendium* in response to a request from Cardinal Federico Borromeo, the archbishop of Milan. The book, published in 1608, draws upon the works of other demonologists and repeats some of the superstitions of the time, including the assertion that Martin Luther was born from the union of the DEVIL and a nun.

Guazzo served as a judge and assessor in witchcraft trials. In 1605, he was sent to Cleves to advise in a case involving the Serene Duke John William of Julich-Cleves. The duke accused a 90-year-old WARLOCK, John, of overlooking and ensorcelling him (see EVIL EYE and SORCERY). John confessed that he used CHARMS and runes to afflict the duke with a wasting sickness and "frenzy." He was found guilty and sentenced to be burned at the stake. Before the sentence could be carried out, John committed suicide by slicing his throat with a knife. According to Guazzo, the Devil himself stood at John's side as he died.

The duke asked Guazzo to assist in other witchcraft cases in Germany, which he did.

The *Compendium* became the leading witch handbook in Italy and has been compared to the *MALLEUS MALEFICARUM*.

FURTHER READING:
Guazzo, Francesco-Maria. *Compendium Maleficarum.* Secaucus, N.J.: University Books, 1974.

Gwydion the Wizard   In Welsh Celtic mythology, the heroic wizard (see WIZARD) and bard of North Wales, whose tales are told in *The Mabinogion.* Gwydion the Wizard was the son of Don, the Welsh goddess who is a counterpart of the Irish Celtic goddess Danu. He was one of three children of Don; the other two were Gofannon the Smith, and a daughter, ARIANROD, a lunar goddess of dawn and the mother of Llew. Gwydion ruled science, light and reason. He is associated with the rainbow and is described as the British Hermes.

He was a skillful magician, a bringer of cultural gifts from the gods to man and a clever thief. He is said to be the father of April Fool's Day, for on April 1 he conjured great armies to fool Arianrod into giving arms to Llew Llaw Gyffes. He helped Math, god of wealth, create a bride for Llew: Blodeuwed, the "flowerlike." Blodeuwed fell in love with another man and betrayed Llew to a treacherous death. The Milky Way is said to be the tracks of Gwydion searching for the dead Llew.

Gwydion used his MAGIC against the men of southern Wales and was punished in return. He used magic illegally to acquire a herd of Pryderi's swine and was made to do penances by Math.

Gwydion eventually slew Pryderi, son of Pwyll, who was ruler of the underworld and the first husband of Rhiannon. In Celtic magic, he plays a role in initiation rites.

Gypsies   Nomadic, dark-skinned people who probably emerged out of northern India around the 10th century and spread throughout Europe, the British Isles and eventually America. Gypsy tradition has little in the way of its own religious beliefs but is steeped in MAGIC and superstition. From their earliest known appearance in Europe in the 15th century, Gypsies have been renowned practitioners of magical arts, and they undoubtedly influenced folk magic wherever they went. During the Renaissance, they were associated with WITCHES and WITCHCRAFT, and many were persecuted and executed as such. In addition, Gypsies were met with hostility and suspicion from populations wherever they went, which added to their persecution, banishment and deportation. In England, it became unlawful to be a Gypsy in 1530; the law was not repealed until 1784.

The first record of Gypsies in Europe is in 1417 in Germany, although it is quite likely that they arrived in Europe much earlier. They came as Christian penitents and claimed to be exiles from a land called "Little Egypt." Europeans called them "Egyptians," which became corrupted as "Gypsies." Their language, Romany, is related to Sanskrit, and many of their customs have similarities to Hindu customs. The Gypsies also absorbed the religious and folk customs of the lands through which they traveled, and many of their practices contain strong Christian and pagan elements. Very little is known about early Gypsy practices; most of the present knowledge comes from observations and records from the 19th century on.

It is not known what led the Gypsies to leave India. Various legends exist as to their origins and why they were condemned to wander the earth: They were Egyptians scattered by Yahweh (Jehovah, or God); they were survivors of Atlantis, left without a homeland; they had refused to help the Virgin Mary during her flight to Egypt; they had forged three nails for Christ's cross of crucifixion. Voltaire proposed that they were descendants of the priests of ISIS and followers of ASTARTE.

The Gypsies' lack of religious creed is explained by an interesting Turkish legend: When religions were distributed to the peoples of the earth a long time ago, they were written down to preserve them. Rather than write in books or on wood or metal, the Gypsies recorded their religion on a cabbage. A donkey came along and ate the cabbage.

The Gypsy universe is populated with various deities and spirits. *Del* is both God and "everything which is above"—the sky, heavens and heavenly bodies. *Pharaun* is a god said to have once been a great pharaoh in the Gypsies' long-lost "Little Egypt." *Beng* is the DEVIL, the source of all evil. Like Christians, Gypsies believe the DEVIL is ugly, with a tail and a reptilian appearance, and has the power to shape-shift. Legends exist of pacts with *Beng*. Moon worship and fire worship are extensive among Gypsies; they apparently have not worshiped the Sun to any significant degree. The MOON is personified by the god *Alako*, defender of Gypsies and taker of their souls after death. *Alako* originally was *Dundra*, a son of God sent to earth to teach humans law, who ascended to the Moon when he was finished and became a god (compare to ARADIA). Fire is considered divine, with the ability to heal, protect, preserve health and punish the evil.

The cult of *Bibi* concerns worship of a LAMIA-like goddess who strangles *gorgio* (non-Gypsy) children by infecting them with cholera, tuberculosis and typhoid fever.

Gypsies also practice phallus worship and an animistic worship of objects, such as anvils. The horse and the bear are regarded as godlike beings.

Gypsies have a strong fear of death and the dead, and numerous taboos govern the way they deal with the dead and dying. All of a dead person's possessions, including his animals, are considered polluted and will haunt the living unless they are destroyed or buried with him. This practice has dwindled since the 19th century, as a result of economic factors and the lessening of the Gypsies' nomadic life-styles. A great fear exists that the dead are angry at being dead and will return as vampires to avenge their deaths. IRON fences sometimes are constructed around graves in order to keep the corpses from escaping. The Gypsies also seek to appease a vampire god by leaving out rice balls and bowls of milk or animal blood. The names of the dead are believed to have magical power and are used in oaths and invocations.

The Gypsy witch is almost without exception a woman; she is called a *chovihani*. She uses her occult powers according to need, to bless and heal or curse and kill. Within the Gypsy community, she is not respected for her magical powers per se but for the money she brings in by servicing the *gorgio* (non-Gypsy) population. The rise in witchcraft and folk-magic activity in Europe and the British Isles in the 15th and 16th centuries probably was influenced by the spread of the Gypsies.

The *chovihani* is said either to inherit her ability or acquire it in childhood through intercourse with a water or earth DEMON while sleeping. Like *gorgio* witches, Gypsy witches are said to have an odd or ugly appearance and to possess the EVIL EYE.

Of all the magical arts, the *chovihani* is best known for DIVINATION and fortune-telling, especially by crystal-gazing or reading palms, the Tarot and tea leaves. The *chovihani* prescribes a multitude of CHARMS to address virtually any situation; many of them involve BLOOD and URINE, two common ingredients in folk magic because of their sympathetic magic properties (see also HAIR AND NAILS). Most illness is ascribed to evil spirits, and the *chovihani* can heal by exorcising these spirits in a trance possession ritual (see SPIRIT EXORCISM).

Bird omens are important. The OWL is a harbinger of death while the swallow, cuckoo and water-wagtail are signs of good fortune.

Magical rites are performed in conjunction with baptisms, marriages and divorces. A newborn infant is unclean. Baptism removes the taboo and protects it from evil. Baptisms consist of immersion in running water, or tattooing. Two names are given, one of which is kept secret in order to fool the Devil and evil spirits. Some baptisms are done within a MAGIC CIRCLE. Baptisms are often repeated for good luck. In marriage ceremonies, the newlyweds sometimes step over a broomstick (see BROOMS) and receive SALT, bread and wine. In divorce, the broomstick ritual is reversed. Another divorce ritual calls for sacrificing a horse by stabbing it in the heart and letting it bleed to death.

FURTHER READING:

Lockhart, J. G. Curses, *Lucks and Talismans*. 1938. Reprint, Detroit: Single Tree Press, 1971.

McDowell, Bob. *Gypsies: Wanderers of the World*. Washington, D.C.: National Geographic Society, 1970.

Trigg, Elwood B. *Gypsy Demons & Divinities*. Secaucus, N.J.: Citadel Press, 1973.

hag An old, ugly woman believed to be a witch or sorceress; also, a supernatural, demonic being whose powers enable her to live an incredibly long time.

The origin of the term "hag" is found in the ancient GODDESS beliefs and myths of the Egyptians, Greeks, Celts and pagan Europeans. The Egyptian *heq* was a matriarchal ruler in predynastic times, one who commanded the NAMES OF POWER. Many Celtic myths feature Gráinne, or "ugliness," the Old and Undying Hag. In Greek mythology, the hag is personified by HECATE, goddess of witchcraft and CROSSROADS; in Norse mythology she is the death-goddess Hel. Old Norse hags may have been sacrificial priestesses, as evidenced by the terms hagi, meaning "sacred grove," *haggen*, meaning "to chop to pieces," and *haggis*, meaning "hag's dish," a dish comprised of organ meats that is still popular in Scotland.

In folklore, hags are sometimes benevolent, wise, beautiful and perpetually young. In Irish and Scottish lore, good hags help with spinning. Supernatural hags haunt the Fen country of Great Britain, working in league with bogeys, spirits of the dead and "creeping horrors" to bring harm to human beings and their animals. The Cailleach Bheur of the Highlands is a lean, blue-faced hag, a supernatural remnant of a Celtic goddess of winter who is reborn each Samhain (All Hallow's Eve, October 31) and turns to stone on Beltane Eve (April 30). The Celts erected sacred standing stones to her. Black Annis, a blue-faced cannibal with iron claws and long teeth, lives in a cave in the Dane Hills. A remnant of the Celtic mother goddess, Anu, Black Annis eats people and animals. Until the 18th century, a ritual was performed in which she was coaxed out of her cave every Easter Monday with a dead cat soaked in aniseed.

In the 16th century, the term *hag* was often substituted for FAIRY. Fairies were reputed to teach their supernatural skills to witches, and the two consorted at night at FAIRY RINGS.

In other lore, succubus hags cause nightmares by sitting on a person's chest and "riding" them through the night, sometimes killing them from exhaustion (see NIGHTMARE). Hags can be prevented from riding by the placement of a pen-knife on one's breast or a table fork under one's head. A sifter placed under the head also prevents riding, for the hag is forced to pass through every hole in it, which takes her all night. Witch-hags are believed to sneak into stables at night and steal horses, riding them all night and returning them sweaty and exhausted. To prevent this, CHARMS and AMULETS are hung in stables.

The term *hag* in relation to witches is still used in Great Britain: *hag stones* mark MAGIC CIRCLES, and *hag tracking* is a means of cursing.

Modern Witches consider the term uncomplimentary, a stereotype of an ugly, disagreeable woman.

FURTHER READING:
Hufford, David J. *The Terror That Comes in the Night.* Philadelphia: University of Pennsylvania Press, 1982.

Leach, Maria, ed., and Jerome Fried, assoc. ed. *Funk & Wagnall's Standard Dictionary of Folklore, Mythology and Legend.* New York: Harper & Row, 1972.

hag stone In folk MAGIC, a stone with a hole in it hung in homes and stables to keep away HAGS or witches, at night. Hung on the bedpost, a hag stone is believed to prevent a hag from riding one's chest and causing a NIGHTMARE. In the stables, it prevents a hag from taking the horses and riding them all night to the point of exhaustion.

See STONES.

hair and nails Hair and nails possess magical attributes that contain the essence of a person, and thus are important ingredients in many magic SPELLS. Hair is associated with strength and virility, and with psychic protection. Abundant hair was considered an asset for many monarchs. The ancient Egyptians believed that a potion made of hair, nail clippings and human BLOOD would give a person absolute power over another.

In folklore, a witch's magical power is bound in her hair. By shaking her hair, the power of a spell is doubled. The shearing off of another's hair is considered an act of degradation, humiliation or punishment. Samson lost his strength when Delilah cut his hair. The Bhils of Central India tortured suspected witches, then cut off a lock of their hair and buried it, thus severing the link between the witches and their magical power. In the witch-hunts, witches were shaved in the belief that it rendered them powerless and more likely to confess; also, they were shaved to be searched for body marks that could be construed as DEVIL'S MARKS.

Nails have been associated with DEMONS and evil; some Jews keep their fingernails as short as possible, and tribes in Madagascar believe the Devil lives under unpared fingernails.

Much Western magical lore about hair and nails can be traced to the *Vendidad,* a Zoroastrian liturgy written in the mid-5th century B.C.E. According to the *Vendidad,* hair and nails are instruments of evil because they grow with a life of their own and can be separated from the body, to be used by witches and WIZARDS for conjuring the dead, bewitching and casting spells. Ahura Mazda gave Zarathustra specific rituals for the safe disposing of hair clippings and nail parings:

> . . . thou shalt take them away ten paces from the faithful, twenty paces from the fire, thirty paces from the water, fifty paces from the bundles of baresma [holy twigs].
>
> Then thou shalt dig a hole, ten fingers deep if the earth is hard, twelve fingers deep if it is soft; thou shalt take thy hair down there and thou shalt say aloud these fiend-smiting words: Out of his pity Mazda made plants grow.
>
> There upon thou shalt draw three furrows with a knife of metal around the hole, or six, or nine, and thou shalt chant the Ahuna Vairya three times, or six, or nine.

> For the nails, thou shalt dig a hole, out of the house, as deep as the top joint of the little finger; thou shalt take the nails down there and thou shalt say aloud these fiend-smiting words: The words are heard from the pious in holiness and good thought.

The practice of burying cut hair and nails persists among many cultures. ALEISTER CROWLEY secretly disposed of his hair and nail clippings throughout his life. In Ozark lore, hair combings are buried, never thrown out. French peasants bury hair; Turks and Chileans stuff hair clippings into walls.

Sorcerers, CUNNING MEN AND WOMEN and witches in many societies have secured the cut hairs of victims to cast spells and break spells. A bewitched victim's hair thrown into a fire supposedly projects the pain of the flames back onto the witch. The hair of a dead man buried under the threshold of an enemy supposedly will cause the enemy to develop ague. In parts of Germany, a small bag of smooth human hair placed on the stomach will tell someone if they have been bewitched. The answer is yes if the hair is tangled after three days.

Hair, particularly pubic hair, is considered a potent ingredient in many love charms. According to legend, JOHN FIAN, a 16th-century Scottish wizard, attempted to make a young girl fall in love with him by making a charm from three of her pubic hairs. However, someone substituted three hairs from a cow's udder, and the lovestruck cow followed Fian all over town. It is still common for lovers to carry lockets of head hair, and in centuries past, young girls often made hair bracelets to give to their lovers to keep them faithful.

RED-haired persons are witches or sorcerers, according to one old belief. Evidence exists to indicate that some ancient pagan sorcerers dyed their hair red for certain rituals. Red hair was common among the Celts, whose traditions were steeped in magic. During the witch hunts red-haired people were often suspected of being witches. Witches were said to shoot hairballs into animals to harm them. These hairballs supposedly lodged in the beasts' stomachs without leaving a mark on the skin.

According to superstition, the cutting of hair must be timed according to the phases of the MOON, depending on how quickly one desires the hair to grow back.

See WITCH BOTTLES.

FURTHER READING:
Cavendish, Richard. *The Black Arts.* New York: Putnam, 1967.
Leach, Maria, ed., and Jerome Fried, assoc. ed. *Funk & Wagnall's Standard Dictionary of Folklore, Mythology and Legend.* New York: Harper & Row, 1972.
Opie, Iona, and Moira Tatem. *A Dictionary of Superstitions.* New York: Oxford University Press, 1989.

hand of glory The severed hand of a hanged murderer, magically preserved, once was used as a CHARM in

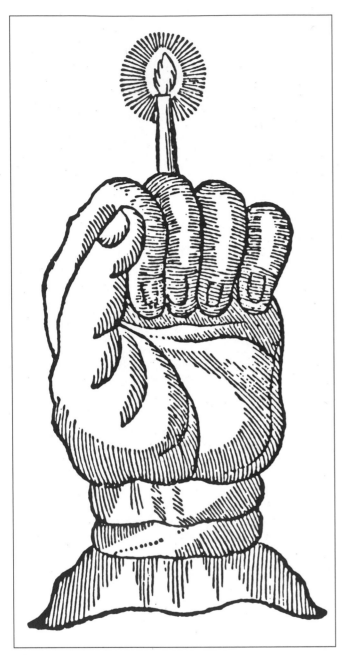

Hand of glory (PETIT ALBERT)

black-magic SPELLS and was believed to aid burglars in breaking into homes and buildings.

The hand of glory was the right hand of a murderer, ideally severed while the corpse still swung from the gallows, or cut during an eclipse of the MOON. It was wrapped in a shroud, squeezed of BLOOD and pickled for two weeks in an earthenware jar with salt, long peppers and saltpeter. It was then either dried in an oven with vervain, an herb believed to repel DEMONS, or laid out to dry in the sun, preferably during the dog days of August.

Once preserved, the hand was fitted with CANDLES between the fingers. The candles, called "dead man's candles," were made from the murderer's fat, with the wick being made from his hair. In another method of curing, the hand of glory was bled, dried and dipped in wax, so that the fingers themselves could be lit as candles.

With candles or fingers burning, the hand of glory supposedly had the power to freeze people in their footsteps and render them speechless. Burglars lit hands of glory before breaking into a house, confident that the charm would keep the occupants in a deep sleep while they plundered the household. If the thumb refused to burn, it meant someone in the house was awake and could not be charmed. According to lore, once a hand of glory was lit, nothing but milk could extinguish it.

As a counter-charm, homeowners made OINTMENTS from the blood of screech OWLS, the fat of while hens and the bile of black CATS and smeared it on their thresholds.

Hands of glory were linked to witches during the witch-hunt centuries. In 1588 two German women, Nichel and Bessers, who were accused of witchcraft and the exhumation of corpses, admitted they poisoned helpless people after lighting hands of glory to immobilize them. JOHN FIAN, who was severely tortured in his witch trial in Scotland in 1590, confessed to using a hand of glory to break into a church, where he performed a service to the DEVIL.

FURTHER READING:

Cavendish, Richard, ed. in chief. *Man, Myth & Magic: The Illustrated Encyclopedia of Mythology, Religion and the Unknown.* New York: Marshall Cavendish, 1983.

de Givry, Emile Grillot. *Witchcraft, Magic and Alchemy.* 1931. Reprint, New York: Dover Publications, 1971.

Leach, Maria, ed., and Jerome Fried, assoc. ed. *Funk & Wagnall's Standard Dictionary of Folklore, Mythology and Legend.* New York: Harper & Row, 1972.

hare   In folklore, a witch's FAMILIAR or a witch metamorphosed in disguise (see METAMORPHOSIS). It is still bad luck in the British Isles for one's path to be crossed by a hare.

Witches were said to be able to change themselves into hares and other animals with magical CHARMS such as the following from the British Isles:

> I shall go into a hare,
> With sorrow and such and muckle care,
> And I shall go in the Devil's name.
> Ay, 'till I come home again.

The hare supposedly was the favorite disguise of ISO-BEL GOWDIE, a Scottish woman who voluntarily confessed to witchcraft in 1662, astonishing her staid community of Auldearne with her wild tales. Once while in the shape of a hare, she said, she had a close call with some dogs. The DEVIL had sent her, as a hare, to carry a message to neighbors. Along the way, she encountered a man and a pack of hounds, which sprang upon her. "I run a very long time," said Gowdie, "but being hard pressed, was forced to take to my house, the door being open, and there took refuge behind a chest." The dogs pursued her into the house, and Gowdie escaped only by running into another room and uttering a "disenchanting" charm:

Hare, hare, God send thee care!
I am in a hare's likeness now;
But I shall be a woman even now——
Hare, hare, God send thee care!

Many stories exist in folklore of hunters shooting hares, only to discover they had killed old hag witches, who resumed their human forms upon death much like the werewolf in disguise. The following Irish folktale, from W. B. Yeats' collection of *Irish Fairy and Folk Tales* (1892), tells of the wounding of a witch hare:

I was out thracking hares meeself, and I seen a fine puss of a thing hopping hopping in the moonlight, and whacking her ears about, now up, now down, and winking her great eyes, and—"Here goes," says I, and the

thing was so close to me that she turned round and looked at me, and then bounced back, as well to say, do your worst! So I had the least grain of life of blessed powder left, and I put it in the gun—and bang at her! My jewel, the scritch she gave would frighten a rigment, and a mist, like, came betwixt me and her, and I seen her no more; but when the mist wint off I saw blood on the spot where she had been, and I followed its track, and at last it led me—whists, whisper—right up to Katey MacShane's door; and when I was at the thrashold, I heerd a murnin' within, a great murnin', and a groanin', and I opened the door, and there she was herself, sittin' quite content in the shape of a woman, and the black cat that was sittin' by her rose up its back and spit at me; but I went on never heedin', and asked the ould——how she was and what ailed her.

"Nothing," sis she.

"What's that on the floor?" sis I.

"Oh," she say, "I was cuttin' a billet of wood," she says, "wid the reaping hook," she says, "an' I've wounded meself in the leg," she says, "and that's drops of my precious blood," she says.

In Norse mythology, the hare is the companion of Freya, goddess of fecundity.

FURTHER READING:
Leach, Maria, ed., and Jerome Fried, assoc. ed. *Funk & Wagnall's Standard Dictionary of Folklore, Mythology and Legend.* New York: Harper & Row, 1972.
Yeats, W. B. *Irish Fairy and Folk Tales.* 1892. Reprint, New York: Dorset Press, 1986.

Hawkins, Jane (17th century) Massachusetts midwife and healer expelled on suspicions of witchcraft in the delivery of a deformed, stillborn fetus. The witchcraft accusations were mixed with a religious controversy affecting Jane Hawkins as well.

Hawkins, married to Richard Hawkins, was well known for her midwifery skills and medical remedies. She also was associated with the Antinomians, a Quaker religious faction that became engaged in political controversy with the dominant Puritans. The Antinomians were led by a woman, Anne Hutchinson.

Hawkins served as midwife to a woman named Mary Dyer, a fellow Antinomian who gave birth in October 1637 to a deformed fetus called a "monster." Authorities declared that it was a sign of God's displeasure with the Antinomians.

Animosity arose against Hawkins, Dyer and Hutchinson. It was said that Hawkins "had familiarity with the Devil" when she had lived in St. Ives, Cornwall, England, and would give young women oil of mandrake to make them conceive. In March 1638, she was ordered "not to meddle in surgery, or physic, drinks, plasters, or oils, not to question matters of religion, except with the elders for satisfaction," according to official records. In June 1638, Hawkins was ordered expelled from Massachusetts Colony

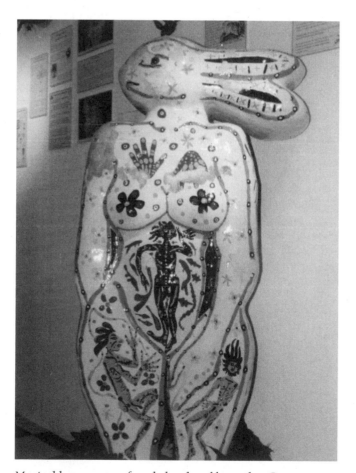

Magical hare woman, found abandoned beneath a Gypsy caravan in England; in the collection of the Museum of Witchcraft in Boscastle, Cornwall (PHOTO BY AUTHOR; COURTESY MUSEUM OF WITCHCRAFT)

or be severely whipped and punished by the court. Her two sons took her away to live in Rhode Island. She returned in 1641 and was banished a second time.

Hutchinson also was banished in 1638. Dyer left, but returned in 1659. She was executed a year later for her Quaker faith.

The association of witchcraft with an unpopular religious practice followed European practices pursued by the Inquisition against heretics and others. The Hawkins case was among the early witchcraft episodes in colonial New England. Had it occurred later, when increasing anti-witch hysteria developed, Hawkins most likely would have been brought to trial and perhaps executed. By the 1650s, Quaker woman missionaries were increasingly linked to witchcraft. Two missionaries, Mary Fisher and Ann Austin, were stripped of their clothing by authorities and searched for WITCH'S MARKS.

FURTHER READING:
Hall, David D., ed. *Witch-hunting in Seventeenth-Century New England: A Documentary History 1638–1692*. Boston: Northeastern University Press, 1991.

Hawthorne, Nathaniel (1804–1864) A native of Salem, Massachusetts, and one of the great masters of American fiction, Nathaniel Hawthorne wrote one of his best-known works, *The House of Seven Gables*, perhaps in part to atone for the role of an ancestor who played a role in the SALEM WITCH hysteria of 1692.

The ancestor, Judge John Hathorne (an earlier spelling of the family name), was a son of Nathaniel's great-great-grandfather, Major William Hathorne. John Hathorne was a respected magistrate of Salem, who heard the trials with two other magistrates. He was not a vindictive man, and he put skeptical questions to the accusers who testified during the lengthy trials. Nevertheless, he believed in witchcraft as an evil and believed in the power to afflict others through MAGIC with POPPETS. He was swayed by the testimony of spectral evidence and allowed it to be admitted in court.

As a young man, Nathaniel Hawthorne was fascinated and deeply affected by a family story that Hathorne had been cursed by one of the convicted witches. One of the condemned, SARAH GOOD, had issued a CURSE as she went to the gallows. Asked by Rev. Nicholas Noyes to confess, she replied, "I am no more a witch than you are a wizard, and if you take away my life, God will give you blood to drink." Noyes reportedly choked on his own blood in 1717. It is not known for certain whether the curse was laid on other officials responsible for the executions, but the Hathorne family apparently came to believe so. Another victim of the Salem hysteria, Philip English, a wealthy merchant and shipper, made no secret of his hate for John Hathorne and Sheriff George Corwin. As a result of the ordeal brought on by charges of witchcraft against them, the Englishes lost all their property and fortune. The health of Mary, Philip's wife, was so impaired that she sickened and died. English bore an open grudge against the authorities, particularly Corwin and Hathorne, neither of whom apparently ever expressed regret over their roles in the sufferings. English refused to forgive Hathorne until just before English died. Ironically, the Hathorne and English families eventually joined in a marriage, which produced the lineage to which Nathaniel Hawthorne was born.

Prior to the witch trials, the Hathorne family had been prosperous in shipping and farming. The family was established in America by Major Hathorne, who left England for Boston in 1630, then moved to Salem in 1636. He became the first speaker in the House of Delegates in Massachusetts colony. In the early 1700s, beginning with Nathaniel's great-grandfather, Captain Joseph Hathorne (born in 1692), the family fortunes began to decline, and the family lost social status in Salem as well.

Nathaniel was born on July 4, 1804, in a gambrel-roofed house in Salem that had been purchased in 1772 by his grandfather, Daniel Hathorne, the youngest son of Captain Joseph. Nathaniel's father, also named Nathaniel, was a sea captain who died of yellow fever while on a voyage to Surinam when the boy was six. Hawthorne spent much of his childhood in Salem and Raymond, Maine, where his mother's family owned property. He preferred to spend time alone in the woods and was described as "fragile."

His family scraped together enough money to send him to Bowdoin College. Prior to his entrance in 1821, Hawthorne wrote to his mother, "What do you think of becoming an Author, and relying for support upon my pen? . . . How proud would you feel to see my works praised by the reviewers, as equal to the proudest productions of the scribbling sons of John Bull. But Authors are always poor Devils, and therefore Satan may take them."

After Nathaniel's graduation from college, one story goes, his older sister convinced him to restore the *w* to Hawthorne, which had been dropped many generations before, in order to separate himself from the infamous Hathorne lineage.

For years, Hawthorne apparently brooded about the witch's curse. He also was fascinated by Puritan sin and suffering. In the introduction to *The Scarlet Letter*, published in 1850, he stated:

> He [Judge Hathorne] made himself so conspicuous in the martyrdom of the witches, that their blood may fairly be said to have left a stain upon him. . . . I know not whether these ancestors of mine be-thought themselves to repent, and ask pardon of heaven for their cruelties. . . . At all events, I, the present writer, as their representative, hereby take shame upon myself for their sakes, and pray that any curse incurred by them . . . may be now and henceforth removed.

Hawthorne used the curse, some real-life figures from Salem and his own gambrel-roofed house in his next novel, *The House of Seven Gables*, written in Lenox, Massachusetts, and published in 1851. Like his own family, the Pyncheon family of the novel suffers from inherited sin related to witchcraft. A piece of property owned by Matthew Maule includes a pure, sweet-water spring. Maule's jealous neighbor, Judge Pyncheon, becomes obsessed with owning it and is driven to have Maule accused of witchcraft. Maule is convicted and sentenced to be hanged. Before he is executed, he curses Pyncheon: "Pyncheon, God will give you blood to drink and quench your greed for eternity." After Maule is buried, Pyncheon buys his land and builds on it the House of Seven Gables. Pyncheon invites his friends over for a housewarming dinner, which he never gets to enjoy: he is found slumped in a chair, dead of a massive throat hemorrhage. The Pyncheon family suffers decline, then is redeemed when young Phoebe Pyncheon marries a descendant of Matthew Maule, and the land and house are restored to their rightful owner.

The malicious character of Judge Pyncheon was modeled on the Rev. Charles Wentworth Upham, mayor and minister of Salem, whose books, *Lectures on Witchcraft* (1831) and *History of Witchcraft and Salem Village* (1867), reveal malice and erroneous moral perspectives but nonetheless established him as an authority on the witch trials. Hawthorne borrowed the Maule name from Thomas Maule, a Quaker merchant who lived in Salem at the time of the trials, and who believed the witch hysteria and favored the executions. Maule's own definition of a witch was anyone who was not a Quaker.

The House of Seven Gables, as Hawthorne's house is now called, remained on its original site near the Salem harbor until 1958, when it was moved to a new location on the harbor. It was opened to the public in 1959 and remains one of Salem's biggest tourist attractions.

FURTHER READING:
Hansen, Chadwick. *Witchcraft at Salem*. New York: New American Library, 1969.
Starkey, Marion L. *The Devil in Massachusetts*. New York: Alfred Knopf, 1950.

hazel   The hazel tree is one of powerful MAGIC, according to ancient beliefs. Hermes' caduceus, a gift from Apollo, was made of hazel. The early Roman naturalist, Pliny, wrote of how to use hazel wands for divining underground springs. The rod of Moses was cut from a hazel tree by Adam in the Garden of Eden. Moses and Aaron used hazel rods to bring plagues into Egypt. In the fourth century, St. Patrick is said to have rid Ireland of snakes by drawing them together with a magic hazel rod and then casting them into the sea.

Hazel wood and hazelnuts are believed to offer protection against witchcraft, DEMONS and fairy bewitchment (see FAIRIES). Hazel breastbands on harnesses have been used to protect horses. In Ireland, the hazel is a symbol of great mystical wisdom. Cattle are singed with hazel rods at Beltane and Midsummer fires in order to keep fairies away. In Scotland, double hazel nuts are thrown at witches.

Hazel nuts also have been used in the casting of SPELLS. In some areas, picking hazel nuts on a Sunday is believed to summon the DEVIL to appear. Hazelnuts are gathered in traditional fall fertility rites in some parts of England.

healing   Contemporary witches and Wiccans view healing as one of their most important functions. They use a wide range of healing techniques, including MAGIC; herbal and folk remedies; body work and energy work; Native American Indian and shamanic techniques (see SHAMANISM); and Western approaches to medicine and psychology. Some Witches are professional healers, trained in Eastern and/or Western medicine and psychology. Witches prefer holistic and natural healing methods that involve healing power of sound, breath, color, touch and movement.

Prior to the scientific age, healing commonly was the province of the village wise woman, CUNNING MAN, witch or WIZARD. Such individuals often were born with the mysterious gift of healing by touch, and many were steeped in herbal lore that had been passed down though generations of their families. Still others said they received their healing ability from FAIRIES. Folk healers diagnosed both human and animal ailments. Some were renowned for determining whether or not haunting fairies or ghosts (see GHOSTS, HAUNTINGS AND WITCHCRAFT) were responsible for illness, and then driving them away.

Witch "inoculating" man by shooting twig through his foot (ULRICH MOLITOR, *DE IANIJS ET PHITONICIUS MULIERBUS*, 1489)

One common remedy for fairy-caused illness was the recitation of Christian PRAYERS followed by a measurement of the patient's girdle to see if the fairy had departed the body (see GIRDLE MEASURING). Other healers diagnosed the patient's urine. Healers dispensed herbal remedies in the form of powders, potions and unguents. They prescribed CHARMS, little prayers comprised of both pagan and Christian elements. They also cast SPELLS. Some folk-magic remedies required procedures on the part of the patient, such as boiling an egg and burying it in an anthill; the disease or condition would disappear when ants had consumed the egg. Healers also made use of gems and semiprecious stones, which have a long history as medicinal objects.

The greatest natural healing knowledge comes from herbalism, the earliest of all healing systems and one used throughout the world. In Western culture, herbalism had been developed to a high art by the ancient Egyptians, Sumerians, Assyrians, Babylonians, Greeks and Romans. Herbal sorcery was renowned in ancient Greece. The greatest collection of ancient plant lore was compiled by Pliny in *Natural History*, a 37-volume work that contains a wealth of information about the medicinal uses of plants, flowers, trees and herbs. For centuries, others built upon Pliny's work, most notably Hildegard of Bingen, a medieval German mystic and abbess, and Nicholas Culpeper, a 17th-century English physician and astrologer who linked herbs to astrological signs.

Plants acquired numerous pagan religious associations, which the Christian Church replaced with Christian associations. *Hypericum perforatum,* for example, blooms during the summer solstice and was an ancient totem of sun worship. The Romans burned it in bonfires in observance of the solstice, which occurs around June 21. The Christian Church associated it with the birth of John the Baptist on June 24, and the plant became known as St. John's wort. Cunning folk, witches and healers often observed both pagan and Christian associations in their charms and recipes.

The church attempted to discredit village healers, for their cures competed with the church, which claimed a monopoly on miracles. Healing by SORCERY was considered fraudulent—and there were many such cases of fraud—and was a civil crime under Roman law. The laws were not strictly enforced, however, for the populace was reluctant to give up local healers. During the witch-hunts, healing by sorcery was considered "white" witchcraft until demonologists began denouncing it as an evil. INCREASE MATHER stated that healing power in a witch was a diabolical gift, not a divine gift from God.

Many contemporary Witches become skilled in the use of herbs to maintain health as well as to cure illness. Some grow and harvest their own herbs, which they use to make salves, syrups, teas, poultices and powders. Herbs also are used in magical healing. For example, a cloth doll called a POPPET is made to represent the patient and is stuffed with the appropriate herbal remedy. The poppet is used in the casting of a sympathetic magic spell for healing.

The ability to heal by a laying on of hands, like healing with herbs, has ancient origins. Prehistoric cave paintings in the Pyrenees indicate that it may have been used as early as 15,000 years ago. Healing by touch has a written history dating back about 5,000 years; it was used in ancient India, China, Tibet, Egypt and Chaldea and appears in both the Old and New Testaments. Gifted individuals are born with the ability for this kind of healing, though it can be learned.

The Christian Church encouraged such miraculous healing within the confines of religion. Outside the church, it was regarded as fraudulent sorcery and witchcraft. The one notable exception, tolerated by the church, was the king's touch, which began in England in the Middle Ages and was popular in England and France until nearly the end of the 17th century. The king's touch was the reputed ability of royalty to heal, especially a type of scrofula called the king's evil. The procedure called for the patient to kneel before the monarch, who lightly touched the face and (usually) invoked the name of God, while a chaplain read from the Gospel of Mark, "They shall lay hands on the sick and they shall recover." The king then hung a gold coin strung on a ribbon around the patient's neck; the coin was reputed to have great magical powers.

The king's touch was begun by Edward the Confessor (r. 1042–66) and was a full ceremony by the time of Henry VII (r. 1485–1509). Charles II (r. 1660–85) gave nearly 91,000 healings. After Charles II the procedure gradually lost favor with monarchs and royal doctors though not with the populace, who searched out wizards and the like as substitutes for the king.

Many contemporary Witches and Pagans are trained in a wide variety of complementary healing modalities involving energy work, body work, shamanic techniques, physical therapy and spiritual counseling. Those who practice spellcraft (perhaps in addition to the above) weave magical spells into their healing work as well.

Hecate   In Greek mythology, a powerful goddess who became the patron of MAGIC and witchcraft. Hecate has three aspects: goddess of fertility and plenty; goddess of the MOON; and queen of the night, ghosts and shades. In her moon-goddess aspect, she is often part of a trinity with SELENE and DIANA/Artemis.

Hecate possesses infernal power, roaming the earth at night with a pack of red-eyed hell hounds and a retinue of dead souls. She is visible only to dogs, and if dogs howl in the night, it means Hecate is about. She is the cause of nightmares and insanity and is so terrifying that many ancients referred to her only as "The Nameless One."

She is the goddess of the dark of the moon, the destroyer of life but also the restorer of life. In one myth, she turns into a bear or boar and kills her own son, then brings him back to life. In her dark aspect, she wears a necklace made of testicles; her hair is made of writhing snakes which petrify, like the Medusa.

Hecate is the goddess of all CROSSROADS, looking in three directions at the same time. In ancient times, three-headed statues of her were set up at many intersections and secret rites were performed under a full moon to appease her. Statues of Hecate carrying torches or swords were erected in front of homes to keep evil spirits at bay.

Hecate has been associated with many incantations, SACRIFICES and RITUALS throughout history. In ancient times, people sought to appease her by leaving chicken hearts and honey cakes outside their doors. On the last day of the month, offerings of honey, onions, fish and eggs were left at crossroads, along with sacrifices of puppies, infant girls and she-lambs. Sorcerers gathered at crossroads to pay homage to her and such infernal servants as the Empusa, a hobgoblin; the Cercopsis, a poltergeist; and the Mormo, a ghoul. One petition for her patronage was recorded in the 3rd century by Hippolytus in *Philosophumena*:

Come, infernal, terrestrial, and heavenly Bombo (Hecate), goddess of the broad roadways, of the crossroad, thou who goest to and fro at night, torch in hand, enemy of the day. Friend and lover of darkness, thou who doest rejoice when the bitches are howling and warm blood is spilled, thou who art walking amid the phantom and in the place of tombs, thou whose thirst is blood, thou who dost strike chill fear into mortal hearts, Gorgo, Mormo, Moon of a thousand forms, cast a propitious eye upon our sacrifice.

As the goddess of all forms of magic and witchcraft, Hecate was far more important in antiquity than the mythical sorceress CIRCE, who was sometimes said to be her daughter, or the witch Medea, also sometimes said to be Hecate's daughter, who helped Jason steal the Golden Fleece.

In modern Witchcraft, Hecate is usually associated with the lunar trinity, the Triple Goddess. She rules over the waning and dark moon, a two-week period that is best for magic that deals with banishing, releasing, planning and introspection. She is invoked for justice.

See GODDESS.

hedge witch   Term coined and popularized by English witch Rae Beth to describe the contemporary yet traditional village witch or wise woman or man who practices alone without a COVEN. Rae Beth describes the hedge witch as "one who 'knows' and worships the Goddess and her consort, the Horned God; one who practices spellcraft for the purposes of healing, and teaches the mysteries."

The contemporary hedge witch is versed in the ways of nature, skilled in herbalism, proficient in the casting of SPELLS and observant of Pagan seasonal festivals (see WHEEL OF THE YEAR).

See CUNNING MAN/CUNNING WOMAN; PELLAR; SOLITARY.

FURTHER READING:
Rae Beth. *Hedge Witch: A Guide to Solitary Witchcraft.* London: Robert Hale, 1990.

Hellfire Club   See BLACK MASS; SATANISM.

Helms Amendment   An attempt in 1985 by two members of Congress, Senator Jesse Helms of North Carolina and Representative Robert Walker of Pennsylvania, to outlaw religious tax exempt status for Witchcraft, Wicca and Pagan churches and organizations. Both measures failed.

The effort was begun by Helms, who queried Secretary of the Treasury James Baker about Witchcraft groups. Baker replied in a letter that several organizations that "espouse a system of beliefs, rituals and practices derived in part from pre-Christian Celtic and Welsh traditions which they label as 'witchcraft'" did indeed have tax-exempt status. Baker also pointed out that any group that is sincere in its beliefs, does not break the law and conforms to "clearly defined public policy" can qualify for tax exemption.

Few Wiccan/Pagan groups apply for tax-exempt status. Most operate on very slim budgets. Nevertheless, the congressmen introduced their bills. Walker's legislative assistant told the press, "If a person is praying for horrible things and sticking pins into voodoo dolls, that is not the kind of religion that should be supported by a tax exemption."

The bills were opposed by the American Civil Liberties Union and numerous Wiccan/Pagan groups, among them the COVENANT OF THE GODDESS, a Berkeley, California, organization that is tax-exempt and represents Witchcraft groups around the country; CIRCLE SANCTUARY, an international Pagan networking organization based near Mt. Horeb, Wisconsin; and the CHURCH AND SCHOOL OF WICCA, then based in New Bern, North Carolina. The ACLU called the bill "the crudest example of First Amendment infringement." Witches, who organized a massive letter-writing and flyer campaign, termed the bills a throwback to the witch-hunts of the Middle Ages. The issue became known as the "Helms Amendment."

Neither the Helms nor Walker measure survived to be incorporated into the sweeping tax-reform legislation passed in 1986.

Hermes   Greek messenger god, swift and cunning, portrayed with winged feet, wearing a winged helmet and carrying a caduceus, a serpent-entwined, magic wand that symbolizes spiritual illumination. Hermes also was a patron god of MAGIC, using his caduceus to cast SPELLS. As god of travelers, his image was erected at CROSSROADS;

he was charged with escorting the souls of the dead to the underworld. The dog is associated with Hermes for its intelligence and devotion.

According to myth, Hermes was born of Zeus and Maia, daughter of Atlas. He was a shrewd thief from his earliest hours. Before nightfall on his first day of life, he stole most of Apollo's heifers. Zeus made him return the heifers. In contrition, Hermes invented the lyre and gave it to Apollo. Hermes continued to play malicious tricks but also was generous in his protection of others: for instance, he saved Odysseus from the magical spells of CIRCE.

Hermes appears in Greek mythology more often than any other deity. The Greeks identified him closely with the Egyptian god of wisdom and magic, Thoth. Hermes is said to have learned the mysteries of the universe, which he sought to teach others. Hermes has been equated with Odin and Wotan in Norse and Teutonic mythology, and with Buddha.

Hermes, along with Thoth, is personified in HERMES TRISMEGISTUS, a mythical figure said to have written the HERMETICA texts of ancient sacred learning and lore.

Hermes Trismegistus   "The thrice greatest Hermes," a mythological blend of the Egyptian god Thoth, who governed mystical wisdom, MAGIC, writing and other disciplines, and was associated with HEALING; and the Greek god HERMES, the personification of universal wisdom and patron of MAGIC, the swift, wing-footed messenger god who carried a magic wand, the caduceus. The ancient Greeks associated Hermes with Thoth so closely that the two became inseparable. "Thrice greatest" refers to Hermes Trismegistus as the greatest of all philosophers; the greatest of all kings; and the greatest of all priests.

Both Thoth and Hermes were associated with sacred writings. As scribe of the gods, Thoth was credited with all sacred books. In some Egyptian writings, he was described as "twice very great" and "five times very great." Hermes was credited with the authorship of 20,000 books by Iamblichus (ca. 250–300 B.C.E.), a Neo-platonic Syrian philosopher, and more than 36,000 by Manetho (ca. 300 B.C.E.), an Egyptian priest who wrote the history of Egypt in Greek, perhaps for Ptolemy I. According to myth, both Thoth and Hermes revealed to mankind the healing arts, magic, writing, astrology, sciences and philosophy. Thoth recorded the weighing of souls in the Judgment Hall of Osiris Hermes conducted the souls of the dead to Hades. Hermes, said Francis Barrett in *Biographia Antiqua,* ". . . communicated the sum of the Abyss, and the divine knowledge to all posterity . . ."

Hermes Trismegistus provided the wisdom of the light in the ancient Egyptian mysteries. He carried an emerald, upon which was recorded all of philosophy, and the caduceus, the symbol of mystical illumination. Hermes Trismegistus vanquished Typhon, the dragon of ignorance and mental, moral and physical perversion.

Hermes Trismegistus (JACQUES BOISSARD, *DE DIVINATIONE ET MAGICIS*)

The surviving wisdom of Hermes Trismegistus is said to be the HERMETICA, 42 books that profoundly influenced the development of Western occultism and magic. These books, probably authored by a succession of anonymous persons date to between the third century B.C.E. and the first century C.E.

FURTHER READING:
Mead, G. R. S. *Thrice Greatest Hermes: Studies in Hellenistic Theosophy and Gnosis.* York Beach, Me.: Samuel Weiser, 1992.

Hermetica   Forty-two sacred books of mystical wisdom attributed to the mythical HERMES TRISMEGISTUS, or "thrice great Hermes," the combined Egyptian and Greek deities of Thoth and HERMES, respectively. The books, which date from somewhere between the third century B.C.E. and first century C.E., had an enormous impact on the development of Western occultism and MAGIC. Many of the spells, rituals and much of the esoteric symbolism contained in Witchcraft folk magic, and contemporary WICCA and PAGANISM are based upon Hermetic material.

The Hermetica may have been authored by one person—according to one legend, Hermes Trismegistus was a grandson of Adam and a builder of the Egyptian pyramids—but probably was the work of several persons in succession. According to legend, the books were initially written on papyrus. Clement of Alexandria, a chronicler of pagan lore, said 36 of the Hermetic books contained the whole philosophy of the Egyptians: four books on astrology, 10 books called the *Hieratic* on law, 10 books on sacred rites and observances, two on music and the rest on writing, cosmography, geography, mathematics and measures and priestly training. The remaining six books were medical and concerned the body, diseases, instruments, medicines, the eyes and women.

Most of the Hermetic books were lost with others in the royal libraries in the burning of Alexandria. According to legend, the surviving books were buried in a secret location in the desert, where they have survived to the present. A few initiates of the mystery schools, ancient secret cults, supposedly know the books' location.

What little was left of the surviving Hermetic lore has been handed down through history and has been translated into various languages. The most important of these

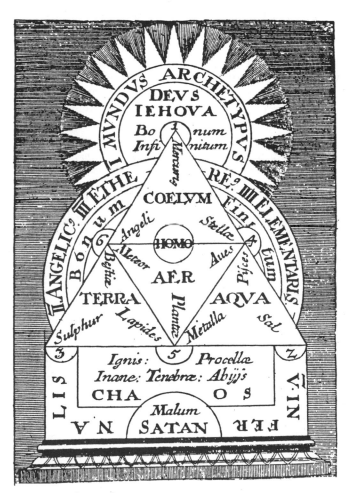

Hermetic scheme of universe (AFTER THOMAS NORTON, *MUSAEUM HERMETICUM*, 1749)

works, and one of the earliest, is *The Divine Pymander*. It consists of 17 fragments collected into a single work, which contain many of the original Hermetic concepts, including the way divine wisdom and the secrets of the universe were revealed to Hermes and how Hermes established his ministry to spread this wisdom throughout the world. *The Divine Pymander* apparently was revised during the early centuries C.E. and has suffered from incorrect translations.

The second book of *The Divine Pymander,* called *Poimandres* or *The Vision,* is perhaps the most famous. It tells of Hermes' mystical vision, cosmogony and the Egyptians' secret sciences of culture and the spiritual development of the soul.

The Emerald Tablet. Also called the *Emerald Table,* the Emerald Tablet is one of the most revered of magical documents in western occultism. Hermes Trismegistus was portrayed in art as holding an emerald upon which was inscribed the whole of the Egyptians' philosophy. This Emerald Tablet was said to be discovered in a cave tomb, clutched in the hands of the corpse of Hermes Trismegistus. According to one version of the legend, the tomb was found by Sarah, wife of Abraham, while another version credits the discovery to Apollonius of Tyana. The gem was inscribed in Phoenician and revealed magical secrets of the universe. A Latin translation of the Tablet appeared by 1200, preceded by several Arabic versions. No two translations are the same, and little of the Tablet appears to make sense.

The significance of the Emerald Tablet, however, lies in its opening: "That which is above is like that which is below and that which is below is like that which is above, to achieve the wonders of the one thing." This is the foundation of astrology and alchemy: that the microcosm of mankind and the earth is a reflection of the macrocosm of God and the heavens.

FURTHER READING:
Hall, Manly Palmer. *The Secret Teachings of All Ages.* Los Angeles: The Philosophi Research Society, 1977.
Mead, G. R. S. *Thrice Greatest Hermes: Studies in Hellenistic Theosophy and Gnosis.* York Beach, Me.: Samuel Weiser, 1992.
Seligmann, Kurt. *The Mirror of Magic.* New York: Pantheon Books, 1948.
Waite, Arthur Edward. *The Hermetic Museum.* York Beach, Me.: Samuel Weiser, 1991.

Hermetic Order of the Golden Dawn   One of the most influential Western occult societies of the late 19th century to early 20th century. Like a meteor, it flared into light, blazed a bright trail and then disintegrated. Members included W. B. Yeats, A. E. Waite, ALEISTER CROWLEY and other noted occultists.

The key founder of the Golden Dawn was Dr. William Wynn Westcott, a London coroner and a Rosicrucian.

In 1887 Westcott obtained part of a manuscript written in brown-ink cipher from the Rev. A. F. A. Woodford, a Mason. The manuscript appeared to be old but probably was not. Westcott himself is believed to be the author. Westcott claimed he was able to decipher the manuscript and discovered it concerned fragments of rituals for the "Golden Dawn," an unknown organization that apparently admitted both men and women.

Westcott asked an occultist friend, Samuel Liddell MacGregor Mathers, to flesh out the fragments into full-scale rituals. Some papers evidently were forged to give the "Golden Dawn" authenticity and a history. It was said to be an old German occult order. Westcott produced papers that showed he had been given a charter to set up an independent lodge in England. The Isis-Urania Temple of the Hermetic Order of the Golden Dawn was established in 1888, with Westcott, Mathers and Dr. W. R. Woodman, Supreme Magus of the Rosicrucian Society of Anglia, as the three Chiefs. The secret society quickly caught on, and 315 initiations took place during the society's heydey, from 1888 to 1896.

An elaborate hierarchy was created, consisting of 10 grades or degrees, each corresponding to the 10 sephiroth of the Tree of Life of the KABBALAH, plus an 11th degree for neophytes. The degrees are divided into three orders: Outer, Second and Third.

One advanced through the Outer Order by examination. Initially, Westcott, Mathers and Woodman were the only members of the Second Order, and they claimed to be under the direction of the Secret Chiefs of the Third Order, who were entities of the astral plane. Mathers' rituals were based largely on Freemasonry.

In 1891 Woodman died and was not replaced in the organization. Mathers produced the initiation ritual for the Adeptus Minor rank and renamed the Second Order the *Ordo Rosae Rubeae et Aureae Crucis,* or the Order of the Rose of Ruby and Cross of Gold (R. R. et A. C.). Initiation was by invitation only.

Mathers was at the very least eccentric and possibly was mentally unstable. He never consummated his marriage with his wife, Mina, who, he said, received teachings from the Secret Chiefs through clairaudience, or supernormal hearing. His finances were erratic, and in 1891 he and his wife were penniless. A rich Golden Dawner, Annie Horniman, became their benefactor. Mathers and his wife moved to Paris, where Mathers set up another lodge. He continued to write curricula materials and send them to London. He was obsessed with jealousy over Westcott and became increasingly autocratic. He devoted a good deal of time to translating the manuscript of *The Book of the Sacred Magic of Abra-Melin the Mage,* which he claimed was bewitched and inhabited by a species of nonphysical intelligence. (The book eventually was published in 1898).

In 1896 Horniman cut off her financial support to Mathers. The same year, Mathers claimed that the Secret Chiefs had initiated him into the Third Order. Horniman disputed his claim and was expelled from the society. In 1897 members began to discover Westcott's questionable role in "discovering" the Golden Dawn. He resigned his post and was succeeded by Florence Farr. By then, irreparable schisms were forming within the Golden Dawn.

Aleister Crowley was initiated in 1898 and rapidly rose up the ranks. In 1899 he went to Paris and insisted upon being initiated into the Second Order. Mathers complied. The London lodge, under Farr, rejected his initiation. In 1900 Crowley went to England as Mathers' "Envoy Extraordinary" and attempted to take control of the quarters of the Second Order. He appeared wearing a black mask, Highland dress and a gilt dagger and stormed the lodge but was turned away.

The Crowley-Mathers alliance was always troubled. Crowley considered himself a superior magician to Mathers. The two supposedly engaged in magical warfare. Mathers sent an astral vampire to attack Crowley psychically, and Crowley responded with an army of DEMONS led by Beelzebub. The London lodge expelled both Crowley and Mathers. Crowley retaliated by publishing some of the Golden Dawn's secret rituals in his magazine, *The Equinox.*

W. B. Yeats took over the Second Order. He attempted to restore unity, but the schisms in the Golden Dawn broke into independent groups. Followers of Mathers formed the Alpha et Omega Temple. In 1903 A. E. Waite and others left, forming a group with the name Golden Dawn but with more of an emphasis on mysticism than magic. In 1905 another splinter group was formed, the Stella Matutina, or "Order of the Companions of the Rising Light in the Morning." The Isis-Uranian Temple became defunct. In 1917 it was resurrected as the Merlin Temple of the Stella Matutina. The Stella Matutina went into decline in the 1940s, following the publication of its secret rituals by a former member, Israel Regardie, Crowley's one-time secretary.

Waite's group, which retained the Golden Dawn name and some of its rituals, declined after 1915 with Waite's departure. Some distant offshoots of the Golden Dawn continue in existence.

During its height, the Hermetic Order of the Golden Dawn possessed the greatest known repository of Western magical knowledge. Second Order studies centered on the Kabbalistic Tree of Life. Three magical systems were taught: the Key of Solomon (see GRIMOIRES); Abra-Melin magic (see ABRAMELIN THE MAGE); and Enochian magic (see JOHN DEE). Materials also were incorporated from the Egyptian Book of the Dead, William Blake's Prophetic Books and the Chaldean Oracles. Instruction was given in astral travel, SCRYING, alchemy, geomancy, the Tarot and astrology.

The key purpose of the order was "to prosecute the Great Work: which is to obtain control of the nature and power of [one's] own being." Some of the texts included Christian elements, such as the establishing of a closer relationship with Jesus, the "Master of Masters." Members circulated various Catholic and Anglican writings and sermons. These were omitted from the materials published by Regardie. Elements of Golden Dawn rituals, Rosicrucianism and Freemasonry have been absorbed into the rituals of modern Witchcraft.

See DION FORTUNE; HERMETICA; MAGIC; FRANCIS ISRAEL REGARDIE.

FURTHER READING:

Gilbert, R. A. *Golden Dawn: Twilight of the Magicians*. Wellingborough, Northhamptonshire, England: The Aquarian Press, 1983.

MacGregor-Mathers, S. L. *The Book of the Sacred Magic of Abra-Melin the Mage*. Wellingborough, England: The Aquarian Press, 1976.

Regardie, Israel. *The Golden Dawn*. 5th ed. St. Paul: Llewellyn Publications, 1986.

———. *What You Should Know About the Golden Dawn*. 3rd ed. Phoenix: Falcon Press, 1983.

Symonds, John, and Kenneth Grant, eds. *The Confessions of Aleister Crowley, An Autobiography*. London: Routledge & Kegan Paul, 1979.

Hermitage Castle Ruined castle near Newcastleton in Roxburghshire, Scotland, reputed to be haunted because of malign black MAGIC and witchcraft practiced by Lord Soulis, its owner and occupant in the 13th century.

Soulis is alleged to have practiced black magic. He kidnapped young farm children, imprisoned them in the castle's dungeon and sacrificed them in dark rites. He had a FAMILIAR Redcap Sly (see REDCAP), who appeared in the form of a horrible old man with vampire-like fangs. Redcap Sly told his master that he could be bound only by a three-stranded rope of sand. Soulis magically made Redcap impervious to weapons. The familiar became so troublesome to him, however, that Soulis resorted to destroying him by boiling him in oil in a brazen pot.

There are different versions of the lord's demise, which sound like variations on the fate of Redcap Sly. According to one story, the enraged parents of the murdered children stormed the castle and attacked Soulis. He was bound in iron chains and a blanket of lead and boiled to death. According to another story, he abducted the Laird of Branxholm, a crime for which he was bound in a sheet of lead and boiled to death.

Ghostly sounds of the young murder victims reportedly are heard coming from within the castle.

FURTHER READING:

Briggs, Katharine. *An Encyclopedia of Fairies*. New York: Pantheon, 1976.

Folklore, Myths and Legends of Britain. London: Reader's Digest Assoc., 1977.

Green, Andrew. *Our Haunted Kingdom*. London: Wolfe Publishing Limited, 1973.

Herne the Hunter A spectral huntsman of English lore, often the leader of the WILD HUNT or the nocturnal processions of the dead. As leader of the Wild Hunt, Herne has lunar associations. His name is associated with another leader of the dead, Herlechin, or Harlequin, also associated with the DEVIL. Herne is portrayed wearing an antlered headdress. In modern Witchcraft, he is associated with the HORNED GOD, and with CERNUNNOS and PAN. Sightings of Herne are still reported in Windsor Forest near Windsor Castle and are associated with Witchcraft activities. Similar spectral horned huntsmen exist in German and French lore.

Hertford Witches (d. 1606) Two women executed for crimes committed by witchcraft in Royston, England. Joan Harrison and her daughter were widely believed to practice malevolent SPELLS and BEWITCHMENT, including deaths.

At the time of Joan Harrison's arrest in the summer of 1606, she had long been regarded as a local witch. Her house was searched and incriminating evidence was found—human bones and hair and a drawing on parchment of a human body and heart. Harrison readily confessed that she used these items to cast spells. By pricking a body part on the drawing, she could cause torment, even death, to a person at a distance. She was aided by two FAMILIARS, she said, one for spells against people and one for spells against cattle.

She confessed to tormenting a neighbor with whom she had argued and who had called her an "old hag." She promised revenge, and soon he fell ill with great bodily pain, as though he were being tortured. Believing himself to be bewitched, he visited Harrison and drew her blood by scratching her (see BLOOD), which brought an end to his torment.

Harrison turned the tables on him by having him arrested and charged for battery. She won her case in court and was awarded five pounds and her trial costs. The man paid her and then suffered a relapse of pains and died.

Later, Harrison was out in a street and passed a house where a young woman was washing clothes with her baby next to her in a cradle. The woman dumped her rinse water just as Harrison was passing, and some of it fell on her. The woman apologized, but Harrison said she would have revenge for the offense. Within a short time, the cradle overturned and shattered, and the woman's baby was killed.

Harrison bewitched a young woman into sickness. The spell was broken by her brother. In revenge, Harrison killed all of his cattle. The brother died soon thereafter.

One of Harrison's final bewitchments was against a drunk at an alehouse who argued with her and called her vile names. After she departed, he felt ill and blamed her. He tracked her down and attacked her, nearly scratching out her eyes.

Soon after this incident, Harrison was arrested, along with her daughter. Harrison was charged with other crimes against people besides the ones recorded. Records do not give the daughter's name or details of her alleged crimes. Mother and daughter were tried in Hertford and were executed by hanging on August 4, 1606.

FURTHER READING:
Rosen, Barbara, ed. *Witchcraft in England, 1558–1618.* Amherst: University of Massachusetts Press, 1991.

hex   A SPELL or bewitchment. The term comes from the Pennsylvania Dutch, who borrowed it from their native German word for "witch," *Hexe,* which in turn is derived from Old High German *hagazussa* or *hagzissa* ("hag"). In common usage, *hex* means an evil spell or CURSE, but among the Pennsylvania Dutch, for example, a hex can be either good or bad. It is cast by a professional witch whose services are sought out and paid for with a donation. Witches also are consulted to break and protect against hexes.

See HEX SIGNS; POWWOWING.

hex death   Also called "voodoo death," hex death is death from a HEX or CURSE resulting from black MAGIC or the breaking of a taboo. The critical factor in hex death is belief. If a person believes that a WITCH or sorcerer can make him die by cursing him or by pointing a finger or bone at him, he probably will expire, and no amount of Western conventional medicine can save him. Hex death may be in part a self-fulfilling prophecy.

In her studies on hex death, anthropologist Joan Halifax-Grof lists four causes: 1) secretly administered poisons or other physical agents; 2) the relationship between physical and emotional factors in the victim; 3) societal reactions in a particular culture; and 4) parapsychological influences. Poisons and physical agents are obvious malfactors; if administered "magically," with plenty of ceremony, they may kill without the victim's knowledge.

The second category refers to the fact that a person literally can die from fright. In stressful situations the adrenaline surges, preparing the body either to fight or escape. If neither is possible, the body could suffer both short- and long-term damage, such as shock, lowering of blood pressure and attacking of the body's immune system. Rage affects the body as well. Finally, if the victim believes his cursed situation to be hopeless, he begins to experience feelings of helplessness, incompetence, despair and worthlessness. Illness sets in, which the victim has no desire to fight, and eventually he succumbs. Psychologists term this situation the *giving up/given up* complex.

Cultural determinants play as large a role in hex death as the victim's own perceptions. Once cursed, the victim may be forced to withdraw from daily community life, becoming almost invisible to his neighbors. The cursed individual becomes despondent, expecting death, and his friends and relatives do not dispute such notions but corroborate them. Eventually, those not cursed see the

victim as already dead, even performing funeral ceremonies over his body, which technically still lives. In Australia, aborigines actually take away food and water from the accursed, since a dead person needs no sustenance. Suffering from starvation and dehydration in the searing Australia bush, the victim indeed dies.

In many cases, however, the victim dies despite the efforts of his friends or family to save him. In such instances, Halifax-Grof speculates that the sorcerer makes a telepathic connection with the victim, somehow influencing his mind. If psychic healing can work, so can psychic killing. One of the most sinister acts of the *obeahman,* or witch doctor, is to steal a person's shadow. By taking a human's spirit and psychically "nailing" it to the sacred ceiba tree, the obeahman has deprived the victim of his spirit and of the need to live.

In Haiti, French anthropologist Alfred Metraux observed a phenomenon called "sending of the dead," in which Baron Samedi, god of the graveyard, possesses the bokor, or sorcerer, and through him commands a client to go to a cemetery at midnight with offerings of food for the Baron. At the cemetery, the client must gather a handful of graveyard earth for each person he wishes to see killed, which he later spreads on the paths taken by the victim(s). Alternatively, the client takes a stone from the cemetery, which magically transforms itself into an evil entity, ready to do its master's bidding. To start the process, the sorcerer throws the stone against the victim's house. Metraux found that whenever a person learned he was a victim of a "sending the dead" spell, he would soon grow thin, stop eating, spit blood and die.

In all these cases, only the reversal of the spell by good magic can save the victim. The mind's capacity for belief and action overpowers all other attempts at conventional logic and scientific rationality.

Sorcerers in various cultures contend that it is possible to cause a hex death without the victim being aware of the hex.

See POINTING; SENDING.

Hexenkopf (Witch's Head)   A rocky hill near Easton, Pennsylvania, in the Lehigh Valley, steeped in witchcraft superstitions and folklore influenced by German immigrants who settled in the area in the 18th and 19th centuries.

The Hexenkopf rises 1,030 feet above sea level and is the highest peak in Northampton County. It is part of a group of rocky hills that are among the oldest exposed rocks in the United States.

Originally, the Hexenkopf was known as Groggy Rustic. One of the early landowners around the hill was Johann Seiler (see SAYLOR FAMILY), who became famous as a powwower, a healer whose remedies included "power" and magical SPELLS. Seiler's son, Peter Saylor, became even more famous as a powwower, and used the Hexenkopf in his magical cures, by casting out illnesses into the rock.

The German immigrants imported their beliefs in witchcraft, witches (*hexerei*), DEMONS and magical healing, called *braucherei* in Germany and then POWWOWING in America. Many of the settlers had come from the Harz Mountains area, where witchcraft beliefs were especially strong. The Harz Mountains were known as the abodes of witches, and the tallest peak, the Brocken, was the site of regular SABBATS and witches' revelries, most notably WALPURGISNACHT. In the Lehigh Valley, the Hexenkopf took over that role. Locals feared the witches' gatherings. The only way a Hexenkopf witch could be killed was to chase her off the hill so that she fell to her death in the valley.

Many stories were told about the evil doings at the Hexenkopf and oral lore accumulated over time, even into present times. The witches were said to be local wives who fooled their husbands by leaving sticks in their beds so that they could escape on their BROOMS to attend their nocturnal gatherings.

After World War I, a man sued for divorce because he discovered his wife was a witch, he claimed to his lawyer. One night he could not sleep, but his wife thought he was asleep and rose from their bed to rub her face with a magical OINTMENT. She mounted her broom, said an incantation, "Uber Stock und uber Stein," and then flew out the window. The curious husband got up and did the same, rubbing his face with the ointment, mounting another broom and uttering the incantation. He said he flew through the air to the top of the Hexenkopf, where an unholy revelry was taking place around a bonfire.

The man's wife was not surprised to see him. She led him through dancers to a table where black men with long tails were giving out a hot drink. He took a few sips and passed out. When he awoke, it was dawn and he was in a neighbor's pigpen.

This was more than enough reason to sue for divorce, the man insisted. But the matter was resolved privately and never went to court.

Lore holds that whenever the Hexenkopf glows at night, the witches and demons are there. The glow may in fact have a natural explanation—the rock has a high mica content, which glints in the right conditions of moonlight.

The Hexenkopf is dubbed "Misery Mountain" for its reputation of bad luck, accidents, suicides, murders, mysterious fires, crop failures and mishaps that happen in the vicinity, even into present times. The vanishing cart or car is prominent in lore. People travel up the steep hill never to come down the other side. One of the old stories tells of an abusive, violent man who mistreated his family and animals. One night he stormed off in a fit of anger to go to a tavern. He hitched up his horse-drawn wagon and mercilessly beat the horses all the way up the hill, giving them no rest. At the summit a mist descended around man and animals, and they were never seen again.

The hill was famous also for its poisonous wind. Powwowing belief held that all diseases and illnesses were caused by the evil actions of the Devil, demons and witches, who were constantly tormenting and harassing people. The evil ones caused a "contagion wind" to blow that brought illness to humans and animals. Such winds could blow off swamps, marshes, graveyards, caves and cellars, but the contagion wind that blew from the Hexenkopf was the most toxic of all. Peter Saylor, a famous powwower, called it "evil poisoning of the air," and said it was Satan punishing the sinful.

Mysterious, charmed animals roamed the Hexenkopf. In the 19th century, a charmed white fox was seen one winter. As long as it was about, hunters could kill no game. They could not kill the fox, either, not even by poison bait. Shots fired at it missed. Locals believed that the fox was the embodiment of all the evil spirits who resided on the hill.

The Hexenkopf also is home to numerous ghosts and hauntings. The ghosts of witches and of the dead who died mysteriously or tragically on or near the hill have been reported seen and heard. On dark and windy nights, a headless man and a headless dog are seen in the area. Fiery, rolling balls of spectral fumes are supposedly the ghosts of two farmers who fought bitterly over property rights. Also seen is the ghost of a peg-legged farmer named Brown who reportedly fell to his death while chasing a witch. On moonless nights, he runs up behind people, making a stumping noise with his peg leg. He has gray hair, a beard and a terrifying face.

The Hexenkopf is under private ownership today. Ruins of old, abandoned homes still exist on it.

FURTHER READING:
Heindel, Ned D. *Hexenkopf: History, Healing & Hexerei.* Easton, Pa.: Williams Township Historical Society, 2005.

hex signs (hexenfoos)　Round magical signs and symbols used by the Pennsylvania Dutch, primarily to protect against witchcraft but also to effect SPELLS. Hex signs are both amuletic and talismanic (see AMULETS; TALISMANS). Traditionally, hex signs are painted on barns, stables and houses to protect against lightning, ensure fertility and protect animal and human occupants alike from becoming *ferhexed*, or bewitched. Hex signs also are painted on cradles, on household goods such as kitchen tools and spoon racks and on wooden or metal disks that can be hung in windows.

Each hex sign has a different meaning. Some of the symbols and designs date back to the Bronze Age—such as the swastika or solar wheel, symbol of the Cult of the Sun—and to ancient Crete and Mycenae. The most common designs or symbols, all enclosed in a circle, are stars with five, six or eight points; pentagrams, or *Trudenfuss* (see PENTACLES AND PENTAGRAMS); variations of the swastika; and hearts. The six-petaled flower/star, a fertility hex sign, is painted on utensils and tools relating to livestock, especially horses, and on linens, weaver's tools, mangling boards and other items. Pomegranates also are used for fertility; oak leaves for male virility; an eagle or rooster with a heart for strength and courage; hearts and tulips for love, faith and a happy marriage.

Hex signs are designed for healing, accumulating material goods and money, starting or stopping rain and innumerable other purposes. A charm or incantation is said as the hex sign is made. Little is known about hex signs, as it is a taboo for the Pennsylvania Dutch to talk about them to outsiders.

The custom of hex signs comes from the Old World and was brought from Germany and Switzerland by the German immigrants who settled in Pennsylvania in the 1700s and 1800s. In the Old Saxon religion, it was customary to paint protective symbols on barns and household items. In Germany, tradition calls for hex signs to be placed on the frames of barns, but not on houses; in Switzerland, it is customary to place the signs on houses. The Pennsylvania Dutch borrowed both practices. Among the Pennsylvania Dutch, regional customs developed in style and placement.

In the 19th century, hex signs proliferated throughout the Pennsylvania Dutch countryside then diminished along with interest in the folk magical arts.

See POWWOWING.

FURTHER READING:
Fandee, Lee R. *Strange Experience: The Autobiography of a Hexenmeister.* Englewood Cliffs, N.J.: Prentice-Hall, 1971.
Mahr, August C. "Origin and Significance of Pennsylvania Dutch Barn Symbols," *The Ohio State Archaeology and Historical Quarterly,* Jan.–Mar. 1945.

Hibbins, Ann (d. 1656) Prominent Boston woman convicted of witchcraft and executed. Her chief crime as a witch seemed to have been a bad temper, which was disliked by her neighbors.

Ann Hibbins was married to William Hibbins, a well-to-do merchant in Boston. She also was the sister of Richard Bellingham, deputy governor of Massachusetts, highly regarded as one of the leading politicians in the colonies. Ann and William Hibbins enjoyed respect and social status and attended the first church established in Boston.

William Hibbins suffered setbacks in business, and the family fortunes declined. According to accounts, that marked the beginning of Ann's "witchcraft." She was said to become increasingly ill-tempered, even toward her husband. She irritated others; the church also censured her, first with admonition and then with excommunication in 1640.

As long as her husband remained alive, Ann enjoyed a certain amount of protection from further prosecution. But after William died in 1654, Ann was soon charged with witchcraft. She declared herself not guilty and agreed to be tried. As part of her interrogation, she was stripped naked and searched for WITCH'S MARKS. Her house was ransacked for POPPETS by which she might have been working her evil SPELLS.

Though a prominent and well-connected woman, others were initially afraid to speak on her behalf, lest they, too, be accused of witchcraft. One prominent citizen, Joshua Scottow, did speak out on her behalf and was swiftly punished. Scottow was forced to write an apology to the court.

Others then also came out in defense of Hibbins, calling her a "saint," not a witch. The defenses did no good, and Hibbins was hanged at the end of May 1656.

FURTHER READING:
Demos, John Putnam. *Entertaining Satan: Witchcraft and the Culture of Early New England.* New York: Oxford University Press, 2004.
Upham, Charles. *History of Witchcraft and Salem Village.* Boston: Wiggin and Lunt, 1867.

Hohman, John George (d. ca. 1845) The most famous *braucher* in the POWWOWING tradition of folk MAGIC, SPELLS, HEXES and healing. John George Hohman (also spelled Homan) was a German immigrant to America and the author of the widely circulated magical text *The Long Lost Friend.*

Little is known about Hohman's life. In 1802, he and his wife, Anna Catherine, and son, Philip (some sources say Caspar), left Hamburg for Philadelphia, arriving on October 12. They had no money and sold themselves as indentured servants. Hohman and his wife were split apart. His wife and son went to Burlington County, New Jersey, and Hohman went to Springfield Township, Bucks County, Pennsylvania.

Hohman lived and worked in a German immigrant community. In his spare time, he made and sold decorated birth certificates and baptismal certificates, a popular custom among the immigrants. In three-and-a-half years, he earned enough money to buy freedom for himself and his family.

The family's home is not known, for Hohman could not afford to purchase land. In 1810, they evidently lived in the Easton area near the HEXENKOPF. Hohman was by then writing books, ballads, hymns, poems and songs, which he published.

By 1815, the Hohmans lived in Reading. Anna Catherine died there in 1832 at age 60. Hohman is believed to have died on April 26, 1845, at age 67 after a "lingering illness."

Hohman gained a wide reputation for his healing ability. In 1818 he published a folk medicine book, *The Field and House Pharmacy Guide,* with remedies for humans and animals. This book contained no magic. In 1820, he published the book that made him famous, *The Long Lost Friend,* a faith-healing text of magical CHARMS and spells that became the bible of powwowing. More than 150 editions have been printed. The book was translated into English in 1850.

There is no evidence that Hohman ever used the term "powwowing" to describe his magical arts. But among the *brauchers,* POWER DOCTORS and powowers, his text was golden, an essential tool for success. Even hex doctors worked black magic with it. Mere ownership conferred power. The belief spread that no one could practice without their own personal copy of *The Long Lost Friend.* The influential SAYLOR FAMILY of folk doctors placed great importance on it.

Hohman and *The Long Lost Friend* gained celebrity status in the early 20th century when a murder was committed over possession of a copy. JOHN BLYMIRE, of York County, Pennsylvania, believed himself to be cursed and was told he had to take possession of the offending witch's copy of *The Long Lost Friend* in order to be cured. Blymire killed the man when he would not give up the book. The story was written in a book *Hex* (1970) by Arthur H. Lewis.

In 1988, a film based on the story was made in Hollywood starring Donald Sutherland. It was originally titled *The Long Lost Friend,* but just prior to release the title was changed to *The Apprentice to Murder.* A German version, *The Night of the Demons,* was produced. Both films performed poorly.

The Long Lost Friend continued to be used until well into the 20th century and still enjoys an audience in present times. More than 500,000 copies have been sold.

FURTHER READING:
Heindel, Ned D. *Hexenkopf: History, Healing & Hexerei.*
    Easton, Pa.: Williams Township Historical Society, 2005.
Lewis, Arthur H. *Hex.* New York: Pocket Books, 1970.

Holda (also Holde, Hulda)   Fierce Germanic goddess of the sky whose nocturnal rides with the souls of the unbaptized dead led to the Christian association of her with the demonic aspects of the WILD HUNT. Holda was beautiful and stately, and bold as a Valkyrie. She also was goddess of the hearth and motherhood and ruled spinning and the cultivation of flax.

As host of the Wild Hunt, Holda was said to be accompanied by WITCHES as well as the souls of the dead. They rode uncontrollably through the night sky, shrieking and crying. The land over which they passed was said to bear double the harvest.

Holda, like other pagan deities, was linked to the DEVIL by Christians. In medieval times, she was transformed from a majestic woman to an old HAG, with a long, hooked nose, long stringy hair and sharp fangs. In folklore, she has been reduced to a bogey, a low-level bad spirit, and a tender of sheep or goats.

Hopkins, Matthew (?–1647?)   England's most notorious professional witch-hunter, who brought about the condemnations and executions of at least 230 alleged witches, more than all other witch-hunters combined during the 160-year peak of the country's witch hysteria.

Hopkins was born in Wenham, Suffolk, the son of a minister. Little is known about him before 1645, when

Matthew Hopkins, his victims and their familiars (OLD WOODCUT)

he took up his witch-hunting activities. Prior to that, he made a meager living as a mediocre lawyer, first in Ipswich and then in Manningtree.

In 1645 he announced publicly that a group of witches in Manningtree had tried to kill him. He abandoned his law practice and went into business to rid the countryside of witches. He advertised that for a fee, he and an associate, John Stearne, would travel to a village and rout them out.

Hopkins knew little about witches beyond reading King JAMES I's *Daemonologie,* but he had no shortage of business. He exploited the Puritans' hatred of witchcraft, the public's fear of it and the political turmoil of the English Civil War (1642–48). Added to this volatile mixture was a rise of feminism among women who, during the Civil War, spoke up about their discontent with their station in life and the way England was being governed. It was not uncommon for politically active Royalist women to become branded as "sorceresses" and "whores of Babylon" by the Parliamentary faction. Some of the witch-hunt victims may have been singled out because they were suspected spies.

Hopkins' method of operation was to turn gossip and innuendo into formal accusations of witchcraft and Devil-worship. Since every village had at least one HAG rumored to be a witch, Hopkins was enormously successful. Most of the accused, however, were merely unpopular people against whom others had grudges. Hopkins dubbed himself "Witch-finder General" and claimed to be appointed by Parliament to hunt witches. He boasted that he possessed the "Devil's List," a coded list of the names of all the witches in England.

His first victim was a one-legged hag, Elizabeth Clark. Hopkins tortured her until she confessed to sleeping with the Devil and harboring several FAMILIARS. She accused five other persons of witchcraft. The inquisitions and extorted confessions mushroomed until at least 38 persons were remanded for trial in Chelmsford. Hopkins and Stearne testified to seeing the imps and familiars of many of the accused appear and try to help them. They were aided by 92 villagers who voluntarily stepped forward to offer "evidence" and "testimony." Of the 38 known accused, 17 were hanged; six were declared guilty but reprieved; four died in prison; and two were acquitted. The fate of the remainder is not certain (see CHELMSFORD WITCHES).

With that success, Hopkins took on four more assistants and went witch-hunting throughout Essex, Suffolk, Huntingdonshire, Norfolk, Cambridge and neighboring counties. His fees were outrageously high, between four and 26 pounds and perhaps much higher; the prevailing wage was sixpence a day. To justify his fees, Hopkins argued that ferreting out witches required great skill, and he denied that he and Stearne profited from their business.

The use of TORTURE in witch trials was forbidden in England, but it was routinely applied in most cases. Hopkins was no exception, but his torture was often excessive. He beat, starved and denied sleep to his victims. His more brutal, and favored, methods included pricking the skin for insensitive spots (see WITCH'S MARK), searching for blemishes as small as flea bites, which could be interpreted as DEVIL'S MARKS, walking victims back and forth in their cells until their feet were blistered, and SWIMMING. In the latter, the victims were bound and thrown into water; if they floated, they were guilty.

When the victims were worn down by torture, Hopkins plied them with leading questions such as, "How is it you came to be acquainted with the Devil?" All he required were nods and monosyllabic answers. He and his associates filled in the colorful details of the alleged malevolent activities. Most of the charges were of bewitching people and their livestock to death; causing illness and lameness; and entertaining evil spirits such a familiars, which usually were nothing more than household pets. He was particularly fond of getting victims to admit they had signed DEVIL'S PACTS.

Not all of his victims were framed. One man, a butcher, traveled about 10 miles to confess voluntarily. He was hanged. Another man claimed to entertain his familiar while in jail; no one else could see the creature.

Later in 1645 Hopkins enjoyed another successful mass witch trial in Suffolk, in which at least 124 persons were arrested and 68 were hanged. One of them was a 70-year-old clergyman, who, after being "walked" and denied sleep, confessed to having a pact with the Devil, having several familiars and to bewitching cattle.

Throughout his witch-hunting, Hopkins constantly searched for evidence that networks of organized COVENS of witches existed. He found nothing to substantiate this belief.

In 1646 Hopkins's witch-hunting career ended almost as abruptly as it had begun. He over-extended himself in greed and zeal. He was publicly criticized for his excessive tortures and high fees and began to meet resistance from judges and local authorities. In the eastern counties, mass witch trials declined, though witches were still brought to trial. Hopkins began to be criticized severely for forcing the swimming test upon people who did not want to take it. He and Stearne separated, with Hopkins returning to Manningtree and Stearne moving to Lawshall.

The fate of Hopkins remains a mystery. There is no trace of him after 1647. Popular legend has it that he was accused of witchcraft and "died miserably." William Andrews, a 19th-century writer on Essex folklore, stated in *Bygone Essex*" (1892) that Hopkins was passing through Suffolk and was himself accused of "being in league with the Devil, and was charged with having stolen a memorandum book containing a list of all the witches in England, which he obtained by means of sorcery."

Hopkins pleaded innocent but was "swum" at Mistley Pond by an angry mob. According to some accounts, he drowned, while others say he floated, was condemned and hanged. No record exists of a trial, if there was one. There is a record of his burial at the Mistley Church in 1647, though there is no tombstone (not uncommon for 17th-century graves). One chronicler of the times said that the burial must have been done "in the dark of night" outside the precincts of the Church, witnessed by no one local. Hopkins' ghost is said to haunt Mistley Pond. An apparition dressed in 17th-century attire is reportedly seen in the vicinity.

According to another story circulated, Hopkins, having fallen out of favor with the public, escaped to New England.

Stearne, however, stated in 1648, "I am certain (notwithstanding whatsoever hath been said of him) he died peacefully at Manningtree, after a long sickensse of a consumption, as many of his generation had done before him, without any trouble of conscience for what he had done, as was falsely reported of him."

See BURY ST. EDMONDS WITCHES.

FURTHER READING:
Deacon, Richard. *Matthew Hopkins: Witch Finder General.* London: Frederick Muller, 1976.
Russell, Jeffrey B. *A History of Witchcraft.* London: Thames and Hudson, 1980.
Thomas, Keith. *Religion and the Decline of Magic.* New York: Charles Scribner's Sons, 1971.

Horne, Fiona (1966–) Australian Wiccan, singer, model and actress.

Fiona Horne grew up in a Catholic home, but by age 13 was disillusioned with the religion. She rebelled by gravitating toward SATANISM, mostly by reading fictional works. When the New Age movement expanded in the 1980s, she expanded her spiritual exploration and discovered Wicca. One of the main reasons it appealed to her is that is recognizes many gods and goddesses and holds that they exist within, not outside of, the individual. Horne was 21 when she initiated herself into Wicca and began practicing as a SOLITARY. She studied naturopathy.

She was 24 when she became the lead singer for the techno-metal fusion band Def FX (1990–1997). Her song lyrics were often occult in nature, but Horne remained quiet about her direct involvement in the Craft. She decided to go public as a Witch in 1998. She wrote an article on Witchcraft for *Australian Marie Claire,* but the article was killed. She decided to expand upon it and publish it as a book, along with her personal experiences, in *Witch: A Personal Journey.*

In 2002, Horne moved to Los Angeles to pursue film and television acting roles. She was the "Alt" in the 2004 Sci Fi Channel reality series *Mad Mad House.* She founded a COVEN in Hollywood.

Horne has written additional books on Witchcraft: *Witch; A Magickal Year* (1999); *Life's A Witch: A Handbook for Teen Witches* (2000); *Witch: A Magickal Journey: A Hip Guide to Modern Witchcraft* (2000); *7 Days to a Magickal New You* (2001); *Magickal Sex: A Witches' Guide to Beds, Knobs, and Broomsticks* (2002); *Witchin': A Handbook for Teen Witches* (2003); *Pop! Goes the Witch: The Disinformation Guide to 21st Century Witchcraft* (2004); *Bewitch a Man: How to Find Him and Keep Him Under Your Spell* (2006); and *L.A. Witch: Fiona Horne's Guide to Coven Magick* (2007).

FURTHER READING:

Horne, Fiona. *Witch: A Magickal Journey: A Hip Guide to Modern Witchcraft.* London: Thorsons, 2001.

Horned God In contemporary Paganism and Witchcraft, the consort of the GODDESS and representative of the male principle of the Supreme Deity. The Horned God is the lord of the woodlands, the hunt and animals. He also is the lord of life, death and the underworld. He is the sun to the Goddess' MOON. The Horned God alternates with the Goddess in ruling over the fertility cycle of birth-death-rebirth. He is born at the winter solstice, unites with the Goddess in marriage at Beltane (May 1) and dies at the summer solstice. His death is a sacrifice to life.

The origin of the Horned God may date to Paleolithic times, as evidenced by a ritualistic cave painting discovered in the Caverne des Trois Freres at Ariège, France. One of the figures is either a stag standing upright on hind legs or a man dressed in stag costume

Satyr family (ALBRECHT DÜRER, 1505)

in a dance. The wearing of animal clothes in rituals to secure game was practiced in Europe for thousands of years.

Among the deities and beings associated with the Horned God are CERNUNNOS, the Celtic god of fertility, animals and the underworld; HERNE THE HUNTER, a specter of Britain; PAN, the Greek god of the woodlands; Janus, the Roman god of good beginnings, whose two-faced visage represents youth and age, life and death; Tammuz and Damuzi, the son-lover-consorts to ISHTAR and INANNA; Osiris, Egyptian lord of the underworld; Dionysus, Greek god of vegetation and the vine, whose cult observed rites of dismemberment and resurrection; and the GREEN MAN, the lord of vegetation and the woodlands.

The horns of the Horned God are associated with his domain of the woodlands, and with the bull and the ram, animal consorts of the Goddess. The horns also symbolize the crescent moon, which is the symbol of the Goddess and represents increase in all things and waxing fertility. In art, the Horned God may be portrayed as half man and half animal, as were Cernunnos and Pan. There is no association between the Horned God and the DEVIL, except in the Christian demonization of pagan deities.

Most traditions in contemporary Witchcraft emphasize the Goddess, though the Horned God is considered important in his role in male-female polarity. He is worshiped in rites, in which he is personified by the high priest, who sometimes wears an antlered headdress or a horned helmet. The Horned God represents sexuality, vitality, the hunt, logic and power, but not in an exploitative fashion. He is considered gentle, tender and compassionate yet is not effeminate.

(See WHEEL OF THE YEAR).

FURTHER READING:
Adler, Margot. *Drawing Down the Moon.* Revised ed. New York: Viking, 1986.
Crowley, Vivianne. *Wicca: The Old Religion in the New Millennium.* Revised ed. London: Thorsons/Harper Collins, 1996.
Valiente, Doreen. *An ABC of Witchcraft Past and Present.* Custer, Wash.: Phoenix Publishing, 1986 (first published 1973).

Horned Women   In Irish legend, 12 horned women, all witches, who take over the household of a rich woman and bewitch her and her sleeping family. No reason for the bewitching is given in the story—perhaps, in times past, no reason was necessary, for witches were believed to bewitch simply because they were witches. The legend tells of how the distressed woman breaks the SPELL.

The bewitchment began late one night, as the woman sat up carding wool while her family and servants slept. A knock came on the door, and she asked who was there. A female voice answered, "I am the Witch of the one Horn."

The woman thought it was a neighbor and opened the door. She was greeted by an ugly woman from whose forehead grew a single horn. The witch held a pair of wool carders. She sat down by the fire and began to card wool with great speed. She suddenly paused and said, "Where are the women? they delay too long."

Another knock came on the door. The mistress of the house, who seemed to be under a spell by now, felt compelled to answer it. She was greeted by another witch, who had two horns growing from her forehead, and who carried a spinning wheel. This witch also sat down by the fire and began to spin wool with great speed.

The house soon was filled with 12 frightful-looking, horned witches, each one having an additional horn, so that the last witch bore 12 horns on her forehead. They worked furiously on the wool, singing an ancient tune, ignoring the mistress, who was unable to move or call for help.

Eventually, one of the witches ordered the mistress to make them a cake, but the woman had no vessel with which to fetch water from the well. The witches told her to take a sieve to the well. She did, but the water ran through the sieve, and she wept. While she was gone, the witches made a cake, using BLOOD drawn from members of the sleeping family in place of water.

As she sat weeping by the well, the mistress heard a voice. It was the Spirit of the Well, who told her how to make a paste of clay and moss and cover the sieve, so that it would hold water. It then instructed her to go back to her house from the north and cry out three time, "The mountain of the Fenian women and the sky over it is all on fire." The mistress did as instructed. The witches shrieked and cried and sped off to the Slivenamon, "the mountains of women," where they lived.

The Spirit of the Well then told the mistress how to break the witches' spell and prevent them from returning. She took the water in which she had bathed her children's feet and sprinkled it over the threshold of the house. She took the blood cake, broke it into pieces and placed them in the mouths of the bewitched sleepers, who were revived. She took the woolen cloth the witches had woven and placed it half in and half out of a padlocked chest. She barred the door with a large crossbeam.

The witches returned in a rage at having been deceived. Their fury increased when they discovered that they could not enter the house because of the water, the broken blood cake and the crossbeam. They flew off into the air, screaming curses against the Spirit of the Well, but they never returned. One of the witches dropped her mantle, which the mistress took and hung up as a reminder of her ordeal. The mantle remained in the family for 500 years.

The legend of the horned women appears to be a blend of pagan and Christian aspects. The well is inhabited by a spirit, a common pagan belief. The horns of the witches symbolize the maternal and nurturing aspect of the GODDESS, who is sometimes represented by a cow. The horns also symbolize the crescent moon, another Goddess symbol. In ancient Greek and Babylonian art, the Mother Goddess often is depicted wearing a headdress of little horns. Yet the horned women of the legend are not maternal and nurturing but HAGS who cast an evil spell, fly through the air and shriek CURSES—the portrayal of witches spread by the Church. The cardinal point of north is associated with power, darkness and mystery in paganism, but in Christianlore it is associated with the DEVIL.

FURTHER READING:
Yeats, W. B. *Irish Fairy and Folk Tales.* 1892. Reprint, New York: Dorset Press, 1986.

horseshoe   AMULET against witches, FAIRIES, the DEVIL, BEWITCHMENT, evil spirits and the EVIL EYE. In earlier times, horseshoes were made of IRON, which in folklore weakens and repels all things evil.

According to English lore, a blacksmith named Dunstan—who later became St. Dunstan—was approached by the Devil to make shoes for the Devil's own hoofed feet. Dunstan tricked the DEVIL by making an iron chain and chaining the Devil to the wall of his shop. The Devil was enraged. Dunstan struck a bargain with him to let him go on condition that he promise never to enter any building or home that had a horsehoe hung over the doorway. The Devil agreed, but only if the horsehoe had its ends pointing up, not down.

A horseshoe placed in a chimney will prevent a witch from flying in on her BROOM. A horseshoe nailed to one's bed will repel nightmares and DEMONS. To be effective, the horseshoe must never be removed once it is installed. In Irish lore, a horseshoe nailed over the threshold of a door keeps fairies out of the house.

In more recent lore, the horseshoe brings good luck.

FURTHER READING:
Cahill, Robert Ellis. *Strange Superstitions*. Danvers, Mass.: Old Saltbox Publishing, 1990.
Opie, Iona, and Moira Tatem. *A Dictionary of Superstitions*. New York: Oxford University Press, 1989.

Huebner, Louise   "The Official Witch of Los Angeles." Louise Huebner made a media splash in the late 1960s and early 1970s with various antics and SPELLS for sexual energy. Huebner, who claimed to be a hereditary witch, wrote two books and made one record, all with a somewhat tongue-in-cheek tone, which portrayed witches as mean, capricious and orgiastic individuals. They included statements such as the following: "And as a witch, I can be a lot meaner than I could have been if I were Jeanne Dixon"; "I always giggle when I'm excited. It's part of being a witch"; "Enchanters need orgies. The orgies will help you generate the electrical and magnetic impulses you will need to cast spells."

According to Huebner, her mother knew she was "different" by the time she was five. Her grandmother was a fortune-teller, and Huebner began practicing fortune-telling at age 10 by reading palms.

In Los Angeles, Huebner established herself as an astrologer and psychic. She authored a newspaper column and had her own horoscope radio show from 1965 to 1969. In 1968 Los Angeles County Supervisor Eugene Debs named her "The Official Witch of Los Angeles" in connection with a Folk Day "happening" at Hollywood Bowl. Huebner, dressed in a long silver robe, passed out red candles, chalk and garlic and led a mass ritual to cast a spell over Los Angeles County to raise its "romantic and emotional vitality." The spell consisted of an incantation: "Light the flame/Bright the fire/Red is the color of desire."

When Huebner began using the "Official Witch" appellation to promote herself, Los Angeles County attempted to stop her from doing so, stating that the title was intended for Folk Day only. Huebner called a press conference and threatened to "despell" Los Angeles County. In the ensuing publicity, the county dropped the matter.

Huebner made numerous radio and television appearances around the country. She dressed in black and carried about a pet black beetle, Sandoz. She also kept a rat and a cat. In 1970 she went to Salem, Massachusetts, where she was received by Mayor Samuel E. Zoll, who gave her a broom inscribed, "May your ride be long and enjoyable." Huebner was quoted by the press as stating the reason for her visit was to forgive Salem "for what they did to those people who were not witches" in Colonial times.

Huebner's books are *Power Through Witchcraft* (1969); *Never Strike a Happy Medium* (1971). Her record is *Moon Magic: A Witch's Guide to Spells, Charms and Enchantments* (1972); *Magical Creatures: The Charming and Mystical Powers of Brownies, Elves, Fairies, Gnomes, Pixies, Sprites and Demons* (1972); *Superstitions: A Witchy Collection of Beliefs About Love, Money, Weather and Much More* (1972); *Love Spells from A to Z: Witchy Spells for Brewing Up Romance* (1972); *Magical Candles, Enchanted Plants ad Powerful Gems: Their Meanings and Uses in the Wild World of Witchcraft* (1972); *Your Lucky Numbers: A Witch's Secrets to Your Personality, Feelings and Relationships Through Numerology* (1972); *Magic Sleep: A Witch's Interpretation of Your Dreams* (1972); *In the Palm of Your Hand: Your Personality and Future in a Witchy Guide to Palmistry* (1972); *Your Future—It's in the Cards: A Witch's Bewitching Scheme Using Standard Playing Cards* (1972); *Seduction Through Witchcraft*.

Huebner's husband, Mentor, died on March 19, 2001. Mentor was an artist who worked on about 250 films and on the designs of theme parks around the world.

Hutton, Ronald (1954–)   Professor of history at Bristol University in England and an authority on the history of Paganism and Witchcraft in Britain.

Ronald Hutton studied history at Pembroke College, Cambridge. He specializes in 16th and 17th-century British history. In the Pagan community, Hutton is best known for his writings on the history of Paganism, Witchcraft, magic, shamanism and the development of Wicca, most notably *The Pagan Religions of the Ancient British Isles: Their Nature and Legacy* (1993); *The Stations of the Sun: A History of the Ritual Year in Britain* (1996); *The Triumph of the Moon: A History of Modern Pagan Witchcraft* (2001); *Shamans: Siberian Spirituality and the Western Imagination* (2001); *Witches, Druids and King Arthur* (2003); and *The Druids: A History* (2007).

ill-wishing A CURSE that is the product of envy, revenge and anger. In earlier times, people commonly blamed their misfortune on the ill-wishing of others. If two people argued and then one suffered a mishap, became ill or had other problems, the other party was suspected of ill-wishing them. Remarks such as "You'll be sorry" were taken seriously as a form of negative witchcraft. If someone enjoyed a great deal of good fortune or prosperity and then suffered a setback, they believed themselves to be the victim of the secret ill-wishing of envious neighbors.

The remedy for ill-wishing was to seek out a witch, a PELLAR or a cunning man or woman (see CUNNING MAN/CUNNING WOMAN) and have the ill-wishing broken or neutralized with a CHARM. If the identity of the ill-wisher was not known, magic or DIVINATION was performed to expose them.

See BLASTING; HEX; SPELL.

imp A small DEMON, often kept inside a bottle or ring and used for magical purposes. Imps are evoked and commanded to carry out tasks and SPELLS.

Witches were said to keep imps that assumed different forms, such as TOADS, rodents and especially flies, spiders and other insects. When accused witches were imprisoned, they were watched closely for any appearances of their imps. Prisons were full of insects and rodents, so it was rare that a cell would not have such visitors. Guards would pounce on them, and if they were killed, it meant they were harmless animals or bugs. But if a fly or spider escaped, it was taken as a sure sign of the witch's imp.

A witch feeds her imps (FROM JOHN ASHTON, *THE DEVIL IN BRITAIN AND AMERICA*, 1896)

Witches were accused of using imps to carry out evil deeds upon innocent people, such as bewitchment, ill fortune, accidents and even death. In return, the witches suckled the imps with their own BLOOD, using their fingers or protuberances on the body. Witch hunters searched bodies for WITCH'S MARKS, usually warts, discolored skin, and unnatural lumps believed to serve as teats or paps.

In some witch trials, the term "imp" was used interchangeably with FAMILIAR.

FURTHER READING:
Upham, Charles. *History of Witchcraft and Salem Village.* Boston: Wiggin and Lunt, 1867.

Inanna Sumerian mother GODDESS, queen of heaven and ruler of the cycles of the seasons and fertility. She was also called Nina; the name Inanna may be a derivative of Nina. She was the most widely known goddess in the later periods of Sumer. The most important legend involving her is that of the sacrifice of the divine king for the fertility of the land, and his descent to the underworld. The myth is similar to that of ISHTAR, the Babylonian and Assyrian mother goddess with whom Inanna became identified.

Inanna's son-lover-consort was Damuzi (also spelled Dumuzi and Daimuz), who, after proving himself upon her bed in a rite of *hieros gamos,* or sacred marriage, was made shepherd of the land by her. Once, Inanna walked down the steps of death to the underworld, the Land of No Return, or Irkalla. She was taken captive by the Gallas, a host of DEMONS, and was freed only by promising that she would substitute another life for her own. She returned to heaven to search for the sacrificial victim. She considered, but rejected, a loyal servant and two minor gods, Shara and Latarrek. When she entered her own temple at Erech, Inanna was shocked to find Damuzi dressed in royal robes and sitting on her throne, instead of out tending his flocks. He seemed to be celebrating her absence rather than mourning it. Enraged, she looked at him with the Eye of Death, and the Gallas dragged Damuzi off to the underworld. Each year, Inanna mourned his death, which brought winter to the land.

From about 2600 B.C.E., to post-Sumerian times, the kings of Sumer mystically identified themselves with Damuzi and were known as the "beloved husbands" of Inanna. At the New Year, an important rite of *hieros gamos* was performed between the king and the high priestess of Inanna, who represented the goddess.

initiation One of the most ancient of rites, initiation marks the psychological crossing of a threshold into new territories, knowledge and abilities. The central themes of initiation are suffering, death and rebirth. The initiate undergoes an ordeal, symbolically dies and is symbolically reborn as a new person, possessing new wisdom.

In contemporary Witchcraft and PAGANISM, initiation marks entry into a closed and traditionally secret society; opens the door to the learning of RITUAL secrets, MAGIC and the development and use of psychic powers; marks a spiritual transformation, in which the initiate begins a journey into Self and toward the Divine Force; and marks the beginning of a new religious faith. While traditional initiation rites exist, Witches and Pagans feel the spiritual threshold may be crossed in many alternate ways. Initiation may be experienced in a group or alone. It may be formal or informal. It may be performed with an old ritual or a new one; it may come as a spontaneous spiritual awakening, in meditation or in dreams. It may occur at a festival.

Newly initiated witches attending Satan at court (GERARD D'EUPHRATES, *LIVRE DE L'HISTOIRE & ANCIENNE CHRONIQUE,* 1549)

Historical Beliefs about Witch Initiations
Historically, a witch's initiation was believed to be dark and diabolic, marked by obscene rituals. During the witch-hunts, stories of offensive initiation rituals were widely believed. Many of them came from confessions made by accused witches who were tortured by inquisitors. The stories varied, but there were common threads to all of them. Some witches were initiated at birth or puberty, claiming their mothers had taken them to SABBATS, presented them to the DEVIL and pledged them to his service. Adult candidates were scouted and recruited by the local officers of covens (see COVEN). After consenting of their own free will to join, they were formally presented to the coven and initiated. Much of the rite was a parody of Christian rites, which fit the prevailing beliefs of the time.

The ceremony, at which the Devil himself was present, took place in a remote location at night. The initiates sometimes brought a copy of the Gospels, which they gave to the Devil. They renounced the Christian faith and baptism by reciting, "I renounce and deny God, the blessed Virgin, the Saints, baptism, father, mother, relations, heaven, earth and all that is the world," according to Pierre de Lancre, 17th-century French witch-hunter. The initiates then pledged a vow of fealty. Scottish witches said they placed one hand upon their crown and the other upon the sole of one foot, dedicating all between the two hands to the service of the Devil. Scandinavian witches reportedly put metal clock shavings and stones in little bags and tossed them in the water, saying "As these shavings of the clock do never return to the clock from which they are taken, so may my soul never return to heaven."

The Devil baptized the initiates, gave them new, secret names, to be used only in the coven, and marked them permanently either by scratching them with his claw or biting them (see DEVIL'S MARK). The new witches were required to kiss the Devil's anus (see KISS OF SHAME), a parody of the kissing of the pope's foot. Sometimes they were made to trample and spit upon the cross. The Devil cut them or pricked their fingers and had them sign pacts (see DEVIL'S PACT.) Finally, he stripped them of their clothing and assigned them one or more FAMILIARS. The coven officer or the Devil recorded their name in a "black book," a membership and attendance record for all coven meetings. Sometimes black fowl or animals were sacrificed to the Devil. After the ceremony, all the witches participated in wild dancing, copulating with the Devil or his demons and feasting upon vile things such as the flesh of roasted, unbaptized babies.

The fantastical, horrible elements of these tales may be ascribed to TORTURE or, in some cases, delusions. Some accounts may have been the result of hallucinatory drug experiences (see OINTMENTS). Witch-hunting manuals such as the *MALLEUS MALEFICARUM* (1486) provided ample material for leading questions to be posed by inquisitors.

Satan baptizing a disciple (R. P. GUACCIUS, *COMPENDIUM MALEFICARUM*, 1626)

However, some family traditions of folk magic and paganism probably existed and may have featured initiatory rites, though nothing resembling the witch-hunter's lurid ideas.

Initiations in Contemporary Witchcraft and Paganism
Contemporary Witchcraft is a mystery religion, providing a context for the initiate to "Know Thyself." Initiatory rites bear no resemblance to the descriptions offered by those early witch-hunters and demonologists. Rites vary according to tradition but generally keep to the universal theme of suffering-death-rebirth in a new spiritual awakening. The following are *not* part of initiation into the Craft or Paganism:

1. There is no renunciation of the Christian faith or any faith.
2. There is no homage to the Devil, including kisses, oaths or pacts. Satan is not recognized by Witches or Pagans.
3. There is no blood sacrifice.

Traditionally, a Witch is not considered a true member of the Craft without formal initiation into a coven, after an apprenticeship period of a year and a day. Women must be initiated by a high priest, men by a high priestess. Among some hereditary Witches, mothers may initiate daughters and fathers, sons as an "adoption into the clan."

In the Gardnerian and Alexandrian traditions, the largest traditions in modern Witchcraft, the initiation is a ceremony conducted within a MAGIC CIRCLE. Both traditions have a system of three degrees of advancement, the entry to each level of which is marked by initiation. There are some differences between the two traditions, but the major aspects are similar. Advancement through the degrees is, like Masonry, advancement through the Mysteries of Western occultism; progressively, more secret teachings are revealed.

In a first-degree initiation, the candidate is blindfolded and bound with cords and challenged outside the magic circle as to the courage to continue. The initiate responds that he or she is ready with "perfect love and perfect trust" to suffer to be purified and learn. Once inside the circle, the candidate maybe ritually scourged (whipped lightly with cords); measured with a cord, which is tied in knots to mark the measures; and administered an oath. In the presence of the Goddess(es), God(s), Guardians, Mighty Dead and Sisters and Brothers of the Craft, the initiate vows to guard and protect the Craft, the Secrets of the Craft, and the brothers and sisters of the Craft, and, in some traditions, to render aid to said brothers and sisters.

The candidate is ritually anointed and kissed; proclaimed a Witch; and presented with a set of magical tools (see WITCHES' TOOLS). The initiate adopts a Craft name. Secret names of the Goddess and God are revealed.

In the Alexandrian tradition, the measure is given back to the Witch. In the Gardnerian tradition, it is customary for the initiator to keep the measure. According to GERALD B. GARDNER, the English Witch for whom the Gardnerian tradition is named, the measure serves as a sort of insurance policy that the oath will be kept.

In the second-degree initiation, the Witch is blindfolded and bound, and renews the oath that it is necessary to suffer to learn and be purified. A ritual scourging may follow. The Witch assumes a new Craft name and is willed the magical power of the initiator. The third-degree initiation, the consummation of the Mysteries, involves the GREAT RITE, a sexual ritual that may be done in actuality or symbolically, with magical tools. All initiations end with a celebration of food and drink (see CAKES-AND-WINE).

Not all Witches follow these same procedures. Many Witches practice as solitaries and do not feel they have to join covens in order to be Witches. They initiate themselves in self-designed rituals. Rites may include ritual baths (a form of baptism), anointing and pledges to serve the GODDESS and use the powers of Witchcraft for the good of others. Other Witches, as well as many Pagans, have a vigil that involves fasting and an all-night experience outdoors, during which the initiate comes into direct contact with the gods, discovers his or her own power and connects with tutelary, totemic or guardian spirits. Still other Witches and Pagans undertake a shamanic initiation, an ecstatic journey to other realms of consciousness (see SHAMANISM).

See LAURIE CABOT; PATRICIA C. CROWTHER; PADDY SLADE.

FURTHER READING:
Crowley, Vivianne. *Wicca: The Old Religion in the New Millennium*. Revised ed. London: Thorsons/Harper Collins, 1996.

Farrar, Janet, and Stewart Farrar. *A Witches Bible Compleat*. New York: Magickal Childe, 1984.

Harvey, Graham. *Contemporary Paganism: Listening People, Speaking Earth*. New York: New York University Press, 1997.

Lea, Henry Charles. *Materials Toward a History of Witchcraft*. Philadelphia: University of Pennsylvania Press, 1939.

Russell, Jeffrey B. *A History of Witchcraft*. London: Thames and Hudson, 1980.

Valiente, Doreen. *An ABC of Witchcraft Past and Present*. 1973. Reprint, Custer, Wash.: Phoenix Publishing, 1986.

Innocent VIII, Pope (1432–1492; r. 1484–1492)

Giovanni Batista Cibo, elected pope in 1484, issued what has been termed one of the most important documents in the history of the Church's fight against witchcraft: the Bull of 1484, *Summis desiderantes affectibus* ("Desiring with supreme ardor"). Though credited with launching the Inquisition full force against witches, it actually followed a long line of earlier bulls inveighing against witchcraft and SORCERY, issued since the 13th century.

The CANON EPISCOPI of 906 had relegated witchcraft to the realm of fantasy, but in the 13th century, popes began to speak out on their beliefs in the reality of witchcraft as an evil against mankind. In his first year as pope, Innocent VIII was approached by Heinrich Kramer and Jacob Sprenger, two Dominican inquisitors, who persuaded him that they were being impeded by local ecclesiastical authorities in their efforts to prosecute witches. They asked for help, and the result was the Bull of 1484, which granted them full authority to carry out their inquisitions and demanded that they receive whatever support was necessary from local officials.

The bull, noted Sir Walter Scott in *Letters on Demonology and Witchcraft* (1830), "rang the tocsin against this formidable, crime [of sorcery], and set forth in the most dismal colours the guilt, while it stimulated the inquisitors to the unsparing discharge of their duty in searching out and punishing the guilty." Its chief object was to transfer the crimes of sorcery to the Waldenses, a religious sect labeled heretics, "and excite and direct the public hatred against the new sect by confounding their doctrines with the influences of the Devil and his fiends."

Text of the Bull of Pope Innocent VIII, 1484

Desiring with supreme ardor, as pastoral solicitude requires, that the Catholic faith in our days everywhere grow and flourish as much as possible, and that all heretical pravity be put far from the territories of the faithful, we freely declare and anew decree this by which our pious desire may be fulfilled, and, all errors being rooted out by our toil as with the hoe of a wise laborer, zeal and devotion to this faith may take deeper hold on the hearts of the faithful themselves.

It has recently come to our ears, not without great pain to us, that in some parts of upper Germany, as well as in the provinces, cities, territories, regions, and dioceses of Mainz, Köln, Trier, Salzburg, and Bremen, many persons of both sexes, heedless of their own salvation and forsaking the catholic faith, give themselves over to devils male and female, and by their incantations, charms and conjurings, and by other abominable superstitions and sortileges, offences, crimes, and misdeeds, ruin and cause to perish the offspring of women, the foal of animals, the products of the earth, the grapes of vines, and the fruits of trees, as well a men and women, cattle and flocks and herds and animals of every kind, vineyards also and orchards, meadows, pastures, harvests, grains and other fruits of the earth; that they afflict and torture with dire pains and anguish, both internal and external, these men, women, cattle, flocks, herds, and animals, and hinder men from begetting and women from conceiving, and prevent all consummation of marriage; that, moreover, they deny with sacrilegious lips the faith they received in holy baptism; and that, at the instigation of the enemy of mankind, they do not fear to commit and perpetrate many other abominable offences and crimes, at the risk of their own souls, to the insult of the divine majesty and to the pernicious example and scandal of multitudes. And, although our beloved sons Henricus Institorus [Kramer] and Jacobus Sprenger, of the order of Friars Preachers, professors of theology, have been and still are deputed by our apostolic letters as inquisitors of heretical pravity, the former in the aforesaid parts of upper Germany, including the provinces, cities, territories, dioceses, and other places, as above, and the latter throughout certain parts of the course of the Rhine; nevertheless certain of the clergy and of the laity of those parts, seeking to be wise above what is fitting, because in the said letter of deputation that aforesaid provinces, cities, dioceses, territories, and other places, and the persons and offences in question were not individually and specifically named, do not blush obstinately to assert that these are not at all included in the said parts and that therefore it is illicit for the aforesaid inquisitors to exercise their office of inquisition in the provinces, cities, dioceses, territories, and other places aforesaid, and that they ought not to be permitted to proceed to the punishment, imprisonment, and correction of the aforesaid persons for the offences and crimes above named. Wherefore in the provinces, cities, dioceses, territories, and places aforesaid such offences and crimes, not without evident damage to their souls and risk of external salvation, go unpunished.

We therefore, desiring, as is our duty, to remove all impediments by which in any way the said inquisitors are hindered in the exercise of their office, and to prevent the taint of heretical pravity and of other like evils from spreading their infection to the ruins of others who are innocent, the dioceses, territories, and places aforesaid in the said parts of upper Germany may not be deprived of the office of the inquisition which is their due, to hereby decree, by virtue of our apostolic authority, that it shall be permitted to the said inquisitors of these regions to exercise their office of inquisition and to proceed to the correction, imprisonment, and punishment of the aforesaid persons for their said offences and crimes, in all respects and altogether precisely as if the provinces, cities, territories, places, persons, and offences aforesaid were expressly named in the said letter. And, fore the greater sureness, extending the said letter and deputation to the provinces, cities, dioceses, territories, places, persons and crimes aforesaid, we grant to the said inquisitors that they or either of them, joining with them our beloved son Johannes Gremper, cleric of the diocese of Constance, master of arts, their present notary, or any other notary public who by them or by either of them shall have been temporarily delegated in the provinces, cities, dioceses, territories, and places aforesaid, may exercise against all persons, of whatsoever condition and rank, the said office of the inquisition, correcting, imprisoning, punishing and chastising, according to their deserts, those persons whom they shall find guilty as aforesaid.

And they shall also have full and entire liberty to propound and preach to the faithful the word of God, as often as it shall seem to them fitting and proper, in each and all the parish churches in the said provinces,

and to do all things necessary and suitable under the aforesaid circumstances, and likewise freely and fully to carry them out.

And moreover we enjoin by apostolic writ on our venerable brother, the Bishop of Strasburg, that, either in his own person or through some other or others solemnly publishing the foregoing wherever, whenever, and how often soever he may deem expedient or by these inquisitors or either of them may be legitimately required, he permit them not to be molested or hindered in any manner whatsoever by any authority whatsoever in the matter of the aforesaid and of this present letter, threatening all oposers, hinderers, contradictors, and rebels, of whatever rank, state, decree, eminence, nobility, excellence, or condition they may be, and whatever privilege of exemption they may enjoy, with excommunication, suspension, interdict, and other still more terrible sentences, censures and penalties, as may be expedient, and this without appeal and with power after due process of law of aggravating and reaggravating these penalties, by our authority, as often as may be necessary, to this end calling in aid, if need be, of the secular arm.

And this, all other apostolic decrees and earlier decisions to the contrary notwithstanding; or if to any, jointly or severally, there has been granted by this apostolic see exemption from interdict, suspension, or excommunication, by apostolic letters not making entire, express, and literal mention of the said grant of exemption; or if there exist any other indulgence whatsoever, general or special, of whatsoever tenor, by failure to name which or to insert it bodily in the present letter the carrying out of this privilege could be hindered or in any way put off,—or any of whose whole tenor special mention must be made in our letters. Let no man, therefore, dare to infringe this page of our declaration, extension, grant, and mandate, or with rash hardihood to contradict it. If any presume to attempt this, let him know that he incurs the wrath of almighty God and of the blessed apostles Peter and Paul.

Given in Rome, at St. Peter's in the year of Our Lord's incarnation 1484, on the nones of December, in the first year of our pontificate.

Immediately upon receipt of the bull, Kramer began a crusade against witches at Innsbruck. He was initially opposed by the local government, though this opposition eventually gave way not only to support but to active participation in witch-hunts. Kramer and Sprenger used the bull at the forefront of their witch-hunter's bible, the MALLEUS MALEFICARUM, published in 1486 and widely circulated throughout Europe. The worst witch hunts and executions took place during the 16th and 17th centuries. In 1523 Pope Adrian VI enforced the Bull of 1484 with a new one, providing for excommunication of "sorcerers and heretics."

FURTHER READING:
Kors, Alan C., and Edward Peters. *Witchcraft in Europe, A Documentary History 1100–1700.* Philadelphia: University of Pennsylvania Press, 1972.

Lea, Henry Charles. *Materials Towards a History of Witchcraft.* Philadelphia: University of Pennsylvania, 1939.

Russell, Jeffrey Burton. *Witchcraft in the Middle Ages.* Ithaca and London: Cornell University Press, 1972.

Inquisition   The Catholic Church's persecution of heretics, lasting several centuries and spreading throughout Europe and even into the New World. The primary objective of the Inquisition was to eliminate religious threats to the Church, especially powerful sects such as the Waldenses, Bogmils, Cathars and Albigenses, as well as Jews and Muslims. As the Inquisition gathered power, it was turned against Gypsies, social undesirables, people caught in political fights—and witches. Historians estimate that between 200,000 and 1 million people, mostly women, died during the "witch-craze" phase of the Inquisition alone.

The roots of the Inquisition start with the First Crusade launched in 1086 by Pope Urban II, a campaign against Muslims to regain territory in the Holy Land. At the same time, the church found itself beset by religious sects growing in power and influence. The church dealt with these sects unevenly, sometimes with tolerance and sometimes with suppression. In 1184, Pope Lucius III issued a bull to bishops to "make inquisition" for heresy. Many bishops were too busy to devote much time to this.

The Inquisition is considered to have begun during the term of Pope Gregory IX, from 1227 to 1233. In 1229, he invited Franciscan monks to participate in inquisitions, a role that expanded for the order for more than two centuries. In 1233 Gregory issued two bulls giving the Dominican order the authority to prosecute heretics. The Dominicans were empowered to proceed against accused heretics and condemn them without appeal, with the help of the secular arm. The Dominicans became the dominant inquisitors for the church.

In 1307, key members of the KNIGHTS TEMPLAR were arrested in France and prosecuted as heretics. The objective of King Philip the Fair was more political than religious; he desired to seize the wealth of the Templars, and he wished to maneuver the church to be subservient to the throne. The Templars were accused of witchcraft and Devil worship as part of their heresy. The first public burning of 54 Templars took place on May 12, 1310, and led to the destruction of the entire order. Many Templars were tortured into confessions.

The Inquisition took another deadly turn in the 13th century with the issuance of several bulls that gave inquisitors increasing powers to arrest, torture and execute. After 1250, Pope Innocent IV issued a series of bulls to aid Dominican inquisitors in carrying out their duties. His final bull, *Ad Extirpa* ("to extirpate"), issued on May 15, 1252, turned Italy into a virtual police state with everyone at the mercy of inquisitors. Anyone who exposed a heretic could have him arrested. The inquisitors had the power to torture people into confessions and sentence them to death by being burned alive at the stake. The bull also put a police force at the disposal of the Inquisition.

Practices of the Inquisition
Manuals. In the early stages of the Inquisition, there were few official guidelines concerning the arrest, questioning and punishment of heretics. In the 1240s, manuals and handbooks for inquisitors began to circulate, which continued into the 17th century. The most influential early handbook was *Practica officii inquisitionis heretice pravitatis*, authored in 1323–24 by the famous inquisitor, Bernard Gui. Another famous handbook was the MALLEUS MALEFICARUM, written in 1488 by two Dominicans, Heinrich Kramer and Jacob Sprenger.

Traits of the ideal inquisitor. Innocent IV issued a bull in 1254 stating that inquisitors should be forceful preachers and "full of zeal for the state." By the early 14th century, inquisitors were required to be at least 40 years of age; most of them were doctors of law trained at universities.

In his influential manual, Gui sets the requirements for a good inquisitor. Essentially, the man must be inflamed with a passion to eradicate all heresy, but show compassion and mercy too:

> The inquisitor . . . should be diligent and fervent in his zeal for the truth of religion, for the salvation of souls, and for the extirpation of heresy. Amid troubles and opposing accidents he should grow earnest, without allowing himself to be inflamed with the fury of wrath and indignation. He must not be sluggish of body, for sloth destroys the vigor of action. He must be intrepid, persisting through danger to death, laboring for religious truth, neither precipitating peril by audacity nor shrinking from it through timidity. He must be unmoved by the prayers and blandishments of those who seek to influence him, yet not be, through hardness of heart, so obstinate that he will yield nothing to entreaty, whether in granting delays or in mitigating punishment, according to place and circumstance, for this implies stubbornness; nor must he be weak and yielding through too great a desire to please, for this will destroy the vigor and value of his work—he who is weak in his work is brother to him who destroys his work. In doubtful matters he must be circumspect and not readily yield credence to what seems probable, for such is not always true; nor should he obstinately reject the opposite, for that which seems improbable often turns out to be fact. He must listen, discuss, and examine with all zeal, that the truth may be reached at the end. Like a judge let him bear himself in passing sentence of corporeal punishment that his face may show compassion, while his inward purpose remains unshaken, and thus will he avoid the appearance of indignation and wrath leading to the charge of cruelty. In imposing pecuniary penalties, let his face preserve the severity of justice as though he were compelled by necessity and not allured by cupidity. Let truth and mercy, which should never leave the heart of a judge, shine forth from his countenance, that his decisions may be free from all suspicion of covetousness or cruelty.

Inquisitors were given full indulgences. They had the power to arrest anyone of any social rank, to seize and sell the property of those they accused and to absolve excommunications. They were both prosecutor and judge. In the early Inquisition, there were many who did their best to pursue truth as they saw it, but many others were corrupted by their power, especially as the Inquisition spread from religious heretics to accused witches.

Arrests and interrogations. In the early Inquisition, accused heretics were given ample opportunity to turn themselves in and repent. They were notified through priests that they should voluntarily convert. Their names were publicly read at sermons. Failing voluntary action, the accused would be arrested and interrogated. If they capitulated, they might be sentenced to penances, fines, whippings, and imprisonment—sometimes for life. A reformed heretic was useful to the church, both as persuasion to others and also for providing the names of other suspects. Unrepentant and relapsed heretics were tortured and sentenced to be burned at the stake.

If an accused heretic died in jail or prior to arrest, the Inquisition did not hold back, but conducted a posthumous trial. If convicted, the body of the accused was dug up and burned.

Torture. Initially inquisitors themselves could not perform the torture. In 1256 Pope Alexander IV gave inquisitors the right to absolve each other and give dispensations, so that they could torture the accused themselves.

By the end of the 13th century, inquisitors throughout Europe were operating under *Ad Extirpa.* Pope John XXII expanded the Inquisition, but did attempt to restrict torture in 1317 by issuing a decree that it should be employed only with "mature and careful deliberation." Torture could not be repeated without fresh evidence against a person. However, zealous inquisitors found ways around restrictions. For example, torture over a period of time was not repeated torture, but torture that was "continued." Confessions were always technically "free and spontaneous," for victims were tortured until they "freely" confessed.

There were six primary methods of torture:

- ordeal by water, in which a person was forced to ingest large quantities of water quickly, which burst blood vessels;
- ordeal by fire, in which the soles of the feet were burned by fire or hot irons;
- the strappado, a pulley, used to hang and drop the accused to dislocate joints;
- the rack, a wooden frame used to stretch a body;
- The wheel, a large cartwheel to which the accused was tied and then beaten with clubs and hammers; and
- the stivaletto, wooden planks and metal wedges used to crush feet and legs.

In addition, the accused were imprisoned, sometimes in dungeons, beaten, starved and psychologically abused.

Details about how these methods were applied are given in the TORTURE entry.

Execution. Burning was seen as the only way to exterminate heretics and discourage participation in religious sects. After the corpse was burned, every bone was broken in order to prevent martyrdom and relics for any followers. The organs were burned, and all the ashes were thrown into water.

Accused witches, who were heretics because they were witches, were burned as well. In England, most witches were hung.

Witchcraft and Sorcery

In the extension of its power as a religious, social and political force, the church had long opposed pagan practices and SORCERY, especially sacrifices to DEMONS. From the 8th century to about the 12th century, the church sought to wipe out paganism. By the 13th century, there was more tolerance, and the church itself even acquired an aura of magical power. Practices of alchemy, MAGIC, sorcery, divination and necromancy were widespread, even in the church. John XXII was well aware of this activity and was a believer himself, using magical talismans for protection. A necromantic plot of sympathetic magic was directed at him and his cardinals. The plot failed, but the pope responded by turning the Inquisition against sorcery.

On July 28, 1319, John XXII ordered the prosecution of two men and a woman who were believed to be consulting with demons and making magical images. He soon followed with another bull directing the Bishop of Toulouse to proceed against sorcerers as if they were heretics. The bishop accused heretics of sacrificing to and worshipping demons and making pacts with the Devil.

John XXII was especially interested in wiping out magical practices among the clergy and prominent people, but his campaigns sometimes backfired, making the victims and their works more popular than ever. In 1330 the pope issued a bull ordering that sorcerer and witch trials be concluded, and no new ones started.

John XXII died in 1334. His successor, Benedict XII, resumed the use of sorcery as a crime of heresy, expanding into small-time practitioners in villages.

In the 14th century, the association between sorcery and heresy took on new dimensions, bringing sorcery and witchcraft into the Inquisition. But nearly 200 years passed before the essential elements of witchcraft as heresy solidified: the DEVIL'S PACT, SABBATS, SHAPE-SHIFTING and MALEFICIA. In 1398, the theological faculty of the University of Paris adopted 28 articles of witchcraft, which became a foundation for subsequent treatises on witchcraft by demonologists. The articles were considered proof of witchcraft, and they established as fact that a Devil's pact was necessary for the performance of all acts of magic and witchcraft. The first reference to sabbats in trials occurred in 1475, but sabbats received scant attention until later in the 15th century. Lurid descriptions were given about witches engaging in ritual feasting, sexual orgies and the ritual murder and cannibalism of infants and children.

Devil's pacts became a central element in the 16th century In the 15th century, the writers of inquisitional handbooks and treatises emphasized sorcery and witchcraft and drew upon the influential writings of St. Thomas Aquinas, who in the late 13th century condemned any kind of invocation of demons and Devil pacts either implicit or explicit.

The campaigns to stamp out sorcery and witchcraft had the effect of whipping up public fears of the powers of magic. People already lived in fear of bewitchment, and the Inquisition intensified it. Ironically, the attention validated the reality of magic and evil powers.

Most accusations against witches concerning evil spell-casting, but diabolical elements were introduced by inquisitors, who sought to prove Devil worship and pacts in order to convict of heresy. Torture also increased in order to secure the necessary "free confessions" to diabolism.

The witch craze raged for nearly three centuries, from the 1500s to the late 1700s, with the most intense persecutions taking place in the 17th century. In the 18th century, the Inquisition lost momentum and finally came to an end.

The Spanish Inquisition

The Inquisition took its own course in Spain and Portugal, where it was turned primarily against Jews and Muslims, religious sects and even Freemasons. Accusations of witchcraft and sorcery were used against many of the accused. The driving force behind the Spanish Inquisition was political unification of the three dominant kingdoms of Spain, Castile, Aragon and Granada, pursued by King Ferdinand, who ascended the throne of Aragon in 1479, and his wife, Queen Isabella, who ascended the throne of Castile in 1474. In 1478, Pope Sixtus IV authorized the examination of Jewish converts to Christianity. The new royals used this against what they perceived as "the Jewish" problem in their own land.

The Spanish Inquisition operated outside the jurisdiction of Rome and had its own organization of councils and inquisitors, overseen by an Inquisitor General. As the first Inquisitor General, Torquemada established rules and procedures. Salaries and expenses of inquisitors were paid from the goods and properties confiscated from the accused, so there was great motivation to target heretics.

The typical procedure against an accused heretic was to read accusations against him from anonymous accusers. The wordings were deliberately vague, and the accused was forced to guess the identity of his accusers and why he was targeted. If he guessed wrongly, he was sent back to prison and recalled again. If he guessed correctly, he was asked why the witnesses accused him of heresy. In that way, the accused were maneuvered into acknowledg-

ing guilt and also naming others who might be dragged into court as well. Throughout, the accused was assigned an "advocate," a sort of public defender, who in actuality did little to defend the accused. Instead, the advocate encouraged the accused to admit guilt.

In many cases, cruel torture was applied. The torture was both physical and psychological. The latter included taking the accused into dark, underground chambers where inquisitors waited with a black-robed and hooded executioner.

Victims were not given formal trials, but rather subjected to long interrogations punctuated by long periods in prison and by torture. Finally the accused was made to appear at an auto-da-fé, at which a sentence was given. The condemned were not always executed; many were sentenced to prison, whippings, scourging, galleys and fines.

Unrepentant or relapsed heretics were sentenced to death by burning at the stake. If they confessed during the auto-da-fé, they were given the mercy of strangulation prior to burning. The executions were spectacular affairs conducted in a public square, attended by royalty. The stakes were about four yards high, with a small board near the top where the condemned were chained. Several final attempts were made to get the condemned to reconcile to Rome. The executions proceeded by first burning the faces of the condemned with flaming furzes attached to poles that were thrust at them. Then dry furzes set about the stakes were set afire.

The Spanish Inquisition did not succumb to the witch craze that swept through Europe, but instead kept most of its focus on religious heretics. The Spaniards extended their Inquisition into the New World, setting up an office in Mexico, whose jurisdiction reached into what later was part of the American Southwest (see SANTA FE WITCHES). The Spanish Inquisition came to a formal end in 1834.

FURTHER READING:
Lea, Henry Charles. *The History of the Inquisition in the Middle Ages.* New York: Macmillan, 1908.
———. *Materials Toward a History of Witchcraft.* Philadelphia: University of Pennsylvania Press, 1939.

iron   In folklore, one of the best charms against witches, sorcerers, DEMONS and other evil spirits. In Europe, folklore holds that witches cannot pass over cold iron, and burying an iron knife under the doorstep of one's house will ensure that no witch will ever enter. In some rural locales, iron has been used to protect entire villages. In India, iron will repel evil spirits; in Scotland, Ireland and Europe, iron also keeps away mischievous and malicious FAIRIES. In some parts, iron keeps ghosts away as well (see GHOSTS, HAUNTINGS AND WITCHCRAFT).

In some cultures, iron has been sacred. The ancient Babylonians, Egyptians and Aztecs believed it came from heaven, perhaps because meteorites are comprised of iron and other metals.

In ancient Greece and Rome, iron was forbidden inside temples and for use by priests. The ancient Saxons would not put IRON rune wands in cemeteries because they feared the iron would scare away the departed spirits.

Iron has been used to make AMULETS to protect against danger, bad luck and the EVIL EYE, as well as against evil spirits and witches. Baylonian and Assyrian men wore amulets fashioned of iron in the belief that they would enhance their virility; the women rubbed themselves with iron powder in order to attract men. Ancient Egyptians inserted iron amulets in the linen wrappings of a mummy in order to invoke the protection of the Eye of Horus. In some parts of Burma, river men still wear iron pyrite amulets as protection against crocodiles.

The 18th-century magnetist, Franz Anton Mesmer, used iron in his attempts to heal illness. Patients sat in tubs filled with water and iron fillings, with protruding iron rods. Mesmer believed the iron conducted animal magnetism, the vital energy he said was in every human body.

See HORSESHOE.

FURTHER READING:
Leach, Maria, ed., and Jerome Fried, assoc. ed. *Funk & Wagnall's Standard Dictionary of Folklore, Mythology and Legend.* New York: Harper & Row, 1972.
Opie, Iona, and Moira Tatem. *A Dictionary of Superstitions.* New York: Oxford University Press, 1989.

Ishtar   The great mother GODDESS of ancient Assyrian and Babylonian mythology. Ishtar was said to be either the daughter of the sky god, Anu, or the MOON god, Sin. Over the course of time, Ishtar absorbed the characteristics of other goddesses and so represents different aspects. Worship of her spread throughout the Middle East, Greece and Egypt. She was an oracle. She ruled over fertility, sex and war and protected man against evil. As the many-breasted Opener of the Womb, she was the giver of all life; as the Destroyer and Queen of the Underworld, she also was the taker of all life. As goddess of the moon, her waxing and waning ruled the cyclical birth and death of the planet. She was the Heavenly Cow, the Green One, the Mistress of the Field.

Her son, Tammuz, also called the Green One, became her lover upon his reaching manhood. Ishtar descended to the realm of the dead to rescue Tammuz, a myth nearly identical to an earlier Sumerian myth of INANNA and Damuzi, and similar to the myth of DEMETER and Kore. When Ishtar descended, both fertility and sexual desire went dormant, to await her seasonal return.

As Queen of Heaven, Ishtar replaced Sin as the moon deity; she rode through the sky at night in a chariot drawn by goats or lions. The Zodiac was known as the "girdle of Ishtar," which also refers to the ancient moon calendar. She was the giver of omens and prophecy through dreams, and through her magic, others could obtain secret knowledge.

Ishtar was associated with the planet Venus. The lion and dove were sacred to her.

Isis   The ancient Egyptian Mother GODDESS, the prototype of the faithful wife and fertile, protective mother. Isis is associated with Sirius, the dog star, the rising of which signals the vernal equinox. Her symbol is the MOON. She is often shown crowned with a lunar orb nestled between the horns of a bull or ram. The worship of Isis was adopted by the Greeks and Romans.

The name *Isis* is the Greek word for the Egyptian hieroglyphic for "throne." She was the sister and wife of the god Osiris. A mortal magician, Isis acquired immortality by tricking the sun god, Ra, into revealing his secret name. She obtained some of his SPITTLE, made a snake from it and left the snake in his path. Ra was bitten and in great agony. She offered to relieve the pain if he would tell her his secret name, and he relented.

Isis (ATHANASIUS KIRCHER, *OEDIPUS ÆGYPTIACUS*, 1652)

When Osiris' treacherous brother, Set (Seth), murdered and dismembered him, Isis scoured the land to find the body parts and used her MAGIC to put them together and breathe life into the body so that she and Osiris could be together one last time before he left to rule the underworld. A son, Horus, was born posthumously and in a virgin birth, and Isis protected the child against Set until Horus was old enough to fight. In art, she was often depicted holding Horus in her arms. After the child was born, Set returned and cut the body of Osiris into 14 pieces, which he scattered along the Nile. Once again, Isis went in search of them, but this time she buried each piece where she found it, so that it would fertilize the land.

Isis of the mysteries and Hermetic wisdom. According to Plutarch, numerous ancient writers believed Isis to be the daughter of HERMES, while others said she was the daughter of Prometheus. Plutarch said her name meant "wisdom." She was known as the goddess of 10,000 appellations. In the Egyptian mysteries, Isis represented the female aspect of the Deity to mankind; she was the Universal Mother of all that lives; wisdom, truth and power. Statues of her were decorated with stars, the Moon and the Sun. Her girdle was joined together with four golden plates which signify the four elements of nature. Her priests were adept at controlling and using the Unseen Forces.

According to Hermetic wisdom, Isis, the Goddess of Women, was schooled by Hermes. With him, she invented the writings of all nations, caused men to love women, invented sailing, gave mankind its laws, ended cannibalism, made justice more powerful than gold or silver, instructed mankind in the mysteries and caused truth to be considered beautiful. An inscription at her temple at Sais read: "I am that which is, which hath been, and which shall be; and no man has ever lifted the veil that hides my Divinity from mortal eyes." The Isis of the mysteries is completely veiled by a scarlet cloth. To initiates who learn her mysteries, she lifts her veil, and they are to remain forever silent about what they have seen.

The Bembine Table of Isis. In 1527, after the sacking of Rome, a bronze tablet measuring 50 by 30 inches and decorated with SILVER and enamel inlay came into the possession of a locksmith or ironworker, who sold it to Cardinal Bembo of Italy. The Bembine Table of Isis, or Isaic Table, is covered with hieroglyphics and inscriptions concerning mystical knowledge and an occult system of sacrifices, rites and ceremonies. It apparently was once used as an altar, perhaps in the chambers where the mysteries of Isis were revealed to initiates. Eliphas Levi believed the tablet was a key to the Book of Thoth, or the Tarot. The tablet is in the Museum of Antiquities at Turin.

Isis as goddess of magic and healing. Isis possessed powerful magic that made even Anubis, god of death, subject to her whims. Therefore, people prayed to her on behalf of the sick and dying. She was goddess of healing and childbirth. At night, she visited the sick, brushing them gently with her wings as she said magical incantations to heal them.

Isis is identified as the Virgin in the constellation Virgo. In Christianity, she has been absorbed by the Virgin Mary. Her image is used in association with magical arts, the occult, thaumaturgy and sorcery.

See HERMETICA.

Island Magee Witches   The last witch trial to occur in Ireland took place in 1711 and involved the mysterious death of a widow, poltergeist activities and the bizarre POSSESSION of a serving girl. The accused witches were not executed but sentenced to a much milder punishment of imprisonment and public ridicule.

The incidents leading to the trial began in September 1710. Anne Hattridge (or Haltridge), widow of the Presbyterian minister at Island Magee, visited the home of her son, James, and his wife. The widow was plagued every night by some unseen force which hurled stones and turf onto her bed (see LITHOBOLY), blew open the curtains, stripped off her nightclothes and snatched the pillows from under her head. Frightened, Mrs. Hattridge finally moved to another room.

But the mysterious activities continued in other forms. On December 11, as Mrs. Hattridge sat by the fire at about twilight, a strange little boy about 12 years old appeared suddenly and sat down beside her. She couldn't see his face, because he kept it covered with a worn blanket, but she observed that he had short black hair and was dressed in dirty and torn clothing. He didn't answer her questions as to who he was or where he'd come from but danced "very nimbly" around the kitchen and then ran out of the house and into the cow shed. The servants attempted to catch him, but the boy had vanished as suddenly as he had appeared.

The apparition did not manifest again until February 11, 1711, when it apparently took a book of sermons that Mrs. Hattridge had been reading. The next day, the boy appeared outside the house, thrust his hand through a glass window and held out the book to one of the servants. He declared Mrs. Hattridge would never get the book back and that the DEVIL had taught him how to read.

The servant, named Margaret Spear, exclaimed, "The Lord bless me from thee!" But the boy laughed and produced a sword, threatening to kill all the occupants of the house. They couldn't prevent him from entering, he said, because the Devil could make him any size or creature he pleased (see METAMORPHOSIS). He threw a stone through the window. When the frightened girl next looked out, she saw the boy catching a turkey cock and making off with it into the woods. The bird managed to escape his grasp.

Then the girl saw the boy begin to dig in the ground with his sword. He announced that he was "making a grave for a corpse which will come out of this house very soon." He flew off into the air (see FLYING).

All was quiet in the Hattridge household until February 15, when Mrs. Hattridge's clothes were moved about her room and then were found laid out on the bed like a corpse. By this time, the news of the supernatural activities had spread throughout town, and numerous people, including the new Presbyterian minister, had come to the house to investigate. No one was able to help. One night, Mrs. Hattridge awoke at midnight complaining of a great pain in her back, as though she'd been stabbed with a knife. The pain persisted and Mrs. Hattridge's condition began to deteriorate, until she died on February 22. During her last days, her clothing continued to be moved mysteriously about various rooms in the house. The townspeople gossiped that Mrs. Hattridge had been bewitched to death.

On February 27 a servant girl named Mary Dunbar came to stay at the house to keep the younger Mrs. Hattridge company. The night she arrived, Dunbar was plagued by supernatural trouble. She found her clothing scattered about and one of her aprons tied into five knots (see KNOTS). She undid them and found a flannel cap that had belonged to the deceased Mrs. Hattridge. On the following day she was suddenly seized with a violent pain in her thigh and suffered fits and ravings.

Dunbar exclaimed that several women were bewitching her; she described them during two fits and gave their names: Janet Liston, Elizabeth Seller, Kate M'Calmond, Janet Carson, Janet Mean, Janet Latimer and "Mrs. Ann." Accordingly, the suspects were arrested and brought to trial. Whenever one of them was brought near Dunbar (usually without Dunbar's knowledge), the young girl fell into fits, hearing and seeing visions of her tormentors and vomiting up great quantities of feathers, cotton, yarn, pins and buttons (see ALLOTRIOPHAGY). She would repeat her conversations with the alleged witches and thrash about so violently that it took three strong men to hold her down. According to testimony by Rev. Dr. Tisdall, vicar of Belfast:

> In her fits she often had her tongue thrust into her windpipe in such a manner than she was like to choak, and the root seemed pulled up into her mouth.

Dunbar claimed her tormentors prohibited her from leaving her room. Whenever she attempted to do so for a while, she fell into fits. One witness claimed he saw a knotted bracelet of yarn appear mysteriously around her wrist. Dunbar also said her tormentors told her she would not be able to give evidence against them in court. During the entire trial, she was struck dumb and sat senseless as though in a trance. Later, Dunbar said she had been possessed by three of the accused witches throughout the proceedings.

According to an account of the trial in MacSkimin's *History of Carrickfergus*:

> It was also deposed that strange noises, as of whistling, scratching, etc., were heard in the house, and that a sulphureous [sic] smell was observed in the rooms; that stones, turf, and the like were thrown about the house, and the coverlets, etc., frequently taken off the beds and made up in the shape of a corpse; and that a bolster [ghost] once walked out of a room into the kitchen with a nightgown about it!

The defendants, none of whom had a lawyer, all denied the charges of witchcraft, and the "one with the worst looks, and therefore the greatest suspect, called God to witness she was wronged." According to court records,

> Their characters were inquired into, and some were reported unfavorably of, which seemed to be rather due to their ill appearance than to any facts provided against them. It was made to appear on oath that most of them had received the Communion, some of them very lately, that several of them had been laborious, industrious people, and had frequently been known to pray with their families, both publickly and privately; most of them could say the Lord's Prayer . . . they being every one Presbyterians.

The trial was short, lasting from six o'clock in the morning until two in the afternoon. In Judge Upton's opinion, there was insufficient evidence to convict the defendants. He had no doubt that Dunbar's affliction was "preternatural and diabolical," but if the defendants really were witches in compact with the Devil, "it could hardly be presumed that they should be such constant attenders upon Divine Service, both in public and private." He instructed the jury that they could not reach a guilty verdict "upon the sole testimony of the afflicted person's visionary images."

The jury felt differently, however, and declared a guilty verdict for all defendants. They were sentenced to a year in jail and to stand in a pillory four times during their incarceration. While pilloried, the "unfortunate wretches" were pelted with eggs and cabbage stalks; one of them was blinded in one eye.

FURTHER READING:
Seymour, St. John D. *Irish Witchcraft and Demonology*. Dublin: Hodges, Figgis & Co., 1913.

jack-o'-lantern A phosphorescent light seen in marsh and swamp areas, which in folklore is either the manifestation of a malicious lost soul or a death omen. Jack-o'-lantern is known by various names, including will-o'-the-wisp and corpse light (England); fairy light and fox fire (Ireland).

According to most legends, the jack-o'-lantern is a wandering soul who has been denied entry into both heaven and hell. Clothed in a luminous garment or carrying a lighted wisp of straw, it drifts about at night, scaring travelers and beckoning them to follow it into the marshes. CHARMS to protect oneself against the spirit include carrying an object made of IRON, which is believed to repel evil spirits, or sticking an iron knife into the ground.

In Ireland, children who are caught outdoors after dark are told to wear their jackets inside-out in order not to be lured astray by a jack-o'-lantern. In Sweden, the spirit is believed to be the soul of an unbaptized child, who tries to lead travelers to water in hopes of receiving baptism. The jack-o'-lantern also appears in American Indian and Appalachian folklore. The Penobscot Indians call it the "fire demon," who has lighted fingertips which it spins in a wheel, and skims the milk at dairies during the night. In the Appalachians, mysterious, firelike balls of light appear in the hills at night and float, move and bob about the countryside. Some are quite large and rise high into the air; others light up the surroundings like daylight. In Africa, the jack-o'-lantern light is called a "witch-fire" and is believed to be the witch herself, flying through the air, or a light sent by the witch to scare wrongdoers. As a corpse light, the eerie glow forecasts death in a household by hovering over a rooftop or even appearing on top of the chest of the person who is about to die.

In American lore, the jack-o'-lantern is associated with witches and the Halloween custom of trick-or-treating. It is customary for trick-or-treaters to carry pumpkin jack-o'-lanterns to frighten away evil spirits.

FURTHER READING:

Leach, Maria, ed., and Jerome Fried, assoc. ed. *Funk & Wagnalls Standard Dictionary of Folklore, Mythology and Legend.* New York: Harper & Row, 1972.

Randolph, Vance. *Ozark Magic and Folklore.* 1947, Reprint, New York: Dover Publications, 1964.

James I (1566–1625) King of Scotland and England who strengthened anti-witch laws in 1604. James' own beliefs about witchcraft reflected the popular views of the day, and while he permitted prosecutions of accused witches, he did not lead the charge against them. When public hysteria threatened to get out of hand, he moved to cool tensions down. "James was not riding the storm like Odin," notes George Lyman Kittredge in *Witchcraft in Old and New England* (1929). "He was only a mortal man, swept off his feet by the tide."

James was born in Scotland in 1566 to Mary Queen of Scots and her second husband, Lord Henry Stuart Darnley, a vicious and dissipated man. In 1567 Darnley was murdered by strangulation. His death was rumored to be the plot of the earl of Bothwell, who then married Mary. The incident caused an uprising among the Scots; Mary abdicated the throne in favor of James, who ruled under regents until 1583, when he began his personal rule as James VI.

The same year, the Scottish clergy, pressured by rising public fears of witchcraft, demanded tougher enforcement of Scotland's witchcraft law, which had been enacted in 1563. James, credulous in his beliefs that witches were evil and posed a threat to Godfearing people, tolerated the increasing witch-hunts.

James was skeptical of the confessions made by accused NORTH BERWICK WITCHES in the trials of 1590–92, even though the confessions involved an alleged plot by witches to murder him and his bride. In 1589 James had agreed to marry by proxy Anne of Denmark, a 15-year-old princess whom he had never met. That same year, she set sail for Scotland from Norway, but her ship was buffeted twice by terrible storms and nearly destroyed. It made port at Oslo, where the passengers were stranded for months. James sailed out to meet the ship. As a result of more storms, he and Anne were forced to remain in Scandinavia until the spring of 1590. On their return to Scotland, they were buffeted by yet more storms but managed to make land safely. The North Berwick witches claimed to have raised these storms. James, however, called them "extreme lyars," until one of the accused convinced him of their supernormal powers by repeating to him the private conversation he had had with Anne on their wedding night. James permitted brutal TORTURES and executions of the accused.

After the North Berwick affair, James made a study of witchcraft on the Continent and read the works of the leading demonologists. He was distressed by the counter-arguments on the "witchcraft delusion" posed by REGINALD SCOT in *The Discoverie of Witchcraft* (1584) and by JOHANN A. WEYER in *De Praestigiis Daemonum* (1563). He wrote his own response, *Daemonologie,* which first appeared in 1597.

Daemeonologie has been blamed for adding to the public hysteria over witches, though Kittredge points out that it added nothing new to the prevailing beliefs about witches. Nevertheless, the book did much to reinforce prevailing beliefs. In it, James acknowledged that witches had the power to raise storms; cause illness and death by burning waxen images; and were followers of "Diana and her wandering court" (see DIANA). He stated that the DEVIL appeared in the likeness of a dog, CAT, ape or other "such-like beast" and always was inventing new techniques for deceiving others (see BLACK ANIMALS; METAMORPHOSIS). He defended SWIMMING as a test for witches and supported the widely held belief that more women were witches than men because women were inherently weak and predisposed to evil. He accepted the execution of a witch as the therapeutic cure for the victim. He advocated the death penalty for clients of CUNNING MEN. He defined a witch as "a consulter with familiar spirits."

By 1597 the witch hysteria in Scotland had reached alarming proportions, and there was evidence that over-zealous WITCH-HUNTERS were indicting people on fraudulent evidence. James reacted by revoking all indictments, and for the remaining years of his rule on the throne of Scotland, executions for witchcraft decreased.

Upon the death of Elizabeth I in 1603, James gained the English throne as James I. His *Daemonologie* was reissued in London the same year, and he ordered copies of Scot's *Discoverie* to be burned.

In 1604 a new Witchcraft Act was passed by Parliament, which stiffened the penalties for witchcraft. The impetus for the new law had already begun years before (see WARBOYS WITCHES) and was neither the idea nor the work of James but of the ruling gentry of England.

The 1604 law closely followed the Elizabethan Witchcraft Act. Under the Elizabethan code, witchcraft, enchantment, CHARMS or SORCERY that caused bodily injury to people or damage to their goods and chattel was punishable by a year in jail with quarterly exposures in the pillory for the first offense and death for the second offense. A sentence of life in jail with quarterly pillory exposures was given for the divining of treasure and the causing of "unlawful" love and intentional hurt. Bewitching a person to death was a capital offense.

The 1604 law punished crimes of witchcraft with death on the first offense instead of a year in jail or life in jail. In addition, the conjuring or evoking of evil spirits for any purpose whatsoever was made a capital offense. However, the law was no tougher than the rest of England's penal code, which mandated death for stealing a sheep or a purse, or breaking into a home. Ironically, the death sentence may have been a blessing: the jails of the time were so abominable and filthy that death might have seemed preferable to life in a stinking, dank, disease-ridden hole.

Passage of the law did not evoke a wave of witch-hunts; the first trials of major importance did not occur until 1612. During James' entire reign of 22 years, fewer than 40 persons were executed for the crime of witchcraft. James pardoned some accused witches because of the weak evidence against them and exposed a number of cases of fraudulent accusations of witches, including the "possession" of a boy in Leicester that sent nine victims to the gallows in 1616. (Unfortunately, James did not uncover the fraud until after the executions. Though he was sorely displeased with the judge and sergeant, he did not punish them.)

The Witchcraft Act of 1604 remained in force until 1736, when it was repealed and replaced by a new law under George II. It was used to prosecute the accused witches in Salem, Massachusetts in 1692. (See SALEM WITCHES.) Some of the worst abuses of witch-hunting in England did not occur until several decades after James' death, when MATTHEW HOPKINS terrorized the countryside in search of victims.

FURTHER READING:

Barstow, Anne Llewellyn. *Witchcraze: A New History of the European Witch Hunts.* San Francisco: Pandora, 1994.

Deacon, Richard. *Matthew Hopkins: Witch Finder General.* London: Frederick Muller, 1976.

Russell, Jeffrey B. *A History of Witchcraft.* London: Thames and Hudson, 1980.

Scot, Reginald. *The Discoverie of Witchcraft.* 1886. Reprint, Yorkshire, England: E. P. Publishing, Ltd., 1973.

Scott, Sir Walter. *Letters on Demonology and Witchcraft.* 1884. Reprint, New York: Citadel Press, 1968.

Trevor-Roper, H. R. *The European Witch-Craze.* New York: Harper & Row, 1957.

Joan of Arc (1412–1431)

Joan of Arc (1412–1431)   A French peasant girl who, spurred on by divine voices and visions, fought the English and secured the coronation of the dauphin Charles as king of France. Contrary to popular belief, she was not executed by the English on charges of witchcraft but for being a relapsed heretic who denied the authority of the Church.

Joan was born a plowman's daughter in Domrémy, a village between the Champagne and Lorraine districts of France. Early in her life, she demonstrated exceptional piety and was hardworking and industrious. She began to hear voices and have visions at age 13 and identified them as the saints Michael, Catherine and Margaret. They told her to go to the dauphin and that she would raise the English siege of Orléans.

At that time, the crown of France was in dispute between the dauphin Charles, son of King Charles VI, and the English, who held control over portions of France. When Joan was 16, her voices led her to Vaucouleurs, a French loyalist stronghold, where she begged a captain to see the dauphin. She was refused; a year later, in 1429, she tried again. She convinced the captain that she was not a witch and that her visions were divine.

Charles received her, and she impressed the superstitious dauphin by telling him his daily personal prayer to God. Her mission, she said, was to defeat the English and get him crowned king of France. He had her interviewed by the clergy; Joan passed their inspection.

The dauphin gave Joan troops, and she led them into battle against the English. True to her visions, she raised the siege of Orléans in May 1429. The dauphin was crowned Charles VII about two months later, on July 17. He ennobled Joan and her family, and she enjoyed enormous popularity among the people as the savior of France.

France, however, was far from unified. Though the English grip was weakened, it was not broken. Paris and parts of Normandy and Burgundy remained loyal to the English. Joan attempted to take Paris but was ordered to retreat before the battle was decided.

On May 23, 1430, Joan attempted to raise a siege of Compiègne. She was unhorsed and captured, and imprisoned in a castle by the Duke of Burgundy, an ally of the English. She unsuccessfully attempted to escape by jumping out of the tower into the moat but didn't hurt herself seriously.

In exchange for 10,000 francs, the Duke of Burgundy turned Joan over to the Bishop of Beauvais, also an English ally. It was the intent of the English to execute Joan, but first they set out to discredit her as a witch and thus weaken Charles VII.

In an informal ecclesiastical hearing, Joan came through exceptionally well. It was verified that she was a virgin, which weakened the case for witchcraft, because all witches were supposed to copulate with the DEVIL, according to belief at the time. Character witnesses painted a shining picture of her piety and virtue. All of this testimony was repressed by the Bishop of Beauvais.

Following the informal hearings, the clergy began interrogations of Joan in her prison cell. She acknowledged that she could see, kiss and embrace her three saints.

Joan was brought to formal trial before 37 clerical judges on 70 charges, among them being a sorceress, witch, diviner, pseudoprophetess, invoker of evil spirits, conjurer and "given to the arts of magic." She was also accused of heresy. Her inquisitors did not torture her, to avoid the appearance of coercion.

The charges of SORCERY and witchcraft could not be substantiated and were dropped. The 70 charges were reduced to 12, the main ones being her heresy in refusing to accept the authority of the Church, her wearing of men's clothing and her ability to see apparitions.

Joan refused to recant, even under the threat of torture or being turned over to the English secular arm for punishment, which was certain execution.

On May 24, 1431, Joan was publicly condemned as a heretic and turned over to the English, who were ready to burn her on the spot. At the last minute, she recanted and signed a hastily written confession renouncing her visions and voices as false, and swearing to return to and obey the Church. This saved her from the pyre, and she was sent to prison for life.

But in prison, she donned men's clothing—allegedly because her voices told her to, but perhaps because her English guards took her women's garb and left her with nothing else to wear. On May 28 she was condemned as a relapsed heretic. She recanted her confession. On May 30 Joan was excommunicated and delivered at last to the English secular arm. She was burned at the stake the same day in Rouen. Legend has it that the executioner was spooked by her death, claiming that her heart refused to burn and he found it whole in the ashes. Throughout her ordeal, Charles VII, to whom she had delivered the crown of France, declined to come to her aid.

In 1450 Pope Calixtus III had her sentence annulled. Joan was canonized in 1920 by Pope Benedict XV. A national festival in her honor is held in France on the second Sunday in May.

FURTHER READING:

Pernoud, Regine. *Joan of Arc: By Herself and Her Witnesses.* New York: Dorset, 1964. First published 1962.

Russell, Jeffrey Burton. *Witchcraft in the Middle Ages.* Ithaca and London: Cornell University Press, 1972.

Jones, Margaret (?–1648)   The first witch to be executed in Massachusetts Bay Colony, on June 15, 1648, in Boston. Margaret Jones was a physician who was accused of witchcraft when patients worsened under her care.

Jones and her husband, Thomas, were among the early settlers in Massachusetts Bay Colony, making their home in Charlestown. According to records of her trial, Jones told some of her patients that if they refused to take her medicines, they would never be healed. Her trial records state, "Accordingly, their Diseases and Hurts continued, with Relapse against the ordinary Course, and beyond the Apprehension of all Physicians and Surgeons."

While her medicines were themselves harmless, the doctor was suspected of bewitching her patients into suffering. Once that thought took hold among her neighbors, she "was found to have such a malignant Touch, as many persons were taken with Deafness, or Vomiting, or other violent Pains or Sicknesses."

Jones was arrested and jailed. A string of witnesses appeared at her trial to testify against her. A jail officer testified that he had seen a little child run from her room, but when he followed it, the child vanished. This was taken as further proof of her being a witch. Jones protested her innocence vigorously and violently, denouncing those who would condemn her, but to no avail. She was sentenced to hang. According to the records,

> . . . her Behavior at her Trial was intemperate, lying notoriously, and railing upon the Jury and Witnesses. In like Distemper, she died. . . . The same Day and Hour she was executed, there was a very great Tempest at Connecticut, which blew down many Trees, etc.

A month prior to Jones' arrest and trial, an order had been passed in Boston requiring that all husbands of accused witches were to be confined to a room and watched for signs of witchcraft themselves. Accordingly, Thomas Jones was accused of being a witch and was jailed. There is no record of his fate.

FURTHER READING:
Drake, Samuel G. *Annals of Witchcraft in New England and Elsewhere in the United States, from their First Settlement.* Boston: W. Elliott Woodward, 1869.
Karlsen, Carol F. *The Devil in the Shape of a Woman: Witchcraft in Colonial New England.* New York: W. W. Norton & Co, 1987.

Juan   In Hispanic lore, any man named Juan has the power to catch witches. To do so, he must draw a MAGIC CIRCLE on the ground and sit inside it. Then he takes off his shirt, turns it inside out and says, "In the name of God I call thee, *bruja.*" Immediately, all witches in the vicinity must appear before him and fall helpless into the circle.

Despite this power, men named Juan were believed to seldom use it, for they knew that witches so summoned would beat them to death.

The turning inside out of the shirt has a curious association with vampire killing folklore in eastern Europe. The vampire hunter would take off his shirt, turn the sleeves inside out and use a sleeve as a telescope to "find" a vampire.

FURTHER READING:
Lummis, Charles. *A New Mexico David.* New York: Charles Scribner's Sons, 1891.

Judith, Anodea (1952–)   American witch, author, artist, songwriter and healer, renowned for her therapeutic work with the chakra system. She is a past president of the CHURCH OF ALL WORLDS, founder of Lifeways, a school for the study of healing and magickal arts, and a founding member of Forever Forests (see GWYDION PENDDERWEN).

Anodea Judith was born Judith Ann Mull on December 1, 1952, in Elyria, Ohio, the youngest of three children and the only daughter (one of her brothers is comedian Martin Mull). From an early age, she was close to

Anodea Judith (COURTESY ANODEA JUDITH)

nature—her grandmother had a farm, where she spent much time communing with the animals and collecting rocks and insects. The seeds for her interest in Paganism and Witchcraft were planted during her early teen years when she read about Greek mythology, which reconstructed her images of God. The strongest religious indoctrination Judith received from her family was Christian Science, which holds that illness is an error in thinking, and may be cured by a wholeness of mind, body and spirit. She learned the healing and beneficial results of positive thinking and mind over matter. Mary Baker Eddy, the founder of Christian Science, could be viewed as a displaced Witch, she says. In high school, Judith was known as a healer. Christianity, however, had no appeal to her, and she looked for another system in which to apply Christian Science principles.

In 1971, Judith enrolled at Clark University, to study psychology and become a therapist, but decided to pursue art instead. In 1973, she moved to California, where she studied at the California College of Arts and Crafts in Oakland and at John F. Kennedy University. For a number of years, she painted environmental murals, which led her to her first discoveries of magic and a connection to primal, racial memories.

In 1975, she underwent a spiritual transformation: she gave up smoking and meat, became bisexual, practiced yoga daily, and did numerous fastings and purifications. Her work became more creative. One day while meditating in a lotus position in her artist's attic in Berkeley, Judith went out-of-body. She saw herself meditating, but looking older than she was. She saw a book fall into her lap, which jarred her back into her body. Its title was *The Chakra System* by A. Judith Mull, the name she was still using at the time. The experience initiated a decade-long study of chakras, acupressure, bioenergetics, gestalt, shamanism, radical psychiatry, ritual magic, healing and psychic reading. The result was the publication of her comprehensive book, *Wheels of Life: A User's Guide to the Chakra System* (1987).

During this formative period, Judith spent a great deal of time in nature, through which she received direct teachings from Goddess. Her given name no longer seemed to fit; she changed it to Anodea ("one of the Goddess") Judith. She met OBERON and MORNING GLORY ZELL, founders of the Church of All Worlds (CAW), and established a long-term friendship that led to Judith's serving as CAW president for seven years (1986–93) and high priestess for 10 years. In addition, she implemented many of its programs, including RING (Requirements Involving Network Growth), the basic training program in CAW, and the CAW guild system, an organizational database for Pagan talents.

Judith was intimately involved for a while with GWYDION PENDDERWEN, founder of Forever Forests and cofounder of Nemeton, helping him develop the Church of All Worlds Sanctuary, known as Annwfn, the home of Forever Forests.

In Berkeley, she worked with ISAAC BONEWITS on *Pentalpha,* a Druidic journal (now defunct), and became friends with fantasy and science fiction author MARION ZIMMER BRADLEY, who is goddess mother to her son. She joined Bradley's Aquarian Order of the Restoration and the Dark Moon Circle, of which Bradley was a founder.

Judith had a brief marriage and bore a son, Alex, in 1982. The marriage dissolved in 1984. Judith and Alex moved to Annwfn, Pendderwen's land in Mendocino County. Pendderwen, who had died in 1982, had named Judith one of five stewards of the land, now owned by the Church of All Worlds. She remained at Annwfn for about 18 months, during which she had profound magical experiences with Goddess. She founded Lifeways in 1983. It was a subsidiary and the teaching arm of CAW.

In 1988 Judith married Richard Ely, a Pagan, Witch and geologist, who has three children from a previous marriage. They live in Sonoma County.

Judith received a master's degree in clinical psychology from the Rosebridge Graduate School of Integrative Therapy in 1989 and a Ph.D. in health and human services from Columbia Pacific University in 1999.

The success of *Wheels of Life* established Judith as a leading teacher on chakras and healing, and she began extensive traveling to present workshops and lectures, especially to non-Pagan audiences. She is a Reiki master and a certified yoga therapist. She wrote *The Sevenfold Journey: Reclaiming Mind, Body and Spirit through the Chakras* with Selene Vega (1993) and *Eastern Body, Western Mind: Psychology and the Chakra System as a Path to the Self* (1996); *Contact: The Yoga of Relationship* (2006); *Waking the Global Heart: Humanity's Rite of Passage from the Love of Power to the Power of Love* (2006); and the booklets *The Truth About Chakras* (2002) and *The Truth About Neo-Paganism* (2002).

Judith defines a witch as a person who takes active control of his or her own life and destiny and who serves Goddess. The religion of the future needs to have a concept of Goddess and an understanding of archetypal thinking, as well as an ecological system. PAGANISM, a religion of the past, is not necessarily the religion of the future, but part of a broader syncretism of various religions that will address mind, body and soul together. Magic, the direction of energy through a sensible system that seeks balance of all things, can assist this syncretic evolution.

Junius, Johannes (1573?–1628)   Burgomaster, or mayor, of Bamberg, Germany, caught with other local leading citizens in one of the most vicious witch persecutions of the INQUISITION. From the early 1600s to about 1630, hundreds of men and women in Bamberg were accused of witchcraft, tortured by the most barbaric means (see TORTURE) and executed. All of the burgomasters of Bamberg fell victim to the inquisitors. The trial of Johannes Junius is of historic importance for the account of his ordeal that he managed to leave behind.

Junius was 55 years old when he was accused of witch-craft by the authorities, who were led by Vicar-General Suffragan Bishop Friedrich Forner and the prince-bishop of Bamberg, Gottfried Johann Georg II Fuchs von Dornheim. Junius had been named by several persons, including the vice-chancellor of Bamberg, Dr. Georg Adam Haan.

On June 28, 1628, Junius was interrogated without torture. He protested his innocence, saying he had never renounced God and was wronged to be so accused. He called the inquisitors' bluff by saying he would like evidence of a single person who had ever seen him at the witch's sabbat (see SABBATS). The inquisitors smugly complied, producing Haan and Hapffens Elsse, who stated in the presence of Junius that they had witnessed his evil activities. Haan swore upon his life that about two years earlier, Junius had attended a witch's sabbat in the electoral council room which he had entered by the left. There, Junius, Haan and others ate and drank. Another man, Hopffens Elsse, testified that he had seen Junius on the Hauptsmoor at a witches' dance, where a holy wafer was desecrated.

Junius vigorously denied the testimony, but the inquisitors told him other "accomplices" had confessed. He was given time to contemplate his situation. In all, six witnesses were brought against him, including Haan's son.

Two days later, on June 30, Junius was asked to confess, but refused. The torture began. First, he was put in thumbscrews. Still he denied renouncing God and being baptized by the DEVIL. The inquisitors noted that he seemed to suffer no pain in the thumbscrews. Such insensitivity to pain was often considered a sign that the Devil was aiding the witch in enduring pain.

The inquisitors then crushed his legs in legscrews. Again Junius protested his innocence, and again the inquisitors noted that he seemed to feel no pain. After the legscrews, the inquisitors had him stripped, shaved and searched for a WITCH'S MARK, which they believed they found in a bluish patch of skin shaped like a clover leaf, which seemed insensitive to pain when pricked three times (see PRICKING).

Finally, Junius was given the strappado, a torture in which the victim's hands are bound by a rope behind his back, which is connected to a pulley. The victim is drawn up to the ceiling and allowed to drop. Junius still protested his innocence. On July 5 the inquisitors again urged him to make a full confession. Exhausted and wracked by incredible pain, Junius gave in and made up a story that he thought would satisfy his persecutors:

He said his dealings with the Devil began in 1624. A lawsuit he had been involved in had cost him 600 florins. One day, he went out to sit in his orchard to contemplate, when a woman who looked like a grassmaid appeared and asked him why he was so sad. He replied that he wasn't. She spoke to him seductively, then turned into a goat which said, "Now you see with whom you have to do.

You must be mine or I will forthwith break your neck." Junius became frightened. The goat grabbed him by the throat and ordered him to renounce God. "God forbid," Junius replied. The goat vanished but shortly reappeared accompanied by a host of people, who threatened him and demanded he renounce God. He did so by saying, "I renounce God in Heaven and his host, and will henceforth recognize the Devil as my God."

Junius was then baptized and christened as Krix, with a paramour named Vixen, an evil spirit. He was congratulated by the other witches, whom he named as residents of Bamberg, and was given a ducat, which later turned into a potsherd.

Whenever he wished to attend a sabbat, a large black dog appeared, and bore him through the air. Vixen promised to give him money.

This tale did not completely satisfy the inquisitors, who allowed Junius more time for "contemplation." On July 7 he was asked to confess further. He obliged them by describing a sabbat and by admitting he attempted murder at the prompting of Vixen. She ordered him to kill his younger son and gave him a gray powder. He could not bring himself to do it and killed his son's horse instead. Vixen also ordered him to kill his daughter. When he refused, she beat him.

Junius also said that the Devil appeared before him as a goat about a week before his arrest and told him he was going to be arrested, but not to worry, that he would be released.

Junius' implication of himself was not enough. The inquisitors took him down the streets of Bamberg, ordering him to name others who were witches. He complied but was tortured again when he did not name enough people.

After this degrading ordeal, Junius was condemned to die at the stake in late July. Also condemned were those whom he falsely had named as Devil-worshipers, including Haan and the others who originally had accused him of the same. While in prison, Junius wrote a letter to his daughter, Veronica, which he managed to have smuggled out and delivered to her. It is written in a shaky hand; that he managed to write it at all is amazing, considering that his hands had been crushed in the thumbscrews and he had been subjected to other torture. Junius' letter provides some of the most damning testimony about the evil excesses of the witch-hunters. An excerpt follows:

> Many hundred thousand good-nights, dearly beloved daughter Veronica. Innocent have I come into prison, innocent have I been tortured, innocent I must die. For whoever comes into the witch prison must become a witch or be tortured until he invents something out of his head and—God pity him—bethinks him of something. I will tell you how it has gone with me. . . . And then came also—God in highest heaven have mercy—the executioner, and put the thumb-screws on me, both hands

bound together, so that the blood ran out at the nails and everywhere, so that for four weeks I could not use my hands, as you can see from the writing. . . . Thereafter they first stripped me, bound my hands behind me, and drew me up in the torture [strappado]. Then I thought heaven and earth were at an end, eight times did they draw me up and let me fall again, so that I suffered terribly agony . . .

When at last the executioner led me back into the prison he said to me: "Sir, I beg you, for God's sake confess something, whether it be true or not. Invent something, for you cannot endure the torture which you will be put to; and even if you bear it all, yet you will not escape, not even if you were an earl, but one torture will follow another until you say you are a witch . . .

And so I begged, since I was in wretched plight, to be given one day for thought and a priest. The priest was refused me, but the time for thought was given . . . at last there came to me a new idea. . . . I would think of something to say and say it. . . . And so I made my confession, as follows, but it was all a lie. Now follows dear child, what I confessed in order to escape the great anguish and bitter torture, which it was impossible for me longer to bear . . .

Then I had to tell what people I had seen [at the sabbat]. I said that I had not recognized them. "You old rascal, I must set the executioner at you. Say—was not the Chancellor there?" So I said yes. "Who besides?" I had not recognized anybody. So he said: "Take one street after another, begin at the market, go out on one street and back on the next. . . . And thus continuously they asked me on all the streets, though I could not and would not say more. So they gave me to the executioner, told him to strip me, shave me all over, and put me to the torture . . .

Then I had to tell what crimes I had committed. I said nothing. . . . "Draw the rascal up!" So I said that I was to kill my children, but I had killed a horse instead. It did not help . . .

Now, dear child, here you have all my confession, for which I much die. And they are sheer lies and made-up things, so help me God. For all this I was forced to say through fear of the torture which was threatened beyond what I had already endured . . .

Dear child, keep this letter secret so that people do not find it, else I shall be tortured most piteously and the jailers will be beheaded. So strictly is it forbidden. . . . I have taken several days to write this: my hands are both lame. I am in a sad plight . . .

Good night, for your father Johannes Junius will never see you more. July 24, 1628.

Junius added a postscript to the margin:

Dear child, six have confessed against me at once . . . all false, through compulsion, as they have all told me, and begged my forgiveness in God's name before they were executed. . . . They know nothing but good of me. They were forced to say it, just as I myself was . . .

See BAMBERG WITCHES.

FURTHER READING:
Kors, Alan C., and Edward Peters. *Witchcraft in Europe, A Documentary History 1100–1700.* Philadelphia: University of Pennsylvania Press, 1972.
Robbins, Rossell Hope. *The Encyclopedia of Witchcraft & Demonology.* 1959. Reprint, New York: Bonanza Books, 1981.

Kabbalah (also Cabala, Kabala, Qabalah) A Jewish system of theosophy, philosophy, science, magic and mysticism founded on the Torah, developed since the Middle Ages and comprising an important part of Western occultism. Kabbalistic studies and magic are part of some traditions of contemporary Witchcraft and PAGANISM.

Kabbalah comes from the Hebrew word *QBL (Qibel)*, meaning "to receive" or "that which is received." "Kabbalah" was first used in the 11th century by Ibn Gabirol, a Spanish philosopher, to describe a secret oral tradition and has since been applied to all Jewish mystical practice. The Kabbalah is a means for achieving union with God while maintaining an active life in the mundane world.

In its role in Western MAGIC, the Kabbalah is the science of letters, the universal language from which all things are created. This science of letters is used to create words and sounds in RITUAL.

According to legend, the Kabbalah was taught by God to a group of angels, who, after the Fall, taught it to man in order to provide man a way back to God. It was passed from Adam to Noah to Abraham, who took it to Egypt, where it was passed to Moses. Moses included it in the first four books of the Pentateuch, but left it out of Deuteronomy. He initiated 70 elders into the Kabbalah, who continued the tradition of passing it down orally. David and Solomon were kabbalistic adepts. Eventually, the wisdom was written down.

The Kabbalah is a body of writings by anonymous authors. The main works are the Sefer Yezirah, or the Book of Creation, and the Zohar, or Book of Splendor. The origins of the Sefer Yezirah date to the eight century. The Zohar is believed to be written by Moses de Leon of Guadalajara, Spain, in the 13th century.

From its beginnings, the mysticism of the Kabbalah was similar to that of gnosticism, including concepts on magic, cosmology and angels. The Kabbalah holds that God is both immanent and transcendent; God is all things, both good and evil; all things make up the whole of an organized universe; and letters and numbers are keys to unlocking the mysteries of the universe (see Gematria).

God, *En Soph or Ain Soph,* is boundless and fills the universe. From God come 10 emanations, called *sephirot,* of angels and men, that form the structure of the Tree of Life and represent aspects of the divine. The Tree of Life shows the descent of the divine into the material world and the path by which man can ascend to the divine while still in the flesh. Each *sephirah* is a level of attainment in knowledge. The *sephirot* are organized in three triangles, with the 10th *sephirah* resting at the base. The triangles represent a portion of the human body: the head, arms and legs; the 10th *sephirah* represents the reproductive organs. The triangles are aligned on three pillars, on the right Mercy (the male principle), on the left Severity (the female principle) and in the middle Mildness, a balance between the two. The *sephirot* and their names and aspects are:

1. Kether, supreme crown
2. Chokmah, wisdom

3. Binah, understanding
4. Chesed, mercy, greatness
5. Geburah, strength, rigor
6. Tiphareth, beauty, harmony
7. Netzach, victory, force
8. Hod, splendor
9. Yesod, foundation
10. Malkuth, kingdom

The cosmos is divided into four worlds: Atziluth, the world of archetypes, from which are derived all forms of manifestation; Briah, the world of creation, in which archetypal ideas become patterns; Yetzirah, the world of formation, in which the patterns are expressed; and Assiah, the world of the material, the plane we perceive with our physical senses. Each *sephirah* is divided into four sections in which the four worlds operate.

The *sephirot* also comprise the sacred name of God, which is unknowable and unspeakable. The Bible gives various substitutes, such as Elohim and Adonai. The personal name of God is the Tetragrammaton, YHVH, usually pronounced as Yahweh, and which appears in the Bible as Jehovah. The four letters of YHVH correspond to the four worlds.

The magical applications of the kabbalah were recognized as early as the 13th century. During the Renaissance,

Kabbalistic tables for calculating the names of good and evil spirits (FRANCIS BARRETT, *THE MAGUS*, 1801)

alchemists and magicians used combinations of kabbalistic numbers and divine names in rituals and incantations. The Tetragrammaton was held in great awe for its power over all things in the universe, including DEMONS. Beginning in the late 15th century, the Kabbalah was harmonized with Christian doctrines to form a Christian Kabbalah, the proponents of which claimed that magic and the Kabbalah proved the divinity of Christ. Cornelius Agrippa von Nettesheim included the Kabbalah in his *De Occulta Philosophia,* published in 1531, which resulted in its erroneous associations with witchcraft. Also in the 16th century, alchemical symbols were integrated into the Christian Kabbalah.

Jewish study of the Kabbalah peaked by the 19th century and then declined. Interest was later revived by non-Jewish Western occultists, such as Francis Barrett, Eliphas Levi and Papus. The Kabbalah formed part of the teachings of the HERMETIC ORDER OF THE GOLDEN DAWN. DION FORTUNE called the Kabbalah the "Yoga of the West." Western occultists linked the Kabbalah to the Tarot and astrology.

In some traditions of Witchcraft and Paganism, the Tree of Life is used for pathworking, magic intended for self-realization.

FURTHER READING:

Bardon, Franz. *The Key to the True Kabbalah.* Salt Lake City: Merkur Publishing, 1996.

Fortune, Dion. *The Mystical Qabalah.* York Beach, Me.: Samuel Weiser, 1984.

Gray, William G. *The Ladder of Lights.* York Beach, Me.: Samuel Weiser, 1981.

Kraig, Donald Michael. *Modern Magick: Eleven Lessons in the High Magickal Arts.* 2nd ed. St. Paul, Minn.: Llewellyn Publications, 2004.

Levi, Eliphas. *Transcendental Magic.* York Beach, Me.: Samuel Weiser, 2001. First published in 1896.

———. *The Book of Splendours: The Inner Mysteries of the Qabalah.* York Beach, Me.: Samuel Weiser, 1984. First published 1894.

Mathers, S.L. MacGregor. *The Kabbalah Unveiled.* London: Routledge and Kegan Paul, 1926.

Scholem, Gershom. *Kabbalah.* New York: New American Library, 1974.

Three Books of Occult Philosophy Written by Henry Cornelius Agrippa of Nettesheim.

Translated by James Freake. Edited and annotated by Donald Tyson. St. Paul, Minn.: Llewellyn Publications, 1995.

Kempe, Ursula   See ST. OSYTH WITCHES.

Keridwen   See CERRIDWEN.

King, Graham   See MUSEUM OF WITCHCRAFT.

kiss of shame   Homage paid to the DEVIL by kissing his posterior. The *osculum infame,* as it was called, was mentioned, in nearly every recorded account of a witches'

Witch giving ritual kiss to Satan (FRANCESCO-MARIA GUAZZO, *COMPENDIUM MALEFICARUM,* 1608)

SABBAT, most confessions of which were extracted under TORTURE. The kiss of shame was regarded as the ultimate act of abasement, though some witches allegedly protested that the Devil had not a common posterior but a second face located there.

The kiss supposedly was given at the beginning of the sabbat, after the Devil had read the rolls of his followers. Sometimes the witches approached him backwards, in true infernal fashion, then turned, bowed and scraped and kissed his fundament. A kiss of shame was always required of new initiates (see INITIATION). Following the kiss, the witches and the Devil commenced their feasting.

Witches also supposedly kissed the posteriors of lower-ranking DEMONS. While the kiss of shame was usually an act of homage, in one case, the NORTH BERWICK WITCHES in Scotland in the 1590–92, the kiss was a penance levied by the Devil. In *Newes from Scotland, declaring the damnable Life of Doctor Fian* (1592), W. Wright reports,

> . . . and seeing that they tarried over long, hee at their coming enjoyed them all to a pennance, which was, that they should kisse his buttockes, in sign of duety to him, which being put over the pulpit bare, every one did as he had enjoyned them.

Accusations of the kiss of shame were often raised in witchcraft and heresy inquisitions and trials. The Cathars and Waldenses (see VAUDOIS), religious sects persecuted for heresy, were thus accused, as were the KNIGHTS TEMPLAR in the 14th century. The Templars were said to require initiates to kiss their superiors on the anus, navel, base of the spine and phallus. Some knights also were said to worship the Devil in the form of a black CAT, which they kissed beneath the tail.

In 1303 Walter Langton, the Bishop of Lichfield and Coventry in England, was accused of SORCERY and ser-

vice to the Devil, which included the kiss of shame; he was able to clear himself of the charges. But one Guillaume Edeline, a doctor of the Sorbonne in France, was not so fortunate. Accused of wizardry (see WIZARD), he confessed to rendering the kiss of shame when the Devil appeared in the shape of a ram. Edeline was executed in 1453.

The Devil also demanded the kiss of shame in other guises besides human and ram. *Errores Haereticorum,* a medieval tract, claims the Cathars took their name "from the term cat, whose posterior they kiss, in whose form Satan appears to them." Tales from the 12th century tell of Satan appearing to his followers in the form of black cats or TOADS and demanding kisses under the cat's tail or in the toad's mouth.

FURTHER READING:
de Givry, Emile Grillot. *Witchcraft, Magic and Alchemy.* 1931. Reprint, New York: Dover Publications, 1971.
Russell, Jeffrey Burton. *Witchcraft in the Middle Ages.* Ithaca and London: Cornell University Press, 1972.

Knights Templar   Also known as The Order of the Temple, the Knights Templar began with lofty ideals of chivalry, crusades and Christian faith, as practiced by an exclusive club of monastic knights. It was founded between 1119 and 1188 by Hugh de Payens of Champagne, France, and a small group of knights, who dedicated themselves to protecting pilgrims to the Holy Land and routing out the infidels from the same. The order accumulated great wealth and power, which two centuries later brought about its downfall amid sordid accusations of heresy, DEVIL-worship, blasphemy and homosexuality.

After its inception, the Knights Templar quickly gained in reputation and respect. Their banner, a white flag with a crimson cross, became symbolic of the Christian war against the infidels, and of the highest ideals. Groups were organized throughout Europe and England, but France remained the stronghold. All members pledged their complete allegiance to a Grand Master. Knights took vows of poverty, humility and chastity, which were strictly enforced. As a religious order, the Templars were not taxed by the Crown and were not subject to the laws of the land; they were answerable only to the pope.

Despite the poverty of the individual knights, the order solicited donations to finance its holy war. Money poured in, and the order grew in power.

The rites of the order were kept in deep secrecy. Over time, this gave rise to much curious speculation and rumor about what really went on in Templar strongholds. For generations, stories were told of blasphemous rites in which Christ was renounced as a false prophet and the cross was spit, urinated and trampled upon. Further, Templars were rumored to engage in homosexual rituals and to worship the DEVIL, who appeared in the form of a black cat, which they kissed beneath the tail (see KISS OF SHAME). They were also said to worship an idol named BAPHOMET, in some versions a stuffed human head, in others a skull or an artificial head with three faces. The Templars, it was said, roasted children and smeared their burning fat upon this idol. For years, no one acted upon these stories.

In the Holy Land, the order used its immense wealth to enter commerce. It lent money and transacted business with the enemy during times of truce. The order's financial power, as well as its immunity to secular law, incurred increasing resentment among the nobility—in particular, King Philip IV of France, who was himself one of the order's debtors.

The collapse of the Crusades did little to harm the order. By the 14th century, it was at its peak of power. Then Philip, coveting the order's vast wealth, set out to seize its riches and lands by accusing the Knights of heresy. The king's willing accomplice was Pope Clement V.

On October 13, 1307, Philip arrested Grand Master Jacques de Molay and 140 Knights in the Paris temple. More arrests followed throughout France. The Templars were subjected to TORTURE en masse. Many confessed to the blasphemies and demonic crimes of which they were accused, though the confessions were so varied that little conclusive proof was amassed. Nevertheless, Philip pursued his wholesale persecution of the order.

On November 22, Philip persuaded Pope Clement to issue a bull ordering all Templars to be arrested and all of their properties seized. Not all countries obeyed as zealously as Philip desired; it took a second papal bull to force King Edward II of England to torture Templars in his dominion. In other countries, leniency was shown toward the Templars, some of whom were acquitted or allowed to join other orders.

In 1310 the public trials of the Templars began in Paris. Those who had survived the brutal torture were brought forward, charged with a long list of crimes and interrogated. Some Knights defended the order. Fifty-four who refused to confess were ordered by Philip to be taken to the suburbs and burned to death. Still, there was no definitive proof of heresy. Accounts of the idol Baphomet varied widely. Many Templars said only that they had heard of such a thing but had never seen it. Nonetheless, opponents of the order claimed the idol was proof that the Templars had adopted the Mahometanism of the infidels. Throughout Europe, Templars were convicted of SORCERY and heresy and burned at the stake.

Clement officially dissolved the order in 1312. The pope specified that all assets were to be turned over to a rival order, the Hospitallers, but this was not universally followed. Assets in France and England were seized by Philip and Edward, both of whom used them for personal ends or lavished them on friends. Elsewhere in Europe, other orders took the assets.

Grand Master de Molay remained in prison for seven years. In 1314 he was placed on a scaffold in Paris and ordered to make a public confession. In exchange, he would be imprisoned for life instead of being executed. To the surprise of the authorities, de Molay angrily denounced his persecution and said he had been tortured into lying. He was, he protested vigorously, innocent of all charges. Enraged, Philip ordered de Molay burned alive. He died at sunset the same day, slowly and painfully in the flames.

According to legend, the dying de Molay declared that as proof of his innocence, Philip and Clement would be summoned to meet him before the throne of God within a year. Both men died within that time.

It is possible that some of the accusations against the Templars had some basis in fact, though no doubt the stories were quite exaggerated. With their exposure to other religions in the Holy Land, the Templars may have absorbed some rites and beliefs into their own system. Some scholars believe they may have adopted aspects of Gnosticism and may have ritualized homosexuality. Many of their secrets will never be known.

FURTHER READING:

Hall, Manly Palmer. *Masonic Orders of Fraternity.* Los Angeles: Philosophical Research Society, 1950.

Russell, Jeffrey B. *A History of Witchcraft.* London: Thames and Hudson, 1980.

Tuchman, Barbara. *A Distant Mirror: The Calamitous 14th Century.* New York: Ballantine Books, 1978.

knots The tying and untying of knots is used to bind and release energy in many folk magic SPELLS and formulas. The ancient Egyptians and Greeks tied knots in cords for love spells. The "knot of Isis," a red jasper AMULET wound in the shroud of royal Egyptian mummies, summoned the protection of ISIS and her son Horus for the dead in the next world. The ancient Romans believed knots could cause impotency, especially if three cords or ropes of different colors were tied in three knots while a couple recited wedding vows. According to Pliny, such marital woes could be prevented by rubbing wolf fat on the threshold of the wedding chamber (see AIGUILLETTE). Other old beliefs about knots hold that the tying of them

Sorcerer selling wind tied in knots to sailors (OLAUS MAGNUS, *HISTORIA DE GENTIBUS SEPTENTRIONALIBUS,* 1555)

prevents pregnancy in a woman, and the untying of them facilitates conception and childbirth. In mainstream religious practices, knotted fringe is believed to confuse and entangle evil spirits, one reason why priests wear collars with no ties, for evil spirits caught in tie knots would disrupt religious services.

Legend has it that the prophet Muhammad was bewitched by an evil man and his daughters, who tied 11 knots in a cord which they hid in a well. The spell made Muhammad ill, and he wasted away nearly to the point of death. To save him, God intervened and sent the archangel Gabriel to reveal where the cord was hidden and how to break the spell. When the cord was brought to him, Muhammad recited 11 verses from the Koran. As he spoke each line, a knot loosened itself. When all the knots were undone, the spell was broken. In Sura CXIII in the Koran, Muhammad calls magicians' work "the evil of [women who] are blowers on knots."

Witches and sorcerers (see SORCERY) were believed to be able to control wind with three knots tied into a rope, or sometimes a handkerchief. When the three knots were tied in the proper magical way, the wind was bound up in them. Sorcerers and witches sometimes sold their magic knots to sailors. The release of one knot brought a gentle, southwesterly wind, two knots a strong north wind and three knots a tempest. In the folklore of the Shetland Islands and Scandinavia, some fishermen are said to command the wind this way. The belief in controlling wind by tying it up goes back to the legends of ancient Greece. Odysseus received a bag of winds from Aeolus to help him on his journey.

In West AFRICAN WITCHCRAFT, the tying of a knot while saying a person's name gives the tier of the knot power over the person named. The power is retained as long as the knot remains tied. In the west of Ireland, an old method for healing sick cattle called for a *worm-knot*, a piece of twine tied in certain knots and dragged over the animal's back. If the twine went smoothly, the cow would recover; if it caught and hitched, the animal would die.

In MAGIC, knots are used to bind and loosen deities and power; as tools in psychic attack and defense; and in magical snares. Magic knots also have the power to kill. According to a medieval formula, a WITCH'S LADDER, made of a string with nine knots, when hidden, causes a victim to die a slow death.

Many contemporary Witches use knots in cord magic. In one method, the Witch ties nine knots while chanting and/or visualizing her objective. By the ninth knot, the spell is complete and the magic power is stored within the knots. According to some formulas, the spell is then effected by the untying of the knots, usually one at a time over a period of nine days; according to others, the cord is tied into a circle. Cord magic is also done by a COVEN as a group. Slip knots are worked in cords, and the magical power is released when the knots are loosened.

FURTHER READING:
Gardner, Gerald B. *The Meaning of Witchcraft*. 1959. Reprint, New York: Magickal Childe, 1982.
Guazzo, Francesco-Maria. *Compendium Maleficarum*. Secaucus, N.J.: University Books, 1974.

Kramer, Heinrich   See *MALLEUS MALEFICARUM*.

Kyteler, Lady Alice (?–ca. 1324)   Lady Alice Kyteler was a wealthy and respected woman and the first person to be tried for witchcraft in Ireland. She was also among the first accused witches of the Middle Ages to be accused of heresy as well. Nearly two more centuries would pass before heresy charges were routine in witchcraft trials. Lady Alice was one of the few accused who ever successfully defied her accusers.

Family jealousies over money apparently were a major factor in the leveling of charges against her. Lady Alice was one of the richest residents of Kilkenny. Much of her wealth had come to her through a succession of husbands. Three of them had died, and Lady Alice had married for a fourth time. When her fourth husband, Sir John le Poer, fell ill with a mysterious wasting disease, he and the stepchildren became suspicious of Lady Alice. Le Poer allegedly found hidden in their home a sackful of vile ingredients for black MAGIC potions and powders. He and the stepchildren accused her of bewitching her first three husbands to death and depriving le Poer of his "natural senses" through the use of her magical concoctions.

The accusations piqued the interest of Richard de Ledrede, the Bishop of Ossory, who may have been interested in confiscating some of Lady Alice's wealth himself. In 1324 de Ledrede made an inquisition and determined that Kilkenny was home to a band of heretical sorcerers, of whom Lady Alice was the head.

De Ledrede indicted Lady Alice and her band on the following seven counts:

1. They had denied the faith of Christ.
2. They sacrificed living animals to various DEMONS, including a low-ranking one named Robin, or son of Art. They dismembered the animals and left them at CROSSROADS. One source said a SACRIFICE consisted of nine red COCKS and the eyes of nine peacocks.
3. They used SORCERY to seek advice from demons.
4. They held nightly meetings in which they blasphemously imitated the power of the church by fulminating sentence of excommunication, with lighted CANDLES, even against their own husbands, from the sole of their foot to the crown of their head, naming each part expressly, and then concluded by extinguishing the candles and by crying, "*Fi! Fi! Fi! Amen.*"
5. They caused disease and death, and aroused love and hatred, by using evil powders, unguents, OINTMENTS and candles. Ingredients included "certain

horrible worms"; dead men's nails; the entrails of cocks sacrificed to demons; the hair (see HAIR AND NAILS), brains and shreds of shrouds of boys who were buried unbaptized; various herbs; and "other abominations." While incantations were recited, the ingredients were cooked in a CAULDRON made out of the skull of a decapitated thief.

6. Lady Alice used sorcery to cause the children of her four husbands to bequeath all their wealth to her and her favorite son, William Outlawe. Also, she bewitched Sir John le Poer to the point where he was emaciated, and his hair and nails dropped off. A maid warned him that he was the victim of witchcraft. He opened some locked chests and found "a sackful of horrible and destestable things," which he turned over to priests.

7. Robin, or Son of Art, was Lady Alice's incubus demon, who appeared as a cat, a hairy black dog or a black man (see FAMILIARS). The demon was the source of her wealth.

It was also charged that Lady Alice took a BROOM and swept the streets of Kilkenny, raking the dirt and filth toward the home of her favorite son, muttering, "To the house of William my sonne/Hie all the wealth of Kilkennie towne."

Bishop de Ledrede sought the arrest of Lady Alice, William and the other unnamed sorcerers. William raised a ruckus, and, because of the family's status, the Bishop was blocked. He decided to handle the matter himself, and excommunicated Lady Alice and cited her to appear before him. She fled to Dublin. Not to be outdone, de Ledrede charged William with heresy.

Lady Alice brought pressure on her influential contacts and had de Ledrede arrested and jailed. He was released after 17 days. His next move was to censure the entire diocese, but he was forced to lift the ban by the Lord Justice, who sided with Lady Alice. De Ledrede tried several more times to bring a civil arrest of Lady Alice and others on charges of sorcery. Lady Alice fled again, this time to England. In Kilkenny, she was condemned as a sorceress, magician and heretic. On the same day, de Ledrede publicly burned her sackful of "abominations."

The only punishment de Ledrede was able to bring against William was a penance of hearing three masses a day for a year, feeding a certain number of poor people and covering a church chancel and chapel with lead. William failed to do these things and eventually was imprisoned.

The Bishop succeeded in arresting Lady Alice's maid, Petronilla, and having her flogged until she confessed to sorcery and orgies that involved Lady Alice. Petronilla was excommunicated, condemned and burned alive on November 3, 1324. Hers was the first death by burning for the crime of heresy in Ireland. Records say that others who were implicated by Petronilla as being members of the band of sorcerers were rounded up; some fled. Some were executed by burning, while others were merely excommunicated, whipped and banished from the diocese.

Lady Alice spent the rest of her life in comfort in England. Bishop de Ledrede was himself accused of heresy and was exiled from his diocese, but he regained favor in 1339. The next witchcraft trial of record in Ireland did not occur until the 17th century.

See ISLAND MAGEE WITCHES.

FURTHER READING:
Lenihan, Eddie. *Defiant Irish Women.* Dublin: Mercier Press, 1991.
Seymour, St. John D. *Irish Witchcraft and Demonology.* Dublin: Hodges, Figgis & Co., 1913.
Thomas, Keith. *Religion and the Decline of Magic.* New York: Charles Scribner's Sons, 1971.

ladder Widely held superstitions that it is bad luck to walk beneath a ladder are related in part to fears about witches, especially during the witch hunt times in colonial America.

Not all witches were burned—for example, in England and in the American colonies, witches were hung. When they dropped, they fell below the ladder leading up to the gallows. It was believed that if a witch touched anyone standing nearby, especially as she or he made a last gasp of breath, that person would soon die.

The superstition was so strong that many people believed that a witch's dying CURSE could linger long after death. Even to walk beneath a gallows ladder long after an execution invited a death curse.

Lady Olwen See WILSON, MONIQUE.

Lady Sheba (d. 2002) Self-described "Witch Queen" who rose to prominence in American Witchcraft in the late 1960s and 1970s. She set a precedent in 1971 by publishing her BOOK OF SHADOWS.

Lady Sheba was born Jessie Bell in the mountains of Kentucky. She said her family had practiced witchcraft for seven generations, and she had inherited her psychic gifts. When she was about six years old, her grandmother introduced her to witchcraft, beginning with stories of Irish leprechauns and little people (see FAIRIES). Every evening, Lady Sheba went with her grandmother to put out a saucer of milk for the little folk. As she grew older,

she learned more and became aware that she was different from most other people. Though a frail child, she knew she possessed powers and knowledge that others did not.

Lady Sheba said she had been granted a "hand of power" that enabled her to protect others. The palm of her right hand supposedly was etched with symbols that could be seen only by other psychics.

Her Craft name came from an inner awareness early in life that, in addition to her family name, she had always been "Sheba," perhaps in a former life. She believed she had lived before in Northern Ireland or Scotland, though she never formally attempted to investigate her past lives.

Lady Sheba said she was initiated as a Witch in the 1930s (see INITIATION). She divided her time between witchcraft and rearing a family. (She and her husband raised four sons and four daughters.) The family moved to Michigan around 1950. In 1971, Lady Sheba founded her own tradition, the American Order of the Brotherhood of Wicca, of which she was high priestess. The tradition combined her own Celtic heritage with American Indian MAGIC. Her RITUALS closely follow the Gardnerian tradition, except that coveners (see COVEN) worship robed rather than skyclad (nude).

As she influenced the forming of additional covens, Lady Sheba said she became "Witch Queen" over them all. Her covens spread over the United States, with a few overseas. Her TALISMAN was a large ruby ring, which she wore on her right index finger as a protector against evil and bringer of good luck. She could see visions in the stone and said others sometimes could see visions, too. She did not allow anyone to touch it, lest the protective power be broken.

Lady Sheba gained attention with the publication of *The Magick Grimoire,* a collection of excerpts from her personal workbook of SPELLS and RITUALS, some of them handed down through her family. Her second book, *The Book of Shadows,* published in 1971, was controversial in the Wiccan community. *The Book of Shadows* comprised laws, revised Gardnerian rituals and descriptions of SABBATS, information traditionally supposed to be kept secret among Witches. By making it public, Lady Sheba was accused of violating that tradition. She defended her decision to publish the book, saying she had been directed by the GODDESS to do so.

In 1973 the Twin Cities Area Council of the American Order of the Brotherhood of Wicca was formed by coven leaders, though all traditions were invited to participate. The Council took an active role in the establishment in 1973–74 of the COUNCIL OF AMERICAN WITCHES. As of the mid-1980s, only a few covens were still part of the Brotherhood.

FURTHER READING:
Adler, Margot. *Drawing Down the Moon.* Revised ed. New York: Viking, 1986.
Lady Sheba. *Book of Shadows.* St Paul: Llewellyn Publications, 1971.

Lancaster (also Lancashire) Witches   Two notable witch trials of England took place in the Pendle Forest area of Lancaster County, in 1612 and 1633. The 1612 trials are noted for the records kept by the court clerk, Thomas Potts, published as a chapbook, which set forth the HAG stereotype of witches. The 1633 trials involved a boy who was coerced by his father into giving false testimony that resulted in more than 30 arrests and 17 convictions.

The 1612 trials. About 20 persons were brought under suspicion of witchcraft in the first major witch trials of northern England. The central figures were two old and decrepit women—Elizabeth Sowthern, alias "Old Demdike," who was about 80 years old, and Anne Whittle, alias "Old Chattox," who was about 60 years old—rivals in the service of wizardry and magical arts to the local population.

In March of 1612 Old Demdike was questioned by a local justice who had received reports that she was a witch. The woman, who was blind, confessed to being a witch and pointed the finger at her granddaughter, Alison Device, and Old Chattox. The three were taken into custody and held in Lancaster castle.

Old Demdike said that about 20 years before, while returning home from begging, she had been stopped in the Pendle Forest by a spirit or DEVIL in the shape of a boy, whose coat was half black and half brown. The Devil said that if she gave him her soul, she could have anything she requested. She asked the Devil's name and was told, "Tibb." Old Demdike agreed. For the next five or six years, Tibb appeared to her and asked what was her bidding, but she repeatedly turned him away. At the end of six years, on one Sabbath morning, while Old Demdike had a child on her knee and was in a slumber, Tibb appeared in the likeness of a brown dog and sucked BLOOD from beneath her left arm. The experience, she said, left her "almost stark mad" for about eight weeks.

Old Demdike also testified that her daughter, Elizabeth Device, had helped out one Richard Baldwyn at his mill just before Christmas in 1611. Led by Alison Device, Old Demdike went to Baldwyn to ask for remuneration. Baldwyn replied, "Get out of my ground, whores and witches, I will burn the one of you, and hang the other," to which Old Demdike retorted, "I do not care for thee, hang thyself." As the women were leaving, Tibb appeared and urged Old Demdike to take revenge. She agreed, and said, "Revenge thee either of him, or his." Tibb vanished and she never saw him again.

Old Chattox confessed that 14 years earlier she had entered into the "devilish abominable profession of witchcraft" through the "wicked persuasion and counsel" of Old Demdike. The DEVIL appeared to her in the likeness of a man, and, at Old Demdike's urging, she promised him her soul and gave him a place near her ribs to suck on. The witches were rewarded with a feast of food and drink. Old Chattox was indicted, according to Potts, for the felonious practice of "diverse wicked and devilish arts called witchcrafts, enchantments, charms and sorceries" to cause the death of one Robert Nutter of Pendle Forest.

Alison Device confessed that after the falling-out with Baldwyn, one of his daughters fell ill the next day, lingered for a year and died. She believed her grandmother bewitched the child to death. Device also was indicted for laming an old peddler.

On Good Friday in April, within a week after the women had been imprisoned in Lancaster castle, Old Demdike's daughter, Elizabeth, called a meeting of her family and that of Old Chattox to discuss a plan to free them. The meeting took place at Malking Tower, the forest home of Old Demdike, and was attended by about 21 persons, 18 of them women. The group devised a plan in which they would kill the jailer and blow up the castle with gunpowder. Following the planning, the group had a feast that included stolen mutton, and bacon and beef. When the justice, Robert Nowell, got wind of the meeting, he had arrested and sent to the castle nine of those involved: Elizabeth Device and her son, James Device; Anne Redfearne, daughter of Old Chattox; Alice Nutter; Katharine Hewit; Jane and John Bulcock, mother and son; Isabel Robey; and Margaret Pearson. Others involved managed to flee.

In all, 20 persons were brought to trial in August. They testified against each other. The principal witnesses were Elizabeth Device's children, Alison, James, who was in his twenties, and Jennet (also given as Jannet), a girl of nine. Both testified against their mother. Jennet said that Elizabeth had an IMP named Ball, which she dispatched to murder anyone who displeased her. James said he had seen Ball in the shape of a brown dog and also had seen his mother making clay images. With the testimony of her children, Elizabeth then confessed. Jennet then implicated James, saying he used another imp in the shape of a dog, Dandy, to bewitch persons to death. James confessed.

Anne Redfearne was acquitted on charges of bewitching Robert Nutter to death. This verdict was so unpopular that Redfearne was retried for bewitching Nutter's father, Christopher Nutter, to death. This time, she was convicted. Alice Nutter, Christopher's wife, was charged with killing one Henry Mytton and was named by the three Devices.

Ten persons were sentenced to hang: Old Chattox, Elizabeth, James and Alison Device; Anne Redfearne; Katherine Hewit; Jane and John Bulcock; and Isabel Robey. Old Demdike died in prison before her trial, and Margaret Pearson was sentenced to a lesser punishment of the pillory and a year in jail. The rest were found not guilty.

In his account of the trials, court clerk Potts described the defendants as the most wretched of hags. Elizabeth Device was an "odious witch," a "barbarous and inhumane monster, beyond example," who was "branded with a preposterous marke in nature, even from her birth, which was her left eye, standing lower then (sic) the other; the one looking down, the other looking up, so strangely deformed, as the best that were present in that honorable assembly, and great audience, did affirm, they had not often seen the like." Old Chattox was "a very old withered spent and decrepit creature, her sight almost gone." Old Demdike was "the rankest hag that ever troubled daylight."

Twenty-one years later, Jennet Device became involved in the second major witch trials of the Pendle Forest area.

The 1633 trials. This episode in witch-hunting history began with a farmer's son, Edmund Robinson, about 10 or 11 years of age, who seemed to have a vivid imagination. According to his story, he was out at the edge of the forest one day and saw two greyhounds, which he thought belonged to a neighbor. He tried to set them on a hare, but when they refused to course, he drew a switch and started to beat them. They turned into a little boy and a woman he knew, Mother Dickenson. Dickenson offered him money to sell his soul to the Devil, but he refused. She took a bridle out of her pocket and put it on the little boy, who turned into a horse. Grabbing Edmund, Dickenson sprang up on the horse and rode over the terrain until they came to a large barn. It was a witches' SABBAT and there were about 50 to 60 persons gathered for a feast. Edmund observed six ugly witches pulling ropes tied to the ceiling of the barn, which brought down meat, butter, bread, milk that fell into basins, hot puddings and other delicacies. Edmund was so frightened that he managed to escape home.

Edmund's father made the boy give a deposition to the authorities. Since Edmund did not know the names of all those present at the sabbat, he was sent around the countryside to churches and public places to identify them by sight. For every witch identified, he would be paid a fee. Such an incentive must have been impossible to resist, and, prodded by his father, Edmund accused more than 30 persons—including Jennet Device. Seventeen of them were found to bear the WITCH'S MARK, were tried and convicted. Among them was Mother Dickenson, a young woman who confessed she had sold her soul to the Devil for money which later vanished and another who was accused of making a pail of water run uphill. The latter apparently was in the habit of rolling her pail downhill and running ahead of it.

The local justices suspected that something foul besides witchcraft was afoot and referred the cases to the King's Council. An investigation by the Bishop of Chester revealed that the elder Robinson had been willing to accept bribes for withholding evidence against the accused. Four prisoners were sent to London, where they were examined for witch's marks, but none were found. Questioned, Edmund finally admitted that during the alleged sabbat, he had been out picking plums. He had been coerced into making up the story by his father, who had sought to make quick money. The prisoners were released (some had died in jail), and Robinson senior was jailed.

FURTHER READING:
Harrison, G. B., ed. *The Trial of the Lancaster Witches.* 1929. Reprint, New York: Barnes & Noble, 1971.
Hole, Christina. *Witchcraft in England.* London: B. T. Batsford Ltd., 1947.
Maple, Eric. *The Dark World of Witches.* New York: A. S. Barnes & Co., 1962.

Lancre, Pierre de (1550?–1631?) Infamous French witch-trial judge who terrorized the Basque region, sent an estimated 600 persons to their deaths at the stake and compiled detailed accounts of alleged infernal activities at witches' SABBATS. Jules Michelet, who relied heavily upon the writings of Pierre de Lancre for his own work, *Satanism and Witchcraft,* called de Lancre "something of a Gascon, boastful and vain of his own achievements . . . a man of wit and perspicacity, and being manifestly in relations with certain young witches, was in a position to know the whole truth." Julio Caro Baroja, in *The World of Witches* (1961), describes de Lancre as "[a man] obsessed with the desire to uncover criminal activities, who accepted religion as the basis for the penal code."

Pierre de Lancre was born Pierre de Rosteguy, sieur de Lancre, between 1550 and 1560. His father was a wealthy winegrower who adopted the surname "de Lancre" upon becoming a royal official. Pierre was given a Jesuit education. He studied law at Turin and in Bohemia, and became a lawyer.

In 1609 two men of Labourd petitioned the French Parlement to ask Henry IV to send judges to deal with witches who were plaguing the region. One of the petitioners was Siegneur de Saint-Pei, Urtubi, who had attended a sabbat and believed a witch was sucking his BLOOD. Henry IV agreed and appointed de Lancre and a man named d'Espaignet (also spelled d'Espagnet). They were given plenary powers subject to no appeal.

De Lancre took his job most seriously. He viewed the people of the Basque country as an irresponsible and immoral lot, easy prey for the DEVIL. By virtue of their geographic locale and their separate language, the Basques were viewed as mysterious and isolated. The men were primarily sailors, who would go off on long fishing ex-

peditions to Canada and Newfoundland, leaving their women behind to run the villages and support themselves and their family. Upon their return, the men would waste their earnings on festivities, wild dancing and drinking. Furthermore, superstitions and beliefs in MAGIC ran high among the Basques. It was no wonder, then, that witchcraft seemed to have infested the population.

De Lancre seemed both fascinated and repulsed by the Basque women. Says Michelet, "the very judge that burns them is all the while charmed by their fascinations." In his writings, de Lancre himself described the Basque women as follows:

> When you see them pass, their hair flying in the wind and brushing their shoulders, so well adorned and caparisoned are they, as they go, with their lovely locks, that the sun glancing through them as through a cloud, makes a flashing aureole of dazzling radiance. . . . Hence

Witches' sabbat according to Pierre de Lancre (PIERRE DE LANCRE, *TABLEAU DE L'INCONSTANCE DES MAUVAIS ANGES ET DEMONS*, 1612)

the dangerous fascination of their eyes, perilous for love no less than for witchery.

The appearance of de Lancre and d'Espaignet in Labourd in May of 1609 caused great alarm. Some residents, anticipating the bloodshed that was to come, fled into the mountains, to Spain and to Newfoundland. Most, however, remained in their homes. Initially, those questioned yielded no information. The dam of resistance was broken by a 17-year-old girl, Margarita, who perhaps thought she could save herself by denouncing others. This she did in great detail, enabling the judges to begin hauling in suspects. They were tortured, pricked for insensitive spots and searched for WITCH'S MARKS. Margarita herself participated in some of the tortures. The confessions implicated others, until hardly a family in Labourd had not been denounced for witchcraft.

De Lancre was undiscriminating in his acquisition of evidence. No person was too young, too old or too feeble in body or brain—he believed them all. He relied heavily upon the testimony of children. Some as young as five years old admitted to attending sabbats and riding on BROOMS and the backs of goats; some testified against their own mothers. De Lancre collected numerous tales of nocturnal sabbats and the brewing of OINTMENTS and POISONS. On the face of the confessions, the Basque witches were the most active and diabolical of all in Europe. They met weekly, sometimes almost daily, at any hour, even during Mass. Crowds of up to 2,000 attended the four major sabbats held during the year. They danced naked, ate corpses, copulated, said BLACK MASSES and worshiped the Devil. They made poisons out of TOADS for ruining the crops, including one incredible mixture of grilled toads and clouds, which ruined fruit trees.

D'Espaignet quit his post in June, leaving de Lancre to carry on alone. De Lancre became convinced that some 3,000 persons, including members of the clergy, bore witch's marks. He said the local priests dispatched sailors to Newfoundland, then imported Devils from Japan who copulated with the wives left behind.

De Lancre pushed through trials and executions. At intervals in the proceedings, he played the lute from the bench and had the condemned witches dance before him. The first group of witches to be burned named many others, which so infuriated the townsfolk that they attacked the condemned as they were being led in carts to the stakes, crying at them to withdraw their accusations. De Lancre relates that on the sabbat after these first burnings, the cowardly Devil did not show up, nor did he for the next three sabbats, but sent an inferior IMP in his stead. Satan allegedly told his followers that no more witches would be burned, but de Lancre proved him a liar.

At one point, de Lancre became convinced that witches and the Devil attempted an attack on him one night while he slept in a castle in Saint Pe. On the night of September 24, the Devil supposedly entered his bedchamber and said a BLACK MASS. Witches forced their way under his bed curtains to poison him but could not do so because he was protected by God. The Devil had sex with one of the witches. According to another version of the story, the Devil and the witches could not gain entrance to the bed chamber but said two Black Masses.

According to de Lancre, when the last witch to be tried and executed was set afire, alive, at the stake, a swarm of toads escaped from her head. The spectators responded with a hail of stones, so that the witch was nearly stoned to death before the flames claimed her. One great black toad, however, managed to avoid stones, sticks and flames, and escaped.

At the end of de Lancre's legal tour in 1610, he was granted a leave of absence and went to Rome, Naples and Lombardy. Sometime between 1612 and 1622, he was rewarded for his great service to the state and was made a state counsellor in Paris. He wrote the details of his trials and investigations in three works: *Tableau de l'inconstance des mauvais anges et démons* (Description of the inconstancy of evil angels) (1612); *L'Incredulité et miscréance du sortilège plainement convaincue* (Incredulity and misbelief of enchantment) (1622); and *Du sortilège* (Witchcraft) (1627). He died in Paris in 1630 or 1631.

FURTHER READING:
Baroja, Julio Caro. *The World of the Witches.* 1961. Reprint, Chicago: University of Chicago Press, 1975.
Michelet, Jules. *Satanism and Witchcraft.* Translated by A. R. Allinson. 1939. Reprint, Secaucus, N.J.: Citadel Press, 1992.
Seligmann, Kurt. *The Mirror of Magic.* New York: Pantheon Books, 1948.

Laveau, Marie (1794?–1881 and 1827–1897) The most famous "voodoo queen" in North America was actually two people: mother and daughter. As leaders of voodoo (the term used at that time) worshipers in New Orleans during the 19th century, both women epitomized a sensational appeal: magical powers, control of one's lovers and enemies, and sex.

Marie Laveau I reputedly was born a free woman of color in New Orleans in 1794. She was of African-American, white and Indian ancestry, and sometimes described as a descendant of French aristocracy or the daughter of a wealthy white planter. Records of her marriage on August 4, 1819, to Jacques Paris, a free man of color from Saint-Domingue (Haiti), report that Marie was the illegitimate daughter of Charles Laveau and Marguerite Darcantel.

Paris was a quadroon—three-fourths white. Not long after the marriage, he disappeared, perhaps returning to Saint-Domingue. About five years later his death was recorded, but there is no certification of interment.

By then Laveau already was calling herself the Widow Paris, and took up employment as a hairdresser to the wealthy white and Creole women of New Orleans. These women confided their most intimate secrets to Marie, about their husbands, their lovers, their estates, their husbands' mistresses, their business affairs, their fears of insanity and of anyone discovering a strain of Negro blood in their ancestry. Marie listened and remembered their confessions, using them later to strengthen her powers as "Voodooienne."

About 1826 Marie took up with Louis Christophe Duminy de Glapion, another quadroon from Saint-Domingue, who moved in with her until his death in June of 1855 (some accounts say 1835). They never married, but he and Marie had 15 children in rapid succession. She quit the business of hairdressing and began to devote all her energies to becoming the supreme voodoo queen of New Orleans.

Blacks had been practicing voodoo secretly around New Orleans ever since the first arrival of slaves from Africa and the Caribbean. Stories circulated of secret rites deep in the bayous, complete with worship of a snake called Zombi and orgiastic dancing, drinking and love-making. Nearly a third of the worshipers were whites, desirous to obtain the "power" to regain a lost lover, take a new lover, eliminate a bad business partner or destroy an enemy.

The meetings became so frequent that white masters feared the blacks were plotting an uprising against them. In 1817, the New Orleans Municipal Council passed a resolution forbidding blacks to gather for dancing or any other purpose except on Sundays and only in places designated by the mayor. The accepted spot was Congo Square on North Rampart Street, now called Beauregard Square, near where Laveau lived. Congo Square reigned as the supreme gathering spot for more than 20 years.

By the early 1830s there were many voodoo queens in New Orleans, fighting over control of the Sunday Congo dances and the secret ceremonies out at Lake Pontchartrain. But when Laveau decided to become queen, contemporaries reported the other queens faded before her, some succumbing to her powerful GRIS-GRIS and some yielding by brute force. A devout Catholic, Laveau added many facets of Catholic worship—like holy water, incense, statues of the saints and Christian prayers—to the voodoo ceremonies.

Laveau turned the Lake Pontchartrain rites into a business, charging fees. She invited the press and police. Other, more secret orgies were organized for wealthy white men looking for beautiful black, mulatto and quadroon mistresses. Laveau then gained control of the dances at Congo Square, entering the gated area before any of the other dancers and performing with her snake for the fascinated onlookers.

Eventually, the information learned in Creole boudoirs, her considerable knowledge of spells and her own style and flair made her the most powerful woman in the city. Whites of all classes appealed to her for help in their various affairs and amours, and the blacks acknowledged her as their leader. Judges paid her as much as $1,000 to help them win elections, and even the most insignificant love powders cost whites $10. Few blacks paid for services. She became so well known that visiting Laveau for a reading became the thing to do while in New Orleans.

Although love provided more business for Laveau than anything else, she was also known for her work with convicted prisoners. She assisted Père (Father) Antoine—New Orleans' popular priest who had married her and Jacques Paris—with yellow fever victims. By the 1850s, she could enter and exit prison with impunity, bringing food and solace to the men in their cells. She donated an altar to the prison chapel and decorated it with her own hands. None of these visits exhibited any outward signs of voodoo, only devout Catholicism.

In 1869, Laveau I presided over her last official voodoo conclave, where the assembled worshipers decided she should retire as she was past 70 years of age. She continued her work at the prison and did not completely retreat from active service until 1875, when she entered her St. Ann Street home and did not leave until her death on June 16, 1881.

Newspaper accounts described her as a saintly figure of 98 (she was 87) who had nursed the sick and prayed incessantly with the diseased and the condemned. Reporters called her the recipient "in the fullest degree" of the "hereditary gift of beauty" in the Laveau family, who gained the notice of Governor Claiborne, French general Humbert, Aaron Burr and even the marquis de Lafayette. The obituaries claimed she had lived her life in piety surrounded by her Catholic religion, with no mention at all of her voodoo past. Even one of her surviving children, Madame Legendre, claimed her saintly mother had never practiced voodoo and despised the cult.

Her daughter and successor was born Marie Laveau Glapion on February 2, 1827, one of the elder Marie's 15 children. It is not known whether she designated her daughter to follow her or Marie chose the role herself. She apparently lacked the compassion of Laveau and inspired more fear and subservience. Like her mother, Marie started her career as a hairdresser, eventually running a bar and brothel on Bourbon Street.

Marie continued the assignations at Maison Blanche (White House), the house her mother had built for secret voodoo meetings and liaisons between white men and women of color. One account says that Marie was a talented procuress, able to provide whatever the men esired for a price. The parties at Maison Blanche offered champagne, food, wine and music, while the young women danced naked for white men only, including politicians and other high officials. The police never bothered her, because they were afraid of crossing her and ending up "hoodooed."

One of the most important events in the New Orleans voodoo calendar was St. John's Eve. An annual gathering in Bayou St. John had started as a religious ceremony but had become a circus under Laveau. St. John's Day corresponds to the summer solstice, celebrated since ancient times. Laveau had presided over it for years; Marie did so on several occasions.

In a newspaper account of St. John's Eve, 1872, the reporter told that after the arrival of Marie, the crowd sang to her then built a large fire to heat a boiling cauldron. Into the cauldron went water from a beer barrel, salt, black pepper, a black snake cut in three pieces representing the Trinity, a cat, a black rooster and various powders. Meanwhile, Marie commanded all present to undress, which they did, singing a repetitive chorus to "Mamzelle Marie." At midnight everyone jumped into the lake for about half an hour to cool off, then came out and sang and danced for another hour. At that time Marie preached a sermon, then gave the celebrants permission for a half-hour's "recreation," or sexual intercourse.

After the rest and recreation, everyone ate and sang some more, until the signal was given to extinguish the fire under the cauldron. Four nude women threw water on the fire, then the contents of the kettle were poured back into the barrel. Marie told everyone to dress again, then she preached another sermon. By now it was daybreak, and everyone went home.

When Laveau died, public interest in her daughter died as well. Marie still reigned over the voodoo ceremonies among the blacks and ran the Maison Blanche, but she never regained much notice in the press. Marie reportedly drowned in a big storm in Lake Pontchartrain in 1897, but some people claimed to see her as late as 1918.

Marie is said to be buried in the family crypt at St. Louis Cemetery No. 1, but the vault does not bear her name. Instead, the inscription indicates that the tomb is the final resting place for "Marie Philome Glapion, deceased June 11, 1897." The tomb still attracts the faithful and the curious. Petitioners leave offerings of food, money and flowers, then ask for Marie Laveau's help after turning around three times and marking a cross with red brick on the stone. The cemetery is quite small, but even so the tomb seems to appear out of nowhere when walking among the crypts.

Others believe Marie Laveau is buried in St. Louis Cemetery No. 2, where another crypt marked "Marie Laveau" bears red-brick crosses and serves as the "Wishing Vault" for young women seeking husbands. Stories place Laveau in cemeteries on Girod Street, Louisa Street and Holt Street as well. Laveau or her daughter still make personal appearances, according to legend, frequenting the areas around the cemetery, the old French Quarter and her voodoo haunts.

See also VODUN.

FURTHER READING:
Rigaud, Milo. *Secrets of Voodoo.* San Francisco: City Lights Books, 1985.
Tallant, Robert. *The Voodoo Queen.* Gretna, La.: Pelican Publishing, 1983.

Leek, Sybil (1923–1983)   English witch and astrologer who moved to America in the 1960s and gained fame by publicizing the renaissance of witchcraft in the Western world. Her trademarks were a cape, loose gowns and a jackdaw named Mr. Hotfoot Jackson who perched on her shoulder. She always wore a crystal necklace, passed on to her, she said, by her psychic Russian grandmother.

Leek claimed to be a hereditary witch and also to have been trained by ALEISTER CROWLEY. Probably much of her witch biography was embellished, intended to create publicity.

Leek was born in the Midlands in England. Her family, she said, came from a long line of hereditary witches that could trace its roots in the Old Religion to 1134 in southern Ireland on her mother's side and to occultists close to the royalty of czarist Russia on her father's side. Leek's mother sported red-gold hair, a color said to be common among witches. Psychic ability ran in all members of her family. Her most famous ancestor, she said, was an English witch named Molly Leigh, who died in 1663. According to Leek, Leigh was buried at the very edge of the local church graveyard. Some time afterward, the vicar and others went to open Leigh's cottage and were shocked to see Leigh, or her apparition, sitting in a chair with her jackdaw perched on her shoulder. The vicar and his company allegedly reopened her grave, drove a stake through her heart, threw the living jackdaw into the coffin and reburied it.

Leek, who claimed an IQ of 164, said she was taught at home by her grandmother until local officials required her to be enrolled in school at age 12. She stayed four years and left at 16.

Leek was nine years old when she met Crowley, supposedly a frequent visitor to the household. She said Crowley would take her out climbing in the rocks and recited his poetry, which encouraged her to write her own poetry. He also gave Leek instruction in the importance of words of power and the power of sound. According to Leek, Crowley announced to her grandmother that little Leek would someday pick up where Crowley would leave off in occultism. The last time she saw him was in 1947, shortly before his death.

However, Crowley left no records indicating that he was acquainted with Leek or her family.

When Leek was 15, she met a well-known pianist-conductor who was 24 years her senior and fell in love. They were married shortly after her 16th birthday and traveled about England and Europe. He died when she was 18. Leek returned home.

Leek said she was initiated into the Craft in southern France, in George du Loup in the hills above Nice, an area that was populated by Cathars in the Middle Ages. According to Leek, her initiation was to replace an elderly Russian aunt, who had been high priestess of a COVEN and had died. Returning again to England, Leek went to live in Burley, a village in the heart of the New Forest. She lived among Gypsies and joined the Horsa coven which claimed to have existed for 700 years. She eventually became its high priestess. She successfully ran three antique shops. At some point, she married a man named Brian and had two sons, Stephen and Julian, who inherited the family's psychic gifts.

In the 1950s, she experienced a mystical vision one spring day while walking alone in the New Forest. She became enveloped in a bright blue light that instilled in her a great sense of peace and the realization that her purpose in life was as an evangelist for the Old Religion.

It was not until 1962 that she began to promote herself as a hereditary witch and coven leader, and by 1963 the press was giving her attention. The death of GERALD B. GARDNER in February 1964 created a vacuum for witch personalities—Gardner was a lover of the media limelight—and Leek stepped in. She announced the founding of the WITCHCRAFT RESEARCH ASSOCIATION (WRA) with herself as president.

She also received a lot of media attention in 1964, when she challenged the academic Rossell Hope Robbins, who had written an encyclopedia on witchcraft and was lecturing against MARGARET MURRAY and her assertions that witchcraft was an ancient religion passed down through generations. Leek attended at least one lecture by Robbins and verbally sparred with him, with her jackdaw giving hoots as well. The media lapped it up and dubbed Leek "Britain's Number One Witch."

The publicity brought tourists and more media to her village. Business at her antique shop declined in the wake of autograph seekers, and her landlord refused to renew her lease unless she publicly denounced witchcraft. She refused, closed up the shop and left the New Forest.

Leek's career as a witch in Britain came to an end in 1964. In 1963–64, churches in Britain were victims of ritualized vandalism, including a Sussex church not far from Leek's home. She claimed that the symbols that defaced the church were directed at her and that the attack had been led by a black magician whom she had healed of illness. Despite her condemnation of the vandalism, the link she made between herself as a witch and black magic cost her supporters. In July 1964 she was forced to resign from the WRA. She moved to the United States.

Leek lived first in New York, but found it a depressing city, and particularly gloomy during the winter. She moved to Los Angeles, where she became acquainted with Crowley's onetime secretary ISRAEL REGARDIE. In her later years, she divided her time between Houston and Florida.

She worked as an astrologer, becoming editor and publisher of her own astrological journal. In 1968, her first book, *Diary of a Witch,* was published. The book described what it was like to be a "modern woman" practicing witchcraft, and it unleashed an enormous public response. Leek made frequent appearances on the media circuit. She met with mixed success, as some of her interviewers expected her to reinforce the stereotypes of witches as evil hags. One of her greatest trials, she said, was learning patience and tolerance in dealing with such situations.

In all, Leek wrote more than 60 books, plus an internationally syndicated column. She liked to say that she never "preached" witchcraft, but sought only to explain the holistic philosophy of the religion and how it differed from satanism. She did not approve of nudity in RITUALS (see skyclad) or of drugs. She believed in cursing, which set her apart from many witches. (See CURSE.)

Leek wrote and spoke a great deal about reincarnation, guided, she said, by the spirit of Madame Helena P. Blavatsky, cofounder of the Theosophical Society. One night as she stood at a lectern to give a talk on psychic phenomena to an audience of the Theosophical Society in St. Louis, Leek was overcome with a shining light, in which she could see the face of an elderly woman. The light seemed to penetrate into Leek. She began her talk, but it was not her original speech, but on reincarnation. She said later she had no awareness of what she was saying.

Afterward, Leek saw a photograph of Blavatsky and recognized her as the woman in her vision. For the rest of her life, Leek said, she felt that Blavatsky had become part of her, using her as an instrument to finish her own work and educate others on reincarnation.

Leek had a particular fondness for snakes and birds. The jackdaw (a relative of the raven) accompanied her to all coven meetings until his death in 1969. Leek had a pet boa constrictor named Miss Sashima.

Leek suffered from illness in her last years and died in Melbourne, Florida, in 1983.

FURTHER READING:

Hutton, Ronald. *The Triumph of the Moon: A History of Modern Pagan Witchcraft.* Oxford: Oxford University Press, 1999.

Leek, Sybil. *The Complete Art of Witchcraft.* New York: World Publishing Co., 1971.

———. *Diary of a Witch.* New York: NAL Signet Library, 1968.

Legba (also Elegguá)   Not the oldest, but perhaps the most important, orisha (god) in the African spirit pantheon is called Legba in VODUN and Elegguá in SANTERÍA. He is the god of doors and entryways, of gates and paths, of CROSSROADS, SORCERY and trickery. Without his permission, the other gods may not come to earth. He has been identified with St. Peter in the Catholic catalogue of saints, since Jesus Christ gave Peter the keys to the Kingdom of Heaven, and like Peter, he serves as the foundation for the cult, or church. He is also associated with a holy guardian angel, St. Michael, St. Martin de Porres or St. Anthony.

In Vodun, Legba is called Papa, or the Father. He is the solar prototype and magical archetype. Vodun worships the sun as a life-giving force, and Legba is the Sun, the Orient, the East, the place where life is created and MAGIC is controlled. As such, Legba is called Legba-Ji, or "god of the creation." His cardinal point in the magical cross is the east. He is greeted first when welcoming the gods or *mystères,* so that he can open the door and let the others enter. Legba-Ati-Bon also represents the "good wood," or sacred trees of the African jungle, symbolized by the wooden center post, or *poteau-mitan,* in the Vodun peristyle. The *poteau-mitan* also acts as a conductor of the spirits into the Vodun ceremonies. Legba forms one-third of the sacred trinity along with Danbhalah-Wedo and Erzulie.

As Legba Grand-Chemin or Maitre Grand-Chemin, Legba is guardian of the crossroads and master of the highways. In occult terms, the crossroads symbolize the joining of the astral vertical forces with the horizontal, so Legba controls the astral-causal magic of the gods. Legba, a cosmic axis, conducts the souls of the faithful to union with the *mystères* and leads the *mystères* down through the center post to the crossroads to receive the SACRIFICE of the worshipers. Some Vodunists believe his associations with CROSSES make Legba the Vodun Christ. But as master of the crossroads, or Maitre Carrefour, Legba also governs SORCERY and is the greatest magician.

Drawings of Legba usually depict him as an old man, bent over with age. He is also associated with water bearers, as Legba controls the fluids of the earth, including blood and circulation. Anatomically, Legba represents vertebrae, bones and bone marrow, symbolized by the center post—the backbone of the peristyle. *Veves,* or symbolic drawings, of Legba incorporate an equal-sided cross. His favorite sacrificial animals are lions and white sheep, his sacred animal is the lizard and his special metal is gold.

In Santería, Elegguá controls all gates and entry-ways, acting as messenger for the gods. After Obatala, father of the gods, Elegguá is the most important; his permission must be gained for any of the other *orishas* to function. Legends tell that Olorun-Olofi, the creator, was ill, and all the efforts of the orishas had had no success. Elegguá, still a child, asked to see Olorun-Olofi and gave him an herb concoction that cured him within a few hours. In gratitude, Olorun-Olofi decreed that Elegguá was the god to be honored first in ceremonies, and he gave Elegguá the keys to all doors and made him owner of the roads.

Elegguá's followers keep his image in their houses, prepared by the Santero according to each individual's temperament and guardian angel. First the Santero gathers earth from a crossroads, an anthill, a churchyard, a hospital, the jail and a bakery, mixing these dirts with herbs sacred to Elegguá, a turtle's head, a stone from an open field and 29 coins of various denominations. This mixture is then added to cement, which has been moistened with wine, honey and *omiero,* a sacred herbal liquid used in initiation ceremonies. Next the Santero forms Elegguá's head, using seashells for the eyes and mouth.

After the cement dries, the Santero buries the head before sunrise at a crossroads to allow Elegguá's spirit to enter and animate the statue. Seven days later, the Santero disinters the head and fills the empty hole with three roosters, whose blood is sprinkled around the inside. Also into the hole go bananas, corn, candies and some of Elegguá's favorite foods, like coconut. He then generously sprinkles rum over the contents and fills the hole with dirt. Back at the house, the Santero sacrifices a mouse or goat; if neither of these animals is available, he substitutes a black chicken. The sacrifice consecrates the statue, and it becomes Elegguá with all his attendant powers.

Devotees keep Elegguá in a small cabinet near the front door. Every Monday, and on the third day of the month, the statue is removed and exposed to the sun for a few hours before noon, then anointed with a special grease called *manteca de corojo* and replaced in the cabinet. The devotee pours a little bit of water three times on the floor in front of the image and then fills his mouth with rum and sprays the stone with it. Next the devotee lights a cigar and blows smoke in Elegguá's face, as the orisha loves cigars, then leaves the lighted smoke by the statue's side. Next, the devotee feeds Elegguá some small pieces of smoked opossum, some coconut and a few grains of corn along with candy. The devotee customarily tells Elegguá—or any orisha, for that matter—what foods he or she is offering the god. A candle is lit by the cabinet door, which is open all day; then the devotee asks Elegguá's protection and help in acquiring a better job, more money or better luck.

Elegguá has 21 different manifestations, some beneficent and some devilish. The oldest Elegguá is Elufe, whose image is carved from a wide, flat stone and kept in the backyard. The guardian Elegguá of cemetery doors is Anagui, who also distributes and adjudicates the work of the other Elegguás. Alaroye lives behind the doors and counts the goddess Oshun among his good friends. Ayeru is messenger to the god Ifá and protector; Baraine is messenger to the god Changó.

But the personae most feared are the Eshus or Echus, considered by many to be incarnations of the Devil. The Eshus live in darkness; on St. Bartholomew's Day, August 24, the Eshus roam the streets and create as much trouble as possible. As a best friend of the God Oggun, Elegguá is called Eshu Ogguanilebbe and is responsible for automobile accidents and railroad derailments. Whenever Oggun is hungry, this Eshu either kills a dog or causes an accident so that bloodthirsty Oggun may feast. Eshu Oku Oro controls life and death, and Eshu Bi is the king of mischief and stands in corners. Eshu Alayiki brings the unexpected. The colors red and black symbolize all the Elegguás.

Many Santeros believe the dark Eshu represents all 21 of Elegguá's personalities. These manifestations of Elegguá fit the Brazilian concept of Exus, horned gods often mistaken for the Devil, who symbolize nature's primal forces. The Exus act as messengers to the gods and are responsible for the world's mischief and trickery. No ceremony in Brazil begins without first asking the Exus for protection and permissions to call on the other gods. Evil spells, or *despachos,* need the Exus' help to succeed, and the practitioners of Quimbanda, or black magic, worship Exu's worst personalities: Exu Mor (death), Exu of the Crossroads and Exu of the Closed Paths.

FURTHER READING:

Davis, Wade. *The Serpent and the Rainbow.* New York: Simon & Schuster, 1985.

Gonzalez-Wippler. *Santeria: African Magic in Latin America.* New York: Original Products, 1981.

Leland, Charles Godfrey (1824–1903)   American folklorist, lecturer and prolific author whose immersion in Gypsy lore and witchcraft played a role in the revival of the latter in the 20th century, especially in America.

Leland was born August 15, 1824, in Philadelphia to a family with Puritan roots. His father, Henry, was a descendant of Hopestill Leland, one of the first white settlers in New England. Family lore maintained that one ancestor was a German sorceress, and Leland always believed that he resembled her in an atavistic way.

Charles Godfrey Leland

The young Leland showed an intense interest in occult subjects, Gypsies and high adventure. He was ambivalent about education; though he graduated from Princeton and studied in Munich and Heidelberg, he later freely acknowledged that he had hated school. Once out of college, he began a lifetime of exotic travel and penetration of the mysterious worlds of GYPSIES, witches and voodoo (see VODUN).

He returned periodically to America, where he had short-lived careers as a lawyer, newspaper editor and article writer. In his thirties he married Isabel Fisher; the marriage lasted more than 40 years, until her death in 1902.

Leland's real love was the occult and folklore, and after his parents died, he took his inheritance and moved to England. From there, he traveled the world. He learned about the Gypsies and also learned to speak their language, Romany. He discovered Shelta, the secret language of the tinkers. The Gypsies took him into their society, calling him a Romany Rye—a non-Gypsy who associates with Gypsies. He collected Gypsy, witchcraft and voodoo artifacts and books, turning his home into a veritable museum.

In 1879 he returned to Philadelphia, where he established the Industrial Art School. He spent several summers with American Indians, learning their spiritual lore. After four years he returned to England, where he began *The Gypsy Journal.* He wrote extensively about the Gypsies in books and articles.

In 1886, while in Italy, Leland met a Florentine Witch whom he referred to only as "Maddalena." He described Maddalena as a hereditary Witch with ancient Etruscan roots. She was born in Tuscany into a family of Witches and was educated by her grandmother, aunt and stepmother in the ways of the Craft.

Maddalena and Leland became close friends. She introduced him to other Witches and divulged many secrets of the Craft to him. The information Leland gleaned from Maddalena was incorporated into a series of books, the best-known of which is *Aradia, or Gospel of the Witches,* published in London in 1889. *Aradia* attempts to establish the antiquity of Witchcraft as a religion. It was the first book of its kind to record specific Witchcraft SPELLS, incantations, beliefs and lore (see ARADIA).

Leland died on March 20, 1903, in Florence, of pneumonia and heart trouble. He had spent the last seven years of his life in ill health, which was further aggravated by his grief at the death of his wife on July 9, 1902. Leland was cremated, and his ashes were returned to Philadelphia for burial.

Leland was known to embellish his folklore accounts, and thus never enjoyed a good reputation with scholars. The authenticity of *Aradia* is disputed.

FURTHER READING:

Adler, Margot. *Drawing Down the Moon.* Revised ed. New York: Viking, 1986.

Clifton, Chas S., ed. *Witchcraft Today: Book One. The Modern Craft Movement*. St. Paul: Llewellyn Publications, 1993.

Farrar, Janet, and Stewart Farrar. *A Witches Bible Compleat*. New York: Magickal Childe, 1984.

Lemp, Rebecca (d. 1590)   One of 32 women convicted of witchcraft and burned in a witch hunt in Nordlingen, Swabia, Germany. The case of Rebecca Lemp is notable for the records of letters left behind about her TORTURE, conviction and death.

The witch hunt was led by the burgomaster, George Pheringer, and two lawyers, Conrad Graf and Sebastien Roettinger. An anti-witch hysteria prevailed, and despite testimony from many people in favor of the accused, 32 were sent to their deaths.

Lemp was the wife of Peter Lemp, an accountant who was well educated and well regarded. She was arrested in April 1590 while her husband was away on business. Initially, she and her six children were confident that the authorities would realize her innocence, and she would soon be set free. Tragically, she was not.

Lemp wrote to her husband, assuring him of her innocence. "Were they to pulverize me and cut me into a thousand pieces, I could not confess anything," she said. "So don't be alarmed. Before my conscience and before my soul, I am innocent. Will I be tortured? I do not believe it, as I am not guilty of anything." Lemp was naïve to think that she would not be tortured—or that she could withstand the torture. She had no conception of the pain and brutality that awaited her.

Lemp was tortured five times before she surrendered and confessed. She then wrote to Peter and once again protested her innocence. She begged him to send her something so that she could end her life, before she died under more torture. Peter sent her poison, but it was intercepted by the authorities.

The court forced Lemp to write to Peter and confess she was a witch. He wrote to the court and insisted she was innocent and petitioned to be allowed to come to her aid. He also asked for the right to confront her accusers, for he believed her confession was forced under torture. He swore that she was honest, chaste and pious and had never entertained an ill or evil thought in her head. She was a good mother who educated her children about the Bible. He asked for her release.

The court's response was to torture Lemp again and then burn her in public on September 9, 1590.

The burnings of Lemp and others incited the witch hysteria to a new intensity. The hysteria reached a peak of insanity in 1594 when Maria Hollin, owner of the Crown tavern in Nordlingen, was arrested and tortured 56 times over the course of 11 months. Authorities from her home town of Ulm interceded and rescued her from jail, claiming they had jurisdiction to try her. She was released. Public sentiment began to turn against witch-hunting, and the hysteria came to an end.

FURTHER READING:

Cawthorne, Nigel. *Witch Hunt: History of a Persecution*. Edison, N.J.: Chartwell Books, 2004.

levitation   A paranormal phenomenon whereby a body or object is raised up into the air in defiance of gravity. Levitation has been reported in cases of bewitchment, hauntings (see GHOSTS, HAUNTINGS AND WITCHCRAFT) and POSSESSION; it also is attributed to saints and holy persons.

In 1550 in Wertet, Brabant, a group of nuns reportedly levitated into the air, climbed trees like cats and were pinched by invisible fingers. A towns-woman was tortured into confessing she had bewitched them. In other cases, beds are said to levitate off the floor. In hauntings, witches, poltergeists and FAIRIES have been blamed for levitating people, animals and objects.

Levitation also has been accomplished by Western psychics and mediums and was a common occurrence—often done fraudulently—at séances in the heydey of Spiritualism. The best-known levitating medium was Daniel Dunglas Home (1833–86), a Scotsman who was expelled from the Catholic Church on charges of SORCERY. Home was reported to levitate many times over a 40-year-period and to control his flights, which were done in trance. On one occasion, witnesses said he flew out of one third-story window in a home and returned through another window. Home was suspected of trickery, but he was never convicted of any fraud.

FURTHER READING:

Summers, Montague. *The History of Witchcraft and Demonology*. London: Kegan Paul, Trench, Trubner & Co. Ltd., 1926.

Lincoln Witches (d. 1618)   Three women accused of deadly witchcraft against an earl and his family in Rutland, England. Mother Joan Flower died before trial, but her daughters Margaret and Philippa confessed to murder by witchcraft and were executed. The case is especially interesting for the details of folk SPELLS described by the accused.

Like many accused witches, the Flower women were believed by their neighbors to be evil witches long before their official trouble. Joan especially was known for her ill temper, rude manners, uncouth behavior, oaths and CURSES. The women worked as domestic servants and, around 1613, Margaret managed to get employment at Belvoir Castle, the home of Sir Francis Manners, the sixth earl of Rutland. Margaret did the laundry and looked after the chickens. She evidently was a poor servant. She stole from the castle, taking things home to her mother, and she also engaged in lewd behavior with men in the castle.

Philippa, meanwhile, fell in love with a man named Thomas Simpson, and bewitched him into loving her—or so he said later.

Margaret fell out of favor with the earl's wife, who fired her and gave her an overly generous severance pay of 40 shillings, a bolster and a mattress of wool. Margaret went home unhappy. According to their later confessions, the Flower women decided to take revenge on the earl and his family by witchcraft. The Devil appeared to them and promised that if they would serve him, he would send them FAMILIARS and they would be able to "easily command what they pleased." They agreed.

Joan sent Margaret back to the castle to obtain the right-handed glove of the earl's oldest son, Lord Henry Rosse (also given as Roos), a small child. Margaret found it in a dunghill. Joan boiled the glove, pricking it often with a knife. She took it out and rubbed it on the back of her cat, Rutterkin—her familiar—instructing the spirit to go and harm the child. She then buried the glove in the yard. Soon the boy fell ill and died and was buried on September 16, 1613. (At a second examination, Margaret said she found the glove on rushes in the castle nursery. Her mother did not bury the glove, but threw it in the fire and burned it at the end of the spell.)

The witches then gleefully bewitched the earl's next son, Lord Francis, who fell severely ill. Francis died, but not until 1619 or 1620. The witches also caused the earl's only daughter, Katherine, to fall seriously ill. They obtained her handkerchief, boiled it and then rubbed it on Rutterkin and ordered the cat to harm her. Katherine managed to survive, marry and have children. Finally, the witches put a curse on the earl and his wife to have no more children. Joan obtained a pair of their gloves. She put the gloves and some of the wool from the mattress into warm water, added some blood (records do not say whose blood), stirred and rubbed the wool and gloves on the belly of Rutterkin while she muttered the curse. The couple in fact had no more children.

The earl suspected the Flower women of witchcraft and ordered them to be arrested around Christmastime 1617 and brought to jail in Lincoln. Before she was taken, Joan undertook a traditional ordeal, to eat bread and butter and swear that it should not pass through her if she were guilty. She did so, did not speak again and fell down and died before she could be taken to jail. Her daughters were arrested and imprisoned.

Margaret confessed that she had two familiars, one white and one black with spots. The white spirit sucked under her left breast and the spotted spirit sucked "within the inward parts of her secrets," or vagina. While in jail, she said that on the night of January 30, 1618, four Devils appeared to her around 11 P.M. or midnight. One had a black head like an ape and stood at the foot of her bed, muttering to her unintelligibly. The other three were Rutterkin, Joan's familiar, and Little Robin and Spirit, presumably her own familiars.

Philippa confessed to seeing Rutterkin leap onto Joan's shoulder and suck at her neck. She said she had her own familiar in the form of a white rat (see RODENTS), which for three or four years had sucked at her left breast. Philippa said that when it first came to her, she promised it her soul in exchange for causing Thomas Simpson to love her.

The earl left the women for trial, asking God to have mercy on their souls. They were executed by hanging on March 11, 1618, in Lincoln.

Three other women were examined on charges of witchcraft at about the same time as the Flower women: Joan Willimott, Anne Baker, and Ellen Green (also Greene). Baker testified that she had been told that the death of young Lord Henry was due to witchcraft and that as his glove rotted in the ground so did his liver.

Willimott said that she had met with Joan and Margaret and had gone to their house, where she saw two familiars, one like a rat and one like an owl. One of them sucked under her right ear. Joan told her that the spirits said she would neither be hanged nor burned. Willimott also said that Joan took some dirt, spit on it (see SPITTLE) and put it in her purse, saying she could not hurt the earl himself, but could harm his son.

Green said she had an association with Willimott. All three confessed to having familiars and performing various acts of MALEFICIA.

FURTHER READING:
Rosen, Barbara, ed. *Witchcraft in England, 1558–1618.* Amherst: University of Massachusetts Press, 1991.

Lipp, Deborah   Gardnerian witch, Druid, author and activist.

Deborah Lipp was born in Philadelphia and grew up in New Jersey, New York and Massachusetts. She was initiated into the Gardnerian tradition in 1981 and became a high priestess in 1986. The same year, she participated in the founding of *ÁR NDRAÍOCHT FÉIN*, a new Druid order, and served on its board of directors for several years. She and founder P. E. I. (ISAAC) BONEWITS married in 1986. The couple had a son, Arthur. They divorced in 1998.

Lipp is active in the media on behalf of Paganism and Wicca. She is the author of *Elements of Ritual: Air, Fire, Water and Earth in the Wiccan Circle* (2003); *Way of Four: Create Elemental Harmony in Your Life* (2004); and *The Ultimate James Bond Fan Book* (2006). With Bonewits, she coauthored *The Study of Witchcraft: A Guidebook to Advanced Wicca* (2007).

Lipp and son Arthur live in Rockland County, New York. In addition to writing, Lipp reads and teaches the Tarot and creates jewelry and other handcrafts.

Lithobolia of New Hampshire, The   A strange case of LITHOBOLY, or stone-peltings, occurred in the late 1600s in the colony of New Hampshire and was attributed to witchcraft. The exact date of the incident is not known, but it was recorded in INCREASE MATHER'S *Providences* in 1684 and in an eyewitness account published in 1698.

The stone-peltings took place over a period of several months at the home of George Walton, a wealthy landowner. The suspected source of the trouble was an elderly woman who was a neighbor of Walton's and was believed to be a witch. She and Walton had a dispute over a piece of land, which Walton claimed belonged to him and which he succeeded in appropriating from her. The bitter woman was overhead to remark that Walton would "never quietly enjoy that piece of ground." Her CURSE apparently came true.

One Sunday night in May at about 10 o'clock, Walton and his family, servants and guests were surprised by the clatter of a great number of stones against the roof and all sides of the house. Walton and several persons ran outside to investigate but could see nothing despite the bright moonlight. Walton found his fence gate torn off its hinges. Before he and the others returned inside, they were pelted by a rain of stones.

They ran back inside the house, where everyone was in an uproar. Stones began flying into the house. Everyone withdrew from the outer rooms, yet stones, some of them as large as fists, continued to fly at them and drop from the ceiling. Stones battered the windows from the inside, punching holes in the leaded glass and forcing out the bars, lead and hasps before ricocheting back into the room. Some of the stones seemed to fly out of the fire and were hot. Stones pelted the brass and pewter ware that was out, sending pots and candlesticks crashing to the floor.

By some miracle, no one was seriously injured by the stones. The occupants of the house immediately assumed preternatural causes. For four hours, stones continued to fly about the house and rain down the chimney. One of the guests grew weary and went back to bed, only to awaken when an eight-pound stone crashed through his chamber door.

The next day, Walton's domestics discovered that various household objects were missing. Some turned up in the yard and other odd places, while others abruptly sailed down the chimney or fell into rooms as though dropped from the ceiling. The men who went to work in the fields found the land littered with stones. A black cat was seen in the orchard and was shot at, but got away (see CATS).

That evening, one of the guests began to play a musical instrument. A "good big Stone" came rumbling in the room, followed by an avalanche of more stones. A hand was seen thrusting out from a hall window, tossing more stones upon the porch, at a time when no one was in the hall.

The stone-throwing and the disappearance of household objects went on for weeks, sometimes stopping for a day or two, then renewing with more force. The stones got larger; two stones weighing more than 30 pounds apiece thundered against one of the guest-room doors. The men at work outside continued to be plagued by stones that rained down and then disappeared from the ground, only to rain down on them again.

On Monday, June 28, came one of the worst stone attacks. Members of the household were eating supper in the kitchen when stones hurled down and broke the table into pieces. R. C. Esq. writes in his account, *Lithobolia: or, the Stone-throwing Devil, etc.* (1698):

> . . . many Stones (some great ones) came thick and three-fold among us, and an old howing Iron, from a Room hard by, where such Utensils lay. Then, as if I had been the designed Object for that time, most of the Stones that came (the smaller I mean) hit me, (sometimes pretty hard), to the number of above 20, near 30 . . . and whether I moved, sit, or walk'd, I had them, and great ones sometimes lighting gently on me. . . . Then was a Room over the Kitchen infested, that had not been so before, and many Stones greater than usual lumbering there over our Heads, not only to ours, but to the great Disturbance and Affrightment of some Children that lay there.

Walton continued to work in the fields with his men, though they were repeatedly pelted by stones. One day Walton said he was struck by more than 40 of them, which injured him so that he suffered chronic pain for the rest of his life. The corn planted in the fields was mysteriously cut off at the roots or uprooted. No agent of the damage was ever seen by anyone. The men said they heard at times an eerie "snorting and whistling" while they worked.

Other strange things continued to happen. A maid was hit on the head by a falling porringer. Hay baled one day was found strewn about the ground the next, with some of it tossed into the trees. One night, a "violent shock of Stones and Brickbats" crashed through a window, toppled books off a case and ripped a foot-long hole in a picture.

Finally, on August 1, Walton had had enough and decided to fight witchcraft with witchcraft. On the advice of someone who claimed to know about such matters, he attempted to cast a SPELL to punish the witch responsible for the harassment. A pot containing URINE and crooked PINS was set on the fire. As it boiled, it was supposed to remove the bewitchment and make the witch suffer. But as the urine began to heat, a stone fell into it and spilled it. The Waltons refilled the pot with more urine and crooked pins. Another stone fell in the pot and spilled the contents again. Then the handles fell off the pot, and the pot split into pieces. The Waltons gave up.

The hails of stones went on. Now more than 100 stones fell on the field while Walton and his men worked. Walton found his tools broken and his fences pulled down.

Walton at last complained to the council in Portsmouth, which summoned both him and the elderly woman for interrogation. En route, Walton was struck by three fist-sized stones, one of which "broke his head," a wound that he showed to the president of the council.

The outcome of the affair is not recorded. Most likely, the stone-throwing stopped after the Portsmouth Council became involved. Walton remained on his land, but his health was ruined.

FURTHER READING:

Mather, Increase. *An Essay for the Recording of Illustrious Providences.* Introduction by James A. Levernier. 1684. Reprint, Delmar, N.Y.: Scholars' Facsimiles and Reprints, 1977.

R. C. Esq. *Lithobolia: or, the Stone-throwing Devil, etc.* London: 1698.

lithoboly   Mysterious hails of stones have been reported from time to time in cases of witchcraft and possession (see POSSESSION; SPIRIT POSSESSION). Victims claim to be pelted by stones which suddenly rain down from the sky, or appear from nowhere inside a room. In folklore, the hails are credited to lithobolia, or stone-throwing DEMONS.

See also THE LITHOBOLIA OF NEW HAMPSHIRE.

Lord's Prayer   A widespread belief from about the 16th to early 18th centuries was that true witches were incapable of reciting the Lord's Prayer from start to finish. The reasoning was that the prayer, or any passage from the Bible, was offensive to the DEVIL, who would not permit his disciples to repeat it. This test was considered virtually infallible both in formal trials and inquisitions and in informal witchhunts. If the accused stumbled or omitted even a few words, she failed the test. Since many accused witches were old, uneducated women, it was likely that a good number of them did not know the prayer or any other bit of Scripture demanded of them; nor would it be surprising that many of them stumbled or forgot lines out of fear. Some, like FLORENCE NEWTON, tried in Ireland in 1661, said they could not remember because of their bad memory and old age. Sometimes a successful recitation of the Lord's Prayer made no difference. Most of the seven women accused of witchcraft in the Island Magee case in Ireland in 1711 had no trouble reciting the Lord's Prayer, yet all seven were found guilty by a jury (see ISLAND MAGEE WITCHES).

The Lord's Prayer has long been considered a powerful charm against witchcraft and the forces of evil (see CHARMS). The theologian St. Augustine (354–430), in his *Sermon Against Fortune-tellers and Diviners,* stated, "But as often as you have to do anything or to go out, cross yourselves in the name of Christ, and saying faithfully the Creed or the Lord's Prayer you may go about your business secure in the help of God." According to the *MALLEUS MALEFICARUM* (1486), reciting the Lord's Prayer was one of a number of remedies guaranteed to drive away incubi and succubi and nullify bewitchments of men and beasts.

The Lord's Prayer is used in EXORCISM of POSSESSION. According to European lore, the prayer also helps ward off vampires.

In some black magic and satanic RITUALS, the Lord's Prayer is recited backwards. An 18th-century magic textbook, the *Grimorium Verum,* instructs that to harm an enemy, one should drive a coffin nail into his footprint and recite the Lord's Prayer backwards.

See PRAYER.

FURTHER READING:

Summers, Montague, ed. *The Malleus Maleficarum of Heinrich Kramer and James Sprenger.* 1928. Reprint, New York: Dover Publications, 1971.

Thomas, Keith. *Religion and the Decline of Magic.* New York: Charles Scribner's Sons, 1971.

lycanthropy   The transformation of a human being into a wolf. There are two types of lycanthropy: a mania in which a person imagines himself to be a wolf and exhibits a craving for blood; and the magical-ecstatic transformation of a person into a werewolf ("man-wolf," from the Old English *wer,* man, plus wolf), usually accomplished with OINTMENTS or magical charm (see CHARMS).

Werewolf lore has existed since antiquity. In some legends, the werewolf is a person born under a CURSE, who cannot prevent himself from his hellish METAMORPHOSIS, which happens on nights of the full MOON. The person, usually a man, but sometimes a woman or a child, acquires the shape of a wolf and all its attributes, and roams about the countryside attacking and eating victims. In most tales, the werewolf is wounded, and the wound sympathetically carries over to the human form and reveals the identity of the werewolf.

In other legends, the werewolf is a sorcerer or witch who deliberately transforms himself at will to do evil and lay waste to his enemies. In South America, shamans, like sorcerers, turn into werewolves and attack and drink the BLOOD of their enemies. Sorcerers also turn into other were-animals (man-animals), including serpents, leopards, panthers, jackals, bear, coyotes, owls, foxes and other feared creatures. But it is the wolf who elicits the most universal fear and is the most dangerous of were-animals. Navajo lore holds that witches become werewolves and other were-animals by donning animal skins, which enables them to travel about at night at great speed. Were-animal witches are said to meet in caves at night, where they initiate new members, plan ritual killings-at-a-distance, practice necrophilia with the corpses of women and eat their victims (see SHAMANISM; SORCERY; WITCHCRAFT).

Werewolf beliefs were strong in medieval times in Europe and the Baltic countries. Later, in the 15th and 16th centuries, it was believed that werewolves, like witches, became servants of the Devil by diabolic pacts (see DEVIL'S PACT), and trials of accused werewolves increased. The cases were characterized by murder and cannibalism. In 1573 in Dole, France, Gilles Garnier was tried and convicted for the murder of several children. He confessed that he killed one victim, a 10-year-old girl, with his teeth and claws, then stripped off her clothing and ate part of her. He took the rest of her flesh home to his wife. He strangled a 10-year-old boy (he did not specify how a wolf can strangle), then bit off a leg and ate the boy's thighs and belly. He was identified when he attacked another victim but was interrupted by several peasants, who thought

Witch turned werewolf attacking travelers (HANS WEIDITZ, 1517)

they recognized Garnier's face, despite his wolf form. He was sentenced to be burned alive.

One of the most celebrated werewolf trials was that of Peter Stubb (also Stube or Stumpf) in 1589 at Bedburg near Cologne. Put on the rack and threatened with torture, Stubb made a lurid confession. He said that he had practiced the "wicked arts" from the age of 12 years and that the Devil had given him a magic belt that enabled him to change into a "devouring wolf." By taking the belt off, he returned to the shape of a man.

For 25 years, Stubb terrorized the countryside at night, stalking children, women, men, lambs, sheep and goats. He was an "insatiable bloodsucker," taking great pleasure in killing. He killed his own son and ate his brains. He killed lambs, kids and other livestock, "feeding on the same most usually raw and bloody." He murdered 13 young children and two pregnant women. He confessed to incest with his daughter, Beell (Bell) and sexual escapades with various mistresses, including a "gossip," Katherine Trompin. His lust remained unsated, so the DEVIL sent him a succubus.

Stubb was finally exposed when some hunters chased him down in wolf form, and he slipped off his belt and was recognized.

In his trial, his daughter and Trompin were judged accessories in some of the murders. Like many condemned witches in Germany, Stubb was sentenced to torture and execution.

One unusual werewolf case resembles that of the BENANDANTI of northern Italy: the werewolves were men who left their bodies and in spirit assumed the shapes of wolves, descending into the underworld to battle the witches. The case was tried in 1692 in Jurgensburg, Livonia, an area east of the Baltic Sea steeped in werewolf lore, and involved an 80-year-old man named Thiess.

Thiess freely confessed to being a werewolf. He testified that his nose had been broken by a man named Skeistan, a witch who was dead at the time he struck Thiess. His story of how it happened was this: Skeistan and other witches prevented crops from growing by carrying seed grain into hell. Thiess was a werewolf, who, with other werewolves, attempted to protect the crops by descending into hell and fighting with the witches to recover what was stolen. Three times a year, on the nights of St. Lucia, Pentecost and St. John (seasonal changes), the battles took place. If the werewolves delayed their descent, the witches barred the gates of hell, and the crops and livestock, even the fish catch, suffered. The werewolves carried iron bars as weapons, and the witches carried broom handles. Skeistan had broken Thiess's nose with a broom handle wrapped in a horse's tail.

The judges, naturally, were shocked to hear that werewolves, who were supposed to be agents of the Devil, could not tolerate the Devil and fought against witches. Asked what happened to werewolves at death, Thiess replied that they were buried like ordinary folk, and their souls went to heaven—another shock for the judges. Thiess insisted that the werewolves were the "hounds of God" who served mankind, preventing the Devil from carrying off the abundance of the earth. If not for them, everyone would suffer. He said werewolves in Germany and Russia likewise fought the witches in their own hells.

Thiess refused to confess that he had signed a pact with the Devil, despite the efforts of the judges. Even the parish priest, summoned to chastise him for his evil ways, failed to sway Thiess. The old man angrily said he was a better man than the priest and that he was neither the first, nor would be the last, werewolf to fight the witches. The judges sentenced him to 10 lashes for acts of idolatry and superstitious beliefs.

FURTHER READING:

Baring-Gould, Sabine. *The Book of Werewolves*. New York: Causeway Books, 1973.

Devlin, Judith. *The Superstitious Mind: French Peasants and the Supernatural in the Nineteenth Century*. New Haven: Yale University Press, 1987.

O'Donnell, Elliott. *Werewolves*. New York: Longvue Press, 1965.

Summers, Montague. *The Werewolf*. 1933. Reprint, New York: Bell Publishing, 1967.

Macbeth Shakespeare's play about intrigue and murder in the royal court of Scotland is one of the most influential literary works in establishing the stereotype of witches as evil, ugly HAGS. The play, written around 1603 and published around 1623, is drawn partly on Raphael Holinshed's *Chronicles of England, Scotland and Ireland* (1577).

Three unnamed witches, sometimes called the "Weird Sisters," are consulted for their prophecies. The play opens with the witches gathered on a barren heath; later, in the famous first scene of Act IV, they stir up a CAULDRON full of vile ingredients and conjure the Greek patron goddess of witchcraft, HECATE, and various spirits. Macbeth's ambition to be king, plus the witches' prophecies, spur him to commit murder. He brings about his own undoing and dies cursing the day he met the witches.

Stated MONTAGUE SUMMERS in *The History of Witchcraft and Demonology* (1926):

> There are few scenes which have so caught the world's fancy as the wild overture to *Macbeth*. In storm and wilderness we are suddenly brought face to face with three mysterious phantasms that ride on the wind and mingle with the mist in thunder, lightning, and in rain. They are not agents of evil, they are evil; nameless, spectral, wholly horrible.

Act IV, Scene I opens with the three witches stirring in their cauldron. Appropriately, thunder roils outside their cavern:

1st Witch: Thrice the brinded cat hath mew'd.
2nd Witch: Thrice, and once the hedgepig whin'd.
3rd Witch: Harpier cries; -'tis time, -'tis 'ime.
1st Witch: Round about the cauldron go;
In the poison'd entrails throw.
Toad, that under cold stone
Days and night has thirty-one
Swelter'd venom sleeping got,
Boil thou first i' the charmed pot.
All: Double, double, toil and trouble;
Fire burn and cauldron bubble.
2nd Witch: Fillet of a fenny snake,
In the cauldron boil and bake;
Eye of newt and toe of frog,
Wool of bat and tongue of dog,
Adder's fork and blind-worm's sting,
Lizard's leg and howlet's wing,
For a charm of powerful trouble,
Like a hell-broth boil and bubble.
All: Scale of dragon, tooth of wolf,
Witches mummy, maw and gulf
of the ravin's salt-sea shark;
Root of hemlock digg'd i' the dark,
Liver of blaspheming Jew,
Gall of goat, and slips of yew
Sliver'd in the moon's eclipse,
Nose of Turk and Tartar's lips,
Finger of birth-strangled babe
Ditch-deliver'd by a drab,
Make the gruel thick and slab:
Add thereto a tiger's chaudron.

Macbeth and Banquo meet the Weird Sisters (WOODCUT FROM HOLINSHED'S *THE CHRONICLES OF SCOTLAND*, 1577)

For th' ingredients of our cauldron.
All: Double, double toil and trouble;
Fire burn and cauldron bubble.
2nd Witch: Cool it with a baboon's blood,
Then the charm is firm and good.
Hecate enters.
Hecate: O, well done! I commend your pains;
And every one shall share in th' gains:
And now about the cauldron sing,
Like elves and fairies in a ring,
Enchanting all that you put in.
Music and song; Hecate exits.

The influence of *Macbeth* on popular opinion about Witches is evidenced in an incident that happened to SYBIL LEEK in the late 1960s. The English Witch had just written her autobiography, *Diary of a Witch,* and was a sought-after guest on the media tour circuit in America. She accepted an invitation to appear on NBC's *Today* show, then hosted by Barbara Walters and Hugh Downs. She expected to have an opportunity to educate *Today's* considerable audience on the Old Religion. Apparently, the NBC programmers expected to entertain viewers with a bit of theater. Leek recounts in her book, *The Complete Art of Witchcraft* (1971):

> I arrived to do the show in the early hours of the morn-
> ing, to find that I was expected to stir a *cauldron* while

mouthing the usual "Double, double, toil and trouble" bit out of Shakespeare, and to look as cackling and as evil as possible.

Leek declined to play the stereotype and managed to salvage some of her appearance on the show with a serious discussion of Witchcraft as a religion.

FURTHER READING:
Leek, Sybil. *Diary of a Witch.* New York: NAL Signet Library, 1968.
Summers, Montague. *The History of Witchcraft and Demonology.* London: Kegan Paul, Trench, Trubner & Co. Ltd., 1926.

Macumba The Brazilian form of VODUN and SANTERÍA, or the worship of the ancient African gods through SPIRIT POSSESSION and MAGIC. There is no "Macumba" religion; the word is an umbrella term for the two principal forms of African spirit worship in Brazil: Candomblé and Umbanda. Macumba sometimes refers to black magic, but that is more properly called Quimbanda.

Black slaves transported to Brazil by the Portuguese in the 1550s found their tribal religion had much in common with the spiritual practices of Indian tribes along the Amazon River. Forced to syncretize the worship of their gods, or *orishas,* into the veneration of Catholic saints to escape persecution, the blacks continued to follow the old ways and rituals in secret. By the time the slaves won their independence in 1888, more than 15 generations of Brazilians—black, white and Indian—had heard the stories of the orishas and how their magical intervention had snared a lover, saved a marriage or a sick baby or eliminated a wicked enemy. Today, some members of all classes and races in Brazil believe in some sort of ancient spiritual communion with the gods while professing Catholicism in public.

Candomblé. Candomblé most closely resembles the ancient Yoruban religions, as does Santería, and retains the Yoruban names of the orishas. Spellings are Portuguese, not Spanish, so *Changó* becomes *Xango, Yemaya* is *Yemanja* or *Iemanja, Oggun* becomes *Ogun* and *Olorun* is *Olorum.* Figures of Catholic saints represent the orishas, although Jesus Christ, also known as *Oxala,* is venerated as a saint on his own.

The term *Candomblé* probably derives from *candombé,* a celebration and dance held by the slaves on the coffee plantations. The first Candomblé center was organized in 1830 in Salvador, the old capital city of Brazil and now the capital of the state of Bahia, by three former slaves who became the cult's high priestesses. The slave women inherited the formerly all-male ceremonial duties when the men were forced to spend their time in slave field labor. The women also served as mistresses to the white Portuguese and claimed that the exercise of their magical rites helped maintain their sexual skill and prowess. These "Mothers of the Saints" trained other women, called "Daughters of the Saints," ensuring that the men were excluded from major responsibilities. Even today, the men perform political rather than spiritual roles.

Candomblé ceremonies follow much the same pattern as those for Santería and Vodun, with invocations to the gods, PRAYERS, offerings and possession of the faithful by the gods. Afro-Brazilian traditions stress the importance of healing the spirit, and devotees of Candomblé believe the moment of greatest spiritual healing occurs when a person becomes one with his orisha during initiation into the cult. Such possession is often intense, requiring constant aid from the other worshipers. The priest may beg the orisha to treat the initiate gently, offering a pigeon or other SACRIFICE to the orisha in return for his or her mercy. The stronger the orisha—gods like Xango or Ogun are considered the strongest—the more violent the possession.

Instead of asking LEGBA or Elegguá to let the spirits in, followers of Candomblé call on the Exus, primal forces of all nature who act as divine tricksters and messengers to the gods. Connections exist between Elegguá/Legba and Exus, however; some of Elegguá's manifestations in Santería are called *Eshus.* They are the gods of mischief, the unexpected and life and death, as well as messengers to the other orishas.

One of the major celebrations to the orisha Yemanja, "goddess of the waters," takes place every January 1. Bra-zilian television broadcasts the event in Rio de Janeiro live to the entire country, although smaller ceremonies occur in other coastal and river towns and cities. More than one million celebrants, dressed in white, wade into the ocean at dusk. A priestess, or *mão de santo* (mother of the saint), lights CANDLES and then purifies and ordains other young priestesses. As the sun sinks behind the mountains, celebrants decorate a small wooden boat with candles, flowers and figurines of the saints. Sometimes doves sail on the boat as well. At midnight, the boat is pushed from shore, and all watch eagerly as the craft bobs in the waves. If the boat sinks, the orisha Yemanja (believed to be the Virgin Mary) has heard her children's prayers and accepts their offering, promising her support and guidance for another year.

Umbanda. Umbanda was not founded until 1904 and has its roots in Hinduism and Buddhism in addition to African tribal religions. The teachings of Spiritism—that communication with discarnate spirits is not only possible but necessary for spiritual healing and acceptance of one's earlier incarnations—also plays a large part in the practices of Umbanda.

The term *umbanda* probably derives from *aum-gandha,* a Sanskrit description of the divine principle. Umbanda incorporates not only worship of the Catholic saints but the beliefs of the Brazilian Indians. The orishas go by their Catholic names and personae, and *Umbandistas* do not call on the gods directly, fearing their intense power. Instead, spirits of divine ancestors act as intermediaries on the worshipers' behalf.

Although followers of Candomblé and Umbanda approach their faiths quite differently, researchers Alberto Villoldo and Stanley Krippner found they share three beliefs:

1. Humans have both a physical and spiritual body.
2. Discarnate entities constantly contact the physical world.
3. Humans can learn to contact and incorporate the spirits for the purposes of healing and spiritual evolution.

Like the devotees of Candomblé, Umbandistas also call on the Exus to protect their temples and let the divine presences enter.

Communication with the spirits of Umbanda resembles very closely the practice of trance channeling. During ceremonies, the Fathers or Mothers of the Saints—either men or women can lead the congregation spiritually in Umbanda—become possessed with a spirit guide, usually of an Amerindian or African, or perhaps of a child who died quite young. The two most popular spirit mediums are the Old Black Man (Preto Velho) and Old Black Woman (Preta Velha), representing the wise old slaves who perished in toil and torture, taking their African wisdom with them into the spiritual world.

As with possession in Vodun and Santería, those receiving the spirits assume the characteristics of their possessors, performing medicine dances of the American Indians, smoking cigars and pipes (tobacco was sacred to the Indians) or bending over from advanced age and labor. Any worshiper can receive the spirits, with help from the priest-mediums. Umbandistas believe that healing of the physical body cannot be achieved without healing the spirit; opening the mind to the entrance of a spirit guide via ecstatic trance is essential to spiritual growth. Spirits enter the body through the head—this is true in Candomblé, Santería and Vodun—and are perceived by the physical body through the "third eye," located in the center of the forehead. Spirits never die but continue on an eternal journey through other worlds, sometimes reincarnating in another physical body. Umbandistas believe the most enlightened spirits teach and heal through the mediums of Umbanda, and mediumship forges a link with these highly evolved minds. Every time a medium receives a spirit guide for teaching and healing, the medium's mind and spirit are raised to another plane of consciousness.

Quimbanda. Umbandista mediums generally refer to "lower" or "mischievous" spirits, rather than "evil" ones, believing that all spirits evolve to higher consciousness. The misbehavers simply need education to set them on the right path.

But the practitioners of Quimbanda or Cuimbanda—black magic—find that evil spirits suit their purposes quite well. Here again the Exus serve, this time as the tricksters, the gods of witchcraft and sorcery. Equated by some with Lucifer himself, "King Exu" receives assistance from Beelzebub and Ashtaroth, known as Exu Mor and Exu of the Crossroads.

Exu of the Closed Paths inspires the most dread. To sicken or destroy an enemy, the Quimbandista prepares a RED satin cloth adorned with mystical symbols and takes it to a CROSSROADS; the magician places upon it four red-and-black crosses. (Red and black are the Exus' colors, as they are for Legba and Eleggua.) Accompanying the crosses are a COCK, plucked and stuffed with red pepper, and other devilish items. Then the Quimbandista lights 13 candles, intoning the name of the enemy and invoking the powers of darkness to do their work. If the Quimbandista is successful, the unlucky victim will find "all paths closed" and will lose his job, become ill, lose his lover and family and eventually dye if not cured by the powers of the orishas.

FURTHER READING:

King, Francis X. *Witchcraft and Demonology.* New York: Exeter Books, 1987.
Laugguth, A. J. *Macumba: White and Black Magic in Brazil.* New York: Harper & Row, 1975.
Villoldo, Alberto, and Stanley Krippner. *Healing States.* New York: Fireside/Simon & Schuster, 1987.

magic   The ability or power to manifest by aligning inner forces with natural and supernatural forces. Inner forces are will, thought and imagination; natural forces are found in nature, such as the elements; and supernatural forces are spirits, deities and the Godhead.

Humankind's awareness of magic and efforts to use it to enhance life are ancient and universal and have been a part of all religious systems. The earliest evidence of magic dates from cave paintings of the Paleolithic Age, some of which suggest that magic RITUALS were employed to secure successful hunts. Magical systems and philosophies have developed around the world, and volumes of literature have been written on them. The discussion here will focus on the development of Western magic and its role in SORCERY and modern WITCHCRAFT and PAGANISM.

The word *magic* comes either from the Greek *megus,* which means "great" (as in "great" science), or from the Greek term *magein,* the science and religion of Zoroaster. Numerous definitions of magic have been offered by many who have practiced and studied it, yet magic eludes precise description. Though systems of magic exist—and some are quite complex—magic remains an

Ritual magic tools, in the collection of the Museum of Witchcraft in Boscastle, Cornwall (PHOTO BY AUTHOR; COURTESY MUSEUM OF WITCHCRAFT)

individualistic experience. Every person who practices magic sees it in a different way.

Magic, like science, works in conformance to the natural laws of the universe. The *Goetia* portion of the *Lemegeton of King Solomon*, a GRIMOIRE, said to be in existence since around 1500, defines magic as

> . . . the Highest, most Absolute, and most Divine Knowledge of Natural Philosophy, advanced in its works and wonderful operations by a right understanding of the inward and occult virtue of things; so that true Agents being applied to proper Patients, strange and admirable effects will thereby be produced. When magicians are profound and diligent searchers into Nature, they, because of their skill, know how to anticipate an effect, the which to the vulgar shall seem to be a miracle.

ALEISTER CROWLEY gave perhaps the most succinct modern definition of magic as "the science and art of causing change to occur in conformity to the will" (*Magick in Theory and Practice,* 1929). Crowley further postulated that "any required Change may be effected by the application of the proper kind of degree of Force in the proper manner through the proper medium to the proper object." He said that "every intentional act is a Magical Act" and that if a magical act failed, it meant the performer had not fulfilled all the requirements for success.

Occultist DION FORTUNE, whose novels have inspired RITUALS for many contemporary Pagans and Witches, defined magic as "the art and science of changing consciousness according to the Will."

P. E. I. ISAAC BONEWITS, in *Real Magic* (1971), defined magic in terms of energy, as

> . . . a science and an art of comprising a system of concepts and methods for the build-up of human emotion, altering the electrochemical balance of the metabolism, using associational techniques and devices to concentrate and focus this emotional energy, thus modulating the energy broadcast by the human body, usually to affect other energy patterns, whether animate or inanimate, but occasionally to affect the personal energy patterns.

Thus magic, when properly performed, changes not only the environment but the magician as well.

Magic is variously described as *white, black* and *gray,* but actually it has no color to its character. Magic is neutral and amoral. It can be bent to good, evil or ambiguous purposes, depending on the intent of the practitioner. The distinction between "white" and "black" magic is modern, according to occultist A. E. Waite, and depends upon sharp contrasts between good and evil spirits. The distinctions were far more obscure in ancient times.

Anthropologist Bronislaw Malinowski stated that magic has three functions—to produce, protect and destroy—and has three elements—the spell or incantation; the rite or procedure; and the state of the practitioner, who usually undergoes a purification process that alters his state of consciousness (fasting, inhaling fumes, taking drugs, chanting, dancing, and so forth).

The simplest form of magic is mechanical SORCERY, in which a physical act is performed to achieve a result. For example, a waxen image is melted over a fire to make a victim die; BLOOD is scattered over a field to ensure a bountiful harvest in the next growing season; KNOTS are tied in a cord to store wind for a sea voyage. Such sorceries, or SPELLS, are performed while reciting magical incantations or CHARMS, to aid the effectiveness of the act. A higher form of sorcery involves petitioning the help of spirits or deities.

Sorcery, out of which grew witchcraft, forms the bulk of the folk magic practiced to affect matters of everyday life, such as ensuring that one's cows give milk, that the butter churns, that one's illness is cured or that one's home is protected from lightning and bewitchment.

James G. Frazer, in *The Golden Bough* (1890), said that all magic is based on the Law of Sympathy, which holds that all things are linked together by invisible bonds. Sometimes sorcery is called *sympathetic magic.* Frazer further divided sympathetic magic into two types. *Homeopathic magic* holds that like produces like: a melted waxen image causes death. *Contagious magic* holds that things once in contact can continue to exert influence on each other, even at a distance. For example, a wound can be magically cured by rubbing ointment on the sword that caused the wound.

These principles are called correspondences: everything in the universe responds to something that corresponds to it. The magician further understands that emotions, thoughts, beliefs, states of mind and the imagination create correspondences and can effect change. "Thoughts are things" and "thoughts create reality" are fundamental to mystical traditions.

Sorcery was practiced extensively in the ancient civilizations of Mesopotamia and the Mediterranean. The ancient Egyptians, Persians, Babylonians, Greeks, Romans and Hebrews had magical systems that greatly influenced later magic in the West. In Egypt, the pharaohs were considered divine kings and were thought to possess innate magical abilities. There were two classes of magicians. The most esteemed were the trained priests, professional magicians who acted as substitutes for the pharaoh, who could not possibly perform all needed magical services. The second class were the lay magicians, the equivalent of folk magicians, healers and WIZARDS. From Egyptian magic came the concept of the power of sacred names, which influenced later European magic (see NAMES OF POWER).

The Greeks developed both a system and philosophies of magic, which were influenced by concepts imported from Egypt, the Middle East and the East. The Greeks envisioned magic as divided into two classes: high and low. High magic, which calls upon the aid of beneficent spirits, is akin to religion. It is called *theurgy,* from *theourgia,* or "working things pertaining to the gods." Theurgic magic was practiced by the Neo-Platonists, adherents to a philosophical and religious system developed in Alexandria in the 3rd century C.E. that was based on a blend of the doctrines of Plato and other Greek philosophers, Oriental mysticism, Judaism and Christianity. Plato believed in a morally neutral natural magic.

Low magic in Greece, *mageia* (sorcery), had acquired an unsavory reputation for fraud by the fifth century B.C.E. Practitioners were not members of the priesthood but individuals who claimed to have magical powers and would help clients for fees. The lowest form of this magic is *goeteia*, which in the classical world was practiced by persons who cast spells, "howled" incantations and concocted PHILTRES and potions.

The Romans used sorcery and counter-sorcery, especially CURSES, to defeat rivals and advance themselves politically and materially. Though sorcery was popular with the public, the private practice of it was greatly feared by those in authority, and harsh laws were passed against it. The Cornelian Law proclaimed, "Soothsayers, enchanters, and those who make use of sorcery for evil purposes; those who conjure up demons, who disrupt the elements, who employ waxen images destructively, shall be punished by death."

The Christian Church separated magic from religion as early as 364, when the Ecumenical Council of Laodicea issued a Thirty-sixth Canon forbidding clerks and priests from becoming magicians, enchanters, astrologers and mathematicians. In 525 the Fourth Canon of the Council of Oxia prohibited the consultation of sorcerers, augurs and diviners and outlawed DIVINATION by wood or bread. In 613 the Council of Tours instructed priests to teach the public that magic to cure illness would not work. The church excommunicated diviners in 692 and renewed its prohibitions against divining in 721. Divining is not magic, because it attempts to interpret omens and understand the future, not influence it, but the proscriptions against diviners indicate the church's overall attitude toward magic, which had a great bearing on the prosecution of sorcerers and witches during the INQUISITION. While the church discouraged the private practice of magic, it absorbed both theurgic and goetic magic elements and Christianized them in its own rites and ceremonies. The goetic magic of sorcerers and witches was said to be evil; witches supposedly derived their magical powers from pacts with the DEVIL (see DEVIL'S PACT).

From about the seventh century to the 17th century, alchemy was in its heyday. Alchemy is not a branch of magic, but many alchemists also were theurgic magicians. Alchemy is based on the HERMETICA and traces its roots to the ancient Egyptians, who, according to the Greeks, believed in the magical properties of metals and alloys and could separate gold and silver from their native matrices.

Alchemists pursued three basic objectives: the transmutation of base metals into gold and silver; the discovery

Doctor Faustus watching a magical disk in his laboratory (REMBRANDT HARMENSZOON VAN RIJN, 1652)

of the elixir of life, which would bestow immortality; and creation of the homunculus, an artificial man. The key to the transmutation and the elixir lay in the discovery of the Philosopher's Stone, an ambiguous material said to be either a stone, powder or liquid that was easy to obtain but recognized only by the initiated. The esoteric purpose of alchemy was mystical and concerned the spiritual regeneration of man.

From about the eighth to 16th centuries, various forms of magic emerged from a renewal of Neo-Platonism, plus Kabbalistic doctrines and Oriental doctrines brought back to Europe by the crusaders. Very little was transcendental. Medieval magic coalesced as a system in the 12th century in Europe. The KNIGHTS TEMPLAR, formed in 1118, developed a magical system learned from the Johannites sect in Jerusalem. Other magicians of Europe were learned men, scholars, physicians and alchemists. Their magic consisted of intricate procedures involving dress, consecrated tools, magical symbols and, most importantly, sacred names of power, which, in incantations, summoned and banished various spirits. The unspeakable name of the Hebrew God, Yahweh, the Tetragrammaton, was the most potent name. The magician worked within a protective MAGIC CIRCLE.

Magicians were not troubled much by the church until the 13th century, with the beginnings of the INQUISITION. In the 13th and 14th centuries, Aristotelian philosophy gained favor over Platonic philosophy. Under Aristotelian thought, no natural magic exists: therefore, magic must be either divine or demonic.

By the 15th century, magicians—seen as competitors with the church—were harassed and hounded, though not to the same degree as sorcerers and witches, who were executed by the thousands for heresy.

Medieval magic reached a peak in the Renaissance in the 16th century under such figures as Agrippa von Nettesheim and PARACELSUS in Europe and John Dee and Robert Fludd in England. Agrippa's *De Occulta Philosophia* dealt with divine names, natural magic and cosmology. Paracelsus stressed the Hermetic doctrine of "As above, so below," which holds that the microcosm of the earth reflects the macrocosm of the universe. Dee, with his partner, Edward Kelly, developed the system of Enochian magic, a language of calls for summoning spirits and traveling in the astral planes. Fludd, a Kabbalist, attempted to reconcile Neo-Platonic and Aristotelian philosophies and to relate Aristotelianism to the Kabbalah. He wrote in defense of the Kabbalah, magic and alchemy.

The 17th and 18th centuries witnessed a popularity of secret esoteric orders, such as the Freemasons and Rosicrucians, whose RITUALS were based on the Hermetica, mystery schools, the Tarot, interpretations of the Kabbalah and astrology. Magical grimoires, containing detailed instructions for magical rites, circulated widely. The most important of these, still used today, is the *Key of Solomon,* whose authorship is attributed to the legendary King Solomon, said to be one of the greatest adepts of mystical wisdom.

During the 17th and 18th centuries, ceremonial magic, developed. Ceremonial magic is a complex art of dealing with spirits. It requires a rigorous discipline and has an intellectual appeal. In ceremonial magic, the magician derives power from God (the Judeo-Christian God) through the successful control of spirits, usually DEMONS, which are believed easier to control that angels. Demons may be good, evil or neutral. In its highest sense, ceremonial magic is a transcendental experience that takes the magician into mystical realms and into communication with the Higher Self. It awakens the magician to the God within.

Magic enjoyed a great revival of interest at the beginning of the 19th century with the publication of Francis Barrett's *The Magus* in 1801; the book borrowed heavily from the works of Agrippa. The revival was greatly influenced by Eliphas Lévi, whose explanation of how magic works, in *Dogma and Ritual of High Magic* (1856), had a lasting impact on the thinking of magicians. Lévi described three laws of magic. The first law was that of will power, which Lévi said was a tangible force, not an abstract concept. The success of magic depends upon the will summoned and directed by the magician. The ceremonial props of medieval magic—the tools, dress, symbols, etc.—had an express purpose, to facilitate the will. The second law was that of astral light, a substance or energy permeating the universe which the magician could access and use to effect changes at a distance. The third law was Lévi's interpretation of the Hermetic axiom, "As above, so below." Any force existing in the universe also existed in the soul of man. Magicians could invoke anything from the macrocosm into themselves and evoke anything from within their own souls into their magical triangle. Other factors contributing to the rise of ceremonial magic were Spiritualism and Theosophy, both of which brought public attention to communication with spirits and the dead.

Perhaps the greatest system of Western ceremonial magic was devised by the HERMETIC ORDER OF THE GOLDEN DAWN, an occult society founded in England by three Rosicrucians, in the late 19th century. The Golden Dawn expanded upon Levi's writings, adding a fourth law, that of the imagination, without which the will was ineffective.

The Golden Dawn influenced Crowley, said to be the greatest magician of the 20th century. Crowley used both Enochian Magic and Abra-Melin Magic in his explorations of the mystical realms, resulting in a popular interest in both systems that has continued into the present (see ABRAMELIN THE MAGE).

Crowley's most significant contribution to magic is the Law of Thelema: "Do what thou wilt shall be the whole of the law," or do what you must and nothing else. In other words, know yourself and be true to yourself.

Another magical group that has influenced modern magic is the Ordo Templi Orientis (O.T.O.), founded around the turn of the 20th century by a German, Karl Kellner, and devoted to sex magic derived from Tantra. Sexual energy is ritually aroused; practitioners identify with the gods and goddesses who personify the sexual principle. Crowley, an O.T.O. initiate, contributed to the rituals. Kellner served as head of its British affiliate and, from 1922 until his death in 1947, as head of the outer order of the organization. Following his death, the O.T.O. fractured. Lodges are in countries around the world.

Members of the Golden Dawn and O.T.O. exported their rituals to North America in the early part of the 20th century. Elements have been absorbed into some forms of contemporary Witchcraft and Paganism.

Components of magic rituals. To be effective, magic should be performed in an altered state of consciousness. Depending upon the practitioner and the type of ritual, the altered state may be a mild one of dissociation or one of trance possession. Sounds, gestures, colors, scents, visual images and symbols all contribute to attaining an altered state. This enables the magician to reach the astral planes, which are inhabited by various entities, and where magical work takes place.

The time for a ritual is set according to astrological auspices. The magician undergoes a rigorous and elaborate preparation, first by purifying his body with fasting and abstinence. He removes himself from distractions and prays, meditates and concentrates on the upcoming ritual. The purification process can last for days. Some magicians attempt to achieve an altered state of mind through food, drink, drugs or sex.

The magician bathes and dons his magical robe, a consecrated garment decorated with magical symbols sigils, words and names. He uses consecrated magical tools, which, ideally, he has made himself according to specific instructions, or purchased new. The principal tools are the wand, sword, knife or dagger, pentacle and chalice, but they can also include a sickle, lancet, hook, lamp, scourge, tripod, cross, spear, crook and other objects. He follows a procedure for drawing and purifying a magic circle. The magician burns incense, the formula of which is appropriate for the ritual. He also uses colors, such as colored CANDLES.

The incantations for invoking spirits are formulae including names of power, recited in a crescendo of intensity, with gesturing of the wand, until the magician directs his entire will and energy into the ritual.

The central part of the ritual is called the pathworking, a complex meditation or visualization. The goal of pathworking is the apprehension of Truth, the uniting of the Self with the One. Popular tools for pathworking are the kabbalistic Tree of Life and the Tarot, the components of which represent archetypal and cosmic forces.

Some ceremonial magic rituals have the express purpose of summoning a particular spirit or deity.

Magic in Contemporary Witchcraft

Contemporary Witchcraft magic is a blend of *theurgy* and *goetia*. It contains elements of folk magic, ceremonial magic and sex magic. (Some Witches also have incorporated non-Western magical elements into their practices.) The Witch works within a magic circle and uses four primary magical tools, which correspond to the ELEMENTS: the athame (or sword)—fire; the pentacle—earth; the chalice—water; and the wand—air. In addition, the Witch uses a censer for the burning of incense and, in most practices, a scourge and cords for tying knots (see WITCHES' TOOLS). Like ceremonial magic tools, the Witch's tools ideally are handmade or purchased new, inscribed with magic SIGILS or runes and consecrated in the four elements (water, candle flame, incense and salt). The Witch invokes the forces of nature, the elements and the elemental spirits that rule the elements (see ELEMENTALS) and appeals to the many faces of the GODDESS and HORNED GOD. Most Witches believe in working with benevolent beings and deities for good purposes. Many spells are derived from pagan sorcery and folk magic, based upon Frazer's Law of Sympathy. The Witch makes use of colors, scents, sounds, movements, symbols and visual images in ritual. Witches do not use BLOOD sacrifices.

GERALD B. GARDNER, the English Witch credited with founding contemporary Witchcraft, the dominant form of which is the Gardnerian tradition, said he received ritual material from his original COVEN of hereditary Witches. He borrowed from the writings of Aleister Crowley and other occult sources, plus drew on his exposure to Eastern occultism (see BOOK OF SHADOWS). Gardner stated eight ways to raise power for magic.

1. *Meditation or concentration.* This corresponds to the ceremonial magician's preparatory period, in which he or she gains a clear idea of the purpose of the ritual, eliminating all other thoughts and distractions and focusing all attention on the task at hand. Gardner may have learned Eastern meditation techniques used in magic and in mysticism during the many years he spent living and working in the East as a British civil servant. Eastern meditation incorporates breath control (*pranayama*), steady and balanced posture (*asana*), finger and hand gestures (*mudra*) and chanting (*mantra*).

2. *Chants, spells, invocations.* Chants are spoken or sung slowly at first, then increased in tempo to shrieks. When the power is at a peak, the Witch releases it and psychically directs it toward the goal. Spells are combinations of movement, gesture and chanted rhymes or charms (the stated purpose of the ritual), designed to bring about the desired effect or change. Invocations are invitations or appeals to the deities for help.

3. *Trance or astral projection.* In astral projection, one leaves the body behind and travels in the astral realms in the astral body, or double, a spirit replica of the physical body. It can pass through physical matter and travel at the speed of thought. It is invisible to most people, though psychically attuned persons may sense its presence or see it. While the double is out of body, the physical form appears to be in deep sleep.

   Gardner advised Witches not to attempt going out of body until clairvoyance was developed. To go out of body, he advocated assuming a kneeling position with arms strained forward and bound, so as to produce a sensation of being pulled forward. The scourge, a whip made of fabric cords, is applied in a light, dragging motion. By traveling astrally, a Witch can arrive at a distant location quickly, communicate with spirit guides or look into the future. Healing work can be done, including the analysis of a problem and the discovery of its solution; attendance to watch over someone; and the delivery of healing energy. It is also possible to use astral projection to influence others while they sleep or to engage in psychic attack; however, most Witches are opposed to harmful or manipulative actions (see WICCAN REDE).

4. *Incense, wine and drugs.* The fumes of incense contribute to the altered state of consciousness, a technique used by both Witches and ceremonial magicians. Gardner said that a moderate amount of wine before and during the ritual aided the raising of power but that too strong or too much drink could cause the Witch to lose control. Some Witches have experimented with drugs.

5. *Dancing.* Witches join hands and dance around the magic circle, speeding up the tempo until the power is at a peak. When the magic is released, they drop to the floor or ground.

6. *Blood control and use of cords.* Binding parts of the body with cords restricts blood flow and alters consciousness, which can facilitate the opening of the third eye for clairvoyance, and astral projection. Cords also are used in knot magic, which binds and releases magical power (see WITCH'S LADDER).

7. *Scourging.* Religious mystics have used flagellation for centuries. In Witchcraft, it ideally is light, slow and steady. Scourging is a milder form of blood control, for it draws blood away from the brain. Not all traditions of Witchcraft practice scourging. Its use in those that do has declined since the 1960s.

8. *The Great Rite.* Sex has been an integral part of magic and religious rites since ancient times. Ritual sexual intercourse between the high priest and high priestess of the coven is said to release tremendous magical power (see GREAT RITE). It requires keeping the mind focused on the purpose of the ritual and ideally releasing the magical power at the moment of climax. The Great Rite often is performed symbolically rather than in actuality.

For many Pagans and Witches, magic is a part of everyday life. The world itself is magical, as is the web of the cosmos. Not all Pagans and Witches practice the same types of magic. Some may prefer ceremonial magic, while others prefer folk magic, and still others prefer "eco-magic," based on natural earth energies and the resident "spirits of the land." Most are mindful of ethical responsibilities when practicing magic. Bringing harm to others is not only unethical, but brings harm to the magician as well. Magic is to be used for growth and betterment.

FURTHER READING:
Cavendish, Richard. *The Black Arts.* New York: Putnam, 1967.
Crowley, Aleister. *Magic in Theory and Practice.* 1929. Reprint, New York: Dover Publications, 1976.
Flint, Valerie I. J. *The Rise of Magic in Early Medieval Europe.* Princeton: Princeton University Press, 1991.
Harvey, Graham. *Contemporary Paganism: Listening People, Speaking Earth.* New York: New York University Press, 1997.
Luhrmann, T. M. *Persuasions of the Witch's Craft: Ritual Magic in Contemporary England.* Cambridge: Harvard University Press, 1989.
Malinowski, Bronislaw. *Magic, Science and Religion.* Garden City, N.Y.: Doubleday Anchor Books, 1948.
Seligmann, Kurt. *The Mirror of Magic.* New York: Pantheon Books, 1948.
Thomas, Keith. *Religion and the Decline of Magic.* New York: Charles Scribner's Sons, 1971.

magic circle   A sacred and purified space in which RITUALS, magical work and ceremonies are conducted. It offers a boundary for a reservoir of concentrated power and acts as a doorway to the world of the gods. The magic circle is an archetypal symbol of wholeness, perfection and unity; the creation of the cosmos; the womb of Mother Earth; the cycle of the seasons and birth-death-regeneration. Within the circle, it becomes possible to transcend the physical, to open the mind to deeper and higher levels of consciousness.

Circles have had a magical, protective significance since ancient times, when they were drawn around the beds of sick persons and mothers who had just given birth to protect them against DEMONS. The remnants of stone circles in Britain attest to the importance of the circle in ancient pagan rites.

Sacred circles used in contemporary PAGANISM and Witchcraft are derived from Western ceremonial magic. There are similarities, but some important differences.

In ceremonial magic, the circle represents a sacred space in which the magician conjures and commands DEMONS and spirits that are dangerous and difficult to control. The circle provides protection against them and must be cast carefully. The magician must never leave the circle during a ritual nor even inadvertently swing his arm outside it, lest a conjured demon grab him and strike him down, or something unpleasant happen.

GRIMOIRES and other magical teachings give detailed instructions for casting the circle with consecrated ritual TOOLS, such as a dagger, sword or wand, during certain astrological conditions and hours of the day or night. The circle is drawn on a floor that has been carefully cleaned; SALT may be sprinkled around its perimeter to reinforce the boundary.

The magician's circle is nine feet in diameter, or a double circle of eight feet within one of 10 feet. The circle is inscribed with magical symbols, words and NAMES OF POWER. In casting the circle, the magician moves DEOSIL, or clockwise, the motion of the sun, MOON and stars through the sky. For negative magic, the magician moves WIDDERSHINS, counterclockwise. He leaves a small opening, then steps inside, closing the opening very carefully to prevent unwanted presences from entering. The magician consecrates the circle with the four elements, Earth, Air, Water and Fire, and invokes the guardian spirits who watch over the four quarters of the sky (the cardinal points) and the four elements. The circle is entered in anticipation of uniting with the gods and the forces of nature in a harmonious relationship, not to conjure or

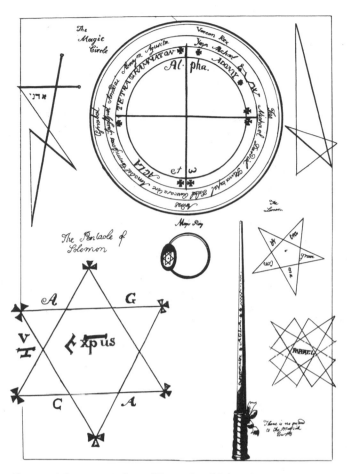

Ceremonial magic circle and Pentacle of Solomon (FRANCIS BARRETT, *THE MAGUS,* 1801)

control spirits. The deities are invited to witness and participate in the rites; all spirits are treated respectfully.

In contemporary Paganism and Witchcraft, circles are cast according to available space, size of group and purpose. They may be traced on a floor or measured out with cord, or may be established by walking the perimeter. Circles outdoors may not be perfect circles.

Negative energy is banished prior to casting a circle. In WICCA, it may be symbolically swept out with a broom by the high priestess. The consciousness of participants is prepared through meditation, visualization, breathing, drumming and other esoteric methods.

The altar and ritual tools—such as a wand, pentacle, censer, cauldron, scourge, athame, chalice, cords and other items—are placed inside the circle area. Witches and Pagans working alone may have fewer tools. Candles, stones or other objects are placed on the floor or ground at the four quarters, or cardinal points.

The circle is ritually cast DEOSIL with an athame, sword or wand. As the circle is cast, a field of psychic energy is visualized. The working space of the circle actually is a three-dimensional sphere. Participants are invited inside

through a gate, which is then closed. The circle is consecrated with the four elements or symbols of the elements. The guardians of the four quarters and elements, called the Lords of the Watchtowers (a Freemasonry term), or the Mighty Ones or the Guardians, are invoked. If the ritual takes place outdoors, nature spirits are invited to participate. God and Goddess are invoked through ritual. Offerings of food, stones, crystals, flowers and so on are made. The purpose of the ritual—such as magic working, a handfasting, or seasonal festival—is stated and the work is carried through. The circle may be opened at any time for exit or entry, then closed again. At the close of rites, food and drink is consecrated, offered to the deities, and shared by all (see CAKES-AND-WINE). As a final release of energy, the spirits and deities are bid farewell, candles are extinguished, and the circle is ritually banished. It is important to close a circle in order not to leave the ritual space psychically active.

Circles can be cast for protection, for example, to ward off psychic attack or protect a home against intruders. Magic circles do not last indefinitely; protective ones must be periodically recharged through ritual.

The term *circle* also refers to Wiccan or Pagan meetings. Some Wiccan covens offer *training circles* for individuals who are in training to become witches and be initiated into the coven.

The Four Quarters
Each cardinal point of the magic circle is associated with a guardian spirit, an element, ritual tool, colors and attributes; correspondences vary among traditions.

North. To ancient pagans, the north was the source of great power. The heavens spun around the North Star, and the ancients aligned their temples and pyramids to the star. North, the cardinal point never touched by the Sun, was associated with darkness, mystery and the unknown.

Perhaps because of the pagan reverence for the north, it became associated with the DEVIL in Christianity. Cemeteries were seldom placed on the north side of a church, which, if used for burial at all, was reserved for unbaptized children, criminals, reprobates and suicides. Many old churches throughout Europe and the British Isles have north doors called "the Devil's door," which were opened after baptisms in order to allow the exorcised demon to escape. Most of these doors have long since been bricked over. The reasons are obscure. Perhaps witches and pagans who were forced to or dared not attend church deliberately entered through the Devil's door. The clergy then blocked the doors in an effort to stamp out lingering paganism.

The north is associated with the element of Earth, the new phase of the Moon, the pentacle, secrecy and darkness, the colors gold or black and death and rebirth. Some traditions of the Craft align their altars to the north. In Masonry, the north represents the condition of the spiritually unenlightened.

East. The quarter of enlightenment, illumination, mysticism and the eternal. It corresponds to the element of Air, the athame or sword, the colors red or white. Traditionally the altar is aligned to the east. When a circle is cast, the high priestess or high priest leaves an opening, sometimes in the northeast portion, depending on the tradition, as the gate for other coveners to enter. The northeast is the symbolic dividing line between the path of darkness (north) and the path of light (east). In Masonry, the east represents mankind's highest and most spiritual consciousness.

South. Solar energy, the Sun, the element Fire, the colors blue or white, and the magic wand are associated with the south. This is the quarter of the will, the direction and channeling of the energy forces of nature and the psychic. South-running water has long been attributed with magical properties, and was used in medieval times by wise women and folk witches in preparing medicine and in anti-witchcraft spells. In Masonry, the south is the halfway meeting point between the spiritual intuition of the east and the rationality of the west. It represents the zenith of intellectuality, as the sun attains its zenith in the southern sky.

West. The quarter of Water, creativity, emotions, fertility and courage to face one's deepest feelings. It is associated with the chalice, the symbol of female creative power and fecundity, the after life, and the colors red or gray. In Masonry, it represents reason, common sense, and material-mindedness.

See CONE OF POWER; DRAWING DOWN THE MOON; ELEMENTS; WITCHES' TOOLS.

FURTHER READING:
Buckland, Raymond. *Buckland's Complete Book of Witchcraft.* St. Paul: Llewellyn Publications, 1986.
Crowley, Vivianne. *Wicca: The Old Religion in the New Millennium.* Revised ed. London: Thorsons/Harper Collins, 1996.
Green, Marian. *A Witch Alone: Thirteen Moons to Master Natural Magic.* London: Torsons/Harper Collins, 1991.
Starhawk. *The Spiral Dance.* Rev. ed. San Francisco: Harper-SanFrancisco, 1989.
Valiente, Doreen. *An ABC of Witchcraft Past and Present.* 1973. Reprint, Custer, Wash.: Phoenix Publishing, 1986.

maleficia   Malicious acts attributed to witches and sorcerers (see SORCERY) in times past that caused harm or death to humans, animals or crops. Since antiquity, witches, sorcerers and magicians have been said to cast negative SPELLS against others out of revenge, spite or malice. During the medieval witch-hunting craze, *maleficia* implied a DEVIL'S PACT and was used to explain virtually any natural disaster, accident, illness or personal misfortune.

Maleficia included damage to crops and illness or death to animals, as well as anything with a negative

Newsletter citing alleged maleficia *and execution of witch Anna Eberlehrin, Augsburg, 1669*

impact upon a person: loss of love, storms, insanity, disease, bad luck, financial problems, lice infestations, even death. Witch-hunters encouraged the blame of accidents and natural disasters upon witchcraft because it enabled them to round up suspects and get convictions.

If a villager muttered a threat or a wish for calamity upon someone and misfortune of any sort occurred to the victim—*maleficia.* If the local wise woman administered a remedy for an illness and the patient worsened or died—*maleficia.* If a hailstorm destroyed the crop, the cows wouldn't give milk or the horse went lame the cause was *maleficia.* In cases of disease, *maleficia* was especially suspect if an illness came on suddenly and violently or if a patient's condition deteriorated rapidly. *Maleficia* was definitely the cause if a priest administered holy ointment and the patient broke out in a sweat.

Witches were believed to effect *maleficia* through a variety of ways: incantations; powders, potions, OINTMENTS and herbs; effigies stuck with thorns and nails; or a HAND OF GLORY. *Maleficia* could be combatted with preventive witchcraft—CHARMS, powders and potions made from certain herbs such as sage or christianwort, and incantations.

Belief in, and the practice of, malefic magic still exists, especially in remote areas. In many cultures various AMULETS and charms are believed to protect one against evil in general, but specific CURSES must be removed with specific remedies, usually by another witch or sorcerer. In contemporary Witchcraft, however, such acts constitute a violation of ethics, which hold that witches should harm no living thing (see WICCAN REDE).

FURTHER READING:

Guazzo, Francesco Maria. *Compendium Maleficarum.* Secaucus, N.J.: University Books, 1974.

Russell, Jeffrey B. *A History of Witchcraft.* London: Thames and Hudson, 1980.

Malleus Maleficarum (The Witch Hammer)

A comprehensive witch-hunter's handbook, the most important treatise on prosecuting witches during the witch hysteria. Published first in Germany in 1486, the *Malleus Maleficarum* proliferated into dozens of editions throughout Europe and England and had a profound impact on European witch trials for about 200 years. MONTAGUE SUMMERS called it "among the most important, wisest, and weightiest books in the world." It was second only to the Bible in sales until John Bunyan's *Pilgrim's Progress* was published in 1678.

The *Malleus Maleficarum* was written by two Dominican inquisitors, Heinrich Kramer and James Sprenger. The two men were empowered by Pope INNOCENT VIII in his Bull of December 9, 1484, to prosecute witches throughout northern Germany. The papal edict was intended to quell Protestant opposition to the INQUISITION and to solidify the case made in 1258 by Pope Alexander IV for the prosecution of witches as heretics. It was the opinion of the church that the secular arm, the civil courts, was not punishing enough witches solely on the basis of MALEFICIA. The effect of both the bull and the *Malleus Maleficarum* spread far beyond Germany, its greatest influence being felt in France and Italy and, to a lesser extent, in England. It was adopted by both Protestant and Catholic civil and ecclesiastical judges.

The full biographies of Kramer and Sprenger are not known, but it is evident that they distinguished themselves in their ecclesiastical careers. Sprenger, born sometime between 1436 and 1438 in Basel, rose rapidly in the Dominican order and was named prior and regent of studies of the Cologne Convent. In 1488 he was named provincial of the Province of Germany.

Kramer was born in Schlettstadt in Lower Alsace (date unknown) and also rose rapidly to become prior of the Dominican House in his hometown. In 1474 he was appointed inquisitor for the provinces of Tyrol, Bohemia, Salzburg and Moravia. There he employed fraudulent tactics to frame people as witches, and subsequently tortured them. The Bishop of Brixen expelled him.

Both men were prolific writers, and by 1485 Kramer drafted a comprehensive manuscript on witchcraft, which was absorbed into the *Malleus Maleficarum*. The book is based generally on the biblical pronouncement. "Thou shall not suffer a witch to live" (Exodus 22:18) and draws on the works of Aristotle, the Scriptures, St. Augustine and St. THOMAS AQUINAS. It maintains that because God acknowledged witches, to doubt witchcraft is in itself heresy.

Karmer in particular exhibited a virulent hatred toward women witches and advocated their extermination. The *Malleus* devotes an entire chapter to the sinful weakness of women, their lascivious nature, moral and intellectual inferiority and gullibility to guidance from deceiving spirits. In Kramer's view, women witches were out to harm all of Christendom.

Scholars have debated the reasons for Kramer's misogyny; he may have had a fear of the power of women mystics of his day, such as Catherine of Siena, who enjoyed the attentions of royalty as well as the church.

The *Malleus Maleficarum* is divided into three parts, each of which raises questions and purports to answer them through opposing arguments. Part I concerns how the DEVIL and his witches, with "the permission of Almighty God," perpetrate a variety of evils upon men and animals, including tempting them with succubi and incubi; instilling hatred; obstructing or destroying fertility; and the metamorphosis of men into beasts. It is

The Malleus Maleficarum *portrayed witches as evil women whose supernatural powers came from the Devil*

the premise of the authors that God permits these acts; otherwise, the Devil would have unlimited power and destroy the world.

Part II discusses how witches cast spells and bewitchments and do their *maleficia* and how these actions may be prevented or remedied. Emphasis is given to the DEVIL'S PACT, considered a key to proving heresy. The existence of witches and their *maleficia* is treated as unassailable fact, and wild stories are presented as truth. Most of the stories of SPELLS, pacts, the SACRIFICE of children and copulation with the Devil came from the inquisitions conducted by Sprenger and Kramer and from material of other ecclesiastical writers on witchcraft.

Part III sets forth the legal procedures for trying witches, including the taking of testimony, admission of evidence, procedures for interrogation and TORTURE and guidelines for sentencing. Judges are instructed to allow hostile witnesses on the reasoning that everyone hated witches. Torture is dealt with matter-of-factly; if the accused did not voluntarily confess, even after a year or so in prison, then torture was to be applied as an incentive. Judges are permitted to lie to the accused, promising them mercy if they confess—it is all done in the best interests of society and the state. The *Malleus* provides for light sentences of penance and imprisonment in certain cases, but the acknowledged purpose of the authors was to execute as many witches as possible, and most of the instructions on sentencing pertain to death.

Some questions are never clearly answered, and contradictions abound. For example, the authors say that the Devil, through witches, afflicts mostly good and just people; they later say that only the wicked are vulnerable. At one point, judges are said to be immune to the bewitchments of witches; at another, the authors assert that witches cast spells over judges with the glance of an eye, and judges are admonished to protect themselves with SALT and sacraments.

The success of the *Malleus Maleficarum* was immediate in Europe. Fourteen editions were published by 1520; another 16 editions appeared by 1669. It became the guidebook by which inquisitors and judges conducted themselves and which subsequent writers used as a foundation for their own works. The book was important in the way it linked witchcraft to heresy.

In England, the book was slower to catch on, perhaps because of the independence of the English Anglican Church. Foreign-language editions surfaced in libraries and among scholars, but no English edition appeared until 1584. Nevertheless, Protestant writers absorbed the material into their own writings. The emphasis in English witchcraft trials was less on heresy and more on *maleficia*.

Kramer and Sprenger piously maintained that God would never permit an innocent person to be convicted of witchcraft. Yet their collaboration, the *Malleus Maleficarum*, provided the blueprint for condemning thousands of innocent people to horrific torture and death.

FURTHER READING:
Barstow, Anne Llewellyn. *Witchcraze: A New History of the European Witch Hunts*. San Francisco: Pandora/Harper Collins, 1994.
Herzig, Tamar. "Witches, Saints and Heretics: Heinrich Kramer's Ties with Italian Women Mystics." *Magic, Ritual and Witchcraft,* vol. 1, no. 1 (Summer 2006): pp. 24–55.
Lea, Henry Charles. *Materials Toward a History of Witchcraft*. Philadelphia: University of Pennsylvania, 1939.
Summers, Montague, ed. *The Malleus Maleficarum of Heinrich Kramer and James Sprenger.* 1928. Reprint, New York: Dover Publications, 1971.
Trevor-Roper, H. R. *The European Witch-Craze.* New York: Harper & Row, 1957.

mandrake   A poisonous perennial herb that grows in the Mediterranean region and that is reputed to have powerful magical properties. Mandrake, part of the nightshade family, has a strong and unpleasant odor. It is highly toxic, though it is used in therapeutic remedies and as an aphrodisiac in love PHILTRES. The magic attributed to mandrake is due to the shape of its thick root, which looks like a man or woman, or sometimes a phallus, and to the phosphorescent glow of its berries in the light dawn. In folklore, a *mandragoras*, a demon spirit resembling a little man with no beard, dwelled in the plant.

According to lore, mandrake shrinks at the approach of a person. Touching it can be fatal. If uprooted, it shrieks and sweats BLOOD, and whoever pulls it out dies in agony. It is safely harvested by digging around all but a small portion of the root, tying a dog to it and leaving. The dog strangles itself pulling out the root in an attempt to follow its master. The death of the dog gives the mandrake root the power to protect against DEMONS. The root also is believed to prophesy the future by shaking its head in answer to questions.

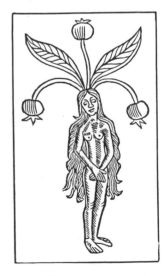

Male and female mandrakes (JOHANNES DE CUBA, *HORTUS SANITATIS*)

In ancient Greece, mandrake was called the plant of CIRCE, the witch goddess who made a juice of the root and used it to transform Odysseus' men into swine. In Greece and Rome it was used medicinally as an anesthetic before cauterization and surgery.

Medieval witches were said to harvest the root at night beneath gallows trees—trees where unrepentant criminals, evil since birth, were supposed to have died. The root purportedly sprang up from the criminal's body drippings. According to Christian lore, the witch washed the root in wine and wrapped it in silk and velvet. She fed it with sacramental wafers stolen from a church during communion, which placed witches in the DEVIL's camp.

Mandrake is reputed to be an aphrodisiac and a fertility pill and is known as *love apples*. In Genesis, the barren Rachel, wife of Jacob, ate mandrake root in order to conceive Joseph. Mandrake is given to women to ensure large families of boys; Arab men wear the root as an AMULET to enhance virility.

FURTHER READING:
de Givry, Emile Grillot. *Witchcraft, Magic and Alchemy.* 1931. Reprint, New York: Dover Publications, 1971.

Martello, Dr. Leo Louis (1931–2000)

American witch, hypnotist, graphologist and activist for civil and gay rights. Leo Louis Martello became a prominent figure in the new Witchcraft of the 1960s until his retirement in the 1990s. Martello was a colorful figure, known for his humor. He kept a boa constrictor beneath his bed.

Martello, who claimed a Sicilian witch heritage, was born in Dudley, Massachusetts, the son of a Sicilian immigrant who owned a farm. He was raised in Worcester and Southbridge. Baptized a Catholic, he was packed off to Catholic boarding school for six years, which he later said were the worst years of his life. He had psychic experiences early in life and in his teens began studying palmistry and the tarot with a Gypsy. By age 16, he was making radio appearances giving handwriting analyses and selling articles.

Martello was educated at Assumption College in Worcester, Massachusetts, and Hunter College and the Institute for Psychotherapy, both in New York City. After moving to New York at age 18 he learned about his ancestral heritage from cousins who said they had been watching him for years for his potential in the Old Religion. He bore a striking resemblance to his paternal grandmother, Maria Concetta, who was renowned in her hometown of Enna, Sicily, as the local *strega,* whom people sought for help when the Catholic Church failed them. She was reputed to be a *jettatore,* one who has the ability to cast the EVIL EYE. She was said to have cursed a mafiosi to his death by heart attack after he beat up her husband and threatened him unless he paid monthly protection money. Secretly, Concetta was a high priestess of the Goddess of the Sikels, who were the founding inhabitants of Sicily.

Dr. Leo Louis Martello (COURTESY LEO LOUIS MARTELLO)

On September 26, 1951, Martello was initiated into his cousins' secret Sicilian coven and became a *mago,* a male Witch. The initiation involved a BLOOD oath to keep the secrets of the coven and its members.

In 1955 Martello was awarded a doctor of divinity degree by the National Congress of Spiritual Consultants. He became an ordained minister (Spiritual Independents, nonsectarian) and served as pastor of the Temple of Spiritual Guidance from 1955–60. He left that position to pursue his interests in Witchcraft, parapsychology, psychology and philosophy and no longer accepted the theology of the National Congress of Spiritual Consultants.

He also did work in hypnographology, the study of handwriting obtained under hypnotic age regression and worked professionally as a graphologist, analyzing handwriting for business clients. He was founder and director of the American Hypnotism Academy in New York from 1950 to 1954 and treasurer of the American Graphological Society from 1955 to 1957.

From 1964 to 1965 he lived in Tangier, Morocco, where he studied oriental Witchcraft. In 1969 shortly before publication of his first book on Witchcraft, *Weird Ways of Witchcraft,* Martello, with the permission of his coven, decided to go public as a witch, in order to promote the truth about Witchcraft. Subsequently, he contacted and was initiated into the Gardnerian, Alexandrian and traditionalist traditions. He was the first public witch to champion the establishment of legally incorporated, tax-exempt Wiccan churches, paid legal holidays for Witches and Wiccan civil rights activities and demonstrations.

In 1969, Martello played a leading role in the first demonstration of the Gay Liberation Front, held against the *Village Voice.*

To further these goals, Martello founded the Witches Liberation Movement and the Witches International Craft Association (WICA). In 1970, he launched publication of the *WICA Newsletter and Witchcraft Digest,* which had a circulation of about 3,500 by the mid-1980s.

Colorful and outspoken, Martello received much publicity in 1970 for his organization of a Witch-In in Central Park on Samhain (All Hallow's Eve). The city parks department at first refused to issue a permit for the Witch-In but relented after Martello secured the aid of the New York Civil Liberties Union and threatened to file a suit for discrimination against a minority religion. The Witch-In, attended by about 1,000 people, was filmed and made into a documentary. Martello then formed the Witches Anti-Defamation League (later renamed the Witches Anti-Discrimination Lobby), dedicated to ensuring Witches' religious rights. By the late 1980s, chapters of the league were established in every state in the United States.

He drafted a Witch Manifesto, which called for a National Witches Day Parade; the moral condemnation of the Catholic Church for its torture and murder of Witches during the Inquisition; a $500 million suit against the church for damages and reparations to the descendants of victims to be paid by the Vatican (see INQUISITION); and a $100 million suit against Salem, Massachusetts, for damages in the 1692 trials (see SALEM WITCHES). He foresaw that the Civil Rights Act of 1964 would enable the establishment of Witchcraft temples and churches.

Martello earned his living primarily as a writer, graphologist and lecturer. He made numerous public appearances to educate others about the Craft and to speak at major Pagan/Wiccan festivals and gatherings. He compared the Craft to an underground spring which has existed for centuries and predates the Judeo-Christian and Muslim faiths and occasionally rises to the surface in small streams and lakes. The modern Craft movement reflects a worldwide rising of this underground spring, coming with such force that it cannot be dammed by enemies. The spiritual force behind the renaissance is comprised of the reincarnated souls of those murdered as Witches by the Inquisition.

Martello defined a witch as a wise practitioner of the Craft, a Nature worshipper and a person who is in control of his or her life. He was of the opinion that too many people enter the Craft with hang-ups from their Judeo-Christian upbringing, and that there is too much emphasis on personalities in the broad neo-Pagan community. The Sicilian tradition teaches that a wrong must be rectified in this life and not left to karma in a future life. The Witch must not permit injustices. His own philosophy, as outlined in *How to Prevent Psychic Blackmail* (1966), was one of "Psychoselfism: sensible selfishness versus senseless self-sacrifice."

Martello's other books are *Witchcraft: The Old Religion; Black Magic, Satanism and Voodoo; Understanding the Tarot; It's Written in the Cards; It's Written in the Stars; Curses in Verses; Witches' Liberation and Practical Guide to Witch Covens; Your Pen Personality;* and *The Hidden World of Hypnotism.* He authored numerous articles. He was the first Witch in America to publish information about Sicilian Witchcraft. Martello was an elder of the Trinacrian Rose church and Grove in Somerville, Massachusetts. In the late 1990s, he retired from his public work. He died in June 2000, and his remains were cremated. Lori Bruno, an elder of Martello's tradition, was executrix of his estate.

FURTHER READING:
Bruno, Lori. "Dr. Leo Louis Martello Memorial Page." Available online. URL: http://templeofdianic.org/Leo.htm. Downloaded November 8, 2007.
"Dr. Leo Louis Martello (1931–2000)." The Witches' Voice. Available online. URL: http://www.witchvox.com/va/dt_va/html?a=usfl&c=homepages&id. Downloaded November 8, 2007.
Martello, Dr. Leo Louis. *Weird Ways of Witchcraft.* New York: HC Publishers, 1969.
———. *Witchcraft: The Old Religion.* Seacaucus, N.J.: University Books, 1973.

Mather, Cotton (1663–1728) Esteemed Puritan minister who helped to fuel witch panics in New England, including the SALEM WITCHES hysteria. "My Hearers will not expect from me an accurate *Definition* of the *vile Thing,*" the Reverend Cotton Mather stated once in a sermon on witchcraft, "since the Grace of God has given me the Happiness to speak without *Experience* of it. But from Accounts both by *Reading* and *Hearing* I have learn'd to describe it so." Thus did Cotton Mather admit his own limitations in dealing with a highly volatile subject.

The son of INCREASE MATHER, a Boston minister and president of Harvard University, Mather was a precocious student, unimpeded by a stutter he suffered. At age 12 he entered Harvard. By age 25 he had assumed a leadership role in his father's North Church in Boston. He viewed himself as one of those chosen by God to ensure the salvation of the Puritans, "a People of God settled in those, which were once the Devil's Territories."

He had an intense interest in the "dark side," including violent crime, the sins of drink, dance and cursing, natural disasters and hell, writing dozens of books on these and other objects over the course of his life. With his father, he investigated cases of alleged witchcraft and POSSESSION of young girls, avowing that prayer and fasting were the only methods of treatment.

Mather accepted without question the writings of WILLIAM PERKINS and others attesting to the existence and evil nature of witches. Even witches who professed to be "white witches" were in fact evil, Mather asserted, and used good deeds to wreak havoc later. As for proof of the existence of witches, Mather often cited references in the Bible, especially to the WITCH OF ENDOR, and the "evidence" amassed at English and European trials, including "voluntary" confessions. A confession, even if unsupported by evidence, was enough to convict, he said.

When witchcraft cases began cropping up in New England in the 1640s, Mather defended the trials and executions. He made his case against witches in *Memorable Providences Relating to Witchcrafts and Possessions,* published in 1689. The book laid the groundwork for the hysteria that was to result from the Salem witch trials in 1692.

Mather was appointed official chronicler of the trials by the colony's governor, Sir William Phips. Mather doubted the validity of spectral evidence, heavily relied upon in the trials, but did little to cool the rising hysteria beyond cautioning the judges. He encouraged identification and punishment of all witches.

Mather believed the Salem trials exposed the Devil's plot against New England: the Puritans were so righteous and virtuous as to enrage the DEVIL and drive him to try to destroy the community. He cited the CURSE of a New England witch, executed about 40 years earlier, who had announced that a "horrible plot" of witchcraft existed against the populace, which would threaten to pull down all the churches if not discovered. That plot, Mather said, was discovered and destroyed at Salem.

Mather attended the hanging of GEORGE BURROUGHS, one of the convicted "witches." Given the infallible test of reciting the LORD'S PRAYER perfectly, Burroughs did so, shaking the faith of the crowd in his conviction. Mather launched a savage, impromptu speech negating the prayer recital and convincing the crowd to carry on with the execution.

Mather's account of the trials, *On Witchcraft: Being the Wonders of the Invisible World,* appeared in 1693. He wrote it in stages, without the help of court documents (which did not arrive in his possession until most of the book was completed), relying instead on his own colored opinions.

When the public backlash to Salem occurred, Mather entrenched himself even deeper in his beliefs. The backlash was so great that Mather's father, Increase, was moved to speak out against the Salem trials, criticizing the spectral evidence and stating that it would be better to let 10 guilty witches go free than to punish one innocent person.

Cotton Mather, however, continued to fan the fires of hysteria. In September 1693 a Boston woman, Margaret Rule, claimed spectral evidence of witchcraft, and Mather declared she was telling the truth. A new panic broke out but was calmed by more reasoned voices.

Mather himself came under fire, most notably from Robert Calef, Boston merchant and author of the book, *Another Brand Pluckt Out of the Burning or More Wonders of*

Title page of the first edition of Wonders, *Boston, 1693*

the Invisible World. Calef presented caricatures of Cotton and Increase Mather as lecherous men who were titillated by young girls whose possessions had lewd overtones. No publisher in New England was willing to touch *More Wonders;* it finally appeared in 1700 in London and made its way back to the Colonies.

The backlash, the credulity of *Wonders* and the mockery of *More Wonders* helped to tarnish Mather's reputation. He was passed over several times for the presidency of Harvard, which left him bitter and prompted him to aid in the founding of Yale University.

Mather defended his views on witchcraft to the end of his life, by which time he was ignored by an increasingly skeptical public.

FURTHER READING:
Boyer, Paul, and Stephen Nissenbaum. *Salem Possessed: The Social Origins of Witchcraft.* Cambridge, Mass.: Harvard University Press, 1974.
Demos, John Putnam. *Entertaining Satan: Witchcraft and the Culture of Early New England.* New York: Oxford University Press, 1982.

Hansen, Chadwick. *Witchcraft at Salem.* New York: New American Library, 1969.

Karlsen, Carol F. *The Devil in the Shape of a Woman: Witchcraft in Colonial New England.* New York: W.W. Norton & Co, 1987.

Mather, Cotton. *On Witchcraft: Being the Wonders of the Invisible World.* Mt. Vernon, N.Y.: The Peter Pauper Press, 1950. First published 1692.

Starkey, Marion L. *The Devil in Massachusetts.* New York: Alfred Knopf, 1950.

Mather, Increase (1639–1723)   Illustrious Puritan minister and intellectual who viewed witchcraft and supernatural happenings as evidence of God's growing displeasure with New England. While his son, COTTON MATHER, became a strident witch-hunter, Increase Mather remained more cautious in evaluating cases and accusations.

Mather was the son of Richard Mather, an English Puritan minister who moved his family to New England in 1635 to escape persecution by the Church of England. Increase was born in Dorchester, Massachusetts. He graduated from Harvard University in 1656 and Trinity College in Dublin in 1658. He worked as a minister for the Church of England until 1661, when, like his father, he returned to Massachusetts for reasons of religious differences. He became pastor of the North Church in Boston and served as president of Harvard from 1685 to 1701.

Mather was an orthodox Puritan, believing firmly in strict fidelity to a covenant with God and strict obeyance of the laws set forth in the Bible. The beginnings of witchcraft cases in the colonies disturbed him; with Cotton, he investigated a number of alleged witchcraft and possession cases.

Mather attributed witchcraft to a decline in religion; he voiced this belief in *An Essay for the Recording of Illustrious Providences,* a collection of supernatural and witchcraft incidents and his views on the subjects in general. Published in 1684, the book was intended to warn people of the need to get their spiritual houses in order, reminding them that as Puritans and Pilgrims, they were players in a cosmic battle between God and Satan for control of the New World and, therefore, of the history of mankind. For reasons known only to God, the DEVIL was permitted to infest the world with legions of DEMONS to test the moral mettle of humans.

Providences immediately captured public interest—perhaps more for its accounts of the supernatural than its moral lectures—and became a best-seller, garnering numerous letters of praise from readers in New England and abroad.

Mather did nothing to prevent the tragedy of the Salem witch hunt (see SALEM WITCHES), but in the wake of the public backlash to the hysteria, he did speak out for greater caution in his *Cases of Conscience Concerning Evil Spirits Personating Men; Witchcrafts, Infallible Proofs of Guilt in such as are Accused with the Crime* (1693). While he acknowledged that spectral evidence alone was insufficient grounds for convicting accused witches, he supported the Salem convictions on the grounds that other, sufficient evidence was given: the testimony of neighbors and the fact that some of the afflicted girls were relieved of their fits when a concoction of rye paste, water and the HAIR AND NAIL clippings of the accused witches was mixed together and set afire. Mather did not personally attend any of the Salem trials except for that of GEORGE BURROUGHS. He would not have acquitted Burroughs, Mather said, because others testified to his diabolical activities.

See LITHOBOLIA OF NEW HAMPSHIRE.

FURTHER READING:

Boyer, Paul, and Stephen Nissenbaum. *Salem Possessed: The Social Origins of Witchcraft.* Cambridge, Mass.: Harvard University Press, 1974.

Demos, John Putnam. *Entertaining Satan: Witchcraft and the Culture of Early New England.* New York: Oxford University Press, 1982.

Hansen, Chadwick. *Witchcraft at Salem.* New York: New American Library, 1969.

Karlsen, Carol F. *The Devil in the Shape of a Woman: Witchcraft in Colonial New England.* New York: W.W. Norton & Co, 1987.

Mather, Increase. *An Essay for the Recording of Illustrious Providences.* Introduction by James A. Levernier. 1684. Reprint, Delmar, N.Y.: Scholars' Facsimiles and Reprints, 1977.

———. *Cases of Conscience Concerning Evil Spirits Personating Men; Witchcrafts, Infallible Proofs of Guilt in such as are Accused with that Crime.* Boston: 1693.

Starkey, Marion L. *The Devil in Massachusetts.* New York: Alfred Knopf, 1950.

Medea   In Greek mythology the "Wise One," a powerful witch who was the niece of the great witch CIRCE and a priestess of HECATE, the GODDESS of witchcraft and MAGIC. Herodotus called Medea the Great Goddess of the Aryan tribes of Parthia. Her magic, according to Pliny, controlled the Sun, Moon and stars.

Medea aided Jason, the adventurer who set out to get the Golden Fleece in order to win a kingdom in Greece that was rightfully his but had been taken over by Pelias. The Golden Fleece was possessed by the King of Colchis in Asia Minor. Medea was his daughter. When Jason and his band of Argonauts appeared, Medea fell madly in love with Jason and helped him win the Golden Fleece.

Medea's father set what he thought was an impossible task for Jason: he could have the fleece if he yoked two bulls with bronze hooves and flaming breath, plowed a field and sowed it with dragon's teeth. The teeth would spring immediately into an army of fierce warriors, all of whom had to be slain.

Medea prepared a magic OINTMENT that made Jason and his men invulnerable for a day. The task was accomplished. Then Medea bewitched the serpent who guarded the Golden Fleece, and she and Jason stole it and, with the Argonauts, fled to Greece. To delay the pursuit of her father, Medea cut the throat of her brother and scattered pieces of his dismembered corpse after them. Jason promised to marry her.

In Greece, they discovered that Pelias had forced Jason's father to kill himself, and Jason's mother had died of grief. Once again, Jason turned to Medea for witchcraft so that he could have revenge. Medea demonstrated her magical powers of rejuvenation by cutting up an old ram and boiling it while she recited incantations. A young lamb sprang up out of the CAULDRON. Medea convinced Pelias' daughters to cut him up so that she could make him young again. This they did, but she vanished without saying the necessary magic words.

Jason and Medea were forced to go to Corinth in exile, where they had two sons. Then Jason fell in love with the daughter of the King of Corinth and married her. Betrayed and enraged, Medea gave the princess a gift of a poisoned robe, and the girl burst into flames as soon as she put it on. Medea killed her two sons and escaped in a dragon-drawn chariot.

Medea was made immortal by Hera, and in Elysium, the afterworld of heroes, she became the wife of Achilles.

megaliths   Large stone structures and groups of standing stones erected in places around the world and believed to have religious or sacred significance or be associated with pagan rites. The term *megaliths* means "great stones" and is derived from the Greek *megas* ("great") and *lithos* ("stone"). Megaliths include any structure made up of large stones, but the term generally refers to those tombs and circular standing structures built in certain parts of North and South America, Asia, Africa, Australia, and Europe.

Who built these structures, how they were built, and for what purposes are questions that have few certain answers. The most widely accepted view is that they were built by Neolithic and early Bronze Age peoples who used them for religious purposes and burial sites and as astronomical observatories for the Sun and other celestial bodies. Special powers have been attributed to megaliths.

Classifications. Megaliths fall into two broad classifications: dolmens and menhirs. Dolmens, also called chambered tombs, usually contained one or more stone-built chambers or rooms where the dead were laid out. Some tombs were long while others were passage-graves, or round tombs with stone passages leading to one or more central rooms. Long tombs are common in parts of Wales, Scotland and England. Passage-graves are most commonly found in Ireland and western parts of Britain. Some tombs are covered with earth, forming mounds or tumuli.

Dolmens apparently served as either tombs of collective graves, in which some remains have been found, or as temples for the dead, in which no human remains have been found. The uncovering of bone shards at some sites has led to the theory that sacrificial rites, even cannibalism, might have taken place. Scholars hold that prehistoric man probably believed that the body's spirit lived in the head; therefore, breaking the head might have been an attempt to free the spirits of the dead. Some investigators believe that the tombs were more than burial sites and were used for religious, social and community gatherings as well.

Menhirs consist of single standing stones and groups of standing stones, sometimes arranged in circles, called cromlechs and henges. The menhirs at AVEBURY, England, form long avenues. Henges are circular arrangements distinguished by a bank or ditch surrounding them, and have one or more entrances. The most famous henge is Stonehenge in Wiltshire, England.

The greatest and oldest of all megalithic remains are the 3,000 menhirs and dolmens at Carnac, Brittany, France. It is believed that the stones originally numbered at least 11,000. One dolmen, covered by a tumulus, has been dated at 4700 B.C.E. The largest single stone is the 350-ton Fairy Stone, originally 20 feet high but now lying in pieces on its side at the end of a Neolithic burial site. It may have been felled by lightning or an earthquake. Astronomical calculations show the Carnac megaliths may have been designed for astronomical observations.

Supernatural powers of megaliths. Standing stones were believed to have the power to heal or hurt. Holed stones required that the ill person climb through the hole to be restored to health. Women hugged stones to stimulate fertility or make a wish come true. The famous Men-an-Tol group of standing stones in Cornwall, England, includes a five-foot-high holed stone that has been reputed for centuries to have healing properties. The stone is nicknamed "The Devil's Eye" and stands between two phallic-shaped boulders. In earlier times, sick children were passed through the hole nine times against the Sun to cure them of their illnesses. Women desiring children passed themselves through the hole, as did the sick who wished to be cured.

FAIRIES were said to inhabit some stones and people left gifts to curry favor with them. Many large, solitary black menhirs have DEVIL legends associated with them.

STONES reputed to have supernatural forces are associated with witches, who were said to practice the occult arts as they gathered around them. In the 1596 trial of the Aberdeen witches of Scotland, the accused confessed to dancing around a gray stone at the foot of Craigleauch hill. The Hoar Stones in Britain's Pendle Forest were said to be the gathering site of the Lancashire witches in the 17th century. Another such site is the Bambury Stone of Bredon Hill. The ROLLRIGHT STONES of the Cotswolds, England, continued to be used as a nocturnal meeting place of witches into modern times.

Other stones were thought to have Earth forces emanating from them. Some psychics fear being near stones after dark because their strange powers disturb them.

Psychic researchers have felt sensations like electric shocks when placing their hands on them, powerful enough to knock them over. Others report feeling tingling and giddiness. Photographs show light radiations emanating from the stones. In dowsing, these forces indicate the source of hidden underground water.

Some stones were believed to move in search of water and even dance. Legends are associated with some stones that brought harm to people who had uprooted them, and the stones themselves are said to be the petrified remains of people who were punished for dancing or playing on the Sabbath.

FURTHER READING:

Burl, Aubrey. *Rites of the Gods.* London: J.M. Dent & Sons Ltd., 1981.

———. *Rings of Stone.* New York: Ticknor & Fields, 1979.

Merlin   Archetypal WIZARD of Arthurian lore. Merlin is a Latinized version of the Welsh Myrddin. His exact origins are lost in myth; he may have been a god, perhaps a version of Mabon or Maponos, the British Apollo, the divine ruler or guardian of Britain. The name *Merlin* may have been given to a succession of wizards. There is no concrete evidence, but it is likely that a Merlin, who was a prophet or a bard, existed toward the end of the fifth century and has become the basis for the Merlin myths.

Merlin's first appearance in literature occurs in the Latin works of Geoffrey of Monmouth, a 12th-century Welsh cleric. *The Prophecies of Merlin,* written in the early 1130s, comprise verses of prophecies made by an alleged man of the fifth century, named Merlin. Monmouth made up many of the prophecies, which stretched beyond the 12th century. In the *History of the Kings of Britain,* which Monmouth finished around 1135–36 and which laid the foundation for the Arthurian legends, Merlin becomes a character, though Monmouth muddles chronology by placing him in both the fifth and sixth centuries. He is a magical boy, born of a union between a mortal woman and a spirit (a *daemon,* which later Christian writers interpreted as the DEVIL). He has great magical powers of prophecy and matures quickly. Merlin uses MAGIC to bring great stones from Ireland to the Salisbury Plain for the building of STONEHENGE and arranges for King Uther Pendragon to seduce Ygerna, who bears the infant Arthur. At that point, Arthur vanishes from Monmouth's story. He reappears in a third poetic work, *The Life of Merlin,* in which he has a sister, Ganieda, who also has prophetic vision. *Vita Merlini,* written by Monmouth around 1150, is a biography of the adult Merlin, but it is also a text of Western magical and spiritual enlightenment. It sets down oral lore of mythology, cosmography, cosmology, natural history, psychology and what are now called archetypes of the human personality.

In 1150 a French poetical version of *History of the Kings of Britain* has Arthur constructing his Round Table under the aegis of Merlin. The best-known portrait of Merlin

Merlin and Viviane in the Forest of Broceliande (EARLY 15TH-CENTURY BOOK COVER)

comes from Sir Thomas Malory's *Le Morte d'Arthur,* published in 1485, a romantic tale in which the infant Arthur is raised by Merlin. Upon the death of Uther Pendragon, Merlin presents the youth Arthur to the knights of the land and has him prove he is heir to the throne by withdrawing the sword Excalibur from the stone in which it is imbedded. Merlin serves as Arthur's magical adviser but disappears from the story early in Arthur's reign. He is brought down by his passion for Nimue, or Viviane, a damsel of the lake who tricks him into revealing the secret of constructing a magical tower of air, which she uses to imprison him.

In contemporary fiction, Merlin usually is presented as a wise old man, despite his youthfulness in early writings. It may be said that he has three aspects: youth, the mature prophet and the wise elder. He has been subject to many interpretations: magician, mystic, shaman, lord of the earth and animals, seer of all things, embodiment of time and trickster. He appears in the form of Mr. Spock of *Star Trek* and Obi Wan Kenobe of *Star Wars*.

FURTHER READING:

Matthews, John, ed. *At the Table of the Grail.* 1984. Reprint, London: Arkana, 1987.

———. *An Arthurian Reader.* Wellingborough, England: The Aquarian Press, 1988.

metamorphosis   The ability of witches, sorcerers (see SORCERY) and other magically empowered persons to transform themselves and other humans at will into animals, birds and insects. In witchcraft trials, people testified that the accused witches had appeared before them or tormented them in some nonhuman shape. For example, in 1663 Jane Milburne of Newcastle, England, did not invite Dorothy Strangers to her wedding supper. Consequently, Milburne alleged, Strangers transformed herself into a CAT and appeared with several other mysterious cats to plague Milburne.

In another English witchcraft case in 1649, John Palmer of St. Albans confessed that he had metamorphosed into a TOAD in order to torment a young man with whom he had had a quarrel. As a toad, Palmer waited for the man in a road. The man kicked the toad. After he returned to the shape of a man, Palmer then complained about a sore shin and bewitched his victim. In areas where witchcraft fears ran high, the sight of nearly any hare or stray dog caused great concern.

Witches were said to transform themselves as they rose up their chimneys on poles and broomsticks to fly off to SABBATS. The most common forms were hegoat, wolf, cat, dog, cow, hare, OWL and bat. Some witches believed that they had done this, perhaps as the result of the hallucinogenic ingredients in some of the OINTMENTS they rubbed on themselves. In 1562 alchemist Giovanni Batista Porta, in his book, *Natural Magick,* told of how hallucinogenic potions caused two men to believe they had metamorphosed into a fish and a goose, respectively:

> . . . the man would seem sometimes to be changed into a fish; and flinging out his arms, would swim on the Ground; sometimes he would seem to skip up, and then dive down again. Another would believe himself turned into a Goose, and would eat Grass, and beat the Ground with his Teeth, like a Goose: now and then sing, and endeavor to clap his Wings.

ISOBEL GOWDIE, a Scottish woman who voluntarily confessed to witchcraft in 1662, said she and her sister witches used incantations to transform themselves into hares, cats, crows and other animals. Sometimes they were bitten by hunting dogs.

Witches were said to use metamorphosis to gain easy entry into a household, in order to cast an evil spell upon an unsuspecting person. An insect crawling on the floor, or a mouse skittering through the door, might be suspect.

Witches also allegedly transformed themselves in order to escape captors. According to one story, a husband tried to prevent his witch wife from attending a sabbat and tied her to the bed with ropes. She changed into a bat and flew off. Another story tells of a witch brought before inquisitors in Navarre in 1547, who was able to smuggle along her magic ointment. She rubbed herself down and turned into a screech owl, escaping certain death.

To torment or punish other humans, witches and sorcerers turned them into beasts. In Greek myth, the sorceress CIRCE turned Ulysses' men into swine. In folktales, wicked sorcerers and witches turned people into frogs or other creatures, who had to wait for the right person to come along and break the evil SPELL.

Demons riding to sabbat (ULRICH MOLITOR, *VON DEN UNHOLDEN ODER HEXEN,* 1489)

One of the most feared metamorphoses was that of wolf. Man-eating wolves who terrorized villages were sometimes said to be witches. The man-wolf condition known as LYCANTHROPY, however, is not the same as metamorphosis, since it is involuntary. According to one 17th-century French tale, a hunter was attacked in the woods by an enormous wolf and was able to cut off one of its paws. Howling, the wolf fled. The hunter took the paw to show to a friend. When he took it from his pocket, he was astonished to see that it had changed into a woman's hand with a ring on one finger, which he recognized as belonging to his wife. He sent for his wife, who was missing one hand. She confessed to being a witch and transforming herself into a wolf in order to attend a sabbat. She was burned at the stake. Another version of the same tale has the wife admitting to lycanthropy.

In 1573 Gilles Garnier, an accused wizard of Lyons, France, was condemned to be burned alive for turning himself into a wolf and attacking and killing children, whom he devoured.

Some demonologists such as JEAN BODIN and Joseph Glanvil accepted metamorphosis as fact, but others denounced it as fallacy. The MALLEUS MALEFICARUM (1486), the leading inquisitor's guide, upheld the latter view, citing saints Augustine and THOMAS AQUINAS as saying that metamorphoses were illusions created by the DEVIL and DEMONS. Such illusions, said authors Heinrich Kramer and James Sprenger, were the result of God punishing some nation for sin. They pointed to verses from the Bible: Leviticus 26, "If ye do not my commandments, I will send the beasts of the field against you, who shall consume you and your flocks," and Deuteronomy 32, "I will also send the teeth of the beasts upon them." As to man-eating wolves, Kramer and Sprenger said they were true wolves possessed by demons. If a person believed himself to have turned into a wolf, it was the result of a witch's illusory SPELL.

INCREASE MATHER called metamorphosis "fabulous" and wondered in awe at the stories that were believed. In *An Essay for the Recording of Illustrious Providences* (1684), Mather says:

> But it is beyond the power of all the Devils in Hell to cause such a transformation; they can no more do it than they can be Authors of a true Miracle. . . . Though I deny not but that the Devil may so impose upon the imagination of Witches so as to make them believe that they are transmuted into Beasts.

Mather recounts a story of a woman who was imprisoned on suspicion of witchcraft and claimed to be able to transform herself into a wolf. The magistrate promised not to have her executed, in case she would turn into a wolf before him. The witch rubbed her head, neck and armpits with an ointment and fell into a deep sleep for three hours. She could not be roused by "noises or blows." When she awakened, she claimed that she had turned into a wolf, gone a few miles away and killed a sheep and a cow. The magistrate investigated and discovered that a sheep and cow in the location described by the witch had indeed been killed. It was evident that the Devil "did that mischief" and that the witch had merely experienced the dreams and delusions created by Satan.

In SHAMANISM, shamans metamorphose (shape-shift) into their guardian animal spirits or power animals (animals from whom they derive their chief power). The shape-shifting is done in an altered state of consciousness.

FURTHER READING:
Baroja, Julio Caro. *The World of the Witches.* 1961. Reprint, Chicago: University of Chicago Press, 1975.

Guazzo, Francesco Maria. *Compendium Maleficarum.* Secaucus, N.J.: University Books, 1974.

Remy, Nicolas. *Demonolatry.* Secaucus, N.J.: University Books, 1974.

Summers, Montague, ed. *The Malleus Maleficarum of Heinrich Kramer and James Sprenger.* 1928. Reprint, New York: Dover Publications, 1971.

mirrors   One of the most ancient forms of DIVINATION is *crystallomancy* or *catoptromancy*, performed with a magic mirror. The Magi of Persia are said to have used mirrors, as well as the ancient Greeks and Romans. In ancient Greece, the witches of Thessaly wrote their oracles in human BLOOD upon mirrors. The Thessalian witches are supposed to have taught Pythagoras how to divine by holding a magic mirror up to the MOON. Romans who were skilled in mirror reading were called *specularii*.

In lore, mirrors are believed to reflect the soul and must be guarded against lest the soul be lost. These fears carry over into superstitious customs, such as covering the mirrors in a house after death to prevent the souls of the living from being carried off by the ghost of the newly departed; and removing mirrors from a sickroom because the soul is more vulnerable in times of illness (see GHOSTS, HAUNTINGS AND WITCHCRAFT). According to another superstition, if one looks into a mirror at night, one will see the DEVIL. In Russian folklore, mirrors are the invention of the Devil, having the power to draw souls out of bodies. The Aztecs used mirrorlike surfaces to keep witches away. A bowl of water with a knife in it was placed in the entrances of homes. A witch looking into it would see her soul pierced by the knife, and flee. According to another belief, witches have no souls, and therefore, like vampires, have no reflections in mirrors.

Medieval and Renaissance magicians often used mirrors, bowls of water, polished STONES and crystals for divination, to see the past, present and future. Village WIZARDS frequently employed mirrors to detect thieves. Whatever the purpose, the magicians would stare into the polished surface until they hypnotized themselves into light trances and saw visions that answered the questions that were put to them. John Dee, England's royal court magician in the 16th century, employed both a crystal egg and a mirror made of polished black obsidian, reportedly taken from Mexico by Cortés. Cagliostro used mirrors, as did the famous 16th-century occultist Agrippa.

According to one legend, Cartaphilus, the Wandering Jew, asked Agrippa in 1525 to produce a vision of his dead childhood sweetheart in his mirror. Agrippa asked the man to count off the decades since the girl had died, and waved his magic wand at each count. Cartaphilus kept counting far beyond the girl's death. At 149, Agrippa felt dizzy but told him to keep counting. Finally, at 1,150, a vision appeared of the girl in ancient Palestine. Cartaphilus called out to her—in disobedience to Agrippa's admonitions—and the vision dissolved. Cartaphilus fainted. Later, he told Agrippa he was the Jew who had struck Christ as he carried the cross and was condemned to wander the earth.

European royalty believed in and used magic mirrors. Catherine de' Medici, a devout believer in the occult arts, had a mirror that revealed to her the future of France. Henri IV also relied on a magic mirror to discover political plots against him.

The medieval magician Albertus Magnus recorded a formula for making a magic mirror: Buy a looking glass and inscribe upon it "S. Solam S. Tattler S. Echogordner Gematur." Bury it at a CROSSROADS during an uneven hour. On the third day, go to the spot at the same hour and dig it up—but do not be the first person to gaze into the mirror. In fact, said Magnus, it is best to let a dog or a cat take the first look.

See SCRYING.

FURTHER READING:
Cavendish, Richard, ed. in chief. *Man, Myth & Magic: The Illustrated Encyclopedia of Mythology, Religion and the Unknown.* New York: Marshall Cavendish, 1983.
de Givry, Emile Grillot. *Witchcraft, Magic and Alchemy.* 1931. Reprint, New York: Dover Publications, 1971.
Opie, Iona, and Moira Tatem. *A Dictionary of Superstitions.* New York: Oxford University Press, 1989.

money   In folklore, money that comes from FAIRIES, witches, sorcerers (see SORCERY) and the DEVIL turns out to be worthless. The victim accepts payment for goods or services and discovers, after it is too late, that the gold coins or currency are actually TOADS, cat claws, shells, lead or other worthless—and sometimes repulsive—objects.

According to legend, Paracelsus, the 16th-century Swiss alchemist, roamed about Europe penniless during his last years, paying innkeepers with gold coins that turned into seashells after he departed. Belief in illusory money parallels another folk belief that livestock purchased unwittingly from witches and fairies would disappear or metamorphose into something undesirable: cows would dissolve in running water, horses would turn into pigs, and so forth.

FURTHER READING:
Evans-Wentz, W. Y. *The Fairy-Faith in Celtic Countries.* 1911. Reprint, Secaucus, N.J.: University Books, 1966.

Moon   Since ancient times, the Moon has been associated with woman and her fertility, monthly cycle, powers of nurturing and powers of darkness. The Moon, ruler of the night and the mysteries of the dark, represents wetness, moisture, intuition, emotion, tides, the psychic, moods and madness. It embodies time, for its phases provided humankind with the first calendar. In contemporary Witchcraft, the Moon is the source of Witches' power, drawn down from the sky; it is the worker of MAGIC. The Great GODDESS, the Mother Goddess, the All-Dewy-One, is at her most formidable and potent as lunar deity.

In the earliest primitive times, the Moon was viewed as the source of fertility of all things. Its light was considered indispensable for abundant harvests, large flocks and herds and human fecundity. It was believed that women were made pregnant by moonbeams. Women who desired children slept under the light of the Moon; those who did not resorted to crude CHARMS, such as rubbing their bellies with spittle to avoid swelling like the waxing of the Moon.

Since antiquity, lunar phases have governed all facets of life. The waxing Moon is auspicious for crop planting and new endeavors, for luck and increasing; the waning Moon is a time of diminishing and destruction. Lunar phases have governed magical rituals for the creation and consecration of magical tools, the summoning of spirits, the preparations of remedies and charms and the castings of SPELLS. One cut one's HAIR AND NAILS, entered into marriages and business arrangements, let blood and traveled according to the phases of the moon. The Moon was believed to govern the humors, the moisture in the body and brain. In 1660 one English astrologer declared that children born at the full Moon would never be healthy but ran the risk of moonstruck madness, or lunacy. Folklore beliefs about the Moon persist to the present day. The Moon still influences magic rites.

The cycle of woman's menstruation is tied to the lunar phases. In many cultures, the words for "Moon" and "menstruation" are the same or very similar (see BLOOD).

The Moon as person and deity. The Moon was primarily a power and a force until about 2600 B.C.E., when it became personified in Middle Eastern civilizations as the Man in the Moon or the Great Man. During his waning, the Man in the Moon was eaten by a dragon and went down into the underworld. He rose anew as his son. The Moon also was believed to incarnate on Earth as a king; some lines of kings claimed to be the representatives of the Moon and wore horned headdresses. Eventually, the Man in the Moon was replaced by the deity of the Moon, who was first a god, then a goddess. The lunar goddess was the Great Goddess, the giver of all things in her waxing phase

Witches and their cat familiars enjoy the full moon (OLD WOODCUT)

and the destroyer of all things in her waning phase. She took on the fertilizing power of the Moon and was the protector of women. As destroyer, she could bring storms, particularly heavy rains, and floods.

The lunar gods and goddesses were portrayed with crescent moons, the auspicious symbol of the waxing and lucky Moon. The Great Goddess was associated with the Cow, goat and bull, whose horns represented the crescent or horned Moon.

To the Greeks, the goddess SELENE once was the sole lunar goddess. Selene was replaced by Artemis (DIANA) and HECATE. The true power of the Moon resided in Hecate, who ruled the waning and dark Moon, the time when the Moon slipped into the underworld and ghosts and spirits walked the earth. Hecate became known as the Three-Headed Hecate, whose triple aspects combined Selene, Artemis and Hecate. The witches of Thessaly were said to be able to draw down the power of the Moon from the sky. In myth, Aphrodite taught her son, Jason, "how to draw down the dark moon" whenever he needed magic.

The Moon in Witchcraft. In contemporary Witchcraft, worship of the Goddess is associated with the Moon. The consort of the Goddess is the HORNED GOD, the god of the woodlands, whose horns represent both the beasts of nature and the horned Moon. The activities and magic workings of a Witch or COVEN are timed according to the phases of the Moon. Most covens meet at the full Moon; some also meet at the new Moon. The Moon is personified by a triple aspect of the Goddess, usually Diana (the Roman name is more common than the Greek name, Artemis), the Virgin, who rules the new and waxing Moon; Selene, the Matron, who rules the full Moon; and Hecate, the Crone, who rules the waning and dark Moon. Magic for healing, gain, luck and increase is done during the waxing Moon. Magical power is greatest on nights of the full moon, particularly at midnight. Magic for binding, banishing and eliminating is done during the waning phase.

The power of the Moon also is drawn down for a trance ritual called DRAWING DOWN THE MOON, in which the high priestess invokes the spirit of the Goddess into her so that She may speak to her followers.

Some feminist witches have a ritual of howling at the Moon in order to connect with the primitive power of the Goddess within.

The Moon is associated with the metal SILVER, favored by Witches for its properties as an amulet (see AMULETS) and as an enhancer of psychic powers.

FURTHER READING:
Crowley, Vivianne. *Wicca: The Old Religion in the New Millennium.* Revised ed. London: Thorsons/Harper Collins, 1996.
Guiley, Rosemary Ellen. *Moonscapes: A Celebration of Lunar Astronomy, Magic, Legend and Lore.* New York: Prentice-Hall, 1991.
Green, Marian. *A Witch Alone: Thirteen Moons to Master Natural Magic.* London: Thorsons/Harper Collins, 1991.
Starhawk. *The Spiral Dance.* Revised ed. San Francisco: HarperSan Francisco, 1989.

Morales Witches (17th century)   Three Pueblo women of San Rafael, New Mexico, famous as witches.

The women—two sisters, Antonia and Placida Morales, and Placida's 17-year-old daughter, Villa—were so feared that they were never punished for any of their alleged witchcraft deeds. Placida was said to have transformed a young man Francisco Ansures of Cerros Cuates into a woman by giving him a cup of bewitched coffee in retaliation for some offense. After drinking it, Ansures said his hair immediately grew two feet and his trousers turned into petticoats. His voice changed in pitch. Ansures remained a woman for several months before he and his wife could afford to pay another witch to lift the CURSE and return him to normal. He said he never did know how he offended Placida.

In 1885, historian and photographer Charles Lummis had the rare opportunity to photograph the three witches standing on the threshold of their adobe hut. People who knew the witches believed that even looking at the photograph would bring bad luck.

The Morales women fared better than another New Mexico witch Marcelina, an old woman who lived in San Mateo. In 1887, Marcelina was stoned to death for turning a man into a woman and making another man lame.

FURTHER READING:
Lummis, Charles. *A New Mexico David.* New York: Charles Scribner's Sons, 1891.
Simmons, Marc. *Witchcraft in the Southwest: Spanish and Indian Supernaturalism on the Rio Grande.* Lincoln: University of Nebraska Press, 1974.

Mora Witches (1669)   Witch hunts in Mora, in central Sweden, in which 85 people were executed for allegedly seducing some 300 children and spiriting them away to satanic SABBATS. Like the SALEM WITCHES trials of 1692–93, the hysteria of Mora was started by children.

The specter of witches first was raised on July 5, 1668, when a 15-year-old boy in Elfdale, Sweden, accused a 17-year-old girl of stealing children for Satan. Others were also accused. All pleaded not guilty except one 71-year-old woman.

That confession sparked concern, and King Charles XI established a commission to redeem the witches by mass public PRAYER instead of TORTURE or imprisonment. Instead, public fears were ignited, and stories of child stealing and devilish activities increased.

The king's commissioners arrived in Mora on August 12, 1669, to investigate, to the relief of the villagers. The following day, the entire population of about 3,000 persons turned out to church to hear a sermon "declaring the miserable case of those people that suffered themselves to be deluded by the Devil." Everyone prayed to be delivered from the scourge.

Children who allegedly had been spirited away to sabbats were assembled and then interviewed one by one. Their stories agreed: they had been snatched sleeping in their beds and spirited away to the most horrid satanic revelries. Some of the children spoke of a white angel who appeared and rescued them, assuring that what was happening to them would not last long but had been permitted "for the wickedness of the people." The children named 70 witches, 15 of whom were other children. Some of them were from the neighboring district of Elfdale. The accused were rounded up, interrogated and tortured. Twenty-three of them confessed immediately.

The witches said they would meet at a gravel pit by a CROSSROADS, where they put vests on their heads and danced "round and round and round about." They went to the crossroads and summoned the DEVIL to take them to an imaginary place called Blockula. According to one account the Devil "generally appeared as a little old man, in a grey coat, with red and blue stockings, with exceedingly long garters. He had a high-crowned hat, with bands of many-colored linen enfolded about it, and a long red beard that hung down to his middle."

After getting their promise to serve him body and soul, the Devil ordered them to steal children, threatening to beat them if they disobeyed. They said they were able to enter the homes because the Devil first removed the window glass. They took the children, promising them fine clothes and other things, and then flying off with them on the backs of beasts, on men whom they had charmed to sleep or astride posts. They admonished the children not to tell anyone. Some who did were "miserably scourged" to death, according to COTTON MATHER, in his book *On Witchcraft, Being the Wonders of the Invisible World* (1693). The judges did find some children with lash marks on them.

The witches said the Devil carried them all away on the backs of horses, asses, goats and monkeys, over the tops of houses, to Blockula, a house with a gate in an infinite green meadow. In a pledge to service of the Devil, the witches cut their fingers and wrote their names in their own BLOOD in his book (see DEVIL'S PACT). The Devil baptized the witches and bade them sit down at a long table for a feast of broth made of coleworts and bacon, bread and butter, milk, cheese and oatmeal. Sometimes the Devil played a harp or fiddle while they ate. Afterwards, they danced in a ring before the Devil, the witches swearing and cursing "most horribly." Sometimes they danced naked.

The Devil caused a terrible dragon to appear and told the witches that if they confessed anything, he would unleash the dragon upon them. He swore he would kill the judges. Some of the witches said they had attempted to murder the trial judges but could not.

The witches also said they had attempted to kill the minister of Elfdale. One witch said the Devil gave her a sledgehammer, which she used to try to drive a nail into the minister's head, but the nail would not go all the way in. The minister complained of a terrible headache at about the same time.

The judges asked the witches to demonstrate their black magic. They were unable to do so, explaining that since they had confessed, they had lost their powers.

All 70 persons accused were condemned to death. The 23 adults who confessed were burned together in one fire in Mora; the following day, 15 children were burned together. The remaining 32 persons were sent to Faluna, where they later were executed.

Milder punishment was meted out to another 56 children who were involved in the escapades. Thirty-six of them, between the ages of nine and 16, were forced to run a gauntlet and were lashed on their hands once a week for a year. Twenty children had their hands lashed with rods for three consecutive Sundays at the church door. Observed Mather, "This course, together with Prayers, in all the Churches thro' the Kingdom, issued in the deliverance of the Country."

The Mora case was long considered to be one of the most convincing pieces of evidence of the prevalence of evil witchcraft.

FURTHER READING:
Baroja, Julio Caro. 1961. Reprint, *The World of the Witches*. Chicago: University of Chicago Press, 1975.

Mather, Cotton. *On Witchcraft: Being the Wonders of the Invisible World.* 1692. Reprint, Mt. Vernon, N.Y.: The Peter Pauper Press, 1950.

Robbins, Rossell Hope. *The Encyclopedia of Witchcraft & Demonology.* 1959. Reprint, New York: Bonanza Books, 1981.

Morgan le Fay   A sorceress or FAIRY who possessed the art of magic herbal HEALING and who was either the sister or half-sister of the legendary King Arthur. According to some legends, Morgan le Fay ("Morgan the Fairy") was the mistress of MERLIN, who taught her MAGIC. Malory said she learned her arts in a nunnery.

Morgan plotted against Arthur to steal his TALISMAN sword, Excalibur or otherwise bring him down. Yet she also came to his aid: when Arthur was mortally wounded in the battle of Camlan, she was one of the four queens who spirited him away to the Isle of Avalon, where she used her magic to save his life.

Sometimes described as a goddess, Morgan seems to be a composite character derived from various Celtic myths and deities. In Welsh folklore, she was related to lake fairies who seduce and then abandon human lovers; in Irish folklore, she lived in a fairy mound from which she flew out in hideous guises to frighten people. In English and Scottish lore, Morgan lived either on Avalon or in various castles, including one near Edinburgh that was inhabited by a bevy of wicked fairies. She also is related to the mermaids of the Breton coast, called Morganes, Mari Morgan or Morgan, who enchanted sailors. Depending on the story, the sailor either went to their deaths or were transported to a blissful underwater paradise. In Italy, mirages over the Straits of Messina are still called the Fata Morganas.

Morgan was sometimes portrayed as an evil HAG or crone, as in the stories of Sir Lancelot and the Lake and *Gawain and the Green Knight.* She is not, however, the "Lady of the Lake" in the Arthurian legend by that name. Morgan was said to have a prodigious sexual appetite and was constantly capturing knights to satisfy her desires.

FURTHER READING:
Briggs, Katharine. *An Encyclopedia of Fairies.* New York: Pantheon, 1976.

Morrigan, the   In Irish mythology, one of three war goddesses, the other two being Neman and Macha. She also was the Mighty Queen, viewed either as a Triple Goddess or the death aspect of the Goddess. Robert Graves gave three aspects of the Morrigan: Ana, Babd and Macha.

In legend, the Morrigan protected the Tuatha de Danaan (see FAIRIES) with a cover of fog and rain so that their boats could land upon the shore of Ireland. On battlefields, she appeared as a raven or scald crow, eating the bodies of the dead. She could present a winsome side that hid her secret intentions of destroying someone, or she could be openly vengeful. She fell in love with Cuchulain, the heroic son of Lugh but was rejected by him. In anger, she harassed him on the battlefield, then tried, in vain, to save his life.

The Morrigan sometimes is associated with the three phases of the MOON—waxing, full and waning—and with the maiden, matron and crone aspects of the Goddess.

See GODDESS.

Mother Redcap A name applied to English ale-wives, wise women and witches. It was also given to FAMILIAR animals.

One Mother Redcap was an elderly woman who lived in a village about 14 miles from Cambridge, England, who was known as a witch. She said she was endowed with her witch powers in circumstances reminiscent of the DEVIL'S PACT legends of medieval centuries. According to an article published in the London *Sunday Chronicle* on September 9, 1928:

> One day a black man called, produced a book and asked her to sign her name in it. The woman signed the book and the mysterious stranger then told her she would be the mistress of five imps who would carry out her orders. Shortly afterwards the woman was seen out accompanied by a rat, a cat, a toad, a ferret, and a mouse. Everybody believed she was a witch, and many people visited her to obtain cures.

Mother Redcap's neighbors apparently viewed her new status as an asset and not something evil, and she was not persecuted. Her story is odd, however, for she claimed to sign the mysterious book without asking what it was or why. In traditional stories of the Devil's pact, the person supposedly knows full well the terms of the deal: their soul in exchange for earthly gain, which places a moral burden squarely upon the shoulders of the individual.

Mother Redcap appeared not to suffer and used her alleged supernatural abilities to help others. She died in 1926.

An Essex Old Mother Redcap lived in a house called Duval's (Devil House) in Wallasea Island, where no traditional witch's familiars such as TOADS, frogs or snakes lived. She would sit in her house peeling potatoes and chanting spells such as "Holly, holly, brolly, brolly, Redcap! Bonny, bonny."

After her death in the 1920s, her house was haunted by the spirit of a familiar and people considered it dangerous to enter. If anyone did and stayed, they were assaulted by a mysterious voice that shouted, "Do it! Do it!" as though to urge them to commit suicide. Cows in the vicinity were stricken with mad cow disease.

The house was bombed into ruins during World War II. In 1953, the ruins were washed away in a tidal wave.

See RED; REDCAP.

FURTHER READING:
Folklore, Myths and Legends of Britain. London: Reader's Digest Assoc. Ltd., 1977.
Pennick, Nigel. *Secrets of East Anglican Magic.* London: Robert Hale, 1995.

Mother Shipton (1488–?) A 15th-century English witch and seer who supposedly prophesied scientific inventions, new technology, wars and politics through several centuries, all written in crude rhymes. The books of her "prophecies" are likely the invention of later writers, among them Richard Head, who published a book of her predictions in 1667; an anonymous writer who published the *Strange and Wonderful History of Mother Shipton* in 1668; and a man named Hindley, who apparently authored Shipton predictions in 1871.

More myth and fabulous tales surround Mother Shipton than fact. Reputedly, she was born Ursula Southeil near Dropping Well in Knaresborough, Yorkshire, in 1488, though the dates 1448 and 1486 also are given in various texts. Her mother, who possessed the powers of HEALING, clairvoyance, STORM RAISING and hexing (see HEX), died in childbirth with "strange and terrible noises." Ursula, who inherited her mother's powers, was raised by a local townswoman. Mysterious things happened around Ursula: furniture moved about on its own, and food disappeared from dinner plates. Once, the townswoman left Ursula alone in her cottage. When she returned with several neighbors, they were attacked by strange forces. A woman was hung by her toes from a staff floating in the air, and men were yoked to the same staff. Other women found themselves dancing in circles; if they tried to stop,

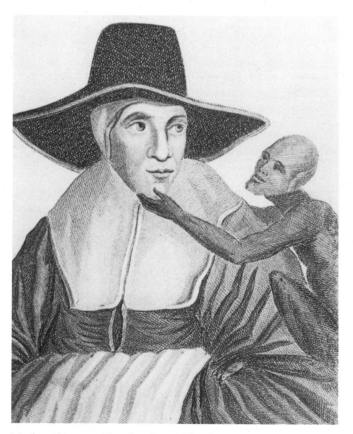

Mother Shipton with a familiar, 19th century

an IMP in the shape of a monkey pinched them to keep them going.

Ursula fit the classic stereotype of HAG. Head described her as follows:

> . . . with very great goggling, but sharp and fiery eyes; her nose of incredible and unproportionable length, having in it many crooks and turnings, adorned with many strange pimples of divers colors, as red and blue mixed, which, like vapors of brimstone, gave such a lustre to the affrighted spectators in the dead time of the night, that one of them confessed that her nurse needed no other light to assist her in the performance of her duty.

In art, she is depicted as wearing a tall, conical, brimmed black hat.

Despite this incredibly ugly appearance, Ursula married Tobias Shipton at age 24. Her husband then disappeared from all records, and Ursula became known as Mother Shipton. She did not like prying neighbors and once took revenge on a group of them by bewitching them at a breakfast party (see SPELLS). The guests suddenly broke into hysterical laughter and ran out of the house, pursued by goblins. For this mischief, Mother Shipton was summoned to court, but she threatened to do worse if she were prosecuted. She then said, "Updraxi, call Stygician Helleuei," and soared off on a winged dragon.

The verses attributed to her vary. One of the best-known is:

> Carriages without horses shall go
> Around the world thoughts shall fly
> In the twinkling of an eye
> Iron in the water shall float
> As easy as a wooden boat
> Gold shall be found, and found
> In a land that's not now known
> A house of glass shall come to pass
> In England, but alas!

Her predictions included automobiles, telephone and telegraph, iron-clad boats, the California gold rush and the Crystal Palace in London. Mother Shipton also is credited with predicting the Civil War in England, the Great Fire of London (1666), the discovery of tobacco and potatoes in the New World, World War II and the women's liberation movement.

Her memorial, Mother Shipton's Cave, is in Knaresborough.

FURTHER READING:

Briggs, Katharine. *British Folktales*. New York: Dorset Press, 1977.

Folklore, Myths and Legends of Britain. London: Reader's Digest Assoc. Ltd., 1977.

Valiente, Doreen. *An ABC of Witchcraft Past and Present*. 1973. Reprint, Custer, Wash.: Phoenix Publishing, 1986.

Murray, Margaret Alice (1863–1963) British anthropologist, archaeologist and Egyptologist best known for her controversial theories on the origins and organization of witchcraft as a religion.

Murray was born July 13, 1863, in Calcutta. She distinguished herself in the British academic world, entering University College in London in 1894. She was named a fellow of the college and specialized in Egyptology. She became a junior lecturer in Egyptology in 1899 and was assistant professor of Egyptology until 1935, when she resigned her post to pursue other studies. She also held other lecturer positions.

Murray did archaeological excavations in Egypt, Malta, Hertfordshire (England), Petra, Minorca and Tell Ajjul in south Palestine. Her interest in witchcraft led her to field studies of the subject throughout Europe, which included an examination of written records of witchcraft trials.

Her first book on witchcraft, *The Witch-cult in Western Europe,* was published in 1921 and caused immediate controversy among her peers. Murray maintained that witchcraft in the Middle Ages and Renaissance was not a phenomenon of Christian heresy but was the remnants of an organized, pagan fertility religion that dated back to Paleolithic times. She also maintained that witchcraft was far more widespread and organized during those centuries than had been generally believed by most historians and anthropologists.

Murray was not the first to put forth this theory. Sir James Frazer had discussed the prehistoric origins of witchcraft rituals and beliefs in his extensive work, *The Golden Bough,* published in 1890. Murray elaborated upon Frazer's work and took her own theories much further.

Murray called witchcraft "the Dianic cult" because of the pagan worship of the goddess DIANA. She believed that most witches were organized into COVENS that always consisted of 12 members plus a leader, either the DEVIL or a man impersonating the Devil, despite the lack of evidence to support such a belief. She also believed that practitioners of witchcraft came from "every rank of society, from the highest to the lowest." Murray remained convinced of the existence of an organized witchcraft religion, despite the lack of evidence to prove it.

In her second book on witchcraft, *The God of the Witches,* published in 1933, Murray discussed the HORNED GOD, or male pagan deity, tracing its origins back to Paleolithic times as well. She portrayed the Horned God as one of power but not evil. A third book, *The Divine King in England,* published in 1954, was perhaps the most controversial of all her works. In it, she asserted that every English king, from William the Conqueror in the 11th century to JAMES I in the early 17th century, was a secret witch and that many of the country's statesmen had been killed in ritual deaths.

For decades, scholars argued over Murray's theories. Her Dianic cult and other views have been widely rejected, including most of her material in *The Divine King in England* and her opinion that the term *sabbat* comes from the French term *s'esbettre,* which means "to frolic" (see SABBATS). Nevertheless, she is recognized for her pioneering work in the field of witchcraft and for shedding light on the continuity of some ancient pagan practices, not only into the Middle Ages but into the 20th century as well.

Murray's theories gave fuel to a movement in England in the 1950s to rediscover Witchcraft as an organized religion. GERALD B. GARDNER expounded upon her theories in his own book, *Witchcraft Today* (1954), for which Murray wrote the introduction. The Dianic cult was an appealing myth that many newly initiated Witches wanted to believe. But by the 1990s, it was acknowledged in Wicca and Paganism that Murray was wrong.

Murray died in London on November 13, 1963, shortly after her 100th birthday.

FURTHER READING:
Adler, Margot. *Drawing Down the Moon.* Revised ed. New York: Viking, 1986.
Murray, Margaret A. *The Witch-Cult in Western Europe.* London: Oxford University Press, 1921.
———. *The God of the Witches.* London: Sampson Low, Marston and Co., Ltd., 1931.
Russell, Jeffrey B. *A History of Witchcraft.* London: Thames and Hudson, 1980.

Murrell, James (1780–1860)   One of England's greatest CUNNING MEN, widely sought for his magical powers for healing, divining lost objects and the future, and casting spells and counter-spells. James Murrell, also known as Cunning Murrell, lived in the Rochford Hundred, an area of southeast Essex widely reputed to be "The Witch Country" because of its numerous and famous men and women witches.

Murrell was born in 1780 in Rochford. He was the SEVENTH SON OF A SEVENTH SON, marking him for a life of magical empowerment. Accordingly, he was the only child in the family to be given an education. Initially, he tried his hand as a surveyor's apprentice and as a chemist's stillman in London. Around 1812, he returned to the Rochford Hundred to settle in Hadleigh in a small cottage and work as a shoemaker. He eventually gave up that career in order to work full time as a cunning man. He married, and fathered 20 children. Not surprisingly, his wife died before he did.

As a cunning man, Murrell's reputation was unsurpassed. Not only locals but wealthy and aristocratic clients sought him out. He possessed a tremendous knowledge of herbal remedies, medicine and astrology. He owned a library of magical tools, books and papers. Although these no longer survive, descriptions of them indicate that perhaps one of his volumes was a magical GRIMOIRE or perhaps *The Magus* by Francis Barrett (1801), from which he learned how to use SIGILS, TALISMANS and AMULETS, and how to invoke various angelic forces at the proper times.

Murrell charged fees for his services, usually a shilling or so, but as much as half a crown for services requiring the summoning of spirits. He would ask his clients if they required "high or low" help. High meant calling on the spirits, while low meant working in the material world. For "high" magic, Murrell would call upon the "good angels" to combat the evil ones.

For divination and to find lost property, Murrell scried in a magic MIRROR that he claimed could see through walls (see SCRYING). He could accurately predict events years into the future. He had a copper talisman with which he determined if a person was honest or not.

He was renowned for his ability to cure sick animals, sometimes by laying on of the hands. He could exorcise DEMONS from people and places. He traveled only at night, sometimes going great distances, and always carried an umbrella as his trademark. He was especially famous for his WITCH BOTTLE counter-spells.

Murrell was often called the "Master of Witches" because it was believed that he could force any witch to do his bidding. One story goes that he confronted a black witch of Canewdon and commanded her to die. She fell dead immediately.

Lore around him built up over the years. He was said to fly at night on a hurdle and to teleport himself over great distances. He also was said to be a smuggler.

Murrell hoped that his powers would be transferred to his sole surviving son, Buck Murrell, according to tradition. Buck, however, was a dull fellow who could do little more than charm warts. Nonetheless, Murrell arranged for him to receive all of his magical objects upon his death.

Near the end of 1860, Murrell became ill and foresaw his own death on December 16. In his final hours, the village curate tried to minister to him, but was driven away by Murrell shouting, "I am the Devil's master!" Upon his death, he was given a proper burial in the Hadleigh churchyard.

Murrell's landlord buried his trunk full of magical books and objects. Son Buck dug it up. The contents survived until 1956, when, unfortunately, they were deemed "worthless" and were destroyed.

One of Murrell's most famous prophecies concerned the survival of witchcraft in Essex: "There will be witches in Leigh for a hundred years, and three in Hadleigh, and nine in Canewdon for ever."

See CANEWDON WITCHES; OLD GEORGE PICKINGILL.

FURTHER READING:
Folklore, Myths and Legends of Britain. London: Reader's Digest Assoc. Ltd., 1977.
Maple, Eric. *The Dark World of Witches.* New York: A.S. Barnes & Co., 1962.
Pennick, Nigel. *Secrets of East Anglian Magic.* London: Robert Hale, 1995.

Museum of Witchcraft   The world's largest collection of paraphernalia and artifacts related to folk magic, witchcraft, WICCA and ritual magic is based in Boscastle, Cornwall, England. The museum was founded by researcher CECIL WILLIAMSON and a version of it was owned for a time by GERALD B. GARDNER.

Williamson's personal interest and research in witchcraft—he also founded the Witchcraft Research Centre—led to his acquisition of thousands of magical objects and items of occult interest. After World War II, he conceived of the idea of opening a witchcraft museum as a way of having his own business and continuing his research. His initial site in 1947 was Stratford-upon-Avon, the birthplace of Shakespeare and a popular tourist destination, but local opposition soon forced him out of town.

Williamson then selected Castletown on the Isle of Man—a summer tourist attraction—as a quieter location. The museum reopened there at Whitsun in 1949 as the Folklore Centre of Superstition and Witchcraft. Gerald Gardner, described in the media as "the resident witch" of Castletown, officiated at the opening and sold his novel,

High Magic's Aid, there. The facility included a restaurant, the Witches Kitchen, for which Williamson had specially made dishes embossed with witches on broomsticks. The restaurant was the idea of Williamson's wife, Gwen, as a way to bring in business.

Gardner purchased the buildings and restaurant from Williamson in 1952, but no exhibits. He placed his own magical and occult objects in it.

Williamson moved his exhibits back to England, establishing a witchcraft museum in Windsor near Windsor Castle in 1952. It was a success with tourists, but local residents took a dim view of it, and Williamson was persuaded to move elsewhere. He relocated to Bourton-on-the-Water in 1954. Local fear of witchcraft received media coverage that helped his business, but Williamson was plagued with ongoing harassment, including SIGILS marked on his door, dead CATS left on his doorstep, and arsonry that destroyed a wing of the museum.

As his collection grew larger, Williamson needed a bigger facility. He moved again, to Loe in Cornwall, and finally in 1960 to Boscastle on the Cornish north coast,

Proprietor Graham King in front of the Museum of Witchcraft in Boscastle, Cornwall (PHOTO BY AUTHOR; COURTESY MUSEUM OF WITCHCRAFT)

Patricia C. Crowther stands before the original Museum of Witchcraft buildings, including the museum, restaurant, ballroom and top of the Witches' Mill, in Castletown, Isle of Man. The photo was taken long after the property had been sold. (PHOTO BY IAN LILLEYMAN; COURTESY PATRICIA C. CROWTHER)

where he established it as the Witches House in the picturesque harbor area of the village.

In 1996, Williamson retired and sold the museum, including several thousand but not all of its exhibits, to Graham King and Liz Crow. King lives in quarters attached to the museum.

King, a Pagan with interests in Witchcraft, had his own business manufacturing specialist cameras in Hampshire but wanted to sell it. He saw a newspaper article that told of the museum being for sale, and if no buyer could be found the collection might be sold as individual lots. He became interested in buying the entire collection and business. The deal was completed at midnight Samhain 1996.

The collection. Williamson's investigations had brought him a wide array of paraphernalia, sometimes purchased, sometimes given to him. Objects included tools for spellcasting, tools for ritual high magic, herbs and other ingredients, POPPETS, potions, DIVINATION tools, clothing, magical jewelry, books and manuscripts, photographs, drawings and paintings, and more. There are TALISMANS made by Gardner, the ritual chalice that belonged to

ALEISTER CROWLEY, swords and an altar slab used by ALEX SANDERS, and artifacts owned by other persons famous in modern Witchcraft and magic.

Perhaps Williamson's most celebrated exhibits were the skeletons of Ursula Kempe, an Essex woman executed as a witch in 1582 (see ST. OSYTH WITCHES), and JOAN WYTTE, the "Fighting Fairy Woman of Bodmin Town," who died in jail in 1813. Williamson kept Kempe's remains for his private collection, but sold those of Wytte as part of the museum's 5,000-plus exhibits.

Williamson never publicly displayed all of his collection, believing that some aspects of the real witch's craft must remain secret.

Gardner's loan. According to Williamson, Gardner did not own enough objects to fill all of his display cases in Castletown, and prevailed upon Williamson to lend him some of his talismans and amulets. Williamson agreed, but took the precaution of making plaster casts and imprints of each metal item. The objects were still in Gardner's possession when he died in 1964. The museum and its contents were inherited by MONIQUE WILSON, who, as Lady Olwen, had been Gardner's high priestess.

Williamson said he asked for the return of his talismans and amulets, but Wilson declined. Williamson decided not to pursue the matter in court, but did pursue a more traditional remedy: a ritual CURSE. He called upon the power of the FAMILIAR spirits to "bring, and to cause, discomforture [sic] to the enemy." Just how much discomfiture the curse caused is not certain. However, Wilson did not keep the exhibits long, but sold them to Ripley's Believe It Or Not in America. Much of the collection has since been dispersed through sale; objects have even been offered over the Internet. Williamson kept the plaster casts and imprints.

Reorganization. King and Crow reorganized the museum and freshened the tableaux, moving some of the more sensational ones, such as a mannequin of a partially clothed woman laid out as an altar for a BLACK MASS. In keeping with Williamson's original vision, most of the exhibits feature historical folk witchcraft and the "wayside witch" or village wise woman or CUNNING MAN. The museum also features modern Witchcraft and ritual magic, and shows the overlaps between Christianity, PAGANISM, Freemasonry, Rosicrucianism, alchemy and so on. King retained a small case on SATANISM, chiefly to educate visitors to the distinction between Satanism and Witchcraft. He added a room that recreates a traditional witch's cottage, with its collection of herbs and divination tools, and a mannequin of a wise woman doing her craft at her table.

Exhibits also show the history of witchcraft and the persecutions, the role of stone circles and sacred sites in rituals, SCRYING and DIVINATION, HEALING, sea witchcraft lore, the HORNED GOD, the HARE and shape-shifting (see METAMORPHOSIS) and working tools of the Witch and magician (see WITCHES' TOOLS).

The museum's policy is to display all aspects of folk and religious witchcraft, including items related to cursing used in the past by village witches. Cursing is not officially condoned in modern Wicca/Paganism.

King removed Wytte's skeleton for a proper burial. Her empty coffin remained on display.

The museum also functions as an information resource center for the media and public, and as an informal gathering place for Wiccans and Pagans. An independent club, "The Friends of the Museum," raises funds for the purchase of new exhibits.

The museum collection continues to grow with donations. Many Witches bequeath their working tools to the museum in their wills, thus ensuring that their possessions are not abused after their death.

On August 16, 2004, Boscastle was hit by torrential rain and a flash flood. The museum suffered damage to some of its exhibits and closed for repairs until March 25, 2005. Supporters donated funds, books and artifacts.

FURTHER READING:

"Museum of Witchcraft." Available online. URL: http://www.witchcraft.co.uk/boscastle.htm. Downloaded November 4, 2007.

names of power Secret names of God or deities, or words substituted for those names, which in MAGIC are used to raise power.

Names of power were used by ancient Egyptians, Greeks, Hebrews, Assyrians and Gnostics, who believed that incredible power could be unleashed by the sound vibrations of the words.

The most powerful of all names of power is the Tetragrammaton, the personal name of God in the Old Testament, usually expressed as YHWH, the transliteration of the Hebrew letters *Yod, He, Vau, He.* The numerical values assigned to these letters add up to ten, which in Hebrew numerology represents the basic organizing principle in the universe. So awesome is the Tetragrammaton that for centuries it was seldom spoken, but was whispered only on Yom Kippur by a high priest. In the scriptures, substitute words were used, such as *Adonai, Adonay* or *Elohim.* The exact pronunciation of the Tetragrammaton is not known; the most accepted is "Yahweh." A variation is "Jehovah."

By using anagrammatical and numerological formulas, numerous names of power have been created for magical purposes. *Agla,* an abbreviation frequently used by rabbis, comes from the first letters of the Hebrew phrase, *Aieth Gadol Leolam Adonai,* which means "Adonai (the Lord) will be great to eternity." *Amen* is a word of power, because in Hebrew it adds up to 91, as does *Jehovah Adonai.*

Some names or words of power are nonsensical, created for their rhythm or their numerical value. The essence of the power unleashed by the words is not in the words themselves but in their intrinsic occult power and the faith of those using them.

Names and words of power appear in all of the major magical GRIMOIRES. In many cases, the origins and meanings of the words have long been lost. For example, the *Key of Solomon* ends a conjuration of DEMONS with the words:

> Aglon, Tetragram, vaycheon, stimulamation, ezphares, retetragrammaton olyaram irion esytion existion eryona onera orasym mozm messias soter Emmanuel Sbaoth Adonay, *te adoro, et teinvoco.* Amen.

Most of the words are unrecognizable, but they probably contribute to the rhythm of the chant, which is important in the attainment of a state of frenzy on the part of the magician.

ALEISTER CROWLEY created AUGMN as an ultimate word of power, which he believed was a mantra of such force that a magician chanting it would be able to control the universe. AUGMN is an expansion of the Buddhist mantra Om, which represents God and the Supreme Reality, the sum total of everything in all creation. The basis for AUGMN is a gematric formula. In Hebrew, the letters of the mantra add up to 100. By breaking down 100 as a sum of 20 and 80, one arrives at the Hebrew letters *kaph* and *pe,* which, transformed into Greek, are the first letters of *kteis* and *phallos,* which correspond to the female and male sexual organs. In *Magick in Theory*

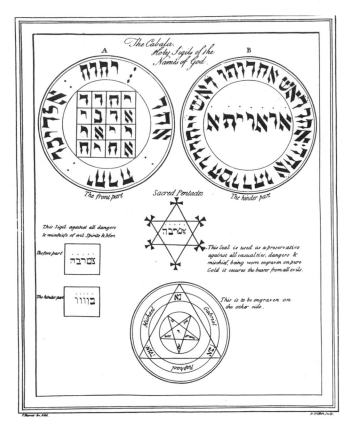

Kabbalistic sigils of the names of God (FRANCIS BARRETT, *THE MAGUS*, 1801)

and Practice (1929), Crowley describes AUGMN as "the Magical formula of the Universe as a reverbatory engine for the extension of Nothingness through the device of equilibrated opposites."

nature spirits   Guardian beings that exist in all life forms in nature, in the plant, animal and mineral kingdoms.

In contemporary Paganism and Witchcraft, nature spirits are treated with respect. Their participation and cooperation is sought to enhance rituals and stimulate communication between humankind and Mother Earth. When sites are selected for outdoor rituals, an effort is made to communicate with nature spirits to secure their cooperation and seek their guidance. Nature spirits manifest themselves through animal and insect noises, a rising of wind, a clearing of sky, the sudden presence of an animal or a flock of birds. They also can be perceived as forms and patterns of light and sound.

necromancy   An ancient art of conjuring the dead for the purpose of DIVINATION. Necromancy is condemned by the Catholic Church as "the agency of evil spirits," and in Elizabethan England it was outlawed by the Witchcraft Act of 1604. Throughout history, necromancy has been feared and reviled as one of the ugliest and most repugnant of magical rites. Necromantic rites are not part of contemporary Paganism and Witchcraft.

Necromancy is not to be confused with conjuring DEMONS or the DEVIL. The spirits of the dead are sought for information because they are no longer bound by the earthly plane and therefore supposedly have access to information beyond that available to the living. Conjured spirits are asked about the future and where to find buried treasure.

Francis Barrett, author of *The Magus* (1801), said necromancy "has its name because it works on the bodies of the dead, and gives answers by the ghosts and apparitions of the dead, and subterraneous spirits, alluring them into the carcasses of the dead by certain hellish charms, and infernal invocations, and by deadly sacrifices and wicked oblations."

There are two kinds of necromancy: raising a corpse itself to life and, more commonly, summoning the spirit of the corpse.

The rituals for necromancy are similar to those for conjuring demons, involving MAGIC CIRCLES, wands, TALISMANS, BELLS and incantations, as prescribed by various GRIMOIRES. In addition, the necromancer surrounds himself by gruesome aspects of death: he wears clothing stolen from corpses and meditates upon death. Some rituals call for the eating of dog flesh, for dogs are associated with HECATE, the patron goddess of witchcraft, and for consuming unsalted and unleavened black bread and unfermented grape juice, symbolic of decay and lifelessness.

Such preparations may go on for days or weeks. The actual ritual itself may take many hours, during which time the magician calls upon Hecate or various demons to help raise the desired spirit. The ritual customarily takes place in a graveyard over the corpse itself. The objective is to summon the spirit to reenter the corpse and bring it back to life, rising and speaking in answer to questions posed by the magician. Recently deceased corpses are preferred by necromancers, for they are said to speak most clearly. If the person has been dead a long time, necromancers try to summon their ghostly spirit to appear. Once the ritual has been performed successfully, the necromancer is supposed to burn the corpse or bury it in quicklime, so that it will not be disturbed again. In the Middle Ages, many believed that necromancers also consumed the flesh of the corpse as part of the ritual.

Some necromancers summon corpses to attack the living. This practice dates back as far as ancient Egypt and Greece and is still done in various parts of the world.

One of the best-known necromancers is the WITCH OF ENDOR, whose conjuring of the dead prophet Samuel for King Saul is recorded in the Bible; Samuel foretold Saul's doom. Apollonius of Tyana gained a great reputation in first-century Greece as a philosopher and necromancer. The 16th-century English magician John Dee and his companion Edward Kelly were reputed necromancers, though Dee never recorded any such activities in his diaries. The 17th-century French magician, Eliphas Lévi, attempted to conjure the spirit of Apollonius, an experience that left him badly shaken and frightened.

Necromancy techniques were taught in medieval Spain, in deep caves near Seville, Toledo and Salamanca. The caves were walled up by Isabella the Catholic, who considered them evil.

The numbers nine and 13 are associated with necromancy. Nine represents an old belief that there were nine spheres through which a soul passed in the transition from life to death. Thirteen was the number of persons who attended Christ's Last Supper, at which he was betrayed; Christ later rose from the dead.

In VODUN, corpses are "raised" from graves in rituals in which appeals are made to Baron Samedi, the scarecrowlike god of graveyards and zombies. In Haiti, the rites take place in a graveyard at midnight. They are performed by the person who is the local incarnation of Papa Nebo, father of death, and a group of followers. A grave is selected and white candles are implanted at its foot and lit. A frock coat and a silk top hat, the symbols of Baron Samedi, are draped on the grave's cross (if the grave has no cross, one is made). A ritual is performed to awaken Baron Samedi from sleep. While the god makes no visible manifestation, he signals his presence and approval by moving or flapping the frock coat or hat.

The necromancers pay homage to the Baron and promise him offerings of food, drink and money, then send him back to sleep by tossing roots and herbs. The corpse is unearthed, and the incarnation of Papa Nebo asks it questions. The answers usually are "heard" only by the Papa Nebo representative.

Newbury Witch (?–1763) An old woman, probably harmless, who was executed as a witch in 1763 by Cromwell's soldiers, near Newbury in Berkshire. The soldiers reportedly saw the old woman sailing on a plank down the River Kennet—by some accounts, the soldiers claimed she was walking on the water—and captured her as a witch and tried to shoot her. According to a 17th-century pamphlet, "with a deriding and loud laughter at them, she caught their bullets in her hands and chewed them." The soldiers then "blooded" her, a custom of the times in which a witch's forehead was slashed in the belief that the bleeding would drain out her power. One of the men put his pistol under her ear and shot her, "at which she straight sank down and died."

FURTHER READING:
Maple, Eric. *The Dark World of Witches.* New York: A.S. Barnes & Co., 1962.

Newton, Florence (ca. mid-17th century) One of the most important witch trials of Ireland was that of Florence Newton, the "Witch of Youghal," who was tried at the Cork assizes in 1661. Newton was accused of bewitching a young girl, Mary Longdon, into fits, and of bewitching one of her jail sentries, David Jones, to death. Unlike many of the witch trials conducted at the time on the Continent, the trial of Florence Newton involved no TORTURE. Some important people were involved in the trial, including the mayor of Youghal, who gave sworn testimony, and Valentine Greatrakes, a noted Irish healer.

Newton was arrested and jailed after Mary Longdon, a maid of John Pyne, claimed Newton had bewitched her. Longdon said Newton had become angry when Mary refused to give her some of her master's beef. Newton "went away grumbling."

A week later, Longdon encountered Newton, who threw herself upon the maid and violently kissed her, saying, "Mary, I pray thee let thee and I be friends; for I bear thee no ill will, and I pray thee do thou bear me none." A few days after the encounter, Mary woke up and saw Newton standing beside her bed with a "little old man in silk cloaths," whom she took to be a spirit. The spirit told Longdon to "follow his advice and she would have all the things after her own heart," to which Longdon replied she would have nothing to do with him, her faith being with the Lord.

A month after being kissed by Newton, Longdon fell ill with "fits and trances." She had shaking fits so violent that three or four men could not hold her down. She repeatedly vomited needles, pins, horsenails, stubbs, wool and straw (see ALLOTRIOPHAGY). She was pelted with mysterious showers of stones that followed her from room to room in her house, and outdoors, from place to place (see LITHOBOLY). Most of the stones vanished when they hit the ground. Longdon grabbed one with a hole in it, knotted a leather throng through it and stuck it in her purse. The stone vanished, but the knot remained in the thong.

Longdon said that during her fits, she saw Newton, who stuck pins in her arms so deeply that men had difficulty getting them out. The maid also said she was levitated out of her bed and carried to the top of the house (see LEVITATION).

Newton was summoned by the authorities. Whenever Longdon was in the accused witch's presence, her fits and discomfort grew worse. Newton was removed to Cork for trial. During the proceedings, whenever Newton was restrained "in bolts," Longdon seemed to be fine; if Newton was let out of bolts, Longdon fell ill, even if she were not in the presence of Newton.

Newton at first denied bewitching Longdon, describing herself as "old and disquieted, and distracted with her [own] sufferings." She mumbled about Longdon suffering, supposedly at the exact times the maid was having fits.

There was a prevailing belief at the time that witches could not recite the LORD'S PRAYER, so the court asked Newton to do this. The old woman stumbled over the prayer, omitting "and forgive us our trespasses." She said the omission was due to her bad memory, but the court was skeptical and appointed a man to try and teach her the prayer; however, she was unable to utter the one line.

Nicholas Pyne, a Youghal townsman, testified that he and two other men had visited Newton in jail and she had confessed her crimes to them. She told them she had not bewitched Longdon but overlooked her with the EVIL EYE, and that there was a vast difference between the two. Newton implicated two other Youghal women, whom she said had the same supernatural powers as she, and she suggested that perhaps one of them had harmed the maid.

Pyne testified that during the visit, they heard noises like a person in chains and bolts running up and down the cell but could see nothing. The next day, Newton confessed the noise was made by her FAMILIAR, which had the shape of a greyhound and went in and out the window.

The famous healer Valentine Greatrakes and two other men gave Newton a test for witchcraft. They sat her on a stool and had a shoemaker try to stick an awl into the stool; he could not do so until the third try. When he attempted to pull the awl out, it broke. There was no mark in the stool where it had been pierced. Then they brought in Longdon and put another awl in her hand. "... [O]ne of them took the maid's hand, and ran violently at the witch's hand with it, but could not enter it, though the awl was so bent that none of them could put it straight again." Finally, the men lanced one of Newton's hands with a cut 1 1/2 inches long and 1/4-inch deep, but the hand did not bleed. Newton's other hand was similarly lanced, and then the two hands bled.

Newton said she was sorry for casting the EVIL EYE on Longdon and causing her harm. The mayor of Youghal rounded up the two women Newton implicated as witches, but before he could subject all three women to the swimming test (see SWIMMING), Newton confessed to overlooking the maid. Longdon said the two women were not guilty, and they were released.

While Newton was in prison, one of her sentries was David Jones, who attempted to teach her the Lord's Prayer. One night she called Jones to her cell and announced she could recite the entire prayer. Once again, she omitted "and forgive us our trespasses." Jones taught the prayer to her again, and Newton, in gratitude, asked to kiss his hand. When Jones went home, he complained to his wife that he had a great pain in his arm and that it was the result of being kissed by the witch.

For the next 14 days Jones grew progressively ill, complaining that the pain was shooting up his arm into his heart, describing symptoms that sound like angina. He told a friend that the hag Newton was pulling off his arm. "Do you not see the old hag, how she pulls me?" Jones said. "Well, I lay my death on her, she has bewitched me." At the end of a fortnight, Jones died.

The surviving records of Newton's trial do not indicate her fate. Longdon apparently covered.

FURTHER READING:
Seymour, St. John D. *Irish Witchcraft and Demonology.* Dublin: Hodges, Figgis & Co., 1913.

nightmare   An ugly DEMON or HAG, who sits on a person's chest during the night, causing great discomfort, a sensation of heaviness and suffocation and bad dreams. It also is the term for the bad dream itself—the definition that prevails in current popular usage.

In centuries past, demons were believed to bring erotic dreams as well as terrifying ones, tempting their victims with forbidden lust. *Mare* is Old English for *incubus*, a male demon. The erotic dreams also could be caused by *succubi*, female demons. In the 16th century, the Swiss alchemist Paracelsus even claimed that menstruation brought on nightmares. More likely, erotic nightmares were a result of repressed sexual desires.

The belief in nightmares as real demons is ancient. The storm god Alu brought nightmares to the Babylonians, while Greeks suffered the onslaughts of the giant, Ephialtes. The Zohar, or "Book of Splendor" in the KABBALAH, asserts that succubi did indeed cause nightmares in men. In medieval times, nightmares were sometimes thought to be caused by SPELLS cast by witches or by POSSESSION. People protected themselves against the dreaded demons by reciting CHARMS and PRAYERS and making the sign of the cross before they went to sleep.

Modern research has found the "Old Hag" syndrome to be commonplace around the world; in the United States, it afflicts about 15 percent of the population. The syndrome is characterized by a person awakening to find himself paralyzed and in the presence of a nonhuman entity, sometimes humanoid in shape and with prominent eyes, which often sits on his chest and causes feelings of suffocation. The experience sometimes is accompanied by musty smells and shuffling sounds. Occultists still attribute such attacks to evil spirits. One scientific theory put forward suggests that the Old Hag syndrome might be a side effect of a poorly understood sleep-pattern derangement, such as narcolepsy.

FURTHER READING:
Hufford, David J. *The Terror That Comes in the Night.* Philadelphia: University of Pennsylvania Press, 1982.

Northampton Witches (d. 1612)   Five men and women who were arraigned and tried on charges of witchcraft and who were all executed by hanging on July 22, 1612, in Northampton, England. The chief evidence against most of them seemed to be public opinion that they were wicked, evil people, and led wicked lives—and so had to be witches.

Several cases were tried separately, but the convicted were all executed on the same day, probably for the convenience of the town.

Agnes Brown and Joan Vaughn or Varnham. Agnes Brown and her daughter Joan Vaughn (also given as Varnham) lived in Guilsborough, Northamptonshire. They were poor and uneducated and Joan was unmarried. They were regarded by their neighbors as ill natured and ill mannered, completely without grace.

Their downfall began one day when Vaughn encountered a gentlewoman, Mistress Belcher. Apparently she was rude, for Belcher struck her. Vaughn retorted that she would remember the injury and would avenge it. Belcher replied that she was not afraid of Vaughn or her mother.

Vaughn went home and told Brown about the incident. It is unknown whether the two vowed revenge. However, Belcher soon fell seriously ill and took to her bed. Her friends blamed Vaughn, and soon Belcher was crying out that her affliction was caused by Vaughn and Brown.

Belcher's brother, Master Avery, came to visit his sister while she was sick. He found that he could not enter the house, as though some malevolent force held him back. After several attempts, he gave up and returned home.

Avery then became tormented with fits like those suffered by his sister. He too blamed his condition on the witchcraft of Brown and Vaughn. He complained to the authorities. A knight, Sir William Saunders of Cottesbrooke, apprehended the women and brought them to the Northampton jail.

Belcher and Avery were convinced that if they could scratch the women and draw blood (see BLOODING), they would be cured. They went to the jail and as soon as they blooded the women, their afflictions ended. The cure was not lasting, for as soon as brother and sister were out of sight of the women, their fits and torments returned, more violent than ever.

On their way home in their coach, Belcher and Avery passed a man and woman riding together on a black horse and acting oddly. The strangers called out a CURSE that either Belcher and Avery or their horses should presently have an accident. The coach horses immediately fell dead.

Once home, Belcher and Avery were cured. The strange occurrence was blamed upon the witchcraft of the jailed women; the horses received the brunt of the Devil's mischief.

Brown and Vaughn were charged with bewitchment of Belcher and Avery and also of bewitching a child to death. They pleaded not guilty. Among the testimonies against them was an account that Brown was seen with two other "witches," Katherine Gardiner and Joan Lucas, all riding on the back of a sow to visit Mother Rhodes, an old witch. Rhodes died before they arrived, but did call out that three of her friends were coming to visit, but too late.

A jury found Brown and Vaughn guilty. While they waited in jail to be executed, neither was heard to pray to God, but only to curse and vilify those who had sealed their doom. This too was taken as proof that they were witches.

Arthur Bill. Arthur Bill was described as a "wretched poor man" of the town of Raunds, whose parents were both known to be witches. Like Vaughn and Brown, he was believed to live an evil life and to bewitch cattle. In May 1612, Bill was accused of bewitching a young woman, Martha Aspines (alias Jeames), to death.

The local authorities apprehended Bill and his parents and subjected them to the SWIMMING test by binding

their hands and feet and tossing them into deep water. All three floated, which meant they were guilty of witchcraft. Son Bill was arrested on May 29 and sent to jail.

Fearing that his father would testify against him, Bill sent for his mother and the two bewitched the father so that he was temporarily unable to speak. He did recover his speech, however, and became the leading witness against his son.

His mother feared that she would be hanged as a witch. Her neighbors urged her to throw herself on God's mercy. Instead, she committed suicide by cutting her own throat, allegedly at the command of her FAMILIAR.

Bill was charged with several other crimes besides murder. At his trial, he was said to have three familiars, named Grizel, Ball and Jack. He pleaded innocent to all crimes, but was found guilty. Bill cried out that the law of the land had convicted an innocent man. He maintained his innocence all the way to the gallows and to his last breath.

Nothing is recorded of the fate of his father. His life might have been spared in exchange for testimony against his son.

Helen Jenkson. Helen Jenkson of Thrapston was widely regarded as a witch who bewitched cattle and caused other mischief. She was accused of bewitching a child to death and was pricked and found to have an insensitive WITCH'S MARK upon her body. The woman who pricked Jenkson, Mistress Moulsho, then had an odd thing happen to her laundry. The maid discovered Moulsho's smock to be covered with images of toads, snakes and other "ugly creatures." Moulsho immediately went to the home of Jenkson and threatened to scratch her eyes out if her linen was not made clean of the foul spots. When she got home, the spots were gone.

Jenkson was arrested and imprisoned on May 11, 1612. She pleaded innocent at her trial, but was found guilty. She too maintained her innocence right up to her death.

Mary Barber. No one had anything but the vilest of words to describe Mary Barber of Stanwick, so perhaps it was inevitable that the cloud of witchcraft would eventually fall upon her. She had "mean parents" and was "monstrous and hideous both in her life and actions." She was licentious, wanton, barbarous, rude and violent.

Barber was accused of bewitching cattle and of bewitching a man to death. She pleaded not guilty. An account of her trial notes only that "good evidence" was presented against her, and she was found guilty.

FURTHER READING:
Rosen, Barbara, ed. *Witchcraft in England, 1558–1618.* Amherst: University of Massachusetts Press, 1991.

North Berwick Witches   An alleged COVEN of WITCHES exposed in 1590–91, providing Scotland with its most celebrated witch trials and executions. King James VI (who became JAMES I of England), a believer in witchcraft, took part in the proceedings himself. The TORTURE

The North Berwick witches plead their innocence before the judges, including King James VI (seated) (WOODCUT FROM *NEWES FROM SCOTLAND*, 1591)

applied to the victims was among the most brutal in Scotland's entire history of witch trials.

The North Berwick witches were accused by a maid named Gillis Duncan, who worked for a man named David Seaton in the town of Tranent. Duncan suddenly began to exhibit strange behavior: a miraculous power to cure virtually any kind of sickness. During the night, she would sneak out of her master's house. Seaton suspected that her nocturnal activities, and her miraculous healing power, were related to the DEVIL.

Duncan was not able to explain to Seaton's satisfaction how she had obtained her power, so he had her tortured. Duncan's fingers were crushed in a vise called the *pillwinkes,* and her head was "thrawed," which consisted of it being bound with a rope that was twisted and wrenched savagely. Still she would not confess to witchcraft. A diligent search of her body was made, and a DEVIL'S MARK was found on her throat. At this incriminating evidence, Duncan confessed to being in league with the Devil.

Duncan was imprisoned and induced to betray others. She named JOHN FIAN, a Saltpans schoolmaster and alleged leader of the coven; Agnes Sampson, a respected and elderly woman of Haddington; Euphemia Maclean and Barbara Napier, two respected women of Edinburgh; and a host of other men and women. Duncan said Maclean had conspired to kill her own husband, and Napier had bewitched to death her husband, Archibald, the last earl of Angus. The suspects were arrested.

. Sampson, who had a reputation as a wise woman, was brought before King James and a council of nobles but refused to confess. Her body was shaved, and a Devil's

mark was found on her genitals. Then she was tortured. She was pinned to a wall of her cell by an iron witch's bridle, which had four sharp prongs that were forced into her mouth, against her tongue and cheeks. Her head was thrawed, and she was deprived of sleep. Finally, she broke down and confessed to 53 counts against her, most of which concerned diagnosing and curing diseases by witchcraft.

According to *Newes from Scotland, Declaring the Damnable Life of Dr. Fian, a Notable Sorcerer,* a pamphlet published in 1591, Sampson confessed to attending a SABBAT with 200 witches on All Hallow's Eve, and that "they together went to sea, each one in a riddle, or cive [seive] . . . with flagons of wine, making merrie and drinking." They landed in North Berwick and danced and sang, with Duncan playing the Jew's harp. The Devil appeared and chastised them for tarrying so, and ordered each of them to kiss his buttocks as penance (see KISS OF SHAME). This the witches did, said Sampson, and made their oaths of allegiance. They asked the Devil why he hated King James, and he answered that the king "was the greatest enemie hee hath in the world." Then the witches went home.

James, though he believed in witchcraft, doubted the confessions and accused the witches of being "extreme lyars." To convince him she spoke the truth, Sampson took the king aside and whispered in his ear the words he and his queen exchanged on the first night of their marriage in Norway.

Sampson also confessed to hanging up a black TOAD by the heels and catching the poison that dripped from its mouth in an oyster shell. She obtained from the king's chamber attendant a piece of soiled clothing worn by the monarch and used it with the toad venom to make a CHARM to bewitch the king into feeling "extraordinary pains as if he had been lying upon sharp thorns and endes of needles."

Finally, Sampson revealed to the king how she and the coven of witches had tried to drown James at sea by raising a storm during his journey to Denmark to fetch his bride-to-be. The Devil told them to catch a CAT for the STORM-RAISING charm. When the victim they chose proved to be too fleet-footed for Fian, the Devil raised Fian up in the air and enabled him to catch the cat. The witches christened it and bound to each of its paws the limb of a corpse. Then, sailing through the air in their riddles and cives, they threw the cat in the ocean, crying *Hola!* A terrible storm arose and sank a boat traveling from Brunt Island to Leith, but the king's vessel was unharmed.

Sampson said the same cat was responsible for a foul wind encountered by the king's ship on his way back from Denmark, while the other ships in his company enjoyed a fair wind. The king never would have arrived safely if his faith in God had not prevailed against the witches' charm, she said.

She described another witches' sabbat, which took place at 11 P.M. one night in the North Berwick church and was attended by more than 100 witches, men and women. The witches paid homage to the Devil by curtsying and then turning WIDDERSHINS, the men doing this nine times and the women six. Fian blew open the church doors with his breath. Surrounded by the light of black candles, the Devil mounted the pulpit and preached a sermon, exhorting them to "not spare to do evil; to eat, drink and be merriye, for he should raise them all up gloriously at the last day." Then the company went out to the cemetery, and Satan showed them which graves to open and which corpses to dismember for body parts for charms.

If Sampson had hoped to save herself by making these confessions, she was sadly mistaken. She was condemned, strangled and burned.

John Fian suffered the most extreme torture. He confessed but then recanted. He was strangled and burned in January 1591.

Euphemia Maclean, the daughter of Lord Cliftonhall and the wife of Patrick Moscrop, a wealthy man, possessed her own considerable estate. She was accused of scheming to kill her husband in order to get another man; of conspiring with the other witches to kill the king by destroying a wax image of him; of conspiring to drown a boat between Leith and Linghorne, in which 60 persons drowned; and "many other monstrous points." She was vigorously defended by half a dozen lawyers, but James insisted on a guilty verdict. Maclean was burned on July 25, 1591, and her lands were forfeited to the king, who gave them to Sir James Sandilands. Maclean's children were relieved of making further forfeitures by an act of Parliament in 1592.

Barbara Napier, wife of Archibald Douglas, was accused of consulting with Richard Graham, a "notorious necromancer," and of killing her husband with witchcraft in 1588. She also was accused of the aforementioned crimes along with the other witches and was condemned to be burnt. According to some accounts, her execution was stayed because she pleaded pregnancy. Later, she was set free.

The witches accused the earl of Bothwell of conspiring with them to drown the king at sea. Bothwell, a reputed necromancer, was an enemy of the king. He was charged with high treason and was imprisoned in Edinburgh Castle, but he eventually escaped.

Richard Graham was convicted of witchcraft and SORCERY and was burned in February 1592.

In all, approximately 70 persons were accused of witchcraft or treason in the North Berwick trials. All were probably imprisoned, but the records are unclear as to how many of the rest of them were executed, left in jail or released.

FURTHER READING:
Hole, Christina. *Witchcraft in England.* London: B.T. Batsford Ltd., 1947.

Sharpe, C. K. *A History of Witchcraft in Scotland.* Glasgow: Thomas D. Morison, 1884.
Summers, Montague. *The Geography of Witchcraft.* London: Kegan Paul, Trench, Truner & Co. Ltd., 1927.

Norton, Rosaleen (1917–1979) New Zealand pantheist and artist of the supernatural, whose eerie works of magical consciousness earned her the title of "the Witch of Kings Cross." Rosaleen Norton's surrealistic Pagan work was greatly misunderstood by the public during her life and was subject to censorship.

Norton was born in 1917 in Dunedin, New Zealand, to a family with conventional religious beliefs. Her father was a captain in the merchant navy. By age three, Norton exhibited artistic talent and was drawing unusual pictures of animal-headed ghosts. At age five, she experienced an apparition of a shining dragon at her bedside.

Her family moved to Lindfield, Australia. Norton was expelled from secondary school in Sydney for her drawings of vampires, werewolves, ghosts and other supernatural beings; the headmistress stated that she had a "depraved nature."

At age 15, she began selling occult short stories. She worked for a while as a cadet journalist and then an illustrator for *Smith's Weekly* but found the work too limiting and left. She studied with artist Rayna Hoff, then took her works to the streets to sell. She supported herself with various low-level jobs. She pursued a study of MAGIC, occultism, metaphysics and psychology.

Norton received her inspiration from what she said were real encounters with Pagan deities, especially those of ancient Greece and Rome. They would appear to her in trance visions, but only if they so desired. In addition, to deities, Norton had encounters with Lucifer, BAPHOMET, DEMONS, astral entities and other beings, some of whom she drew as nude half-animal, half-human beings.

In 1949 Norton exhibited paintings at Melbourne University. They shocked and offended many and were treated as obscenities.

In 1952 publisher Walter Glover of Sydney published *The Art of Rosaleen Norton,* a collection of her works accompanied by poems written by Gavin Greenlees, Norton's lover. The book was attacked by critics as "blatant . . . obscenity," and the Post Master General threatened to prosecute Glover for an indecent publication. A magistrate fined the publisher five pounds plus costs for including in the book two illustrations deemed "offensive to public chastity and human decency." The offending works were blacked out of subsequent copies.

Copies shipped to the United States were confiscated and burned by U.S. Customs. Glover had difficulty advertising the book. Serious financial problems developed, and in 1957, Glover declared bankruptcy.

In 1955 Norton's reputation was further damaged by charges that she was "the black witch of Kings Cross" and had participated in Satanic cult activities. The charges were made by a 19-year-old waitress who had been arrested on vagrancy charges and later admitted her accusations against Norton were based on hearsay. Norton attempted to make a public explanation of how PAN, one of her favored deities, was not Satan, but the episode nevertheless was played up sensationally in the press. A month after the arrest of the waitress, Norton and Greenlees were arrested in their basement tenement flat by the vice squad.

Norton and Greenlees endured nearly two years of protracted court hearings, which received a great deal of media attention. The two had been filmed in ceremonial garb performing a ceremonial ritual to Pan. It was alleged that they had engaged in an "unnatural sex act" and that the film supposedly was evidence of a Kings Cross witch cult. There was testimony about the "lewd" and "lustful" nature of Norton's work. Norton and Greenlees eventually were fined 25 pounds each for assisting in the production of obscene photographs.

After the conclusion of the court hearings, Norton retired from public view. She died in 1979.

In 1981 Glover, back in business, received the copyright to Norton's book from the Official Receiver in Bankruptcy. He reissued it in 1982, to a more sympathetic audience.

FURTHER READING:
Drury, Neville. *Pan's Daughter.* Sydney: Collins Australia, 1988.

Nurse, Rebecca (1621–1692)   Accused witch executed in the SALEM WITCHES hysteria in Massachusetts in 1692–93.

Rebecca Nurse and her husband Francis were two of the most prominent and well-respected citizens of Salem. They had established a prosperous farm compound that was almost self sufficient, supporting a large extended family of several generations. Their prosperity was envied, and they angered some of the residents by their involvement in a land dispute.

However, the Nurses were regular churchgoers, and Rebecca was known for her meek demeanor and good deeds; she was saintlike. Of all the people who might be candidates for witchcraft, she was probably the least likely. By the time of the hysteria, she was old and infirm as well, suffering from stomach problems and weakness that kept her confined for days to her home.

Historians have speculated that had she been the first to be accused, few would have believed the charges, and the hysteria might have died an early death with no, or perhaps few, casualties. But the hysteria of the girls by then were believed by too many residents. When the girls cried out against Nurse, their charges were taken seriously by many. Envy of the Nurses' prosperity and status, and simmering resentments over the land dispute, may have played a role in the fate of Rebecca. It is possible that the accusing girls picked up on gossip against Rebecca and her family. She also was vocal in her criticism of the examinations and upheld the innocence of the first women accused. Soon the girls were muttering against Rebecca as a witch.

Some of the Nurses' friends paid a visit to the Nurse farm to warn Rebecca. There they found her in ill health, sick for about a week with a stomach ailment. Nurse voluntarily raised the issue of the hysteria and how badly she felt for Reverend Samuel Parris and his family. She said she believed the girls were indeed afflicted by an "evil hand," but that the accused were innocent. When told that she was being cried out against as a witch herself, Nurse was astonished. She replied, "If it be so, the will of the Lord be done . . . I am as innocent as the child unborn; but surely, what sin hath God found out in me unrepented of, that he should lay such an affliction upon me in my old age?"

On March 23, 1692, a warrant was issued for Nurse's arrest. She was questioned the following day before a public audience that included the girls. When told that several of the girls claimed she had harmed them by beating and afflicting them with pain, Nurse said God would declare her innocence. It appeared that she might be set free. Then Ann Putnam Sr., worked into an emotional frenzy, declared that Nurse had appeared to her with the "black man," the DEVIL, and tempted her. Putnam's charge incited the crowd. When Nurse then beseeched God to help her, the girls fell into terrible fits, claiming that Nurse and her FAMILIARS were harming them.

There was more damning testimony. A neighbor Sarah Houlton claimed that Nurse had cursed her husband to death because his pigs got loose on the Nurse farm. Another neighbor, Henry Kenney, said Nurse bewitched him so that he could not breathe properly whenever he was near her.

Hathorne had Nurse examined for WITCH'S MARKS. Several were found. Nurse protested that any older person such as herself would have growths on their body.

Judge John Hathorne questioned Nurse at length. She either repeated her innocence or said she could make no reply. The latter answer seemed most troubling to the magistrates and the crowd. The girls mimicked every body movement that Nurse made and fell into repeated fits. Nurse acknowledged that she thought the girls were bewitched. Even more damning to herself was her answer that she thought the Devil could indeed appear in her shape. Ann Putnam went into such violent fits that she had to be carried from the meeting house. Nurse was sent to jail to await further examination, which took place on April 11.

Sentiments about Nurse were mixed. Even Hathorne was doubtful that such a pious woman could be in league with the Devil. Thirty-nine of her friends signed a petition in her favor—including even Jonathan Putnam, who had been one of her original accusers.

Nurse was tried in the Court of Oyer & Terminer on June 30 with four others. Ann Putnam Jr. testified that Nurse had killed six children, and Houlton retold the story of her husband's cursed death.

Despite the testimony against her, Nurse was the only one found not guilty by the jury. The accusers fell into fits in protest. Not all of the judges were happy with the verdict, and William Stoughton said he would seek a new indictment against her. Accused witch Abigail Hobbs was brought out from jail to testify against Nurse. Rebecca recognized her as "one of us." She probably meant as a fellow prisoner and accused, but the court took her words to mean a fellow witch. Asked to explain herself, Nurse remained silent. The jury changed the verdict to guilty.

Nurse's friends appealed to Governor William Phips, who granted Nurse a reprieve. It did no good. Nurse's church in Salem excommunicated her on July 3. Nurse was executed by hanging on July 19. Her death demonstrated that no one was safe from the accusations of witchcraft.

FURTHER READING:
Demos, John Putnam. *Entertaining Satan: Witchcraft and the Culture of Early New England.* New York: Oxford University Press, 2004.
Hansen, Chadwick. *Witchcraft at Salem.* New York: New American Library, 1969.
Upham, Charles. *History of Witchcraft and Salem Village.* Boston: Wiggin and Lunt, 1867.

oak apples Oak apples are galls formed on oak trees by the larva of a type of wasp. In folk MAGIC, they are used as a means of divining whether or not a child has been bewitched or struck by the EVIL EYE. To determine bewitchment, three oak apples are cut from a tree and dropped into a bowl or pail of water that is placed beneath the child's cradle. If they float, the child is safe; if they sink, he or she is bewitched. The procedure requires strict silence or it will not be accurate.

See DIVINATION.

obsession Although the terms *obsession* and *possession* have been used interchangeably, obsession, from the Latin *obsidere*, technically refers to "besieging" or attacking a person or personality from without. POSSESSION, on the other hand, refers to being completely taken over by the DEVIL, DEMONS or other spirits from within. Medieval theologians distinguished between the two states, although in neither case was the victim responsible.

Saints could not be possessed, but could be obsessed by devils and evil thoughts. Usually such torments afflicted monks and hermits who lived ascetic, celibate lives, often in the desert. The *Life of St. Hilary* tells how the saint's "temptations were numerous; . . . how often when he lay down did naked women appear to him." And when St. Anthony tried to sleep, the Devil assumed the form of a woman and tried to seduce him with feminine gestures. Other holy or biblical figures, such as Saul, also suffered obsessive spirits, not total possession.

In the 17th century a young Spanish nun, Doña Micaela de Aguirre, was obsessed by the Devil. Irritated by Doña Micaela's perfection, the Devil began tormenting her, appearing one night in the shape of a horse. He stood on Micaela with his full weight, kicking and trampling her and leaving her badly bruised. Sometimes the Devil immersed Doña Micaela in the convent well up to her neck, leaving her there all night. In the end, according to her biographer, Doña Micaela triumphed: "Mocking his

Man obsessed by Devil (JOHANNES LICHTENBERGER, *PROGNOSTICATIO,* 1500)

cunning she bade him fetch an axe and chop wood. And the enemy could not disobey her [for she was a saint]; he took the axe and chopped the wood up with all haste and departed in confusion, roaring with anger at being defeated by a young nun."

In modern psychiatry, obsession means being totally dominated by a fixed idea that controls or affects all other actions, such as constantly checking to see if a door is locked, or believing that deadly germs are everywhere. Most physicians do not believe that a person can become totally possessed by demons from within.

oils (also anointing oils)   Perfumed and floral oils have played an important role in magical and religious rites throughout history. Their efficacy is based on the belief that odors and scents have the power to affect people and objects. In ancient Egypt, magical SPELLS to assure the well-being of the dead called for the magician to anoint himself with certain oils. The Catholic Church uses sacred oils in baptisms, confirmations and the ordination of priests. In contemporary Witchcraft, scented oils are used to perfume the air prior to rituals, to create a pleasing atmosphere for the gods, and scented and plain oils are used in anointing in INITIATION, self-blessings, Wiccaning and magical spells. Oils also are common in folk magic and in the magical spells of VODUN and SANTERÍA.

The formula for oils depends upon their purpose. The oil itself should be pure and virgin; olive oil is ideal, but other vegetable oils are also used. The oils are mixed with various herbs, flowers, roots and essences. As the Witch works, she chants over them a CHARM related to the oils. The bottles or vials are left in the dark for several days to increase the potency of the oils.

Anointing oils are rubbed on various parts of the body, such as the palms, forehead, heart, genitals and chakras; are placed in shoes; and are rubbed onto ritual tools. They also are rubbed onto CANDLES, which are then burned in spells and rites; and onto effigies and POPPETS.

Oils are made for numerous purposes, such as to attract love, money, protection and luck; to ward off negative influences, the EVIL EYE and illness; to cast or break CURSES; to bless, confuse and influence others; to enhance psychic powers and "dream true"; to gain success and win victory in legal disputes.

Examples of formulas are as follows: to attract health, mix two ounces of virgin oil with a single scent, either rose, gardenia, carnation, grated lemon peel or lemon flowers. A blessing oil for ritual tools and altar consists of two tablespoons of a mixture of two parts frankincense and one part benzoin gum, added to two ounces of oil.

FURTHER READING:
Marlbrough, Ray L. *Charms, Spells & Formulas.* St. Paul: Llewellyn Publications, 1987.

ointments (also unguents)   Grease-based preparations have been used in magical, healing and oracular rites since ancient times. The ancient Egyptians used magical and sacred ointments for numerous purposes, such as embalming mummies and stimulating prophetic dreams. According to the instructions on a third-century magical papyrus, divining dreams could be induced in an elaborate rite, part of which called for the smearing of a magical ointment on the eyes. The ointment was made from the flowers of "the Greek bean," which could be purchased from a garland seller. The flowers were sealed in a glass container and left for 20 days in a dark and secret place. When the container was opened, it would reveal a phallus and testicles inside. The container was resealed for another 40 days, after which the genitals would become bloody. The ointment made from this was kept on a piece of glass in a pot that was hidden, and was rubbed on the eyes when an answer to a question was desired from one's dreams.

In folklore, witches were reputed to use ointments— also called *sorcerer's grease*—for two purposes: FLYING and to kill others. Some ointments also were said to enable witches to shape-shift into animals and birds (see METAMORPHOSIS). Recipes for ointments have been handed down through the centuries and have been published in magical GRIMOIRES. The recipes contain vile ingredients such as baby's fat and bat's BLOOD, or bizarre ingredients such as the filings of BELLS. Many also call for herbs and drugs that are toxic and/or hallucinogenic, such as belladonna (the "Devil's weed"), hemlock, hellebore root, *cannabis,* hemp, MANDRAKE, henbane and aconite. Such drugs produce dizziness, confusion, shortness of breath, irregular heartbeat, delirium and hallucinations.

According to lore, witches of old brewed the ointments in their CAULDRONS. For flying, they rubbed the ointments on themselves and the BROOMS, pitchforks, chairs, poles or beanstalks that they used to ride through the air. Some accused witches confessed in trials that they were given magic ointments by the DEVIL. Five women brought to trial in Arras, France, in 1460 said they had been given such an ointment by Satan, which they rubbed on small poles and "straightway flew where they wished to be, above good towns and woods and waters, and the Devil guided them to that place where they must hold their assembly."

Legends tell of people who found pots of ointment, rubbed themselves with it and instantly found themselves transported to the scene of wild witch revelries.

While witches often insisted they had indeed flown through the air with the help of their ointments, most demonologists, as early as the 15th century, believed the effects to be imaginary and not real. In some tests conducted by investigators, a witch rubbed herself down with the ointment and then fell into a deep sleep. Upon awakening, she insisted she had been transported through the air to a SABBAT, when in fact she had been observed not

Witches concocting flying ointment before the sabbat (HANS BALDUNG GRIEN, 1514)

moving for hours. In a tale from 1547, a witch summoned before the INQUISITION of Navarre secretly brought along a jar of magic ointment, which she managed to rub on herself. In front of the judges, she turned into a screech owl and flew away.

One recipe published in REGINALD SCOT's *Discoverie of Witchcraft* (1584) calls for sium, *Acarum vulgare* (probably sweet flag), cinquefoil, bat's blood, oil and *Solanum somniferum,* combined with fat or lard, which the witches were supposed to rub vigorously into their skin "till they look red and be verie hot, so as the pores may be opened and their flesh soluble and loose."

Scot also offered another flying recipe, which called for the fat of young children to be boiled in water and combined with "eleoselinum" (probably hemlock), aconite, poplar leaves and soot. Still another recipe called for aconite, poppy juice, foxglove, poplar leaves and cinquefoil, in a base of beeswax, lanoline and almond oil.

Like demonologists of his time, Scot believed that the ointments affected the brain and did not really enable witches to fly.

In modern times, Dr. Erich-Will Peuckert of the University of Göttingen, West Germany, tested a medieval flying-ointment recipe on himself and a colleague. The ingredients included deadly nightshade, thornapple, henbane, wild celery and parsley in a base of hog's lard. The ointment caused the two men to fall into a trancelike sleep for 20 hours, during which each had nearly identical dreams of flying through the air to a mountain top and participating in erotic orgies with monsters and DEMONS. Upon awakening, both men had headaches and felt depressed. Peuckert was impressed with the intense realism of the dreams. In light of his experiment, it is probable that medieval witches who used such ointments believed that they actually had such experiences, which accounts for the similarities in many "confessions."

The following killing ointment was recorded by JOHANN WEYER, 16th-century demonologist:

Hemlock, juice of aconite,
Poplar leaves and roots bind tight.
Watercress and add to oil
Baby's fat and let it boil.
Bat's blood, belladonna too
Will kill off those who bother you.

It is possible that some medicinal ointments, concocted by village wise women and wise men for deadening pain and healing, contained an imbalance of toxic ingredients that proved fatal.

Another kind of ointment supposedly made witches invisible. Medieval witches were said to rub themselves down with it before leaving their homes for secret sabbats. The chief ingredient was the herb VERVAIN, associated with invisibility, which was crushed and steeped overnight in olive oil or lard, then squeezed through a cloth to remove the leaves. Sometimes mint was substituted for vervain.

GERALD B. GARDNER, the father of contemporary Witchcraft, said he knew of no 20th-century Witches who used any kind of ointments. Gardner believed medieval witches did use ointments but said such preparations most likely were applied to help keep naked witches warm in outdoor rites or to make them slippery if they were caught, both of which are dubious. Some ointments, he said, contained perfumes that were released in dancing as the skin grew hot.

FURTHER READING:
Baroja, Julio Caro. *The World of the Witches.* 1961. Reprint, Chicago: University of Chicago Press, 1975.
Gardner, Gerald B. *Witchcraft Today.* London: Rider & Co., 1954, 1956.
Remy, Nicolas. *Demonolatry.* Secaucus, N.J.: University Books, 1974.
Scot, Reginald. *The Discoverie of Witchcraft.* 1886. Reprint, Yorkshire, England: E.P. Publishing, Ltd., 1973.

Old Dorothy Clutterbuck See CLUTTERBUCK, OLD DOROTHY.

Old Shuck See BLACK ANIMALS.

ordeal by touch A means of identifying a witch. Ordeal by touch was used in the interrogation and trial of accused witches in Europe, the British Isles and the American colonies.

The ordeal called for the accused to touch a victim, someone who claimed to have been bewitched or afflicted by the accused. If the fits or problem vanished, that meant the accused was guilty because they had taken the CURSE back into themselves.

Order of the Garter The highest order of knights in Great Britain, founded by King Edward III in 1350, it was linked to the witch cult by British anthropologist MARGARET A. MURRAY. Her evidence is dubious, though there are some curious aspects to this chivalric Order.

Edward conceived the Order in 1344 and formally created it on St. George's Day, April 23, 1350, in honor of the Holy Trinity, the Virgin Mary, St. Edward the Confessor and St. George, the patron saint of England. The Order is sometimes called The Order of St. George.

According to legend, the Order resulted from an episode at court. While the king danced with the Countess of Salisbury, her garter fell to the floor. The king swooped it up and placed it on his own leg, saying, *"Honi soit qui mal y pense"* ("Shame on him who thinks evil of it"). The remark became the Order's motto. The official emblem was a dark blue ribbon edged in gold, bearing the motto in gold letters; this ribbon was worn below the left knee.

The Order originally numbered 26: 12 knights led by Edward, plus 12 knights led by the Prince of Wales. Beginning in 1786 the Order was opened to admit others. In modern times, the order has a dean and 12 canons.

In *The Witch-cult in Western Europe* (1921), Murray reads a great deal of significance into the numbers of the Order. The original groups of 13—12 plus a leader—equate with the supposedly traditional number in a witches' COVEN. THIRTEEN is still represented in the modern structure: a dean plus 12 canons. Murray also points out that Edward's mantle, as Chief of the Order, bore 168 garters. He wore another garter on his leg, and the total of 169 equals 13 times 13.

According to modern witch lore, GARTERS were worn as a secret means of identification. GERALD B. GARDNER, in *Witchcraft Today* (1954), suggested that the countess of Salisbury was a witch and that Edward immediately recognized her dropped garter as her secret identification and gallantly saved her from being exposed and brought to trial. Garters, however, were in fashion at the time, and it was not unusual for ladies of the court to be wearing them.

Gardner further speculated that a Black Book, containing the Order's original constitution, was spirited away after Edward's death in 1377.

Most likely, the purpose of the Order of the Garter was nothing more than what Edward publicly intended it to be: purely one of chivalry. Thanks largely to Murray, a "tradition" of garters for witches was created.

FURTHER READING:
Murray, Margaret A. *The Witch-Cult in Western Europe.* London: Oxford University Press, 1921.

owls   The owl is associated with death, SORCERY and the dark underside of life. To the ancient Egyptians, the owl represented night, death and cold. The Bible (Leviticus) says the owl is an unclean bird. The ancient Greeks, however, viewed it as the sacred symbol of wisdom, for the owl was the constant companion of Athena, goddess of wisdom.

The ancient Romans considered the bird a bad omen, presaging death; Caesar's murder was announced by the screeching of owls. Besides death, the hooting of an owl foretells illness, bad weather and the loss of virginity of a village girl. In European and American folklore, various CHARMS could counteract the owl: throwing SALT in a fire, turning one's pockets inside out or tying KNOTS in a handkerchief.

The Aztecs equated owls with evil spirits, including one regarded as the enemy of the human race, whose name

A boy watches a witch shape-shift into an owl (18TH-CENTURY WOODCUT)

was "Rational Owl." In Africa, owls are feared because they are instruments of sorcerers (see AFRICAN WITCH-CRAFT). To North American Indians, the owl is a bird of ill omen, either the harbinger of death or a messenger from the dead. The Sauk believe that if an owl is seen at night, it will cause facial paralysis. Chippewa medicine men stuff the skin of an owl with magic ingredients and direct it to fly to a victim's house and cause starvation. Folk healers in Peru use owls to combat negative sorcery. In Peruvian myth, the "owl woman" is associated with shamanistic rituals and magical curing (see SHAMANISM).

DEMONS in the forms of owls supposed attended witches, accompanying them on their broomstick flights and running errands of evil for them. Magicians and healers used owl feathers as a charm to lull people to sleep.

In some cultures, the owl has long been respected. In India, eating owl eyeballs is said to give a person night vision. The Kiowa Indians of North America believe medicine men turn into owls at death.

FURTHER READING:

Leach, Maria, ed., and Jerome Fried, assoc. ed. *Funk & Wagnall's Standard Dictionary of Folklore, Mythology and Legend.* New York: Harper & Row, 1972.

Opie, Iona, and Moira Tatem. *A Dictionary of Superstitions.* New York: Oxford University Press, 1989.

Pagan Federation   International organization based in London that provides information on PAGANISM, counters misconceptions about the religion and works for the rights of Pagans to worship in freedom. The Pagan Federation also provides networking help among Pagans and "genuine seekers of the Old Ways" and aids in the contact and dialogue among the various traditions of Paganism worldwide. Its mission statement is "to promote and defend the Pagan traditions."

Originally called the Pagan Front, the federation was founded in 1971 by members of the four branches of the Old Religion of Wisecraft. One of the key founders was JOHN SCORE, also known as *M*, who served for years as editor of the influential periodical, *The Wiccan*, which became the newsletter of the federation. *The Wiccan* evolved into a quarterly magazine called *Pagan Dawn*.

The Pagan Federation works with institutions, governmental bodies and the public to present accurate information on Pagan religious views and rights. It seeks to uphold Article 18 of the Universal Declaration of Human Rights, to which Britain is a signatory, which states:

> Everyone has the right to freedom of thought, conscience and religion; this right includes freedom to change his religion or belief, and freedom, either alone or in community with others and in public and private, to manifest his religion or belief in teaching, practice, worship and observance.

Membership is open to anyone 16 years of age (the age was lowered from 18 to 16 in 2007) who agrees with these three principles, stated as:

1. Love and kinship with Nature. Reverence for the life force and its ever-renewing cycles of life and death.
2. The Pagan Ethic: *If it harm none, Do what thou wilt.* This is a positive morality, expressing the belief in individual responsibility for discovering one's own true nature and developing it fully, in harmony with the outer world and community.
3. Honoring the Totality of Divine Reality, which transcends gender, without suppressing either the female or male aspect of Deity.

The Pagan Federation sponsors events for members and for the public. It has prison, hospital, community service and interfaith activities. It is a member of PEBBLE.

FURTHER READING:
The Pagan Federation Web site. Available online. URL: http://www.paganfed.org/about.php. Downloaded November 4, 2007.

Paganism   Contemporary Earth-based spiritual traditions and paths blending elements of pre-Christian, Christian and non-Christian religions. The PAGAN FEDERATION defines Paganism as a "polytheistic or pantheistic nature-worshiping religion."

A women's ritual celebrated at a Pagan gathering, sponsored by Circle Sanctuary of Wisconsin (COURTESY CIRCLE SANCTUARY)

Paganism is one of the fastest-growing new religions. A 2007 report in the United Kingdom estimated the number of Pagans in Britain at approximately 43,000, with approximately 2,000 in Scotland. Dozens of Pagan paths exist all over the world, and new ones are always in creation. WITCHCRAFT comprises the largest segment of Paganism.

Pagan is a Latin term meaning "country-dweller." In the early days of Christianity, which was largely a religion of cities, "pagan" was applied to those who adhered to their old religious beliefs. As the Christian Church grew in strength and eradicated and absorbed old religions and rival sects, pagan became a derogatory term. It implied that one was unsophisticated and uneducated and worshiped false gods.

In contemporary times, Pagan as a proper noun refers primarily to practitioners of traditions reconstructed from early classical and European roots and also to traditions created from shamanic and tribal traditions. Some practitioners prefer the term "Neo-Pagan," first used in the United States by OBERON ZELL-RAVENHEART, a principal founder of the CHURCH AND SCHOOL OF WICCA.

Paganism flowered in the 1960s as an outgrowth of the new Witchcraft founded by GERALD B. GARDNER, aided by liberal interests in feminism, Goddess spirituality, ecology, Gaia, New Age spirituality and a desire for personal direct and transcendent experience of the Divine. A connection to and reverence for Nature is common to all of the diverse traditions within Paganism. At its core, Paganism emphasizes direct experience of the divine of a mystical or magical nature.

Paganism has three central characteristics. It is polytheistic and recognizes a plurality of divine beings. It views the material world as a theophany, a manifestation of divinity. It recognizes the divine feminine.

Paganism means different things to different followers: it is a religion, a philosophy and a way of life. As a movement, it is not unified, centralized, structured or highly organized, which is one of its key appeals. There is no bureaucracy, dogma or orthodoxy. There are few "churches" and paid clergy. Practitioners are free to design and follow their own unique ways of experiencing and worshiping the divine. Some Pagans belong to groups, but the majority prefer to practice as SOLITARIES.

Paganism appeals primarily to white middle-class individuals. Many are attracted to it because of deeply moving or mystical experiences they had involving Nature. They also may find the Judeo-Christian God remote, inaccessible and intangible. They may have become alienated over dogma and orthodoxy and institutional insistence that clergy must mediate between them and the divine.

Others find Paganism through a study of religions, philosophy, folklore, archeology, mythology or the classics or through environmental concerns and politics. One does not "become" a Pagan so much as "come home to" Paganism.

Scholar RONALD HUTTON identifies four "direct lines of connection" between the paganism of the past and the Paganism of the present: 1) high ritual magic; 2) "hedge," or folk, witchcraft; 3) the general and continuing interest in the art and literature of the ancient world; and 4) folk rites, such as those observed at seasonal festivals.

In his study of the pagan religions of the British Isles, Hutton observes that contemporary people know very little about the old pagan religions of the ancient British Isles (which are looked to as sources for much of modern Paganism). Much information has been demonstrated to be wrong or cannot be proved.

Contemporary Paganism makes little or no claim to represent ancient religions. Rather, Pagans draw upon a heritage of history, folklore, mythology, literature, art, archaeology and even science fiction and fantasy to reconstruct the essence of ancient Paganism for contemporary interests and needs.

Three principles reflect the core beliefs of many Pagans:

Love for and kinship with Nature. Pagans do not seek to dominate Nature, but live in harmony with it, revering the life force and the eternal cycle of birth-death-rebirth. Divinity is immanent in the realm of Nature, as it is in all things in creation. The planet has its own living consciousness. The cycles of Nature are celebrated in seasonal festivals (see WHEEL OF THE YEAR) and RITUALS are observed around the phases of the MOON. Many Pagans are environmental activists.

The Pagan Ethic. "Do what thou wilt but harm none" is the same ethic as the WICCAN REDE. It places responsibility on the individual to develop self-knowledge and truth and express it in harmony with all things.

The Divine Masculine and Feminine. Divine Oneness is expressed in the divine feminine and masculine, which engage in an eternal cosmic dance of creation. Pagans honors the "totality of divine reality," which transcends gender and does not suppress either the male or female aspect of Deity. The aspects of Deity, expressed through many gods and goddesses, are for many practitioners real beings who share the world with human beings. The divine is also expressed in the forces of nature and within individuals.

Most Pagans believe in the "threefold effect," which, like the Witches' THREEFOLD LAW OF RETURN, holds that an individual's actions are returned to him or her magnified three times. RITES OF PASSAGE are an important part of Paganism. Most believe in some form of reincarnation.

There are dominant traditions within Paganism, but as a whole the movement has grown increasingly eclectic. As mentioned earlier, Witchcraft is the largest tradition. Among others are:

Druidry. The second largest tradition within Paganism, Druidry is oriented around the Sun, as opposed to the Moon for Witchcraft. Little is known about the Druids of antiquity, who apparently were the priestly caste of the Celts. The Romans annihilated them. In the 18th century in Britain, a revival of interest in Druids produced various ceremonial orders that purported to reconstruct Druidic rites. Contemporary Druidry is also a reconstruction.

Some orders of contemporary Druids are divided into the three orders of antiquity: the Bards, or poets; the Ovates, or seers: and the Druids, or priestly politicians. The tradition is reconstructed from Celtic rites and the ancient bardic tradition of preserving laws, myth and culture in poetry and storytelling.

Contemporary Druidry is both esoteric and exoteric. It does not recognize a creator; P. E. I. ISAAC BONEWITS observes that the universe "just is," and no one know where it came from or why. One of the primary purposes of Druidry, and of Paganism in general, says Bonewits, is to save the planet by making people more ecologically responsible.

Not all Druids consider themselves Pagan; some are decidedly Christian and see Druidry more as a philosophy and way of life rather than a religion. Non-Celtic traditions have been absorbed into Druidry (as well as other Pagan traditions), such as Native American sweat lodges, shamanic journeying, Eastern meditation and kabbalistic teachings.

Heathenism. A group of traditions identified particularly with Germanic and Scandinavian traditions. Among the best-known are Odinism, Northern Tradition, Asatru and Vanatru. Deity is recognized in its personifications from northern mythologies. The Aesir are the deities of the sky and the Vanir are the deities of the Earth. The runes are an important tool for accessing the mysteries. Some Heathens prefer not to blend elements of other traditions with the Northern cosmology.

Men's and women's mystery traditions. Numerous groups pursue self-knowledge through the mysteries surrounding the GODDESS and HORNED GOD. They offer initiations drawn from antiquity, such as the rites of Mithras or the rites of ISIS, perhaps combined with magic. The most prominent of the women's groups are Dianic, named after the independent goddess DIANA. They are inspired by the ideas of matriarchy and feminism.

Shamanism. Shamanic traditions and paths are attracting increasing numbers of Pagans who desire direct contact with the spirit world achieved through altered states of consciousness. Healing is especially important in Pagan Shamanism.

Though diverse, Pagan traditions share many common values and practices. Diversity is important, and Pagans tend to be more open-minded than the general public on such topics as gay, lesbian, bisexual and group marriage lifestyles. Pagans value sensuality and sexuality as part of their spiritual experience.

Pagans are more open to paranormal experience, and more likely to have paranormal experiences than the general public. For Pagans, all things are interconnected; there is no such thing as random coincidence.

Freedom of choice in spiritual pursuits is highly valued. Many Pagans are ambivalent about Paganism becoming more socially acceptable in the mainstream. On one hand, it means less prejudice and harassment. However, many Pagans feel that mainstream acceptance will dilute Paganism.

Magic is not practiced by all Pagans, but when it is, it is emphasized as a force for healing and benefit, not for harm. Much of the magic practiced emphasizes self-realization rather than SPELL-casting.

Rituals vary, but share some common elements drawn from English-based magical practices, such as the uses of ritual tools, the casting of MAGICAL CIRCLES, the drawing down or evocation of spiritual power, and so forth.

Paganism continues to flourish, as first-generation Pagans have children who opt also for Pagan paths. As in Witchcraft, there are tensions and debates over such issues as to how much institutionalization and structure are desirable; whether or not a professional priesthood should be created; whether or not it is appropriate for spiritual teachers and students to engage in sex; and how to raise Pagan children. Many Pagans see Paganism as "the" religious calling for the 21st century. Most mainsteam people, however, prefer religion with structure and orthodoxy—the very antithesis of Paganism.

Trends include

- An increase in the visibility and social acceptance of Paganism
- An increase in Pagan scholarship and academic studies
- An increase in high-profile Pagan professionals and artisans, who are creating a substantial body of Pagan literature, art, film, performing arts and music with mainstream appeal
- An increase in Pagan journals, books and information (including on the Internet) for dissemination to the public
- An increase in social services tailored especially for Pagans
- An increasing willingness to legally fight discrimination and harassment
- The development of a body of standard Pagan rituals and rites of passage
- An increase in religious freedom networking and interfaith dialogue
- An increase in the number of cross-tradition Pagan festival gatherings and Pagan representation at international congresses of religions

See CIRCLE SANCTUARY; PAGAN WAY; PEBBLE.

FURTHER READING:

Adler, Margot. *Drawing Down the Moon*. Rev. ed. New York: Viking, 1986.

Berger, Helen A., Evan A. Leach, and Leigh Shaffer. *Voices from the Pagan Census: A National Survey of Witches and Neo-Pagans in the United States*. Columbia: University of South Carolina Press, 2003.

Crowley, Vivianne. *Phoenix from the Flame: Pagan Spirituality in the Western World*. London: Aquarian, 1994.

———. *Principles of Paganism*. London: Thorsons/HarperCollins, 1996.

Harvey, Graham. *Contemporary Paganism: Listening People, Speaking Earth*. New York: New York University Press, 1997.

Harvey, Graham, and Charlotte Hardman, eds. *Paganism Today*. London: Thorsons/HarperCollins, 1996.

Hopman, Ellen Evert, and Lawrence Bond. *Being a Pagan: Druids, Wiccans and Witches Today*. Rochester, Vt.: Destiny Books, 2002.

Hutton, Ronald. *The Pagan Religions of the Ancient British Isles: Their Nature and Legacy*. Oxford: Blackwell Publishers, 1991.

Kemp, Anthony. *Witchcraft and Paganism Today*. London: Michael O'Mara Books, Ltd., 1993.

Pagan Way Contemporary Pagan movement that emerged in America in 1970 in response to a rapidly rising interest in PAGANISM, WITCHCRAFT and MAGIC. Existing Witchcraft covens, with traditional intensive screening programs and "year-and-a-day" probationary periods, were unable to accommodate the large number of inquiries and applicants. Pagan Way provided an alternative with an open, nature-oriented system that emphasized celebration of nature over magic and that had no formal INITIATION or membership requirements.

One of the central figures in the development of Pagan Way was Joseph B. Wilson, an American witch who founded a popular journal, *The Waxing Moon*, in 1965. While stationed with the U.S. Air Force in England in 1969, Wilson began and coordinated correspondence among 15 to 20 groups and persons interested in establishing an esoteric form of Paganism. Among other key figures were ED FITCH, an American and high priest in the Gardnerian tradition, at the time stationed with the U.S. Air Force in North Dakota; Fred and Martha Adler, American witches in California; JOHN SCORE (also known as M) of England, who wielded considerable influence on both sides of the Atlantic through his newsletter, *The Wiccan;* the leaders of the Regency and Plant Bran covens in Britain; Tony Kelly, British poet; and Susan Roberts, journalist and author of *Witches U.S.A.*

After four to five months of round-robin correspondence, the founders decided upon basic principles for the new movement and conceived ideas for rituals. Fitch and Kelly began writing introductory materials. Fitch composed group and solitary rituals based on Celtic and European folk traditions, with some Gardnerian influence. In addition, he composed material for an Outer Court, an introduction to Witchcraft. The material first appeared in *The Waxing Moon,* the publication of which Wilson turned over to Fitch and Thomas Giles, of Philadelphia, in 1969.

Fitch and Giles set up mailing centers in Minot, North Dakota, and Philadelphia. The Pagan material was so enthusiastically received that Fitch and Giles approved the establishment of additional, independent mailing centers.

The rituals, lore and background material were never copyrighted but were placed in the public domain in order to gain the widest possible distribution. Over the years, they have been republished several times by various occult houses as *The Rituals of the Pagan Way, A Book of Pagan Rituals* and perhaps under other titles as well.

In the 1970s Pagan Way groves spread across the United States, primarily in major cities but also in some small communities. Many followers were solitaries. Pagan Way appealed to two main audiences: those just getting started in Witchcraft, and those interested in attending Pagan ceremonies and structuring social and civic activities around them, much like mainstream churches. According to Fitch, the movement never was intended to address the esoteric audience of mystery seekers. Eventually, adaptations were made for those who wanted more esoteric aspects: initiation rites were added by Cole, Enderle and others, and secret, closed Outer Courts were formed which gave more emphasis to magic.

In 1971 Wilson resumed editorship of *The Waxing Moon;* Fitch and Giles renamed their journal *The Crystal Well* and published separately.

Pagan Way groves thrived during the 1970s. The founders and early organizers let the movement take its own course. No central organization was formed; the groves and mailing centers remained autonomous and loosely affiliated. By 1980 what little there was of the organization had fallen apart, and groves dwindled in size and number. An ever-changing scene of new groups emerged out of Pagan Way. The Pagan Way rituals, however, endured, and continue to be used and adapted by numerous succeeding Pagan groups.

In the United Kingdom, the movement evolved separately from the American movement with the founding in 1971 of the Pagan Front, which later changed its name to the PAGAN FEDERATION.

Pan   Greek pastoral deity of flocks and herds, who was half man and half goat, with the legs, horns and beard of a goat. He was the offspring of either HERMES and Penel-ope, or Hermes and Dryope, daughter of King Dropys, whose flocks he tended. His cult was centered in Arcadia, where he haunted the woodlands, hills and mountains, sleeping at noon and then dancing through the woods as he played the panpipes, which he invented. As a lusty leader of satyrs, he chased the nymphs; he later was incorporated into the retinue of Dionysus. His symbol was the phallus, and he was invoked for the fertility of flocks, or an abundant hunt. Every region in Greece had its own Pan, who was known by various names, and Pan eventually came to symbolize the universal god. He is recognized in PAGANISM and contemporary Witchcraft and is an aspect of the HORNED GOD.

Parsons, Hugh (mid-17th century)   One of the few trials in the early American colonies of a man accused of witchcraft was that of Hugh Parsons, which took place in 1651 in Springfield, Connecticut. A successful sawyer and bricklayer, Parsons enjoyed a reputation as an "honest, sensible laboring" man, according to the records of his trial. He was one of the first settlers in the Springfield area.

Parsons married a young woman, Mary Lewis, on October 27, 1645. Mary had a sharp tongue and did not get along with some of her neighbors. Furthermore, she had swings in mood and temper. At some point in the marriage, Mary accused Goodwife Marshfield of bewitching the children of Mr. Moxon, the settlement's minister. Goody Marshfield sued for libel and won. Parsons made no secret of his opinion that the verdict was due to false testimony, but he paid the fine of 24 bushels of corn plus 20 shillings.

Sometime later, Parsons had another run-in involving Moxon. The dispute concerned an alleged agreement to replace the bricks in Moxon's chimney. Parsons conceded to Moxon's terms and did the job, muttering that now Parsons "would be even with" Moxon, and "this will be the end of it."

Such incidents stirred up resentment against Parsons and his wife among the townspeople. Furthermore, the area had been plagued since 1641 by bad fortune and mischief attributed to witches. Evidently, the townspeople finally decided to put a stop to their troubles by prosecuting a witch, and Parsons provided them with the ideal victim.

On October 4, 1649, the Parsonses had their first child, Samuel, who died a year later. On October 26, 1650, a second son, Joshua, was born. Shortly after the baby's birth, Mary's mental and physical health began to deteriorate. She neglected her baby, which languished and died on March 11, 1651. Mary was declared permanently insane, having been rendered so by witchcraft. Her condition and the deaths of her two infants were taken as legal evidence that both she and Parsons were witches. The records state, "the clamor against the Father increased and he was denounced as a Witch on all Sides."

Parsons was brought to trial in Springfield first. There was no shortage of "evidence" against him, including the testimony of the vengeful Moxon and Goody Marshfield. A jury convicted him of bewitching his second child to death.

Mary was sent to jail in Boston on May 1. She went to trial on May 7 facing two charges: having familiarity with the DEVIL as a witch, and "willfully and most wickedly murdering her owne Child." She was found not guilty on the first charge, due to insufficient evidence. She confessed she was guilty of the second charge and was condemned to death.

On May 27 Mary confessed that she was a witch. The Springfield court reluctantly reversed the verdict against Parsons. He was not, however, a free man. More charges were brought against him of having familiarity with the Devil to hurt "diverse Persons." The jury was convinced that even though Parsons did not bewitch his second child to death, he did practice witchcraft on his neighbors. The incriminating "evidence" was little more than his habits of cutting boiled puddings longitudinally, filing his saws at night and other "amusements." After a long and tedious trial in Springfield, Parsons was sent to jail in Boston. There is no record of his final fate, but he never returned to Springfield.

Paxson, Diana L. (1943–   )   Pagan, Wiccan and author of fantasy fiction and Pagan nonfiction. Diana L. Paxson has been a leader in Pagan and Wiccan activities.

Paxson was born in 1943 and grew up in California. In 1964, she graduated from Mills College, and in 1966 she earned a master's degree in comparative literature from the University of California.

Paxson was a founder of the Society of Creative Anachronism in 1966 and also was a first officer of the COVENANT OF THE GODDESS.

Paxson's sister-in-law was MARION ZIMMER BRADLEY, whose ceremonial lodge gave Paxson her first Pagan INITIATION. In 1978, Paxson joined Bradley as a founder of the Darkmoon Circle, from which came the Fellowship of the Spiral Path. In 1982, Paxson was consecrated as priestess of the Fellowship.

Paxson has been especially active in the Heathen tradition of Asatru; she is the founder and *gydhja* (female equivalent of a *godhi*, the Asatru spiritual leader) of the *Hrafnar* tradition in Berkeley, California, and is an elder and board director of the Troth (formerly the Ring of Troth), an international Heathen organization. She edits Troth's journal, *Idunna*. Her nonfiction Pagan books center on the Heathen tradition, *Taking Up the Runes* and *Essential Asatru*.

Paxson has published more than 70 fantasy short stories and numerous novels, including nine historical fantasies. Her best-known works are the Chronicles of Westria novels and books in the Mists of Avalon series, which she took over from Bradley. She served as the western re-

gional director of the Science Fiction & Fantasy Writers of America. With Z BUDAPEST, a longtime friend and collaborator, she coauthored *Celestial Wisdom for Every Year of Your Life* (2003), an astrological guide.

In addition, Paxson plays the folk harp and composes music and designs and sews period costumes. She lives in her literary household, Greyhaven, in Berkeley.

PEBBLE   The Public Bodies Liaison Committee for British Paganism. PEBBLE is a network organization to promote Pagan interests, community services and civil rights, especially to British government agencies.

PEBBLE was formed in 1988 originally to lobby for access rights to Stonehenge. It has since expanded its activities. Partners include more than 20 orders, groups and individuals, among them the PAGAN FEDERATION, the Pagan Network, the Pagan Association, Heathens for Progress, the Druid Network, Derbyshire Pagans and the Council of British Druid Orders.

Some of the projects undertaken by PEBBLE are to get Paganism listed as a religious selection in the 2011 British census and to get Pagan terminology in new editions of the Oxford Dictionary.

pellar   In English folk MAGIC and WITCHCRAFT, a healer, diviner and breaker of SPELLS. The term is probably a corruption of *expel,* as in the repelling or expelling of spells. A pellar would be sought out if a person thought he or she had been bewitched or cursed.

Sometimes the mere mention of "going to the pellar" was sufficient for stolen goods to be returned, or restitution made for grievances. It also was customary to make annual visits to a pellar just to have one's "protection" renewed against bad luck and any acts of witchcraft that might be directed one's way. This trip customarily was done in the spring, as it was believed that the increasing of the Sun's rays magnified the power of the pellar. A trip to see a famous pellar was often a considerable undertaking, with long waits upon arrival.

Despite their importance in rural society, few pellars made their living solely upon their magical craft. Most were poor, and held other jobs while they performed their magical services on the side.

Like CUNNING MEN/WOMEN, white witches, wizards, conjurers and so on, pellars were believed to acquire their gifts through heredity or supernatural means. In Cornwall, pellars were said to be descended from Matthew Lutey of Cury, whose spell-breaking powers reputedly were bestowed upon him by a mermaid whom he rescued and returned to sea.

Pellars made CHARMS for their clients from herbs, powders, ointments, potions, stones, and perhaps teeth, bones and dirt taken from graves. These were placed in little bags to be worn about the neck as an AMULET. Sometimes powders and earth from graves was to be thrown over children, cattle or other livestock as a way

A pellar (OLD WOODCUT)

of protecting them against bewitchment and the EVIL EYE (see also BLASTING).

Or, the clients might be given bits of paper or parchment inscribed with mysterious words or astrological signs copied from magical texts (see GRIMOIRES). ABRACADABRA was commonly used, as was the term *Sator Arepo Tenet Opera Rotas* or *Nalgah* or *Tetragrammaton*. Written charms were folded and worn around the neck in little bags as well.

Whatever the remedy, a great deal of secrecy surrounded it, and clients were admonished not to talk about any of the proceedings between the pellar and client.

Pellars, as well as their folk magic counterparts, were active well into the 19th century. A few still can be found in rural locations in modern times.

FURTHER READING:
Bottrell, William, in Kelvin I. Jones, ed., *Cornish Witches & Cunning Men*. Penzance: Oakmagic Publications, 1996.

Penczak, Christopher (1973–)   Witch and popular author of books on Witchcraft and MAGIC.

Christopher Penczak was born on May 10 in Lawrence, Massachusetts. He was raised a Catholic and spent 12 years in Catholic school. Some early paranormal experiences helped to set the stage for his later conversion to Witchcraft.

Penczak was in the fourth grade when he had a spontaneous out-of-body experience in class. To others, it appeared as though he fainted, then revived. He watched the entire experience out of body. Years later, he had another intense paranormal experience an after-death visitation of his great aunt Mary. About a week after Mary's death, he was at school and saw her image in a glass. The image spoke to him and sent him into a mild trance state. Others explained the experience as a grief-induced daydream, but Penczak knew it was more, that he had had a genuine visitation from Mary.

Catholicism provided no satisfactory answers for these early paranormal experiences, nor did it help him with his realization at a young age that he was gay. Penczak went through a stage of agnosticism and then began studying Eastern spirituality through the practice of yoga.

In 1991, Penczak enrolled in University of Massachusetts at Lowell. A woman who was a family friend introduced him to Witchcraft. At first, he felt simultaneously repulsed and fascinated by it, but the more he learned and experienced, the more the Craft appealed to him. He attended a full moon RITUAL that brought the power of the Craft home to him in a vivid way. The ritual took place outdoors under a cloudy sky. His friend, the high priestess, called upon the GODDESS of the MOON to part the clouds so that the Moon could shine down. The clouds parted, and the sky remained open until she closed the ritual, and the clouds covered the sky again. At this ritual, he also had the opportunity to do a healing spell for a friend, and the result of that spell impressed him so much that he decided to pursue further study in Witchcraft.

Penczak's friend became his first mentor in the Craft. She introduced him to the work of her teacher, LAURIE CABOT, through Laurie's book *The Power of the Witch,* cowritten with Tom Cowan. His mentor encouraged him to take Cabot's courses on the art, science and religion of Witchcraft in Salem, Massachusetts. The Craft helped him to explore and celebrate his sexual nature.

He formed an informal COVEN with his mother and a college friend, both of whom also studied with Laurie, and began doing rituals for all the Moon observances, the WHEEL OF THE YEAR, healing and SPELL work. The coven remained intact through is college years and became the nucleus of later magickal groups.

After college, Penczak pursued a career in the music industry as a rock singer, worked in A&R administration in a Boston-area studio-turned-record-company known as Fort Apache, and continued his personal studies in Witchcraft. When he was laid off work, he turned to teaching classes in Witchcraft, the start of his success in the Craft.

In 1999, he became a reiki master and a certified flower-essence consultant. In 2000, he was ordained as a non-denominational minister by the Universal Brotherhood Movement, Inc., of Florida. In 2002, he graduated from a medicinal herbal-apprentice program.

Penczak lives in New Hampshire with his husband, Steve Kenson, a designer and developer of role-playing games. He works full time as a writer, teacher, presenter and healer. He is a part time faculty member at the North Eastern Institute of Whole Health and a founding member and past secretary of the Gifts of Grace Foundation, a nonprofit community service organization in New Hampshire. He is owner of HelioLuna Flower Essences.

In his teachings, Penczak emphasizes Witchcraft as temple work, a spiritual path of truth and responsibility, healing, empowerment, and individual relationship with the divine. It is important to have a foundation in metaphysics, psychic ability and the principles of magic before one can learn effective applications in rituals.

An eclectic at heart, he teaches no lineage tradition. His four temple books on Witchcraft teach Witchcraft as a mystery tradition devoted to spiritual development, direct contact with the divine, inner planes work and self-empowerment. These teachings reflect trends in Witchcraft and Paganism toward a deeper exploration of the mysteries, rather than traditional spellcraft, and an ongoing merging of Witchcraft and Paganism with other spiritual traditions. Penczak's goal is to bring together mainstream metaphysical practices, such as reiki, and Theosophy, and ascension with occultist, Witchcraft and shamanic traditions. His personal spiritual practice involves intellectual research, divine inspiration, meditation and inner journey work.

Penczak is a prolific author, and his books have received numerous awards. In 2002, his book *City Magick* won Best Magic Book from the Coalition of Visionary Retailers. In 2003, he won the same award for *The Inner Temple of Witchcraft*. In 2004, he received multiple awards from the Coalition of Visionary Retailers, including a tie for Best Book of the Year for *The Outer Temple of Witchcraft*.

He wrote one of the first mainstream books for gay Witches, *Gay Witchcraft: Empowering the Tribe* (2003), as an outgrowth of his own search for meaning in a spiritual tradition oriented to a masculine-feminine polarity. He discovered many gay/lesbian/bisexual/transgender themes in mythology and early paganism and applied them to his own evolving spiritual practice. He wanted to bring these early roots to light, to counter some of the existing prejudice against homosexuality that he encountered within the Craft and Paganism. The book has become instructional for the Pagan community at large.

Other books include *Spirit Allies: Meet Your Team from the Other Side* (2002); *The Witch's Shield: Protection Magick and Psychic Self-Defense* (2004); *Magick of Reiki* (2004); *Magick of Reiki: Focused Energy for Healing, Ritual, & Spiritual Development* (2004); *Temple of Shamanic Witchcraft* (2005); *Instant Magick: Ancient Wisdom, Modern Spellcraft* (2006); *Sons of the Goddess: A Young Man's Guide to Wicca* (2006); *The Mystic Foundation: Understanding and Exploring the Magical Universe* (2006); *Ascension Magick: Ritual, Myth & Healing for the New Aeon* (2007); and *The Living Temple of Witchcraft, Volume One: The Descent of the Goddess* (2008). *The Living Temple of Witchcraft, Volume Two: The Journey of the God* was scheduled for 2009.

FURTHER READING:

Christopher Penczak official Web site. URL: http://www.chistopherpenczak.com. Downloaded October 20, 2007.

Penczak, Christopher. *Gay Witchcraft: Empowering the Tribe.* York Beach, Me.: Samuel Weiser, 2003.

———. *The Inner Temple of Witchcraft: Magic Meditation and Psychic Development.* St. Paul: Llewellyn Publications, 2003.

———. "An Interview with Christopher Penczak." By Lisa Braun. Available online. URL: http://www.llewellyn.com/bookstore/article.php?id=448. Downloaded November 6, 2007.

Christopher Penczak

Pendderwen, Gwydion (1946–1982) Celtic bard whose legacy to the contemporary Pagan movement includes a collection of moving writings, rituals, music, songs and poetry; the Faery (Feri) Tradition, which he confounded; and two organizations: Nemeton, originally a networking group and Forever Forests, dedicated to reforestation work. Pendderwen devoted much of his life to a spiritual search and artistic expression. He was witty, eloquent and highly respected but also given to outbursts of temper that made some of his personal relationships difficult. He spent some of his later years in a spartan, solitary life in Mendocino County, California, on a homestead called Annwfn, now a Pagan retreat; prior to his death, he was active in the Pagan antinuclear movement (see PAGANISM).

Pendderwen was born in Berkeley, California, on May 21, 1946. He was 13 when he met VICTOR ANDERSON, a witch, seer and poet with whom he cofounded the Faery Tradition of Witchcraft. He studied with Anderson until he was in his early twenties, learning about the Craft, Celtic folklore and other systems, such as the Huna tradition of Hawaii and Haitian and West African VODUN. He was particularly influenced by Robert Graves' theories of GODDESS as muse and poet as sacred king. Pendderwen and Anderson developed and wrote much of the liturgical material for their tradition.

Pendderwen's magical practices were based on trance, poetry and communication with NATURE SPIRITS and FAIRIES. He often retired early and spent much of the night in solitude in trance.

He attended California State University at Hayward, where he majored in theater and earned a bachelor of arts degree. He enrolled in the master of fine arts program but apparently did not complete it. He disliked modern theater, preferring *dromenon*, drama in its original form as religious or mystical ritual. He learned Welsh, which led to a long correspondence with a friend in Wales, who interested him in Celtic nationalism. He was active in historically oriented groups, including the Society for Creative Anachronism (SCA), serving as Court Bard for the society's Kingdom of the West.

With Alison Harlow, an initiate of the Faery Tradition and a fellow member of the SCA, Pendderwen founded Nemeton in 1970 in Oakland. Nemeton, which means "sacred grove" in Welsh, originally served as a Pagan networking organization. In 1974 Nemeton published three issues of *Nemeton* magazine, then folded. Regional secretariats of the Nemeton organization spread across the United States, playing a key role in early Wiccan and Pagan networking and growth there. In 1978 Nemeton merged with the CHURCH OF ALL WORLDS and became the church's publishing arm.

In 1972 Pendderwen's first recording, *Songs of the Old Religion*—songs for each SABBAT, the seasons and love songs to GODDESS—brought him fame within the Pagan community. He was married briefly, then divorced.

He earned his living working for the Internal Revenue Service and the Department of Health, Education and Welfare but did not enjoy the restrictions of federal bureaucracy. On a vacation to the British Isles, Pendderwen reached a turning point in his life. He met his Welsh correspondent, Deri ap Arthur, and others active in the Wiccan movement, including ALEX SANDERS and STEWART FARRAR. It is likely that Sanders or other members of the Alexandrian tradition shared an Alexandrian BOOK OF SHADOWS with Pendderwen, for he and Anderson later incorporated Alexandrian material into the Faery Tradition.

At the Eistedffodd in Wales—a regular gathering of bards for artistic competition in Welsh music, poetry and drama—he was profoundly moved by being honored onstage as a foreigner of Welsh descent. In Ireland he experienced a terrifying vision of the MORRIGAN, one of the forms taken by the ancient Irish war goddess, Badb, upon Tara Hill; it made him identify more strongly with the archetypal sacred king.

Pendderwen quit his job upon his return to the United States and began homesteading at Annwfn in Mendocino County. He lived in a cabin with no electricity and only a cat for company. He learned carpentry and gardened, and pursued his artistic work. He identified with a new archetype, the GREEN MAN, and started to hold tree plantings every winter on his own and nearby land. The outgrowth was Forever Forests, formed in 1977 to sponsor annual tree plantings and encourage ecological consciousness as a magical process in harmony with Mother Earth.

He emerged from seclusion in 1980 to appear in concert and ritual at the first Pagan Spirit Gathering. He spent the last two years of his life active in public, sponsoring and organizing Pagan gatherings and tree plantings, and participating in antinuclear demonstrations. He was arrested for civil disobedience, along with members of Reclaiming (see STARHAWK), at a demonstration at Lawrence Livermore Laboratory in California in 1982.

Pendderwen tried to establish an extended family on Annwfn, but personal differences with friends and a constant shortage of money impeded him. In the fall of 1982 he was killed in an automobile accident.

Pendderwen's published works, all through Nemeton, include: *Wheel of the Year* (1979), a songbook of music and poems produced with the help of P. E. I. (ISAAC) BONEWITS, Craig Millen and Andraste; *The Rites of Summer* (1980), two musical fantasies performed at the 1979 Summer Solstice gathering at Coeden Brith, a 200-acre piece of wilderness owned by Nemeton and adjacent to Annwfn; and *The Faerie Shaman* (1981), songs of trees, country life, British Isles history and Pendderwen's love for Wales.

Much of his poetry, rituals and liturgical material remains unpublished.

In 1978 Forever Forests merged with the Church of All Worlds (CAW). CAW took over the magical and ritual work in 1987, leaving the activities of Forever Forests limited to tree plantings and environmental and reforestation projects.

See ANODEA, JUDITH.

FURTHER READING:
Adler, Margot. *Drawing Down the Moon*. Revised ed. New York: Viking, 1986.

pentacle and pentagram The pentacle, a five-pointed star with a single point upright, is the most important symbol of contemporary Witchcraft. It is both a religious symbol, as the cross is to Christianity and the six-pointed star is to Judaism, and a symbol of the magical craft of Witchcraft. A written or drawn pentacle is called a pentagram. In Craft rituals and MAGIC, the pentacle is a round disk made of clay, wax or earthenware (or, in some traditions, copper or SILVER) which is inscribed with a pentagram and other magical SIGILS and symbols and is used to consecrate the MAGIC CIRCLE, ground energy and cast SPELLS. In rituals such as DRAWING DOWN THE MOON, the high priestess may assume the pentacle position—standing with arms and legs outstretched—the symbol of birth and rebirth.

Many Witches wear a pentacle pendant or ring as a sign of their religion, or as an AMULET or TALISMAN. Most are made of silver, the metal of the MOON and psychic forces, but some are made of gold, the metal of power and energy. Some COVENS use the pentacle as the sigil of Witches initiated into the second degree.

In ritual, pentagrams are drawn in the air with the sword or athame. The methods of drawing a pentagram are precise and vary according to purpose. Pentagrams to invoke are drawn differently than pentagrams to banish. In magic, the pentagram is the Witch's symbol of protection and positive power and is used to control the elemental forces. Pentagrams also are used in Craft meditation exercises, in which each point of the star is associated with a specific quality, attribute, concept, emotion or the name of a Pagan deity.

Magician's pentacle. The magician's pentacle is a round disk or circle inscribed, customarily, with a five-pointed star. It is also called the Pentacle of Solomon and is an important and powerful magical symbol of divine power. According to various interpretations, it represents God or man and the four elements of nature; the five senses; the five wounds inflicted on Christ on the cross; and the five points of man in an outstretched position: head, arms and legs. The magician embroiders pentacles on his robes and inscribes them inside and outside the magic circles used in ceremonies and rituals. Pentacles are engraved on rings. As an amulet, the pentacle protects the magician against attack from demons and spirits; as a talisman, it enables him to conjure and command them.

Some pentacles are symbols other than the five-pointed star: circles, semicircles, squares and crosses, inscribed with the names of angels or DEMONS, or the magical names of God (see NAMES OF POWER). These symbols act as talismans to achieve a specific purpose, such as wealth, love or revenge.

Pentalpha, sign of recognition used by Pythagoras and disciples (MEDIEVAL DRAWING)

Inverted pentacle. The sacred symbol of Witchcraft often is misunderstood because of associations of the inverted pentacle, with single point down and double points up, with the infernal. If an upright five-pointed star represents God or the deity, then the reverse is said to represent Satan. In the 19th century, Eliphas Levi described the inverted pentacle as representing the horns of the goat of the witches' SABBAT. "It is the goat of lust attacking the Heavens with its horns. It is a sign execrated by initiates of a superior rank, even at the Sabbath," Lévi said in Key of the Mysteries.

The Church of Satan, founded in 1966 in America, adopted as its symbol the BAPHOMET, an encircled inverted pentacle inscribed with a goat's head and kabbalistic symbols spelling "Leviathan," an infernal serpent associated with the DEVIL (see SATANISM).

In Europe, some modern Witches used the inverted pentacle to denote the second-degree rank. This use declined, because of the association of the symbol with Satanism.

FURTHER READING:
Adler, Margot. *Drawing Down the Moon*. Revised ed. New York: Viking, 1986.
Farrar, Janet, and Stewart Farrar. *A Witches Bible Compleat*. New York: Magickal Childe, 1984.

Pentacle Quest A nearly 10-year effort by Witchcraft and Pagan organizations and families to require the U.S. Department of Veterans Affairs (VA) to allow PENTACLES to be placed on the grave markers of military veterans.

The VA, which recognized 38 religious symbols, had repeatedly denied recognition of the pentacle, the religious symbol of Witchcraft and Wicca. The VA was sued in U.S. District Court by the Washington, D.C., based American United for Separation of Church and State, representing CIRCLE SANCTUARY, the AQUARIAN TABERNACLE CHURCH, the COVENANT OF THE GODDESS, other Wiccan and Pagan organizations and families of veterans.

A verdict in favor of the plaintiffs was rendered on April 23, 2007. The VA also was ordered to pay $225,000 in legal costs to the plaintiffs.

During his first campaign for president, George W. Bush stated that he was opposed to Wiccan soldiers practicing their faith at Fort Hood, Texas. "I don't think witchcraft is a religion, and I wish the military would take another look at this and decide against it," he said. It is believed that his remarks influenced the VA.

One of the first pentacle-inscribed headstones was dedicated on December 1, 2007, on the grave of PFC Stephen P. Snowberger III, who was killed in action in Iraq on May 11, 2006. Snowberger was buried in a family cemetery near Lexington, North Carolina. SELENA FOX, founder of Circle Sanctuary, was among the Wiccan clergy leading the interfaith ceremony.

Among other Wiccan and Pagan churches and organizations participating were the House of Akasha (North Carolina), Clann Caladvlwch (North Carolina), Path of the Moon Collective (North Carolina), Sylvan Hearth Pagan Temple (South Carolina) and Gaia's Rising Covenant of Unitarian Universalist Pagans (South Carolina).

FURTHER READING:
Cooperman, Alan. "Administration Yields on Wiccan Symbol." Available online. URL: http://www.washingtonpost.com/wp-dyn/content/article/2007/04/23/AR2007042302073.html. Downloaded December 8, 2007.

"National Dedication & Memorial of North Carolina's first VA-issued Pentacle Gravestone honors Wiccan Soldier killed in Iraq." Available online. URL: http://bbsnews.net/article.php/20071130180218617. Downloaded December 8, 2007.

Pentreath, Dolly (1692–1777)   Wise woman, witch and PELLAR of great repute in Cornwall, England.

Dolly (Dorothy) Pentreath was born in the parish Paul in Cornwall in 1692. She never married, but bore a son in her twenties. She lived in Mousehole and worked as a fishmonger, and was renowned for her skill in fortune-telling, CHARMS, DIVINATION, expelling bewitchments and so on. She is credited with a rudimentary knowledge of astrology, as it was said that she knew the hours, days and minutes that were right for conjuring and the casting of SPELLS.

Except when people needed her for magical skills, Pentreath was generally avoided, perhaps because of her illegitimate child, and also because she was "dirty about her person and habits and very coarsely spoken when she chose," according to one description of her.

Pentreath was fluent in Cornish, a language that even then was disappearing from society. When excited, she would let loose a torrent of Cornish, which, unintelligible to others, sounded like fearsome cursing. According to one story, a man named Mr. Price was riding a skittish horse past Pentreath and her cowl full of fish one day. He accidentally upset the cowl, spilling the fish into a ditch. Pentreath screamed at him in Cornish while heaving mud and rocks at him. Every sentence ended with *cronnack an haga dhu,* which sounded to Price like a curse.

He offered money to Pentreath to learn the meaning of what she was saying. She said, "Give me the money first then, and I must call ye a fool for your pains; all I said was to call ye a fool for your pains; as all I said was to call ye the ugly black toad that ye art."

At that, Price threatened to horsewhip her. Pentreath retorted that if he did so, she would lay a SPELL on him that would cause his arm to rot from the shoulder. Price sped off.

Pentreath was also credited with good deeds. She once gave refuge to a deserter sailor, hiding him in a cavity of the chimney of her house. She lit a fire, put a kettle of water on to boil and got out a keeve, or basin, for washing. Soon enough, a naval party burst in and demanded to search the premises for the deserter. They found Pentreath sitting on a stool at the keeve with her skirts hiked up. She screamed at them that she was about to wash her feet and cursed them in Cornish. When they would not leave, she ran to her door and screamed out to her neighbors that the men were going to ransack all the houses. The men left. Later that night, the deserter escaped on a fishing boat.

By her late eighties, Pentreath was partially deaf and severely bent with age, but was in good enough health to regularly walk several miles even in bad weather. When she died on December 26, 1777, she was buried in the churchyard of the parish Paul.

FURTHER READING:
Jones, Kelvin I. *Seven Cornish Witches.* Penzance: Oakmagic Publications, 1998.

Perkins, William (1555–1602)   England Puritan and demonologist, a Fellow at Christ's College in Cambridge, whose views on WITCHES and WITCHCRAFT greatly shaped public opinion in the last decade of the 16th century and the beginning of the 17th century.

Perkins' work, *Discourse on the Damned Art of Witchcraft,* was published posthumously in 1608 and surpassed JAMES I's *Daemonologie* as the leading witchhunter's bible. He accepted completely the witch dogma of other demonologists. He divided witchcraft into two types—"divining" and "working." The second type included STORM RAISING, the poisoning of air (which brings pestilence), the BLASTING of corn and crops and the "procuring of strange passions and torments in men's bodies and other creatures, with curing of the same." He said that witches should get a fair trial, but he favored the use of TORTURE. Of DEVIL'S PACTS, Perkins said:

> When witches begin to make a league, they are sober and sound in understanding, but after they once be in the league, their reason, and understanding may be depraved, memory weakened, and all the powers of the soul blemished, they are deluded and so intoxicated that they will run into a thousand of fantastical imaginations, holding themselves to be transformed into the shapes of other creatures, to be transported in the air, to do many strange things, which in truth they do not.

Perkins set forth "safe" ways for discovering witches, which COTTON MATHER endorsed and summarized in *On Witchcraft: Being the Wonders of the Invisible World* in 1692. These ways were not sufficient for conviction but raised conjecture that a suspect was a witch:

1. Notorious defamation as a witch, especially by "men of honesty and credit."
2. Testimony by a fellow witch or magician.
3. A cursing, followed by a death.
4. Enmity, quarreling or threats, followed by "mischief."
5. Being the son or daughter, servant, familiar friend, near neighbor or old companion of a known or convicted witch, since witchcraft is an art that can be learned.
6. The presence of a Devil's mark.
7. Unconstant or contrary answers to interrogation.
8. Recovery from scratching [see PRICKING] and SWIMMING.
9. The testimony of a wizard who offers to show the witch's face in a glass.
10. A deathbed oath by a victim that he has been bewitched to death.

The following were deemed sufficient for conviction:

1. A "free and voluntary confession" of the accused.
2. The testimony of two "good and honest" witnesses that the accused has entered into a pact with the Devil or has practiced witchcraft.
3. Other proof of a Devil's pact.
4. Proof that the accused has entertained familiar spirits.
5. Testimony that the accused has done anything to infer entering into a Devil's pact, using enchantments, divining the future, raising tempests or raising the form of a dead man.

FURTHER READING:
Hansen, Chadwick. *Witchcraft at Salem.* New York: George Braziller, 1967.
Mather, Cotton. *On Witchcraft: Being the Wonders of the Invisible World.* 1692. Reprint, Mt. Vernon, N.Y.: The Peter Pauper Press, 1950.

philtre Magical potion that causes a person to fall in love with another. Philtres, also called love potions, have been common in MAGIC, folk magic and myth since antiquity. Important in the Middle Ages, they declined in popularity in the 17th and 18th centuries in favor of SPELLS and CHARMS. Philtres are still brewed in modern times in various folk-magic traditions.

A philtre consists of wine, tea or water doctored with herbs or drugs. For best results, according to lore, it should be concocted only by a professional witch. When drunk, the philtre supposedly makes the recipient fall in love with the giver, which means great care must be taken that it is administered properly. In the tale of *Tristan and Isolde,* Isolde's mother obtains a philtre that will make her unwilling daughter fall in love with her betrothed, King Mark of Cornwall. Thinking it is poison, Isolde shares it with Tristan, the king's knight who is escorting her to Cornwall. They fall irrevocably in love, which proves fatal to both of them.

There is at least one story of a philtre producing not love but insanity. According to the Roman biographer Suetonius (69–140), the emperor Caligula (12–14) went mad after drinking a love philtre administered by his wife, Caesonia—thereby providing an excuse for the emperor's irrational behavior.

The most common ingredient in philtres has been the smelly MANDRAKE root, also called "love apples," a poisonous member of the nightshade family. Orange and ambergris added a little flavor and pleasant aroma. VERVAIN, an herb, was also used a great deal and still is used in the 20th century. Other common ingredients are the hearts and reproductive organs of animals, such as the testicles of kangaroos, used by Australian aborigines, and the testicles of beavers, used by some North American Indians. In India, betel nuts or tobacco are added to philtres. A simple formula from Nova Scotia calls for a woman to steep her hair in water and then give the water to her intended to drink.

Herbs and plants are common additives: briony (similar to mandrake) and fern seed in England, the latter of which must be gathered on the eve of St. John's Day. The Chinese use shang-luh, a plant that resembles ginseng. In Germany, a red gum called dragon blood is used.

One medieval philtre recipe called for grinding into a powder the heart of a dove, the liver of a sparrow, the womb of a swallow and the kidney of a hare. To that was added an equal part of the person's own blood, also dried and powdered. This was mixed into a liquid and offered as a drink, with "marvellous success" promised.

In the 16th century, Girolamo Folengo offered this formidable recipe in his *Maccaronea:*

> Black dust of tomb, venom of toad, flesh of brigand, lung of ass, blood of blind infant, corpses from graves, bile of ox.

Since philtres depend upon convincing someone to drink a brew that may not taste or smell pleasant, they

Witches brewing magical potions (HANS WEIDITZ, 1517)

are no longer as popular as other charms, such as GRIS-GRIS, dolls or POPPETS and spells. Even in the Middle Ages, the limitations of philtres were recognized. One alternative recipe recommended rubbing the hands with vervain juice and touching "the man or woman you wish to inspire with love."

In modern Witchcraft, the concoction of any love charm for the purpose of forcing love or manipulating an unsuspecting person is considered unethical by many Witches. It is preferable to make love charms to enhance love that already exists between two persons. Love charms also are acceptable if caveats are added, such as "for the good of all," "if they are right for each other" and "if no one is harmed" (see WICCAN REDE).

FURTHER READING:
Marlbrough, Ray L. *Charms Spells & Formulas.* St. Paul: Llewellyn Publications, 1987.
Thomas, Keith. *Religion and the Decline of Magic.* New York: Charles Scribner's Sons, 1971.

Pickingill, Old George (1816–1909) Legendary English CUNNING MAN and a controversial figure to many contemporary Witches.   According to the English folklorist Eric Maples, Old George Pickingill claimed to be descended from a line of hereditary witches dating back

to the 11th century. He was born in 1816, the oldest of nine children to Charles and Susannah Pickingill, in Hockley, in Essex in East Anglia. Like his father, George was a farm laborer and worked in the Canewdon district. He was viewed by his neighbors as a mysterious, ill-tempered man who practiced magic and employed a fleet of IMPS to plow his fields for him while he relaxed.

Pickingill claimed his original witch ancestor was a woman named Julia, the "Witch of Brandon," a village north of Thetford in Norfolk. In 1071, according to family legend, Julia was hired to make magical chants to the troops of Hereward the Wake, inspiring them in battle against the enemy Normans. Her chants also were supposed to befuddle the Normans. Nevertheless, the Normans set fire to the village, and Julia was burned to death. Ever since, according to legend, members of each generation of the Pickingill family served as priests in the Old Religion.

The Pickingill witches worshiped the HORNED GOD. George Pickingill was vehemently anti-Christian, and openly advocated the overthrow of the Christian Church. To that end, he collaborated with ceremonial magicians, Witches, Satanists, Rosicrucians and Freemasons, in the hopes of spreading beliefs that would replace the church.

Over a 60-year period, Pickingill established a group of covens known as the Nine Covens, located in Hertfordshire, Essex, Hampshire, Sussex and Norfolk. He selected leaders who had hereditary connections to the Craft. Initiates included both men and women, but all RITUALS were performed entirely by women. Pickingill also was said to be the leader who controlled a coven of female witches called the Seven Witches of Canewdon. Pickingill terrorized the local farmers and extorted beer from them by threatening to stop their machinery with magic.

Called a Master of Witches, Pickingill reputedly could make nine secret witches declare themselves simply by whistling. He was alleged to sit by his hedge and smoke his pipe while his army of IMPS harvested his fields in half the time it would have taken men. No one went to his house without invitation, and even then did so in fear. At his death, his imps appeared in the form of white mice. After his death, they haunted his cottage, and passersby could see their RED eyes glowing in the dark.

In 1974, more information surfaced about Pickingill, from a source who claimed to be the front for a group of anonymous hereditary Witches who wanted the truth to be known about him. From 1974 to 1977, a series of articles about Pickingill were published in the British magazine *The Wiccan*, the newsletter of the Pagan Front (now the PAGAN FEDERATION), edited by JOHN SCORE. The author was E. W. "Bill" Liddell, who used the pseudonym "Lugh." He said that he had been inducted into a number of "Old Style Craft covens" between 1950 and 1961 and then had retired to New Zealand. From 1977 to 1988, Liddell published more articles in another publication, *The Cauldron*.

Liddell said that Pickingill's correct patronymic was Pickingale, and that he had Romany kin and was raised as a Gypsy. His hereditary tradition used many rituals imported from Middle Ages Europe and adapted to East Anglia. Rites of worship of the Horned God were conducted by women and involved ritual nudity and sexual inductions. Pickingill divined that the Craft revival would be activated in 1962, and reintroduced GODDESS rituals into his coven to launch Wicca.

According to Liddell, ALEISTER CROWLEY was initiated into one of Pickingill's Nine Covens in 1899 or 1900, but was soon expelled because of his deplorable behavior. However, Liddell said that he absorbed the Pickingill rituals, some of which came from France and the Netherlands, and used them in constructing his own rituals. Crowley, however, makes no mention of this in any of his extant writings.

GERALD B. GARDNER's New Forest coven was supposedly one of Pickingill's Nine.

When Crowley met Gardner in 1947, he allegedly agreed—or volunteered—to use "magical recall" to remember the exact Pickingill rituals and write them down for Gardner, who then used them in constructing his own

BOOK OF SHADOWS. If Crowley did, this document either cannot be found or no longer exists.

In one of his more controversial claims, Liddell also asserted that Pickingill had collaborated with pseudo-Rosicrucians to write the rituals for the HERMETIC ORDER OF THE GOLDEN DAWN.

Critics of The Lugh material cite the lack of supporting documentation or evidence to validate these claims as reason for dismissal of them.

See CANEWDON WITCHES.

FURTHER READING:
Hutton, Ronald. *The Pagan Religions of the Ancient British Isles: Their Nature and Legacy.* Oxford: Blackwell Publishers, 1991.
Kelly, Aidan A. *Crafting the Art of Magic Book I: A History of Modern Witchcraft, 1939–1964.* St. Paul: Llewellyn Publications, 1991.
Liddell, E. W., and Michael Howard. *The Pickingill Papers: The Origin of the Gardnerian Craft.* Chieveley, England: Cpall Bann Publishing, 1994.
Maple, Eric. *The Dark World of Witches.* New York: A.S. Barnes & Co., 1962.
Valiente, Doreen. *The Rebirth of Witchcraft.* London: Robert Hale, 1989.

pins   Pins are used in some magical SPELLS and in sympathetic MAGIC. Stray pins always should be picked up, according to superstition; otherwise a witch will pick them up and use them in magic. Witches were said to throw crooked pins into their brews to cast evil spells and also to break evil spells. To bless a friend with happiness and prosperity, a witch plucked a lemon at midnight and recited an incantation while sticking the fruit full of pins of various colors. To curse an enemy (see CURSE), the witch took the lemon, uttered a different incantation and stuck it with at least several black pins among other colors.

In the witchcraft trials of earlier centuries, pins were used to prick the bodies of the accused in order to locate spots insensitive to pain. Such spots, called DEVIL'S MARKS, were considered proof that the accused was a witch.

In English lore, a witch's power could be destroyed by pricking a pigeon with pins or by sticking pins in the heart of a stolen hen.

In cases of POSSESSION, pins are often vomited by the victims, along with other strange objects (see ALLOTRIOPHAGY).

In folk magic, crooked pins are tossed into magic wells to help effect both curses and wishes. In VODUN, SANTERÍA, MACUMBA, folk magic and various tribal and other cultures, pins are stuck into effigies and POPPETS to cause discomfort, pain and even death. The victim supposedly feels the distress in the part of the body that has been pierced by the pin. Such magic is proscribed by the tenets of modern Witchcraft, which hold that magic is not to be used to harm or manipulate others (see WICCAN REDE).

FURTHER READING:

Leach, Maria, ed., and Jerome Fried, assoc. ed. *Funk & Wagnall's Standard Dictionary of Folklore, Mythology and Legend.* New York: Harper & Row, 1972.

Opie, Iona, and Moira Tatem. *A Dictionary of Superstitions.* New York: Oxford University Press, 1989.

pointing   Witches and sorcerers (see SORCERY) are believed to have a fatal power to kill by pointing. The Malaysian *pawang,* or magician, points his *kris,* a type of dagger with wavy blade, which begins to drip with BLOOD. Many North American Indian tribes have legends of the killing of animals by pointing. The underlying principle of pointing is the belief that magicians have the power to use their will as a weapon and direct it against others. The deadly, magical energy streams out of their fingers toward the victim. If they send hatred and death, that energy attracts the necessary dark forces to accomplish the goal. If a victim knows he has been pointed at, and believes in the power of the sorcerer, he may bring about his own demise as self-fulfilling prophecy.

See CURSE.

poisons   Dexterity with poisons has been ascribed to witches and sorcerers (see SORCERY) since ancient times. The knowledge to kill is the reverse side of the knowledge to heal, and the village sorcerer or wise woman who was skilled with herbs had the power to do both. Sorcerers knowledgeable in herbs and poisons were believed to exist in Cro-Magnon times, according to anthropologists' conclusions based on cave paintings. In classical times, witches were consulted for poisons—the best way to get rid of an enemy—as often as for love potions. In ancient Rome, 170 women were once condemned for poisoning under the pretense of incantation. During the European witch-hunts, accused witches were commonly believed to poison humans and animals as part of their ongoing MALEFICIA against Christians. They allegedly poisoned wells and barber's flour and smeared lethal OINTMENTS on door handles.

In modern Witchcraft, poisoning, or causing any harm to any living creature, violates the primary law of the Craft (see WICCAN REDE), which holds that Witches must use their skills for healing and good. In other cultures, particularly tribal ones, illness and death is sometimes blamed on poisoning by witchcraft.

Poisons, used as covert and highly selective weapons, have no peer. They are discreet, hard to trace and can be administered either in deadly doses or in small doses over a period of time, leading to slow illness and death. Some of the most innocuous-looking plants and animals contain fatal poisons, which can be incorporated into OILS, foods or powders. Many poisons have no taste or smell, making them especially insidious.

Plant and animal poisons. Native Africans and Indians of the New World have long been experts in the use of

Witches exhuming corpses from graves to obtain body parts for magical spells (WOODCUT FROM FRANCESCO-MARIA GUAZZO'S *COMPENDIUM MALEFICARUM,* 1608)

poisons. Curare, the infamous plant poison traditionally used on arrows and darts, acts as a muscle relaxant, causing eventual asphyxiation. Curare's main component, D-tubocurarine, works so well as a muscle relaxant that it now appears in various anaesthetics used in conventional surgery. Strychnine, a poison from the *nux vomica* plant, has the opposite effect, stimulating the nervous system to the point of severe spasms and death. Poisonous mushrooms, containing toxic alkaloids, such as muscarin and phalloidin, also appear in native concoctions.

Plants of the Solanaceous, or nightshade, family—like belladonna, henbane and MANDRAKE—allegedly have been used by witches for centuries, producing hallucinations and death. One particularly effective method for ingesting nightshades is topically, through the moist tissues of the vagina. Other popular witch poisons included hemp and hemlock.

One nightshade, datura, is so highly hallucinogenic and dangerous that even researchers are afraid of it. Also called "the holy flower of the North Star," datura and its derivatives, which produce a very deep sleep, have been the preferred drugs of criminals and black magicians for centuries. The name supposedly originates in ancient India, where bands of thieves called *dhatureas* used the drug to incapacitate their victims. Portuguese explorers to India found that Hindu prostitutes were so adept at using datura that they knew exactly how many seeds were necessary in a dose to keep their clients unconscious for hours. A 17th-century traveler to India reported that Indian women, seething with passion for the light-skinned Europeans but held in check by their husbands, gave the men datura, then made love in front of them while the husbands sat stupefied with their eyes open.

The Yaqui Indians of northern Mexico used to rub a salve containing datura on their genitals, legs and feet and believe they were flying. Wives and slaves of dead kings among the Chibcha Indians of Colombia received doses of datura before being buried alive with their masters. Quechua Indians in Peru called the plant *huaca,* or "grave," because they believe persons intoxicated with the drug can locate the tombs of their ancestors. Togo witch doctors mixed datura with fish poison and administered it to reputed witches to determine guilt. Some West African women still raise beetles, feed the beetles on datura, then mix the beetles' feces in food to eliminate unnecessary husbands or unfaithful lovers.

Animals, too, such as venomous snakes and lizards, provide poisons. Cleopatra died from the bite of a poisonous asp, and as early as Roman times women used poisonous TOADS to remove unwanted husbands or lovers. [The fungus gets its name because Europeans believe toads ingested their venom by eating poisonous mushrooms, hence *toadstool.*] Medieval soldiers wounded their enemies by discreetly rubbing the secretions of *Bufo vulgaris,* the common toad, into the skin. When boiled in oil, the bufo easily secreted venom which could be skimmed off the top. Sixteenth-century Italians learned how to extract toad poison with salt, which could then be sprinkled on the victim's food. Toad venom was so highly regarded that by the 18th century, weapons makers added it to explosive shells—if the gunpowder and shrapnel didn't kill the enemy, the toad toxin would.

The *Bufo marinus,* or bouga toad, a native of the New World, reached the old one not long after Columbus and was immediately recognized by those familiar with poisons as a handy little beast. The Choco Indians of western Colombia milked poisonous toads by placing them in bamboo tubes suspended over open flames, then collecting the exuded yellow venom into ceramic jars. The main toxic ingredients of the toad's glands are bufogenin and bufotoxin, 50 to 100 times more potent than digitalis and causing death by rapid heartbeat leading to heart failure. The *bufo marinus* also contains bufotenine, a hallucinogen.

The Chinese were most expert with the *bufo marinus.* They collected the venom and condensed it into smooth, dark disks, like pills, called *ch'an su,* dispensing it for the treatment of toothache, canker sores, sinus inflammations and bleeding gums. Taken orally, the pills worked on the common cold. Of course, the toad's toxic properties were not forgotten in labyrinthine Chinese politics.

Other poisonous sea creatures include two varieties of tropical fish, the *fou-fou,* or *Diodon hystrix,* and the sea toad, or *Sphoeroides testudineus.* Both are commonly called blowfish or puffer fish, describing their ability to puff up their spiny bodies to dissuade predators. Such procedures are unnecessary, as the puffer fish contains tetrodotoxin in its skin, liver, ovaries and intestines—a poison 500 times stronger than cyanide, 150,000 times more potent than cocaine. Ancient Egyptians appreciated the puffer fish at least 5,000 years ago, and the presence of deadly puffers in the Red Sea led to the Old Testament injunctions against eating scaleless fish, outlined in the book of Deuteronomy. The puffer is a modern delicacy in the Orient. Prepared correctly, it is harmless; prepared incorrectly, it is fatal, which turns a puffer fish meal into a sort of Russian roulette.

Poison and justice. Long before the Europeans raided the coasts of Africa looking for slaves, WITCH DOCTORS and certain tribes specialized in the administration of poisons to determine the existence of witches and a suspect's guilt or innocence. The Efik tribespeople along the Niger River became famous for their secret societies, which were responsible for keeping order among their neighbors through various horrible punitive methods. One of the Efik's most powerful weapons was the poison test, in which the accused was forced to drink a potion made from eight seeds of the highly toxic Calabar bean, whose main component is physostigmine. Such a huge dose sedates the spinal cord, causing progressive paralysis from the feet to the waist, and eventually leads to loss of all muscular control and death by asphyxiation.

The victim, after drinking the poison, had to stand before a judicial gathering of the Efik until the poison began to take effect, then walk toward a line drawn ten feet away from the tribunal. If the accused vomited up the poison, he was declared innocent. If he reached the line but had not vomited, he was also innocent and was quickly given an antidote of excrement mixed with water that had been used to wash a female's external genitalia. Most died horribly, however, wracked with convulsions. The guilty did not receive burial, either, but had their eyes gouged out and their bodies cast naked into the forest.

Peoples of nearly all African cultures used poisons to eliminate the guilty. In certain regions chiefs ordered criminals to be executed by pricking their skin with lances or needles dipped in toxic plant juices. In West Africa, the son and heir of a chief had to undergo two poison ordeals to see if he possessed the superhuman qualities necessary to become the new chief; if he failed, the line was broken and another family became royal leader.

To purge communities of witchcraft, witch doctors would prepare poisons and force all the citizens to drink them. One witch doctor prepared a concoction containing poisonous bark from the *Leguminosae* tree, along with a powder made from the dried hearts of previous victims, ground glass, lizards, toads, crushed snakes and human remains. This disgusting liquid was left to ferment for a year, at which time the entire village drank a draught during a great festival. Up to 2,000 people died every year. When Africa was carved up into European imperial colonies, such practices were outlawed.

Africans also use poison tests on animals to divine a human's innocence or witch-inspired guilt. The *benge* test involves giving poison to chickens while reading a list of suspects. When a chicken dies at the same instant a name is called, that suspect is found guilty (see AFRICAN WITCHCRAFT).

Witches and poisonous retribution. As Europeans grew more sophisticated with medicines and chemicals, metal-based poisons like lead, arsenic and mercury derivatives became popular. Socially accepted doctors, primarily male, suffered little suspicion about poisoning, but the female midwives, healers and abortionists continually battled indictments as witches. Perhaps the doctors saw such condemnation as a way to eliminate competition.

Nevertheless, the fear of witchcraft was rampant, particularly in the 16th and 17th centuries, when anything unexplainable was attributable to the DEVIL. Midwives were especially vulnerable, since they were blamed for murdering children and for using their bodies to obtain ingredients for poisons. Even high officials were not above suspicion; when the Milanese Commissioner of Health was observed wiping his ink-stained hands on a wall in 1630, he was accused of spreading plague. Intense interrogation and TORTURE gave rise to the Commissioner's full confession and names of accomplices. All involved were torn with hot pincers and burned at the stake.

In the 17th-century French court of Louis XIV, the Chambre Ardente case revealed a ring of poisoners who allegedly supplied witches and abortionists all over France. Poisons and love potions were common at court, used to dispose of unwanted lovers and attract new ones. After an enormous investigation accompanied by torture, evidence surfaced that the poisoners had been the cause of an unknown number of murders, including some 2,500 unwanted babies who were secretly buried in a garden at Villeneuve-sur-Gravois. The ringleader, Catherine Deshayes, called La Voisin, and her confederates were accused not only of poisoning but also of Devil-worship and practice of the BLACK MASS. They suffered brutal torture and died at the stake. The entire case would have run on its own hysteria for years if King Louis had not intervened in 1680, outlawing fortune-tellers and mandating legal controls over poisons.

See FLYING; ALICE KYTELER; ZOMBIE.

FURTHER READING:
Evans-Pritchard, E. E. *Witchcraft, Oracles and Magic Among the Azande* (abridged). Oxford: Clarendon Press, 1983.
Hughes, Pennethorne. *Witchcraft.* New York: Penguin Books, 1965.
Kluckhorn, Clyde. *Navaho Witchcraft.* 1944. Reprint, Boston: Beacon Press, 1967.
Lea, Henry Charles. *Materials Toward a History of Witchcraft.* Philadelphia: University of Pennsylvania, 1939.
Summers, Montague, ed. *The Malleus Maleficarum of Heinrich Kramer and James Sprenger.* 1928. Reprint, New York: Dover Publications, 1971.

Pope (c. 1630–1690)   Tewa Pueblo medicine man of San Juan, New Mexico, who used SORCERY to lead a rebellious fight against Spanish settlers. Pope claimed to be the representative of *el Demonio,* the DEVIL.

When the Spaniards settled along the Rio Grande in New Mexico in the late 16th century, they established an imperialistic rule and subjugated the native Pueblo. They overtook the Pueblo villages and began forcing the natives to convert to Christianity. They confiscated Pueblo goods and food, forcing many into starvation. European diseases took their toll. Pueblo began abandoning their villages. Pueblo leaders and medicine men tried to hold their villages and culture together by emphasizing their traditional ways and beliefs.

Around 1650, Spanish Franciscan friars became alarmed at the increasing influence of Pueblo medicine men. The missionaries believed their work was being obstructed by diabolical SPELLS and HEXES. They began a program of persecution in an attempt to discredit the medicine men. The friars summoned royal troops to raid their homes and confiscate their magical tools, which were publicly burned. These acts infuriated the medicine men and made them more determined than ever to turn their people against the missionaries.

The Spaniards retaliated in turn, flogging, imprisoning and executing Pueblo medicine men and leaders. A crisis occurred in 1675, when four Pueblo were hanged and 47 were publicly whipped. Many others were jailed. The charges were witchcraft murders of several missionaries and the bewitchment of a church inspector. All of the accused were found guilty of witchcraft, idolatry, communion with the Devil and plotting a rebellion with neighboring Apache.

Outraged, a large contingent of Pueblo chiefs and warriors descended upon Santa Fe, where they confronted the Spanish governor and demanded the release of those still in jail. They offered in return choice hides, chickens, eggs, beans, hay and tobacco. The governor complied.

By then the action was too little too late. One of the whipped medicine men was Pope, who dedicated himself to overthrowing the Spaniards. Declaring himself the representative of *el Demonio,* Pope set up headquarters in Taos, 70 miles north of Santa Fe, where he conducted magical rites in an underground kiva, or ceremonial room. He let it be known that he was conspiring with the Devil himself in order to fan superstitious fears. He was said to travel about on a whirlwind. His strategy worked, and he united the pueblo communities that were still independent, along with some Hopi and Zuni.

Pope communicated with the village chiefs by sending messengers bearing knotted ropes. The chiefs were to untie a KNOT every day. When the last knot was untied, the Indians were to rise up in a united rebellion and attack the Spaniards. Word leaked out to the Spaniards, and Pope had to advance his timing by several days and got the message to the chiefs.

On August 10, 1680, the Pueblo and their allies attacked and killed 21 priests and more than 400 soldiers and government officials in northern New Mexico. Many Spaniards fled south to El Paso, and others banded together in Santa Fe to fight back. The Pueblo won their independence. It was a humiliating blow for Spain. The missionaries were banished.

Pope systematically destroyed Christian churches and missions in an attempt to obliterate the Spanish from the landscape. He became leader of several Tewa villages, which he ruled with a harsh hand. Internal opposition arose, weakening the Pueblo force, which the Spaniards were able to exploit. The Pueblo also were vulnerable to raids and attacks by Navajo, Apache and Ute forces.

Pope died in 1690, and the Pueblo united front crumbled. In 1692, the Spaniards retaliated, led by General Diego de Vargas. Spain reclaimed its territory, and Franciscan missions reopened. Santa Fe attracted an influx of settlers and new towns were founded. The missionaries, however, never returned to their strident denunciation of the Pueblo medicine men, and witchcraft beliefs along the Rio Grande remained strong.

FURTHER READING:
Simmons, Marc. *Witchcraft in the Southwest: Spanish and Indian Supernaturalism on the Rio Grande.* Lincoln: University of Nebraska Press, 1974.

poppet   A magical doll made for spell-casting and ritual magic.

In spell-casting, the doll substitutes for the person who is the object of the spell. The doll is carefully made in a state of concentration that focuses on the purpose of the spell. Ideally, the doll has things belonging to the subject, such as bits of clothing and snippets of HAIR AND NAIL clippings. The latter especially are believed to magically link the person to the spell because they contain the living essence of a person. In earlier times, if personal items were not available a kite would be flown over the subject's chimney to catch the soot, or essence, of the occupants. The soot would then be placed inside the poppet as a substitute. Animal hair also was used for poppet stuffing.

Life is breathed into a poppet by blowing into the doll's mouth through a straw. Thus the poppet takes on a magical life of its own and activates the spell.

If the spell is a CURSE, such as illness, misfortune or death, or a binding spell to stop someone from a particular activity, the poppet is pierced with pins, nails or shards of glass, or bound with cord, covered with burning candle wax or even hung by the neck. Sometimes poppets are buried after being activated. Photographs can substitute for a doll and be similarly mutilated. A poppet to stop an illicit love affair might have its heart and genitals pierced and legs bound together.

In the SALEM WITCHES trials, several of the accused were said to have made use of poppets to harm and kill others. GEORGE BURROUGHS supposedly made Abigail Hobbs stick pins into poppets he gave her. BRIDGET BISHOP, Goody Hawkes and Hawkes' slave, Candy, supposedly stuck pins in poppets to inflict pain at a distance on their victims.

Chimney poppet for protection of the home, in the collection of the Museum of Witchcraft at Boscastle, Cornwall (PHOTO BY AUTHOR; COURTESY MUSEUM OF WITCHCRAFT)

Judge John Hathorne ordered Candy to produce one of her poppets in court. It was made mostly of rags and grass. He made Candy eat the grass, and then he burned the rags. One of the afflicted girls screamed that her hand was being burned at the same time, so the flames were put out.

Two men who worked on Bishop's house testified that they found several poppets inside a wall. They were made of rags and hog bristles, with headless pins stuck into them. The poppets seemed to validate testimony that Bishop had bewitched people to death and had caused many problems with her evil spells.

Not all poppets have negative purposes. For example, they are made for healing, prosperity and love spells as well. A healing poppet might be attached with certain herbs, stones or crystals intended to facilitate the healing.

The MUSEUM OF WITCHCRAFT in Boscastle, Cornwall, England, has an extensive poppet collection that includes a good luck and protection poppet made for the home. The poppet had been walled into a chimney of a cottage and was discovered during restoration work. The chimney, as part of the hearth, represents the heart and well-being of the home.

In ritual magic, poppets are substitutes for aspects of God and Goddess and used in rituals and to activate certain energies. One of the most common poppets for such purposes is the Biddy or Bridie Doll, made at Imbolc (see WHEEL OF THE YEAR) in honor of St. Bride and to welcome spring. There are variations of the ritual, such as those described below.

The Bridie Doll is made as much as possible from natural materials, for example twigs and straw for the body, pinecone for the head, rushes for hair, pebbles for eyes, silk for the dress and shells for decorations. Traditionally, this construction is done by women.

When the doll is made, a Bride song is sung to call in Goddess energy for fertility and healing, especially of the land. The doll is then placed in a decorated carriage and taken to a home adjacent to her final destination, where she will be given to the land. All of the ritual participants enter the home except the one who carries the doll. The door is knocked upon THREE times and the doll is welcomed in three times, entering upon the third. She remains in the home overnight and then is given to the land.

In Glastonbury, England, the ritual has been done by placing the doll in a darkened room. Children, each carrying a candle, enter the room and a welcome song is sung to the doll. The doll is taken to the Chalice Well garden, a natural springs area associated with the legend of the Holy Grail.

See CORN DOLLY; MAGIC; SPELLS.

possession   A complete takeover of one's personality by a malevolent entity, allowing the entity to dominate; the victim becomes, even somewhat physically, that demonic being. Possession has been blamed on bewitchment, though causes probably were hysterical fantasies, physical and mental disorders and repressed sexual desire. In modern times, possession is still sometimes attributed to witchcraft, CURSES and the interferences of DEMONS.

Early Christians enjoyed a much more intimate relationship with Christ and God, so consequently they feared personal, active intervention by the forces of evil. PRAYER, CHARMS and AMULETS were employed to keep the DEVIL at bay, since he was constantly on the prowl for unsuspecting victims.

Later Christian theology considered the idea of spirit possession heretical, so anyone found showing signs of unusual behavior or a different personality was automatically possessed (*energumenus*; the possessed person is an *energumen*) by the DEVIL.

During the witch hunts, there were two acknowledged ways to become possessed by the Devil: either the Devil passes directly into a person, or someone—usually said to be a witch or WIZARD—working with the Devil sends a demon into a victim through bewitchment. Many unfortunates were branded as witches or evil ones simply because they were old, ugly or on the social fringe (see HAG). Noted Julio Caro Baroja in *The World of the Witches* (1961):

Hanging of farm woman convicted of being possessed by demons (RAPPRESENTATIONE DELLA ASSIONE, 1520)

there is a deep-rooted belief in various parts of Europe in the existence of people who quite involuntarily bring "bad luck" (*mal fario*) . . . or have the "evil eye." . . . panish writers of the 16th and 17th centuries worked out theories that the "evil eye" was the result of the presence of certain harmful properties in the eye or in other parts of the body of certain types of people . . . more particularly through those of elderly spinsters, cripples and certain types of sick people.

Such evil body parts were not necessarily the result of the unfortunate's own free will (see EVIL EYE). Terrible deformities, especially of the face, also led the general populace to believe the sufferer was marked by the Devil, much as the Elephant Man of 19th-century London was feared and mocked.

Most medieval thinkers, however, firm in their belief in man's sinfulness, assumed that the Devil used one of his human henchmen to torment the innocent. Every time a child sickened or had seizures—which now probably would be diagnosed as epilepsy—or livestock died, or crops failed, sufferers looked for a witch responsible. The witch usually was a poor old woman, angry with her station in life, argumentative with her neighbors and quite likely a midwife.

The witch was believed to transmit the demon through some tangible object, often a potion, CHARM or amulet. The most common means of sending the Devil to an innocent victim was through food. In his *Dialogues*, Pope Gregory the Great tells the story of a possessed servant girl. She apparently ate some lettuce leaves from the garden, and a Devil had been sitting on one when she consumed it. The demon complained about such treatment of an innocent bystander, but he was exorcised anyway.

HENRI BOGUET, a great demonologist and witch judge in 17th-century France, found that APPLES, a treat in which the Devil could easily hide and that raised no alarm in the eater, were the best food for transmission. "In this, Satan continually rehearses the means by which he tempted Adam and Eve in the earthly paradise," Boguet commented in *Discours des sorciers* (1602), his authoritative legal textbook on demonology. He reported an incident at Annecy, Savoy, in 1585 where townspeople pushed an apple that was giving out a "great and confused noise" into the river. Boguet said that the apple was no doubt full of devils and that the citizens had successfully foiled a witch's attempt to possess someone.

Many modern occultists believe that people become possessed by evil spirits today by toying with the supernatural, such as through automatic writing. The spirits that are attracted usually take unpleasant shapes.

The Jesuit professor Malachi Martin, in *Hostage to the Devil* (1976), outlined the stages of possession: the actual entry point, when the evil spirit first enters the victim; a stage of erroneous judgments by the possessed in vital matters, perhaps including the making of unethical choices; the voluntary yielding of control by the possessed person to the invading spirit, even though he knows the spirit is alien to his personality; and finally, perfect possession. Although Martin acknowledged the original innocence of the victim, he stressed that possession cannot occur without the consent, however subliminal, of the possessed.

The Catholic Church defines the true signs of possession as displaying superhuman strength, often accompanied by fits and convulsions; having knowledge of the future or other secret information; being able to understand and converse in languages previously unknown to the victim; and revulsion toward sacred objects or texts. Early Puritan ministers and later Protestant clergy agree on these same signs, adding the complete ignorance of the possessed person about his fits and behaviors. In a treatise written in Rouen in 1644, in response to the possession of nuns at a Louviers convent, the author lists 11 indications of demonic possession, which would alert a priest to look for the sure signs:

1. To think oneself possessed.
2. To lead a wicked life.
3. To live outside the rules of society. (Many accused witches led mildly scandalous lives.)
4. To be persistently ill, falling into heavy sleep and vomiting strange objects (see ALLOTRIOPHAGY). Some theologians described such symptoms as merely illusions caused by a witch, not signs of possession.
5. To blaspheme.
6. To make a pact with the Devil. (Most demonologists found pact-makers were accused witches, not possessed victims; see DEVIL'S PACT.)
7. To be troubled by spirits.
8. To show a frightening and horrible countenance. (The thinking was that since God and his angels were beautiful, man made in God's image, and not the Devil's, would be beautiful, too.)
9. To be tired of living (and probably contemplating suicide, a sin).
10. To be uncontrollable and violent.
11. To make sounds and movements like an animal. (Many medieval sufferers believed they were vicious animals, most often wolves. Some resorted to running on all fours and even tearing at their victims with their teeth. From such stories arose the myths of LYCANTHROPY, or werewolves.)

To this list may be added the practice of lewd and obscene acts—or even just sexual thoughts—and the classic picture of a possessed person emerges. Many possessed victims smelled horrible as well, either of foul bodily odors or of sulphur, associated with the Devil's fiery home.

Other signs of possession include a complete change in body features, such as a distended stomach, wrenching of the face into horrible expressions or rapid weight loss. The victim may seem so wasted that death appears inevitable. The voice usually changes also, to a deep, rasping, menacing, guttural croak. Sometimes the evil spirit expresses itself through automatic writing. Other possessed victims levitated.

Examined in the light of modern medicine, the convulsions and seizures, the manifestations of another personality and even the paranormal experiences are most likely symptoms of epilepsy, hysteria, schizophrenia or some other psychological problem. Possession is not the automatic answer for unexplained behavior, nor is EXORCISM the preferred treatment. For the Catholic Church, only when the indications of possession are accompanied by striking paranormal phenomena and extreme revulsion toward sacred objects should they be considered manifestations of the Devil.

Even during the height of the witchcraft hysteria in the 16th and 17th centuries, debate raged over the existence of witches and whether they could cause people to be possessed by the Devil. "Celebrity" possession victims like Jeanne des Anges in Loudun were sometimes tricked into convulsing at the sight of a "holy" relic, when in fact the item was just a piece of wood or plain water. Ten years after Urbain Grandier's death for his role at Loudun, a Frenchman named Monconys visited Jeanne des Anges at the convent and found that the "blood" of her stigmata was merely red paint.

Famous cases of possession in the 16th and 17th centuries include Nicole of Laon, who used her possession by Beelzebub to indict French Huguenots; the possessions of nuns at the convents of Aix-en-Provence (see AIX-EN-PROVENCE POSSESSIONS), Louviers, Lille and Loudun; the WARBOYS WITCHES; and the witchcraft hysteria in Salem (see SALEM WITCHES). Exorcism of possessing demons continues today.

See SPIRIT POSSESSION.

FURTHER READING:
Ebon, Martin. *The Devil's Bride, Exorcism: Past and Present.* New York: Harper & Row, 1974.
Huxley, Aldous. *The Devils of Loudun.* New York: Harper & Brothers, 1952.
Martin, Malachi. *Hostage to the Devil.* New York: Harper & ow, 1976.

power doctor   In the Ozarks region of the United States, power doctors are backwoods healers who use CHARMS, AMULETS, incantations and MAGIC to cure illness. They are similar to the powwowers of the Pennsylvania Dutch in function, performing services without charging fees but accepting "gifts" and "voluntary offerings" instead (see POWWOWING). Unlike the powwowers, power doctors must learn their craft from a person of the opposite sex who is *not* a blood relative. They believe that they may in turn teach two or three others, but to spread the word to more than that means losing their ability.

Power doctors are called upon to "charm off" warts, sores and boils and to cure various minor maladies, such as colds, headaches and body aches. Hundreds of recipes exist for charming off warts. One method calls for killing a TOAD and rubbing its intestines on the offending growth. Another and more exotic formula requires killing a black CAT and taking it to a graveyard at night, where it must be placed on the grave of a person who has been buried the same day. If a person led a "wicked life," the wart will disappear that much quicker. Most power-doctor cures prescribe similar measures, all of which must be carried out in secrecy lest the cure will not take effect. Charms must also not be mentioned to others for the same reason.

Each power doctor has his or her own favored charms, methods and incantations. Many incantations come from the Bible or are loosely adapted from it—they are called "old sayin's"—while other incantations are nonsense, such as "bozz bozzer mozz mozzer kozz kozzer." There is no formal handbook.

Blood stopping is a service performed by power doctors. Persons who suffer deep cuts and wounds from hunting accidents or from knives and axes used in farm labor are rushed to a power doctor to stop the heavy bleeding.

Rabies may be stopped with "madstones," a treatment once common in many parts of the United States. The stones resemble porous volcanic ash, but the hill folk claim they are taken from the entrails of a deer. They are passed down from father to son, never sold, but often lent to someone who is bitten by a rabid animal. The stone is applied to the wound and supposedly draws out the poison. When it falls off, it is immersed in warm milk, which turns green. The stone is applied to the wound repeatedly and immersed in milk until the milk no longer turns green. At that point, the rabies is supposed to be cured.

Some power doctors claim to be able to cure serious disease and illness, such as cancer. In addition to mum-bled charms and prescriptions for KNOTS, burned mole feet, pricked beetles and other strange ingredients, the power doctors may practice a laying on of hands. Their faith healing is considered different from that of religious faith healers.

See CUNNING MAN/CUNNING WOMAN; WIZARD.

FURTHER READING:
Randolph, Vance. *Ozark Magic and Folklore.* 1947. Reprint, New York: Dover Publications, 1964.

powwowing   Oral traditions of magical and spiritual healing concentrated in German-American Pennsylvania culture. German settlers who colonized the interior of Pennsylvania in the 1700s and 1800s brought with them their Old World beliefs in witchcraft and MAGIC. The Pennsylvania Dutch (*Dutch* is a corruption of the German word for "German," *Deutsch*) clustered in the verdant rural farmland of York, Dauphin, Lancaster, Schuylkill, Carbon, Lehigh, Berks, Bucks and other surrounding counties, which reminded them of their former homeland. They kept to themselves, retained their German language (which became mixed with English over time to form the Pennsylvania Dutch dialect) and remained suspicious of outsiders. The healing practices became known as "powwowing."

The term was derived from the settlers' observations of Indian powwows, meetings for ceremonial or conference purposes. Much of the Germans' practices centered around cures and HEALING. The settlers enlisted the help of the Indians in finding native roots and herbs that could be used in their medicinal recipes. They discovered that, like themselves, the Indians used CHARMS and incantations. They were intrigued by the powwows conducted to drive out evil spirits. They adopted the term powwow to apply to their own magical healing.

Powwowing has survived into modern times. Some of the charms and incantations used date back to the Middle Ages, probably to the time of Albertus Magnus, a magician, alchemist and prolific author whose feats were often called witchcraft. Powwowing charms also include kabbalistic and biblical elements (see KABBALAH).

The most skilled practitioners of powwowing are born into it and inherit such paranormal abilities as clairvoyance and precognition, as well as the ability to heal by a laying on of hands. Both women and men are powwowers; in fact, some of the most powerful are men. According to tradition, the SEVENTH SON OF A SEVENTH SON inherits unusual powers. The offspring of powwowers are schooled verbally in the lore only by family members. In some families, the knowledge is passed from one gender to another, while in others it is passed along the same gender lines. The apprentice powwowers may "try for" their first cures while still children. Other names for powwowers are hex doctor, witch, *hexenmeister* and *braucher*. A hexenmeister deals in spirit-conjuring, spells and hexes, while a braucher deals with healing. Powwowers consider themselves staunch Christians who have been endowed with supernatural powers, both to heal and to harm. "Divine Truth" is considered the active ingredient in all healing.

Most powwowers work quietly, attracting clients by word of mouth. Many run their powwowing as a side business, seeing clients in the evenings and weekends; others work at it full-time. Most accept "voluntary offerings" and suggest certain amounts for various kinds of services. They will help clients who cannot afford to pay anything, perhaps in the certainty that the grateful clients are bound to return when funds are available. Some charge for their services.

Most of a powwower's business concerns minor health complaints, such as removing warts, "stopping blood" (stopping bleeding by touch) and relieving a host of infections, aches and pains. Other common complaints include a malady called "the liver grow'd" and opnema, a wasting away usually due to malnutrition. Some powwowers treat cancers and diseases of the organs.

Powwowers also offer charms for protecting the household, livestock and crops from misfortune, witchcraft and evil spirits, and for success in virtually every kind of endeavor, from hunting to games to lawsuits to love.

Another power is the casting and removing of hexes (see HEX) or SPELLS. In superstitious areas such as Pennsylvania's "hex belt" (as the areas heavily populated by Pennsylvania Dutch are called) it once was common to blame bad crops, illness, bad luck and other misfortunes on hexes, or CURSES cast by enemies. A person who believed he was hexed consulted a powwower, who identified the person responsible for the hex and then offered a charm for breaking the spell.

The power of a hex rises and falls in direct proportion to the reputed power of the witch who casts it. A powerful spell can only be broken by a powerful witch. Sometimes, several visits to a witch are required before a spell can be broken. (See PELLAR.)

Powwowers memorize their charms, incantations and recipes. Several books have served as important sources. The most significant book is *Pow-wows, or Long Lost Friend* (1820), a slim volume written by JOHN GEORGE HOHMAN, a powwower who lived near Reading. Hohman and his wife, Catherine, immigrated to Pennsylvania from Germany in 1802. He was a devout Roman Catholic and a great believer in faith healing, but he proved to be mediocre as a practitioner of it. He also failed at farming. He finally achieved modest financial success by collecting various charms and herbal remedies that had existed for centuries in oral tradition and publishing them as a sort of handbook. The *Long Lost Friend,* as it became known in powwowing country, was not a book of hexes, Hohman emphasized. It was for healing, not destroying. While the book did not make him rich, it remains in print to the present day.

The *Long Lost Friend* mixes magic and healing formulas from a variety of sources dating back to antiquity, including Germany, the British Isles and Egypt. It also includes wisdom from the GYPSIES and the Kabbalah. Hohman includes his own testimonials of successfully cured persons and notes in his introduction:

> There are many in America who believe neither in a hell nor in a heaven; but in Germany there are not so many of these persons found. I, Hohman, ask: Who can immediately banish the wheal, or mortification? I reply, and I, Hohman, say: All this is done by the Lord. Therefore, a hell and a heaven must exist; and I think very little of any one who dares deny it.

Hohman also promises his readers:

> Whoever carries this book with him, is safe from all his enemies, visible or invisible; and whoever has this book with him cannot die without the holy corpse of Jesus Christ, nor drowned [sic] in any water, nor burn up in any fire, nor can any unjust sentence be passed upon him. So help me.

To prevent witches from bewitching cattle, or evil spirits from tormenting people in their sleep at night, Hohman offers the following charm, to be written down and placed either in the stable or on the bedstead:

> Trotter Head, I forbid thee my house and premises; I forbid thee my horse and cow-stable; I forbid thee my bedstead, that thou mayest not breathe upon me; breathe into some other house, until thou hast ascended every hill, until thou hast counted every fence post, and until thou hast crossed every water. And thus dear day may come again into my house, in the name of God the Father, the Son, and the Holy Ghost. Amen.

To stop blood, Hohman recommends consulting the first book of Moses, second chapter, verses 11–13, for the names of the four principal waters of the world which flow out of Paradise—Pison, Gihon, Hedekial and Pheat—and writing them down. "You will find this effective," he states.

Another important book of powwowing is the anonymous SIXTH AND SEVENTH BOOKS OF MOSES, drawn from material from the Talmud, Kabbalah and Old Testament. According to this book, one may break a hex by wearing a special AMULET that consists of herbs wrapped in specially prepared parchment inscribed with Bible verses or charms. Another method directs the hexed to avoid direct sunlight, stay indoors when the MOON is full, hold the ears at the sound of a BELL and absolutely never listen to the crowing of a COCK.

One does not have to be a powwower to possess or use these two books. They were once a staple in Pennsylvania Dutch households. But the charms were believed to be most effective when prescribed and recited by a bona fide powwower, followed by the requisite three signs of the cross.

Powwowers use a variety of techniques in their craft. Some clients may require only a laying on of hands, a murmured incantation and the sign of the cross. Others may be given special potions or powders. A well-reputed powwower at the turn of the century, Charles W. Rice, who lived in York, specialized in curing blindness with "sea monster tears," which he dispensed at $2.50 per drop.

One of the most common charms once was the *Himmels-brief ("heaven letter")*, a verse or guarantee or protection which the powwower writes on a piece of parchment or paper, to be hung in the house or barn or carried on the person. *Himmels-briefs* protected homes against fire, lightning and pestilence, and persons against murderers, robbers, mad dogs and all assaults with a deadly weapon, in war or peace. Doubters were told, "Whosoever doubts the truth of this may attach a copy of this letter to the neck of a dog and then fire upon him, and he will be convinced of its truthfulness." *Himmels-briefs* cost anywhere from $25 to hundreds of dollars, depending on the reputation of the powwower and the purpose of the charm. They were popular with soldiers in World War I, who carried them into battle hoping for protection from injury and death.

In earlier times, some powwowers were known to advocate violence, even murder, as the way to break a hex when charms and doses of dove's blood failed. A number of murders in the history of Pennsylvania have been attributed to witchcraft, even the murders of witches themselves, such as the 1928 case of Nelson Rehmeyer, the "Witch of Rehmeyer's Hollow," and the 1934 case of Susan Mummey, "the Witch of Ringtown Valley."

Powwowing is declining, replaced by other forms of healing and complementary medicine.

See JOHN BLYMIRE; POWER DOCTOR.

FURTHER READING:
Hohman, John George. *Pow-wows, or Long Lost Friend*. 1820. Reprint, Brooklyn, N.Y.: Fulton Religious Supply Co., n.d.
Gandee, Lee R. *Strange Experience: The Autobiography of a Hexenmeister*. Englewood Cliffs, N.J.: Prentice-Hall, 1971.
Kriebel, David W. *Powwowing Among the Pennsylvania Dutch*. University Park: Penn State University Press, 2007.
Lewis, Arthur H. *Hex*. New York: Pocket Books, 1970.

prayer As part of its efforts to stamp out rival religious practices, the church Christianized and absorbed many of their customs. One such practice was the use of magical CHARMS, or little prayers, verses and incantations recited to achieve a goal, cure illness or ward off evil. Charms were associated with MAGIC, and the WIZARDS, sorcerers (see SORCERY), witches, and CUNNING MEN AND WOMEN who practiced magic. The church opposed using magical charms but sanctioned the use of Christian prayer in their place for the same purpose.

It was acceptable and proper to recite Christian prayers—but not pagan or folk-magic charms—while gathering medicinal herbs in order to enhance their effectiveness, and in the application of medicine for illness.

Prayer was believed to protect against witchcraft (WOODCUT FROM FRANCESCO-MARIA GUAZZO'S *COMPENDIUM MALEFICARUM*, 1608)

The Christian prayer became an all-purpose spiritual shield: for example, a nine-day regimen of holy bread or water accompanied by the recitation of three Paternosters and three Aves in honor of the Trinity and St. Herbert would protect against all disease, witchcraft, mad dogs and Satan.

By muddying the distinction between magical charms and Christian prayers, the church may have made it more difficult to abolish the former. Many magical healers used Christian prayers or debased versions of Christian prayers as their own charms, but the church claimed that the source—the magician—rendered such charms ineffective. It was not always a successful argument; to be on the safe side, many people relied both on magic and the church.

During the witch-hunts, Christian prayer was said to be one of the best defenses against the DEVIL and his DEMONS and witches. Prayers said every morning would protect a person against witchcraft throughout the day. Witches were supposed to be unable to recite certain prayers, especially the LORD'S PRAYER; this was used as a test in many witch trials.

Prayers are part of the Catholic Church's ritual of EXORCISM.

FURTHER READING:
Lea, Henry Charles. *Materials Toward a History of Witchcraft*. Philadelphia: University of Pennsylvania, 1939.
Thomas, Keith. *Religion and the Decline of Magic*. New York: Charles Scribner's Sons, 1971.

pricking A common method of discovering witches in the 16th and 17th centuries was to prick their skin with needles, pins and bodkins, which were daggerlike instruments for drawing ribbons through loops or hems, or punching holes in cloth. It was believed that all witches had a WITCH'S MARK, a patch of skin or blemish that was insensitive to pain or that would not bleed when pricked. The discovery of such a spot alone was not sufficient proof to convict a person but was added to the evidence against her. Pricking was done throughout Europe but was most widespread in England and Scotland.

It was not uncommon for professional witch finders, who earned good fees by unmasking witches from town to town, to use fake bodkins in order to falsify evidence. Some of these instruments had hollow wooden handles and retractable points, which gave the appearance of penetrating the accused witch's flesh up to the hilt without pain, mark or BLOOD. Other specially designed needles had one sharp end and one blunt end, which was used by

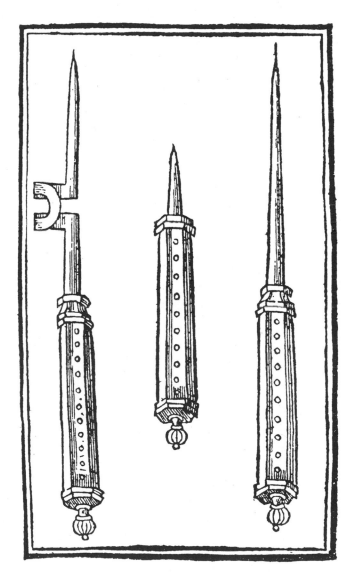

Bodkins used to prick accused witches (FROM REGINALD SCOTT'S *THE DISCOVERIE OF WITCHCRAFT*, 1584)

sleight of hand to draw blood in "normal" spots and have no effect on "witch's marks."

MATTHEW HOPKINS, England's notorious witch-hunter of the 17th century, used pricking as one of his methods. In 1650 the officials of Newcastle-on-Tyne offered another witch-hunter 20 shillings for each witch he uncovered. The man, not named in the records, examined and pricked suspects, and succeeded in getting one man and 14 women executed. One woman was saved by Lieutenant-Colonel Hobson of Newcastle, who ordered her repricked.

The pricker had forced the woman to stand in front of a group of witnesses, naked to the waist. Then he ordered her to pull her skirt up over her head while he appeared to ram a pin in her thigh. It drew no blood. Hobson suspected the woman had no reaction to the pin out of fright and shame, and because the blood was rushing to another part of her body. He had her brought to him and the test was done again. This time, the wound bled, and the woman was released.

The pricker collected his fees and left Newcastle but later was discovered to be a fraud. He fled England for Scotland but soon was captured and sentenced to hang. He confessed he had falsely caused the deaths of 220 persons in order to collect fees ranging from 20 shillings to three pounds.

FURTHER READING:

Barstow, Anne Llewellyn. *Witchcraze: A New History of the European Witch Hunts.* San Francisco: Pandora, 1994.

Deacon, Richard. *Matthew Hopkins: Witch Finder General.* London: Frederick Muller, 1976.

Remy, Nicolas. *Demonolatry.* Secaucus, N.J.: University Books, 1974.

Thomas, Keith. *Religion and the Decline of Magic.* New York: Charles Scribner's Sons, 1971.

Proctor, John and Elizabeth (17th century) Victims of the SALEM WITCHES trials in 1692–93.

John and Elizabeth Proctor (also spelled Procter) were well-to-do farmers in Salem Farms (now Peabody) when the witch hysteria erupted in Salem Village, Massachusetts. John Proctor was openly critical of the trials and of the fits of the girls who cried out against their neighbors as witches. His criticism backfired tragically on him and his wife.

After REBECCA NURSE was examined by the magistrates on charges of witchcraft, Proctor went home in anger, declaring that the girls should all be put to the whipping post before everyone was accused of witchcraft. One of the girls who had fits allegedly caused by the witches was Mary Warren, one of Proctor's servants. On the morning of Nurse's examination by the magistrates, Proctor went home in a rage over the injustice of it. He told Warren that if she were indeed afflicted, then he wished her to be more afflicted, because she and the other girls were accusing innocent people. When Warren went into fits, he threatened to thrash her to beat the fits out of her—a common treatment for hysterical and mad behavior at the time.

On April 11, 1692, Elizabeth Proctor was cried out against as a witch and arrested. John went to her public examination to defend her. Reverend Samuel Parris' manservant, John Indian, testified that Elizabeth had appeared to him in spirit, attempted to choke him and had tried to get him to sign her devil's book.

Abigail Williams and Ann Putnam testified that Elizabeth had appeared to them many times and had caused them great afflictions. She had asked them to sign her book too. Mary Warren said that Elizabeth forced her to sign the book.

When Elizabeth denied the accusations, the girls fell into fits and screamed that they saw Elizabeth's apparition sitting on a beam above them. The girls then cried out against John Proctor as a WIZARD, making him the first man to be accused of witchcraft in the Salem hysteria. The girls said they saw his apparition approach other women who were present at the hearing. Those women, Goodwife Pope and Goodwife Bibber, responded by immediately falling into fits. The next day, both John and Elizabeth were sent to prison along with several other victims.

As soon as they were sent to jail, deputies of the court went to the Proctor farm and seized all of the valuable assets. The cattle were sold or slaughtered for shipment to the West Indies. Beer and soup were emptied from their containers so that the deputies could take the containers. They left nothing for the Proctors' two children, William and Sarah.

The Proctors were tried together on August 5 in the Court of Oyer & Terminer and condemned to death. Elizabeth "pleaded her belly," meaning that she was pregnant. According to law, a pregnant woman could not be executed, because her unborn child was considered to be innocent. Execution would still take place, but after the child was born. John Proctor was sentenced to be hanged.

Their children, William and Sarah, also were accused of witchcraft. William protested his innocence and was tortured by having his neck tied to his heels until his blood gushed forth from his nose.

In desperation, John wrote a petition to the court protesting the innocence of himself and Elizabeth and likening the trials to the Spanish Inquisition. Thirty-one of their former neighbors in Ipswich and 20 of their friends in Salem signed a petition attesting to their virtuous characters and lives. The petition had no influence.

John soon realized that they could not get fair trials with the girls' hysterical fits being allowed as testimony. A few days before the Proctors' own trials—and four days after the execution of Nurse—John wrote to INCREASE MATHER and four other leading Boston ministers, asking them for a change of venue to Boston, or, if that were not possible, then to proceed in Salem with new magistrates who were less likely to be swayed by the hysterical girls.

He complained that the accused were already being condemned before they were put on trial. He also protested the torture of his children.

Mather was not swayed, answering on August 1 that "the Devil may sometimes represent an innocent person."

John was sent to the gallows with the others on August 19. Reverend Nicholas Noyes refused his request for PRAYER, on the grounds that he did not confess that he was a witch. John went to his death with dignity.

Elizabeth gave birth in January 1693. By then, the witch hunts were over, and she was spared her death sentence. However, she had no legal rights and could not reclaim any of the property owned by her husband. In 1696 she petitioned the court for a reversal of her verdict in order to restore her civil rights, but without success. In 1711, the judgments were reversed for 22 survivors and their families, and small amounts of restitution were paid.

FURTHER READING:
Hansen, Chadwick. *Witchcraft at Salem.* New York: New American Library, 1969.
Upham, Charles. *History of Witchcraft and Salem Village.* Boston: Wiggin and Lunt, 1867.

Puck   The personal name of a nature spirit in the folklore of Britain, Ireland and Wales known for his mischievous and trickster ways. In medieval times, under the influence of Christianity, Puck was associated with the DEVIL, as were all pagan deities and spirits.

In folklore, *puck* is a term; for a type of spirit. Shakespeare popularized it as the name of a character in his play *A Midsummer Night's Dream.* A puck is also known as a *puca, pouk, phouka* and *pwca* (Welsh). Puck's traits correspond also to those of the pixie or piskey of England's West Country lore.

Puck is a shape-shifter and is often seen as a black animal or a black half-animal. He is most often depicted as a misleader, especially leading travelers astray. When he is so inclined, he favors humans by enabling them to understand animal speech and by protecting them from evil spirits. If treated well, household pucks, like brownies, will clean up the house during the night and also do yard work. Ungrateful people invoke Puck's wrath. He also bedevils grave robbers.

In Christianized English lore, Puck was viewed as having a particularly malicious nature and was equated with the Devil. Hell was called "Puck's Pinfold." Puck is also known as Robin Goodfellow, another type of BOGEY, or wicked spirit, who was popular in England in the 16th and 17th centuries. Rudyard Kipling, however, portrayed him as a nature spirit in "Puck of Pooks Hill."

To contemporary Witches, Puck is seen more in his original form as an "Old One" and a spirit of the land. English Witch PADDY SLADE, who has a special relationship with Puck, says of him:

Puck is the Lord of the Greenwood, the Spirit of Albion, the Spirit of the Island of Graymayre. He is probably the last of the Old Ones, those who inhabited the Island in the days before the users of iron came. He keeps the Old Faith and does not suffer fools, which is why he is thought of as tricky; but is a good and true friend to all who try to keep the Old Ways honestly. He *will* teach the language of the wild creatures and of the trees, but he must trust you first.

Slade's "Wild Rite of the Mother" features Puck. He speaks the following words (the first two sentences are taken from Kipling; the remainder is Slade's composition):

I am the Old One. My voice is deeper than three cows lowing.

I keep the Wild Magic. I am Pan. I am Herne. I am the Lord of the Greenwood, Friend of Trees and Wild Creatures. I come with the Wolf, the first teacher to this rite. I bring the Stag of Seven Tines to stand Watch Ward.

(*The rite then describes the music of the Earth.*)

Deep in the rocks; deep in the Woods; Underground and Overground. Under the sky and beneath the Sea, the Pulse is Beating. The Earth Sings.

You can hear it if you listen. The Crystals in the rocks tune to it. The Plants and Trees grow to it. The waters flow to it.

See FAIRIES; NATURE SPIRITS.

quirin (also quirus) In folklore, a stone said to have the powers of a truth serum and highly valued by witches and magicians. When placed beneath a pillow, the quirin causes a person to talk in his sleep and confess his "rogueries." The stone allegedly is found in the nests of either the lapwing or the hoopoe, two Old World species of birds often confused in earlier centuries. The lapwing, a species of plover, exists in Europe and Asia, while the hoopoe, related to the kingfisher, lives in Europe, Asia and Africa. Both are crested but they are differently colored: the lapwing is predominantly gray and white, while the hoopoe is orange-gold, black and white.

See STONES.

Ravenwolf, Silver (1956–) American Witch and author, known especially for her books on the Craft for teenagers.

Silver Ravenwolf—her Craft name—was born Jenine E. Trayer on September 11, 1956. Her father was a Lutheran, and her mother attended the First Christian Church Disciples of Christ, a Baptist offshoot. Ravenwolf was 14 when her 20-year-old cousin Tess gave her a deck of Tarot cards and also introduced her to the concept of reincarnation and to the Craft via *Diary of a Witch,* the autobiography of SYBIL LEEK.

By age 17, Ravenwolf was involved in the Craft. She received her first degree INITIATION in November 1991 from Bried Foxsong of Sacred Hart. She received second and third degree initiations in the Temple of Hecate Triskele of the Caledonii Tradition. On June 29, 1996, she was eldered by Lord Serphant at the Puff Gathering in North Carolina. She heads the Black Forest Circle and Seminary, a North American organization of 38 clans, each of which includes several COVENS. Her hearthstone coven is Coven of the Omega Wolf.

Ravenwolf has written more than 28 nonfiction and fiction books. She also paints, makes jewelry and crafts, does professional photography and professional astrology. Her breakout book was *To Ride a Silver Broomstick: New Generation Witchcraft,* published in 1994. *Teen Witch: Wicca for a New Generation* was published in 1998 and tapped a growing interest in the Craft among young people.

Other nonfiction books written by Ravenwolf are *Hex Craft: Dutch Country Pow-wow Magick* (1995); *To Stir a Magic Cauldron: Witch's Guide to Casting and Conjuring* (1996); *The Rune Oracle* (1996); *Angels: Companions in Magick* (1996); *American Folk Magick; Charms, Spells and Herbals* (1999); *To Light a Sacred Flame: Practical Witchcraft for the Millennium* (1999); *The Rune Mysteries* (1999); *Silver's Spells for Prosperity* (1999); *Halloween: Customs, Recipes and Spells* (1999); *Witches Runes Kit* (1999); *Teen Witch Kit: Everything You Need to Know to Make Magic!* (2000); *Silver's Spells for Love: Getting It. Keeping It. Tossing It.* (2001); *Solitary Witch: The Ultimate Book of Shadows for the New Generation* (20010: *Silver's Spells for Abundance* (2005); *A Witch's Notebook: 9 Lessons in Witchcraft* (2005); and *Mindlight: Secrets of Energy, Magic and Manifestation* (2006).

Read, Margaret (d. 1590) One of three women ever to be executed by burning in England on charges of witchcraft. Margaret Read lived in King's Lynn, East Anglia, England.

Read was convicted of murdering her husband by witchcraft, a crime considered to be petty treason and punishable by burning rather than the more traditional hanging. She was burned in the Tuesday Market in King's Lynn. Her heart exploded, splattering the wall of a nearby house with her blood. A heart in a carved Egyptian diamond pattern was made on the wall to commemorate the event.

red   The color of BLOOD, health, vigor, sexual passion and aggression, red has had magical significance since the time of ancient Egypt. Egyptians linked red to death and to an evil dragon, Typhon; they mocked redheaded men in certain religious rites. Red is the color of the Greek and Roman phallic god, Priapus, and the god of war, Mars. The Old Testament links sin to the color scarlet: "Though your sins be scarlet . . ." (Isaiah 1:18). Because it is the color of blood, red is used in the trappings of ritual blood SACRIFICE.

Red is also associated with witches. It is a widespread folk belief that witches have red hair, perhaps because red hair is unusual. In some places, it is unlucky to see people with red hair: fishermen in Scotland and Ireland believe they will catch no fish if they spot a red-haired woman on the way to their boats. In old Irish lore, witches were believed to don red caps before flying through the air to their SABBATS. They could turn pieces of straw into red pigs, which they sold at the market to unsuspecting customers. If the pigs crossed running water as they were driven home, they changed back into straw. According to another folk belief, a witch's soul pops out of her mouth in the form of a red mouse.

Red works in CHARMS against witches. The Pennsylvania Dutch draw red lines around barns to keep witches out (see HEX). In Bohemia, it is believed that a charm tied in a red cloth and hung around the neck will protect one from bewitchment. Other charms to repel witches include red-painted carts and wreaths of rowan tied with red threads. Braided red cords or ropes hung in stables force witches to stop and count each thread before they can harm animals, according to one popular folk belief.

With its biblical association with sin, red figures prominently in old tales of witches' sabbats and Black Masses (see BLACK MASS). Abigail Williams, one of the accused SALEM WITCHES in 1692, said witches consumed "red drink and red bread" at their sabbats. The priests who officiated at blasphemous Black Masses often wore red garments and slippers and read from red-and-black books. In 1895 Prince Scipio Borghese of Italy was discovered to have a chamber in his palace which was devoted to satanic masses, furnished with crimson-and-gold chairs and scarlet-and-black silk curtains (see SATANISM).

In contemporary Witchcraft, red is associated primarily with health, vigor and passion. In healing it is called "the great energizer" and is said to stimulate the blood. Red CANDLES and cords (see KNOTS) are used in magic spells.

Redcap   One of the most malignant and vampire-like goblins of the folklore of the border counties between England and Scotland. Redcap lives in various old and ruined castles and peel towers, where he takes delight in wreaking evil upon unwitting visitors. He keeps his cap dyed red from human blood.

One description of Redcap is as follows: ". . . a short thickset old man, with long prominent teeth, skinny fingers armed with talons like eagles, large eyes of a fiery red color, hair streaming down his shoulders, iron boots, a pikestaff in his left hand, and a red cap on his head."

If one encountered Redcap, it was useless to try to resist him by brute human strength. He could be repelled, however, by making the sign of the cross or reciting Biblical scripture.

Lord Soulis of HERMITAGE CASTLE reputedly had a Redcap as a FAMILIAR. In European lore, redcaps have a milder nature and are more like the helpful household brownies, who clean and do chores.

See MOTHER REDCAP; RED.

Regardie, Francis Israel (1907–1983)   Occultist, psychotherapist and one-time secretary of ALEISTER CROWLEY.

Born in England on November 17, 1907, Francis Israel Regardie (he dropped the use of his first name later on) spent most of his life in the United States, emigrating there at age 13. He became fascinated with occultism and the activities and writings of Crowley and secured a position as Crowley's secretary in 1928. From that year to 1934, Regardie traveled around Europe with Crowley. Like many of Crowley's friends and associates, Regardie eventually suffered a falling out with him.

Regardie's works are important influences in WITCHCRAFT and PAGANISM. He wrote numerous books on occultism, the first of which were *The Tree of Life* and *The Garden of Pomegranates*, both of which were published in 1932. In 1934, the year of his falling-out with Crowley, he joined the Stella Matutina temple of the HERMETIC ORDER OF THE GOLDEN DAWN. He left after a few years and violated his oath of secrecy by publishing the complete rituals of the Golden Dawn in a four-volume encyclopedia, *The Golden Dawn: an Encyclopedia of Practical Occultism,* between 1937 and 1940. The work has been revised and reissued several times. Regardie broke his oath because he believed the teachings of the Golden Dawn should be revealed to the public. The Golden Dawn material has been incorporated into numerous Pagan and Wiccan rituals.

Regardie became a chiropractor. He served in the U.S. Army during World War II, then settled in southern California, where he worked as a psychotherapist. He authored a biography of Crowley, *The Eye in the Triangle,* and coauthored, with P. R. Stephenson, another Crowley associate, *The Legend of Aleister Crowley,* both of which appeared in 1970. Regardie always acknowledged Crowley's faults but defended Crowley as "a great mystic, sincere, dedicated and hard working."

Regardie's other books include: *My Rosicrucian Adventure* (1936; 1971); *Middle Pillar* (1945; 1970); *The Romance of Metaphysics* (1946); *The Art of Healing* (1964); *Roll Away the Stone* (1964); *Tree of Life; A Study in Magic* (1969); *What is the Qabalah?* (1970); *To Invoke Your Higher Self* (1973); and *Twelve Steps to Spiritual Enlightenment* (1975).

Rémy, Nicholas (1530–1616) French lawyer, demonologist and determined witch-hunter who claimed to have sent 900 witches to their deaths over a 10-year period in Lorraine. So convinced was Rémy of the evil and doings of witches that he compiled his "facts" into a book, *Demonolatry,* which became a leading handbook for witch-hunters.

Rémy was born in Charmes to a family of distinguished lawyers. He followed the family tradition and studied law at the University of Toulouse. He practiced in Paris from 1563 to 1570, when he was appointed Lieutenant General of Vosges, filling a vacancy created by his retiring uncle. In 1575 he was appointed secretary to Duke Charles III of Lorraine. Besides being a lawyer, Remy also was a historian and poet and wrote several works on history.

As a youth, Rémy had witnessed the trials of witches, which may have shaped his later opinions. It was not until 1582 that he took up his own personal crusade against witches. Several days after refusing to give money to a beggar woman, his eldest son died. Rémy was convinced the woman was a witch and successfully prosecuted her for bewitching his son to death. Like his contemporary JEAN BODIN, Rémy believed in DEVIL'S PACTS, wild SABBATS and MALEFICIA against men and beasts. He was credulous, believing the most fantastic stories about DEMONS raising mountains in the blink of an eye, making rivers run backwards, putting out the stars and making the sky fall. Like Bodin and other authorities, he also believed that witches should suffer and be burned as punishment.

In 1592, after a decade of prosecuting witches, Rémy retired to the countryside to escape the plague. There he compiled *Demonolatry,* which was published in 1595 in Lyons. The book includes notes and details from his many trials and his assertions about witches' black MAGIC and SPELLS, the various ways in which they poisoned people (see POISONS) and their infernal escapades with demons and the DEVIL. He devoted much space to describing satanic pacts and the feasting, dancing and sexual orgies that took place at sabbats. He described how the Devil threw people into his service, first with cajoling and promises of wealth, power, love or comfort, then by threats of disaster or death. He backed up his statements with "evidence" obtained from confessions, such as the following:

At Guermingen, 19th Dec., 1589, Antoine Welch no longer dared oppose the Demon in anything after he threatened to twist his neck unless he obeyed his commands, for he seemed on the very point of fulfilling his threat . . . Certainly there are many examples in pagan histories of houses being cast down, the destruction of the crops, chasms in the earth, fiery blasts and other such disastrous tempests stirred up by Demons for the destruction of men for no other purpose than to bind their minds to the observance of some new cult and to establish their mastery more and more firmly over them.

Therefore we may first conclude that it is no mere fable that witches meet and converse with Demons in very person. Secondly, it is clear that Demons use the two most powerful weapons of persuasion against the feeble wills of mortals, namely, hope and fear, desire and terror; for they well know how to induce and inspire such emotions.

Rémy's claim of sending 900 witches to their deaths cannot be corroborated by existing records; he cites only 128 cases himself in his book. Nevertheless, his accumulated "facts" seemed reasoned and beyond refute to the audience of his day. *Demonolatry* was an immediate success and was reprinted eight times, including two German translations. It became a leading handbook of witch-hunters, replacing the *MALLEUS MALEFICARUM* in some parts of Europe.

While he influenced the unhappy fate of countless innocent victims, Remy continued in the comfortable service of the Duke until his death in 1612, secure in the righteousness of his work.

FURTHER READING:
Baroja, Julio Caro. *The World of the Witches.* 1961. Reprint, Chicago: University of Chicago Press, 1975.
Lea, Henry Charles. *Materials Toward a History of Witchcraft.* Philadelphia: University of Pennsylvania, 1939.
Rémy, Nicolas. *Demonolatry.* Secaucus, N.J.: University Books, 1974.

rings AMULETS of power, strength, divinity, sovereignty and protection. In legend, they are also TALISMANS of MAGIC, enabling their wearers to perform supernatural feats or become invisible. The origins of magic rings are not known, but they appear in ancient mythology. Marduk, the champion of the Babylonian gods, holds a ring in his portrayal as a warrior; in Greek myth, Jove released the Titan Prometheus from his chains but required him to wear one link on his finger.

The legendary King Solomon had a magic ring, etched with a hexagram and the real name of God, which enabled him to conjure the djinn (demons) and force them to work for him. One of Satan's fiercest DEMONS, Asmodeus, craftily convinced Solomon to lend him the magic ring, whereupon Asmodeus threw Solomon out of Jerusalem and set himself up as king. He threw the ring into the sea. Solomon recovered it from a fish's belly and restored himself to his throne. He imprisoned Asmodeus in a jar.

Ancient Egyptians and Hebrews used signet rings, which were inscribed with names or magic words or phrases (see NAMES OF POWER). The signet ring is still a symbol of authority in both church and state. In the Middle Ages, rings inscribed with magic formulas were popular amulets to ward off illness. In England, from the early Middle Ages to the 16th century, "cramp rings" were popular as cures for epilepsy and related disorders. Originally, the rings were fashioned from the coins given by the monarch in Good Friday devotions. Later, rings were simply made and then blessed and rubbed by the monarch. Some cramp rings were exported to Europe. In

World War I, German soldiers wore rings inscribed with runes as protection against wounds and death.

Rings set with semiprecious and precious STONES, cast in a precious metal, are amulets bearing the particular properties of the stone. Red jasper, for example, is associated with BLOOD, and soldiers in ancient times wore rings of red jasper to prevent bleeding to death from wounds. AMBER is one of many stones that protect against the EVIL EYE, while cat's eye and ruby protect against witchcraft. Many stones are medicinal amulets that protect against various diseases and disorders.

Many modern Witches wear silver rings bearing runic inscriptions, the names of deities, a pentacle, a crescent moon, images of GODDESS or other representations of the Craft.

FURTHER READING:
Budge, E. A. Wallis. *Amulets and Superstitions.* New York: Dover Publications, 1978. First published 1930.
de Givry, Emile Grillot. *Witchcraft, Magic and Alchemy.* 1931. Reprint, New York: Dover Publications, 1971.

rites of passage   The contemporary Pagan and witchcraft communities create their own RITUALS for life's important transitions: birth, death, marriage, divorce, coming of age and entering elderhood. A rich variety of prayers, songs, chants, meditations, rituals, poetry and other creative works is in continual evolution as Pagans draw on different traditions and heritages to meet their own spiritual needs.

These rites affirm the sacred wheel of birth-death-rebirth, the sacredness of the body, the human connection to nature, and oneness with the divine, expressed by the various aspects of the GODDESS and God. There are rites that honor the newly and ancestral dead and for animals. Of particular importance are rites of puberty and of aging, two stages of life largely ignored in Western society and mainstream religion. Puberty rites for both boys and girls are conducted. For elders, there are croning rituals for women and saging rituals for men.

Equally important are rites for dying, which address the spiritual needs to accept death as part of the cycle of life, rather than deny it. Death is celebrated as a rebirth, not only on a spiritual plane, but as preparation for return to Earth in another life.

Marriage rites in contemporary Paganism and Witchcraft are called handfastings, pledged to last as long as does love. In some traditions, the couple jumps over a broomstick for good luck. Divorce rites—another transition largely ignored from a ceremonial standpoint in Western society—are called handpartings.

"Wiccaning" and "Paganing" are child-blessing rites similar to a Christening, in which an infant is presented to the elements and Goddess/God and ritually blessed. In contemporary Witchcraft traditions, the child may be given a secret Craft name, which is used until the child is old enough to select his or her own name, if so desired.

Wiccaning and Paganing do not commit a child to a particular spiritual path; the child is free to choose his or her own path when the appropriate time comes.

FURTHER READING:
Farrar, Janet, and Stewart Farrar. *A Witches Bible Compleat.* New York: Magickal Childe, 1984.
Fitch, Ed, and Renee, Janine. *Magical Rites from the Crystal Well.* St. Paul: Llewellyn Publications, 1984.
Harvey, Graham. *Contemporary Paganism: Listening People, Speaking Earth.* New York: New York University Press, 1997.
Starhawk, M. Macha NightMare and the Reclaiming Collective. *The Pagan Book of Living and Dying.* San Francisco: HarperSanFrancisco, 1997.

ritual   A prescribed form of ceremony to achieve a transformation of consciousness. All religions and spiritual, mystical and magical traditions have their own rituals, which are the means by which to contact divine or supernatural will or forces. Rituals help the individual define him-/herself in relation to the cosmos, and mark progress through life and spiritual unfolding.

In MAGIC, rituals are used to change consciousness and to bring desired things into being: to invoke the presence of entities, spirits or energies; to release energies; to honor and celebrate deities, nature and sacred times; and to manifest change. Rituals in folk magic or witchcraft are spell-castings (see SPELLS), usually for luck, healing, fertility, protection, EXORCISM, hexing, "unwitching," and so on. In high magic, rituals are akin to those in religious ceremonies. In addition, there are sacred/societal rituals of transition, passage and INITIATION.

Ritual has played an important role in the development of human consciousness since the beginnings of history. It exists in all facets of life. It is part of the cosmic fabric that weaves everything together in a harmonious whole. Daily life is structured around rituals—personal habits, meals, activities at certain times, and so on.

Ritual helps the human consciousness tap into unseen forces: forces of the inner self, forces of nature, forces of the cosmos. Hsun Tzu, a Chinese philosopher of the third century B.C.E., said that ritual makes for harmony in the universe and brings out the best in human beings—it is the culmination of culture.

In his classic work *The Rites of Passage,* Arnold Van Gennup described three parts to a ritual: separation, in which there is withdrawal from the world; transition; and incorporation, in which change is integrated into life. Anthropologist Victor Turner described the phase of transition as "liminality," the "betwixt and between" worlds. He said rituals foster *communitas,* or a bond that goes beyond words.

When ritual changes consciousness, a space for inner knowing is created; archetypal energies are activated. A new awareness or knowledge may arrive in a dream, flashes of inspiration, signs in the material world or other synchronistic events.

Herb spirit blessing ritual (PHOTO BY SELENA FOX; COURTESY OF CIRCLE SANCTUARY)

The most effective rituals, even if they are simple, engage the senses as much as possible. Involving the senses alters consciousness and opens the gateway to visionary thinking. This is accomplished through recitation, chanting, singing, prayer and invocation; dancing, movement or postures, or reenactment of mystery dramas; costumes or special dress; incense, smoke, candles or fire; offerings or sacrifices; consumption of food and drink (or, conversely, fasting); purifications; use of sacred objects, relics, tools, images and symbols. These elements create physical and psychological changes intended to help achieve the goal of the ritual.

All elements of a ritual should be observed correctly to ensure success.

Rituals are done both individually and collectively. There is greater power in a group, where all energies are focussed on the same objective.

Carl Jung was critical of the moribund state of ritual in modern Western society. Ritual has all but evaporated from daily life and holds little meaning for many in dry religious services. Ritual is emphasized in WICCA and PAGANISM, and contemporary witches and Pagans have drawn upon traditional pagan sources to create meaningful rituals for modern times. Rituals are observed in all

worship services, magical workings, SABBATS and personal rites of passage.

See CONE OF POWER; WHEEL OF THE YEAR.

FURTHER READING:

Bonewits, Isaac. *Real Magic.* Revised ed. York Beach, Me.: Samuel Weiser, 1989.

Crowley, Vivianne. *Wicca: The Old Religion in the New Millennium.* Revised ed. London: Thorsons/Harper Collins, 1996.

Driver, Tom F. *The Magic of Ritual.* San Francisco: HarperSanFrancisco, 1991.

Eliade, Mircea. *Patterns in Comparative Religion.* New York: New American Library, 1958.

Van Gennep, Arnold. *The Rites of Passage.* 1908. Chicago: University of Chicago Press, 1960.

Rivera, Luis de (17th century)   Mule drover accused of bewitching cattle and mules to stampede. The case of Luis de Rivera illustrates how problems of all kinds were once easily blamed on WITCHCRAFT.

In 1628, de Rivera signed on as a mule drover with a supply wagon train traveling from Mexico to New Mexico. Enroute, the cattle and mules went into a stampede that resulted in serious financial losses. The other hands immediately suspected that a witch must be among them.

De Rivera, who had suffered a long run of bad luck in other matters, broke down and confessed that he must be the culprit.

As soon as the wagon train arrived in Santa Fe, de Rivera was turned over to the INQUISITION and sent back to Mexico City for trial by the church. There he once again confessed his guilt and begged for mercy, saying he was foolish and was not trying to commit sin or renounce the Christian faith. The court let him off with a light sentence of penance.

FURTHER READING:
Simmons, Marc. *Witchcraft in the Southwest: Spanish and Indian Supernaturalism on the Rio Grande.* Lincoln: University of Nebraska Press, 1974.

rodents   Rats and mice once were considered to be among the leading FAMILIARS of witches. Seventeenth-

The Pied Piper leads a town's rats away (FROM THE FAIRY TALE "THE RATCATCHER" IN ANDREW LANG'S *THE RED FAIRY BOOK*)

century Quakers called rodents "the devil's disciples" and said that they were carriers of the devil's lies and deceits.

A house or ship infested by rodents had to be exorcized, according to Quaker belief. The method was to write a stern letter ordering them to leave under threat of death. Supposedly, the rodents would find it, eat it and then leave. It was necessary for them to eat the letter in order to understand it.

A 19th-century rat EXORCISM letter found in the cellar of a Quaker home in Cape Cod, Massachusetts, calls the rats "spirits of the bottomless pit" and warns, "Begone, or you are ruined! We are preparing water to drown you; fire to roast you; cats to catch you; and clubs to maul you." The letter then instructs the rat to go to a neighbor's house.

In other lore, rats are said to be the embodiment of evil spirits and will haunts houses. Since ancient times, rats have been associated with the human soul. Their sudden disappearance from a ship or a house forewarns of death, doom and disaster.

FURTHER READING:
Cahill, Robert Ellis. *Strange Superstitions.* Danvers, Mass.: Old Saltbox Publishing, 1990.
Radford, E. and M.A. *The Encyclopedia of Superstitions.* Edited and revised by Christina Hole. New York: Barnes & Noble, 1961.

Rollright Stones   In the Cotswolds in England, a group of prehistoric standing stones associated in popular legend with a witch. The Rollright stones, which are estimated to be older than Stonehenge, are located between Chipping Norton and Long Compton, on a high, windy ridge overlooking Long Compton. The area has a long history of witchcraft activities.

The original purpose of the Rollright Stones is not known, but it may have served as a ritual gathering site.

According to legend, an unnamed Danish king and his army once invaded England. At Rollright, they encountered a witch, and the king sought her supernatural knowledge, asking if he would conquer England. She told him to walk seven strides to the top of the ridge. If he could see the village of Long Compton below, then he would become king of England.

The king eagerly followed her instructions. But at the seventh step, he discovered that the view of the village was blocked by a barrow. At that instant, the witch cried,

Sink down man, and rise up stone!
King of England thou shalt be none.

The king and all his men were suddenly turned to stone. The king became the solitary King Stone. Nearby, his soldiers formed a cromlech, or circle, called the King's Men. The witch prepared to turn herself into an elder tree, but before she did, she backtracked to four of the king's knights, who had lagged behind, whispering and plotting against the king. She turned them to stone, and today they are called the Whispering Knights.

Originally, the King's Men numbered 11 stones, but some have been broken into pieces. The cromlech measures about 100 feet across. The stones are believed to date to the Bronze Age; the Whispering Knights are most likely part of a burial mound.

Legend has it that at midnight, the stones come alive and turn into men again. They join hands and dance, and anyone unfortunate enough to gaze upon them either goes insane or dies. According to 18th-century lore, village maidens would go to the Whispering Knights one by one on Midsummer's Eve and listen carefully, hoping to hear in the whisperings their future and fate.

Until 1949 the Rollright Stones were regularly used as the site of Witches' gatherings. Sometimes local people liked to sneak up and spy on the Witches. One such person was CHARLES WALTON, who was murdered in 1945 in what appeared to be a ritual killing. In 1949 a SABBAT was observed by two outsiders, and the resulting press publicity forced the Witches to go elsewhere. In 1964 a London COVEN held a special gathering at the Rollright Stones for a magazine article. The stones have been vandalized by teenagers, and access to them is now restricted to daylight hours.

FURTHER READING:
Bord, Janet, and Colin Bord. *Ancient Mysteries of Britain.* Manchester, N.H.: Salem House Publishers, 1986.

sabbat In earlier times, a diabolical gathering of witches. In modern times, a seasonal celebration observed by Wiccans and Pagans.

The belief that witches convened in sabbats, assemblies characterized by obscene behavior, dominated the witch hunts from the 14th and 15th centuries. The origins of the sabbat are a blend of seasonal pagan rites still in existence—most notably the great festivals of Beltane (observed May 1) and Samhain (observed October 31)—and the belief that heretics held obscene rites. The sabbat also may be related to the Bacchanalian and Saturnalian rites of the ancient Greeks and Romans. The term *sabbat* is Old French and is derived in part from the Hebrew *Shabbath,* "to rest," pertaining to the seventh day of the week designated by the Ten Commandments as the day of rest and worship.

Some historians say that *sabbat* as it was applied to heretics and witches was anti-Semitic, for Jews were among the heretics. Similarly, heretics, and sometimes witches, were said to meet in synagogues, a term that also was used synonymously with sabbats. The sabbat became much more prominent in continental Europe during the witch-hunts than it did in England, where there is no record of a witch sabbat prior to 1620, except for an innocuous feast that was termed a sabbat in the Lancaster witch trials of 1612 (see LANCASTER WITCHES).

The assemblies of heretics were described as including sexual orgies, gluttonous feasting, worship of the DEVIL, blasphemous and diabolical rites and copulation with DEMONS. As witchcraft became heresy, these activities were attributed to witches.

The first mention of a sabbat in a trial of the INQUISITION occurred in Toulouse in 1335. The term *sabbat* (also *sabbath*) for these meetings was not applied regularly until about the mid-15th century. Once the sabbat appeared in trials, however, it quickly assumed a certain form. Sabbats invariably took place at night in remote locations, such as

Witches roasting babies in preparation for the sabbat (WOODCUT FROM FRANCESCO-MARIA GUAZZO'S *COMPENDIUM MALEFICARUM,* 1608)

mountains, caves and deep forest areas. The best-known gathering place for sabbats was the Brocken in the Harz Mountains of Germany, where the greatest activity took place on WALPURGISNACHT (beltane), April 30. To get to a sabbat, witches flew through the air, sometimes on the backs of demons that had metamorphosed into animals, or astride broomsticks or poles (see FLYING). The witches themselves sometimes changed into animals (see META-MORPHOSIS) and were accompanied by their FAMILIARS. The Devil usually appeared in the shape of a he-goat, ugly and smelly, though at times he was said to arrive as a TOAD, crow or black CAT. He presided over the sabbat while sitting on a throne. The witches took off their clothes and paid homage to him by kissing his backside (see KISS OF SHAME). Unbaptized infants were offered up in SACRIFICE. New witches were initiated by signing his black book in BLOOD, renouncing Christianity, taking an oath and trampling upon the cross (see INITIATION). The Devil marked his initiates with his claw (see DEVIL'S MARK). There followed a great feast, with much drinking and eating, although demonologists often noted that the food tasted vile and that no SALT was present, for witches could not abide salt. If infants had been sacrificed, they were cooked and eaten. After the feasting came dancing and indiscriminate copulation among the witches and demons. On occasion, the witches would go out into the night and raise storms or cause other trouble (see STORM RAISING). The witches flew home before dawn. The nights of the sabbats varied. Some witches said they attended weekly sabbats, while others said they went only once or twice a year.

In 1659 a French shepherdess gave this description of a sabbat that occurred on the summer solstice, observed by her and some companions:

> [They] heard a noise and a very dreadful uproar, and, looking on all sides to see whence could come these frightful howlings and these cries of all sorts of animals, they saw at the foot of the mountain the figures of cats, goats, serpents, dragons, and every kind of cruel, impure and unclean animal, who were keeping their Sabbath and making horrible confusion, who were uttering words that were most filthy and sacrilegious that can be imagined and filling the air with the most abominable blasphemies.

It is doubtful that such organized, malevolent activities took place. Most likely, the witches' sabbat was a fabrication of the witch-hunters, who seized upon admission of attendance at a gathering, meeting or feast and twisted it into a diabolical affair. Victims who made such confessions were pressed to name others who had attended the sabbats. In this manner, sometimes entire villages became implicated in Devil-worship.

Contemporary Witches and Pagans use the term *sabbat* to describe their seasonal holidays, but increasingly prefer terms such as *seasonal celebrations* or *seasonal festivals* which do not carry the stereotyped image of *sabbat*.

See WHEEL OF THE YEAR.

Witches' sabbat meal (ULRICH MOLITOR, *VON DEN UNHOLDEN ODER HEXEN,* 1489)

FURTHER READING:

Baroja, Julio Caro. *The World of the Witches.* 1961. Reprint, Chicago: University of Chicago Press, 1975.

Barstow, Anne Llewellyn. *Witchcraze: A New History of the European Witch Hunts.* San Francisco: Pandora/Harper Collins, 1994.

Ginzburg, Carlo. *Ecstasies: Deciphering the Witches' Sabbath.* New York: Pantheon Books, 1991.

Lea, Henry Charles. *Materials Toward a History of Witchcraft.* Philadelphia: University of Pennsylvania, 1939.

Marwick, Max, ed. *Witchcraft and Sorcery.* New York: Viking Penguin, 1982.

Michelet, Jules. *Satanism and Witchcraft.* Reprint. Secaucus, N.J.: Citadel Press, 1939.

Summers, Montague. *The History of Witchcraft and Demonology.* London: Kegan Paul, Trench, Trubner & Co. Ltd., 1926.

Trevor-Roper, H. R. *The European Witch-Craze.* New York: Harper & Row, 1957.

sacrifice   An offering of a gift, especially to a deity or being, in petition, thanksgiving or appeasement. The most common offerings are food, drink, the fruits of harvest and the BLOOD sacrifice of animals and fowl. The highest sacrifice is that of human life, a practice now rare. Sacrifices can be made to the ELEMENTS, the sun and MOON, the cardinal points, sacred landmarks (mountains, lakes, rivers and so on), the dead and supernatural beings.

In contemporary Witchcraft and PAGANISM offerings are cakes, drinks, fruits, flowers, poems, handicrafts, incense, nuts and other items. Blood sacrifice is considered unnecessary for worship. In Witchcraft rituals, an offering of food and drink is presented at the altar or sprinkled about the outdoors as an offering.

Blood sacrifice. Ritual blood sacrifice is an ancient custom of propitiation to the gods. Animals, fowl and humans have long been sacrificed in various religious rites to secure bountiful harvests and secure blessings and protection from deities. Blood consumed in ritual sacrifice is believed to give the drinker the soul and attributes of the blood of the deceased, whether it be human or animal. The Celts and Druids reportedly drank the blood of their sacrificed human victims. The Aztecs cut the hearts out of human sacrifices with flint knives; the still-beating heart was held aloft by the priest, then placed in a ceremonial receptacle. The body was often dismembered and eaten in an act of ritual cannibalism. The Khonds of southern India impaled their victims on stakes and cut off pieces of their backs to fertilize the soil.

The sacrifice of first-born children was once a common custom in various cultures, particularly in times of trouble. During the Punic Wars, the nobility of Carthage sacrificed hundreds of children to Baal by rolling them into pits of fire.

The early Hebrews practiced blood sacrifices of animals. The book of Leviticus in the Old Testament lays out instructions for all kinds of sacrifices, including animals and fowl. In Genesis, Cain offers the fruits of his harvest, which does not please the Lord, and Abel offers one of his flock, which does please the Lord. Also in Genesis, God tests Abraham by instructing him to sacrifice his son. Abraham is stopped at the last moment, and a ram is substituted.

The Paschal Lamb, eaten at Passover, is a sacrifice commemorating the deliverance of the Israelites from Egypt. Christ obviated the need for blood sacrifice by shedding his own blood on the cross, thus securing eternal redemption for mankind. The Eucharist and communion services are nonbloody sacrifices, in which bread and wine or grape juice substitute for the body and blood of Christ.

Divine sacrifice is an important theme in mythology. For example, Osiris, Dionysus and Attis are dismembered in sacrifice for rebirth.

During the witch hunts, witches were said to sacrifice COCKS and unbaptized children to the DEVIL. They also were charged with cannibalism of infants and children. The cock sacrifices most likely relate to the pagan custom of sacrificing cocks as the corn spirit in harvest festivals, or in folk-magic SPELLS, in order to ensure an abundant crop the following year. The accusations of sacrifice and cannibalism of children were most likely the result of the TORTURE applied during inquisitions and trials of accused witches. It also is in keeping with the historical trend of similar accusations leveled by one religious group against another. The Syrians accused the Jews of human sacrifice and cannibalism, much as the Romans accused the Christians and the Christians accused the Gnostics, Cathars, Waldenses and Albigenses.

In MAGIC, blood sacrifice releases a flash of power, which the magician uses for a SPELL or conjuration. The old GRIMOIRES call for killing animals and using their skins to make parchment used in drawing the magical symbols needed. Animals offered should be young, healthy and virgin, for the maximum release of energy. The letting of blood, and the fear and death throes of the victim, add to the frenzy of the magician.

ALEISTER CROWLEY, in *Magick in Theory and Practice* (1929), said that "The ethics of the thing appear to have concerned no one; nor, to tell the truth, need they do so." Crowley sacrificed animals and fowl in his rituals, within a MAGIC CIRCLE or triangle, which prevented the energy from escaping. He considered the torturing of the animal first, in order to obtain an elemental slave, as "indefensible, utterly black magic of the very worst kind," although in the next breath he said that he had no objection to such black magic if it was "properly understood." Crowley also noted that a magician could effect a blood sacrifice without the loss of life by gashing himself or his assistant.

Animals are sacrificed in various tribal religions and in VODUN and SANTERÍA. the animal sacrifices of Santería—usually fowl and sometimes lambs or goats—have raised much opposition in America from animal-rights groups and offended individuals who consider the custom barbaric. The issue has been exacerbated by the practice of some Santeríans of leaving their beheaded and mutilated sacrifices in public places for others to find. Charges of stealing pet dogs and cats for sacrifice have been levied against the groups. Santeríans in the U.S. counter that the Constitution protects their right to worship as they see fit. They defend animal sacrifice by pointing to its ancient roots.

Satanic groups, which are not connected to Pagans or Witches, also may practice blood sacrifice (see SATANISM).

FURTHER READING:

Russell, Jeffrey Burton. *Witchcraft in the Middle Ages.* Ithaca and London: Cornell University Press, 1972.

Thomas, Keith. *Religion and the Decline of Magic.* New York: Charles Scribner's Sons, 1971.

St. Osyth Witches A witch hunt that swept through a remote coastal area of Essex, England, in 1582 brought indictments against 14 women. Despite lurid and flimsy testimony of the kind that quickly led to convictions and executions elsewhere, all but two of the women went free. The hysteria took place in St. Osyth, not far from Chelmsford, where a major witch hysteria had occurred about 14 years earlier.

The hunt began against Ursula Kempe of St. Osyth, a poor woman who made a meager living by midwifery, harlotry and white witchcraft, chiefly "unwitching," that is, removing bad SPELLS that people believed had been cast against them. A woman named Grace Thurlowe had a son who became strangely ill with convulsions. Kempe and some neighbors came to see him. Kempe took him by the hand, muttered incantations, and told Thurlowe that the boy "would do well enough." The child was healed almost immediately.

Thurlowe, suspicious of witchcraft, then would not let Kempe nurse her newborn daughter. The infant fell out of its crib and broke its neck. Thurlowe and Kempe quarreled violently, and "Ursley" threatened Thurlowe with lameness. Soon, Thurlowe was severely crippled with arthritis that was so bad she could scarcely drag herself around on hands and knees. (By another account, Kempe treated Thurlowe for her arthritis, but Thurlowe refused to pay Kempe's fee of 12 pence, after which her arthritis flared up again.)

Thurlowe worked for a county session judge, Bryan Darcy, and complained to him about Kempe. Darcy investigated, and coerced Kempe's illegitimate eight-year-old son Thomas to "confess" to incredible stories about his mother. He told Darcy that his mother "hath foure seuerall spirits, the one called Tyffin, the other Tittey, the third Pigine, and the fourth Iacke: and being asked what colors they were, saith that Tyttey is like a little grey Cat, Tyffin is like a white lambe, Pygine is black like a Toad, and Iacke is black like a Cat." Thomas said he had seen these FAMILIARS come at night and suck blood from his mother at her arms and other places on her body. He also said that the spirits had been given to "Godmother Newman" (Alice Newman) in an earthenware pot. Darcy also found a man who claimed Kempe had bewitched his wife to death.

Kempe denied these stories, but Darcy tricked her by falsely promising her leniency if she confessed. Fearful for her life, Kempe confessed to having familiars and consorting with other St. Osyth witches, whom she named: Elizabeth Bennet, Alice Hunt and her sister Margery Sammon, as well as Alice Newman. Hunt and Sammon were daughters of "old Mother Barnes," a witch of notorious repute who allegedly had bequeathed to them her familiars, "two spirites like Toades, the one called Tom and the other Robbyn."

These accused women in turn named others, hoping for mercy from the court. Hunt confirmed her sister Mar-

Accused St. Osyth witch sends a familiar to seek revenge for a quarrel, 16th century

gery as a witch, as well as Joan Pechey. Newman confirmed Bennet. Soon 14 women were "exposed." Most of them were disreputable and/or poor. Hunt's eight-year-old stepdaughter claimed that she had two little things, one black and one white, "the which shee kept in a little lowe earthen pot with woll, color white and black . . . and saith, that shee hath seene her mother to feede them with milke."

Bennet admitted that she had two spirits, "one called Suckin, being blacke like a Dogge, the other called Lierd, beeing red like a Lion." Another accused woman, Annis Herd, was charged by her seven-year-old illegitimate daughter of having six avices or blackbirds as her IMPS, and six more who lay in a box lined with black and white wool.

The accused elaborated stories on each other, especially about their familiars. In Darcy's own account, he reported:

The sayd Ursley Kemp had foure sprytes, viz. their names Tettey a hee like a gray cat, Jack a hee like a black cat, Pygin a she like a black toad, and Tyffin a she like a white lambe. The hees were to plague to death, and the shees to punish with bodily harme, and to destroy cattell.

Tyffyn, Ursley's white spirit, did tell her always (when she asked) what the other witches had done: and by her the most part were appelled, which spirit telled her always true. As is well approved by the other withes confession.

The sayd Ales Newman had the sayd Ursely Kemps spirits to vse [use] at her pleasure. Elizabeth Bennet had two spirits, viz. their names Suckyn, a hee like a blacke dog: and Lyard, red lyke a lyon or hare.

Ales Hunt had two spirits lyke colts, the one blacke, the other white.

Margery Sammon had two spirits lyke toads, their names Tom and Robyn.

Cysley Celles had two spirits by seurall names, viz. Sotheons Hercules, Jack, or Mercury.

Ales Manfield and Margaret Greull had in common by agreement, iiii spirits, viz. their names Robin, Jack,

Will, Puppet, alias Mamet, whereof two were hees, and two were shees, lyke vnto black cats.

Elizabeth Eustace had iii impses or spirits of color white, grey, and black.

Annis Herd had vi impes or spirites, like aiuses and black byrdes, and vi other like kine, of the bygnes of rats, with short hornes; the aiuses shee fed with wheat, barley, otes, and bread, the kine with straw and hay.

The women were charged with crimes of bewitching animals, bewitching brewing, baking and butter churning, striking people with wasting sickness and bewitching people to death. Some accounts of the hysteria, such as by REGINALD SCOT, place the number of accused at 17 or 18, going to their deaths. Historian Rossell Hope Robbins, citing more recent research of records, placed the number at 14, with two executions.

With lurid stories and "confessions" abounding, it seems that convictions would have been certain of many of the accused. However, two women were not indicted at all. Strangely, one of these was Sammon, who confessed. Two women were imprisoned but denied charges of bewitching cattle and two people to death. They were not indicted and released.

Four women who went to trial—three of them on charges of bewitching people to death—pleaded not guilty and were acquitted. Testimony against them came from children.

Four others accused pleaded not guilty, were tried and convicted, and then reprieved. One of them was Newman, who was charged with bewitching to death four persons plus her husband. Agnes Glascock and Cicely Celles similarly were charged with bewitchment to death. Joan Turner was charged with bewitchment by over-looking (see EVIL EYE), and did spend a year in prison.

The only two hanged were Kempe and Bennet. Kempe was charged with bewitching three people to death between 1580 and 1582. She confessed to the crimes. Bennet was charged with killing a man and his wife.

The remains of Ursula Kempe were exhumed by researcher CECIL WILLIAMSON, and placed on display in an open elm coffin lined with purple satin in his MUSEUM OF WITCHCRAFT. The exhumation was televised. Williamson discovered that Kempe's body had been driven through with iron spikes, an old custom intended to keep restless ghosts and vampires from leaving their graves to haunt the living. Kempe's remains were kept by Williamson for his personal collection when he sold the museum in 1996.

See CHELMSFORD WITCHES; CUNNING MAN/CUNNING WOMAN.

FURTHER READING:

Robbins, Rossell Hope. *The Encyclopedia of Witchcraft & Demonology*. 1959. Reprint, New York: Bonanza Books, 1981.

Scot, Reginald. *The Discoverie of Witchcraft*. 1886. Reprint. Yorkshire, England: E.P. Publishing, Ltd. 1973.

Summers, Montague. *The Geography of Witchcraft*. London: Kegan Paul, Trench, Trubner & Co. Ltd., 1927.

Salem "Old Witch" Jail   The jail that housed the accused SALEM WITCHES during the witch hysteria of 1692–93 was a cold, foul, rat-infested dungeon located near the North River. It was used to house Indians, pirates and criminals, most of whom were condemned to die; the conditions in which such persons spent their last days were of little concern. It also housed debtors: people jailed because they could not pay their debts and those who were unable to pay the fees levied for keep in the jail.

Construction of the dungeon was approved in 1683 by the town of Salem. It succeeded two earlier prisons, one built in 1663 on the seized lands of Quakers, and another built in 1669. The new jail, built in 1684, was constructed of large, hand-hewn oak timbers and siding, and measured 70 by 280 feet. There were no bars, for Puritan prisoners accepted their punishment. Those who did not and managed to escape were either caught or killed by Indians or wild animals.

The prisoners were fed salted foods and drink mixed with herring-pickle, for which they had to pay. This caused a constant, dreadful thirst, which made them more likely to confess in order to get relief.

Despite its grim conditions, the jail was a social gathering place. The jailkeeper sold grog to visitors who came in the evenings to play chess and other games. For a bond of one pound, a prisoner was released during the day to visit family and friends, and then returned at night.

During the witch hysteria of 1692, the jail housed four lots of accused victims. The jailers routinely stripped the women of their clothing to examine and prick them in search of witch is WITCH'S MARKS (see PRICKING). They—and members of their families—were tortured for confessions (see TORTURE). One of the accused, Elizabeth Cary, was locked in leg irons and placed in a room with no bed. "The weight of the irons was about eight pounds," wrote her husband, Captain Nathaniel Cary. "These irons and her other afflictions, soon brought her into convulsion fits, so that I thought she would die that night." Cary bribed the jailer with his life's savings in order to get his wife freed.

Elizabeth Cary was not the only accused witch to suffer convulsions; many of the other victims suffered hysterical fits from the conditions and their treatment at the hands of the jailers. Two victims, Sarah Osborne and Ann Foster, died in jail. Foster's son was assessed a fee of two pounds, 16 shillings for permission to remove his mother's body for burial.

The salaries and expenses of the sheriff and his staff, the magistrates, the hangman and all persons concerned with the court were paid by the accused, who were each assessed one pound, 10 shillings. In addition, the prisoners were billed seven shillings and sixpence for their fetters, chains and cuffs, and an extra fee for being searched for witch's marks. The hangman's substantial fee was charged to the victims' estates or families. Those who had money fared the best. Captain John Alden, jailed on witchcraft charges, escaped by bribing the jailkeeper five pounds; he hid in New York until 1693, when the hysteria ended.

After victims were condemned, they were taken from the jail by oxcart out to GALLOWS HILL. Their corpses, swaying from the limbs of the locust trees, could be seen from the center of town.

In 1764 the jail was expanded with the addition of second and third stories. It was discontinued as a jail in 1813 and subsequently passed into private ownership and was used as a residence. In 1863 it was purchased by Abner Cheney Goodell, state historian; it was later acquired by his son, Abner Cheney Goodell, Jr.

The jail was given little historical attention until 1934, when Mrs. Goodell, Jr., found in an old sealed closet a jailer's bill for the keep of paupers, some of whom were victims in the Salem trials. In response to public inquiries about the dungeon, the Goodells opened the jail to the public in 1935. The original jail was closed sometime later and re created in a museum, the Salem Witch Dungeon.

FURTHER READING:
Goodell, Alfred P. "The Story of the Old Witch Jail." Undated manuscript, Essex Institute, Salem, Mass.

Salem Witches   One of the last outbreaks of WITCH-CRAFT hysteria, and certainly the largest in the New World, occurred in Salem, Massachusetts, from 1692 to 1693. During the course of the trials, 141 people were arrested as suspects, 19 were hanged and one was pressed to death. Those afflicted by the witches were mostly young girls, yet their "child's play" led not only to the deaths of innocent people but also to total upheaval in the colonial Puritan Church.

Scores of studies have examined the causes of the Salem witchcraft trials: some dealing with the political and social problems of Salem Village (now Danvers, Massachusetts), others with repressed sexual, generational or racial hostility; revolt by the disenfranchised; repression of women; regional feuds brought over from England; or ergotism, a food poisoning in the bread flour that may have led to hallucinations. Some studies have concentrated solely on the overly zealous nature of the parishioners. Whatever the reasons, there is little doubt that all those who were involved believed totally that witchcraft posed a serious threat to the health and spiritual well-being of the colony.

Divisions in the town. The Puritans who left England and settled in Salem in 1626, under the leadership of Roger Conant, hoped they would find peace in the new land. The settlement originally was named Naumkeag, the Indian term for "land of three rivers." Sometime before July 24, 1629, the name was changed to Salem from the Hebrew term *shalom,* meaning "peace." By 1692, however, peace was far from the order of the day.

For years, the community of Salem Village had chafed under the administration of neighboring Salem Town, which held legal, church and taxing authority over the more rural village. Villagers were required to attend services in the town, although the distance for some residents was more than 10 miles. As early as 1666, village

Witch flying over Salem (BERT POOLE, 1895; ESSEX INSTITUTE)

residents petitioned the town and the colony's General Court for permission to build a meetinghouse and hire a minister, which they finally accomplished in 1672.

That permission alone did not make them a full-fledged community, however, but more a parish within the juris diction of Salem Town. The 17th-century Puritan "Church" was not the building, minister or attendees but an "elect"—those select few who had been filled with divine grace, given testimony to God's power and were allowed to receive communion. Church members attending services in Salem Village still had to travel to their real churches for communion. Continued discontent among Salem Villagers about their situation, coupled with disputes over who in the village had the power to select ministers, was described as a "restless frame of spirit" a—moral defect in the villagers' characters—instead of a legal issue. By the time Samuel Parris arrived to be the fourth minister in Salem Village in 1689, the community was irreparably split between those who wished to maintain ties with Salem Town and those who believed the village was best served by autonomy. Parris vocally supported the separatist interests. Eventually, the village divided between those who stood behind Parris and those who did not.

Beginning of the hysteria. In some ways, Rev. Parris caused the witch hysteria, however unknowingly. Before becoming a minister, Parris had worked as a merchant in Barbados; when he returned to Massachusetts, he brought back a slave couple, John and TITUBA Indian (Indian was probably not the couple's surname but a description of their race). Tituba cared for Parris' nine-year-old daughter Elizabeth, called Betty, and his 11-year-old niece, Abigail Williams. Especially in winter, when bad weather kept the girls indoors, Tituba most likely regaled the girls with stories about her native Barbados, including tales of voodoo (see VODUN).

Fascinated with a subject that the Puritans found shocking, the girls soon became dabblers in the occult. Joined by other girls in the village who ranged from 12 to 20—Susannah Sheldon, Elizabeth Booth Elizabeth Hubbard, Mary Warren, Mary Walcott, Sarah Churchill, Mercy Lewis and Ann Putnam, Jr. (Ann Putnam Sr. was her mother)—they began telling each other's fortunes. Making a primitive crystal ball by floating an egg white in a glass of water, the girls tried to ascertain the trades of their future husbands. One reportedly saw the likeness of a coffin, representing death; what had begun as a fun game had now turned into dangerous magic.

The girls, beginning with Betty Parris in January 1692, began having fits, crawling into holes, making strange noises and contorting their bodies. It is impossible to know whether the girls feigned witchcraft to hide their involvement in Tituba's magic or whether they actually believed they were possessed (see POSSESSION). In any case, Rev. Parris consulted with the previous Salem Village minister, Rev. Deodat Lawson, and with Rev. John Hale of nearby Beverly. In February he brought in Dr. William Griggs, the village physician and employer of the now-afflicted Elizabeth Hubbard. Griggs had no medical precedent for the girls' condition, so he diagnosed bewitchment.

Seventeenth-century Puritans believed in witchcraft as a cause of illness and death. They further believed the accepted wisdom of the day that witches derived their power from the DEVIL. So the next step was to find the witch or witches responsible, exterminate them and cure the girls. After much prayer and exhortation, the frightened girls, unable or unwilling to admit their own complicity, began to name names.

Right before this, Mary Walcott's aunt, Mary Sibley, tried to use magic to find the witches. She requested that Tituba make a witch cake out of rye meal mixed with the urine of the afflicted girls. The cake, taken from a traditional English recipe, was then fed to the dog. If the girls were bewitched, one of two things were supposed to happen: either the dog would suffer torments too, or as her FAMILIAR, he would identify his witch. Rev. Parris furiously accused Mary Sibley of "going to the Devil for help against the Devil," lectured her on her sins and publicly humiliated her in church. But the damage had been done: "the Devil hath been raised among us, and his rage is vehement and terrible," said Parris, "and when he shall be silenced, the Lord only knows."

Crying out against the witches. The first accused, or "cried out against," were Tituba herself, SARAH GOOD and Sarah Osborne. Goodwife (usually shortened to Goody; Mistress or Mrs. was reserved for women of higher rank) Good's husband William did not provide for his family, and she defiantly begged and looked out for them herself. Goody Osborne, old and bedridden, had earlier caused a scandal by allowing her servant to live in her house before she married him. Tituba was a natural suspect. Suspicious neighbors were not surprised that any or all three were witches, and none was a member of the church.

Warrants for their arrest were issued, and all three appeared in the ordinary, or public house, of Nathaniel Ingersoll before Salem Town magistrates John Hathorne and Jonathan Corwin on March 1. The girls, present at all of the interrogations, fell into fits and convulsions as each woman stood up for questioning, claiming that the woman's specter was roaming the room, biting them, pinching them and often appearing as a bird or other animal someplace in the room, usually on a particular beam of the ceiling. Hathorne and Corwin angrily demanded why the women were tormenting the girls, but both Sarahs denied any wrongdoing.

Tituba, however, beaten since the witch cake episode by Rev. Parris and afraid to reveal the winter story sessions and conjurings, confessed to being a witch. She said that a black dog had threatened her and ordered her to hurt the girls, and that two large CATS, one black and one RED, had made her serve them. She claimed that she had

Accused witches pilloried in New England (OLD WOODCUT)

ridden through the air on a pole to "witch meetings" with Goody Good and Goody Osborne, accompanied by the other women's familiars: a yellow bird for Good, a winged creature with a woman's head and another hairy one with a long nose for Osborne. Tituba cried that Good and Osborne had forced her to attack Ann Putnam Jr. with a knife just the night before, and Ann corroborated her statement by claiming that the witches had come at her with a knife and tried to cut off her head.

Most damningly for Salem, Tituba revealed that the witchcraft was not limited to herself and the two Sarahs: that there was a COVEN of witches in Massachusetts, about six in number, led by a tall, white-haired man dressed all in black, and that she had seen him. During the next day's questioning, Tituba claimed that the tall man had come to her many times, forcing her to sign his Devil's book in BLOOD, and that she had seen nine names already there (see DEVIL'S PACT).

Such a story, frighteningly real to the Puritans because of rumors that had circulated a few years earlier that a conspiracy of witches would destroy Salem Village, beginning with the household of the minister. Hathorne, Corwin and Rev. Parris were pushed to begin an all-out hunt for the perpetrators of such crimes. All three women were taken to prison in Boston, where Good and Osborne were put in heavy iron chains to keep their specters from traveling about and tormenting the girls. Osborne, already frail, died there.

The politics of witchcraft. Complicating the legal process of arrest and trial was the loss of Massachusetts Bay's colonial charter. Massachusetts Bay was established as a Puritan colony in 1629 and was enjoying self rule when the English courts revoked its charter in 1684–85, restricting the colony's independence. The high-handed Sir Edmund Andros, the first royal governor, was overthrown in 1688 when William and Mary of Orange took away the English throne from James II in the Glorious Revolution. Since that time, Massachusetts Bay had had no authority to try capital cases, and for the first six months of the witch hunt, suspects merely languished in prison, usually in irons (see SALEM "OLD WITCH" JAIL).

But more than the legal ramifications, the loss of Massachusetts' charter represented to the Puritans a punishment from God: the colony had been established in covenant with God, and prayer and fasting and good lives would keep up Massachusetts' end of the covenant and protect the colony from harm. Increasingly, the petty transgressions and factionalism of the colonists were viewed as sins against the covenant, and an outbreak of witchcraft seemed the ultimate retribution for the colony's evil ways. Published sermons by COTTON MATHER and his father, INCREASE MATHER, and the long-winded railings against witchcraft from Rev. Parris' pulpit every Sunday, convinced the villagers that evil walked among them and must be rooted out at all cost.

More witches are named. Relying on the spectral visions of the afflicted girls, the magistrates and ministers pressed them to name more witches if they could, and Ann Putnam Jr., with the help of her vengeful mother, cried out against MARTHA COREY, a member of the Salem Village congregation and wife of local landowner GILES COREY. Before arresting her, Ann's uncle Edward Putnam and Ezekiel Cheever rode to the Corey home to speak with Martha. The men pressed Ann to reveal what clothes Martha was wearing, hoping to prove that such a godly churchwoman was innocent. Ann claimed she could not, as Martha had temporarily removed her spectral sight.

When the men arrived, Martha calmly said she knew why they had come and even taunted them by asking, "Does shee tell you what clothes I have on?" They were shocked to think Martha had preternatural knowledge of the earlier conversation. And when Martha visited the Thomas Putnam home to see young Ann, the girl fell into terrible fits, claiming she saw Martha's specter roasting a man over a fire. Mercy Lewis said other witches joined Martha's specter, urging her to sign the Devil's book. Martha steadfastly maintained her innocence later before the magistrates, but the girls' torments and anguish in court convinced the judges she was a witch. Every time she said something or made a gesture, the girls mimicked her. If she bit her lip, the girls shrieked in pain, showing teeth marks on their arms and hands. Even her husband, Giles, testified against her and asked her to confess to witchcraft.

The next woman named as a witch was REBECCA NURSE, one of the most outstanding people of her community and a church member. If the girls had named Rebecca Nurse or Martha Corey as witches first, instead of Sarah Good and Sarah Osborne, their accusations probably would have been dismissed as folly. But by now, the magistrates were willing to believe anything the girls claimed. Even close family members of the accused believed in the women's guilt, refusing to believe that the magistrates or girls would accuse anyone who was not a witch.

Rebecca's accuser was Ann Putnam, Sr., who had joined the ranks of "the afflicted," as the accusing girls were known, by claiming that the specters of Corey and Nurse had come to her and tortured her hellishly, urging her to sign the Devil's book. Abigail Williams, Mary Walcott and Elizabeth Hubbard agreed that Nurse had come to them, too, wanting them to sign. Rebecca was old and ill, but she was forced to stand before the magistrates and the girls. Ann Putnam, Jr. claimed Nurse's specter had beaten her, and Ann Sr. cried out that Nurse had brought the "black man" with her. Rebecca defended herself as best she could, but she too was sent to prison.

Joining Rebecca in prison was four-year-old Dorcas Good, whom the afflicted girls had claimed was a witch, learning her evil trade from her mother Sarah. Dorcas was chained like all the others.

The next victims of witch hysteria were JOHN AND ELIZABETH PROCTER, tavern-keepers and vocal opponents of the proceedings. Mary Warren, one of the original afflicted girls and Procter's maid, earlier had been "cured" of her fits when Procter threatened to beat her if she persisted. Knowing of the Procters' opposition, the girls were eager to eliminate any who would dispute them.

But before the Procters were arrested, Sarah Cloyce, the sister of Rebecca Nurse, stormed out of church in disgust when Rev. Parris' sermon implied the guilt of her sister and all the other accused witches. Such a display of anger made her a convenient target, and the girls cried out against Cloyce and Elizabeth Procter together. John Procter accompanied his wife to support her before the magistrates, who had moved the proceedings to the Salem Town meetinghouse and were joined by Deputy Governor Thomas Danforth and Captain Samuel Sewell. Tituba's husband John had joined the afflicted, and he,

---

The Wonders of the Invisible World:

Being an Account of the

TRYALS

OF

Several Witches,

Lately Executed in

NEW-ENGLAND:

And of several remarkable. Curiosities therein Occurring.

Together with,

I. Observations upon the Nature, the Number, and the Operations of the Devils.

II. A short Narrative of a late outrage committed by a knot of Witches in *Swede-Land*, very much resembling, and so far explaining, that under which *New-England* has laboured.

III. Some Councels directing a due Improvement of the Terrible things lately done by the unusual and amazing Range of *Evil-Spirits* in *New-England*.

IV. A brief Discourse upon those *Temptations* which are the more ordinary Devices of Satan.

By COTTON MATHER.

Published by the Special Command of his EXCELLENCY the Governour of the Province of the *Massachusetts-Bay* in *New-England*.

Printed first, at *Boston* in *New-England*; and Reprinted at *London*, for *John Dunton*, at the *Raven* in the *Poultry*. 1693.

Title page of London edition of Cotton Mather's witch pamphlet, 1693

along with Mary Walcott, Abigail Williams, Ann Putnam, Jr. and Mercy Lewis all claimed that the witches' specters tortured them, urging them to sign the Devil's book and drink victims' blood. During the interrogation, Abigail and Ann Jr. saw John Procter's specter sitting on a ceiling beam and tormenting the girls.

Abigail accused Elizabeth Procter of forcing her maid, Mary Warren, to sign the Devil's book, a shrewd defense against Mary's reluctance to testify against her employer. By doing so, the girls named Mary a witch and gave notice to the other afflicted that hesitation or denial would result in their being named witches. During her own interrogation, Mary had no choice but to confirm the girls' accusations and rejoin their ranks.

Arrested along with Mary Warren were Giles Corey, BRIDGET BISHOP and Abigail Hobbs. Bishop entertained people in her home with liquor and games to all hours, dressed in flashy red outfits and had scandalized Salem for years. Accusations of witchcraft were not far behind. Abigail Hobbs, mentally unbalanced, readily confessed to witchcraft and told Hathorne of her bargain with "the old boy" that allowed him to appear to the afflicted girls in her shape. Instead of dismissing her story as that of an insane person, the magistrates believed every word and found vindication in it for the girls' spectral attacks.

Eighty-year-old Giles Corey, Martha's husband, described as powerful and brutal, resolutely denied any involvement with witchcraft. But the girls' usual performance, claiming spectral pinching and other torments, sealed his fate as a wizard.

On April 21 Abigail Hobbs' wild tales led to the arrests of nine more people: a very old man named Nehemiah Abbot; Abigail's parents, William and Deliverance Hobbs; Bridget Bishop's stepson Edward and his wife Sarah; Mary Esty, sister of Rebecca Nurse and Sarah Cloyce; a Negro slave named Mary Black; Sarah Wilds; and Mary English, wife of the wealthy Salem merchant Philip English. Up to now, all the accused had lived in the Salem vicinity, but five of these suspects were from Topsfield. Eventually, witches were sought in 22 other communities.

The interrogations before Hathorne and Corwin followed the usual pattern, with the magistrates badgering the accused and the girls throwing fits and claiming spectral violence. But for the first time, they recanted their accusations against a victim, and Nehemiah Abbot was acquitted. If their change of heart was intentional, it was judged a shrewd move: the girls would not charge an innocent person and could tell witches from godly people.

The others were not so lucky. Edward and Sarah Bishop were guilty by association with his mother. Deliverance Hobbs first denied involvement but then succumbed to the magistrates' bullying and confessed signing the Devil's book, brought to her by Sarah Wilds. Such confessions brought the girls temporary relief. Her husband obdurately held onto his innocence but was carried off to prison just the same. Mary Black, the slave, denied prick-

ing dolls and said she just pinned her collar. But when the magistrates asked her to pin her collar, the girls screamed in pain, and Mary Walcott appeared so badly pricked that she bled. Sarah Wilds's meek denials did not save her, either.

Villagers considered Mary Esty a likely witch since her sisters were already accused. But her adamant protestations of innocence impressed even Hathorne, leading him to demand of the girls that they be sure. Naturally, spectral evidence found Goody Esty guilty. When Hathorne, angry at what he thought was Esty's lying, asked her if she believed the girls bewitched, she is reported to have replied, "It is an evil spirit, but wither it be witchcraft I do not know." Over the next few weeks, the girls—all but Mercy Lewis—began to doubt they had seen Esty's specter, and she was freed. But then Mercy fell into terrible convulsions and claimed that Esty's specter was choking her because she alone maintained the woman was a witch. Esty was returned to prison.

On April 30 six more people were arrested: Sarah Morey, Lydia Dustin, Susannah Martin, Dorcas Hoar, merchant Philip English and Rev. GEORGE BURROUGHS. Morey was eventually acquitted, and Dustin died in prison. Dorcas Hoar and Susannah Martin, independently minded, had long been accused of witchcraft; Martin even had the temerity to laugh at the antics of the girls. Philip English escaped to Boston with his wife Mary, also accused, until the affair died down. He saved their lives but lost most of his property.

Rev. Burroughs, however, had been brought to Salem from his home in Wells, Maine. A minister at Salem Village before Parris, he had alienated many of the parishioners, especially Ann Putnam Sr., and witchcraft was a convenient vehicle for her vengeance. Ann Jr. actually first accused Burroughs, screaming that a minister was offering her the Devil's book. The specter told young Ann that his name was Burroughs, that he had murdered several people while in Salem and that "he was above witch for he was a conjurer." All agreed that Burroughs was the coven leader that Tituba had described.

Given Burroughs' station and occupation, the magistrates decided a more discreet examination would be in order. He was interrogated at Ingersoll's ordinary by Hathorne, Corwin, Captain Sewall and William Stoughton, a man vigorously in favor of rooting out witchcraft. After the private questioning, various citizens stepped forth and accused Burroughs, a small man, of feats of superhuman strength and cruelty, and the girls writhed as always. The magistrates sighed collectively at the capture of the witches' ringleader.

Unfortunately, Burroughs still had followers unapprehended. John Willard, who had earlier helped in the arrests, was himself accused and caught after he refused to issue any more warrants. His damning evidence was his inability to recite the LORD'S PRAYER, viewed as certain proof of the Devil's handiwork; only the godly can recite the Lord's word. George Jacobs, an early opponent of the proceedings, was arrested with Willard and Jacobs' granddaughter Margaret. Jacobs could not recite the Lord's Prayer either, and his maidservant, Sarah Churchill, said she had seen his name in the Devil's book.

Like Mary Warren, Churchill had second thoughts about the girls' games when Jacobs, her employer, stood accused. But the girls turned on her as well, saying she had signed. She confessed, but later recanted. Haunted by her false confession, Churchill complained that everyone believed her accusations, but no one believed her when she said someone was innocent. None of this impaired her qualifications as an accuser of others, and Churchill remained in company with the other afflicted girls.

Prosecution, condemnation and execution. As noted earlier, no trials could be held until Massachusetts obtained a new charter, and so all the accused remained in prison without a formal trial. Finally, in May of 1692, the new royal governor, Sir William Phips, arrived with a charter. Unwilling to concern himself with the witchcraft mess, Phips established a Court of Oyer and Terminer ("to hear and determine") to try the witches. Sitting on the court were now Lt. Governor William Stoughton as chief justice, Bartholomew Gedney, Jonathan Corwin, John Hathorne, Nathaniel Saltonstall, Peter Sergeant, Wait Still Winthrop, Samuel Sewall and John Richards. All were among the most respected men in the colony, but many were the same men already sending accused witches to prison.

By May's end, approximately 100 people sat in prison based on the girls' accusations. Three of the more memorable were Elizabeth Cary, Martha Carrier and John Alden, the son of John and Priscilla Alden of Plymouth. Judge Gedney was shocked to find Alden, a respected sea captain, accused of witchcraft, but when the girls shrieked and cried out in pain, Gedney pressed Alden to confess. He refused and was led away; he later escaped to New York. Elizabeth Cary came of her own free will to the court when she heard she had been accused, and she learned that her specter did no harm to the girls until they were sure it was she.

Martha Carrier was the first accused from Andover, Massachusetts, which eventually named 43 witches in its citizenry. Defiantly, Carrier denied tormenting the girls or seeing any black man, but the more she stood firm, the more the girls writhed. Finally, Carrier's hands and feet were bound to keep her specter from torturing the girls further, for the wisdom of the day said a witch in bondage could harm no one.

The Court of Oyer and Terminer first sat on June 2 and lost no time in trying and sentencing the accused witches. Bridget Bishop was first on the docket and was found guilty. Chief Justice Stoughton signed her death warrant on June 8, and she was hanged two days later. The body was casually placed in a shallow grave on Salem's GALLOWS HILL, for witches did not deserve Christian burial.

Justice Saltonstall resigned from the court not too long thereafter, disgusted at the entire affair and uncomfortable at the total reliance on the girls' spectral evidence. His opposition later earned him an accusation of witchcraft.

The question of spectral evidence had dominated the proceedings from the beginning. The problem was not whether the girls saw the spectral shenanigans but whether a righteous God could allow the Devil to afflict the girls in the shape of an innocent person. If the Devil could not assume an innocent's shape, the spectral evidence was invaluable against the accused. If he could, how else were the magistrates to tell who was guilty? Turning to the colony's clergy, the court asked for an opinion, and on June 15 the ministers, led by Increase and Cotton Mather, cautioned the judges against placing too much emphasis on spectral evidence alone. Other tests, such as "falling at the sight," in which victims collapsed at a look from a witch, or the touch test, in which victims were relieved of their torments by touching the witch, were considered more reliable. Nevertheless, the ministers thanked the court for its diligence and pushed for "the vigorous prosecution of such as have rendered themselves obnoxious."

Chief Justice Stoughton firmly believed until his death that God would not allow the Devil to assume an innocent's shape, and so the court pressed on. The next to appear were Susannah Martin, Sarah Good and Rebecca Nurse. Martin and Good were condemned, but Nurse was originally acquitted. The girls, present as always, went into terrible fits at the news, and Stoughton calmly asked the jury if it was certain of her innocence. The jury reconsidered and found her guilty. Again, Nurse's friends tried to save her, petitioning Governor Phips to reprieve her. He did but later rescinded his order.

On June 30 the court tried and condemned Sarah Wilds and Elizabeth How. How, of Topsfield, had cured John Indian's fits by touching him, and others accused her of bewitching their children and animals. Interestingly, during the trials one of the afflicted accused Rev. Samuel Willard, pastor of the Old South Meeting House in Boston. Because he was minister for three of the justices, the court protected Willard, reprimanded the accuser and explained to the public that she had meant John Willard, already imprisoned.

The executions of Nurse, How, Martin, Sarah Good and Sarah Wilds took place July 19. Rev. Noyes, present as a witch-hunter from the beginning, urged Sarah Good to confess, but she defiantly cursed him, saying, "I am no more a witch than you are a wizard, and if you take away my life, God will give you blood to drink." Noyes died in 1717, supposedly of an internal hemorrhage, choking on his own blood. All but Nurse remained in the shallow grave on the hill; her family secretly removed the body that night to give it a decent burial.

Witchcraft in other communities. By now the girls' power was so great that they were celebrities in the colony and were believed to be invincible. Consequently, citizens of

Trial of George Jacobs (ESSEX INSTITUTE)

neighboring towns requested that the girls look at their communities with their spectral vision and find the witches responsible for whatever problems existed: illness, poor crops, dead livestock. Most affected was the town of Andover, which the girls found to be crawling with witches. The problem with these later hotbeds of witchcraft was that the girls knew no one by name and had to identify the criminals by fits in front of individuals or the touch test. Many confessed to witchcraft in Andover, because all had realized that those who confessed were spared execution. Lying was preferable to hanging.

The girls began naming very prominent people as witches, including Andover's justice of the peace, Dudley Bradstreet, the son of the colony's former governor. His brother John was also accused. The brothers and their wives fled the colony before they could be arrested. Two

dogs were executed as witches in Andover as well. One man accused by the girls, described as a "worthy Gentleman from Boston," turned the tables on them and issued a warrant for their arrest for slander, demanding £1000 in damages. The afflicted balked and quickly went on to scrutinize other towns.

The executions continue. The next group condemned by the Court of Oyer and Terminer consisted of Elizabeth and John Procter, John Willard, George Burroughs, George Jacobs and Martha Carrier. The court granted Elizabeth Procter a stay of execution because she was pregnant, a delay that saved her life. Carrier's own sons confessed to witchcraft, but their confessions were obtained after torture. Jacobs' granddaughter Margaret also testified he was a wizard but later retracted her testimony. No one believed her, but she was later acquitted.

Willard, Jacobs, Carrier, Burroughs and John Procter went to Gallows Hill on August 19. Before Burroughs died, he shocked the crowd by reciting the Lord's Prayer perfectly, creating an uproar. Demands for Burroughs' freedom were countered by the afflicted girls, who cried out that "the Black Man" had prompted Burroughs through his recital of the prayer. It was generally believed that even the Devil could not recite the Lord's Prayer, and the crowd's mood grew darker. A riot was thwarted by Rev. Cotton Mather, who told the crowd that Burroughs was not an ordained minister and that the Devil was known to change himself often into an angel of light if there was profit in doing so. When the crowd was calmed, Mather urged that the executions proceed, and they did. As before, the bodies were dumped into a shallow grave, leaving Burroughs' hand and chin exposed.

Fifteen more witches were tried and convicted in September. Of those, four confessed and escaped execution to save their souls. Three more avoided death either by pregnancy, confession or outright escape from prison. The remaining eight—Martha Corey, Mary Esty, Alice Parker, Ann Pudeater, Margaret Scot, Wilmott Redd, Samuel Wardwell and Mary Parker—were hanged on September 22.

Alice Parker, Ann Pudeater and Wilmott Redd were all hanged based on the spectral evidence of the girls. Mary Parker of Andover had passed the touch test in court and had caused a pin to run through Mary Warren's hand and blood to run out of her mouth. Samuel Wardwell, completely intimidated, confessed to signing the Devil's book for a black man who promised him riches. He later retracted his confession, but the court believed his earlier testimony. Wardwell choked on smoke from the hangman's pipe during his execution, and the girls, ever-present, claimed it was the Devil preventing him from finally confessing.

Giles Corey was pressed to death on September 19 for refusing to acknowledge the court's right to try him. A landowner, Corey knew that as a convicted witch his property would be confiscated by the Crown. He reasoned that if he did not acknowledge the right of trial, he could not be tried and convicted, and without conviction his property remained his. In frustration, the court sentenced Corey to a "punishment hard and severe." He was taken to a Salem field, staked to the ground and covered with a large wooden plank. Stones were piled on the plank one at a time, until the weight was so great his tongue was forced out of his mouth. Sheriff George Corwin used his cane to poke it back into Corey's mouth. Corey's only response to the questions put to him was to ask for more weight. More stones were piled atop him, until finally he was crushed lifeless. Ann Putnam Jr. saw his execution as divine justice, for she claimed that when Corey had signed on with the Devil, he had been promised never to die by hanging.

The hysteria subsides. The crowd didn't know it in late September, but these were the last executions. The col-

ony's ministers, long skeptical of the spectral evidence, finally took a stand against such proof, casting doubt on the decisions of the court. The number of accusers had grown to more than 50 people, leading even dedicated witch-hunters like Rev. John Hale to question such large numbers of witches and bewitched in so small a colony. And the afflicted girls, giddy with power, had gone so far as to accuse Lady Phips, wife of the royal governor. That was the last straw; on October 29 Governor Phips dissolved the Court of Oyer and Terminer.

But the prisons were still overflowing with accused witches, so Governor Phips asked the General Court to establish a Superior Court to finish the business. Sitting on the Superior Court in January 1693 were William Stoughton, again as chief justice, John Richards, Wait Still Winthrop, Samuel Sewall and Thomas Danforth. All but Danforth had been on the Court of Oyer and Terminer, but except for Stoughton, they had confided to the governor their uneasiness over the convictions and their desire to try again. He agreed. The trials were no longer held exclusively in Salem but traveled to the seat of each witch's county. Most importantly, spectral evidence was no longer admissible.

Without spectral evidence, juries acquitted most of the accused. Only three were convicted, and Stoughton quickly signed their death warrants and those for five more convicted in September. But Governor Phips, tired of Stoughton's intransigence, reprieved all eight. The Superior Court again sat on April 25 and for the last time on May 9; all those tried were acquitted, and Massachusetts' witchcraft nightmare was over. Tituba was released from jail in May and was sold as a slave to cover her prison expenses.

The aftermath. Throwing out spectral evidence placed the colony in a grave dilemma: either the state admitted it was wrong and had committed murder, threatening the political system, or the men involved confessed their sins before God and protected their Puritan covenant. If spectral evidence was inadmissible, could witchcraft ever be proven?

Eventually, the prosecutions were seen as one more trial placed on God's covenant with New England—not so much a judicial miscarriage as a terrible sin to be expiated. Those who had participated in the proceedings—Cotton and Increase Mather, the other clergy, the magistrates, even the accusers—suffered illness and personal setbacks in the years following the hysteria. Samuel Parris was forced to leave his ministry in Salem, while Ann Putnam Jr. publicly begged forgiveness before the village in 1706. Long before that, the Puritan clergy had called for an Official Day of Humiliation on January 14, 1697, for fasting and public apology. Samuel Sewall heard his confession of guilt read that morning from the pulpit of his church.

By 1703 the Massachusetts colonial legislature began granting retroactive amnesties to the convicted and executed. Even more amazing, they authorized financial restitution to the victims and their families. In 1711 Massachusetts Bay became one of the first governments ever to compensate voluntarily persons victimized by its own mistakes.

As early as 1693 Increase Mather wrote in *Cases of Conscience Concerning Evil Spirits Personating Men* that finding a witch was probably impossible, because the determination rested on the assumption that God had set humanly recognizable limits on Satan, but Satan and God are beyond human comprehension. Summing up, Rev. John Hale, an early supporter of the witch hunt, wrote in his *Modest Enquiry into the Nature of Witchcraft* (1697) that "I have had a deep sence of the sad consequences of mistakes in matters Capital; and their impossibility of recovering when compleated." He went on to say that the people involved meant well, but "such was the darkness of that day, the tortures and lamentations of the afflicted, and the power of former presidents [precedents], that we walked in the clouds, and could not see our way."

Giles Corey, who died the most unusual death of the Salem victims, was memorialized in a ballad:

Giles Corey was a Wizzard strong,
    And a stubborn Wretch was he,
And fitt was he to hang on high
    Upon the Locust Tree.
So when before the Magistrates
    For Triall did he come,
He would no true Confession make
    But was compleatlie dumbe.
"Giles Corey," said the Magistrate,
    "What hast thou heare to pleade
To these that now accuse thy Soule
    Of Crimes and horrid Deed?"
Giles Corey—he said not a Worde,
    No single Worde spake he;
"Giles Corey," sayeth the Magistrate,
    "We'll press it out of thee."
They got them then a heavy Beam,
    They laid it on his Breast;
They loaded it with heavie Stones,
    And hard upon him prest.
"More weight," now said this wretched Man,
    "More weight," again he cryed,
And he did no Confession make,
    But wickedly he died.

One interesting footnote to the Salem witch hysteria is that the American author NATHANIEL HAWTHORNE, a descendent of magistrate John Hathorne, added the *w* to his name to expunge some of the Puritan guilt by association. The trials also served as an allegory for the communist purges in America during the 1950s; the most notable example of this is Arthur Miller's play *The Crucible*.

Modern Salem's legacy. The witchcraft hysteria of 1692 still attracts many tourists to Salem and the neighboring town of Danvers each year. Gallows Hill, the once remote site where the victims were executed and buried in shallow graves, has long been built over with residential dwellings. Legend has it that the ghosts of the victims haunt the area. The Witch House, the restored Salem home of Judge Jonathan Corwin, is open for tours; visitors see the small upper chamber where the magistrates subjected nervous townsfolk to the questioning that determined whether or not they would be charged and tried. The original jail no longer exists, but the dungeon has been re-created in the Witch Dungeon Museum. The entire witch episode is re-created in a narrated, multisensory presentation in the Witch Museum, located in a former church, which draws more than 140,000 visitors a year.

FURTHER READING:
Boyer, Paul, and Stephen Nissenbaum. *Salem Possessed: The Social Origins of Witchcraft.* Cambridge, Mass.: Harvard University Press, 1974.
Demos, John Putnam. *Entertaining Satan: Witchcraft and the Culture of Early New England. Rev. ed.* New York: Oxford University Press, 2004.
Hansen, Chadwick. *Witchcraft at Salem.* New York: New American Library, 1969.
Karlsen, Carol F. *The Devil in the Shape of a Woman: Witchcraft in Colonial New England.* New York: W.W. Norton & Co, 1987.
Mather, Cotton. *On Witchcraft: Being the Wonders of the Invisible World.* 1692. Reprint. Mt. Vernon, N.Y.: The Peter Pauper Press, 1950.
Mather, Increase. *Cases of Conscience Concerning Evil Spirits Personating Men; Witchcrafts, Infallible Proofs of Guilt in such as are Accused with that Crime.* Boston: 1693.
Starkey, Marion L. *The Devil in Massachusetts.* New York: Alfred Knopf, 1950.

salt   Preservative linked to luck and protection against evil. Salt superstitions have a long history going back to ancient times.

Folklore. Salt is essential to health, as well as a preservative of food, and in ancient times it was more valuable than gold. Roman soldiers were often paid in salt; hence the phrase that someone is "worth his salt." The word *salary* is derived from *salt*.

Sharing a person's salt is symbolic of establishing a deep bond between people. When a new home was occupied, salt was often one of the first things to be brought across the threshold in order to drive away evil influences and establish good energy and luck. A pinch of salt was sprinkled before any job or task in order to ensure the same.

Salt was used in divination. At Halloween, every person in a house turned over a thimbleful of salt upon a platter. Whoever's pillar fell apart by the next day would die within a year. At Christmas, omens for the coming year were read from the dryness or moistness of salt.

Because of the high value of salt, spilling it has long been considered bad luck. To counter the bad luck, spilt salt should be thrown over the left shoulder, for that is where evil spirits can be found lurking. Spilling salt can make a person vulnerable to the Devil. In FAIRY lore, spilt salt should be thrown into the home fire so that the household brownies can lick it.

In Christianity, salt is symbolic of incorruptibility, eternity and divine wisdom. Early Christians began using salt in christenings and baptisms as a purification and protection. Church sites were consecrated with salt and holy water. The Catholic ritual of the benediction of salt and water ensures physical health. Oaths sometimes were taken on salt instead of the Bible.

Demon and witch lore. As a preservative, salt is contrary to the nature of demons, who are intent upon corrupting and destroying. Salt is sometimes thrown at weddings, to preserve marital happiness and also to repel evil spirits who might be intent upon wreaking havoc with the newlyweds. Salt was placed in coffins as a preservative for the soul after death and to protect it against assaults by evil spirits. Salt was used in pagan sacrifices. It was placed in the cribs of infants to protect them against evil spirits.

Salt and salted water, especially blessed, are used to cleanse premises believed to be infested by demons. Salted water is washed around mirrors, windows and doorways and sometimes washed over entire walls and ceilings.

Witches as well as demons are repelled by salt. In medieval times, it was believed that witches and the animals they bewitched were unable to eat anything salted. Inquisitors who interrogated accused witches were advised by demonologists to first protect themselves by wearing a sacramental AMULET made of salt consecrated on Palm Sunday and blessed herbs, pressed into a disc of blessed wax. One means of torturing accused witches was to force-feed them heavily salted food and deny them water.

An old recipe for breaking an evil spell calls for stealing a tile from a witch's roof, sprinkling it with salt and urine and then heating it over fire while reciting a CHARM. Such antidotes were still in use in modern times in rural parts of Europe to remove spells from stables and homes and to cure illness. In American Ozark lore, women who complain of food being too salty are suspected of being witches. One Ozark way to detect a witch is to sprinkle salt on her chair. If she is a witch, the salt will melt and cause her dress to stick to the chair.

Salt neutralizes the EVIL EYE cast by witches.

Magic. Salt is used in SPELLS and magical rituals as a representative of the element of earth. It also purifies and defines magical boundaries. For example, salt might be sprinkled around a MAGIC CIRCLE as an added protection.

Alchemy. In alchemy, all things, including the four elements, are composed of a divine trinity that includes salt, mercury and sulphur. Salt represents the body, female and earth aspects, and was a crucial ingredient in alchemic recipes for making gold. One 17th-century formula for potable gold, believed to be an antidote for poison, a cura-tive of heart disease and a repellent of the Devil, included gold, salt, red wine vinegar, the ashes of a block of tin burnt in an iron pan, wine and honey.

FURTHER READING:
Cahill, Robert Ellis. *Strange Superstitions.* Danvers, Mass.: Old Saltbox Publishing, 1990.
Radford, E. and M.A. *The Encyclopedia of Superstitions.* Edited and revised by Christina Hole. New York: Barnes & Noble, 1961.

Salt Lane Witches   In English folklore, two white witches who once lived in Castle Street, Worcester, in medieval times. They were considered white witches because instead of bewitching others to their harm, they used their MAGIC to free the carts that frequently became stuck in the mud near their cottages. For sixpence, one witch would stroke and bless the horse while the other would stroke the cartwheels.

One day a wagoner tried to bargain with the witches and noticed a piece of straw on his horse's back. Thinking it was part of their magic, he cut it in half. Immediately, the witch who was stroking the horse screamed and fell dead, severed in two. The cart was freed, and the wagoner fled. The second witch lived on and later turned a troop of soldiers into stone, when they appeared in town to collect taxes. According to legend, their petrified figures once stood at what is now the main road that passes through Worcester. A local merchant tried to break the spell of the figures, but one of the stones turned into a giant horse which reared up and pawed the air, frightening him off.

FURTHER READING:
Folklore, Myths and Legends of Britain. London: Reader's Digest Assoc. Ltd., 1977.

Sanders, Alex (1926–1988)   Self-proclaimed "King of the Witches" in his native England, Alex Sanders rose to fame in the 1960s, founding a major tradition bearing his name: the Alexandrian tradition. A gifted psychic with a flamboyant style, he was for years the most public witch in Britain, gaining headlines for his reputed sensational acts of MAGIC. Some called him the enfant terrible of British witchcraft, whose life was surrounded by more myth than fact.

Sanders was born in Manchester, the oldest of six children. His father was a music hall entertainer and suffered from alcoholism. By Sanders' own account, he was seven when he discovered his grandmother, Mary Bibby, standing naked in the kitchen in the middle of a circle drawn on the floor. She revealed herself as a hereditary Witch and initiated him on the spot. She ordered him to enter the circle, take off his clothes and bend down with his head between his thighs. She took a knife and nicked his scrotum, saying, "You are one of us now."

According to Sanders, Mary Bibby gave him her BOOK OF SHADOWS, which he copied, and taught him the rites

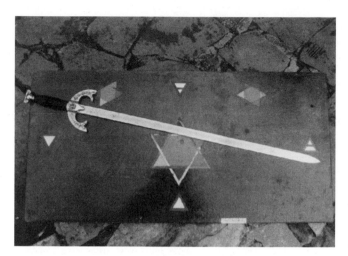

Altar slab and ritual sword belonging to Alex Sanders, in the collection of the Museum of Witchcraft in Boscastle, Cornwall (PHOTO BY AUTHOR; COURTESY MUSEUM OF WITCHCRAFT)

and magic of witches. He discovered his own natural psychic gifts for clairvoyance and healing by touch. He worked as an analytical chemist at a laboratory in Manchester, where he met and married a 19-year-old coworker, Doreen, when he was 21. They had two children, Paul and Janice, but the marriage rapidly disintegrated. Doreen took the children and left Sanders when he was 26.

Sanders then entered a long period of drifting from one low-level job to another, drinking and indulging in sexual flings with both men and women, according to his account of his life. He decided to follow the left-hand path and use magic to bring him wealth and power. For a time, he worshiped the DEVIL and studied Abra-Melin magic. He apparently attracted people who supported him financially. He formed his first COVEN, began getting media attention, attracted more followers and by 1965, claimed to have 1,623 initiates in 100 covens, who then "persuaded" him to be elected King of the Witches. Although he emphasized that the title of king pertained only to his own Alexandrian tradition, the media treated it otherwise, as though he were king of all Witches.

Sanders boasted about his alleged feats of magic. He claimed to create a flesh-and-blood "spiritual baby" in a rite of ritual masturbation, with the help of a male assistant. Sanders said the baby disappeared shortly after its creation, and "grew up" as a spirit that took over him in his trance channeling. Michael, as the spirit was called, supposedly was responsible for "forcing" Sanders to carry on at wild parties, insult others and otherwise act abominably. Eventually, Sanders claimed, Michael simmered down and became a valuable spirit familiar, offering advice in healing matters. Sanders also channeled a FAMILIAR entity, Nick Demdike, who said he had been persecuted as a witch in the Lancaster trials of the 17th century. (See LANCASTER WITCHES.)

Sanders reportedly got rid of warts by "wishing them on someone else, someone who's already ugly, with boil marks I can fill up with the warts." He claimed to cure a man of heroin addiction, and cure cystitis in a woman by laying his hands on her head and willing her affliction away. He also said he cured a young woman of stomach cancer by sitting with her in the hospital for three days and nights, holding her feet and pouring healing energy into her.

He effected other cures by pointing at the troubled spots on the body and concentrating. Pointing, he said, never failed. He claimed he gave magical abortions by pointing at the womb and commanding the pregnancy to end.

One of Sanders' more famous alleged cures concerned his daughter, Janice, who was born in dry labor with her left foot twisted backwards. Doctors said nothing could be done until the child was in her teens. Sanders received an "impression" from Michael to take olive oil, warm it, and anoint Janice's foot. Sanders did so, then simply twisted Janice's foot straight. The foot remained corrected; Janice walked normally, except for a slight limp in cold, damp weather.

In the 1960s, Sanders met Maxine Morris, a Roman Catholic and 20 years his junior, whom he initiated into the Craft in 1964 and handfasted in 1965. Maxine became his high priestess. In 1968, They married in a civil ceremony and moved to a basement flat near Notting Hill Gate in London, where they ran their coven and taught training classes. They attracted many followers and initiated people into the Craft. Their daughter, Maya, was born the same year. (See MAXINE SANDERS.)

Sanders was catapulted into the national public spotlight by a sensational newspaper article in 1969. The publicity led to a romanticized biography, *King of the Witches*, by June Johns (1969), a film, "Legend of the Witches," and numerous appearances on media talk shows, and public speaking engagements. Sanders enjoyed the publicity and was adept at exploiting it, to the dismay of other Witches who felt he dragged the Craft through the gutter press.

Curiously, Sanders always appeared robed or clad in a loincloth in photos of himself in RITUALS, while other witches with him were naked. He explained this by saying that "witch law" required the elder of a coven to be apart from the others and easily identifiable.

Sanders' accounts of his INITIATION into the Craft by his grandmother, his magical escapades, and the extent of his "kingdom" are dubious. Years after his publicity peaked, it was revealed that he passed off the writings and teachings of others as his own. STEWART FARRAR, a journalist who was initiated by Sanders, said Sanders used material from the Gardnerian BOOK OF SHADOWS, written by GERALD B. GARDNER and DOREEN VALIENTE, and either took credit for it himself or passed it off as inherited material. He also passed off material written by occultist Eliphas Lévi and Franz Bardon as his own, sometimes after making slight changes in it, and other times not bothering to make any changes at all.

According to some Gardnerian Witches, Sanders created his Alexandrian tradition after he was refused initiation into various Gardnerian covens, having obtained a copy of the Gardnerian book of shadows. However, there is some evidence in Gardner's correspondence papers that Sanders was a Gardnerian initiate. He was initiated by a high priestess whose Craft name was Medea and who was described as "the Derbyshire priestess."

In 1972, Alex and Maxine had a son, Victor. In 1973, they separated. Sanders moved to Sussex, where he was less active and away from the media limelight. Maxine remained in the London flat, where she continued to run a coven and teach the Craft. Sanders took his teaching to Continental Europe.

Sanders died on April 30, 1988 (Beltane), after a long battle with lung cancer. His funeral was a media event. Witches and Pagans from various traditions attended to pay their respects. A tape recording was played in which he declared that Victor should succeed him as "King of the Witches." According to Maxine, Victor had no desire to do so, and had gone to live in the United States. A "Witchcraft Council of Elders" said no other successor would be elected. (Some Witches say the council was a fabrication of followers of Sanders.)

The Alexandrian tradition took hold in other countries. In the United States, it did not gain as wide a following as the Gardnerian tradition, and was hurt by negative publicity about Sanders. By the 1980s, none of the Alexandrian covens had any connection with Sanders himself. The tradition became much stronger in Canada, where it was more firmly established. In subsequent years, as the Craft evolved, fusions were made between the Gardnerian and Alexandrian traditions.

Despite Sanders' media grandstanding, he is recognized for making a substantial contribution to the overall evolution of modern Witchcraft. Following Sanders' death, Stewart Farrar observed: "Alex was a born showman; but the fact remains that he made a major contribution to the Craft, in his own often bizarre way, and many people (including ourselves [Stewart and wife Janet Owen Farrar]) might never have been introduced to it but for him."

See VIVIANNE CROWLEY.

FURTHER READING:

Farrar, Janet, and Stewart Farrar. *A Witches Bible Compleat*. New York: Magickal Childe, 1984.

Johns, June. *King of the Witches: The World of Alex Sanders*. New York: Coward-McCann, Inc., 1969.

Russell, Jeffrey B. *A History of Witchcraft*. London: Thames and Hudson, 1980.

Sanders, Maxine (1948–) Prominent English Witch once married to the late ALEX SANDERS. Maxine Sanders helped to found the Alexandrian tradition of contemporary Witchcraft in the 1960s in England.

She was born Arline Maxine Morris in Manchester, England, and received a Catholic education at St. Joseph's Convent there. Her mother was intensely interested in esoteric studies, Subud and Theosophy. Maxine was withdrawn as a child; according to her own account, she was clairvoyant and very sensitive to the thoughts and feelings of others. She withdrew further in astral projection. Her mother used her to view remotely her father's gambling.

Maxine said she was initiated into the Egyptian mysteries at a young age. In 1962, at age 14, she met Alex Sanders at an esoteric soirée hosted by her mother. She had met him previously as a young child; her mother and Sanders had been friends since before Maxine's birth and worked at the same pharmaceutical center.

Maxine was drawn to the magnetic Sanders, who talked about Witchcraft. Two years later, while attending secretarial college, she was initiated into his COVEN. They were handfasted in 1965 and legally married in 1968. Maxine became Alex's high priestess.

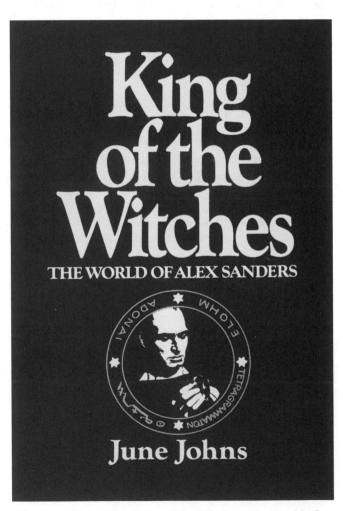

The cover of June Johns' King of the Witches: The World of Alex Sanders

In 1967 Maxine and Alex left Manchester and moved to a flat in the Notting Hill Gate area of London, a place full of counterculture ferment. They offered classes and conducted RITUALS. Alex, who had a flair for showmanship, was an immediate media sensation. The couple and their coven conducted rituals skyclad—in the nude—for the press. Oddly, everyone but Alex himself was unclothed; he always wore a robe or loincloth.

Life with Alex was a roller coaster of publicity. Many of the newly public witches in Britain opposed the Sanders' willingness to be in the limelight, but support was received from others, such as SYBIL LEEK and JANET AND STEWART FARRAR; the latter two were initiated into the Alexandrian tradition.

The Sanders had two children, Maya, born in 1968, and Victor, born in 1972. In 1973, Maxine and Alex separated. Alex moved to Sussex, and Maxine remained in the Notting Hill Gate flat. The couple worked together until Alex's death from lung cancer in 1988.

Maxine Sanders continued her work as a high priestess, initiating, teaching, consulting and speaking. In 2002, she moved to a tiny stone cottage, Bron Afron, in the Snowdonia National Park in Wales. She has retired from active public life. Her autobiography, *Fire Child,* was published in 2007.

FURTHER READING:
Maxine Sanders official Web site. Available online. URL: http://www.maxinesanders.co.uk. Downloaded November 12, 2007.
Sanders, Maxine. *Fire Child: The Life and Magic of Maxine Sanders "Witch Queen."* Oxford: Mandrake, 2007.
The Wiccan/Pagan Times. "TWPT Takes to Maxine Sanders." Available online. URL: http://www.twpt.com/sanders.htm. Downloaded November 12, 2007.

Santa Fe Witches (17th century)   Two women accused of murder by bewitchment who were tried by the INQUISITION.

The charges were made in Santa Fe, New Mexico, by Spanish immigrants against a Mexican Indian, Beatriz de Los Angeles, and her daughter, Juana de la Cruz, a half-breed. Both women, especially de Los Angeles, were feared by many in Santa Fe for their alleged diabolical powers. It was rumored that de Los Angeles had poisoned two of her servants to death in order to test out a new recipe for a potion. Another servant told stories of her mistress casting evil SPELLS with POPPETS that she buried beneath her hearth or hung from trees.

De Los Angeles was rumored to have poisoned to death one of her lovers, Diego Bellido, who beat her during an argument. The poison was mixed in a bowl of cornmeal gruel. Bellido fell ill with severe abdominal pain and died within a few weeks. She also put a death HEX on a royal officer, Hernando Martinez, because he slept with her daughter.

De la Cruz was said to have the EVIL EYE, causing children and animals to fall ill and sometimes die. She flew about at night inside an egg to spy on her lovers. When she discovered that her husband was unfaithful, she gave him some poisoned enchanted milk and killed him.

The anxiety over the women reached such a pitch that an officer of the Inquisition was informed of their evil deeds. After a thorough investigation, however, Father Estéban de Perea concluded that there was no evidence of witchcraft and that the women were the victims of malicious gossip. The case against them was closed.

Had the case arisen in Europe, where the witch hysteria was much stronger, the two women most likely would have been tortured, tried and executed.

FURTHER READING:
Simmons, Marc. *Witchcraft in the Southwest: Spanish and Indian Supernaturalism on the Rio Grande.* Lincoln: University of Nebraska Press, 1974.

Santería   Similar in practice to VODUN, Santería centers around the worship of the ancient African gods who have been assimilated as Catholic saints. *Santería* comes from the Spanish word *santo,* meaning "saint"; practitioners are called Santeros (female: Santeras).

Like Vodun, Santería came to the Americas with the millions of black slaves from West Africa, principally from the Yoruban tribes along the Niger River. Forced to convert to Catholicism, the slaves continued their religion in secret, passing along ancient traditions either orally or in handwritten notebooks that came to be called *libretas.* Gradually, the Yorubans began to see what they believed were the incarnations of their gods in the Catholic saints and syncretized the two faiths. The slaves' Spanish and Portuguese masters eventually grew fascinated with Yoruban magic and began to practice it themselves. Today, any city with a large Hispanic population probably boasts as many Santeros as devout Catholics, since many of the devotees practice both. New York, Miami, Los Angeles and the nations of Cuba and Jamaica all have Santería strongholds. Brazilians also practice Santería but under the names of Candomblé, Umbanda and Quimbanda (see MACUMBA).

The orishas. In the ancient Yoruban tongue, gods were called *orishas,* and that is the term still used today. Just like the Vodun *loa,* the orishas have complex human personalities, with strong desires, preferences and temperaments. When they possess their "children," the devotees assume the orishas' supernatural characteristics, performing feats of great strength, eating and drinking huge quantities of food and alcohol and divining the future with great accuracy.

Santeros also believe there was a supreme creator of heaven and earth, but like the Gran Met in Vodun, he is unapproachable. In the beginning was Olodumare, a being incomprehensible to mortals, who was composed of three spirits: Nzame, Olofi (also called Olorun) and Baba Nkwa. Nzame created all the stars, planets, earth, plant and animal life, then made Omo Oba, a man, at the suggestion of the other two, to rule over all creation. Such power went to Omo Oba's head, causing Olodumare to order Nzalam, the lighting bolt, to destroy the earth in flames. But Omo Oba's immortality saved him; he hid deep underground, changed his name to Olosi and only resurfaces to tempt men to break Olodumare's laws—much like the story of Lucifer as a fallen angel. Afterward, Olodumare took pity on the scorched earth, and so Nzame, Olofi and Baba Nkwa again gave it life, this time creating a mortal man, Obatalá. At this second creation, Olofi took over provenance of earth, and the other two went off to create life elsewhere. As the first ancestor, Obatalá is the father of the gods and the first orisha.

Depicted as a white man on horseback, Obatalá is associated with all things white and represents peace and purity. His wife, Oddudúa, is a black woman who is usually shown breastfeeding an infant and represents maternity. Obatalá and Oddudúa had two children: a son Aganyú and a daughter Yemayá. Aganyú and Yemayá married and had a son Orungán, who was so handsome that Aganyú died of envy. Orungán forced himself incestuously upon his mother, a beautiful woman of yellow skin who is the goddess of the MOON and womanhood. She cursed him and he died. Completely overcome with her sorrows, Yemayá climbed a mountain, where she delivered 14 gods conceived by Orungán in a single birth and then died. The waters released when her abdomen burst caused the deluge—the Flood—and the place where she died became the holy city of Ile Ife, the same sacred place worshiped in Vodun.

Tragic Yemayá remains a popular goddess in Santería, whose colors are light blue and white. The 14 deities born to Yemayá include Changó, the god of fire, thunder and lightning. Young, virile and handsome, Changó also governs the passions. His colors are red and white, and he is one of the most popular deities in Santería. His wife, Oba, is goddess of the Oba River. Continually jealous and suspicious of her philandering husband, she follows him and has him watched.

Oyá, goddess of the Niger River, is wife of the god Oggún, but also is Changó's favorite concubine. She gives him power over fire, which is holy to her. Oyá controls memory and is the patroness of justice. She also governs death and cemeteries, and maroon is her favorite color. Alefi, the wind, is Oyá's messenger. Oshún, the goddess of the Oshún River, also enjoys Changó's favors. She is the goddess of love and marriage and loves fans, mirrors and seashells. Also the goddess of gold and money, Oshún prefers the color yellow. Pumpkins are sacred to her. She is a very popular deity.

Ochosi is the god of hunters, birds and wild animals and also watches over jails, perhaps as cages for humans. He likes lavender and black and chooses the bow and arrow as his symbols. Olokun lives on the ocean floor with the mermaids, watching over the seas. He is a her-maphrodite and has very long hair. His favorite mistress is Olosa, who aids fishermen and employs the crocodile as her messenger. Orisha-Oko governs the fields and harvests and brings fertility to land and families. Oke rules over the mountains and protects those who live in high places.

Chankpana, the god of smallpox, appears as an old man nursing a lacerated leg. He uses flies and mosquitoes as his messengers. Dada governs unborn children and gardens. Ayé-Shaluga rules fortune and good luck. The last two of the 14, Orun, god of the Sun, and Ochu, goddess of the Moon, have few followers.

Other important orishas include Eleggúa (called LEGBA in Vodun), the god of entrances, doorways and roads, who allows the other orishas to enter the sphere of man. All homes keep an image of Eleggúa behind the door as he is the most powerful orisha after Obatalá. One of Eleggúa's best friends, Oggún, governs war and iron, all weapons (including sacrificial knives) and the treatment of tumors and skin diseases. He prefers black dogs as sacrifices (see SACRIFICE) and has many followers in Santería. Orúnla owns the Table of Ifá, the sacred system of DIVINATION, and also shares great friendship with Eleggúa. Babalu-Ayé is patron of the sick. Symbolized by a pair of crutches, he appears as an old man accompanied by two dogs.

Aroni is the god of medicine, while Osachin is the patron god of doctors. Ayé or Ayá is the midget goddess of the jungle, and Oyé rules storms. Ochumare serves as goddess of the rainbow. Homes come under the protection of Olarosa, while Olimerin guards the entire village. The twin gods Ibeyi watch over infants. Ifá is the patron of impossible things and the god of fertility and palm trees. He was the first owner of the Table of Ifá. Chiyidi controls nightmares and used to be an evil entity (see NIGHTMARE). Iku is the spirit of death. Rounding out this partial list is Bacoso, the king and founder of the Yoruba dynasty and the holy city of Ife. Each of the orishas appears in many forms, and only the priest best knows what manifestation to invoke, depending upon the situation. Extremely difficult cases may necessitate calling upon the Seven African Powers, a combination of Obatalá, Eleggúa, Orúnla, Changó, Oggún, Yemayá and Oshún.

Saints identified with the orishas may be of either sex and not necessarily of the same gender as the orisha. Santeros do not dare question such arrangements, explaining the situation by saying that after the gods' mystical deaths, they were reincarnated in new bodies. A partial list of the saints identified with the orishas of Santería follows:

Olorun/Olofi, God the Creator	The Crucified Christ
Obatalá	Our Lady of Mercy
Oddudúa	Saint Claire
Aganyú	Saint Joseph

Yemayá	Our Lady of Regla
Orungán	The Infant Jesus
Changó	Saint Barbara
Oyá	Our Lady of La Candelaria; also St. Theresa and St. Catherine
Oshún	Our Lady of La Caridad del Cobre
Ochosi	Saint Isidro
Dada	Our Lady of Mount Carmel
Ochumare	Our Lady of Hope
Oggún	Saint Peter, St. Anthony or Joan of Arc
Babalú-Ayé	Saint Lazarus
Eleggua	Holy Guardian Angel, St. Michael, St. Martin de Porres, St. Peter
Orúnla	Saint Francis of Assisi
Ifá	Saint Anthony of Padua
Bacoso	Saint Christopher

Rites and practices. Although all worshipers of Santería could be called Santeros, the term usually refers to the priests or priestesses. The highest order of priest is a *babalawo,* who has power not only to heal the sick and punish the unjust but to divine the future through the Table of Ifá. All babalawos are male, as Orúnla, god of the Table of Ifá, is male. Within the order of babalawo are various degrees, ranging from high priest to the one responsible for a particular orisha's sacrifice. Following the babalawo are the priests of orishas who govern the sick or healing, and the priests or priestesses of Orisha-Oko, the god of agriculture. Priests consecrated to lesser orishas or human deities also fall in this third category. The power of the babalawo is limitless, as he wears the hats of healer, diviner, judge, pastor, matchmaker and magician.

The babalawo's second-most important duty is sacrificing animals as offerings to the orishas. Common sacrificial animals include all types of fowl—chickens, roosters, pigeons, doves and other birds—goats, pigs and occasionally bulls. In Cuba, Santeros may obtain government meat-ration cards because they have to buy so many live animals. In some parts of the United States, animal-rights groups oppose ritual SACRIFICE on the grounds that animals may be tortured and pets may be stolen and slaughtered. The Santeros counter that animal sacrifice, if done humanely, is legal in many states; they deny that cats and dogs are sacrificed. Those practicing black MAGIC, however, reputedly use cats and dogs as ingredients for evil SPELLS.

Reading the seashells (*los caracoles*) of the Table of Ifá is the paramount DIVINATION procedure in Santería. Santeros who specialize in Table readings are called *italeros* and are often babalawos consecrated to the service of Orúnla. Reading the Table is also known as *diloggun* or *mediloggun.* The Table has 18 shells, but the italero uses only 16. The shells may be bought in any *botánica* (a store where Santería and Vodun paraphernalia and herbs are sold) by anyone, but uninitiated users, *aleyos,* may use only 12. The smooth, unbroken sides of the shell are filed

until the serrated sides appear, showing what appears to be a tiny mouth with teeth. As such, the shells are the "mouthpieces" of the orishas.

During a consultation, called a *registro,* the italero prays to the gods, rubs the 16 shells together, then throws them onto a straw mat (*estera*). The shells are read according to how many of them fall with their top sides, or "mouths," uppermost. The italero interprets the pattern in which they fall, called an *ordun,* then repeats the procedure four times. Each ordun has a name and number and "speaks" for one or more of the orishas. Like the Chinese system of I Ching, the divinations rely on ancient proverbs associated with each ordun and require the italero to interpret for the particular situation.

Very often the babalawo finds the questioner has been put under an evil SPELL, or *bilongo,* by an enemy. Such action requires placing an *ebbo,* or counteracting spell, on the guilty party. If the ebbo does more damage to the enemy than the enemy's original spell, it only increases the prestige of the babalawo. The greater the babalawo's accuracy in divination and response, the larger his clientele. Remedies range from herbal baths to complicated spells involving various oils, plants and intimate waste products of the intended victim. Babalawos commonly prescribe a *resguardo,* or protective TALISMAN. A typical resguardo is a small cloth bag filled with various herbs, spices and other ingredients, dedicated to a certain orisha, which will keep the owner from harm.

Another popular divinatory method, normally used to consult Eleggua, is called *darle coco al santo* ("give the coconut to the saint"), or reading coconut meat. Coconuts are used in all major Santería ceremonies and form the main ingredient for several spells. To prepare a coconut for divination, the reader must break its shell with a hard object, never cracking the nut on the floor, as that would offend Obi, the coconut's deity. The meat—white on one side and brown on the other—is then divided into four equal pieces. The pieces are thrown on the floor, and one of five patterns results.

Readings of the Table of Ifá by the babalawo help determine all of the important characteristics of a person's life and how he or she should deal with each event as it occurs. Upon the birth of a child, the parents consult the babalawo to find the infant's assigned orisha, plant, birthstone and animal. In Santería, birthstones have no relation to the birth month. Good-talisman animals include goats, elephants and turtles; noxious ones are many reptiles, venomous insects, some types of frogs, all birds of prey, rats, crocodiles, lizards and spiders.

WATER has great spiritual powers as a defensive measure for the Santero, as it does in other religions and magical systems. Since evil spirits dissolve in water, all devotees keep a small receptacle of water under their beds to clean away evil influences, which must be changed every 24 hours. The "dirty" water must never fall onto the floor or go down the kitchen sink.

Other protective agents against evil are GARLIC and brown sugar. To be really safe, a Santero burns brown sugar and garlic skins in a small pan over hot coals. The thick smoke, called *sahumerio,* fills the house, seeping even into closets and corners where evil spirits can hide. Evil beings also dislike black rag dolls.

Healing and magic.   Santeros are accomplished herbalists, since plants, and especially herbs, are sacred to the orishas. Most plants serve dual purposes, as curatives and as magic ingredients, and can be obtained in any good botanica. Garlic lowers high blood pressure, coconut water acts as a diuretic, anise seed alleviates indigestion, sarsaparilla cures rheumatism, nerves and syphilis and indigo works on epilepsy. *Higuereta,* which produces castor oil, has been used by the Santeros on cancerous tumors for centuries with amazing results.

Cuttings from *escoba amarga* bushes are used in purifying baths and to drive away the *abikus,* mischievous spirits that reincarnate in a child who dies very young. According to the older Santeros, the only way to drive out an abiku is to beat it with a branch of the bush, usually on a Wednesday. If a child dies young, the Santero makes a mark on its body, often by cutting off a piece of the child's ear before burial. Following the birth of another child, the Santero searches for the mark, which he claims he often finds. To keep the abiku from taking the second child, the baby is "tied" to the earth by placing a small chain on its wrist or ankle. The chain is not removed until the child is well past puberty.

The *bombax ceiba* tree, or five-leaf silk-cotton tree, gives the Santero curative or magical powers from almost every part. Sacred to Santería, the ceiba is worshiped as a female saint; worshipers will not even cross the tree's shadow without first asking permission. Teas from the ceiba's roots and leaves aid in curing venereal disease and urinary tract infections. The leaves also work on anemia. Ceiba-bark tea helps cure infertility. The tree trunk and the ground around it help cast evil spells; if a Santero wishes harm upon someone, he must walk naked around the ceiba tree several times at midnight and brush the trunk with his fingertips, softly asking the tree to help him against his enemy. Even the shade attracts spirits, giving strength to spells cast there.

Santería has been described as African magic adapted for the West and for city life. It is ruled by the laws of similarity (that like produces like) and contact (that things that have been in contact with each other continue to affect one another even after contact has been broken). The magic of similarity is *homeopathic,* or *sympathetic.* The Santero can affect situations by acting out the scene beforehand or by using natural objects in alliance with or resembling the intended victim; e.g., a wax doll. Another common sympathetic practice is to take a small stone and name it after the victim, then kick it under a bed and concentrate very hard on the named person.

Magic by contact is *contagious.* The magician procures items that have been in contact with the victim—clothing, nail parings, hair clippings (see HAIR AND NAILS), even dirt from under the feet (see FOOTPRINTS) or air from the victim's home—and uses them to effect the spell.

The Santero wields enormous power, having knowledge that can change a person's life either through his own skill or by the help of the orishas. The decision to use that power for good or evil rests with the Santero alone.

Santeros fear the EVIL EYE, knowing that the eye's harmful magic can come from anyone. Children wear a tiny jet hand and a bit of coral on a gold bracelet to protect them; adults may be similarly protected or wear a small glass eyeball pinned to the chest (see AMULETS).

Black magic. Most magic in Santería comes under the "white" classification: spells for wayward lovers, good luck, money and cures. Santeros who deal exclusively in black magic—*brujería* or *palo mayombe*—come primarily from Congo tribal ancestry and are called *mayomberos,* or "black witches." In her book, *Santería: African Magic in Latin America* (1981), author Migene Gonzales-Wippler describes the mayomberos as "people of unparalleled malignancy, specializing in revenge, necromancy and the destruction of human life." Ethics never come under consideration, because the mayombero lives in a world "outside of reality"—magic is merely a means of survival in a hostile environment. Retribution can be avoided by magic and by "paying" the demonic forces through offerings of food, liquor, money and animal sacrifice.

Before a novice can become a full-fledged mayombero, he must sleep under a ceiba tree for seven nights. At the end of the week, he takes a new set of clothes and buries them in a previously chosen grave in the cemetery. While his clothes are buried, the novice takes a series of purifying herbal baths; at the end of 21 days, or three successive Fridays, the candidate digs up his clothes, puts them on and goes with his teacher back to the ceiba tree. Other mayomberos join them there as witnesses, invoking the spirits of the dead and that of the ceiba to approve the initiation. The candidate is crowned with ceiba leaves, which represent the spirits of the dead taking possession of the new mayombero. Finally, the mayomberos place a lighted candle in a white dish in the initiate's hands and give him his scepter, or *kisengue:* a human tibia bone wrapped in black cloth. He is now ready to call on the powers of darkness.

Making the nganga. Once the mayombero has been initiated, his next project is the making of the *nganga,* or CAULDRON, that contains all his magical potions and powers. When the MOON is right—no WITCHCRAFT can be accomplished during a waning Moon, since that period signifies death—the mayombero and an assistant return to the cemetery to a preselected gravesite. The chosen grave is usually fairly recent, since the mayombero desires a corpse with a brain still inside the skull, no matter how decayed. The mayombero also knows the identity of the corpse, called the *kiyumba*. Choice kiyumbas were violent persons in life, preferably criminals or the insane. The still-extant brain helps the kiyumba to think and better act on the mayombero's evil purposes. The bodies of whites are also favored, since some mayomberos believe whites take instruction better than blacks. Other mayomberos hedge their bets by taking a brain from corpses of both races, ensuring that their evil spells will work on either.

The mayombero sprinkles rum in the shape of a cross over the grave, then opens it. The corpse is raised, and the mayombero removes the head, the toes, the fingers, ribs and the tibias of the kiyumba, wrapping them in black cloth and taking them home. Once there, the mayombero lies on the floor, and his assistant covers him with a sheet and lights four tapers around the body as if the mayombero were dead. A knife is placed near the mayombero, and on the blade are seven little heaps of gunpowder called *fula*. As the kiyumba takes possession of the mayombero, he becomes rigid and then goes into convulsions. The assistant asks the kiyumba if it will do the bidding of the mayombero; if the answer is yes, the gunpowder ignites spontaneously. If no, the body parts must be returned to the cemetery.

If the spirit agrees, the mayombero writes the kiyumba's name on a piece of paper and places it in the bottom of a big, iron cauldron together with a few coins in payment to the kiyumba. He adds the remains, along with some earth from the gravesite, then cuts a small incision in his arm with a white-handled knife and lets a few drops of blood fall into the cauldron to "refresh" the kiyumba. Some mayomberos sacrifice a rooster to the kiyumba instead, fearing the spirit could become too fond of the mayombero's BLOOD and turn into a vampire.

To the blood, the mayombero adds wax from a burned candle, a cigar butt, ashes, lime and a piece of bamboo sealed at both ends with wax. The bamboo contains sand, seawater and quicksilver, to give the kiyumba the speed of quicksilver and the persistence of the ever-moving tides. Next, the mayombero puts in the body of a small black dog to help the kiyumba track its victims, along with various herbs and tree barks. The rest of the recipe calls for red pepper, chili, garlic, onions, cinnamon, rue, ants, worms, lizards, termites, bats, frogs, Spanish flies, a tarantula, a centipede, a wasp and a scorpion. If the mayombero plans to create good spells from his nganga, a splash of holy water is added at the end. If the cauldron will be used for both good and evil, no baptism is necessary.

After combining all these ingredients, the mayombero takes the cauldron back to the cemetery, where it is buried and left for three successive Fridays. At that time, the mayombero disinters the cauldron and reburies it beside a ceiba or other magical tree for another three Fridays. At the conclusion of the 42 days, the mayombero hauls the cauldron home, where he adds some rum with pepper,

dry wine, Florida water (a popular cologne in the Caribbean) and fresh blood. The nganga is ready.

Occasionally the mayombero does not use a cauldron, choosing instead to place the ingredients, called *boumba*, in a sheet and then tie it up in a burlap sack. The sack, known as a *macuto*, then hangs from a ceiling beam in the darkest room of the mayombero's house. The nganga or macuto forms a small world completely at the bidding of the mayombero, with the kiyumba controlling the animals and plants inside the nganga with it and obeying the orders of the mayombero like a faithful slave, always willing and ready.

The nganga must pass two tests before the mayombero trusts its powers. For the first trial, the mayombero buries the nganga under a tree and tells the kiyumba to dry all the tree's leaves within a certain length of time. If the nganga passes, then the mayombero orders the kiyumba to kill a specific animal. If the kiyumba succeeds again, the mayombero takes the nganga home.

There are two other types of ngangas: the *zarabanda* and the *ndoki*. The mayombero makes a zarabanda in the traditional manner but invokes the spirit of the Congo deity Zarabanda to work directly with the kiyumba. The ndoki ranks as perhaps the most infernal preparation in the mayombero's repertoire. First, a black CAT is tortured and boiled alive. The mayombero then buries the cat for 24 hours. Upon disinterment, he adds a few of the cat's bones to seven phalanx bones from the little fingers of seven corpses, along with the dust from seven graves. These ingredients are placed in the cauldron with garlic and pepper; then the mayombero sprinkles rum over the pot and blows cigar smoke over it. The cauldron stays in the woods overnight, and then it is ready. Considered the property of the DEVIL, the *ndoki* is used to kill and destroy its victims in the most fearsome and horrible ways.

Santeros fear the nganga's powers so much that they will not even speak of them except in whispers. Making a nganga is illegal, needless to say, punishable with a fine or imprisonment, but few mayomberos worry about trifles like legal codes or police officers. They operate with impunity, wielding death and destruction on behalf of anyone for a price.

See AFRICAN WITCHCRAFT; GRIS-GRIS; ZOMBIE.

FURTHER READING:
Gleason, Judith. *Oya: In Praise of the Goddess.* Boston: Shambhala, 1987.
Gonzalez-Wippler. *Santeria: African Magic in Latin America.* New York: Original Products, 1981.

Satanism   The worship of Satan, or the DEVIL, the god of evil in Christianity. During the witch hunts, witches, along with heretics, were accused of worshiping the Devil. Many confessed to it, probably coerced by TORTURE. In popular lore, witches are still believed to worship the Devil. In contemporary PAGANISM and Witchcraft, or WICCA, there is no belief in nor worship of the Devil.

Satanism has been far less common throughout history than many would believe. The inquisitors and witch-hunters of earlier centuries tried to persuade the populace that Devil-worshipers were everywhere and posed a serious threat to their well-being. For about 250 years, from the mid-15th century to the early 18th century, the height of the witchhunts, that argument worked. It is possible that some Devil-worship may have actually existed in those times, as an act of defiance among those who opposed the authority of the Christian Church.

Satanism as an organized activity did not exist much before the 17th century. As early as the seventh century, however, the Catholic Church was condemning priests who subverted the magical powers of the Holy Mass for evil purposes. The *Grimoire of Honorious,* a magical textbook first printed in the 17th century, gave instructions for saying masses to conjure DEMONS. In the 17th century, satanic activities were conducted by Christians who indulged in the magical/sexual rites of the BLACK MASS, presided over by defrocked or unscrupulous priests. The most notorious of these escapades took place in France during the reign of Louis XIV, engineered by the king's mistress, Madame de Montespan, and led by an occultist named La Voisin and a 67-year-old libertine priest, the Abbé Guiborg.

There is no reliable evidence of satanic activity in the 18th century. In England, the Hellfire Club, a society founded by Sir Francis Dashwood (1708–1781), has often been described as satanic, but in actuality it was little more than a club for adolescent-like men to indulge in drinking, sexual play with women called "nuns" and outrageous behavior. The Hellfire Club, or the "Medmenham Monks," as they called themselves, met regularly between 1750 and 1762 in Dashwood's home, Medmenham Abbey. The members were said to conduct Black Masses, but it is doubtful that these were serious satanic activities. Similar groups were the Brimstone Boys and Blue Blazers of Ireland.

Perhaps the most famous satanist of the 19th century was the Abbé Boullan of France, who became the head of an offshoot of the Church of Carmel and allegedly practiced black magic and infant SACRIFICE. The Church of Carmel was formed by Eugene Vintras, the foreman of a cardboard box factory in Tillysur-Seulles. In 1839 Vintras said he received a letter from the archangel Michael, followed by visions of the archangel, the Holy Ghost, St. Joseph and the Virgin Mary. He was informed that he was the reincarnated Prophet Elijah, and he was to found a new religious order and proclaim the coming of the Age of the Holy Ghost. The true king of France, he was told, was one Charles Naundorf.

Vintras went about the countryside preaching this news and acquiring followers, including priests. Masses were celebrated that included visions of chalices filled with BLOOD, and blood stains on the Eucharist. By 1848 the Church of Carmel, as the movement was known, was condemned by the Pope. In 1851 Vintras was accused by a former disciple of conducting Black Masses in the nude, homosexuality and masturbating while praying at the altar.

Shortly before his death in 1875, Vintras befriended Boullan, who formed a splinter group of the Church of Carmel upon Vintras' death. He ran the group for 18 years, until his death, outwardly maintaining pious practices but secretly conducting satanic rituals.

Boullan seems to have been obsessed with Satanism and evil since age 29, when he took a nun named Adele Chevalier as his mistress. Chevalier left her convent, bore two bastard children and founded with Boullan the Society for the Reparation of Souls. Boullan specialized in exorcising demons by unconventional means, such as feeding possessed victims a mixture of human excrement and the Eucharist (see EXORCISM). He also performed Black Masses. On January 8, 1860, he and Chevalier reportedly conducted a Black Mass in which they sacrificed one of their children.

By the time Boullan met Vintras, Boullan was claiming to be the reincarnated St. John the Baptist. He taught his followers sexual techniques and said the original sin of Adam and Eve could be redeemed by sex with incubi and succubi. He and his followers also were said to copulate with the spirits of the dead, including Anthony the Great.

Boullan's group was infiltrated by two Rosicrucians, Oswald Wirth and Stanislas de Guaita, who wrote an exposé, *The Temple of Satan.* Boullan and de Guaita supposedly engaged in magical warfare. Boullan and his friend, the novelist J. K. Huysmans, claimed to be attacked by DEMONS. When Boullan collapsed and died of a heart attack on January 3, 1893, Huysmans believed it was due to an evil spell cast by de Guaita, and said so in print. De Guaita challenged him to a duel, but Huysmans declined and apologized.

In his novel, *La-bas,* Huysmans included a Black Mass, which he said was based on his observations of one conducted by a satanic group in Paris, operating in the late 19th century. He said the Mass was recited backwards, the crucifix was upside down, the Eucharist was defiled and the rite ended in a sexual orgy.

In the early 20th century, ALEISTER CROWLEY was linked to Satanism. Although he called himself "the Beast," used the words "life," "love" and "light" to describe Satan and once baptized and crucified a toad as Jesus, he was not a satanist but a magician and occultist.

The largest movement of modern Satanism began in the 1960s in the United States, led by Anton Szandor LaVey (born Howard Stanton Levey), a shrewd man with a charismatic persona and an imposing appearance. LaVey founded the Church of Satan in San Francisco in 1966, the activities of which became the object of great media attention.

LaVey devised or re-created rituals from historical sources on the KNIGHTS TEMPLAR, the Hellfire Club, the

HERMETIC ORDER OF THE GOLDEN DAWN and Aleister Crowley. LaVey apparently enjoyed the theatrics of the rituals; he dressed in a scarlet-lined cape and kept skulls and other odd objects about. He viewed the Devil as a dark force hidden in nature, ruling earthly affairs. Man's true nature, he claimed, is one of lust, pride, hedonism and willfulness, attributes that enable the advancement of civilization. Flesh should not be denied but celebrated. Individuals who stand in the way of achieving what one wants should be cursed.

On WALPURGISNACHT (April 30) in 1966, LaVey shaved his head and announced the founding of the Church of Satan. He recognized the shock value of using the term *church* for worshiping the Devil and recognized people's innate need for ritual, ceremony and pageantry. He performed satanic baptisms, weddings and funerals, all of which received widespread media coverage. He used a semi-nude woman (partially covered by a leopard skin) as an altar.

LaVey preached antiestablishmentarianism, self-indulgence and all forms of gratification and vengeance. Enemies were to be hated and smashed. Sex was exalted. He opposed the use of drugs, saying they were escapist and unnecessary to achieving natural highs. He also deplored the use of black magic in criminal activity. He did not include a Black Mass in his rituals, because he believed the Black Mass to be out of date.

The Church of Satan organized into grottoes. A reversed pentacle containing a goat's head, called the BAPHOMET, was chosen as the symbol. LaVey used Enochian as the magical language for rituals and espoused the Enochian Keys used by Crowley.

LaVey authored *The Satanic Bible* (1969) and *The Satanic Rituals* (1972). A third book, *The Compleat Witch*, was published in Europe.

In 1975 the church suffered a serious loss of members, who left to form a new organization, the Temple of Set. In the mid-1970s the Church of Satan reorganized as a secret society and dissolved its grottoes. The headquarters remain in San Francisco. LaVey became inactive and then went into seclusion. He reappeared in the media in the 1990s, and in 1992 authored a new book, *The Devil's Notebook*. LaVey suffered from heart problems for years. He died on October 30, 1997, at the age of 67.

Claims have been made about the numbers of persons involved in Satanism, and their various activities, including alleged human sacrifice. Some of these claims are based on "recovered memories." Many such claims have been discredited. Satanic groups exist—they appeal to alienated youths—but there is no proof of ritual human sacrifice (the Church of Satan and Temple of Set say they do not practice or condone blood sacrifice).

Contemporary Witches and Pagans often are wrongly blamed for satanic activities. Various organizations carry on public relations and education programs for the media and members of the law-enforcement community to counteract such accusations.

FURTHER READING:
Boulware, Jack. "Has the Church of Satan Gone to Hell?" *Gnosis,* no. 50, Winter 1999, pp. 25–33.
LaVey, Anton Szandor. *The Satanic Bible.* New York: Avon Books, 1969.
Russell, Jeffrey Burton. *The Prince of Darkness.* London: Thames and Hudson, 1989.
Terry, Maury. *The Ultimate Evil.* New York: Doubleday, 1987.

Sawyer, Elisabeth (?–1621) A poor Englishwoman framed and executed for witchcraft.

Elisabeth Sawyer, the "Witch of Edmonton," was accused of bewitching her neighbors' children and cattle because the neighbors refused to buy her BROOMS. She was also accused of bewitching to death a woman, Agnes Ratcliffe, who allegedly had struck one of Sawyer's sows for eating some of her soap. The same evening, Ratcliffe became fatally ill; according to her husband, she was "extraordinarily vexed, and in a most strange manner in her sicknesse was tormented . . . she lay foaming at the mouth and was extraordinarily distempered."

Sawyer was arrested and searched for a WITCH'S MARK. She denied the accusations and cursed her accusers. She was harassed by Reverend Henry Goodcole, of Newgate Prison, into finally confessing that she had sold her soul to the DEVIL. The Devil appeared to her in the form of a DEMON and a dog that was usually black but would be white if it appeared while she was praying. As a dog, he wagged his tail happily whenever Sawyer would scratch his back. Sawyer also confessed that she had prayed in Latin at the Devil's request.

According to Goodcole, she told him that the dog "demanded of mee my soule and body; threatning then to teare me in pieces if I did not grant unto him my soule and my bodie when he asked of me . . . to seale this my

The Witch of Edmonton (WOODCUT, 1658)

promise I gave him leave to sucke of my blood, the which he asked of me."

Apparently the dog deserted her once she was arrested, for Sawyer also told Goodcole that it had not visited her in jail.

At her trial, three women testified that they had examined her body, and had found "a private and strange marke," which was said to be the teat by which the demon dog suckled her BLOOD. Other "evidence" against her was her crooked and deformed body, and her perpetual depression, all of which had made her an outcast in her own village. Goodcole maintained that she had turned to witchcraft out of "malice and envy" toward her neighbors.

Sawyer was hanged at Tyburn on April 19, 1621, two days after her confession. Her execution was one of only five during the last nine years of the reign of JAMES I, an ardent witch-hunter. Her accusing neighbors, who were rumored to also be in league with the Devil, were not bothered by authorities.

The story, based on Goodcole's account written just days after Sawyer's execution, quickly became grist for a play by poets William Rowley, Thomas Dekker and John Ford. It is the first play to give a sympathetic portrayal of a witch. The plot revolves around illicit love and murder, with Sawyer as the bewitching agent who goads the protagonist into killing. Sawyer's alleged FAMILIAR, the black dog, is the play's villain. A clownish character named Cuddy Banks befriends the dog, who has the power of speech, and is not affected by the dog's evil. The play is moralistic, showing how the Devil attempts to seduce people into selling their souls, and how Sawyer foolishly fell victim to him.

FURTHER READING:

Harris, Anthony. *Night's Black Agents: Witchcraft and Magic in Seventeenth-Century English Drama.* Manchester: Manchester University Press, 1980.

Maple, Eric. *The Dark World of Witches.* New York: A.S. Barnes & Co., 1962.

Saylor Family (19th century)   Family of prominent German powwowers, or folk doctors who practiced magical medical arts. The Saylor Family were influential healers for about two centuries in the Lehigh Valley area of Pennsylvania.

The American branch of the Saylor family was founded by Johann Peter Seiler, born on September 26, 1721. He was orphaned. With his brother, he immigrated to America in 1738 and worked off the cost of his passage as an indentured servant. He settled first in New Jersey and married Anna Margaret Maurer of Greenwich. A daughter, Elizabeth, was born in 1750. The couple had 10 children in all.

The Seilers moved to Raubsville, Pennsylvania. Johann established a successful folk medicine practice using herbal remedies, CHARMS, magical SPELLS and a lay-

ing on of hands. By 1779, he owned 200 acres of land. In the 1780s he bought more tracts near the HEXENKOPF and surrounding areas. He had a large library of books, a still for preparing herbal concoctions and beehives. In the Revolutionary War, Seiler served as a lieutenant colonel in the army, and three sons served as privates.

Seiler was among the first practitioners to be called a powwower. He treated both whites and Indians; the latter called him "the great powwow man."

Seiler died on January 8, 1803. His tombstone bears a carving of a HEXENFOOS, a six-pointed flower drawn with a compass, intended to keep evil spirits away.

Seiler's son Jacob became well known as a powwower and so did Jacob's son Johannes and Johannes' son John Henry.

But the star of the Saylor family was Seiler's youngest son, Peter, born in 1770. Peter inherited the family estate and his father's medical practice. By then, the spelling of the family name had changed to Saylor. Peter developed his own unique brand of witchy medicine, spurred on by the popularity of the handbook *The Long Lost Friend* (1820) by JOHN GEORGE HOHMAN, another famous powwower. Peter lived to the age of 91 and devoted himself to his medical arts, practiced out of the family estate, where he built a splendid stone house. Saylor's Lane, leading to the house, was often lined with the carriages and carts of patients waiting their turns.

Peter was a formidable figure, and stories circulated about his magical prowess. It was said that he once butchered a hog and left it hanging inside one of his magical circles. A man tried to steal the hog but, upon entering the circle, became unable to move until Peter arrived and set him free. Peter also was said to be able to tie knots in threads with his tongue.

In powwowing, disease and illness are caused by the DEVIL and the DEMONS and WITCHES who serve him. Illness is cast out, based on the model set by Jesus in the New Testament, when he exorcized demons into a herd of swine. Similarly, powwowers of the 19th century cast out illness into animals.

Peter was especially known for his ability to cast out illness, and his favored receptacle was not animals, but the HEXENKOPF, a large rocky hill that had the profile of a witch's head. The German immigrants had brought witch lore with them, and they associated the Hexenkopf with witch activities; Peter's activities increased the witch lore and the fear of the hill. He was known to cast MAGIC CIRCLES on the ground and stand within them, uttering his incantations to "call down power." He and other powwowers in his family—as well as in the tradition in general—believed that his magical powers waxed and waned with the MOON. The best and most powerful day was the first Friday following a full moon; the most difficult cases were treated then.

Peter trained his son Peter Jr. and his nephew Jacob in powwowing. Shortly before he died in 1862, Peter instructed his son to take certain witchcraft books out of his library, weight them down with stones and throw them in the Delaware River because he wished that the books be never more used. Peter Jr. complied. The instruction evidently was conditional for him to inherit the family estate and the medical practice.

Peter Jr. changed the spelling of his last name to Sailor. He was 53 when his father died, and he was able to practice powwowing for only six years before he was paralyzed by a stroke on August 22, 1868. He died on September 3. He was a bachelor and had no children to train, but he did instruct John Henry Wilhelm.

Jacob Saylor moved to Bethlehem Township and established his practice. He also began writing down some of the remedies, but the collection was never published. It survives as a manuscript at Franklin and Marshall College in Lancaster, Pennsylvania.

After 1868, the Saylor male line of powwowers ended, and the calling was pursued by the Wilhelms, who were related to the Saylors by marriage. John Henry and his brother, Eugene, were the most famous. Their father, Jacob Wilhelm, also was a renowned healer and wrote a detailed book of his cures.

The old Saylor home reportedly is haunted by unknown spirits or ghosts. Disembodied voices have been heard, and a repairman once insisted that the furnace turned on by itself. The nearby Wilhelm home no longer exists, having burned to the ground in 2002.

FURTHER READING:
Heindel, Ned D. *Hexenkopf: History, Healing & Hexerei.* Easton, Pa.: Williams Township Historical Society, 2005.

School of Wicca   See CHURCH AND SCHOOL OF WICCA.

Score, John (d. 1979)   Also known as M, John Score was an influential figure in Britain during the formative years of the re-emergence of PAGANISM and Witchcraft, the latter of which Score preferred to call the Old Religion of Wisecraft.

Score, of Wimborne, Dorset, served in the Royal Air Force from 1931 to 1946, retiring with the rank of Flight Lieutenant (Signals). In 1948 he organized and directed the telecommunications for the Olympic Games, held in London that year, work that earned him a bronze medallion.

In 1968 he became editor of *The Wiccan.* Under his direction, *The Wiccan* rose to prominence in both Britain and the United States as one of the leading Pagan journals. With a group of persons from Britain and America, Score played a role in the formation of the PAGAN WAY in America. In 1971 he was a key founder of the Pagan Front in Britain, which evolved separately from the American group, later changing its name to the PAGAN FEDERATION. *The Wiccan* became the newsletter of the Pagan Front/Federation.

In establishing the Pagan Front, Score sought to defend the religious freedom of all Pagans and to protect Paganism from undesirable exploitation and the infiltration of black-MAGIC elements. To these ends, he was often controversial.

Throughout his life, Score maintained a deep interest in the occult and what he called the Ancient Wisdom. He delved into all forms of natural healing and earned a Naturopathic Doctor degree in the United States. He studied reincarnation and experienced memories of his own past lives in ancient Egypt and Atlantis. He also researched ways to use his technical knowledge with help from his spirit guides to develop an instrument for communicating with spirits without the need for a human medium. His work was done independently of other researchers in what eventually became known as the "electronic voice phenomenon," the recording of spirit voices directly onto magnetic tape. Score believed he achieved some success on his own, but poor health forced him to leave his work incomplete.

Score suffered from ill health through much of his life, particularly in his later years. He died in December 1979, survived by his wife and two sons.

Scot, Michael (ca. 1175–1234)   Reputed Scottish magician whose life is surrounded by as much legend as fact. Scot was respected as a mathematician, physician, astrologer and scholar. He was outspoken in his condemnation of MAGIC and NECROMANCY, yet he seemed to know so much about these subjects that most of his peers considered him both a sorcerer and a necromancer. Legends grew up around him, transforming him into a magician with great supernatural powers.

Little is known about Scot's early life, including his exact birthplace. It is believed that he may have come from Balwearie in Fife. His family evidently was affluent, for he studied at Oxford.

After Oxford, Scot traveled to various centers of learning in Europe: the Sorbonne in Paris; Bologna; Palermo; Toledo and Sicily. In Sicily, he was an astrologer to King Ferdinand II, whose court included many adepts in magic, alchemy and the occult arts.

Scot entered the clerical order at some point in his life and enjoyed great esteem in the eyes of the Pope. In 1223 the Archbishopric of Cashel in Ireland became vacant, and the Pope nominated Scot to fill it. He declined because he did not know the Irish language.

In 1230 Scot went to England, where he is erroneously credited with having introduced the works of Aristotle, which he translated.

He wrote extensively, mixing science and the occult. His book on physiognomy, the study of man's face, held that the stars and planets marked life's events upon the face. His book on astronomy included astrological PRAYERS and conjurations. As was typical of the time, Scot believed in alchemy, DIVINATION and the magical properties of precious STONES and herbs as sciences.

In particular, Scot wrote on magic and necromancy, fully describing practices and rituals. The publication of such magic acts customarily was prohibited out of fear that people would be encouraged to perform them. It was said that Scot performed them himself, disguising his magic rituals as scientific experiments.

According to legend, Scot commanded a retinue of FA-MILIARS, which he dispatched to raid the kitchens of the Pope and French and Spanish royalty, and transport their food back to him by air. He also was said to ride through the sky on a demonic horse; to sail the seas in a demonic ship; and to ride on the back of some fantastical sea beast. He supposedly could make the BELLS of Notre Dame ring with a wave of his magic wand.

The DEVIL was said to help Scot in his philanthropic undertakings, such as the building of a road in Scotland within a single night.

A recipe for making gold that is attributed to Scot calls for "the BLOOD of a ruddy man and the blood of a red owl," mixed with saffron, alum, URINE and cucumber juice.

Dante called Scot a fraud and placed him in eternal torment in the eighth circle of the *Inferno*. He is said to be buried in Melrose Abbey in Scotland. According to legend, a "wondrous light" burns within his tomb to chase away evil spirits and will continue to burn until the day of doom.

FURTHER READING:
Folklore, Myths and Legends of Britain. London: Reader's Digest Assoc. Ltd., 1977.
Sharpe, C. K. *A History of Witchcraft in Scotland.* Glasgow: Thomas D. Morison, 1884.

Scot, Reginald (ca. 1538–1599) During the darkest days of the witch persecutions, Reginald Scot was among the few voices of reason to be heard. In 1584 he self-published *The Discoverie of Witchcraft,* in which he refuted many of the beliefs concerning the power of WITCHES and denounced their persecution as the "extreme and intolerable tyranny" of the INQUISITION.

Scot was drawn to the subject of WITCHCRAFT not by profession—he was not a judge, scholar or demonologist—but by his own sense of personal outrage at the TORTURE and execution of people he considered to be innocent of any wrongdoing. In the 1886 edition of *Discoverie,* Dr. Brinsley Nicholson writes in the introduction that Scot saw himself

> . . . engaged in a righteous work, that of rescuing feeble and ignorant, though it may be too pretentious and shrewish, old women from false charges and a violent death, and in a noble work endeavoring to stem the torrent of superstition and cruelty which was then beginning to overflow the land.

Scot was born to the genteel family of Sir John Scot near Smeeth in Kent, in or around 1538. He was sent to Oxford at age 17 but left school without earning a degree and returned to the family lands. He was thoughtful, bright and reflective, and he enjoyed studying "obscure authors that had by the generality of Scholars been neglected," according to Nicholson. He worked for a time as a subsidies collector for the government, served a year in Parliament and tended to hop gardening, which was the subject of his first book, *The Hop Garden,* published in 1574.

He married in 1558, but his wife, Jane, died and left him childless. A second marriage also yielded no children. Scot was supported by his cousin, Sir Thomas Scot, whose estate he managed.

In composing *Discoverie,* Scot drew upon his knowledge of superstition in rural life, the law and literature. He also drew upon the writings of numerous scholars, theologians and experts in various fields, even those who disagreed with his own views. He was heavily influenced by the writings of JOHANN WEYER, a German physician who opposed the witch-hunts.

Scot's book became a compendium of the beliefs of the day, a classic in witchcraft literature, covering such topics as ghosts (see GHOSTS, HAUNTINGS AND WITCHCRAFT), POSSESSION, CHARMS, DIVINATION, FAIRIES, SPELLS, MAGIC, witchcraft itself and the practices of the DEVIL.

Scot defined four categories of witches:

1. the falsely accused innocent;
2. the deluded and crazy who convinced themselves they were in a pact with Satan;
3. the true, malevolent witch who harmed by poisoning but not by supernatural power; and
4. imposters who collected fees for false spells, cures and prophecies.

Scot allowed that the last two categories were those that the Bible had said should not be suffered to live. But he resolutely denied that any witch derived supernatural power from the Devil, whom he said had no physical power of his own.

Scot also maintained, among his various arguments, that the manifestations of spirits were delusions due to mental disturbances in the beholder and that the incubus was a natural disease. He denounced the Pope, who "canonized the rich for saints and banneth the poor for witches."

He included his own beliefs, such as the healing powers of unicorn horns and precious gems, and the power of a carp's head bone to staunch bleeding.

Scot was not alone in his condemnation of the witch persecutions; his writing was part of a continuing skepticism about witchcraft that persisted in England. *Discoverie* did have a favorable impact upon the clergy in England, but King JAMES I was violently opposed to it. He ordered copies burned and wrote his own refutation, *Daemonologie.*

See WITCH OF ENDOR.

FURTHER READING:
Kors, Alan C., and Edward Peters. *Witchcraft in Europe, A Documentary History 1100–1700.* Philadelphia: University of Pennsylvania Press, 1972.

Lea, Henry Charles. *Materials Toward a History of Witchcraft.* Philadelphia: University of Pennsylvania, 1939.

Scot, Reginald. *The Discoverie of Witchcraft.* 1886. Reprint, Yorkshire, England: E.P. Publishing, Ltd., 1973.

scrying The ancient art of clairvoyance achieved by concentrating upon an object—usually one with a shiny surface—until visions appear.

The term *scrying* comes from the English word *descry,* which means "to make out dimly" or "to reveal." The services of a scryer typically are sought for predictions of the future, answers to questions, solutions to problems and help in finding lost objects and in identifying or tracking down criminals. In earlier times, a scryer was likely to be a wise woman or wise man—perhaps also called a witch—who was naturally gifted with second sight.

Scrying is not limited to crystal balls but includes any smooth and shiny object that makes a good speculum. Many early scryers simply gazed into the still water of a lake or pond at night. Most scryers use objects with reflective surfaces, such as mirrors, polished STONES or metals and bowls of liquid. Egyptian scryers used ink, BLOOD and other dark liquids. In the 16th century, Nostradamus used bowls of water to see the visions from which he produced his famous prophecies. John Dee, the royal court magician in 16th-century England, used a crystal egg and a piece of obsidian said to have been brought from Mexico by Cortés. Like many other magicians, ALEISTER CROWLEY used a precious gem for scrying. Crowley's speculum was a topaz set in a wooden cross of six squares, painted vermilion.

Few witches throughout history have used crystal balls, which are heavy and expensive. Glass-ball fishing floats are commonly used, as are WITCH BALLS, colored glass balls intended to be hung in homes to keep out witches and the EVIL EYE. A favored speculum is the magic MIRROR with a concave side painted black. Witches may make magic mirrors themselves, painting and decorating them with magic SIGILS during the waxing of the MOON and consecrating them in RITUALS like other working tools (see WITCHES' TOOLS). GERALD B. GARDNER practiced scrying with a mirror in an old picture frame he found in a London junk shop. The glass was slightly curved and had been coated gray-black on the concave side.

Another scrying tool used by witches is a CAULDRON painted black on the inside. The witch fills the cauldron with water and drops in a silver coin to represent the Moon in the night sky.

Scrying may be done within a MAGIC CIRCLE. The best results are obtained at night, when the reception of psychic impressions is believed to be clearer. Methods vary, but after a period of concentration upon the speculum, the scryer either sees visions upon its surface or receives mental images and impressions. Sometimes the visions are symbolic and must be interpreted. Practice is necessary to learn the meanings behind the symbols seen.

See DIVINATION.

FURTHER READING:

Farrar, Stewart. *What Witches Do: A Modern Coven Revealed.* Custer, Wash.: Phoenix Publishing Co., 1983.

Valiente, Doreen. *An ABC of Witchcraft Past and Present.* 1973. Reprint, Custer, Wash.: Phoenix Publishing, 1986.

sea witches The sailing trade in Britain has been steeped for centuries in folklore, including belief in sea witches, who allegedly have the power to control a man's fate out on the waves. Sea witches are said to lurk up and down the coast, ready to curse ships and cause them to wreck upon the rocks or founder in a storm. Some sea witches are phantoms, the ghosts of dead witches (see GHOSTS, HAUNTINGS AND WITCHCRAFT). According to legend, Sir Francis Drake sold his soul to the DEVIL in order to become a skilled seaman and admiral. The Devil sent Drake phantom sea witches, who helped him raise a storm at sea and defeat the Spanish Armada in 1588 (see STORM RAISING). The witches are still said to haunt the land near where the battle took place: Devil's Point, which overlooks Devonport.

Selene A Greek goddess of the MOON, Selene is a winged, silvery woman who presides over night skies, sailing along in her chariot pulled by shining, winged white horses, cows or bulls (whose horns represent the crescent moon). Sometimes she sits astride a bull, horse or mule. In contemporary Witchcraft, Selene is one aspect of the Triple Goddess, along with DIANA (Artemis) and HECATE.

Selene's role in Greek mythology is minor. She is the daughter of Theia and Hyperion. In some myths she is the daughter of Theia and Helios, the sun god, and is the sister of Phoebus Apollo, who succeeded Helios as the sun deity. Other names for Selene are Phoebe and Mene, the latter of which refers to her changing shape during the course of the lunar month.

The Greeks worshiped Selene at new and full moons, believing her to influence the fecundity of all life forms on earth. During the Hellenistic era, Selene (the Moon) was the destination of the souls of the dead.

The most significant myth of Selene is that of her fascination with her lover, Endymion, a magnificent youth who is a king, hunter or shepherd. In the version recorded by Theocritus, a 3rd-century poet, Endymion falls asleep on Mount Latmus and is observed by Selene, who falls in love with his beauty. She comes down from the sky and kisses him, bewitching him into immortal, deathless sleep so that she can visit him night after night into eternity. In other versions, Endymion wakes and is equally enchanted with Selene. He begs Zeus to grant him immortality so that he can continue to love Selene, and Zeus does so on the condition that Endymion remain asleep forever.

As an aspect of the Triple Goddess, Selene presides over the full moon, a seven-day period that lasts from three days before fullness to three days after, when certain kinds of MAGIC are at their greatest strength. It is Selene's aspect that is invoked in the DRAWING DOWN THE MOON ritual. Witches sometimes call upon her in magic related to finding solutions to problems.

See GODDESS.

sending   Sorcerers in many cultures send animals, birds, insects, spirits, animated objects and allegedly even bewitched corpses to carry out CURSES—usually of death—against victims (see SORCERY). The animal may be the sorcerer's own FAMILIAR or a creature suited to the curse. Navajo and Hindu sorcerers often use dogs, but if the curse calls for destroying crops, they will send grasshoppers, locusts, caterpillars and other insects. The Chippewa lay a curse of starvation by stuffing an OWL skin with magical substances and causing it to fly to the victim's home. Shamans send familiars—usually in the form of an animal or bird—out to battle for them, but if the familiar dies, so does the shaman (see SHAMANISM). New Guinea sorcerers favor snakes and crocodiles for sending, while in Malay, the familiar is usually an owl or badger passed down from generation to generation. New Guinea sorcerers also send disease-causing objects, such as pieces of magical bone and coral, to lodge in bodies. In Africa, the Kaguru witches send anteaters to burrow under the walls of their victims' huts, and the Gisu send rats in pairs to collect hair and nail clippings of victims for use in black-magic SPELLS (see AFRICAN WITCHCRAFT; HAIR AND NAILS).

Spirits dispatched on magical errands may be DEMONS or entities summoned by the sorcerer, or they may be artificial ELEMENTALS or THOUGHTFORMS, created by MAGIC. Rather than relying on familiars, the sorcerer may send his or her own *fetch*, or astral body, which is projected out from the physical body.

The Zulus' familiars are said to be corpses dug up and reanimated with magic; they are sent out on night errands to scare travelers with their shrieking and pranks. Corpses also are sent in VODUN, with an invocation to St. Expedit, whose image is placed upside-down on the altar:

> Almighty God, my Father, come and find (name) that he may be disappeared before me like the thunder and lightning. Saint Expedit . . . I call on you and take you as my patron from today, I am sending you to find (name); rid me of . . . his head, rid me of his memory . . . of all my enemies, visible and invisible, bring down on them thunder and lightning. In thine honour Saint Expedit, three Paters.

Sending is most common among tribal societies of the Pacific islands, Africa, Siberia and North America but also is known among the folk witches of Scandinavia, Iceland and the Baltic countries. In European and English lore, witches were believed to send their familiars, usu-

ally CATS, dogs, TOADS, HARES or owls, to carry out evil spells against their neighbors.

FURTHER READING:
Leach, Maria, ed., and Jerome Fried, assoc. ed. *Funk & Wagnall's Standard Dictionary of Folklore, Mythology and Legend.* New York: Harper & Row, 1972.

seventh child of a seventh child   In folklore, people who possess magical powers.

Seven is the most mystical and magical of numbers. Since the Middle Ages, the seventh son of a seventh son is supposed to have formidable magical and healing powers: He is clairvoyant and can see DEMONS and witches that no one else can see. He is capable of casting powerful SPELLS, and he possesses the ability to heal by a laying on of hands. The Pennsylvania Dutch hold in high regard the seventh son of a seventh son who is born into a family of witches, for his spells are considered more powerful than those of other witches and more difficult to break. The seventh daughter of a seventh daughter or a seventh son is supposed to be born with the powers of a witch, but with no connection to the devil. She can foretell the future and can heal the sick.

shamanism   The oldest system of HEALING in the world, shamanism is prevalent in tribal cultures which, though isolated from one another, have developed beliefs and techniques with startling similarities. A shaman enters an ecstatic altered state of consciousness, which enables him to communicate with guardian and helping spirits and draw upon sources of enormous power. The primary purpose of shamanism is the healing of body and mind. It also is used for DIVINATION and to ensure good hunts and prosperity for a tribe or village.

According to archaeological and ethnological evidence, shamanism has been practiced for some 20,000 to 30,000 years. It may be much older, perhaps as old as the human race. It is found all over the world, including very remote portions of the Americas, Siberia and Asia, Australia, northern Europe and Africa.

Shamanic systems vary greatly, but most share basic similarities. The shaman must function comfortably in two realities, the ordinary reality of the everyday, waking world, and the nonordinary reality of the shamanic state of consciousness. The nonordinary reality is attained in trance which varies from light to deep coma and enables the shaman to see and do things that are impossible in ordinary reality. Once in trance, the shaman enters the lowerworld by slipping into a hole or opening in the earth. In the lowerworld, he sees the cause of disease in a patient and knows its cure, and sees his guardian spirit and spirit helpers. He can shape-shift into these spirits and fly through the air (see METAMORPHOSIS). He performs his cures and can see into the future. When his shamanic work is done, he reemerges from the lowerworld back into ordinary reality. Shamans are also said to ascend to the sky in spirit boats or astride the spirits of sacrificed horses.

The nonordinary reality is as real to the shaman as is the ordinary reality. The things he sees are not hallucinations but are externalized. The shamanic state of consciousness is induced through drumming, rattling and dancing or, in some societies, by ingesting hallucinogens.

Most shamans are men, though women also can become shamans; some women shamans are extraordinarily powerful. In some cultures, shamans are involuntarily chosen by the spirits. They realize their calling in a transformational experience, often a serious illness that brings them close to death and is self-cured. In other cultures, persons with natural shamanic gifts are selected at a young age, trained and initiated (see INITIATION).

The shaman must obtain a guardian spirit, which is the source of his spiritual powers. The guardian spirit also is called a power animal, tutelary spirit, totemic animal or FAMILIAR. A common method of discovering and connecting with the guardian spirit is the solitary, all-night vigil outdoors. The guardian spirit usually manifests as an animal, bird, fish or reptile but may also appear in human form. It is both beneficent and beneficial and brings to the shaman the powers of an entire species. The shaman invites the guardian spirit into his body; it protects him from illness and from unfriendly forces in the lowerworld. Guardian spirits change over the years as the shaman's needs change.

After a guardian spirit is acquired, healing and divination may be performed. Healing techniques vary. A shaman may collect spirit helpers, which are the causes and cures of illness. Spirit helpers are represented by plants, insects, small objects, worms and the like. When the shaman sees, in trance, the cause of an illness, he places one of these objects in the back of his mouth and one in the front. He then begins to "suck" the illness out of the body of the patient. The energy that causes the illness is absorbed by the spirit helpers in his mouth who protect the shaman from absorbing the illness himself. The helper in the back of the mouth acts as a backup, in case the illness gets past the helper in front.

In other techniques, the shaman descends to the lowerworld, or the realm of the dead, to bring back the soul of a patient or to retrieve a patient's guardian spirit. Some shamans exorcise disease-causing spirits in séancelike procedures or by invoking or cajoling them to leave the patient.

Sleight-of-hand tricks are sometimes used, but do not necessarily negate a healing.

Some traditions of contemporary Paganism and Witchcraft incorporate shamanic practices. Most of these concern raising energy, Otherworld journeys and healing. Some Witches, such as STARHAWK, consider Witchcraft a shamanistic religion because raising energy, Otherworldy contact and healing are fundamental to it. Some Pagans say the same about various forms of contemporary Paganism. Pagan/Wiccan shamanism fosters a closer connection to the Earth and plays a role in the environmental and ecological interests of many individuals. It also plays a significant role in the creation of healing therapies especially tailored to Pagan and Wiccan spirituality.

FURTHER READING:

Eliade, Mircea. *Shamanism.* Revised and enlarged ed. Princeton, N.J.: Princeton University Press, 1974.

Harner, Michael. *The Way of the Shaman.* New York: Bantam, 1982.

Harvey, Graham. *Contemporary Paganism: Listening People, Speaking Earth.* New York: New York University Press, 1997.

Kalweit, Holger. *Dreamtime & Inner Space: The World of the Shaman.* Boston: Shambhala Publications, 1984.

shape-shifting   See METAMORPHOSIS.

sigils   Symbols linked to names and sets of ideas, by which spirits or deities may be called into awareness and controlled. The term comes from the Latin *sigillum,* which means "seal." A sigil alone does not call forth spirits but serves as a physical focus through which a practitioner achieves a desired state of mind. Sigils represent the secret names of spirits and deities, which reveal themselves differently to each magic practitioner. Once a spirit or deity has been summoned in magic, it may be controlled, if necessary, by subjecting its sigil to fire or thrusts with the magical sword.

Sigils also represent complex concepts or contain the entire essence of a SPELL. The pentacle (see PENTACLE AND PENTAGRAM) is the most powerful sigil for contemporary Witchcraft. Sigils are also used as identifying logos of organizations. An individual may adopt a sigil, such as a runic letter, to inscribe on magical tools (see WITCHES' TOOLS). Sigils may serve as AMULETS, TALISMANS or meditational tools.

Sigils may be geometric shapes, astrological signs, alchemical symbols, CROSSES and signs associated with deities. They are created through intuition, inspiration and meditation.

A sigil is energized in a RITUAL with chanting and visualization. When it is charged, it is "sent" to do its work. Meditation upon a sigil enables one to access everything the sigil represents without consciously thinking about it.

FURTHER READING:

Barrett, Francis. *The Magus.* London: Lackington, Allen and Co., 1801.

Tyson, Donald. *The New Magus.* St. Paul: Llewellyn Publications, 1988.

A Table shewing the names of the Angels governing the 7 days of the week with their Sigils, Planets, Signs, &c

Sunday	Monday	Tuesday	Wednesday	Thursday	Friday	Saturday
Michaïel	Gabriel	Camael	Raphaël	Sachiel	Ana'el	Caffiel
name of the 4.ᵗʰ Heaven	name of the 1.ˢᵗ Heaven	name of the 5.ᵗʰ Heaven	name of the 2.ⁿᵈ Heaven	name of the 6.ᵗʰ Heaven	name of the 3.ʳᵈ Heaven	15 Angels ruling above the 6.ᵗʰ Heaven
Machen.	Shamain.	Machon.	Raquie.	Zebul.	Sagun.	

Sigils of the angels of the week, in column below names (FRANCIS BARRETT, *THE MAGUS*, 1801)

silver   The favored metal of contemporary Pagans and Witches for its associations with GODDESS, moon MAGIC, the female principle and the Goddess in winter. Silver reputedly possesses protective powers against negative influences and evil spirits and has been used since ancient times for AMULETS. The metal also is said to enhance psychic faculties. Some Witches prefer to wear all silver jewelry; many who wear gold also wear at least one piece of silver at the same time.

Silver, which appears in nature in a pure state and is an excellent conductor of electromagnetic energy, has always been valued in various societies and has long been used for magical and sacred purposes. The ancient Egyptians revered silver more than gold, for silver is not found in Egypt. The god Ra was said to have bones of silver. Egyptians used the metal to make scarabs, RINGS and other objects used in magical SPELLS.

Silver has a long association with the MOON. The Incas considered silver to be a divine quality rather than a metal substance. They associated silver with the luster of moonlight and called it the tears of the moon. In alchemy, the symbol of silver is a crescent moon; alchemists called the metal Luna or DIANA, after the Roman goddess of the Moon. In China, the Moon is known as the silver candle and the Milky Way is called the silver river.

Silver amulets repel evil spirits from persons, houses and buildings. In the folklore of parts of France, couples who are going to be married encircle themselves in a silver chain in order to avoid being bewitched en route to the church.

FURTHER READING:

Guiley, Rosemary Ellen. *Moonscapes: A Celebration of Lunar Astronomy, Magic, Legend and Lore.* New York: Prentice-Hall, 1991.

Leach, Maria, ed., and Jerome Fried, assoc. ed. *Funk & Wagnall's Standard Dictionary of Folklore, Mythology and Legend.* New York: Harper & Row, 1972.

Sixth and Seventh Books of Moses   A magical text of SPELLS and CONJURATIONS especially popular in the POWWOWING tradition among German settlers in America.

The *Sixth and Seventh Books of Moses*—also called the "Mystery of all Mysteries"—have more than 125 MAGIC CIRCLES, seals, TALISMANS and HEXENFOOS for summoning spirits and working spells such as luck, wealth, necromancy, healing, protection, CURSES and other magical purposes.

The text, based on kabbalistic magic, supposedly was written by Johann Scheibel, who lived in the late 18th century and was published posthumously in 1849 in Stuttgart, Germany. According to lore, the book was dictated by God to Moses on Mount Sinai but was omitted from the Old Testament because of its power. The book was passed down to Aaron, Caleb, Joshua, David and the magically powerful King Solomon.

German-language editions of the text were brought to America by immigrants and were translated into English by the early 19th century. They were favored by many powwowers, along with JOHN GEORGE HOHMAN's *The Long Lost Friend.*

Folk tales from Germany portray the book as powerful but dangerous if it falls into the wrong hands or is misused. One tale holds that no more magic or WITCH-CRAFT exist because the *Sixth and Seventh Books of Moses* is safely locked up in Wittenberg, Germany.

See BOOK OF SHADOWS; GRIMOIRES.

FURTHER READING:
Heindel, Ned D.. *Hexenkopf: History, Healing & Hexerei.* Easton, Pa.: Williams Township Historical Society, 2005.

Skelton, Robin (1925–1997)

Poet, author, professor and prominent Pagan in British Columbia, Canada. Robin Skelton also was known for his ghost investigations.

Skelton was born in 1925 in Easington, Yorkshire, England. His father, Cyril Skelton, was the headmaster of the village school. Robin was educated at Leeds University and Cambridge University. During World War II, he served in the Royal Air Force in India and Ceylon. Upon his return to England, he took a teaching position at Manchester University. There he founded the Peterloo group of artists and the Manchester Institute of Contemporary Arts.

In 1963, he emigrated to British Columbia and joined the English department of the University of Victoria. He was appointed professor in 1966. He founded and directed a creative writing program that became popular with poets. In 1967, he founded, with John Peter, *The Malahat Review,* now one of Canada's major literary journals.

Skelton was drawn to PAGANISM and used Pagan imagery in his own writing and poetry. He sometimes wrote under the pseudonym of a "French poet" Georges Zuk.

His involvement as an elder in Paganism earned him the title "Canada's Merlin." He died in 1997.

Skelton wrote more than 100 books during his career, among them books on Paganism, MAGIC, SPELLS, WITCH-CRAFT and ghosts. Some of his titles are *The Practice of Witchcraft Today: An Introduction to Beliefs and Rituals of the Old Religion* (d.n.); *A Gathering of Ghosts: Haunting and Exorcisms from the Personal Casebook of Robin Skelton and Jean Kozocari* (1989); *The Practice of Witchcraft* (1990); *Earth, Air, Fire, Water: Pre-Christian and Pagan Elements in British Songs, Rhymes and Ballads* (1991); *The Magical Practice of Talismans* (1993); *Spellcraft: A Handbook of Invocations, Blessings, Protections, Healing Spells* (1995); and *The Practice of Witchcraft Today: An Introduction to Beliefs and Rituals* (1995).

Slade, Paddy (1939–   )

English village witch or wise woman in the old hereditary tradition.

Paddy Slade was born Patricia Hadlow near Canterbury, Kent, on September 29, 1939, to Robert and Rose Hadlow. Her father was a sailor. She was the youngest of seven children, with three brothers and three sisters. She was nicknamed Paddy by her father.

Slade's mother—a Highland Scot—and her father's parents quietly practiced the old ways of the village witches or cunning men and women (see CUNNING MAN/CUN-NING WOMAN), which were absorbed by the young Paddy. Evidently destined for the path of the Witch, Slade had an initiatory visionary experience at the age of nine.

At the time, World War II was under way, and Canterbury was subjected to a 14-night blitz by the German Luftwaffe. Residents were evacuated as the city burned, and Slade's family went into the woods to sleep in tents. Slade describes the experience that happened one night:

> I don't know if it was a dream or it actually happened. It was very clear then and it is very clear to me now. I went out of the tent and started walking through the woods, which kept changing character. I came to a place where there was a stream. You don't get water on high chalk land, but here was this stream. All around were all the flowers that were ever seen in the woods, from the early spring right through the year. There were lots of animals—weasels, badgers, foxes and all sorts. I looked at them and at all the flowers, wondering why there were violets and briar roses at the same time.
>
> Then I became aware of a great figure on the other side of the stream. It seemed to me that he was dressed in black leather. He had magnificent antlers. I looked up at him and said, "Are we going to die?" He said, "No, you've got far too much to do and learn." He sat on the other side of the stream for awhile, telling me what I should know. Then he said, "I want you to meet somebody else."
>
> He took me across the stream and put me in front of him on his horse, and off we went, up into the sky, such a long way. We came to a lovely place. There was a beautiful woman sitting on a stone. She started telling me more about what I needed to know and learn. When she finished, I was put back on a horse and brought back to my little bed in the tent.
>
> In the morning I told only my mother about it. She said, "You've been lucky—you have met the Horned God and the Goddess. But you are only nine. You have got

Paddy Slade (COURTESY PADDY SLADE)

to go to school, you have got to live with other people. Don't forget about it, but keep it in the back of your mind. You are a very lucky girl."

Slade did not share the experience with others until much later in life. She told it to her husband, Pete, who said, "I think you met your God."

Slade went to Cambridge, graduating with a bachelor's degree in medieval history and English. After college, she joined the Signals branch of the Women's Royal Air Force.

While in the service, Slade met her husband, Philip (Pete) Slade. They married in 1955, and had two sons: Robert, born in 1956, and Peter, born in 1957. Military service took them abroad for several years to Singapore and Fiji.

After returning to England, husband Pete suffered a heart attack and died in 1962. As relatives and friends pressed her about what to do with her life, Slade decided to isolate herself by moving around to remote locations in the English countryside. For a time, she had no telephone. In 1982, she settled in a small village near Bath in Somerset, where she has remained to the present.

Immediately after Pete's death, Slade lived on Dartmoor. There she had a second profound visionary experience that was her self-initiation as a witch. Although interested in the old Craft ways all of her life, she had not overtly practiced as a "witch." One night she went out to the moor and found a natural magical circle with a standing stone. There she stayed all night and through the next day, having visionary encounters with a host of beings, including the HORNED GOD and GODDESS again; PUCK, who became her dominant guide; the spirits of the ELEMENTS; and other spirits.

The experience, she said, "shattered" her and left her significantly changed. She discovered an ability to attune to animals and trees, and to understand them (in folk tradition, the gift of understanding animals is bestowed by Puck when he takes a liking to a person). This especially aided her natural affinity with horses.

Slade embarked upon her path, developing her own methods for working magic. While she learned much from various teachers, including Dolores Ashcroft-Nowicki, her greatest teachers were nature and otherworldly beings. Education on the inner planes is characteristic of initiations in all great mystery traditions.

Slade advocates thoroughly experiencing the elements before practicing any kind of SPELLS or magic. Some of this must be done naked and alone for very short periods in order to relate to the elements in the depths of one's being. When one is thoroughly familiar with the elements and the rhythms of nature—it takes a year or two—then one is ready to learn magic. (She differentiates this nudity from the skyclad ritual nudity made popular by GERALD B. GARDNER, which Slade considers a modern invention and not true to the old ways.)

As for modern WICCA and Witchcraft as a religion, Slade feels that most individuals who enter this path are well-intentioned, but some do not know what they're doing, because they have not taken the time to educate themselves to the ways of nature: they get more caught up in artificial trappings and procedures than in real magic. Modern craft lore about covens, hierarchies, working tools and so on has little, if anything, to do with traditional witchcraft.

Slade has taught her craft to many students, offering a course in "the Old Wild Magic." She is sought for herbal and magical remedies. In recent years, she has decreased her teaching and concentrated on her private path, working magic with a few individuals.

Slade is the author of *To Thomas Monk with Grateful Thanks* (1972), a biographical and historical work; *Encyclopedia of White Magic* (1990); *Natural Magic* (1990), a book about old-fashioned magic with the elements; *Seasonal Magic: Diary of a Village Witch* (1997), a revision of *Natural Magic* that follows her original vision for the book, and *Tales Round the Cauldron* (2004).

See HEDGE WITCH; SOLITARY.

Slater, Herman (1938–1992) American Wiccan high priest and occult-bookstore proprietor and publisher, whose flamboyant style and out-spokenness earned him both admirers and critics. He viewed his role as "telling the truth" about WITCHCRAFT and PAGANISM "within the context of today's lifestyles."

Born in 1938, Slater grew up in a lower-middle-class Jewish neighborhood of New York. At an early age, he became aware of anti-Semitism on the part of the Catholic Church, which became one of the influences that led him to Witchcraft. He also was influenced to become politically active after seeing Frank Sinatra portray a politically strong figure in *The House I Live In*.

Slater studied business administration at New York University, liberal arts at Hunter College and traffic management at the Traffic Management Institute in New York. He completed a full course at the United States Navy Personnel School in Bainbridge, Maryland.

From 1958 to 1969 he worked in a series of business jobs in management, traffic expediting and insurance-claims investigation. In 1969 he was forced to quit work because he was suffering from tuberculosis of the bone, which cost him a hip bone and required three years of recuperation.

Slater began experiencing paranormal phenomena, including clairvoyance and a mysterious LEVITATION. The levitation occurred during his recuperation, in which he spent one year in bed in a body cast that weighed 300 pounds. One morning, he awoke and found himself, in his cast, stretched across a chair on the opposite side of the room. His paranormal experiences led him to the Craft, and in 1972 he was initiated (see INITIATION) into the New York Coven of Welsh Traditional Witches, of which Ed Buczynski was high priest.

Slater and Buczynski became public advocates for Witchcraft and opened a bookstore in Brooklyn, the War-

Herman Slater (COURTESY HERMAN SLATER)

lock Shop. For several years they published a periodical, *Earth Religion News*. Through an affiliate organization, Friends of the Craft, they presented awards to the Inquisitional Bigot of the Year. In 1972 Slater presented the award to NBC during a guest appearance on the *Today* show, for an episode of *Macmillan and Wife* that had taken Witchcraft rituals and corrupted them into Devil-worship rituals for the plot. The outraged *Today* crew had Slater physically removed from the set.

In 1974 Slater was initiated into the Gardnerian tradition (see GERALD B. GARDNER). He assumed leadership of the COVEN in the late 1970s and moved it and the bookstore to Manhattan. The coven was renamed Earthstar Temple, practicing a blend of Welsh and Gardernian traditions. The bookstore was renamed the Magickal Childe.

Slater devoted a great deal of time to educating others about Witchcraft. He was a frequent guest lecturer in area colleges. He starred in his own video, *An Introduction to Witchcraft and Satanism*, in which he appears in his ceremonial robe and antler headdress, along with his FAMILIAR, a snake named Herman. For awhile he hosted a weekly cable television show aired in Manhattan, *The Magickal Mystery Tour,* which featured interviews, rituals, music, occultism and magic instruction. Slater loosely defined

it as an "Earth religion 700 Club" because it spreads the word on the Old Religion and asked for donations.

A self-professed conservative who opposed drugs, promiscuity and love magic, he was blunt in his criticism of Witches and Pagans who indulged in drugs and sex magic—practices that began to wane in the 1980s. He acknowledged that such bluntness made him unpopular.

Slater is the author of *A Book of Pagan Rituals, The Magickal Formulary* and *The Magickal Formulary II.* He divided his time between Manhattan where he lived with three dogs, a cat and the snake and Ft. Lauderdale, Florida. His Craft name was Govanan.

He died on July 9, 1992, of AIDS.

solitary   A contemporary Pagan or Witch who practices a tradition and worships alone rather than as a member of a COVEN or group. During the early public years of Witchcraft (the 1960s into the 1970s), membership in covens was emphasized. To be considered a Witch, one had to be initiated by another Witch, and that usually meant joining a coven (see INITIATION). As Craft traditions changed and became more liberal, it became acceptable to initiate one's self. Some Witches feel initiations are ceremonial only and are not necessary to becoming a Witch or Pagan. Many solitaries have belonged to various covens or groups and have decided they prefer being alone; others opt to be solitaries to protect their privacy. The number of solitaries is not known.

See HEDGEWITCH.

sorcery   Systems of MAGIC, DIVINATION and SPELL-CASTING. The distinction between sorcery and witchcraft is often murky. Both have been nearly universal throughout history and have been defined with different shades of meaning. In many cases, the terms *sorcery* and *witchcraft* have been used interchangeably. During the witch hysteria in Europe, however, *witchcraft* was regarded as different from *sorcery*.

The word *sorcery* comes from the French *sors*, for "spell," and refers to the casting of SPELLS or the use of CHARMS to influence love, fertility, luck, health and wealth. The French word for "witch" is *sorcier*. In many societies, the assumption is made that spells have an evil purpose and that sorcerers cast spells against others for whom they have an unjustified hatred. Conversely, sorcery provides protection against other sorcery. Counter-sorcerers, WITCH DOCTORS or medicine men may be sought out to cast protective spells against the evil spells of other sorcerers, or to break evil spells.

Sorcery fulfills various needs in society, such as protecting people and livestock against disaster, outsiders and enemies; redressing wrongs and meting out justice; controlling the environment; and explaining frightening phenomena.

Sorcery is low MAGIC: it is not a set of beliefs, like high magic, but is mechanistic and intuitive. Some societies still make distinctions between sorcery and witchcraft. Many African tribes view witchcraft as thoroughly evil, while sorcery is close to religion. It is benevolent when performed for the good of society, such as protecting a village or tribe from the evil of enemy sorcerers or from natural disasters, but it is evil if performed for the gain of one individual at the expense of another. The Lugbara, however, view sorcery as more evil than witchcraft, for sorcerers use medicines against others, while witches direct only hostile emotions against others (see AFRICAN WITCHCRAFT). The Navajo associate witchcraft with death and the dead and sorcery with enchantment by spells; sorcerers, however, also kill others and participate in witches' SABBATS.

DIVINATION is related to sorcery. In some societies it is viewed as completely separate—performed by oracles, card readers, palm readers and the like—while in others it is considered a form of sorcery and is performed by sorcerers or witches.

Sorcerers, like witches, have long been accused of other evil, offensive behaviors: holding orgiastic nocturnal sabbats, conjuring the dead (see NECROMANCY), shape-shifting (see METAMORPHOSIS), cannibalism, night riding (see NIGHTMARE), owning and having sex with FAMILIARS and vampirism.

Anthropologists have attempted to distinguish sorcery from witchcraft by defining sorcery as harmful magic, usually illegitimate, that is performed by a professional, the sorcerer. The witch, on the other hand, is a person, usually female, who is believed to be inherently evil, born with the power to commit evil against others, and filled with anger and envy. Such a person has some physical characteristic to distinguish her as a witch, such as a mark, a substance within the body or the EVIL EYE. This definition stems from E. Evans-Pritchard, an anthropologist who did one of the first systematic studies of sorcery, among the Zande of Africa, in the early 20th century. The definition does not hold up for sorcery and witchcraft in all societies, and it does not fit contemporary Witchcraft.

In its simplest form, sorcery is magic by the manipulation of natural forces and powers to achieve a desired objective. Neolithic cave paintings depicting rituals for successful hunts give evidence that primitive peoples had a grasp of magic and practiced sorcery. One of the most famous examples is the *Sorcerer of Trois Frère* cave painting in France, a depiction of an antlered half-man half-beast or man in animal costume performing a ritualistic walk or dance. The figure may represent a sorcerer or a shaman preparing for a hunt or the god spirit of the forests or animals. The ancient Greeks believed that sorcerers called upon *daimones*, intermediary spirits between heaven and earth, to help them in their magic. Originally, *daimones* were neither good nor evil but could be swayed to either purpose (see DEMONS). Demons began to take on the aspects of evil with Plato's pupil, Xenocrates, who believed that the gods embodied good and *daimones* embodied evil.

By the sixth century B.C.E., sorcery was associated with fraud. As Christianity developed, sorcery became entangled with demonology, the system of demons who served the DEVIL.

European witchcraft grew out of sorcery, the casting of spells and divination. Until the INQUISITION, sorcery was considered a civil crime, punishable under civil law. By the 14th century, the church succeeded in linking sorcery to heresy, making sorcery an ecclesiastical crime. The most odious form of heretical sorcery was witchcraft, the performing of MALEFICIA in service to the DEVIL. The *MALLEUS MALEFICARUM* (1486), the leading witch-hunter's handbook of the INQUISITION, further strengthened the connection between sorcery and heresy and attributed most witchcraft to women.

During the late Middle Ages and Renaissance, the term *sorcerer* was also applied to men of high learning, such as alchemists and physicians, some of whom were believed to derive their knowledge from supernormal sources. Their conjuring of demons for knowledge or riches was not considered the same as a witch's conjuring of demons for *maleficia*. Royalty and popes were reputed to practice sorcery.

The European view of witchcraft as Devil-worship sorcery has lasted to present times. Contemporary Witches, who define their Witchcraft as GODDESS worship and benevolent magic for the good of others have sought to re-educate the public, which has proved to be a difficult task.

FURTHER READING:
Malinowski, Bronislaw. *Magic, Science and Religion*. Garden City, N.Y.: Doubleday Anchor Books, 1948.
Marwick, Max, ed. *Witchcraft and Sorcery*. New York: Viking Penguin, 1982.
Rush, John A. *Witchcraft and Sorcery*. Springfield, Ill.: Charles C. Thomas, 1974.
Russell, Jeffrey Burton. *Witchcraft in the Middle Ages*. Ithaca and London: Cornell University Press, 1972.

Spare, Austin Osman (1888–1956)   English artist and magician, known for his strange and sometimes frightening art. Austin Osman Spare was called a genius in art, but he turned away from a conventional artist's career to create images of DEMONS and atavisms, spirits raised up from deep levels of consciousness.

Spare was born on December 31, 1888, in London; his father was a City of London policeman. He left school at age 13 and worked for a time in a stained-glass factory. He obtained a scholarship to the Royal College of Art in Kensington and enjoyed success as an artist by 1909.

The seeds for Spare's occult life were sown early in childhood. Alienated from his mother by age 16, he gravitated toward a mysterious older woman named Mrs. Margaret Paterson. They met in 1902 when Paterson was working as a fortune-teller in London. She claimed to be a hereditary witch descended from a line of Salem witches who escaped execution during the witch trials in 1692, which was unlikely. Spare called her his "witch-mother." Later, he said that she possessed great skill in DIVINATION and had the ability to materialize spirits and her thoughts at will for long periods of time. According to Spare, Paterson would sometimes mentally project visions of the future that she saw for clients. The visions would be visible in a dark corner of the room. He said they always came true.

Spare said Paterson could change her shape from an old woman to a beautiful, seductive young woman. He did nude paintings of her in both guises. (See METAMORPHOSIS.)

Paterson taught Spare how to visualize and evoke spirits and ELEMENTALS and how to reify his dream imagery. She also initiated Spare in a witches' SABBAT, which he described as taking place in another dimension, where cities were constructed of an unearthly geometry. Spare said he attended such sabbats several times.

Under further tutelage of Mrs. Paterson on the MAGIC of SIGILS, Spare developed his own system of magic, based heavily on will and sex—his own sex drive was quite intense—and the works of ALEISTER CROWLEY.

Spare believed that the power of will is capable of fulfilling any deeply held desire. The formula, simpler than ceremonial magic, was in his unpublished GRIMOIRE, *The Book of the Living Word of Zos*. The formula called for creating sigils or TALISMANS in an "alphabet of desire." The desire is written down in full. Repeating letters are crossed out and the remaining letters are combined into a sigil like a sort of monogram. The sigil is impressed upon the subconscious by staring at it. The original desire is then let go so that the "god within" can work undisturbed toward the desired end.

According to one story, Spare once told a friend he would conjure freshly cut roses to fall from the air. His magic involved creating some symbolic drawings, which he waved in the air while repeating "roses." He got results, but they were unexpected—the plumbing in the room overhead burst, and Spare and his friend were dowsed by sewage.

In his strange art, Spare is best known for his atavisms, the reifying of primal forces from previous existences, drawn from the deepest layers of the human mind. This too was a product of his education from Paterson. According to another story, one of his atavisms caused the suicide of one witness and the insanity of another.

Despite his ability to paint the spirits and images he saw, Spare was occasionally at a loss for words to describe some of his more bizarre experiences. Some of his visions put him into a place that he was able only to describe as "spaces beyond space." He said he was never able to duplicate Paterson's exceptional ability to manifest.

Spare spent most of his life as a recluse, living in poverty in London. He was remote and detached, preferring the company of his cats to that of human beings. He is considered a source of modern chaos magic.

In 1941, during World War II, his studio received a direct bomb hit and was destroyed. Spare was severely injured. He was paralyzed on his right side and lost the use of both arms. Within six months, he had regained the use of his right arm, and he resumed his art. For the rest of his life, he struggled with physical impairment and failing health, yet enjoyed one of his best periods as an artist.

In 1956, Spare was contacted by GERALD B. GARDNER for his help in a magical war with Kenneth Grant, a protégé of Crowley's. Gardner believed that Grant was stealing his witches for his own New Isis Lodge, and he decided to launch a magical attack on him and reclaim his witches. In particular, Gardner wanted back a self-proclaimed "water-witch" named Clanda. It was the last year of Spare's life, and by then he was living in dire poverty and obscurity, eking out a living by painting portraits in local pubs.

Using his "alphabet of desire," Spare created a talisman for Gardner that would "restore lost property to its rightful place," which Spare himself described as "a sort of amphibious owl with the wings of a bat and talons of an eagle." Gardner did not give Spare specific information as to the exact nature of the "lost property"; he knew that Spare and Grant were on friendly terms.

During a Black Isis rite at the New Isis Temple, Clanda experienced the apparent negative effects of the talisman. Her role was to lie passively on the altar. Instead she sat up, sweating and with a hypnotized and glazed look in her eyes. She behaved as though in the grip of terror, convulsing and shuddering. Later she described what she experienced: the appearance of a huge bird that gripped her in its talons and carried her off into the night. She struggled and broke free, falling back onto the altar. The attending magicians saw none of this, but they did hear what sounded like the talons of a large bird scrabbling against the wind, and they felt a cold wind rush about the room. Talon marks were found on the window frame, and the windowsill was covered with a strange, gelatinous substance that seemed to breathe on its own. A strong odor of the sea permeated the temple for days.

Clanda did not return to Gardner. Instead, she moved to New Zealand, where she later drowned.

Spare died on May 15, 1956, in a London hospital.

Some of Spare's work appears in two quarterly art review magazines he edited, *Form* and *Golden Hind*. He wrote three books that were published: *The Book of Pleasure (Self-love), the Psychology of Ecstasy* (1913), and *The Focus of Life* (1921), both of which dealt with his magic system, and *A Book of Automatic Drawing*, published posthumously in 1972.

FURTHER READING:
"Austin Osman Spare." Available online. URL: http://www.fulgur.co.uk/authors/aos/. Downloaded November 20, 2007.
"Austin Osman Spare Obituary." Available online. URL: http://www.fulgur.co.uk/authors/aos/articles/obit/. Downloaded November 20, 2007.

Grimassi, Raven. *The Encyclopedia of Wicca & Witchcraft.* 2nd ed. St. Paul, Minn.: Llewellyn Publications, 2003.

Guiley, Rosemary Ellen. *The Encyclopedia of Witches and Witchcraft.* 2nd ed. New York: Facts On File, 1999.

King, Francis. *Megatherion: The Magickal World of Aleister Crowley.* New York: Creation Books, 2004.

Spee, Friedrich von (1591–1635)   German Jesuit and poet who, in the course of serving as confessor to witches during the trials in Würzburg, became revolted by the TORTURE and execution of innocent people. Spee wrote and anonymously published *Cautio Criminalis,* an exposé of the fraud in witch trials, which may have influenced the decline of witch-hunts in subsequent years.

Spee was born in Kaiserwerth. He was educated at the Jesuit College in Cologne and entered the order in 1611. Further studies included philosophy in Würzburg and theology in Mainz. In 1624 Spee was sent to Paderborn as a preacher; in 1627 he was sent back to Würzburg, where he worked as a professor.

During the 1620s the witch hysteria was reaching its peak in Germany, especially in the communities of Bamberg, Würzburg, Mainz, Cologne, Baden and Brandenburg. The prince-bishops of Würzburg and Bamberg were particularly zealous about hunting down and burning witches and, encouraged by the Jesuits, they executed about 1,500 persons between them (see BAMBERG WITCHES).

It was Spee's duty to serve as confessor to the condemned in Würzburg. He began his job believing that real witches, servants of the DEVIL, did exist. But in the course of watching one after another victim be condemned with no hope of a fair trial, Spee began to change his views. While he continued to believe that a few witches did exist, he became convinced that none of them had been found in Würzburg. The flimsy evidence and brutal torture sickened him. By the time he was 30, his hair was nearly white—"through grief," he explained, "over the many witches whom I have prepared for death; not one was guilty."

Spee observed that the slightest hint of witchcraft was sufficient to condemn a person to death and that once the accusation was made, there was no hope of escape. If the accused had led an unpious life, she was certainly a witch; if she had led a good life, she also was a witch, because witches deceived others by appearing to be virtuous. If the defendant broke down readily under torture, it was proof of witchery; if she didn't, that was proof, too. If she died under torture, it was said that the Devil broke her neck, and that also was proof. Spee said:

> Often I have thought that the only reason why we are not all wizards is due to the fact that we have not all been tortured. And there is truth in what an inquisitor dared to boast lately, that if he could reach the Pope, he would make him confess that he was a wizard.

Spee also was concerned about the ever-widening ripple effects of the trials. Victims were always forced to name accomplices, and Spee feared that, as the trials mounted, "there is nobody in our day, of whatsoever sex, fortune, rank, or dignity, who is safe, if he have but an enemy and slanderer to bring him into suspicion of witchcraft."

On 1631 Spee anonymously published *Cautio Criminalis* ("Precautions for Prosecutors"), in which he savagely attacked the witch-hunters and exposed their methods. He pointed out that there was great incentive among the inquisitors to condemn as many persons as possible, since they were paid a fee per witch burned, plus whatever they could confiscate from the victims' assets. He exposed the claims of confessions without torture as lies; "no torture" in fact meant light torture, and while that in itself was severe, it was nothing compared to the torture that would follow if a victim persisted in a claim of innocence. Spee wrote:

> She can never clear herself. The investigating committee would feel disgraced if it acquitted a woman; once arrested and in chains, she has to be guilty, by fair means or foul.
>
> Meanwhile, ignorant and headstrong priests harass the wretched creature so that, whether truly or not, she will confess herself guilty; unless she does so, they say, she cannot be saved or partake of the sacraments.

Although *Cautio Criminalis* was published anonymously, Spee's authorship was generally known within Jesuit circles, and the book was denounced by many of his order. Despite attempts to suppress it, the book was translated into French, Dutch and Polish and disseminated throughout the Continent. Witch trials continued at a fevered pace for some 30 years after the book's first appearance, then began to abate.

Spee was sent to Treves as a parish priest. He died on August 7, 1635, just 44 years old, a victim of the plague.

FURTHER READING:
Midelfort, H. C. Erik. *Witch Hunting in Southwestern Germany 1562–1684.* Stanford, Calif.: Stanford University Press, 1972.

Trevor-Roper, H. R. *The European Witch-Craze.* New York: Harper & Row, 1957.

spell   A spoken or written formula that, in an act of MAGIC, is intended to cause or influence a course of events. Belief in and use of spells have been universal since ancient times and have been an integral part of religious practices. Methods vary according to culture, but all spell work is based on RITUAL.

Spells are closely related to PRAYER, which is a ritual consisting of a petition to a deity or deities for a desired outcome, and which involves visualization of the goal, statement of desire for the goal and ritualized movements or body positions (e.g., bowing of head, folding or clasp-

The Devil gives poppets to witches for spell-casting, 15th century

ing of hands, closing of eyes). Spells are also related to various methods of mind power such as "creative visualization," "positive thinking" and "positive imaging," all of which emphasize mental images, identification with mental images, a clear goal, repetition of one's intent to achieve this goal, projection of will and invocation of the aid of spirits, deities or the Divine Force.

Spells may be beneficial or harmful, and they may be worked on people, animals and nature. The purposes are limitless and include healing, love, money, success, fertility, longevity, protection from disaster, ill fortune and evil, exorcism of ghosts and spirits (see SPIRIT EXORCISM), victory in battle, truth in DIVINATION, weather control and accomplishment of supernatural feats. When directed against enemies, spells are used to cause illness, destruction, loss of love, impotence, barrenness, failure and even death. One may cast a spell for oneself, or one may direct a spell against another person. A positive spell is a blessing. Archaic terms for spells include bewitchment and enchantment; negative spells generally are called hexes or curses. A binding spell is one intended to prevent harm or disaster, or to stop someone from performing particular act: for example, stopping murder or rape, as in the case of serial criminals, or even stopping the spread of gossip.

Witches, sorcerers (see SORCERY), WITCH DOCTORS, and other magically empowered persons cast both beneficial and harmful spells, according to need. In contemporary Paganism and Witchcraft, ethics prohibit CURSES. Pagans and Witches are divided as to the acceptability of binding spells (see WICCAN REDE).

Anatomy of a spell. An act of magic requires a practitioner; a RITUAL; and a spell. The spell consists of words or incantations (sometimes called a CHARM or rune); the rit-

ual is a set of actions done while the words are being spoken. The ancient Egyptians believed words were so powerful that speaking them would bring about the desired goal. Words and NAMES OF POWER were vital to Egyptian magic and had to be pronounced correctly and with the proper intonation. In Western magic, the ultimate NAME of power is the Tetragrammaton, YHWH (Yahweh), the sacred name of God.

A spell-casting ritual raises power through a combination of visualization, meditation, identification, body movement, incantation (statement of goal), petition to deities and projection of will. The success of a spell rests on the power and will raised and the skill with which they are focused and projected. Words, chants, songs, movements and use of objects such as ritual tools, effigies, POPPETS, cords, CANDLES, or HAIR AND NAILS facilitate spell casting.

In ancient India, many spells were sung. Ancient Jain wizards had numerous spells named after various animals and fowl; presumably by uttering a spell, a WIZARD could change a person into that animal or bird. The Indians of South America use powerful chants in virtually every magical ritual; certain spells are believed to assume human shape and carry out orders.

In contemporary Witchcraft, spell casting is done within a MAGIC CIRCLE. Many covens work spells as part of their regular meetings, and each coven is likely to have its own techniques. The goal of the spell is stated; some Witches write it down. The act of writing down a desired goal, which is emphasized in positive-thinking techniques, helps to bolster the will to achieve the goal. Preparations are made for the ritual, such as the lighting of colored candles or the mixing of magical OILS. In a healing or love ritual, an herb-filled poppet, or cloth doll, may be used. The doll is identified with the person who is the object of

Witches setting a village afire (WOODCUT FROM FRANCESCO-MARIA GUAZZO'S *COMPENDIUM MALEFICARUM,* 1608)

the spell so that it becomes the person during the ritual. To aid the identification, the doll may be marked with the person's name or astrological sign or have attached to it hair clippings from the person. Photographs also are used. If there is no object, a thought-form, or mental image, is created. If the spell is cast by a group, all must agree upon the image and hold it firmly in their minds.

Power is raised in various ways, including CHANTING, dancing, tying KNOTS in cords or hand clapping. Drums and rattles may be used. Witches invite higher forces to work with them in implementing the spell, usually an aspect of the GODDESS or HORNED GOD, and the forces of the ELEMENTS. An aspect of the deity is chosen that best fits the nature of the spell. For example, a spell for money might be addressed to Math, god of wealth and increase.

Spells and charms are contained in many books on Witchcraft, folk magic and magic. While they may be effective, most Witches feel that words composed from the heart are best. The recitation of a chant or charm alone will not successfully cast a spell.

While performing the ritual, the Witch focuses intense concentration and will in achieving the goal, visualizing it and believing it is already accomplished. When the psychic power is at its peak, it is released and directed toward the goal. The spell work ends with a psychic cleanup ritual to banish remnants of psychic energy. The Witch thanks the deity and forces of the elements.

See CONE OF POWER.

FURTHER READING:
Buckland, Raymond. *Buckland's Complete Book of Witchcraft.* St. Paul: Llewellyn Publications, 1986.
Farrar, Janet, and Stewart Farrar. *A Witches Bible Compleat.* New York: Magickal Childe, 1984.
Luhrmann, T. M. *Persuasions of the Witch's Craft: Ritual Magic in Contemporary England.* Cambridge: Harvard University Press, 1989.

spider   In folk MAGIC, a black spider eaten every morning between two slices of buttered bread will endow one with great strength and power. According to lore, witches could raise storms at sea by catching spiders in pots (see STORM RAISING).

Spiders are ingredients in numerous folk remedies around the world. Spiders caught while weaving are considered all-around AMULETS against disease. In English lore, a spider carried in a silk bag around the neck will help ward off contagious diseases. Old ague remedies prescribed ingesting live spiders that were rolled in either butter, molasses or cobwebs.

The weaving of the spider is associated with creativity, imagination, destiny and the waxing and waning of the MOON. In some myths, the Moon is portrayed as a spider.

In some cultures, it is considered very unlucky to kill spiders. Tahitians believe spiders are the shadows of gods and take great care never to harm them.

FURTHER READING:
Leach, Maria, ed., and Jerome Fried, assoc. ed. *Funk & Wagnall's Standard Dictionary of Folklore, Mythology and Legend.* New York: Harper & Row, 1972.
Opie, Iona, and Moira Tatem. *A Dictionary of Superstitions.* New York: Oxford University Press, 1989.

spirit exorcism   Dismissal or expulsion of an interfering spirit. SPIRIT EXORCISMS are performed in many cultures when human problems are deemed to be caused by spirits, including the dead. "Spirit releasement" is a modern term preferred by many in the West, as it avoids religious connotations.

Spirit exorcists may perform several "persuasive departures" in one day, depending on the intuitive ability and strength of the exorcist. Working with spirits, the exorcist comes to realize the sensations associated with such restless entities, usually described as vibrations or a feeling of cold. Some entities emit odors, like stale flowers or worse.

The late Dr. Carl A. Wickland was one of the most famous Western practitioners of persuasive exorcism. Wickland believed that possession occurred when a discarnate entity blundered, confusedly, into a living person's aura and became trapped. Using the services of his wife Anna, a medium, Wickland coaxed the spirit out of its victim and into his wife, through whom he communicated with it.

Witches sometimes are called upon to perform releasement, of ghosts and remnants of unwanted psychic or spiritual energy. Spirit exorcisms, as cures to illness and solution to a wide range of personal problems, are common throughout the world.

FURTHER READING:
Crabtree, Adam. *Multiple Man, Explorations in Possession and Multiple Personality.* New York:Praeger, 1985.
Rogo, D. Scott. *The Infinite Boundary.* New York: Dodd, Mead & Co., 1987.
Wickland, Carl. *Thirty Years Among the Dead.* 1924; Reprint, N. Hollywood: Newcastle Publishing Co., 1974.

spirit possession   Unlike demonic possession, in which a person is taken over by devils or evil spirits for harm, spirit possession is a voluntary, culturally sanctioned displacement of personality. The spirits—which may be deities, angels, DEMONS, "advanced" entities or the dead—are invited to enter a human being to communicate with the living. Mediumship and channeling are forms of spirit possession. The person may maintain awareness or be in a deep trance.

In some societies, spirit possession is practiced by oracles and prophets, who go into trance and become possessed by deities in order to see the future. In certain shamanic traditions, shamans become possessed for prophecy and healing, the latter of which involves driving or sucking evil spirits out of the sick. Most shamans, however, control spirits rather than allow themselves to become possessed by them (see SHAMANISM).

In Witchcraft the rituals of DRAWING DOWN THE MOON and Drawing Down the Sun are a form of TEMPORARY spirit possession. The rituals involve the invoking of the GODDESS (Moon) into the high priestess and the God (Sun) into the high priest, who may then speak in trance.

For many people, the concept of possession by various gods serves as an important part of religious worship. To be possessed means that the god has found a person worthy to receive the spirit of the god. In India, possession by spirits permeates daily life. Most often the possessed person is a woman, who attributes all sorts of personal problems—menstrual pain, the death of children, barrenness, miscarriage, her husband's infidelities—to the intervention of the spirits. In many cases the woman has little family support and perhaps suffers harsh treatment from her husband, father or brothers, and so possession by a spirit gains her sympathy instead of condemnation for her troubles.

Others find they can control their relatives, large crowds, and even gain for themselves gifts of money, food or liquor. In some cases, subservient women use the possessed state to castigate their husbands and make them act more kindly. In such cultures, possession provides liberation for the women, allowing them to ask for more material goods and attention, air grievances, be more sexual and achieve some parity in their male-dominated societies (see AFRICAN WITCHCRAFT).

In VODUN, the possession of the faithful by the various gods is called "mounting the horse"—the horse being the victim who "manifests" the spirit, who "rides" him or her. Spirit possessions usually last only as long as the ceremonies, brought on by the feverish excitement of fast-beating drums and chanting. Similar possessions take place in SANTERÍA and MACUMBA. In Haiti, if someone becomes recurrently possessed, at any time and any place, he or she is not considered to be filled with the spirit of the gods but to be psychologically unbalanced.

Spirit possession also occurs in Christianity. The word *enthusiastic* originally meant being filled with the holy spirit. After the crucifixion and resurrection of Jesus Christ, on the first day of Pentecost, the Apostles were said to be possessed by the Holy Spirit. Fire appeared above their heads, and they spoke in different languages, or tongues, than those they knew. Speaking in tongues in an ecstatic state characterized early Christian worship, but by the Middle Ages it represented demonic possession more often than saintly enthusiasm.

In modern Christian worship, the Pentecostal movement has revived interest in speaking in tongues and ecstatic communion with God. The movement began on January 1, 1901 (the first day of the 20th century), when a group of Bethel College, Topeka, Kansas, reportedly received the Spirit. Various sects have sought communi-cation with the Lord in this manner, with the so-called Holy Rollers being perhaps the most famous in the first part of this century. Worshipers rolled and writhed on the floor, putting themselves in a state of self-induced hypnosis, and prayed that the Spirit would come to them. The congregation considered those who received the Spirit as blessed, much like the worshipers during a Vodun rite praise those who have been mounted by a god. Earlier critics of such worship would have found the participants possessed. The largest group of Pentecostals in the United States is the Assemblies of God, with thousands of members worldwide.

In Spiritualism, some trance mediums allow themselves to be possessed by spirits who speak through them. In some Spiritualist churches, spirit-possessed mediums deliver sermons in trance, as well as messages from the dead to members of the congregation. Channeling involves the invoking of highly evolved entries, who "possess" the channeler in order to speak to a human audience.

FURTHER READING:

Crabtree, Adam. *Multiple Man, Explorations in Possession and Multiple Personality*. New York: Praeger, 1985.
Rogo, D. Scott. *The Infinite Boundary*. New York: Dodd, Mead & Co., 1987.
Wickland, Carl. *Thirty Years Among the Dead*. 1924. Reprint, N. Hollywood: Newcastle Publishing Co., 1974.

spittle   A key ingredient in many SPELLS and CURSES. One way to throw a curse is to spit on a stone and rub it while reciting the curse. In Lapland lore, illness and misfortune can be brought upon a person by spitting three times upon a knife and then rubbing the knife on the victim. Another Lapland spell for dooming someone to destruction calls for tying three KNOTS in a linen towel in the name of the DEVIL, spitting on them and naming the victim.

Marquesan sorcerers spit into leaves and bury them while reciting incantations against enemies. Malay sorcerers place spit, BLOOD, URINE and excrement on clay effigies, which they roast to curse a victim to death (see SORCERY). Necromancers sometimes spit as part of their rituals for conjuring the spirits of the dead (see NECROMANCY).

In other folk MAGIC beliefs, the saliva of the victim is believed to boost the power of the spell. Therefore, some people believe it is unwise to spit indiscreetly, as it enables DEMONS to capture one's saliva and use it for evil purpose. Among the tribes of East Africa, South Africa and New Zealand, spittle is hidden lest it fall into the hands of a sorcerer.

European witch-hunters believed that witches could not shed tears but would try to fool inquisitors by smearing their cheeks with spittle.

In folk magic, spitting is a universal defense against the EVIL EYE, bad luck, illness and witchcraft. Practices that date back to early Roman times include spitting in the right shoe every morning; spitting into the toilet after urination; spitting on the breast or on the ground three times; and spitting while passing any place where danger might exist. Pliny records the effectiveness of spittle against various disorders, such as boils, eye infections, epilepsy and leprosy.

Spittle is especially potent in protecting infants and children against fascination (another term for evil eye). In Italy, persons who are suspected of overlooking children (casting the evil eye on them) are asked to spit in their faces to nullify the harm done.

The custom of spitting into the hands before a fight in order to make the blows stronger dates back to early Roman times. Spitting salted water at haunted locations protects one from any negative presences.

FURTHER READING:

Leach, Maria, ed., and Jerome Fried, assoc. ed. *Funk & Wagnall's Standard Dictionary of Folklore, Mythology and Legend.* New York: Harper & Row, 1972.

Mickaharic, Draja. *A Century of Spells.* York Beach, Me.: Samuel Weiser, 1988.

Parrinder, Geoffrey. *Witchcraft European and African.* London: Faber & Faber, 1970.

Sprenger, James   See MALLEUS MALIFICARUM.

sprite trap   Magical device used to entangle and entrap troublesome or harmful spirits, ghosts and the unquiet dead. The sprite trap is made of a blackthorn stave and copper wire that has never carried electricity. In a magical procedure, the wire is bound to the stave with RED thread and the stave is marked with a Dag (or D) rune. At night, the trap is set at the entrance to a home, church, graveyard or other location where disturbances take place. A cleft blackthorn stave with a lighted candle is set in front of the trap to attract the undesirable entity.

When the trap has ensnared a spirit, it is removed and the thread is cut with a consecrated knife. The thread is placed into a prepared WITCH BOTTLE. If the purpose of the bottle is to imprison the spirit, a spell such as this is recited while the thread is placed in it:

> Thread, tie up this sprite,
> Free us from its spite,
> Tangel up the bane,
> Let not a jiece [small piece] remain,
> Ka!

The bottle is then corked and sealed with red wax. It is buried and a thorn bush is planted on the site. The bottle must never be opened or broken, lest a very angry spirit escape.

FURTHER READING:

Pennick, Nigel. *Secrets of East Anglican Magic.* London: Robert Hale, 1995.

Stacker Lee (also Stagolee, Stackerlee, Stackalee)   In American folklore, a black man who entered into a DEVIL'S PACT and brought about his own undoing. By selling his soul, Stacker Lee obtained a magical Stetson hat, which enabled him to metamorphose into various shapes, from animals to mountains (see METAMORPHOSIS); to have great prowess with women; and to have mastery over fire: he could walk on hot slag and eat flames. But the supernatural powers swelled Stacker Lee's ego to the point where even the Devil found him to be unbearably obnoxious, and so the Devil arranged for him to lose his hat. The hat was stolen in a barroom by Billy Lyon (also Billy Lion or Billy Galion). In a rage, Stacker Lee shot Billy to death and ultimately went to hell himself.

FURTHER READING:

American Folklore and Legend. Pleasantville, N.Y.: Reader's Digest Assn., 1978.

Stamford Witches (1692)   Witch trials in Stamford, Connecticut, in which a servant girl accused six women of afflicting her with fits. Nevertheless, two of the accused came close to being put to death on slender "evidence," in the zeal of officials to avoid a panic of the type that had occurred at Salem.

The ordeal of the Stamford Witches began in the spring of 1692, when Katherine Branch, a 17-year-old French servant of Daniel Wescot, was seized with severe fits. It is possible that she suffered from epilepsy, but such fits were blamed on witchcraft at that time.

In late April, Branch had been out gathering herbs when she experienced a "pinching and pricking at her breast," according to case records. She went home and burst into tears. Upon Wescot's questioning, she said she had seen a CAT who had promised her "fine things" if she would go with it. Several days later, she saw ten cats who threatened to kill her for telling about her experience in the fields.

Visions and fits continued for 13 days, until Branch denounced Goodwife Elizabeth Clauson as a witch who was causing Branch's troubles. Clauson was a highly respected pillar of the community but had been involved in a long, ongoing dispute with Mrs. Wescot over a quantity of spun flax.

Wescot summoned a midwife, who said Branch's fits might be due to a natural cause. But when the girl did not respond to treatments, which included burning feathers under her nose and bleeding, the midwife became convinced she was bewitched.

Thus encouraged, Branch cried out against five other women: Mercy Disborough, Mary and Hannah Harvey, Mary Staples and Goody Miller. Wescot's wife suspected Branch of fabricating elaborate lies; nevertheless, a court of inquiry into the matter began hearings on May 27, 1692.

The accused women emphatically denied that they were witches. Goody Miller fled to New York Colony in order to avoid being arrested. The two prime suspects, Clauson and Disborough, were searched more than once for WITCH'S MARKS). Nothing was found on Clauson save a wart that was judged normal, but Disborough exuded several "unnatural" excrescences that were held in evidence against her. Meanwhile, Branch continued having her fits.

The matter was deemed serious enough for a special trial, and the women were jailed while testimony was gathered. Two ministers questioned Branch, who cried out against Clauson, "You kill me, you kill me."

The trial opened on September 14, and Clauson and Disborough were swiftly indicted by a grand jury which proclaimed, "by the law of God and the law of the Colony, thou deseruest [deserve] to dye." The two women pleaded not guilty.

Staples and the two Harvey women were considered to be only under suspicion of witchcraft. The court invited people to step forward and testify against them, but only two persons did, and the three were acquitted.

Disborough insisted on being given the swimming test, which was not commonly administered in American witchcraft trials. She and Clauson were bound and thrown into water. Both floated "like a corck," a sign of guilt (see SWIMMING).

The prosecution presented numerous depositions it had collected, all against the two accused, which was not surprising in light of the prevailing belief that to testify on behalf of an accused witch meant being in league with the Devil as well. However, two longtime neighbors of Clauson's did step forward and testify in her favor.

Perhaps encouraged by this bravery, others stepped forward in Clauson's defense. Seventy-six Stamford residents signed a petition attesting to her good character and behavior.

The jury deliberated long and hard and was unable to reach a verdict. A committee of five prominent ministers was called in to examine the trial records and evidence. In their formal opinion, they stated that swimming was sinful and unlawful and could not be used as evidence; that Disborough's excrescences should not be allowed as evidence unless so decreed by "some able physitians"; that they suspected Branch of lying; and that Branch's fits might be related to the same condition that afflicted her mother.

The jury was reconvened in Fairfield on October 28 and heard additional testimony. By this time, 19 accused witches had been hanged in Salem, 100 were in jail and some 200 more had been accused of witchcraft, all of which must have had some effect on everyone concerned in the trial. They jury convicted Disborough and sentenced her to die but did find Clauson not guilty. Clauson was set free from jail and returned to Stamford, where she lived with her family until her death, at age 83, in 1714.

After the trial, friends of Disborough petitioned the court, claiming the second part of the trial was illegal because one of the original jurors had been missing. An investigating committee reprieved Disborough.

FURTHER READING:
Marcus, Ronald. *"Elizabeth Clawson, Thou Deseruest to Dye."* Stamford, Conn.: Communication Corp., 1976.

Starhawk (1951–)   American Witch, feminist, and peace activist whose popular books have influenced thousands of people to discover their inner power and spirituality and to join WITCHCRAFT and PAGANISM. Starhawk is cofounder of Reclaiming, an activist branch of Paganism.

Starhawk holds a master's degree in psychology from Antioch West University. She was taught Witchcraft while she was a student in college. Most of Starhawk's awakening and spiritual knowledge came in shamanic fashion from her own dream and trance experiences.

Starhawk had a Jewish upbringing (her grandparents were Orthodox Jews) that emphasized intellectual freedom. By the 1960s, she saw no future for women in Judaism—there were not yet any women rabbis. In the late 1960s, while attending college, she undertook an anthropology project on witchcraft. She met women who practiced Celtic Witchcraft and realized that Witchcraft reflected her own beliefs.

In 1975, she moved to San Francisco, where she met VICTOR ANDERSON, founder of the Faery tradition, at a COVENANT OF THE GODDESS meeting. She asked to study with him and later was initiated by him into the Faery tradition.

She practiced as a SOLITARY for years before forming her first COVEN, Compost, from a group of men and women

Starhawk (COURTESY STARHAWK)

who attended a class in Witchcraft that she taught at the Bay Area Center for Alternative Education in the San Francisco area. After organizing, the coven performed a formal initiation ceremony.

She formed another coven, Honeysuckle, comprised entirely of women. Rituals for both covens were based on the Faery tradition. Though feminist, her rituals included men and led to an increasing contact between feminist women and men in Witchcraft and Paganism.

Starhawk has taught at several Bay Area colleges. From 1993 to 1996 she was a lecturer at the Institute for Culture and Creation Spirituality at Holy Names College in Oakland, run by a Dominican priest Matthew Fox. In 1988, Cardinal Joseph Ratzinger attempted to have her ousted from the faculty as part of the silencing of Fox for his nonconformist views on creation spirituality.

Starhawk campaigns for a new political agenda for sacred values: peace, a community that honors diversity, family unity, self-determination, sound environmental practices, and social justice. She lives part-time in San Francisco and part-time in Sonoma County, where she practices permaculture (permanent agriculture). She travels internationally to lecture and give workshops. With Penny Livingston-Stark and Erik Ohlsen, she cote-aches EAT, Earth Activist Training, a seminar on permaculture, political activism, and Earth-based spirituality. She sees environmentalism as vitally important to Paganism, which celebrates the sacred embodied in the Earth and the human community.

Her first book, *The Spiral Dance: A Rebirth of the Ancient Religion of the Great Goddess* (1979), was based on the Faery tradition and was widely acclaimed throughout Paganism. Special editions were published for the book's 10th and 20th anniversaries, in which Starhawk discussed the evolution of the broader Pagan movement and compared it to similar traditions among Native Americans, African-Americans, and indigenous peoples.

Her other published nonfiction books are *Dreaming the Dark* (1982); *Truth or Dare: Encounters of Power, Authority and Mystery* (1987), which won the Media Alliance Meritorious Achievement Award for nonfiction in 1988; *Circle Round: Raising Children in the Goddess Tradition,* with Anne Hill and Diane Baker (1998); *The Twelve Swans: A Journey to the Realms of Magic, Healing and Action* (2000), coauthored with Hilary Valentine; and *The Earth Path: Grounding Your Spirit in the Rhythms of Nature* (2004). *Webs of Power: Notes from the Global Uprising* (2003) is a collection of her political essays that won the Nautilus Award from the trade association NAPRA in the year it was published. She is a contributor to the anthology *The Pagan Book of Living and Dying* (1997).

Film and documentary credits include her work as a consultant for *Goddess Remembered* and *The Burning Times,* and coauthorship with Donna Read of the commentary for *Full Circle,* all produced by the National Film Board of Canada. Starhawk and Read formed their own film company, Belili Productions. Their first film, *Signs Out of Time* (2004), featured the life of archaeologist Marija Gimbutas.

Her fiction credits include *The Fifth Sacred Thing* (1993), winner of the Lambda award for best Gay and Lesbian Science Fiction in 1994, and *Walking to Mercury* (1997). In addition Starhawk has recorded several CDs based on her teachings. She has written songs and chants used by others in RITUALS.

FURTHER READING:
Hopman, Ellen Evert, and Lawrence Bond. *Being a Pagan: Druids, Wiccans and Witches Today.* Rochester, Vt.: Destiny Books, 2002.

Starhawk official Web site. Available online. URL: http://www.starhawk.org. Downloaded November 2, 2007.

stones   Stones are credited with many MAGIC, HEALING and lucky properties. Semi-precious stones are used in AMULETS to ward off the EVIL EYE, illness and death, to bring the wearer good luck and fortune or to cure various ailments. Sardonyx and cat's eye, for example, are considered protection against witchcraft, while coral wards off the evil eye and prevents sterility.

In folk magic, stones with certain shapes and characteristics are considered supernatural or lucky. Legend has it that Coinneach Odhar, a 17th-century Scottish seer, got his gift of second sight with the help of a stone with a hole in it. While cutting peat one day for a farmer, he stopped to take a nap and woke up with the stone on his chest. He looked through the hole and saw a vision of the farmer's wife bringing him a poisoned meal. When the woman brought him his meal, he fed it to a dog, which died.

Stones with holes in them are female symbols and have been used in many fertility rites throughout history. In witch lore, a stone with a hole in it is a special sign of the favor of the goddess DIANA and will bring the finder good fortune and luck. A round stone, large or small, is also considered lucky, but only if the finder recites an incantation and throws the stone in the air three times. To give such a stone away brings disaster upon the finder. In India, a holed dolmen has healing power.

In the Ozarks, a stone with a hole in it found in running water is especially lucky, to be collected and placed in a box beneath the front porch or doorstep. Oval or round stones found in parts of Ireland are called cursing stones and are turned counterclockwise (WIDDERSHINS) in cursing SPELLS. The famous Blarney Stone in southern Ireland, a four-foot block of limestone, was a gift of a witch, according to some legends. Kissing the stone is believed to endow one with a great gift of oratory. The real origin of the stone is unknown. Another legend holds that the stone was brought to Ireland from the Holy Land.

Small stones or pebbles scattered about on a floor are said to prevent witches from entering a house. In cases of demonic POSSESSION and CURSES, hails of stones reportedly have rained down on the accursed, following them wherever they go. The stones seem to come from nowhere, even raining down from ceilings inside rooms (see LITHOBOLY).

FURTHER READING:

Budge, E. A. Wallis. *Amulets and Superstitions.* 1930. Reprint, New York: Dover Publications, 1978.

Evans-Wentz, W. Y. *The Fairy-Faith in Celtic Countries.* 1911. Reprint, Secaucus, N.J.: University Books, 1966.

storm raising The ability of witches to cause tempests, hailstorms and lightning, according to lore, especially during the witch-hunts. By whipping up the elements of nature, witches struck homes and crops, sank ships and killed men and animals, all allegedly with great delight. Church authorities said God permitted the DEVIL and witches to do these MALEFICIA as punishment upon the world.

After a SABBAT, witches were said to mount their BROOMS and fly out to sea, where they would stir up a tempest by dumping the vile contents of their CAULDRONS into the water or by throwing their hair into the sea. From their brooms, they would hurl lightning bolts at ships. If they raised a storm over land, they would throw lightning at men, animals and buildings on the ground (see FLYING).

Witches also caused storms by stirring water poured into holes in the ground, urinating into holes, reciting magical formulas, drawing magical diagrams and shutting up toads and spiders in pots. Spanish witches caused hailstorms to destroy fruit crops by scattering a magic powder over the fruit.

Witches brought on rain by sacrificing COCKS in their cauldrons. Witches could control wind by tying three KNOTS in a rope or whip and unloosing them one by one. One old Scottish recipe for storm raising called for dipping a rag in water and beating it three times on a stone in the name of Satan, while reciting the following:

> I knock this rag upon this stone
> To raise the wind in the devil's name
> It shall not lye till I please again.

Witches raising storm at sea (OLAUS MAGNUS' *HISTORIA DE GENTIBUS SEPTENTRIONALIBUS,* 1555)

Control of the elements, including the ability to raise storms and cause rain, has been attributed to magicians, shamans, sorcerers and witches since ancient times around the world (see MAGIC; SHAMANISM; SORCERY). In ancient Egypt, magicians used waxen images and SPELLS to raise winds and storms against enemy invaders. As early as 700, the Church was prosecuting sorcerers for causing storms, sentencing them to penance.

During the height of the witch hysteria, natural disasters were attributed to witchcraft, and many people were blamed, tried and executed for being the alleged perpetrators. In Ratisbon (now Regensburg), Germany, in the 15th century, a violent hailstorm destroyed all the crops, fruits and vines in a mile-wide swath. The townsfolk blamed the storm on witches and demanded an official inquiry. There was no shortage of suspects, but the field was narrowed to two women, who were separately imprisoned and interrogated. At first, both denied responsibility. They were tortured—one was hung by her thumbs—until they confessed not only to being witches and causing the storm but to copulating with incubi for 18 and 20 years, respectively. The day after they confessed, they were burned at the stake.

In the village of Waldshut on the Rhine, there lived a witch who was so despised by the townsfolk that she was pointedly not invited to a wedding celebration, as was nearly everyone else. Angry, she conjured up a Devil and asked for a hailstorm to pelt the merrymakers. He raised her up and transported her to a hill near the town, where she was seen by shepherds. She made a trench, urinated into it and stirred the urine with her fingers. The Devil lifted the liquid up and turned it into a violent hailstorm which pelted the dancers and wedding party and guests. The shepherds told the bewildered villagers about the witch, whereupon she was arrested. She confessed she had caused the storm because she had not been invited to the wedding. For this and other alleged acts of witchcraft, she was burned.

The most famous storm attributed to witches was recorded in the trial of Scotland's JOHN FIAN in 1591. He and his alleged COVEN of NORTH BERWICK WITCHES were accused of raising a sea tempest to try to drown James VI (JAMES I) and Queen Anne on their way from Denmark. A storm did arise and slowed the ship down, but no one was drowned.

Remedies against storm raising. The Church prohibited superstitious remedies against WITCHCRAFT such as storm raising, because of their pagan associations. What the Church recommended, however, was little more than superstition with a sacrament thrown in, and rituals that replaced magic incantations with Christian ones. In essence, they were pagan remedies trussed up with Christian window dressing.

PRAYER, sacraments and the invocation of the name of God were all said to be the most effective weapons. If a person had faith in God and kept the commandments, revered the rites of the Church and protected himself with the sign of the CROSS, then he would be immune from storms and tempests.

The MALLEUS MALEFICARUM (1486) reports the testimony of one witch who was asked by a judge what could be done to stop a storm. She said the townspeople should recite:

> I adjure you, hailstorms and winds, by the five wounds of Christ, and by the three nails which pierced His hands and feet, and by the four Holy Evangelists, Matthew, Mark, Luke and John, that you be dissolved and fall as rain.

But most peasants were loath to give up their superstitions, and the church also sanctioned such remedies as the ringing of church bells during a storm, which was supposed to drive the storm devils away, and the placing in fields of CHARMS made from flowers consecrated on Palm Sunday. If a storm struck, the charm would protect the owner's crops, even though the surrounding land and crops would be damaged.

Another remedy was throwing three hailstones into a fire during the storm. This had to be accompanied with an invocation of the Holy Trinity, the LORD'S PRAYER and the Angelic Salutation, all repeated two or three times, followed by the Gospel of St. John, "In the beginning was the word." The sign of the cross had to be made in each of the four directions, and then "The Word was made Flesh" was repeated three times. Finally, the ritual was ended with, "By the words of this Gospel may this tempest be stopped." Church officials said that while it was the holy words that really did the job, casting the hailstones into the fire added further torment to the DEVIL.

Contemporary Pagans and Witches may do weather rituals, such as for rain to end a drought, but do not believe in using weather magic to cause harm or suffering.

See TEMPESTARII

FURTHER READING:
Barstow, Anne Llewellyn. *Witchcraze: A New History of the European Witch Hunts.* San Francisco: Pandora, 1994.
Larner, Christina. *Enemies of God.* London: Chatto & Windus, 1981.
Lea, Henry Charles. *Materials Toward a History of Witchcraft.* Philadelphia: University of Pennsylvania, 1939.
Thomas, Keith. *Religion and the Decline of Magic.* New York: Charles Scribner's Sons, 1971.

striga (also stria, strix) A BLOOD-drinking night spirit of classical antiquity, which became known as a witch in folklore. The *striges* (plural) were said to be terrible women who could turn themselves into dreadful birds of prey, with huge talons, misshapen heads and breasts full of poisonous milk. Like the lamiae, and succubi, they preyed upon unprotected sleeping men and children. With men, they turned into women, had sexual intercourse, then drank the men's blood. To children, they offered their poisonous milk. They were associated with screech OWLS, birds of SORCERY whose feathers are used in magical spells in classical myth.

Ovid proposed three theories as to the origin of *striges*: they were born that way; they were enchanted; they were HAGS who had been put under a SPELL. Petronius claimed that *striges* were wise women of the night who possessed the power to overthrow the natural order of things.

After the fall of the Roman Empire, *striges* endured in folklore, and the term became low Latin for "witch." As Christianity spread, the *striges*, along with other pagan spirits, became associated with demonolatry. The Synod of Rome in 743 outlawed offerings to such spirits. In 744 a "List of Superstitions" drawn up at the Council of Leptinnes renounced "all the works of the demon . . . and all evil beings that are like them." Various laws were passed forbidding belief in *striges* and other pagan spirits, such as one in Saxony in 789, which punished such belief with execution.

By the Middle Ages, the *striges* were identified in Christianity as servants of Satan and his DEMONS. They were defined as women witches who practiced sorcery and flew through the air. The *striges'* association with screech owls gave rise to the term *owlblasted*, which referred to the effects of a wasting-away spell cast upon a man (see BLASTING). This expression remained in popular use in Britain through the 16th century.

FURTHER READING:
Lea, Henry Charles. *Materials Toward a History of Witchcraft.* Philadelphia: University of Pennsylvania, 1939.
Russell, Jeffrey Burton. *Witchcraft in the Middle Ages.* Ithaca and London: Cornell University Press, 1972.

Summers, Montague (1880–1948) English author who wrote extensively on WITCHCRAFT, demonology, vampires and werewolves (see LYCANTHROPY). He believed that Satan and his DEMONS were real and that they exerted a powerful hold over witches, who were evil. He was credulous of the dark, supernatural worlds he explored. Nevertheless, his books, some of which were still in print in the late 20th century, offer an interesting look at popular stories and beliefs of earlier times.

Summers was born Alphonsus Joseph-Mary Augustus Montague Summers on April 10, 1880, in Clifton, near Bristol. He was the youngest of seven children in a family headed by a banker and justice of the peace. He was raised an Anglican but later converted to Catholicism.

Early in life, Summers was drawn to drama and literature, subjects on which he wrote books later in life. He studied at Trinity College in Oxford and then at Lichfield Theological College. He earned both bachelor and master of arts degrees by 1906.

While working as a curate in Bath, he and another clergyman were charged with pederasty. Summers was acquitted and the charges were dropped.

In 1909 he entered the Roman Catholic Church and became a priest. From 1911 to 1926 he taught at various schools and wrote books on literature, drama, witchcraft and the supernatural. In his later years he lived at Oxford, studying the thousands of books he had collected over the years. He was considered an odd man by his peers.

Summers devoted more than 30 years to an intense study of witchcraft, which he felt had been neglected by serious English historians. He reviewed the works of older demonologists, men such as JEAN BODIN, NICHOLAS RÉMY, FRANCESCO-MARIA GUAZZO and many others. He translated into English the MALLEUS MALEFICARUM, first published in 1486 and the most influential guide in the persecution, TORTURE and execution of alleged witches during the entire witch hysteria. He exalted the book's authors, James Sprenger and Heinrich Kramer, as brilliant men. He also translated or edited the works of leading demonologists, including Henri Boguet, Guazzo, Rémy, REGINALD SCOT, RICHARD BOVET and Ludovico Sinistrari.

Summers believed in witches and felt they deserved the punishment they got, but he disagreed with British anthropologist MARGARET A. MURRAY in her assertion that witchcraft was an organized religion in the Middle Ages. That, said Summers, was "a most ingenious . . . but wholly untenable hypothesis."

In his book *The History of Witchcraft and Demonology* (1926), Summers maintained that witchcraft was not necessarily a product of the Middle Ages but did rise up at that time with sufficient force to threaten the very peace and salvation of mankind. He believed the confessions of witches to be not the products of hysteria and hallucination but "to be in the main hideous and horrible fact."

Summers embraced every belief about the evil and vileness of witches. In the introduction of *History*, he told his readers:

> In the following pages I have endeavored to show the witch as she really was—an evil liver; a social pest and parasite; the devotee of a loathly and obscene creed; an adept at poisoning, blackmail and other creeping crimes; a member of a powerful secret organization inimical to Church and State; a blasphemer in word and deed; swaying the villagers by terror and superstition; a charlatan and a quack sometimes; a bawd; an abortionist; the dark counsellor of lewd court ladies and adulterous gallants; a minister to vice and inconceivable corruption; battening upon the filth and foulest passions of the age.

Summers wrote *The Geography of Witchcraft* (1927) and *A Popular History of Witchcraft* (1937). His books on vampires and werewolves—which some critics say are filled with unsubstantiated old wives' tales—are *The Vampire: His Kith and Kin* (1928); *The Vampire in Europe* (1929); and *The Werewolf* (1933).

Summers died on August 10, 1948, the same year in which a new edition of his translation of the *Malleus Maleficarum* was issued.

FURTHER READING:
Baroja, Julio Caro. *The World of the Witches*. 1961. Reprint, Chicago: University of Chicago Press, 1975.

Russell, Jeffrey Burton. *Witchcraft in the Middle Ages*. Ithaca and London: Cornell University Press, 1972.
Summers, Montague. *The History of Witchcraft and Demonology*. London: Kegan Paul, Trench, Trubner & Co. Ltd., 1926.
———. *The Geography of Witchcraft*. London: Kegan Paul, Trench, Trubner & Co. Ltd., 1927.

swimming   A test of guilt or innocence for witches was trial by water, or swimming, a method that was used up until the 19th century. Accused witches were bound and thrown into water to see if they would float or sink. It was believed that the guilty floated and the innocent sank.

Trial by water was used by Hammurabi (1792–1750 B.C.E.), king of Babylonia, whose laws comprised one of the great ancient codes. Hammurabi declared that if a person was accused of black MAGIC but not proven guilty, he was to be plunged into a river. If he drowned, his accuser got his property. If he survived, his accuser would be executed, and he would take over the dead man's property.

Swimming, or ducking, as trial by water came to be known in some witchcraft trials, appeared in Europe, the British Isles and America in the 16th through 18th centuries but never gained widespread acceptance among judges as irrevocable proof of guilt or innocence. Swimming was declared illegal in England in 1219 by Henry III, but that didn't stop witch-hunters from doing it.

The accused witch was bound by either the right thumb to the right toe, or right thumb to left toe ("cross bound") and plunged into a river or lake. Innocence seldom mattered, for the victim often sank and drowned before he or she could be pulled out. Sometimes the accused had no chance at all to survive, because he or she was sewn into a sack before being tossed into the water.

Swimming was endorsed by JAMES I of England, who stated in *Daemonologie* (1597) "that God hath appointed (for a supernatural signe of the monstrous impietie of Witches) that the water shall refuse to receive them in her bosome, that have shaken off them the sacred Water of Baptisme, and wilfully refused the benefite thereof." England's leading witch-hunter, MATTHEW HOPKINS, "swam" many of his accused victims, though he said he never used it as evidence in trials. In Europe, the chief champion of swimming was a Hessian schoolmaster named William Adolf Scribonius, who wrote a book in 1588 on how to identify and punish witches.

In the American colonies, two accused witches in Hartford, Connecticut, were "swum" in 1633 and were judged guilty because they floated; they were hanged. In 1706 a Virginia woman named Grace Sherwood agreed to be swum to prove her innocence. In chronicling the case in *Annals of Witchcraft* (1869), Samuel Drake stated that "few more disgraceful Scenes were ever enacted in the Prosecutions for Witchcraft" in the Colonies.

Sherwood was accused of witchcraft by a man and his wife; a warrant was issued for her to appear before court. Sherwood failed to show, was arraigned and was searched

Swimming an accused witch (OLD WOODCUT)

for WITCH'S MARKS. Two "things like Titts on her private Parts, of a black coller, being blacker than ye Rest of her Body," were found, along with several other "Spots." However, the court had no specific crime with which to charge Sherwood, merely suspicion of witchcraft. Reluctant to acquit her, the court decided to use the "old English Test" of water. Sherwood, who had little to say in her own defense, agreed. Ironically, the court ordered the sheriff to take care not to expose her to rainy weather before she was "swum," as "she might take cold." Sherwood floated in the test, was plucked out and examined again for marks. Surviving records do not tell what became of the unfortunate woman. The place where the water trial took place, an inlet of Lynnhaven Bay in Princess Anne County, became known as "Witch Duck."

Swimming failed to become an ironclad means of unmasking witches because it could be manipulated by either accuser or accused. Many witch-hunters found ways to make certain their victims floated; some victims succeeded in sinking themselves long enough to be declared innocent. The records of various witch trials show that some victims requested the swimming test in order to clear their names, and some of them, unfortunately, floated despite their most valiant efforts to sink.

INCREASE MATHER strongly disapproved of swimming and railed against it in his book, *An Essay for the Recording of Illustrious Providences* (1684). Mather tore apart King James's argument that WATER, being an instrument of baptism and therefore holy, would reject witches, by saying that such a notion would apply only to those who were baptized. That meant anyone who was not baptized would float, regardless of whether or not he or she was a witch, Mather said.

Furthermore, Mather said, morality has nothing to do with body weight. He cited cases of the guilty going free and the innocent being condemned. Some people who were "swum" more than once both floated and sank.

Local jurisdictions throughout the Continent and the British Isles prohibited swimming. It was outlawed throughout all of England in 1712, and those who did it faced murder charges if their victim drowned. Nevertheless, it continued to be employed in lynch-mob situations. Swimming eventually died out in the 19th century.

In Russia, swimming was used in a different way. Persons suspected of witchcraft were taken to the deep side of a river, tied around the waist with rope and lowered in. If they sank, they were quickly pulled out. If they floated, they were hauled out and branded with a red-hot iron in the shape of a cross to warn others that they were witches. It was believed that the branding nullified the witches' power.

FURTHER READING:

Deacon, Richard. *Matthew Hopkins: Witch Finder General.* London: Frederick Muller, 1976.

Hole, Christina. *Witchcraft in England.* London: B.T. Batsford Ltd., 1947.

Macfarlane, A. D. J. *Witchcraft in Tudor and Suart England.* London: Routledge & Kegan Paul Lt., 1970.

Mather, Increase. *An Essay for the Recording of Illustrious Providences.* 1684. Reprint, Delmar, N.Y.: Scholars' Facsimiles and Reprints, 1977.

talismans Objects that possess magical or supernatural power of their own and transmit them to the owner. Talismans often are confused with AMULETS, objects that protect their wearers from evil and harm. Talismans usually perform a single function and enable powerful transformations. The magic wand of a sorcerer or FAIRY, King Arthur's sword Excalibur, seven-league boots and Mercury's helmet of invisibility are all talismans.

A talisman can be any object, but in MAGIC can be endowed with supernatural power only by the forces of nature, by God or the gods or by being made in a ritualistic way. Precious STONES have always been considered talismans, for example, each having its own magical or curative powers endowed by nature.

Talismans are universal in all periods of history. They were common in ancient Egypt and Babylonia, where they were used to try and alter the forces of nature. In the Middle Ages, holy objects were valued as talismans for their ability to cure illness. Witches and thieves made talismans out of the severed hands of criminals (see HAND OF GLORY).

Alchemists followed elaborate rituals to make talismans: they waited for auspicious astrological signs, then recited incantations to summon spirits who would imbue the talismans with power. The most sought-after talisman was the elusive Philosopher's Stone, which alchemists believed would transform base metals into gold and silver.

The GRIMOIRES offer instructions for making talismans of engravings upon stones or parchment under aus-

Talismanic seals (FRANCIS BARRETT, *THE MAGUS,* 1801)

picious astrological signs. There are talismans for making fortunes, winning in gambling, preventing sudden death, improving memory and even making good speeches.

Catherine de' Medici, queen consort of Henry II of France, always carried with her a talisman that was a medal allegedly made from metals that had been melted together under astrologically favorable signs, plus human and he-goat BLOOD. The original was broken upon her death, but a copy exists in the Bibliothèque Nationale in Paris. One side of the medal is engraved with the god Jupiter, the eagle of Ganymede and a demon with the head of the Egyptian god, Anubis; the other side bears a Venus figure believed to be Catherine, which is flanked by the names of DEMONS. The queen believed the talisman conferred upon her clairvoyance and sovereign power.

FURTHER READING:
Cavendish, Richard, ed. *The Encyclopedia of the Unexplained.* New York: McGraw-Hill, 1974.
Thomas, Keith. *Religion and the Decline of Magic.* New York: Charles Scribner's Sons, 1971.

tasseomancy Also called *tasseography,* tasseomancy is the divinatory art of reading tea leaves and coffee grounds (see DIVINATION). Like PALMISTRY, it is particularly associated with WITCHES and GYPSIES, who popularized it, but it has lost popularity to other methods. The roots of tasseomancy date to the Middle Ages, when diviners interpreted the symbols formed by blobs of melted max, molten lead and other substances. In the 17th century, tea was introduced from the Orient to the West by the Dutch, and tea drinking quickly became a widespread habit. The shapes and symbols formed by the dregs in the bottom of the cup seemed natural for divination.

In a tea-leaf reading, the client drinks a cup of tea, preferably made from coarse leaves in a cup that is broad and shallow. A tiny amount of liquid is left in the cup, just enough to swish the dregs around. The cup is upturned on the saucer. The reader picks up the cup and examines the dregs, which may form letters, numbers, geometric patterns, straight or wavy lines or shapes that resemble animals, birds and objects. Symbols have certain meanings; for example, straight lines indicate careful planning and peace of mind, while a cup shape indicates love and harmony. Time frames are estimated by the proximity of the leaves to the rim. Dregs closest to the rim and the handle represent the immediate future, while those at the bottom indicate the far future. Some readers say they can predict only 24 hours into the future.

Coffee grounds are less commonly used for divination. Italians in the 18th century claimed to have invented coffee-ground divination, and they believed the prophecies were caused by demons. Diviners who used this method recited incantations during the procedure, such as *"Aqua boraxit venias carajos," "Fixitur et patricam explinabit tor-*nare,"* and *"Hax verticalines, pax Fantas marobum, max destinatus, veida porol."* If the incantations were done incorrectly, the reading would be inaccurate.

Tasseomancy is still done in England, Ireland and Europe. In America, it is done primarily in large cities, in "Gypsy tearooms" and restaurants that have a back room for fortune-telling services.

tears According to folk belief, witches are unable to shed tears. The origins of this belief may be found in the tears shed over the crucifixion of Christ and a statement by St. Bernard (1091–1153) that the tears of the humble could penetrate heaven and conquer the unconquerable. Therefore, the reasoning went, tears were an offense to the DEVIL, who would do whatever was necessary to prevent his witches from crying.

This "truth" was repeated in medieval witch-hunters' guides such as the MALLEUS MALEFICARUM (1486) and by leading demonologists of the 16th century, such as JEAN BODIN. In *De la Demonomanie des Sorciers* (1580), Bodin stated that witches and WIZARDS can neither cry nor look a man directly in the eye. JAMES I of England (James VI of Scotland) wrote in *Daemonologie* (1597):

. . . threaten and torture them [witches] as ye please, while first they repent; (God not permitting them to dissemble their obstinacie in so horrible a crime,) albeit the woman-kind especially be able otherwayes to shed teares at every light occasion, when they will, yea, although it were dissembingly, like the crocodiles.

An accused witch's inability to cry during her interrogation, TORTURE, or trial was taken as proof that she was a witch. The possibility that a person might be beyond tears due to terror or pain was never considered; a defendant was damned if she didn't cry, and damned if she did. The *Malleus Maleficarum* instructs judges to take particular note of tears:

For we are taught both by the words of worthy men of old and by our own experience that this is a most certain sign, and it has been found that even if she be urged by solemn conjurations to shed tears, if she be a witch she will not be able to weep.

Judges were warned that witches, knowing that the absence of tears as proof of their guilt, might try to fake crying by smearing their cheeks with SPITTLE. Defendants were to be watched closely at all times for this trick.

The *Malleus Maleficarum* notes that while witches will not cry in the presence of judges, or during their interrogation, they will weep while in their cells. This was not to be taken seriously, however, because it was most likely a trick of the Devil, "since tearful grieving, weaving and deceiving are said to be proper to women."

If an accused witch was able to cry, she was supposed to be discharged, unless there still existed a "grave suspicion" that she was indeed a witch. Naturally, many defendants who cried were nonetheless convicted of witchcraft, as there were plenty of other ways to prove guilt.

In passing sentence, a judge might give a defendant one last chance to prove her innocence by crying. According to the *Malleus,* he would place his hand upon her head and pronounce:

> I conjure you by the bitter tears shed on the Cross by our Saviour the Lord Jesus Christ for the salvation of the world, and by the burning tears poured in the evening hour over His wounds by the most glorious Virgin Mary, His Mother, and by all the tears which have been shed here in this world by the Saints and Elect of God, from whose eyes He has now wiped away all tears, that if you be innocent you do now shed tears, but if you be guilty that you shall by no means do so. In the name of the Father, and of the Son, and of the Holy Ghost. Amen.

By the time sentence was passed, many victims were incapable of tears. Some had been tortured to the point where they were barely conscious; others had had their will to live broken. Crying might only mean a return to torture; refusal to cry could bring a speedier, and therefore merciful, death.

FURTHER READING:
Lea, Henry Charles. *Materials Toward a History of Witchcraft.* Philadelphia: University of Pennsylvania, 1939.
Summers, Montague, ed. *The Malleus Maleficarum of Heinrich Kramer and James Sprenger.* 1928. Reprint, New York: Dover Publications, 1971.

technopaganism   See PAGANISM.

Tedworth, Drummer of   See GHOSTS, HAUNTINGS AND WITCHCRAFT.

Tempestarii   In medieval lore, witches who specialized in STORM RAISING for the mythical dwellers of a land in the sky called Magonia. When huge storm clouds rolled over the land, they were said to be the ships of the Magonians. The Tempestarii aided the Magonians by whipping up the wind and creating lightning and thunder. By maliciously dumping their cargoes overboard, the Magonians sent hail to pelt the crops below. Then they would land their ships and, with the further help of the Tempestarii, steal the beaten-down crops. Often they would streak back into the sky without paying the Tempestarii and the witches would give chase, which the peasants below saw as the wispy clouds in the sky that follow a storm.

thirteen   In superstition, the number of bad luck and evil power. According to lore, witches' COVENS always number 13 members, although there has never been sufficient evidence in history to substantiate it. That myth was given fuel by British anthropologist MARGARET A. MURRAY, who stated in her book *The Witch-cult of West-*

ern Europe (1921) that WITCHES in the Middle East formed in groups of 12 plus 1 leader. In support of her theory, she cited trial records that mentioned 18 covens with 13 members between 1567 and 1673: five in England, nine in Scotland and one each in France, Germany, Ireland and America. The data were discredited by other scholars, who said the number 13 had been obtained by TORTURE or arrived at by error. In some cases, it was the number of witches arrested; far more than 13 were then implicated in the trials. Some accused witches claimed to have 13 members in their covens, such as ISOBEL GOWDIE, tried in Scotland in 1662, and Ann Armstrong, of Newcastle-on-Tyne, England, tried in 1673. Some modern covens may have 13 members, but most range in size from four to 20 members. Covens usually conduct their meetings at the full MOON, which occurs 13 times a year.

Thirteen has been considered an unlucky number since ancient times. It is an unstable number, being just one beyond the number 12, which is the divine number of grace and perfection: there are 12 signs in the Zodiac, 12 hours in the day and 12 tribes of Ancient Israel. In Christianity, 13 is a parody of the last Supper, at which Christ and his apostles totaled 13 (Judas the betrayer was the first to rise from the table.) It is still considered unlucky to have 13 people at dinner.

So unlucky is 13 that it is omitted from addresses and floors of buildings. In the case of the latter, people may live or work on the 13th floor but feel better because it is called the 14th floor. The fear of the number 13 is called *triskaidekaphobia.* It is not uncommon for superstitious people to cancel trips on the 13th day of the month.

Friday the 13th packs a double wallop of bad luck, since Friday, the day Christ was crucified, is an unlucky day to enter into contracts, start new ventures or get married. In 1969 a 13-year-old Eton schoolboy, S. R. Baxter, proved mathematically that the 13th day of the month was more likely to fall on Friday than any other day. There is at least one Friday the 13th every year; the most that can occur is 3, as happened in 1987.

In the 19th century, the Thirteen Club was formed by 13 men in New York City to flout the bad-luck lore of the number. Appropriately, the charter dinner meeting took place on Friday the 13th, January 1882, in room 13 of Knickerbocker Cottage, from 13 minutes past eight until the 13th hour (1 A.M.). The members decided to dine on the 13th of every month. Lifetime membership in the club cost $13; the initiation fee was $1.13, and monthly dues were 13 cents. At the meetings, the members thumbed their noses at other superstitions, such as spilling SALT and breaking MIRRORS. The club was so successful that a sister club was formed in London.

In the Major Arcana of the Tarot deck, the 13th key, or card, is Death. If the card appears rightside-up, it signifies transformation. Upside-down, it signifies disaster, upheaval, inertia and anarchy.

Despite its bad-luck associations in superstition, the number 13 is regarded much more positively in esoteric traditions. It is the number of mystical manifestation. The teachings of Jesus are centered on the formula of 1+12 (Jesus plus his 12 disciples). One added to 12 creates the unlimited number of 13, according to Pythagoras. It is through this formula that such miracles as the multiplication of the loaves and fishes take place. Thirteen is the all-or-nothing cosmic law of destiny: death through failure and degeneration, or rebirth through regeneration. It is also the number of the Great Goddess, represented by 13 lunar cycles to a year. In the kabbalistic system of gematria, in which numerical values are assigned to letters, 13 is equated with "love of unity," because the Hebrew letters for "love" and "unity" both total 13.

Contemporary Witches consider thirteen to be a lucky number.

FURTHER READING:

Hoffman, Paul. "Friday the 13th." *Smithsonian,* Feb. 1987, n.p.

Thomas, Keith. *Religion and the Decline of Magic.* New York: Charles Scribner's Sons, 1971.

Valiente, Doreen. *An ABC of Witchcraft Past and Present.* 1973. Reprint, Custer, Wash.: Phoenix Publishing, 1986.

Thomas Aquinas, St. (1226–1274) A Dominican and one of the greatest theologians of the Christian church, Thomas Aquinas had a profound effect on the witch-hunts of the INQUISITION. His revolutionary philosophy was cited by demonologists and inquisitors for centuries as a basis for their persecutions.

Born at his family's castle near Roccasecca, Italy, Aquinas was educated by the Benedictines at Monte Cassino. He studied liberal arts at the University of Naples and then entered the Dominican order. He was sent to Paris and Cologne for training. In Cologne he met the famous alchemist, Albertus Magnus, and became his pupil in 1244, gaining a great deal of knowledge about alchemy. He is said to have performed magical feats, but these are legends.

In 1252 Aquinas returned to Paris to the Dominican St. James Convent. In 1256 he was appointed professor of theology at the University of Paris. In 1259 he traveled to Italy, where he spent nine years teaching, writing and lecturing at the papal court. He was recalled to Paris in 1268, then back to Italy in 1272. In 1274 Pope Gregory X appointed him consultant to the Council of Lyons, but Aquinas died en route, on February 7, at the Benedictine monastery of Fossanova.

During his career, Aquinas produced voluminous works that revolutionized Christian theology, most notably *Summa Contra Gentiles* and *Summa Theologica.* His philosophy had a major impact on the church's view of witchcraft and on the transformation of SORCERY into the heresy of witchcraft: heresy, even if the product of ignorance, was a sin because ignorance is the product of criminal negligence. Aquinas also stated that the practice of MAGIC was not virtuous and was practiced by "men of evil life."

He believed in the DEVIL as a tangible person with the senses of man. While he did not believe in formal pacts with the Devil, he did believe in implicit pacts (see DEVIL'S PACT). A heretic, just by virtue of being a heretic, could be assumed to have somehow given himself over to the Devil, whether or not the thought had even crossed his mind. He also believed in transvection, METAMORPHOSIS, STORM RAISING and ligatures (see AIGUILLETTE). He was among the clerics and demonologists who refuted the *CANON EPISCOPI,* which attributed such phenomena to delusion.

DEMONS, Aquinas said, do assail man and do so with the explicit permission of God. Demons and the Devil tempt man with pseudomiracles and are responsible for all sin and sexual impotence. Witchcraft, he declared, is permanent in the world, not to be remedied by more witchcraft, but only by the cessation of sin and sometimes by exorcisms performed by the church (see EXORCISM).

See *MALLEUS MALEFICARUM.*

FURTHER READING:

Kors, Alan C., and Edward Peters. *Witchcraft in Europe, A Documentary History 1100–1700.* Philadelphia: University of Pennsylvania Press, 1972.

Russell, Jeffrey Burton. *Witchcraft in the Middle Ages.* Ithaca and London: Cornell University Press, 1972.

three The number three plays a prominent role in myth, mysticism, the mystery traditions, folklore, alchemy, RITUAL and MAGIC.

Three is the numerical vibration that opens the gateways to the higher planes, the realm of the gods. It is the number of bringing something into manifestation in the material world.

Pythagoras said that three is "a triple Word, for the Hierarchical Order always manifests itself by Three." All the great religions recognize the expression of the Godhead in trinities. For example, in Christianity it is Father-Son-Holy Spirit. In Hinduism the trinity is Brahman-Shiva-Vishnu. There are three pillars to Zen Buddhism. The ancient Egyptians' holy trinity was Osiris-Isis-Horus. The Great Goddess of contemporary Witchcraft has a threefold expression of Virgin-Mother-Crone. In Jewish mysticism there are three pillars to the Tree of Life, which is a blueprint for the descent of the divine into matter and the return ascent to the Godhead. The top three *sephirot,* or stations, of the Tree of Life, are the mystical steps to unity: Understanding, Wisdom and Humility. In the *Sefer Yetzirah* (Book of Formation) of the KABBALAH, three is expressed in the Three Mothers, Aleph, Mem and Shin, which form the foundation of "all others." Aleph, Mem and Shin are letters of the Hebrew alphabet that mean, respectively, "breath," or vital spirit; "seas," or water; and "life-breath of the Divine Ones," or "Holy Spirit."

The Western mystery tradition and alchemy are based on the legendary teachings of HERMES TRISMEGISTUS or "Thrice-Greatest Hermes." Three is the ascent of consciousness, represented by the upward-pointing triangle and the face of the pyramid. It represents the unification of body-mind-spirit and heart-will-intellect and eyes-ears-mouth (what we see, hear and speak as products of our spiritual consciousness). The Three Wise Men of the Bible represent the enlightened consciousness. The Great Work of alchemy— the attainment of material and spiritual gold— takes place in three main stages.

The Greek philosopher Anatolius observed that three, "the first odd number, is called perfect by some, because it is the first number to signify the totality—beginning, middle and end." Thus, we find in mythology, folklore and fairy tales the recurrent motif of the triad: three wishes, three sisters, three brothers, three chances, blessings done in threes, and SPELLS and CHARMS done in threes ("thrice times the charm").

Three is also the number of wisdom and knowledge in its association with the Three Fates and the past, present and future, and the ancient sciences of music, geometry and arithmetic.

FURTHER READING:
Guiley, Rosemary Ellen. *Dreamwork for the Soul.* New York: Berkley Books, 1998.
Heline, Corinne. *Sacred Science of Numbers.* Marina de Rey, Calif.: DeVorss & Co., 1991.

Threefold Law of Return (also Threefold Law of Karma)
An ethic more than a law of uncertain origin that emerged in the Gardnerian tradition (see GERALD B. GARDNER) of contemporary Witchcraft and that has been adopted by some witches in other traditions. It is derived from the Eastern concept of karma.

Karma is the cosmic principle of cause and effect, which holds that for every action in life, there is a reaction; good is returned by good, evil is returned by evil. Karma is the sum total of causes set in motion through a series of incarnations, and it influences the spiritual progress of the soul toward Divine Consciousness. Karma is not a law of punishment, though it has been interpreted as such by some schools of Western esoteric thought, such as Theosophy.

The Threefold Law of Return, however says that an action is not returned in equal measure but magnified three times, which defies the metaphysical laws of the universe. According to this concept, a Witch who uses her powers for good gets triple good in return. The law is a significant incentive not to use MAGIC to curse others or even manipulate them, for the evil will return in triple strength as well. Some Witches say the return is sevenfold.

The origin of the Threefold Law of Return in Witchcraft is not known. References to returning persecution twofold appear in the legend of ARADIA, as recorded in the late 19th century by CHARLES GODFREY LELAND. in

the legend of DIANA, the Greek goddess and patroness of witches, sends her daughter, Aradia, to earth to teach witches their art. Diana instructs Aradia:

And when a priest shall do you injury
By his benedictions, ye shall do to him
Double the harm, and do it in the name
Of me, *Diana,* Queen of witches all!

Gerald B. Gardner, for whom Gardnerian Witchcraft is named, was a believer in karma and promoted the ethic that Witches must not use their power for anything that brings harm to another. There is no evidence that he conceived of the threefold return, though P. E. I. (ISAAC) BONEWITS notes that Gardner did specify threefold return in RITUAL scourging (light whipping). Three may have gotten attached to the concept of karma simply because it is a magical number; incantations often are repeated THREE times ("three times is the charm"). Three is perfect and lucky, and in contemporary Witchcraft it is associated with the Triple Goddess (see GODDESS).

The first known reference in print to the Threefold Law of Return appeared in 1970 in *Witchcraft Ancient and Modern,* by RAYMOND BUCKLAND, who was initiated into the Craft by Gardner and was instrumental in introducing Gardnerian Witchcraft into the United States. Buckland observes that with the retribution under the Threefold Law, "there is no inducement for a Witch to do evil."

The law of cause and effect is watched over by higher entities called the Lords of Karma, a concept from Theosophy that is drawn from the Hindu *lipikas,* the "scribes," whose job it is to record karma, and the *devarajas,* who rule over the cardinal points (and also are associated with the elements) and are said to be karmic agents during a person's life on earth. According to STEWART FARRAR, the Lords of Karma do not override the law of karma but can help push people in the right karmic direction.

Most contemporary Witches believe in reincarnation and the cause and effect of karma, but some do not take the Threefold Law of Return literally in terms of a triple return. They believe in using their powers for good and not evil (see WICCAN REDE).

FURTHER READING:
Buckland, Raymond. *Buckland's Complete Book of Witchcraft.* St. Paul: Llewellyn Publications, 1986.
Weinstein, Marion. *Earth Magic: A Dianic Book of Shadows.* Revised ed. Custer, Wash.: Phoenix Publishing, 1998.

Tituba (Indian)   West Indian slave in Salem who was instrumental in starting the SALEM WITCHES hysteria of 1692–93.

Tituba and her husband, John, both known by the surname Indian, were brought to the American colonies by Reverend Samuel Parris, who lived for a time in the Spanish West Indies. Parris went to Salem to preach in 1689. "Indian" was not their real last name, but one given to them as a descriptor of their origins. The couple were slaves in the Parris household. Tituba looked after Parris' nine-year-old daughter, Betty, and her 11-year-old cousin, Abigail Williams.

Tituba undoubtedly brought with her the local folklore, superstitions and folk magic practices of her homeland. Some of these she may have practiced quietly in the Parris household.

In 1691–92, during the long and cold winter, Tituba entertained Betty, Abigail and their friends by teaching them simple divination games. It was all innocent fun until one of the girls saw a death omen, and everyone became frightened. Hysterical fits started and drew the attention of adults. The girls claimed they were being afflicted by witches in Salem. When asked to identify the witches, the girls were reluctant to do so. Tituba was prevailed upon by Mary Sibley, the aunt of one of the afflicted girls, to do some folk magic that would reveal the identities: She was to make a "witch cake" and feed it to the family dog. The dog would suffer fits if the girls were bewitched and might reveal the culprit. Parris beat Tituba when he found out and criticized Sibley. The girls then named Tituba, Sarah Good and Sarah Osborne as the witches.

Questioned by authorities, Tituba at first protested her innocence, but then quickly confessed to being a witch. She told outlandish stories that fed the hysteria, playing into the prevailing fears that witchcraft was a serious danger in New England. The DEVIL had come to her and told her to hurt the children, but she had refused. Four witches, including the two Sarahs, were responsible. She said she did not know who the other two were. The witches and the Devil had hurt Tituba until she in turn had hurt the children. She was instructed to kill the children. She pledged to do no more harm.

The Devil had sometimes appeared in the form of a man, a hog and a black dog. He had with him sometimes a yellow bird, a black cat and a red cat, FAMILIARS that told her to serve them. She refused. Sarah Good had a yellow bird familiar that sucked between her fingers. Osborn had two familiars, a hairy thing with two legs and a thing that had the head of a woman, two legs and wings. Tituba also said that she and the other witches rode through the air on poles. She fell into fits like the girls.

It was an artful confession, for it turned attention away from Tituba and on to other suspects and saved her life. Tituba was jailed, where she languished for more than a year. Parris refused to pay her jail charges. She eventually was sold and released.

Meanwhile, her husband John became an accuser too and rolled about on the floor "like a hog" when in the presence of alleged witches. He too was spared execution.

The lies Tituba told to save herself condemned others and ruined lives. More than 100 people were arrested and questioned, 19 died. The reputations of many others were permanently destroyed, turning them into social outcasts.

FURTHER READING:
Hansen, Chadwick. *Witchcraft at Salem.* New York: New American Library, 1969.
Karlsen, Carol F. *The Devil in the Shape of a Woman: Witchcraft in Colonial New England.* New York: W.W. Norton & Co, 1987.
Upham, Charles. *History of Witchcraft and Salem Village.* Boston: Wiggin and Lunt, 1867.

toads   Toads are associated with witches both as ingredients in brews and as FAMILIARS. Toad skins are covered with glands that secrete a thick, white poison when the toad is provoked or injured. The poison, *bufotenin,* also called *toads' milk* in popular lore, is hallucinogenic. Depending on the species of toad, the poison may simply taste bad or it may kill (see POISONS).

Toad lore. Since the time of Zoroaster, ca. 600 B.C.E., toads have been linked to evil; Zoroaster declared that for this reason, they should all be killed. The toad is the infernal opposite of the frog, which for the ancient Egyptians symbolized fertility and resurrection. In medieval and later times, toads were regarded as satanic creatures. Witches were believed to be able to disguise themselves as toads. Toads also were familiars, housing DEMONS who were assigned by the DEVIL to be servants to witches. Witches were said to send their toad familiars out to poison others and cause mishaps and mayhem. Toads also accompanied them to SABBATS.

Toads were common ingredients in various magical recipes. According to lore, witches decapitated and skinned them and then threw them into their CAULDRONS along with other bizarre ingredients. A lotion made of toad's SPITTLE and sowthistle sap could make a witch invisible. In folk MAGIC remedies, the ashes of a burned toad mixed with brandy was believed to be an effective cure for drunkenness.

Toads also were used as CHARMS in NECROMANCY and black magic. To kill an enemy, a witch or sorcerer baptized a toad with the enemy's name and then tortured the toad to death. The victim supposedly suffered the same fate.

It was believed that toads carried a jewel, called a *toadstone,* that would detect poison by becoming hot in its presence. The toadstone was either extracted from the toad's head or was vomited up by the toad.

In fantastic tales of witches' SABBATS during the witch hunts, witches were said to bite, mangle and tear apart toads in their worship of the Devil. By stamping his foot, the Devil could send all toads into the earth.

Toads in contemporary Witchcraft. Some contemporary Witches consider toads good familiars, noting that the creatures are intelligent, easy to tame and easy to care for. They also are said to have psychic qualities. Reportedly, Witches have methods of collecting toad's milk without harm to the toad.

See CHARLES WALTON.

FURTHER READING:
Thomas, Keith. *Religion and the Decline of Magic.* New York: Charles Scribner's Sons, 1971.
Valiente, Doreen. *An ABC of Witchcraft Past and Present.* 1973. Reprint, Custer, Wash.: Phoenix Publishing, 1986.

Toad-Witch A special kind of self-initiated witch in English folklore. Toad-Witches, or Toadsmen and Toadswomen as they are also called, were powerful and feared, especially for their ability to "overlook" or cast the EVIL EYE. Toadsmen had power over horses, pigs and women, while Toadswomen had power over horses, pigs and men. Being a Toad-Witch was considered dangerous, as one was likely to go insane because of the tremendous supernatural power, and to die a violent death.

Stories about Toad-Witches have been passed down through oral tradition, and were published in England by the turn of the 20th century. In her published account in 1901, Tilley Baldrey of Huntingtoft, a self-professed Toad-Witch, told how she had acquired the powers.

Baldrey caught a type of hopping toad called a natterjack (now rare) and carried it in her bosom until it rotted away to the backbone. She then held the bones over running WATER at midnight. The supernatural forces pulled her over the water, and she initiated herself by saying, "Then you be a witch." Baldrey thus was empowered to overlook, bind men and animals, to kill without disease, see in the dark like an animal and drive in mud where other vehicles would get mired.

Baldrey said that her husband, Dola, ran off with another woman, Neoma Cason, and went to live in a village about 16 miles away. She magically forced him to return to her by making him walk backwards the entire distance. This reportedly was witnessed by four persons.

Then Baldrey exacted revenge upon her rival. She took a lock of Cason's hair and burned it in a RITUAL to curse her. Cason was terrified when she learned of this, and sought the help of a CUNNING MAN to undo the CURSE. He told her that in order to do so, she must obtain the ashes of her hair— which, of course, was impossible. Doomed, she went into decline and soon died. Baldrey attended her funeral and threw the ashes of her hair on the coffin as it was being lowered into the ground.

There were other ways for aspiring Toad-Witches to get the toad's bones for INITIATION. Dead toads were placed in anthills to be eaten away to the bones. The bones were then taken at midnight to a stream that ran from north to south and cast into the water. Those that floated upstream against the current were the magical bones (north traditionally is associated with the dark powers). These bones often were worn as amulets and carried in special pouches, especially for horse charming.

Acquiring the power to overlook and to kill was sometimes said to require nine toads, all tied together with string and left to die. The power was acquired after the toads were buried.

FURTHER READING:
Pennick, Nigel. *Secrets of East Anglican Magic.* London: Robert Hale, 1995.

torture During the height of the witch-hunts, a period between the mid-14th and mid-17th centuries, the cruelest, most savage torture was used against accused witches in order to make them confess and name accomplices. The MALLEUS MALEFICARUM (1486) observes, "common justice demands that a witch should not be condemned to death unless she is convicted by her own confession." To that end—confession and execution—torture was considered an acceptable means.

By the time the INQUISITION added witchcraft to its list of heresies in 1320, torture was an ancient institution. It was legal under Roman law and over the centuries had been regularly applied to criminals and innocents of all sorts. Numerous devices and procedures had been invented to inflict the most pain and torment without killing the victim. Many of these were turned upon accused witches.

Between about 1435 and 1484, the hunting down of witches spread like a plague throughout Europe. At least 28 treatises on the evil of witchcraft were written by clerics and demonologists. With Pope INNOCENT VIII's issuance of his papal bull against witches in 1484, the persecution of people as witches increased. The worst tortures and wholesale exterminations occurred on the Continent, particularly in Germany, as well as in France, Italy and Switzerland, at the hands of both Catholic and Protestant inquisitors. Scotland, during the reign of King James VI (see JAMES I), was also witness to brutal tortures. Torture was far less prevalent and extreme in England, Ireland, and Scandinavia and was eventually outlawed in England. Torture was not extensively employed in the American colonies; the accused in the Salem trials in 1692 were tortured, but mildly compared to what was done on the Continent.

An inestimable number of victims were tortured and executed during the 16th and early 17th centuries. The inquisitors generally followed procedures and guidelines set forth in books such as the *Malleus Maleficarum,* written by Heinrich Kramer and James Sprenger, the Dominican inquisitors to Pope Innocent VIII. At first, the accused was urged to confess. She was stripped naked, shaved, pricked for insensitive spots and examined for blemishes that could be construed as DEVILS' MARKS. The *Malleus* cautions that most witches, at this point, would not confess. Then they had to be put to the "engines of torture."

Before torture began, the torturer usually took the victim aside and explained the torture and the effect it would have. He urged the victim to confess. Sometimes, the threat of torture was enough to induce a confession, which was considered voluntary and added weight to the Inquisition's case against the prevalence of witches. Sometimes the victim broke down after light torture, which was also considered a "voluntary" confession.

The *Malleus* notes that a witch who refused to talk, even under torture, was being aided by the DEVIL, who had the power to render her "so insensitive to the pains of torture that she will sooner be torn limb from limb that confess any of the truth. But torture is not to be neglected for this reason, for they are not all equally endowed with this power."

While the victim was tortured, the inquisitor repeated questions, while a clerk recorded what was said. The potential for error was great, especially if an uneducated victim spoke and understood only dialect. In many cases, clerks resorted to *etc.* instead of recording all details. Sometimes the victim's exact response was not recorded at all, but questions, usually accusatory, were noted merely as *affirmed.*

The torture went on until the victim confessed. The torturer had to take great care not to kill the victim but to relent when she was spent and beyond comprehension. She was taken back to her cell, where she was allowed

Head restraint and leg shackle used to imprison accused witches in England, in the collection of the Museum of Witchcraft, Boscastle, Cornwall (PHOTO BY THE AUTHOR; COURTESY MUSEUM OF WITCHCRAFT)

to rest the regain sufficient strength to endure another round of torture in a few hours or the next day. Each subsequent round of torture was more brutal than the last. For this the torturer and other court officials were paid, usually out of seized funds belonging to the victim. If the victim had no money, her relatives were forced to pay the costs, which included not only the actual torture but the torturer's meals, travel expenses, "entertainment" and hay for his horse. If he had assistants, those were paid as well.

While the victims screamed, the torturers and other court officials carried on like children frightened of the dark. They sprayed their instruments of torture with holy water and inscribed them with the words *Soli Deo Gloria* ("Glory be only to God"), which supposedly would protect them from being bewitched. They wore AMULETS of blessed wax and herbs and constantly crossed themselves, lest the witch harm them with evil MAGIC. They forced the victims to drink witch broth, a concoction made of the ashes of burnt witches, which was supposed to prevent the victims from harming their torturers.

If a victim endured an exceptional amount of torture without confessing, court officials looked for the Devil's intervention. The *Malleus* cites an example of a witch in the town of Hagenau, Germany, who allegedly was able to maintain silence with the help of a powder she had made by killing a newborn, first-born male child who had not been baptized, roasting it in the oven with certain other ingredients and grinding it all to powder and ash. Any witch or criminal who carried such a powder was unable to confess crimes. The exact methods of torture varied according to locale. The rack, for example, was not used in Scotland or England but was applied on the Continent, especially in France. In 1652 in Rieux, France, Suzanne Gaudry was stretched horribly on the rack while she "screamed ceaselessly" that she was not a witch, according to records. She finally confessed and was hanged and burned. Her torturer was paid four *livres,* 16 *sous.*

Victims were routinely horsewhipped. The spider, a sharp iron fork, was used to mangle breasts. Red-hot pincers were used to tear flesh, even breasts, off the body. Red-hot irons burned flesh and were inserted up vaginas and rectums. In extreme cases, the *Malleus* recommended the red-hot-iron test, in which a witch was forced to grab the hot iron; if she could hold it, she was guilty. Often by the time this test was administered, the victim was insensitive even to excruciating pain.

A device called the turcas was used to tear out fingernails. In 1590–91 JOHN FIAN was subjected to this and other tortures in Scotland. After his nails were ripped out, needles were driven into the quicks.

The boots, also called bootikens (cashielaws in Scotland), was a savage device of wedges that fitted the legs from ankles to knees. The torturer used a large, heavy hammer to pound the wedges, driving them closer together. At each strike, the inquisitor repeated the question.

The wedges lacerated flesh and crushed bone, sometimes so thoroughly that marrow gushed out and the legs were rendered useless.

Similarly, the thumbscrews, or pinniewinks, did the same damage to thumbs and toes, crushing them at the roots of the nails so that blood spurted out. In 1629 a woman in Prossneck, Germany, was left to suffer in the thumbscrews from 10 A.M. to 1 P.M., while the torturer and other court officials went out to lunch.

Other tortures included thrawing, in which the head was bound with ropes and jerked from side to side; the application to armpits and groins of burning feathers dipped in sulphur; immersion of fingers and hands in pots of boiling oil and water (it was believed that witches, protected by the Devil, would be unharmed by this, but if they were harmed it was due to deception by the Devil); and the gouging out of eyes with irons. Alcohol was poured on the head and set afire. Bodies were broken on the wheel. One common procedure was to blood the victim by cutting the flesh above the nostrils. BLOODING was believed to nullify a witch's power.

The water torture involved forcing great quantities of water, sometimes boiling, down the throat of the victim, along with a long knotted cloth. The cloth was then violently jerked out, which tore up the bowels. In another form of water torture, victims were fed only salted foods and briny water.

One of the most vicious torture methods, usually reserved for last, was the strappado, in which the victim's hands were bound behind her back and attached to a pulley. She was drawn to the ceiling and then dropped, and the jerk of the rope dislocated the shoulders, hands and elbows. This method was made more severe with the addition of weights to the victim's feet, increasing the pain and dislocating the hips, feet and knees as well. In France, stones weighing 40 to more than 200 pounds were used; one case involved 660-pound weights.

In many instances, there was no limit to the savagery of the torture used against accused witches. Anything was allowed as long as it got the desired results, and some inquisitors were openly sadistic. Many victims confessed in order to avoid great suffering.

After confession, however, came more torture as part of the sentence. Victims were usually condemned to death; in rare instances, they were released or banished. En route to the gallows or stakes, the condemned were flogged, burned, branded, squeezed with red-hot tongs and subjected to the hacking off of fingers and hands and the cutting out of tongues. The severed body parts were nailed to gallows, a grisly chore that netted the executioner an extra fee.

One insidious means of torture was to torture the victim's family while the victim watched helplessly. In 1594 Alison Balfour of Orkney was forced to watch her aged husband, son and seven-year-old daughter be tortured; she quickly confessed.

In England, painful physical torture was more isolated than widespread; instead, induced torture was employed. One of the most common methods was watching or waking, in which the victim was deprived of sleep until a hallucinatory state set in and the victim confessed. Walking also was common and was a favorite technique of England's most famous witch-hunter, MATTHEW HOPKINS. The victim was walked to and fro to the point of utter exhaustion. When witch-hunters could get away with it, they subjected victims to SWIMMING, in which they were bound hand and foot and thrown in water to see if they floated or sank. Floating meant guilty. If the innocent victim sank and drowned, it was simply too bad. Swimming was also employed on the Continent; a few cases were recorded in the American colonies.

In the mid-17th century, the torture and execution of witches began to collapse. Horrified at the excesses, dukes, princes and government officials moved to stop or at least limit torture and commute death sentences to life in prison or banishment. In Germany, the duke of Brunswick and the archbishop and elector of Menz were so shocked at the cruelty of the torturers, and the fact that judges accepted confessions made under torture, that they abolished torture in their dominions and influenced other rulers to do the same.

To demonstrate the barbarism and absurdity of such procedures, the duke of Brunswick invited two Jesuit priests to hear the confession of an accused witch who was incarcerated in a dungeon. Both priests were strong opponents of witchcraft; one was FRIEDRICH VON SPEE. Unknown to the priests, the duke had instructed the torturers to induce a certain confession from the woman. When the priests and the duke arrived, the torturers began applying pain and questions. In anguish, the woman at last broke down and confessed to attending many SABBATS on the Brocken, a notorious mountain rendezvous of witches. Furthermore, she claimed she had seen two Jesuit priests there, who had shocked even the witches with their abominations. The priests had assumed the shapes of goats, wolves and other animals and had copulated with the witches, who bore up to seven children at a time, all with heads like toads and legs like spiders. Asked to name the Jesuits, she said they were the two men in the torture room, watching.

Spee and the other priest were profoundly upset. The duke of Brunswick then explained how he had arranged the confession to demonstrate how torture would induce a person to admit to anything suggested by questions. Spee was so affected that he became a strident critic of the witch trials, exposing their horrors in *Cautio Criminalis* ("Precautions for Prosecutors"), published anonymously in 1631.

Other critics and skeptics spoke out against the witch mania, including REGINALD SCOT and Thomas Hobbes in England, Michel de Montaigne in France and Alfonso Salazar de Frias, the grand inquisitor of Spain. Laws

The tortures and executions of accused German witches (WOODCUT FROM TENGLER, *LAIENSPIEGEL*, 1508)

against torture were passed in 1649 in Scotland; 1654 in Brandenburg; 1652 and 1662 in England; and 1682 in France. From the second half of the 17th century on, witch panics died down to sporadic bursts.

FURTHER READING:

Barstow, Anne Llewellyn. *Witchcraze: A New History of the European Witch Hunts.* San Francisco: Pandora/Harper Collins, 1994.

Deacon, Richard. *Matthew Hopkins: Witch Finder General.* London: Frederick Muller, 1976.

Henningsen, Gustav. *The Witches' Advocate: Basque Witchcraft & the Spanish Inquisition.* Reno: University of Nevada Press, 1980.

Larner, Christina. *Enemies of God.* London: Chatto & Windus, 1981.

Thomas, Keith. *Religion and the Decline of Magic.* New York: Charles Scribner's Sons, 1971.

Trevor-Roper, H. R. *The European Witch-Craze.* New York: Harper & Row, 1957.

transvection   see FLYING.

trials by ordeal   Methods used in trials, including witchcraft trials, to determine guilt or innocence. Trials by ordeal involve a physical test. In England, such trials were introduced by the Saxons. English law gave the accused the right to choose trial by ordeal or trial by jury.

Ordeal by touch. The custom of touching the corpse of a murder victim was used throughout Europe and Britain and was imported to the American colonies. If a murder suspect touched the corpse and caused it to bleed, he was guilty.

According to lore, the custom originated in Denmark when a man was stabbed to death in a brawl. The king made all the participants touch the chest of the corpse and swear they were innocent. When the guilty man did so, the corpse gushed blood from the stab wound and through the nostrils. The guilty man broke down and confessed. He was beheaded.

A variation of the ordeal by touch holds that when touched by the guilty, the murdered corpse does not bleed but opens it eyes.

In Herefordshire, England, under the reign of King Charles I (r. 1625–49), Johan Norkett, wife of Arthur Nor-

kett, was found dead of apparent suicide. A month after her burial, suspicions abounded that she was in fact murdered. Her body was dug up, and four suspects were made to touch it. When they did so, according to the story, the body regained its lifelike color, sweated, opened its eyes, and dripped blood from the marriage-ring finger. Three of the four were found guilty and executed. The fourth, a woman, was imprisoned.

Also in the 17th century, in Scotland, Christina Wilson was accused of murdering her brother by SORCERY. The corpse bled when she touched it, and she was convicted. Ordeal by touch was used in the 17th century to convict Rebecca Ames of Massachusetts of witchcraft. Seventy-seven years later, an attempt was made in court in Salem, Massachusetts, to force an ordeal by touch in the murder case against John Ames of Boxford. Ames was accused of murdering his wife, Ruth, by poisoning. Ames was defended by John Adams, who would become the second president of the United States. Adams refused to let the test be done, claiming that it was "nothing but black arts and witchcraft." The magistrates backed down, and Ames was declared innocent and went free.

Ordeal by food. The accused were made to swallow large pieces of bread over which mass had been said. If they could do so without choking, they were innocent. The slightest cough meant they were guilty. Sometimes cheese was added to the bread.

Ordeal by water. Similar to the ordeal by food, the accused were forced to swallow huge quantities of water quickly. No ill effects meant innocence. However, the ordeal sometimes killed the accused, by causing veins to burst and hemorrhage.

The ordeal of hot water involved sticking a hand into a pot of boiling water. If there were no burns, the accused was innocent. Sometimes oil was used instead of water.

Another type of ordeal by cold water was known as SWIMMING, in which the accused, bound hand and foot, was tossed into deep water. Sinking (and usually drowning) meant innocence. Floating (and thus rejection by the pure water) meant guilt.

Ordeal by hot iron. The accused were forced to walk or sit on red-hot irons. If they were able to do so, they were guilty.

unguents See OINTMENTS.

urine Like nail clippings and hair (see HAIR AND NAILS), urine is a potent ingredient in folk CHARMS and counter-charms. Its potency is attributed to its personal connection to an individual and to the belief that urine influences health.

By the 16th century, physicians recognized that symptoms of disease showed up in a patient's urine, which would appear cloudy, discolored or foul-smelling. Some physicians believed they could diagnose illness solely by urine, without having to see the patient himself. Astrologers also made medical diagnoses from urine, based on the positions of the planets and stars at the time the urine was voided or delivered to them for examination.

Alchemists used urine in their experiments as well. Paracelsus, the 16th-century Swiss alchemist, wrote that urine, BLOOD, hair, sweat and excrement retained for a time a vital life essence called *mumia*. These ingredients could be used to make a *microcosmic magnet*, which, through the *mumia*, would draw off disease.

The WIZARDS and CUNNING MEN AND WOMEN who flourished during the 16th and 17th centuries, practicing their magical remedies, used urine both for diagnosing and curing illnesses—especially those caused by witchcraft.

A handbook published in England in 1631 gave this means of diagnosing a patient's prospects for recovery: take a urine sample and immerse a nettle in it for 24 hours. If the nettle remains green and healthy, the patient will live. If the nettle drys up, the patient will die.

In folk MAGIC, boiling a person's urine helps determine if and how bewitchment has occurred. Urine is then used to effect cures, usually by boiling, baking, burying or throwing it upon a fire. Ann Green, a witch or cunning woman of northeast England, said in 1654 that she cured headaches caused by BEWITCHMENT by putting a clipping of the victim's hair in his own urine, boiling it and throwing it on a fire. The fire was supposed to destroy the spell.

Boiled urine also was said to cure nephritis. Urine boiled in a pot containing crooked PINS was a common remedy for bewitchment.

A case in Yorkshire in 1683 involved a sick man whom a doctor said suffered from bewitchment. To break the spell, the doctor prescribed a cake made of the patient's urine and hair, combined with wheat meal and horseshoe stumps. The cake was to be tossed in a fire.

Edible "witch's cakes" were baked in the early American colonies in the 17th century to cure smallpox. Ingredients included rye, barley, herbs, water and a cup of baby's urine. The cake was fed to a dog, and if the dog shuddered while eating it, the patient would recover.

One of the most effective counter-charms against witchcraft was to secure the witch's own urine: if it was bottled and buried, the witch would be unable to urinate. During the Salem witch trials of 1692 (see SALEM

351

WITCHES), a local doctor named Roger Toothaker claimed his daughter had killed a witch with urine. The daughter spied on the witch until she saw the woman go to her outhouse. The daughter collected the witch's urine and boiled it in a pot until the foul-smelling smoke blocked the chimney flue. The next morning, the witch was dead. In another case cited during the Salem trials, a Mrs. Simms of Marblehead said she had been cursed by her witch neighbor, Wilmot "Mammy" Reed, never to urinate again. Mrs. Simms testified she had been unable to urinate for weeks after being cursed. Reed was hanged on September 22, 1692.

In Ozark superstition, it is unlucky to eat while urinating, because it is "feeding the Devil and starving God."

See WITCH BOTTLES.

FURTHER READING:
Pennick, Nigel. *Secrets of East Anglican Magic*. London: Robert Hale, 1995.
Thomas, Keith. *Religion and the Decline of Magic*. New York: Charles Scribner's Sons, 1971.

Valiente, Doreen (1922–1999) English high priestess and one of the most influential Witches in the Witchcraft revival and emergence of WICCA. An early initiate of GERALD B. GARDNER, doreen valiente wrote and coauthored with Gardner the basic RITUALS and other materials that shaped the evolution of Witchcraft/Wicca as both craft and religion. Gardner gets the credit for launching the Witchcraft revival, but Valiente deserves the credit for giving it an appealing and enduring depth and texture.

Valiente was born Doreen Edith Dominy on January 4, 1922, in Mitcham, south London, to a devout Christian couple, Harry Dominy, an architect and quantity surveyor, and his wife, Edith. She was given an Irish first name, perhaps because her parents had been to Ireland before she was born. In early childhood, she lived nearly Horley in Surrey, where she had a mystical experience while gazing at the MOON. She saw that behind ordinary reality was a reality far more potent, which she later described as "the world of force behind the world of form." This new perception connected her years later to Witchcraft.

After Surrey, Doreen's family moved to the West Country, where she became fascinated by the magical folklore. As a teenager, she began casting her own SPELLS and even did a spell to stop harassment of her mother, who worked as a housekeeper for an ill-tempered woman. Doreen persuaded her mother to obtain a few strands of the woman's HAIR. She wound the hair around a POPPET containing herbs and pricked with black-ended PINS and cast a spell of protection for her mother. The woman then suffered harassment by a blackbird and stopped harassing Doreen's mother.

Her parents tried repeatedly to steer her toward Christianity and sent her to a convent school. She left at age 15 and never went back. By her late teens and early 20s, she was very aware of her own psychic abilities. She read extensively in occult literature, including the Theosophists and ALEISTER CROWLEY and especially admired DION FORTUNE.

At age 19, Doreen went to work as a secretary in Barry, South Wales. There she met Joanis Vlachopoulos, 32, an illiterate seaman with the merchant navy based in Cardiff. They were married on January 31, 1941. Six months later, Vlachopoulos was reported missing at sea and presumed dead, a casualty of World War II. Doreen remained for a while in Wales and then moved to London.

On May 29, 1944, Doreen married Cosimo Valiente, a convalescing refugee from the Spanish civil war, who had gone on to fight with the Free French Forces, was wounded and sent to England to recover.

After the war, Valiente and her husband moved to Bournemouth near the New Forest. In 1951, the Witchcraft Act outlawing witchcraft was repealed in Britain and was replaced by the Fraudulent Mediums Act. On July 29, 1951, Valiente's attention was caught by a newspaper article about CECIL WILLIAMSON and his opening of his Folklore Centre of Superstition and Witchcraft (see MUSEUM OF WITCHCRAFT) on the Isle of Man. The article, headlined "Calling All Covens," mentioned a coven in the New Forest. Valiente wrote to Williamson for information, and he passed her letter on to GERALD B. GARDNER. After a period of correspondence, Gardner invited Valiente to meet him for tea one afternoon at the home of DAFO, the woman who had initiated Gardner into the New Forest coven.

Gardner did not press Valiente to join his coven but gave her a copy of his novel, *High Magic's Aid*. It was his test of potential initiates, to see how they would react to the descriptions of ritual nudity (skyclad). Valiente was not put off, and so passed the test.

On Midsummer's Eve 1953, Gardner initiated her into his coven. He conducted the ritual at the home of Dafo in Christchurch, Hampshire, where he stopped en route to Stonehenge for a Druid solstice ritual. Valiente took the Craft name of Ameth. Her husband had no interest and did not join but accepted her involvement in the Craft. To other members of her family, Valiente explained that she had joined a Druid order, which was considered respectable.

For the initiation, Gardner used his own BOOK OF SHADOWS, a collection of ritual and Craft material he said came from his New Forest coven. Valiente, by then well read in occult literature, recognized portions of the rite as coming from ALEISTER CROWLEY's *Gnostic Mass* and CHARLES GODFREY LELAND's *Aradia*.

Gardner gave Valiente his book of shadows and other ritual material that he claimed came from the hereditary New Forest witches. Valiente recognized more material from Crowley and Leland and also from Rudyard Kipling, freemasonry, and the *Key of Solomon*. She politely accepted Gardner's assertion that it had been handed down over a long lineage of Witches practicing Witchcraft as a pagan religion, but privately she always believed that he was rankled to know she saw through the story. Valiente told Gardner that the Crowley material especially should come out because of Crowley's unsavory reputation.

From 1954 to 1957, Valiente collaborated with Gardner in reworking the book of shadows, using her considerable poetic gifts to improve and flesh out the material. The book of shadows served as the basis for what became the Gardnerian tradition, still the dominant tradition in contemporary Witchcraft.

Some of Valiente's contributions are considered the most beautiful in the Craft and have passed into common use, most notably THE CHARGE OF THE GODDESS (reworked from Crowley and Leland) and "The Witches' Rune."

Valiente is credited with increasing the emphasis on the GODDESS, which helped to transform the Craft into a full-fledged Pagan religion. Valiente said that the God and Goddess elements were already present when she received the material from Gardner.

Gardner was not an easy person to work with. His egotism and publicity-seeking tried the patience of members of his coven, including Valiente, who became high priestess. Splits developed in the coven over Gardner's relentless pursuit of publicity and over his fabricated "ancient" Craft laws, which chauvinistically gave dominance to the God and required the high priestess to retire when she got to be too old.

By 1957, Valiente and others who had had enough of "the gospel according to Gerald" departed the coven. Valiente and another coven member, Ned Grove, formed their own coven. Eventually, she patched up her friendship with Gardner and remained friends with him until his death, although she never worked with him again.

After Gardner died in 1964, Valiente was initiated into the CLAN OF TUBAL CAIN by ROBERT COCHRANE, a flamboyant man who claimed to be a hereditary witch practicing a tradition handed down through his family. Valiente fell out with him after determining that his story was more fiction than fact. She also did not like his open disdain of Gardnerians and his drug habits. Cochrane apparently committed "ritual suicide" with belladonna in 1966.

From 1964 to 1966, Valiente received a series of spirit communications from a spirit who said he was "Jack Brakespeare," a "traditional witch." The communications began one night as Valiente was in a hypnagogic state (the borderline between wakefulness and sleep), in which she saw a group of robed people engaged in a ritual in the corner of a field by moonlight. She began to communicate with Brakespeare, whose small coven lived in Surrey around the early 19th century. The communications were sporadic. Valiente surmised that the purpose behind them was to pass on information about the old ways.

Cosimo died in April 1972. Valiente began to spend more time writing and published her first book, *An ABC of Witchcraft,* in 1973. That was followed by *Natural Magic* (1975) and *Witchcraft for Tomorrow* (1978), which incorporate material from her Brakespeare communications. *Witchcraft for Tomorrow* was written in response to years of plagiarism and distortion of her creations for the book of shadows. The book includes *Liber Umbrarum: The Book of Shadows,* a new and simplified book of shadows for persons interested in initiating themselves and organizing a coven. Valiente wrote her autobiography, *The Rebirth of Witchcraft,* published in 1989. In addition to her books, Valiente wrote numerous articles.

During the 1970s, the British parliament considered reinstating a version of the Witchraft Act making witchcraft illegal. Valiente lobbied against this. New laws were never passed.

In 1980, Valiente initiated a search for OLD DOROTHY CLUTTERBUCK, the high priestess whom Gardner said initiated him in 1939. So little was known about Clutterbuck that historian Jeffrey B. Russell implied in his book, *A History of Witchcraft: Sorcerers, Heretics and Pagans* (1980), that Clutterbuck may have never existed at all. Valiente made a diligent search through records and, by 1982, discovered Clutterbuck's birth and death records and her will, which are now published on the Internet.

Valiente's account of her research is related in *A Witch's Bible* by JANET AND STEWART FARRAR, and in Valiente's autobiography.

In 1995, Valiente became a patron of the Centre for Pagan Studies, founded by her high priest, John Belham-Payne. In 1997, her partner, Ron (Cookie) "Dusio" Cooke died. In her later years, Valiente was openly critical of WICCA and its internal politics. She preferred to call Witchcraft "the Old Craft," and favored a certain amount of secrecy on the part of covens. She said that distinctions among traditions do not matter, for "a witch is a witch is a witch." She opposed organized religion as "an unmitigated curse to humanity." Much of the promising future for Paganism, she said, lies in feminism and the green movement.

Valiente also was critical of Gardner and some of the elements he introduced into Witchcraft. For example, she said that the THREEFOLD LAW OF RETURN was an invention of Gardner's. She said she did not believe that Gardner ever expected the enormous response he got. However, proving just how much of Witchcraft came from the hereditary New Forest witches or Gardner's imagination may never be determined.

Valiente believed in reincarnation and felt a great affinity with ancient Egypt.

Valiente was stricken with cancer in her later years. She died in a nursing home in Brighton, Sussex, on September 1, 1999, attended by Belham-Payne and his wife, Julie. Belham-Payne performed a simple Pagan service at her funeral, attended by friends. The rites are published on the Internet.

Valiente had no children. She left an extensive collection of personal papers, possessions, artifacts and copyrights to all her writings to Belham-Payne. The collection includes items made for her by Gardner and his and her original books of shadow. In keeping with her last wishes, Belham-Payne published a book of her poetry, *Charge of the Goddess*, in 2000.

FURTHER READING:

"D. Valiente on Gardner." Hecate's Cauldron. Available online. URL: http://www.hecatescauldron.org/Valiente%20%20Gardner. htm. Downloaded September 12, 2007.

Official Doreen Valiente Web site. Available online. URL: http://www.doreenvaliente.com. Downloaded September 12, 2007.

Thorn, Michael. "FireHeart Interviews Doreen Valiente." Interview published in 1991. *FireHeart* no. 6. Available online. URL: http://www.earthspirit.com/fireheart/fhdv1. html. Downloaded September 12, 2007.

Valiente, Doreen. *The Rebirth of Witchcraft*. London: Robert Hale, 1989.

Vaudois   The Vaudois area of the Alps was a hotbed of Catholic heresy in the 12th century. The Valdenses (Waldenses) were followers of Peter Valdo (Waldo): early Protestants against Catholic ritual and for the purity of the biblical gospel. Both the Dominican order of friars and the INQUISITION had been organized to root out this supposed abomination. Inquisitors believed that the heresy was accompanied by the practice of witchcraft, making the religious crime one against both God and nature.

By the 15th century, the Valdenses were no longer a theological threat, having been eliminated, but the connection with witchcraft remained: in the Alps, in the Lyonnais region and in Flanders, witches are called *Waudenses* and their gatherings are known as *Valdesias* or *Vauderye*.

vervain   An herb sacred since ancient times and used in both witchcraft and antiwitchcraft CHARMS, PHILTRES and potions. Vervain grows throughout Eurasia and North America. It was said to be revered by the DRUIDS because it resembles the oak, which was sacred to them. Druids gathered it on moonless nights in the spring when the Dog Star, Sirius, rose in the sky, being careful not to touch it as they collected it into IRON containers. The ancient Greeks and Romans considered vervain sacred as well. In Rome, it was consecrated for the purification of homes and temples and was used in medicinal remedies for a variety of ailments. Early Christians called vervain "herb-of-the-cross" because it was believed to have staunched Christ's BLOOD as he hung on the cross.

Because of its association with Christ, vervain was said to be an effective charm against WITCHES, evil SPELLS and DEMONS. People hung it in their homes, over their stable doors, among their crops and around their necks. Witches used it freely in their potions, ointments and brews and in the preparation of a HAND OF GLORY.

In Italian witch lore, vervain is sacred to DIANA, patron goddess of witches. Contemporary Witches use it as an ingredient in ritual purification baths.

Vervain is a common ingredient in folk-magic love philtres, because of the belief that its undiluted juice can bring about any wish. Vervain also reputedly can bestow immunity to disease, the gift of clairvoyance and protection against bewitchment.

Among its many medicinal uses are as a cure for toothaches, ulcers, heavy menstrual flow, gout, worms, and jaundice. Early Americans wore vervain around their necks and touched it for good cures and good health.

See HEALING.

Vodun (also Voodoo)   Vodun, recognized as a religion, bears little resemblance to the lurid snake-and-sex orgies, complete with pin-stuck dolls and zombielike followers depicted in the movies. An estimated 50 million worshipers worldwide believe that the work of the gods appears in every facet of daily life and that pleasing the gods will gain the faithful health, wealth and spiritual contentment. The gods "speak" to their devotees through SPIRIT POSSESSION but only for a short time during ceremonies. Vodun is almost synonymous with Haiti, but the rites also flourish in New Orleans, New York, Houston and Charleston, South Carolina.

Etymologists trace the origins of the word *vodun* to the term *vodun,* meaning "spirit" or "deity" in the Fon language of the West African kingdom of Dahomey, now part of Nigeria. Eighteenth-century Creoles (whites born in the New World, usually of Spanish or French ancestry, but also meaning native-born persons of mixed ancestry), masters of the Dahomean slaves, translated the word into *vaudau.* The Creole language derives from French, with definite African patterns of phonetics and grammar. Eventually, the word became *voudou, voudoun, vodun, voodoo* or even *hoodoo.* Most current practitioners of the ancient rites regard the terms *voodoo* and *hoodoo* as pejorative, however, preferring one of the other spellings. To the faithful, Vodun is not only a religion but also a way of life.

Vodun came to the New World—especially to the Caribbean islands of Jamaica and Saint-Domingue, now divided into the nations of Dominican Republic and Haiti—with the millions of black African slaves, encompassing members of the Bambara, Foula, Arada or Ardra, Mandingue, Fon, Nago, Iwe, Ibo, Yoruba and Congo tribes. Their strange religious practices perhaps first amused their white masters, but soon fearful whites forbade their slaves not only from practicing their religion but also from gathering in any type of congregation. Penalties were sadistic and severe, including mutilation, sexual disfigurement, flaying alive and burial alive. Any slave found possessing a FETISH (a figurine or carved image of a god) was to be imprisoned, hanged or flayed alive.

To save the blacks from the "animal" nature they were believed to possess, the masters baptized the slaves as Catholic Christians, which only forced native practices underground. In front of whites, blacks practiced Catholicism, but among each other, the gods of their ancestors were not forgotten. Rites held deep in the woods, prayers transmitted in work songs and worship of saints while secretly praying to the gods preserved the old traditions while giving them a new twist.

What evolved was syncretism: the blending of traditional Catholic worship of saints and Christ with the gods of Africa. Blacks could beg for intercession from St. Patrick, who banished the snakes from Ireland, and really be calling on their serpent god, Danbhalah-Wedo. Fetishes became unnecessary: even the masters tolerated a "poor idiot slave" keeping a tame snake or lighting candles for the "saints." Vodunists do not view such blending as profaning Christianity or Vodun but as enrichment of their faith.

Serving the loa. The Vodun pantheon of gods, called *loas* or *mystères,* is enormous and can accommodate additional local deities or ancestral spirits as needs arise. Vodunists acknowledge an original Supreme Being, called Gran Met, who made the world, but he has long since finished his work and returned to other worlds or perhaps to eternal contemplation. His remoteness precludes active worship. Devotees are those "who serve the *loa,*" and depending on the rites observed, the *loas* can be kind, beneficent, wise, violent, sexual, vindictive, generous or mean.

The "father" of the *loas* is Danbhalah-Wedo, or the Great Serpent (also called Danbhallah or Damballah), which brought forth creation. Prior to the days of slavery, Africans worshiped a large python, called Danh-gbwe, as the embodiment of gods. The snake was harmless to humans, and devotees believed that any child touched by the serpent had been chosen as a priest or priestess by the god himself. After transportation to the Americas, the blacks found a substitute in a type of boa. Danbhalah is the oldest of the ancestors and does not speak, only hisses. *Langage,* the sacred language of Vodun, which represents long-forgotten African liturgy, originated with Danbhalah's hissing. Danbhalah governs the waters of the earth and is also associated with LEGBA, the god of the sun and the way of all spiritual communion.

Aida-Wedo, the Rainbow, which arose from the waters of earth serves as the many-colored way of the gods' message to earth and is Danbhalah's wife. She, too, is a serpent: a short coiled snake who feeds upon bananas and lives mainly in the water. Her bright spectrum decorates Vodun temples, especially the central support pole. Aida-Wedo is only one manifestation of the goddess Erzulie, the deity of beauty, love, wealth and prosperity. Normally referred to as Maîtresse Erzulie, she is the lunar wife of Legba, the Sun. And as the MOON, Erzulie is pure, virginal. Contact with her heated husband burned her skin, so Erzulie is usually depicted as a beautiful, dark-skinned Ethiopian. There are many different Erzulies, encompassing not only the better virtues of love and good will but also the vices of jealousy, discord and vengeance. She can be vain, likes pretty jewelry and perfume and angers easily.

According to the creation myth, Danbhalah, the Serpent, and Aida-Wedo, the Rainbow, taught men and women how to procreate, and how to make BLOOD sacrifices so that they could become the spirit and obtain the wisdom of the Serpent.

Although Danbhalah represents the ancestral knowledge of Vodun, no communion of god and worshiper can take place without the offices of Legba. He is the Orient, the East, the Sun and the place the Sun rises. He governs gates, fences and entryways; no other deity may join a Vodun ceremony unless Legba has been asked to open the "door." He controls the actions of all other spirits. Depicted both as a man sprinkling water and as an old man walking with a stick or crutch, Legba personifies the ritual waters and the consolidation of Vodun mysteries. He is called *Papa,* and through syncretization has become identified with St. Peter, the gatekeeper of heaven and the man to whom Christ gave the keys to the Kingdom. Others see Legba as Christ, a mulatto man born of the Sun and the Moon. Legba also guards CROSSROADS, and as

Maître Carrefour (master of the four roads, or crossroads) is the patron of SORCERY.

Other important deities—all of whom have various manifestations—include Ogou Fer or Ogoun, the god of war and armor, iron and metalworking, wisdom and fire, who is associated with St. James; Agwe or Agoueh, the spirit of the sea, who presides over all fish and sea life and those who sail upon it; Zaka, the god of agriculture, who manifests himself in the clothes and coarse speech of the peasant; and Erzulie Freda, the goddess's most feminine and flirtatious persona. As Venus was Mars' lover, so Ogou takes Erzulie Freda. The total pantheon of Vodun *loas* encompasses hundreds of gods and goddesses and grows each time the spirit of an ancestor becomes divine.

A separate classification of *loas* are the Guedes, the various spirits of death and dying, debauchery and lewdness, graveyards and grave diggers. As sexual spirits, the Guedes also govern the preservation and renewal of life and protect the children. Depictions of the Guedes, usually referred to as Guede Nibbho or Nimbo, Baron Samedi (Saturday, the day of death) or Baron Cimetière (cemetery), show the *loa* in a dark tailcoat and tall hat like an undertaker. His symbols are coffins and phalluses. Those possessed by Baron Samedi tell lewd jokes, wear dark glasses and smoke cigarettes or cigars. They eat voraciously and drink copious amounts of alcohol. Entire cults of Vodun revolve around the worship of the Guedes.

Rites and practices. Each tribal rite, whether Rada (Arada), Congo, Petro, Ibo, etc., has its own manifestations of the *loas* and different rituals and ceremonies, although most of the primary *loas* appear in each one. The Guedes, using many names to hide their true personalities or intents, move freely among each Vodun division. The two main rites of Vodun worship are Rada and Petro or Pethro. Rada rites follow more traditional African patterns and emphasize the gentler, more positive attributes of the *loas*. Devotees wear all-white clothing for the ceremonies. Animals sacrificed—the "partaking of the blood"—include chickens, goats and bulls (see SACRIFICE). Three oxhide-covered drums provide the rhythms for the CHANTING, representing three atmospheres of the Sun, or Legba: the largest, called Manman, related to the chromosphere; the next, called simply Second, related to the photosphere; and the smallest one, called Bou-Lah, which is the solar nucleus. These drums provide the most resonant combinations of musical rhythm of any rite and are struck with drumsticks. The drummers are called *houn'torguiers*.

The Petro rites appear to have originated in Haiti during the slavery days. The *Petro* allegedly comes from Don Juan Felipe Pedro, a Spanish Vodun priest and former slave who contributed a rather violent style of dance to the ceremonies. Many of the Petro practices, including more violent worship services and the use of RED in ceremonial clothing and on the face, come from the Arawak and Carib Indians who then lived on Saint-Domingue. Petro *loas* tend to be more menacing, deadly and ill-tempered than other *loas;* many of their names simply have the appellation Ge-Rouge (Red Eyes) after a Rada name to signify the Petro form. Pigs are sacrificed for the benefit of Petro *loas.*

Petro devotees use only two drums, and they are covered in goatskin and struck only with the hands. Rigaud reports that the drums are considered cannibalistic, even demonic, and their syncopated rhythms are difficult to control in MAGIC operations, rendering them dangerous. The first drum is identified with thunderbolts and their patron, Quebiesou Dan Leh; the second and smaller with Guinee, or the extremity of the world that receives the thunderbolt.

Guinee, or *lan* Guinée or Ginen, represents the symbolic homeland of the Africans in diaspora. The sacred city of Guinée is Ifé, the Mecca of Vodun. An actual Ifé exists in southern Nigeria, but the Ifé of Vodun is a legendary place where the revelations of the *loas* descended unto the first faithful. Vodun devotees refer to themselves as sons or daughters of Guinée: "ti guinin." Vodunists believe all aspects of life—administrative, religious, social, political, agricultural, artistic—originated in Ifé, but most especially the art of DIVINATION. Since Africa is east of the New World, Ifé represents the celestial position of the Sun. Devotees gain spiritual strength from Ifé; when the sacred drums need divine refreshment, they are "sent to Ifé" in a very solemn ceremony signifying death, burial and resurrection.

Some aspects of Vodun worship appear fairly constant, with local alterations, for all rites. The temple, which can be anything from a formal structure to a designated place behind the house, is called a *hounfour, humfo* or *oum'phor.* Within the temple, also known as the "holy of holies," are an ALTAR and perhaps rooms for solitary meditation by initiates. The altar stone, called a *pe,* is covered in candles and *govis,* small jars believed to contain the spirits of revered ancestors. Offerings of food, drink or money may grace the altar, as well as ritual rattles, charms, flags, sacred STONES and other paraphernalia. Years ago, the sacred snakes symbolizing Danbhalah lived in the *pe's* hollow interior, but no longer.

The walls and floors are covered in elaborate, colored designs symbolizing the gods, called *veves.* These drawings can be permanent or created in cornmeal, flour, powdered brick, gunpowder or face powder just before a ceremony. They are quite beautiful and incorporate the symbols and occult signs of the *loa* being worshiped: a *veve* for Legba shows a cross, one for Erzulie a heart, Danbhalah a serpent, and Baron Samedi a coffin. Usually drawn around the center post or the place of sacrifice, the *veve* serves as a ritual "magnet" for the *loa's* entrance, obliging the *loa* to descend to earth.

Ritual flags may hang on the walls or from the ceiling. There are usually pictures of the Catholic saints, believed to be incarnations of lower Vodun deities. Most *hounfours* even display photographs of government officials. Since every chief of state is the gods' representative on earth, portraits of former dictators Papa Doc and Baby Doc Duvalier use to occupy important positions. A model boat completes the decorations, representing Maîtresse Erzulie and the ritual waters.

Outside the main temple is the *peristyle,* the roofed and sometimes partially enclosed courtyard adjacent to the holy of holies. Since the *hounfour* probably cannot accommodate all the Vodun participants and onlookers, most ceremonies are conducted in the open-air peristyle, as is treatment of the sick. A low wall encircles the area, allowing those who are not dressed properly or are merely curious to watch less conspicuously. The peristyle's floor is always made of hard-packed earth without paving or tile.

Holding up the peristyle is the *poteau-mitan,* or center post. The *poteau-mitan* symbolizes the center of Vodun, from the sky to hell, and is the cosmic axis of all Vodun magic. Usually made of wood and set in a circular masonry base called the *socle,* the post bears colorful decorations and designs representing the serpent Danbhalah and his wife Aida-Wedo. The *poteau-mitan* also symbolizes Legba Ati-Bon ("wood of justice," or Legba Tree-of-the-Good), the way of all Vodun knowledge and communion with the gods. Geometrically, the placement of the center post forms perfect squares, circles, crosses and triangles with the *socle* and the roof of the peristyle, adding to its magical powers. All Vodun temples have a *poteau-mitan,* or center, even if the post exists only symbolically.

Outside the peristyle, the trees surrounding the courtyard serve as sacred *reposoirs,* or sanctuaries, for the gods. Vodun devotees believe all things serve the *loa* and by definition are expressions and extensions of God, especially the trees. They are revered as divinities themselves and receive offerings of food, drink and money. Like cathedrals, they are places to be in the presence of the holy spirit; banana trees are particularly revered.

Calling the loas. True communion comes through divine possession. When summoned, the gods may enter a *govi* or "mount a horse"—assume a person's mind and body. The possessed loses all consciousness, totally becoming the possessing *loa* with all his or her desires and eccentricities. Young women possessed by the older spirits seem frail and decrepit, while the infirm possessed by young, virile gods dance and cavort with no thought to their disabilities. Even facial expressions change to resemble the god or goddess. Although a sacred interaction between *loa* and devotee, possession can be frightening and even dangerous. Some worshipers, unable to control the *loa,* have gone insane or died.

The *loas* manifest to protect, punish, confer skills and talents, prophesy, cure illness, exorcise spirits, give counsel, assist with rituals and take sacrificial offerings.

The priest or priestess, called *houngan* and *mambo,* respectively, acts as an intermediary to summon the *loa* and helps the *loa* to depart when his or her business is finished. The *houngan* and *mambo* receive total authority from the *loas,* and therefore their roles could be compared to that of the Pope, says Rigaud. Indeed, the *houngan* is often called *papa* or *papa-loa,* while the mambo is called *manman,* or *mama.* The *houngano* and *mambo* serve as healers, diviners, psychologists, musicians and spiritual leaders.

Like a ruler's scepter, the most important symbol of the *houngan*'s or *mambo*'s office is the *asson,* a large ritual rattle made from the calabash, a type of squash with a bulbous end and a long handle. Symbolically, the *asson* represents the joining of the two most active magic principles: the circle at the round end and the wand at the handle. The handle also symbolizes the *poteau-mitan,* or vertical post. Inside the dried calabash are sacred stones and serpent vertebrae, considered the bones of African ancestors. Eight different stones in eight colors are used to symbolize eight ancestor gods (eight signifies eternity). Chains of colored beads, symbolizing the rainbow of Aida-Wedo, or more snake vertebrae encircle the round end of the calabash. When the vertebrae rattle, making the *asson* "speak," the spirits come down to the faithful through Danbhalah, the oldest of the ancestors. Once the *houngan* has attracted the *loa* through the deity's symbol, or *veve,* appealed to Legba for intercession and performed the water rituals and prayers, shaking the *asson* or striking it upon the *veve* releases the power of the *loas* and brings them into the ceremony.

Other important members of the worship service include *la place* or *commandant la place,* the master of ceremonies, who orchestrates the flag-waving ceremonies, the choral singing and chanting and the drum beating. *La place* carries a ritual sword made of the finest iron and sometimes decorated with geometric designs and symbols. The sword's name is *ku-bha-sah,* which means "cutting away all that is material." Brandishing his sword from east to west during the ceremonies, *la place* cuts away the material world, leaving the faithful open for the divine presences. *La place*'s sword also symbolizes the *loa* Ogou, god of iron and weaponry.

The chorus or *canzo,* composed of fully initiated Vodun members called *hounsihs* or *hounsis,* performs under the direction of the *hounguenicon* or *hounguenikon,* usually a woman and the second-most powerful member after the *houngan* or *mambo.* By sending the chants to the *loas* in the astral plane, the *hounguenicon* calls the *loas* and demands their presence on earth.

Novices not yet completely in the *loas*' power are called *hounsih bossales.* The initiate who obtains the sacrificial animals is the *hounsih ventailleur,* and the sacrificial cook is the *hounsih cuisiniere.* The *hounguenicon quartier-maitre* oversees distribution of sacrificial food not reserved for the loas.

Vodun and magic. Magic, for both good and evil purposes, is an integral part of Vodun. Unlike the dichotomy of good and evil expressed in Judeo-Christian philosophy, evil in Vodun is merely the mirror image of good. The magic of the spirits is there to be used, and if that is for evil, then so be it. A *houngan* more involved in black-magic sorcery than healing is known as a *bokor* or *boko,* or "one who serves the *loa* with both hands."

Dating back to the days of slavery and probably beyond to the tribal kingdoms of Africa, the real Vodun power resided in the secret societies. Membership in the societies means total commitment to Vodun and complete secrecy about its practices and rituals. Oaths are made in BLOOD, and like the Sicilian code of *omerta,* or silence, transgressors can expect death if they reveal any of the society's secrets.

The most feared secret society is the Bizango, a sect that dates back to the bands of escaped slaves, called Maroons, hiding in the mountains. Also called Cochon Gris (Gray Pigs), Sect Rouge and Vrinbrindingue or Vin'Bain-Ding (Blood, Pain, Excrement), the Bizango reputedly meet at night, secretly, recognizing the other members through elaborate rituals and passwords. All through the night, according to some reports, Bizango initiates travel through the countryside, picking up members as they go, then hold frenzied dances dedicated to Baron Samedi, the *loa* of the graveyard. A nocturnal traveler who cannot give the password supposedly becomes the sect's human sacrifice—a "goat without horns"—or a candidate for zombification. Some members of these red sects believe that Legba, the Vodun Jesus, died upon the cross to serve as an edible human sacrifice, symbolized by the sacraments, "This is My Body . . . This is My Blood. Take and eat in remembrance of Me."

Politics and Vodun. Few understood the political nature of the Vodun societies better than Haitian dictator François (Papa Doc) Duvalier, a physician who was president of Haiti from 1957 until his death in 1971. Allying himself with the *houngan,* he used the trappings of Vodun to secure his power base, such as changing the Haitian flag to red and black, the Bizango colors, from its original red and blue. Papa Doc dressed in black suits with narrow black ties, the traditional clothing of Baron Samedi, until the people began to believe he *was* the *loa.* Stories circulated that Papa Doc could read goat entrails, that he slept in a tomb once a year to commune with the spirits and that he kept the head of an enemy on his desk.

When a Graham Greene story about Haiti, *The Comedians,* was made into a movie in 1967, Papa Doc reputedly stuck pins into effigies of actors Richard Burton, Elizabeth Taylor and Alec Guinness because he hated the film's discussion of his role in Haiti and Vodun. One story says that Papa Doc sent an emissary to collect a pinch of earth, a withered flower and a vial of air from John F. Kennedy's grave at Arlington National Cemetery so that he could capture the late president's soul and control U.S. foreign policy. Even Papa Doc's secret police, the Tonton Macoutes, depended on folk tales and fears of the spirits: children were told that unless they were good, their uncle, or *ton ton,* would carry them off in his *macoute,* or knapsack. Thousands of people were spirited away to be tortured and never seen again.

When Papa Doc died in 1971, his son Jean-Claude, called Baby Doc, declared himself President for Life and managed to hold on until his overthrow in February 1986. Because the Duvaliers had such intricate ties to the Vodun societies, many *houngan* and *mambos* were murdered or forced to publicly recant their beliefs and become Christians following his departure. Yet many Haitians believe that the societies finally grew sick of Baby Doc and his excesses; when they turned the spirits against him, he had no other options but to go. One of the new junta's first acts was to reinstate the old red and blue flag. Vodun was declared an official religion in Haiti by a decree of President Jean-Bertrand Aristide's on April 4, 2003.

See GRIS-GRIS; MARIE LAVEAU; SANTERÍA; MACUMBA; ZOMBIE.

FURTHER READING:

Davis, Wade. *The Serpent and the Rainbow.* New York: Simon & Schuster, 1985.

Hill, Douglas, and Pat Williams. *The Supernatural.* London: Aldus Books, 1965.

Rigaud, Milo. *Secrets of Voodoo.* San Francisco: City Light Books, 1985.

Waldenses   See VAUDOIS.

Walpurgisnacht   In German witch lore, the greatest of the pagan festivals celebrating fertility and one of the major SABBATS observed by witches. Walpurgisnacht is the same as Beltane or May Eve and is celebrated on the night of April 30 in observance of the burgeoning spring. Walpurgisnacht became associated with Saint Walburga, a nun of Wimbourne, England, who went to Germany in 748 to found a monastery. She died at Heidenheim on February 25, 777. She was enormously popular, and cults dedicated to her quickly sprang into existence. In Roman martyrology, her feast day is May 1.

During the witch hunts, Walpurgisnacht, or Walpurgis Night, was believed to be a night of witch revelry throughout Germany, the Low Countries and Scandinavia. Witches mounted their BROOMS and flew to mountaintops, where they carried on with wild feasting, dancing and copulation with DEMONS and the DEVIL. MONTAGUE SUMMERS observes in *The History of Witchcraft and Demonology* (1926), "There was not a hill-top in Finland, so the peasant believed, which at midnight on the last day of April was not thronged by demons and sorcerers."

In Germany, the Brocken, a dominant peak in the Harz Mountains, was the most infamous site of the witch sabbats. The Harz Mountains are in a wild region of northern Germany (now part of the German Democratic Republic), a fitting locale for the reputed witch gatherings. So common was the belief in the sabbats that maps of the Harz drawn in the 18th century almost always depicted witches on broomsticks converging upon the Brocken.

St. Walpurga was a gentle woman who lived a life of exceptional holiness. Yet the festival that carries her name, like other sabbats celebrated by witches, became associated with diabolic activities.

Contemporary Pagans and Witches observe the holiday with traditional festivities of dancing, rituals and feasting, none of which are associated with the Devil.

See WHEEL OF THE YEAR.

FURTHER READING:
Baroja, Julio Caro. *The World of the Witches.* 1961. Reprint, Chicago: University of Chicago Press, 1975.
Russell, Jeffrey Burton. *Witchcraft in the Middle Ages.* Ithaca and London: Cornell University Press, 1972.
Thomas, Keith. *Religion and the Decline of Magic.* New York: Charles Scribner's Sons, 1971.

Walton, Charles (1871–1945)   A man with second sight who was renowned as a witch in his village of Lower Quinton, England. Charles Walton was brutally murdered in 1945 in what was labeled a ritual witch killing, despite the lack of evidence that witches or occultists were responsible. The murder was never solved, despite the efforts of Scotland Yard.

The village of Lower Quinton lies in Gloucestershire in the Cotswolds, an area of England with a long history of witches and WITCHCRAFT. Nearby are the ROLLRIGHT STONES, strange, ancient monoliths said to be a Danish

Witch riding he-goat Devil to Walpurgisnacht sabbat, goaded by amoretti (ALBRECHT DÜRER)·

king and his army that were stricken by a local witch. The area is rife with superstitions.

Walton was an odd, reclusive man who worked as a field laborer and lived in a thatched cottage with his niece, Edith Walton. He was widely known to have clairvoyant powers and claimed he could talk to birds and direct them to go wherever he wanted, simply by pointing. He also claimed to have a lesser control over animals, except dogs, which he feared. He bred large TOADS of a type called *natterjack,* which runs rather than hops.

Walton's clairvoyancy began in his youth, and it changed his personality from extrovert to introvert. For three nights running, he saw a phantom black dog running on nearby Meon Hill, a particularly "witchy" site. On the third night, the dog changed into a headless woman, and the following day, his sister died.

For the remainder of his 74 years, Walton withdrew into himself. He worked for meager wages, seldom drank in public and was left alone by his neighbors. It was whispered by the villagers that he would steal out to the mysterious Rollright Stones nearby and watch witch RITUALS.

On the morning of February 14, 1945, Walton arose early and set out into the fields with a stick, a pitchfork and a bill hook. He had been hired by a farmer whose land lay near Meon Hill. About midday, the farmer saw Walton at work, trimming hedges with the bill hook.

But Walton never returned home. His worried niece contacted her uncle, and the two of them, along with the farmer, set out to search for the old man. They found his body lying faceup beneath a willow tree on Meon Hill. A pitchfork had been driven through his throat with such force that it had nearly severed his head; the prongs were embedded about six inches into the earth. A cross-shaped wound had been slashed on his chest with the bill hook, which was stuck into his ribs. Walton's face was contorted in terror. A few days later, a black dog was found hanged on Meon Hill.

Scotland Yard sent Detective Superintendent Robert Fabian to investigate. Fabian expected to solve the case quickly. However, he received little cooperation from the residents of Lower Quinton, who insisted Walton had been killed by some unknown person because he was a witch.

The witchcraft aspects of the case attracted a great deal of attention, including that of anthropologist MARGARET A. MURRAY, who said she believed Walton had been killed in a blood-sacrifice ritual. The case also was investigated by a writer, Donald McCormick, who wrote a book on it, *Murder by Witchcraft.* Despite the lack of evidence, some odd facts and stories came to light.

The date of Walton's murder, February 14, was the date that ancient Druids allegedly made blood-sacrifice rituals for good crops, in the belief that if life force is taken out of the earth, it must be returned. The crops of 1944 had been poor, and the spring of 1945 did not look promising, either. Walton was known to harness his huge toads to toy ploughs and send them running into the fields. In 1662 a Scottish witch, ISOBEL GOWDIE, confessed to doing the same in order to blast the crops (see BLASTING). Perhaps someone thought Walton was using witchcraft to blast his neighbor's crops.

Significantly, Walton's blood had been allowed to drain into the ground. According to old beliefs, a witch's power could be neutralized by "blooding." Many accused witches bled to death from cutting and slashing, usually done to the forehead. The practice was done in certain parts of England from the 16th century up to the 19th century (see BLOOD).

In 1875 a suspected witch in Long Compton, not far from Lower Quinton, was killed in almost the exact manner as was Walton. The murderer was the village idiot, John Haywood, who was convinced that 75-year-old Ann

Turner was one of 16 witches in Long Compton, and had bewitched him. The local crops were poor as well. Haywood confessed to pinning the old woman to the ground with a pitchfork and, with a bill hook, slashing her throat and chest in the form of a cross.

For Fabian, the case grew even more mysterious. He saw a black dog run down Meon Hill, followed by a farmhand. The dog ran out of sight. Fabian asked the farmhand about the dog, but the terrified man claimed there had been no dog. Later the same day, a police car ran over a dog. The next day, a heifer died in a ditch.

Fabian and his men took 4,000 statements and 29 samples of hair, clothing and blood, and still came to a dead end. The murderer of Charles Walton was never discovered.

See HEXENKOPF.

FURTHER READING:
Cavendish, Richard, ed. *The Encyclopedia of the Unexplained.* New York: McGraw-Hill, 1974.
Wilson, Colin. *The Occult.* New York: Vintage Books, 1971.

Warboys Witches   The story of the Throckmorton (also Throgmorton) children in Huntington, Essex, England, in 1589, is the first well-known case of allegedly possessed young people and the successful destruction of witches based on the evidence of minors (see POSSESSION).

Squire Robert Throckmorton of Warboys and his wife had five daughters: Joan, Elizabeth, Mary, Grace and Jane. As a wealthy landowner, Throckmorton supported many of his poorer neighbors, among them the Samuels. Alice Samuel and her daughter Agnes frequently visited the Throckmorton household and were well known to the girls.

In 1589 the youngest, Jane, began having sneezing fits and convulsions and fell into a trance. Her frightened parents consulted a Cambridge physician, Dr. Barrow, and a Dr. Butler. Looking only at Jane's URINE, both doctors diagnosed BEWITCHMENT. When the 76-year-old Alice Samuel came to offer her sympathies, Jane cried out against her, accusing the old woman of witchcraft. Within two months, all the other sisters were suffering hysterical fits, and the eldest, Joan, predicted that there would eventually be 12 demoniacs in the house. Sure enough, the maidservants fell victim to the SPELLS; if any left Squire Throckmorton's employ, their successors also became possessed. All pointed to Mrs. Samuel as the source of their torments.

Like other demoniacs, the girls shrieked and contorted if the person attempted prayer or read from the Bible, especially the beginning of the Gospel of St. John. Such actions are generally accepted as the signs of true possession but may also have been a convenient way for the girls to avoid pious exercises. In the only account of the Throckmorton possession, probably written by the girls' uncle, Gilbert Pickering, Elizabeth would throw fits to avoid religious lessons, only to come out of a tantrum if someone played cards with her, and to clench her teeth unless she ate outdoors at a particularly pretty pond.

Squire and Mrs. Throckmorton doubted the girls' possession, since they had only lived in the area a short time and no one had any motive for bewitching the family. They ignored the girls' accusations and tauntings of Mrs. Samuel.

In September 1590 the Throckmortons were visited by Lady Cromwell and her daughter-in-law. Lady Cromwell was the wife of Sir Henry Cromwell (grandfather of Sir Oliver Cromwell), the richest commoner in England. When she saw Mrs. Samuel, who was one of the Cromwell's tenants, Lady Cromwell angrily ripped the old woman's bonnet from her head, denounced her as a witch and ordered her hair burned. Horrified, Mrs. Samuel beseeched Lady Cromwell, "Madame, why do you use me thus? I never did you any harm, as yet."

Back home, Lady Cromwell experienced a terrible nightmare, in which she dreamed that Mrs. Samuel had sent her cat to rip the flesh from her body. Lady Cromwell never fully recovered; her health gradually declined, and she died a lingering death 15 months later, in July 1592.

By this time, the girls were afflicted, only when Mrs. Samuel was absent, not present. Mrs. Samuel then was forced to live with the Throckmortons for several weeks in order to determine her effect on the children. Mrs. Samuel, her daughter Agnes and another suspected witch also were scratched by the girls, a custom similar to PRICKING. The girls constantly exhorted Alice to confess her dealings with the DEVIL and delivered pious speeches that moved onlookers to tears. Giving in to the constant pressure, Alice confessed just before Christmas 1592.

Not too long after Christmas, however, Mr. Samuel and Agnes convinced Mrs. Samuel to recant, and she again claimed her innocence, only to reconfess before the bishop of Lincoln and a justice of the peace in Huntington on December 29. All three Samuels were jailed, although Agnes was released on bail to allow the girls to extract incriminating evidence from her through more scratchings. Mrs. Samuels confessed to having familiars, devils who were far inferior to the princes Beelzebub or Lucifer. She identified them as Pluck, Catch and White and the three cousins Smackes. The DEMONS often appeared as chickens.

The Samuels were not connected to the death of Lady Cromwell until the Throckmorton children accused Mrs. Samuel of bewitching her to death, thus placing her in jeopardy of capital punishment as a murderer under the Witchcraft Act of 1563.

The Samuels were tried on April 5, 1593, on charges of murdering Lady Cromwell by witchcraft. The court accepted the testimony of the Throckmorton girls, as well as several other persons who claimed that the Samuels had bewitched their livestock to death over the years. The jury took only five hours to convict all three.

Mrs. Samuel, Agnes and Mr. Samuel were hanged, and afterwards the Throckmorton girls returned to perfect health. Since Lady Cromwell had allegedly died due to the black offices of Alice Samuel, her husband, Sir Henry Cromwell, received all of the Samuels' goods. He used the money to establish an annual sermon at Queens' College, Cambridge, to "preache and invaye against the detestable practice, synne, and offence of witchcraft, inchantment, charm, and sorcereye." The sermons lasted until 1812.

The Warboys case had a significant impact on public belief in witchcraft and the EVIL EYE. The case was widely publicized, in part due to the impressionable judge, Edward Fenner, who, in collaboration with several others, produced a broadsheet, *The Most Strange and Admirable Discoverie of the Three Witches of Warboys,* published in 1593. The case also left an impact on the governing class. The Cromwells served in the Parliament of JAMES I, who gained the throne in 1603. In response to public pressure for more stringent actions against witches, the Parliament passed a new Witchcraft Act in 1604, which stiffened punishment for some witchcraft offenses.

FURTHER READING:

Robbins, Rossell Hope. *The Encyclopedia of Witchcraft & Demonology.* 1959. Reprint, New York: Bonanza Books, 1981.

Summers, Montague. *The Geography of Witchcraft.* London: Kegan Paul, Trench, Truner & Co. Ltd., 1927.

warlock   A term for male witches, though most men in contemporary Witchcraft prefer to be called Witches or Wiccans like their female counterparts. The word has negative connotations; it stems from the old Anglo-Saxon word *waerloga,* which means traitor, deceiver or liar. Tra-

Warlock riding to sabbat (ULRICH MOLITOR, *DE IANIJS ET PHITONICIUS MULIERIBUS,* 1489)

ditionally, a warlock is a sorcerer or WIZARD who has gained supernatural power and knowledge through a DEVIL'S PACT. (Such pacts are not part of contemporary Witchcraft.)

Since the revival of Witchcraft in the 1950s, few Witches have referred to male Witches as warlocks; SYBIL LEEK once commented that use of the word was a rarity, except among outsiders.

water   Water has ancient associations with the pure and holy. The Celts were particularly fascinated by its powers of life, HEALING, cleansing, regeneration and destruction and established numerous water deities and cults of rivers, streams, lakes and wells. Many water deities are female; water is linked to the MOON, a female force that governs the tides and female body fluids, and the moisture of wombs and birth. These positive associations of water with the female force are honored in contemporary Witchcraft; yet, in centuries past, water was used as a weapon against witches by the Catholic Church and zealous witch-hunters of both Catholic and Protestant faith.

During the witch hunts, suspected witches were bound and thrown into water to see if they would float or sink. It was believed that water, the medium of holy baptism, would reject an agent of the DEVIL; witches would float (see SWIMMING). According to another popular belief, witches and DEMONS were unable to cross running streams. If one was pursued by a witch or "fiend," the safest thing to do was cross a stream (see FORTRESS OF DUMBARTON).

Holy water—water mixed with SALT and blessed by a priest—was considered one of the Catholic Church's most powerful weapons against "the Fiend" and his subjects, who are supposed to be allergic to it. Holy water was sprinkled aroma houses to drive away evil spirits and "pestilential vapours," on crops to promote fertility and protects them from being blasted by witches and on farm animals to protect them from bewitchment (see BLASTING). The holy-water carrier came by regularly like a medieval milk man, making sure than no one was ever caught short of divine protection. When storms hit—stirred up by witches, no doubt—villagers raced to the local church to get extra holy water to protect their homes against lightning and to drive the witches away.

Inquisitors in the witch hunts were advised to keep holy water at hand to fend off SPELLS and evil looks. Holy water was also touted as protection against vampires; both vampires and witches supposedly recoiled at contact with the blessed liquid.

In medieval times, holy water was reputed to have miraculous medicinal powers. A dose of it would prevent one from being stricken by the plague. It was poured down the throats of sick animals who were diagnosed as suffering from a witch's curse and taken by humans for virtually all illnesses and diseases. Ironically, holy water was frequently prescribed by the very people often accused of witchcraft—the village wise women or healers. One such witch in 15th-century England prescribed a diet of holy bread and holy water for horses to prevent them from being stolen.

In the medieval stories about blasphemous witches' SABBATS and BLACK MASSES, holy water supposedly was replaced by URINE. Sometimes the Devil was said to urinate into a hole in the ground then dip it out and sprinkle it on his witches and demons.

Protestant reformers challenged the supernatural power of holy water, saying it was good for cooking but little else. By the end of the 16th century in England, the Church of England had abolished it from all rituals, along with most other Catholic sacraments.

Holy water is used in of EXORCISM, and to protect places against demonic forces.

In MAGIC, holy water is used to purify the MAGIC CIRCLE and to consecrate the tools of the magician, such as the sword, wand and knife (see WITCHES' TOOLS).

In contemporary witchcraft, salted water is used in rituals to anoint participants and to consecrate and purify objects, tools and the boundaries of the magic circle itself. The element of water is associated with fecundity, nurturing, emotions, love and compassion.

FURTHER READING:
Opie, Iona, and Moira Tatem. *A Dictionary of Superstitions.* New York: Oxford University Press, 1989.

Webster, Mary (d. 1696)   Massachusetts woman accused of bewitching a man to cause him ill health. Mary Webster was indicted and acquitted at trial, but a gang nearly tortured her to death after the verdict.

Webster and her husband, William Webster, lived in Hadley, Hampshire County. They were poor and depended on the townspeople for aid. One man who helped them was Philip Smith, a man of about 50 years who was a prominent citizen. But when Smith fell mysteriously ill in 1683, he and others accused Webster of bewitching him because she was unhappy with the amount of help he had given her and her husband.

According to Smith, Webster had expressed her unhappiness to him, and he had some fear that she might cause him problems. Smith's health went into sudden decline. He soon took to bed, delirious and speaking in what seemed to be strange languages. He said he was in great pain from being pricked with what felt like hundreds of pins, especially on his arms and toes. He cried out against Webster and others, claiming that he could see them before him, though they were invisible to others.

COTTON MATHER later reported that Smith's home was sometimes filled with the strange smell of musk and sounds of a mysterious scratching were heard. A supernatural fire was seen on his bed, and a mysterious form like a big cat appeared on the bed as well.

While Smith languished, Webster was examined on suspicion of witchcraft by the county magistrates, appearing before them on March 27, 1683. She was indicted on May 22, 1683, and was sent to jail pending trial. Webster was accused of having a DEVIL'S PACT and of having a FAMILIAR in the form of a *warraneage,* an Indian word for "black cat." An examination of her body revealed that she had teats of DEVIL'S MARKS in her "secret parts" where her various IMPS suckled.

On June 1, 1683, Webster was tried. Smith testified against her, but a jury found her not guilty. The verdict was unsatisfactory to some of the local residents. That winter, a gang of youths seized Webster, dragged her out of her house and hung her until she was nearly dead. Then they cut her down, rolled her in the snow, buried her in it and left her. She survived.

Smith died in 1684. The night of his death, according to Mather, a witness said the bed moved and shook of its own accord. On the second night, when the corpse had been prepared for the funeral, witnesses said there were unexplained noises in the room, as though furniture were being shoved about. Mather declared that these phenomena and the circumstances of death were "unquestionable" proof of witchcraft.

FURTHER READING:
Hall, David D., ed. *Witch-hunting in Seventeenth-Century New England: A Documentary History 1638–1692.* Boston: Northeastern University Press, 1991.
Mather, Cotton. *Memorable Providences, Relating to Witchcrafts and Possessions.* Boston: n.p., 1689.

Weinstein, Marion   American Witch, author, entertainer and media spokesperson. Marion Weinstein is especially known for her teachings on the positive applications and ethics of magic—she is called the "Ethics Witch." As an entertainer, she offers Wicca-based stand-up comedy.

Weinstein grew up in the 1950s. She said she knew from early childhood—by age three—that she was a Witch. Born in New York City on a new moon in the sign of Taurus (with moon in Gemini), she has always felt an affinity with Diana, the aspect of GODDESS who rules the new and waxing MOON. As a young child, Weinstein called her dolls "witches." She knew instinctively the basics of magic: that reality can be changed by specific, intense concentration. She felt a profound connection to Halloween (Samhain) that went beyond a child's interest in trick-or-treating; to her, this most mysterious of Pagan holidays was filled with magic and beauty.

The oldest of three daughters in a Jewish family, Weinstein became interested in Jewish mysticism, but was disappointed to find the KABBALAH closed to women. At an early age, she realized she had a psychic link with her mother, the experience of which encouraged her to develop her intuition.

In school, she was fascinated by fairy tales, certain they were truth that had become fictionalized. Fairy

Marion Weinstein (COURTESY MARION WEINSTEIN)

tales launched her on a lifelong pursuit of her Witchcraft heritage.

In early adulthood, Weinstein began to piece her intuitions and research together. At age 19, she visited Pompeii and felt a strong, instinctive connection to classical PAGANISM.

She graduated from Barnard College with a bachelor's degree in English literature. Witchcraft played a prominent part in her creative life. She wrote a Rogers-and-Hart-style musical comedy about Witchcraft, *The Girl from Salem,* which was produced on campus. After graduation, she took several courses in film at Columbia University, then went to Los Angeles to work as a commercial artist and animator. After two years, she returned to New York, studied acting, dance and voice and joined an improvisational theater troupe.

At the same time, she pursued her spiritual research and formed a group of people interested in MAGIC and Witchcraft. The group quickly recognized itself as a coven, with an eclectic tradition, meeting regularly on the Witchcraft holidays, and devoted to—among other traditional goals—sending positive energy toward world peace and nourishment of the planet.

In 1969, Weinstein connected with WBAI-FM radio, a liberal station in New York City. Her audition tape became the Halloween show that same year. That led to "Marion's Cauldron," her own program. Weinstein decided to "come out" as a Witch live on air, figuring she would be supported by the station's liberal staff. Many reacted negatively, however, and Weinstein had a difficult time for several years before being accepted as a Witch.

Weinstein interviewed experts, taught occult techniques, conducted group RITUALS and discussed topics such as psychic phenomena and dream research, as well as Witchcraft. Her show lasted 14 years. She concluded her work at WBAI-FM as she had begun, on Halloween.

During 20 years of research, Weinstein compiled a treasury of material on Witchcraft and magic, which she integrated into her first book, *Positive Magic* (1978 and revised in 1981).

While she was working on *Positive Magic,* her own personal theology crystallized into a system of working with five aspects of the Deity: DIANA, SELENE and HECATE as the Triple Goddess, complimented by CERNUNNOS and PAN, which she correlates to the five points of the pentagram, the religious symbol of Witchcraft. Weinstein developed this system in her second book, *Earth Magic: A Dianic Book of Shadows* (1979). The book was published by her own company, Earth Magic Productions, founded the same year, and initially was intended for a small audience of Witches. Its success led to several revised editions.

Weinstein has always advocated the practice of magic only for beneficial purposes, both with the public and inside the Wiccan/Pagan communities. Her stand on this led to the informal title of the "Ethics Witch." Ideally, an ethics spokesperson shouldn't be necessary, she believes, because magical practice should be understood as inherently ethical.

Weinstein began working professionally as a stand-up comic in nightclubs in 1978, using Witchcraft as the basis for her routines. Every Halloween, she appears in a New York City comedy club to deliver her annual routine about Witchcraft and to lead people in a ritual of positive magic. She appears on numerous radio and television shows and presents lectures and workshops about practical magic.

From 2001 to 2005, she had a radio show on Voice of America, "Marion Weinstein Live!"

Weinstein's guiding belief about Witchcraft is that a Witch's job is to help the community and to restore magic to daily life. Her personal definition of magic is transformation. She teaches personal self-transformation—always for the good of all and according to free will—as an ongoing way to help the individual self and the global community. A self-avowed "city Witch" in a modern world, she believes the ancient traditions translate well to fulfill current needs. *Earth Magic* notes the integration of Witchcraft into mainstream religious, political, environmental and social concerns and the "discovery" of new physics that show that the universe is indeed a magical place.

Weinstein sees Witchcraft not only as a religion, but also as a philosophy and a way of life, springing from a personal inspiration that comes from within. Her guiding tenet is the THREEFOLD LAW OF RETURN. She encourages people to develop their own groups and traditions in accordance with their inner guidance and their cultural and karmic roots, rather than to follow rules set by someone else. Her own system of Dianic Witchcraft evolved before the term became synonymous with feminist Witchcraft, and relates to her affinity with Diana. She believes it is helpful for women to identify with one particular aspect of the Goddess and embody the attributes associated with that deity, and for men to align similarly with God.

Her personal pantheon of deities has expanded from the original five to include Ceres, Goddess of the grain and rebirth; Neptune, God of the seas; Isis, Osiris and Horus, the holy trinity of the ancient Egyptians; and Cerridwen, Celtic Goddess of the Cauldron of Transformation.

Weinstein lives on Long Island with her pets and FAMILIARS. Some of her pets and familiars have reincarnated, and she maintains an animal family of wild and "non-wild" animals. She is involved in animal rescue work of lost, abandoned and mistreated dogs and cats and is developing her interspecies communication with animals.

Through Earth Magic Productions, Weinstein has created audio and video products from some of her radio interviews, instructional material and workshops. Her other book credits include *Racewalking,* with William Finley (1986), an exercise guide to the sport; *Magic for Peace* (1991); *The Ancient/Modern Witch* (1991, revised in 1993); *Positive Magic: Ancient Metaphysical Techniques for Modern hints,* revised edition (2002); and *Earth Magic: A Book of Shadows for Positive Witches,* revised edition (2003). She offers rituals on the Internet.

FURTHER READING:

Marion Weinstein Web site. Available online. URL: http://www.marionweinstein.com. Downloaded September 12, 2007.

"The Wiccan/Pagan Times Talks with Marion Weinstein." Available online. URL: http://www.twpt.com/weinstein.htm. Downloaded September 12, 2007.

Weir, Thomas (ca. 1600–1670) One of the most respected citizens of Edinburgh, Scotland, Major Weir shocked the entire city in 1670 by voluntarily confessing to black MAGIC. For all 70 years of his life, Weir had been a model citizen: a devout Presbyterian, a soldier who served Parliament in the Civil War and a respected civil servant. His secrets could have gone to the grave with him, yet for some unfathomable reason—perhaps overwhelming guilt—he was suddenly seized with the need to unburden himself before the public. Like ISOBEL GOWDIE eight years before, he voluntarily confessed to activities largely sexual in nature.

Weir said he had long practiced black magic and owned a black magic staff. His chief crime was incest with his sister, Jean, with whom he had sexual relations from the time she was a teenager until she was about 50. Then, disgusted with her wrinkles, he had turned to other young girls: Margaret Bourdon, the daughter of his dead wife, and Bessie Weems, a servant. He had also committed sodomy with various animals, including sheep, cows and his mare.

Despite public disbelief, Weir continued to broadcast his confessions, forcing the Lord Provost of the city to order an investigation.

Weir and his sister were brought to trial on April 29, 1670, charged with sexual crimes. While in prison, Weir cursed the doctors and clergy who tried to help him, and said, "I know my sentence of damnation is already sealed in Heaven . . . for I find nothing within me but blackness and darkness, brimstone and burning to the bottom of Hell." Weir was convicted of adultery, incest, one count of fornication and one count of bestiality. He was condemned to be strangled at a stake between Edinburgh and Leith on Monday, April 11, 1670, and his body burned to ashes.

Jean voluntarily confessed to incest. Perhaps in an effort to save herself, she laid the blame on her brother's witchcraft. He and she had signed a pact with the DEVIL, she said (see DEVIL'S PACT). She described going to a meeting with the Devil in Musselburgh on September 7, 1648, traveling in a coach drawn by six horses. She also confessed to consorting with witches, FAIRIES and necromancers (see NECROMANCY) and to having a familiar (see FAMILIARS) who spun huge quantities of wool for her and helped her carry out various evil acts.

Jean was sentenced to be hanged on April 12 in the Grassmarket in Edinburgh. To the end, she was contemptuous of the court and the citizenry.

The shocked citizens of Edinburgh were inclined to think the Weirs merely insane. But, in the climate of the times, stories of the Weirs's witchcraft easily became embellished. Weir's house, Bow Head, was said to be haunted, and sounds of spinning could supposedly be heard there at night.

FURTHER READING:

Sharpe, C. K. *A History of Witchcraft in Scotland.* Glasgow: Thomas D. Morison, 1884.

Summers, Montague. *The Geography of Witchcraft.* London: Kegan Paul, Trench, Truner & Co. Ltd., 1927.

Weschcke, Carl Llewellyn (1930–) Magician, Tantric, Pagan and former Wiccan high priest, Carl Weschcke is chairman of Llewellyn Worldwide, one of the largest publishers of New Age body, mind and spirit books in the United States. Weschcke played a leading role in the growth of the Wiccan and Pagan religions during their formative years in the 1970s. In the late 1970s, he reduced his public role in witchcraft to devote more time to his family and his growing publishing enterprise.

Weschcke was born on September 10, 1930, in St. Paul, Minnesota, to a Roman Catholic and Pagan family. Early on, he was exposed to metaphysics and the occult. He was fascinated by astronomy, religion and the occult and was most influenced by his paternal grandfather, who was vice president of the American Theosophical Society and believed in reincarnation. When Weschcke turned 12, his present from his grandfather was his own astrological chart. Weschcke's parents practiced mind reading, which they often discussed. And one of their houses was full of thumpings that they attributed to the ghost of the deceased former owner.

Weschcke graduated from St. Paul Academy in 1948 and went on to attend business school at the Babson Institute in Massachusetts. Upon graduating in 1951, he went to work in the family pharmaceuticals business, but found it unfulfilling. Instead, he wanted to be a publisher. He returned to school to study for a doctorate in philosophy at the University of Minnesota—which he did not have time to complete—and began looking for publishing opportunities.

During the 1950s and into the early 1960s, Weschcke was active in the civil rights and civil liberties movements, holding office in the St. Paul branch of the National Association for the Advancement of Colored People (NAACP) and the Minnesota branch of the American Civil Liberties Union (ACLU). He played a major role in bringing about fair housing legislation in St. Paul.

In 1960, he purchased Llewellyn Publishing Company, a small mail-order house selling mostly astrology books, almanacs and calendars, based in Los Angeles. The founder, Llewellyn George, had died six years earlier. Weschcke moved the business to St. Paul and began publishing and distributing a complete line of astrology and occult books. He purchased books from all over the world, at one time carrying nearly 10,000 titles for both retail and wholesale distribution. In the late 1970s, he decided to completely devote the company to publishing and dropped the distribution of other publishers' titles.

In 1964, Weschcke bought a large, stone mansion on Summit Avenue in St. Paul as both home and place of business. The house was reputed to be haunted, and Weschcke had numerous odd experiences. He was awakened by cold drafts coming in open windows, which had been closed when he had gone to sleep, and he heard footsteps. He saw apparitions of a man and a woman, which he believed were not true spirits, but the vibrations of former occupants that had been recorded into the psychic dimensions of the house.

A newspaper story about the haunting created an avalanche of public attention, paving the way for his media prominence in the emerging Witchcraft/Paganism movement.

Weschcke opened the Gnostica Bookstore and School of Self-Development in Minneapolis in 1970. It was a popular gathering place for people interested in the occult and alternative religions. A year later, a local convention manager suggested that Minneapolis could benefit from a Woodstock-style festival, and Weschcke took the opportunity to host it.

The first of several annual festivals was held in 1971. Initially called The First American Aquarian Festival of Astrology and the Occult Sciences, and later called Gnosticon, the festivals drew witches, pagans, magicians, astrologers, Christians and others from all over the world. Witchcraft rituals and group meditations were conducted. Weschcke led meditations for peace and the healing of Earth. Some attendees came costumed. At times, the festivities got a little wild, such as in 1974, when a group of about 20 pagans leaped into the hotel swimming pool at midnight to go skinny-dipping.

Carl Weschcke (COURTESY LLEWELLYN PUBLICATIONS)

Weschcke himself was initiated into the American Celtic tradition of witchcraft in 1972 by LADY SHEBA. He rose to high priest and held coven meetings in his Summit Avenue home.

In 1972, Weschcke married Sandra Heggum, a priestess in the same tradition, in a highly publicized handfasting ceremony at the winter solstice. The wrote their own vows from old witch rituals. Guests drank from a large cauldron filled with fruit, wine and flowers.

Weschcke remained open about his witchcraft faith and activities, which brought him continual media publicity. He published a popular Pagan journal, *Gnostica,* edited for a time by Isaac Bonewits. In the fall of 1973, Weschcke helped organize the COUNCIL OF AMERICAN WITCHES, then became its chairperson. For the council, he drafted "The Thirteen Principles of Belief" statement, one of his proudest accomplishments in the Craft. The statement was later incorporated into the U.S. Army's handbook for chaplains.

In the mid-1970s, Weschcke began to wind down his public activities. In 1973, his son, Gabriel, was born. In 1976 he sold the haunted house and moved to the country and began to devote more time to his family. He restructured his business by closing the bookstore, dropping *Gnostica* and the festivals and increasing the number of book titles published. During the same period, he adopted Llewellyn as a middle name, to use both in business and in magic. By the late 1980s, Llewellyn published 30 to 50 titles a year, plus audio- and videotapes, computer software and a popular "catazine," a combination magazine and catalog, *The New Times,* since renamed *New Worlds of Body, Mind & Spirit.*

The Weschckes raised their son in the Unitarian church. Gabriel, who holds a master's degree in publishing science from Pace University, New York, became regional sales manager and then vice president for Llewellyn. His wife, Michele, also works for Llewellyn as a business analyst and corporate secretary.

The Weschckes support the Wiccan/Pagan communities primarily through publishing; many of their authors are sent to organizational conferences and activities. Most of their time has been taken up by the demands of the business, which by the mid-1990s had grown to a midsize publishing house issuing about 100 new titles a year spanning a general spirituality/new age market. *Fate* magazine, a holding of Llewellyn, was sold in 2000. A downturn in business after 9/11 led to a corporate restructuring, followed by a rebound in 2003. In 2005 Llewellyn built a combined 80,000-square-foot office and warehouse in Woodbury, Minnesota, and publishes an average of 150 new titles annually, and employs 103 people. Llewellyn has further diversified by publishing alternative health, green lifestyle and self-help titles and has two fiction imprints: Midnight Ink, publishing mystery fiction, and FLUX, publishing young adult fiction.

Weschcke sees Wicca/Paganism and indeed the entire span of Astrology, tarot, magic, Kabbalah, shamanism, and spirituality, in a vital resurgence—a true "New Age"— widely influencing contemporary culture. Personally, he believes spirituality cannot be separated from daily life and that practicing Magick means accepting responsibility for one's thoughts and actions in all areas.

Weschcke holds two honorary doctorates, one in magic. He served for a time as grandmaster of Aurum Solis, an international magical order established in Great Britain in 1897, now based in Canada with affiliates in Europe and the United States.

Weyer, Johann (1515–1588)

A German physician and demonologist. Johann Weyer became so moved by the brutal persecution of accused witches that he spoke out strongly against the witch-hunters. Most witches, he said, were merely mentally disturbed, melancholic women who were incapable of harming any creature.

Weyer was born to a noble Protestant family in Brabant. He was a student of Agrippa von Nettesheim, who had successfully defended an accused witch and earned a bad reputation for doing so. Weyer studied medicine in Paris and became a physician, serving as a court physician to the Duke of Cleves in the Netherlands.

Weyer was alarmed by the mounting persecutions and brutal tortures of accused witches. He believed in the DEVIL and his legions of DEMONS but denied that the DEVIL gave witches power to inflict harm upon mankind.

He thought belief in witchcraft was caused by the DEVIL and that the Church was playing into Satan's hands by promoting belief in the evil power of witches.

Weyer set down his views in his book, *De Praestigiis Daemonum,* published in 1563. In it, he said most witches were deluded old women, the outcasts of society, who were fools, not heretics. Some might wish harm on their neighbors but could not carry it out. If harm occurred coincidentally, they believed, in their delusion, that they had brought it about.

Weyer acknowledged that there were witches who made pacts with Satan (see DEVIL'S PACT) but said that Satan, not the witches, caused harm. If such a witch killed cattle, for example, she did so by poison, not by supernatural means. He acknowledged that there were sorcerers who entered into demonic pacts for their own personal gain, but he believed that they were not the same as the helpless outcasts who were being persecuted by the Church.

Witches, he said, should be forgiven or, at the most, fined if they repented. He deplored the TORTURES and executions of victims and said that their confessions of

Johann Weyer (IOANNIS WIERI, DE LAMIIS LIBER, 1577)

SABBATS, FLYING through the air, STORM RAISING and such were meaningless.

Weyer was able to discourage witch-hunting in much of the Netherlands until he was forced out by the Catholic governor, the duke of Alba. Though he intended to inject a voice of reason into the witch hysteria, his book, unfortunately, had almost the opposite effect. Weyer was savagely denounced by critics such as JEAN BODIN and JAMES I, who believed in evil witches and advocated their extermination. Bodin said copies of Weyer's book should be burned. Books were written in refutation of Weyer and helped to stimulate further witch-hunts.

In 1568 Weyer published the *Pseudo-Monarchy of Demons,* an inventory and description of Satan's legions. Weyer claimed that there were 7,405,926 devils and demons organized in 1,111 divisions of 6,666 each. Later, the Lutheran Church thought his estimate way too low and raised the census of the demonic population to 2,665,866,746,664.

See REGINALD SCOT.

FURTHER READING:

Lea, Henry Charles. *Materials Toward a History of Witchcraft.* Philadelphia: University of Pennsylvania, 1939.

Trevor-Roper, H. R. *The European Witch-Craze.* New York: Harper & Row, 1957.

Wheel of the Year   In contemporary PAGANISM and Witchcraft, the life cycles of continual birth, death and renewal as expressed in the changing seasons. The Wheel of the Year is marked by eight seasonal festivals that are tied to the natural transitions of seasons and to the old Celtic agricultural calendar. The Sun, which rules the seasons, is symbolized by a wheel, and Earth turning around the Sun also is a wheel. Observing the seasonal festivals brings celebrants into an awareness of the turning of the cosmic wheel, and of the individual's relationship to Earth.

The seasonal festivals also are known as SABBATS, a term which has declined in use because of its association with the demonic orgies described in the literature of the European witch-hunts. Contemporary Pagan seasonal rites are drawn from earlier traditions of agricultural observances.

The celebration of the seasons has provided opportunities for creative expression through poetry, music, dance, song and drama. Festivities include both old Pagan customs and newly created rituals. There is no orthodox liturgy in Paganism and Witchcraft, and observances are as different and as creative as the many who participate in them. The Wheel of the Year honors the GODDESS, God and Nature, and provides a means for giving thanks for the bounties of the earth. The festivals are times of rejoicing, feasting, dancing and gaiety. Generally they are held outdoors, and may last over two or more days.

Not all traditions or individuals observe each of the eight festivals. Each tradition follows its own customs and rituals. Beltane and Samhain are the most universally observed.

Winter Solstice Eve (Yule). The winter solstice marks the longest night of the year. The Goddess awakens from her sleep and finds she is pregnant with the Sun God. It is a time for reflection and an awakening from the dark. Solstice rituals, for both winter and summer, are universal, and are intended to help the Sun change its course in the sky.

Samhain. An ancient Celtic festival that celebrates the beginning of winter, marked by death, and the beginning of the Celtic New Year. It is observed on October 31. "Samhain" (pronounced sow-ain) is an Irish term for "end of summer." According to tradition, home fires were extinguished and relit from the festival bonfire. Samhain marks the third and final harvest, and the storage of provisions for the winter. The veil between the worlds of the living and the dead is at its thinnest point in the year, making communication easier. The souls of the dead come into the land of the living. Cakes are baked as offerings for the souls of the dead.

Samhain is a time for taking inventory of life and getting rid of weaknesses and what is no longer desired.

Samhain is known popularly as All Hallow's Eve, or Halloween, and a multitude of games and customs have evolved in its observance. It is possible that the custom of trick-or-treating originated with an old Irish peasant practice of going door to door to collect money, breadcake, cheese, eggs, butter, nuts, apples, etc., in preparation for the festival of St. Columb Kill. Apples appear in many rites, especially as ingredients in brews. Apple dunking may once have been a form of divination.

Dancing at a seasonal rite (OLD WOODCUT)

Imbolc (Imbolg). A winter purification and fire festival, often called the "Feast of Lights." It is observed on February 1 "Imbolc" or "Imbolg" (pronounced iv-olc), which in Irish means "in the belly," or "lactation," and signifies the growing of life in the womb of Mother Earth. It celebrates Brigid (Brigit), Irish Celtic goddess of fire, fertility, crops, livestock, wisdom, poetry and household arts. Imbolc provides the first glimmers of life in the darkness of the Earth. The Goddess prepares for the birth of the Sun God. "Candlemas" is the Christian name for this festival, which also is known as St. Brigid's Day.

Spring Equinox (Ostara). Day and night, and the forces of male and female, are in equal balance. The spring equinox observed on or about March 21, paves the way for the coming lushness of summer. It is a time for nurturing new growth and launching new projects. Dionysian rites may be performed.

Beltane. One of the great Celtic solar festivals, celebrated in earlier times with bonfires. It is observed May 1. *Beltane* is an Irish term meaning "great fire." Beltane rites celebrate birth, fertility and the blossoming of all life, personified by the union of the Goddess and Sun God, also known in Christianized lore as King Winter and Queen May. Celebrants jump over broomsticks and dance around maypoles, both symbols of fertility. Great bonfires are lit. Offerings are left for the FAIRIES.

Beltane bonfires were believed to bring fertility to crops, homes and livestock. People danced deosil, or clockwise, around the fires or crept between fires for good luck and protection against illness. Cattle were driven through fires for protection against illness. In Druidic times, the Druids lit the fires on hillsides as they uttered incantations.

Midsummer. One of the most important and widespread solar festivals of Europe, and universal around the world. The Sun God dies. In European tradition, the night before the solstice on or about June 21, is a time of great magic, especially for love charms. Certain herbs picked at midnight will bring luck and protect against ill fortune. Contact with the fairy realm is easier. Bonfires are lit to help the Sun change its course in the sky, and rites resemble those for Beltane. Burning wheels are rolled downhill, and burning disks hurled at the Sun. The peak of power of the Sun God is manifested in the flourishing of crops and livestock. Celebrants jump over fires.

Selena Fox, center left, and Dennis Carpenter, to her left, lead a spring equinox candlelight ritual sponsored by Circle Sanctuary in Wisconsin (COURTESY CIRCLE SANCTUARY)

Circle Sanctuary community members and the Oak Apple Morris Dancers do a traditional English Morris dance to celebrate Beltane at Circle Sanctuary in Wisconsin (PHOTO BY SELENA FOX; COURTESY CIRCLE SANCTUARY)

Lughnasadh (Lammas). A great festival of games and dance, named for Lugh, the Irish Celtic solar god. It is observed August 1. *Lughnasadh* relates to words meaning "to give in marriage," and was once associated with marriage contracts. Nine months away is the next Beltane, the birth of summer and life. According to medieval legend, the festival celebrates the Irish god Lugh's marriage to the Sovranty of Ireland, the goddess Eriu. A hag, Eriu is transformed into a beauty by the marriage, and personifies the land of Ireland. First harvests are made, accompanied by thanksgivings and rites to ensure the bounty of the next year's crops. Some traditions observe the death of the Sacred King as a sacrifice to ensure the fertility of next year's crops. In old Pagan customs, the blood of a cock would be scattered on the fields.

Lammas, from the Old English terms for "loaf" and "mass," is a Christianized name for an old Saxon fruit and grain festival coined by the early English Church. The holiday was celebrated with the first harvests, the ripening of apples and winter wheat, the latter of which, according to tradition, was made into loaves and blessed in the church. Lammas Day also was a day of accounts. In Scotland, tenant farmers took their first grain harvests to their landlords on August 1 to pay the rent.

Autumn Equinox (Mabon). Once again, day and night and male and female forces are equal. The autumn equinox, observed on or about September 21, is the time of second harvests, of balancing the accounts of life, and preparing for the winter. Traditionally, the Eleusinian Mysteries are observed in rites and dramas. "Mabon" is a name introduced in the 1970s to give the festival a Celtic trait.

FURTHER READING:
Crowley, Vivianne. *Principles of Wicca.* London: Thorsons/Harper Collins, 1997.
Harvey, Graham. *Contemporary Paganism: Listening People, Speaking Earth.* New York: New York University Press, 1997.
Hutton, Ronald. *The Pagan Religions of the Ancient British Isles: Their Nature and Legacy.* Oxford: Blackwell Publishers, 1991.
———. *The Stations of the Sun: A History of the Ritual Year in Britain.* Oxford: Oxford University Press, 1996.
Starhawk. *The Spiral Dance.* Rev. ed. San Francisco: HarperSanFrancisco, 1989.

Wicca   An alternate, and sometimes preferred, name for the religion of contemporary Witchcraft. Some witches prefer to call themselves Wiccans rather than Witches and say they practice Wicca, rather than Witchcraft, because the words do not carry the negative stereotypes attached to *Witch* and *Witchcraft*. The terms *Wicca* and *Wiccan* distinguish practitioners of contemporary Witchcraft the religion from practitioners of folk MAGIC and other forms of witchcraft as sorcery. They signify an organized religion with a set of beliefs, tenets, laws, ethics, holy days and rituals.

Some Wiccans believe that *Wicca* is derived from the Old English terms *wita*, which means "councilor," or *wis*, which means "wise." *Wicca* is Old English for "witch," as is the Old English term *wicce*. *Wiccian* means "to work sorcery" and "to bewitch." Still another Old English term, *wican*, means "to bend." In the sense that Witches use magic to influence events, *Wicca* and *Wiccan* are therefore appropriate terms.

See WITCHCRAFT.

Wiccaning   See RITES OF PASSAGE.

Wiccan Rede   The creed of contemporary PAGANISM and Witchcraft is expressed simply:

Eight words the Wiccan Rede fulfill;
An' it harm none, do what ye will.

The Wiccan Rede acknowledges the right of all people to choose their own paths, as long as their choices do not bring injury to another. The term *Wiccan Rede* is derived from the Old English terms *wicca* ("witch") and *roedan* ("to guide or direct"). *An* is Old English, short for *and*. Some Witches erroneously believe it is an archaic term for *if*.

The exact origin of the Wiccan Rede is uncertain. According to GERALD B. GARDNER, the creed is derived from the legendary Good King Pausol, who declared, "Do what you like so long as you harm no one," and apparently was adhered to by successive generations of witches. It probably has more recent origins, dating to the 1940s and 1950s, the early years of what was to become the "Gardnerian tradition" of modern Witchcraft. Gardner, who borrowed from the writings of ALEISTER CROWLEY, may have composed the Wiccan Rede by modifying Crowley's Law of Thelema: "Do what thou wilt shall be the whole of the Law." Crowley believed that if people knew their true wills and followed them, they would harmonize with the universe.

The Rede may originally have been intended to help make modern Witchcraft more acceptable to the public. It has since become interpreted very conservatively by most Witches and influences the casting of SPELLS. Some witches feel the Rede should be interpreted more liberally.

Witches espouse a deep and abiding respect for the sanctity and free will of all living creatures and do not believe they should use their powers to interfere in that free will. They believe it is unethical to use MAGIC to harm or manipulate; even a love SPELL is manipulative if it is an attempt to sway affections against one's free will. Rather than cast a love spell aimed at a particular person, for example, a Witch casts a spell directed at attracting the right and perfect love, for the good and free will of all. Many Witches believe they should not cast any sort of spells on others without first obtaining their permission—even HEALING spells.

It is believed that violators of this interpretation of the Wiccan Rede will suffer a karmic boomerang effect and bring negativity or evil upon themselves.

This interpretation of the Rede seems extreme to some in the Craft, for it means that spells should not be cast against wrongdoers: a Witch could make no effort to stop a rapist or a crime magically, because that would be manipulation of the criminal's free will. Those who favor the conservative interpretation argue that they can instead cast spells to protect victims.

Other Witches advocate casting "binding" spells; that is, spells that stop or prevent evil. A binding spell on a serial murderer, for example, would not be a CURSE upon the murderer but would be aimed at getting him caught. One celebrated binding spell was cast in 1980 in the San Francisco Bay Area, against the Mt. Tam Murderer, a serial killer who ambushed and shot joggers, most of them women. A group of Witches led by Z BUDAPEST conducted a public "hexing" (their term for binding) ritual, calling for the murderer, who had been at large for nearly three years, to bring himself down through his own evil and mistakes. Within three months, the killer made enough mistakes to lead to his arrest; he was later convicted and given the death sentence.

Many Witches also cast binding spells to help causes, such as antinuclear movements, environmental concerns and animal welfare—to stop the killing of whales, for example. Binding spells are also cast against troublemakers, destructive gossips and annoying, meddlesome persons. In some of these situations, judgment is subjective. Casting a binding spell upon a coworker with whom one is having conflicts may be considered ethical by some Witches but not so by others. In an effort to be ethically consistent, some Witches cast spells that are directed not at persons but at situations. For example, instead of binding a troublesome person in order to solve a problem, the Witch casts a spell directed at solution of the problem by unspecified means "for the good of all." Or, instead of casting a love spell on a specific individual, the Witch casts a spell to attract "the right and perfect love."

Still other Witches feel the interpretations of the Wiccan Rede have become too convoluted and have stripped Witches of their magical effectiveness, reducing them to a harmless level of "Bambi magic." They say that if it is morally responsible to stop a crime physically, then it should be morally responsible to stop it magically. Some Witches do practice cursing when they feel it is warranted, but are quiet about it.

In other cultures where witchcraft plays a different role, the issue would not exist: a magician or sorcerer who refused to curse an enemy would be useless to society. But contemporary Witches seek to dispel age-old negative beliefs about Witches. Despite occasional allowances for "white witches" in popular lore, the witch has been perceived throughout history as one who uses supernatural forces and powers especially for evil. Contemporary Witches define themselves differently, as agents of good and as healers.

See THREEFOLD LAW OF RETURN.

FURTHER READING:
Buckland, Raymond. *Buckland's Complete Book of Witchcraft.* St. Paul: Llewellyn Publications, 1986.
Crowley, Vivianne. *Wicca: The Old Religion in the New Millennium.* Revised ed. London: Thorsons/Harper Collins, 1996.
Valiente, Doreen. *An ABC of Witchcraft Past and Present.* 1973. Reprint, Custer, Wash.: Phoenix Publishing, 1986.

widdershins (also withershins) A counterclockwise, circular movement used in the casting of binding and banishing SPELLS and CURSES, and in the casting of some MAGIC CIRCLES. The term *widdershins* comes from the Anglo-Saxon term *with sith,* "to walk against." The Irish equivalent is *tuatal or tuathal,* which means "a turning to the left"; it is the "unholy round" in Irish folklore. The opposite of widdershins is DEOSIL, moving clockwise.

Widdershins refers to walking against the sun and generally represents the unnatural and negative. In the casting of a black magic spell against the occupants of a house, for example, a witch or sorcerer would walk around the house counterclockwise. Widdershins motions and movements also are used in spells to get rid of negative spells or undesirable situations. It is used in necromantic rituals (see NECROMANCY).

In contemporary Witchcraft, once a MAGIC CIRCLE is cast deosil, a small section of it may be opened for access and egress with a widdershins motion with a sword or athame (see WITCHES' TOOLS), then reclosed deosil.

Wild Hunt In Celtic and Germanic folklore, a furious bunch of ghosts of the restless dead who ride through the sky on their phantom horses accompanied by their spectral hounds, shrieking and making wild noises (see GHOSTS, HAUNTINGS AND WITCHCRAFT). The hounds and horses are black, with hideous eyes. In various medieval versions of the Wild Hunt, witches join the phantoms, and the ghostly train is led by pagan goddesses-turned-devils (by Christianity), including DIANA, HOLDA, Herodias, HECATE and Berchta. A Cornish version of the Wild Hunt, Devil's Dandy Dogs, is the most diabolical of ghostly packs, hunting the countryside for human souls. The Sluagh, or the Host, is a band of the unforgiven dead of the Highland fairy folk (see FAIRIES). Diana's night train punished the lazy and wicked but were generous on occasion: if a peasant left out food for them, they ate it and magically replenished it before they left.

The Wild Hunt is still seen flying over the countryside on Samhain, All Hallow's Eve.

FURTHER READING:
Russell, Jeffrey Burton. *Witchcraft in the Middle Ages.* Ithaca and London: Cornell University Press, 1972.
Thomas, Keith. *Religion and the Decline of Magic.* New York: Charles Scribner's Sons, 1971.

Williamson, Cecil Hugh (1909–1999) Researcher, occultist and founder of The Witchcraft Research Centre and the MUSEUM OF WITCHCRAFT in England. Cecil Hugh Williamson was acquainted with GERALD B. GARDNER and ALEISTER CROWLEY during the formative years of the Witchcraft revival. He was in his own right an accomplished wise man and magician.

Williamson was born on September 18, 1909, in Paignton, South Devon, England, to a well-to-do family. His father had a career in the fleet air arm of the Royal Navy. In childhood he was introduced to the by through being involved in what he terms "a major public act of witchcraft" at North Bovey, Devonshire, where he spent holidays with his uncle. In 1916, at the age of six, Williamson witnessed an old woman reputed to be a witch being stripped of her clothing and beaten. He ran to her defense and was beaten himself. The woman befriended him and taught him about witches. These events were followed five years later by another witchcraft incident in which the power of spellcraft was demonstrated to him. An odd, elderly woman showed him how to cast a SPELL against a boy who was bullying him at school. The bully soon had a skiing accident that left him crippled and unable to return to school.

These incidents had a dramatic and lifelong impact upon his way of life and led eventually to his meeting and

Cecil Williamson (AUTHOR'S COLLECTION)

associating with leading mediums and psychics working in London. He took part in their seances by playing the role of the "young, silent virgin boy in white."

Williamson attended prep school in Norfolk and then Malvern College in Worcestershire. He spent summers in Dinard, France, with his grandmother and her medium friend, Mona Mackenzie. After graduation, his father sent him to Rhodesia to learn how to grow tobacco. There he had as houseboy, Zandonda, a retired witch doctor who taught him about African magic.

In 1930, Williamson returned to London and entered the film industry, doing production work at several studios. He continued to collect information on folk witches and their craft. In 1933, he married Gwen Wilcox, niece of film producer and director Herbert Wilcox. Gwen worked as a makeup artist for Max Factor of Hollywood.

Williamson's study of the occult brought him substantial knowledge and a network of impressive contacts, among them Egyptologist E. A. Wallis Budge, historian MONTAGUE SUMMERS and anthropologist MARGARET MURRAY. His expertise came to the attention of the British government's MI6 prior to World War II. In 1938, he was asked, and agreed, to help the MI6 intelligence section of the Foreign Office collect information about Nazi occult interests. He formed The Witchcraft Research Centre for this purpose.

His tasks included such things as identifying who in the Nazi power structure was interested in astrology, predictions (especially those of Nostradamus), graphology and so on. He played an instrumental role in using phony Nostradamus predictions to lure Rudolf Hess to Scotland. The predictions were planted in an old book in France that found its way to Hess. He was arrested in Scotland.

Williamson said he was involved in a famous "witches' ritual" to put a CURSE on Hitler and prevent him from invading England. The ritual was staged in Ashdown Forest, Crowbourgh, Sussex, as a hoax to fool Hitler. Aleister Crowley and Crowley's son, Amado, were part of the operation. Gerald Gardner was not present, although he later said he and his New Forest coven were involved and that the event took place in the New Forest (see CONE OF POWER).

After the war ended, Williamson found himself without work but with a little cash. He decided to go into business for himself and hit upon the idea of setting up a witchcraft museum. He selected Stratford-on-Avon as the site in 1947, but local antagonism ran him out of town. He moved to Castletown on the Isle of Man, where in 1949 he opened the Folklore Centre of Superstition and Witchcraft and Witches Kitchen restaurant at The Witches Mill. He filled it with magical objects he had collected over the years. He was described in the press as a "witchcraft consultant." He said his proficiency in the magical arts—such as spell-casting and the making of POPPETS—was both professional and academic.

In 1951, he opened a museum addition and employed Gardner as the "resident witch." The repeal of the Witch-craft Act the same year enabled Williamson to get a lot of media attention and publicity. Soon after the repeal, Williamson advertised for witches via the media. On July 29, 1951, he was featured in newspapers in an article headlined "Calling All Covens." He described the Old Religion and how witches observed four SABBATS, Samhain, Candlemas, Beltane and Lammas. He said he had connections to witches and invited others to contact him. One who did was DOREEN VALIENTE. Williamson passed her letter on to Gardner. In 1952, he sold the museum buildings to Gardner and moved his collection back to England. He relocated several times, including to Royal Windsor and Bourton-on-the-Water in the Cotswolds. Local residents were not pleased. In Bourton-on-the-Water, Williamson received death threats and was bombed. Dead CATS were hung in trees as warnings to him. An arson attack destroyed part of the museum. Williamson moved an, finally settling at Boscastle, a tiny seaside village on the north coast of Cornwall in 1960–61. During that time, he operated other museums in various locations, such as the Museum of Smuggling at Polperro and the Museum of Shellcraft at Buckfast.

Relationship with Gerald B. Gardner. Williamson met Gardner in 1946 when he happened to visit the Atlantis occult bookshop in London and was introduced to him as he was giving an informal talk. Gardner apparently was keen to establish a relationship because of Williamson's network of occult contacts. The relationship between the two was strained at times and ended on bad terms.

Williamson described Gardner as vain, self-centered and tight with money and more interested in having outlets for his nudist and voyeuristic interests than in learning anything about authentic witchcraft. Nonetheless, he was a colorful character, and Williamson saw him frequently prior to his move to the Isle of Man.

At the time of their meeting, Gardner was running a coven in Bricketts Wood outside St. Albans. He had a cottage on the grounds of a nudist club. His altar, said Williamson, consisted of an "Anderson," an air raid shelter table with a metal top. Here the GREAT RITE was performed. The coven had far more men than women, about an 80–20 percent split, since the sexual ritual was not favored by many women who joined. At one point, Williamson said, Gardner resorted to hiring a London prostitute to fill the role of the high priestess and engage in sex. Williamson said he participated as an observer in some of the coven's activities.

Williamson took Gardner to visit Aleister Crowley on several occasions (Gardner did not drive a car). Gardner signed up for a lesson course from Crowley, ostensibly to learn more magical craft for his budding witchcraft tradition. It was a short-lived project, for he did not study the lessons as Crowley wished. The last time Williamson saw Crowley was in 1946, when Crowley was ill and living in Hastings. According to Williamson, Gardner wanted to patch up the relationship with Crowley and so they paid a visit to him. Crowley was only cordial, not conciliatory, and later privately warned Williamson to be careful of Gardner.

Crowley offered Williamson his Baphomet magical ring for his museum, although the ring was pawned. Williamson redeemed it and gave it back to Crowley, but Crowley insisted that he keep it.

When Gardner discovered Williamson's interest in establishing his museum on the Isle of Man, he urged him to buy the Bricketts Wood cottage and dismantle it and take it with him. Williamson bought only the exhibits inside.

After Williamson and his wife moved to Castletown on the Isle of Man, Gardner unexpectedly showed up on their doorstep to visit. He was having money trouble with a family trust fund and stayed for three months, until lawyers straightened the matter out. Gardner officiated at the opening of the museum, where he also sold copies of his privately printed novel, *High Magic's Aid*. While staying with Williamson, he also worked on his BOOK OF SHADOWS and his version of the history of witchcraft, published as *Witchcraft Today* in 1954. Gardner moved to Castletown and purchased a house near the museum.

Over the years, Williamson followed Aleister Crowley's advice to stay clear of cult groups. He did not belong to any occult group or society. He saw the services of the folk witch as valuable and necessary to society, especially to lower classes who could not afford fancy medical treatment and who were often persecuted or victimized by authorities and the upper classes. He disdained the revivalist Pagan religion of modern Witches, criticizing them for "being nonproductive of results."

Later years. Once back in England, Williamson continued his active research of the occult, acquiring pieces for his collections and adding information to his data bank for the Witchcraft Research Centre. He also turned to investigating survival after death. According to his records, between 1930 and 1997 he took part as a spectator or "operative" in 1,120 witchcraft cases that produce beneficial results and had known, met with and been taught by 82 wise women. He said the days of the genuine witch and her craft were coming to an end, as fewer and fewer people turned to witches for resolution of problems.

Williamson retired in 1996. On October 31, at midnight, he sold the Museum of Witchcraft to Graham King and Elizabeth Crow. He retired to Witheridge, Tiverton, in Devon. He retained some of the museum artifacts, as well as his extensive collection of occult objects that are part of the Witchcraft Research Centre, such as the skeleton of URSULA KEMPE, executed for witchcraft in the 16th century in the ST. OSYTH WITCHES case.

Williamson's health declined and in 1999 he suffered a stroke. He died at his home on December 9, 1999, at age 90. At his request, there was no funeral service. He left instructions that people who wished to observe his passing conduct their own RITUAL on December 18 at 10 P.M. GMT.

Some of Williamson's letters, personal magical items and artifacts are at the Museum of Witchcraft.

will-o'-the-wisp   See JACK-O'-LANTERN.

willow   The bark of the willow contains salicin, which has analgesic properties. These properties, which were discovered by the Druids, make willow bark an important ingredient in the herbalist's pharmacopoeia. In ancient Greece, the willow was highly revered by witches and was sacred to the goddesses HECATE, CIRCE and Persephone. In folklore it is called "witches' aspirin" and the "tree of enchantment" and is associated with the MOON. Contemporary Witches use it in HEALING rituals; the soft branches are knotted (see KNOTS) in the casting of SPELLS. Willow also is used to bind birch twigs onto an ash branch to form a "Witch's broom," also used in rituals. A willow planted in the garden, especially if it is near a spring or river, will bring the blessings of the Moon to the occupant and will guard the home. In some parts of England, the willow has a dark side according to love: it is said to stalk travelers at night, muttering low noises.

Wilson, Monique   English Witch known as Lady Olwen, a high priestess with GERALD B. GARDNER, the namesake of the Gardnerian tradition of contemporary Witchcraft. In 1963 she initiated RAYMOND BUCKLAND into the Craft; Buckland became the chief spokesperson for the Gardnerian tradition in the United States.

Upon Gardner's death later in 1964, Wilson and PATRICIA C. CROWTHER were designated the chief heirs to his estate. Wilson was the prime beneficiary, inheriting Gardner's Witchcraft Museum (the Witches' Mill) in Castletown on the Isle of Man, his collection of swords, daggers and magical tools and objects, his notebooks and papers and the copyrights to his books. For a few years, Wilson and her husband, "Scotty," an ex-pilot, held weekly COVEN meetings at Gardner's cottage in Castletown, ran the museum and kept up an international correspondence with Witches.

Wilson then sold the museum to Ripley's International, a move that earned her the disfavor of many Witches. Ripley's dispersed the contents in museums in Canada and the United States, including the Ripley's Museum of Witchcraft and Magic on Fisherman's Wharf in San Francisco. Many Witches feel the exhibits sensationalize and cheapen Witchcraft and are not a fitting end to Gardner's possessions.

See MUSEUM OF WITCHCRAFT.

Windsor Witches (d. 1579)   Four women accused and hung as witches for a variety of crimes in Windsor, England. One of their chief offenses was alleged to be bewitchment by POPPET, a type of witchcraft greatly feared at the time by Queen Elizabeth I. In August 1578, three female waxen dolls with bristles stuck into their hearts were found in a dunghill in London, causing great concern in royal circles over the use of witchcraft in treason. The alleged use of waxen dolls by the Windsor women focused more attention on the case than might have otherwise been warranted.

The principal figure in the case was Elizabeth Stile, alias Rockingham, a widow of 65 years. She was regarded as "lewd, malicious and hurtful" by her neighbors and was arrested on charges of witchcraft. She was forced to walk the 12 miles from Windsor to Reading, where she was imprisoned.

Stile made an extensive confession and said she had a rat for a FAMILIAR (see RODENTS) named Philip that she fed with her own BLOOD from her right wrist. She said she had allowed a DEVIL'S MARK to be made by the Devil on her right side. She named other witches and said they all met and conspired to bewitch cattle and bewitch several people to death, some through SPELLS cast with poppets in the shape of waxen images.

The other witches were:

Father Rosimond and his daughter, of Farnham, both witches and enchanters who could shape-shift. Father Rosimond was seen in the shapes of an ape and a horse.

Mother Dutten, who seemed to have had psychic powers and could give people messages when they visited. She kept a TOAD familiar in her garden, which she fed with blood from her right side.

Mother Devell, a poor woman whose familiar was a black CAT named Jill, which she fed with a mixture of milk and her own blood.

Mother Margaret, an old woman who hobbled about on crutches and kept a kitten familiar named Jenny, which she fed with crumbs and her own blood. Mother Margaret, said Stile, gave her money and told her not to divulge the witches' secrets.

The crimes Stile admitted to, committed by her and the other witches, were the bewitchment deaths of:

- a farmer named Langford
- Master Gallis, the former mayor of Windsor
- a butcher named Switcher
- a man named Saddock, who reneged on his promise to give Stile his cloak

Stile said the witches killed Langford, Gallis and Switcher by making images of red wax and sticking them in the hearts with bristles or hawthorn thorns. She killed Saddock by clapping him on the shoulder; he went home and died soon after.

The witches bewitched, or did "overspeak," several other people who sickened but did not die:

- a butcher named Mastlin
- a fisherman named William Foster
- the wife of a baker named Willis
- George Whitting, the servant of Matthew Glover of Eton
- a man named Foster

Furthermore, the busy witches killed cattle by bewitchment and also cast malevolent spells against anyone who angered them.

Stile said she was led into witchcraft by Mothers Dutten and Devell. The three would meet at 11 o'clock at night to pledge themselves to service to the DEVIL.

At the trials of the four women, testimony was given attesting to their witchcraft. An ostler who had given aid to Stile fell ill after she expressed unhappiness with the amount of his alms. He went to Father Rosimond, who cured him and told him there were many evil witches in Windsor. The ostler drew Stile's blood and got more relief from his aching body.

A boy who went to get water at a well next to Stile's home had an unpleasant encounter with her. He threw a stone at her house, and she said she would get even with him. She took away his pitcher. The boy went home and suffered the reversal of his hand, causing him great pain. The hand was restored by either Father Rosimond or Mother Devell.

While in jail, Stile said that Mother Devell was bewitching her and the other two women, causing all sensation to be gone from her hands and feet. Her toes rotted off, and she was carted to court in a barrow.

Stile and Mothers Dutten, Devell and Margaret were found guilty of witchcraft but not of treason. They were hanged on February 29, 1579. Rosimond apparently was not charged or tried.

FURTHER READING:
Rosen, Barbara, ed. *Witchcraft in England, 1558–1618.* Amherst: University of Massachusetts Press, 1991.

witch   See WITCHES.

WITCH   A feminist organization that sprang into existence in the late 1960s in America and flourished briefly among young women at college campuses across the country. WITCH originally stood for Women's International Terrorist Conspiracy from Hell, though on occasion the name changed to fit various political activities. The organization was formally launched in 1968 on Samhain, All Hallow's Eve, the SABBAT most strongly associated with witches in the public mind. The year was a peak for protest movements: civil rights, the war in Vietnam and women's liberation. In that year, Martin Luther King and Robert Kennedy were assassinated. College campuses were hotbeds of demonstrations against the military, big business, big government and authority in general. Interest in mysticism, the occult and witchcraft was high.

WITCH was strongly feminist and viewed itself as a political, revolutionary, guerrilla organization. Witches and GYPSIES, the WITCH literature stated, were the original guerrilla fighters against the oppression of women and of the oppression of all. Dressed in rags and pointed, conical hats, and carrying brooms, members of WITCH conducted demonstrations.

Some outsiders saw the group as more comic than serious. Andrew Greeley, Roman Catholic priest, novelist, lecturer on sociology at the University of Chicago and program director of the National Opinion Research Center at the university, called WITCH "a combination of the put-on and the serious, the deliberately comic and the profoundly agonized, of the bizarre and the holy." When three members of WITCH appeared in the university's social-science building to shriek CURSES upon the sociology department ("A hex on thy strategy!"), Greeley himself responded in comic fashion by offering to sprinkle holy water in the departmental office. His offer was turned down.

WITCH was not regarded as legitimate by many other Witches. WITCH maintained that any woman could become a Witch by saying "I am a Witch" three times and thinking about it—rather than being initiated by another Witch (see INITIATION)—and that any woman could start a COVEN of Witches simply by declaring so.

FURTHER READING:

Adler, Margot. *Drawing Down the Moon.* Revised ed. New York: Viking, 1986.

witch balls   Decorative glass balls made in England from the 18th century onward, often hung in windows to ward off witches's SPELLS or ill fortune. They appeared in America in the 19th century. Witch balls measure up to seven inches in diameter and are predominantly green or blue, though some are decorated in enameled swirls and stripes of varying colors. Others are silvered to act as convex mirrors. Because they are similar to the glass balls used by fishermen on nets, witch balls are associated with many sea superstitions and legends.

In the Ozarks, a witch ball is made of black hair rolled with beeswax into a hard pellet about the size of a marble. It is used in CURSES. If a witch wishes to harm or kill someone, she makes a hair ball and tosses it at the victim. In Ozark folklore, it is said that when someone is killed by a witch's curse, the witch ball is always found near the body.

Witch ball is also a term for a puffball fungus found in parts of America, which burns for a long time. Indians used it to carry fire from one camp to another.

See AMULET.

witch bottle   A CHARM used in folk MAGIC to protect against evil spirits and magical attack, and to counteract SPELLS cast by witches. Witch bottles were prevalent in Elizabethan England, especially in East Anglia, where superstitions and beliefs in witches were strong, although their use has continued into modern times.

The witch bottle was a little flask about three inches high and made of green or blue glass. Some were larger and rounder, about five to nine inches in height; these were known as Greybeards or Bellarmines. The Bellarmines were named after a fearsome Catholic inquisitor who persecuted Protestants and was called a DEMON by his victims. The Greybeards and Bellarmines were made of brown or gray stoneware, glazed with SALT and embossed with bearded faces. Both the salt and severe face were believed to scare off evil.

The witch bottle was prepared magically by a witch or CUNNING MAN or WOMAN, who placed into it the victim's URINE, HAIR AND NAILS, or RED thread from SPRITE-TRAPS. When the bottle was buried beneath the house hearth or threshold, the spell was nullified and the witch supposedly suffered great discomfort. Sometimes the bottles were thrown into a fire; when they exploded, the spell was broken or the witch was supposedly killed. If urine was used as a counter-charm, then the witch became unable to urinate; thus, she was exposed for her MALEFICIA. Witch bottles were especially used to nullify the EVIL EYE.

Witch bottles were hung in chimneys as charms to prevent witches from flying down and entering a house. They were also hung near doors and windows and plastered into walls above door lintels to protect the threshold. Commercial buildings, rail lines, bridges and other structures were often given witch bottles as a general prophylactic against evil and disaster.

Joseph Glanvil described the making of a witch bottle in his book *Sadducimus Triumphatus—or Full and Plain Evidence Concerning Witches and Apparitions* (1681). According to Glanvil, the wife of William Brearly, a priest and fellow of Christ's College, Cambridge, became ill when the couple took lodgings in Suffolk County. She was haunted by an apparition in the shape of a bird. A cunning man prescribed a witch bottle containing her urine and PINS, needles and nails. The bottle was to be corked and set by the fire. The evil was removed, and the WIZARD who bewitched her allegedly died.

England's great cunning man JAMES MURRELL was famous for his witch bottles. Some were made of IRON. According to lore, the local blacksmith had great difficulty in forging the first iron bottle for Murrell, who had to say a prayer in order for the fire to draw. Another story holds that a boy was made to drink beer from this first bottle without knowing what it was. When he learned it was a witch bottle, he went home in dread and died.

As Murrell often instructed his clients to heat his witch bottles in the fire, the blacksmith wisely made a tiny hole in the top of the iron ones so that steam could escape and the bottles would not lethally explode. The hissing steam made Murrell think that the spirits of the witches he was battling were escaping.

A witch bottle cure from Murrell follows along the lines of this story from the 1850s:

A young woman discovered an old Gypsy in a barn drinking beer left by the harvesters. She ordered the old woman out and was cursed by her. Almost immediately, the girl began having fits and acting alternately like a CAT and a dog.

Her family consulted Murrell, who prepared a witch bottle containing the girls' urine and BLOOD, herbs and pins. The bottle was heated in a fire in a darkened room with locked doors. The family was instructed to remain silent or the counter-spell would not work.

Soon footsteps sounded outside the door, then furious knocking. A woman's voice said, "For God's sake, stop. You're killing me." Instantly the witch bottle exploded, and the voice faded away. The girl recovered. In the morning, the Gypsy's badly burned body was discovered in the road three miles away.

See BIDDY EARLY.

FURTHER READING:

Maple, Eric. *The Dark World of Witches.* New York: A.S. Barnes & Co., 1962.

Pennick, Nigel. *Secrets of East Anglican Magic.* London: Robert Hale, 1995.

witch boxes   In Britain, CHARMS placed in a house to protect the occupants from witch's SPELLS and to prevent witches from entering. Witch boxes were popular in the 16th and 17th centuries. They usually were a small wooden box with a glass front, filled with herbs, bits of rowan, pieces of human bone and odds and ends, over which a magic spell of protection had been cast. The boxes often were sold by witch-hunters who went from town to town whipping up hysteria about witches.

witchcraft   Belief in witchcraft is universal, but there is no universal definition of it, for the term has different meanings in different cultures and has had different meanings at different times in history.

Witchcraft has both negative and positive connotations. It is a form of SORCERY, the magical manipulation of supernormal forces through the casting of SPELLS and the conjuring or invoking of spirits, for either good or bad purposes. MAGIC and sorcery have been used by mankind since prehistoric times in an effort to control the environment and enhance daily life. In most societies, however, witchcraft has been considered harmful.

Anthropologists define witchcraft as an innate condition, the use of malevolent power by psychic means without need of RITUAL or CHARM. Witchcraft also involves the use of supernormal powers, such as invisibility, shape-shifting, flying, ability to kill at a distance, clairvoyancy and astral projection. Most witchcraft is regarded with fear and uncertainty, though it provides a necessary social function by enabling others to seek redress of wrongs and grievances and alleviation from stress and troubles.

During the INQUISITION, witchcraft was viewed as evil magic, heresy and Devil worship. The associations with evil and the DEVIL linger in modern Western culture.

Since the 1950s, Witchcraft (capital W) has been practiced as an organized, Pagan religion that worships the GODDESS and HORNED GOD and stresses the use of magic only for benevolent purposes. Religious Witchcraft represents but a small portion of the types of witchcraft still practiced around the world.

The History of Western Witchcraft
Western concepts of witchcraft evolved from magical beliefs and practices in ancient Egypt, the Middle East and the classical and hellenistic worlds. Spell-casting and interaction with intermediary spirits were part of daily life. The Greeks and Romans made wide use of CURSES, usually written on lead tablets, to gain advantage in love, business and sport. The intermediary spirits were not servants of evil, but a host of beings who mediated and interfered in human affairs with a variety of agendas. The Greek *daimon,* for example, could be good or bad.

Magic, the *daimones* and intermediary spirits of the air became increasingly associated with the Devil in the early centuries of Christianity, as the church sought to establish itself as the only source of power and access to the divine. Magicians, diviners and sorcerers who consulted spirits were increasingly seen as traffickers in evil.

The Inquisition.   The Christian Church's determined campaign to eradicate heretics was turned on witches by the middle of the 15th century. For nearly 250 years, witches were hunted down and executed as heretics, accused of worshiping the Devil. Most of the witch hunts in Europe were conducted by the church, both Catholic and Protestant. In Britain, witchcraft was considered largely a civil crime, and witches were prosecuted by the state.

The association of witchcraft with heresy occurred slowly over a period of centuries. Prior to the Middle Ages, witchcraft and sorcery were considered essentially the same. Sorcery was a civil crime, and witches and sorcerers were punished under civil law, which usually called for fines, imprisonment and banishment. Heresy, on the other hand, was punishable by death under civil law as early as 430, even though such laws were not rigorously enforced. Under Roman law, distinctions were made between white witchcraft, or sorcery, and black witchcraft. White witchcraft, which consisted largely of magical healing and divination, was not considered a crime, while black witchcraft, or harmful magic, was a crime. White witchcraft was tolerated and usually considered beneficial; it served a useful function in society and was defended by the public. White witchcraft could become black witchcraft, however, if a cure resulted in the death of a patient. Under canon law, the distinctions between white and black witchcraft began to disappear, until both were punished as heresy.

From the eight century on, sorcery was increasingly associated with harmful witchcraft, and witchcraft was increasingly associated with heresy. Beginning in the 11th century, heretics were sentenced with increasing frequency to death by burning. The church directed its efforts against the religious sects of the Albigenses, which flourished in eastern Europe and southern France; the Cathars, which spread over much of Europe; and the

Waldenses (Vaudois), which appeared in the late 12th century in southern France. These religious sects were also accused of sorcery, SABBATS and Devil-worship. In 1184, the church's efforts became more formal with the direction of Pope Lucius III to bishops to investigate all deviations from church teachings. The Inquisition was established between 1227 and 1233. In 1233, Pope Gregory IX issued a bull that decreed that inquisitors would be Dominicans and would be answerable only to the pope.

During the same period, however, ecclesiastical belief in witchcraft was at a low due to the *CANON EPISCO-PI*, which held that witchcraft was an illusion and belief in it was heresy. This was reversed by a series of papal bulls against sorcery and the influence of the writings of demonologists and theologians who became increasingly obsessed with witchcraft. One of the most influential theologians was THOMAS AQUINAS, who in the 13th century refuted the *Canon Episcopi* and endorsed beliefs that witches copulated with DEMONS, flew through the air, shape-shifted, raised storms and performed other MALE-FICIA. Aquinas believed such acts implied a pact with the Devil. He also believed heretics should be burned.

The demonification of witchcraft received an additional boost in the 13th and 14th centuries from the growing favor of Aristotelian philosophy over Platonic philosophy. Platonic philosophy provides for the existence of natural magic that is neither black nor white, but morally neutral. Under Aristotelian thought, no natural magic exists; therefore magic must be either divine or demonic.

Bulls against sorcery and witchcraft were issued through the mid-15th century, some of which instructed inquisitors to distinguish between sorcery/witchcraft and heresy. Sorcery was first linked to heresy by Sixtus IV in bulls issued in 1473, 1478 and 1483. The bull that turned the full force of the Inquisition against witches—as heretical sorcerers—was that of INNOCENT VIII in 1484. Two years later, the inquisitors Heinrich Kramer and Jacob Sprenger published the *MALLEUS MALEFICARUM*, which carried the bull as an introduction and set forth rules for identifying, prosecuting and punishing witches. The *Malleus* quickly spread throughout Europe and was considered the primary witch-hunters' reference as the Inquisition gained force. By this time, the characteristics of witchcraft had been established as a DEVIL'S PACT, secret, orgiastic sabbats, infanticide, cannibalism, renunciation of Christianity and desecration of the cross and Eucharist.

In 1522, Martin Luther called sorcerers and witches "the Devil's whores" and criticized lawyers for wanting too much proof to convict. In 1532, the *Carolina*, the criminal code enacted under Charles V for the Holy Roman Empire, distinguished between white and black witchcraft, but provided punishment for both. Injurious witchcraft was punishable by death by burning, as was homosexuality and sex with animals. Witchcraft that did not cause injury or damage was punished according to the magnitude of the crime. Fortune-telling by sorcery or other magical arts called for torture and imprisonment. In 1572, a Saxon law code was enacted that called for the death penalty for all forms of witchcraft.

Accusations of witchcraft usually started with simple sorceries—spells perceived to harm others. The accused usually had had an argument with a neighbor or had been overheard muttering complaints or CURSES. They were often tortured, sometimes in the most cruel and barbaric manner, until they died or confessed to witchcraft and worshiping the Devil. Inquisitors also forced them to name accomplices. Whole villages were sometimes implicated, and mass executions took place. The most common form of execution in Europe was burning at the stake. If the victim was lucky, he or she was strangled first. Many were burned alive.

Many trials probably were motivated by the desire of the inquisitors to seize the properties of the accused. This was a factor in areas that suffered the most savage persecutions, such as Germany. The majority of victims were of the lower classes, poor and often beggars. Most also were women: The *Malleus Maleficarum* had firmly linked women to witchcraft. Many were social outcasts.

The activities of the Inquisition were strongest in Germany, France and Switzerland in the 15th and 16th centuries, spreading into Scandinavia in the 16th and 17th centuries. Fewer inquisitional activities against witches took place in Spain or Portugal. The circumstances that touched off witch hunts in various areas cannot be generalized. Political and social unrest were factors; trials increased in Germany and elsewhere in Europe during the Thirty Years' War from 1618 to 1648. Bad crops, plagues and infectious diseases also contributed to searches for scapegoats.

In the 16th century, the witch hysteria was countered by demonologists, such as JOHANN WEYER, who questioned the validity of beliefs about witches and opposed the tactics of witch hunters. The witch hysteria peaked between 1560 and 1660, then tapered off during the next 90 years.

Witchcraft in Britain and the American Colonies. Witch-hunting in Britain bloomed later than in Europe. Throughout the witch hysteria, witchcraft was treated largely as a civil crime. The emphasis was not on a witch's heresy by virtue of a pact with the Devil, but upon her power to bring misery to others with her spells and curses.

Prior to 1542, witchcraft was considered sorcery in England, punishable by secular and ecclesiastical laws as early as 668. Witches usually were tried by the church and given moderate punishment by the state. If nobles were involved in charges of sorcery or witchcraft, the crime had the potential of becoming a charge of treason, if sorcery had been used against the throne or to divine the political future.

In 1542, Henry VIII passed the first witchcraft act, which provided for witches to be tried and punished by the state. The statute of 1542 made a felony of the conjuring of spirits, divining and casting of false or malicious spells and enchantments. Such offenses were punishable by "death, loss and forfeiture of their lands, tenants, goods and chattels." Records exist of only one case brought to trial under the law; the accused was pardoned. The law was repealed in 1547 by Edward VI.

A second witchcraft act was passed in 1563 under Elizabeth I. This act was the result of ecclesiastical pressure to address rising public fears of witchcraft. It increased penalties: death for murder by witchcraft; a year in jail and the pillory for less serious witchcraft; and forfeiture of property for second convictions of divination, attempted murder and unlawful love spells.

A similar act was passed in Scotland the same year. During the reign of James VI (1567–1602), brutal witch hunts took place in Scotland, involving barbaric torture and burning at the stake (see NORTH BERWICK WITCHES). Though James feared witches and permitted the witch hunts, he did act to cool the hysteria when it threatened to get out of hand. In 1603, he became JAMES I of England and ruled the united kingdoms of England and Scotland until his death in 1625. In 1604, the Elizabethan Witchcraft Act was repealed and a third and tougher act was passed for England and Scotland. It called for death by hanging for the first conviction of malefic witchcraft, regardless of whether or not a victim had died. The penalty for divining, destroying or damaging property and the concoction of love philtres remained a year in jail plus the pillory. The act also made it a felony to conjure, consult, entertain, covenant with, employ, feed or reward any evil spirit for any purpose, thus introducing Devil's pacts into the law.

The Act of 1604 remained in force until 1736. England's witch hysteria peaked under its force in the 1640s, also a time of political and social strife caused by the civil war. Witch-hunting was a profitable profession, and witch finders such as MATTHEW HOPKINS made good fees by identifying witches by pricking them and discovering DEVIL'S MARKS. Convicted witches in England usually were hung, not burned.

Most of the witch trials in England and Scotland concerned witches accused of being in league with the Devil. The "white witches"—the CUNNING MEN AND CUNNING WOMEN, WIZARDS, diviners and healers—were seldom prosecuted by the courts, despite the fact that their sorceries were illegal. The church courts prosecuted them, for their magical miracles were in direct competition with the clergy, many of whom also practiced white witchcraft. Punishments usually were light, a marked contrast from Europe.

The *Malleus Maleficarum* had little impact in England. It was not translated into English until 1584, 98 years after it had been written. England had its own 17th-century Protestant demonologists who wrote treatises on identifying and punishing witches, including WILLIAM PERKINS, John Cotta, Thomas Potts, Richard Baldwin and other learned men. These opinion-shapers held that white witches were far more dangerous than black witches and deserved to be prosecuted all the more.

Ireland remained free of much of the witch hysteria. Only about eight trials are recorded between 1324 (see ALICE KYTELER) and 1711 (See ISLAND MAGEE WITCHES). Except for the Kyteler trial, they all involved Protestants against Protestants. A law against witchcraft was passed in 1587 and was repealed in 1821.

Witch problems in the American colonies did not begin until the 1640s, just as the hysteria was peaking in England, and never reached the magnitude of the witch hunts elsewhere. The first hanging of a convicted witch occurred in 1647 in Connecticut. INCREASE MATHER and his son, COTTON MATHER, ministers and leaders in Massachusetts, were influenced by the demonologists of England—Cotton Mather cited Perkins in his own treatises on witchcraft—and believed that a conspiracy of witches who were in league with Satan threatened the survival of New England. The mass trials of SALEM WITCHES in 1692, the most spectacular witch case in America, were tried under the 1604 statute. Elsewhere in the colonies, trials were scattered. Besides the Salem victims, there are records of only a dozen or so executions of witches in New England, plus a number of lighter punishments of whippings and banishment. Pennsylvania law under William Penn was tolerant, thus making it possible later for the German immigrant powwowers (wizards or cunning folk) to establish their culture (see POWWOWING).

In the 16th century, the Spanish Inquisition, which had an office in Mexico City, prosecuted Native American accused witches in the southwest territory of New Mexico (see POPE; SANTA FE WITCHES).

The end of the witch hysteria. Church and state persecutions of witches came to a halt in Europe, Britain and America by the 1730s, though cases in Germany continued to be tried for several more decades. The last witch trial occurred in 1711 in Ireland, resulting in sentences of jail and the pillory. In England, Jane Clarke and her son and daughter were the last to be indicted as witches in 1717. Despite the willingness of 25 people to testify against them, the case was thrown out of court. In Scotland, Janet Horne was the last to be tried and burned in 1727. In the American colonies, Grace Sherwood of Virginia was accused of witchcraft in 1706, and the SWIMMING test was employed, but the case evidently was dropped. In Jura, a beggar woman was burned as a witch in 1731. Persecutions lingered in France and Germany, where the greatest witch-hunting had taken place during the height of the Inquisition. In France, the last executions took place in 1745. In Bavaria, Anna Maria Schwagel was the last accused witch to be executed in 1775 by beheading.

Political and social changes and backlash against the persecutions made witch-hunting both undesirable and unnecessary. In Germany, the threatened destruction of entire populations necessitated a cooling of accusations and trials. Throughout Europe, the evolution from feudalism to capitalism during the 17th and 18th centuries changed attitudes toward the instability created by the threat of heresy and the subsequent confiscations of property. In England, the Civil War drastically changed society by establishing a republican commonwealth, paving the way for a middle class and improving religious toleration. In the American colonies, public disgust was so great after Salem that leaders criticized the methods of the court. Salem repented, and in 1711 the general court restored the civil rights of 22 of those convicted in 1692 (the rights of the remaining victims were restored in 1957).

The Industrial Revolution and age of science brought shifts to urban population centers, changes in livelihood and more education. Among learned men, the skepticism of science took hold, and it became unfashionable to believe in witchcraft and magic. One influential critic was Francis Hutchinson, an English clergyman who wrote his sharply critical *Essay Concerning Witchcraft* (1718), which exposed the false accusations, evidence and political motivations of many trials.

In 1736, under George II in England, the Witchcraft Act of 1604 was repealed and replaced with a new statute that removed penalties for witchcraft, sorcery, enchantment and conjuration. However, the new law punished those who pretended to use witchcraft, sorcery, enchantment and conjuration in fraudulent fortune-telling and divining. Punishment was a year in jail with quarterly appearances in the pillory.

Witchcraft receded as heresy and returned to its former state of sorcery and folk magic. The public still perceived a witch as a malevolent person in league with the Devil, but continued to rely heavily upon cunning folk, powwowers, witch doctors, sorcerers, white witches and the like for healing, fertility, luck, prosperity and divination. The trade of white witchcraft flourished during the 18th century and most of the 19th century. Among rural, uneducated populations, anti-witch sentiment continued. In England, Europe and even America, there were outbreaks of violence against suspected witches all through the 19th century and into the early 20th century (see JOHN BLYMIRE and CHARLES WALTON). The violence sometimes was turned on white witches whose magic failed to work. Stories in the press were published periodically about witches, magical charms and rumors of nocturnal meetings in forests.

In the latter half of the 19th century, Spiritualism spread quickly on both sides of the Atlantic. In England, the Witchcraft Act of 1736 and the Vagrancy Act of 1824 were used to prosecute mediums on charges of conjuring spirits and fraudulent fortune-telling. A campaign to rescind the 1736 statute was mounted by Spiritualists in 1950, after the law had been used against a medium who defrauded a widow. In 1951, the Witchcraft Act of 1736 and a section of the Vagrancy Act of 1824 were replaced by the Fraudulent Mediums Act. For the first time in more than 300 years in Britain, witchcraft was no longer a crime.

Witchcraft, women and misogyny. The witchcraft defined and attacked by church and state during the witch craze focused on women. Christianity holds women accountable for sin, so it was naturally presumed that they were predisposed to the evils of witchcraft and Devil-worship. The *Malleus Maleficarum* is replete with misogyny. Authors Heinrich Kramer and Jacob Sprenger, Dominican inquisitors, state that "all witchcraft comes from carnal lust, which in women is insatiable." They said that men are protected from succumbing to witchcraft because Jesus was a man.

Furthermore, they said that women are "chiefly addicted to Evil Superstitions" because they are feeble-brained, "intellectually like children," weak in body, impressionable, lustful, have weak memories and are by nature liars. Much of the offensive behavior attributed to witches was sex-related: uninhibited copulation with demons and FAMILIARS, sexual attacks upon men in the form of succubi, the causation of impotency and infertility and, incredibly, the theft of male sexual organs.

Most of the women accused of witchcraft were social outcasts, beyond the immediate control of men: they were spinsters and widows. The patriarchal societies of Europe and Britain were openly hostile to such women. The hostility was only exacerbated by old age, poverty, handicaps and ugliness.

Women had no rights of their own and no say in their own destiny. Most went from being the property of a father to the property of a husband. The majority were stuck in lives of grinding poverty and misery. It is possible that women were more likely to turn to sorcery in an effort to improve their plights or redress their grievances, which would make them more vulnerable to accusations of witchcraft. The tales of imaginary flights to sabbats seem more like desperate attempts to relieve boredom and unhappiness than intentions to indulge in evil (see ISOBEL GOWDIE).

Non-European witchcraft. In non-European societies, witchcraft is commonly, but not always, associated with women. Most African tribes believe that witchcraft is inherited and can be passed to either sex; the Tellensi of northern Ghana believe that witchcraft is passed only by the mother. The Navajo associate more men with witchcraft than women, but women witches are invariably old or childless, which corresponds to the European portrait of spinsters and widows.

Ancient legends among the Ona and Yahgans of Tierra del Fuego bear a chilling resemblance to the European witch hunts. According to the Ona legend, witchcraft and the magical arts were known only to women in the old days of Ona-land. The women kept their own lodge, which was closed to men. They had the power to cause sickness and death, and the men lived in total fear of them. Finally, the men decided they had had enough tyranny and that a dead witch was better than a live witch. They massacred all the women and adolescent girls. They spared only the smallest girls who had not yet begun their training in witchcraft so that the men eventually would have wives again. To prevent the girls from banding together and reasserting their power when they grew up, the men formed a secret society and lodge that excluded women. The lodge was protected by fierce demons. The men kept their dominance over women from then on.

The Yahgans, neighbors of the Ona, also have a legend of the ancient rule of men by women who used witchcraft and cunning. The Yahgan men also deposed the women, not through massacre but apparently by mutual consent.

Witchcraft, a Pagan religion. In the 1950s, Witchcraft was re-created as a Pagan religion, centered on the worship of the GODDESS and her consort, the HORNED GOD, and the practice of benevolent magic. The father of this revival was GERALD B. GARDNER, an English civil servant whose interest in the occult led, he said, to his INITIATION in 1939 into a COVEN of witches in England. It is difficult to say whether Gardner intended to create a new religion or whether it grew spontaneously from public interest in his writings and activities.

Gardner said his coven was descended from a long line of hereditary witches, who practiced both a magical craft and a Pagan religion, "The Craft of the Wise" and "The Old Religion." Other covens scattered about England have claimed the same; most remain rather secretive, and it is unknown exactly how far back their lineages go or exactly what has constituted religious Witchcraft over the centuries.

In the latter part of the 19th century, American folklorist CHARLES GODFREY LELAND said he discovered a hereditary heritage of witches in Tuscany, who worshiped ARADIA, daughter of DIANA. In the 1920s, British anthropologist MARGARET A. MURRAY advanced the idea that the witches who were persecuted during the witch hysteria were organized pagan religious cults who worshiped the Horned God. Both Leland and Murray have been criticized by historians, and the idea that witches maintained a lineage of organized religion was discredited.

Isolated groups and cults did keep alive various pagan rites and customs, especially those related to health and fertility, such as seasonal festivals (see WHEEL OF THE YEAR). There is evidence of a flourishing cult of Diana in western and central Europe in the fifth and sixth centuries, which apparently survived to the Middle Ages. The *BENANDANTI*, an agrarian cult of nocturnal witch-fighters, survived in northern Italy to the 16th and 17th centuries. The *strigoi* of Romania, witches both living and dead, possessed supernatural powers and fought each other at night. Another Romanian cult, the Calusari, was a secret society of cathartic dancers whose patronness was the Queen of the Fairies, or Diana/Herodia/Aradia.

At the time of Gardner's initiation, Murray's theory had not been put to rest. Gardner accepted her theory of a European witch cult. He feared that Witchcraft was in danger of dying out due to a lack of young members and wanted to publicize it. He had been given a framework of rituals, including initiations and a system of greater and lesser Sabbats by his coven. He obtained additional ritual material from ALEISTER CROWLEY, whom he met in 1946. Because the Witchcraft Act of 1736 was still on the books, his coven allegedly discouraged him from writing openly about Witchcraft. Instead, he wrote a novel *High Magic's Aid* under the pseudonym "Scire," published in 1949. The book contained the rituals and beliefs Gardner had been given by his coven.

After the repeal of the Witchcraft Act in 1951, Gardner broke away from the coven and formed his own coven. To flesh out his rituals, he apparently borrowed from Leland, the Ordo Templi Orientis (O.T.O.), of which he was a member, masonry, the Hermetic Order of the Golden Dawn, Rosicrucianism, Eastern mysticism and magic (Gardner had spent many years in the East), folklore and mythology. In 1953, he initiated DOREEN VALIENTE, with whom he collaborated in writing and revising the rituals. According to Valiente, Gardner's material showed heavy influence by the O.T.O. and Crowley, which she removed and rewrote in simpler form. Gardner never acknowledged Crowley's exact role in his rituals. He maintained that Crowley belonged to the "witch cult" and may have had some hand in reconstructing the rituals, but had kept his oaths of secrecy.

Gardner wrote two nonfiction books about Witchcraft, *Witchcraft Today* (1954) and *The Meaning of Witchcraft* (1959), which described the Craft as he saw it and put forth the Murray theory. The books captured a public

Witch and wizard riding to sabbat (ULRICH MOLITOR, *HEXEN MEYSTEREY,* 1545)

proposal that was not adopted. Gardner apparently revised it in a false archaic English. The 161 "Ancient Craft Laws" were said to date back to the 16th century, but were of modern authorship. They cover conduct, secrecy, coven meetings and territories and discipline. Valiente never considered the document to be authentic. The laws have been published in various versions.

A huge growth spurt of Witchcraft took place in the 1960s and 1970s, during a revival of interest in occultism. Most early converts were women and came from the ranks of the white middle class, followed by those in creative arts, academia and professions. Gardner's revival of Witchcraft spread to other countries, including the United States, Canada, Australia, France, Germany and Japan.

In the initial boom, there were suddenly more would-be Witches than covens to initiate them; initiation was required in order to consider oneself a Witch. Many people were attracted for the wrong reasons—a fad or manipulation of others. Most of these eventually dropped out of the movement; some splintered off in their own directions. Gardner's Witchcraft became known as Gardnerian, and other "traditions" were created or came to light. ALEX SANDERS, an Englishman who claimed to be a hereditary Witch, founded the Alexandrian tradition, based heavily on the rituals of Gardner.

Some traditions claimed ancient, hereditary lineages; some of these claims were soon proved to be false. Numerous traditions were born, lived brief lives and died, while others grew, survived and evolved. Emphasis on the Goddess appealed to many women in the feminist movement and others who felt shortchanged and disenfranchised by Christianity and other mainstream religions.

By the 1980s, most Witches no longer believed that the Craft was an unbroken religious tradition since pagan

Devil seducing witch (ULRICH MOLITOR, *VON DEN UNHOLDEN ODER HEXEN,* 1489)

fancy and revived an interest in Witchcraft. In 1957, Valiente "hived off" to form her own coven.

In revising Gardner's ritual material, Valiente increased the emphasis on the Goddess. She said the Goddess was part of the Craft at the time she joined it. However, witchcraft trial records emphasize the alleged worship of the Devil, not the Goddess, and Gardner's *High Magic's Aid* does not mention the Goddess. In following Murray, Gardner at first emphasized the role of the Horned God. The Goddess gradually assumed more importance, thus elevating the role of the high priestess to leader of the coven.

During the 1950s, Craft laws and ethics took shape. The WICCAN REDE, "An' it harm none, do what ye will," stipulates that Witches may use their magical powers only for good, never to harm any living thing. The need was seen for a set of written rules, and "Ned," who left Gardner's coven with Valiente, is said to have drafted a

Mass executions of Haarlemites as devil-worshipers, under Fernando Álvarez de Toledo, duke of Alba, after conquest of Haarlem, 1573 (MICHAEL AISTINGER, *DE LEONE BELGICO*)

times. Many felt ancient rites and beliefs have been reconstructed to suit modern times; in this way, they preserve an ancient heritage.

From England and the United States, Witchcraft spread around the world, with dozens of traditions being founded. The movement has not been unified or cohesive. Autonomy, diversity and change are valued.

Witches still find themselves the victims of prejudice, hate and fear. Many are secretive about their involvement in the Craft, while others feel it is essential to seek publicity in order to gain acceptance by society. Organizations and networks have been formed to help educate the media and public and fight for civil rights.

Some Witches use the term "Wicca" to distinguish modern religious Witchcraft from folklore witchcraft. Others feel it is important to use the word "Witchcraft" and continue to educate the public that not all witches are evil.

Modern Traditions of Witchcraft

Witchcraft is an autonomous religion constantly reinvented by its practitioners to suit changing needs. There are no central authority, clergy, dogma and liturgy. It is oriented to small groups, members of whom are all priests and priestesses, with authority centered in the group's high priestess/high priest.

Different traditions have their own rituals, philosophies and beliefs. Witchcraft embraces diversity, including gay, lesbian, transgender and bisexual people, some of whom have founded their own traditions. Witchcraft is eclectic, drawing on a variety of magical/mystical/religious philosophies and practices. Though folk witchcraft is not shamanic in nature, shamanistic elements of trance, out-of-body journeying and healing have increased in rituals and practice. Some traditions give emphasis to ceremonial magic and to kabbalistic mysteries.

New rituals, songs, chants and poetry are continually created. Witches view change and flexibility as positive, a guarantee that their religion will never grow stale with obsolete ideas.

All traditions share a deep respect for nature and all living things. Most Witches are pantheists, believing the divine force to be immanent in nature. Many are polytheists, in the sense that they believe the divine force manifests in multiple forms, recognized as Pagan deities. The Goddess generally is given supremacy over the Horned God. Rituals are colorful, creative and energizing. Witches believe in enjoying sensual and sexual pleasures without guilt. Magic, whether performed individually or in a coven, should be directed toward a good purpose, not to harm.

Devil carrying witch off to hell (OLAUS MAGNUS, *HISTORIA DE GENTIBUS SEPTENTRIONALIBUS*, 1555)

Within traditions, covens and groups are autonomous, some fiercely so. Each customarily has a secret BOOK OF SHADOWS, which includes the tradition's laws, ethics, rituals, administrative rules and other material, including personal material and material relating to the coven. Most traditions have formal initiation procedures. It has become increasingly acceptable to initiate oneself into the Craft and practice alone as a SOLITARY rather than as part of a coven.

Many covens belong to organizations that lobby for Pagan rights and provide forums for discussion, unity and community.

Witchcraft features many traditions and, within them, subtraditions. Practitioners across the spectrum see Witchcraft as progressive and evolutionary, rather than static and bound to past beliefs and practices. JANET FARRAR and GAVIN BONE have been instrumental in advancing progressive concepts of the Craft that incorporate ceremonial magic, old pagan practices, folk magic, shamanism, ecstatic mysteries and Eastern mysticism and philosophy.

Some of the major traditions are

Gardnerian. The revived Witchcraft named after Gerald B. Gardner remains the dominant tradition worldwide, but no longer holds a monopoly in the Craft. It has been subject to much criticism and reinterpretation. It is centered on worship of the Goddess and her consort, the Horned God, represented in the coven by the high priestess and high priest. It emphasizes polarity in all things manifest in the universe, fertility and the cycles of birth-death-rebirth.

Nature is honored, and one accepts oneself and all other living things as part of her. Eight seasonal Pagan sabbats are observed. The WICCAN REDE of harming no living thing is the guiding principle.

Formal INITIATION into a coven by a high priest or high priestess is stressed, though there are rituals for self-initiation. One enters the Craft in "perfect love and perfect trust," which means complete trust of fellow coveners. In initiation into a coven, a woman must be initiated by a man and a man by a woman. Initiates trace their lineage back to Gardner or Lady Olwen, his high priestess. Many receive lineage papers.

The Gardnerian hierarchy has three degrees of advancement, traditionally separated by a minimum of a year and a day. Only a third-degree witch may become a high priestess or high priest. The high priestess is the titular head of the coven. Some covens emphasize the Goddess more than the Horned God, while others put the male and female aspects on a par. The deities are called by a multitude of Pagan deity names, depending on the coven and the rituals being performed. Rituals are performed within a MAGIC CIRCLE. Witches work with a set of tools: an athame or ritual knife, wand, sword, cords, censer, pentacle and chalice.

One of the original hallmarks of the Gardnerian tradition is worship in the nude, which Gardner called "skyclad." He enjoyed nudist camps in England and believed that nudity was healthy. Gardnerians hold that worshiping in the nude brings them closer to nature and keeps all coveners equal. The nudity was sensationalized in the media. Many Gardnerian covens have broken away from this practice and worship robed.

Another original hallmark of the Gardnerian tradition is ritual scourging, the light flogging of coveners with cords as a means of purification and symbolic suffering and raising psychic energy. This practice has declined in American Gardnerian covens, replaced by other energy-raising techniques such as ecstatic dancing, drumming and trance.

Gardner also espoused ritual sexual acts between high priestess and high priest, called the GREAT RITE. The rite can be performed symbolically with a chalice and blade.

Magic in the tradition is theurgic, that is, performed with the aid of beneficent spirits.

The Gardnerian tradition was introduced to the United States in the 1960s by RAYMOND BUCKLAND and his wife, Rosemary, natives of England who were initiated into the craft in 1963 by Gardner's high priestess, Lady Olwen (MONIQUE WILSON). The Bucklands moved to America and established a coven and museum on Long Island.

Alexandrian. Named after its founder, Alex Sanders, the British self-proclaimed "King of the Witches," the Alexandrian tradition was the second largest tradition to come out of England. The tradition is based heavily upon the Gardnerian tradition, with greater emphasis on cord magic (see KNOTS) and ceremonial magic. Sanders adopted Gardner's skyclad practice. The Alexandrian tradition declined with Sanders' retirement from the limelight in the 1970s and death in 1988. Sanders' wife, Maxine, remained active on her own for more than a decade. The Alexandrian tradition is practiced by covens around the world, and elements of it have been absorbed into newer traditions. (See VIVIAN CROWLEY; JANET AND STEWART FARRAR.)

Dianic/Feminist. A broad tradition that includes covens that are feminist and/or strongly matriarchal in orientation. The name is taken from Diana, Greek goddess of the moon and the hunt, and one of the principal names for the Goddess aspect in Witchcraft. The Goddess is worshiped exclusively or nearly so. The emphasis is on rediscovering and reclaiming female power and divinity and consciousness-raising. Some covens are all-female, while others admit men. The Dianic tradition espouses a feminist spirituality sisterhood that opposes an oppressive, patriarchal society and works to bring about positive social and political changes for all.

Dianic Witchcraft emerged from the feminist consciousness movement and had its strongest origins in the United States. One of the first Dianic covens was formed in Dallas, Texas, by Morgan McFarland and Mark Roberts in the late 1960s. Originally, McFarland had no name for her coven; the name Dianic came to her later. Rituals revolved around the phases of the MOON and were steeped in ancient matriarchal myth and power. Some years later, McFarland and Roberts split, but the Dianic tradition was continued by other covens. Among the most notable leaders who have shaped Dianic Witchcraft are Z BUDA-PEST and STARHAWK. Budapest, a founder of the Susan B. Anthony coven in 1971, once said Dianic Witchcraft is a "Wimmin's Religion" not open to men. Starhawk, an initiate of the Faery Tradition (see below), integrated men into Dianic Witchcraft.

Rituals are eclectic; some are derived from the Gardnerian and Faery traditions, while others have been created new. Many feminist covens do not have a handed-down book of shadows.

Many Dianic Witches are political activists for women's and civil rights, environmental issues and peace and antinuclear issues.

Hereditary/Family. Witchcraft traditions that blend folk magic, some of which has Christianized elements, and ethnic traditions, often handed down through family lineages. People who inherit the training often have in-

Newsletter concerning burning of three witches at Derneburg, October 1555

nate psychic and healing abilities. Examples are the POW-WOWING *brauchers* (healers) and *hexenmeisters* (witches) of Germanic-Pennsylvania Dutch traditions and various Italian traditions.

In the early days of Witchcraft, it was important to claim a secret hereditary lineage. Some claims were exaggerated or even made up in order to establish legitimacy. Presently, traditions incorporating ethnic and family traditions are flexible and fluid and may mix elements from other traditions and pagan practices.

Faery/Faerie/Fairy Tradition. An ecstatic and magical Craft religion founded and developed by VICTOR ANDERSON and GWYDION PENDDERWEN. Initially small and secretive, many of the fundamentals of the Tradition have reached a wide audience through the writings of Starhawk, a Faery Tradition initiate.

Like all Craft traditions, the Faery Tradition honors nature and reveres the deities who personify the forces of nature, life, fertility, death and rebirth. It is polytheistic rather than dualistic, and while it recognizes the male-female polarity and other polarities, it does not emphasize polarities as much as the Gardnerian tradition. The Faery Tradition emphasizes pragmatic magic, self-development and theurgy.

There is no standard secret book of shadows, but rather an eclectic approach to working the Craft and living life. Some aspects remain secretive, while most are taught openly. The Faery Tradition provides for a passing of power upon initiation, which links the initiate to the power of the group and those who have gone before.

The tradition identifies different currents of energy within the universe, that are used in magic. "Faery power" is an ecstatic energy of attunement that is beautiful and sensual but goes beyond the senses: One fills the senses with beauty to go beyond the senses. There is an awareness of the unseen reality, a respect for the wisdom of nature, and acceptance of oneself and others as part of nature and a sensual mysticism that involves a celebratory embracing of life and a love of beauty.

Metaphysical teachings and secret words and names are handed down in the tradition. Two key teachings center on the IRON and pearl PENTAGRAMS, meditation tools to bring oneself into balance with the universe and to explore the self. The points of the iron pentagram represent Sex, Self, Passion, Pride and Power. The points of the pearl pentagram represent Love, Wisdom, Knowledge, Law and Power.

Shamanic. Some of the fastest-growing traditions in Witchcraft incorporate shamanic elements of trance and healing. One of the earliest blendings was created by SELENA FOX, high priestess of CIRCLE SANCTUARY near Mt. Horeb, Wisconsin. Fox combined Witchcraft, transpersonal psychology and crosscultural shamanistic traditions.

Witches cavorting with demons (OLD WOODCUT)

Shamanic elements include the discovery of one's personal relationship with the spirits of nature and finding one's power animals and plants, which become allies in healing. Respect is paid to one's genetic and spiritual human ancestors, to all life-forms and to the Earth. The initiatory experience is the vigil, a night spent alone in nature without fire, shelter or food. The vigil, undertaken after a period of training, brings the individual face to face with deep, primal fears and provides for an intense self-examination.

Goth. One of the newer traditions or movements, Goth Craft blends Witchcraft and Goth culture, emphasizing the dark aspects of deities and exploration of the shadow side of spirituality. Goth Witchcraft features BLOOD magic, death magic, NECROMANCY, and self-expression through the dark arts (see RAVEN DIGITALIS). Confrontation with one's shadow side and integration of it are important parts of the path to wholeness as envisioned by Carl G. Jung and also proponents of transpersonal psychology.

FURTHER READING:

Adler, Margot. *Drawing Down the Moon.* Rev. ed. New York: Penguin, 2006.

Bonewits, Isaac. *Bonewits's Essential Guide to Witchcraft and Wicca.* New York: Citadel Press Books, 2006.

Briggs, Robin. *Witches & Neighbors: The Social and Cultural Context of European Witchcraft.* New York: Viking, 1996.

Buckland, Raymond. *The Witch Book: The Encyclopedia of Witchcraft, Wicca, and Neo-paganism.* Detroit: Visible Ink Press, 2002.

Farrar, Janet, and Gavin Bone. *Progressive Witchcraft: Spirituality, Mysteries & Training in Modern Wicca.* Franklin Lakes, N.J.: New Page Books, 2004.

Flint, Valerie, and Richard Gordon, Georg Luck, and Daniel Ogden. *Witchcraft and Magic in Europe: Ancient Greece and Rome.* London: The Athlone Press, 1999.

Grimassi, Raven. *The Encyclopedia of Wicca & Witchcraft.* 2nd ed. St. Paul, Minn.: Llewellyn Publications, 2003.

Hutton, Ronald. *The Triumph of the Moon: A History of Modern Pagan Witchcraft.* Oxford: Oxford University Press, 1999.

Lipp, Deborah, and Isaac Bonewits. *The Study of Witchcraft: A Guidebook to Advanced Wicca.* York Beach, Me.: Weiser Books, 2007.

Rabinovitch, Shelley, and James Lewis. *The Encyclopedia of Modern Witchcraft and Neo-Paganism.* New York: Citadel Press, 2002.

Witchcraft Research Association (WRA)   Organization founded in February 1964 by SYBIL LEEK with the purpose of uniting witches in Britain.

Leek established herself as president, but only for a few months, stepping down in July 1964 in the face of backfired self-promotion and publicity. Leek moved to America, and DOREEN VALIENTE stepped in as her successor. The association had a journal, the *Pentagram,* edited by a friend of ROBERT COCHRANE, who also contributed articles.

On October 3, 1964, the WRA hosted a dinner at which Valiente urged all witch traditions to come out of secrecy and join together. Among the approximately 50 attendees were Cochrane and PATRICIA CROWTHER. Cochrane was introduced as a hereditary witch, and Valiente and Crowther made a toast to the HORNED GOD together.

In the first issue of *Pentagram,* Valiente wrote about her dream to see the WRA become the United Nations for witches. All traditions, she said, should make themselves known and accept one another. This dream was never realized, for the *Pentagram* became the battleground between supporters of GERALD B. GARDNER, among whom Crowther and her husband, ARNOLD CROWTHER, were leading voices, and anti-Gardnerians, including Cochrane and his associate, Taliesin. By 1966, the *Pentagram* folded, and the WRA ceased soon after.

FURTHER READING:

Hutton, Ronald. *The Triumph of the Moon: A History of Modern Pagan Witchcraft.* Oxford: Oxford University Press, 1999.

Valiente, Doreen. *The Rebirth of Witchcraft.* London: Robert Hale, 1989.

witch doctors   Witch doctors, also called *jujumen, obeahmen, root doctors, conjure men* and *leaf doctors,* serve as priests and physicians to African tribal members and to believers in VODUN, SANTERÍA, the MACUMBA cults in Brazil and those who seek the healing powers of herbs.

As their name suggests, witch doctors in Africa treat patients for witch-induced sickness, divining the witch responsible for a victim's illness or misfortune and curing the patient by sending a counteracting SPELLS. As their power grows, the witch doctors can control entire villages, convincing members they know the sources of evil and how to use them. Among the old Zulu and Ashanti tribes, women often served as witch finders, adorning themselves in feathers and furs and smearing paint and white clay for fierceness on their faces. After reaching a hysterical frenzy brought on by drum beating and CHANTING, the witch finders would point to the witch perpetrators, resulting in the condemned's immediate execution (see AFRICAN WITCHCRAFT).

A witch-doctor general practitioner is called a *nganga,* the same word used by the black WITCHES in Santería for their evil-spirit CAULDRONS. The nganga divines the source of a victim's misfortunes by casting the *hakata,* or bones (the "bones" may be seeds, dice, shells or actual bones), interpreting the lay of the throws and offering prophecies of good health or evildoing (see DIVINATION). Ngangas supposedly use their power only for good, but they must be familiar with witchcraft's evil practices in order to combat them. If a witch sends a *ngozi,* or grudge-bearing spirit, to harm someone, then the witch doctor must know how to send an even more powerful ngozi to the witch.

POISONS provide powerful weapons for the witch doctor, used to detect witches and perform spells. In a poison test, the witch doctor administers a poisonous drink to a suspect; if he sickens and vomits, he is innocent, but if he tolerates the drink, he is an evil witch. Suspects die during the ordeal, but their deaths are viewed as divine justice. A variation on the ordeal is the *benge,* in which poisons are given to chickens as the suspects' names are read; if a chicken dies while a name is called, that suspect is guilty.

Used in SPELLS, poisons can bring about the desired effects promised by the witch doctor. One famous case involved a root doctor, or specialist in herbal medicines, named Dr. Bug. For $50, Dr. Bug guaranteed his patients that they would fail their physicals when drafted into the armed services. The willing clients took a potion and then suffered from "hippity-hoppity heart syndrome," thereby escaping the draft. Doctors were amazed to find so many sufferers of the condition, until one draftee took a double dose to make sure he would fail the physical and died. His autopsy showed the potion contained a mixture of oleander leaves, which contain digitalis, and rubbing alcohol, mothballs and lead.

Witch doctoring did not die with the modernization of Africa. Now often called "traditional healers" to remove the negative connotations of "witch doctor," native practitioners dispense herbal medicines, divine futures and seek alternative methods of treatment for their clients, many of whom have embraced other Western styles and attitudes. In some cases, the healers, also called *jujumen* (from the African *juju,* or FETISH), have scored remarkable successes, especially for chronic illnesses like high blood pressure, asthma, mental illness and venereal disease.

In the Deep South region of the United States and in Haiti, healers are known as *root doctors, conjure men* or *leaf doctors* (*dokte feuilles* in Creole French). These people practice herbal medicine, administering potions and preparations to cure a variety of diseases, especially the more mundane ones: colds, aching joints, headaches, gastrointestinal complaints and minor "female complications." Although well respected for their knowledge, the leaf doctors have no special access to the gods and cannot treat the more serious illnesses brought on by spirit intervention, spiritual disharmony and witchcraft.

The most famous conjure man in America was DOCTOR JOHN, a free black witch doctor in 19th-century New Orleans. One of MARIE LAVEAU's early mentors, Doctor John controlled most of the blacks and a good deal of the whites in the city with his powders, love potions and amazing knowledge about their lives—usually gained through a network of well-placed spies. He amassed a large fortune by dispensing GRIS-GRIS but ended his life in poverty after losing his property through fraud. His peers said Doctor John had been "fixed," or been the victim of spells greater than his.

In his research on Jamaican native healers, called *obeahmen,* Joseph K. Long asked why many people prefer witch doctors to trained physicians. In some cases, he postulated, witch doctors seem more sympathetic, gearing their treatments to the societal norms of the community. In others, the disease may be more a form of community hysteria, and once fears are calmed, the disease dissipates. Ultimately, however, he found that among peoples who believe in MAGIC, magic works.

In rural Appalachia, a witch doctor is one who breaks the spells of witches. If one is troubled by bewitchment, one seeks out the witch doctor, just as one would go to a medical doctor for a physical ailment.

FURTHER READING:
Evans-Pritchard, E. E. *Witchcraft, Oracles and Magic Among the Azande.* Abridge. Oxford: Clarendon Press, 1983.

Mair, Lucy. *Witchcraft.* New York: McGraw-Hill World University Library, 1969.

Middleton, John, ed. Magic, *Curing & Witchcraft.* Austin: University of Texas Press, 1967.

Parrinder, Geoffrey. *Witchcraft European and African.* London: Faber & Faber, 1970.

witches   Practitioners of witchcraft. According to tradition, witches are skilled in SORCERY and MAGIC. Belief in witches, sorcerers and magicians has existed universally since prehistoric times. A witch can be either male or female. Most have been feared and abhorred because they are believed to be vindictive, cast evil SPELLS upon others and consort with evil spirits. Witch with a capital W applies to contemporary followers of a Pagan religion, who advocate use of magical skills only for good.

Origin of witch.   The word "witch" comes from the Middle English word *witche,* which is derived from the Old English terms *wicca, wicce* and *wiccian,* which mean "to work sorcery, bewitch." The Indo-European root of these terms is *weik,* which has to do with magic and religion.

Witches in non-Western cultures.   Outside of the West, most witches are viewed as evil. In Navajo lore, men and women become witches to gain wealth, hurt others out of envy and wreak vengeance. Initiation into Witchery Way requires killing a person, usually a sibling. Witches rob graves, shape-shift into animals, hold nocturnal SABBATS, eat corpses and shoot alien substances into the bodies of victims to cause illness. They then charge the victims a fee for a cure. More men than women are witches, but the women are usually old or childless. Among the Shawnee, Fox and other tribes of eastern North America, male and female witches organize into societies with their own rites, which include cannibalism.

African beliefs about witches are similar. Witches are at the least unsociable and irritable and at the worst thoroughly evil. Mandari witches dance on the graves of their victims, while Lugbara witches dance naked—the

ultimate outrageous behavior. Lugbara witches also have other extraordinary behaviors, such as walking on their hands instead of their feet. The Dinka believe witches have tails. Some tribes, such as the Mandari, Nyakyusa and Zande, believe that witchcraft is inherited and that a person cannot help committing the antisocial and evil acts that are part of witchcraft.

Witches in Western beliefs. The Western concepts of witches evolved from the sorcery and magic beliefs of the ancient Assyrians, Babylonians, Akkadians, Hebrews, Greeks and Romans. An ancient Assyrian tablet speaks of the bewitching powers of witches, WIZARDS, sorcerers and

Condemned witches burning in St. Peter's Port, Guernsey, 1700

sorceresses. In ancient Greece and Rome, witches were renowned for their herbal knowledge, magical potions and supernatural powers. Thessaly, a region in Greece, was particularly "notorious for witchcraft" and "universally known for magic incantations," according to Apuleius, a Roman poet of the Second century. Thessalian witches reputedly had the power to bring the moon down from the sky (see DRAWING DOWN THE MOON). Pythagoras is said to have learned from them how to divine by holding up a polished silver disc to the moon. So potent was their power that the Roman poet Horace of the First century B.C.E. posed, "What witch, what magician will be able to free you from Thessalian sorceries?"

The Roman poets Ovid and Statius described witches as having long, flowing hair and going about barefoot. In *Amores,* Ovid describes a "certain old hag" named Dipsas:

> She knows the Black Arts and the spells of Aenea [Circe] and by her skill turns back the waters to their source.
>
> She knows what herbs, what the threads twisted by the magic circle, what the poison of the loving mare [a love philtre] can do. At her will, the clouds mass in the entire heavens. At her will, the day shines in the clear sky. I have sent the stars dripping with blood—if you may believe me—and the face of the moon glowing red with blood. I suspect that she flits through the shades of night,

and that her aged body is covered with feathers. She summons from the ancient tombs her antique ancestors, and make the ground yawn open with her incantation.

In his novel *Metamorphoses,* Apuleius describes Meroe, an old witch who owns an inn:

> She is capable of bringing down the sky, suspending the earth, making springs dry up, sweeping away mountains, conjuring the spirits of the dead. She can weaken the gods, put out the stars, light up Hell itself.
>
> When a neighboring innkeeper would not return her love, she changed him into a frog. A lawyer who prosecuted her she turned into a ram.

Classical witches were said to possess the EVIL EYE. Pliny wrote of those who killed by looks, Tully wrote of women who had two "apples" in one eye, and Ovid and Plutarch wrote of poison in the eyes.

Witchcraft, witches, sorcerers, "them that have familiar spirits," charmers and wizards "that chirp and mutter" are mentioned in the Bible (see WITCH OF ENDOR). The most famous biblical quotation cited by the witch-hunters of the INQUISITION was Exodus 22:18: "Thou shalt not suffer a witch to live." However, it was pointed out as early as 1584, by Reginald Scot in *Discovery of Witchcraft,* that Hebrew words translated as "witch" usually referred to diviners, astrologers, poisoners and jugglers (manipulators), and not "witches" as defined by Christian demonology. According to the historian Henry Charles Lea, the witchcraft denounced most often by the Bible was merely DIVINATION. The Hebrews practiced magic and sorcery, which included herbal formulas, conjurations, the evil eye, AMULETS and TALISMANS, NECROMANCY and divination, but did not consider them diabolical or malevolent, as the Christians later did. Hebrew DEMONS, which included evil spirits, were absorbed into Christian demonology.

During the European witch craze from the mid-15th century through the 18th century, witches were viewed as heretics who worshiped the DEVIL and engaged in abominable practices, such as MALEFICIA, shape-shifting, orgiastic dances, copulation with demons, cannibalism, vampirism and flying through the air. "The Scriptures assert that there are devils and witches and that they are the common enemy of mankind," said INCREASE MATHER in *Cases of Conscience* in 1693. John Wagstaffe, a writer well known in England and New England in the late 17th century, defined witches in terms of Jezebel, the Phoenician princess who, according to the Bible, married King Ahab in the ninth century B.C.E. and promoted the worship of her own gods, Baal and Asherah. A disgusted priest threw her out a window to her death, and God's only recourse was to destroy the house of Ahab. Stated Wagstaffe, "Thus you shall often meet in the Bible with fornication and witchcraft joined together. By fornication and whoredom is meant idolatry and by witchcraft the art of engaging men in it. The whoredom of Jezebel was her idolatry, and her witchcraft was the maintaining of Baal's priests."

The four witches (ALBRECHT DÜRER, 1497)

Demonologists divided witches into classes. Witches also were called diviners, consulters with familiar spirits, wizards, necromancers, charmers and enchanters. Gypsies, exorcists, astrologers, numerologists and other fortune-tellers also were classed as witches. William West wrote in 1594:

> A witch or hag is she which being eluded by a league made with the Devil through his persuasion, inspiration, and juggling, thinketh she can design what manner of things soever, either by thought or imprecation, as to shake the air with lightnings and thunder, to cause hail and tempests, to remove green corn or trees to another place, to be carried of her familiar with hath upon him the deceitful shape of a goat, swine, calf, etc. into some mountain far distant, in a wonderful space of time. And sometimes to fly upon a staff or fork, or some other instrument. And to spend all the night after with her sweetheart, in playing, sorting, banqueting, dalliance, and diverse other devilish lusts, and lewd desports and to show a thousand such monstrous mockeries.

West said other kinds of witches included enchanters and charmers, jugglers, soothsaying wizards, divinators and magicians.

Some distinctions were made between "white" witches and "black" witches. White witches were those who cured illness, divined lost property, exposed thieves, enhanced fertility and drove away bad weather. Black witches were those who used their magic only for the harm of others. White witches often were called other names, such as cunning folk, wise folk, wizard, sorcerer and witch doctor.

Witch-hunters did not prosecute white witches—chiefly the healers and diviners—with the same fervor as black witches, for they were perceived as serving a vital need in the community. As much as the public feared bad witches as a menace to body and soul, they valued the village sorcerer who would cure their sicknesses and help them in times of trouble.

As the witch mania intensified, demonologists, witch-hunters and the learned men who shaped public opinion began calling for prosecution of white witches as well. It was said that good witches really were a menace because of their capability of doing evil. Their supernatural gifts did not come from God, but from the Devil. In England, Perkins and Thomas Cooper of Oxford were among those who believed good witches were far more dangerous than bad witches, and that both needed to be extirpated. This view was endorsed by COTTON MATHER in Massachusetts. George Giffard, an Oxford preacher, said that all witches should be put to death not because they kill others, but because they deal with devils. "These cunning men and women which deale with spirites and charmes seeming to do good, and draw the people into manifold impieties, with all others which have familiarity with devils, or use conjurations, ought to bee rooted out, that others might see and feare," Giffard stated.

Witch and queen, from the fairy tale "The White Duck" in Andrew Lang's The Yellow Fairy Book

It was believed that witches could be identified by certain tell-tale signs: insensitive spots or marks on the body, called DEVIL'S MARKS (almost any mole qualified); the inability to shed TEARS; and supernumerary teats or excrescences for suckling IMPS, called WITCH'S MARKS. The evil eye was a sign, but was not infallible, said Increase Mather. Others described witches as invariably ugly and deformed (see HAG). Many of the accused witches were outcasts or on the fringes of society, looked down upon by their neighbors because of their unmarried status, handicaps, homely appearances, ill temper or poverty. Not all victims were such: some were married, young and prosperous.

"Witch" was a devastating accusation. If arrested and taken before a court or inquisitor, one was often assumed to be guilty. TORTURE was applied until one confessed. Families of accused witches were shunned, and it was not uncommon that they abandoned the victim. Such was the pathetic case of a woman burned at the stake in 1649 in Lauder, Scotland. As she faced death, she declared to the crowd:

All you that see me this day! Know ye that I am to die as a Witch, by my own Confession! And I free all Men, especially the Ministers and Magistrates, from the guilt of my Blood, I take it wholly on my self, and as I must make answer to the God of Heaven, I declare that I am as free from Witchcraft as any Child, but being accused by a Malicious Woman, and Imprisoned under the Name of a Witch, my Husband and Friends disowned me, and seeing no hope of ever being in Credit again, through the Temptation of the Devil, I made that Confession to destroy my own Life, being weary of it, and shusing (sic) rather to die than to Live.

Religious Witches. Contemporary Witches who practice Witchcraft as a religion face a powerful, negative stereotype of the witch: a hag with a large, warty nose, a pointy chin, scraggly hair and a cone-shaped black hat, who lives alone with her animals—usually black CATS—who casts evil spells on others, and who is in league with the Devil. This stereotype has been reinforced for centuries in literature, drama, the popular press and film and television.

The term *Witch* was used by GERALD B. GARDNER in the 1950s, in his revelation that he had been initiated by a CO-VEN of hereditary Witches in England, who practiced "the Old Religion." There is doubt that those people called themselves Witches; most likely, they were a Rosicrucian group. The religion that Gardner forged became Witchcraft.

Contemporary Witches define themselves as healers, servants of the community and servants of the GODDESS and HORNED GOD. They believe in respecting the sanctity of all life and being in harmony with all living things and with the forces of the universe. They strive to attune themselves to nature and the elements, forces that can be influenced in the working of magic. They develop their psychic abilities and seek to raise their spiritual consciousness through study, worship, the practice of their Craft and observance of a moral and ethical lifestyle, in accordance with Craft laws and tenets. Magic and worship are carried out in rituals. Most Witches believe in using magic for good, not harm. Some Witches endorse using CURSES and binding spells under certain conditions.

Since the rise of Witchcraft as a religion in the 1950s, Witches have worked to eradicate their negative stereotype and reeducate the public. The task is complicated by the diverse practices of contemporary Witches, not all of whom identify with the laws and ethics of the religious Craft. The average layperson who knows little about Witchcraft lumps all witches together under the stereotype.

Most Witches feel strongly that the word *Witch* should not be abandoned, though some use the term *Wiccan* to describe modern religious practitioners and to distinguish themselves from folklore witches.

FURTHER READING:

Adler, Margot. *Drawing Down the Moon.* Rev. ed. New York: Penguin, 2006.

Briggs, Robin. *Witches & Neighbors: The Social and Cultural Context of European Witchcraft.* New York: Viking, 1996.

Farrar, Janet, and Gavin Bone. *Progressive Witchcraft: Spirituality, Mysteries & Training in Modern Wicca.* Franklin Lakes, N.J.: New Page Books, 2004.

Flint, Valerie, and Richard Gordon, Georg Luck, and Daniel Ogden. *Witchcraft and Magic in Europe: Ancient Greece and Rome.* London: The Athlone Press, 1999.

Malinowski, Bronislaw. *Magic, Science and Religion.* Garden City, N.Y.: Doubleday Anchor Books, 1948.

Starhawk. *The Spiral Dance.* Rev. ed. San Francisco: HarperOne, 1999.

Witches League of Public Awareness   International educational organization based in Salem, Massachusetts, which works to end prejudice and bigotry against Witches and Witchcraft, especially in the media.

The Witches League of Public Awareness (WLPA) was organized in 1986 by Salem Witch LAURIE CABOT to protest the filming of John Updike's novel *The Witches of Eastwick.* The novel concerns three "witches" who are involved with the Devil.

The League networks with major witch groups around the world. It also works with the American Civil Liberties Union regarding religious freedom interests, and with police departments concerning occult crimes not committed by Witches but automatically blamed on them. The WLPA exposed "File 18," a secret newsletter compiled in the 1980s by a police officer, which constituted an "occult hit list" for police, falsely naming individual Witches and Craft organizations as those who could be suspected of occult crimes.

The WLPA maintains a network of "Information Resource People" who act as resource contacts for media and the public and who monitor the media in its portrayal of Witches. Where there are inaccuracies and misrepresentations, the League responds by sending the appropriate educational and legal information.

The WLPA does not handle individual discrimination cases.

witches' light   A light emitted or carried by witches that enables them to be detected by others, especially at night.

According to the folklore of the Azande of Africa, a witch releases a spirit to murder others while they sleep, much as medieval witches were believed to dispatch DEMONS in the shape of animal FAMILIARS. This spirit, or essence of witchcraft, may be seen at night, glowing like sparks kicked off from a fire. In daytime, the light is visible only to those who are witches or WITCH DOCTORS.

Effutu witches of southern Ghana use a spiritual "web" or "wire" by which they travel in search of victims. As they move across this web at night, they are visible as bright flashes of light (see AFRICAN WITCHCRAFT).

The Pueblo of New Mexico, and the Bantu and Gusii of Africa, maintain that witches travel by night, carrying lights that alternately flare up and down. The Gusii say the changes in brightness are due to the witches removing and replacing the lids of the fire-pots which they carry with them.

Among the Dobu Islanders of the western Pacific, the *kainana*—the fire emitted by the pubes of flying witches—may be seen at night. To ward off danger, the villages gather together around fires which are kept burning all night. No one returns home until dawn. These beliefs are comparable to the European lore that witches fly by night on BROOMS lit by CANDLES in the besoms.

FURTHER READING:
Evans-Pritchard, E. E. *Witchcraft, Oracles and Magic Among the Azande.* Abridged. Oxford: Clarendon Press, 1983.

witches' tools   The magical working tools in contemporary Witchcraft are associated with the forces of the ELEMENTS. The tools and their uses are derivative of some Hermetic magical practices (see HERMETICA). Before they can be used in RITUALS, all magical tools must be consecrated in rites that involve exposure of the tools to the four elements of Nature, by immersing or sprinkling them with salted WATER; passing them through or over a flame; passing them through incense smoke; and touching them with a disk of earth or baked clay, or plunging them into the earth. The consecration rituals are similar to those in *The Key of Solomon*, a magical grimoire attributed to the legendary King Solomon (see GRIMOIRES) and translated into English in 1888, to which Pagan elements have been added.

Magical tools customarily are inscribed with Runes, SIGILS and symbols. Ideally, the tools are handmade, for the act of construction helps to imbue them with the Witch's personal power. Or, tools can be bought and personalized through inscription, consecration and ritual. Magical tools serve a variety of purposes in rituals and are used in the consecration of MAGIC CIRCLES and of other magic tools.

Athame. A Witch's personal, magical knife, traditionally double-bladed with a black hilt, and fashioned of steel or iron. The blade may be magnetized. Magical knives were said to be used by witches in the Middle Ages.

According to the Gardnerian tradition, the athame is used only for ritual purposes, such as casting the magic circle, and never for cutting. Other traditions call for using the knife to cast and cut in the belief that its power increases with use. In some rituals, the athame takes on phallic symbolism; it is plunged into a chalice filled with juice or wine, signifying the union of male and female forces (see GREAT RITE).

The athame is associated with the element of fire (in some traditions, with air). In some traditions, it is interchangeable with the sword.

Among some hereditary Witches in England, metal is never used in ritual tools because it interferes with energy in the earth. Athame blades are therefore made of flint.

Some Witches use a white-hilted knife for cutting and inscribing. Knives are never used for sacrifices, which are not condoned.

Censer. A small dish or container is used to burn incense, herbs, chemicals, wood or other substances, to cleanse and purify the air before rituals. Censing, which represents the element of air, exorcises and keeps unwanted energies away from the magic site; offers sweet air to GODDESS and God; raises vibrational rates and summons energies; relaxes the senses; and contains and concentrates power. The formulas used depend on the purpose of the ritual. The burning of incense as protection and offering is an ancient religious practice found around the world.

Cup (also chalice, goblet). The cup is associated with the female forces in the universe: fertility, beauty, the womb, earth, emotion, love, compassion, receptivity, instinct, intuition and the subconscious mind. It is the receptacle of spiritual forces. It is associated with the element of water. Held upright, the cup is an open womb, ready to receive. Held inverted, it symbolizes birth and realization. The cup holds water or wine, which is consecrated and used in rituals or shared among coveners (see COVEN).

Pentacle. Symbol of the earth, the pentacle is a disk or square of metal (usually copper or silver), wax, baked clay, earthenware or wood, and is inscribed with Craft symbols. It is generally associated with female energy. Among its uses are to ground energy and to serve food shared at the end of a coven's working session. See also PENTACLE AND PENTAGRAM.

Sword. Not all Witches use a sword; some covens have a single sword for the entire group. The sword serves the same function as the athame, used for ritual purposes such as casting the circle but not for cutting. It is considered more authoritative than the athame. The sword is associated with the element fire (in some traditions, with air). Gardner made his own swords.

Wand. The wand is the instrument of invocation of spirits. It represents the element of fire (in some traditions, air) and symbolizes the life-force within the Witch. The wand dates back to prehistoric times and is mentioned in the Bible; both Moses and Aaron use rods to bring the plague to Egypt. The Greek god HERMES is represented with a caduceus, a wand entwined with snakes and winged at the top, a symbol of power, wisdom and healing.

HAZEL has always been considered the best wood for wands, followed by ash, rowan and WILLOW; 18 inches is considered a good length. The wood should be cut when the moon is waxing or full. In certain Witchcraft rituals, tipped phallic wands are used. Some Witches use wands made of crystal, silver, carved ivory or ebony, and gold. In some cases, a wand may be used to cast magic circles.

Cauldron. Some traditions use a cauldron to represent the fifth element of Spirit and the Mystic Center.

Other Tools

Some traditions also employ the following tools:

Cords. Cords of silk, other natural materials or nylon are used primarily in the Gardnerian and Alexandrian traditions. A single, nine-foot RED cord is used in a Witch's initiation into the Craft (see INITIATION). In magic work, cords are knotted by Witches either individually or in a group, while they chant a spell (see KNOTS; SPELLS). The knots are tied in certain patterns or orders and are left tied until the right moment for untying, which releases the magic energy and effects the spell. A system of colors is used for different spells. Cords also are used in binding parts of the body to reduce BLOOD circulation, as a means of achieving an altered state of consciousness in the raising of psychic power.

Divination items. Runes, Tarot cards, crystals, the I Ching and other systems of DIVINATION are important working tools.

Prayer beads. Pagan prayer beads are strands or necklaces of colored beads, each of which represents a different prayer. They are used like meditation beads or a rosary.

Scourge. Light beating with a scourge made of knotted strands of silk or other light materials is done primarily in the Gardnerian and Alexandrian traditions. It was favored by Gardner in INITIATIONS, to symbolize the need to learn through suffering and as a way to raise psychic power and gain "the Sight" (clairvoyance). For the latter purpose, Gardner said scourging excites both body and soul but allows one to retain control over the power raised. The scourging should not be strong enough to break the skin but should be strong enough to draw blood to that part of the body and away from the brain. If done long enough, it induces drowsiness.

Scourging has fallen out of favor with many Witches and some covens have abandoned the practice. Others scourge very lightly.

FURTHER READING:
Adler, Margot. *Drawing Down the Moon.* Revised ed. New York: Viking, 1986.
Crowley, Vivianne. *Wicca: The Old Religion in the New Millennium.* Revised ed. London: Thorsons/Harper Collins, 1996.
Farrar, Stewart. *What Witches Do: A Modern Coven Revealed.* Custer, Wash.: Phoenix Publishing Co., 1983.
Starhawk, M. Macha NightMare and the Reclaiming Collective. *The Pagan Book of Living and Dying.* San Francisco: HarperSanFrancisco, 1997.

witch-finder An expert at examining and identifying witches. Witch-finders were especially important during the height of the witch hunts in the 16th and 17th centuries.

In Britain, every town and county had its witch-finder, who was kept busy investigating all mishaps and accidents, which usually were believed to be caused by witchcraft and sorcery. Even acts of nature, such as hailstorms that destroyed crops, were blamed on the MALEFICIA of witches.

Witch-finders identified suspects and prepared them for judicial examination and trial. They carefully examined bodies for WITCH'S MARKS. Many witch-finders pricked suspects with needles and sharp instruments. If the suspect did not cry, or moles and warts did not bleed, the suspect was a witch. If they could not recite the LORD'S PRAYER without stumbling, they were witches. Ownership of cats, dogs, TOADS and other creatures were taken to be FAMILIARS. Some said they could identify witches simply by looking at them. Witch-finders might give suspects special diets to counteract whatever magical CHARMS they might have ingested to hide their identities or to become invisible and escape.

Witch-finders were well paid for their services, and many traveled about the countryside for hire. They were paid per person fees for every suspect found guilty. Most were not above torturing suspects into confessions in order to enhance their fees and reputations. One of the most highly paid witch-finders was MATTHEW HOPKINS of England. Many clergymen were witch-finders for hire. In Scotland in the 17th century, ministers competed with one another to secure the condemnation of the most witches. If professional witch-finders were not available, communities hired witches and WIZARDS themselves.

FURTHER READING:
Grant, James. *The Mysteries of All Nations: Rise and Progress of Superstition, Laws Against and Trials of Witches, Ancient and Modern Delusions, Together With Strange Customs, Fables and Tales.* Edinburgh: Leith, Reid & Son, n.d.

witching hour The hour of midnight on the night of the full MOON. This is a time of transformation and change and the height of witches' spell-casting powers. The roots of this notion go back to ancient times, to the worship of goddesses associated with the Moon, fertility and witchcraft. As the Moon waxes in its phases, so do the powers associated with it and its deities, until they culminate at the full moon.

Witch of Edmonton See SAWYER, ELISABETH.

Witch of Endor According to the story related in Samuel I of the Old Testament, the Witch of Endor was a pythoness and necromancer who raised the spirit of Samuel at the request of King Saul of Israel (see NECROMANCY). Although she is called a "witch," it is likely not an accurate description of her.

The Bible relates that Saul was afraid of an impending attack by a mighty army of Philistines, who had been joined by his rival, David. He gathered up the Israelites and camped at Mount Gilboa. He sought advice from prophets and divination by sacred lot and from the Lord, but he received no answer as to his fate or the action he should take.

Saul instructed his servants, "Seek me a woman that hath a familiar spirit, that I may go to her, and enquire of her." His servants directed him to the pythoness at Endor, whose name is never given.

Saul disguised himself and went to the witch the same night. At first, she was frightened that he had come to expose her as a witch: "Behold, thou knowest what Saul hath done, how he hath cut off those that have familiar spirits, and the wizards, out of the land: wherefore then layest thou a snare for my life, to cause me to die?"

Saul assured the woman he meant her no harm and instructed her to conjure Samuel from the dead. She performed her ritual and claimed to see gods rising out of the earth, followed by a spirit like an old man, wrapped in a robe. Saul, who could see nothing, believed the old spirit was Samuel and prostrated himself on the ground.

Samuel was not pleased to be disturbed from the grave. Saul said he faced war and had been abandoned by God. But Samuel's reply was not what Saul wanted to hear: that God was displeased with Saul for his disobedience and had torn his kingdom from his hand and given it to David. "Moreover, the Lord will also deliver Israel with thee into the hand of the Philistines: and tomorrow shalt

Witch of Endor conjuring Samuel for Saul (JOSEPH GLANVIL, *SADUCISMUS TRIUMPHATUS,* 1681 ED.)

thou and the sons be with me: the Lord shall also deliver the host of Israel into the hand of the Philistines."

Upon hearing this condemnation, Saul fell into a faint. The spirit of Samuel vanished. The woman went to Saul and offered him food for strength, but he refused. His servants and the witch helped him get up. She killed a fatted calf she had and cooked it, and made some unleavened bread. Before he left, Saul relented and ate the meal she offered him.

The next day, the Philistines attacked the Israelites, who fled in terror and were slain. Saul's sons Jonathan, Abinadab and Malchishua were slain, and Saul was badly wounded. Saul ordered an armor-bearer to kill him with his sword, but the soldier refused. Saul took his sword and fell upon it.

When the Philistines found his body, they cut off the head, fastened his body to the wall of Beth-shan and put his armor in the temple of ASTARTE. His headless body was removed by the inhabitants of Jabesh-gilead, who burned the body and buried the bones. David succeeded Saul as King of Israel.

Among those who considered the conjuration of Samuel to be a hoax was REGINALD SCOT, the 16th-century English writer who attempted to debunk beliefs about witchcraft in his book, *The Discoverie of Witchcraft.* Scot devoted several chapters to a discussion of the story, asserting that the distraught Saul was taken for a fool by a clever woman whose familiar was a "counterfeit":

> When Saule had told hir, that he would have Samuel brought up to him, she departed from his presence into hir closet, where doubtles she had hir familiar; to wit, some lewd craftie preest, and made Saule stand at the door like a foole (as it were with his finger in a hole), to hear the cousening [deceitful] answers, but not see the counsening [sic] handling thereof, and the couterfetting [sic] of the matter.

The witch, Scot said, knew who Saul was despite his disguise. She played out her incantations, lied about seeing gods or angels ascending from the earth and about seeing the spirit of old Samuel. Scot discounts that such a spirit could have been Samuel, for it was clothed in a new mantle such as he was buried in and surely would have been rotted by the time he was conjured.

Theologians such as Augustine and Tertullian, and the French demonologist, JEAN BODIN (a contemporary of Scot's), said a spirit was conjured, but it was the DEVIL, not Samuel. Scot disagreed, saying the Devil would have been banished by the word "God" or "Jehovah," spoken five times during the conjuration. Furthermore, Scot said, the Devil would not appear to rebuke and punish someone for evil but to encourage them to do more evil.

The witch, said Scot, was a ventriloquist, "that is, Speaking at it were from the bottome of her bellie, did cast herself into a transe [sic] and so abused Saule, answering to Saule in Samuels name, in his counterfeit hollow voice."

FURTHER READING:
de Givry, Emile Grillot. *Witchcraft, Magic and Alchemy.* 1931. Reprint, New York: Dover Publications, 1971.
Hill, Douglas, and Pat Williams. *The Supernatural.* London: Aldus Books, 1965.

witch pegs   In rural areas of the Ozarks, CHARMS for keeping witches away from a home, made from cedar pegs with three prongs, driven into the ground in the path to the door. Folklore belief holds that the prongs are associated with the Trinity. It is considered bad luck to step on or disturb a witch peg.

witch's butter   In old Swedish lore, the yellow vomit of witches' cats found in gardens. In centuries past, it was believed that the DEVIL gave witches CATS, called *carriers*. The witches sent the cats out into the neighborhood to steal food. The cats were wont to gorge themselves on the stolen food, which they then vomited in their neighbors' yards.

Witches' butter also refers to a genus of the lowest group of freshwater algae, *Nostoc*, also called *star spittle*. After summer rain, *Nostoc* swells suddenly to a gelatinous mass, giving the appearance of having fallen from the sky.

witch's cradle   A means to torture accused witches. A witch was tied up in a sack, string the sack over a tree limb and set it swinging. The rocking motion of this witch's cradle, as it was called, caused profound disorientation and helped induce confessions. Most subjected to this also suffered profound hallucinations, which probably added color to their confessions (see TORTURE).

The term witch's cradle also applies to modern sensory-deprivation techniques and devices used to induce altered states of consciousness.

witch's hat   The stereotypical image of a witch is that of an ugly, old HAG wearing a tall, black, pointed hat with a broad brim. The origin of this stereotype is not certain.

In medieval woodcuts, witches are shown wearing various costumes of the times, including headscarves and hats of different fashions. Many are shown bareheaded, with locks flying in the wind.

It is possible that the witch's hat is an exaggeration of the tall, conical "dunce's hat" that was popular in the royal courts of the 15th century or the tall but blunt-topped hats worn by Puritans and the Welsh. No matter what the fashion, pointed hats were frowned upon by the Church, which associated points with the horns of the DEVIL.

Brimless, conical hats have been associated with male WIZARDS and magicians. It is possible that an artist, somewhere along the way, added a brim to make the hats more appropriate for women. By Victorian times, the tall, black, conical hat and the ugly crone became readily identifiable symbols of wickedness in illustrations of children's fairy tales.

Another possibility is that the witch's hat may indeed go back to antiquity. Ancient Etruscan coins from the city of Luna have a head on one side which may be the goddess DIANA, who is associated with witches. The head wears a brimless, conical hat.

Most contemporary Witches go bareheaded or wear ritual headwear such as headbands with a crescent moon or other religious symbol positioned on the forehead. In rituals in which GODDESS and HORNED GOD are represented, the high priestess may wear a headband crown, and the high priest a helmet with horns or antlers.

witch's ladder   A string of 40 beads or a cord with 40 KNOTS, used in MAGIC. The beads or knots enable a Witch to concentrate on repetitive chants or incantations without having to keep count. This enables the Witch to focus will and energy on the desired goal.

In lore, a witch's ladder was a rope or cord of nine knots. It was believed that witches of old could cast a death SPELL over a person by tying the knots and then hiding the cord.

Witch's ladders are used in self-healing work.

See WITCHES' TOOLS.

witch's mark   In witch lore, an extra treat or nipple on witches for suckling FAMILIARS and IMPS, who were said to crave human BLOOD. Extra nipples appear naturally in a small percentage of the population, but in earlier times, they had an infernal association. Any wart, mole, tumor, protuberance or discoloration of the skin was thought to be a witch's mark, particularly if it secreted fluid or blood. When accused witches were arrested, their bodies and cavities were searched for any irregularities. Red spots, bumps under the tongue and fleshy bumps and folds in the vagina were considered paps for familiars.

In witchcraft trials, "prickers" pricked the skin of the accused to determine insensitive areas (see PRICKING), which also were called witch's marks. Out of fear, some people cut off their warts, moles and lumps, but the resulting scars were also taken as proof of being a witch and trying to hide it. The term *witch's mark* is often used interchangeably with DEVIL'S MARK, which was considered proof of a covenant with Satan.

Witch's marks also are described as unusual birthmarks. SYBIL LEEK believed in witch's marks and said she and other women in her family line were born with them.

INITIATION rituals in some traditions of contemporary Witchcraft call for symbolic witches' marks in an X-shaped cross to be made with anointing OILS on the body of the candidate. According to the BOOK OF SHADOWS for the Gardnerian tradition, the crosses are traced over the third eye, the heart and the genitals, symbolizing the freeing of mind, heart and body.

In rural Appalachia, a witch mark is a star, similar in shape to a Maltese cross, that is etched or drawn over the doorway of a home or barn, to keep witches away. It is also carved out of wood and nailed over the door.

FURTHER READING:
Guazzo, Francesco-Maria. *Compendium Maleficarum*. Secaucus, N.J.: University Books, 1974.

Summers, Montague, ed. *The Malleus Maleficarum of Heinrich Kramer and James Sprenger.* 1928. Reprint, New York: Dover Publications, 1971.

wizard   Old term used to describe male magicians, sorcerers or witches, but seldom used in modern times. The word wizard is derived from the Middle English term *wis*, which means "wise." It first appeared in 1440 and was synonymous with *wise women* and *wise men*. In the 16th and 17th centuries—the height of popularity of the European village magician—it applied to a high magician but also to cunning men, cunning women, charmers,

Wizards arrive in town to cause trouble (NEWES OF SCOTLAND, 1592)

blessers, sorcerers, conjurers and witches. After 1825, wizard became almost exclusively synonymous with witch, but its usage died out during the 20th century.

Most villages and towns in Britain and Europe had at least one wizard, who usually was respected and feared by the local folk. The wizard specialized in a variety of magical services, such as fortune-telling; finding missing persons and objects; finding hidden treasure; curing illnesses in people and animals; interpreting dreams; detecting theft; exorcising GHOSTS and FAIRIES; casting SPELLS; breaking the spells of witches and fairies; making AMULETS; and making love PHILTRES. Because he was deemed the diviner of the guilty in crimes, the word of the wizard often carried great weight in a village or town (see DIVINATION). The wizard's CHARMS were part folk magic and part Christian in origin.

Wizards were "commonly men of inferior rank," as Sir Thomas Browne described them in 17th-century England. Most earned paltry fees from their services and worked at other jobs to make a living. They claimed to get their powers from God, the archangels, ancient holy men of the Bible or the fairies. Thomas Hope, a Lancashire wizard, said in 1638 that he had gotten his healing powers from being washed in special WATER at Rome.

In England, wizards were prosecuted for crimes by both the state and the church. The Witchcraft Acts of 1542, 1563 and 1604 made felonies of popular forms of magic, such as fortune-telling, divination to find lost or stolen goods, conjuring spirits and making love charms. Prosecution by the state was erratic, due in part to the defense wizards enjoyed from their clientele, their lack of records and the general popularity of folk magic. Wizards suspected or accused of harmful magic were prosecuted as witches. The church considered sorcery and divination to be diabolical acts for the Devil.

The high magician wizard was an intellectual who pursued alchemy, the Hermetic wisdom (see HERMETICA) and Neoplatonic philosophy. They read the GRIMOIRES, invoked spirits in RITUALS and scryed in crystals (see SCRYING).

In the 17th century, wizardry of both folk and high magic declined in prestige, retreating from urban population centers to the countryside. In the 19th century, interest in high magic revived, but folk-magic wizardry continued to be predominantly a rural phenomenon.

Wookey Hole   A series of limestone caves near Wells, England, which were carved away over time by the River Axe. In pagan times, the winter death rites of the GODDESS may have been celebrated here. Such rites, performed at Samhain (observed October 31), included the sacrifice of oxen in observance of the dying of the earth (see SABBAT). The Goddess was represented by a high priestess.

The cave also may have been used to initiate women into a pagan priesthood (see INITIATION). In 1912 excavations at the site uncovered the bones of a Romano-British woman. Nearby were the bones of a goat and a kid, as well as a comb, dagger and a round stalagmite that resembled a crude crystal ball.

According to legend, a bloodthirsty "Witch of Wookey" lived in the cave. In one version, the witch had once been spurned in love and in revenge cast SPELLS on the villagers of Wookey and demanded human SACRIFICE. The terrified villagers appealed to the Abbot of Glastonbury, who dispatched a monk to confront the witch in the depths of the cave. Her evil spells were of no avail against the monk. The witch tried to escape, but the monk succeeded in sprinkling her with holy water, turning her into stone. In another version, the witch directed her MALEFICIA against lovers throughout Somerset. She cast a spell that ruined one couple's wedding plans. The would-be groom took holy vows and became a monk. He exacted revenge by sprinkling the witch with holy water and turning her to stone.

A 20-foot high stalagmite inside the cave is said to be the preserved remains of this witch.

FURTHER READING:
Bord, Janet, and Colin Bord. *Ancient Mysteries of Britain.* Manchester, N.H.: Salem House Publishers, 1986.
Folklore, Myths and Legends of Britain. London: Reader's Digest Assoc. Ltd., 1977.

Wytte, Joan (1775–1813)   Cornish woman known as "The Fighting Fairy Woman of Bodmin," renowned as a witch.

Joan Wytte was born in 1775 in Bodmin to a family of weavers and tawners (makers of white leather). Small in stature, she reputedly could communicate with FAIRIES and spirits.

Wytte was clairvoyant, and people sought her services as a seer, diviner and healer. She was known to visit a local holy well called Scarlett's, where she did SCRYING and tied clouties on the branches of the trees. (A cloutie, pronounced kloo-tee, is a type of CHARM that is a strip of cloth taken from the clothing of a sick person. As it decays on the tree limb, the limbs of the sick person heal in a form of sympathetic magic. Clouties, consisting of strips of cloth and ribbons, are still tied to the trees at holy wells in modern times.)

Sometime in her twenties, Wytte developed a serious tooth decay that eventually caused a painful abscess, for which there were few dental remedies at the time. The pain of this condition changed her behavior, and she became more ill-tempered. She shouted at people and picked fights, and turned to drinking. She suffered bouts of delirium and muttered in her sleep, causing others to think that she was possessed by the DEVIL.

One day Wytte became involved in a fight with several people and demonstrated almost supernatural strength by picking them up and hurling them around and beating upon them so seriously that they were injured. She was arrested and taken to Bodmin jail.

Wytte languished in jail for years, suffering the fate of other prisoners who had no wealth by which to procure their release. Eventually, the bad diet, damp and dreadful conditions—especially working the treadmill, the fate of all prisoners—caused her to become ill with pneumonia, and she died. Her body was dissected by the jail's surgeon, and the skeleton was placed in a prison storeroom.

A new prison governor arrived, William Hicks, who decided to use Wytte's skeleton for amusement in a seance for friends. The skeleton was placed in a coffin and a bone put in it for her spirit to use in answering questions. Two persons were given bones, which would be rapped. One was for receiving yes answers and one was for receiving no answers. Offstage Hicks secreted a person who also had a bone, and would play the part of Wytte. According to lore, the seance took an unexpected turn of events. The coffin lid allegedly flew open, and, with a great whooshing sound, the bones were yanked from all three people and sent flying about the seance room, beating upon the heads and shoulders of those present. The violence then stopped as abruptly as it had started.

Wytte's bones remained in the jail storeroom. In 1927, after the jail was closed, her skeleton was acquired by a doctor in north Cornwall. It eventually passed into the hands of an antique dealer, and was acquired by CECIL WILLIAMSON, founder of the MUSEUM OF WITCHCRAFT. Williamson put the bones on display in a coffin in the museum.

When the museum, in Boscastle, Cornwall, was sold in 1996, the new owners, Graham King and Liz Crow, experienced poltergeist phenomena associated with the skeleton. They consulted a witch from St. Buryan, Cassandra Latham, who told them the spirit of Wytte did not want to be on public view and would not rest until she had been given a proper burial. The bones were removed for that purpose. The empty coffin remained on display, along with an account of the tragic story of Wytte.

FURTHER READING:
Jones, Kelvin I. *Seven Cornish Witches*. Penzance: Oakmagic Publications, 1998.

Zell-Ravenheart, Morning Glory (1948–) American Pagan and Goddess historian and a principal in the CHURCH OF ALL WORLDS along with her husband, OBERON ZELL-RAVENHEART. Morning Glory Zell-Ravenheart has followed a mystical path in the Craft and Paganism. She describes her life as the story of a shaman: one who, by virtue of physical weakness or other characteristics, does not fit into society, undergoes a struggle for identity that goes into the realm of spirit and emerges stronger and with a new identity. She is a practitioner of Celtic Pagan shamanism and has dedicated herself to working for a pantheistic, ecology-conscious, "Living Goddess" world.

Morning Glory was born Diana Moore in Long Beach, California, on May 27, 1948, to a lower middle-class family with Irish and Choctaw Indian blood. Her parents were from Mississippi and moved to California during World War II so that her father could work in an aircraft factory. Three of her great-grandmothers were Choctaws who married white men in order to avoid the Trail of Tears when the Choctaw reservation was abolished in 1908. One of her grandmothers was an Irish milkmaid who immigrated to America during the Irish potato famine and married a well-to-do southern planter.

Morning Glory believes she was, or at least a portion of her was, an Indian child who died young in a previous life. She had early memories of walking the Trail of Tears, being hungry and seeing nothing but red dust. When she learned to talk, she told her mother she was not her real mother, that her real mother was somewhere in Oklaho-

ma. Also at an early age, Morning Glory began to experience clairvoyant dreams, which earned her the sobriquet of "witch" as she grew older.

Her mother, a devout Pentecostal who married young, came from a family of 13 children and wanted a large family herself; she was able only to have one child. She was a devoted mother and raised her daughter in what Morning Glory jokingly describes as "totalitarian Christianity."

On Morning Glory's father's side, one grandfather was a Methodist minister and a supporter of the Ku Klux Klan. At a young age, Morning Glory would debate the Bible with him. A lover of dinosaurs, she was a Darwinist at an early age and defended evolution. As a child, she attended Methodist services by herself, though her mother did not approve. Between the ages of 10 and 12 she became disenchanted with the Methodists and became deeply involved in the Pentecostal church.

Unhappy at home, Morning Glory visited her Pentecostal pastor to seek help and advice. She was told that she and her mother were subordinate to men; that this was the destiny of women; that they must be obedient to the will of God; and that if they bore their suffering with fortitude, they would "get a gold crown in heaven some day."

This sent Morning Glory, a budding feminist, off on a comparative religion quest between the ages of 13 and 16. She found the various denominations of Christianity to be the same in one respect: women were not in positions of power and were not accorded the right of controlling their own destiny. She studied Buddhism and Zen Buddhism and joined the Vedanta Society, but she found that they also had a predominantly male perspective on the order of the cosmos. The Vedanta Society did introduce her to the Goddess, and she still maintains an altar to various Hindu goddesses, most importantly the Mother Goddess, Lakshmi.

She made her formal break with Christianity at about age 14, following a dialogue with her Methodist minister grandfather, who insisted that animals have no souls and did not go to heaven. As an animal lover, who had spent much of her free time with both domestic animals and wild creatures of the woods, Morning Glory could not accept this. Her comparative religion search had included Greek mythology, which connected her to Paganism and her namesake, Diana. At night, Morning Glory would go outside and sing to the moon and try to call it down. She felt the Goddess, as huntress and protectress of all wild things, was speaking to her. The Goddess entered her life as a vital force, and Morning Glory became a Pagan.

Around age 17 and after graduating from high school, Morning Glory initiated herself into Witchcraft following a three-week vigil at Big Sur, California. As part of the ritual, she dove off a cliff into a pool of water and recognized herself as a Witch as she swam out.

She changed her name to Morning Glory at age 19. In her studies of Diana, she learned that as the Greek Artemis, the Goddess had demanded great personal sacrifices from her human daughters, including celibacy. Morning Glory wanted someday to marry and have children and felt that keeping her given name might be a negative influence.

She enrolled in a community college but dropped out after one semester, following Timothy Leary's advice to "turn on, tune in and drop out." With her pet boa constrictor, she traveled to Eugene, Oregon, to join a commune and fell in love with a hitchhiker, Gary, whom she met enroute. Gary went to the commune with her, and they were married when she was 21. A year later, a daughter, Rainbow (now Gail), was born. The marriage, which was open, lasted about four years, until Morning Glory met her present husband, Oberon (at that time known as Tim "Otter" Zell).

Around 1971 Morning Glory had a vivid, precognitive dream that she was going to meet a man who would change her life; she saw the man clearly in her dream. She told Gary about it. In 1973 she attended the Gnosticon Aquarian festival in St. Paul and listened to Oberon give the keynote address. When she saw him, she recognized him as the man in the dream. "The universe parted, bells rang and lights lit up" when she and Oberon looked at each other, she recalls. After the talk, she approached him, and both knew they had found their soul mate. In Morning Glory's words, "It was like electric lightning. We had this silent communion. We held hands and looked into each other's eyes and telepathically conveyed our en-

Morning Glory and Otter Zell-Ravenheart (COURTESY MORNING GLORY AND OTTER ZELL-RAVENHEART)

tire lives. It was powerful and indescribable. We knew we would never be separated."

Morning Glory called Gary from the festival and told him she had finally met the man in her dream. She took her daughter and went to live with Zell in St. Louis and obtained a divorce. (Rainbow eventually returned to Eugene to live with her father.) In 1974, Morning Glory and Oberon were married.

Morning Glory trained for the traditional year and a day to become a priestess of the Church of All Worlds (CAW). In 1974 she became coeditor with Oberon of the church's flagship publication, the *Green Egg*, until it went out of print in 1976. When the publication was revived in 1988, she resumed coeditorship with Oberon for several years.

Morning Glory and Oberon left St. Louis and the central nest of the CAW in 1976 and spent a number of years traveling, living in monastic retreat, and undertaking exotic adventures. In 1985 they settled in Ukiah, California.

Morning Glory oversees one of the church's subsidiaries, the Ecosophical Research Association, which she and Oberon founded in 1977. Both volunteer for Critter Care, a wildlife animal rescue organization. She serves the aspect of the Goddess known as Potnia Theron, Our Lady of the Beasts.

She has pursued studies in mythology, history, comparative third world religions, zoology, natural history, ethnobotany and the magical and psychic arts. One of her major interests, the history and mythology of the Goddess, led to the creation of Mythic Images in 1990, a business that offers Goddess and mythology products, and for which Oberon sculpts originals. She writes and lectures on the Goddess.

Morning Glory has written nonfiction, fiction and poetry. Some of her fantasy stories were published in MARION ZIMMER BRADLEY's "Swords and Sorceresses" anthologies and in comic book form.

Morning Glory and Oberon have always had an open marriage. From 1984 to 1994, they had a triad and, when that ended, took three new members into their intentional family. Morning Glory coined the term "polyamory" in her 1990 article, "A Bouquet of Lovers," to describe the intentional family lifestyles of multiple lovers.

In 2005 Morning Glory experienced a setback in health when broken bones from a fall sent her to the hospital. She was discovered to have cancer of the bone marrow and blood, a treatable but incurable illness. She underwent surgery, chemotherapy and radiation. Oberon and others organized magical healing RITUALS and an Internet healing circle forum for her. In 2007 her health improved dramatically, so that she could continue her work.

FURTHER READING:
Church of All Worlds official Web site. Available online. URL: http://www.caw.org. Accessed March 13, 2008.
Mythic Images Collection. Available online. URL: http://www. MythicImages.com. Downloaded March 13, 2008.

Zell-Ravenheart, Oberon (1942–)   American Pagan, visionary and author and the key founder of the CHURCH OF ALL WORLDS. Oberon Zell-Ravenheart (formerly Tim Zell, Otter G'Zell and Otter Zell) has played a leading role in PAGANISM. A self-described modern wizard, Zell has worn many hats in his career: transpersonal psychologist, naturalist, metaphysician, mystic, shaman, theologian, teacher, author, artist, lecturer and ordained Priest of the Earth-Mother, Gaea.

He was born Timothy Zell on November 30, 1942, in St. Louis, Missouri. His father served in the armed forces in the South Pacific during World War II. A year before his birth, Zell's maternal grandfather died at home. Zell believes he reincarnated aspects of his grandfather's personality. As a child, he experienced dreams of dying and going into a void. He exhibited many personality characteristics of the man he never knew, and at an early age he developed a love for spending time in the woods with nature—just as his grandfather had loved to do.

After his father's return from the war, the Zell family moved to Clark Summit, a small town outside Scranton, Pennsylvania. As a child, Oberon kept to himself and spent virtually all of his free time in the woods behind the family home. He would sit motionless and let the wildlife come around him. Perhaps because of this solitary time, he became telepathic at a young age and could

hear the thoughts of those around him. As a consequence, he shunned large groups of people, because the telepathic commotion was too much to handle. His early years were fraught with serious illnesses (including a nervous breakdown), which he says "erased and reprogrammed" his mind several times.

During Oberon's teenage years, his father was promoted and the family moved to Crystal Lake, northwest of Chicago, Illinois. Oberon took naturally to the lake, as he had to the woods. He learned instinctively to swim "like an otter," folding his arms by his side and wiggling through the water. Otter became his nickname. He was introspective, read a wide range of literature, and delved into science fiction and fantasy.

He enrolled at Westminster Fulton College in St. Louis, where, in the early 1960s, he met Richard Lance Christie, an association that eventually led to the formation of the Church of All Worlds. Zell shaped the church to his personal vision: Religion should not be concerned merely with personal salvation, a goal overwhelmingly insignificant within the total context of the cosmos, but should be primarily focused on connecting with all time and space, the lifeflow of the universe and the oneness of all things. He coined the term "Neo-Pagan."

Under Oberon's leadership, the church, which filed for incorporation in 1967 and was formally chartered in 1968, attracted a following of intellectuals. It and Oberon played major roles in the coalescing and networking of the budding Pagan movement and the alliance of Paganism with the environmental movement. Oberon edited the church's journal, the *Green Egg*, and made featured appearances at Pagan festivals and science fiction conventions. Sometimes he carried his pet boa constrictor, Histah, on his shoulders as he gave addresses.

In 1963, Zell married his first wife, Martha, with whom he had a son, Bryan, his only child. That relationship ended in 1971.

Between 1965 and 1968, Zell earned undergraduate degrees in sociology/anthropology and clinical psychology, a teaching certificate and a doctor of divinity from Life Science College. He entered, but did not complete, the doctoral program in clinical psychology at Washington University.

In 1970, Oberon formulated and published "the thealogy [sic] of deep ecology," which later became known as The Gaea Hypothesis, the concept of Mother Earth as a sentient being who, in order to survive, needs the harmonious balance of all things on the planet. He preceded James Lovelock, whose similar "Gaia hypothesis" was published in 1974 and gained a popular acceptance.

Oberon was invited to give a keynote address at the 1973 Gnosticon Pagan festival in Minneapolis on "Theagenesis: The Birth of the Goddess," his ideas about Oneness with Earth. In the audience was Morning Glory Ferns (see MORNING GLORY RAVENHEART-ZELL). In a dramatic moment, the two recognized each other as soul mates and experienced a profound, telepathic intimacy. Oberon took Morning Glory back to his home in St Louis. Six months later, they were legally married in a spectacular Pagan handfasting ceremony at the 1974 Gnosticon festival at Easter.

In 1976, Tim and Morning Glory left St. Louis and the central nest of the Church of All Worlds. They bought an old school bus and drove it to Illinois, where they converted it into a mobile home. They visited Coeden Brith in Mendocino County, California, land belonging to Alison Harlow, a cofounder of the Pagan organization Nemeton (see GWYDION PENDDERWEN). They then went to Eugene, Oregon, where they taught classes on Witchcraft and shamanism and third world religions at a local community college.

In the fall of 1976, Zell underwent a profound mystical vision quest that proved to be a watershed in his life. For two weeks, he fasted alone in the wilderness near a hot spring by the Mackenzie River, with no clothes and only a knife and a sleeping bag. He learned to be completely in tune with nature, meditated, kept a journal and smoked marijuana. He emerged from the experience completely transformed: his old identity as an urban social psychologist had been obliterated, and he was now a mountain man, ready to embark on new paths, live in the woods and become a priest of Gaea. With Morning Glory, he performed a ritual baptism, and initiated himself into the Eighth Circle of the Church of All Worlds.

For the next eight years, Zell did little public work. In 1977, he and Morning Glory returned to Coeden Brith and shared with Harlow their secret: that they had discovered how to create unicorns from baby goats. Harlow offered them a contract to live on the land as caretakers. They created a monastic homestead and a Pagan retreat, conducted seminars in the community, raised wild animals and ran the Church of All Worlds as an umbrella organization for several Pagan subsidiaries. Through one subsidiary, the Ecosophical Research Association, they embarked on various projects, including the breeding of unicorns and a hunt for mermaids off Papua New Guinea.

In 1979, Zell decided to change his name from Tim. He had been dissatisfied with it since leaving St. Louis, for everywhere he went, he seemed to find a prominent person named Tim, and it made him feel awkward. He tried to forge new names without success. In March of that year, he and Morning Glory sat by the banks of the river that flows through Coeden Brith and discussed Oberon's identity crisis. Morning Glory suggested his nickname, Otter. Zell rejected it, saying he wanted a name with more "flash" that would be taken seriously by urban folk, with whom they planned to do business with the unicorns. Morning Glory then suggested asking the Mother for a sign, which Zell did. At that moment, an otter popped up out of the water, climbed on a rock, looked at them, twirled around and dove back into the water. Zell had never before seen an otter in the wild and has not seen

one since. "I hear and obey," he said. He changed his last name to G'Zell, a contraction of "Glory" and "Zell," a style borrowed from science fiction. For a time, the couple were known as Otter G'Zell and Morning G'Zell.

From the beginning, the Zells had formed an open marriage. Indeed, it was Morning Glory who later coined the term *polyamory*. In 1984, they included a third primary partner, Diane Darling, in their relationship.

In 1985, Harlow asked the couple to leave Coeden Brith to make way for other plans; they moved to Ukiah, where they lived for the next 11 years with their animals and extended family near a bend in the Russian River. Family members include Oberon's son, Bryan, and Darling and her son, Zack. Oberon emerged from retreat to resume public appearances, including lectures, workshops and classes. He and Morning Glory began to reactivate the Church of All Worlds, which had shrunk to a small, mostly California, base. Morning Glory and Diane resurrected the *Green Egg* at Beltane in 1988.

Otter also worked as a freelance graphic artist and computer operator. He is a prolific writer and artist. Since the late 1960s, he has illustrated fantasy and science fiction magazines and books and has designed posters, record album covers and T-shirts. He illustrated ANODEA JUDITH's book *Wheels of Life,* and drew a Darkovan Bestiary for MARION ZIMMER BRADLEY's science fiction series.

In the '80s, Otter began sculpting museum-quality replicas of Goddess figurines, and in In 1990, the Zell formed Mythic Images, a business offering goddess and gods, jewelry, and other mythology products. The business is now run as a Ravenheart family enterprise, Theagenesis, LLC.

Otter officially changed his first name to Oberon in the fall of 1994, following ritual and personal experiences in which he understood that he had to come to terms with his inner underworld, the shadow side. The new name was taken in a river baptism.

The triad marriage with Diane Darling ended in the summer of 1994, and three new persons joined the family: Wolf Stiles, Liza Gabriel, and Wynter Rose. They adopted *Ravenheart* as the extended family name, and all moved in together in a succession of two large homes. In 1997, the Ravenhearts were featured in a television show, *Strange Universe,* and in a documentary in 2000, *The Love Chronicles: Love in the '60s.* In 1999, the Ravenheart family moved to Sonoma County, California. There, Oberon began a new career as a book author. His first book, *Grimoire for the Apprentice Wizard,* was published in 2004. As a contributing and advisory counsel for this remarkable work, Oberon gathers together many of the most respected and well-known leaders, founders, elders and teachers in the worldwide Pagan community into The Grey Council.

The instant success of the *Grimoire* inspired Oberon to create his most ambitious project to date: the online GREY SCHOOL OF WIZARDRY, which opened its virtual doors in

August of 2004. With dozens of faculty members and hundreds of classes—in 16 departments, at seven "year-levels"—the Grey School offers the most comprehensive apprenticeship in magickal practice and arcane lore that has ever been offered in one place. Graduates are certified Journeyman Wizards.

Since 2005, Oberon has been supportive of Morning Glory's recovery from cancer and has continued his work with CAW, the Grey School, and other projects. Following the *Grimoire,* he has published *Companion for the Apprentice Wizard* (2006), *Creating Circles & Ceremonies* (with Morning Glory; 2006), and *A Wizard's Bestiary* (with Ash DeKirk; 2007).

FURTHER READING:
Church of All Worlds. Available online. URL: hrrp://www.caw.org. Downloaded October 12, 2007.
Green Egg magazine. Available online. URL: http://www.GreenEggzine.com. Downloaded October 12, 2007.
The Grey School of Wizardry. Available online. URL: http://www.GreySchool.com. Downloaded October 12, 2007.
The Mythic Images Collection. Available online. URL: http://www.MythicImages.com. Downloaded October 12, 2007.
Oberon Zell Web site. Available online. URL: http://www.OberonZell.com. Downloaded October 12, 2007.

zombie   A dead person brought back to life by a magician, but not to the life the person previously knew. Believed dead by all who knew him, and by himself as well, the zombie becomes more like a robot than a human being, staring ahead and blindly following the magician-leader, doing his every bidding.

The word *zombie* probably comes from the African Congo word *nzambi,* which means "the spirit of a dead person." Yet a truly dead person—one who has lost bodily functions, whose cells have decayed—cannot be returned to life. To unlock the mystery of zombies Harvard ethnobotanist Wade Davis went to Haiti in 1982. Davis reasoned that the zombie ("zombi," as he preferred to spell it) was a person buried alive, who only seemed dead. Such a person had to be drugged to appear dead, exhibiting no life at all, but could come out of his trance and resume living. He talked to two people who claimed to be zombies: a man named Clairvius Narcisse and a woman known as Ti Femme. They told how they died, how they witnessed their burials and how the *bokor,* or black-magic Vodun *houngan* (priest) lifted them from the grave.

After months of study and conversations with various *hougans,* Davis confirmed his suspicions. The "zombies" were created by the administration of a powerful poison to an open wound or into the victim's food, guaranteeing its entrance into the bloodstream. The poison contains various pharmacologically active plants and animals and usually ground human remains, but the most important ingredient is the puffer fish, which contains *tetrodotoxin.* These fish, of the species *Sphoeroides testudineus* and *Diodon hystrix,* are so poisonous that a tiny drop of tetro-

dotoxin is fatal. Most importantly, tetrodotoxin exhibits two very strange characteristics: the body becomes completely paralyzed, the eyes glazing over and becoming completely unresponsive, mimicking death; and one can recover from a highly controlled dose without any aftereffects. Even trained doctors cannot tell if the victim has truly died from the poison.

The ingredients of zombie poison as determined by Davis are as follows:

First a bouga toad (*Bufo marinus*) and a sea snake are buried in a jar until they "die from rage," say the Vodun preparers; or in other words, the toad secretes venom from its glands in its desperate state. Then ground millipeds and tarantulas are mixed with plant products: *tcha-tcha* seeds, or *Albizzia lebbeck,* which causes pulmonary swelling; consige seeds, from a tree in the mohagany family with no known poisonous attributes; leaves from *pomme cajou,* or the cashew nut (*Anacardium occidentale*); and *bresillet* leaves (*Comocladia glabra*). The last two plants are in the poison ivy family and cause severe dermatitis. All of these plant and animal products are ground into a powder, placed in a jar and buried for two days.

Next the preparer adds *tremblador* and *desmembre,* plants that Davis was unable to identify botanically. At the third stage, the preparer adds four more plants that produce severe topical irritations. The itching from these plants could cause the sufferer to break the skin while scratching, making it easier for the applied "zombie powder" to enter the bloodstream. To work, the poison must enter through an open wound or be ingested into the stomach. These plants are *maman guepes* (*Urera baccifera*) and *mashasha* (*Dalechampia scandens*), both members of the stinging nettle family. The hollow hairs on the plants' surface act like syringes, injecting a chemical similar to formic acid (the compound responsible for ant-bite stings) into the skin.

Also included is *Dieffenbachia seguine,* known as "dumbcane," which contains oxalate needles that act like ground glass. During the nineteenth century, masters forced slaves to eat *Dieffenbachia* leaves, which irritated the larynx, making breathing difficult and speaking impossible, hence the appellation "dumb." The fourth plant is *bwa pine* (*Zanthoxylum matinicense*), used for its sharp spines.

The animals added at this point complete the poisonous picture. Skins of the white tree-frog (*Osteopilus dominicencis*) are ground with two species of tarantulas, then added to another bouga toad and four species of the deadly puffer fish: *Sphoeroides testudineus, Sphoeroides spengleri, Diodon hystrix* and *Diodon holacanthus.* For dramatic effect, the powder can be mixed with ground human remains, preferably a skull.

Once the *bokor* raises the zombie from his tomb, the victim is force-fed a concoction of cane sugar, sweet potato and *Datura stramonium,* or "zombie's cucumber," which causes hallucinations and disorientation. The *bokor* announces the zombie's new name and new "life," and completely confused, the zombie follows the *bokor* wherever he leads him. Tribal Africans believe that slothful persons in life risk being made zombies after death, condemned to work for the *bokor* into eternity.

Traditionally, zombies work the fields, although some believe they are responsible for other work performed at night, like baking bread. A few zombies reportedly have served as bookkeepers, and even shopclerks. Becoming a zombie was a slave's worst nightmare, since death provided no release from unremitting labor. Zombies require little food, but care must be taken not to give them SALT. Considered a magical, purifying substance since medieval times, salt can give the zombie back his powers of speech and taste, releasing a homing instinct that calls the zombie back to his grave. Once there, he burrows deep into the ground, away from the *bokor's* influence, and resumes his eternal rest.

There is no antidote to "zombie poison," since too many of its components have no recourse. But the Vodun preparers make what they call an antidote, made of various leaves from plants with no pharmacological properties, the liquor clairin, ammonia and lemon juice. Other possible ingredients include mothballs, seawater, perfume, rock salt and a mysterious liquid available from Vodun apothecaries known as *magic noire,* or "black magic."

Although making a zombie requires detailed knowledge of the poisons—and cannot work without tetrodotoxin's peculiar properties—the entire process requires belief in magic and the faith that zombies are real. In Vodun, zombies are made by sorcerers, who have captured the soul—the *ti bon ange* ("little good angel") of the deceased. When a person dies, the Vodunist believes the *ti bon ange* hovers about the cadaver for seven days, during which time the soul is most vulnerable to sorcery. If the *bokor* captures it, he can make not only a zombie of the flesh, as described above, but a "zombie astral": a ghost or spirit who wanders at the command of the *bokor.*

Through SORCERY, the *bokor* controls those who were alive either in the body or the spirit. To guard against such a fate, relatives of the deceased "kill" the body again, stabbing a knife through the heart or decapitating it. Others place a dagger in the deceased's coffin to stab the *bokor* or sew up the deceased's mouth so he cannot answer the *bokor* when he calls. Another trick is to place seeds in the coffin, which the *bokor* must count before taking the body. Such a tedious task can take too long, and dawn could break before the *bokor* can remove the body. And no black magic is performed during daylight.

Davis, who wrote *The Serpent and the Rainbow* (1985), also found that zombification was no random act of evil or criminality but a means of capital punishment. Dating back to the secret Maroon societies—groups of escaped slaves hiding in the mountains of Saint-Domingue—and beyond to the secret tribal societies of Africa, blacks have always established their own judicial tribunals for keeping their communities under control. By means of

poisons, magic and extreme secrecy, these organizations surrounded their neighbors with a cloak of fear, administering swift retribution to any who broke the codes. In the days of slavery, blacks used poisons to fight back against their white masters. Poisons worked well, too, against any black who betrayed his brother or sister slaves. Stories of people who banded together to eat human flesh, to dance in cemeteries and raise the dead inspired enough dread to cause any lawbreaker to think twice.

FURTHER READING:
Davis, Wade. *The Serpent and the Rainbow.* New York: Simon & Schuster, 1985.
Hill, Douglas, and Pat Williams. *The Supernatural.* London: Aldus Books, 1965.
Rigaud, Milo. *Secrets of Voodoo.* San Francisco: City Lights Books, 1985.

Zugarramurdi Witches　As part of their efforts to stem public hysteria over witches and sorcerers (see SORCERY), Spanish inquisitors conducted mass trials of accused witches in the Basque village of Zugarramurdi from June 10 to November 8, 1610. For all the hue and cry mounted by the local folk and the lurid testimony given at the lengthy trials, only six persons went to the stake.

Zugarramurdi, a Navarre town on the border of the Labourd region, where the infamous witch-hunter PIERRE DE LANCRE was scouring the countryside for witches, provided a rich setting for superstitious villagers. Nearby was a large, subterranean cave, cut through by a river called the Infernukeorreka, or "stream of Hell," a perfect place for witches to gather and practice their alleged cult of Satan and various pagan rites.

The Supreme Inquisition appointed Don Juan Valle Alvarado as inquisitor in charge of the investigation at Zugarramurdi. Alvarado spent several months gathering testimony, which cast suspicion of witchcraft crimes upon nearly 300 persons, not counting children. The testimony of wild diabolical activities was accepted without question. Alvarado determined that 40 of the suspects were obviously guilty. He had them arrested and taken to Logrono for trial before three judges.

According to the testimony given at the trials, the Zugarramurdi witches were organized in a hierarchy. At the top were senior sorcerers and witches, followed by second-grade initiates who served as tutors of novices. First-grade initiates were responsible for making POISONS and casting SPELLS. Child recruits included those under the age of five who were taken to SABBATS by force; those from age five or six up who were induced to attend sabbats with false promises or goodies; older novices who were preparing to renounce Christianity; and neophytes who had made their renunciation. The entire lot of them were said to worship an ugly, gargoylelike DEVIL.

Detailed descriptions were given of renunciation ceremonies. The novice was presented to the Devil and formally renounced God, the Blessed Virgin, the saints, baptism and confirmation, parents and godparents, Christianity and all those who follow it. The novice kissed the Devil's hind end (see KISS OF SHAME). The Devil marked the novice with his claw, drawing BLOOD, which was caught in a bowl or cup, and also marked the novice in the pupil of the eye with a shape of a TOAD (see DEVIL'S MARK).

The novice, now an initiate, was bound over as a slave to a master or mistress, who was paid in SILVER by the Devil. According to testimony, the silver vanished if not spent within 24 hours (see MONEY). The initiate was given a toad as his or her FAMILIAR, which had been tended by a master or mistress, and instructions for evildoing. After a satisfactory trial period, the initiate was given complete control of the toad and was allowed to make poisons.

Child recruits were bound over to instructors and given many toads to care for.

The witches were said to meet every Friday night and to hold special masses on the night before major Christian holy days. On these occasions, the Devil preached sermons.

The Zugarramurdi witches also were accused of the usual MALEFICIA attributed to witches elsewhere:

Metamorphosis. They changed into animals in order to frighten and hurt others.

Spells. They sabotaged flourishing crops with powders and poisons made from snakes, lizards, toads, newts, slugs, snails and puffballs. The witches metamorphosed into animals and, led by the Devil, sprinkled their poisons over the crops while intoning, "Powder, powder, ruin everything," or "Let all [or half] be lost with the exception of anything that belongs to me." These spells usually were cast during an early autumn southerly wind called *sorguin aizia* or "the wind of the witches." The witches also raised storms (see STORM RAISING) to destroy crops. They allegedly poisoned animals and murdered human beings by administering poisonous powder or OINTMENTS which caused people to become ill and die.

Vampirism. Villagers claimed witches stole children out of their beds at night, carried them off and consumed their blood and flesh. Some cases of vampirism of adults also were given at court.

Of the 40 accused witches, 18 confessed and tearfully asked for mercy, and were reconciled with the church. Six were burned at the stake, including Maria Zozaya, an elderly woman who was said to be one of the senior witches. Five of the accused died during the trials; effigies of them were burned along with the six who were executed. The remaining 11 presumably were not convicted.

FURTHER READING:
Henningsen, Gustav. *The Witches' Advocate: Basque Witchcraft & the Spanish Inquisition.* Reno: University of Nevada Press, 1980.

ꙸ BIBLIOGRAPHY ꙸ

Adler, Margot. *Drawing Down the Moon.* Rev. ed. New York: Penguin, 2006.

Amber, K. *Coven Craft.* St. Paul, Minn.: Llewellyn Publications, 2003.

Anderson, William, and Clive Hicks. *The Green Man: The Archtype of Our Oneness with the Earth.* San Francisco: HarperSanFrancisco, 1991.

Anglo, Sydney, ed. *The Damned Art, Essays in the Literature of Witchcraft.* London: Routledge & Kegan Paul Ltd., 1977.

Ankarloo, Bengt, and Gustav Henningsen, eds. *Early Modern European Witchcraft: Centres and Peripheries.* Oxford: Clarendon Press, 1990.

Baldwin, Richard. *A Revelation of Several Hundreds of Children & Others that Prophesie and Preach in Their Sleep, etc.* London: n.p., 1689.

Barber, Chris. *Mysterious Wales.* London: Granada Publishing, 1983.

Bardon, Franz. *The Key to the True Kabbalah.* Salt Lake City: Merkur Publishing, 1996.

Baring-Gould, Sabine. *The Book of Werewolves.* New York: Causeway Books, 1973.

Baroja, Julio Caro. *The World of the Witches.* Chicago: University of Chicago Press, 1975 (first published 1961).

Barrett, Francis. *The Magus.* London: Lackington, Allen and Co., 1801.

Barstow, Anne Llewellyn. *Witchcraze: A New History of the European Witch Hunts.* San Francisco: Pandora/Harper Collins, 1994.

Berger, Helen A., Evan A. Leach, and Leigh Shaffer. *Voices from the Pagan Census: A National Survey of Witches and Neo-Pagans in the United States.* Columbia: University of South Carolina Press, 2003.

Bias, Clifford. *Ritual Book of Magic.* York Beach, Me.: Samuel Weiser, Inc., 1981.

Bonewits, P. E. I. *Real Magic.* New York: Samuel Weiser, 1989.

———. *Bonewits' Essential Guide to Witchcraft and Wicca.* New York: Citadel Press Books, 2006.

Bonfanti, Leo. *The Witchcraft Hysteria, Vols. I & II.* Wakefield, Mass.: Pride Publications Inc., 1971, 1977.

Bord, Janet, and Colin. *Ancient Mysteries of Britain.* Manchester, N.H.: Salem House Publishers, 1986.

Bottrell, William. *Cornish Witches & Cunning Men.* Kelvin I. Jones, ed. Penzance, England: Oakmagic Publications, 1996.

Boyer, Paul, and Stephen Nissenbaum. *Salem Possessed: The Social Origins of Witchcraft.* Cambridge, Mass.: Harvard University Press, 1974.

Bracelin, J. L. *Gerald Gardner: Witch.* London: Octagon Press, 1960.

Brier, Bob. *Ancient Egyptian Magic.* New York: William Morrow, 1980.

Briggs, Katharine. *The Fairies in Tradition and Literature.* London: Routledge & Kegan Paul, 1978.

———. *British Folktales.* New York: Dorset Press, 1977.

———. *An Encyclopedia of Fairies.* New York: Pantheon, 1976.

Briggs, Robin. *Witches & Neighbors: The Social and Cultural Context of European Witchcraft.* New York: Viking, 1996.

Brown, David C. *A Guide to the Salem Witchcraft Hysteria of 1692.* Self-published, 1984.

Buckland, Raymond. *The Witch Book: The Encyclopedia of Witchcraft, Wicca, and Neo-paganism.* Detroit: Visible Ink Press, 2002.

———. *Buckland's Complete Book of Witchcraft.* St. Paul, Minn.: Llewellyn Publications, 1986.

———. *Anatomy of the Occult.* New York: Samuel Weiser, 1977.

———. *Witchcraft from the Inside.* 2nd ed. St. Paul, Minn.: Llewellyn Publications, 1975.

———. *Ancient and Modern Witchcraft.* Secaucus, N.J.: Castle Books, 1970.

———. *A Pocket Guide to the Supernatural.* New York: Ace Books, 1969.

Budapest, Zsusanna. *The Holy Book of Women's Mysteries, Vol. I (revised) and Vol. II.* Oakland, Calif.: 1986, 1980.

Budge, E. A. Wallis. *Amulets and Superstitions.* New York: Dover Publications, 1978. First published 1930.

———. *Egyptian Magic.* New York: Dover Publications, 1971. First published 1901.

Bullfinch's Mythology. New York: Avenel Books, 1984.

Burl, Aubrey. *Stonehenge.* London: Constable, 2006.

———. *Rites of the Gods.* London: J.M. Dent & Sons Ltd., 1981.

———. *Rings of Stone.* New York: Ticknor & Fields, 1979.

Burman, Edward. *The Inquisition: Hammer of Heresy.* New York: Metro Books, 1984.

Burr, George Lincoln, ed. *Narratives of the Witchcraft Cases 1648–1706.* New York: Charles Scribner's Sons, 1914.

———. *New England's Witches and Wizards.* Peabody, Mass.: Chandler-Smith Publishing House, 1983.

Cahill, Robert Ellis. *Strange Superstitions.* Danvers, Mass.: Old Saltbox Publishing, n.p.r., 1990.

———. *The Horrors of Salem's Witch Dungeon.* Peabody, Mass.: Chandler-Smith Publishing House, 1986.

Calef, Robert. *Another Brand Pluckt out of the Burning or More Wonders of the Invisible World.* Boston: 1697.

Campbell, Joseph. *The Way of the Animal Powers Vol. I: Historical Atlas of World Mythology.* London: Times Books, 1984.

———. *The Masks of God Vol. II: Oriental Mythology.* New York: Viking Penguin, 1962.

———. *The Masks of God Vol. I: Primitive Mythology.* New York: Viking Penguin, 1959.

Carr-Gomm, Philip. *Druidcraft: The Magic of Wicca and Druidry.* London: Thorsons, 2002.

Carr-Gomm, Philip, ed. *The Druid Renaissance.* London: Thorsons, 1996.

Case, Paul Foster. *The Tarot.* Richmond, Va.: Macoy Publishing Co., 1947.

Cassirer, Manfred. *Medium on Trial: The Story of Helen Duncan and The Witchcraft Act.* Standstead, England: PN Publishing, 1996.

Cavendish, Richard. *A History of Magic.* New York: Taplinger, 1977.

———. *The Powers of Evil.* New York: G.P. Putnam's Sons, 1975.

———. *The Black Arts.* New York: G.P. Putnam's Sons, 1967.

Cawthorne, Nigel. *Witch Hunt: History of a Persecution.* Edison, N.J.: Chartwell Books, 2004.

Chamberlain, Rev. N. H. *Samuel Sewall and the World He Lived In.* Boston: De Wolfe, Fiske & Co., 1897.

Chippindale, Christopher. *Stonehenge Complete.* London: Thames and Hudson, 2004.

Christie-Murray, David. *A History of Heresy.* New York: Oxford University Press, 1976.

Clifton, Chas S., ed. *Witchcraft Today: Book One The Modern Craft Movement.* St. Paul, Minn.: Llewellyn Publications, 1993.

Cochrane, Robert and Evan John Jones. *The Robert Cochrane Letters: An Insight into Modern Traditional Witchcraft.* Somerset, Eng.: Capall Bann Publishing, 2001.

Crabtree, Adam. *Multiple Man, Explorations in Possession and Multiple Personality.* New York: Praeger, 1985.

Crowley, Aleister. *Magic in Theory and Practice.* New York: Dover Publications, 1976. First published 1929.

Crowley, Vivianne. *Principles of Wicca.* London: Thorsons/Harper Collins, 1997.

———. *Principles of Paganism.* London: Thorsons/HarperCollins, 1996.

———. *Wicca: The Old Religion in the New Millennium.* London: Thorsons/Harper Collins, 1996.

———. *Phoenix from the Flame: Pagan Spirituality in the Western World.* London: Aquarian, 1994.

———. *Witch Blood!* New York: House of Collectibles, Inc., 1974.

Crowther, Patricia. *From Stagecraft to Witchcraft: The Early Years of High Priestess.* Milverton, Eng.: Capall Bann Publishing, 2002.

———. *Lid off the Cauldron: A Wicca Handbook.* York Beach, Me.: Samuel Weiser, 1989.

Crowther, Patricia, and Arnold. *The Witches Speak.* New York: Samuel Weiser, 1976.

Cunningham, Scott. *Cunningham's Encyclopedia of Crystal, Gem & Metal Magic.* St. Paul, Minn.: Llewellyn Publications, 1987.

———. *Cunningham's Encyclopedia of Magical Herbs.* St. Paul, Minn.: Llewellyn Publications, 1985.

———. *Earth Power.* St. Paul, Minn.: Llewellyn Publications, 1983.

———. *Magical Herbalism.* St. Paul, Minn.: Llewellyn, 1982.

Cunningham, Scott, and David Harrington. *The Magical Household.* St. Paul, Minn.: Llewellyn Publications, 1987.

Daly, Mary. *Beyond God the Father.* Rev. ed. Boston: Beacon Press, 1985.

———. *The Church and the Second Sex.* Boston: Beacon Press, 1985.

———. *Gyn/Ecology.* Boston: Beacon Press, 1978.

Davis, Wade. *The Serpent and the Rainbow.* New York: Simon and Schuster, 1985.

Deacon, Richard. *Matthew Hopkins: Witch Finder General.* London: Frederick Muller, 1976.

de Givry, Emile Grillot. *Witchcraft, Magic and Alchemy.* New York: Dover Publications, 1971.

Demos, John Putnam. *Entertaining Satan: Witchcraft and the Culture of Early New England.* New York: Oxford University Press, 2004.

Devlin, Judith. *The Superstitious Mind: French Peasants and the Supernatural in the Nineteenth Century.* New Haven, Conn.: Yale University Press, 1987.

Digitalis, Raven. *Goth Craft: The Magickal Side of Dark Culture.* St. Paul, Minn.: Llewellyn Publications, 2007.

Di Stasti, Lawrence. *Mal Occhio/The Underside of Vision.* San Francisco: North Point Press, 1981.

Drake, Samuel G. *Annals of Witchcraft in New England and Elsewhere in the United States, from Their First Settlement.* Boston: W. Elliott Woodward, 1869.

Driver, Tom F. *The Magic of Ritual.* San Francisco: HarperSanFrancisco, 1991.

Drury, Neville. *Pan's Daughter.* Sydney: Collins Australia, 1988.

Ebon, Martin. *The Devil's Bride, Exorcism: Past and Present.* New York: Harper & Row, 1974.

Eliade, Mircea. *From Primitives to Zen: A Thematic Sourcebook of the History of Religions.* San Francisco: Harper & Row, 1977.

———. *Occultism, Witchcraft and Cultural Fashions.* Chicago: University of Chicago, 1976.

———. *Shamanism.* Rev. ed. Princeton, N.J.: Princeton University Press, 1974.

———. *Patterns in Comparative Religion.* New York: New American Library, 1958.

Elworthy, Frederick Thomas. *The Evil Eye.* Secaucus, N.J.: University Books/Citadel Press, 1895.

Encyclopedia of Superstitions, Folklore, and the Occult Sciences of the World. Chicago: J.H. Yewdale & Sons, 1903.

Endicott, K. M. *An Analysis of Malaysian Magic.* Oxford: Oxford University Press, 1970.

Epstein, Pearl. *Kabbalah: The Way of the Jewish Mystic.* Boston: Shambhala, 1988.

Evans-Pritchard, E. E. *Witchcraft, Oracles and Magic Among the Azande.* Oxford: Clarendon Press, 1983.

Evans-Wentz, W. Y. *The Fairy-Faith in Celtic Countries.* Secaucus, N.J.: University Books, 1966. First published 1911.

Farrar, Janet, and Gavin Bone. *Progressive Witchcraft: Spirituality, Mysteries & Training in Modern Wicca.* Franklin Lakes, N.J.: New Page Books, 2004.

Farrar, Janet, and Stewart. *The Witches' Way: Principles, Rituals and Beliefs of Modern Witchcraft.* Custer, Wash.: Phoenix Publishing, 1988.

———. *A Witches' Bible Compleat.* New York: Magickal Childe, 1984.

Farrar, Stewart. *What Witches Do: A Modern Coven Revealed.* Custer, Wash.: Phoenix Publishing Co., 1983.

Filotas, Bernadette. *Pagan Survivals, Superstitions and Popular Cultures.* Toronto: Pontifical Institute of Mediaeval Studies, 2005.

Finucane, R. C. *Appearances of the Dead: A Cultural History of Ghosts.* Buffalo, N.Y.: Prometheus Books, 1984.

Fitch, Ed, and Janine Renee. *Magical Rites from the Crystal Well.* St. Paul, Minn.: Llewellyn Publications, 1984.

Flint, Valerie I. J. *The Rise of Magic in Early Medieval Europe.* Princeton: Princeton University Press, 1991.

Flint, Valerie, Richard Gordon, Georg Luck, and Daniel Ogden. *Witchcraft and Magic in Europe: Ancient Greece and Rome.* London: The Athlone Press, 1999.

Fortune, Dion. *The Mystical Qabalah.* York Beach, Me.: Samuel Weiser, 1984.

———. *Psychic Self-Defense.* 6th ed. York Beach, Me.: Samuel Weiser, 1982.

Foxfire 6. Garden City, N.Y.: Anchor Books/Doubleday, 1980.

Foxfire 2. Garden City, N.Y.: Anchor Books/Doubleday, 1973.

Frazer, Sir James G. *The Golden Bough.* New York: Avenel Books, 1981. First published 1890.

French, Peter J. *John Dee: The World of an Elizabethan Magus.* London: Routledge & Kegan Paul, 1972.

Frost, Gavin, and Yvonne. *The Magic Power of Witchcraft.* West Nyack, N.Y.: Parker Publishing, 1976.

Gandee, Lee R. *Strange Experience: The Autobiography of a Hexenmeister.* Englewood Cliffs, N.J.: Prentice-Hall, 1971.

Gardner, Gerald B. *The Meaning of Witchcraft.* New York: Magickal Childe, 1982. First published 1959.

Gardner, Gerald B. *Witchcraft Today.* London: Rider & Co., 1954, 1956.

Gauld, Alan, and A. D. Cornell. *Poltergeists.* London: Routledge & Kegan Paul, 1979.

Gibson, Walter B. *Witchcraft.* New York: Grosset & Dunlap, 1973.

Gilbert, R. A. *Golden Dawn: Twilight of the Magicians.* Wellingborough, Northhamptonshire, Eng.: The Aquarian Press, 1983.

Ginzburg, Calor. *Ecstasies: Deciphering the Witches' Sabbath.* New York: Pantheon Books, 1991.

———. *Night Battles, Witchcraft & Agrarian Cults in the Sixteenth & Seventeenth Centuries.* New York: Penguin Books, 1983.

Glanvil, Joseph. *Saducimus Triumphatus: Full and Plain Evidence Concerning Witches and Apparitions.* London, 1689.

Glass, Justine. *Witchcraft, the Sixth Sense.* Hollywood, Calif.: Melvin Powers Wilshire Book Co., 1965.

Gleason, Judith. *Oya: In Praise of the Goddess.* Boston: Shambhala, 1987.

Godwin, John. *Occult America.* New York: Doubleday, 1972.

Goodell, Alfred P. *The Story of the Old Witch Jail.* Undated manuscript, Essex Institute, Salem, Mass.

Gonzalez-Wippler. *Santeria: African Magic in Latin America.* New York: Original Products, 1981.

Grant, James. *The Mysteries of All Nations: Rise and Progress of Superstition, Laws Against and Trials of Witches, Ancient and Modern Delusions, Together With Strange Customs, Fables and Tales.* Edinburgh: Leith, Reid & Son, n.d.

Graves, Robert. *The White Goddess.* New York: Farrar, Straus and Giroux, 1966.

Gray, William G. *The Ladder of Lights.* York Beach, Me.: Samuel Weiser, 1981.

Green, Andrew. *Our Haunted Kingdom.* London: Wolfe Publishing Limited, 1973.

Green, Marian. *A Witch Alone: Thirteen Moons to Master Natural Magic.* London: Thorsons/HarperCollins, 1991.

———. *The Gentle Arts of Aquarian Magic.* Wellingborough, Northamptonshire: The Aquarian Press, 1987.

Green, Miranda. *The Gods of the Celts.* Gloucester, Eng.: Alan Sutton, 1986.

Grimassi, Raven. *The Encyclopedia of Wicca & Witchcraft.* 2nd ed. St. Paul, Minn.: Llewellyn Publications, 2003.

Guazzo, Francesco-Maria. *Compendium Maleficarum*. Secaucus, N.J.: University Books, 1974.

Guiley, Rosemary Ellen. *Dreamwork for the Soul*. New York: Berkley Books, 1998.

———. *Harpers Encyclopedia of Mystical and Paranormal Experience*. San Francisco: HarperSanFrancisco, 1991.

———. *Moonscapes: A Celebration of Lunar Astronomy, Magic, Legend and Lore*. New York: Prentice Hall, 1991.

———. *Tales of Reincarnation*. New York: Pocket Books, 1991.

Gummere, Amelia Mott. *Witchcraft and Quakerism: A Study in Social History*. Philadelphia: The Biddle Press, 1908.

Hadingham, Evan. *Circles and Standing Stones*. New York: Anchor Books, 1976.

Hall, David D., ed. *Witch-hunting in Seventeenth-Century New England: A Documentary History 1638–1692*. Boston: Northeastern University Press, 1991.

Hall, Manly P. *The Secret Teachings of All Ages*. Los Angeles: The Philosophical Research Society, Inc., 1977.

Hamilton, Edith. *Mythology*. New York: New American Library/Mentor, 1942.

Hansen, Chadwick. *Witchcraft at Salem*. New York: New American Library, 1969.

Harding, M. Esther. *Women's Mysteries Ancient and Modern*. New York: Harper & Row, 1971.

Harner, Michael. *The Way of the Shaman*. New York: Bantam, 1982.

Harrington, David, and Regula deTraci. *Whispers of the Moon: The Life and Work of Scott Cunningham*. St. Paul, Minn.: Llewellyn Publications, 1996.

Harris, Anthony. *Night's Black Agents: Witchcraft and Magic in Seventeenth-Century English Drama*. Manchester, Eng.: Manchester University Press, 1980.

Harrison, G. B., ed. *The Trial of the Lancaster Witches*. New York: Barnes & Noble, 1971. First published 1929.

Harvey, Graham. *Contemporary Paganism: Listening People, Speaking Earth*. New York: New York University Press, 1997.

Harvey, Graham, and Charlotte Hardman, eds. *Paganism Today*. London: Thorsons/HarperCollins, 1996.

Hawkins, Gerald S. *Beyond Stonehenge*. New York: Harper & Row, 1973.

———. *Stonehenge Decoded*. New York: Dorset Press, 1965.

Heindel, Ned D. *Hexenkopf: History, Healing & Hexerei*. Easton, Pa.: Williams Township Historical Society, 2005.

Henningsen, Gustav. *The Witches' Advocate: Basque Witchcraft & the Spanish Inquisition*. Reno: University of Nevada Press, 1980.

Heselston, Philip. *Wiccan Roots*. Milverton, Eng.: Capall Bann, 2000.

Hill, Douglas, and Pat Williams. *The Supernatural*. London: Aldus Books, 1965.

Hitching, Francis. *Earth Magic*. New York: William Morrow and Co., 1977.

Hohman, John George. *Pow-wows or Long Lost Friend*. Brooklyn, N.Y.: Fulton Religious Supply Co., n.d. First published 1820.

Hole, Christina. *Witchcraft in England*. London: B.T. Batsford Ltd., 1947.

Hope, Murray. *The Psychology of Ritual*. Longmead, Dorset: Element Books Ltd., 1988.

Hopman, Ellen Evert, and Lawrence Bond. *Being a Pagan: Druids, Wiccans and Witches Today*. Rochester, Vt.: Destiny Books, 2002.

Hori, Ichiro. *Folk Religion in Japan*. Chicago: University of Chicago, 1968.

Horne, Fiona. *Witch: A Magickal Journey: A Hip Guide to Modern Witchcraft*. London: Thorsons, 2001.

Howey, M. Oldfield. *The Cat in Magic, Mythology, and Religion*. New York: Crescent Books, 1989.

Huebner, Louise. *Never Strike a Happy Medium*. Los Angeles: Nash Publishing, 1971.

Hueffner, Oliver Maddox. *The Book of Witches*. Totowa, N.J.: Rowman & Littlefield, 1973. First published 1903.

Hufford, David J. *The Terror That Comes in the Night*. Philadelphia: University of Pennsylvania Press, 1982.

Hughes, Pennethorne. *Witchcraft*. New York: Penguin Books, 1965.

Hunt, Robert. *Cornish Legends*. Redruth, England: Tor Mark Press, 1997.

Hutton, Ronald. *The Triumph of the Moon: A History of Modern Pagan Witchcraft*. Oxford: Oxford University Press, 1999.

———. *The Stations of the Sun: A History of the Ritual Year in Britain*. Oxford: Oxford University Press, 1996.

———. *The Pagan Religions of the Ancient British Isles: Their Nature and Legacy*. Oxford: Basil Blackwell Publishers, 1991.

Huxley, Aldous. *The Devils of Loudun*. New York: Harper & Brothers, 1952.

Hyatt, Victoria, and Joseph W. Charles. *The Book of Demons*. New York: Simon and Schuster, 1974.

Iglehart, Hallie Austen. *WomanSpirit*. San Francisco: Harper & Row, 1983.

Jameson, J. Franklin, ed. *Narratives of the Witchcraft Cases 1648–1706*. New York: Charles Scribner's Sons, 1914.

Johns, June. *King of the Witches: The World of Alex Sanders*. New York: Coward-McCann, Inc., 1969.

Jones, Evan John, and Charles. Clifton. *Sacred Mask, Sacred Dance*. St. Paul, Minn.: Llewellyn Publications, 1997.

Jones, Evan John, and Robert Cochrane. *The Roebuck in the Thicket: An Anthology of the Robert Cochrane Tradition*. Somerset, England: Capall Bann Publishing, 2002.

Jones, Kelvin I. *Seven Cornish Witches*. Penzance: Oakmagic Publications, 1998.

———. *Witchcraft in Cornwall*. Penzance: Oakmagic Publications, 1995.

Jordan, Michael. *Witches: An Encyclopedia of Paganism and Magic*. London: Kyle Cathie Ltd., 1996.

Judith, Anodea. *Wheels of Life*. St. Paul, Minn.: Llewellyn Publications, 1988.

Kalweit, Holger. *Dreamtime & Inner Space: The World of the Shaman*. Boston: Shambhala Publications, 1984.

Karlsen, Carol F. *The Devil in the Shape of a Woman: Witchcraft in Colonial New England*. New York: W.W. Norton & Co, 1987.

Kelly, Aidan A. *Crafting the Art of Magic Book I: A History of Modern Witchcraft, 1939–1964*. St. Paul, Minn.: Llewellyn Publications, 1991.

Kemp, Anthony. *Witchcraft and Paganism Today*. London: Michael O'Mara Books, 1993.

Kerr, Howard, and Charles L. Crow, eds. *The Occult in America: New Historical Perspectives*. Urbana: University of Illinois Press, 1983.

King, Francis. *Megatherion: The Magickal World of Aleister Crowley*. New York: Creation Books, 2004.

———. *Witchcraft and Demonology*. New York: Exeter Books, 1987.

Kittredge, George Lyman. *Witchcraft in Old and New England*. Cambridge: Harvard University Press, 1929.

Kluckhorn, Clyde. *Navaho Witchcraft*. Boston: Beacon Press, 1967. First published 1944.

Konstantinos. *Nocturnal Witchcraft: Magic After Dark*. St. Paul, Minn.: Llewellyn Publications, 2002.

Kors, Alan C., and Edward Peters. *Witchcraft in Europe, A Documentary History 1100–1700*. Philadelphia: University of Pennsylvania Press, 1972.

Kraig, Donald Michael. *Modern Magick: Eleven Lessons in the High Magickal Arts*. 2nd ed. St. Paul, Minn.: Llewellyn Publications, 2004.

Kriebel, David W. *Powwowing Among the Pennsylvania Dutch*. University Park: Penn State University Press, 2007.

Lady Sheba. *Book of Shadows*. St. Paul, Minn: Llewellyn Publications, 1971.

Larner, Christina. *Enemies of God*. London: Chatto & Windus, 1981.

Larrington, Carolyn, ed. *The Feminist Companion to Mythology*. London: Pandora/HarperCollins, 1992.

Laugguth, A. J. *Macumba: White and Black Magic in Brazil*. New York: Harper & Row, 1975.

LaVey, Anton Szandor. *The Satanic Bible*. New York: Avon Books, 1969.

Lea, Henry Charles. *Materials Toward a History of Witchcraft*. Philadelphia: University of Pennsylvania Press, 1939.

———. *The History of the Inquisition in the Middle Ages*. New York: Macmillan, 1908.

Leach, Maria, ed., and Jerome Fried, assoc. ed. *Funk & Wagnall's Standard Dictionary of Folklore, Mythology and Legend*. New York: Harper & Row, 1972.

Leadbeater, C. W. *Ancient Mystic Rites*. Wheaton, Ill.: Theosophical Publishing House, 1986. First published 1926.

Leek, Sybil. *Sybil Leek's Book of Curses*. Englewood Cliffs, N.J.: Prentice Hall, 1975.

———. *The Complete Art of Witchcraft*. New York: World Publishing Co., 1971.

———. *Diary of a Witch*. New York: NAL Signet Library, 1968.

Leland, Charles G. *Aradia: Gospel of the Witches*. Custer, Wash.: Phoenix Publishing, 1990.

Lenihan, Edmund. *Defiant Irish Women*. Dublin: Mercier Press, 1991.

———. *In Search of Biddy Early*. Dublin: Mercier Press, 1987.

Levi, Eliphas. *Transcendental Magic*. York Beach, Me.: Samuel Weiser, 2001. First published 1896.

———. *The Book of Splendours: The Inner Mysteries of the Qabalah*. York Beach, Me.: Samuel Weiser, 1984. First published 1894.

Lewis, Arthur H. *Hex*. New York: Pocket Books, 1970.

Liddell, E. W. and Michael Howard. *The Pickingill Papers: The Origin of the Gardnerian Craft*. Chieveley, Eng.: Capall Bann Publishing, 1994.

Lipp, Deborah, and Isaac Bonewits. *The Study of Witchcraft: A Guidebook to Advanced Wicca*. York Beach, Me.: Weiser Books, 2007.

Lockhart, J. G. *Curses, Lucks and Talismans*. Detroit: Single Tree Press, 1971. First published 1938.

Loewe, Michael, and Carmen Blacker. *Oracles and Divination*. Boulder, Colo.: Shambala, 1981.

Luhrmann, T. M. *Persuasions of the Witch's Craft: Ritual Magic in Contemporary England*. Cambridge, Mass.: Harvard University Press, 1989.

Lummis, Charles. *A New Mexico David*. New York: Charles Scribner's Sons, 1891.

Macfarlane, A. D. J. *Witchcraft in Tudor and Suart England*. London: Routledge & Kegan Paul Lt., 1970.

MacGregor-Mathers, S. L. *The Book of the Sacred Magic of Abra-Melin the Mage*. Wellingborough, Eng.: The Aquarian Press, 1976.

Mackay, Charles, L.L.D. *Extraordinary Popular Delusions and the Madness of Crowds*. New York: L.C. Page, 1932. First published 1852.

Mair, Lucy. *Witchcraft*. New York: McGraw-Hill World University Library, 1969.

Malinowski, Bronislaw. *Magic, Science and Religion*. Garden City, N.Y.: Doubleday Anchor Books, 1948.

Maple, Eric. *The Dark World of Witches*. New York: A.S. Barnes & Co., 1962.

Marcus, Ronald. *Elizabeth Clawson, Thou Deservest to Dye*. Stamford, Conn.: Communication Corp., 1976.

Marlborough, Ray L. *Charms Spells & Formulas*. St. Paul, Minn.: Llewellyn Publications, 1987.

Marriott, Alice, and Carol C Rachlin. *American Indian Mythology*. New York: Thomas Y. Crowell, 1968.

Marron, Kevin. *Witches, Pagans & Magic in the New Age*. Toronto: Seal Books/McClelland-Bantam Inc., 1989.

Martello, Dr. Leo Louis. *Witchcraft: The Old Religion*. Seacaucus, N.J.: University Books, 1973.

———. *Weird Ways of Witchcraft*. New York: HC Publishers, 1969.

Martin, Malachi. *Hostage to the Devil*. New York: Harper & Row, 1976.

Mathers, S. L. MacGregor. *The Kabbalah Unveiled*. London: Routledge and Kegan Paul, 1926.

Marwick, Max, ed. *Witchcraft and Sorcery*. New York: Viking Penguin, 1982.

Mather, Cotton. *On Witchcraft: Being the Wonders of the Invisible World*. Mt. Vernon, N.Y.: The Peter Pauper Press, 1950. First published 1693.

———. *Memorable Providences, Relating to Witchcrafts and Possessions*. Boston: n.p., 1689.

Mather, Increase. *Cases of Conscience Concerning Evil Spirits Personating Men; Witchcrafts, Infallible Proofs of Guilt in such as are Accused with that Crime*. Boston: n.p., 1693.

———. *An Essay for the Recording of Illustrious Providences*, with introduction by James A. Levernier. Delmar, N.Y.: Scholars' Facsimiles and Reprints, 1977. First published 1684.

Matthews, John, ed. *An Arthurian Reader.* Wellingborough, Eng.: The Aquarian Press, 1988.

Matthews, John, ed. *At the Table of the Grail.* London: Arkana, 1987. First published 1984.

McDowell, Bob. *Gypsies: Wanderers of the World.* Washington, D.C.: National Geographic Society, 1970.

Mead, G. R. S. *Thrice Greatest Hermes: Studies in Hellenistic Theosophy and Gnosis.* York Beach, Me.: Samuel Weiser, 1992.

Michaelsen, Scott, ed. *Portable Darkness: An Aleister Crowley Reader.* New York: Harmony Books, 1989.

Michelet, Jules. *Satanism and Witchcraft.* Secaucus, N.J.: Citadel Press, 1939 (reprint).

Mickaharic, Draja. *A Century of Spells.* York Beach, Me.: Samuel Weiser, 1988.

Middleton, John, ed. *Magic, Curing & Witchcraft.* Austin: University of Texas Press, 1967.

Midelfort, H. C. Erik. *Witch Hunting in Southwestern Germany 1562–1684.* Stanford, Calif.: Stanford University Press, 1972.

Monter, E. William, ed. *European Witchcraft.* New York: John Wiley & Sons, Inc., 1969.

Monter, E. William. *Witchcraft in France and Switzerland.* New York: Cornell University, 1976.

Moore, R. Laurence. *In Search of White Crows.* New York: Oxford University Press, 1977.

Murray, Margaret A. *The God of the Witches.* London: Sampson Low, Marston and Co., Ltd., 1931.

———. *The Witch-Cult in Western Europe.* London: Oxford University Press, 1921.

Nauman, St. Elmo Jr. *Exorcism Through the Ages.* Secaucus, N.J.: Citadel, 1974.

O'Donnell, Elliott. *Werewolves.* New York: Longvue Press, 1965.

Ogden, Daniel. *Magic, Witchcraft, and Ghosts in the Greek and Roman Worlds: A Sourcebook.* New York: Oxford University Press, 2002.

O'Grady, Joan. *The Prince of Darkness: The Devil in History, Religion and the Human Psyche.* New York: Barnes and Noble Books, 1989.

Opie, Iona, and Moira Tatem. *A Dictionary of Superstitions.* New York: Oxford University Press, 1989.

Parrinder, Geoffrey. *Witchcraft European and African.* London: Faber & Faber, 1970.

Penczak, Christopher. *Gay Witchcraft: Empowering the Tribe.* York Beach, Me.: Samuel Weiser, 2003.

Penczak, Christopher. *The Inner Temple of Witchcraft: Magic Meditation and Psychic Development.* St. Paul, Minn.: Llewellyn Publications, 2003.

Pennick, Nigel. *Secrets of East Anglian Magic.* London: Robert Hale, 1995.

Pepper, Elizabeth, and John Wilcock. *Magical and Mystical Sites.* New York: Harper & Row, 1977.

Pernoud, Regine. *Joan of Arc: By Herself and Her Witnesses.* New York: Dorset, 1964. First published 1962.

Piggott, Stuart. *The Druids.* London: Thames and Hudson, 1975.

Potter, Carole. *Knock on Wood and Other Superstitions.* New York: Bonanza Books, 1984.

Rabinovitch, Shelley, and James Lewis. *The Encyclopedia of Modern Witchcraft and Neo-Paganism.* New York: Citadel Press, 2002.

Radford, E., and M. A. Radford. *The Encyclopedia of Superstitions.* Edited and revised by Christina Hole. New York: Barnes and Noble, 1961.

Rae, Beth. *Hedge Witch: A Guide to Solitary Witchcraft.* London: Robert Hale, 1990.

Randolph, Vance. *Ozark Magic and Folklore.* New York: Dover Publications, 1964. First published 1947.

R.C. Esq. *Lithobolia: or, the Stone-throwing Devil, etc.* London: 1698.

Regardie, Israel. *The Golden Dawn.* 5th ed. St. Paul, Minn.: Llewellyn Publications, 1986.

———. *What You Should Know About the Golden Dawn.* 3rd ed. Phoenix: Falcon Press, 1983.

———. *Ceremonial Magic: A Guide to the Mechanisms of Ritual.* Wellingborough, Northamptonshire, Eng.: The Aquarian Press, 1980.

Remy, Nicolas. *Demonolatry.* Secaucus, N.J.: University Books, 1974.

Rhodes, H. F. T. *The Satanic Mass: A Sociological & Criminological Study.* New York: Citadel Press, 1955.

Rigaud, Milo. *Secrets of Voodoo.* San Francisco: City Lights Books, 1985.

Robbins, Rossell Hope. *The Encyclopedia of Witchcraft & Demonology.* New York: Bonanza Books, 1981. First published 1959.

Rogo, D. Scott. *The Infinite Boundary.* New York: Dodd, Mead & Co., 1987.

Rosen, Barbara, ed. *Witchcraft in England, 1558–1618.* Amherst: University of Massachusetts Press, 1991.

Royston, Richard. *An Advertisement to the Jury-men of England Touching Witches. Together with a Difference Between an English and Hebrew Witch.* London: n.p., 1653.

Rudwin, Maximilian. *The Devil in Legend and Literature.* La Salle, Ill.: Open Court Publishing Co., 1931, 1959.

Rush, John A. *Witchcraft and Sorcery.* Springfield, Ill.: Charles C. Thomas, 1974.

Russell, Jeffrey Burton. *The Prince of Darkness.* London: Thames & Hudson, 1989.

———. *Lucifer: The Devil in the Middle Ages.* Ithaca and London: Cornell University Press, 1984.

———. *A History of Witchcraft.* London: Thames and Hudson, 1980.

———. *The Devil.* Ithaca and London: Cornell University Press, 1977.

———. *Witchcraft in the Middle Ages.* Ithaca and London: Cornell University Press, 1972.

Saletore, R. N. *Indian Witchcraft.* Atlantic Highlands, N.J.: Humanities Press, 1981.

Sanders, Maxine. *Fire Child: The Life and Magic of Maxine Sanders "Witch Queen."* Oxford: Mandrake, 2007.

Savramis, Demosthenes. *The Satanizing of Woman: Religion Versus Sexuality.* Translated by Martin Ebon. Garden City, N.Y.: Doubleday & Co., Inc., 1974.

Scholem, Gershom. *Kabbalah.* New York: New American Library, 1974.

Scot, Reginald. *The Discoverie of Witchcraft.* Yorkshire, Eng.: E.P. Publishing, Ltd., 1973; 1886 ed.

Scott, Sir Walter. *Letters on Demonology and Witchcraft.* New York: Citadel Press, 1968. First published 1884.

Seligmann, Kurt. *The Mirror of Magic.* New York: Pantheon Books, 1948.

Seymour, St. John D. *Irish Witchcraft and Demonology.* Dublin: Hodges, Figgis & Co., 1913.

Seznec, Jean. *The Survival of the Pagan Gods.* Princeton: Princeton University Press, 1981.

Shallcrass, Philip. *Druidry.* London: Piatkus Books, 2000.

Sharpe, C. K. *A History of Witchcraft in Scotland.* Glasgow: Thomas D. Morison, 1884.

Simmons, Marc. *Witchcraft in the Southwest: Spanish and Indian Supernaturalism on the Rio Grande.* Lincoln.: University of Nebraska Press, 1974.

Sjoo, Monica, and Barbara Mor. *The Great Cosmic Mother.* San Francisco: Harper & Row, 1987.

Southern, R. W. *Western Society and the Church in the Middle Ages.* Harmondsworth, Middlesex, Eng.: Penguin Books, 1970.

Starhawk. *The Spiral Dance.* Rev. ed. San Francisco: HarperOne, 1999.

Starhawk, M. *Macha NightMare and the Reclaiming Collective. The Pagan Book of Living and Dying.* San Francisco: HarperSanFrancisco, 1997.

Starkey, Marion L. *The Devil in Massachusetts.* New York: Alfred Knopf, 1950.

Stephenson, P. R., and Israel Regardie. *The Legend of Aleister Crowley.* St. Paul, Minn.: Llewellyn Publications, 1970.

Stewart, R. J. *Living Magical Arts.* Poole, Dorset, Eng.: Blandford Press, 1987.

Stoller, Paul, and Cheryl Olkes. *In Sorcery's Shadow.* Chicago: University of Chicago, 1987.

Stone, Merlin. *Ancient Mirrors of Womanhood.* Boston: Beacon Press, 1984. First published 1979.

Stone, Merlin. *When God Was a Woman.* San Diego: Harcourt Brace Jovanovich, 1976.

Stutley, Margaret. *Ancient Indian Magic and Lore.* Boulder, Colo.: Great Eastern Book Co., 1980.

Summers, Montague. *The Werewolf.* New York: Bell Publishing, 1967. First published 1933.

———. *The Geography of Witchcraft.* London: Kegan Paul, Trench, Trubner & Co. Ltd., 1927.

———. *The History of Witchcraft and Demonology.* London: Kegan Paul, Trench, Trubner & Co. Ltd., 1926.

Summers, Montague, ed. *TheMalleus Maleficarum of Heinrich Kramer and James Sprenger.* New York: Dover Publications, 1971. First published 1928.

Suster, Gerald, ed. *John Dee: Essential Readings.* Wellingborough, Northamptonshire, Eng.: Crucible, 1986.

Symonds, John, and Kenneth Grant, eds. *The Confessions of Aleister Crowley, an Autobiography.* London: Routledge & Kegan Paul, 1979.

Tallant, Robert. *The Voodoo Queen.* Gretna, La.: Pelican Publishing, 1983.

Terry, Maury. *The Ultimate Evil.* New York: Doubleday, 1987.

Thomas, Keith. *Religion and the Decline of Magic.* New York: Charles Scribner's Sons, 1971.

Three Books of Occult Philosophy Written by Henry Cornelius Agrippa of Nettesheim. Trans. by James Freake. Ed. and annot. Donald Tyson. St. Paul, Minn.: Llewellyn Publications, 1995.

Trevor-Roper, H. R. *The European Witch-Craze.* New York: Harper & Row, 1957.

Trigg, Elwood B. *Gypsy Demons & Divinities.* Secaucus, N.J.: Citadel Press, 1973.

Tuchman, Barbara. *A Distant Mirror: The Calamitous 14th Century.* New York: Ballantine Books, 1978.

Upham, Charles. *History of Witchcraft and Salem Village.* Boston: Wiggin and Lunt, 1867.

Valiente, Doreen. *The Rebirth of Witchcraft.* London: Robert Hale, 1989.

———. *Witchcraft for Tomorrow.* Custer, Wash.: Phoenix Publishing, 1985. First published 1978.

———. *An ABC of Witchcraft Past and Present.* Custer, Wash.: Phoenix Publishing, 1986. First published 1973.

Villoldo, Alberto, and Stanley Krippner. *Healing States.* New York: Fireside/Simon & Schuster, 1987.

Waite, Arthur Edward. *The Hermetic Museum.* York Beach, Me.: Samuel Weiser, 1991.

———. *The Book of Black Magic and of Pacts.* York Beach, Me.: Samuel Weiser, 1972.

Walker Barbar G. *The Woman's Dictionary of Symbols & Sacred Objects.* San Francisco: Harper & Row, 1988.

———. *The Crone.* San Francisco: Harper & Row, 1985.

———. *The Woman's Encyclopedia of Myths and Secrets.* San Francisco: Harper & Row, 1983.

Walker, D. P. *Unclean Spirits: Possession and Exorcism in France and England in the Late Sixteenth and Early Seventeenth Centuries.* Philadelphia: University of Pennsylvania Press, 1981.

Weinstein, Marion. *Earth Magic: A Dianic Book of Shadows.* Rev. ed. Custer, Wash.: Phoenix Publishing, 1998.

———. *Positive Magic.* Rev. ed. Custer, Wash.: Phoenix Publishing, 1981.

Weisman, Richard. *Witchcraft, Magic and Religion in Seventeenth Century Massachusetts.* Amherst: University of Massachusetts Press, 1984.

Weltfish, Gene. *The Lost Universe: The Way of Life of the Pawnee.* New York: Ballantine Books, 1965.

Wickland, Carl. *Thirty Years Among the Dead.* Hollywood, Calif.: Newcastle Publishing Co., 1974. First published 1924.

Williams, Howard. *The Superstitions of Witchcraft.* London: Longman, Green, Longman, Roberts & Green, 1865.

Williams, Selma R., and Pamela J Williams. *Riding the Nightmare: Women and Witchcraft.* New York: Atheneum, 1978.

Wilson, Colin. *Mysteries.* New York: Perigee/G.P. Putnam's Sons, 1978.

———. *The Occult.* New York: Vintage Books, 1971.

Wilson, Ian. *All in the Mind.* New York: Doubleday, 1982.

Yeats, W. B. *Irish Fairy and Folk Tales.* New York: Dorset Press, 1986. First published 1892.

⁂ INDEX ⁂

Boldface page numbers indicate major treatment of a topic. *Italic* page numbers indicate illustrations.